THE NEW COLLEGEVILLE
BIBLE COMMENTARY

NEW TESTAMENT

THE NEW COLLEGEVILLE BIBLE COMMENTARY

NEW TESTAMENT

SERIES EDITOR
Daniel Durken, O.S.B.

LITURGICAL PRESS
Collegeville, Minnesota

www.litpress.org

Nihil Obstat: Reverend Robert Harren, J.C.L., *Censor deputatus.*
Imprimatur: ✠ Most Reverend John F. Kinney, J.C.D., D.D., Bishop of St. Cloud, Minnesota, June 28, 2008.

Design by Ann Blattner.

Cover illustration: *Baptism of Jesus* (detail) by Donald Jackson. Copyright 2005 *The Saint John's Bible* and the Hill Museum & Manuscript Library at Saint John's University, Collegeville, Minnesota.

Excerpts from the *New American Bible with Revised New Testament and Psalms* Copyright © 1991, 1986, 1970 Confraternity of Christian Doctrine, Inc., Washington, DC. Used with permission. All rights reserved. No part of the *New American Bible* may be reproduced by any means without permission in writing from the copyright owner.

© 2009 by Order of Saint Benedict, Collegeville, Minnesota. All rights reserved. No part of this book may be reproduced in any form, by print, microfilm, microfiche, mechanical recording, photocopying, translation, or by any other means, known or yet unknown, for any purpose except brief quotations in reviews, without the previous written permission of Liturgical Press, Saint John's Abbey, P.O. Box 7500, Collegeville, Minnesota 56321-7500. Printed in the United States of America.

Library of Congress Cataloging-in-Publication Data

The new Collegeville Bible commentary. New Testament / series editor, Daniel Durken.
    p.   cm.
  ISBN 978-0-8146-3260-4
  1. Bible. N.T.—Commentaries.   I. Durken, Daniel.

BS2341.52.N49   2008
225.7—dc22

2008027534

CONTENTS

PREFACE ix
   Daniel Durken, O.S.B.

ABBREVIATIONS xi

MAPS xii

   The Gospel According to Matthew   1
      Barbara E. Reid, O.P.

   The Gospel According to Mark   91
      Marie Noonan Sabin

   The Gospel According to Luke   215
      Michael F. Patella, O.S.B.

   The Gospel According to John   309
      Scott M. Lewis, S.J.

   The Acts of the Apostles   369
      Dennis Hamm, S.J.

THE PAULINE LETTERS   436
   Vincent M. Smiles

   The Letter to the Romans   439
      Robert J. Karris, O.F.M.

   THE LETTERS TO THE CORINTHIANS   479
      Marie A. Pascuzzi

   The First Letter to the Corinthians   486
      Marie A. Pascuzzi

Contents

> The Second Letter to the Corinthians 547
> *Marie A. Pascuzzi*
>
> The Letter to the Galatians 581
> *Robert J. Karris, O.F.M.*
>
> The Letter to the Ephesians 602
> *Vincent M. Smiles*
>
> The Letter to the Philippians 620
> *Vincent M. Smiles*
>
> The Letter to the Colossians 635
> *Vincent M. Smiles*
>
> The First Letter to the Thessalonians 651
> *Vincent M. Smiles*
>
> The Second Letter to the Thessalonians 667
> *Vincent M. Smiles*
>
> The First Letter to Timothy 678
> *Terence J. Keegan, O.P.*
>
> The Second Letter to Timothy 699
> *Terence J. Keegan, O.P.*
>
> The Letter to Titus 714
> *Terence J. Keegan, O.P.*
>
> The Letter to Philemon 723
> *Terence J. Keegan, O.P.*
>
> The Letter to the Hebrews 731
> *Daniel J. Harrington, S.J.*

THE GENERAL LETTERS 767
Patrick J. Hartin

> The Letter of James 768
> *Patrick J. Hartin*

The First Letter of Peter   784
  Patrick J. Hartin

The Second Letter of Peter   797
  Patrick J. Hartin

THE LETTERS OF JOHN   807
  Scott M. Lewis, S.J.

  The First Letter of John   809
    Scott M. Lewis, S.J.

  The Second Letter of John   818
    Scott M. Lewis, S.J.

  The Third Letter of John   820
    Scott M. Lewis, S.J.

  The Letter of Jude   822
    Patrick J. Hartin

  The Book of Revelation   828
    Catherine A. Cory

Preface

Anticipating by five years the Second Vatican Council's urging that "all the Christian faithful learn by frequent reading of the divine Scriptures the 'excelling knowledge of Jesus Christ' (Philippians 3:8)," Liturgical Press pioneered the publication of a popular commentary on all the books of the Bible. Beginning in 1960 the Press produced forty-six booklets, the *Old and New Testament Reading Guides*, that contained biblical texts and commentaries written by leading Scripture scholars. In his *Seventy-Five Years of Grace: The Liturgical Press 1926–2001*, Mark Twomey writes, "These *Guides* came to be regarded as one of the most outstanding teaching and generally informative tools to be prepared in modern times on the Bible."

Two decades later the need for a revised edition of these *Guides* produced the *Collegeville Bible Commentary*. Between 1983 and 1986 Liturgical Press published eleven booklets of the New Testament series and twenty-five booklets of the Old Testament series in the familiar and best-selling format of biblical text accompanied by its commentary.

With over two million copies sold and the passing of yet another two decades, it was time to bring forth the new edition of these commentaries, the *New Collegeville Bible Commentary*. This book brings together the twelve New Testament volumes published between 2005 and 2007. These commentaries, as Gregory W. Dawes states in his introductory volume to this series,

> deal with one or more of the books that form the biblical library. In studying that book, it will ask [and answer] precisely these questions. What sort of book is this? When was it written? By whom was it written and for what purpose? How does it organize its material and present its message? It is important to try to answer such questions if we are to read biblical books intelligently.

It is especially appropriate that this volume is published in the Year of Paul 2008–2009. In the Second Letter to Timothy, attributed to the prolific and profound Paul, we are reminded that "all scripture is inspired by God and is useful for teaching, for refutation, for correction, and for training in righteousness" (3:16). May these commentaries, together with frequent reading of Scripture, inspire you and lead you to greater knowledge and love of Jesus Christ.

Daniel Durken, o.s.b.
Series Editor

ABBREVIATIONS

Books of the Bible

Acts—Acts of the Apostles
Amos—Amos
Bar—Baruch
1 Chr—1 Chronicles
2 Chr—2 Chronicles
Col—Colossians
1 Cor—1 Corinthians
2 Cor—2 Corinthians
Dan—Daniel
Deut—Deuteronomy
Eccl (or Qoh)—Ecclesiastes
Eph—Ephesians
Esth—Esther
Exod—Exodus
Ezek—Ezekiel
Ezra—Ezra
Gal—Galatians
Gen—Genesis
Hab—Habakkuk
Hag—Haggai
Heb—Hebrews
Hos—Hosea
Isa—Isaiah
Jas—James
Jdt—Judith
Jer—Jeremiah
Job—Job
Joel—Joel
John—John
1 John—1 John
2 John—2 John
3 John—3 John
Jonah—Jonah
Josh—Joshua
Jude—Jude
Judg—Judges
1 Kgs—1 Kings

2 Kgs—2 Kings
Lam—Lamentations
Lev—Leviticus
Luke—Luke
1 Macc—1 Maccabees
2 Macc—2 Maccabees
Mal—Malachi
Mark—Mark
Matt—Matthew
Mic—Micah
Nah—Nahum
Neh—Nehemiah
Num—Numbers
Obad—Obadiah
1 Pet—1 Peter
2 Pet—2 Peter
Phil—Philippians
Phlm—Philemon
Prov—Proverbs
Ps(s)—Psalms
Rev—Revelation
Rom—Romans
Ruth—Ruth
1 Sam—1 Samuel
2 Sam—2 Samuel
Sir—Sirach
Song—Song of Songs
1 Thess—1 Thessalonians
2 Thess—2 Thessalonians
1 Tim—1 Timothy
2 Tim—2 Timothy
Titus—Titus
Tob—Tobit
Wis—Wisdom
Zech—Zechariah
Zeph—Zephaniah

Other Abbreviations

Ant.—*Antiquities of the Jews*
Apoc. Bar.—Syriac Greek Apocalypse of Baruch
H.E.—Eusebius, *Historia Ecclesiastica*

KJV—King James Version
LXX—Septuagint
NAB—New American Bible
T. Moses—*Testament of Moses*

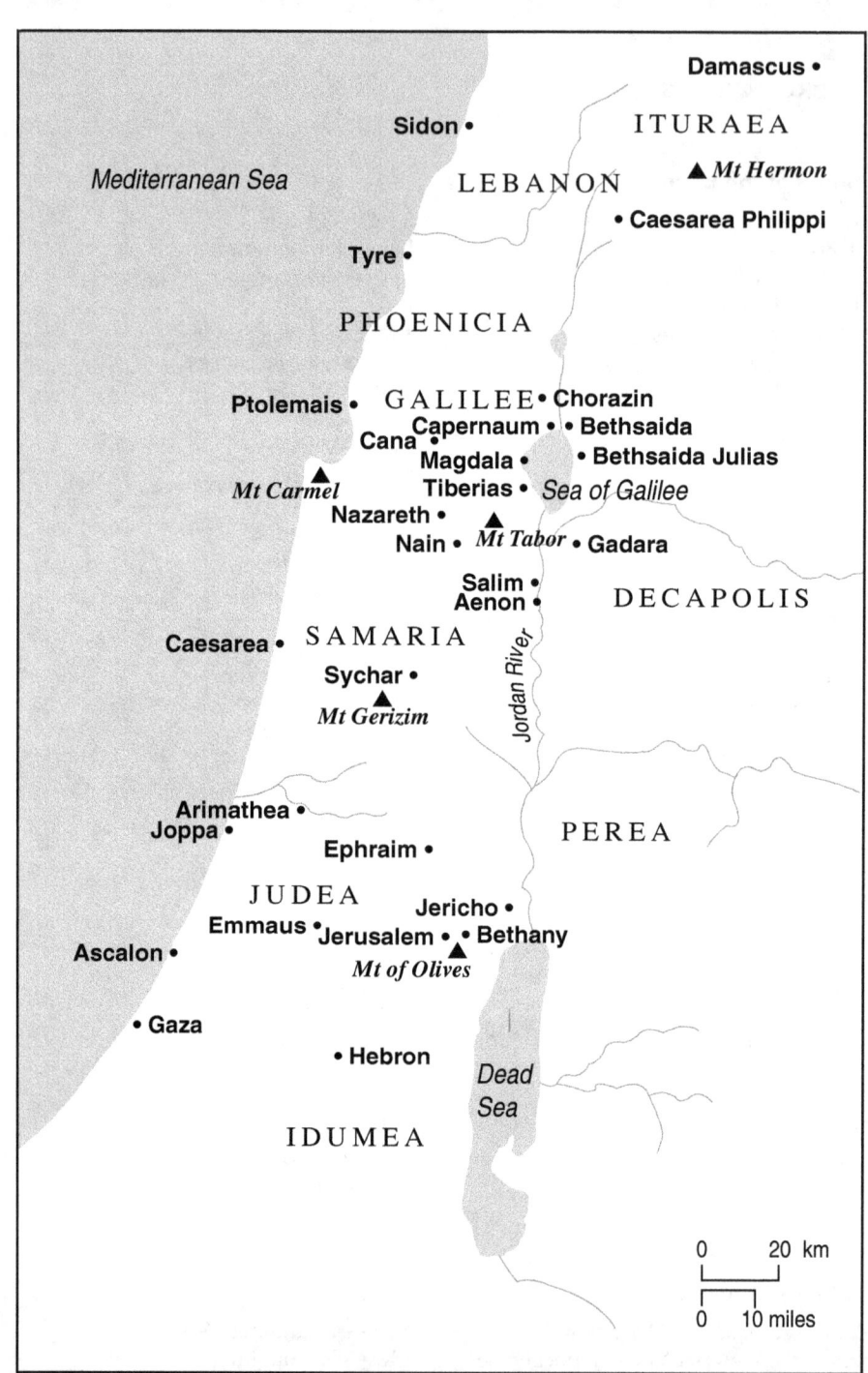

Palestine in the Time of Jesus

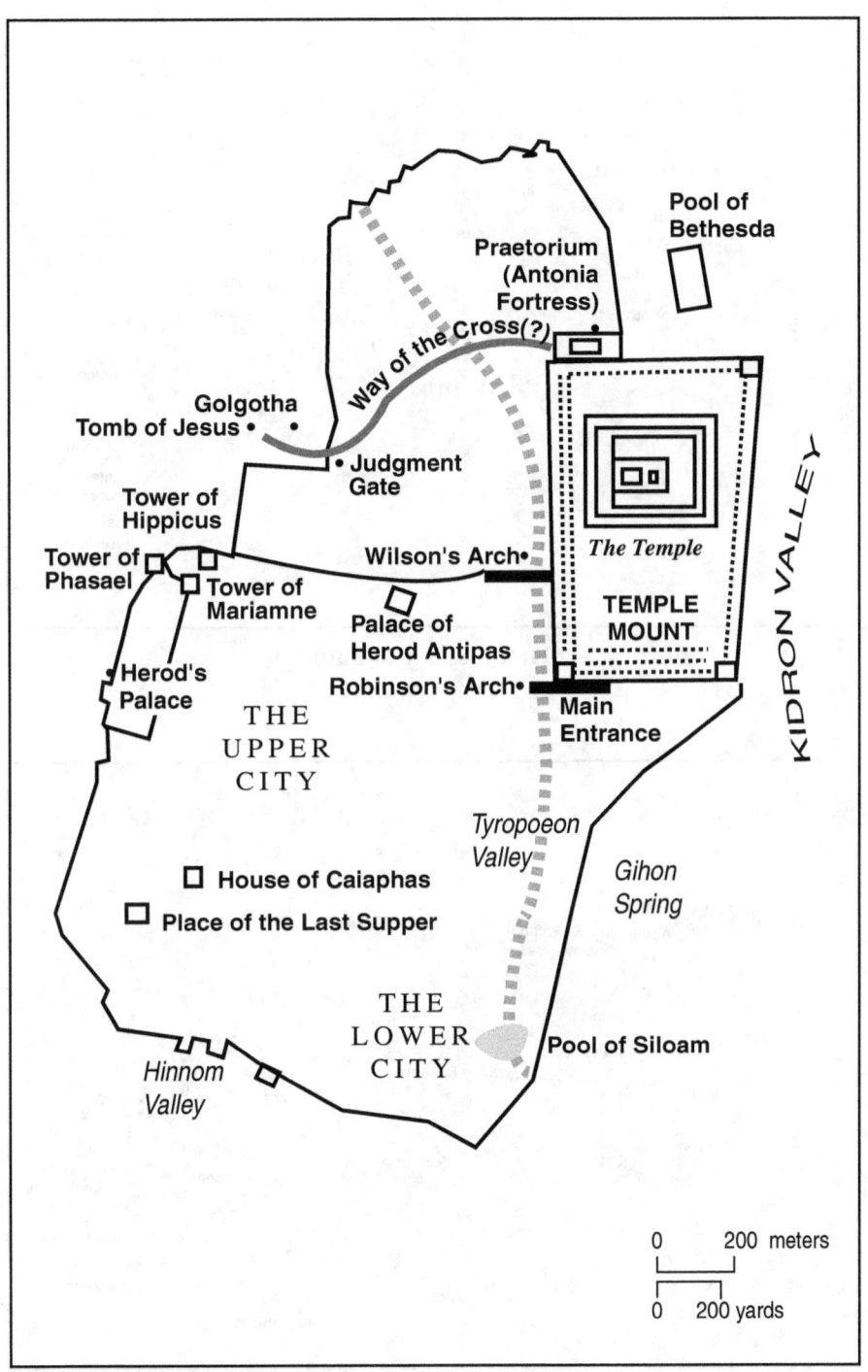

Jerusalem in the Time of Jesus

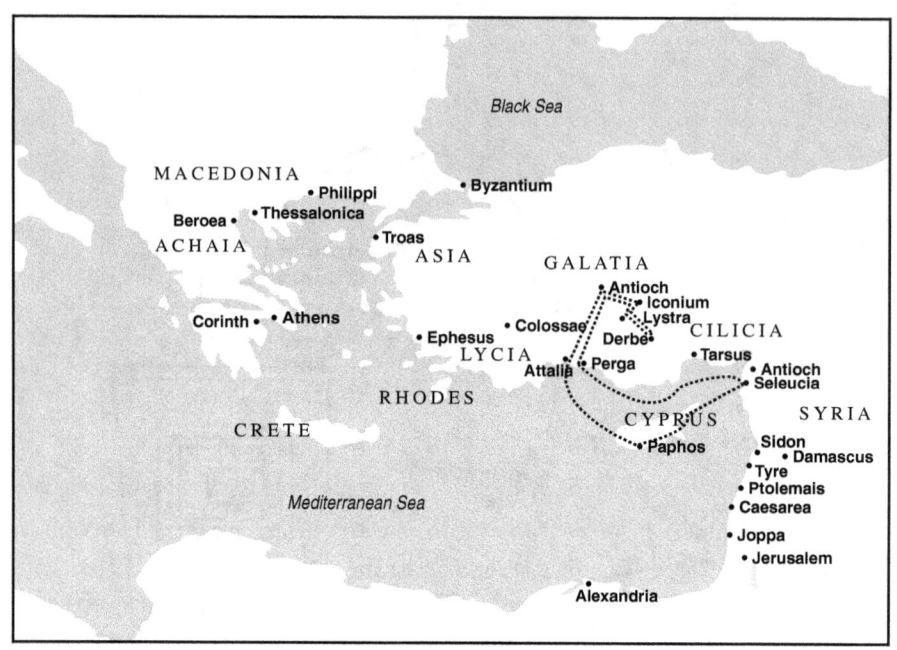

First Journey of Paul

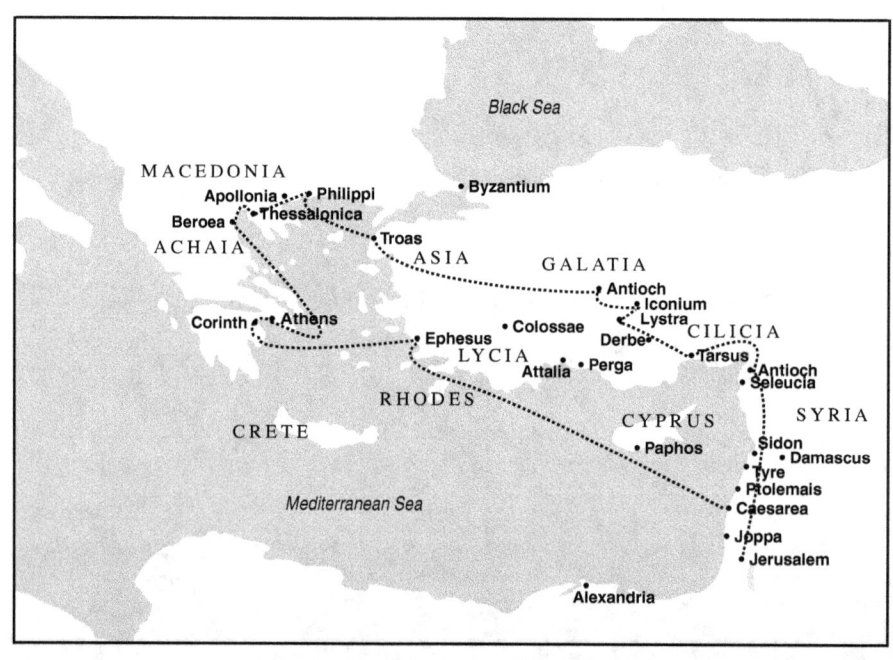

Second Journey of Paul

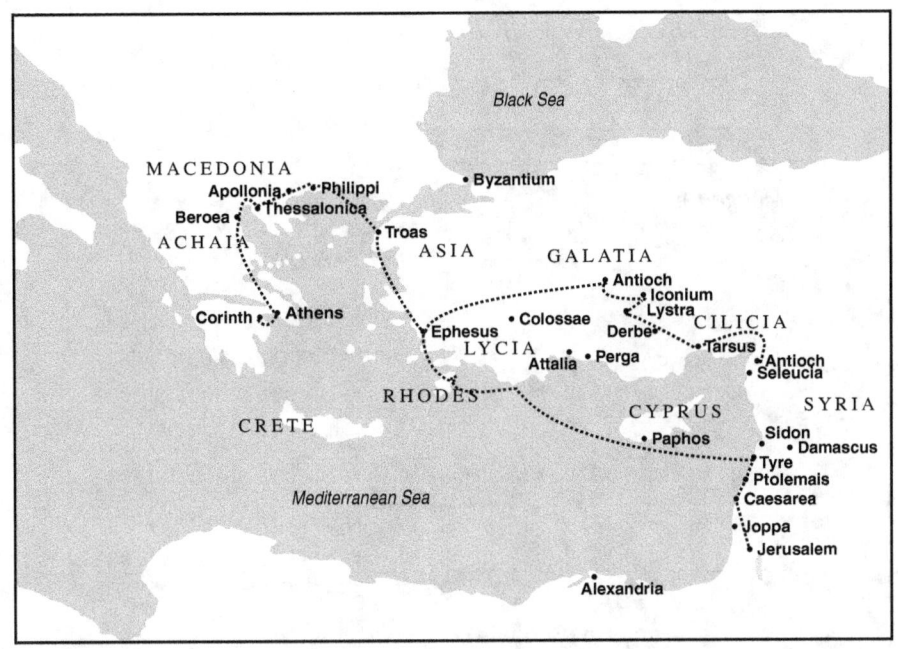

Third Journey of Paul

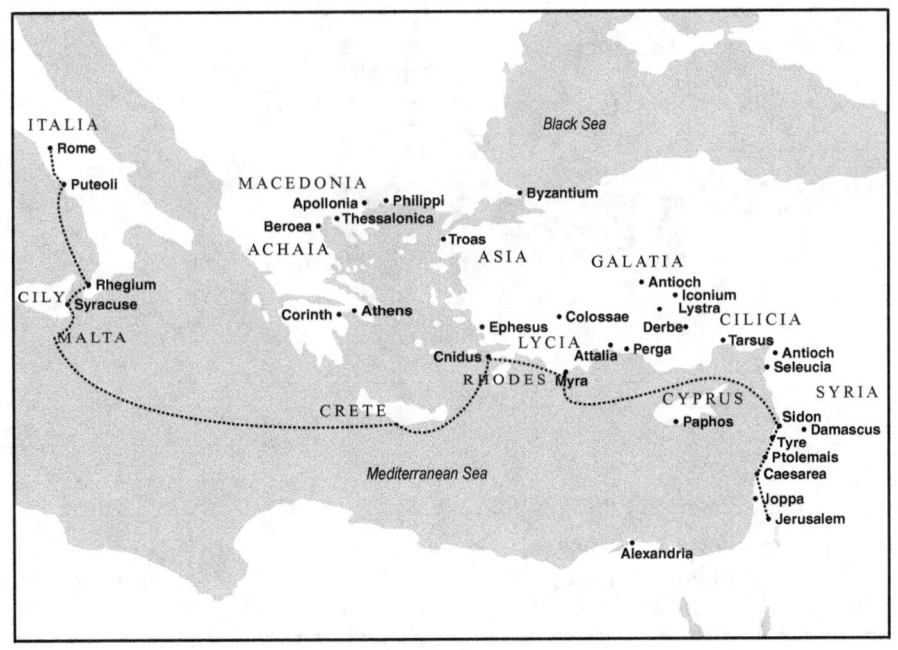

Paul's Journey to Rome

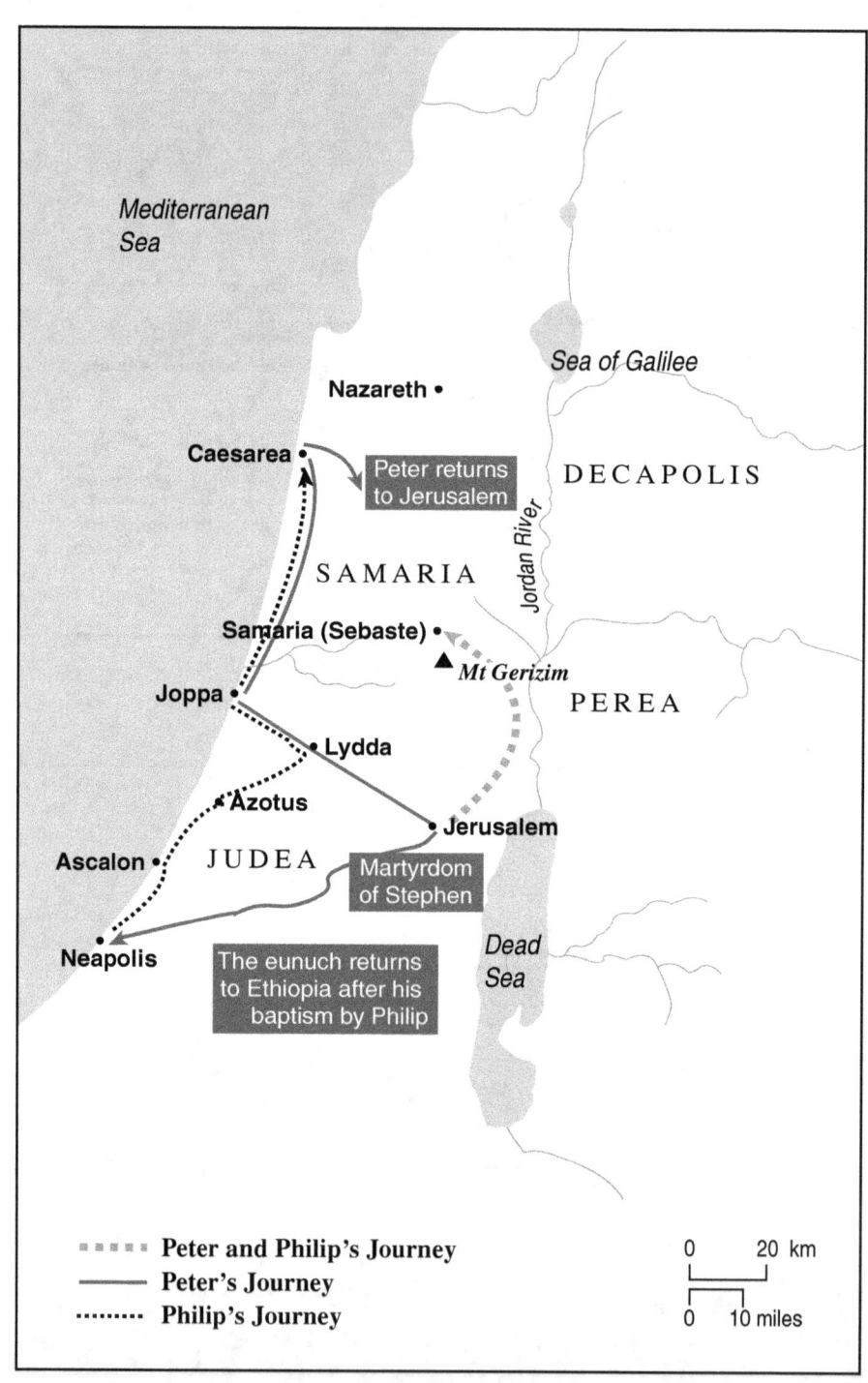

Journeys of Peter and Philip

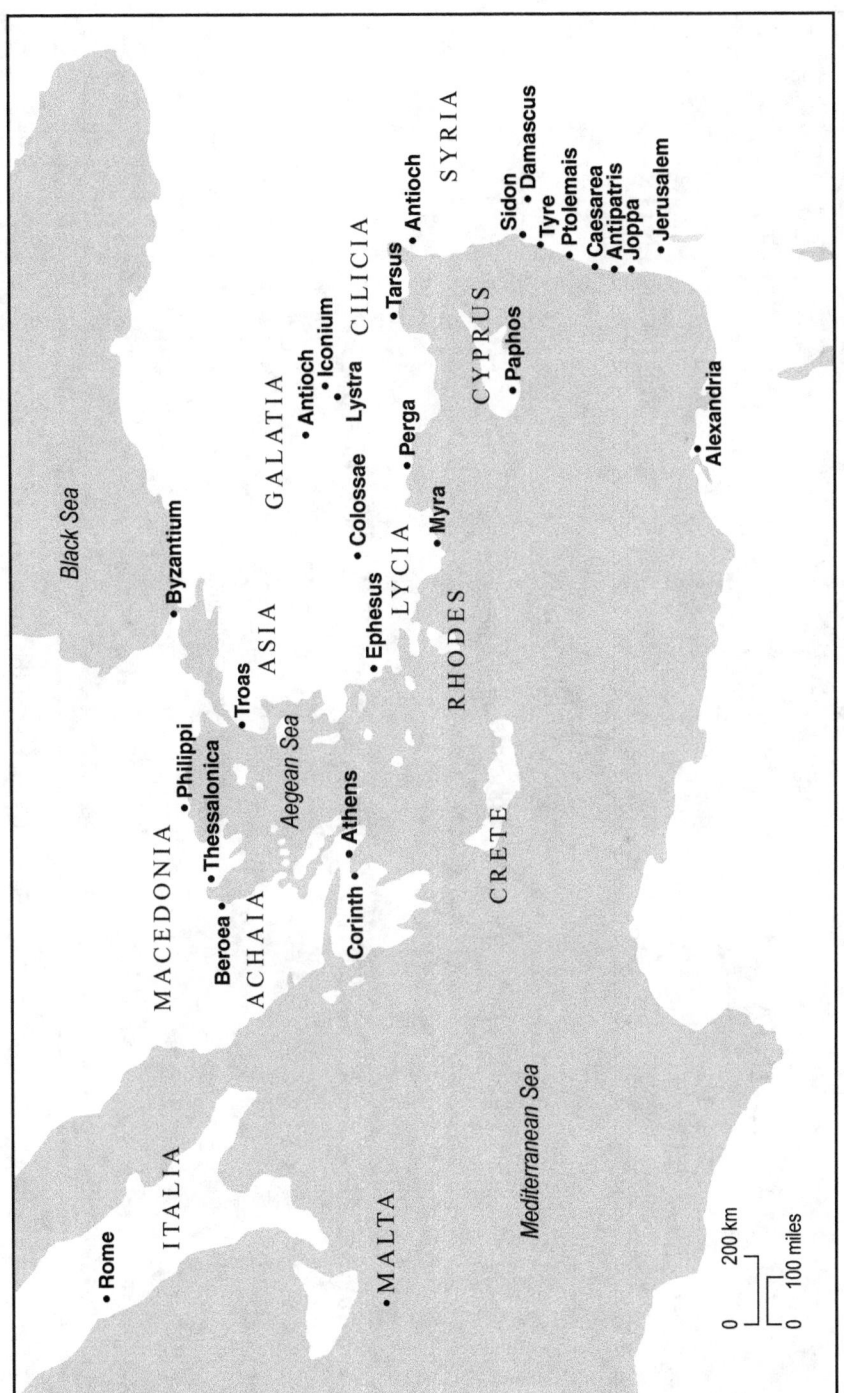

The World of Paul

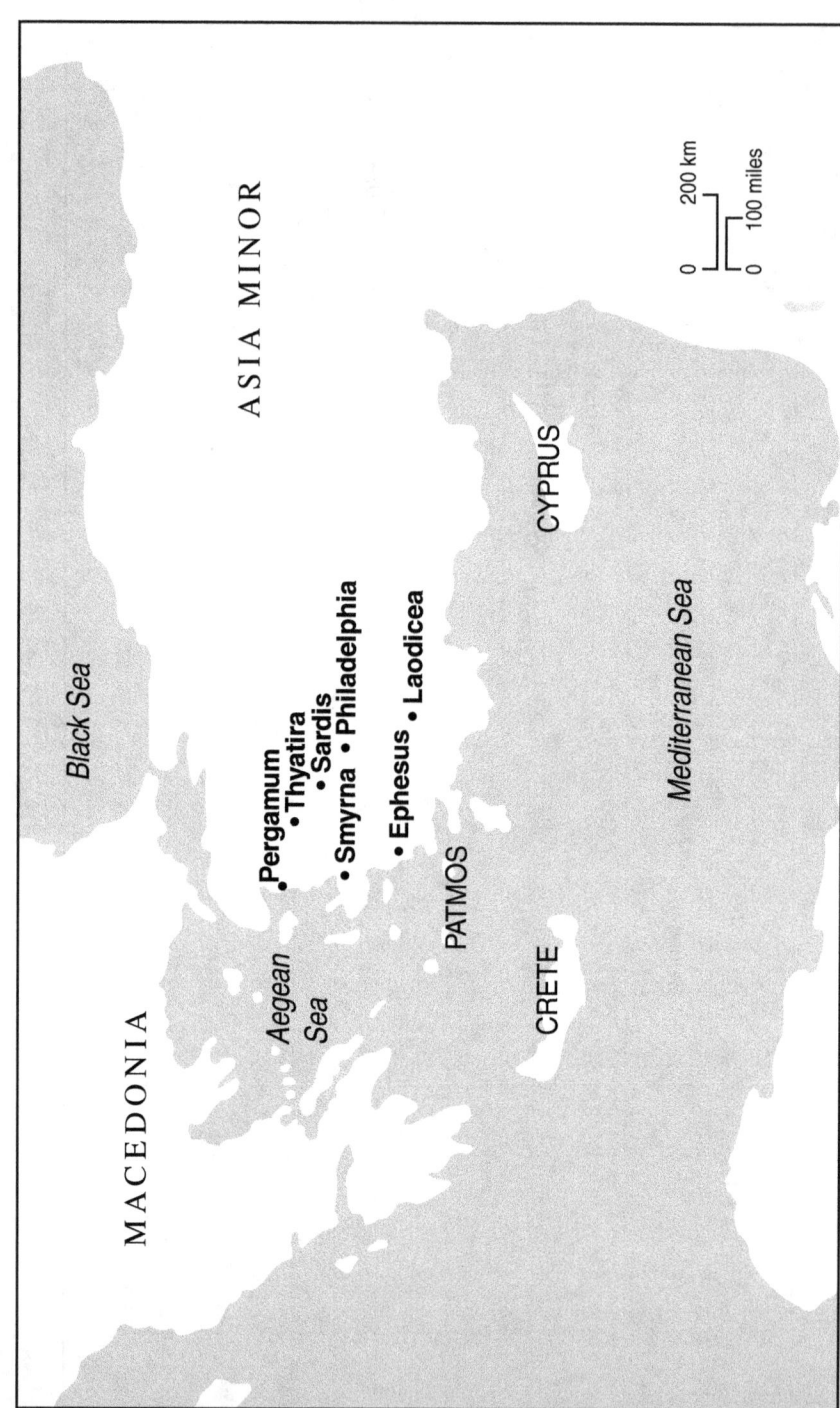

Seven Churches of the Revelation

The Gospel According to Matthew

Barbara E. Reid, O.P.

INTRODUCTION

In many ways the Gospel of Matthew holds primacy of place for Christians. It is the first book in the New Testament, and in patristic times it was thought to have been the first Gospel written. It was the Gospel most used in worship in the early church. And it has been the one most commented upon and preached, beginning with the first known commentary on the Gospel of Matthew by Origen (ca. A.D. 185–254).

Some of the best-loved passages in Scripture, as well as some of the most difficult sayings and teachings of Jesus, are found in this Gospel. This Gospel is distinctive for its emphasis on the Jewishness of Jesus, as authoritative teacher, whose life and ministry fulfill the Scriptures. Wisdom motifs also mark Matthew's presentation of Jesus. The assurance that Jesus is Emmanuel, "God-with-us," frames the whole Gospel (1:23; 28:20).

Author

Traditionally, the author of the First Gospel has been identified as Matthew, the tax collector who was called by Jesus (Matt 9:9) and sent out as an apostle (10:3). But, like many ancient authors, the evangelist nowhere identifies himself. The apostle Matthew may have been responsible for an earlier stage of the Gospel tradition, or he may have been a missionary to the area where this Gospel was composed. But most scholars agree that he was not the author of the Gospel. The composer copied extensively from the Gospel of Mark; an eyewitness would have told the story in his own words. It is also doubtful that a tax collector would have the kind of religious and literary education needed to produce this Gospel. Finally, the theological concerns in this Gospel are those of second-generation Christians. For the sake of brevity, however, we continue to refer to the author as "Matthew."

The evangelist was likely a Jewish Christian, writing for a community that was predominantly Jewish Christian. The author had extensive knowledge of the Hebrew Scriptures and a keen concern for Jewish observance and the role of the Law. A few scholars hold that Matthew was a Gentile because of his fierce anti-Jewish polemic, especially in chapter 23. In addition, he seems to have been unfamiliar with distinctions between Pharisees and Sadducees (e.g., 16:5-12; 22:23). He also appears to have misunderstood the Hebrew parallelism in Zechariah 9:9, thinking that the prophet is speaking of two beasts (21:1-9).

These, however, are not sure indicators that the evangelist was a Gentile. The anti-Jewish polemic can be explained as part of a Jewish Christian's attempt to define his community in relation to other Jews who have not followed Jesus. Matthew's juxtaposition of "Pharisees and Sadducees" is simply a generic phrase for the religious leaders at a time when Sadducees were no longer functioning. And the apparent misinterpretation of Zechariah 9:9 does not negate the evidence that the evangelist had a thorough knowledge of the Hebrew Scriptures, seen in his frequent biblical citations and allusions.

Date

Allusions to the destruction of the temple in Jerusalem (21:41-42; 22:7; 24:1-2) indicate that Matthew wrote after A.D. 70. A date of approximately A.D. 85 would allow time for circulation of the Gospel of Mark, one of Matthew's sources, which was composed close to A.D. 70.

Setting

We do not know the precise locale of the Matthean community, but a prosperous urban setting is likely from the twenty-six times that Matthew uses the word *polis*, "city" (cf. Mark, four times; Luke, sixteen times) and the twenty-eight times he mentions gold and silver (cf. Mark, one time; Luke, four times). Matthean Christians, like those of other locales, were women and men of diverse social and civic status, ethnic identities, and levels of wealth. They comprised only a small percentage of the total population. It was a mixed community of Jews and Gentiles, striving to work out their identity as the New Israel.

The oldest tradition, and still the most frequently suggested locale for the Matthean community, is Antioch of Syria. As the third largest city of the empire, it had a sizable Jewish population. It was an important center of emerging Christianity (Acts 11:19-26; 13:1-3), where Jewish and Gentile Christians struggled to work out their new relationship in Christ (Gal

2:11-13). Other possible settings include Caesarea Maritima, Sepphoris, Alexandria, Edessa, Tyre, and Sidon.

Jews and Christians

The relationship of the Matthean community to their Jewish counterparts is not entirely clear. Pointing to a rupture between the two groups are references to "their synagogues" (4:23; 9:35; 10:17; 12:9; 13:54), "your synagogues" (23:34), "their scribes" (7:29), "the Jews to the present [day]" (28:15), Jewish persecution of Jesus' followers (10:17; 23:34), and bitter denunciation of the scribes and Pharisees (ch. 23). There are stories of exemplary faith of those who are not Jews: the magi (2:1-12); a Roman centurion (8:5-13); a Canaanite woman (15:21-28); a Roman soldier (27:54). That Jesus' message is for Gentiles is seen clearly in the final commission (28:19) and more subtly in the inclusion of Ruth and Rahab in Jesus' genealogy (1:5); the coming of the magi to worship Jesus (2:11); the saying "in his name the Gentiles will hope" (12:21); the faith of a Canaanite woman (15:21-28); and in the parables of the tenants (21:33-43) and the marriage feast (22:1-10).

Yet, at the same time Matthew stresses a specific outreach to Israel. Only in Matthew does Jesus tell his disciples to confine their mission to the towns of Israel (10:5-6, 23; 15:24). And Matthew's Gospel, overall, is strongly Jewish in tone, emphasizing the abiding validity of the Law and fulfillment of the Scriptures.

This Gospel is designed to offer Matthew's Jewish Christians an account of Jesus' life and mission that enables them to relate to the two loyalties that pull them. On the one hand, they are Jews who are trying to define themselves in relation to other Jews who have not accepted Jesus. The latter see them as disloyal to the Mosaic covenant, engaged in dangerous partnership with pagans. On the other hand, they are Christians trying to relate to a community in which the majority is now Gentile, for whom the continued adherence of Jewish Christians to Jewish Law and customs would prove problematic. Matthew's Gospel tries to defend and define Jewish Christianity, on the one hand, and unity with Gentile Christians, on the other. It validates the community's continuity with the past promises to Israel, while at the same time justifies their new allegiance to the person of Christ and his mission.

A prime pastoral concern is the impact that Christian use of the Gospel of Matthew has had on Jewish-Christian relations. Statements in the Gospel that reflect the historical tensions of an emerging Jewish Christian community struggling to define itself in relation to other Jews need to be clearly explained as such so that they are not used to fuel anti-Judaism in contemporary contexts.

The Gospel According to Matthew

Composition

Eusebius, our earliest source of information on Matthew, quotes Papias of Hierapolis (ca. A.D. 125) as saying, "Matthew compiled the Sayings *(logia)* in the Hebrew language, and everyone translated them as well as they could" (*H.E.* 3.39.16). Irenaeus and Origen understood Eusebius's statement to mean that Matthew composed the Gospel in Hebrew or Aramaic. There is no firm evidence, however, that Papias was in a position to know the facts of the evangelist's method of composition. Moreover, his statement is full of ambiguities, and there is no indisputable evidence from the Greek text of the Gospel that it was translated from a Hebrew or Aramaic original.

Most modern scholars think that Matthew relied on the Marcan tradition as one of his prime sources. Matthew has retained some 600 of Mark's 660 verses, often streamlining the story and converting narration into dialogue. He follows Mark more closely from chapter 13 onward than in the first twelve chapters. Matthew adds infancy narratives and resurrection appearance stories, and recasts Jesus' teaching into five large blocks of discourse. He adapts the story to his predominantly Jewish Christian community by omitting explanations of Jewish customs (e.g., Matt 15:2; cf. Mark 7:3-4). Matthew also emphasizes more explicitly Jesus' fulfillment of the Scriptures, often citing specific texts from the Old Testament, particularly from the prophet Isaiah (e.g., 3:3; 4:14; 8:17). He gives more attention to the question of the Law and its observance (5:17-48).

Matthew, as well as Luke, also used a source called "Q" (for *Quelle*, German for "source") for some two hundred sayings of Jesus. Although no copy of this collection of sayings has yet been found, its existence can be supposed, due to the similarity in the wording and order of these sayings in the two Gospels. Finally, Matthew also relied on oral and written traditions, designated "M," that are unique to his Gospel.

The evangelist's own words capture well his method of composition: "every scribe who has been instructed in the kingdom of heaven is like the head of a household who brings from his storeroom both the new and the old" (13:52). Matthew both faithfully transmits and creatively shapes the tradition.

Structure

There are various ways to delineate the structure of Matthew's Gospel. Many think that Matthew's organizing principle was to present Jesus as the New Moses, giving five blocks of teaching, corresponding to the five books of the Pentateuch. A concluding formula, "When Jesus finished these words" (7:28; 19:1; cf. 11:1; 13:53; 26:1), marks off each section of narrative and discourse. Framing the whole are the infancy narratives and the passion-resurrection account. Benjamin W. Bacon was the first to propose this structure (*Studies in Matthew* [London: Constable, 1930]):

I. Infancy Narratives: 1:1–2:23
II. Five Books of Narratives and Discourses
    1. The Son Begins to Proclaim the Kingdom
       A. Narrative: Beginnings of the Ministry: 3:1–4:25
       B. Discourse: The Sermon on the Mount: 5:1–7:29
    2. The Mission of Jesus and His Disciples in Galilee
       A. Narrative: The Cycle of Nine Miracle Stories: 8:1–9:38
       B. Discourse: The Mission, Past and Future: 10:1–11:1
    3. Jesus Meets Opposition from Israel
       A. Narrative: Jesus Disputes with Israel: 11:2–12:50
       B. Discourse: Parables: 13:1-53
    4. The Messiah Forms the Church and Prophesies His Passion
       A. Narrative: The Itinerant Jesus Prepares for the Church by His Deeds: 13:54–17:27
       B. Discourse: Church Life and Order: 18:1-35
    5. The Messiah and the Church on the Way to the Passion
       A. Narrative: Jesus Leads His Disciples to the Cross as He Confounds His Enemies: 19:1–23:29
       B. Discourse: The Last Judgment: 24:1–25:46
III. Climax: Passion, Death, and Resurrection: 26:1–28:20

One problem with this structure is that it relegates the infancy and passion narratives to a marginal position, when, in fact, they are central to Matthew's story. Not all scholars agree that the motif of Jesus as the New Moses is the central organizing theme.

Some scholars see a chiastic pattern, with chapter 13 as the hinge (e.g., Peter Ellis, *Matthew: His Mind and His Message* [Collegeville: Liturgical Press, 1974]):

```
a     Narratives          chs. 1–4
 b     Sermons            chs. 5–7
  c     Narratives        chs. 8–9
   d     Sermons          ch. 10
    e     Narratives      chs. 11–12
     f     Sermon         ch. 13
    e'    Narratives      chs. 14–17
```

         d'   Sermons   ch. 18
      c'   Narratives   chs. 19–22
   b'   Sermons   chs. 23–25
a'   Narratives   chs. 26–28

In this configuration, Matthew 13:35 is the turning point: before it Jesus addresses all Jews; after it he devotes his attention solely to those who have already become his disciples.

Not all scholars see Matthew's structure in such neat patterns. Another approach is to regard Matthew more as a storyteller whose structure has more seams and turns and is determined by his retelling of Mark's story (e.g., Donald Senior, *What Are They Saying About Matthew?* [rev. ed.; New York/Mahwah: Paulist Press, 1996] 34–37):

I. 1:1–4:11 Origin of Jesus
II. 4:12–10:42 Galilean ministry of teaching (chs. 5–7) and healing (chs. 8–9) as a model for disciples' ministry (ch. 10)
III. 11:1–16:12 Varying responses to Jesus (rejection by Jewish opponents, faith of disciples)
IV. 16:13–20:34 Jesus and his disciples on the way to Jerusalem
V. 21:1–28:15 Jerusalem; Jesus' final days of teaching in the temple
VI. 28:16-20 Finale: Back to Galilee; disciples sent to the whole world; Jesus' abiding presence

This outline delineates the major movements and theological motifs of the Gospel, taking into account the fluid nature of narrative, and is the outline adopted in this commentary.

Purpose

This Gospel, with its emphasis on Jesus as authoritative Teacher and its stress on the ethical implications of discipleship, is a powerful catechetical tool. The evangelist may have composed it with the idea of providing a handbook for church leaders to assist them in preaching, teaching, and leading worship. This text is a particularly useful guide for helping believers discern what to keep from tradition and what to let go in changing circumstances. Its strategies for peace-making, reconciliation, and formation of community make this Gospel a potent pastoral aid. In every age it continues to bring new vision and hope to Christians in mission, inviting them into ever deeper relationship with Jesus, who remains always with them (1:23; 28:20).

Matthew 1

The commentaries in this booklet are all primarily based on the Greek text rather than the New American Bible translation. Accordingly, the translation of words or phrases in the commentaries sometimes differs from the translation provided at the top of the page. It is hoped that these complementary translations will enhance understanding of the Gospel.

COMMENTARY

THE ORIGINS OF JESUS

Matt 1:1–4:11

The opening chapters set the stage for the whole Gospel. Matthew, like Luke, begins with two introductory chapters of infancy narratives. The differences between the two accounts indicate that they did not share the same sources for this portion of the story. Matthew tells the story of Jesus' origins, the unusual circumstances surrounding his birth, and the threat to Jesus' life by Herod from the perspective of Joseph. Luke, in contrast, makes Mary central. Beginning with the infancy narratives, Matthew calls attention to the fulfillment of Scripture through Jesus' life and ministry. In the opening two chapters he highlights Jesus' Davidic descent and presents Jesus as recapitulating in his own life important events in the history of Israel. Matthew then situates Jesus in relation to John the Baptist, followed by his account of Jesus' testing in the desert in preparation for his public ministry.

1:1 Book of origins

The title verse introduces motifs that run throughout the whole of the Gospel. The opening phrase, "book of the genealogy *(biblos geneseōs),*" can also be translated "account of the birth" or "book of origin." This same phrase begins the account of creation in Genesis 2:4 (LXX) and the list of descendants of Adam in Genesis 5:1. Matthew narrates a new creative act of God. Three important titles follow. Jesus is *christos,* "messiah," the "anointed" of God. This term designates one who is set apart by God for particular service, such as kings (Pss 2:2; 89:20); priests (Lev 4:3, 5); prophets (1 Kgs 19:16). Some Jewish writings spoke of a coming messiah who would carry out God's purposes in a new way. Expectations surrounding this figure were by no means uniform. "Son of David," one of Matthew's favorite designations of Jesus (1:1, 20; 9:27; 12:23; 15:22; 20:30, 31; 21:9, 15; 22:42-45), underscores Jesus' royal status and also recalls God's choice of unlikely persons for important

7

roles in salvation history. "Son of Abraham" relates Jesus to the prime figure in Israel's history, the one whose struggle to be obedient to God brought blessing for all the peoples on earth.

1:2-17 The genealogy of Jesus (cf. Luke 3:23-38)

The genealogy functions not as a historical record but as a way to situate Jesus in relation to the memorable characters in Israel's history. It tells who he is by recounting who his people are. Drawing on 1 Chronicles 1:28-42; 3:5-24; Ruth 4:12-22, Matthew outlines Jesus' ancestors in three schematized sections of fourteen generations each (v. 17). The progression is from Israel's origin in Abraham to its glorious days under David (vv. 2-6a), then to the disastrous time of the Babylonian exile (vv. 6b-11), and finally to the hope-filled future with the birth of the Messiah (vv. 12-16). The number fourteen is symbolic. Some think that it represents the numerical value of the name David ($d + v + d = 4 + 6 + 4 = 14$), but more likely it signifies fullness or completion, being double the number seven, which symbolizes perfection in the Bible. A problem is that the last section has only thirteen generations. Matthew simply may have miscounted, or a name may have dropped out in the transmission.

The linear progression of thirty-nine male ancestors is broken at four points by the names of women. They are not the ones who would immediately come to mind as great figures from Israel's past. Each has an unusual twist to her story. Tamar (v. 3), after being widowed, took decisive action to coerce her father-in-law, Judah, to provide an heir for her (Gen 38). She conceived Perez and Zerah, who continued the Davidic line. Tamar is the only woman in the Hebrew Scriptures who is called righteous (Gen 38:26), a term that is of central importance to Matthew. Rahab (v. 5), a prostitute in Jericho (Josh 2), risked disobeying the orders of the king of Jericho and sheltered spies sent from Joshua to reconnoiter the land. She subsequently gave birth to Boaz, the great-grandfather of David. Ruth (v. 5), a Moabite woman, returned with her mother-in-law, Naomi, to Bethlehem, rather than stay with her own people after her husband Mahlon died. In Bethlehem, Ruth presented herself to Boaz at the threshing floor and conceived Obed, who carried forth the Davidic line. Finally, the wife of Uriah (v. 6) is the one who bore David's son Solomon after David arranged to have Uriah killed in battle (2 Sam 11).

Each story speaks of how women took bold actions outside the bounds of regular patriarchal marriage to enable God's purposes to be brought to fruition in unexpected ways. Not only were the circumstances unusual, but some of these women were also outsiders to Israel. Remembering their stories prepares for the extraordinary circumstances of Jesus' birth and the salvation he will ultimately extend to those outside Israel (28:19). The women's presence in the midst of the male ancestors of Jesus also signals the integral role that women disciples play in the community of Jesus' followers. They remind the reader that women are not marginal to the history of Israel or of Christianity.

1:18-25 The birth of Jesus

Both the genealogy and the account of the birth of Jesus stress the theme of continuity and discontinuity. The same faithful God of Israel continues to act with saving grace toward the New People of God in surprising ways. Verses 18-25 explain how Jesus is son of God through the holy Spirit and "son of David" through legal adoption by Joseph.

Marriage in first-century Palestine, usually arranged by the elders of the two families, took place in two steps. There was a formal betrothal before witnesses that was legally binding. The bride remained in her father's home for another year or so until the ceremony of her transfer to the home of her husband. Jesus' conception occurs between these two stages. The agency of the holy Spirit (v. 18) is not sexual; rather, the Spirit is God's life-giving power evident in creation (Gen 1:2; Ps 104:30) and in prophetic speech (22:43). It is the divine power at work in Jesus (3:16; 12:18, 28) and his disciples (10:20).

Joseph is faced with an impossible dilemma (v. 19). He is a righteous *(dikaios)* man, that is, one who is faithful to the demands of the Law. The Law prescribed death for adulterers (Deut 22:23-27). But Joseph is unwilling to publicly denounce his betrothed. A secret divorce is not possible; two witnesses are needed, and Mary's pregnancy would be known by all her relatives and townspeople. Joseph decides on a middle course: he will divorce her quietly (Deut 24:1), without stating the reasons. He will not initiate a public trial (Num 5:11-31). This solution, however, does not prevent Mary from being exposed to public shame. The only way to prevent this would be for Joseph to complete his marriage to her and adopt the child as his own. This is what the angel instructs him to do in a dream (v. 20).

This is the first of four instances in the infancy narratives in which an angel communicates with Joseph through a dream (see also 2:13, 19, 22). This is a common means of divine revelation in biblical tradition (see Gen 16:7-14; 37:5-11), especially to announce the birth of important figures in Israel's salvation (Ishmael, Gen 16:7-12; Isaac, Gen 17:1-19; Samson, Judg 13:3-22). There are usually five elements in annunciations: (1) the angel appears; (2) the person is afraid; (3) the angel gives reassurance, announces

Matthew 1

the birth, tells the child's name and its meaning, and foretells his great deeds; (4) the person objects; (5) the angel gives a sign. The angel assures Joseph (v. 20) that this child is of God, and not from any act of unfaithfulness. God asks Joseph and Mary to complete their commitment to each other in difficult circumstances. But they also have the promise that God will be with them throughout (v. 23). The angel pronounces and interprets the name of the child, Jesus (v. 21). This derivative of the name Joshua (in Hebrew, *Yeshua* or *Yeshu*) was common in the first century. It means "God helps" but came to be associated with the verb *yšʿ*, which means "God saves." Jesus' saving mission of forgiveness is enacted in healing stories (9:2-8) and is confirmed in his words to his disciples at his final supper with them (26:28).

The first of Matthew's quotations of the Hebrew Scriptures (vv. 22-23) is from Isaiah 7:14. As in 2:15, 17, 23; 4:14; 8:17; 13:35; 21:4; 26:56; 27:9, the citation begins with the formula "this took place to fulfill what the Lord had said through the prophet" (see also the Old Testament citations without this exact formula in 2:5; 3:3; 12:17; 13:14). In Isaiah 7:14 the oracle to King Ahaz refers to the birth of a royal son in the near future who will be a sign of hope to Judah. The Hebrew word *ʿalmâ*, "young woman," refers to the mother's age, not her sexual status (*betulah* is the Hebrew word for "virgin"). The Septuagint, the Greek translation, however, renders this *parthenos*, "virgin." Isaiah is predicting a birth that will come about in a normal way, but Matthew applies it to the virginal conception of Jesus. The promise of Emmanuel, "God is with us" frames the whole Gospel (1:23; cf. 28:20).

Joseph follows the angel's commands and completes the marriage ceremony with Mary (v. 24) and names her son Jesus (v. 25). Again Matthew underscores Mary's virginity at the time of Jesus' conception and birth. Verse 25 is ambiguous; it neither affirms nor denies Mary's perpetual virginity.

In this opening chapter Jesus' identity is established in relation to God, to the royal line of David, and to notable figures of Israel's past. He embodies the faithfulness and startling creativity of God, the kingliness of David, and the bold and socially questionable righteousness of the women in his ancestry and of his legal father, Joseph. In the next chapter the focus is on positive and negative responses to Jesus. Place names figure prominently, linking Jesus with significant events of Israel's history.

2:1-12 Herod and the magi

Matthew does not relate details about Jesus' birth (cf. Luke 2:1-7). What is of interest is the place and the initial reactions to him. Jesus' birth in

Bethlehem, the place where David was anointed king (1 Sam 16:1-13), highlights his royal Davidic identity. The reigning king is Herod the Great, who was appointed by the Roman senate to rule Judea in 40 B.C. A power struggle will ensue between Jesus and the Herodian kings over who bears the title "king of the Jews" (v. 2; see 27:11, 29, 37, 42).

The first visitors to the newborn Jesus are exotic characters from the East. The term "magi" originally referred to a caste of Persian priests, who served their king. They were not kings or wise men, but were adept at interpreting dreams. Here they appear to be astrologers who can interpret the movement of the stars. Magi were often associated with sorcery and magic, and were not always held in high regard (e.g., the magicians of Pharaoh, Exod 7–8). Matthew, however, portrays them very favorably. These Gentiles who respond positively to Jesus stand in stark contrast to Herod, the chief priests, and scribes (v. 4), foreshadowing the inclusion of non-Jews in the Jesus movement and the rejection of Jesus by many Jews.

There is much speculation whether the episodes in Matthew 2 have a historical basis or whether they are creations of Matthew to serve his theological purposes. With regard to the star, some think it was Halley's comet, which appeared in 12–11 B.C., others the convergence of Jupiter and Saturn in 7–6 B.C. Alternatively, Matthew may have created it in conformity with the belief in antiquity that royal births are marked by astrological phenomena. Or Matthew may have intended an allusion to the story of Balaam, a sorcerer from the East, who predicted that a star would come out of Jacob (Num 24:17).

The Scripture quotation in verse 6 is a conflation of Micah 5:1 and 2 Samuel 5:2. Matthew customarily adapts the biblical citations to fit his context and purposes. As Jesus' birthplace, Bethlehem is no longer "too small to be among the clans of Judah" (Mic 5:1), but now is "by no means least among the rulers of Judah" (Matt 2:6). And just as God called David from Bethlehem to shepherd Israel (2 Sam 5:2), so Jesus is shepherd to God's people (9:36; 26:31).

The response of the magi to Jesus matches that of disciples. The magi are overjoyed at the sign of Jesus' birth (2:10), just as disciples' initial acceptance of Jesus is marked by joy (13:20, 44) and is promised as an end-time reward (25:21, 23). The magi bow down in homage to Jesus (v. 11; cf. Herod's insincere desire to do so in v. 8), as do the disciples after the storm (14:33), the Canaanite woman pleading for her daughter (15:25), and the women disciples (28:9) and the Eleven (28:17) when they meet the risen Christ. The magi give to Jesus the most precious gifts they have (v. 11), just as disciples offer him their very selves (4:22; 8:15; 10:37-39). Finally, the magi, like Joseph, are obedient to divine commands conveyed in dreams (v. 12), just as disciples are to obey the covenant and Jesus' word (5:19).

The text does not say how many magi there were or exactly from where they came. The traditional number of three magi is derived from the three gifts that they bear (2:11). It is possible that Matthew has in mind Psalm 72:10, which speaks of the kings of Arabia and Sheba bringing gifts to the newly anointed king. Or he may have intended an allusion to Isaiah 60:6: "All from Sheba shall come / bearing gold and frankincense, / and proclaiming the praises of the LORD." In any case, Matthew sets the stage for all who will come from east and west to dine in the realm of God (8:11; 22:1-14).

2:13-15 The flight into Egypt

Each of the Gospels tells of those who not only reject Jesus but who actively seek to destroy him from the beginning of his ministry. Matthew begins this theme even earlier. From Jesus' very infancy Herod tries to kill him. As an intended victim of violence, the Matthean Jesus teaches his disciples how not to respond in kind to violence, to love their enemies, and to pray for their persecutors (5:38-48). There are circumstances, however, when flight is the necessary course of action (2:13-15).

Joseph takes center stage once again as he obediently fulfills the divine command conveyed in a dream (as also in 1:20-24; 2:19-20, 22). He takes Jesus and his mother to Egypt, a traditional place of refuge for Israelites (Gen 42–48; 1 Kgs 11:40; 2 Kgs 25:26; Jer 26:21; 41:16-18; 43:1-7).

The quotation from Hosea 11:1, "Out of Egypt I called my son" (2:15), seems odd, for the holy family is just going into Egypt. What Matthew presumes is that they will, indeed, leave Egypt, and by doing so Scripture is fulfilled in one more way. The text alludes to the Exodus and identifies Jesus with the paradigmatic saving event for Israel. Here begins Matthew's portrait of Jesus as a Moses-like figure, the authoritative Teacher of the Law.

2:16-18 The slaughter of the children

There is no verification of this event in historical records, but sources do attest to the cruelty of Herod. Josephus (*Ant.* 15; see also *T. Moses* 6:2-7) tells of how Herod, in his paranoia about his power, killed members of his own family. He also ordered the murder of one son from each of the leading families of Judea to ensure that there would be mourning at his funeral. The episode of the slaughter provides another parallel between Jesus and Moses, recalling Pharaoh's murder of the male Hebrew children (Exod

1:15-22). Just as God protected Moses through the actions of Moses' mother and sister and Pharaoh's daughter (Exod 2:1-10), so divine protection surrounds Jesus through the obedient actions of Joseph.

Once again, a citation from the Old Testament underscores the fulfillment of Scripture (2:17-18). Matthew adapts the quotation from Jeremiah 31:15 to fit his context and purpose. Rachel, who died en route from Bethel to Ephrath (which is identified with Bethlehem, Gen 35:16-21), is weeping for all the descendants of Israel who were marched off into exile. Ramah, about five miles north of Jerusalem, was on the route of the exile. Whereas Matthew uses this text to express the bitter lamentation of Israel over its slaughtered children, in Jeremiah it is part of an oracle that promises an end to the suffering and the return of the exiled Israelites (Jer 31:16).

2:19-23 A home in Nazareth

Just as Moses received a divine command to return home after the rulers who sought his life had died (Exod 4:19), so Joseph follows the angel's directive to go home to Israel with his family. Although Herod the Great is dead, his son Archelaus still poses a menace. Archelaus was the eldest of Herod's three sons among whom the kingdom was divided. He ruled Judea, Samaria, and Idumea for ten years (4 B.C.–A.D. 6), while Philip governed the area north and east of the Sea of Galilee, and Herod Antipas (14:1-12) controlled Galilee and Perea. Archelaus followed in his father's footsteps when it came to cruelty, but he did not have his father's administrative ability.

Joseph, once again directed by a dream, takes his family to Galilee (2:22), which enjoyed greater peace than Judea. They settle in Nazareth, some four miles from the city of Sepphoris, which Herod Antipas was building as his capital. It is possible that the availability of work for Joseph, an artisan (13:55), was also a motivating factor for their choice of Nazareth as their new home. Matthew, however, sees this as one more way in which Scripture is fulfilled. There is actually no text in the Scriptures that says "He shall be called a Nazorean" (v. 23). Most likely Matthew sees a wordplay with *nēṣer*, "shoot" or "branch," and intends an allusion to Isaiah 11:1, "A shoot shall sprout from the stump of Jesse." This reference to a Davidic royal heir once again highlights Jesus' identity as king in the line of David (see Rom 15:12; 1 Pet 4:14; Rev 5:5, which also interpret Isaiah 11:1 in relation to Jesus as Messiah). Another possibility is that the wordplay is with *nāzîr*, meaning "one dedicated to God." Nazirites, like Samson (Judg 13:5-7), took a vow, did not cut their hair, and did not drink wine (Num 6:1-21) as a sign that they were set apart for God. Matthew may have in mind an allusion to Isaiah

4:3, "he . . . will be called holy." In any event, this final verse of the infancy narratives rounds out the portrait of Jesus as the fulfillment of all God's promises to Israel.

3:1-12 The proclamation of John the Baptist

The scene switches now to a desert area of Judea, east of Jerusalem, where John is baptizing and preaching repentance. The precise locale of John's ministry is not known. The arid region in the vicinity of the Dead Sea, along the Jordan River (3:6), is likely. John prepares the way, proclaiming the identical message as Jesus, "Repent, for the kingdom of heaven is at hand!" (3:2; 4:17).

The phrase "kingdom of heaven," unique to this Gospel, occurs thirty-two times. While Mark and Luke speak of the "kingdom of God," Matthew avoids using the divine name, much as Jews reading the Torah substitute "Adonai" ("Lord") for "YHWH." The expression "kingdom of heaven" does not connote a geographic area, nor does it refer to something that will be manifest only at a later time in the transcendent realm. The term *basileia*, "kingdom," means "kingly rule" or "reign," not a territory. God's reign is already present and visible here and now with the coming of Jesus (3:2; 4:17; 12:28), though it awaits completion (6:10, 33; 16:27-28).

In the context of first-century Palestine, this proclamation of God's reign was a direct challenge to Roman imperial authority. Jesus and John offer an alternate vision of power—not one based on domination and exploitation, but one in which forgiveness, healing, and well-being are offered to all. "God-with-us" means divine authoritative power over all and empowerment of all who become disciples. It is difficult to find an adequate way to express this in English. The metaphor "kingdom" falls short, evoking an image of male monarchical rule. Other ways to translate *basileia* include "rule," "reign," "realm," or "kin-dom," expressing this powerful and empowering relatedness of God's people in terms that are more inclusive.

John prepares people to recognize this embodiment of God's saving power in Jesus by adapting the words of the prophet Isaiah (40:3). In its original context the prophecy referred to the return of Israel from exile in Babylon, through the desert, to their homeland. Matthew also wants to portray John in the likeness of Elijah, with his ascetic clothing and diet (3:4; 2 Kgs 1:8). Many expected that Elijah would return as precursor and messenger before the end time (Mal 3:1; 4:5-6; Sir 48:10-11). Matthew makes this identification of John with Elijah even more explicit at 11:10, 14; 17:11-13.

With hyperbole, Matthew depicts the response to John as overwhelmingly positive (v. 5). The baptism John offers differs in several ways from

Jewish ritual washing: it is a one-time ritual, not repeated; it is not self-administered, but performed by God's prophet; and it is not for the removal of ritual impurity, but signifies repentance from sin (vv. 2, 6).

Unique to Matthew is the naming of Pharisees and Sadducees among those who come to John to be baptized (v. 7). The Pharisees were lay religious leaders active in Palestine from the second century B.C. until the first century A.D. Their name probably derives from the Hebrew word *perushîm*, "separated ones." They differed from the Sadducees in their oral interpretation of the Law, their more progressive theology, such as belief in resurrection (Matt 22:23; Acts 23:8), and in their accommodation to Hellenism. Sadducees were priests, from a more elite class, based in Jerusalem, whose role disappeared after the fall of the temple in A.D. 70. Their name may have come from the high priestly family of Zadok (1 Kgs 1:26) or from the word *ṣaddîqîm*, "just ones." The Sadducees had influence over the temple personnel and the political elite, whereas the Pharisees appealed to ordinary laypeople, advising them how to live everyday life in faithfulness to the Torah.

Matthew's introduction of these two groups of religious leaders brings onto the stage the prime opponents of Jesus. The Sadducees have a limited role in the Gospel, mentioned again only at 16:1, 6-12, while the Pharisees appear at every turn, challenging Jesus on his table practices (9:11; 15:1), fasting (9:14), the source of his power (9:34; 12:24), sabbath observance (12:2), and his interpretation of the Law (19:3). The Pharisees are the prime movers in the conspiracy to destroy Jesus (12:14; 21:46; 22:15). John's fierce accusation here reveals their insincerity in coming to be baptized and prepares for Jesus' denunciation of their hypocrisy in chapter 23. John insists that anyone who is serious about repentance must demonstrate this visibly in his or her deeds (v. 8), a theme in Jesus' teaching as well (7:21-23). Birth into the people of God is not sufficient for salvation (v. 9). A note of urgency is struck in verse 10. The time for producing "good fruit" (one of Matthew's favorite expressions; see 7:15-20; 12:33-37; 13:8, 22-26; 21:19, 43; 26:29) is now.

After painting numerous parallels between John and Jesus, Matthew now clearly distinguishes the two (vv. 11-12). Jesus is more powerful than John; the baptizer is not even worthy to perform the task of a slave, to carry Jesus' sandals (v. 11). The reference to Jesus baptizing is best understood as a metaphor for his whole ministry of forgiveness, healing, and reconciliation. Only the Fourth Gospel mentions Jesus baptizing (John 3:22; 4:1-2).

Jesus' mission is one that refines with fire (see Zech 13:9; 1 Cor 3:13-15) and empowers people with the holy Spirit. And as a farmer separates wheat from chaff by tossing the harvested grain into the air with a winnowing fork, so Jesus will separate the righteous from the unrepentant at the end time (v. 12; see Jer 15:7). Unquenchable fire metaphorically expresses the unending pain of those whose choices separate them eternally from the love of God (similarly 13:30, 40-43, 49-50).

3:13-17 The baptism of Jesus

This episode further elaborates the relationship between Jesus and John and builds on the identification of Jesus as Son of God that was set forth in the infancy narratives. Only in Matthew's Gospel is there a dialogue between John and Jesus (vv. 14-15). It reflects the difficulties that the early Christians had with Jesus' undergoing John's baptism of repentance. First, if Jesus is greater than John (as John asserted in verse 11), then why does he appear subordinate here? A second problem is that as Christians came to believe in Jesus' sinlessness from birth, they struggled to explain why he would have sought John's baptism of repentance.

In Jesus' reply (v. 15) we find two key Matthean terms: "fulfill" and "righteousness." The theme of fulfillment of God's promises to Israel in the person of Jesus has been stressed from the outset with citations of Scripture (1:22-23; 2:5-6, 15, 17-18, 23) and in the way Jesus' life has replicated the history of his people. Matthew introduced his theme of righteousness when he applied the term to Joseph (1:19); now he affirms Jesus' righteousness. This is also a quality expected of disciples of Jesus (5:6, 10, 20; 6:33). The term *dikaiosynē*, "righteousness," denotes right relationship with God, self, others, and all creation. From a Jewish perspective, righteousness is accomplished through faithfulness to the demands of the covenant, which the Matthean Jesus affirms (5:17-20).

A divine revelation further interprets the happening (vv. 16-17). "Rend[ing] the heavens" is a familiar expression from prophetic literature (Isa 63:19; cf. Ezek 1:1). People in Jesus' day imagined that the world is divided into three tiers: the heavens, the earth, and the underworld. An opening of the heavens signals a moment when human beings are in direct communication with the divine. The descent of the Spirit recalls the messianic prophecies of Isaiah: "the Spirit of the LORD shall rest upon him" (11:2; cf. 61:1) and "the spirit of God" that swept over the waters at creation (Gen 1:2; the Hebrew *rûaḥ ʾelohîm* can also be translated "a mighty wind," as in the NAB).

A heavenly voice (v. 17) is the counterpoint to the voice of John in the desert (v. 3). While in the Gospels of Mark (1:11) and Luke (3:22) the voice is directed only to Jesus: "*You* are my beloved Son," in Matthew the revelation is to all: "*This* is my beloved Son" (v. 17; emphasis added). This declaration carries multiple meanings. In the Hebrew Scriptures "son of God" occurs with three different nuances: (1) a chosen servant of God (the Hebrew *'ebed*, "servant," is rendered *pais* in the LXX, which can also be translated "child") who will play a saving role for Israel and who will suffer for it (Isa 42:1; see 12:18-21, where Matthew explicitly presents Jesus as fulfilling this text); (2) a royal Davidic son (see Psalm 2:7, a coronation psalm, in which God assures the Davidic king, "You are my son"); (3) Israel is God's firstborn son (Exod 4:22-23). The filial relationship between God and Israel is now personified in Jesus. There is also an echo of Genesis 22:2, where God instructs Abraham, "Take your son Isaac, your only one, whom you love" to the land of Moriah to offer him up. There is a foreshadowing that the sacrificial act that God interrupted with Isaac will be fulfilled with Jesus.

Vivid metaphors of the heavens opening, the Spirit descending, and the voice of God speaking (see also 17:5) bring to a dramatic climax a scene that further establishes Jesus' identity as Son of God and Son of David. The baptism scene also points ahead to Jesus' death, where the centurion and his companions affirm, "Truly, this was the Son of God!" (Matt 27:54).

4:1-11 Testing in the wilderness

This is the final episode of the first section of the Gospel, which tells of Jesus' origins, establishes his identity, and sets the stage for the beginning of his public ministry. Matthew, like Luke (4:1-13), draws both from Mark's brief notice of Jesus' testing in the desert (Mark 1:12-13) and Q (see p. 8), which supplies a dialogue between Jesus and the devil. There is a mythical quality to the scene, as the evangelist has telescoped into one episode temptations that Jesus likely faced repeatedly throughout his life (Heb 4:15). There are also echoes of Israel's sojourn in the desert. But unlike Israel, who proved unfaithful during that time by grumbling against Moses, and testing God, Jesus stays steadfastly faithful to God's word. The fast for forty days and nights (v. 2) echoes that of Moses (Deut 9:18; so also Elijah, 1 Kgs 19:8). The motif of the mountain (v. 8) calls to mind Moses' encounter with God on Mount Sinai. Matthew uses this motif frequently (5:1–8:1; 15:29-31; 17:1-8; 28:16-20) to present Jesus as the authoritative interpreter of the Law.

While the first three chapters clearly establish Jesus' identity as "Son of God" for the reader, the tester (4:3) articulates three fundamental doubts. "*If* you are the Son of God . . ." (vv. 3, 6; emphasis added) functions both to confront the readers about any lingering doubts about what it means for Jesus to be beloved child of God and also demands that they examine their own answers to these tests as followers of God's own beloved. Each cuts to the core of what it means to be faithfully centered on God.

The first temptation is to be intent on gratifying one's own hungers (v. 3). Jesus counters with a quotation from Deuteronomy 8:3. In subsequent episodes Jesus enacts God's care for hungry people by feeding them with both physical and spiritual food (5:1–7:29; 14:31-21; 15:32-39; 26:26-30).

The second test concerns the desire for a showy display of power to prove God's might (v. 5). The devil takes Jesus to the parapet (literally, the "wing") of the temple and urges him to jump off to prove God's ability to rescue. He quotes Psalm 91, which assures that God's angels will let no evil befall the beloved. Jesus counters with another text from Deuteronomy (6:16). As the Gospel continues, Jesus remains true to his mission as "God-with-us," meeting people in their human needs and bringing them healing and empowerment. He does not compel people to believe through flashy displays of power, but in the paradoxical manner of God in human flesh.

The third test concerns idolatrous misuse of power (vv. 8-9). A human face is put on this temptation when Jesus makes the same reply, "Get away, Satan!" (v. 10), to Peter when he rejects Jesus' prediction of his passion (16:21-23). Here Jesus invokes Deuteronomy 6:13, bringing the focus again to true power and worship, which centers on God alone. The same verb, *proskyneō*, "prostrate," (v. 9) is used of the magi's adoration of the infant Jesus (2:2, 8), and of the women disciples' worship at the feet of the risen Christ (28:9).

Although the devil departs at the conclusion of this episode (v. 11), Matthew indicates that these tests haunted Jesus to the end. Even as he was dying a variation on these temptations surfaces: "He trusted in God; let him deliver him now if he wants him. For he said, 'I am the Son of God'" (27:43). The ministrations of angels (4:11) signal that divine protection and power always surround God's beloved ones, no matter how intense the trial.

THE BEGINNINGS OF THE GALILEAN MINISTRY
Matt 4:12–10:42

In the second main section of the Gospel, Matthew narrates the beginnings of Jesus' ministry in Galilee. After his opening proclamation of his mission (4:12-17), Jesus calls the first of his disciples (4:18-22) and begins to preach and heal multitudes of people (4:23-25). Then follows his magisterial teaching in the Sermon on the Mount (5:1–7:28), a series of healing stories (8:1–9:37), and the sending of the disciples in mission (10:1-42).

4:12-17 The announcement of the nearness of God's reign

Matthew, following Mark (1:14), links the beginning of Jesus' public ministry with John's arrest (4:12). He gives a fuller account of John's death at the hands of Herod Antipas at 14:3-12. It seems odd that Jesus would go to Galilee upon news of John's arrest; it may be that Jesus intended to take up the mission where John left off (see John 3:22-23; 4:1-3). The expression "withdrew to Galilee" (v. 12) clashes with Jesus' preaching in public (v. 17), and hints at the danger Jesus faces by ministering there.

Jesus resettles in Capernaum (see also 8:5; 9:1), a fishing village at the northwest corner of the Sea of Galilee. It lay along an important trade route, the *Via Maris*, "the Way of the Sea." This would have ensured a greater audience for his ministry than the tiny village of Nazareth (see 13:53-58, where Jesus is rejected in his hometown). For Matthew, the reason for Jesus' relocation is to fulfill Scripture (vv. 14-16). He adapts an oracle from the prophet Isaiah (9:1-2) to announce the hope that lies beyond death with the coming of Jesus. The oracle was originally addressed to Galilee after the Assyrian invasion in 732 B.C. To make the link, Matthew reminds the reader that Capernaum was in the general region of the territory allotted to the tribes of Zebulun and Naphtali (Josh 19:10-16; 19:32-39). The Matthean Jesus stresses at the outset that his mission is only to Israel (10:5; 15:24). But here again, as in the story of the magi (2:1-12), with the expression "Galilee of the Gentiles" (v. 15) there is a foreshadowing of the expansion of Jesus' mission to the Gentiles (28:16-20).

Jesus' opening proclamation of his mission (v. 17) matches that of John the Baptist (3:2). (See above, at 3:2, for comments on the meaning of "the kingdom of heaven.") The phrase "at hand" translates a word (*engiken*) that is ambiguous in Greek. It can mean "has arrived" or "has drawn near." Matthew (as also Mark 1:15) expresses that there is a new inbreaking of God's reign with the arrival of Jesus, but it is not yet fully accomplished. The expression "from that time on" (v. 17) marks an important transition in the story, as also at 16:21, where the phrase signals a new focus on Jesus' coming passion in Jerusalem.

4:18-22 The call of the first disciples

In this stylized account of the call of Jesus' first followers, Matthew introduces key characteristics of discipleship, which help readers reflect on their own response to Jesus. First, the invitation is initiated by Jesus. Unlike disciples of rabbis, who would seek out the one with whom they wanted to study, these disciples of Jesus are invited by him. They are going about their everyday work, casting their nets into the sea and making repairs to them when Jesus encounters them at the seaside. Far from being "uneducated, ordinary men," as the polemical reference to Peter and John in Acts 4:13 states, these fishermen were savvy businessmen who managed employees (Mark 1:20) and located their industry in an advantageous tax district. Philip and Andrew were originally from Bethsaida (John 1:44), in the territory ruled by Philip. It is likely that they relocated to Capernaum for a tax break.

Jesus' invitation is to an active mission. Discipleship does not entail merely intellectual assent, but following Jesus in every respect, becoming "fishers" of other persons (see Jer 16:16). There is a stress on the totality and immediacy of the response of these first disciples. The radical changes that the life of discipleship demands are symbolized in the leaving of their nets, their boat, and their father. In the story there is no preparation for this encounter with Jesus. There is something so compelling about his person and message that Peter, Andrew, James, and John immediately follow him.

The communal dimension of discipleship is emphasized by the coming of the call to two sets of brothers. That the call can be rejected is shown in the story of the rich young man (19:16-22). The inclusion of marginalized people in Jesus' entourage is exemplified in the call of the toll collector Matthew (9:9-13). Others for whom there is no call story but who are clearly disciples of Jesus include the women "who had followed Jesus from Galilee, ministering to him" (27:55), among whom were "Mary Magdalene and Mary the mother of James and Joseph, and the mother of the sons of Zebedee" (27:56). Another latecomer in the Gospel is Joseph of Arimathea, whom Matthew also identifies as "a disciple of Jesus" (27:57).

4:23-25 The spreading of Jesus' fame

A summary statement of Jesus' successful ministry of teaching, preaching, and healing makes a bridge between the opening proclamation and initial formation of disciples to the advanced teaching (chs. 5–7) and further healing (chs. 8–9) that precede the sending out of the disciples on mission (ch. 10). Unlike the Gospel of John, which shows Jesus moving between Galilee and Jerusalem, in the Synoptic Gospels Jesus' ministry first centers only on Galilee (v. 23). He makes only one fateful trip to Jerusalem, which begins at Matthew 19:1. Characteristic of Matthew's emphasis on the primacy of Jesus' mission to Israel (10:5; 15:24) is that Jesus teaches in synagogues (v. 23). The expression "their synagogues" reflects the tension in Matthew's day between his predominantly Jewish Christian community and Jews who have not chosen to follow Jesus (see above, "Jews and Christians," in the introductory comments, p. 7).

The geographical sweep indicates those places from which Matthean Christians hailed or places in which the Gospel first circulated. Syria (v. 24) most likely refers to the Roman province by that name, which included

Palestine and the other places listed in verse 25. "Decapolis, Ten Cities," most of which were on the east side of the Jordan River, were cities in which Hellenistic culture flourished and which were thought of as Gentile regions. The names thus hint at a mixture of Jews and Gentiles. This great multitude becomes the audience for Jesus' Sermon on the Mount.

THE SERMON ON THE MOUNT
Matt 5:1–7:28

This is probably the best known and most quoted part of the Gospel. Luke has a comparable sermon, but sets it on a plain (6:17-49). Matthew's setting on a mountain (5:1; also at 4:8; 15:29-31; 17:1-8; 28:16-20) makes Jesus a Moses-like figure, but one who exceeds Moses as authoritative Teacher of the Law. This is the first of five major discourses in the Gospel (followed by 10:1–11:1 on mission; 13:1-53 on parables; 18:1-35 on church life and order; 24:1–25:46 on the last judgment). It may have originated as a collection of the core teachings of Jesus, specifically aimed at Jewish Christians, helping them relate their new faith to their Jewish heritage. The emphasis on fulfillment of the Law and the prophets (5:17; 7:12) encircles the whole.

Several ways of outlining the structure of the sermon are possible. The Beatitudes (5:1-12) and parabolic sayings about publicly living and proclaiming them (5:13-16) lead off. Then follow six antithetical statements about the rigorous demands of discipleship (5:17-48). Jesus' interpretation of the Law is more stringent than that of the scribes and Pharisees (5:20). Next are teachings about various attitudes and actions incumbent on disciples (6:1–7:12). A highlight in this section is the Our Father (6:9-15). Rounding out the sermon are concluding exhortations and warnings (7:13-28).

5:1-12 The Beatitudes

The summary statement in 4:23-25 has brought on stage a great multitude who have been healed by Jesus and have heard his teaching. This crowd, along with Jesus' disciples, are now the recipients of detailed instruction. Throughout the Gospel the crowds are generally favorable to Jesus, but at the passion narrative they become adversarial (27:20-26). Jesus assumes a sitting position, typical of teachers (5:1; Ezek 8:1) and of rulers (Matt 27:19).

The Beatitudes have echoes in Wisdom literature and the prophets (e.g., Prov 3:13; 28:14; Sir 25:7-9; 48:1-11; Isa 30:18; 32:20). Matthew casts them in eight parallel statements of blessing and promise in the third person plural

Matthew 5

(vv. 3-10) and concludes with a ninth beatitude in the second person plural (v. 11). Luke structures them into four blessings followed by four "woes" (6:20-26). Matthew relegates the woes to an extended denunciation of the scribes and Pharisees in 23:13-23. The rewards assured to disciples are already experienced to a degree in the present time ("Blessed *are* . . ."; emphasis added) but await fulfillment at the end time.

In the first blessing (v. 3), *ptōchos* denotes "beggar," that is, one who is destitute. The theme of God's care for the poor is found abundantly in the Old Testament (e.g., Exod 22:25-27; Deut 15:7-11; Isa 61:1). That wealth is an obstacle to discipleship surfaces again in Jesus' teaching at 19:16-30. Matthew's addition of "in spirit" (cf. Luke 6:20) likely reflects the struggle of those in the community with greater material wealth to live as disciples. The assurance of the "kingdom of heaven" frames the Beatitudes (vv. 3, 10).

The second beatitude (v. 4) speaks of comfort to those who mourn. This recalls the comfort Isaiah gives to Zion when mourning the destruction of the temple (Isa 61:1-3). It also points forward to the women who perform the rites of mourning for Jesus surrounding his death (26:6-13; 27:55-56, 61; 28:1-10) and the joy they experience in encountering him once again alive (28:8).

The third beatitude, "Blessed are the meek" (v. 5), does not teach disciples to be shrinking violets; rather, the word *praeis* connotes those who are not overly impressed by their own self-importance—in other words, those who are appropriately humble and considerate. This beatitude echoes Psalm 37:11, where the Hebrew word for meek, ʿanāwîm, is essentially equivalent to "poor in spirit." The promise of land has an echo in 1 Enoch 5:7, where the eschatological promise refers not only to Israel but to the whole earth.

In the fourth beatitude there is an allusion to Psalm 107:5, 8-9, in which God satisfies those who hunger and thirst. Matthew adds one of his key terms, "righteousness" (see also 1:19; 3:15; 6:33), that is, right relation with God, self, others, and all creation. Disciples are to seek it actively, "hunger and thirst" for it (v. 6), through faithfulness to the demands of the covenant (5:17-20). However, there is a sober warning in the eighth beatitude that they will be persecuted for the sake of righteousness (v. 10).

The fifth beatitude assures those who exercise mercy that the same will be shown to them (v. 7). A similar assertion is made about forgiveness in the prayer Jesus teaches his disciples (6:12; see also 18:23-35). Twice in conflictual situations Jesus admonishes his opponents to learn the meaning of mercy (9:13; 12:7). At 23:23 Jesus lists mercy, along with judgment and fidelity, as the weightier matters of the Law.

In Psalm 24:4, a hymn for processing into the temple, the "clean of hand and pure of heart" are those who are not idolaters and who have not sworn falsely. They are the ones who are able to stand in the holy place and receive blessings and justice from God. In the sixth beatitude (v. 8) the promise of "seeing God" refers not to encountering God in the temple in Jerusalem (as in Pss 11:7; 17:15; 27:4; 42:3), but is an eschatological promise to be in God's presence face to face (cf. Exod 3:6; 19:21; 33:20, 23, reflecting the belief that human beings could not see God and live).

The seventh beatitude (v. 9) assures those who devote themselves to peacemaking that they will be sons and daughters of God. As Jesus has been shown to be Son of God (1:1; 2:15; 3:17), so too disciples who learn his ways of forgiveness and reconciliation share in the same intimate relationship with God. Jesus gives concrete strategies for peacemaking in 5:38-48 and 18:1-35. In the ears of Jewish Christians, this beatitude would also be evocative of God's gift of *shālôm*, not just the absence of strife, but a pervasive well-being in every arena of life.

The eighth beatitude (v. 10) circles back to the fourth one, regarding righteousness (v. 6), and promises attainment of the reign of God, as does the first (v. 3). The kinds of persecution that Matthean Christians likely faced were economic harassment, conflicts with Jews who did not join them, struggles over the degree of accommodation to Hellenistic culture, and the like. Jesus speaks to his disciples more concretely about the kinds of persecution they may face when he first sends them out on mission (10:16-42).

The ninth beatitude (v. 11) speaks of verbal abuse that disciples suffer because of Jesus. They are to find joy in the midst of such trials through hope in a heavenly reward and from the assurance that they are being prophetic—a ministry that always entails rejection by some (v. 12; 23:29-34).

5:13-16 Salt and light

With two metaphors Jesus speaks to his followers about how they already are salt of the earth (v. 13) and light of the world (v. 14). The first word, *you*, is emphatic in both verses, contrasting Matthean Christians with their counterparts in the synagogue. Salt was a critical necessity in the ancient world (Sir 39:26). It was used for seasoning, preservation, and purifying (2 Kgs 2:19-22). It was used to ratify covenants (Num 18:29; 2 Chr 13:5) and in liturgical functions (Exod 30:35; Lev 2:13; Ezek 43:24; Ezra 6:9). To eat salt with someone signifies a bond of friendship and loyalty (Ezra 4:14; Acts 1:4). Salts in the soil are needed for its fecundity, but soil that is "nothing but sulphur and salt" is a desert wasteland (Deut 29:22; similarly

Ps 107:34; Job 39:6; Jer 17:6; Zeph 2:9). Salt scattered on a conquered city symbolically reinforced its devastation (Judg 9:45).

In telling his disciples "You are the salt of the earth," Jesus can draw on any of these symbols. Disciples preserve, purify, and judge, drawing out the savor of God's love in the world. The puzzle about how salt may lose its taste is probably best answered by salt being diluted or dissolved. Coming on the heels of Jesus' exhortation to rejoice when persecuted (vv. 11-12), it is likely a warning to disciples not to let their ardor dissipate under the rigors of persecution.

Disciples are also "the light of the world," like a city set on a mountain that cannot be hidden (v. 14). The metaphor has a political twist, since Cicero (*Cataline* 4.6) described Rome as a "light to the whole world." It is Jesus' beatitudinal way of life that is light to the world, not the imperial domination system. Just as the city on a mountain cannot be hidden, a lamp is not lit and then immediately extinguished (v. 15). One does not waste precious fuel oil this way. Using a vessel (*modios*, literally, a "bushel basket") to put out the light would prevent dangerous sparks from spreading.

These two images speak of the all-encompassing nature of the witness of disciples: as salt and light they influence the whole world. These metaphors also show that the disciples do not draw attention to themselves. Just as salt is most effective when it is not noticed in well-seasoned food and a lamp serves to illumine the other objects in the room, so the effect of disciples' good works is to point to God, who is glorified. In verse 16 Matthew gives the first of many references to God as "Father." See remarks at 6:9-16.

5:17-20 The Law and righteousness

These verses clearly set forth Jesus' relationship to the Law. He is a thoroughly observant Jew who is devoted to keeping the Law. He does not replace the Law, nor does he break it; rather, he fulfills it, bringing it to its intended purpose. He is authentic interpreter of the Law for a changed situation.

5:21-26 On anger

This is the first of six antithetical statements (5:21-48), each of which begins with "You have heard that it was said . . . ," followed by a command introduced with the formula "But I say to you . . ." In each instance Jesus declares a former understanding of the Law inadequate as he places more stringent demands on his disciples. Each of the six examples addresses an aspect of right relation among people in a covenantal faith community. The word *adelphos* in verse 22 refers not only to blood relations but to a Christian "brother or sister."

Killing another person is the epitome of broken relationships. The Law given to Moses forbids killing (Exod 20:13; Deut 5:18). Jesus' command is to defuse anger and work toward reconciliation before the rupture in the relationship reaches a murderous stage. He gives three concrete examples. The first is to avoid insulting one another. *Rēqāʾ* is an Aramaic word meaning approximately the same thing as *morē* in Greek, which is "you fool" (v. 22). Second, liturgical sacrifices do not cover over broken relationships. One must attempt face-to-face reconciliation before making ritual offerings (vv. 23-24; see similar injunctions in Isa 1; Prov 15:8; 21:3, 27; Sir 34:21-27; 35:1-4). The third example warns against letting conflicts escalate to the point of litigation in court (vv. 25-26). For disciples, it is imperative to defuse anger and attempt reconciliation, so that no conflict becomes murderous. One who lets anger simmer and grow will face judgment (v. 22) before God.

The Sanhedrin, Gehenna, and prison are all ways of speaking about judgment. The Sanhedrin was the highest Jewish judicial council (see 26:57-68). Gehenna comes from the Hebrew *gê hinnōm*, "Hinnom valley," which runs south-southwest of Jerusalem. It came to represent the place of fiery judgment, because there the fires of the Molech cult burned, and later, smoldering refuse. Prison was not used to hold debtors or other offenders long term, as verse 26 implies. Once guilt was determined, one would be executed, deported, or sold into slavery. The point is that the consequences for not working at reconciliation are dire. It is not enough for Jesus' disciples to avoid killing; they must actively seek to defuse anger and pursue right relation with all. Here Jesus is not addressing righteous anger, that is, outrage at injustice that gives energy to work toward change.

5:27-30 On adultery

Just as anger is prohibited (vv. 21-26) as the first step toward murder, so the lustful look is condemned as the prelude to adultery. The Law forbids not only adultery (Exod 20:14; Deut 5:18) but also covetousness (Exod 20:17) of another person's spouse and of their possessions. Vivid metaphors of tearing out one's eye and cutting off a hand convey the seriousness of the sin of lust. On Gehenna, see verse 22.

5:31-32 On divorce

The third example builds on the previous one, adding that divorce is also a form of adultery. It is addressed to males and reflects the Jewish custom that only they could initiate divorce. The process for doing so is found in Deuteronomy 24:1. A fuller elaboration of Jesus' teaching on divorce is found in Matthew 19:1-12. Here the reasoning is not given, simply the prohibition, along with the exception for *porneia* (v. 32). Scholars are divided over whether this word connotes sexual misconduct, that is, adultery, or whether it refers to marriage to close kin, which was forbidden in Jewish law (Lev 18:6-18; see also Acts 15:20, 29).

5:33-37 On taking oaths

Now the focus shifts to address honesty in relationships. Whereas Leviticus 19:12 admonished, "You shall not swear falsely by my name, thus profaning the name of your God," Jesus insists that relations among Christians be so transparent as to end the need for taking oaths at all. Just as Matthew uses *the reign of heaven*, avoiding the use of "God" (see comments at 3:2), so here he employs "heaven" (v. 34), "earth" (see Ps 24:1), and "Jerusalem" (v. 35) as euphemisms for God. Verse 36 makes an ironic reference to coloring one's hair, a practice already used in antiquity. Christian integrity must be such that there is no need to swear in order to make another believe the veracity of their word.

5:38-42 On nonretaliation

The fifth unit concerns the *ius talionis* (Lev 24:20), which was based on the principle of equal reciprocity. The Law placed limits on retribution, so as to curtail escalating cycles of vengeance. As in the previous four examples, Jesus demands more, thus going to the core of the attitudes and actions necessary to adequately fulfill what the Law intends. The principle is articulated in verse 39a, and four concrete examples follow in verses 39b-42. Verse 39a is best translated "do not retaliate against the evildoer." The verb *antistēnai* most often carries the connotation "resist violently" or "armed resistance in military encounters" (e.g., Eph 6:13).

A command not to resist evil makes little sense on the lips of Jesus, when the whole Gospel shows him doing just the opposite. The issue here is *how* the disciple is to confront evil. The examples that follow show how nonretaliation is a strategy that breaks cycles of violence in confrontations between persons of unequal power and status. In the first three the person addressed is a victim of an injustice inflicted by a more powerful person. Retaliation by the injured party is not a realistic option. The expected response is submission. There is an alternate way to respond by actively confronting the injustice with a positive and provocative act that can break the cycle of violence and begin a different one in which gestures of reconciliation can be reciprocated.

The first example (v. 39b) involves a backhanded slap (only the right hand would be used for striking another), meant to insult and humiliate.

Turning the other cheek is a creative response that robs the aggressor of the power to humiliate and shames the one who intended to inflict shame. It interrupts the cycle of violence, which is the first step toward restoration of right relation. It could begin to move the aggressor toward repentance, leading to reconciliation.

In a similar way, a debtor who stands naked in court, after handing over both under and outer garments to a creditor (v. 40), performs a shocking act that places shame on the creditor. See Genesis 9:20-27, which asserts that it is the one who views another's nakedness who is shamed. Isaiah (20:1-6) made use of this strategy. This tactic exposes the injustice of the economic system to which the creditor subscribes and opens the possibility that he may repent, perceiving the common humanity that unites him with those he had exploited.

The third illustration (v. 41) envisions a situation in which a Roman soldier compels one of the subject people to carry his pack. Seizing the initiative, the subjugated person can destabilize the situation, creating a dilemma for the soldier, who worries that he would face punishment for exacting service for excessive distances.

The last example (v. 42) is addressed to the person in a superior economic position. In context it implies a situation in which there is indebtedness due to some injustice. Nonretaliation on the part of the lender would be foregoing the demand that the money or goods be returned.

Each of these illustrations gives an example of how to restore justice by interrupting cycles of violence and enmity and initiating new cycles of generosity that invite reciprocity. In this way the intent of the Law is fulfilled.

5:43-48 Love your enemy

The sixth and last in the series of antitheses deals with the command to love the neighbor (Lev 19:18). Love, as a commandment, concerns not feelings but deeds that reflect faithfulness to the covenant. Nowhere in the Scriptures is there a command to hate the enemy. It was generally understood, however, that Israelites were obliged to practice deeds of covenant fidelity toward one another, but such was not required toward those outside the covenant community. "Hate," *miseō,* not only denotes active hostility but also connotes "love less" (as Matt 6:24). For Jesus this is an inadequate interpretation of the Law. He requires the same treatment for both those inside and outside the covenant community. Concrete ways to love enemies include praying for persecutors (v. 44) and welcoming outsiders (v. 47). "Persecut[ors]" likely refers to fellow Jews who opposed Christian missionaries, as in 10:23;

Matthew 5

23:34. The verb *aspazomai*, "greet," in verse 47 connotes welcome and a wish for well-being, not simply a salutation.

While in previous examples the motive was to avoid punishment (vv. 21-26, 29, 30), the reason given for loving enemies (vv. 45-48) is that God acts this way, treating both the just and the unjust with the same gratuitous bounty (v. 45). Giving loving treatment only to one's own people does not adequately fulfill the Law. Verse 48 sums up: "There must be no limits to your goodness, as your heavenly Father's goodness knows no bounds" (cf. NAB: "So be perfect, just as your heavenly Father is perfect"). The word *teleios*, usually translated "perfect," connotes not so much moral perfection as completeness, full maturity, as the Hebrew *tāmîm* does (Deut 18:13).

6:1-18 Almsgiving, prayer, and fasting

There is a shift now away from the antithetical structure of 5:21-48 as this next section addresses three practices that are pillars of Jewish spirituality: almsgiving (vv. 2-4), prayer (vv. 5-15), and fasting (vv. 16-18). All the material, except the Lord's Prayer (vv. 9-13), which stands at the center, is unique to Matthew. Verse 1 sounds the theme and ties this section to the previous one. As recipients of God's limitless graciousness and mercy (5:43-48), disciples are to respond in kind, with generous deeds of righteousness (see 3:15; 5:6, 10, 20) that express and establish right relation. The emphasis in each instance is on the interior disposition. The thread of "who sees" (vv. 1, 4, 5, 6, 16, 18) and the theme of reward (vv. 1, 2, 4, 5, 6, 16, 18) run throughout the section.

6:2-4 On almsgiving

Care for the poor is frequently enjoined in the Scriptures (e.g., Deut 24:19-22; Isa 58:6-8; Prov 25:21; Sir 3:30). In performing deeds of mercy, disciples are not to call attention to themselves. The exaggerated metaphors "blow a trumpet before you" (v. 2) and "do not let your left hand know what your right is doing" (v. 3) underscore the point that almsgiving should be done in an unobtrusive manner. Ostentatious givers already receive the reward of praise from others (v. 2). But such displays further shame the recipient, thus preventing right relation from becoming a present reality. Jesus contrasts the desired behavior of his disciples with that of hypocrites. *Hypocritēs* is the term for an actor who dons a mask (see Jesus' accusation of the Pharisees as hypocrites in 23:13, 15, 23, 25, 27, 29). It is aptly used here for those who pose as something they are not. The polemic between Matthew's community and the synagogue surfaces again at verses 2 and 5. Hypocrites are found in every religious group, and Christians are no exception. Staying centered on God is the key, as the next section on prayer elaborates.

6:5-15 On prayer

Jesus continues his denunciation of ostentatious shows of pious practices. It is not a critique of praying in a standing position, which was the normal prayer stance both for Jews and early Christians. Nor is Jesus advocating private prayer over communal. In fact, he teaches his disciples a communal prayer to *our* Father (v. 9). As in verse 2, the problematic aspect is the showiness of prayers done to attract the attention of others. Such behavior makes prayer impossible. The purpose of prayer is communication with God, for which one needs to shut out other concerns ("close the door," v. 6) and reach into the depths of spirit ("go to your inner room," v. 6). The reward is deeper communion with God (v. 6) rather than empty praise of human admirers (v. 5).

Furthermore, prayer is not a one-way street, nor does it require multiple words. Matthew stereotypes the prayer of pagans as babbling and criticizes them for thinking that they can manipulate God by deluging God with voluminous words. Jesus emphasizes that God already knows the needs of those who pray and implies that God stands ready to meet those needs (v. 8). Moreover, prayer of petition is only one kind of prayer. Jesus exemplifies prayer that flows from God's gracious initiative and responds in deeds of right relation (14:23; 19:13; 26:36-46). Jesus then teaches his disciples how to pray (vv. 9-13; see also 18:19; 24:20).

As in the rest of this section, the emphasis is on the interior disposition, "how" to pray (v. 9), not the words that are to be used. Luke 11:2-4 has a shorter version. Each evangelist tailors the prayer to his community's needs. The address "Our Father in heaven" is common in Jewish prayers. The pronoun "our" stresses the communal dimension of faith and the oneness of all children of God across all boundaries of difference. Calling God "Father" was not unique to Jesus; there are texts from the Hebrew Scriptures, Qumran, Philo, Josephus, and rabbinic literature in which this metaphor is used of God. Although it is the most frequently used metaphor (fifty-three times) by the Matthean Jesus, it is not the only one. See, for example, 13:33, where Matthew speaks of God as a bakerwoman, or 23:37, where Jesus applies to himself the metaphor used of God in Psalm 91, namely, that of a bird that gathers her fledglings under her wings. For the early Christians, "Father" expressed not so much intimacy as God's power and providence. By addressing God as "Father," they challenged the emperor's claim to be "father of the nation," asserting that only God is the supreme power.

Matthew 6

The first three petitions (vv. 9-10) focus on God and are essentially reiterations of one desire, expressed in three ways. "Hallowed be your name" echoes Leviticus 22:32; Deuteronomy 32:51; Isaiah 8:13; 29:23; and is similar to a line from the Jewish *Kaddish* prayer: "May thy great name be magnified and hallowed." God's name is hallowed when people recognize and give praise for divine saving deeds (Isa 29:23) and when they keep God's commands (Lev 22:32). The reign of God is already inaugurated (3:2; 4:17); disciples pray for God to bring it to eschatological fulfillment, according to God's will for salvation and well-being for all realms of creation, "on earth as in heaven" (see 7:21 on God's will).

The remaining petitions (vv. 11-13) ask for divine assistance in satisfying human needs for sustenance, forgiveness, strength in the final testing, and deliverance from evil. "Bread" refers to both spiritual nourishment (e.g., Wisdom's banquet, Prov 9:1-6) and physical nourishment. The meaning of *epiousios*, "daily" or "for the coming day," is ambiguous. It may refer to the food one needs to survive each day, or it may allude to the eschatological Day of the Lord. The prayer recalls God's providing of manna to the Israelites (Exod 16:12-35) and cultivates in disciples this same kind of trust. There are also eucharistic overtones for Christians.

Matthew's keen interest in forgiveness and reconciliation (5:38-48; 18:1-35) is reflected in his expansion of the petition for forgiveness (vv. 12, 14-15). He draws a clear link between one's ability to forgive others and one's ability to be forgiven by God. The two flow from and into each other. Divine forgiveness comes first (18:23-35). After receiving unearned forgiveness from God, disciples are obliged to offer forgiveness to others. And when disciples forgive others, they are forgiven by God (6:14-15; 18:35). Matthew uses the term *opheilēmata*, "debts," (cf. *hamartias*, "sins," in Luke 11:4), a term that reminds disciples that offenses against others include monetary inequities from systemic injustices. See Deuteronomy 15 for prescriptions for relaxation of debts in the sabbatical year.

The final petition (v. 13) is for God's protection and deliverance both now and at the end time. Until God's purposes are completely accomplished, evil will still exist, ever testing the disciple to be faithful. The language of testing *(peirasmos)* is used not in the sense of God sadistically toying with people, looking for ways to determine their fidelity, but rather it acknowledges the struggle against evil in which disciples engage (as did Jesus, 4:1-11) throughout their earthly sojourn. Jesus teaches his disciples to rely on God's power and faithfulness to bring them through every trial and emerge victorious over evil (*ponēros* can be understood as "evil" or "the evil one," that is, Satan). In Matthew's apocalyptic outlook, there will be a final end-time crisis that will bring this testing to conclusion (chs. 24–25). The whole prayer has an eschatological dimension as well as a present one. Disciples rely on God's power and protection to provide for and save them for all eternity, a reality already tasted in the present.

6:16-18 On fasting

As with almsgiving and prayer (vv. 1-6), Christians who fast are not to call attention to their pious practice. The verb *aphanizō*, "neglect their appearance," literally means "disfigure" or "render unrecognizable." It may refer to covering one's head with a cloth (Jer 14:4) or with ashes (1 Macc 3:47), or neglecting to wash (v. 17). The point is that adulation is its own reward, and no further benefit will accrue to one who is ostentatious in fasting.

6:19–7:12 Ethical sayings

The next sayings are loosely connected by catchwords. Almost all of them have parallels in Luke. They make dualistic contrasts between earth and heaven, light and darkness, love and hate. Such clean separation does not exist in real life. What these pairs underscore is the choice disciples must make to be wholly centered on God while moving toward light, love, and heaven. The prevailing motif is trust in God's providence. The first saying (vv. 19-21) contrasts the corrosive nature of material things with the security of devotedness to God. Treasure on earth, such as clothing and linens, can be consumed by moths or insects or stolen by thieves. They also consume one's attention and one's heart. The lasting treasure is the heart centered on God, which cannot be dislodged.

In this context the saying about the eye being the lamp of the body (vv. 22-23) points out the dangers of eyeing the possessions of others, which incites covetous desire. Evil-eyed envy is one of the attitudes that is most destructive of community. Not only the individual but the whole body of believers is affected by such "darkness." The next saying (v. 24) reprises verses 19-21 with a different image. A word play makes the point all the more sharply. "Mammon," "wealth," is derived from the root *'mn*, "trust," the same root from which "amen" comes. God is the only one to whom disciples say "amen."

The last section (vv. 25-34) builds on these sayings, illustrating God's care for birds, wild flowers, and grass of the field, and assures disciples that God knows their needs and provides for them. This passage does not advocate passivity, that is, doing nothing and expecting that God will provide. Nor does it make a judgment on the faith of those whose daily reality is a desperate struggle to survive. The point is that when disciples' whole attention is centered on seeking God's reign and right relation with all creation (5:6, 10, 20; 6:1), then those who have enough of life's necessities do not become obsessed with the quest for material possessions. Rather, they cooperate with God in providing for others (6:1-4), in supplying their daily bread (6:11). Likewise, those who are in desperate straits can let go of their worry. Neither obsessive anxiety about subsistence nor fixated desires on excessive accumulation have a place in the realm of God. Both are reflective of little faith (see also 8:26; 14:31; 16:8).

The present imperative "Stop judging" (7:1) not only warns about avoiding judging others but commands the listeners to desist from what they are in fact doing. As with forgiveness (6:14-15), peoples' actions redound to them in kind. It is not the case that disciples should overlook wrongdoing by another member of the community (*adelphos*, "brother," vv. 3-5). What is forbidden is hypocritical fault-finding. A wooden beam in the eye (v. 3) is a hyperbolic way of depicting an evil eye (6:23).

The saying in 7:6 is unique to Matthew and somewhat enigmatic. What is holy ("hallowed") in 6:9 is God's name. A pearl can signify the realm of God (see 13:45-46). "Dogs" is likely a reference to outsiders (see also 15:26), since Jews did not keep dogs indoors as house pets. Swine were unclean animals for Jews. So the saying is best understood as an admonition not to preach about the reign of God to Gentiles or pagans, but to concentrate the mission within Israel (similarly 10:5-6). If persecution can be expected in the mission to Israel (5:10; 10:16-36), all the more would such be anticipated with outsiders.

Verses 7-11 circle back to the theme of petitionary prayer. There is a reprise of the image of God as Father (6:9), as the sayings assure that just as human fathers provide good things to their children, so does God. The emphasis (as in 6:25-34) is on God's loving providence. Humans do not manipulate God into giving them what they want, nor does God need reminding of their needs. God does not give stones for bread (Matt 4:3; 6:11; 14:13-21; 26:26-30). When disciples seek foremost God's reign and right relation (6:33), this is readily granted. Askers receive, seekers find, and the door is opened to those who knock, even if the specific things disciples ask for are not always granted.

This loosely connected group of ethical sayings reaches its climax with the "golden rule" (v. 12). There are numerous parallels to this saying in both Jewish and Greco-Roman literature. In the Old Testament there are variations such as "love your neighbor as yourself" (Lev 19:18; see Matt 5:43) and "do to no one what you yourself dislike" (Tob 4:15). Admonitions about forgiveness (6:14-15) and judging (7:1-3) have already been framed in terms of getting back in kind what you do. Now this is offered as the guiding principle that sums up the whole of how disciples are to live according to the Scriptures. It closes the section that began with 5:17-20, on Jesus' fulfillment of the Law and the prophets.

7:13-29 Exhortations and warnings

The final group of sayings and parables are mostly from Q. Using dualistic contrasts, they warn about end-time consequences for doing or not doing what Jesus teaches. The notion of two ways was a common one in Judaism and early Christianity (e.g., Deut 30:15-20; Ps 1:6; Sir 15:14-17). The "narrow gate" (v. 13) and the "constricted road" (v. 14) express the difficulties involved in choosing the way of Jesus. Moreover, there are teachers or pastors ("false prophets" and "ravenous wolves," v. 15) who would lead believers astray. But it is not difficult to determine the right leaders to follow. The effects ("fruits") of their teaching and preaching easily reveal the correctness of their words (vv. 16-18, 20). The theme of bearing good fruit is a favorite of Matthew (see references at 3:10), as is fiery destruction for one who fails to do so (vv. 19; 3:10, 12; 13:40; 18:8; 25:41).

Every major discourse in Matthew's Gospel ends with a warning to put Jesus' teaching into practice (5:2-27; 13:36-43, 47-50; 18:23-35; 24:37–25:46). This is the focus of the sayings in verses 21-23 and the parable of the two builders (vv. 24-27). Saying "Lord, Lord" (vv. 21, 22), either as a cry for help (8:2, 6, 8, 25; 9:28; 14:28, 30; 15:22, 25, 27; 17:15; 20:30, 31, 33) or as a liturgical acclamation (Rom 10:9; 1 Cor 12:3; Phil 2:11) is not sufficient; one must not only acknowledge Jesus' power but also engage it in doing deeds like his own (i.e., doing "the will of my Father in heaven" v. 21; on God's will see also 6:9-10; 12:50; 18:14; 26:39, 42, 44). The opposite is also true. Those who do mighty deeds like those of Jesus must be in intimate relationship with him, or else they risk him declaring at the end time, "I never knew you" (v. 23).

In the parable of the two builders (vv. 24-27) the point is similar. One who hears and puts Jesus' words into practice is like one who builds on a rock foundation (v. 24). This image is often used of God (e.g., Deut 32:4, 18, 31; Pss 18:2; 28:1; Isa 17:10). Now it is applied to Jesus and at 16:18 to Peter. The emphasis on hearing and doing echoes Israel's response at the giving of the Law, "All that the LORD has said, we will heed and do" (Exod 24:7; see also Deut 31:11-12). The emphasis in the parable is on Jesus as authoritative interpreter of the Law—"these words of *mine*" (vv. 24, 26; emphasis added). The conflicts with other religious leaders, both in Jesus' day and in Matthew's, lurk beneath the surface of this parable.

The Sermon on the Mount concludes with the same formula as each of Matthew's major discourses does, "When Jesus finished these words" (7:28;

Matthew 7

cf. 11:1; 13:53; 19:1; 26:1). The next major section focuses on Jesus' healing ministry.

8:1–9:38 Compassionate healing

Matthew returns to the Markan source, gathering in this section stories of Jesus healing every kind of illness. Two segments dealing with discipleship punctuate these (8:18-27; 9:9-17) and prepare for the commissioning in chapter 10. The healing stories generally have the same form with the following elements: (1) the setting is described; (2) the sick person approaches Jesus and requests healing; (3) the gravity of the illness is depicted, highlighting the healing power of Jesus; (4) Jesus pronounces a word of healing and often touches the person; (5) there is a demonstration of the cure; (6) onlookers react with amazement. The healing stories focus on Jesus' power, but they do not compel people to believe. Some persons are tentative in their requests (8:2), some have great faith before Jesus heals (8:10; 9:22, 29), and others have little faith (8:26). Some reject him (8:34), and others glorify God (9:8) and preach throughout the land about him (9:31).

8:1-4 A person with leprosy

There are three healings in the initial cycle. First is a person with leprosy (vv. 1-4), who prostrates himself before Jesus (see also 2:2, 8, 11; 14:3; 15:25; 28:9). Having just instructed his disciples about doing the will of God (7:21), Jesus now enacts God's will to heal and shows that his own will is one with God's. In Leviticus 13–14 there are detailed prescriptions for dealing with leprosy (a term applied to various kinds of skin ailments, not only what is known today as Hansen's disease). Once again Jesus is intent on fulfilling the Law and sends the healed man to complete the rituals for reincorporation into the community of believers. The detail about telling no one (v. 4) is one that Matthew has preserved from Mark, but the theme of secrecy does not function in Matthew as it does in Mark. In Matthew the crowds are still with Jesus (v. 1), and Jesus' identity has been made public from the start.

8:5-13 A centurion's servant

In the second healing story, set in Capernaum (4:13; 9:1), an officer of the Roman army in charge of one hundred soldiers approaches Jesus, appealing on behalf of his servant (*pais* could also mean "child"). Unlike the episode with the Canaanite woman (15:21-28), Jesus does not rebuff this Gentile. As with her (15:28), Jesus praises the faith of this non-Jew and even contrasts his great faith with that of Israel (v. 10). It is a foreshadowing of the inclusion of Gentiles from all corners of the earth (see Isa 2:2-4; Mic 4:1-4; Zech 8:20-23).

Reclining with Israel's ancestors at the eschatological banquet (v. 11) is a frequently used image for the joys of the life that lies beyond (22:1-14; Isa 25:6). Matthew uses his favorite image of "outer darkness, where there will be wailing and grinding of teeth" (vv. 12, cf. 13:42, 50; 22:13; 24:51; 25:30) to contrast the fate of those for whom the eschatological banquet has been prepared but who do not accept Jesus. One unique element in this story is that Jesus heals at a distance and does not personally encounter the sick person. It highlights Jesus' authority (*exousia*, v. 9) but also may reflect a concern for ritual purity by not having Jesus enter a Gentile house.

8:14-15 Peter's mother-in-law

Third in the series of healing stories is the cure of Peter's mother-in-law. There are also elements of a call story. Unlike other healing stories, in which the sick person approaches Jesus, here Jesus takes the initiative. He sees her (*eiden*, v. 14), just as he sees Matthew when he calls him to be a disciple (9:9). Her response, "she rose and waited on *(diakonein)* him" (v. 15), also characterizes discipleship. The verb *diakonein* is used throughout the New Testament for a variety of ministries: table service (Acts 6:2), ministry of the word (Acts 6:4), financial ministry (Luke 8:3; Acts 11:29; 12:25), apostolic ministry (Acts 1:25). Also, in Matthew's version her service is to Jesus alone (cf. Mark 1:31, where she waits on "them"). See 27:55, where the many Galilean women who followed and ministered to Jesus keep vigil at the crucifixion. It is possible that Matthew has blended the story of this woman's healing with that of her call as a disciple. That Simon's mother-in-law may have played a significant role in the early community of disciples is likely from the fact that she is identified (though not by name), whereas other persons who are healed remain completely anonymous.

8:16-17 Summary

Matthew, like Mark, sets this first cycle of healings in one powerful day, rounding it off with a summary statement of all the other cures Jesus did. Typically, he cites Isaiah, drawing attention to how Jesus' healing ministry fulfills the Scriptures. This text (Isa 53:4) is from the Suffering Servant songs and points ahead to the Passion.

8:18-22 The rigors of discipleship

The link between healing and ministry is hinted at in the healing of Simon's mother-in-law (vv. 14-15; see also 9:31). But discipleship demands far more than an attraction to Jesus because of his mighty deeds of healing. To a scribe who wants to follow him, Jesus speaks soberly about the itinerant nature of discipleship (vv. 19-20). For other favorable references to scribes, see 13:52; 23:34. Jesus reminds those who have already become disciples that commitment to following him takes precedence over all other obligations and ties, even to family members. (See Tob 1:16-20 on the obligation to bury the dead; cf. 1 Kgs 19:20.) Jesus' homelessness recalls that of Woman Wisdom (Prov 1:20; Sir 24:7; see other parallels with Wisdom at Matt 11:16, 25-30; 23:34-39).

This is the first instance of the title "Son of Man" in the Gospel. This enigmatic expression is found only on the lips of Jesus. It occurs in contexts where Jesus speaks of his earthly ministry (9:6; 11:19; 12:8, 32; 13:37; 16:13), his passion (12:40; 17:9, 12, 22; 20:18, 28; 26:2, 24, 45), and his future coming and role as judge at the end time (10:23; 13:41; 16:27, 28; 19:28; 24:27, 30, 37, 39, 44; 25:31; 26:64). The phrase *ho huios tou anthrōpou* ("son of man") is found in Daniel 7:14 and in 1 Enoch 37–71 for an end-time agent of salvation and judgment. It may reflect a Semitic expression, *ben ʾādām* in Hebrew, or *bar ʾĕneāsh* in Aramaic, "son of humanity," designating a single member of the human species. Jesus may have used this phrase as a way of speaking of himself simply as a human being. It could be translated as "a certain person" or "someone" or, when used as a self-designation, simply "I." Whatever the provenance and original meaning of the expression, it is clearly used as a christological title in the Gospels.

8:23-27 Stormy fears

Having given orders at verse 18 to cross to the other side of the lake, Jesus now does so with his disciples in tow. These are ones who are willing to give up ties to home and family. But further difficulties lie ahead, symbolized by the "violent storm," literally, *seismos megas*, "a great earthquake" (see 24:7; 27:51; 28:2). The "earthquake" points ahead to the difficulties for disciples surrounding Jesus' passion. Initial enthusiasm for following Jesus can quickly give way to paralyzing fear for one's own life. But Jesus' power to preserve life, already demonstrated in his authority over disease, illness, and demons, now extends even to natural forces (see Pss 65:8; 89:10; 93:3-4; 107:29 for God's power over the threatening waters). The "little faith" of fearful disciples (see also 6:30; 14:31; 16:8; 17:20) gives way to amazement as they focus, not on the seemingly overwhelming obstacles, but on the person of Jesus.

8:28-34 Ministry at the margins

In the next healing story Jesus ventures out on the other side of the lake, which Matthew regards as Gentile territory. Demons and death ("tombs,"

v. 28) epitomize the forces of evil. Matthew has made the locale Gadara (cf. Gerasa in Mark 5:1), which is some five miles away from the sea. Despite the logistical difficulties, the image of swine (unclean animals) rushing down the steep bank to their watery demise vividly conveys the point. Jesus' power extends over all forces of evil, especially to those on the margins. The deeds expected at the end time (v. 29) are already begun in his earthly ministry. Unlike the story of the Samaritan woman who brings her whole town to believe in Jesus (John 4:39), the swineherds' report to their townspeople causes the opposite reaction (vv. 33-34). Jesus then returns to his home territory (9:1), where he receives a favorable reception (9:8).

9:1-8 Forgiveness with healing

Matthew preserves a tradition from Mark (2:1-12) that reflects the ancient belief that sickness and sin are related. In other New Testament texts (e.g., John 9:3) Jesus clearly asserts that sickness or disability is not due to any one individual person's sin. In a broader sense, sin can be thought of as the mortal condition that holds all people bound, from which only God can liberate. Thus when Jesus forgives the sin of the paralyzed man, some scribes accuse him of blasphemy. A scribe is portrayed favorably in 8:19, but for the remainder of the Gospel scribes are mainly adversaries of Jesus (7:29; 9:3; 12:38; 15:1; 16:21; 20:18; 21:15; 23:13-29; 26:57; 27:41). Blasphemy ordinarily refers to misusing the divine name (Lev 24:15-16; Num 15:30), but here it refers to Jesus arrogating to himself a power that belongs only to God. This is a charge that resurfaces when Jesus is interrogated by the high priest (26:65).

Not only does Jesus pronounce divine forgiveness, but he also reads others' thoughts (v. 4), another power that belongs only to God (Jer 11:20; Ps 7:9). This episode affirms another dimension of Jesus' power, while also heightening the conflict with Jesus' opponents. In addition, it portrays the important role of the faith community in bringing a person to wellness. It is the faith of the man's friends which Jesus sees (v. 2) and which causes him to act. Finally, it reflects a holistic approach to the person. Jesus heals both body and spirit, allowing the person to arise to a new life (*egeirein*, "rose," v. 7, the same verb used of Jesus' resurrection at 28:6). The crowd reacts (v. 8) in a manner similar to that of 7:28-29.

9:9-13 The call of Matthew

Interjected in a cycle of healing stories that began with Jesus ministering to outsiders (8:28-34) is the call of a tax collector, a marginalized Jew. Matthew has taken the story from Mark (2:13-17), where the tax collector's name is Levi. The change to the name Matthew brings forward the authoritative figure behind this Gospel, one of the Twelve (10:3). As in the call of the first disciples (4:18-22), the response is immediate and total. The remaining verses center on Jesus' close association with many marginalized people (v. 10).

Tax collectors were ostracized by observant Jews for a number of reasons. They were looked upon as collaborators with the Romans, and their work brought them into continuous contact with Gentiles. Moreover, they had a reputation for dishonesty, as they would try to charge more than the amount prescribed (Luke 3:13). "Sinners" (v. 10) refers to Gentiles, who do not know the Law, as well as Jews who miss the mark in keeping the Law, either by immoral acts or because of their profession (tax collectors, shepherds, wool dyers, etc.). Eating with such people was particularly offensive (v. 11), since a shared meal signified intimate relationship. In addition, meals with Jesus foreshadow inclusion in the eschatological banquet (14:32-39; 22:1-14; 26:26-30). Dining with Jesus is not only a social event but also a means of healing (v. 12) and forgiveness (v. 13). Matthew adds a quotation from Hosea 6:6 (v. 13; see also 12:7), which reflects conflict between his community and other Jews about ritual purity. With this story the evangelist legitimates the presence and participation of all kinds of marginalized people in the community of Jesus' followers. Discipleship is offered to all who hunger and thirst for righteousness (5:6); those who think of themselves as already righteous find it difficult to be open to the call (v. 13).

9:14-17 Old and new

Inclusive sharing at table was not the only practice of early Christians that proved problematic. The question of why Jesus did not fast (see also 11:18-19) needed to be explained, as well as why Christians resumed the practice. Jews were obliged to fast only on the Day of Atonement (Lev 16:29; 23:27), but they also fasted in tandem with prayer (Ps 35:13), penance (2 Sam 12:13-25; 1 Kgs 21:27), mourning (2 Sam 1:12; 3:36), and divine revelation (Dan 10:3). The *Didache* (8:1; from the first half of the second century) notes that Pharisees fasted on Mondays and Thursdays (see Luke 18:12), so Christians took up the practice on Wednesdays and Fridays. While the bridegroom (a metaphor used of God, e.g., Hos 2:19; Isa 54:3-6; Jer 2:2, and used again of Jesus in Matt 25:1-13) is still present with the guests, it is not the time for fasting. "The days will come" (v. 15b) is a phrase often used to introduce an oracle of woe (Amos 7:2; Jer 38:31) and hints at the death of Jesus. It echoes Isaiah 53:8, where the Suffering Servant "was taken away." After the death of Jesus it is appropriate for his disciples to fast (see 6:16-18). Metaphors of

Matthew 9

new cloth and new wine symbolize the new way of Jesus. Yet there is no abandoning what went before. Matthew preserves from the Markan tradition the theme of the incompatibility of the old and the new but adds "and both are preserved" (v. 17).

9:18-26 Tenacious faith

A third cycle of healing stories begins with an account that weaves together the cure of a woman who had suffered from a hemorrhage for twelve years and that of a twelve-year-old girl who has died. Matthew trims away many of Mark's descriptive details (cf. Mark 5:21-43) and adds some that heighten the Jewish ambiance: flute players at the deathbed of the young girl (v. 23), as prescribed for funerals for even the poorest of Jews (*m. Ketub* 4:4); and "tassels" (v. 20) on Jesus' cloak, worn by Jews to help them remember to keep all God's commandments (Num 15:38-41).

In both stories the healing power of Jesus and the faith of the petitioners is central. The official, despite the fact that his daughter is already dead, prostrates himself before Jesus (as do other characters in 2:2-11; 8:2; 14:3; 15:25; 28:9). And even after twelve years of suffering, the woman with the hemorrhages still musters courageous faith. Jesus, like Elijah (1 Kgs 17:17-24) and Elisha (2 Kgs 4:32-37), has the power to resuscitate those who have died, an act that prefigures his own resurrection.

There are a number of similarities between Jesus and these two women that point ahead to his passion. Like the woman with the hemorrhage, he too suffers, bleeds, does not cry out, stays steadfast in faith, and attains salvation (the Greek word *sōzein*, v. 22, means both "healed" and "saved") by his courageous act. As the child of the ruler, at the time of her death, is surrounded by an unruly crowd, who ridicule Jesus for saying she is not dead, so Jesus, the child of God, is taunted by crowds of passersby, religious officials, and those crucified with him, for his trust in God to bring life from death (27:39-44). And as news spread throughout the land that Jesus had raised up the girl (v. 26), so the Galilean women will spread the news that Jesus has been raised (28:6-8).

9:27-31 Efficacious faith

Matthew brings the cycle of powerful healing stories to a climax as he doubles the number of men (also at 8:28; cf. Mark 5:2) who are blind (cf. Mark 10:46-52; see also Matt 20:29-34) and turns Jesus' question not only toward the ones seeking healing in the narrative but to the reader as well: "Do you believe that I can do this?" (v. 28). A disciple will need to answer this question with a strong affirmative before being able to call on that same

Matthew 9

power in mission (ch. 10). The men address Jesus with Matthew's favorite messianic title, "Son of David" (v. 27; 1:1; 12:23; 15:22; 20:30, 31; 21:9, 15). The warning not to tell anyone (v. 30) is a holdover from Mark's version; the theme of secrecy does not function in Matthew as it does in Mark (see also 8:4).

9:32-34 Healing and conflict

The final brief healing story reflects ancient belief that disability and illness were caused by demon possession (see also 8:28-34). Matthew keeps the focus on Jesus' mission to Israel (v. 33, as also 10:6; 15: 24). The divided response to Jesus (as in 9:1-8) is a theme that keeps building. The crowds continue to react favorably to him until his passion (27:20-26), while the Pharisees take the role of prime opponents (see 3:7; 5:20; 9:11, 14).

9:35-38 Compassionate shepherd

Concluding this section is a summary statement (as 8:16-17) of Jesus' successful ministry of preaching, teaching, and healing. His focus remains on ministry to his own people (v. 35). This is one of the few times that Matthew does not make the reference to synagogues polemical. The stress is on Jesus' heartfelt compassion for his people. The image of shepherd as religious leader is a familiar one for God (Pss 23; 100; Isa 40:11) and for religious leaders (Ezek 34:8-12) and occurs twice more in the Gospel (10:6; 18:14-16). The metaphor shifts abruptly into agricultural imagery (vv. 37-38), as the image of laborers for the harvest leads into the mission discourse.

10:1-4 Called for mission

The mission discourse is the second of the five major blocks of teaching. It begins with the call and sending of the twelve disciples (vv. 1-15), followed by sober warnings about coming persecutions (vv. 16-25), reassurances about God's protection (vv. 26-33), and further sayings about repercussions, conditions, and rewards of discipleship (vv. 34-42). The central place of this discourse conveys to the reader that all discipleship has a missionary dimension to it. The number twelve is symbolic for the whole of the new Israel, recalling the twelve tribes that constituted the people of the covenant. "Disciples" (*mathētai*, v. 1) designates a wide group of followers (73 times in Matthew). The term "apostle" (*apostolos*, v. 2) means "one sent" and is used only here in the Gospel of Matthew. Jesus' bestowing his authority on his disciples to heal recalls Moses' imparting his spirit to the elders of Israel (Num 11:24-25). The commission to teach comes to disciples only at 28:20.

Matthew relies on Mark (3:13-19) for the list of the Twelve. There are slight variations in the names in Luke 6:12-16 and Acts 1:13. Matthew orders the names in six pairs and adds the designation "the tax collector" to Matthew (v. 3). About many of these figures little is known. Simon Peter always stands at the head and Judas Iscariot at the end. The Twelve (who appear again in 11:1; 19:28; 20:17; 26:14, 20, 47) do not play a major role in this Gospel.

10:5-15 Commissioning

The instructions given to the Twelve speak to all itinerant Christian missionaries as well as to those who receive and support them. They tell Jesus' envoys where and how to travel, how to approach people in new places, what to say and do, and how to handle rejection. For the community that offers hospitality to missionaries, they also provide a way to identify false prophets (7:15-23). Matthew is unique in stressing the mission to Israel (also 15:24). While a few episodes foreshadow a Gentile mission (2:1-12; 8:5-13, 28-33; 15:21-28), this does not become explicit until 28:16-20. Jesus himself likely understood his mission to be only for the renewal of his own people, while his followers subsequently understood it as intended for Gentiles as well.

Christian missionaries make the same proclamation as Jesus (4:17) and John the Baptist (3:2), and they perform the same healing deeds as Jesus (chs. 8–9). By so doing, Christians are the human face of Christ still at work in the world, bringing hope and healing wherever there are illness, death, and manifestations of evil. Missionaries are to present themselves as completely vulnerable—without money, luggage, extra clothing, footwear, or weapons (a walking stick was often used to fend off beasts). They are not self-sufficient; rather, they are totally reliant on God's providence, demonstrated in their dependence on the hospitality of others. While missionaries deserve to be paid (v. 10; similarly 1 Cor 9:14), Jesus instructs them to minister without charge so that the poor are not excluded and so that they are able to proclaim the Gospel with integrity (v. 8b; similarly 2 Cor 11:7). The message cannot be tailored to what those who will give money want to hear. Missionaries are not to move around seeking better accommodations. They are to remain in one house, a visible sign of "God-with-us" (1:23; 28:20), offering peace (see above on 5:9) to all within. Like Jesus, missionaries face acceptance by some and rejection by others. When rejected, they are not to respond violently, but rather they symbolically shake off the vestiges of their encounter. Not to accept the bearers of the Gospel has dire consequences. For the story of Sodom and Gomorrah (v. 15), see Genesis 19.

Matthew 10

10:16-42 The cost of missionary life

In addition to the self-imposed rigors outlined in 10:5-15, missionaries also face dangers from without (vv. 16-25). They may be "handed over" (v. 17; as is Jesus in 27:2, 18) to local councils of Jewish leaders, the Roman prefect, or the Herodian king. They may be flogged (v. 17; see 20:19; 23:34; Acts 22:19; 2 Cor 11:24-25) and hated by all (v. 22). Worst of all, members of one's own family or apostates from the Christian community ("brothers" and "sisters"; see v. 21) may denounce them to the authorities.

In response to such perils, missionaries must first remember that they are heralds of the messianic reign of peace, when sheep and wolves can dwell together (Isa 11:6). Even so, they are not naïve about their opponents. When possible, they are to flee persecution (v. 23). When brought before the authorities, they can rely on the Spirit for the words by which they will bear witness. They are to endure "to the end" (v. 22), probably a reference to the eschatological coming of the Son of Humanity rather than to martyrdom. Regarding persecution, see above on 5:10-11. All these tribulations should come as no surprise to Christian missionaries, since they are following in the footsteps of their teacher (vv. 24-25). On Beelzebul (v. 25), see 12:22-37.

Three times Jesus reassures those he sends out not to be afraid (vv. 26, 28, 31). They are to proclaim boldly and openly, since the Gospel is meant for all; it is not esoteric teaching (vv. 26-27). Further, even if their life is taken, it is only their body *(sōma)* that is destroyed, not their soul *(psychē)*. Moreover, they are so highly prized in God's sight that God's providential care will never falter (vv. 29-31). One who publicly professes commitment to Jesus can depend on the same unwavering commitment from God through Jesus (v. 32). The only cautions are that there is one who can destroy the whole person in Gehenna (v. 28; see 5:22), and there are eschatological consequences for apostasy (v. 33).

A disparate collection of sayings (vv. 34-42) rounds out the mission discourse. These apply more widely to all disciples. In verses 34-37 Jesus returns to the topic of family divisions that result from allegiance to Jesus. Previously Jesus pronounced peacemakers blessed (5:9) and outlined concrete strategies of nonretaliation of violence (5:38-48). At his arrest he prohibits the use of a sword in his defense (26:52). Verse 34 does not contradict these but rather speaks about the effect of his mission. Jesus' purpose is not to create division, but his coming has provoked opposing responses (see also 4:22; 8:21-22). The "sword" may be an allusion to Ezekiel 14:17, where the prophet speaks of a sword of discrimination that goes through the midst of the people, separating out those destined for destruction from those who will have mercy.

The sayings in verses 37-39 underscore the utter attachment to Jesus that is demanded of a disciple. A disciple who does not love his or her own family members and who does not recognize God's love revealed in those closest at hand will not be able to share that divine love with outsiders. But disciples, especially those called to go away from home on mission, must be willing to subordinate their attachment to what they love best—family and even their own life—for the sake of Jesus and his mission. Taking up one's cross (v. 38) does not refer to accepting suffering in general but refers specifically to the persecutions and sacrifices one endures for the sake of the mission. The paradoxical reward for such self-renunciation is finding life (v. 39).

The last sayings in the discourse shift focus to the receiving communities. Those who accept prophets, righteous ones, and "little ones" (see vv. 40-42; see also 18:6, 10, 14) among the disciples can expect to share in the grace of the one offering such gifts. On reward or punishment for offering a drink, see 25:35, 42.

VARYING RESPONSES TO JESUS
Matt 11:1–16:12

11:1-19 Jesus and John the Baptist

Matthew concludes the second block of teaching (10:1-42) with a transitional sentence, "When Jesus finished . . ." (as in 7:28; 13:53; 19:1; 26:1). Unlike Mark (6:30), Matthew does not recount the return of the Twelve and the success of their first missionary excursion; rather, he focuses on the divided responses to Jesus' mission, which his disciples also experience. The disciples do not always understand, but they, along with the crowds, continue to follow him, while opposition from the religious leaders increases.

This section begins with John's query about Jesus' identity (vv. 2-6), followed by Jesus' testimony about John (vv. 7-11), and concludes with a parable about the rejection both experience (vv. 12-19). The sayings are mostly from Q (parallel in Luke 7:18-35). Matthew noted at 4:12 that John had been arrested, and he will recount the story of John's death at 14:1-12. John's uncertainty about whether Jesus is the "one who is to come" (v. 3) seems to be at odds with the baptismal scene (3:13-17), where John appeared to know that Jesus is the "one coming after" him and is mightier than he is (3:11). The scene in 11:2-6 functions to clarify for the reader that the healings and teaching of Jesus in the previous chapters confirm his messianic identity. The kinds of deeds listed in verse 5 echo Isaiah 35:5-6. Although

Matthew 11

there is no explicit mention of the Messiah in Isaiah 35, these promises in a postexilic context are heralds of the dawning messianic era. An alternative interpretation is that Jesus is redefining what is to be expected of the Messiah. If some are looking for a military and political leader of the Davidic line such as the *Psalms of Solomon* 17-18 describe, then Jesus corrects their mistaken expectation. It is important to remember, however, that there was a variety of messianic expectations in Jesus' day. The beatitude in verse 6 underlines the paradoxical nature of Jesus' messiahship, at which many will take offense (*skandalizomai*, literally, "be scandalized"; see also 13:21, 57; 15:12; 26:31, 33).

Verses 7-15 shift the focus to Jesus' estimation of John. John is no flighty figure who runs after every would-be messiah who blows into town; rather, he is the one who has correctly identified God's anointed. He is the expected Elijah-like prophet (v. 14; see 17:10-12), the forerunner of the messianic reign. In verse 10 Matthew combines Malachi 3:1 and Exodus 23:30 to show the fulfillment of God's promise to send a messenger (John) to prepare the way for the one who heralds God's reign (Jesus). There may be an implied contrast in verses 7-8 between John and Herod Antipas, as the latter had coins minted with the symbol of a reed at the founding of Tiberias (A.D. 19). John's Elijah-like clothing (3:4) was nothing like Herod's luxurious dress.

John is a hinge figure who both prepares the way for the new era of God's reign (v. 11) and is also part of the reign, as both he and Jesus proclaim its arrival (3:2; 4:17) and suffer violence for its sake (11:12). John's imprisonment is an example of how the reign of God suffers violence at the hands of the violent who attempt to overpower it (v. 12). "The violent" who attempt to lay waste God's rule include not only human opponents, like Herod and those of his ilk, but also the demonic forces with which Jesus contends in his exorcisms and healings. The theme of having "ears . . . to hear" (v. 15) points ahead to the parables discourse (13:9, 13-17, 43).

The parable in verses 11-16 likens "this generation" (a pejorative phrase, as also at 12:39-42; 16:4; 17:17; 23:36) to a group of children who stubbornly refuse to play with another group, whether it is a comic game or a tragic one. Not responding to John's "dirge" nor Jesus' "flute," they instead sit (v. 16) in judgment (see 27:19). Such was also the reception accorded to Woman Wisdom, who called out her invitation to eat and drink (Prov 1:20-21; 9:3-5). But just as Wisdom is rejected by the foolish (Prov 1:23-25; Sir 15:7-8; Wis 10:3; Bar 3:12), so too John and Jesus are rejected. The accusation "glutton and drunkard" (v. 19) alludes to Deuteronomy 21:20, where it connotes a rebellious son. Verse 19b refutes this charge: Jesus is Wisdom incarnate who is vindicated (Prov 8:8, 20) by her works. For other parallels between Jesus and Wisdom, see 8:18-22; 11:25-30; 23:34-36, 37-39.

11:20-24 Consequences of rejection

To reject Jesus' invitation carries weighty consequences. The "mighty deeds" he has done (esp. chs. 8–9) should lead to repentance with understanding that he is the "one who is to come" (11:3) and Wisdom incarnate (11:19b). Capernaum, where Jesus makes his home (4:13; 8:5; 9:1; 17:24), Chorazin, and Bethsaida are villages near the Sea of Galilee. Previously Capernaum had given Jesus a favorable reception (9:8), although after his first powerful deed done there, he already spoke of his rejection by Israel (8:10-12). It is here that Jesus first clashes with the religious leaders (9:3, 11). A taunt to the king of Babylon (Isa 14:12-20) is redirected to Capernaum (v. 23). The coastal cities Tyre and Sidon were frequently denounced by the prophets for their corruption (Isa 23:1-12; Jer 25:22; Ezek 28:11-23). For the story of Sodom (vv. 23-24), see Genesis 19.

11:25-30 The revealer's yoke

This prayer is akin to the *Thanksgiving Hymns* from Qumran and uses language like that of the Fourth Gospel. It stresses the intimate relationship between Jesus and the Creator and Jesus' unique role as revealer. These verses are not to be taken as speaking of predestination or as anti-intellectualism; rather, they speak of how those who are vulnerable and marginalized are the most receptive to the revelation Jesus offers. The word *hēpioi*, "infants," (v. 25) connotes both the dependence of one who is needy as well as the inexperience of the fledgling disciples who have welcomed Jesus' teaching and his saving deeds.

In verses 28-30 Jesus, like Woman Wisdom (Sir 51:23-30), invites those who are oppressed by the yoke of sin, suffering, economic distress, and hard physical labor to take upon themselves his yoke. Rather than taking up the yoke of oppressive rulers such as Egypt (Lev 26:13) or Babylon (Isa 47:6), Israel is to take upon itself that of Yahweh (Jer 2:20). God's "yoke" is study of and obedience to Torah (Jer 5:5). To take up Jesus' yoke is not to reject Torah; rather, it is to live by his interpretation of it (5:17-20). The lightness of Jesus' yoke is not a lax interpretation of the Torah—quite the contrary (5:21-48; 10:16-23)! Accepting its more stringent demands paradoxically leads to liberation from all that oppresses. This is the opposite of what the Pharisaic interpreters do (23:4). "Rest[ing]" connotes that all the created order is in right relationship, and the believing community together delights in its goodness (as God does in Genesis 2:1-3).

Matthew 12

12:1-14 Sabbath controversies

Two conflicts between Jesus and the Pharisees advance the theme of rejection and culminate with a death threat (v. 14). In the first conflict Jesus defends his hungry disciples for plucking heads of grain on the sabbath. Deuteronomy 23:25 allows hungry persons to take grain from a neighbor's field, but they may not use a sickle. This saves poor persons from having to beg, while at the same time guaranteeing that they will not take undo advantage of the owner of the field.

The issue in Matthew 12:1-8, however, is that the disciples are breaking the sabbath. Jesus defends his disciples' action by citing two texts of the Torah. In verses 3-4 Jesus interprets 1 Samuel 21:1-6 as an illustration of how an act of compassion to respond to a human need must take precedence over cultic observance. This is reiterated in verse 7 with a quotation from Hosea 6:6. In verse 5 Matthew makes reference to the instructions on the duties of priests described in Leviticus 24:8 and Numbers 28:9-10. Jesus does not dismiss the Law (see also 5:17), but when there are differing interpretations of the Law, it is he who is the authoritative interpreter of the Law.

The second controversy (vv. 9-14), involving a cure on the sabbath, takes place in a synagogue. The question put to Jesus in verse 10 is a trap. Jesus cleverly replies, arguing from the lesser to the greater (as also 6:25, 26, 30; 10:31). His accusers readily recognize that they would rescue a sheep in danger on the sabbath. How much more valuable is a person in need, Jesus advances. The point of debate is whether or not the need is life-threatening, thus warranting saving action on the sabbath, which is allowed. Again, this episode highlights Jesus' authority to interpret the Law and the deadly hostility which that claim provokes.

12:15-21 Approved by God

At the center of the controversy stories in chapter 12 is Matthew's longest fulfillment quotation, that is, the use of citations from the Old Testament to interpret what he is saying about Jesus. The main point of the citation from Isaiah 42:1-4 is to underscore Jesus' identity as the one approved of and chosen by God, even as human authorities reject him and seek to do away with him. There are echoes of God's affirmation of the beloved Son at his baptism (3:17) and transfiguration (17:5). The emphasis is not on the suffering of the servant, but on his meekness and gentleness (11:29; 21:4-5). That Jesus has the spirit of God (v. 18) prepares for the ensuing controversy in 12:22-32.

Matthew 12

12:22-37 Power from the Spirit of God

This episode begins with a healing very similar to that in 9:32-34. This time the controversy centers on the source of Jesus' power. The crowd continues to react favorably, though they are uncertain about Jesus' identity (v. 23). The religious leaders, however, continue their offensive, this time accusing Jesus of exorcising by the power of Beelzebul. The etymology of this disdainful name for Satan is uncertain. Most likely it derived from "Baalzebub," "Lord of the Flies," a Philistine deity (2 Kgs 1:2). The impact of Jesus' reply is that since his deeds of power are destroying Satan's realm, he cannot be using Satan's power. He then turns the tables and suggests that it is his opponents who are in the grip of Satan's power (v. 27). Returning to his own defense, Jesus spells out that it is by the spirit of God that he performs exorcisms (v. 28)—clear signs of the inbreaking of God's realm. Jesus, the stronger one (see 3:11), binds up Satan (v. 29) by his deeds of power.

A series of loosely connected sayings follows. First there is a warning that one cannot stay neutral in this power struggle (v. 30). Then follow ominous sayings about blasphemy against the Spirit (vv. 31-32). This unforgivable sin is attributing to Satan what is truly of God. This is a warning to the religious leaders. They knowingly pit themselves against God by opposing Jesus. By so doing, they close themselves off from God's boundless offer of forgiveness. It is not that God refuses to forgive, but that they have consciously refused to accept forgiveness (see 5:43-48; 18:23-35). Then Matthew uses a favorite metaphor, bearing fruit (vv. 33-37; see also 3:8, 10; 7:16-20; 13:23; 21:19), to unmask further the wickedness of the religious leaders. Their deeds, and especially their spoken opposition to Jesus, reveal their true nature.

12:38-47 An evil generation

A shift of scene brings scribes and Pharisees asking for a sign from Jesus. The many signs Jesus has already performed have not led them to faith; more of the same will likewise have no effect on those who have already chosen evil (v. 39). One final sign remains: that of Jesus' death and resurrection. But even this mighty deed will not convince everyone (27:62-63; 28:17). The theme of outsiders who respond more favorably than Israel, particularly its leaders, surfaces once again (similarly 2:1-11; 8:10-12; 11:20-24), as even Ninevites and the Queen of the South (1 Kgs 10:1-13) will participate in judging the unrepentant.

The saying about the roaming unclean spirit (vv. 43-45) warns that in addition to initial repentance ("swept clean," v. 44), one must become filled

Matthew 12

with Jesus, allowing him to take possession and dwell within. The religious leaders appear to have everything in order (v. 44), when in fact, they are empty within (similarly 23:27-28). In addition to renouncing evil Jesus' disciples must have a full heart (12:34) that actively seeks the realm of God and a life that produces good fruit.

12:46-50 True family

The final vignette in this section brings Jesus' mother and siblings onto the scene. Matthew does not give a motive for their wanting to speak with him. Are they for him or against him? At 10:34-39 Jesus has spoken about the family divisions that disciples face. Is that the case with his own family? This is the last mention of Jesus' family members. Those bound to Jesus in discipleship are as family to him and to one another.

13:1-53 The parables discourse

The third major block of teaching comprises seven parables, two allegorical explanations (vv. 18-23, 36-43), and a theory on Jesus' use of parables (vv. 10-17, 34-35, 51-52). These puzzling stories use figurative language to speak in everyday terms about the realm of God. Yet there is usually a twist, so that they do not simply tell how life is but challenge the hearer to convert to how life can be in God's realm. They are usually open-ended, allowing for a variety of interpretations.

13:1-9 Parable of the sower, seed, soil, harvest

The scene shifts from the controversies with religious leaders to a large crowd eager for Jesus' teaching (vv. 1-2). Matthew's rendition closely follows that of Mark (4:1-9). A different message comes forth, depending on which "character" is the focus: the sower, the seed, the soil, or the harvest. The sower is usually thought to represent God or Jesus, while the seed is the word of God (vv. 18-23). When focusing on the sower, the central point concerns how the farmer acts: he indiscriminately sows seed on every type of ground, offering the word to everyone, regardless of their potential for accepting it (similarly 5:45). The exhortation in verse 9 recalls the *Shemaʾ*, ("Hear O Israel," Deut 6:4-5), prayed each day by observant Jews. This prayer underscores Israel's unique relationship with God, while Jesus' parable widens the invitation to all.

When the seed is the focus, the point shifts to the reliability of the seed to bring forth a yield, even though it first seems that there will be no harvest. The parable echoes Isaiah 55:10-11, assuring that God's word does accomplish its purpose, even though much of it falls on deaf ears. Shifting attention to the harvest, the point is the assurance not only that the work will eventually bear fruit but that the harvest will explode in staggering proportions. The huge amounts in verse 8 are hyperbolic and propel the hearer into an eschatological scenario. The image of harvest is often used to speak of the end time (see also 13:30, 39; 21:34, 41). A good harvest yields up to tenfold. One that produces one hundred or sixty or thirtyfold is unimaginable. Fulfillment at the end time will far exceed all that we know here and now. Finally, if one focuses on the soil, the message concerns the quality and conditions needed for the word to be nurtured and come to fruition in the lives of disciples. The explanation in verses 18-23 elaborates this interpretation.

13:10-17 The reason for speaking in parables

Matthew, in contrast to Mark (4:1-12), draws a clear division between Jesus' disciples and the crowd. Rather than ask Jesus to explain the parable to them, the disciples ask why Jesus speaks to the crowd in parables (v. 10). Jesus explains that disciples have been given a gift from God to understand the "mysteries of the kingdom of heaven" (v. 11), that is, the presence of God's realm in Jesus and his ministry. Verses 13-17 emphasize human responsibility to respond to God's gift. The effect of the quotation from Isaiah 6:9-10 is to place the blame for not understanding on those who deliberately block their ears to God's word, in contrast to the blessedness of those who do respond to God's grace (vv. 16-17).

13:18-23 Explanation of the parable of the soil

Rarely in the Gospels are parables explained. This and the explanation of the weeds and wheat (13:36-43) are exceptions. Ordinarily parables are open-ended, requiring the hearer to wrestle with their enigmatic challenges. Most likely 13:18-23 represents an interpretation by the early church rather than words from Jesus' lips. The allegorical explanation focuses on the varying levels of receptivity of the four different types of soil, that is, the four types of hearers of the word. The emphasis is on the hearer; each is exhorted to cull out all impediments to becoming "rich soil." The parable also helps explain why some hearers of the word "bear fruit" and others don't.

13:24-30 Weeds among the wheat

This parable, unique to Matthew, wrestles with the questions of who is responsible for evil (vv. 27-28a) and what is to be done about it (vv. 28b-30). The first question is easily answered: an enemy is responsible (v. 28). The more difficult question is what is the best course of action to take with regard to the weeds. The householder's reply is startling, since the best method is to eradicate the weeds as early as possible. To try to separate the two at harvest is difficult and not totally effective. Moreover, to let the two grow together poses danger to the wheat seedlings as they compete for water and nutrients.

The parable does not tell whether the householder's plan succeeded. If one presumes that it did, then the parable assures that the forces of good can withstand the forces of evil, and it advocates patient trust in the One whose job it is to do the separating at the end time. Alternatively, if the householder is seen as a foolish absentee landlord who greedily thinks that even the weeds can bring him benefit as fuel, then the parable speaks of good news to peasants who watch exploitive landowners brought down by one of their own. One other twist may be that the parable invites nonretaliation against an enemy (as 5:43-48), an action that is vindicated in the end time.

13:31-32 Mischievous mustard

The most common interpretation of this parable is that just as a tiny mustard seed grows into a large tree, so the realm of God grows enormously from its small beginnings. But this explanation misses the possible twist and the call for conversion that may lie beneath the surface. That the mustard becomes a large tree *(dendron)*, a botanical impossibility, may point to a burlesque of the image in Ezekiel 17, 31, and Daniel 4. Rather than think of the coming reign of God as a majestic cedar tree imported from Lebanon, Jesus uses the image of a lowly garden herb that grows right in one's own backyard. God's realm is not like a dominating empire, but its power erupts out of weakness. Its transformative power comes from unpretentious ventures of faith by Jesus' disciples. Moreover, the uncontrollable growth of mustard, crossing over boundaries to mix with other crops, offers an image for the manner in which Gentile Christians were growing exponentially and intermingling with Jewish believers in the Matthean community.

13:33-35 Hiding leaven

Important to the meaning of this parable is that in every other instance in Scripture in which leaven occurs, it represents evil or corruption (Exod 12:15-20, 34; Mark 8:15; Luke 12:1; 1 Cor 5:6-7; Gal 5:9). The startling message is that the reign of God is like a batch of dough that has been permeated by "corruptive" agents. It offers both hope to those who have been on the margins or excluded and a challenge to those who are in a privileged position. An odd detail is that the woman hides *(kryptō)* the leaven in the dough, which brings out again the paradox of hiddenness and revelation with regard to Jesus and his message (10:26; 11:25; 13:35, 44). It is also important to note that it is the work of a woman that is the vehicle for God's revelation. The amount of flour also indicates a revelation of God is in the offing. Every time a character in the Scriptures bakes with three measures of flour (approximately fifty pounds!), it is in preparation for heavenly visitors (Gen 18:6; Judg 6:19; 1 Sam 1:24). In verses 34-35 Matthew quotes Psalm 78:2 to explain again (as in 13:10-17) that Jesus' disciples have a privileged place of understanding, while the message remains hidden to the crowds.

13:36-43 The weeds and wheat explained

The allegorical explanation of the parable in 13:24-30 is likely not from the lips of Jesus but represents how the early Christians made sense of it (as with 13:18-23). The audience shifts from the crowds to Jesus' disciples (v. 36), as they become privy once again to special understanding. Each detail is given a symbolic meaning. The tone is apocalyptic as evildoers are separated once and for all from the righteous and their opposite fates are sealed. A warning is sounded to anyone who will listen that they be found among the "children of the kingdom" and not among the "children of the evil one." There is a shift from 13:16, where the disciples were blessed *because* they see and hear; now the possibility lies open that a disciple may not hear (v. 43).

13:44-53 Treasure found, stored, and shared

The parables of the buried treasure (v. 44) and the pearl of great price (vv. 45-46) offer two different ways of coming upon the reign of God: finding it unexpectedly or after a diligent search. Both speak of the total response required (as also 4:18-22; 9:9). The emphasis, however, is not on how much one has to give up, but on the immense joy that comes from the complete investment of self and resources in God's realm. The parable of the net (vv. 47-48) and its explanation (vv. 49-50) mirrors that of the weeds and the wheat and its interpretation (13:24-30, 36-43), both in wording and message.

The final verses (51-52) tie together the whole parable discourse in chapter 13. The disciples have a certain privileged level of understanding (13:11-12, 16-17), but their comprehension is by no means complete. The saying about scribes who have been instructed is often thought to be a self-portrait of the evangelist, but it actually characterizes the educated disciple, schooled in Jesus' interpretation of the Law, thus knowing how to preserve what is essential from the old for a new reality.

13:54-58 Rejected prophet

The divided responses to Jesus' teaching play out not only with disciples and crowds, as in the previous discourse on the parables, but also with his own family and neighbors. In a close-knit village, everyone presumes to know everything about Jesus, yet he startles them with his wisdom and mighty deeds. As they puzzle over the source of Jesus' power, the reader is led to supply the answer with a response of faith. The reference to Jesus' siblings has been understood in various ways: as other children of Mary and Joseph, cousins of Jesus, or Joseph's children from an earlier marriage. It is not clear whether Matthew knew the tradition about Mary's perpetual virginity (see 1:25).

14:1-12 Death of John the Baptist

The theme of the rejection of Jesus by his own is heightened as Jesus' likeness to John is voiced by Herod (see also 16:14). John's arrest was the catalyst for Jesus to begin his ministry in Galilee (4:12) and to reveal himself as the coming One and Wisdom incarnate (11:2-19). Like John, Jesus too will be executed and buried by his disciples. Matthew follows Mark 6:14-29 in retelling John's death. He shortens and simplifies the account, shifting the spotlight more toward Herod, not his wife, as the responsible one.

14:13-21 Feeding of the five thousand

In contrast to Herod's deadly banquet, where the king seeks to satisfy his own desires, Jesus hosts a vast multitude, healing and feeding them until they are all satisfied (v. 20). From the midst of his own grief at the death of his mentor (v. 13), his wounded heart fills with compassion for others who are suffering (v. 14). The same faithful God who provided manna and quail for Israel in the wilderness wandering (Exod 16; Num 11:31-35) and who worked through Elisha to feed a hungry crowd (2 Kgs 4:42-44) acts now through Jesus to bring well-being to the people. Jesus' saying that many would come from east and west to eat with Israel's ancestors in the realm of God (8:11) is enacted here. The parable of the great banquet (22:1-10) will also return to this theme. The parallels with the Last Supper (26:26) are unmistakable as Jesus takes, blesses, breaks, and gives the bread. There are also overtones of the eschatological banquet envisioned by Isaiah (25:6-10). In contrast to the disciples' solution to have all in the crowd take care of themselves, Jesus points them toward the abundance—even surfeit—of resources that are already in their midst to be shared (see also 15:32-39). Matthew makes it explicit that the participants in this feast are women and children as well as men (v. 21).

14:22-36 Walking on water

This is the second time that Jesus demonstrates his mastery over the water. In 8:23-27 Jesus calmed the sea and the disciples' dread in the midst of a storm. In this episode Jesus shows himself to be like God, both in his ability to tread on the water (e.g., Ps 77:19; Job 9:8; 38:16) and in his self-identification as *egō eimi*, literally "I am" (v. 27), the self-designation of God to Moses (Exod 3:14). While in the Markan episode the disciples remain uncomprehending and resistant to this epiphany (6:45-52), Matthew adds a poignant vignette that captures the faltering attempts of the disciples, represented by Peter (see also 16:18-19), to overcome their fears and to step out with Jesus in faith. His power to save (1:21; 8:25) takes them beyond their little faith (also 6:30; 8:26; 16:8; 17:20) to the ability to proclaim him "Son of God" (see 3:17; 16:16; 17:5; 27:54).

Jesus continues his saving ministry to all those who are sick. As a pious Jew, he is wearing tassels as a reminder to keep God's commandments (Num 15:38-40; Deut 22:12). Those who want to touch these are expressing their desire to live in the way that is faithful to God, through Jesus (as also the woman with a hemorrhage, 9:20-22). All who do so are saved (the verb *diesōthēsan*, v. 36, means both "saved" and "healed").

15:1-20 Blind guides

This section begins with a confrontation between Jesus and the religious leaders (vv. 1-9), followed by a declaration of Jesus to the crowd (vv. 10-11), then a discussion between Jesus and his disciples (vv. 12-20). Matthew follows Mark (7:1-23) but makes substantial changes. He tones down Mark's sweeping critique of Jewish practices (7:13), although he does heighten the censure of the Pharisees with his addition of verses 13-14. In contrast to Mark's mostly Gentile community, Matthew's community probably still observed many of the Jewish practices and did not find these incompatible with Jesus' teaching.

The "tradition of the elders" (v. 2) refers to customs and regulations passed down orally, interpreting how to live the Law in everyday life. These began to be codified in written collections around A.D. 200. The debate over the level of authority such traditions carried was a lively one both in Jesus' day and in Matthew's. Jesus denounces those whose interpretation is not in accord with God's intent (vv. 3, 6). As examples, he cites the imposition of purity practices (v. 2), meant only for priests (Exod 30:19; 40:12); distorted use of *korban*, the custom of declaring something dedicated to God (vv. 3-9); and giving cultic purity (regarding unclean foods) priority over moral purity (v. 11). Purity of the heart is fundamental (vv. 17-20); from this all authentic ritual practice flows.

Matthew 15

The quotation from Isaiah 29:13 (vv. 8-9) is an invitation to the hearers to open their hearts to Jesus (similarly 13:15, 19). In contrast to Jesus, who leads the blind to sight and faith (9:27-31; 20:30-34), his opponents are blind guides (see also 23:16, 17, 19, 24, 26), taking themselves and others toward disaster and judgment.

15:21-28 Tenacious faith

This is one of the most disturbing episodes in the Gospel. In no other story does Jesus ignore and then insult a person who comes to him in need. Matthew does not say why Jesus is headed toward the pagan coastal region; it is not to extend his mission beyond his own people (v. 24; see also 9:36; 10:6; 18:12). There are two tensions in this story: they involve crossing both ethnic and gender boundaries. The cry of the Canaanite woman, *eleēson me*, "Have pity on me," recalls Psalm 109:26 and the pleas of the blind men (9:27; 20:30, 31) and the father of the boy with epilepsy (17:15). This is also a liturgical formula, which may reveal tensions in Matthew's community not only over Gentile inclusion but also over the role of women in the liturgical and theological life of the community.

Jesus' retort (v. 26) may allude to Isaiah 56:10, where those who are blind and without knowledge are like "dumb dogs." Or it may allude to the tension between Galileans and coastal peoples, as the Galileans often saw their grain exported to Tyre and Sidon, leaving themselves without enough (see Acts 12:20). The woman's clever response displays her great and tenacious faith (v. 28), which contrasts with that of the disciples, whose fearfulness so often displays their "little faith" (6:30; 8:26; 14:31; 16:8; 17:20). Perhaps Jesus' confrontation with this woman was a turning point in his understanding of his mission to all peoples (28:19).

15:29-39 Healing and feeding more multitudes

This episode replays 14:15-21 with slight differences. Unlike the Markan feeding stories (6:34-44; 8:1-10), where the first takes place in Jewish territory and the second on the Gentile side of the lake, Matthew makes no such distinction. For him, Jesus' mission is still restricted to Israel (10:5; 15:24). As in 14:15-21, the feeding is linked with healing. This time there is also a didactic element. Jesus sits on a mountaintop (v. 29), a teacher akin to Moses (see also 5:1; 17:1; 28:16). The disciples seem to have progressed in their understanding. This time they do not propose to Jesus that the crowd be sent away to find food for themselves. They are ready with seven loaves, and, as before, they help Jesus distribute them. While the same theological motifs are in play as in 14:15-21, there is slightly more emphasis on messianic fulfillment, as the kind of healings Jesus does echo those of the messianic age described in Isaiah 35:5-6. Also, the messianic banquet is to be set on a mountaintop (Isa 25:6-10).

16:1-12 The leaven of the Pharisees and Sadducees

That the feedings of the multitudes were meant to be teaching moments for Jesus' disciples is clear from the dialogue in verses 5-12. This conversation is preceded by a confrontation between Jesus and the religious leaders. By the time Matthew is writing, the Sadducees are no longer an entity. After the destruction of the temple in A.D. 70, their priestly ministry and power base disappeared. Matthew's linking of Pharisees and Sadducees (as at 3:7-10) is a sweeping expression to include all rival religious leaders. Jesus' denunciation of them reflects the conflicts in Matthew's day between the followers of Jesus and those still adhering to synagogue affiliation. The rival religious leaders question Jesus not with sincerity but with the intent to test *(peirazō)* him, as the devil did (4:1, 3). Even though they have signs, they are predisposed not to respond with faith. See 12:38-47 on the sign of Jonah as a reference to Jesus' death and resurrection.

The disciples, in contrast, struggle to move from "little faith" (v. 8; similarly 6:30; 8:26; 14:31) to understanding and belief. Jesus' query about their not remembering (vv. 5, 9) is not so much pointing out a lapse in memory as it is an accusation of disobedience. Unfaithfulness to the covenant is repeatedly spoken of in the Old Testament as forgetfulness of God or of the commandments (e.g., Deut 4:9; 8:11; 9:7; Isa 17:10; Jer 18:15). The symbol of leaven for corruption occurs often in the Scriptures (see 13:33). In contrast to Mark's version of this episode (8:1-10), Matthew's disciples do finally grasp what it is that Jesus, the authoritative teacher, is telling them (v. 12).

JESUS AND HIS DISCIPLES ON THE WAY TO JERUSALEM
Matt 16:13–20:34

16:13-28 Following the Messiah to the cross

This episode constitutes a major turning point in the Gospel. It begins in the northernmost region of Israel, Caesarea Philippi, a city given to Herod the Great by Augustus and rebuilt by Herod's son Philip, who renamed the city after himself and the emperor. The scene moves from the question of Jesus to his disciples about his identity (vv. 13-20), to the first prediction of the passion (vv. 21-23; reiterated at 17:22-23; 20:17-19), to Jesus' instructions to his disciples about taking up the cross (vv. 24-28). The expression "From that time on" (v. 21) signals a major shift in the story. This same phrase, which introduces Jesus' public ministry in Galilee (4:17), now points attention to Jesus' ministry and death in Jerusalem.

On Jesus' identity as "Son of Man" (v. 13) see the comments on 8:20; for his relationship with John the Baptist and Elijah, see 3:1-17; 4:1-11; 9:18-26; 11:1-19; 14:1-12; 17:9-13. Matthew is unique in drawing parallels between Jesus and Jeremiah through his explicit quotations of the prophet (2:17; 27:9) and his allusions to him (7:15-23; 11:28-30; 23:37-39). The declaration of Jesus' messiahship (v. 16) is not a new revelation in Matthew (see 1:1, 17, 18; 11:2). But the nature of Jesus' messiahship as entailing his suffering and death (v. 21) is articulated here for the first time.

As frequently in Matthew, Peter takes a prominent role as spokesperson for the disciples (see also 14:28; 15:15; 17:4, 24-27; 18:21; 19:27; 26:33). The blessing of Peter in verses 17-19 is unique to Matthew. It plays on the meaning of his name, *Petros* ("rock") in Greek, *Cephas* in Aramaic (1 Cor 15:5), and counters the worship for which Caesarea Philippi was known. It had a sanctuary for the god Pan, with a large rock-faced cliff with carved niches that held statues. Jesus' blessing of Peter exalts the emerging rock-like faith, not only of Peter but of the whole community of disciples. This is the unshakable foundation (see 7:24-27) for those who cling to the "stone that the builders rejected" (21:42; Ps 118:22). Jesus assures the community that God will stand behind their decisions about membership, regulations, and forgiveness (see 18:18, where all the members are given the power to "bind" and to "loose").

Peter's reaction to Jesus' prediction of the passion highlights the fact that the formation of the disciples is not yet complete. The "rock" falters when confronted with the stumbling block (*skandalon*, 18:6, 7) of the passion. Jesus then builds on the instructions begun at 10:38-39 in the mission discourse. To be his disciple entails willingness to lose even life itself. To take up one's cross does not refer to enduring whatever suffering comes in life; rather, it refers specifically to the willingness to suffer the consequences for proclaiming and living the Gospel. So it is not a saying that encourages persons who are victimized or suffering to simply bear it as their way of identifying with Jesus.

As we have seen in the Gospel, Jesus always healed and alleviated the suffering of all such persons. Likewise the saying about denial of self is not simply self-denial in the sense of choosing to giving up certain pleasures; rather, it concerns the disciples' choice to lose themselves entirely in Christ—to take on his way of life and mission and his very identity as one's own. Paradoxically, this is the way that truly leads to life. A reminder about judgment and the imminent coming of the Son of Humanity (vv. 27-28) underscores that the choice to follow Jesus or not carries eternal consequences.

17:1-13 The transfiguration of Jesus and the coming of Elijah

The question of Jesus' identity and what that means continues to loom large in this episode. On the heels of Jesus' teaching that he must suffer and die and then be raised up (16:21), the reader is given utter assurance that Jesus' execution does not mean that he is accursed (Deut 21:23) or in any way rejected by God. The brilliance of his face and clothing (v. 2) indicates his righteousness (see 13:43). The voice from heaven (v. 5) reaffirms the message heard at Jesus' baptism (3:17): he is God's beloved one. The instruction "listen to him" (v. 5) echoes Deuteronomy 18:15 and insists that Jesus is the correct interpreter of the Law and the Prophets, signified by the figures of Moses and Elijah (v. 3).

Matthew further highlights the portrait of Jesus as the new Moses with the details of the high mountain (v. 1; see also 5:1; 15:29; 28:16), Jesus' shining face (v. 2, like that of Moses after his encounter with God on Mount Sinai, Exod 34:29), and the overshadowing cloud (v. 5, like that which signaled God's presence with Israel in their sojourn to freedom, Exod 16:10; 19:9, etc.). Matthew specifically labels this experience a vision (v. 9), and the disciples react in much the same way as Daniel did to his apocalyptic visions (Dan 8:17-18; 10:7-9).

The discussion about Elijah (vv. 9-13) reflects a debate about the correct interpretation of Malachi 4:5 (3:23 Hebrew), which speaks about the coming of Elijah before the Day of the Lord. For Christians this has taken place in the person of John the Baptist (see also 3:1-17; 9:18-26; 11:1-19; 14:1-12).

17:14-20 The power of little faith

The tragic situation of a child who suffers from what is probably epilepsy (the Greek word *selēniazomai* literally means "moonstruck") becomes an occasion for further training for the disciples. The father's plaintive "Lord, have pity" echoes the pleas of other sufferers in the Gospel (8:2, 5-6, 25; 14:30; 15:22, 25; 20:30-31). While the disciples have been given the authority to cure every disease and illness (10:1), Matthew has not yet reported that they were ever able to do so (cf. Mark 6:13, 30). Jesus' harsh words for the disciples echo those of Moses as he voiced his exasperation with Israel (Deut 32:5). Jesus redirects the disciples away from focusing on what they lack, toward claiming and exercising the power they do have with their little faith (see also 6:30; 8:26; 14:31; 16:8; 21:21-22). See 13:31-32 for the parable of the mustard seed.

Matthew 17

17:22-23 Second prediction of the Passion

The reaction of the disciples to this second prediction of Jesus' death and resurrection is not denial, as in 16:21-23, but overwhelming grief. Their progress in comprehension and acceptance advances as they move with Jesus toward Jerusalem (contrast Mark 9:2).

17:24-27 The temple tax

This story is peculiar to Matthew's Gospel. The issue is the payment of a yearly tax of a half-shekel that was obligatory for all Jewish males over twenty years old (Exod 30:11-16). This served for the upkeep of the temple, as well as a sign of solidarity among Jews both within Israel and in the Diaspora. Controversy over this payment may have stemmed from disapproval over the manner in which the money was used by the Sadducees or the shaming of those who were too poor to contribute. Jesus' exchange with Peter makes it clear that as children of God, whose house the temple is, they are exempt from taxes for the temple. Nonetheless, for the sake of not causing scandal, Jesus pays the money. The fantastic detail of finding a coin in the mouth of a fish gives the story the air of a folktale.

18:1-14 Greatness in God's realm

The fourth great block of teaching concerns life in community. The first section (18:1-14) focuses on the need for humility and for the care of the most vulnerable. The second (18:15-20) outlines a procedure for reconciling aggrieved members of the community, followed by a parable (18:21-35) about unlimited forgiveness. While these teachings are addressed to "the disciples" (v. 1), the nature of the instruction is to those with leadership responsibility, not to the "little ones."

In the first part (vv. 1-5) Jesus teaches leaders to cultivate humility by consciously identifying themselves with the concerns of the least important in the community. Children are certainly valued in families, but they are the most vulnerable and the least able to contribute to the sustenance of the group, at least until they are older. A second way to exercise humility is by showing hospitality toward those who are "nobodies" (v. 5). Lavishing care on them with the same attentiveness and openness that one would show to an important guest is the way of true leadership. Finally, leaders must be wary of putting any stumbling block (*skandalon*, vv. 6-9) in the way of a "little one." The consequences for doing so are dire. Matthew does not spell out precisely who the "little ones" are. They may be new converts or those whose faith is not yet strong. At 10:42 they are Christian missionaries. One's treatment of "the least" is the basis for reward or punishment at the last judgment (25:40, 45).

A further lesson in prizing each of the "little ones" is presented in the parable of the shepherd who goes to extraordinary lengths to recover a lost sheep (vv. 10-14). Christian leaders are to emulate God's care for Israel (Ps 23; Isa 40:11) and Jesus' compassion for people who are "like sheep without a shepherd" (9:36). They are not to be like the shepherds that Ezekiel (34:12) denounces for placing their own welfare above that of the "flock." They are to seek out the "lost sheep of the house of Israel" (10:6). The emphasis in Matthew's version of the parable is not on the repentance of the sheep (cf. Luke 15:7), but rather on the urgent task of the shepherd who follows God's will and experiences great joy in finding the lost (vv. 13-14).

18:15-20 A process for reconciliation

This section presents steps to be taken in the community when one member sins against another. The first step is direct confrontation, begun by the one who is offended (v. 15) and approaches the other with a willingness to forgive. The best case scenario is that this first confrontation brings about the needed repentance, and then reconciliation results. If it fails, however, the next step is to involve one or two others from the community (v. 16). The aim is to establish the truth, relying on impartial witnesses or facilitators. If this does not work, then the matter is brought before the whole community (*ekklēsia*, "church," used only here and in 16:18 in the Gospels). If that fails, then the person is to be treated like "a Gentile or a tax collector" (v. 17). It is not clear whether this means to exclude the person or to emulate Jesus' practice of befriending such people (see 8:5-13; 9:9-13; 11:19; 15:21-28).

Here Jesus may be advocating that Christians be willing to sit and break bread together, even while they are working toward resolving their differences. Note that Matthew does not indicate the nature of the offense. Such a strategy would not work for every kind of sin. Note that the whole community has a role in binding and loosing offenses (18:18), and the whole body is involved in praying for reconciliation.

18:21-35 Forgiveness aborted

The process sketched above is lengthy and arduous. Peter asks Jesus how often you have to do all this—as many as seven times? In biblical terms, seven is a perfect number, signifying here an endless number of times. Jesus' exhortation to forgive seventy-seven times (v. 22) contrasts with the threat of Lamech, who vowed vengeance "seventy-sevenfold" (Gen 4:24).

The parable plays out in three acts. In the first (vv. 23-27) a king decides to call in his "loan" (*daneion*), that is, the money due him from a slave who

Matthew 18

is a high-level bureaucrat (indicated by the amounts of money with which he deals, v. 24). This slave is evidently responsible for exacting tribute from other subjects. He builds networks and works the system to his and the king's advantage. The king, in a pure display of power, wants to collect ten thousand talents, approximately six to ten thousand days' wages. His purpose is to remind the servant of his subservience. The slave's response is exactly what the king wanted (v. 26). He does homage to the king and acknowledges his dependence and loyalty. The king is satisfied and returns him to his position. Word will spread both of the king's power and his generosity.

In the second act (vv. 28-30) the forgiven bureaucrat replicates the king's actions with his subordinates. This one owes him one hundred times less than the amount he owed the king. The point is not the difference in amount but that both are unable to pay. Although the second underling responds in exactly the same way his master did to the king, the latter carries through his threats with a vengeance instead of forgiving the debt.

In the final part (vv. 31-34) the fellow servants report everything to the king, who becomes enraged. If his servant has understood the meaning of his previous actions, then he should have replicated them. If the slave wants loyalty, adulation, and recognition of his power, the king has shown him how to exact it. Instead, he has shamed the king by not imitating him. He has said by his actions that the king's method of exerting power is not effective. If the slave thinks that physical abuse, debasing another, and brutal imprisonment are the ways to gain power, then the king will show him just that. The conclusion (v. 35) was likely added by the evangelist.

As with all metaphors, the king is both like and unlike God. Unlike the monarch in the parable, God does not work for his own self-aggrandizement, but for the well-being of all creation. But like the king, God, through Jesus, has graciously forgiven all debt of sin (for which Jesus teaches the disciples to pray in 6:12). The only response to such mercy is to let it transform one's heart so as to be able to act with the same kind of graciousness toward others. This kind of power is through vulnerability and a willingness to forgo vengeance to work toward reconciliation. Those who do not learn to imitate godly ways in their dealings with one another will be treated by God in the way they have treated others.

19:1-15 Teaching on divorce and blessing of children

In his journey toward Jerusalem, Jesus takes the route along the eastern side of the Jordan River, as did most Jews, to avoid going through Samaria

(v. 1). As at 16:1, rival religious leaders put a question to Jesus to test him (*peirazō*, as also 4:1, 3). Jesus' teaching on not divorcing was already introduced in the Sermon on the Mount (5:31-32). Now the question centers on whether there are any exceptions (v. 3). The exchange is cast as a rabbinical debate, such as the one between the first-century rabbis Shammai and Hillel. The latter held that a man could divorce his wife even for spoiling a dish for him, whereas the former argued that only sexual misconduct was grounds for divorce.

In his reply Jesus first cites Genesis 1:27 and then Genesis 2:24, arguing that God's intention from creation is for man and woman to remain united. Jesus' opponents, also citing Scripture, come back with a text from Deuteronomy 24:1-4, where Moses permits a man to divorce his wife by handing her a written bill of divorce. Jesus distinguishes between God's positive command in Genesis, which reveals God's intent, and Moses' concession to Israel because of their inability to achieve the ideal. As at 5:32, Jesus characterizes divorce as adultery, unless the basis for separating is *porneia* (v. 9). The meaning of this word is not certain. It may refer to sexual misconduct, such as adultery or marriage to close kin, which was forbidden in Jewish law (Lev 18:6-18; see also Acts 15:20, 29). If it is the latter, then the question concerns some Gentile converts who wished to become Christian but who were in such forbidden marriages. Would they first have to divorce to enter the community?

The reaction of Jesus' disciples reveals the radical nature of his teaching. "It is better not to marry" (v. 10) is akin to the hyperbole in 18:8-9, which states that it is better to cut off a hand or foot or eye rather than cause a little one to sin. Jesus acknowledges that not all can accept this teaching. It has long been debated whether the saying in verse 12 refers to those who choose to remain celibate or to those who do not remarry after the death or divorce of a spouse. In Jewish tradition marriage was the norm, although some groups, such as the Therapeutae and the Qumranites, evidently practiced celibacy.

The reason why a Christian might make such a choice is for the sake of the mission. Many widows in the early church chose to live together and to devote themselves to ministry rather than remarry (see Acts 9:39, which may refer to such a situation, and 1 Timothy 5:3-16 for regulations regarding them). For women in Jesus' day, his stricter teaching on divorce may often have served a compassionate end, safeguarding women from being cast aside for no good reason and from being placed in a vulnerable position socially and economically. By the same token, painful decisions about divorce in a contemporary context must take into consideration Jesus' prime concern for the well-being of each person as a valued son or daughter of God in the community of believers.

In verses 13-15 the lens widens to the most vulnerable members in the family unit. When linked to the previous scene, Jesus' blessing and prayer for the little ones recognize that they may be the ones who suffer most when the parents are contemplating divorce. A reason why the disciples wanted to prevent the children from coming to Jesus is not given. In a pronouncement reminiscent of 18:3, Jesus speaks about their importance in God's realm.

19:16-30 Discipleship and possessions

The exchange between Jesus and the rich young man and the ensuing discussion with the disciples speak soberly about the obstacle that possessions can pose for discipleship. In Matthew's account (cf. Mark 10:17-31; Luke 18:18-30), the rich man asks Jesus about doing good, one of the evangelist's favorite themes (5:16; 7:17-19; 12:12, 33-35; 13:23, 24; 26:10). Keeping the commandments is a first step in doing good. The young man's question, "Which ones?" rings false, since all the commandments must be kept equally. Jesus' invitation to him to go beyond simply keeping the commandments and to "be perfect" (*teleios*, as also at 5:48) concerns becoming "whole" or "complete." As at 5:48, this is not an invitation for a select few, nor is it presenting a contrast between Judaism and Christianity. In the Old Testament, although riches are regarded as a sign of God's blessing (Deut 28:1-14), there are also the same dire warnings about the corrosiveness of riches (Ezek 7:19; Amos 6:4-8; Prov 15:16).

In Matthew's perspective, being a disciple of Jesus entails faithfulness to the Jewish Law as interpreted by Jesus, which demands radical attachment to him. It is as difficult for a rich person to do this as it is for a camel to squeeze through the eye of a needle (v. 24). The popular interpretation that there was a gate so named in Jerusalem has no basis. Jesus' response to the disciples' astonishment (similarly, 19:10) is to refocus their attention on God's initiative and power with them, enabling them to do what is good—the question with which the rich man began (v. 16). See also the beatitude of the poor in 6:3 and the admonitions that the heart lies where the treasure is (6:21) and that one cannot serve both God and mammon (6:24). The treasure to seek above all is the realm of God (13:44). The theme of reward for disciples runs throughout the Gospel (5:12, 46-47; 6:1-6, 16, 18; 10:39-42; 25:21, 23, 34). Here the focus is eschatological. Disciples share in the glory and the final judgment by the Human One, as their self-emptying for God's realm has prepared them to receive the eternal inheritance God wills for all.

Matthew 20

20:1-16 Justice in the vineyard

This parable and the previous episode conclude with the same saying about reversal (19:30; 20:16). This is a floating proverb that is tagged on to various New Testament passages in diverse contexts (see also Mark 10:31; Luke 13:30). It does not supply the meaning for the parable. In the story the first hired are paid last because the point of the story depends on their seeing what the last hired receive. The complaint of the workers in verse 12 voices what is so puzzling about this parable. Does not justice demand that those who worked more earn more? The vineyard owner has promised that he will pay what is just (*dikaios*, v. 4) and insists that he is doing no injustice (*ouk adikō se*, v. 13). He then asks, "Am I not free to do as I wish with my own money? Are you envious because I am generous?" (v. 15).

Two important points are made in the landowner's reply. If he is a figure for God, his actions show that God's generosity, which is not merited, is freely lavished on those most in need. God's generosity does no injustice, but neither can it be calculated or earned. The story *is* about people getting what they deserve: all have the right to eat for the day. From the position of the day laborers, who are on the lowest economic rung and who stand waiting all day (v. 6), wanting to work but not hired, the wage given them enables them to feed their family for one more day. Less than a denarius would be useless. From their perspective, those who were hired at the beginning of the day, though they have worked longer and harder, at least had the satisfaction of knowing all day that come sundown they would be able to feed their families. In God's realm, justice means that all are fed as a sign of God's equal and inclusive love; it does not mean getting what we deserve, either in terms of retribution for wrongdoing or recompense for good deeds.

The second point is that "evil-eye" envy is the most destructive force in a community. The question in verse 15 is, literally, "Or is your eye evil that I am good?" In a first-century worldview of limited good, anyone's gain means another one's loss. While the grumblers focus on their perceived loss, they miss the limitless goodness and generosity of the landowner. Linked with the previous discussion about the danger of riches, this parable challenges those disciples who have enough to meet their daily needs to reject acquisitiveness and attend to the needs of those who are in desperate straits.

20:17-28 To drink the cup

The third prediction of Jesus' passion is more detailed than the others and occurs as Jesus and his disciples near Jerusalem. In the first prediction

(16:21-23) Jesus told his disciples that he would be killed at the hands of the elders, chief priests, and scribes. In fact, the Jewish leaders did not have the authority to carry out capital punishment (see John 18:31). Jesus will actually be handed over to the Gentiles (v. 19), who will put him to death (cf. the second prediction, where Jesus spoke in general terms of being betrayed into human hands, 17:22-23).

It is jarring to have the disciples bickering over the places of honor in the kingdom after this sober prediction. Matthew redacts the story (cf. Mark 10:35-45), so that the mother of James and John makes the request, thus softening the critique of the disciples and making their mother the ambitious one. It is ambiguous whether the other ten are indignant at the audacity of the request or whether they are upset that these two beat them to it (v. 24).

The metaphor "cup" is used often in the Scriptures to speak of the suffering of Israel (Isa 51:17; Jer 25:15; 49:12; 51:7; Lam 4:21; *Mart. Isa.* 5:13). In 26:39 Jesus implores God to let "this cup" pass him by. Jesus then instructs the disciples on the manner of leadership they are to exercise. They are not to "lord it over" any others; rather, like Jesus himself, they are to serve the rest of the community. Jesus' service is service to the death, a giving of his life as ransom for all. The word *polys*, "many," does not exclude anyone. It reflects a Semitic expression where "many" is the opposite of "one," thus the equivalent of "all." The notion of Jesus giving his life as ransom draws on the image of a slave who buys back his freedom for a price. These last verses of the Gospel are aimed at leaders who have some degree of power, privilege, status, and choice. Their choice to take the lowly position of service is liberating when accompanied by empowerment of those who are otherwise powerless. These sayings must not be used to reinforce the servitude of those who are enslaved in whatever way.

20:29-34 A final healing

This is the last healing story in the Gospel. It mirrors the one in 9:27-31, where two blind men also cried out to Jesus, "Son of David, have pity on us!" (see also 12:23; 15:22). After having instructed his disciples on servant leadership (20:25-28), Jesus demonstrates for them the kind of descendant of King David he is. As in 9:27-31, Jesus engages the two men in conversation; he does not merely touch them and keep going. Jesus treats them not simply as objects of compassion but with dignity, as people who are able to articulate their need (v. 32). These two who see and follow (v. 34) model the response needed of disciples as Jesus now prepares to enter Jerusalem as Son of David (21:9, 15) to begin the ordeal that will culminate in his reign with God.

Matthew 21

JERUSALEM; JESUS' FINAL DAYS OF TEACHING IN THE TEMPLE

Matt 21:1–28:15

21:1-11 Entry into Jerusalem

Jesus' journey to Jerusalem, begun at 16:21, climaxes with his enthusiastic reception by a very large crowd (vv. 1-11), and his action in the temple (vv. 12-17). Both scenes are eschatological in tone and are heavily interlaced with quotations from the prophets, so that the significance in terms of fulfillment of Scriptures is most evident. Jesus enters the city from the east. The Mount of Olives, according to Zechariah 14:4 is the place where the final eschatological struggle will take place. Matthew seems to speak of two animals (v. 2), but he is preserving the parallelism of Zechariah 9:9 (quoted in v. 5), which actually describes only one beast. The prophet tells of the Messiah entering the city "riding on an ass, / on a colt, the foal of an ass." Jesus' action is a parody of that of a conqueror over a vanquished city. The Hebrew word *hôši'ânā'* means "save, please!" Here it is not so much a plea for help as an acclamation of praise. The shouts of adulation of the crowd (echoing Ps 118:26 in v. 9) contrast with the mounting antagonism of the Jewish leaders. The reaction described in verse 10, "the whole city was shaken *(eseisthē),*" points ahead to the aftermath of the death of Jesus, when "the earth quaked *(eseisthē,*" 27:51).

21:12-17 Confrontation in the temple

In Matthew's account, Jesus' entry into Jerusalem culminates with his action in the temple (cf. Mark 11:15-19, where Jesus waits until the next day). Scholars still speculate on the nature of the abuse that Jesus was protesting. The interpretation of each evangelist differs slightly. In Matthew's account, Jesus interrupts the commercial activity in the temple area (v. 12). Buying and selling of animals was necessary for temple sacrifice. Doves were the poor woman's offering after childbirth (Lev 12:6-8; Luke 2:24). Greek and Roman coins had to be changed into Tyrian shekels, not because they lacked an offensive image, but because they had the highest silver content.

Matthew interprets Jesus' action (v. 13) by combining quotations from Isaiah 56:7 and Jeremiah 7:11. The first speaks of the messianic ideal of the temple being a perfect place of prayer for all peoples (though Matthew omits that last phrase; cf. Mark 11:16). The second was a warning to the people of Judah, who continued trusting in the efficacy of temple worship while their deeds toward one another were rampantly unjust. Jeremiah warned that their corruption was defiling their "hideout," the temple, and predicted its destruction. In verses 12-13 Matthew's Jesus is a fiery prophet

Matthew 21

bent on rectifying abuse. In verses 14-17, unique to Matthew, Jesus is the compassionate healer of those who are least welcome in the temple (see Lev 21:18, where the blind and the lame are forbidden to offer sacrifices).

Jesus fulfills the messianic promise of Isaiah 35:5-6, where all, including those who are blind and lame, are healed and march exultantly into Jerusalem. Typically, the response to Jesus is divided. The leaders become indignant, while the children (see also 18:1-4; 19:13-15) sing "Hosanna to the Son of David" (see the use of this title in healing stories at 9:27; 12:23; 15:22; 20:30, 31). Jesus responds by quoting from Psalm 8:3.

21:18-22 The withered fig tree

This strange story may have evolved from the parable of the fig tree in Luke 13:6-9. Fruitful figs and vines are a symbol of peace and prosperity (1 Kgs 4:25), and Matthew frequently uses the metaphor "bear fruit" to speak of doing righteous deeds (cf. 3:8; 7:15-20; 12:33-37; 13:23; 21:19, 33-43). In the Matthean setting, there are strong eschatological overtones from chapter 21 forward. The time has arrived when there must be evidence of "good fruit," or else there will be destruction of the temple and condemnation of those who lead people astray (see also Jer 8:13; Hos 9:10, 16). The last two verses shift emphasis, so that the story becomes one about the power of faith (see also 7:7-11; cf. 6:30; 8:25, 26; 14:30, 31; 16:8; 17:20, where Jesus chides the disciples for their lack of faith). Jesus does not promise that the object of every prayerful request will be granted; rather, he assures believers that when they pray with faith in God's gracious goodness, God will always be with them (1:23; 28:20). God's power is at work in believers, even when they confront the most insurmountable obstacles.

21:23-27 The authority of Jesus

Throughout Matthew's Gospel, Jesus is portrayed as the authoritative teacher whom many people follow but whom the leaders reject. Now there are open confrontations between Jesus and the religious authorities. The chief priests and elders (v. 23) are the leading opponents in the passion narrative (the Pharisees drop out of view after chapter 23). Their trap backfires, and they themselves are trapped by Jesus' question. Three parables follow, the first two of which indirectly answer the question about the source of Jesus' authority.

21:28-32 Saying and doing

The technique Jesus uses is like that of Nathan (2 Sam 12:1-12), whereby the hearers are asked for their opinion and end by pronouncing judgment on themselves. The parable seems a simple one at first. Both children (the word in verse 28 is *teknon*, "child," not *huios*, "son") fall short of the ideal. But the one who appeared to *do* the father's will was the first.

However, in a culture that highly prizes honor, the answer is not so clear. In some manuscript variants of this parable, the one who gives the correct answer is the second child. The first child shamed the father publicly, a worse fault than failing to carry through on one's word. At 7:21-27 Jesus insisted to his disciples that saying *and* doing are necessary; now he directs this message to religious authorities who do not practice what they preach (23:3). Verses 31-32 contrast the leaders, who should most exemplify righteousness, with those who are thought least able to do so. But there is still time for the leaders to repent. Those who initially refuse to say yes to Jesus and do the will of God can still change their minds.

21:33-43 Treacherous tenants

Matthew reworks Mark's version (12:1-12), making the parable more allegorical and more pointedly christological. It is a familiar story, echoing Isaiah 5, but with a new ending. In Isaiah 5 Yahweh decides to destroy the vineyard after disappointment over the yield of sour grapes from Israel, the carefully cultivated vine. In Jesus' parable the tenants are destroyed; the vineyard remains and is entrusted to others. The eschatological time (*kairos*, v. 34) demands that fruit be evident now (see 21:18-22). The repeated sending of the servants (vv. 34-39) is like God's repeated sending of the prophets to Israel. Prophets were called "servants" of God (Jer 7:25; 25:4; Amos 3:7; Zech 1:6), and their fates match those in the parable (see Jer 20:2; 26:20-23; 2 Chr 24:21).

The sequence of actions in verse 39 corresponds to the details of Jesus' passion. He is seized (26:50), taken outside the city limits (27:31-32), and then killed (27:35). The murderous plans of the tenants in the vineyard match the intent of the chief priests and Pharisees (21:46; 22:15) toward Jesus. The chief priests and elders pronounce their own self-condemnation (v. 41), but the future tense verbs show that the possibility is yet open so the Jewish leaders can still change their minds (as also 21:29, 32). They could still be among those "other tenants" to whom the vineyard will be entrusted.

Jesus' question in verse 42 (see also 12:3, 5; 19:4; 21:16) underscores the conflict between Jesus' interpretation of Scripture and that of the opposing religious leaders. The quotation from Psalm 118 in verse 42 recalls God's unlikely choice of David as king, the prototype for the Messiah, and points toward the leadership of the new Israel as coming from those rejected as unimportant. At the conclusion (vv. 45-46) the chief priests and Pharisees clearly understand the parable (cf. 13:51), but instead of heeding Jesus' invitation, they plot his arrest.

22:1-14 Dressed for the feast

This is the third of three parables that Jesus addresses to the religious leaders in Jerusalem after they challenged his authority (21:23-27). The parable is highly allegorized and has a number of unrealistic details. The image of a wedding banquet recalls Matthew 9:15, where Jesus was likened to a groom, whose presence demands feasting, not fasting. This metaphor is frequently used in the Scriptures to signify God's abundant care, both now and at the end time (e.g., Isa 25:6-10; 55:1-3). The repeated invitation is reminiscent of the multiple envoys in 21:33-46 and has an echo of Lady Wisdom inviting all to her banquet (Prov 9:5). The custom of a double invitation (see Esth 5:8; 6:14) allowed the potential guest to find out who the other guests were and whether all was being arranged appropriately. It also gave them time to decide if they would be able to reciprocate. The time lapse also allowed the host to determine the amount of food needed.

Unlike Luke 14:15-24, there are no detailed excuses offered by the invitees. Their mistreatment and killing of the king's servants (vv. 5-6) and the king's enraged response (v. 7), are allegorical allusions to the killing of John the Baptist and the prophets and the destruction of Jerusalem in A.D. 70. The king's retaliation can be expected in an honor-and-shame system, in which one responds in kind to an affront. But his second response (vv. 8-10) is shocking. In a first-century Mediterranean world likes eat with likes, since eating together signifies sharing of values and of social position. The king sends his servants out to the places where the main road cuts through the city boundary, going out to the countryside (v. 10). This is where the poorer people lived, while the elite (5 to 10 percent of the population) lived in the center of the city. Like the parables in 13:24-30, 47-50, both "good" and "bad" are gathered in, and then there is sorting out.

The last scene (vv. 11-14) is entirely unrealistic but highlights Matthew's ethical concern: one must be ready at all times for the end-time banquet, clothed with good deeds (similarly Rom 13:14; Gal 3:27; Col 3:12). More is required of a disciple than initial acceptance of the invitation to be a "friend of God and prophets" (Wis 7:27). See also 20:13, where the grumbler is called "friend," as is Judas at the moment of betrayal (26:50). In the Matthean narrative context, the parable is a warning to the religious leaders who are offered repeated invitations to accept Jesus. The seriousness of their refusal is painted with vivid metaphors: they will be cast into the outer

Matthew 22

darkness (see also 8:12; 25:30), where there is weeping and gnashing of teeth (8:12, 13:42, 50; 24:51; 25:30). The proverbial saying in verse 14 does not entirely capture the meaning of the parable. The focus is on how those who are expected to respond to the invitation (the religious leaders) refuse, while the unexpected invitees (the socially marginal) have accepted.

22:15-22 Taxes to Caesar

This is the first of four more controversies between Jesus and the religious leaders. Their flattering words (v. 16) are true but insincere, as they proceed to lay a deliberate trap (v. 15). The question is a sticky one. Since the Roman occupation of Palestine in 63 B.C., Jews were obliged to pay tribute, or a head tax, in Roman coinage, on each man, woman, and slave. If Jesus opposes this payment, he would be advocating revolt against Rome. If he advocates payment, then he would be seen as a collaborator with the enemy. Jesus sees the malice and hypocrisy of his questioners, who have set this trap (v. 18). His clever response can be understood in one of three ways: (1) one should pay nothing to Caesar because everything belongs to God (Lev 25:23); (2) one should pay the emperor because he is God's representative (as Rom 13:1-7; 1 Pet 2:13-17); (3) one can pay Caesar but recognize that his authority is relative and that loyalty to God takes precedence. The last is the most likely meaning. As in 17:24-27, Jesus advises paying the tax, but this is not a vote of support for the occupying power. The amazed response (v. 22) of the Pharisees' disciples (see also 8:27; 9:33; 15:31; 21:20) underscores Jesus' skill in outwitting his opponents.

22:23-33 The question of resurrection

In this second controversy the Sadducees pose a question that derides belief in the resurrection. Ideas about the afterlife were diverse in Jesus' day. The notion of resurrection of the dead first appears in the book of Daniel (12:2), written in the second century B.C., and was accepted by the Pharisees but not the Sadducees (see Acts 23:6). The situation posed by the Sadducees, citing Deuteronomy 25:5-10, is absurd (although see Tobit 3:8; 6:14, where Sarah, the daughter of Raguel, outlives seven husbands). Like the previous question, it is set up to try to make Jesus contradict his own teaching or the Scriptures. It is a Bible battle in which Jesus emerges as authoritative teacher.

Jesus responds by accusing his opponents of not knowing the Scriptures or the power of God. He cites Exodus 3:6, 15-16 to argue that Israel's ancestors, who were physically dead at the time that God spoke to Moses, continued to be in relationship with God, and so they were in some sense among the living. Jesus also asserts that the Sadducees do not understand the nature of resurrection. By God's power new life will be created that is continuous in some way with the life we have known, yet it will be brought to fullness in ways we do not yet know.

22:34-40 The greatest commandment

In Mark's account (12:28-34; cf. Luke 10:25), the scribe's question is sincere, but in Matthew it leads to another controversy. The Pharisees gather together (v. 34), signaling a plot against Jesus (see 2:4; 22:41; 26:3; 27:17, 27; 28:12; possibly this also alludes to Ps 2:2). The question they pose is meant to test him (see also 22:15). All commandments are important; all must be kept. The query is not whether some laws can be disregarded, but whether Jesus, like some teachers, would sum up the Torah in a simple statement, as did Rabbi Hillel: "What is hateful to you do not do to your neighbor" (b. Šabb. 31a).

Jesus summarizes the whole of the Law in two commandments (see also 7:12). The first, the *Shemaʿ* (Deut 6:4-9), was recited twice a day by Jews. It enjoins love of God with one's whole heart, soul, and strength. The heart *(kardia)*, was considered the seat of all emotions, the soul *(psychē)*, the center of vitality and consciousness, and strength *(ischys)* denotes power or might. The second command, love of neighbor, is from the Holiness Code (Lev 19:18), which asserts that love of God is manifest in love toward the neighbor. The modern Western notion of the necessity of self-love would have been a foreign concept to people of the biblical world. They did not understand themselves in individualistic terms, but rather as enmeshed in a particular family, clan, and religious group. Dependent on others for their sense of self-identity, love of self and love of others are inseparable.

22:41-46 David's son

In the fourth and final controversy, Jesus is the one who initiates the questioning. Again, the debate centers on the correct interpretation of Scripture. The text in question is Psalm 110:1, a coronation psalm, in which God assures the new king of special honor (sitting at the right hand) and a vanquishing of his enemies (making them subservient, "under your feet"). The speaker in the psalm is David, who says that the "Lord" *(kyrios)*, meaning Yahweh, is speaking to "my lord" *(kyrios)*, meaning the new king.

Jesus stumps his opponents by asking that if David, inspired by the Spirit, calls the new king (here equated with the messiah) "lord," then he must be more than simply his son. The notion that the messiah would be a "son of David" is found in Isaiah 11:1, 10; Jeremiah 23:5. Although this is a favorite Matthean title for Jesus (1:1; 9:27; 12:23; 15:22; 20:30, 31; 21:9, 15), "Son of David" is not adequate to express all that Jesus is. This text brings together several important christological titles intimating that Jesus is also Messiah, Son of God, and Lord. The silence of Jesus' opponents indicates a victory for him. There will be no further exchanges with the leaders until the passion narrative, as he speaks now only with the crowds and his disciples.

23:1-12 Warning against hypocrisy

The whole of this chapter is a stinging denunciation by Jesus of the scribes and Pharisees, who have been cast as his opponents throughout the Gospel. Matthew expands a brief critique of scribes from Mark 12:38-40, weaving in material from Q and Luke 11:37-52. In the New Testament, scribes are religious leaders who are learned in Torah. Pharisees, lay religious leaders, differed from Sadducees in their belief in resurrection (see 22:23-33) and in oral interpretation of the Law. The excoriating tone of Jesus' rebuke reflects the vehemence of the conflict between the Christians of Matthew's community, who were predominantly Jewish, and the Jews of emerging rabbinic Judaism.

Jesus takes on the role of a prophet, much like Amos (5:18-20; 6:1-7) or Isaiah (5:8-10, 11-14), who uses the classic "woe" form to denounce the wrongdoing of a group of his own people, with the intent to turn them from evil and toward right relation with God. Jesus' words are a warning to the crowds and his disciples (v. 1) not to follow the hypocritical practices of these leaders, who do not practice what they teach (v. 3). In contrast to Jesus, whose burden is light (11:30), they lay heavy loads on people's shoulders (v. 4). They make their phylacteries and fringes noticeable to all (v. 5). (Phylacteries are leather boxes containing the parchment texts such as Exodus 13:1-16; Deuteronomy 6:4-9; 11:13-22, which are strapped to the forehead and arm during morning prayer.) Wearing "tassels" or "fringes" at the corners of the outer garments reminds a Jew to observe all God's commands (Num 15:38-39; Deut 22:12; Matt 9:20; 14:36). Jesus also criticizes the leaders' love of places of honor and deferential titles (vv. 6-10)—only he and God are to bear these titles. Like many other reform movements, there was an impulse in early Christianity toward egalitarianism and status reversal (vv. 11-12; see also 18:1-4; 19:13-15; 20:20-28).

23:13-36 Seven woes

In the seven woes that ensue, the religious leaders are repeatedly called "hypocrites"—a term that originally referred to an actor, one who put on

Matthew 23

a mask to assume another personage. In the first woe (vv. 13-14), Jesus denounces the scribes and Pharisees not only because they fail to enter into God's realm themselves but, worse yet, they block the way for others. The image of unlocking and locking the way to heaven recalls Matthew 16:19, where Peter is given the keys to God's realm. For Matthew's community, Peter and the leaders of the emergent Christian community are the authorities to be heeded rather than those of the synagogue.

The second woe (v. 15) is an accusation that the Gentile converts to Pharisaism are twice as zealous and twice as misguided as their teachers. Jesus warns that in the end they will be "child[ren] of Gehenna" rather than "children of God" (e.g., Matt 5:9, cf. 45). The name "Gehenna" derives from "The Valley *(gē)* of Hinnom," which runs south-southwest of Jerusalem. It represented the place of fiery judgment, because it was there that fires of the cult of Molech and later, smoldering refuse, were located.

In the third woe (vv. 16-22), Jesus critiques the meaningless distinctions the Pharisees invented in their oath-taking. In Jesus' world, binding obligations were set not by contracts but with one's word, by public swearing. For the most serious agreements, God's name would be invoked. But devout Jews objected to speaking God's name aloud. Just as Matthew substituted "the reign of heaven" for "the reign of God" (see 3:2), so Pharisees would swear on the gold or the gifts of the temple, objects associated with God, as a way to avoid saying the divine name. Jesus says that these fine distinctions are useless; the effect is the same. See Matthew 5:33-37 on not taking oaths at all.

In the fourth woe (vv. 23-24), Jesus accuses the leaders of not being able to distinguish between what is important and what is not. The texts on tithing (see Lev 27:30-33; Num 18:21-32; Deut 14:22-29) prescribe giving one-tenth of one's produce, flocks, wine, grain, and oil to support the temple, the Levites, and the poor. They do not mention herbs, such as mint, dill, and cumin. Jesus teaches his disciples that their observance of the Law must go beyond what is written (Matt 5:21-48), but the point is to arrive at more complete harmony with God and all that God has created (5:20, 48). The Pharisees, by contrast, engage in intensified practices of keeping the Law that lead them away from deeds of justice, mercy, and faith. Thus they become "blind guides," not seeing the way clearly themselves and leading others onto a destructive path. The outrageousness of their practice is captured in the hyperbole "swallow the camel."

The fifth woe (vv. 25-26) contrasts outer practices with inner dispositions. Jesus uses a strong term, *harpagēs*, "pillage, plunder," to speak of the corrupt inner state of the scribes and Pharisees, who misuse their power to exploit others. He also accuses them of *akrasia*, "lack of self-control" and "want of power" (see v. 25). The reference is to sexual activity or intemperance in general. By contrast, the interior disposition Jesus has taught his disciples is purity of heart (5:8), the ability to forgive from the heart (18:35), and love of God with all one's heart (22:37).

The sixth woe (vv. 27-28) continues in the same vein as the fifth. The Pharisees and scribes present a lovely exterior, seeming to be in right relation with God and others, while their interior disposition is rotten with hypocrisy and evildoing. Like white-washed sepulchers, they hide putrid decay within. White-washing sepulchers made them easily visible, so that Jews could avoid contact with them and thus maintain ritual purity (see Lev 21:1, 11).

In the seventh and last woe (vv. 29-36), the Pharisees and scribes pretend to honor the prophets and righteous ancestors with decorated monuments and protest that had they been alive earlier, they would never have done what their ancestors did to the prophets. In truth, Jesus says, they are no different from their forebears. They will kill the prophet Jesus just as their ancestors rid themselves of the pesky prophets who denounced their unrighteousness. They show themselves to be not children of God but children of Gehenna (v. 15) and children of murderers (v. 31), linked to all the innocent blood shed from Abel to Zechariah, the first victim of murder in the Bible (Gen 4:8) to the last. There is some confusion about the identity of Zechariah. The Old Testament prophet Zechariah was the son of Barachiah (Zech 1:1), but as far as we know, he was not murdered "between the sanctuary and the altar" (v. 35), as was Zechariah, son of Jehoiada (2 Chr 24:20-22).

The theme of responsibility for innocent blood is an important one in the passion narrative as Judas tries to return the blood money (27:4), Pilate tries to wash himself of guilt for Jesus' blood (27:24), and the people say to Pilate, "His blood be on us and on our children" (27:25). At the Last Supper Jesus offers to his disciples his "blood of the covenant" (26:28) for the forgiveness of sins.

23:37-39 Lament over Jerusalem

The tone shifts from vehement denunciation of the leaders to profound sadness for the city which destroys God's messengers and which, by Matthew's day, lies in ruins. The poignant image of a mother bird yearning to gather her rebellious young under her wings is a common metaphor in the Scriptures for God's loving care (Deut 32:11; Ruth 2:12; Pss 17:8; 36:7; 57:1; 61:4; Luke 13:34-35). But like a mother who never abandons even the most

Matthew 23

wayward child, Jesus, quoting Psalm 118:26, holds out the promise that they will see him again when they can receive him as did the disciples when he first entered Jerusalem (21:9).

The denunciations and woes in this chapter must always be read in the context of a bitter internal family dispute between the Jewish Christians and Jews who did not join them in Matthew's day. Jesus is a prophet admonishing his own leaders and inviting them to a change of heart. His words still sound a warning against hypocrisy to any religious leaders.

24:1–25:46 The apocalyptic discourse

Jesus has been teaching his disciples and warning and disputing with other religious leaders since 21:23. He now leaves the temple area and directs his instruction only to his disciples (24:1, 3). He speaks of the calamities that presage the coming of the Human One (24:1-33) and tells three parables (24:45–25:30) that emphasize the need for watchfulness. The parable of the final judgment (25:31-46) brings this last block of teaching to a climax.

24:1-14 The beginning of the end

The tension between Jesus and the temple leadership has been mounting. He has performed a prophetic action of purification in the temple (21:12-17), he has engaged in debates with the temple leadership (21:23–22:46), and he has warned his disciples about their hypocrisy (23:1-36). This comes to a head as Jesus now predicts the very destruction of the temple (24:1-2), an occurrence that Jeremiah (7:1-15) associated with the messianic age. In Matthew's day this has already occurred. At his interrogation before the Jewish leaders, false witnesses accuse Jesus of making threats against the temple (26:61) and passers-by deride him about this in the crucifixion scene (27:40).

Jesus then speaks about the signs of the end times. He is seated, as authoritative teacher (see also 5:10; 15:29), on the Mount of Olives, the place associated with the final judgment (Zech 14:4). As in the parable discourse (13:10-17), Jesus' disciples receive private instruction. He paints a picture of massive chaos and destruction, with a proliferation of false messiahs, wars, famines, earthquakes, persecution, hatred because of Jesus' name, sin, betrayal, deception, lawlessness, and loss of fervor. Strife comes both from within and from without.

In almost every age people see these signs and wonder if they herald the end. A similar theme is found in the mission discourse (10:16-25, 34-39), where Jesus also assured his disciples not to fear anything because of God's constant care for them (10:26-33). Here as well, Jesus tells them that if they persevere to the end, they will be saved (v. 13). These birthpangs (v. 8) are the prelude to new life. For Matthew, this end is not imminent—the Gospel must first be preached throughout the whole world (see also 28:16-20).

24:15-31 Signs of the coming of the Human One

There will be unmistakable signs when the end actually does come. It will be as evident as lightning across the sky (v. 27) or vultures circling over a corpse (v. 28). One sign will be like the one spoken of by Daniel, the "desolating abomination" (v. 15; Dan 9:27; 11:31; 12:11). In Daniel this referred to the statue that Antiochus IV Epiphanes placed in the temple in 167 B.C., which sparked the Maccabean revolt. Still fresh in the memories of Matthew's community is that the emperor Caligula threatened a similar action in A.D. 40.

A future event of this caliber will signal the end. This is a time when immediate flight is the response to the danger (as in 2:12-13, 10:23). As is so often the case, it is mothers and children who are the most adversely affected. The disciples are to pray that it not happen at a time when the hardship would be intensified, such as winter or the sabbath. Fleeing on the sabbath (v. 20) may have drawn attention to the community and put them at risk. Or it could be a cause of division if some thought flight would break sabbath observance.

Cosmic signs (as in Isa 13:10; 34:4; Ezek 32:7; Joel 2:10, 31; 3:4; 4:15; Amos 8:9; Hag 2:6, 21) preface the final sign before the coming of the Human One (see comments at 8:20). Why mourning (v. 30) will accompany this sign is not clear—is it because of the tribulations or because people are repenting? The motif of God gathering in the elect at the end time is a common one (Deut 30:3-4; Isa 11:11-12; Ezek 37:21; 39:27-29; Zech 2:6-12).

24:32-51 Parables of watchfulness

A series of parables and figurative sayings exhorts disciples to watchfulness. The fig tree (vv. 32-35), which is different from other trees in Palestine (most are evergreens), sheds all its leaves in winter. Just as its budding is a sign of the arrival of summer, the signs in the previous verses alert disciples to the coming of the Human One. There is a tension between verse 34, which assures that the end is imminent, and verse 14, which asserts that the Gospel first has to be preached to the whole world. Disciples need to be both ready and steadfast, trusting in Jesus' words, which will never pass away (similarly the Torah, 5:18). The timing of the end is unpredictable, so disciples need to stay awake (see also 26:38, 40, 41).

While the previous verses emphasize watchfulness for the coming of the master, the parable of the faithful servant (vv. 45-51) exhorts to vigilance in day-to-day tasks that must be fulfilled in the in-between time. One of these is the daily distribution of food (v. 45). This detail may be an allusion to the difficulties in the early church over food and eating, such as conflicts over Gentile and Jewish Christians eating together (Gal 2:11-14) or having people of differing social status at the same table (22:1-14). Alternatively, giving food may be understood as a metaphor for teaching (so 1 Cor 3:2; John 6:25-33), and the parable as an exhortation to leaders to exercise their teaching ministry well. The warning to those who gorge themselves on the resources meant for the community is dire; such a one will be dismembered (*dichotomēsei*, literally, "cut in two," v. 51) as a condemned person.

25:1-13 Ready maidens

A second parable advising preparedness for the coming of the Human One casts Jesus in the role of a bridegroom (as 9:15; see Isa 54:5; Jer 31:32; Hos 2:16, where Yahweh is the bridegroom of Israel). In Jesus' day, weddings took place in two stages. First was the betrothal ceremony at the home of the father of the bride, at which the groom presented the marriage contract and the bride price to his future father-in-law. The bride continued to live in her father's house until the second step, when she would move to the home of her husband, about a year later. This is the stage depicted in the parable. The maidens are waiting while the groom and the bride's father hammer out the final negotiations. Upon reaching a final agreement, the wedding party would go in procession to the house of the groom, where the feasting would commence.

The waiting women are friends of the groom; the bride is never mentioned in the story. The word *parthenos* refers to a virgin, a young woman of marriageable age (twelve or in her early teens). The contrast between wise and foolish recalls the builders in 7:24-27. It is not clear whether the women are carrying torches (the usual connotation of *lampades*) wrapped with oil-soaked rags or hand-held oil lamps with lighted wicks. Matthew 5:14-16 provides a clue to interpreting why the women cannot share their oil. There light is equated with good deeds that are visible to others and lead to praise of God. Similarly, at Matthew 7:24-27 the wise are those who hear and act on Jesus' words. Just so, the wise maidens in this parable are those who have faithfully prepared for the end time. No one can supply this preparation for another. One is either ready or not at the eschatological moment.

25:14-30 Investing talents

This parable is often interpreted as an exhortation to use all one's God-given gifts to the full. However, the Greek word *talanton* has no other connotation than a monetary unit or weight measurement. In the parable it denotes a very large sum of money. What the parable depicts are two servants who invest and double the money with which they are entrusted, which wins them their master's approval, a share in his joy, and further responsibility. The third servant, by contrast, buries the money, which was considered the best way of safeguarding valuables in antiquity. Yet he earns harsh punishment from the master.

Key to understanding the parable is that Jesus did not live in a capitalist system, where it was thought that wealth can be increased by investment. Rather, people had a notion of limited good: there is only so much wealth, and any increase to one person takes away from another. The aim in life for a peasant was to have enough to take care of his family. Anyone amassing large amounts for himself would be seen as greedy and wicked. In the parable, then, if the master is not a figure for God, it is the third servant who is the honorable one—only he has refused to collaborate with his master in his unfettered greed. The parable warns rich people to stop exploiting those who are poor, and it encourages poor people to take courageous measures to expose greed for the sin that it is. The last verse is sobering, depicting what can happen to those who oppose the rich and powerful. It can encourage disciples to find ways to stand together as they confront unjust systems. There is still opportunity, since the end time has not yet arrived.

25:31-46 Final judgment

This is the last of Matthew's parables and is unique to this Gospel. The time of judgment has arrived as the Human One comes in his glory (v. 31). This scene is intimately linked with 28:16-20, where Jesus instructs his followers to make disciples of all nations (*panta ta ethnē*, 28:19), a command that this parable presumes has been fulfilled. All the nations (v. 32) are now assembled to render account. The reason why the sheep are separated from the goats is not clear. Both were very valuable. Nor is there any evidence that after pasturing them together during the daytime, a shepherd would separate the two at night. (See 3:12; 13:24-30, 47-50; 24:40-41; 25:1-13 for other images of end-time separation.) Since most people were right-handed and developed greater strength and skill with this hand, the right side came to symbolize favor, blessing, and honor.

The image of Jesus shifts from shepherd to king (v. 34; see 2:2; 21:5). And, like Moses, who laid out before the Israelites the choice of blessing or curse (Deut 11:26), Jesus separates those "blessed by my Father" (v. 34) from those "accursed" (v. 41). This is not predestined; rather, God's invitation

Matthew 25

goes out to all (5:45; 13:3-9), and the choice to accept or reject it rests with each. For those who accept the invitation, which is visible in their deeds, blessing and inheritance in God's realm await.

In light of the saying at 24:14, it is likely that Matthew envisions the completion of the great commission (28:16-20); all people, including Israel, Gentiles, and Christians, have heard the Gospel and are now judged according to their deeds. The "least brothers" (v. 40) and "least ones" (v. 45) most likely refer to other Christians rather than to just any person in need. See 11:11; 18:6, 14, where "little ones" and "least" refer to vulnerable members of the Christian community, and 10:41-42, where Jesus promises the reward of a righteous person for those who receive the needy ones sent out on mission. The basis of judgment, then, is how one receives Jesus through his followers who proclaim the Gospel (see 10:40).

26:1–27:66 The passion and resurrection

Matthew's usual formula at the end of a block of teaching, "When Jesus finished . . ." (26:1, as also 7:28; 11:1; 13:53; 19:1), marks the transition to the passion narrative. There is also an echo of Deuteronomy 32:45, where Moses finished his instruction to Israel and then prepared for his death. In these final scenes Matthew follows Mark closely, while adding his own unique touches. Jesus is portrayed as knowing what will happen and as being in control of the events. As Matthew is wont to do, he interprets each action as fulfilling the Scriptures.

26:1-16 Preparation for death:
Treacherous plotting and prophetic anointing

For the fourth and last time (16:21; 17:22-23; 20:18-19), Jesus predicts his death. The prime movers are the chief priests and elders (v. 3), along with the high priest, Caiaphas (v. 3), who held office from A.D. 18 to 36. The Pharisees and scribes, who have been Jesus' opponents up to this point in the narrative, drop out of view until 27:62. The people are still basically favorable toward Jesus (v. 5).

In strong contrast to the leaders' treachery is the action of an anonymous woman who anoints Jesus in the home of Simon the leper. This takes place in Bethany, a village just east of Jerusalem, over the Mount of Olives. In the Gospel of John this is identified as the home of Martha, Mary, and Lazarus (John 11:1–12:12). By anointing Jesus' head, the woman takes on the role of priest and prophet. She both prepares Jesus for burial (v. 12) and commissions him as messianic king (see Sam 16:12-13; 1 Kgs 1:39). Jesus affirms her action, over the objection of the disciples. There is no question of a lack of concern for the poor by Jesus (see 5:3, 42; 6:2-4, 24; 19:21; 25:31-46); rather, the issue is the timing and the woman's recognition of Jesus' fate. She embodies the understanding and loyalty of the women disciples who, in contrast to the others (26:56), remain to see the crucifixion (27:55-56), keep vigil at the tomb (27:61), and are the first to encounter the risen Christ (28:1-10). Her pouring of oil on Jesus' head (v. 6) prefigures Jesus' pouring out of his blood for all (v. 28). While her action is remembered (v. 13), her identity is not.

In strong contrast is the act of Judas (vv. 14-16), who negotiates with the chief priests to hand Jesus over to them. No motive is given (cf. John 12:6). Once again Matthew interprets this deed through Scripture. Thirty pieces of silver is the worth of a slave (Exod 21:32). But probably the allusion is to Zechariah 11:12-13, where this is the amount of a shepherd's wage, which Judas casts back into the treasury (see 27:3-10).

26:17-35 The Last Supper

As the woman prepared Jesus for his passion, so now Jesus prepares his disciples. In the first scene (vv. 17-19), the disciples approach (*prosēlthon*, the reverential stance also of the woman in v. 7; also 4:3, 11; 5:1; 8:2) Jesus and ask about Passover preparations. Jesus' reply has an apocalyptic nuance, as Matthew uses both *kairos*, "appointed time" (8:29; cf. 13:30; 16:3; 21:34), and *engiken*, "draws near" (cf. 3:2; 4:17; 10:7; 21:34; 24:32-33) in reference to the end time.

The meal begins with a notation that Jesus is with his disciples (v. 20). His words and actions interpret for his intimate followers ("Twelve" is symbolic for all, as also 10:1-4) how he is still present with them ("Emmanuel," 1:23; cf. 28:20), even when his earthly life ends. Tragic predictions of betrayal (vv. 20-25) and denial (vv. 31-35) by his closest disciples frame Jesus' eucharistic words and actions (vv. 26-30). In verses 20-25 there is a contrast between the obedience of Jesus (v. 24) and the disobedience of Judas, who calls Jesus "Rabbi" (vv. 25 and 49), after Jesus has instructed his disciples not to use that address (23:8). The allusion to Psalm 41:10 in verse 23 captures the anguish of betrayal by an intimate friend. Typically, Matthew signals the dire consequences of not acting justly with a pronunciation of woe (as 11:21; 18:7; 23:13, 15, 16, 23, 25, 27, 29; 24:19). Unique to Matthew is the personal exchange between Judas and Jesus (v. 25; also 26:49-50). Jesus' enigmatic "you have said so" is the same response he gives to the high priest (26:64) and to Pilate (27:11).

The institution of the Eucharist (vv. 26-29) is the core and climax of this section. Jesus' gift of self in the form of bread is reminiscent of the feedings of the multitudes (14:13-21; 15:32-39) and of the similar actions by Elijah and Elisha (1 Kgs 17: 8-16; 2 Kgs 4:42-44), as well as of God's provision of manna in the desert for Israel (Exod 16). The cup in which all participate symbolizes both his death (see 20:22; 26:39, 42) and a ratification of a renewed life in covenantal fidelity. Blood, as the symbol of life (Deut 12:23), was sprinkled by Moses on the altar and on the people (Exod 24:8) to seal the covenant.

A unique element in Matthew's account is the interpretation that this action is "on behalf of many, for the forgiveness of sins" (v. 28). This is an allusion to the servant in Isaiah 53:4-12 (see also 12:17-21; 20:28). The "many" *(pollōn)* is a Semitic expression meaning "all"; no one is excluded from the saving effects of Jesus' death (see 1:21). Forgiveness is possible even for those who hand Jesus over to death. The gift of bread and wine also sounds an eschatological note, as the messianic banquet of Isaiah 25:6-9 is in view. Jesus assures his disciples that while the intimacy of eating and drinking together, which they shared during his earthly life, is ending, they will yet experience this with him in the realm of God (v. 29).

The scene shifts to the Mount of Olives (v. 31; see 24:3), where jubilant singing (Psalms 114–118 are sung at the conclusion of the Passover meal) gives way to a sober prediction by Jesus that all the disciples will have their faith shaken *(skandalizesthai,* literally, to find Jesus a "stumbling block" or "obstacle." See also 11:6; 13:57; 15:12). A quotation from Zechariah 13:7 that speaks of the disintegration of the community is accompanied by a promise of its renewal. Galilee is the place where Jesus first gathered disciples (4:18-22) and commissioned them (10:1-42) and where he appears to them for the last time, sending them to the whole world (28:16-20). Peter, representative of the whole (see 16:16-23), boasts that this will never happen (vv. 33-35). The irony is strong, as in the next scene the disciples sleep instead of keeping watch (vv. 36-46) and flee (v. 56), while the women disciples stay the course (27:55-56, 61; 28:1-10).

26:36-46 Prayer at Gethsemane

Arriving at Gethsemane (meaning "olive press") with his disciples (v. 36; see 26:20), Jesus separates himself from them to pray, taking along Peter and the sons of Zebedee, namely, James and John. These three were among the first called and sent (4:18-22; 10:2) and were privileged witnesses at the Transfiguration (17:1-8). They are also singled out as the ones who struggled most to understand Jesus' passion (16:22; 20:20-23). The separation of Jesus from the rest of the disciples may be an allusion to Genesis 22:5, where Abraham tells his servants to stay back while he and Isaac pray. While

Abraham is exemplary in his faithfulness, he misinterprets what action God desires. Jesus is both faithful to God and understands what action will bring liberation for his people. For him there will be no rescuing angel (26:53).

Three times Jesus implores God (on the metaphor of "Father" for God, see the comments on 6:5-15) to let the cup (a metaphor for death; see 20:22; 26:27) pass from him without drinking it. His grief is extreme (quoting lament psalms 42:4-5; 43:5 at v. 38), and his struggle is real. Jesus is not a puppet in the hand of God. His death is not inevitable. He wrestles with the final choice to proceed with handing over his life.

Jesus' faithfulness in seeking and following God's direction stands in contrast with the frailty of his disciples. They fail to keep watch (see chs. 24–25) and do not pray, as Jesus had instructed (v. 41 and 6:13), to be delivered from the test *(peirasmos)*—both the present crisis and the eschatological trial. Yet they will be restored and empowered by the risen Christ (28:7, 16-20). The final scenes of intimacy between Jesus and his followers began with Jesus noting at the supper that his appointed hour was at hand (26:18). They now close with his declaration that both the hour and the one handing him over are at hand (vv. 45-46).

26:47-56 Jesus' arrest

Jesus' words are immediately fulfilled with the arrival of Judas and a large, armed crowd, who come on the authority of the chief priests and elders. With so many people in the city for the feast, Judas has prearranged a signal so that there will be no confusion. A kiss, normally given by a disciple to a teacher as a sign of respect, turns treacherous. And as at the Last Supper (26:25), Judas addresses Jesus as Rabbi (v. 49), against Jesus' instructions (23:8). The tone of Jesus' response (v. 50) is not clear. It can be understood as an ironic question, "Friend, why are you here?" (KJV) or an instruction that emphasizes Jesus' control of the scene: "Friend, do what you have come for" (NAB). Or, by addressing Judas as "friend," he reminds him of their intimate relationship and holds out to him the possibility of forgiveness, recalling that Judas has partaken in the cup of his blood that is shed for forgiveness of sins (26:28).

A desperate attempt on the part of a disciple to halt the arrest (v. 51) serves to underscore once again a lack of understanding. Jesus has taught his followers not to counter violence with violence (5:38-48), which he reinforces here with a pronouncement unique to Matthew: "all who take the sword will perish by the sword" (v. 52; similarly Rev 13:10). Moreover, Jesus withstands the temptation to call upon angelic rescuers (v. 53, as at 4:6). As always, Matthew explains that all these seemingly incomprehensible events happen to fulfill the Scriptures (v. 54, 56). The fallibility of the disciples culminates with their desertion and fleeing (v. 56; but see 27:55-56, 61; 28:1-10, where the Galilean women continue to follow and serve).

26:57-68 Interrogation before the Sanhedrin

The arresting party brings Jesus to the high priest, scribes, and elders (the Pharisees have dropped from view in the passion narrative and only reappear at 27:62). The mention of Peter (v. 58) prepares for the next scene, in which he denies Jesus (vv. 69-75). The Jewish leaders do not have authority to put a person to death (John 18:31). While Matthew gives the scene the aura of a trial, it is more a strategy session to prepare the case they will present to Pilate. In Christian tradition, the blame for Jesus' death increasingly has been taken off the Romans and put on the Jewish leaders. Matthew paints the Jewish leaders as vile, seeking *false* testimony (v. 59; cf. Mark 14:55) against Jesus.

Two witnesses are necessary for a death sentence (Deut 17:6). The accusation that Jesus said he can destroy the temple and rebuild it (v. 61) is both false and ironically correct. Although he performed a prophetic act in judgment on the temple (21:1-17) and remarked about its coming destruction (24:2), he did not say that he himself would destroy it. But since destruction and restoration of the temple were thought to be a sign of the messianic age, the accusation is actually true. Jesus' initial silence toward the high priest (v. 63) recalls that of the servant in Isaiah 53:7. At 27:40 the charge will be made again by passers-by reviling the crucified Jesus.

The high priest shifts the focus, demanding that Jesus respond under oath to the charge that he is Messiah, Son of God (v. 64). That Jesus is Messiah has been affirmed from the opening line of the Gospel (1:1, 17, 18; 2:4; 11:2; 16:16; 22:42; 23:10). "Son of God" underscores his unique relationship with God (2:15; 3:17; 11:25-27; 17:5), his healing power (8:29), and his authority (see 14:33; 16:20, where the two titles occur in tandem). Jesus had taught his disciples not to take oaths (7:33-37). He replies to the high priest with the same enigmatic phrase, "You have said so" (v. 64), that he had said to Judas (26:25) and to Pilate (27:11). His further response underscores his identity as the coming Human One. Blending Psalm 110:1 and Daniel 7:13, he moves the discussion to an eschatological plane. At this the high priest accuses Jesus of blasphemy, that is, abusing the divine name or insulting God (v. 65), an offense the leaders deem worthy of death (v. 66). They themselves begin to abuse Jesus (cf. Mark 14:65, where it is an anonymous "some") and mock his identity as prophet and Messiah (vv. 67-68), an element unique to Matthew.

26:69-75 Peter denies Jesus

The utter failure of Peter is not unexpected; Jesus has warned that this will happen (26:31-35). Peter has been in the lead as one of the first disciples called (4:18-22) and was a privileged witness at the Transfiguration (17:1-8). He was the spokesperson for the disciples in declaring Jesus "messiah" (16:16), and the one to whom Jesus entrusted the "keys to the kingdom of heaven" (16:19). But he has also been the prime example of a disciple who struggles to understand and fails miserably (16:22-23; 26:33-35). Not once but three times he denies being with Jesus, and he does so with an oath (see 5:33-37, where Jesus forbids oath-taking). Matthew adds that Peter makes the denial "in front of everyone" (v. 70; cf. 5:16; 10:32-33). This is the last mention of Peter in Matthew's Gospel. Presumably his bitter tears (v. 75) are tears of repentance, and he is among the disciples to whom the women announce the good news (28:7-10) and among those who are commissioned to preach to all the nations (28:16).

27:1-2 The council hands Jesus over

After a night of interrogation and abuse, the chief priests and elders fulfill what Jesus had predicted at 20:18-19. They hand Jesus over (*paradidōmi*, 10:4; 26:15, 25; 27:3, 18, 26) to the Roman governor, Pontius Pilate, who ruled from A.D. 26 to 36.

27:3-10 The death of Judas

Seeing Jesus condemned prompts a change of heart in Judas. Ordinarily the verb *metanoein* is used for repentance, whereas here it is *metamelētheis*, "deeply regretted" (v. 3). But it is likely that Judas' words in verse 4 indicate true repentance and not simply regret. Judas, like the leaders Jesus warned in 23:35-36, is responsible for shedding innocent blood. (See 27:24, where Pilate will try to make himself innocent of Jesus' blood.) The leaders dissociate themselves from Judas' attempt to return the money (see 27:24 for Pilate's use of the same phrase, "Look to it yourselves"). In desperation, Judas flings the money into the temple and tragically ends his life. A rather different version is found in Acts 1:15-20. The quotation in verses 9-10 interpreting the purchase of the "Field of Blood" is actually an adaptation of Zechariah 11:12-13, although Matthew attributes it to Jeremiah. Perhaps Matthew makes the association because of a similarity with the slaughter of the innocents (2:17-18), interpreted with Jeremiah 31:15. Or Matthew may mean to recall Jesus' critique of the temple and its leadership (21:13, quoting Jer 7:11). Alternatively, he may be alluding to the story of the potter's field in Jeremiah 18–19.

Matthew 27

27:11-14 Trial before Pilate

Resuming the action begun at verse 2, Matthew now tells of the interrogation by the Roman governor. His question is different from that of the Jewish authorities and concerns Jesus' kingship. Once again Jesus answers enigmatically, "You say so" (v. 11; see 26:64), and then remains silent when the chief priests and elders testify against him (as also 26:63). Jesus' silence is evocative again of the servant of Isaiah 53:7, whose appearance caused amazement (Isa 52:14-15; v. 14).

27:15-26 Choice of Barabbas

Beyond the Gospel references, there is no other evidence of a custom of releasing a prisoner at Passover. The choice, according to Matthew, is between Jesus Barabbas and "Jesus called Messiah" (v. 17). Matthew heightens the notoriety of the former (v. 16) and names envy as the motive for handing Jesus over (v. 18). Three other unique elements in Matthew serve to shift the blame away from Pilate and onto the Jewish leaders. The first is the dream of Pilate's wife, who urges her husband to "have nothing to do with that righteous man" (v. 19). In the opening chapters, dreams are the means by which Joseph, a "righteous man" (1:19), learns God's desire and by what actions he is to preserve the life of Jesus and his mother (1:20; 2:13, 19, 22). A second element found only in Matthew is Pilate's handwashing (v. 24), a futile attempt to declare his own innocence and to dissociate himself from Jesus' death (similarly the chief priests with Judas, 27:4). A third unique feature of the Matthean account is the climactic cry of the whole people, "His blood be upon us and upon our children" (v. 25).

Until this point the crowds have been basically favorable toward Jesus. Now they demand his crucifixion (vv. 22, 23), and the people as a whole (*laos*, as at 1:21) take upon themselves the responsibility for his blood (v. 25; see Lev 20:9-16; Josh 2:19-20; 2 Sam 1:16; 14:9; Jer 51:35). This verse has been interpreted as a curse upon all Jewish people for all time. This is a grave misinterpretation that Christians have a serious obligation to counter (see the Vatican II document *Nostra Aetate* 4). In the context of Matthew's Gospel, "the whole people" refers to those who opposed Jesus during his lifetime as well as Jewish opponents of the early Christian community. Verse 25 reflects the inner family conflict and the struggle of Jesus' disciples to understand why all Jews did not follow Jesus (similarly Matthew 13; Romans 9–11). Matthew sees a connection between the rejection of Jesus and the events that unfold in the decades following Jesus' death ("upon our children"), particularly the destruction of the temple. The scene concludes with Pilate releasing Barabbas, having Jesus scourged to weaken him, and handing him over (*paradidōmi*, 10:4; 20:18; 26:15, 25; 27:2, 3, 18, 26) for the last time to the soldiers to crucify him.

27:27-31 Mockery by the soldiers

Just as the interrogation before the chief priests and elders ended with them abusing Jesus (26:67-68), so the Roman trial concludes with abuse by the soldiers of the governor inside the praetorium, the governor's official residence. A cohort consisted of six hundred men; in verse 27 it likely refers to simply a large group of soldiers. These would have been local men employed by the Romans. They mock Jesus' kingship, arraying him in scarlet, with a pseudo-crown and scepter. In Mark 15:17 the robe is purple, a color worn by royalty and the rich (see, e.g., Luke 16:19), but Matthew's detail is more realistic. Roman soldiers wore red cloaks; they simply adorn Jesus in one of their own. The crown of thorns was not so much to inflict pain as to imitate that of an emperor with its rays. The acclamation (v. 29) simulates the greeting toward the emperor, "Ave, Caesar!" The derisive mockery turns to physical abuse (v. 30) and ends with Jesus being led to crucifixion.

27:32 Simon of Cyrene

On the way to the site of crucifixion, Simon of Cyrene (a North African city in present-day Libya) is pressed into service to help Jesus carry the cross. Likely he was visiting Jerusalem for the Passover feast. While Jesus has said that those who wish to be his follower must take up their cross (16:24), discipleship motifs are not entirely clear in this scene, especially since Simon is forced into carrying the crossbeam. At the same time, the presence of this Simon is a poignant reminder of the absence of Simon Peter, who has struggled to accept the fact that Jesus would die (16:21-23), then declared he would follow Jesus to the death (26:33-35), but has fled (26:56) and denied that he was ever with Jesus (26:69-75).

27:33-44 Crucifixion and mockery

The place of crucifixion, Golgotha, "Place of the Skull," gets its name either because the hill is skull-shaped or because of the executions that took place there. It was customary to give the condemned person a drink mixed with a narcotic to ease the pain. Matthew makes it wine mixed with gall, so that the action corresponds to what is said in Psalm 69:21.

No details are narrated about the crucifixion itself (v. 35). Matthew's readers are well familiar with what other contemporary writers describe as the most cruel and painful of all punishments. It was used on slaves, violent criminals, and political rebels. Carried out in a public place, it was meant to be a deterrent. Matthew focuses on how to make meaning of this horrible death. He uses the Scriptures, primarily the lament psalms, to interpret each action. In verse 35 the division of Jesus' clothing alludes to Psalm 22:18. The wagging heads of the mockers (v. 39) recalls Psalm 22:7.

For the third time (26:67-68; 27:27-31) Jesus endures mockery. First the passers-by (vv. 39-40) resurrect the charge made before the Sanhedrin (26:61) about the destruction of the temple, an event that Matthew connects with the death of Jesus (21:41, 43). Their taunt, "If you are the Son of God," recalls the same tempting words of Satan (4:3, 6), who urges Jesus to throw himself from the pinnacle of the temple and let God's angels rescue him to prove he is truly God's Son. Both scenes reflect the struggle of believers to explain how Jesus can be the beloved Son of God (2:15; 3:17; 17:5) and yet die such a horrendous death. The taunt of the chief priests, scribes, and elders is a variation of the same (vv. 41-42). The paradox of saving life by losing life (16:25) is visibly played out. It is through losing his life that Jesus "saves his people from their sins" (1:21). While the placard over the cross (v. 37) carries the title "King of the Jews" (the charge made by Pilate, 27:11, and his soldiers, 27:29), the religious leaders use the more messianically charged phrase "King of Israel" (v. 42). Verse 43, unique to Matthew, employs Psalm 22:8 and Wisdom 2:18 to align Jesus with the righteous sufferer whom God will vindicate. Finally, even the bandits crucified with Jesus join in the abuse (v. 44; cf. Luke 23:40-43).

27:45-56 Death of Jesus

An apocalyptic tone is set as darkness spreads over the land for three hours (see Amos 8:9). Jesus cries out in a loud voice (v. 46), once again using the words of Psalm 22. He has been deserted and opposed by Judas (26:14-16, 48-49), the disciples (26:56), Peter (26:69-75), the religious leaders (26:57-68), the crowds (27:21-22), the Roman authorities (27:1-31), and now even God seems to have abandoned him. His anguished prayer is that of a righteous sufferer. While the end of the psalm, which moves to a note of confident hope in God's power to save, is not spoken, the Gospel will indeed end with Jesus' vindication.

The bystanders either misinterpret or deliberately mock Jesus (v. 47) and think he is calling on Elijah. There was an expectation that Elijah would return before the final judgment (Mal 4:5; Sir 48:10). But John the Baptist has already played this role (Matt 11:14; 17:10-13). It is not entirely clear what prompts the offer of *oxos*, a cheap, sour wine used by the lower classes (v. 48), or whether this is a compassionate or mocking gesture. Most likely Matthew includes it as one more way in which Scriptures (Ps 69:21) are fulfilled. As terse as the notice of Jesus' crucifixion (v. 35) is the statement he "gave up his spirit" (v. 50). This is not a reference to the Holy Spirit but to the life-breath (*pneuma* means both "spirit" and "breath") that Jesus hands back to God. Matthew portrays Jesus not as an unwilling victim but as faithful Son of God who consciously returns to God.

Four apocalyptic signs follow immediately, powerful demonstrations that God did not abandon Jesus:

1) The curtain of the temple, probably the inner veil in front of the holy of holies (Exod 26:31-35), is torn (the passive voice designates this as God's doing) from top to bottom. This can be understood as a portent of the destruction of the temple or as opening access to the God of Israel to all the Gentiles.

2) The earth quakes, a portent of the end of the present age and the beginning of the new (4 Ezra 6:13-16; 2 *Apoc. Bar.* 27:7; 70:8; Zech 14:4-5; Matt 24:7). Cosmic signs accompany the momentous events of Jesus' birth (2:2), his death, his resurrection (28:2), and his return in glory (24:27-31).

3) Many of the holy dead emerge from their tombs and appear to people in Jerusalem (vv. 52-53). In verse 52, Matthew, in language akin to that of Ezekiel 37, asserts that it is Jesus' death that makes possible the resurrection of the holy ones. The sequence of events becomes confused in verse 53 because Matthew makes a correction: the resurrection of others cannot happen until the resurrection of Jesus, which Matthew has not yet narrated.

4) The centurion and those with him, who had participated in crucifying Jesus, come to believe in Jesus and declare, "Truly this was the Son of God!" (v. 54; cf. vv. 40, 43). This is all the more significant when their employer, the emperor, allocated this title to himself, seeing himself as agent of the gods.

Not only has God not abandoned Jesus but the many Galilean women disciples have also remained faithful to him (vv. 55-56). They are steadfastly keeping watch (as Jesus exhorts disciples to do in chapters 24–25), after having followed Jesus from Galilee and having ministered (*diakonousai*) to him (see 8:15 for various meanings of this verb). Mary Magdalene heads the list (v. 56; as in Matt 27:61; 28:1; Mark 15:40, 47; 16:1, 9; Luke 8:2; 24:10; cf. John 19:25; 20:1-2, 11-18). No information is given about her before this point in the narrative. Only Luke 8:2-3 introduces her before the passion account. The common confusion of her with a prostitute or a sinner has no basis in the Scriptures. The other Mary accompanying her is the mother of James and Joseph (cf. Mark 15:40). At Matthew 13:55 there is the mention of Jesus having siblings named James and Joseph. Possibly Matthew is alluding to the mother of Jesus (cf. John 19:25), but if so, he does not develop the significance. The third figure is the mother of the sons of Zebedee, who at 20:20-21 had wanted places of honor for her sons in Jesus' realm. She drops out of the list in 27:61 and 28:1.

Matthew 27

27:57-66 Witnesses at the tomb

Another disciple emerges, a rich man (see 19:16-26, where Jesus elaborates on how difficult it is for a rich person to be a disciple) who offers his tomb for Jesus' burial. There is no mention of Joseph having been part of the Sanhedrin that condemned Jesus (cf. Mark 14:53). There are many limestone quarries in Jerusalem, some of which were used secondarily as cemeteries. A body would be laid in a niche carved in the rock until the flesh decomposed. Then the bones would be gathered into an ossuary ("bone box"), and the niche could be reused for another family member. A tomb complex would have a number of niches. The stone is rolled across the entrance to prevent grave robbers or animals from entering. No anointing of Jesus' body is narrated, since he has already been anointed for burial by an unnamed woman (26:6-13).

Keeping vigil at the tomb (v. 61) are Mary Magdalene and the "other Mary," presumably the mother of James and Joseph named in verse 56. They come again in 28:1 to see the tomb. These witnesses serve to verify that Jesus is truly dead and that there is no mistaking the place of his burial.

Unique to Matthew is the request of the chief priests and the Pharisees (who have been absent since 23:39) to Pilate to set a guard at the tomb (vv. 62-66). Their recollection of Jesus' prediction that after three days he would rise (16:21; 17:23; 20:19) sets the stage for the empty tomb and the resurrection appearances. Their fear of the impact of the disciples' proclamation that Jesus was raised from the dead (v. 64) is ironic, since this is exactly what occurs. The charge that Jesus was an "imposter" (v. 63) and that his disciples stole the body (v. 64) likely reflects the kinds of arguments Matthew's community encountered from their opponents.

28:1-15 The empty tomb

The same two women who witnessed Jesus' crucifixion (27:55-56) and who kept vigil at his burial (27:61) return once again to the tomb. As at the death of Jesus, an earthquake (27:51, 54; see also 24:7), an apocalyptic sign, occurs, accompanied by the descent of an angel from heaven. In the opening chapters an angel conveyed to Joseph the divine interpretation of the puzzling events surrounding Jesus' birth. Similarly, an angel communicates the meaning of the extraordinary aftermath of Jesus' death. In an ironic play on words and images, the guards who were supposed to secure the dead body, themselves become like dead men (v. 4).

The angel assures the women not to fear and announces that Jesus has been raised as he said (16:21; 17:22-23; 20:18-19). The passive voice "he has been raised" (v. 6) connotes that God performs the action. The angel then commissions the women to go quickly to give the message to the disciples and to instruct them to go to Galilee, where they will see him (fulfilling Jesus' words in 26:32). Matthew does not explicitly mention Peter (cf. Mark 16:7; Luke 24:12, 34), though he is presumably among the disciples (v. 7) and the Eleven (v. 16). The women do exactly as instructed; with fear and great joy, they run to announce the message to the disciples (v. 8; cf. Mark 16:8, where they say nothing because of their fear).

Unique to Matthew are verses 9-10, where Jesus meets the women on the way. That they seize his feet is a detail that attests to the reality of his person and his tangibility. He is not a ghost or a spirit; nor is it simply the memory of Jesus that lives on with them. The women worship *(proskynein)* Jesus (see also 2:8, 11; 14:33; 15:25; 28:17). Jesus' repetition in verse 10 of the message they have already received from the angel (v. 7) is significant in that the women are commissioned directly by Jesus, giving them credentials as prime witnesses and apostles. Matthew's account represents a strand of Christian tradition in the same line as that of John 20:1-2, 11-18, where Mary Magdalene goes to the tomb alone and there encounters the risen Christ and is commissioned to announce the good news to the community of brothers and sisters (20:17). By contrast, in Mark 16:1-8 and Luke 24:1-12 the women do not encounter Jesus but only the angel. Peter is given primacy of place by Luke (24:12, 34) and Paul, who does not list the women among those to whom the risen Christ appeared (1 Cor 15:3-8).

Rounding out the story of the guard at the tomb (27:62-66) is their report to the chief priests of all that had happened (28:11-15). Along with the elders, they gather and take counsel (as 27:1). Just as money figured in the plan to hand Jesus over to death (26:14-16; 27:3-10), so did money figure in the false interpretation of his resurrection (v. 12; see 6:19-34; 10:8-9; 13:22; 19:16-30 for warnings about the dangers of money). The ongoing polemics into Matthew's day between followers of Jesus and their opponents are reflected in the remark in verse 15.

FINALE: BACK TO GALILEE; COMMISSION TO THE WHOLE WORLD; JESUS' ABIDING PRESENCE

Matt 28:16-20

28:16-20 The Great Commission

In a scene unique to Matthew, the thread of the story of the women's witness, which left off at verse 10, is resumed. It presumes that they have fulfilled their commission to tell the news of the resurrection to the other disciples and that these have believed them. The juxtaposition of "eleven"

Matthew 28

with "disciples" creates a tension in the narrative. "Eleven" is a reminder that one of "the Twelve" (see 10:1-4) is no more. Yet "the disciples" (referred to seventy-three times in Matthew) comprised a group larger than the Twelve, among whom were most notably the Galilean women who followed and ministered (27:55). While Matthew has depicted the women as apostles who are commissioned in 28:7-10, he excludes them from the commission to preach to all the nations.

The mountaintop setting (as at 4:8; 5:1; 15:29; 17:1) evokes the image of Jesus as the new Moses. Like the women (28:9), the Eleven worship Jesus, though unlike them, they (it is not clear in the Greek whether it is all or some of them) doubt or hesitate before the challenge (*distazō*, v. 17; also 14:31). Until this point in the Gospel, Jesus had insisted that the mission was restricted to the "lost sheep of the house of Israel" (10:6; 15:24); now the disciples are to go to "all nations" (*panta ta ethnē*, v. 19; see 25:32). Some understand Matthew to be saying that the mission is to be directed from now on to the Gentiles exclusively (i.e., that the mission to Israel has ended). But more likely Matthew's heavily Jewish Christian community sees that Israel is still included among "all [the] nations" to whom they reach out. The mission is to make disciples, to baptize, and to teach.

A liturgical formula from early Christian tradition has been placed on Jesus' lips (v. 19). As Jesus has been depicted as Teacher par excellence, so are his disciples to follow in his footsteps with his authority (v. 18; see 10:1).

The final verse of the Gospel reiterates the assurance given at 1:23 and 18:20: despite the "little faith" and the failures of his followers, Jesus remains always with the community that gathers and ministers in his name. Not even death can break that bond—ever.

The Gospel According to Mark

Marie Noonan Sabin

INTRODUCTION

Author

The actual author of the Gospel of Mark, like those of all the Gospels, is unknown to us. The manuscripts that survived date from the fourth century; the names of the evangelists were added sometime in the second century. There is reason to believe that the early church was less interested in knowing the actual authorship than in connecting the Gospel narratives with apostolic witnesses. They found the names "Matthew" and "John" within their respective Gospels, and the name "Luke" as one mentioned by Paul as his traveling companion. For Mark they relied on a fragment written by a second-century bishop named Papias, who spoke of Mark as the "interpreter" of Peter. This suggestion dovetailed with the observation in Acts that Peter had visited the home of someone in Jerusalem named "John who is called Mark" (Acts 12:12). Some also found support in the reference in the first letter of Peter to "Mark, my son" (1 Pet 5:13). Not all scholars accept these inferences, yet the link with Peter is supported by internal evidence.

Audience

Since we do not know for certain who wrote the Gospel of Mark, we also cannot be certain of its intended audience. The link with Peter has led some scholars to speculate that it was addressed, like Peter's first letter, to the church in Rome. But there are many other bases for speculating both about Mark's Gospel and Peter's letter. Among them is the fact that Peter is known in Acts as the head of the Jerusalem church; an argument could be made that Mark was a member of that early Jewish-Christian community.

Language

Language offers some internal clues as to both the author and his intended audience. Mark's manuscript, like the other Gospels, has come down to us as a Greek text. Why, one might wonder, would the evangelists have written in Greek instead of in Hebrew or Aramaic, the Semitic idiom common in Galilee? The most probable reason is that from the time that Alexander of Greece conquered the Mesopotamian world, three centuries before the time of Jesus, Greek was the language of educated people. In fact, in the time of Alexander, the Jews translated their Bible into Greek. They called it the "Septuagint" (meaning "seventy"), because they developed a legend that seventy scribes had been asked to do the translation in isolated cells and all came up with identical words, thus proving the inspiration of God. Educated Jews knew the Bible in Greek as well as in Hebrew and Aramaic. There is good evidence that when the evangelists quote or refer to the Jewish Bible, they are following the Septuagint.

Mark's Gospel is not written in fluent Greek, however. Indeed, it contains numerous "semitisms," that is, phrases that are awkward in Greek but would read well if translated into Hebrew or Aramaic. The overall impression it leaves, therefore, is that of an author who thought in one language and was trying to write in another. In addition, Mark's Gospel is the only one that uses Aramaic phrases at key moments of the narrative: *Talitha koum,* meaning "Little girl, rise up!*" (Mark 5:41); *Ephphatha*, meaning "Be released"* or "Be opened" (Mark 7:34); *Abba*, meaning "Father" (Mark 14:36); and *Eloi, Eloi,* meaning "My God, my God" (Mark 15:34).

Date and historical setting

The date of Mark's Gospel is also a matter of speculation. Most, although not all, scholars believe that Mark's was the earliest of the Gospels, written around 70 C.E. and followed in the eighties by Matthew and Luke, and in the nineties by John.

The year 70 was significant for all Jews, including the Jewish followers of Jesus, because it was the year that the Romans destroyed the Temple in Jerusalem. The destruction was the traumatic end to the four-year revolt of the Jews against Rome. The Temple had been destroyed once before by Babylon, six centuries earlier, and the effect had been devastating. The Roman destruction was also a watershed in Jewish history.

This time the Temple was never rebuilt. The leaders of the revolt (the Zealots), along with the temple leaders (priests and Sadducees), disappeared or scattered. Judaism itself might have disappeared had it not been for the Pharisees. The Pharisees' reputation in the New Testament as rigid legalists is ill-deserved. They were, in fact, a devout lay group who had

---

* Translation from the original Greek. In sections where the same words appear multiple times, only the first reference is noted.

The Gospel According to Mark

developed a flexible and creative approach to the interpretation of Scripture and had also fostered ways of bringing the prayers of the Temple into Jewish homes. When the Temple was lost, they provided the foundations for a continuing and vital Judaism. As the ancestors of modern rabbinic Judaism, they deserve the respect of modern Christians.

Why, then, are the Pharisees vilified in the New Testament? The answer does not lie in the time of Jesus. Indeed, many of the teachings of Jesus are so close to those of the Pharisees that some scholars have proposed that he is shown arguing with them because he was a member of their school. Judaism before the fall of the Temple was tolerant of many different forms of expression, and historical studies suggest that Christianity did not begin as a consciously separate religion, but as a new formulation of the ancient Jewish faith. After the Temple fell, however, Judaism regrouped, and the Pharisaic leaders became less tolerant of diversity within their ranks. In that new atmosphere, Jewish followers of Jesus were regarded with suspicion and put out of the synagogues. The Christian-Jewish community responded with anger. In the context of the post-seventies, the Pharisees appeared hostile to Jesus, and it is that hostility (and their own anger) that the evangelists retroactively projected into their accounts of Jesus' time.

Modern Judaism and modern Christianity may have developed along clearly different paths, but readers of the Gospels need to understand that Jesus and his disciples, as well as the evangelists Mark, Matthew, and John (Luke was Gentile), saw themselves as faithful Jews. Matthew's diatribes against "the scribes and the Pharisees" and John's scornful use of "the Jews" must be understood in the context of their own times, not that of Jesus.

The way each Gospel expresses its attitude toward Jews and Judaism is one criterion for dating it. John's denunciation of "the Jews" is one reason for placing his Gospel at the end of the century. Luke's way of distancing Christianity from Judaism (especially in Acts) suggests that he is not writing in its earliest moments. The Gospels of Mark and Matthew, on the other hand, are clearly composed in the context of a deep regard for Judaism itself. So, while all the Gospels are steeped in the Jewish Scriptures, Mark and Matthew especially present Jesus in the light of them.

The relevance of the "Old Testament" to the New Testament

It is helpful to know that in the first century all Jewish thought about God was centered in Scripture. Jews believed that the Bible contained all of God's revelation but that no one person or one faith community could grasp all of that revelation at any single time. It was a pious habit of mind to seek to understand every new and significant person, teaching, and

The Gospel According to Mark

event in Judaism through the lens of Scripture. At the same time, it was a religious task to consider how these new persons, teachings, and events brought to the surface new depths in Scripture hitherto unseen. It was, in fact, considered important for each new generation to reopen the Scriptures and search for new meanings in the light of its own time. The new meanings that surfaced were not considered replacements of older interpretations but enrichments of them.

Christians reading the New Testament today will miss much of its meaning and most of its richness if they are unfamiliar with the references to the "Old" or First Testament that form its framework and substructure. This commentary, therefore, tries to present the reader with all the scriptural quotes, allusions, and echoes that provide the basis of Mark's theological thought. Some explanation of the full context of these biblical references is always given. For readers who desire more complete understanding, the biblical citations are offered as well.

Readers of Mark's Gospel need to be aware that Genesis is always in the background. Mark is always thinking of God as the Creator, whose primary concern is to create, sustain, and restore life. His Gospel is filled with reminders of "the beginning." It is structured around the idea that God desires to lead us back to the original Garden. Particularly important to Mark is God's creation of human beings in God's image (Gen 1:27). He presents Jesus as a new Adam ("son of man") and as image of the divinity ("son of God").

Mark also connects Jesus to the central prophets of Jewish tradition—Moses and Elijah. In terms of narrative structure, Jesus' relationship to John the Baptist is patterned after the Elijah-Elisha cycle in the two books of Kings, a cycle which, in its own way, echoes biblical narrative from Genesis to Kings. The miracles that Mark shows Jesus performing have their connections to Elijah's raising up a young man from death (1 Kgs 17:17-24), to Elisha's multiplication of loaves (2 Kgs 4:42-44), and to his cleansing of a leper (2 Kgs 5:1-14). When Mark shows Jesus in his state of transfigured glory, he shows him in conversation with Moses, the giver of God's word, and with Elijah, the prophet who, according to biblical legend, never died but was taken up to heaven.

Mark also places Jesus in the tradition of the prophets seeking the reform of the Temple. By means of interweaving quotations from Scripture, Mark links Jesus to the warnings of Jeremiah and the vision of Isaiah. He shows Jesus warning that the Temple would be destroyed unless the Temple authorities gave up their idolatrous connections with foreign power and wealth. At the same time, he shows Jesus sharing Isaiah's vision of a sacred space where all peoples will join together in worshiping the one God.

When Mark composes the narrative of Jesus' death, he makes use of a range of Scriptures that depict God's righteous servant put to death by evil forces. First and foremost, he interprets Jesus' death through the lens of Isaiah's "Suffering Servant." In certain passages known as "The Songs of the Suffering Servant" (Isa 42:1-4; 49:1-7; 50:4-11; 52:13–53:12), Isaiah draws a portrait of God's faithful servant who is tortured, mocked, and killed by the obtuse kings of the world, who do not understand the identity of the one whom they are killing. They also are slow to understand that his death atones for their sins and that after death he will be raised up and exalted by God.

Mark also draws on similar patterns in the Psalms. And he surely had in mind the opening of the Wisdom of Solomon, where "godless men" put "the righteous one" to death because his goodness makes their lives uncomfortable and because "he styles himself a child of the Lord" (Wis 2:13) and "boasts that God is his Father" (Wis 2:16). In this work, the righteous one is not only exalted by God but given immortality as well (Wis 2:23).

In general, the most significant background comes from the Wisdom writings. In Catholic tradition, there are seven Jewish Wisdom writings: Proverbs, Psalms, Job, Ecclesiastes, the Song of Songs, Sirach, and the Wisdom of Solomon. Each of these works is distinct, yet they share certain significant things in common. They are all set in domestic situations and everyday life. Many of them use a pithy, aphoristic style of speech. They are all focused on how to live a wise and holy life. They all agree that "fear of the Lord [in the sense of holy awe] is the beginning of wisdom." Most important, three of them (Proverbs, Sirach, and the Wisdom of Solomon) imagine God's Wisdom as a personified attribute that walks on earth and dwells among human beings. God's Wisdom was there from the beginning and created the world and all that is in it. God's Wisdom is imagined as a maternal figure—life-giving, nurturing and healing, restorative and transfiguring. When Mark wanted to communicate the significance of Jesus, it was quite natural for him to present him as God's Wisdom made flesh.

Genre

A grasp of Mark's overriding reference to Scripture should keep the reader from regarding his Gospel as an eyewitness account or as any conventional form of biography or history. What Mark gives us is far richer. In keeping with the Jewish practices of his time, Mark interprets Jesus in the light of the Hebrew Bible. He uses Scripture as an interpretive framework. At the same time, he shows Jesus reinterpreting Scripture. Out of this two-way exchange, Mark offers us a Wisdom book.

Like other Wisdom books, Mark's Gospel derives its meaning from the Hebrew Bible. It takes place, for the most part, in the everyday settings of sea and synagogue, home and table. Its central figure, Jesus, offers wisdom in parables, riddles, and short pithy sayings called aphorisms. At the same time, Mark shows Jesus to be not only a teacher of Wisdom but Wisdom itself. Jesus calls his followers to an unconventional wisdom, a way of living (and a way of dying) that he himself exemplifies.

In modern terms, Mark's work is theological. As such, it is purposefully put together. An attentive reader cannot fail to notice Mark's craft: the repetition of certain significant words and the shaping of the narrative into symbolic events and meaningful patterns. There is a theological focus to his overall design.

Key words

Mark is given to the repetition of certain key words or phrases. For example, he uses some form of the verb "release" to indicate both the forgiveness of sin and the healing of a disease. In chapter 1 he says that John the Baptist was "proclaiming a baptism of repentance for the *release** of sins" (1:4). Later in the same chapter, when Jesus cures Simon's mother-in-law, Mark says, "the fever *released** her" (1:31). In chapter 2, when Mark describes Jesus' healing of the paralytic, he notes that Jesus said, "Child, your sins are *released*" (2:5). The word is not translated this way because it is not idiomatic English, but the literal meaning conveys two aspects of Mark's interpretation of Jesus. First, it suggests an equation between healing and forgiveness. Second, it indicates Mark's view that Jesus continually sets people free. At the end of chapter 7, when Mark shows Jesus engaged in a healing action that summarizes much of what has gone before, he calls attention to the importance of the episode by quoting Jesus in Aramaic: *Ephphatha!*—that is, "Be opened" or, literally, "Be *released*"* (7:34).

In chapter 15, Mark returns to the theme, using it in an ironic way as part of the speech of Pilate. As Pilate strives to please the crowd, he keeps asking them which prisoner he should "release" to them (15:9, 11) until he finally "releases" Barabbas (15:15). When Jesus dies, however, Mark says he "released" his last breath (15:37), thus implying that in dying, Jesus himself is set free.

The various forms of "rise up" or "be raised" are significant because together they form a running refrain that points to Jesus' resurrection. Mark uses the phrase "raised up" repeatedly. In chapter 6, for example, when Herod is speculating on the identity of Jesus, he says, "It is John whom I beheaded. He has been raised up" (6:16). By using the word here, Mark hints at the future "raising up" of Jesus. In chapter 14, Mark notes that Jesus says to his disciples, "After I have been raised up, I shall go before you to Galilee" (14:28). At the end of his Gospel, Mark indicates that an angel repeats these words to the women who came to the tomb: "He has been raised; he is not here" (16:6). In other places, Mark consistently uses some form of the same verb to denote the effect of Jesus' healing miracles. Unfortunately, English translations often blur this meaningful refrain by using synonyms. As a consequence, this commentary will go out of its way to call the reader's attention to its presence.

When Jesus heals Simon's mother-in-law, for example, Mark says he "raised her up"* (1:31). When Jesus cures the paralytic, Mark notes that Jesus said, "Rise up"* (2:11). Jesus uses the exact same words to the man with the withered hand (3:3) and to Jairus's daughter, the little girl whom everyone had given up for dead (5:41). By using this word again and again, Mark suggests that Jesus' healing miracles are related to the great miracle of his resurrection.

Another word that is important to Mark is "straightway." The word sounds odd to modern ears, and most English translations, including the New American Bible, either translate it as "immediately" or "at once" or omit it entirely. But it echoes the message of the prophetic voice in chapter 1 that cries out in the desert, telling the people to prepare for God's coming by making "straight" his "ways" (1:3). Mark was so intrigued by this pun (which works in both Greek and English) that he uses it forty-three times in his Gospel.

In the first part of his Gospel (chs. 1–8), Mark uses the word to signal an act of moral urgency. In the first chapter alone, Mark uses this word eleven times. Mark says that Jesus ascended from the baptismal waters "straightway"* (1:10). The Spirit drives Jesus into the desert "straightway" (1:12). When Jesus calls Andrew and Simon, they leave their nets "straightway" (1:18), and Jesus calls to James and John "straightway" (1:20). He goes into the synagogue "straightway" (1:21), where "straightway" he is approached by a man with an unclean spirit (1:23). Jesus' reputation spreads everywhere "straightway" (1:28). When he leaves the synagogue, Jesus proceeds "straightway" to the house of Simon's mother-in-law (1:29), where "straightway" Simon and Andrew tell Jesus about her sickness (1:30). When Jesus touches the leper, "the leprosy left him *straightway*" (1:42), and "being deeply moved," Jesus "*straightway* sent him forth" (1:43). In the first chapter everything happens as it should, and God's ways are made straight.

In the passion narrative of the Gospel, Mark uses the word sparsely and ironically. Judas arrives to betray Jesus "straightway"* (14:43) and approaches him with a kiss "straightway" (14:43). After he has denied Jesus three times, Peter hears the second cockcrow "straightway" (14:72). The high priest calls the council to condemn Jesus "straightway" (15:1). If one recalls Mark's earlier use of the word, the irony here seems heavy. At the same time, by using it Mark is signaling a larger irony by which, in spite of all appearances, God's plan is going straight.

Another key word translated literally in this commentary is *ecstasy*. If one analyzes the elements of this word, one sees that it is made up of two parts—*ek,* which means "out" in Greek, and *stasis*, which is related to the Greek word for "stand." Thus to experience ecstasy means to "stand outside" oneself, to be outside one's normal state of being. Mark uses one form of this word when he wants to indicate that someone is "out of his mind." When Jesus cures the paralytic, for example, Mark first describes his cure as a kind of resurrection, saying that the man *"rose up,* picked up his mat straightway, and went away in the sight of everyone"* (2:12a). He then says, "They were all *out of their minds** and glorified God, saying, 'We have never seen anything like this'" (2:12b). A similar use occurs in chapter 3 when Mark says that those close to Jesus thought that Jesus was *"out of his mind"* (3:21).

Mark uses a different form of the same word to indicate moments when something Jesus does or says causes people to experience an abnormal state of awareness and joy. He uses both forms of the word to describe the scene in which Jesus raises up the daughter of Jairus. When Jesus arrives, people are already lamenting her death. Then, Mark tells us, "[He] said to her, *'Talitha koum,'* which means 'Little girl, *rise up*!'"* Then Mark describes the reaction of those witnessing this event: "The girl, a child of twelve, *rose up straightway** and walked around. At that, they were *out of their minds with ecstasy*"* (5:41-42).

At the end of the Gospel, when three women come to Jesus' tomb to anoint him, they discover that his body is not there, and a young man in white tells them, "He has been raised" (16:6). Mark then describes their response as one of "trembling and *ecstasy"* (16:8). Mark has prepared his readers for this response by the earlier episodes. Like the crowd that witnessed the paralytic rise up from his mat and the crowd that saw the dead child come back to life, the women are overwhelmed by joy.

By means of these episodes, linked by the word "ecstasy," Mark indicates the way in which realization of God's power to restore life transforms the human consciousness.

Patterns and design

Mark shapes his narrative in patterns of twos and threes. The reader will be first aware of doublets. Sometimes this is a matter of repeating episodes; sometimes it is a matter of echoing words. There are, for example, two instances in Mark when Jesus calms the sea (chs. 4 and 6). Twice he multiplies bread for a hungry crowd (chs. 6 and 8). There are two occasions when people discuss who Jesus is (chs. 6 and 8). There are two instances in which Jesus gives specific instructions to his disciples (chs. 6 and 8). And there are numerous other examples, which this commentary will point out along the way.

At the end of chapter 8, Mark seems to give a reason for his method when he describes Jesus' healing of a blind man in two stages. Here he dramatizes the idea that the blind man cannot shift from darkness to vision all at once; he needs to go through a process of coming to sight. In the same way, careful readers will find that each repetition enlarges their understanding. At the conclusion of the commentary, we will talk about how Mark's whole Gospel is divided into two parts and how Mark has worked out this structure to shift the reader's perceptions from a conventional to an unconventional way of seeing.

Mark also likes to pattern things in threes. There are three healing miracles, for example, in chapter 1, three questions asked of Jesus in chapter 2, three seed parables in chapter 4. Jesus makes three predictions of his death (in chs. 8, 9, and 10). Three times Mark shows Jesus being called "the beloved son" (in chs. 1, 9, and 12). Jesus has three chief disciples (Peter, James, and John), whom he takes with him on three key occasions (the raising of Jairus's daughter in chapter 5, his transfiguration in chapter 9, and his agony in the garden in chapter 14). There are also three key anonymous women who are healed in the first part of the Gospel (in chs. 1 and 5). In the second part, three women (two Marys and Salome) follow Jesus to Jerusalem, watch where he is laid in the tomb, and then come to anoint him (chs. 15 and 16).

As with the doublets, there are numerous other examples, which we will note as we go along. If readers become alert to this pattern, they will see that Mark always uses the middle of these triads to shed light on the other two. Again at the conclusion of the commentary, we will suggest how Mark's whole Gospel might also be viewed as having three parts. The middle of this large triad, shedding light on both sides, is the scene of Jesus' transfiguration.

Transfiguration at the center

Given Mark's careful choice of words and patterns, it is surely no accident that he places the scene of Jesus' transfiguration exactly in the middle of his Gospel (9:2). The transfiguration of Jesus is Mark's way of imaging his resurrection. On one side of this scene, Mark shows the ecstatic response of those who see the paralytic rise up from his mat and those who witness a little girl rise up from her deathbed. On the other side, he shows the ecstatic response of the women who have come to realize that Jesus himself has been "raised up." The scene of Jesus' transfiguration overshadows both parts of the Gospel, emphasizing God's creative, transforming, transfiguring power to restore life.

Mark's Gospel is sometimes called "the Gospel of the Cross," so it is worth noting that the Transfiguration overshadows the cross. Mark arranges events so that the scene of transfiguration follows right after Jesus speaks to his disciples about taking up the cross, and it completes his meaning. Jesus says: "Whoever wishes to come after me must deny himself, take up his cross, and follow me. For whoever wishes to save his life will lose it, but whoever loses his life for my sake and that of the gospel will save it" (8:34-35). Mark does not explain this saying but dramatizes the paradox it contains by following this call to "lose" one's life with this scene of transfigured life. Mark does not show Jesus elevating the cross for its own sake, but rather embracing it as a means to Transfiguration. In Mark, the whole teaching of Jesus is death-*and-resurrection*, cross-*and-Transfiguration*.

Conclusion

Rich in Scripture, theological in purpose, and brilliant in design, Mark's Gospel invites its readers to become followers of Jesus' transfiguring wisdom.

NOTES ON THE TRANSLATION

Literal or root meanings

The Church encourages translators to return to "the original texts of the sacred books" (*Dei verbum, The Dogmatic Constitution on Sacred Revelation*, #22). That recommendation has been followed scrupulously in this commentary, to the point where the commentator often renders the meaning of the biblical words in a more literal way than the New American Bible translation printed above it. In each instance, the reader should be aware that the commentator has looked at the root meaning of the original word and consciously chosen a more literal translation over one that is more conventional or even more idiomatic. This kind of conscious choice is particularly evident in the four key words listed in the Introduction: "release," "rise up" or "raised up," "straightway," and "ecstasy" or "ecstatic." Liturgical Press believes that its readers will be enriched by being offered these alternative translations.

Mark 1

Capitalization

In some instances, the difference between the commentator's translation and that of the NAB involves capitalization. The reader should know that we have no original manuscripts of the Gospels, and that of those we do possess, the best were written entirely in capital letters called "uncials." Thus all modern capitals are the choice of a later editor. Such editorial emendations are, like translations, forms of interpretation. This commentator has chosen not to capitalize certain words in order to highlight what she believes to be Mark's theological view.

For example, she does not capitalize "son of man" because she believes that it is not used by Mark as a special title, but rather in its usual Hebrew sense of *ben 'adam*, which literally means "son of Adam" or "human being." (She also sees it as sometimes following the Aramaic custom of using it as an alternative to "I.") She believes that Mark's habit of constantly associating the term with Jesus expresses his theological perception of Jesus as a second Adam. She does not capitalize "messiah" because she wants to emphasize that Mark redefined that term in the process of using it, and she would like to encourage the reader to reflect on that redefinition. She does not capitalize "holy spirit" because she wants to remind the reader of its use throughout the Hebrew Bible. While the modern Christian of course sees this phrase in relation to the Trinitarian understanding of the fourth-century creed, Mark's first-century audience would have heard it in terms of the biblical tradition they knew. Again Liturgical Press hopes that the reader's grasp of the depth of Mark's text will be enhanced by these alternative understandings.

COMMENTARY

BEGINNING

Mark 1:1-45

1:1 Beginning

In the Greek text of Mark, the word "beginning" has nothing in front of it, neither "the" nor "a"; the Gospel starts abruptly with the simple word "Beginning." By this device Mark calls attention to this word and emphasizes it. In this way he recalls the opening of the Hebrew Bible—"In the beginning"—the moment of Creation. In Jewish tradition the word "beginning" was equated with Wisdom, because in the book of Proverbs personified Wisdom says, "The LORD made me *the beginning* of his way" (Prov

Mark 1

8:22). So some Jewish teachers paraphrased Genesis 1:1 to read, "In *Wisdom* God created the heavens and the earth." Mark's opening is thus rich in meaning, identifying the gospel (or "good news") of Jesus with Wisdom, and that Wisdom with a new Creation.

1:2-3 As it is written

Mark brings together here three voices from the Hebrew Scripture. The messenger who "goes ahead" suggests the angel God sent to lead his people to freedom in the story of the Exodus (23:20). The messenger sent to "prepare the way" suggests the figure whom God promises through the prophet Malachi and who will purge the people of their sins (Mal 3:1). The "voice of one crying out in the desert" is the herald described by Isaiah who is to give "comfort" to God's people (Isa 40:1). In just two verses Mark sums up a biblical tradition whereby angelic or human figures are sent to draw the people to God through preparation, through purgation, and through comfort. The messenger here is John the Baptist, who appears, in the next verse, as Isaiah's "voice . . . crying out in the desert."

1:4-8 John the Baptist

The description of John in 1:6 makes him resemble Elijah, who is similarly dressed in the Second Book of Kings (1:8). It was said that Elijah never died but ascended to heaven in a fiery chariot (2 Kgs 2:11). By interpreting John as another Elijah, Mark indicates John's greatness as a prophet. Elijah passed on his gift as a prophet to a successor, Elisha; so here, Mark introduces Elijah as a prophet who will be succeeded by another—Jesus. In the Elijah-Elisha stories, however, Elijah is pictured as the greater prophet; here, John's proclamation about Jesus reverses that order. The Elijah-Elisha context places Jesus in the tradition of the prophets, with their long habit of pressing for religious reform.

1:9-11 The baptism of Jesus

The scene that Mark portrays reinforces the idea that Creation is happening again: as in Genesis 1, God's spirit hovers over the waters. In describing the opening of the heavens, Mark uses an unusual word for that opening that means "rend"* or "split apart"*; he uses the word again near the end of his Gospel when he describes the splitting open of the sanctuary veil after Jesus' death (15:38). The echoing word links the two scenes, suggesting that Jesus is opening up God's dwelling place.

In a Jewish writing of the time *(The Testament of Judah)* the heavens are opened "to pour out the spirit as a blessing of the holy Father." Here

God's spirit descends "like a dove," a term used for the beloved in the Song of Songs. The idea of God's beloved becomes explicit here in the "voice from the heavens" saying, "You are my beloved Son; with you I am well pleased."

The phrase "beloved Son" also brings to mind the story of Isaac, where God asks Abraham to "take your son, your only son, your beloved son" and offer him up as a sacrifice (Gen 22:2). In ancient Passover liturgy, Isaac's sacrifice is referred to as a voluntary act on Isaac's part; Isaac merges with the Passover lamb as it is said that Isaac's blood was placed on the doorposts so that the angel of death would spare the Israelites. So the echo here points to Jesus' sacrificial death and its saving consequences.

1:12-13 Temptation in the desert

As the baptism scene recapitulates the opening of Genesis, so the reference to temptation for "forty days in the desert" encapsulates the key experience of Israel in the book of Exodus. There is no suggestion here, however, that Jesus' encounter with Satan involves a struggle. Rather, Mark gives us a static picture, the human figure of Jesus steadfast between "wild beasts" and ministering angels. It is an icon of original humanity, only this time not sinning.

1:14-15 "The gospel of God"

Jesus' ministry picks up where John's leaves off; "the gospel of God" suggests their continuity. While we tend to restrict the term "gospel" to the story of Jesus, Mark uses the term to refer to the broader narrative of all God's deeds among his people; it is the gospel or "good news" of God that both John and Jesus proclaim. Jesus, like John, calls the people to repentance. In both Greek and Hebrew the word translated here as "repent" carries the sense of "turning" or change of heart. Jesus calls people to this change not as a warning but as a promise: it is the "time of fulfillment," the time of God's "kingdom." In biblical thought, God's kingdom is not a particular place but a condition of living according to God's will. While it tends to be projected into the future, it can also denote a timeless state of being. Similarly, the "time of fulfillment" is not restricted to a particular moment but designates a realization of God's presence. Both these ideas are further unfolded in Mark's story.

1:16-20 The call of the first disciples

In the ancient world, it was not customary for teachers to seek their disciples; on the contrary, teachers attracted disciples. Jesus' action here is therefore

Mark 1

striking, for it suggests the action of personified Wisdom, who, in the book of Proverbs, does go about calling her followers. Wisdom calls those who are in need of her—"the simple ones" (Prov 1:22). So Jesus here calls simple fishermen. As Wisdom promises her followers a higher life, so Jesus promises his disciples that they will do a more advanced kind of "fishing."

The response of those called is equally striking. Without inquiry or hesitation, they leave both livelihood and family. Their quickness to respond is enhanced by a word omitted in most translations: Mark says that *"Straightway** they left their nets and followed him" (1:18). As we noted in the Introduction (pp. 11–12), the word "straightway" echoes the message of the voice crying in the desert, telling the people to prepare for God's coming by making "straight" his "ways" (1:3). The ready commitment of Simon and Andrew, James and John is thus shown to be the ideal response of anyone called by God. It is worth noting that we never see any of these disciples make this ideal response again. Throughout most of Mark's Gospel they are singularly slow to understand or to follow Jesus. But Mark sets up this opening scene to suggest their ideal capabilities.

1:21-45 Three miracles of healing

Studies of the structure of Mark's Gospel have shown that he likes to link events, teachings, and sometimes words together in a pattern of three. When he does so, the middle event, teaching, or word always functions as the key one, shedding light on the other two. So here, at the conclusion of Mark's opening chapter, when we find three miracles of healing, it is important to notice how and for what purpose they are linked together.

1) The casting out of "an unclean spirit" (1:21-28). Although the NAB caption speaks of the "cure of a demoniac," Mark's text does not use the word "demon" here but "unclean spirit." The use of this term indicates the perception that possession by evil is an unnatural or pathological state, a perception that predominates in Mark's Gospel. In chapter 3, as we will see, Jesus implicitly contrasts possession by an unclean spirit with possession by God's holy spirit (3:29-30). Here in the synagogue, it is because he sees the man's natural state to be a holy one that Jesus heals the man by simply commanding the unclean spirit to leave him.

The unclean spirit, for its part, knows itself to be destroyed by the simple confrontation of "the Holy One of God" (1:24). It is significant that Jesus commands the unclean spirit to depart with the same word that he later uses to command the storm to "be still" (4:39).

The incident is enclosed in descriptions of the people's reaction to Jesus' power. They speak of his act of exorcism as "a new teaching" (1:27). Mark seems to imply that there is something new in Jesus' perception that possession by evil is reversible.

The word that Mark then chooses to describe the crowd's state at seeing the cure (here in verse 27 translated simply as "amazed") is also part of a pattern of three. Mark uses it again to describe the feelings of the crowd that sees Jesus immediately after his transfiguration (9:15) and again to describe Jesus' own disturbed emotions in Gethsemane (14:33). It might best be translated as a state of "shock" or enhanced consciousness.

2) The raising up of Simon's mother-in-law (1:29-31). Short as this incident is, it is the middle and therefore key event of these three healings. Unfortunately, its full drama is obscured by the translation. The Greek word used to describe the woman's condition (1:30) is frequently used to describe someone already dead, and the Greek word used to describe her cure (1:31) is best translated "raised up."* (It is the same word used to describe Jesus' own resurrection in 16:6.) Finally, the phrase translated as "waited on them" would more accurately be rendered "served"* or "ministered to"* them (the Greek verb used is related to the word for "deacon"). So translated, the incident distills the essence of what Jesus is about: he takes a dead woman by the hand and raises her up, not only to new physical health but to a new spiritual status. Throughout the Gospel of Mark, Jesus says repeatedly that he has come "not to be served but to serve." This woman is the first person in the Gospel to act as Jesus does.

3) The healing of the leper (1:40-45). In his first miracle Jesus heals a man within the synagogue; here he heals a man who has been ostracized from the synagogue because of his illness. Jesus' relation to the synagogue here is complicated. On the one hand, by touching the leper he violates a religious prohibition against touching the "unclean"; on the other hand, Jesus sends the man back to the priests and the prescribed rituals for lepers. To complicate matters further, Jesus tells the healed man to "tell no one anything" (1:44) and yet suggests that the man's healed body will serve as a "proof" or "witness." And in fact the man does become a witness, spreading the word of Jesus' action. Jesus thus heals more than the man's body—he restores him to his community and changes him from someone who was alone and alienated to one who, it seems, cannot help bearing witness to God's healing power.

Summary of the healing miracles (1:21-45)

In the first instance, the unclean spirit within the man cries out upon being confronted by Jesus' holiness; in the second instance, friends bring Jesus to the woman who is sick; in this third incident, the sick man himself

Mark 1

approaches Jesus and asks for help. Both the first and last healings involve bringing someone back to acceptance within the synagogue. In the first, Jesus touches uncleanness within; in the last, he touches uncleanness without.

The first and last healings involve people who, because they are considered "unclean," are forced to live on the fringe of Jewish religious society. What point, then, is Mark trying to make by placing the miracle of Simon's mother-in-law in between them? Is he not suggesting that the place of women in this society is on a par with them? The woman, it may be noted, does not even have a name; she is only known by her relationship to a man—in this case, not even her son but her son-in-law. Situated between a demoniac and a leper, the caricature of "the mother-in-law," we might guess, was an ancient joke. But Jesus, we have noted, not only cures her but changes her: he "raises her up."* By his use of this language, Mark signals to us that all of these miracles of healing are forerunners of Jesus' resurrection. Or to put it another way, Jesus' resurrection comprehends the raising up of all humanity.

1:32-39, 45b A rhythm of healing, preaching, and prayer

In between the healing of the mother-in-law and the leper, Mark tells us that Jesus continually healed the sick and drove out demons, and, when he could, withdrew to "a deserted place" to pray. Yet he also tells us that when Simon and others came to tell him that everyone was looking for him, he returned to the villages to preach, noting that this was his purpose. In this way, Mark indicates a tension in Jesus' life between outreach and withdrawal, or a rhythm of action and prayer. In the last part of the final verse, Mark suggests that this division collapses and that even in the desert Jesus is not away from the crowds that need healing.

Summary of chapter 1

In chapter 1, Mark sets out the framework for his whole Gospel: the traditions of Creation and Wisdom. He indicates that in Jesus, God is initiating a new beginning, a new creation. Through Jesus' connection with John and John's resemblance to Elijah, Mark suggests that Jesus is not, however, breaking off from Jewish tradition or the Jewish Bible but is acting in continuity with the prophets. Indeed, Mark suggests in many ways that Jesus is reenacting the history of Israel. In the scene of Jesus' baptism, Mark shows Jesus to be God's "beloved son," as Israel always named itself, and like Isaac, who also represents Israel in Jewish legend, to be a son destined for a sacrificial death that will be saving for many. Through the brief scene of

Jesus' being tempted in the desert, Mark recalls the Israelites' experience of the Exodus.

Mark also shows that Jesus embodies the Wisdom traditions. Through his dramatization of Jesus' calling of his disciples, he suggests the figure of God's Wisdom calling the simple to be her followers. Through his presentation of Jesus as a healer, Mark expands upon the idea of Wisdom as one who seeks to restore God's creation. Although Mark describes Jesus as teaching and preaching, what he actually shows us is Jesus totally given over to making people whole. Through the language of "raising up"* in a key miracle, Mark indicates that he sees resurrection as the ultimate act of Wisdom's way of restoration or re-creation.

JESUS' ACTS OF RESTORATION AND RE-CREATION
Mark 2:1-28

2:1-4 Breaking through the roof

As chapter 1 concludes with the description of a crowd coming to Jesus even in "deserted places," so chapter 2 opens with so many people gathered in Jesus' home that "there was no longer room for them, not even around the door" (2:2). As a consequence, Mark tells us, the four friends bringing a paralytic to Jesus resort to opening up the roof above him (2:2-4). Although the vocabulary is not identical, there is an interesting parallel here to the heavens opening up at Jesus' baptism; it is typical of Mark's theological slant to suggest that Jesus continually opens things up. In the rest of this chapter, Mark shows Jesus opening up new meanings in sinfulness and forgiveness.

2:5-7 "Your sins are released"

It is in keeping with this view that Mark shows Jesus telling the paralytic that his sins are "released"* or "let go."* The word is not translated that way because it is not idiomatic English, but it is literally correct and more accurately reflects Mark's view that evil binds but God sets free. The same verb is used by Mark to describe John's baptism "for the *release** of sins" (1:4), the action of Simon and Andrew in *letting go** of their nets (1:18), and the fever *letting go* of Simon's mother-in-law when Jesus raises her up (1:31).

2:6-7 "Who but God alone can forgive sins?"

This reflection of the scribes is sometimes taken as Markan irony—that is, it is suggested that by phrasing it the way he does, Mark makes the challenge of the scribes unwittingly point to Jesus' special and divine powers. But another possible interpretation is that Mark is making the scribes

Mark 2

raise an old theological question so that he can then show Jesus answering it in an unconventional way. When we read the Gospels as eyewitness accounts, we often miss the carefully constructed rhetorical patterns common in the ancient world. It is worth reflecting that from Plato on, it was a common teaching technique to construct a dialogue between a master teacher and an obtuse listener; the questions of the obtuse listener serve to draw out the thought of the master teacher. So here, the question of the scribes serves as a catalyst for Jesus' teaching on forgiveness. And Jesus teaches more than once in Mark's Gospel that human beings are called to forgive one another in imitation of God's forgiveness of them. If one argues to the contrary that only God can forgive, one could use this idea to dodge the obligation to forgive others.

2:9 "Which is easier to say . . . ?"

In typical Jewish fashion, Jesus often answers a question with a question. The question he raises here is something of a riddle, for while forgiving sins is clearly the harder thing to do, it is by far the easier thing to say because it requires no visible proof. (No one can check on whether or not sins have been forgiven, but the cure of paralyzed limbs is either seen or not seen.)

By means of quoting this riddle, Mark also suggests that Jesus equates the act of forgiveness with the act of healing—that is, he shows that Jesus taught that to forgive someone is to heal them. Mark thus implies that all of Jesus' acts of healing are theological symbols of God's desire to forgive us and make us whole. The miracles of healing have a theological dimension.

In the ancient world, moreover, people often believed (as indeed, some people still do) that illness or injury was a punishment inflicted by God for some sin. By coupling forgiveness with healing, Mark shows how Jesus taught that it is God's will to forgive rather than to punish, to heal rather than to hurt.

2:10 "The son of man"

What does Jesus mean by saying that "the son of man has authority to forgive sins on earth"? Many scholars have noted that in Mark, "the son of man" is the way Jesus most often refers to himself; they have then interpreted this phrase as a special title. But recent scholarship has pointed out that in Hebrew and Aramaic the phrase simply means "human being," as in Psalm 8:5:

> What is man that you should be mindful of him,
>   or *the son of man* that you should care for him?

It has also been noted that in Aramaic the phrase was often used as a form of self-reference. Still others note that in Hebrew the phrase literally equals "son of Adam." All these facts suggest that in using it, Mark was not giving Jesus a special title but rather emphasizing his common humanity. If he attaches any special role to it, it is not that of apocalyptic agent but rather that of second Adam, a representative of humanity giving us all a fresh start.

When Mark quotes Jesus saying that "the son of man has authority to forgive sins on earth," he seems to be suggesting that all human beings have the power to forgive and that Jesus as the second Adam is modeling this role for all of us. This function of the phrase "son of man" needs to be kept in mind when we see it again at the end of this chapter (2:27).

2:11-12a "Rise, pick up your mat, and go home"

Once again Mark chooses the same verb for "rise up"* in a healing miracle that he will use to describe the raising up of Jesus. The immediate response of the paralytic is intensified in Mark's text by the additional word "straightway"*; the straightening of the man's limbs is presented as one more instance of "making straight the way of the LORD."

2:12b "They were all astounded . . ."

The word translated here as "astounded" is literally "out of their minds"* or ecstatic. This response of the crowd is echoed in the later response of those who witness the raising up of a little girl (5:42) and, at the very end of the Gospel, in the response of the three women who come to realize the implications of the empty tomb (16:8). The experience of being ecstatic thus forms a pattern in Mark. Its implications need further exploring.

2:13-17 The calling of tax collectors and sinners

This is the second time in Mark's Gospel that Jesus calls disciples to himself; there will be a third calling in chapter 3. The calling of disciples is thus a Markan triad, and knowing the pattern, we can anticipate that the middle incident—which is this one—will be key, shedding light on the meaning of the other two. We have seen that in the first, the disciples respond in ideal fashion ("straightway"). In the third calling (3:13-19), Jesus not only calls disciples to himself but sends them out "to preach and to drive out demons" (3:14-15). We are also given the names of the twelve apostles, including that of Jesus' betrayer. In this middle incident, Mark dramatizes the fact that Jesus calls not saints but sinners.

2:13-14 Levi

The first to be called is Levi, "sitting at the customs post." To understand the implications of this call and why Levi would have been regarded as a public sinner, it is necessary to know something of the history of the Jerusalem Temple and the Jewish priesthood in the time of Jesus and of Mark.

From the eighth century before the time of Jesus until the time of the Gospels, every major power in the Mediterranean world conquered the Jews and occupied Jerusalem: Assyria, Babylon, Persia, Greece, and Rome. Babylon destroyed Solomon's Temple in the sixth century. Under the Persian king Cyrus, the Jews were allowed to rebuild it. In the first century, Herod expanded it, but the Romans destroyed it again in the year 70. Both the Greeks and the Romans were especially hostile to the Jewish faith because they felt that it detracted from their secular power. The Greeks under Alexander III began to undermine the power of the Temple by appointing the high priests. No longer was the priesthood the sacred legacy of Aaron, no longer was it handed down to the special tribe of Levi. It became a political appointment, a job up for sale like any other appointment in the world of power and money.

The most anti-Jewish of the Greek rulers was a man named Antiochus IV. His attempt to wipe out Judaism through the banning of circumcision together with acts of sacrilege in the Temple occasioned the revolt of the Maccabees (whose victory and purifying of the Temple is still celebrated each year at Hanukkah). At the time of Jesus and of Mark, the Romans had taken up where the Greeks left off. They continued the practice of appointing the high priests, and they also attempted to desecrate the Temple in other ways.

In this context, tax collectors were hated, not just because they took money but because they took it from the Jewish people for the benefit of Rome. Levi, "sitting at his customs post," is an apt symbol of the Roman corruption of the Jewish priesthood. Instead of being a religious leader as Levites had originally been destined, this Levi has sold out to the enemy and collects taxes for them.

2:15-28 Three questions of Wisdom

1) "Why does he eat with tax collectors and sinners?" (2:15-17). Modern readers sometimes regard this question as one that reveals the Pharisees' legalism and rigidity, but we should recognize it instead as one that is not unnatural for any pious member of a religious community. We might ask ourselves: How readily would today's churchgoers welcome an enemy collaborator into their midst? It also helps our understanding to realize that because the dietary laws were well defined in Judaism, eating with non-

Jews was complicated and potentially an occasion for religious backsliding. The question, then, does not reflect so badly on the Pharisees; yet Jesus' response does emphasize his radical inclusiveness.

Jesus' response ("Those who are well do not need a physician, but the sick do," 2:17) is designed by Mark to reveal more of his identity. His reply here is the kind of pithy aphorism that one finds in the book of Proverbs and other Wisdom writings. By showing Jesus speaking in this style, Mark is dramatizing Jesus as a teacher of Wisdom. Even more, when he quotes Jesus as saying, "I did not come to call the righteous but sinners," he is placing Jesus in the role of Wisdom herself, who seeks out all those who have need of her, especially the unwise or the sinner.

Modern readers sometimes interpret Jesus' statement by saying that he really meant the "*self*-righteous." How, they think, could he possibly exclude the righteous? But their thinking betrays a certain literalism. If we realize that Mark is intent upon presenting Jesus to us as God's Wisdom incarnate, then we can hear these words, not as those of an ordinary religious leader, but as the speech of Wisdom herself—Wisdom seeking out the foolish sinner.

2) Feasting or fasting? (2:18-22). The second question asked of Jesus here comes not from the Pharisees but from the people. The question is typical of all people who have made a religious commitment, because it is natural for pious folk to assume that there is a right way and a wrong way of doing things. If they see two religious leaders whom they respect doing things differently, they naturally want to know which one is right. Jesus' indirect reply (again a question answered by a question) suggests that there are no absolutes here but simply seasons of appropriateness. His response is again reminiscent of the Wisdom writings—this time, of Ecclesiastes:

> There is an appointed time for everything . . . .
>   A time to weep, and a time to laugh;
>   A time to mourn, and a time to dance (Eccl 3:1, 4).

The point is bolstered by two more Wisdom sayings: "No one sews a piece of unshrunken cloth on an old cloak" (2:21) and "No one pours new wine into old wineskins" (2:22).

Like so many of the concise truths of Proverbs, these sayings are homey, seeming to arise from close observation in a domestic setting. They are not in themselves profound, but they support the perspective implicit in the reply about fasting or feasting that there are seasons in the spiritual life. This pair of sayings also suggests that there can be a tension if we try to force a new style upon an old one.

Mark 2

Many Christians have been tempted to read in here a contrast between the "Old Testament" and the New Testament or between Judaism and Christianity, but such contrasts would have made no sense to Mark. At the time Mark was composing, there was no division between testaments; what we now call the "Old" or First Testament constituted all the Scripture there was. There was, moreover, not yet an established Christian church that sharply distinguished itself from Judaism. So the tension between "old" and "new" here cannot be taken as a Jewish-Christian conflict; it is simply a wise observation about the unsettling effects of new patterns upon old ones. It is worth noting, moreover, that Jesus suggests here that his disciples will eventually and appropriately return to fasting (2:30). The time of the bridegroom is not here permanently—at least, not yet.

The image of the bridegroom suggests the Song of Songs as well as the marriage feast between God and humanity described in Isaiah, some of the other prophets, and some of the psalms. The new clothing and the new wine go along with the image of this feasting. Through this series of aphorisms Mark seems to be suggesting two different time frames—one present and one future. Jesus as "bridegroom" anticipates humanity's future with God, and to the extent that his followers perceive him as such, they feast in the light of this future promise. But that future has not yet arrived, and the dissonance between that future promise and the present reality is experienced as the tension of new cloth pulling at old or new wine causing familiar containers to burst open.

3) "Why are they doing what is unlawful on the Sabbath?" (2:23-28). The third question comes like the first from the Pharisees, and also like the first, it expresses moral outrage. This time the outrage comes from Jesus' direct violation of the Sabbath laws, which forbade all work of any kind, from picking grain to cooking it. Modern Christian readers tend to dismiss these laws as superficial and again condemn the Pharisees as legalists. But the Sabbath laws were designed to foreshadow the end time, when, according to God's promise, there would be no work, no war, no illness, and no distinctions in authority and power, but all—male and female, slave and free—would sit down together as equals at God's banquet and share in God's rest. This "rest" was not conceived of as the mere absence of work but as a joyous sharing in God's timeless presence. One did not heal on the Sabbath because symbolically the Sabbath was a time without illness.

Once again Mark uses a question that gives him the opportunity to set forth Jesus' teaching on the Sabbath. Jesus' teaching indirectly reminds the Pharisees that the essential purpose of the Sabbath is to anticipate and celebrate the wholeness for which God originally created human beings. Thus, he implies, satisfying human hunger is more in keeping with the purpose of the Sabbath than all the rules and rituals, even the sacred bread.

Jesus' final saying, "The Sabbath was made for man, not man for the Sabbath," sums up this idea of original humanity as the apex of God's creation. The final saying, "The son of man is lord even of the Sabbath," should thus not be taken to mean that only Jesus is lord of the Sabbath; rather, it summarizes Jesus' role throughout the Gospel of Mark as the second Adam, the representative of humanity restored to its original wholeness. It is saying that God made the Sabbath for human beings as a symbol of their final destiny—a love feast with him and with one another.

Summary of chapter 2

In chapter 2, Mark dramatizes the way that Jesus, like Wisdom, restores human beings to wholeness, both physical and spiritual. In the opening incident, he shows Jesus equating forgiveness with healing. He next shows Jesus, again like Wisdom, seeking out sinners to be his followers. In particular, he shows Jesus singling out Levi, who stands for all the Jewish religious leaders who were selling out to Rome and thus weakening Jewish faith. By calling him to be his follower, Jesus/Wisdom is implicitly calling him, and Israel in general, to turn away from worldly power and back to the wisdom of their fathers.

Mark then sets up three questions asked of Jesus by perplexed people around him. These questions give Mark the opportunity to set forth Jesus' teaching on sin and forgiveness, religious behavior, and the purpose of the Sabbath. Mark shows Jesus responding in the style of Wisdom, both in terms of his aphoristic speech and in terms of his active seeking out of those who need him. The middle question about fasting or feasting gives Mark the opportunity to indicate the tension Jesus causes by his unconventional ways and how that unconventionality is the result of Jesus' anticipation of the future of humanity, when humankind, restored to original wholeness, will be gathered at the marriage feast of God. By means of the final question, Mark sets forth Jesus' teaching on the Sabbath. In his response Jesus teaches that the Sabbath was created for the benefit of humanity and as a sign and foretaste of its eternal banquet with the divine.

By these means, Mark develops the themes of Wisdom and Creation he introduced in the first chapter. In the second chapter he shows Jesus acting and speaking like God's Wisdom, God's co-creator in Proverbs (Prov 8:30), restoring people to wholeness, unsettling people from their familiar ways, and teaching that human wholeness is central to God's purpose.

Mark 3

JESUS' CHALLENGE OF CONVENTIONAL WISDOM
Mark 3:1-35

3:1-3 Healing the man with a withered hand

The image of something "withered" is a repeated one in Mark; it is part of his Creation theme, contrasting the withering of created things with their intended fruitfulness. In chapter 4, for example, the seed sown in shallow soil withers up (4:6); in chapter 9, "withering away" is one of the effects of an unclean spirit (9:18); in chapter 11, it becomes one of the seasons of the cursed fig tree (11:20-21).

In curing this man's withered arm, Jesus is acting out the restorative role of God the Creator, a role usually assigned to God's Wisdom. Jesus' first act here is to ask the man to "rise up"* (a resurrection word again) and to come forward "into the midst"* of the community. The implication is that the withered arm of the man had alienated him (like the leper) from the religious community, or at least put him on the fringes of it. Jesus' action here thus defies the conventional shunning of the physically disabled; it is doubly restorative.

3:4-5 The purpose of the Sabbath

This scene of healing is also used by Mark as an extension of Jesus' teaching on the sabbath. Mark implies that many who witnessed this healing in the synagogue were once again more concerned about the Sabbath rules than about the purpose of the Sabbath. He shows Jesus challenging them explicitly: "Is it lawful to do good on the Sabbath rather than to do evil, to save life rather than to destroy it?" (3:4) The large and absolute terms Jesus uses here seem to echo the moment in Deuteronomy when God sets before his people the large issues of life and death: "I have set before you life and death. . . . Choose life, then, that you and your descendants may live" (Deut 30:19). Jesus' question here, in other words, is framed so as to echo this proclamation of God. His argument is clearly not a small one over specific rules but a large one over the purpose of human worship.

Mark goes on to describe Jesus as "looking around them with anger and grieved at their hardness of heart" (3:5a). This particular mixture of anger and grief is also reminiscent of God's feelings as they are frequently portrayed in the Hebrew Bible. God is not portrayed there as unmoved and immovable, but as loving, jealous, angry, grieving, and forgiving. "Hardness of heart," on the other hand—the unmoved and immovable heart—is a common phrase the Hebrew Bible uses to express the human condition of sinfulness.

Further, when Mark shows Jesus in the actual act of curing the man, he quotes him as saying, "Stretch out your hand" (3:5b), a phrase that echoes the moment in Exodus when God tells Moses to stretch forth his hand over the sea to prepare a path for the Israelites' escape (Exod 14:16). The echo here is evocative, suggesting that Jesus not only cures the arm but gives the man new freedom. In all these different ways, Mark describes Jesus as a reflection of God.

3:6 The Pharisees and the Herodians

Mark sets up these two groups as particularly in opposition to Jesus. It is a surprising combination. The Pharisees were laypeople and scholars of the Bible. In spite of their later Christian reputation, they were in fact flexible interpreters of Scripture, believers in resurrection, and devoted to the cause of bringing Temple holiness into the home. The Herodians, on the other hand, were nominally Jews, but, in practice, collaborators with Rome; they were successively appointed by Rome to be tetrarchs of Palestine. The Romans called each tetrarch "the king of the Jews." The Herodians were obvious opponents of Jesus, but the Pharisees were not. Some scholars have even wondered if Jesus is shown arguing so much with the Pharisees because he belonged generally to their school of thought.

It is worth noting that the Pharisees do not show up again in Mark's description of Jesus' arrest and death. Judas makes his deal with "the chief priests" (14:10), with whom the Pharisees were not connected. It is true that the Pharisees do reappear with the Herodians here, trying to entrap Jesus by their question about paying taxes to Caesar (12:13). Yet Mark, more than any other evangelist, seems to implicate Rome in Jesus' death. We know that Matthew's anger against the Pharisees is directed not to those of Jesus' time but to those of Matthew's day who were putting the Jewish followers of Jesus out of the synagogues. It is possible that the same phenomenon accounts for their characterization here. Thematically, of course, the plotting of Jesus' death signals their negative response to the choice set before them between death and life.

3:7-10 The crowds that follow Jesus

In between key episodes and teachings, Mark interweaves passages about the crowds that follow Jesus. These passages serve to balance the picture of a few Jewish leaders plotting against Jesus with the picture of the large Jewish crowds who push to be close to him.

Mark 3

3:11 The unclean spirits that proclaim Jesus "Son of God"

Throughout the Gospel of Mark, the unclean spirits recognize Jesus' holiness, and even before he commands them to leave, they feel instantly displaced by his presence. We have already heard one such spirit cry out, "What have you to do with us, Jesus of Nazareth? Have you come to destroy us?" (1:24). It is part of Mark's irony that he shows the unclean spirits to have such clarity about Jesus' identity, while he shows the human followers of Jesus to be confused and uncertain. The fact that Mark shows them calling Jesus "Son of God" should not be taken as a proclamation of Jesus' role in the Trinity, because that doctrinal formulation was not arrived at until the fourth century. Rather, Mark is indicating that the spirit world saw Jesus clearly as God's image. (There is an early Jewish tradition that when God showed the angels the first human being, they saw God's reflection so clearly that they knelt in worship.)

3:12 "He warned them sternly not to make him known"

Much has been made by some readers of Mark over the repeated way he shows Jesus trying to silence those who recognize his holiness. This has been interpreted by some to mean that Jesus wanted to keep his identity hidden, and this theory is referred to in some books as "the messianic secret." But such an interpretation assumes that Mark is simply recording what Jesus said and did; it gives no credit to Mark as a shaping author and theologian. If, on the contrary, we assume that Mark has a theological purpose in mind, then we will hear these admonitions to silence differently. They serve two theological functions. First, by showing Jesus repeatedly asking others not to talk about his holiness or his ability to heal, Mark sets Jesus off from the typical hero who demands recognition of his powers. Second, Mark makes the spread of Jesus' reputation even more significant because it grows in spite of him.

3:13-19 The third calling of disciples

As the last of a triad, this calling should be read in connection with the other two (1:16-20; 2:13-17). As we noted before, in the first calling episode, the disciples appear to be saints responding in an ideal way, but in the second calling scene, it is clear that Jesus is seeking out sinners. This time Mark expands upon the scene by suggesting the purpose of Jesus' calling and by giving us the names of those called. Mark tells us that Jesus "appointed twelve" in order that "he might send them forth to preach and to have authority [or power] to drive out demons." When Mark describes Jesus ascending a mountain to do this, he evokes the memory of Moses;

when he emphasizes the number twelve, he evokes the twelve tribes of Israel. He thus implies that Jesus' gathering and sending forth of twelve followers is an act in continuity with Jewish tradition. The actions of preaching and casting out of demons are in continuity with the prophets.

Some of the names of the twelve are also significant. Peter, James, and John are the three whom Jesus will take to see the raising up of a child (5:37), his transfiguration (9:2), and his distress in Gethsemane (14:23). They also are given different names, always a signal in the Hebrew Bible of an inner transformation. Yet at the end we are also given the name of his betrayer. So Mark, in giving us a list of names, is giving us more than practical information. He is confirming what he suggested in the first two calling episodes, namely, that Jesus' disciples are a mixed lot, with one who would ultimately betray him and others who would ultimately be transformed by him. The reappearance of these four in other episodes of Mark's Gospel is worth tracking.

3:20-21 "He is out of his mind"

Once again Mark links episodes with a comment about the crowds pressing in on Jesus, this time to the point where no one could eat. Mark then comments that Jesus' relatives (literally, "those who were close to him," so perhaps his disciples) "set out to seize him, for they said, 'He is out of his mind.'" The Greek word that is translated "out of his mind" literally means "out of himself"; it is related to the Greek word for "ecstasy," on which we have commented before (see 2:12b). By using it, Mark suggests that Jesus has a more heightened consciousness than those around him.

3:22-30 Satan, forgiveness, and the holy spirit

By quoting the protests of the scribes to Jesus' exorcisms, Mark presents more of Jesus' teaching on forgiveness. The scribes say that Jesus himself must be possessed by Satan in order to drive out demons. Implicit in their statement is the idea that good and evil are so distinct and opposite that the "good" person should not go anywhere near "evil" persons. This thought is a logical extension of the idea that if Jesus were truly a person of God, he would not eat with sinners.

Jesus refutes this point of view in several ways. First he asks the commonsense question, "How can Satan drive out Satan?" He goes on to make the observation that "A kingdom divided against itself cannot stand" (3:23-24). Next he uses the analogy of "the strong man": "But no one can enter a strong man's house to plunder his property unless he first ties up the strong man. Then he can plunder his house" (3:27). Some interpretations of this analogy

Mark 3

assert that "the strong man" is Satan, and Jesus is the one who ties him up. But this would turn Jesus into a plunderer as well as a violent enforcer of his will—roles that violate everything we know of Jesus' teachings. Rather, it makes more sense to see that the violent intruder is Satan, and "the strong man" is the normally good person who is bound and robbed by him.

This view is borne out by Jesus' final words here about forgiveness—that "all sins and all blasphemies" will be forgiven except the blasphemy "against the holy spirit" (3:29). What Jesus means by "the sin against the holy spirit" has been puzzled over for centuries. The problem probably arose from capitalizing "holy spirit" and then assuming that "the sin against the Holy Spirit" was a special offense. But Mark would not have been thinking in terms of a Trinitarian formula. He would have been using "holy spirit" to mean simply God's spirit, as it appears in Psalm 51:11:

> Cast me not out from your presence,
> and your holy spirit take not from me.

The clue to Jesus' meaning here lies in the final explanation Mark gives: "For they had said, 'He has an unclean spirit'" (3:30). By means of this explanation, Mark stresses the opposition between an "unclean spirit" and God's "holy spirit." As Psalm 51 attests, it was common Jewish belief that every human being naturally possesses God's holy spirit. Jesus is teaching that the opposite of this state, that is, possession by an "unclean spirit," is thus unnatural or pathological. The "blasphemy against the holy spirit" is the denial of the fact that possession of God's holy spirit is every person's natural state. There is therefore no clearcut division, such as the scribes have implied, between good and evil persons; there are only people in varying states of pathology or wellness.

So Jesus, by driving out the unclean spirits, can restore people to their original wholeness. Sinners are invaded and bound by Satan; Jesus sets them free.

3:31-35 Jesus' "brother and sister and mother"

In the final section of chapter 3, Mark shows Jesus redefining the meaning of family. Mark first shows the crowd around Jesus using the conventional meaning of "family" as those who are related in blood. Mark sets up this usual understanding so that he can present Jesus' unconventional teaching that "whoever does the will of God" is his "brother and sister and mother." This statement does not, of course, denigrate his blood relatives but simply elevates the essential quality of their kinship with him.

Mark initiates here what will become a growing theme in his Gospel, namely, that people cannot be labeled according to prefixed assumptions; they can only be defined by what they do. So no one can presume who constitutes a member of Jesus' family according to some external criterion. Jesus' brothers and sisters are simply those who act like him in relation to God and others. Later in his Gospel, Mark will show that this existential relationship with Jesus also applies to discipleship.

Summary of chapter 3

In chapter 3, Mark shows how Jesus challenges conventional ways of wisdom. Instead of shunning the man who is alienated from the religious community by his physical disability, Jesus summons him to the midst of the synagogue. In curing the man, he not only restores him but restores the Sabbath to its original purpose of celebrating God's creation of human life. Instead of fighting with unclean spirits and demanding their subservience to his powers, Jesus treats them as a human pathology, and once having cast them out of a person, he asks for their silence. For his disciples, he calls together a mixed lot of people, including his future betrayer. He seeks out closeness with people to the point where his family or his disciples consider him "out of his mind." He asserts that all sins will be forgiven except the sin of thinking that the holy spirit is not the natural possession of every human being. He finds his family not in blood bonds but in spiritual kinship. In all these ways, Mark shows Jesus to be at once the restorer of human wholeness and the challenger of conventional wisdom.

JESUS AS WISDOM TEACHER

Mark 4:1-41

4:1-34 The three seed parables

Parables are common to the style of the Wisdom writings, so it is in keeping with Mark's presentation of Jesus that he shows him teaching by means of them. It helps to know that in Jewish tradition a "parable" was a set form with a set purpose, not just an illustrative story. Most often it was a succinct way of suggesting what God, or God's kingdom, is like. And very often it formed this comparison by weaving together small pieces or echoes of Scripture. The suggestive analogy that emerged was one that interpreted the Bible passages at the same time that it used them to point to God's kingdom. The rabbis described parables as "making handles for the Torah," meaning that parables were intended to open up the meaning of the Bible—to help people "get a handle" on it.

Mark 4

Because parables were generally considered interpretations of the Bible, it was common practice for Jewish teachers to place several parables on the same theme next to each other so that the student could reflect on different possibilities of meaning. It was said that they placed them together "like pearls on a string." So when we see three parables on seeds placed together, we should assume that they are intended to be read in relationship to one another. This interrelated reading becomes even more urgent in view of Mark's habit of expressing himself in triads.

4:3-9 The parable of the sower
This parable is based on the common biblical image of God as a farmer sowing his seed. For example, in Isaiah 55:10-11, God says:

> For just as from the heavens
>   the rain and snow come down
> And do not return there
>   till they have watered the earth,
>   making it fertile and fruitful,
> Giving seed to him who sows
>   and bread to him who eats,
> So shall my word be
>   that goes forth from my mouth;
> It shall not return to me void,
>   but shall do my will,
>   achieving the end for which I sent it.

And underlying the poetic description of Genesis 1 is a similar image of God creating the whole universe by his word alone. God has only to say "Let there be light" and "there was light" (Gen 1:3). In these passages, God is a sower and his word is the fertile seed that creates the world.

In the parable that Mark shows Jesus telling first, the sower's seed is only partially successful. Unlike God's word in either Genesis or Isaiah, the seed does not entirely "achieve the end" for which God sends it. It is thwarted by birds (4:4), by "rocky ground" (4:5), and by "thorns" (4:7). Only when it falls on "rich soil" does it produce fruit (4:8). This divided result is at odds with the purpose of the Creator in Isaiah and in Genesis.

The vocabulary used to describe these results, moreover, intensifies the division. The birds "consume" the seed (4:4); the sun "scorches" it, so that it "withers" (4:6); the thorns "choke" it (4:7). On the other hand, the seed that falls on good soil yields a superabundant harvest—"thirty, sixty, and a hundredfold" (4:8). The clearcut and exaggerated difference in results suggests an apocalyptic scenario—that is, a frightening view of the end time in which all people are revealed to have been predetermined to either eternal damnation or eternal bliss. Is that the teaching of Jesus here? We need to suspend our judgment until we have read the other two seed parables.

4:26-29 The parable of the seed that grows by itself

This parable is unique to Mark's Gospel. If we read it in connection with the first seed parable, we find that it offers a picture so opposite that it is comic. In this scenario, the seed is so fertile it sprouts no matter what. Even while the farmer sleeps, the seed goes on growing, "he knows not how" (4:27). The words suggest something that has its own rhythm—"night and day" (4:27)—and cannot be stopped. Indeed, the phrase rendered here as "of its own accord" is literally in Greek "automatically"* (4:28). On automatic, the seed grows larger and larger until "the harvest has come" (4:29).

The first parable would make us wary and worried about our final destiny. This second parable reassures us that all shall be well. This kind of uncalculating trust in God suggests the wisdom that "the Preacher" arrives at in Ecclesiastes, when he says:

> One who pays heed to the wind will not sow,
>   and one who watches the clouds will never reap.
> Just as you know not how the breath of life
>   fashions the human frame in the mother's womb,
> So you know not the work of God
>   which he is accomplishing in the universe.
> In the morning sow your seed,
>   and at evening let not your hands be idle:
> For you know not which of the two will be successful,
>   or whether both alike will turn out well (Eccl 11:4-6).

The first parable presents the scary, apocalyptic view of an end time in which souls are predetermined to eternal bliss or damnation. The second presents the reassuring perspective of Wisdom that in spite of our limited ways, God is making all things work together for good.

This perspective is further emphasized by the fact that the line about wielding the sickle to cut the ripe harvest (4:29) actually echoes a passage in the prophet Joel where the harvest is sin and the sickle represents God's vengeance (4:13). Joel is giving the harvest imagery an abnormal, almost perverse meaning. Mark is reversing this reversal and turning the harvest imagery back into something positive and good.

Mark 4

As the middle parable, this second one is the key to the meaning of the triad. To understand the fullness of what Mark is presenting here as the teaching of Jesus, we need to look at the last one.

4:30-32 The parable of the mustard seed

The mustard seed as "the smallest of all the seeds" was proverbial in Palestine. What grows from it, however, while large for a plant (about eight feet), is not very tall in comparison with a tree. So the oft-repeated interpretation of this parable, that it is about a tiny seed growing into a huge tree, is misleadingly simplistic. Jews in Mark's audience would have been struck by several other aspects of this parable. First, they would have been surprised that anyone would have bothered to plant the mustard seed at all because it was so common. Mustard seed bushes grow all around the Lake of Galilee. Second, in the description of branches large enough to give shade to "the birds of the sky," they would have heard a direct echo of passages in Ezekiel and Daniel.

This echo, in fact, would have given them the real clue to the parable's meaning. In Ezekiel, God plants "a noble cedar" so grand that "beasts and birds dwell in its shade" (Ezek 17:22-23). In context, this grand tree is clearly a symbol of the Davidic kingdom. In the Book of Daniel, King Nebuchadnezzar asks Daniel to interpret a dream that includes this description of a tree:

> I saw a tree of great height at the center of the world. It was large and strong, with its top touching the heavens, and it could be seen to the ends of the earth. Its leaves were beautiful and its fruit abundant, providing food for all. Under it the wild beasts found shade, in its branches the birds of the air nested; all men ate of it (Dan 4:7b-9).

The tree echoes the forbidden tree of Genesis 2, while its heaven-reaching top and nourishing of all flesh suggest "the tree of life" sealed off in the Garden.

By means of these echoes of Ezekiel and Daniel, the parable connects the common mustard seed plant with David's kingdom and with the tree of life in the first Garden. The real surprise in the parable is not the shift from small to large, but the paradoxical joining of the common and the ordinary with the divinely appointed grandeur of David and the divinely created nourishment of the original Garden. Through this imagery from the Bible, the parable suggests that the kingdom of God is analogous to something very common transformed into something grand and divinely life-giving.

Summary of the three parables

If we now read the three parables as a connected unit, we can see how they form a conversation about God's kingdom. The first parable presents a view of God's kingdom that was typical of apocalyptic writing of the time—that is, it suggests that God has created many people in this world but not all of them will be saved or arrive at God's kingdom. Some are destined to be lost. The labored allegorical explanation that is given in 4:14-20 may or may not be Mark's; many scholars think that it was added later. But whether it was or not, the parable itself invites that kind of exposition; it makes salvation the responsibility of the individual soul (or soil). The soil (or soul), moreover, appears predestined. There is no suggestion that the soil could change or that God's grace might intervene.

The second and third parables, however, present an entirely different point of view. The second parable, in fact, as we have seen, functions as a direct, almost comic refutation of the first, suggesting that no matter what, God's seed will grow and God's harvest will come. Its insistence on the unstoppable dynamism of God's seed prepares the way for the third parable, in which God's kingdom grows surprisingly out of common and ordinary seed.

It is worth noting that only the second and third parables are compared to God's kingdom (4:26, 30). As Mark presents Jesus' teaching, he does not introduce the first parable the same way. If we assume that all three parables must be read as a connected whole, then it appears that Jesus is not affirming the apocalyptic view here, but is going to some lengths to refute it. He is doing this in a way that is not familiar to us but would have been to a Jewish audience. He strings together three parables about seeds so his listeners will know they are interconnected. In the first, he gives the view that many of his day believed; in the next two, however, he undermines that view and offers some refuting wisdom. Through the second parable, he reminds his listeners of the wisdom of not trying to control everything, but to let go and trust in God's providence. Through the third parable, he reminds them that God created every human being (not just a few special ones) for the fullness of life.

4:10-13, 21-25 The purpose of the parables

In two different places in the chapter, Mark shows Jesus talking about his reason for teaching in parables. His first response seems almost perverse. He seems to be saying that he teaches in parables because he does not want everyone to understand him. But what he is actually doing is quoting Isaiah, and to understand his meaning, we have to know the context there.

The quotation comes from what is called Isaiah's "call story"—that is, it comes from the place in Isaiah where he recalls how he was first called by God to be a prophet. Every prophet has a similar story, and the stories follow a similar pattern. The prophet is always taken by surprise or put off balance by God's call. He accordingly always resists. Then God acts in some powerful way that makes the prophet realize that he has no choice. In Isaiah's case, he is first given a vision of God seated on a throne, worshiped by seraphim, who cry out, "Holy, holy, holy" while "the frame of the door shook and the house was filled with smoke" (Isa 6:3-4). Isaiah's first response is fear: "Then I said, 'Woe is me, I am doomed! For I am a man of unclean lips, living among a people of unclean lips; yet my eyes have seen the King, the LORD of hosts!'" (Isa 6:5). God then sends one of the seraphim to him with an ember to purge his unclean lips. After that, God asks, "Whom shall I send?" and Isaiah answers, "Here I am . . . . send me" (Isa 6:6-8). At that point, God tells him to "Go and say to this people":

> Listen carefully, but you shall not understand!
>   Look intently, but you shall know nothing!
> You are to make the heart of this people sluggish,
>   to dull their eyes and close their ears;
> Else their eyes will see, their ears hear,
>   their heart understand,
>   and they will turn and be healed (Isa 6:9-10).

In context, God's words are clearly ironic. He is sending the prophet to the people because he wants them to "turn and be healed"; his saying the opposite only underscores how much he wants it. So when Mark shows Jesus quoting that passage here, we should also understand it as irony. Jesus' quotation of Isaiah links him to the prophet's mission and indicates that he, like Isaiah, is speaking so as to touch and heal hearts. He teaches in parables for that purpose.

Mark makes Jesus' intentions clearer a bit later when he has him compare his teaching to a lamp (4:22-25). In the Bible, a "lamp" is frequently used as a metaphor for God's word. The psalmist sings, "Your word is a lamp for my feet" (Ps 119:105), and the author of Proverbs says about one of the commandments, "The bidding is a lamp, and the teaching a light" (Prov 6:23). So here, when Jesus asks if anyone would put a lamp under a bushel basket or a bed, he is suggesting that no one would try to hide God's word. Further, he is indicating that he certainly is not doing so. By implication, he is suggesting that the parable is a "lampstand" that will show off the light of God's word. The rabbis also speak of the parable form as a kind of lamp by which one can read the Bible more clearly.

When Jesus then goes on to say that "there is nothing hidden except to be made visible" and "nothing is secret except to come to light" (4:22), he appears to be expressing the Jewish view that the Bible contains God's revelation and nothing is hidden in the Bible except to be made clear.

The two proverbial sayings that follow—"The measure with which you measure will be measured out to you" (4:24) and "To the one who has, more will be given; from the one who has not, even what he has will be taken away" (4:25)—have a parallel in the Talmud, the most significant collection of the Jewish oral tradition. In the Talmud, it is clear that what is being talked about is the measure of one's understanding of God's word.

4:34-41 Jesus himself as parable

The parable section of the chapter appears to close with Mark telling us that "Without parables he [Jesus] did not speak to them [the crowd], but to his own disciples he explained everything in private" (4:34). The implication of this seems to be that Jesus did not use parables in teaching his disciples. It appears to confirm the earlier statement that Mark quotes Jesus as saying to his disciples: "The mystery of the kingdom of God has been granted to you. But to those outside everything comes in parables" (4:11). Yet the assertion is puzzling, because so far in his Gospel, Mark has not shown us Jesus teaching any other way.

What kind of distinction is Mark trying to make between Jesus' teaching of the crowd and his teaching of his disciples? In what special way has "the mystery of the kingdom of God" been granted to Jesus' disciples? In the closing verses of chapter 4, Mark seems to provide an answer. He shows Jesus himself to be a living parable. That is to say, in the final episode of Jesus' stilling the sea, Mark reveals that the person of Jesus provides an analogy to what God is like.

As in the parables that Jesus tells, this parable that he enacts is composed of echoes of Scripture. In this case, the direct echo is of some of the psalms that reflect on God's power over creation:

> LORD, God of hosts, who is like you? . . .
> You rule the raging sea;
>   you still its swelling waves (Ps 89:9a, 10).
>
> You still the roaring of the seas,
>   the roaring of their waves (Ps 65:8).

Mark 4

> [The LORD] hushed the storm to a murmur;
> the waves of the sea were stilled (Ps 107:29).

Mark, steeped in the Hebrew Bible himself, surely assumed that when he quotes the disciples saying, "Who then is this whom even wind and sea obey?" (4:41), his audience would have heard the answer in their memory of these psalms.

In the first part of chapter 4, Mark shows Jesus teaching in the style of a teacher of Wisdom, teaching in parables. At the end, however, he shows Jesus teaching by his actions. He shows Jesus stilling the sea as God stills the sea in the psalms. He shows Jesus to be "like God." He shows Jesus to be in himself a Wisdom parable. Those who are his disciples have been granted a direct encounter with "the mystery of the kingdom of God."

Summary of chapter 4

In chapter 4, Mark focuses on Jesus' teaching about the kingdom of God. He shows him teaching in the style of a Wisdom teacher, using parables to shed light on God's revelation in Scripture. He does so by following a method common to other Jewish teachers. He strings together three parables linked by the image of seeds. They are all based on the biblical image that expresses God the Creator as God the sower. Yet each one imagines God's sowing and the results differently. The first parable imagines God sowing some seeds that will bear fruit and some that will not. The second parable imagines God's word as a seed that will come to fruition no matter what. The third parable imagines God's word as a seed that is common and accessible, yet grows to be shade and shelter for all creatures.

In between the parables, Mark shows Jesus commenting on the purpose of parables. He first quotes the passage in Isaiah where God (by ironically saying the opposite of what he means) indicates how much he wants his word to touch and heal the human heart. He next suggests that the parable form is like a lampstand that shows off the light of God's word. He indicates that he speaks in parables in order to bring to light what is hidden in God's revelation.

Mark shows Jesus asking the question of how to find an analogy for God's kingdom. The second and third parables form one kind of answer. But in the final episode of the chapter, when Mark shows Jesus stilling the sea, he provides a different kind of answer. He shows Jesus himself acting the way God does in the psalms. He suggests that Jesus himself is a kind of parable, a living likeness of God. As a parable, he is like a lampstand that makes more visible the light of God's word. He is a living metaphor that serves to bring to light what is hidden in God's revelation.

THE TRANSFORMING EFFECT OF JESUS/WISDOM

Mark 5:1-43

5:1-20 The transformation of the Gerasene demoniac

No one knows exactly what Mark had in mind by "the territory of the Gerasenes," but it was clearly pagan territory, being on "the other side of the sea" from Galilee and inhabited by people who tended pigs (an unclean and forbidden animal to Jews). There are fascinating echoes of Isaiah's description of a pagan people who, he says, were "living among the graves," "eating swine's flesh," and "crying out, 'Hold back, do not touch me!'" (Isa 65:4-5a). So we find here in Mark's narrative a man "dwelling among the tombs" whom "no one could restrain" (5:3), and who was "always crying out" (5:5). He is not said to be "eating swine's flesh," but swine do figure prominently in the story. In Isaiah, these pagan practices enkindle God's wrath (Isa 65:5b). Here, however, Mark shows Jesus treating them as evidence of unclean spirits, a pathological state that can be cured.

The narrative is also suggestive of Jesus' metaphor of "the strong man" in chapter 3. You may remember that there, Jesus observes, "No one can enter a strong man's house to plunder his property unless he first ties up the strong man" (3:27). Here in fact is a strong man, powerful enough to have pulled apart his physical chains (5:4), but nonetheless invaded and plundered by unclean spirits. Jesus' response is not to bind but to free him.

The exchange between Jesus and the unclean spirits reveals something about Mark's view of the nature of evil. First of all, like the unclean spirit in 1:24, the unclean spirits here cry out in protest at Jesus' appearance (5:7). Once again Mark indicates that they feel diminished by Jesus' very presence. Second, it should not be passed over that the name of these unclean spirits, "Legion," is the name of a unit in the Roman army. Surely a Jewish audience would have been amused by this piece of wit at their enemy's expense. Even more, they would have found it a joke that these Roman demons ask to be placed inside a herd of pigs. The final act in this rhetorical comedy is the scene of the pigs rushing headlong into the sea.

The serious side of this story is the pointed suggestion that those who were currently occupying Palestine and meddling with the Temple belong to the devil. At the time that Mark's Gospel was written down (probably the year 70), it would not have been safe or prudent for anyone to have said

Mark 5

such a thing directly. But here and elsewhere, as we shall see, Mark insinuates his view of Rome.

After the unclean spirits leave him, the man who had been possessed reappears "clothed and in his right mind" (5:15). The details suggest that before, he had been naked and crazy; in ridding him of his demons, Jesus has restored him to himself. This restoration is such a profound change that it seems like a transformation. The ultimate sign of his transformation appears in the man's going off "to proclaim in Decapolis what Jesus had done for him" (5:20). Like the cured leper in 1:45, this man is transformed from an alienated human being into one who spreads the word of God's goodness.

5:25-34 The transformation of the menstruating woman

The narrative of the woman who was suffering for twelve years from a menstrual disorder is interjected into the story of the twelve-year-old girl who appears to be dead. This structure of interlocking stories is a device Mark uses for a purpose. We will consider later what that purpose is.

The narrative of this woman is striking because in it Mark shows Jesus dealing openly and compassionately with a female condition that was taboo. Menstruating women were considered ritually unclean and excluded from Temple gatherings. Menstruating women were considered sexually unclean, so husbands were forbidden to have intercourse with them. In biblical writings, a menstruating woman is used as a symbol of idolatry. Thus, to describe a woman who had suffered from a flow of menstrual blood over a period of twelve years is to hold up for consideration a woman who in every way sums ups "the unclean" within Judaism—ritually, sexually, and religiously. Her healing contact with Jesus thus has significance far beyond the immediate miracle. Mark suggests that she was changed in two different ways: first, "she felt in her body that she was healed of her affliction" (5:29), and second, she receives an affirmation of her faith (5:34).

There are details in the scene worth noting. First, Mark underlines the spiritual significance of the story by his repeated use of "straightway." He tells us that "*Straightway** her flow of blood dried up" (5:29) and "*Straightway* Jesus was aware that power had gone out from him" (5:30).

Second, Mark says that the woman approached Jesus "in fear and trembling" (5:33). The phrase anticipates the description of the three women before the empty tomb and should be kept in mind as a clue to its meaning. Clearly, the woman here is trembling because she has sensed the power that has healed her body; she is not frightened but in awe of it. When we read later that the women at the tomb were also "trembling" (16:8), we should remember that Mark has used the word here to signify the holy state of being overwhelmed by God's power. Mark confirms this meaning when he quotes Jesus as saying, "Daughter, your faith has saved you" (5:34a). Mark confirms this further by showing Jesus bestowing on her a traditional Jewish blessing: "Go [or walk] in peace . . . ." (5:34a). The woman has been transformed by Jesus from someone who was ostracized as "unclean" into a model of faith.

5:21-24, 35-43 The transformation of the synagogue leader's daughter

After the story of Jesus' transformation of the possessed man in the pagan, Gentile world of the Gerasenes, Mark says that Jesus crossed the Sea of Galilee again, back to the Jewish side (5:21). Here Mark begins the story of Jairus, the synagogue official who begs for help for his dying daughter (5:22-24). Mark interrupts that narrative to tell the one of the menstruating woman, then returns to it after she has been healed and sent off in peace. The interruption serves two purposes: first, it provides a narrative reason for Jesus' delay in going to see the little girl, an interval that appears to be fatal (5:35), so that, dramatically, Jesus' miracle here has greater dimensions than a simple healing. Second, it makes the story of the older woman shed light on the meaning of the little girl's, and vice versa. Intertwined as narratives, they are also intertwined in meaning. In both cases, a female person is brought back from the brink of death.

Mark shapes the narrative of the little girl so as to show that this is a story of resurrection—one that anticipates Jesus' own. He quotes Jesus as saying three things in the course of the story, each of them pointing to the story's ultimate significance. Jesus says to the synagogue official, "Do not be afraid; just have faith" (5:36). He says to the weeping crowd, "The child is not dead but asleep" (5:39). And he says to the child herself, "Rise up!"* (5:41).

Each one of these comments is geared toward transforming common attitudes toward death. To the synagogue official, death was not only an occasion of sadness but of fear, because it was believed at the time that death rendered the human body "unclean" and so made anyone who touched it ritually unclean. To the crowd "weeping and wailing loudly" (5:38), death was final, and to the child herself, life seemed over. Against these views, Jesus' comments exchange fear for faith, suggest that death is but a temporary and reversible phase, and call the child back to life.

Once again, as in the healing of Simon's mother-in-law (1:31) and the healing of the paralytic (2:11), Mark uses the same word here for "rise" that he uses for Jesus' resurrection. Mark also uses key words to describe the reaction of the witnesses. What is translated here as "They were utterly

Mark 5

astounded" (5:42b) is literally "They were out of their minds [or "beside themselves"] with ecstasy."* The phrase "out of their minds" echoes Mark's earlier description of those who witnessed the paralytic rise up (2:12b) and the place where those close to Jesus think he is "out of his mind" (3:21). Mark will use the word "ecstasy" again at the end of his Gospel to describe the experience of the women overwhelmed by God's power to overcome death.

Summary of chapter 5

In this chapter, Mark shows Jesus having a transforming effect on different states considered "unclean" within Judaism: demon possession, menstruation, and death. Considering these three episodes as another Markan triad, we need to explore how the middle episode is key. The first transforming miracle takes place in the Gentile world; the last is set in the home of a synagogue leader. The first frees a man from his demons and restores him to himself; the last raises up a child thought dead and restores her to her parents. In the middle is the transformation of a Jewish woman whose physical condition has alienated her as completely from Temple and synagogue as demons or death. In curing her, Jesus restores her both to herself and to her religious community. In effect, he brings her back to life.

THE RECOGNITION OF JESUS/WISDOM

Mark 6:1-56

6:1-6 Jesus as too familiar

In the preceding chapters, Mark has repeatedly dramatized how people around Jesus are challenged by his unconventional ways. They are challenged by his "new teaching" (1:27) that possession by demons is a pathological state that can be cured (1:21-28; 3:22-30); by his transforming outreach to "the unclean" (1:40-45; 5:1-43); by his "raising up"* of women (1:29-31; 5:21-43); by his calling of sinners (2:13-17) and his views on sin and forgiveness (3:22-30); by his seeming indifference to religious rules (2:18-28); by his priorities—by the way he continually places human need first (3:1-5); by his redefining the meaning of "family" (3:31-35); by his teaching in parables (4:1-34); by his easy command of demons and storms (1:25; 4:39; 5:8).

At the beginning of chapter 6, Mark dramatizes the opposite: he constructs a scene in which the people in Jesus' hometown find him too familiar to teach them anything. The questions that Mark quotes them as asking are typical of all people who expect (or want) their encounter with the divine to be unusual and spectacular.

Since Mark has been presenting Jesus to his readers as Wisdom herself, there is particular irony in their question "What kind of wisdom has been given him?" (6:2). With further irony, Mark uses their questions to set up Jesus' Wisdom-saying, "A prophet is not without honor except in his native place and among his own kin and in his own house" (6:4). In this pithy observation, Mark shows Jesus also hinting at the destiny of his disciples.

6:7-13, 30-31 The commissioning of the disciples of Jesus/Wisdom

Mark shows that the disciples are instructed to imitate Jesus in preaching repentance, driving out demons, and curing the sick (6:12-13). By implication, the instruction to be detached from their possessions (6:8-9) also reflects the simple lifestyle of Jesus/Wisdom, a point Mark will develop in chapter 10. Mark links this narrative to the scene in Nazareth by showing that Jesus tells them to expect rejection (6:11). Later in the chapter, Mark shows how the disciples return to report and how Jesus invites them to follow him further by withdrawing for prayer (6:30-31).

6:14-29 The death of John the Baptist

As in chapter 5, Mark interweaves different narratives, so that each one comments on the other. As we have seen, one narrative strand is concerned with the disciples—how they are sent forth to be like Jesus and how they return to report. In between we hear the story of John the Baptist. Although at first hearing the transition may seem abrupt and the stories unconnected, with hindsight we can see that Mark has set up the narrative about John and his followers to foreshadow the narrative of Jesus and his disciples. Mark builds upon the original connections he has made between John and Jesus (1:14; 2:18) to achieve this effect.

Mark uses the device of a conversation about Jesus and John to set up the connections. First we hear people in general comparing Jesus with John (6:14), and then we hear Herod making the same comparison (6:16). In both instances, these voices speak of John as "raised from the dead." It is only then, and in retrospect, that we hear how and why John was murdered by Herod.

The story is complex, dramatizing the convergence of many causes. The root cause is classic: a prophet (John) "speaks truth to power." Nonetheless, we are told, Herod himself would not have injured John on that account, because he "feared John" and "liked to listen to him" (6:20). His wife, Herodias, however, angered at being denounced as unlawful, "harbored a grudge" and looked for the chance to avenge herself (6:19). The opportunity

Mark 6

presents itself in the form of Herod's birthday party, a seemingly innocuous celebration (6:21). There the dance of a young girl (the daughter of Herodias) leads to Herod's extravagant and thoughtless vow: "I will grant you whatever you ask of me, even to half of my kingdom" (6:23). The plot concludes in a dizzying series of ironies: the young girl acts like a dutiful and docile daughter in repeating to Herod her mother's murderous request for "the head of John the Baptist" (6:24). The king, although "deeply distressed," accedes to the request out of a sense of fidelity to his word (6:26). The girl, dutiful to the end, took the prophet's head and "gave it to her mother" (6:28).

Mark has told the story of John's death in a way that illuminates how it results from a tragic and ironic mixture of vengeful hatred, chance opportunity, filial devotion, and vacillating weakness. As Mark tells the story, it is clear that while there is certainly some real evil at work (the unlawful marriage to begin with, and then the desire for revenge on the part of Herodias), the murder would never have been accomplished without Herod's weak ambivalence. Even though he knew John "to be a righteous and holy man," he had him imprisoned (6:17, 20), and even though he was "deeply distressed" (6:26) by the girl's savage request, he gave the order for John's beheading (6:27).

Mark's narrative and theological purpose in telling this story is revealed in the conclusion: "When his disciples heard about it, they came and took his body and laid it in a tomb" (6:29). Mark has put the story of John's death here as a foreshadowing of Jesus' death. The two stories are not, of course, exactly the same, but there are parallels. In the second part of his Gospel, Mark will show Jesus speaking some unwelcome truths to those in power, and he will suggest how some leaders (both Roman and Jewish) were resentful of this criticism, and so looked for a way to get rid of him. He will show the collaboration between these vengeful people and the opportunist Judas (14:10-11). But above all, he will show how it is Pilate's weakness, especially his desire "to satisfy the crowd," that results in his condemnation of Jesus (15:15).

Mark also uses this story to illuminate the difference between John's disciples and those of Jesus. Unlike John's disciples, Jesus' disciples do not come as a group to ask for his body and bury it. One person, Joseph of Arimathea, does come, but he is a member of the council that condemned Jesus and so a new and unexpected disciple. All the others have fled. It is with pointed irony that Mark makes this story of John and his faithful disciples part of the narrative in which Jesus' disciples receive their instructions.

Finally, Mark uses this story to foreshadow Jesus' resurrection. He does this through the opening speculation by the people and by Herod that Jesus may in fact be John "raised up." Before this, Mark has introduced the motif of resurrection through the vocabulary of "rising up" and "raised up" that he uses for so many of Jesus' miracles. Here Mark makes the resurrection theme explicit.

It is also worth noting that Mark sets up a structure here that he will repeat in connection with Jesus. He gives a hint of John's resurrection before he tells us about his death, just as he will tell of Jesus' transfiguration before he gives an account of his passion. In this way, too, Mark uses John's story to foreshadow that of Jesus.

6:31-44 The feeding of the five thousand

The motif of food and of eating is a recurring one in Mark's Gospel. It causes criticism when Jesus is seen eating with sinners and tax collectors (2:16). It raises questions when Jesus and his disciples feast rather than fast (2:18-19). It occasions moral outrage when Jesus allows his disciples to pick grain on the Sabbath, and the outrage in turn provides the opportunity for Jesus to teach that God's intent for the Sabbath is human wholeness (2:23-28).

All this concern with nurture is part of Mark's portrayal of Jesus as Wisdom—a womanly figure in Proverbs (and elsewhere), who ceaselessly invites guests to the divine banquet. In keeping with these motherly characteristics, Mark shows Jesus' first concern for Jairus's daughter, once he has brought her back to life, is that "she should be given something to eat" (5:43). That verse, which is the conclusion of chapter 5, prepares for Jesus' concern here for feeding the five thousand who have followed him.

Mark constructs a transition from the narrative of Jesus and the disciples to this narrative by noting that they were surrounded by so many people that "they had no opportunity even to eat" (6:31). There is an echo here of the earlier scene where "the crowds gathered, making it impossible for them even to eat" (3:20). In the earlier instance, Mark tells us that those close to Jesus said, "He is out of his mind" (3:21). In this instance, Mark says that Jesus and his disciples set off "to a deserted place" (6:32) but could not keep the crowds away. Mark then describes a repetition of what happened at the end of chapter 1 when Jesus "remained in deserted places," and yet "people kept coming to him from everywhere" (1:45b). Here again Mark dramatizes that Jesus cannot escape the crowds. They arrive at his destination on foot before he arrives at it by boat (6:32-33).

In the scenes that follow, Mark suggests in several different ways that Jesus is acting the way God acts in the Hebrew Bible. When Mark tells us that Jesus' heart was "moved with pity for them, for they were like sheep without a shepherd" (6:34), he is echoing the place in Ezekiel where God pities the hungry sheep and promises to shepherd them himself (Ezek 34:11-15).

When Mark tells us that Jesus ordered the people to "sit down in groups," the words literally are "meal-sharing groups"* (6:39). This phrasing is suggestive of God's instructions for sharing the Passover meal: "If a family is too small for a whole lamb, it shall join the nearest household in procuring one and shall share in the lamb" (Exod 12:4).

Through the threefold repetition of "deserted place" (6:31a, 32, 35), Mark emphasizes that the setting is similar to the wilderness setting of the Exodus journey.

Mark thus tells the story of Jesus' miraculous feeding of the five thousand in the desert in such a way that it would remind his audience of God's miraculous way of providing his people with manna in the desert. In this context, Jesus' invitation to come to the desert ("Come away . . . and rest a while," 6:31a) is suggestive of God's command not even to gather manna on the seventh day but to share his Sabbath rest (Exod 16:23).

The overall thrust of the book of Exodus is God's providential care for his people, not only in leading them out of slavery but in leading them into a space and time apart from ordinary concerns—into a desert place and Sabbath time where they could learn to become dependent on God for food and life itself. By echoing this crucial time in the history of God's people, Mark suggests how Jesus reflects this nurturing aspect of God.

6:45-52 Walking on water

In describing Jesus' "walking on the sea" (6:48b), Mark shows Jesus acting like God in Job (9:8 and 38:16) and Sirach (24:5-6). Other miraculous actions of Jesus have some precedent in one of the prophets: Elisha multiplies bread (2 Kgs 4:42-44) and cures the leper Naaman (2 Kgs 5:1-14); Elijah raises a young man from the dead (1 Kgs 17:17-24). But no prophet walks on water. In describing this scene, Mark is dramatizing his perception that Jesus resembles God himself. Mark intensifies this perception by showing Jesus still the waters once again as he did at the end of chapter 4. There we noted that Mark, through echoes of Psalm 84, suggests that Jesus is a living parable of what God is like. When Mark repeats the scene here, he makes that likeness clear.

The reaction of the disciples, however, to this second incident of Jesus' stilling the sea is markedly less perceptive than the first time around. This time, when they see Jesus walking to them on the water, they are not awed but terrified. (Here Mark uses a verb that means "fright," not "holy fear.")

Mark 6

When the wind dies down, they do not ask, as they did before, "Who then is this, whom even wind and sea obey?" (4:41). In the earlier incident, Mark suggests that they might be coming to a deeper understanding of Jesus' identity. In this scene, however, he says that "they had not understood the incident of the loaves. On the contrary, their hearts were hardened" (6:52).

"Hardness of heart," as we have noted before, is a typical way for the Hebrew Bible to express the obstinate resistance of the sinner to God's outreach. Mark has used it before in his Gospel to describe the Pharisees' cold reaction to Jesus' healing of the man with a withered hand (3:5). It is striking that he uses the same phrase here to describe the obtuse response of Jesus' own disciples.

6:53-56 Recognition of Jesus at Gennesaret

Mark concludes the chapter with a sharply contrasting description of the ordinary crowds. Most telling is the phrase "people straightway* recognized him" (6:54). It is striking because the chapter opens with Mark dramatizing a scene in Jesus' hometown in which people who "know" him cannot recognize him as anything more than "the carpenter, the son of Mary" (6:3).

The importance of the recognition here is underlined by Mark's use of the word "straightway." While Jesus' own disciples fail to understand anything significant in Jesus' feeding of the five thousand, the crowds scurry to bring their sick, and like the woman with the disordered flow of blood (5:28), they "begged him that they might touch only the tassel on his cloak" (6:56).

Summary of chapter 6

In this chapter, Mark dwells on the theme of people recognizing or not recognizing Jesus as God's Wisdom. In the opening scene, he shows people in Jesus' hometown not recognizing him as anyone special because he is so familiar. In the last scene of the chapter, Mark shows ordinary crowds elsewhere recognizing him "straightway." These two extremes frame the chapter.

In between, Mark dwells on the role of the disciples and their variable responses to Jesus and to his actions. Again there is a framework of two extremes: early in the chapter we see the disciples sent forth to imitate Jesus in his preaching, healing, and exorcising of demons, yet at the end of the chapter we find that "their hearts were hardened," so that they remember neither Jesus' miracle of the loaves nor his earlier command of the sea.

Mark 6

The complicated, uncertain nature of the disciples is further dramatized through Mark's device of interweaving the story of John the Baptist into their story. The narrative of John's death and the possibility of his being "raised up" function as a foreshadowing of the death and resurrection of Jesus. At the same time, Mark sets up the courageous, faithful disciples of John as a contrast to the disciples of Jesus, who, in the end, will become frightened (as they are here) and run away.

And even while he is showing the disciples as repeatedly unable to grasp who Jesus is, Mark is dramatizing more and more clearly that Jesus is the image of God. Jesus feeds the crowds with bread in the desert as God fed the Israelites with manna in the wilderness; he walks on water as God does in Job and Sirach.

JESUS' REDEFINING OF THE "UNCLEAN"
Mark 7:1-37

7:1-13 Discussion of the sacred and the profane

In Jewish tradition, there are clear boundaries between the sacred and the profane, between what is to be consecrated to God and what is to be regarded as secular or "common." The Jewish people see themselves as consecrated to God in accordance with God's blessing of them in Exodus 19:6: "You shall be to me a kingdom of priests, a holy nation." The Ten Commandments of the covenant, as well as the subsidiary laws designed to support and protect them, are considered a gift to be cherished.

The laws concerning food are part of this larger context. Eating kosher food and using kosher dishes are an acknowledgment that all life, as well as the nourishing of it, is sacred to the Lord. The whole discussion in this chapter should be regarded in that context and not as an argument over trivial rules. The Jewish custom of washing their hands before eating, and the vessels before using them, was originally more than good hygiene. They were also acts of ritual purification, signaling Jewish desire to consecrate this most basic of human activities.

Unfortunately, verses 3 and 4, which try to give an explanation for these washing rituals, are flawed in the original manuscript. Verse 3 literally reads, "For the Pharisees and all the Jews do not eat unless they have washed themselves *with the fist** . . . ." Verse 4 literally reads, "And they do not eat from the marketplace unless they immerse themselves, and there are many other traditions they carry out, the immersing of cups and pots and bronze vessels *and beds.**" No translator knows what to do with "the fist" in verse 3 or the "beds" of verse 4. No commentator notes that the

Mark 7

word "immerse" here is *baptizo* in Greek. It's a word that Mark uses for baptism but is ill-suited to this context. Many scholars think that this curious explanation of Jewish customs was probably added to Mark's manuscript after the first century. Vincent Taylor, one of the best of these scholars, recommends skipping verses 2-4 entirely.

In any case, Mark uses a favorite device here: he cites a question by the Pharisees in order to set up Jesus' teaching on what is and is not sacred. The Pharisees challenge the eating customs of Jesus' disciples, just as earlier they had challenged their picking grain on the Sabbath (2:24). The language of this challenge highlights what is at stake: "Why do your disciples . . . eat the bread with unclean hands?" (7:5). The word translated "unclean" here could also be translated "common." What is "common" is profane and ordinary, not consecrated and sacred. It is a consistent theme of Mark's that Jesus is like Wisdom, who, in Proverbs, goes into the marketplace to find her followers. Like Wisdom, Jesus does not shun the common and ordinary but seeks to transform it.

In 7:6-7, Jesus critiques his challengers in the language of Isaiah 29:13. In context, Isaiah is expressing God's frustration that the people of Jerusalem do not trust that God will save them from besieging enemies. God finds the root cause in the fact that the people honor him with their lips, not their hearts. Their worship has become merely "routine observance of human precepts."

In 7:8, Jesus carries this accusation even further, saying, "You disregard God's commandment but cling to human tradition." In 7:10-12, Jesus gives a concrete example of this practice. He notes how some fail to honor their parents by withholding support for them on the grounds that the money is *"qorban,"* or dedicated to God. How much this was actually done is difficult to determine. But the point of Jesus' criticism is clearly part of the larger theme of the chapter. Jesus is pointing out that human relationships are what is truly sacred, and no religious formula can ration-alize that sacredness away.

7:14-23 What defiles a person

Just as Mark uses a question by the Pharisees to set the stage for Jesus' teaching on what is sacred, so here he uses a question by the disciples to open up Jesus' teaching on what is defiling. Jesus says to the crowd that "Nothing that enters one from outside can defile that person" (7:15). Mark calls this a "parable" or "riddle" (7:17), indicating that it is a saying whose full meaning needs to be unpacked.

At first glance, Jesus' saying appears to challenge the Jewish dietary laws. After all, if nothing that one takes in is defiling, then why refuse to eat certain

Mark 7

foods? The parenthetical comment "Thus he declared all foods unclean" was probably added later and was intended as just such an explanation. We know, however, from Acts 10:1-11 that the question of which foods were unclean went on being debated in the early church. And as Jesus goes on teaching here, we see that he is presenting something more morally complex. The complexity is contained in what comes "from within people, from their hearts" (7:21). If we grasp the saying as a whole, we realize that the emphasis is not on dismissing what enters a person but on demonstrating the greater evil of "what comes out" (7:20). As in much of Jesus' teaching, his intent appears not so much to disregard external rules as to focus on internal realities.

7:24-30 Jesus and the Syrophoenician woman; the healing of the daughter with an unclean spirit

Mark dramatizes Jesus' point here by showing him in pagan or "unclean" territory. Here Jesus converses with a pagan woman and exorcises the unclean spirit that has possessed her daughter. In so doing, Mark is showing Jesus engaged in activities that other pious Jews of his time would have found unconventional, even shocking. Mark softens the shock value of Jesus' outreach to the Gentiles by indicating his reluctance to become involved.

First, Mark tells his audience that Jesus "wanted no one to know about" his journey to Tyre. Second, when the woman asks Jesus to cure her daughter, Mark says that Jesus first put her off by saying, "Let the children be fed first. For it is not right to take the food of the children and throw it to the dogs" (7:27). Jesus' language here indicates that he saw Israel as his priority over the Gentiles. The "children" are the children of Israel. The term "dogs" was a common and insulting way for Jews of the time to refer to Gentiles.

The woman responds in a bold and witty way by accepting these terms and turning them back to Jesus through a play on words and ideas. She says: "Lord, even the dogs under the table eat the children's scraps" (7:28). This kind of playfulness with words is typically Jewish. Mark perhaps wanted to dramatize that even someone as "unclean" as a Gentile woman with a possessed daughter was capable of parrying on equal terms with a Jew. The healing of her daughter (7:30) is linked to Mark's way of showing her, not as unclean Gentile, but as a partner in wit.

There is precedent in Hebrew Scripture for Jewish outreach to the Gentiles. In the Second Book of Kings we hear how Elisha the prophet cured the Syrian king of leprosy (2 Kgs 5:1-19). But Mark uses language that indicates that Jesus' exchange with this woman has more meaning than a simple cure. When the woman first comes to Jesus, Mark says she heard of him "straightway"* (7:25). The word is translated above as "soon," but as we have suggested before, "straightway" is Mark's particular way of indicating moral urgency.

The words of the exchange between Jesus and the woman may also be weighted with special meaning. It was a common Jewish idiom to speak of God's word as "bread." And the word translated here as "food" is literally "bread"* (7:27), so we might understand Jesus to be saying, "It is not right to take God's word [the "bread"] and throw it to the dogs" [that is, to those who do not know how to understand it]. When Mark shows Jesus conceding to the woman's wish, he may be indicating Jesus' willingness to extend God's word to the Gentiles.

7:31-37 Jesus' healing of the deaf-mute

Mark shows that Jesus continued his ministry in Gentile territory, this time on the other side of the Sea of Galilee, in Decapolis. In language that echoes the healing of the paralytic (2:3), Mark tells us that "They brought to him a man that was deaf and mute and begged him that he might lay a hand on him." Mark then describes Jesus' curing the man through a series of ritual actions known to have been used by both Greek and Jewish healers. The Aramaic phrase *ephphatha* literally means "be released,"* which links it to Jesus' saying to the paralytic that his sins are "released" (2:5).

Mark indicates that this healing has moral significance through his use of the word "straightway"* (translated above as "immediately"): "And straightway his ears were opened and his tongue was loosed from chains and he began to speak straight" (7:35).

By the use of the word "straightway," together with the repetition of "straight,"* Mark indicates that more is happening here than a simple cure. The whole event echoes ideas and language in Isaiah, some of which Mark showed Jesus alluding to in 4:10-13. We have noted before that when Jesus is speaking about the purpose of parables, he quotes the place in Isaiah where God says ironically:

> You are to make the heart of this people sluggish,
> > to dull their eyes and close their ears;
> Else their eyes will see, their ears hear,
> > their heart understand,
> > and they will turn and be healed (Isa 6:9-10).

And as we said earlier, of course God actually hopes the people will see and hear, understand and be healed. In a later book in Isaiah, when God is promising to save his people, God says:

Mark 7

> Then will the eyes of the blind be opened,
>   the ears of the deaf be cleared;
> Then will the lame leap like a stag,
>   then the tongue of the mute will sing (Isa 35:5-6).

In this concluding episode of chapter 7, Mark shows Jesus doing what God has promised. By showing Jesus healing the deaf-mute, Mark is suggesting that Jesus is opening up people to God's word.

Summary of chapter 7

In this chapter, Mark develops the theme of Jesus' relationship to the "unclean. " It is a theme that Mark touched on in Jesus' first healing of the man with the unclean spirit (1:21-27); in his cure of the leper (1:40-45); in his eating with sinners (2:13-17); in the accusation that Jesus himself has an unclean spirit (3:30); in Jesus' exorcism of the Gerasene demoniac (5:2); and in the power Jesus gives his disciples to drive out unclean spirits (6:7).

This chapter has a triad structure. A homily by Jesus that redefines what makes a person "unclean" (7:14-23) is framed by two conversations on the subject. Before the homily, Jesus has a conversation with men of traditional piety about what is sacred and what is "unclean" or profane (7:1-14). After the homily, he has an unconventional dialogue with a pagan woman and drives out an unclean spirit from her daughter (7:24-30). Mark shows Jesus responding to the challenge of those who think in conventional terms by redefining what is "unclean." Mark dramatizes this redefinition by showing Jesus' outreach to the Gentile woman and her daughter.

In the concluding episode Mark indicates the significance of Jesus' redefinition by showing him engaged in healing a deaf-mute, an action that symbolizes the opening of people's ears to the meaning of God's word.

SECOND SIGHT—A SHARPER FOCUS

Mark 8:1-38

8:1-10 The second feeding of a crowd

Mark designs his Gospel so that themes, images, and even events are repeated more than once. With hindsight the reader becomes aware of a pattern of doublets. There is a theological purpose to this design that chapter 8 points to, which we will discuss later. The doublet at the beginning of chapter 8 is striking: once again a large and hungry crowd is gathered around Jesus, and once again he feeds them with scant supplies. Once again there are baskets left over. (Compare 6:34-44.)

There are also some interesting details of difference. In the first scenario, Jesus is "moved with pity" for the crowd because they "were like sheep without a shepherd" (6:34); his initial compassion is for their spiritual hunger. Here Jesus is concerned about the crowd because they have been with him "for three days and have nothing to eat" (8:2). In the first scene, the disciples approach Jesus about the situation (6:35); here Jesus approaches them (8:1-3). In the first scene, they distribute "five loaves and two fish" (6:38); here they distribute seven loaves and "a few fish" (8:6-7). In both instances, Jesus orders the crowd to sit down to be fed, but in the first one he suggests that they form "meal-sharing groups" (6:39), a detail that is omitted here. In both instances Jesus prays over the bread and then breaks it, but in the first scene Mark specifically says that he "said the blessing" over it (6:41), while in the second, Mark says he "gave thanks" (8:6). In both cases, Mark tells us that the people ate "and were satisfied" (6:42; 8:8). In both scenes, the disciples gather up baskets of leftovers, but in the first instance it is twelve (6:43), while in the second there are seven (8:8).

Is there any significance to these small differences? Many scholars have suggested that the first feeding is suggestive of God feeding his people with manna, while the second is suggestive of the Eucharist. To arrive at this conclusion, they note that the "three days" of chapter 8 suggests Jesus' three days in the tomb; that saying a blessing over the bread is the conventional description of the Jewish grace before meals, while the giving of thanks over it suggests the Eucharist (which literally means "thanksgiving"); that the number twelve in the first episode suggests the twelve tribes of Israel, while the number seven suggests the sacraments of the church. Yet there are many flaws in these arguments: "three days" was a conventional biblical way of indicating a long period of time; the Jewish blessing over food is in fact a prayer of thanksgiving; and the sacraments of the church were not numbered for many centuries. So it would seem that to call the first miracle Jewish and the second one Christian is strained. What is clear is that Mark wanted his audience to be aware of a miraculous event that repeated itself.

8:11-21 Double failures to understand

What follows are two episodes in which first the Pharisees and then Jesus' disciples fail to get the point of the miracle he has just performed. Although they are usually treated separately, it is important to see that they are designed to be parallel. They are also equal in irony.

If one is reading the Gospel as a literal account, one could, of course, shrug off the Pharisees' request for "a sign from heaven" (8:11) by saying that there is no reason to think that the Pharisees were present at the

Mark 8

miraculous feeding. But if one agrees that Mark has a theological design, then one perceives the juxtaposition of the feeding miracle and the Pharisees' request for "a sign from heaven" as Mark's way of indicating the Pharisees' obtuseness. When Mark goes on to say that Jesus' response was to sigh "from the depth of his spirit" (8:12), the reader shares that sense of exasperation.

The episode that follows (8:14-23) shows that the disciples have a parallel obtuseness. Mark dramatizes this in several ways. First, he quotes Jesus warning them against "the leaven of the Pharisees and the leaven of Herod" (8:15). Conventionally, "leaven" was considered to be a symbol of puffery or pride, so Jesus is apparently cautioning them against being too self-sufficient to trust in God. The disciples' response misses the point completely. Taking his words literally, "They concluded among themselves that it was because they had no bread" (8:16).

In describing how Jesus reproached them, Mark uses words that repeat earlier moments in the Gospel. At the end of chapter 6, when the disciples are frightened by seeing Jesus walk on the water and still the storm (6:49-51), Mark tells us, "They had not understood the incident of the loaves. On the contrary, their hearts were hardened" (6:52). So here, when Mark shows Jesus saying, "Why do you conclude you have no bread? Do you not yet understand or comprehend? Are your hearts hardened? . . . And do you not remember when I broke the five loaves for the five thousand . . . ?" (8:17-19), we hear a repetition of that earlier moment when the disciples missed the point. The repetition serves to underline the disciples' obtuseness.

8:22-26 The two-stage healing of the blind man

Like the healing of the deaf-mute at the end of chapter 7, the healing of the blind man here has symbolic significance. Particular elements of that earlier healing are repeated here. In both instances, Mark tells us that Jesus took the person aside (7:33; 8:23); in both, Mark indicates a laying on of hands (7:32; 8:25); in both, Mark says that Jesus used spittle as a means of healing (7:33; 8:23). The repeating details are enough to alert the reader to the fact that one healing is linked to the other. On a deeper level, they are linked in terms of the context of Isaiah:

> Then will the eyes of the blind be opened,
>   the ears of the deaf be cleared;
> Then will the lame leap like a stag,
>   then the tongue of the mute will sing (Isa 35:5-6).

In the earlier healing, Mark shows Jesus clearing the ears of the deaf and opening his mouth; here he shows Jesus opening the eyes of the blind.

The episode here also sheds light on Mark's structural habit of repeating incidents. The blind man does not see clearly right away; it takes a second laying on of hands before he "could see everything distinctly" (8:25). In the same way, Mark repeats incidents so that the reader can see more readily what he is about. So he describes two episodes that show Jesus is in command of the sea (4:35-41; 6:45-51); he twice describes Jesus miraculously feeding the people in the desert; he offers two healing incidents that dramatize how Jesus enacts the words of Isaiah.

This kind of structure may be related to the structure of Hebrew verse, which often repeats an initial thought in varied words. In Psalm 19, for example, we read:

> The law of the LORD is perfect,
>   refreshing the soul.
> The decree of the LORD is trustworthy,
>   giving wisdom to the simple (Ps 19:8).

The second verse repeats but varies the idea of the first, thereby enriching it. One commentator has described this structure as giving us "A, and what's more, B." In the same way, Mark's second, repeating episodes vary and enrich the significance of the first, making us grasp their meaning more clearly. We will discuss later the way in which the whole second half of Mark's Gospel (chs. 9–16) functions as a second verse, clarifying and enriching the teachings and actions of Jesus in the first half (chs. 1–8).

8:27-33 A second discussion of the identity of Jesus

The question that Mark shows Jesus raising here, "Who do people say that I am?" (8:27), is also a repetition. We have heard it before, although indirectly. In chapter 6, Mark tells us that people are talking about who Jesus is and offering various opinions: "John the Baptist has been raised from the dead . . . . He is Elijah . . . . He is a prophet like any of the prophets" (6:14-15). When Mark gives the disciples' response to Jesus' question here, he shows them repeating these opinions verbatim: "They said in reply, 'John the Baptist, others Elijah, still others, one of the prophets'" (8:28). Mark then shows Jesus asking the question directly of his disciples (8:29).

The response that Mark shows Peter making—"You are the Messiah" (8:29)—is strikingly different from the other speculations. Most Christians accept that response in the light of their own faith today. They also tend to perceive it through the lens of Matthew, who first adds to Peter's confession, "the Son of the living God" (Matt 16:16), and who then shows Jesus responding, "Blessed are you, Simon son of Jonah. For flesh and blood has not revealed this to you, but my heavenly Father. And so I say to you, you are Peter, and upon this rock I will build my church" (Matt 16:17-18). But readers who see the four evangelists as four different theologians will be sensitive to the different nuances in Mark's dramatization of what happens next.

In Mark's version, Jesus does not commend Peter for his reply. Instead, he charges the disciples not to speak about him (8:30) and goes on to tell them, for the first time, how he will suffer, die, and be raised up again (8:31). Mark then describes Peter as so unable to accept this prediction that he "rebuke[s]" Jesus (8:32). Although Mark does not spell it out, the implication seems to be that Peter cannot accept the idea of Jesus' suffering and death; it does not fit his idea of a "messiah." Mark indicates that Jesus, in turn, cannot accept Peter's interpretation of who he is and that he rebukes him in radically strong language: "Get behind me, Satan. You are thinking not as God does, but as human beings do" (8:33).

Matthew also describes this second exchange between Jesus and Peter, but only after Jesus has commended Peter and told him that he will found his church upon him. What are we to make of this radical difference? If one is reading the Gospels as literal eyewitness accounts, one must resort to examining sources and speculating on how one evangelist took from one source and the other from another. But if one is reading the Gospels as theology (which the church now encourages us to do), one concludes that Mark had a different theological interpretation of this event than Matthew. Since Mark's is the earliest Gospel, one might then conclude that Mark and Matthew were each responding to the theological needs of their own time and respective faith-communities. In Matthew's time (probably a decade later than Mark's), the Christian community was beginning to emerge as a church. (Indeed, the word is used for the first time here in Matthew 16.) Moreover, it was undergoing persecution and needed to be affirmed as a community under God's care. In Mark's time, the Jesus-community saw itself as part of Judaism. The pressing issue was not, therefore, God's providence (which would have been taken for granted), but why Jesus was so important to them and what they meant in calling him "Messiah."

Contrary to popular belief, recent scholarship has shown that there was no single, fixed concept of "the Messiah" within Judaism of the first century. The term, which in Hebrew simply means "the anointed one," was used variably, both in the Hebrew Bible and in other Jewish writings that were contemporaneous with Jesus and Mark. Within the Hebrew Bible, it is most often applied to a king, but also to a high priest or a patriarch. Isaiah applied it to the Persian king Cyrus, who allowed the Jews to go home to Jerusalem from captivity in Babylon (Isa 45:1). In the Jewish writings outside the Bible, the term is variously applied to a teacher, a warrior, and a judge. The Dead Sea Scrolls anticipated the coming of two messiahs, a king and a high priest. In short, one cannot pin the term down to a particular definition but must acknowledge that it was generally used to indicate any figure whom the faith-community saw as God's representative, someone who was doing God's work on its behalf.

The one constant in all these variations was that a "messiah," as God's agent, was always imagined as victorious in his work. When Mark shows Peter rebuking Jesus for telling them he would die, he is showing Peter reacting on the basis of this assumption of victory and triumph. By the same token, when Mark shows Jesus rebuking Peter, he is indicating that Jesus was rebuking him for this assumption. Nowhere in Judaism before Jesus is there evidence of a suffering messiah. (Isaiah's "Suffering Servant" [Isa 52:13–53:12] was not considered messianic.) Only after Christianity was established did the idea begin to develop within Judaism. Here it is Peter's rejection of a suffering messiah that Jesus labels human-minded and not God-minded (8:33).

8:34-38 The second commissioning of Jesus' disciples

Mark shows that in the first commissioning of his disciples, Jesus sends them out to imitate him in preaching repentance, driving out demons, and curing the sick (6:7-13). We noted earlier that when Mark interleaves the story of John the Baptist between this commissioning and the disciples' return from their first efforts (6:14-29), he subtly suggests the destiny of both Jesus and Jesus' disciples. The death of John the Baptist is a foreshadowing of Jesus' death. Since Jesus has just instructed his disciples to imitate him, the placement of John's narrative at this point suggests that they will also be called to imitate him in the yielding of their lives. Here in chapter 8 this indirect suggestion is made clear. Mark shows us Jesus speaking plainly about what is involved in being his disciple: "Whoever wishes to come after me must deny self, take up the cross, and follow me" (8:34).

The chapter concludes with Mark indicating that death, however, is not the end of the story. He has just shown Jesus asserting the paradox that "Whoever wishes to save his life will lose it, but whoever loses his life for my sake and the sake of the gospel will save it" (8:35). Mark develops the implications of this paradox by indicating that at the end of time, Jesus will determine his followers accordingly: "Whoever is ashamed of me . . . the

Mark 8

son of man will be ashamed of when he comes in his Father's glory with the holy angels" (8:38). Some would like to read "son of man" here as the title of triumphant, apocalyptic figure, but as in 2:10, it makes sense to read it instead as the Aramaic form of self-reference. The use of the word "ashamed" emphasizes the fact that the cross is not only a painful death but a shameful one, and the followers of Jesus need to be prepared for worldly shame as well as physical suffering. Yet Mark also shows how Jesus implied that the shame of the cross would one day be replaced by the glory of the Father's presence. Mark thus prepares the reader for the transfiguration of Jesus, which follows in chapter 9.

Summary of chapter 8

In this chapter, Mark repeats some earlier events, images, and ideas. In doing so, he does not present exact repetitions but offers variations on the theme. It is a chapter of doublets. The chapter opens with a second episode in which Jesus feeds a great crowd in a deserted place. It is followed by the double misunderstanding of the miracle both by the Pharisees and by the disciples. It concludes with a second discussion of Jesus' identity and with a second commissioning of his disciples. In describing the disciples' failure to understand, Mark shows Jesus asking, "Are your hearts hardened?" (8:17) thus echoing the language of Jesus' dismay in chapter 6.

In presenting a second discussion of Jesus' identity and a second commissioning of the disciples, Mark sharpens the readers' focus. In the earlier discussions of chapter 6, Mark only hints that suffering and death will be significant parts of their destiny. Mark's main focus is on Jesus' power to heal and restore and on his passing on this power to his disciples. The emphasis is on Jesus as a miracle-worker and his disciples as potentially like him.

In chapter 8, however, Mark reverses the emphasis and begins to show that Jesus sees himself and his disciples as destined for a shameful death. Mark has shown Jesus speaking in parables and riddling sayings before. Here he shows him offering the ultimate paradox of losing one's life in order to save it.

This shift and sharpening of focus is symbolized in the two-stage healing of the blind man, itself a variation on the symbolic healing of the deaf-mute in chapter 7. Both healings take their meaning from the passage in Isaiah where God promises the ultimate healing and restoration of his people. Beyond that, the healing of the blind man has special significance because of the way Mark tells the story. By dramatizing the cure of the blind man in two stages, Mark indicates the theological purpose of his structure of doublets. The second time around, Mark strives to make the meaning of Jesus clearer. In the same way, the whole second half of Mark's Gospel (chs. 9–16) serves to clarify the first. The hinge between the two lies here at the end of chapter 8. When Mark shows Jesus speaking of a time of future glory, he prepares the reader for the scene of Jesus' transfiguration.

TRANSFIGURATION—NEW PERCEPTIONS
Mark 9:1-50

9:1-7 The Transfiguration

Mark opens this chapter by quoting Jesus' promise that some of those around him will see the kingdom of God before they die (9:1). This assertion is often interpreted to mean that Jesus promised that the end of the world would come soon, or at least that the first followers of Jesus believed that was to happen. But such an interpretation comes from reading the text as a literal account. If instead one sees Mark's shaping hand here, one sees that he was preparing his readers for the transfiguration scene that comes immediately afterward. The Transfiguration does in fact present an imaginative rendering of what God's final kingdom will be like.

The word that is conventionally translated "transfigured" is actually "metamorphosed,"* which indicates not just a change in appearance but a changed state of being. There is a sense of new beginnings. The time frame of "six days" (9:2) is suggestive of the six days of Creation before God's Sabbath rest. Mark intensifies the sense of a new creation when he describes God's voice saying to Jesus the very same words he spoke at the moment of his baptism (compare 9:7 with 1:11).

The reference to "six days" also recalls the period Moses waited before the divine voice called to him on the mountain of Sinai (Exod 24:12-18). Mark further links Jesus to Moses by describing Jesus talking with him. It is significant that Jesus is pictured conversing with the two greatest figures of Jewish tradition, Moses and Elijah (9:4), representatives of the Law and the Prophets. Jesus, whom Mark has shown to be God's Wisdom, is in conversation with the traditional figures of Jewish wisdom. It is a timeless moment. Mark emphasizes that he sees Jesus as one of them. He perceives Jesus to be a continuation of the wisdom of Israel.

This trio of great figures is matched by a trio of disciples. They are the same three disciples Mark shows Jesus taking with him to witness the raising up of the little girl (5:37); they will be the same three that Mark will show Jesus taking with him into the garden of Gethsemane (14:33). In terms of Markan structure, these episodes form a triad, and the middle or key incident is here in chapter 9. By noting that Jesus took them "up a high mountain" and "apart" (9:2), Mark indicates that Jesus is trying to lead them into his transfigured state. And as Mark describes the scene, they, too, for a brief moment, are changed.

Peter's desire to build three tents (or "booths"*) may seem puzzling unless one is aware of the Jewish feast of Booths (or "Tabernacles"). It is a feast that follows the Jewish New Year and is intended to celebrate the natural harvest as a sign of God's final harvest. It is a feast of the end time. It takes its name from the fact that it is observed by the construction of temporary outdoor huts or "booths," which are decorated with the fruits of the harvest. When Mark shows Peter wanting to build three booths here, he is indicating Peter's perception that he has entered the end time of God's final kingdom.

Unfortunately, this meaning of Peter's question is obscured by the translation "tents." It is also canceled out by the conventional translation, "He hardly knew what to say, they were so terrified" (9:6). The word translated as "terrified" here would be better translated "filled with awe."* If it were, one would hear the echo of the end of chapter 4, where the disciples ask each other, "Who then is this whom even wind and sea obey?" (4:41). That Mark intends to signal awe rather than fright is indicated by the first statement he shows Peter saying: "Rabbi, it is good that we are here!" (9:5). A feeling of goodness is compatible with awe but not with terror. Mark's suggestion that Peter was overwhelmed by the goodness of God's presence is also his way of indicating that Peter, too, has been transfigured, however briefly. As Jesus' transfiguration looks forward to his resurrection, so Peter's state here gives promise of his future glory.

The words Mark uses to describe Jesus' clothing are suggestive of the prophet Malachi's description of God's messenger when he comes at the end of time to judge, purify, and gather God's people (Mal 3:1-3). In that passage God says:

> Lo, I am sending my messenger
>   to prepare the way before me;
> And suddenly there will come to the Temple
>   the LORD whom you seek,
> And the messenger of the covenant whom you desire.
>   Yes, he is coming, says the LORD of hosts.
> But who will endure the day of his coming?
>   And who can stand when he appears?
> For he is like the refiner's fire
>   or like the fuller's lye.

> He will sit refining and purifying,
>   and he will purify the sons of Levi,
> Refining them like gold or silver
>   that they may offer due sacrifice to the LORD.

As we noted at the time, Mark alludes briefly to this passage in the very opening of his Gospel (1:2). Here he comes back to it by describing Jesus' garments as "dazzling white, such as no fuller on earth could bleach them" (9:3). By emphasizing that Jesus' clothing is whiter than "the fuller's lye," Mark links him to Malachi's prophet of the end time.

9:8-10 The descent from the mountain

The vision of future glory fades abruptly: "Suddenly, looking around, they no longer saw anyone but Jesus alone with them" (9:8). Jesus charges them not to tell what they have seen until after he has risen from the dead (9:9). And these disciples, who were the very ones to witness Jesus' raising up of the little girl (5:37), question one another about the meaning of the term "rising from the dead" (9:10). Their descent from the mountain is not only physical but spiritual. They have returned from a brief moment of insight to their usual state of dulled understanding.

9:11-13 Elijah

Elijah is a recurring figure in Mark's Gospel. As we noted earlier, Mark describes John the Baptist in a way that makes him resemble Elijah (1:6). Biblical legend had it that Elijah never died but was taken up to heaven in a fiery chariot (2 Kgs 2:11) and would return some day to prepare God's people for the end time (Mal 3:23). In chapter 6, Mark tells us that people speculated that Jesus might be Elijah come back (6:15). In chapter 8, he indicates that some of the disciples thought the same (8:28). But in the transfiguration scene, Mark shows Jesus talking with Elijah, thus suggesting that Jesus is compatible with Elijah and yet distinct from him.

As further clarification, Mark shows an exchange about Elijah between Jesus and his disciples. The disciples ask why Elijah had to come first (that is, before the end time). Jesus' response falls into three parts. First he echoes the prophecy of Malachi that Elijah has to come "and restore all things" (9:12). Then he turns the question about and asks why he himself ("the son of man") has to suffer. Finally he declares that "Elijah has come and they did to him whatever they pleased" (9:13).

There are gaps in this reply. Nonetheless, Mark seems to be using it to clarify both the similarities and dissimilarities between Jesus and Elijah.

First he shows Jesus acknowledging Elijah as a forerunner. At the same time, he shows Jesus comparing his own sufferings to come with those of Elijah.

The reference to Elijah's suffering makes no sense in terms of the narratives concerning Elijah in the Second Book of Kings. The reference only makes sense as an identification of Elijah with John the Baptist. So the exchange serves to confirm what Mark has been doing throughout his Gospel: he has identified John the Baptist with Elijah and shown him to be the forerunner of Jesus, not only in his drawing people to God but also in his unjust suffering and death.

We suggested earlier that in chapter 6 Mark inserts the story of John the Baptist's death into the narrative of the disciples' mission as a subtle forewarning of what they themselves should expect (6:19-29). Here Mark makes the connection clear.

9:14-29 The healing of the boy with a mute and deaf spirit

This healing recapitulates and incorporates a number of healings that Mark has shown Jesus performing in the first half of the Gospel. The exorcism of a "mute and deaf spirit" (9:25) recalls the healing of the deaf-mute in 7:33-37. The violently destructive effects of the unclean spirit (9:18-26) are reminiscent of the demonic possession of the man among the tombs in 5:1-20. Jesus' "rebuke" of the spirit (9:25) echoes his first exorcism of the man in the synagogue (1:25). The corpse-like appearance of the boy and the bystanders' insistence that "He is dead" (9:26) recall the apparent death of Jairus's daughter (5:38-43). And Jesus' gesture of taking the boy by the hand and raising him up (9:27) repeats Jesus' way of raising that little girl and bringing her back to life (5:41). The attentive reader has a sense of déjà vu.

Mark does not simply provide a repetitive incident, however. He adds to it a whole discussion of how unclean spirits can be driven out. Mark tells us first that the crowd, some scribes, and the disciples were all arguing about it (9:14). He notes that the disciples, although commissioned by Jesus to drive out demons (6:7), have failed in this instance. He shows the disciples asking Jesus why they have failed (9:28), and he provides Jesus' answer as the climax to the episode: "This kind can only come out through prayer" (9:29).

Accordingly, Mark places great emphasis here on the importance of faith as part of the healing process. He shows Jesus sighing over the disciples' lack of faith (9:19). He gives Jesus' reply to the boy's father: "Everything is possible to one who has faith" (9:23). He dramatizes the father praying, "I do believe; help my unbelief!" (9:24).

In the first part of his Gospel, Mark shows Jesus performing one miracle after another easily and, as it were, automatically. But here he indicates that miracles are not automatic events; rather, he indicates that healings are a process that involves faith and prayer.

9:30-32 Jesus' second prediction of his death and resurrection

This prediction is the middle of a triad of predictions. The first occurs in 8:31; the third will occur in 10:33-34. The language is almost identical in each case, but not quite. In the first prediction, Mark shows Jesus speaking of being rejected "by the elders, the chief priests, and the scribes" and then being killed. The passive voice used here does not indicate the agent of the killing. In the third prediction, Mark shows Jesus telling his disciples that he will be "handed over to the chief priests and the scribes" who will, in turn, "hand him over to the Gentiles" who will put him to death. In this middle and key version, Mark quotes Jesus as saying that he will be "handed over to human beings and they will kill him." In this key version, Mark suggests that all humanity rather than a particular agent is responsible for Jesus' death. Mark makes a point of saying that the disciples do not understand (9:32).

9:33-37 "Who is the greatest?"

Mark underlines the disciples' lack of understanding in the next episode. We have seen how twice before, Mark has shown Jesus telling these disciples that he must be rejected, suffer, and die (8:31; 9:31). He has shown Jesus making an explicit connection between his cross and their discipleship (8:34-35). And yet here they are, "discussing among themselves . . . who was the greatest" (9:34).

Mark indicates that they had some sense of the inappropriateness of their discussion by noting that they did not answer Jesus' question but "remained silent" (9:34). Mark then uses their question to set up further teaching by Jesus: "If anyone wishes to be first, he shall be the last of all and the servant of all" (9:35).

It is worth noting that Jesus "called the Twelve" before giving this teaching. This is the third time that Jesus summons and instructs the Twelve; in effect, it is another Markan triad. The first time, Jesus sends them out as apostles "to preach and to have authority to drive out demons" (3:14-15); the second time, he instructs them "to take nothing for the journey but a walking stick" (6:8); here he instructs them to be servants. Mark shows Jesus progressively teaching his disciples how to give up the pursuit of worldly power. He dramatizes Jesus' point by showing him elevate the child (9:36-37).

Mark 9

9:38-40 "Whoever is not against us is for us"

Mark continues in the next episode to stress Jesus' instruction on the yielding of power. He uses the reactions of the disciples as a foil for this teaching. In this scene, the disciples ironically exhibit a worldly sense of competition about the spiritual ministry of exorcism: "Teacher, we saw someone driving out demons in your name, and we tried to prevent him because he does not follow us" (9:38). Mark gives Jesus' response (9:39-40) as further instruction in being one who serves others, not one who seeks to be superior.

9:41-42 The reward of a cup of water

At this point, the text indicates that Jesus said, "Anyone who gives you a cup of water to drink because you belong to Christ . . . will surely not lose his reward." This saying does not seem to fit in here. Instead, it would seem to fit logically after Jesus' statement "Whoever receives one child such as this in my name, receives me" (9:37). This placement is supported by the fact that the phrase that is translated here as "you belong to Christ" literally reads "because in name you are Christ's."

Mark has been showing how Jesus tried to teach his disciples that being like him means being like a child in powerlessness. And so it follows that whoever receives a child in his name—that is, welcomes the powerless in his name—welcomes him. It would make sense for Jesus to then turn it about and speak of his disciples as the "children" being welcomed by others. Assuming that his disciples will become the powerless he has asked them to be, Jesus goes on to say that anyone who welcomes them in his name (even with as little as a cup of water) will be rewarded.

This rearrangement of verses would also make more sense out of Jesus saying, "Whoever causes one of these little ones who believe [in me] to sin, it would be better for him if a great millstone were put around his neck and he were thrown into the sea" (9:42).

The disciples' complaint about someone outside their group driving out demons in Jesus' name (9:38) would then take on even greater irony. Mark would be showing that instead of getting Jesus' point about powerlessness, the disciples (one more time!) had missed the point and latched on to the phrase "in my name" as the key one. Thus the protest against someone driving out demons in Jesus' name who isn't one of "them."

9:43-48 Being ready to give up everything

The list that follows then makes sense as a continuing part of Jesus' instruction to give up things that most people cling to—even, if necessary, one's very limbs. The terse style in which these teachings are phrased is typical of the Wisdom writings, as is the rhythmical pairings of contrasts: "It is better [to do such and such] than to [do this or that]."

9:49-50 Being salted

Being salted "with" fire is a bit puzzling, but there is precedent in the Hebrew Bible for linking both elements with purification. We have already noted the passage in Malachi where he speaks of the final messenger of the covenant being like "the refiner's fire" (Mal 3:2). In both Leviticus and Ezekiel, salt is connected with sacrificial offerings that are burned on the altar. Leviticus speaks of the "salt of the covenant": "Every offering of grain that you present to the LORD shall be seasoned with salt. Do not let the salt of the covenant of your God be lacking from your grain offering" (Lev 2:13). Similarly in Ezekiel, God asks for purifying sacrifices that involve both salt and fire: "When you have finished the purification, bring an unblemished young bull and an unblemished ram from the flock. And present them before the LORD. The priests shall strew salt on them and offer them to the LORD as holocausts" (Ezek 43:23-24).

Mark has just shown Jesus teaching his disciples to be ready to sacrifice their own bodies, if necessary, in order to be his disciples. It would seem to be in keeping with those demands that he speaks of their purifying themselves with salt and fire. When Mark shows Jesus saying in conclusion, "Keep salt in yourselves" (9:50), he would seem to be referring to both "the salt of the covenant" and the fire of self-sacrifice that he himself will model.

Summary of chapter 9

The chapter shifts the readers' focus and makes plain things hidden before. The scene of Jesus' transfiguration begins this shift by revealing the inner and future glory of both Jesus and his disciples. Mark designs this revelation to come before the narrative of Jesus' shameful death so that it will overshadow it. It points to Jesus' resurrection.

At the same time, the chapter is unified by a new perspective on power. The Transfiguration reveals a splendor that will transform the ignominy of rejection and death. The casting out of demons is revealed to be not a matter of super power but of simple faith and prayer. The servant and the child are held up as the greatest. God's power is declared to be inclusive and not restricted to an inner circle. Jesus teaches that it is better to be crippled for God than to remain strong and not be for him. In conclusion, Jesus teaches that the "fire" of sacrificing oneself may be the "salt" needed to season the kingdom.

Mark 10

RETURN TO THE BEGINNING

Mark 10:1-52

10:1-12 "From the beginning of creation"

This discussion of divorce is usually treated apart from Mark's whole Gospel. Abstracted in that way from its context, Jesus' words on marriage appear to be stricter and less flexible than the present teachings of the church. But if the passage is read in its whole setting, a different sense emerges. In the preceding chapter, Mark has shown Jesus elevating a child (9:36-37), and in the passage that immediately follows this one, Mark shows Jesus saying, "Whoever does not accept the kingdom of God like a child will not enter it" (10:15). In fact, the whole of chapter 10 (as we are about to show) is focused on how to live with childlike simplicity. In this passage on marriage, Mark sets up this focus by giving Jesus' reference to "the beginning of creation" (10:6). "The beginning of creation" is the frame for the whole chapter.

In Jewish thought about the end time (that is, the projected moment when, it was believed, the will of God would entirely prevail), there were two distinct strains of thought. One view held that God would prevail as judge, destroying the wicked and preserving the good. The other view held that God would act as a healer and redeemer, restoring his people and leading them back, as it were, to their original state in the Garden of Eden. In the Prophets, one hears a lot about God's judgment on Israel; it is associated with the destruction of Jerusalem and especially the Temple, as well as the defeat and captivity of Israel. In the prophetic imagination, however, God's final judgments are rendered only on the nations that besiege and corrupt Israel. God's judgments on Israel itself are temporary. The prophet always envisions that in the end time God will restore his people to virtue, his Temple to its original state as a house of prayer, and the land to its original condition of abundance and fertility.

In the Wisdom writings, the prevailing imagery is of the Garden. The Psalms sing of how God created human beings for glory ("You have made him a little less than the angels," Ps 8:6); how God preserves his people from destruction (They shall be "like a tree / planted by running water, / That brings forth its fruit in due season," Ps 1:3); how God restores them after a time of wandering or distress ("Beside restful waters he leads me; he refreshes my soul," Ps 23:2-3). The Song of Songs imagines the Garden as the setting for the love affair between God and humanity. The book of Sirach associates the Garden imagery of the Song with the feminine figure of God's Wisdom. The book of Job, for all its tragic disaster, concludes with a reminder of the majesty of creation, the restoration of Job, and a new beginning. The cynical preacher in Ecclesiastes changes from finding that "all is vanity" to a new trust in God's power to create. The author of the Wisdom of Solomon takes the idea of restoration a step further by perceiving that Wisdom in the human soul is a reflection of God's immortality. In all of these writings, while God's judgment on evil is certainly assumed and articulated, there is also a sense that the true human destiny is to return to the original Garden. To say that Mark shows "the beginning of creation" to be the framework for Jesus' teachings is to imply his reference to this whole tradition.

It is this tradition that Mark shows at work here when he tells us that Jesus quoted Genesis 2:24 (10:7-8) and contrasted its ideal of married oneness with the bill of divorce that Moses allowed as a concession to the "hardness of your hearts" (10:5).

Mark has used the phrase "hardness of heart" twice before—once to describe the Pharisees when they begrudge Jesus' healing on the Sabbath (3:5) and again to describe the disciples when they fail to understand the miracle of the loaves (6:52). In all three instances, the phrase does not indicate the commitment of a sin but the failure to measure up to an ideal standard. So here, we may infer, Mark shows Jesus using this phrase to indicate a falling away from the ideal human state.

10:13-16 Children as the ideal members of God's kingdom

In describing Jesus' blessing of the children here, Mark echoes and develops the scene in the previous chapter (9:36-37) where Jesus embraces a child and says, "Whoever receives one child such as this in my name, receives me." As we noted before, in that context Jesus seems to be teaching his disciples the value of powerlessness. This idea seems to be confirmed and clarified by what Mark shows Jesus saying here: "Whoever does not accept the kingdom of God like a child will not enter it" (10:15).

10:17-31 The poor as ideal members of the kingdom

The story of the rich man who cannot follow Jesus is of a piece with this emphasis. The man affirms that he has kept the Ten Commandments from his youth (10:20), a declaration that indicates his essential goodness. And Mark goes on to say that Jesus "loved him" (10:21). Nonetheless, Mark shows Jesus asking more of him: "You are lacking in one thing. Go, sell what you have, and give to the poor, and you will have treasure in heaven; then come, follow me" (10:21).

Just as in the teachings about being faithful in marriage and about becoming childlike, Mark shows Jesus holding up an ideal. It is an ideal that

Mark 10

is in keeping with Jesus' other teachings on detachment. Just as Mark shows Jesus teaching his disciples to detach themselves from power by becoming like children, so here he shows Jesus teaching them to detach themselves from possessions. By showing that despite his goodness, this rich man cannot follow Jesus' instruction (10:22), Mark indicates that Jesus is setting up a norm for holiness that demands far more than the conventional one. In the discussion with the disciples that follows (10:23-33), Mark further dramatizes the unconventionality of Jesus' request.

Mark does this by setting up a dialogue between Jesus and his disciples, in which Jesus repeatedly stresses "how hard" it is for the wealthy to enter God's kingdom, while the disciples repeatedly express their astonishment at what he is saying (10:23-26). (Jesus' statement that "It is easier for a camel . . . " has a rabbinic parallel—"It is easier for an elephant . . ."—and so should not be seen as a special riddle of Jesus, but simply as an exaggeration typical of first-century Jewish teachers.)

The climax of this dialogue occurs when the disciples ask, "Then who can be saved?" and Jesus responds, "For human beings it is impossible, but not for God. All things are possible for God" (10:26-27). In this pithy exchange, Mark shows that Jesus was asking his followers to commit themselves to a way of living that could not be accomplished without God's grace. He was shifting the burden from their need for self-sufficiency to their need for total dependence on God. This acknowledgment of total dependence is, of course, the ultimate poverty, the ultimate detachment.

10: 28-31, 35-45 The disciples' failure to understand

In the exchange that follows between Peter and Jesus (10:28-31), Mark shows how little Peter has understood. Peter's response to Jesus' request for this total detachment is to protest that he has already accomplished it: "We have given up everything and followed you" (10:28). Jesus' reply is indirect, not directly disagreeing, and indeed promising rewards in this life and "eternal life in the age to come" (10:30). Yet among his promises, Mark shows Jesus slipping in "persecutions," a reminder that following Jesus will involve following him in the way of suffering. Jesus' final assertion, "Many that are first will be last and [the] last will be first" (10:31), is also a reminder of the paradox of the cross.

Mark particularly dramatizes the disciples' failure to grasp that final lesson when he shows James and John asking to be first in glory (10:37). Mark introduces this ironic question by showing James and John talking to Jesus as if he were their servant: "We want you to do for us whatever we ask of you" (10:35). And he shows Jesus accepting this role: "What do you wish [me] to do for you?" (10:36). In the exchange that follows between Jesus and his disciples, Mark shows the extent of the gap in the disciples' understanding.

The reply that Mark shows Jesus giving here is central to Mark's interpretation of Jesus' theology. First, he shows Jesus speaking cryptically of his "cup" and his "baptism" (10:38-39). In the Psalms, "cup" is figuratively linked to one's inheritance or destiny ("Lord, my allotted portion and my cup," Ps 16:5) and to salvation ("I will raise the cup of salvation and call on the name of the Lord," Ps 116:13). "Baptism" is not a word used in the Hebrew Bible, although the ritual immersion that it connotes was part of Judaism and signified (as it does in Mark) a change of heart. These words take on additional meaning here. Jesus' use of the word "cup" suggests the cup of wine that he will later designate as the cup of his blood (14:24), and his use of the word "baptism" also suggests a link with his death.

Paul emphasizes this link when he asks, "Are you unaware that we who were baptized into Christ Jesus were baptized into his death?" (Rom 6:3). When Mark shows James and John being quick to accept this "cup" and "baptism" (10:39), he indicates that they are not making these same connections with death. Mark confirms this lack of awareness when he shows Jesus saying, "You do not know what you are asking" (10:38).

By giving the ironic request of James and John, Mark sets the stage for a fuller illumination of Jesus' teaching on worldly power (10:42-45). He shows Jesus here giving his disciples the plainest explanation of what he is about. Mark first shows Jesus distancing himself from the worldly, Gentile conventions of power, in which "those who are recognized as rulers . . . lord it over" others and "make their authority . . . felt" (10:42). Then Mark shows Jesus directly rejecting this approach: "It shall not be so among you" (10:43). Next, he shows Jesus telling them how they should act: "Whoever wishes to be first among you will be the slave of all" (10:43-44). Last, and most important, Mark shows Jesus explaining that by so doing, they will truly be his disciples, because he came expressly "not to be served but to serve" (10:45). Beyond that, Mark suggests by his final phrase that Jesus has come to offer the ultimate service of giving up his life for the sake of others.

The phrase "to give his life as a ransom for many" is a quote from Isaiah 53:11, where God is speaking about his chosen servant, who will offer his life as an atoning sacrifice for the sins of others. This is the last of those passages in Isaiah known as the "Songs of the Suffering Servant." In Isaiah, the Servant is identified as Israel—God's righteous servant among the nations, who is put to death by the kings of the world because they do not understand Israel's God-blessed nature or mission. By quoting this phrase as part of Jesus' self-understanding, Mark suggests that Jesus can be understood through the same lens: he is God's righteous servant; he will be put to death by Gentile powers that fail to understand him; he will offer his life as an atonement for the sins of others; he will ultimately be exalted by God.

10:32-34 Jesus' third prediction of his death

Mark interweaves Jesus' third prediction of his own suffering in between the episodes that show the failure of Peter, James, and John to understand that as Jesus' disciples they have been called to dispossession, service, and death. It is a structure we have seen Mark use before. Just as he placed the story of John the Baptist's death in the middle of the first sending forth of the disciples (6:14-29), so here he places the prediction of Jesus' death between the episode showing Peter's confidence that he has already given up everything and the episode of the request of James and John for glory.

Mark, moreover, shows Jesus being explicit here in a way that he never has been before. In the first prediction, Mark quotes Jesus speaking vaguely about how he must "suffer greatly . . . be rejected . . . be killed . . . and rise after three days" (8:31). In the second prediction, Mark shows Jesus adding the element of betrayal, but generalizing everything else: "The son of man is to be handed over to human beings and they will kill him, and three days after his death he will rise" (9:31). Here Mark shows Jesus speaking specifically about "going up to Jerusalem" and about how he will be handed over "to the chief priests and the scribes," who will, in turn, "hand him over to the Gentiles, who will mock him, spit upon him, scourge him, and put him to death" (10:33-34). If we look at these three predictions as one of Mark's triads, the middle prediction is key, indicating that "human beings" in general are responsible for Jesus' death. But within Mark's narrative, the concreteness of the third prediction is Mark's way of sharpening the irony of the disciples' lack of understanding.

10:46-52 The symbolic cure of the blind man

This is another miracle of healing that has a symbolic and summarizing function. In 8:22-26, Mark shows Jesus healing a blind man in two stages. We noted that the miracle echoes the earlier healing of the deaf-mute (7:33) and completes Jesus' relationship to the passage in Isaiah where "the ears of the deaf" are "cleared" and "the eyes of the blind" are "opened" (Isa 35:5-6). At the same time, the two-stage process alerts the reader to the meaning behind Mark's doublet structure. In the next miraculous healing (9:14-29), a deaf-mute is cured again. In describing this cure, Mark incorporates a number of elements that have been part of several earlier miracles, so that this miracle incorporates what has gone before. In the same way, this cure of the blind man Bartimaeus appears to be a doublet, and more than a doublet, of the cure of the blind man in chapter 8.

Within the immediate narrative, the story of the blind beggar reverses that of the rich man. The rich man could not become a disciple of Jesus because of his many possessions. The beggar has no possessions except his cloak, and he immediately casts that away to come to Jesus (10:50). In the end, the blind man not only receives his sight from Jesus but "followed him on the way" (10:52).

Beyond that, the name Bartimaeus literally means "son of the unclean" in Hebrew, so the name alone has a summarizing function. In the first part of his Gospel, Mark has shown Jesus to be in constant association with "the unclean" of his society—demoniacs, lepers, tax collectors, sinners, a woman with a flow of blood, and a dead body. When Mark shows Jesus healing someone who is named "son of the unclean," he is reminding his readers of them all.

Mark also shows this blind man to have other distinctive characteristics. Unlike the first blind man, who was brought to Jesus by others, this one calls out to him (10:47). Mark shows him addressing Jesus, moreover, as "son of David," a title that indicates he recognizes Jesus as God's chosen agent. There is a certain irony, therefore, in his request to see (10:51), because he seems to already be seeing more than many sighted folk around him. Mark shows Jesus confirming this when he says, "Go your way; your faith has saved you" (10:52). In showing Jesus' cure of Bartimaeus, Mark sums up how Jesus can heal and restore all "the unclean" who have faith in God's outreach to them.

In this summarizing incident, Mark echoes certain words from the first part of his Gospel. When he says that the blind man "began to cry out" (10:47), we hear an echo of the unclean spirit in chapter 5, who also cried out to Jesus (5:5). The intent, however, is the reverse: the unclean spirit wanted Jesus to go away; the blind man wants him to come near. When Mark describes the disciples' telling the blind man to "take courage" (10:49), he uses the same word that he shows Jesus saying to his frightened disciples in chapter 6 (6:50). But again there is a difference: the disciples remain fearful; the blind man seems to need no encouragement, for he springs up and goes to Jesus (10:50). The phrase that is translated here as "get up" (10:49) is in fact *"rise* up"* and thus an echo of Jesus' words to the dead child in chapter 5 (5:41). Jesus' final words to the blind man, "Your faith has saved you" (10:52), repeats his final words to the woman healed of her flow of blood (5:34). In ending this narrative, Mark says that *"Straightway**

Mark 10

[translated here as 'immediately'] he received his sight" (10:52). In short, there are enough key words in this short episode to suggest that Mark is loading it with particular significance. It is as though Mark wanted to suggest the possibility of all people—whether blinded by demons or by fear or by "uncleanness" or even by death—to be restored, to have their lives "made straight" again.

Summary of chapter 10

In this chapter, Mark shows Jesus pointing to "the beginning of creation" as revealing God's intended destiny for human beings, and trying to teach his disciples how to return to that state of original simplicity. Mark shows Jesus doing this in several ways. First, he shows Jesus referring to the beginning unity between man and woman as the norm for human relationships. Then he shows him holding up children as models of the detachment from power necessary to enter the kingdom. Next, through setting up a dialogue between Jesus and a rich man, he shows Jesus teaching his disciples that they need to divest themselves of all possessions and learn to depend totally upon God's providence. Mark then indicates the disciples' failure to understand these teachings by showing parallel episodes that involve the three key disciples—Peter first, then James and John. Mark sharpens the irony of the disciples' obtuseness by placing in between these episodes Jesus' third and most explicit prediction of his own suffering and death.

In conclusion, Mark shows the healing of a blind beggar who, out of his powerlessness and poverty, is ready to become a disciple of Jesus. He is a beggar whose name means "son of the unclean" and whose cure, as Mark constructs the story, echoes and summarizes many of Jesus' earlier miracles. When Mark ends this narrative by saying, "Straightway* he received his sight and followed him on the way" (10:52), he affirms the potential for every human being to follow Jesus' way of return to the beginning.

JESUS AND THE TEMPLE AUTHORITIES— NEW UNDERSTANDINGS OF POWER

Mark 11:1-37

11:1-11 Jesus' entry into Jerusalem

In this opening scene, Mark picks up on the cure of the blind beggar by showing the people spreading their cloaks on the ground (11:8) and crying out, "Blessed is the kingdom of our father David that is to come!" (11:10). Their cry also echoes the first proclamation of John the Baptist, "One mightier than I is coming after me" (1:7). Yet Mark modifies the impression of triumphant entry by describing Jesus riding on a colt.

In the whole next section of his Gospel, Mark shows Jesus acting out the new understandings of power he has been trying to teach his disciples. Mark also shifts his style, showing Jesus, like many of the prophets, engaged in symbolic or parabolic action. To begin with, by showing the lengths to which Jesus goes to ride into Jerusalem on a colt (11:1-7), Mark calls attention to the relationship between Jesus and the words of Zechariah:

> See, your king shall come to you;
>   a just savior is he,
> Meek, and riding on an ass,
>   on a colt, the foal of an ass (9:9).

In Zechariah, the predicted king is unknown and mysterious. One of the most striking details in Zechariah's description is this picture of him entering Jerusalem on "the foal of an ass." The choice of the donkey not only suggests humility but peacemaking; in ancient times war was associated with the horse. Zechariah goes on to say that this king will "banish the horse from Jerusalem" along with "the warrior's bow," and "he shall proclaim peace to the nations" (9:10). The passages that follow in Zechariah are complex, but essentially the coming of this peace-loving king begins the restoration of Jerusalem.

At the same time, Mark echoes, through the images of the people spreading "leafy branches" and crying out "Hosanna" (11:8), the description in the first book of Maccabees of Simon Maccabeus entering Jerusalem "with praise and palm branches" to take back the Temple from the Greek tyrant Antiochus IV (1 Macc 13:47-52).

We have spoken before about how different foreign conquerors of Jerusalem tried to take over the Temple and weaken Jewish religion. One of the most despised was Antiochus IV, a Greek ruler of Palestine two centuries before the time of Jesus. He tried to virtually eradicate Jewish faith in a number of ways. He ordered the substitution of the Greek constitution for the Hebrew Bible. He forbade circumcision, and if mothers violated his edict, he killed their babies and hung the dead infants around their necks. He erected a statue of himself in the Temple. This statue of Antiochus is referred to in Daniel 12:11 as "the abomination of desolation" or "the desolating sacrilege" (a phrase that is used by Mark, as we will see, in chapter 13).

It was the last straw for the Jewish people. They rose up in revolt, led by the seven Maccabee brothers. Their success in restoring the Temple is

Mark 11

still celebrated in the annual feast of Hanukkah. The first book of Maccabees records that Simon Maccabeus "cleansed the Temple" of Antiochus's statue and all his other profanities (1 Macc 13:50b).

By using language that would remind his readers of both Zechariah's peace-loving king and of Simon Maccabeus, Mark offers a complex picture of Jesus. Both scriptural passages converge in showing someone who took action to restore the Temple to its original state as a place of worship. Yet there is a tension between the two. As Mark develops his portrait of Jesus' relationship to the Temple, he also continues to show this tension.

11:15-19 Jesus' "cleansing of the Temple"

It is interesting to note that the phrase "cleansing of the Temple" is not used by Mark. The caption is an editor's choice; one can only speculate that the editor was thinking of the book of Maccabees. In any event, the episode that follows, like the opening one of the chapter, is constructed out of interweaving echoes of the Hebrew Scripture. The key echoes occur in what Mark shows Jesus teaching:

> My house shall be called a house of prayer for all peoples.
> But you have made it a den of thieves (11:17).

The first line here is a direct quote from Isaiah 56:7, while the second comes from Jeremiah 7:11. The passage in Isaiah is expressing his vision of a time when God will welcome foreigners to the Temple:

> All who keep the Sabbath free from profanation
>   and hold to my covenant,
> Them I will bring to my holy mountain
>   and make joyful in my house of prayer (56:6-7).

The passage from Jeremiah comes from what is known as his "Temple sermon." It is a long passage in which the prophet expresses God's anger at the people's breaking of the covenant and his demand for their moral reform:

> Put not your trust in the deceitful words: "This is the Temple of the LORD! The Temple of the LORD! The Temple of the LORD!" Only if you thoroughly reform your ways and your deeds; if each of you deals justly with his neighbor; if you no longer oppress the resident alien, the orphan, and the widow; if you no longer shed innocent blood in this place, or follow strange gods to your own harm, will I remain with you in this place . . . . Are you to steal and murder, commit adultery and

perjury, burn incense to Baal, go after strange gods that you know not, and yet come to stand before me in this house which bears my name, and say, "We are safe; we can commit all these abominations again"? Has this house which bears my name become in your eyes a den of thieves? (Jer 7:4-7, 9-11).

In interweaving these two passages, Mark is juxtaposing two very different strands in biblical tradition. The passage from Jeremiah expresses a warning about being corrupted by foreigners who will not only encourage burning incense to a foreign god but will also foster the weakening of covenant commitments. The passage from Isaiah expresses the vision of a time when foreigners will want to join Israel in worshiping the one God, and all people will be joyfully one in prayer. By showing Jesus quoting both these passages at once—indeed, even making one sentence out of them—Mark again suggests a tension and a complexity in Jesus' attitude toward the Temple. On the one hand, the quotation from Jeremiah places him in the tradition of the reforming prophets seeking to purify Temple worship of foreign influences. On the other hand, the quotation from Isaiah places him in the tradition of the visionary prophets seeking to bring all people together by welcoming foreigners into God's house.

When Mark shows Jesus driving out "those selling and buying" and overturning "the tables of the money changers" and not permitting "anyone to carry anything through the Temple area" (11:15-16), these actions must be understood in the context of these prophetic traditions. In the light of these traditions, it does not make sense to assume (as many have) that Mark was indicating that Jesus' actions were hostile to the Temple per se. Nor does it make sense to assume that Jesus was expressing anger at a Temple system that allowed money on the premises.

Some historical background sheds light on the latter. It was customary for Jews to purchase an animal to sacrifice in the Temple, and while they ordinarily used Roman coins in their business transactions, they did not think that appropriate for sacred matters. The Temple authorities accordingly allowed them to exchange their Roman coin for a special Temple coin, which could then be used for their sacrifice. Such a system was no more scandalous than the money collections taken up today in Christian churches.

The prophetic tradition, exemplified in Jeremiah, of criticizing the gap between Temple worship and moral behavior, explains Mark's intent in showing Jesus' anger at the "buyers and sellers" in the Temple. Mark is not suggesting that Jesus was reacting to the custom of money exchange or that he wanted to overturn the whole Temple. Rather, Mark is suggesting that, like reforming prophets before him, Jesus wanted to purify the Temple of the foreign influences that had commercialized it. Under Rome, this commercialization had taken the specific form of turning the priesthood into a political job. The high priests were appointed by Rome and collaborated with the Romans. Some who might have been committed to the Temple became committed instead to collecting taxes for the empire. It is this overall picture of Jewish faith corrupted by venal interests that Mark conveys here. It is opposition to this corruption of faith that Mark shows Jesus symbolizing by overturning the tables of the money changers.

Mark's perspective is signaled by the scriptural contexts he provides for Jesus' action: Maccabees, Jeremiah, Isaiah. By alluding to Maccabees, Mark indicates that Jesus is "cleansing the Temple," as Simon Maccabeus did, from the idolatrous perversion of Jewish worship caused by foreign occupiers. By quoting Jeremiah, Mark indicates that Jesus is angry, as Jeremiah was, at the weakening of the covenant. But by also quoting Isaiah, Mark indicates that Jesus has a countering prophetic vision of a time when foreigners would be included in the covenant.

11:12-14, 20-28 The fig tree

Two episodes involving the fig tree enclose the symbolic action in the Temple. It is a typical Markan structure and indicates a relationship between the scenes. To understand them, it helps to know the symbolism of the fig tree in first-century Jewish thought. First of all, the fig tree was considered to be the tree that was forbidden in the Garden of Eden. (It is an interpretation that makes sense when you consider that fig trees are indigenous to that part of the world, and that Genesis 3:7 says that Adam and Eve sewed together fig leaves for their first form of clothing.) Second, a fig tree in bloom was considered to be a sign of the end time, of God's final kingdom.

It is also important to consider that Jesus' curse of the fig tree is related to God's curse of the ground when Adam and Eve leave the Garden (Gen 3:17). In Genesis, God tells Adam and Eve that the ground will only bring forth "thorns and thistles" for them (Gen 3:18). In Isaiah, however, this curse is explicitly reversed, and God says he will make the cypress grow instead of the thornbush, and the myrtle instead of nettles (Isa 55:13). Jesus' curse is often translated (as it is here) in such a way that it seems irreversible. But some scholars have suggested that the phrasing is more accurately rendered, "May no one ever eat fruit from you *to the end of this age.**" Such a translation leaves open the possibility of a future reversal, and Mark, in a later chapter, refers to the fig tree in bloom (13:28). The possibility of such a reversal also fits better with one of the first things Mark says about the tree: "It was not the season for figs" (11:13). As we have noted before, the Wisdom writings are especially attuned to the idea that human matters are not permanent but seasonable.

The conversation that Mark gives between Jesus and Peter regarding the tree (11:20-25) gives hope for a different season. Peter says, "The fig tree that you cursed has withered" (11:21). Jesus' response, "Have faith in God" (11:22), is usually taken to mean that Jesus is telling Peter he could have the same power as Jesus. If one has been following Mark's view of Jesus, one sees that he always shows Jesus' power directed toward healing. So here it seems right to understand Jesus' reply as encouragement to have faith in the fig tree's restoration.

Such an understanding is bolstered by two things. First, the term "withered" should remind Mark's readers of the episode where Jesus healed the man with a withered arm (3:1-5). Second, Mark shows Jesus going on here to recommend not only prayer but forgiveness (11:24-25). By providing the context of forgiveness, Mark suggests the possibility of a renewed tree. And as we have just noted above, Mark shows us a renewed fig tree later on.

11:27-32 "By what power . . . ?" (11:28)

The chapter concludes with Mark giving a direct question from the Temple authorities about the source of Jesus' power. Mark then shows Jesus replying with a question that is also something of a riddle: "Was John's baptism of heavenly or of human origin?" (11:30). By showing the authorities' confusion in trying to answer it, Mark indicates their mistake in trying to divide the "human" from the "heavenly." Implied is Mark's view that the figure and actions of Jesus show that they belong together.

Summary of chapter 11

In chapter 10, Mark has shown Jesus teaching his disciples that they should not seek worldly power but rather should follow him in seeking "not be served but to serve." In this chapter, Mark shows the kind of power Jesus does possess. He shows him to be at once forceful and humble.

In the opening verses, Mark shows Jesus entering Jerusalem to the acclaim of crowds, yet riding on a donkey. Through the language he uses to describe Jesus, Mark relates him both to Zechariah's peacemaking king and to Simon Maccabeus in his act of taking back the Temple. Through his description of Jesus' actions in the Temple, Mark further indicates Jesus' relationship to Simon's "cleansing" of the Temple. Through his quotations from Jesus' teaching, Mark places Jesus simultaneously in the tradition of prophetic reform of the Temple (like Jeremiah) and in the tradition of the prophetic vision of restoration of the Temple and universal prayer (like Isaiah).

Mark 11

By enclosing the symbolic action in the Temple with two episodes involving the fig tree, Mark further symbolizes the relationship between Jesus and power. In the first episode, Mark shows Jesus cursing the tree in much the same way that God cursed the ground in Genesis. It is another episode in which Mark shows Jesus reflecting God's action in the Hebrew Bible. Yet in the second episode, Mark shows Jesus encouraging Peter to "have faith" in its restoration. Mark's view is parallel to Isaiah's view of God reversing the original curse and restoring the earth.

Through this conversation with Peter, Mark indicates that Jesus is pointing to the power to move or transform things through faith and prayer and, above all, forgiveness. Through the further exchange between Jesus and the Temple authorities, Mark suggests how it is God's power, especially the power to forgive, that unites the human and the heavenly.

JESUS AS WISDOM IN THE TEMPLE

Mark 12:1-44

12:1-13 Parable of the vineyard

It is striking that Mark shows Jesus once again speaking in parables, a style he has not shown him using since chapter 4. This parable is clearly an allegory, but it is also shaped by pieces of interweaving Scripture. The vineyard as a metaphor for Israel occurs in Isaiah, Jeremiah, Ezekiel, Hosea, and the Song of Songs. In this long tradition, God creates a vineyard that he loves. He is sometimes angry at it, but in the end God always restores it. The opening verses here echo, in a condensed way, the "Vineyard Song" in Isaiah:

> My friend had a vineyard
>   on a fertile hillside;
> He spaded it, cleared it of stones,
>   and planted the choicest vines;
> Within it he built a watchtower,
>   and hewed out a wine press.
> Then he looked for the crop of grapes,
>   but what it yielded was wild grapes (Isa 5:1-2).

In Isaiah's song, the "friend" is God, and "the vineyard of the LORD of hosts is the house of Israel" (Isa 5:7). God is angry at his vineyard for only yielding "wild grapes," and he threatens to destroy it (Isa 5:5-6). Much later in Isaiah, when God proclaims a "new heavens and a new earth," he also promises a new vineyard (Isa 65:17-21).

Mark 12

It is important to realize that although Mark is clearly alluding to the first passage in Isaiah, he is not repeating it. There are key differences: the vineyard here is not yielding "wild grapes" but a good harvest. The anger of the vineyard owner is therefore not directed at the vineyard, but at the tenants who are keeping him from gathering it (12:8b). What we have in Mark is thus not the same plot line as in Isaiah but a rather different story. We cannot hastily conclude (as many have) that it is about God's anger at Israel, because if we are reading carefully, we see that the vineyard (Israel) is not the cause of God's distress.

At the conclusion of the parable, Mark tells us that Jesus said that the owner of the vineyard would "put the tenants to death and give the vineyard to others" (12:9). Mark then shows Jesus quoting Psalm 118:22:

> The stone that the builders rejected
> has become the cornerstone.

Christians of a later time came to identify "the cornerstone" with Christ, and so they interpreted this parable to mean that God would take his vineyard from Jews and give it to Christians. But in the tradition flourishing in Mark's time, the psalm was sung at Passover as a way of rejoicing that Israel, the enslaved people, had become the cornerstone of a nation covenanted to God. Knowing this fact, we need to carefully reexamine all the terms of the parable.

First of all, who are the tenants? The word "tenants" suggests those who have a commercial interest in the property, not a personal one. They are distinguished in the story from the landlord's "servants," whom they beat up and send away, and from his "beloved son," whom they kill. In biblical tradition, a prophet is usually described as God's servant. Israel itself is known as God's servant and also as God's beloved son. The "tenants" are hostile to the servants and the son, and obstructionist in regard to the vineyard. In short, they are hostile to Israel.

The parable, then, is not directed against Israel but against those who would destroy it. Israel, as God's vineyard, is fruitful, but hostile hirelings are preventing God's harvest. God promises to take back the vineyard from them and give it to others who will allow it to come to harvest.

Mark then says, "They were seeking to arrest him, but they feared the crowd, for they realized that he had addressed the parable to them" (12:12). Mark does not explicitly identify whom he means by "them," and there is no direct antecedent. In the following verse, Mark says that "They sent some Pharisees and Herodians to him . . . ." (12:13), so we know that he could not mean either of those two groups. The only plausible group left are the Temple authorities who were questioning Jesus in chapter 11—"the chief priests, the scribes, and the elders" (11:27). In terms of what we know of the historical situation of the Temple in the time of Jesus, the parable is a transparent allegory of the corruption of the Temple by Rome and its Jewish collaborators—that is, the chief priests and some of their associates who had sold out to Rome.

In addition, the reference to the landowner's "beloved son," of course, also suggests Jesus himself, who has been referred to by this phrase twice before at key moments in Mark's Gospel—at his baptism and his transfiguration (1:11; 9:7). In the baptism scene, we have suggested, Jesus is God's "beloved son" in the sense of being a "second Adam," giving hope for a renewed humanity. In the transfiguration scene, Mark shows Jesus addressed by God as "my beloved son" in terms of his inner radiance, which images God's own. At the same time, it is a scene in which Mark shows Jesus in conversation with Elijah and Moses, that is, he shows him in conversation with the greatest prophets of Jewish tradition.

We have noted before that in a Markan triad, the middle episode is the most illuminating one. The transfiguration scene seems to imply that Jesus represents the teachings of Israel in the same way as Moses and Elijah did. So here in this vineyard parable, Jesus stands allied with religious Israel. In predicting the death of "the beloved son" at the hands of outsiders hostile to Israel, the parable is predicting simultaneously the death of Jesus and the destruction of the Temple. By means of this parable, Mark shows how both were destroyed by perverted power. The parable is a fitting conclusion to the discussion of power that runs through both chapters 10 and 11.

12:13-37 The four questions

In this section, Mark shows Jesus answering four questions about the Torah, the first five books of the Bible, or the teachings of Moses. In biblical thought, the Torah was equated with Wisdom. We have spoken earlier about how, in many different ways, Mark presents Jesus as God's Wisdom. So here, as he shows Jesus in the Temple answering questions about the Torah, Mark suggests that he is responding as Wisdom itself.

It is worth noting, moreover, that the questions involve different schools of thought within Early Judaism—Pharisees, Sadducees, and scribes. David Daube, a Jewish scholar, has suggested that they also represent the four questions asked by four sons in an ancient family liturgy for Passover. The first question is asked by a righteous son on a point of law. The second question is a mocking one, asked by a wicked son. The third question comes from a pious son. Finally, the father of the family gives instruction to a fourth son, who does not know how to ask.

12:13-17 The first response: "Whose image?"

Jesus' response to the Pharisees' question about the lawfulness of the Temple tax is often treated as a statement on the separation of church and state. One of the main causes of Jewish anger at the Caesars was their attempt (like Antiochus IV before them) to put their own image in the Temple. Jesus' response implies that Caesar's image has no place there.

More important, however, is how Mark uses this question (as he has earlier in his Gospel) to illumine Jesus' teaching on some key passage in the Bible. In this case, when Jesus responds to the Pharisees' question with his own question, "Whose image and inscription is this?" (12:16), there is more at stake than money. Mark shows Jesus using language that would have reminded his audience of the most important verse in Genesis: "God created human beings in God's image" (1:27).

What the response implies is this: Caesar's image may be on the coin, but God's image is inscribed on every human being. Jesus' response is first of all a theological one. The theological answer, moreover, touches the core of Mark's Gospel, because Mark has shown Jesus himself to be the image of God.

12:18-27 The second response:
"He is not God of the dead but of the living"

The Sadducees were a group particularly in league with the Temple priests. Unlike the Pharisees, they questioned belief in immortality, and their narrative here is designed to make that belief seem ridiculous. Mark shows Jesus responding in a way that emphasizes God as the Creator. First, he shows Jesus pointing to "the scriptures" and "the power of God" (12:24). Then he shows Jesus spelling out what he has in mind by quoting God's words to Moses at the burning bush: "I am the God of Abraham, [the] God of Isaac, and [the] God of Jacob" (12:26). The meaning of the reply is not obvious, and one has to read between the lines. But Jesus' response implies that by speaking of the patriarchs in the present tense, God indicates that they are still alive, because "He is not God of the dead but of the living" (12:27). Mark shows Jesus suggesting that belief in the Scriptures would lead one to belief in resurrection. Mark also quotes Jesus as saying twice to the Sadducees, "You are misled" (12:24, 27). He implies that not to believe in resurrection is to limit God's power.

Mark 12

To further unpack this passage, Jesus' response seems to be saying that if one believes that God had the power to create life, one should believe that God has the power to re-create it. This point of view is in keeping with the way Mark has depicted Jesus, throughout his Gospel, as healing and restoring life. It is in keeping with the transfiguration scene, in which Mark shows Elijah and Moses fully alive. It is in keeping with the way Mark continually points to Jesus' own resurrection.

12:28-34 The third response: "You shall love the Lord your God . . . ."

The third question is asked by "one of the scribes" (12:28), a group particularly versed in Scripture. The scribe asks the most basic question: "Which is the first of all the commandments?" (12:28).

In his reply, Mark shows Jesus weaving together three essential parts of Judaism. The first part, "Hear, O Israel! The Lord our God is LORD alone" (12:29), is the central "creed" of Judaism, that is, it is an assertion of Jews' central belief in one God. It has always been at the heart of Jewish worship. The second part, "You shall love the Lord your God with all your heart, with all your soul, with all your mind, and with all your strength" (12:30), is a direct quotation from Deuteronomy (6:4). The third part, "You shall love your neighbor as yourself" (12:31), is a direct quotation from Leviticus (19:2).

By interweaving these three parts, Mark shows Jesus speaking as a scribe himself, that is, as a teacher of Scripture. Mark shows Jesus using a method typical of Jewish Scripture scholars and Wisdom teachers of the first century. The effect of this interweaving is to suggest that love of God implies love of neighbor and that both together are what constitute true worship.

It is striking that Mark shows Jesus and the scribe to be in perfect agreement. He shows the scribe repeating what Jesus has said, only adding another quotation from Scripture to further support it: "'To love your neighbor as yourself' is worth more than all burnt offerings and sacrifices" (12:33).

The last part of the scribe's comment is an allusion to Psalm 40:7-9:

> Sacrifice and offering you do not want . . . .
> Holocausts and sin-offerings you do not require;
> So I said, "Here I am . . .
> To do your will is my delight."

Mark shows that the scribe uses the same method as Jesus, bringing together different parts of the Hebrew Bible to illuminate their meaning.

Mark further indicates the harmony between Jesus and the scribe when he quotes Jesus saying to him approvingly, "You are not far from the kingdom of God" (12:34). The incident stands out because through it Mark shows that Jesus was not at odds with *all* the scribes and Temple authorities. On the contrary, Mark shows Jesus to be in perfect agreement with one who taught the central tenets of Judaism.

12:35-37 The fourth response: "How is he [the messiah] his [David's] son?"

In this passage, Mark shows Jesus posing a riddle about the meaning of "the messiah." He does so by continuing to juxtapose one Scripture passage with another. In this instance, he juxtaposes the tradition based on God's promise to David in the second book of Samuel with a popular interpretation of Psalm 110. In the passage from 2 Samuel, God says to David:

> I will raise up your heir after you, sprung from your loins, and I will make his kingdom firm. It is he who shall build a house for my name. And I will make his royal throne firm forever. I will be a father to him, and he shall be a son to me. . . . Your house and your kingdom shall endure forever before me; your throne shall stand firm forever (2 Sam 7:12b-14, 16).

In the first century, all the psalms were popularly attributed to David, so he was considered the speaker in Psalm 110. In its opening verse, the words "my lord" were interpreted as a reference to a coming messiah who would be victorious for Israel. Mark shows Jesus putting these two things together and suggesting that they don't add up—that is, he is asking: If the coming messiah is a son of David, how come David calls him "my lord"?

There is no answer to this riddle. By having Jesus pose this riddle, Mark is not intent on giving answers but on raising questions. The riddle raises a question about popular understandings of "the messiah." Earlier in his Gospel, Mark shows that Peter has an understanding that Jesus does not share. Peter thinks that if Jesus is "the messiah," he cannot suffer and die. And as we have seen, Jesus reproaches him (8:29-33). Here Mark shows Jesus using Scripture to reveal the fault line in the tradition. By this means, Mark shows how Jesus raised questions in the minds of his audience. Mark shakes up the popular definition of "the messiah" so that he can dramatize that Jesus is a "messiah" in an unconventional sense.

12:38-44 The rich and the poor in the Temple

Mark concludes the chapter with a contrast between those who use the Temple for their own profit and those who give to it their last coin. The episode sums up and illumines the theme of wealth versus poverty that has run throughout the last three chapters.

We have just noted that Mark shows Jesus in perfect agreement with one of the scribes. But here he shows Jesus denouncing those scribes who use their religion for self-aggrandizement. It is important to see that the scribes who seek "seats of honor" are not unlike James and John, who asked to sit at Jesus' right and left in his glory (10:37). By means of the echo, Mark reminds us of Jesus' teaching that "whoever wishes to be first among you will be the slave of all" (10:44). In addition to seeking glory, we learn, these Temple authorities make venal profit off the needs of poor widows (12:40). The language that Mark shows Jesus using to describe their action—"they *devour* the house of widows" (emphasis added)—suggests that their greed is the reverse of the nurturing habits of Jesus himself.

The episode of the poor widow has several functions. First of all, it clarifies Jesus' anger at the money changers (11:15-17). By showing Jesus' approval of the widow's contribution to the Temple treasury, Mark indicates that it was not money in the Temple per se that caused Jesus' anger. Rather, as the condemnation of the greedy scribes shows, Jesus was angered by those who used the Temple money for themselves.

At the same time, when Mark shows Jesus praising the poor widow because "she, from her poverty, has contributed all she had" (12:44), he also shows him echoing his instruction to the rich man to sell all he has (10:21). The widow's total self-giving embodies the commandment to "love the Lord your God with all your heart, with all your soul, with all your mind, and with all your strength" (12:30).

Summary of chapter 12

The chapter is unified around the theme of wholehearted love of God versus religion perverted by greed and hypocrisy. The parable of the vineyard contrasts the venal tenants of the vineyard with the vineyard owner's servants and "beloved son." It is a transparent allegory, contrasting the present authorities in the Temple—the Romans and their hirelings—with the prophets and with Jesus.

The parable makes use of the vineyard tradition in the Hebrew Bible, especially Isaiah, to indicate the similarities and differences between Israel's situation now and in the past. As in the past, God is not able to reap from his vineyard (Israel) the harvest he wants from it. Unlike the past, the cause of this is not the vineyard itself but the obstructions placed in the way by the greedy and hostile occupier of the vineyard (Rome).

These "tenants" want whatever "inheritance" there is for themselves. The narrative of the killing of the beloved son, together with the image of the ungathered harvest, suggests that those who now occupy the vineyard are responsible both for the killing of Jesus and for the destruction of the Temple. The quotation from Psalm 110 in the conclusion of the parable suggests that God will vindicate his people (Israel) as he has before.

When Jesus tells this parable, Mark depicts him again as a Wisdom teacher. In the rest of the chapter, Mark shows Jesus engaged in interpreting the meaning of Scripture to various groups of Jewish scholars in the Temple. By doing this, Mark suggests (as he has earlier) that Jesus is Wisdom itself.

As Wisdom in the Temple, Jesus responds to four types of questions about Jewish teaching. The first question puts forward the relationship between the Temple and worldly power. Jesus' response suggests that worldly power does not belong in the Temple. It also suggests that human beings, as bearers of God's image, belong wholly to God. The second question puts forward the relationship between God and death. Jesus' response indicates that God is concerned with life, not death. God the Creator has the power to go on creating. The third question puts forward the relationship between love of God and love of neighbor. Jesus and the scribe agree that they are inextricably woven together. Love of neighbor (as the Psalms and Prophets have said) is the truest way of loving God. The last question takes the form of a riddle that Jesus himself asks about the meaning of God's "messiah." The riddle raises questions about the conventional understandings of the term and so prepares for an unconventional one.

All of Jesus' responses bear on his identity in Mark's Gospel. Mark presents Jesus as image of God, as one who lives beyond death, as one who has come "not to be served but to serve" (10:45), and as unconventional messiah.

These responses also indicate the kind of Temple reform Jesus stands for. In conclusion, Mark sums up that reform by the contrast Jesus makes between the venal and hypocritical Temple authorities, who use the Temple for their own purposes, and the poor widow, who gives all that she has to sustain it.

JESUS AS PROPHET IN THE TEMPLE

Mark 13:1-37

13:1-2 The prophecy of the destruction of the Temple

In chapters 11 and 12, Mark has shown Jesus pointing to the spiritual devastation of the Temple. Here he speaks of its coming physical destruction. Both kinds of speech belong to the role of the prophet. We have a tendency today to restrict the word "prophet" to one who makes predictions about the future. But the biblical prophets were not soothsayers. They were messengers of God, reminding the people of God's past word in Scripture and, in the light of it, conveying God's present word on human behavior. They were, in fact, preachers.

The prevailing theme of the prophets is the need for Temple reform. By this they did not so much mean reform of liturgical practices but of people's way of living. They were constantly calling the people back to their commitment to the covenant. They identified the breaking of any of the commandments with idolatry. For example, Jeremiah's "Temple sermon" (see p. 162) equates adultery and perjury with the worship of Baal. They always preached, moreover, in times when Israel was in crisis—either under attack by foreign powers or actually occupied by them. Every foreign power that conquered Jerusalem also took over the Temple. So in such times (which constituted most of Israel's biblical history), the danger of idolatry from within was compounded by foreign influences from without. As a consequence, the prophets warned the people again and again about succumbing to false gods as well as about neglecting their obligations to love their neighbors as themselves.

The Temple building functioned as a key image in these warnings. The prophets expressed God's displeasure with the people by saying either that God would destroy the Temple or that God would leave the Temple. Many scholars think that these imaginative warnings were not so much predicting disaster to the Temple as reflecting on it after the fact. Take Jeremiah, for example. The Temple was destroyed by Babylon in 586 B.C.E., the time of Jeremiah, and the people lived in exile from Jerusalem until 539. When Jeremiah, therefore, tells the people that it is God's will for them to submit to Babylon, is he looking ahead, or is he trying to reassure the exiles that God had a plan in allowing their disaster? Many scholars think it was the latter.

All this background is relevant to the prophecy that Mark shows Jesus making here. For the second time in Jewish history, the Temple was destroyed—this time by the Romans in the year 70 C.E., forty years after the death of Jesus but in the lifetime of Mark. It had a traumatic effect on everyone associated with the Jewish community, including those Jews who were followers of Jesus. Most scholars date the Gospel of Mark around that time, either just before or just after. Mark portrays Jesus, as we have seen, in the role of a prophet, preaching about the corruption of Temple worship. The prophetic tradition raises this question: When Mark shows Jesus saying that the Temple would be destroyed, is he suggesting that Jesus in fact predicted its destruction, or is he imaginatively projecting how Jesus as prophet reflected on its meaning?

In any case, the chapter is carefully designed. Mark opens the chapter by citing the disciples' admiration for the Temple. Their wonder at the great buildings expresses a long tradition of reverence for the Temple as the dwelling place of God. Mark cites Jesus' reply without indicating his tone of voice. Many have assumed that Mark shows Jesus to be angry at the Temple, but we have seen that his anger is tempered by the prophetic vision of reform.

13:4 and 13:32 "When will this happen?"

At the time that Mark was composing, there was a large body of Jewish writings known as "apocalyptic." They were characterized by a number of things. They warned of a final disaster that in some way took the form of a battle between good and evil, that is, directly between God and Satan, or between good and evil nations, or between good and evil forces. (For example, the Dead Sea Scrolls speak of a final clash between "the sons of darkness" and the "sons of light.") They made precise predictions about the time that the world would end. They also projected that there would be particular signs that the end was about to happen. The question raised by the disciples here—"Tell us, when will this happen, and what sign will there be when all these things are about to come to an end?" (13:4)—is typical of these writings. Mark does not give Jesus' reply for many verses, and when he does, he shows him giving an answer that does not fit the apocalyptic perspective: "But of that day or hour no one knows, neither the angels in heaven, nor the Son, but only the Father" (13:32). This exchange functions as the frame for the chapter.

13:5-13 Instructions to the disciples

Mark shows that instead of replying right away to the disciples' question, Jesus instructs them on how to behave in the face of coming disaster. These instructions are a mixture of many things, and they need to be looked at carefully.

Some of what Mark shows Jesus saying are generalized clichés taken from contemporary writing about the end of time. These include the warnings about "wars and reports of wars" (13:7), about nation rising against nation (13:8a), about "earthquakes" (13:8b), about how "brother will hand over brother to death" (13:12).

But most of the warnings Mark places in Jesus' mouth are ones that would only have had meaning for Mark's own community in the year 70 or later. For example, Jesus' warning that "Many will come in my name saying, I am he" (13:5) makes most sense after Jesus' death. Indeed, earlier Mark has shown Jesus refusing to stop someone healing in his name, saying, "Whoever is not against us is for us" (9:40). Similarly, Jesus' warning that "They will hand you over to courts. You will be beaten in synagogues. You will be arraigned before governors and kings because of me" (13:9) does not apply to the disciples of Jesus' time but to his later followers.

It becomes clear that Mark is speaking to his own time when he shows Jesus saying, "But the gospel must first be preached to all the nations" (13:10). So, too, the advice that immediately follows this statement makes sense if it is seen as directed to Mark's community: "When they lead you away and hand you over, do not worry beforehand about what you are to say. But say whatever will be given to you at that hour. For it will not be you who are speaking but the holy spirit" (13:11). Finally, the warning "You will be hated by all because of my name" (13:13a) suggests what was happening in Mark's time, not in that of Jesus.

It is important to realize that Mark is addressing two different periods of time. Otherwise, we might think that the hatred and persecution of Jesus' followers happened while Jesus was still alive. But we know historically that this was not the case. And in other parts of his Gospel, Mark has shown that while some of those in power were hostile to Jesus, the crowds followed him. It is Mark's community, living after the double trauma of the death of Jesus and the destruction of the Temple, that needs encouragement to "persevere to the end" (13:13b).

13:14-27 An apocalyptic end?

This description of the end again makes use of phrases used in apocalyptic writings of the time. These include the warning to flee to the mountains (13:14), and not to go back to one's house (13:16), the lament for those who are pregnant "in those days" (13:17), and the admonition to "Pray that this does not happen in winter" (13:18).

The reference to "tribulation such as has not been" (13:19) is taken verbatim from Daniel 12:1, where it is indeed predicting a final disaster that will bring about an eternal separation of the good from the wicked:

> Some shall live forever,
>   others shall be in everlasting horror and disgrace (Dan 12:2).

As in other apocalyptic literature, this moment of doom is precisely timed. In this case, the doom is related to "the abomination of desolation": "From the time that the daily sacrifice is abolished and the abomination of desolation is set up, there shall be one thousand two hundred and ninety days" (Dan 12:11).

The "abomination of desolation" is Daniel's veiled way of speaking about Antiochus's sacrilegious act of placing an image of himself in the Temple. Mark clearly shows Jesus referring to the same act when he uses the very same phrase (13:14a) and then emphasizes that the reference is to a written work ("let the reader understand," 13:14b). By showing that Jesus quotes the book of Daniel, Mark suggests that Jesus, too, perceives sacrilege in the Temple as the cause of the tribulations to come. Only in Mark's time, the veiled reference to sacrilege would have been to that of the Romans.

But Mark also shows that Jesus' perspective is different from that of Daniel and the other apocalyptic writings. He does this in many different ways. First, while Jesus warns, in typical apocalyptic language, of "wars" and "earthquakes" and "famines" (13:7-8), he also comments, "These are the beginnings of the labor pains" (13:8b). The image of "labor pains" or "birth pangs" was often associated with a time when God's kingdom would prevail.

Second, Mark shows Jesus reassuring his followers that God will shorten the days of tribulation (13:20). The description that follows of a darkened sun and stars "falling from the sky" (13:25) also has apocalyptic parallels, but the edge is softened here by the suggestion that this shaking of the heavens is part of God's act of mercy.

Third, Mark shows Jesus telling his disciples that he, the second Adam ("son of Adam" or "son of man"), will return in glory to gather his elect "from the end of the earth to the end of the sky" (13:26-27). Mark has shown Jesus speaking before about his own rising from the dead, but it is the first time that he has shown him promising his disciples some future glory.

In all these ways, Mark shows that while Jesus uses some apocalyptic terms, he does not share that perspective. In chapter 4, we looked at the way Mark shows Jesus telling an apocalyptic parable (the sower), and then two more parables that reverse its meaning (the seed growing secretly and the mustard seed). In the same way here, Mark shows Jesus using the apocalyptic language of some contemporary writers in order to show how he differs from their point of view.

In Mark's Gospel, Jesus does not predict a final battle between good and evil, and he does not believe that anyone can calculate when the end will come. Instead, he says that the suffering to come should be understood as "labor pains" (13:8). He says that God will shorten the suffering (13:20). He says that beyond the suffering there will be glory (13:26). And he says that no one but God the Father can know the time of the end (13:32). Jesus also expresses a non-apocalyptic point of view in his reference to the fig tree and in his parable of the returning lord of the house.

13:28-31 The fig tree blooms again

In chapter 11, Mark shows Jesus first cursing a fig tree that was not in season (11:12-14), and later exhorting Peter to "have faith" in God's power to restore it (11:20-23). These episodes, we suggested, are best understood in terms of God's actions in the Hebrew Bible. In Genesis 3, God curses the ground, but in Isaiah, God reverses that curse (Isa 55:12-13; 65:17-25). Following a similar pattern, Mark shows Jesus speaking here of the fig tree once more in bloom. This image is particularly significant in the light of contemporary Jewish thought, where the fig tree coming back into bloom was considered a sign of God's kingdom.

13:32-37 The lord of the house returns

Mark shows Jesus telling a parable that has significance both for the time of Jesus and for the end time. It has immediate significance for Jesus' disciples because it warns of the lord of the house returning to his servants at "cockcrow" (13:35), a clear foreshadowing of the cockcrow that wakens Peter to remorse for having denied any knowledge of Jesus (14:30, 72).

This parable also bears a significant relationship to the parable of the vineyard (12:1-9). In that parable, the owner of the vineyard goes away and allows hired hands to tend his vineyard. In this parable, the owner also goes off, but he leaves his house in the charge of trusted servants. In both parables, the owner stands for God, and the vineyard or house represents the sacred space where God dwells. In the first parable, the sacred space is violated by hirelings; in the second parable, "the lord of the house" is on his way back home. The parable ends, as it were, with a question: What will the lord of the house find when he returns? And it explicitly ends with the advice to "watch" (13:33, 35, 37), an exhortation that belongs to the Wisdom traditions.

The exhortation to watchfulness appears three times in this chapter. It appears first when Jesus tells the disciples to "Watch out for yourselves" in regard to those who might deceive them (13:9). It occurs a second time in the context of Jesus' warning about "false messiahs and false prophets" (13:22-23). And it is repeated three times in connection with this parable— once at the beginning and twice at the end (13:33, 35, 37).

The word "watch" is the key word of the chapter. It belongs to the Wisdom traditions, because it is in those traditions that the acknowledgment of uncertainty is prized. It is wise to know what one does not know. So here Mark shows Jesus acknowledging that only God the Father can know when the end will come. Not knowing, one must be always on the watch.

Summary of chapter 13

The chapter is unified by the question about "signs." It is framed by the disciples' question that seeks definite signs as to when the end will come and by Jesus' reply that "No one knows," so they must always "watch." An apocalyptic question receives a non-apocalyptic reply.

In between, Mark shows Jesus countering what were conventionally considered the signs of God's coming judgment (war, earthquake, famine, family betrayal, death, and cosmic turmoil) with images that bring hope: giving birth, a merciful shortening of suffering, a glorious ingathering of the elect, a new season in which the fig tree blooms again. In this way, Mark shows Jesus countering the conventional fears of a coming apocalypse with suggestions of a new beginning.

The specific reference to "the beginning of God's creation" (13:19), even though it is made in the context of predicted suffering, is a reminder of God's purpose in creation to "look at everything [that God] had made" and find it "very good" (Gen 1:31). The very word "beginning" reminds Mark's readers of his persistent images of a new creation. The parable of the fig tree in bloom is one more of these images. It is a sign of return to the original Garden.

The glorious ingathering of Jesus as the "son of man" reinforces this sign. We have suggested before that the phrase "son of man" is best understood as "son of Adam." Jesus as "son of Adam" is also a second Adam. Mark presents him as a representative of humanity who has not fallen. As such, he is a representative who perfectly reflects human beings as God intended them to be at the beginning—as image of God.

The central "sign" of the chapter, of course, is the Temple itself. In chapters 11 and 12, Mark has shown Jesus using the language of the prophets to point to its corruption and to hope for its restoration. In this chapter, he shows Jesus borrowing the veiled words of the book of Daniel ("the abomination of desolation") to point to the sacrilegious use of the Temple by the Romans. In the parable of "the lord of the house" returning home, he gives hope that God will come back to his dwelling place.

That hope, without certainty, brings the chapter to its concluding key word, the key word of Wisdom—"Watch!"

Mark 14

THE PASSION NARRATIVE, PART I: PREPARATIONS FOR DEATH AND LIFE

Mark 14:1-52

14:1-2 Preparation for betrayal

In these opening verses, Mark introduces the theme of betrayal that he interweaves throughout the chapter. The Feast of Passover, designed to celebrate the freedom of the people of God, is the setting for the plot to kill Jesus. By means of the plotters' remark that they had better not kill Jesus at the feast (14:2), Mark suggests the tension both between the feast and the plot and between the Temple authorities and the people.

14:3-9 Anointing: preparation for death and life

The next few verses present a counter theme. The setting is "the house of Simon the leper" (14:3). Mark introduces this figure without explanation. The reader only knows the name "Simon" in association with Peter (1:16, 29-30; 3:16). The only leper to appear before is the one cured in 1:40-45. Does Mark intend the reader to make some connection between this Simon and Simon Peter or between this leper and the one who was healed?

The mystery of the scene is compounded by the entry of an anonymous woman carrying an alabaster jar (14:3). Again, Mark makes no attempt to identify this woman. The reader, however, may have a subliminal memory of having encountered before this particular pairing of anonymous woman and leper. In Mark's account of Jesus' first miracles, he tells of Jesus healing "Simon's mother-in-law" (1:29-31), and then a leper (1:40-45). The name "Simon," transposed here to the leper, adds to the impression of déjà vu.

We noted earlier that Mark's language suggests that Jesus did not merely heal the woman physically but "raised her up"* (1:31) to a new status of ministry. It is one in which she "served"* others (1:31). And serving others is how Jesus describes his own way of life (10:45). The leper, too, receives more than a physical cure. Mark tells us that Jesus sent him back to the priest and so to his community. Once there, Mark says, he spread the word of Jesus to such an extent that Jesus could not "enter a town openly" (1:45).

Could it be, then, that Mark intends his readers to regard the woman and leper here as these two persons in their changed state? That supposition is supported by the fact that they act here in unconventional and extraordinary ways. Unlike most lepers, "Simon the leper" is able to open his home to a social gathering. Even more remarkable, Mark shows Jesus saying that what the anonymous woman has done will always be part of the gospel proclamation (14:9).

The leper disappears from the narrative while the woman preoccupies it. It is important to look carefully at how Mark describes her actions. A jar made of "alabaster" suggests something rare and valuable. The perfumed oil that it contains is described by two words, one of which is hard to translate. The first word means "pure"* (translated above as "genuine"). The other word does not appear in any other piece of writing; it is closest to the Greek word for "faith."* Mark is presenting his readers with a highly symbolic narrative in which the woman is bearing the costly oil of faith.

The woman proceeds to break the jar and pour out the oil (14:3b). The word Mark chooses for "break" here is no ordinary word, but one that means to "shatter" or "to destroy completely." By using it, Mark calls attention to the action. He suggests that this is not a casual or conventional sort of breaking. The word for "poured" has the sense of "poured out." In its root form, it is related to the word associated with a cultic pouring out of blood. Mark uses a variant of it later in the chapter when he describes Jesus saying, "This is my blood of the covenant, which is poured out for many" (14:24). In fact, with hindsight one can see that the woman's gestures here of "breaking" and "pouring out" anticipate the gestures Mark shows Jesus making at the Last Supper. Mark makes the woman's extravagant gestures of breaking and pouring a symbolic foreshadowing of Jesus' extravagant gestures of giving his body to be broken and his blood to be poured out.

By showing the narrow-minded response of some present who view this extravagance as a "waste" (14:4-5), Mark sets the stage for Jesus' praise of this woman's act (14:8-9). Given the symbolic nature of the narrative, every word here is important. When Mark shows Jesus rebuking the protestors by saying, "Let her alone" (14:6), we hear an echo of the scene where Jesus rebukes those who were keeping back the children (10:13-14). When Mark shows Jesus saying, "She has done what she could" (14:8a), we hear an echo of Jesus' praise of the poor widow: "[She] contributed all she had" (12:44).

When Mark shows Jesus saying, "She has anticipated anointing my body for burial" (14:8b), we are forced to consider the different meanings of "anointing." Jesus speaks of anointing here in the context of consecrating the body for death. At the same time, Mark's readers would have been aware that Jesus was referred to as "messiah," a Hebrew word that means "the anointed one." In the Bible and other writings of the time, that term generally referred to someone who was sent to do God's work, and so it was a title associated with glory. But we have already seen that Mark shows Jesus rebuking Peter for making that association (8:29-33). Mark shows

Mark 14

Jesus consistently teaching that God's anointed one should be associated instead with suffering and even death. In this episode in chapter 14, Mark dramatizes that meaning. Jesus becomes "the anointed one" in the context of death.

When Mark shows Jesus saying, "Wherever the gospel is proclaimed to the whole world, what she has done will be told in remembrance* of her" (14:9), what does Mark have in mind? We have suggested that Mark intends a connection between the woman's extravagant gestures of breaking and pouring and Jesus' gestures (later in this chapter) that symbolize his death. In other words, Mark makes her gestures anticipate the eucharistic gestures of Jesus. And those gestures of breaking and pouring are the very ones that, according to Paul, Jesus asked his followers to do *"in remembrance"* of him (1 Cor 11:24-25, emphasis added).

The phrase expresses a concept important to Passover celebrations and also to celebrations of the Eucharist. In both instances, it conveys the sense of doing more than recalling a past event. Rather, it suggests a reliving of a past event in such a way that God's grace is not just recalled but made present. At the end of every Passover meal, the leader prays that God may grant the grace of freedom to every Jew here and now. In the same way, the presider at the Eucharist prays that the freeing grace of Jesus may be made present here and now. The eucharistic act of "remembrance" is not an act of recalling what Jesus did but of making it present once again.

When Mark gives his own account of the first Eucharist (14:22-26), his wording is close to that of Paul's account in First Corinthians. It is therefore striking that Mark does not put the phrase "in remembrance" there. The fact that it is here confirms Mark's intention to link this woman's gestures to the Eucharist. In preparing Jesus' body for burial, she has prepared his body for a death that will be life-giving. It is for her eucharistic gestures that she will be kept *"in remembrance."*

14:10-11 Preparation for betrayal continued

These two verses connect Judas with the plot to kill Jesus. They reintroduce the theme of betrayal. Mark consistently uses the phrase "hand over" to express betrayal. That use carries ironic overtones, because "hand over" can also mean *hand on,* as of a tradition. By his persistent repetition of the phrase, Mark suggests that Jesus is *handing on* the tradition of being *handed over.* It is the same word that Paul uses with the same double meaning when he says that he is *"handing on"* to the Christian community at Corinth what he knows about Jesus' institution of the Eucharist "on the night that he was *handed over"* (1 Cor 11:23).

14:12-16 Preparations for the Passover Supper

The details of this episode again seem both mysterious and symbolic, like the details of the anointing scene. Mark does not identify which disciples were sent or the man "carrying a jar of water" (14:13). Nor does he tell us how the man knows to lead the disciples to the right place. Mark also doesn't identify "the master of the house" nor tell us why he has already prepared a room for Jesus' Passover (14:14-15). The narrative's lack of realistic concreteness suggests that it is also intended to be symbolic.

In fact, many details suggest that Mark intends this narrative to symbolize the Eucharist. By referring to the Passover supper as "the Feast of Unleavened Bread" (v. 12), Mark stresses a detail that would be significant to a eucharistic community. When Mark notes that the disciples set off to prepare the supper on the day "when they sacrificed the Passover lamb" (14:12), he is calling attention to the sacrificial implications of the meal to come.

When Mark speaks of an anonymous man carrying a pottery water jar, the image seems to echo and complement the anonymous woman carrying an alabaster jar of costly ointment. We have noted that the alabaster jar indicates that it contains something precious and that the pouring out of its ointment anticipates Jesus' pouring out of the wine that he calls his blood. The pottery (or earthenware) jar is humble in comparison, and the water is ordinary compared with the precious ointment. One may think of Paul saying, "We hold this treasure in earthen vessels, that the surpassing power may be of God and not from us" (2 Cor 4:7). In any case, by presenting his readers with these different but echoing images, Mark suggests the pairing of water and wine that is part of the eucharistic celebration and proclaims, for the believer, the meeting of humanity with divinity.

In that context, the "large upper room furnished and ready" (14:15) is perhaps suggestive of the house churches that were developing in Mark's time to accommodate the eucharistic gatherings of the early Christian communities. Once again, Mark seems to be projecting his own time frame into the narrative. He is trying to give the reader his own awareness that this last Passover meal of Jesus was also the first Eucharist.

14:22-26 The Passover/Eucharist

In between predictions of betrayal, Mark places his account of the meal that he describes as both Passover and Eucharist. The blessing and breaking of bread, together with the blessing and giving of the cup (14:22-23), suggest the opening prayers of every Passover meal. (These read: "Blessed are you, O God, king of the universe, creator of the fruit of the vine.") It is also usual to conclude the Passover Seder, as they do here, with the singing of a hymn (14:26). What is strikingly different is Jesus' identification of the bread as his body and the wine as his blood (14:22-24). Mark also shows Jesus speaking of his blood as that "of the covenant" (14:24a). That reference suggests both the blood of the Passover lamb that saved the Israelites from destruction (Exod 12:13) and the sacrificial blood that ratified the covenant (Exod 24:8).

In addition, Mark shows Jesus quoting from Isaiah when he speaks of his blood being "shed for many" (14:24b). That phrase is also an echo of what Mark has shown Jesus saying earlier to his disciples about the purpose of his life: "The son of man did not come to be served but to serve and to give his life as a ransom for many" (10:45). In both instances, the phrase is an echo of Isaiah's description of God's justification of his "Suffering Servant":

> Through his suffering, my servant shall justify many,
>   and their guilt he shall bear (Isa 53:11).

By showing Jesus repeating this phrase, Mark interprets Jesus' death in that tradition of atoning sacrifice. It is also a tradition in which God raises up his servant and exalts him. Like the episode of Jesus' anointing, it is a suggestion of hope in this chapter so seemingly concentrated on betrayal and death.

Another suggestion of hope is given in Jesus' further words that he will not drink "the fruit of the vine" again until the day when he drinks it new "in the kingdom of God" (14:25). Although in one sense it suggests that he is moving toward death, in another sense it offers hope that there will be another time, a new time, in which God's kingdom will at last prevail. And by showing that Jesus speaks of this time as one in which there will be "fruit of the vine" to drink, Mark also suggests that there will be a time when the fruit of God's vineyard will be accessible again to God.

14:17-21, 27-31 Predictions of betrayal

Mark frames the narrative of this Passover/Eucharist with predictions of Jesus' betrayal. The scene he describes before the supper (14:18) echoes a verse in Psalm 41 where the speaker recalls a time when friends as well as foes turned against him:

> Even the friend who had my trust,
>   who shared my table, has scorned me (v. 10).

When Mark then shows Jesus saying that his betrayer will be "the one who dips with me into the dish" (14:20), he brings to mind both the dipping gesture characteristic of the Passover Seder and the dipping posture of baptism. By suggesting both simultaneously, Mark suggests that the experience of being betrayed is the tradition of God's servants. (Being *handed over* is being *handed on*).

When Mark shows Jesus saying, "For the son of man indeed goes, as it is written of him" (14:21), he indicates how much his narrative uses Scripture to shape and interpret the story of Jesus' passion. The foretelling of the disciples' betrayal (14:27) is preceded by a passage from Zechariah:

> [I will] strike the shepherd
>   that the sheep may be dispersed (Zech 13:7).

In the context of Zechariah, God is saying that he will strike the shepherd *so that* the sheep may be dispersed. God says that he will purge Israel of false prophets and false shepherds so that he can preserve the remnant and make Jerusalem holy again. In Mark, the prophecy is used to indicate how all the Twelve, including Peter, will scatter and leave Jesus without their support.

When Mark shows Jesus making this prediction to Peter, it is even more precise: "Amen, I say to you, this very night before the cock crows twice you will deny me three times" (14:30). Mark thus links Jesus' warning to Peter to his general admonition to "watchfulness" in chapter 13: "You do not know when the lord of the house is coming, whether in the evening, or at midnight, or at cockcrow . . . " (13:35). The vehemence of Peter's refusal to accept himself as a possible betrayer (14:29, 31) intensifies the enormity of his eventual act of betrayal (14:66-72).

Yet even in this context of betrayal, Mark shows Jesus predicting once again that he will be raised from the dead (14:28). In this instance, Mark shows him speaking not only about his being raised but about his life beyond death: "I shall go before you to Galilee." It is striking because his words do not suggest ascension to heaven (like Elijah), but a return to ongoing ministry. And this phrase is the one the women at the tomb are sent to repeat to the disciples after Jesus' death (16:7).

14:32-52 Betrayal in the garden

This betrayal has two parts: (1) betrayal by the three key disciples (14:32-42), and (2) betrayal by Judas (14:43-52).

14:32-42 Betrayal by the disciples. The first part is conventionally labeled "Agony in the Garden," although in fact there is no explicit mention of a garden; the garden setting is inferred from knowledge of Gethsemane. The image of betrayal in a garden fits in with the fact that Creation provides Mark's overall frame of reference. In that context, there is particular irony in Mark showing Jesus, second Adam, betrayed in a garden.

There is also irony within the scene itself. We have noted before that Mark shows Jesus taking these same three disciples with him at three key moments in the Gospel: at the raising up of Jairus's daughter (5:37); at the transfiguration of Jesus (9:2); and here. The first two episodes point toward Jesus' resurrection. In fact, in terms of the overall structure of Mark's narrative, the transfiguration scene takes the place of a resurrection scene. In this scene in the garden, all the elements of the transfiguration scene are reversed. Mark tells us that instead of being radiant and dazzling (9:3), Jesus is "troubled and distressed" (14:33). Instead of ascending up a mountain (9:2), Jesus falls to the ground (14:35). Instead of being blessed by the Father (9:9), Jesus cries out to the Father to take away his coming suffering and death (14:36). Peter, who is so roused by the moment of transfiguration that he wants to celebrate it (9:5), falls asleep (14:37). It is also significant that Mark shows Jesus not addressing him here as "Peter" but reverting to "Simon," the name he had before he became a disciple.

Mark connects this scene to others in his Gospel as well. By showing that Jesus refers to his suffering as "this cup," Mark links this scene to Jesus' question to James and John: "Can you drink the cup that I drink . . . ?" (10:38). The word is, of course, also linked to the Passover/Eucharist Mark has just described and to the cup of Jesus' blood (14:23-24).

By showing that Jesus cries out "Abba," the Aramaic word for "father" (14:36), Mark indicates the importance of this moment. He shows Jesus using Aramaic only in three other key places: when Jesus raises up the little girl from death (5:41); when Jesus symbolically heals the deaf-mute (7:34); and when Jesus cries out to God from the cross (15:34).

Most important, Mark shows Jesus using the word "watch" three times in this brief episode (14:34, 37, 38). Like the "cockcrow" (14:30), this refrain links this moment to the warnings at the end of chapter 13 (13:33, 35, 37). There, at the conclusion of the parable of the returning lord of the house, Jesus says to his disciples, "May he not come suddenly and find you sleeping. What I say to you, I say to all: 'Watch!'" (13:36-37). Here Jesus comes back to his disciples three times and finds them asleep.

Jesus' announcement that "the son of man is to be handed over to sinners" (14:41b) picks up the theme of being "handed over." It is full of irony in view of the fact that throughout the Gospel Mark has shown Jesus reaching out to sinners.

The phrase translated above as "Get up!" (14:42) is literally "You are raised up!"* It is again ironic. By means of it, Mark indicates the distance between what the disciples ought to be and what in fact they are.

14:43-52 Betrayal by Judas. The betrayal by Judas follows upon the more subtle betrayals by the three key disciples. It is signaled by Mark's word for moral urgency, "straightway"* (omitted in the translation given here for 14:43). Judas comes as the agent of the Temple authorities—"the chief priests, the scribes, and the elders" (14:43). The crowd that accompanies him is the reverse of "the crowd" we have seen earlier that follows after Jesus. The "sign" that Judas has arranged with them (14:44) is doubly ironic. It is ironic because of the earlier episode where the Pharisees sought "a sign from heaven" (8:11). It is ironic because the sign of betrayal is a kiss (14:44).

Mark's irony continues as he says that Judas approached Jesus "straightway" (again translated as "immediately" above) and addressed him by the honorific "Rabbi" before he kissed him (14:45).

When Mark goes on to say, "they laid hands on him and arrested him" (14:46), the reader hears an ironic echo of Jesus' "laying his hands" on the sick to cure them (6:5).

When Mark shows Jesus asking, "Have you come out as against a robber?" (14:48), the reader hears an ironic echo of Jeremiah's sermon that reproaches the Temple authorities for turning the Temple into "a den of thieves" (11:17).

The reference to the fulfillment of the Scriptures (14:49) should be understood in terms of the passage from Zechariah quoted earlier in this chapter (14:27):

> [I will] strike the shepherd,
>   that the sheep may be dispersed.

Mark shows its fulfillment here by the terse statement "And they all left him and fled" (14:50).

The episode concludes with Mark's description of a young man who started to follow Jesus until the crowd seized hold of him; then he left behind the linen cloth on his body "and ran off naked" (14:51-52). The incident dramatizes the kind of situation warned about earlier in 13:14-16: "When you see the desolating abomination . . . a person in a field must not return to get his cloak." By this dramatic image, Mark suggests that the "tribulation" warned about in chapter 13 has begun.

Mark 14

Summary of the passion narrative, Part I (14:1-52)

Part I of the passion narrative interweaves two contrasting themes, one of which leads to death and the other to life. The episodes of the chapter show preparations being made for both.

The negative theme, that of betrayal, appears to dominate. The chapter opens with chief priests and scribes plotting to kill Jesus, and it concludes with his arrest in the garden. In the middle verses, Mark shows Judas joining the conspiracy to kill Jesus. Mark's account of the Last Supper is framed by Jesus' predictions of the betrayals by Judas and Peter. The scene in the garden reverses all the elements of the Transfiguration: Jesus "falls to the ground," while the three key disciples—Peter, James, and John—fail to "watch" with him. After Jesus' arrest, all his disciples desert him. From the point of view of plot, the preparation for Jesus' death appears to be advancing inevitably.

Yet, interwoven into this death-leading plot are events that suggest Jesus' continued life in the Eucharist. First, Mark tells us of an anonymous woman who anoints Jesus for his death. Mark describes her gestures in such a way that they anticipate the Eucharist. The Eucharist is further symbolized by the pairing of this anonymous woman with her alabaster vase of ointment and the anonymous man with his earthenware jar of water. The woman "shatters" the vase and "pours out" the precious ointment. Her extravagant gestures prepare for Jesus' extravagant gestures of breaking and pouring out. The anonymous man with his earthen vessel leads Jesus' disciples to a large room already prepared to receive them. Together, they suggest the early eucharistic communities meeting in house churches and reliving Jesus' gestures "in remembrance" of him.

These episodes introduce the description of the Passover meal in which Jesus speaks of the bread as his body and the wine as his blood. In its introductory blessings and its final hymn, it is a traditional Passover meal, celebrating God's act of freeing his people from slavery. In the midst of this traditional framework, Jesus speaks of his body as the bread to be broken and of the wine as his blood to be "shed for many." In this way he links his blood to the saving blood of the covenant and to the atoning blood of Isaiah's Suffering Servant. He reverses the effect of the vineyard parable by predicting a future day when the vineyard's fruit will again be accessible and God's kingdom will prevail. His words imply the paradox of a death that will be life-giving. After the supper, even while he is predicting the scattering of his disciples, he speaks of his life beyond death.

In Mark's telling of it, Part I of the passion narrative presents episodes and scriptural echoes that prepare simultaneously for Jesus' death and for his new life. The plot seems to be moving inevitably toward his death, but the framework of Passover freedom, together with hints of the kingdom to come, life beyond death in Galilee, and a eucharistic community holding him "in remembrance," points to a dramatic irony in which what looks like the end may in fact be a new beginning.

THE PASSION NARRATIVE, PART II: THE IDENTITY OF JESUS ON TRIAL
Mark 14:53–15:15

14:53-65 Jesus before the high priest

As we read this account, it is important to remember the place of the high priest in Judaism at the time of Jesus. As we explained earlier, the high priest at this time was appointed by the Romans and did not represent the religious leadership of the Jews. The "chief priests and the elders and the scribes" who accompany the high priest here (14:53) should also be understood as part of a group that were collaborating with Rome. Their plot to kill Jesus, therefore, together with their questions and their response to him, must be seen in this context. (Mark has earlier shown Jesus' total agreement with a different sort of scribe in 12:28-34.)

Mark establishes the injustice of the trial by noting that from the outset "the chief priests and the entire Sanhedrin kept trying to obtain testimony against Jesus in order to put him to death, but they found none" (14:55). Mark notes that not having found any valid evidence against Jesus, they offered "false witness" (14:56a). This testimony is further invalidated by the fact that the witnesses did not agree (14:56b, 59). (Having at least two witnesses who agree is a requirement of Deuteronomy 19:15.) The false witness that they offer has to do with the Temple: "We heard him say, 'I will destroy this Temple made with hands and within three days I will build another not made with hands'" (14:58). Mark has earlier given the reader an account of what Jesus said about the Temple (ch. 13), so the reader can judge how false this statement is.

Of course, the reader familiar with the interpretation given in John—"But he was speaking about the Temple of his body" (John 2:21)—may read this false accusation as containing an ironic truth, but within the framework of Mark's Gospel, Jesus has spoken only of the Temple being destroyed (13:2). Yet the reader who knows the end of the story may be haunted anyway by the ironic mixture here of uncanny truth with deliberate falsehood.

The questions of the high priest also have ironic elements. When the high priest asks, "Are you the Anointed One [the Messiah], the son of the Blessed

Mark 14

One?" (14:61), he is asking the key questions of Mark's narrative about Jesus' identity. Mark has earlier shown Jesus reproving Peter for identifying him as a triumphant, non-suffering messiah (8:32). Mark has just shown Jesus becoming "the Anointed One" in the context of death (14:8). He has also just shown that for Jesus, the implication of being "the son of the Blessed One" is acceptance of the Father's will, even to the point of death (14:36).

Jesus' response here, however, does not stress his death but his glory. Mark shows him quoting Daniel 7:13 when he describes himself as "son of man . . . coming with the clouds of heaven." In Daniel's context, the phrase describes an angelic figure who comes in human form ("One *like* a son of man") and who represents the people of God in contrast to worldly kingdoms, described as beasts. We have noted before that Mark shows Jesus applying this phrase to himself as a way of indicating that he represents all humanity. Mark uses the phrase to suggest that Jesus is a second Adam, giving all of us a second chance.

Mark shows Jesus adding to that reference the image of himself "seated at the right hand of the Power" (14:62). The image of someone seated "at the right hand" of God comes from the first verse of Psalm 110, where God is reassuring his anointed king that he will protect him from his enemies:

> The LORD says to my lord:
>   "Take your throne at my right hand,
>   while I make your enemies your footstool."

In chapter 12, Mark has shown Jesus quoting this psalm in order to raise questions about the nature of the Messiah or Anointed One (12:35-39). Here Mark shows Jesus implicitly identifying himself with this figure. Yet Mark has also shown, through Jesus' rebuke of Peter (8:33), that Jesus defines "messiah" differently from those who associate the term with triumphant power in this world.

Mark shows the high priest responding in a way that reveals he does not share Jesus' understanding of the terms "messiah" or "son of the Blessed One." The high priest responds by tearing his garments and calling Jesus' reply a "blasphemy" (14:64). The high priest implies that it is blasphemous to refer to oneself by either of these terms. But in Jewish law, that was not the case. "Blasphemy" is defined in Leviticus as "cursing" God (Lev 24:15-16), not anything else. Being called "messiah" means being called the one anointed to do God's work; it is hardly a term hostile to God. And being "son of God" was a claim that any pious Jew might make. By this reply, Mark shows the high priest to be either ignorant of Jewish law and custom or indifferent to it. Mark is thus dramatizing the fact that the high priest of that time was not a religious leader but a worldly one. In league with Rome, he did not know or care about Jewish piety.

In addition, Mark constructs the scene of Jesus' trial by interweaving echoes of Scripture that reveal how much it is the pattern for God's just one to be misunderstood and condemned by the powers of the world. First of all, Mark seems to be reenacting the scene in the Wisdom of Solomon where "the wicked" set out to "beset the just one" (Wis 2:12) because "he professes to have knowledge of God and styles himself a child of the LORD" (Wis 2:13) and "boasts that God is his Father" (Wis 2:16b). The "wicked" in the Wisdom of Solomon also go on to condemn the just man "to a shameful death" (Wis 2:20).

Second, by saying that "Some began to spit on him" and "struck him" (14:65), Mark seems also to be summoning up the third song of Isaiah's "Suffering Servant" figure:

> I gave my back to those who beat me,
>   my cheeks to those who plucked my beard;
> My face I did not shield
>   from buffets and spitting (Isa 50:6).

Like "the just one" of the Wisdom of Solomon, the Suffering Servant is mocked and condemned by the obtuse powers of the world, who do not understand his identity as God's servant. By echoing both those works, Mark is providing an interpretive framework for understanding the condemnation and death of Jesus.

14:66-72 Peter denies knowing Jesus

Mark shows the two trials to be about Jesus' identity. He bridges these two trials with the episode in which Jesus' key disciple denies knowing who Jesus is. Peter's presence "in the courtyard" (14:66) picks up an earlier point in Mark's narrative (14:54). The structure is the typical Markan "sandwich" we have noted before, for example in Mark's placement of the story of John the Baptist's death (6:17-29) and in his narrative of the healing of the woman with a menstrual disorder (5:25-34). In each instance, the middle section sheds light on the parts it separates. So here the episode of Peter's denial of Jesus illuminates the trials that center on Jesus' identity.

Both the high priest and Pilate condemn Jesus by misrepresenting his identity as one that claims power. They both function as false witnesses to Jesus. At the other extreme, Mark shows Peter refusing to witness at all.

Ironically, one of the high priest's maids bears witness to Peter's identity ("You too were with the Nazarene, Jesus," 14:67b). This identification of Peter is repeated two more times (14:69-70). Mark creates a triad of true identifications of Peter that balance the triad, under Pilate, of false identifications of Jesus. Peter's denials are incrementally more vehement. The narrative reaches its climax when the cock crows a second time (14:72) and Peter remembers the prediction of Jesus, "Amen, I say to you, this very night before the cock crows twice, you will deny me three times" (14:30). The second cockcrow is prefaced by the key word "straightway"* (translated above as "immediately"). Mark notes that upon hearing it, Peter "broke down and wept" (14:72b). Mark is dramatizing the fact that in denying Jesus, Peter has been denying himself. In Mark's account, Peter's identity is bound to the identity of Jesus. Ironically, too, Peter's denial of himself is not the kind of self-denial that Jesus asked of his followers (8:34). Rather, Mark shows it is the opposite: Peter denies knowing Jesus because he is trying to save himself from a similar fate. Mark's narrative dramatizes the truth of Jesus' wisdom: "Whoever wishes to save his life will lose it" (8:35). The other side of that truth remains for now only in the reader's mind.

15:1-15 Jesus before Pilate

As we have seen, Mark shows the high priest falsely accusing Jesus of blasphemy. His accusation serves to reveal both his ignorance of Jewish religious law and his underlying fear of Jesus' power. Mark shows that he does not understand the terms "messiah" and "son of the Blessed" in a spiritual sense but sees them as a threat to his worldly power. Mark emphasizes the concern of the high priest for worldly power by structuring Jesus' trial before Pilate as a parallel to it. In both instances, Mark shows that the one interrogating Jesus is not interested in what Jesus has done but in who he is and how his identity may threaten their own.

Mark shows Pilate's main concern to be whether Jesus considers himself "the king of the Jews." In Mark's account, Pilate repeats this phrase three times, like a refrain. The first time, Pilate asks the question directly of Jesus (15:2). The second time, he uses the term in a question to the crowd: "Do you want me to release to you the king of the Jews?" (15:9). The third time, Pilate uses it to address the crowd about Jesus' fate: "Then what [do you want] me to do with [the man you call] the king of the Jews?" (15:12).

To grasp the full effect of this refrain, it is helpful for the modern reader to know that the term was in fact a title that the Romans applied to their designated tetrarchs. At the time of Jesus, Herod Antipas was tetrarch of Galilee, while Judea was directly under the administration of Roman procurators like Pilate. Needless to say, ordinary Jews of the time did not like the idea of a Roman appointee being called their "king." Pilate's reference to Jesus by this term was therefore politically charged. By showing Pilate's repeated use of it, Mark indicates that Pilate fired up the crowd to think that Jesus either was a tool of Rome or had claimed such an alliance for himself. While on the surface Mark's narrative seems to suggest that Pilate turned over Jesus' fate to the Jewish crowd, at a more subtle level Mark is showing how Pilate incited the crowd to anger.

Just as Mark shows the high priest trying to turn the religious community against Jesus on the false claim that he had committed some kind of blasphemy, so he shows Pilate trying to turn the crowds against Jesus on the false claim that he had taken to himself a title of Roman power.

The scene has other ironic details worth noting. In the opening verse, Mark says that "the chief priests with the elders and the scribes" held a council about Jesus *"straightway"** (a word omitted in the translation above). Mark repeats the key word of the theme of betrayal by saying they *"handed him over* to Pilate" (15:1b, emphasis added). The word for "release," which Mark has associated before with Jesus' acts of freeing people from physical ailments or from sin, appears here in the question of Pilate: ""Do you want me to release to you the king of the Jews?" (15:9). This question is the middle one of the triad of references to Jesus as "the king of the Jews," thus stressing its irony.

Summary of the passion narrative, Part II (14:53–15:15)

Part II of Mark's passion narrative focuses on the identity of Jesus. There are two balancing scenes in which the identity of Jesus is put on trial. Each trial is characterized by a falsification of who Jesus is; in each case, Jesus is condemned on false grounds. In the trial before the high priest, Jesus is condemned as a blasphemer, although he has said nothing that would constitute blasphemy according to Jewish law. In the trial before Pilate, Jesus is condemned as a would-be "king of the Jews," although he had never claimed that Roman title or sought that Roman power.

In between these matching trials and false witnesses, Mark gives an account of Peter's refusal to witness to Jesus at all. As Mark tells the story, Peter's denial of Jesus is also a denial of himself.

In Mark's narrative, the high priest, Pilate, and Peter are alike in trying to save themselves. As a consequence, each one betrays himself: the high priest betrays that he is not truly a religious leader of the Jews; Pilate betrays that he is not truly an administrator of justice; Peter betrays that he is not truly a disciple of Jesus. Their false witness to Jesus is pivotal to their own identities.

THE PASSION NARRATIVE, PART III: THE DEATH OF JESUS

Mark 15:6-47

15:6 The death sentence

We have already suggested that Mark shows Pilate inciting the crowd by referring to Jesus repeatedly as "the king of the Jews" (15:2, 9, 12). But in fact, Mark is more precise than that. He indicates that Pilate used that title to arouse the chief priests, because "he knew that it was out of envy that the chief priests had handed him over" (15:10). After that, Mark says, "the chief priests stirred up the crowd to have him release Barabbas for them instead" (15:11).

The release of Barabbas is further Markan irony. It is ironic from the point of view of the Roman trial because Barabbas, Mark tells us, is a known insurgent against Rome and a murderer as well (15:7). And it is ironic from the point of view of the Jewish trial because the name Barabbas means in Hebrew "son of the Father." Jesus, who has no plans to strike against Rome, is put to death, while a convicted rebel against Rome is released. Jesus is condemned for calling himself "son of the Blessed," while one whose very name means the same thing is released.

The word "released" is also used by Mark as an ironic refrain, being repeated three times in this short episode (15:9, 11, 15). The theme that Mark has repeatedly associated with Jesus' acts of forgiveness and healing is repeatedly used here in connection with Jesus' sentence of death.

Mark tells the story of the death sentence in such a way that everyone is implicated: the crowd that shouts "Crucify him" (15:13-14); the chief priests, who have stirred them up to this (15:11); and Pilate, who, "wishing to satisfy the crowd" (15:15), handed Jesus over to be crucified. Although Mark reports the involvement of the crowd, he shapes the narrative to place the greatest blame on the chief priests and Pilate—that is, the agents of Rome. In particular, he indicates the moral weakness of Pilate by showing that he knows Jesus is innocent (15:14) and nonetheless condemns him, just "to satisfy the crowd" (15:15).

15:16-20 The mockery of Jesus

In this description of the Roman soldiers' mockery of Jesus, Mark dramatizes the irony of calling Jesus "king of the Jews" (15:18). He expands upon the image of Isaiah's "Suffering Servant," to which he had alluded earlier (14:64):

Mark 15

> I gave my back to those who beat me,
>> my cheeks to those who plucked my beard;
> My face I did not shield
>> from buffets and spitting (Isa 50:6).

Here the "buffets and spitting" accompany the elaborate mockery of the purple cloak and crown of thorns (15:17), the mocking salutation (15:18), and posture of kneeling (15:19).

The whole scene also expands upon the brief suggestion in the Wisdom of Solomon of "the wicked" torturing "the just one":

> With revilement and torture let us put him to the test
>> that we may have proof of his gentleness
>> and try his patience.
> Let us condemn him to a shameful death;
>> for according to his own words, God will
>>> take care of him (Wis 2:19-20).

The mock homage also ironically recalls three earlier instances in Mark's Gospel where some knelt in all seriousness before Jesus: the leper seeking to be healed (1:40); the demons who recognized him as "son of God" (3:11); and the woman who touched him and was overwhelmed by her cure (5:33).

15:21 Simon forced to take up the cross

The reappearance of the name "Simon" here has symbolic significance. Mark has just shown us Simon Peter denying Jesus while refusing to "deny himself and take up his cross." (The language of denial here explicitly repeats the language of 8:34.) Like Simon the leper, this Simon also functions as his alter ego, forced into doing what Simon Peter the disciple has not been able to do.

The other names in this brief incident are significant as well. "Simon" was a Jewish name, and Cyrene was apparently a Greek colony where many Jews had settled. The names "Alexander" and "Rufus" are, respectively, Greek and Roman. Through these names, Mark suggests how Jesus' followers were eventually to include the Greek and the Roman world.

15:22-32 Crucifixion

Mark translates the name "Golgotha" as "Place of the Skull." His Jewish audience would have known the legend that it was the burial place of Adam's skull. Thus even as he shows Jesus being led to his death, Mark

Mark 15

calls attention to the fact that Jesus is a second Adam. Mark thus suggests the cosmic irony of his death.

The "wine drugged with myrrh" (15:23) echoes the distress expressed by the psalmist, who says "I have become an outcast to my kin" because "zeal for your house consumes me" (Ps 69:9-10). In his anguish, he cries out:

> Insult has broken my heart, and I am weak.
> I looked for compassion, but there was none,
> for comforters, but found none.
> Instead, they put gall in my food;
> for my thirst they gave me vinegar (Ps 69:21-22).

Similarly, the detail about the soldiers' dividing Jesus' clothes (15:24) recalls the agony of the innocent one in Psalm 22:

> They stare at me and gloat;
> they divide my garments among them;
> for my clothing they cast lots (Ps 22:18b-19).

The passers-by who shake their heads at Jesus (15:29), along with their mocking taunts to "save yourself" (15:30), also recall Psalm 22:

> All who see me mock me;
> they curl their lips and jeer;
> they shake their heads at me (Ps 22:8).

The gesture of head-wagging also echoes the mockery of Jerusalem in the Book of Lamentations:

> All who pass by
> clap their hands at you;
> They hiss and wag their heads (Lam 2:15).

Mark is clearly summoning up a long biblical tradition in which the servants of God are mocked. He interweaves scriptural references into his narrative as a way of communicating the meaning of Jesus' death.

In this context, it is significant that Mark speaks of the title "the king of the Jews" as an "inscription" on Jesus' cross (15:26). It was common Jewish idiom to speak of Scripture as "what is written" or "what is inscribed." Mark thus suggests that the mockery of Jesus is, in its own right, a "Scripture." He sees Jesus' way of the cross as part of the long tradition of righteous prophets and psalmists who suffered for their zeal for God.

When Mark notes that "With him they crucified two revolutionaries, one on his right and one on his left" (15:27), his phrasing reminds the reader that James and John had once asked to be in those positions (10:37). They thought that being on Jesus' right and left would be places of glory. Mark uses the same phrasing here to reveal to his audience the irony of their request. He shows that unwittingly they had asked to be placed in the tradition of suffering servants.

Mark shows Jesus being taunted by everyone present: the passers-by (15:30), the chief priests (15:31), and even those crucified with him (15:32). Mark shapes their taunts to underscore the irony of Jesus' plight. The passers-by repeat the earlier false testimony (14:57-58) that Jesus said he "would destroy the Temple and rebuild it in three days" (15:29). Both they and the chief priests ironically suggest that he should "save" himself by "coming down from the cross" (15:30, 32). Mark chooses language that reminds his audience that Jesus has said the opposite: "Whoever wishes to come after me must deny himself, take up his cross, and follow me. For whoever wishes to save his life will lose it, but whoever loses his life for my sake and that of the gospel will save it" (8:34-35). The ultimate irony of Mark's narrative lies in the way he shows that in spite of the appearances of death and defeat, Jesus is accomplishing what he set out to do.

15:33-40 Death

Mark's account of Jesus' death gives details that suggest Creation in the process of being reversed. Light is created at the beginning of Genesis 1; Jesus' death brings darkness (15:33). The loss of light also echoes Jesus' description of the great tribulation, when "the sun will be darkened" (13:24).

Mark next says that Jesus cried out to God (15:34). Significantly, Mark uses Aramaic for the fourth time in the Gospel. The other three times are the raising up of the little girl from death (5:41), the healing of the deaf-mute (7:34), and Jesus' anguished cry to his Father in Gethsemane (14:36)—all key turning points in Mark's Gospel. The words here constitute the opening of Psalm 22, and their significance increases if one knows the whole psalm. It is a psalm in which the speaker begins in despair and moves to an encounter with death, but then is rescued by God, and concludes with thanksgiving and praise. If one knows the whole structure, then the opening verse recalls not only the speaker's initial agony but also his eventual rescue and restoration.

Mark goes on to say that the bystanders are confused by the Aramaic word for "my God" *(Eloi)* and think that Jesus is calling Elijah (15:35). It is worth noting that this is the third time the bystanders have had a place in Mark's account. Each reference indicates a different attitude toward Jesus. The first reference is to Simon of Cyrene, who is forced to help carry the cross (15:21). The second is to the bystanders who revile and taunt Jesus (15:29). In this third reference, the bystanders are simply confused. Their confusion of the word for God with that for Elijah recalls earlier places in Mark's narrative where people confused Jesus' identity with that of Elijah (6:15; 8:28). By repeating the confusion here, Mark suggests that confusion about Jesus' identity remained right up to the end. The episode also serves to clarify the kinship and distinction between Jesus and Elijah. Mark stresses that while Jesus may be like Elijah in many ways, they are not the same.

The next verse repeats the detail, already given in verse 23, of the sour wine offered to Jesus to drink. It is a detail that echoes, as we have noted before, the plight of God's servant in Psalm 69:22. Here this detail is combined with a taunt: "Wait, let us see if Elijah comes to take him down" (15:36). Again the mockery echoes that of the just one in the Wisdom of Solomon:

> Let us see whether his words be true;
>   let us find out what will happen to him.
> For if the just one be the son of God, he will defend him
>   and deliver him from the hand of his foes (Wis 2:17-18).

The precise words that Mark uses to describe the moment of Jesus' death are significant: "Then Jesus, releasing a loud voice, breathed out"* (15:37). This literal translation is not as idiomatic as the conventional one, but it serves to highlight Mark's ultimate use of the theme of *release*. When Jesus cures Simon's mother-in-law, Mark says that "the fever *released** her" (1:31b). When Jesus forgives the paralytic, he says, "Your sins are *released*" (2:5). When Jesus heals the deaf-mute, he says in Aramaic, "Be *released*!" (7:34). And we have just seen how Mark shows Pilate ironically releasing a murderous rebel, but not Jesus, from death (15:6, 9, 15). So it is dramatically effective that Mark uses the verb again here, suggesting that Jesus' final breath is freeing.

The splitting of the sanctuary veil (15:38) must be seen in this context. (The translation "torn" is misleading.) The word that Mark uses for "split"* here is an unusual one. He has used it once before in his Gospel, when he described the heavens opening up at the moment of Jesus' baptism (1:10). By repeating it here, Mark suggests that a similar event is taking place. In his death, Jesus is opening up the heavens.

This interpretation is strengthened by two details. First, the phrase idiomatically translated here as "top to bottom" is literally "from above to below"*—a wording suggestive of God's creation of the dome of the sky to separate the waters "above" and "below" in Genesis 1:6-8. Second, the unusual word for "split"* is also used in a significant place in the Septuagint (the Greek translation of the Hebrew Bible that the evangelists followed). It appears in a prayer of Isaiah that asks God to split the heavens and come down and take back his sanctuary from Israel's enemies who have trampled it (Isa 63:18–64:1). If we put these details together, we see that Mark's choice of wording suggests that through his death, Jesus is opening up the sacred place of God's dwelling. He is making it accessible.

By immediately following the split veil with the centurion's proclamation of faith in Jesus as "the son of God" (15:39), Mark confirms this understanding. He is suggesting that even the Roman soldier—someone disposed to pollute the Temple with false gods—has come to see the divine image in Jesus' humanity. In his death, Jesus has opened up the heavens even to the Romans.

15:40-41 The watchful women

Before he presents the passion narrative, Mark gives the last word of Jesus to his disciples as "Watch!" (13:37). Mark then shows how Jesus' disciples, particularly his three key disciples, fail to do this (14:32-42). Here Mark introduces a balancing trio of women who do what Jesus has asked. At the same time that Mark shows that all the men have fled (14:50), he also shows that there were women who did not flee but were "seeing* from a distance" (15:40). The verb that Mark uses for "seeing" here is one that implies spiritual insight. The watchful "seeing" of these women stands in contrast to the betrayal by Judas, the denial of Jesus by Peter, and the flight of the other disciples. The women are not labeled "disciples," but Mark describes them acting in the way Jesus has asked his disciples to do. Mark also tells us that they had "followed" Jesus in Galilee and "ministered to him" (15:41a). Mark names three but says there were also many others (15:41b).

The three names that Mark gives are vaguely identified. The first is Mary Magdalene, known in all the Gospels as the first witness to Jesus' resurrection, but not yet called that here. (The idea that she was a "sinful woman" is not in Mark.) The last is Salome, about whom we know nothing. We do know that "Salome" was the name of the daughter of Herodias, who danced for the head of John the Baptist, but in Mark's account of that event, her name is not given (6:17-29). Did Mark assume that his audience knew her name and intended them to infer that she reappears here transformed? The middle woman, described only as "the mother of the younger James and of Joses," is presumably (on the basis of 6:3) the mother of Jesus. It is striking that Mark does not single her out; he treats these women as a generic group. Yet Mark suggests that this generic group of women, in their "following" and "ministering" and, above all, in their watchful "seeing," act in the ways to which Jesus has called all his disciples.

15:42-47 Burial

Mark loads every detail of the burial scene with significance. First, he tells us that "it was the day of preparation, the day before the Sabbath" (15:42). This is usually understood as just a simple reporting of fact. But given Mark's tendency to emphasize symbolic detail, one might surmise that he wants his readers to consider that the burial of Jesus was "a day of preparation" for his resurrection. The "preparation" theme of chapter 14 is being brought to a climax.

Joseph of Arimathea (15:43) is another disciple hitherto unknown in the Gospel, like the anonymous woman and man at the beginning of chapter 14 (14:3-16). He, like they, appears in the narrative suddenly, just as he is needed. Strikingly, he is described as a member of the council that has just condemned Jesus. His action in asking for the body of Jesus (15:43) suggests a transformation in his understanding of Jesus, just as much as the centurion's proclamation (15:39). Together, the Roman centurion and the Jewish member of the Sanhedrin reverse the judgments of the trials against Jesus.

Mark also characterizes Joseph by saying that he was "awaiting the kingdom of God" (15:43). It is the seventh time that the phrase "kingdom of God" has appeared in Mark's Gospel. The first time is in the preaching of Jesus (1:15). The second, third, and fourth times occur in the chapter containing the seed parables (4:11, 26, 30). The fifth time is when Jesus says approvingly to the scribe, "You are not far from the kingdom of God" (12:34). The sixth time is at the Last Supper, when Jesus says he will "not drink again the fruit of the vine until the day when I drink it new in the kingdom of God" (14:25). "The kingdom of God," in other words, is an important theme throughout the Gospel. When Mark says that Joseph was "awaiting" it, he also picks up on the themes of "watching" and "preparation." Through showing his action of seeking to honor Jesus in death, Mark implies that Joseph now links Jesus with the kingdom.

Pilate's response—wanting to make sure that Jesus was really dead (15:44-45)—confirms the characterization of Pilate that Mark has already given. By means of this detail, Mark again suggests the non-spiritual level on which Pilate exists. In view of Mark's hints of resurrection to come, it is also ironic.

The linen cloth in which Joseph buries Jesus (15:46) is significant because of the way it recalls the young disciple who left his linen cloth behind when he fled the scene of Jesus' arrest (14:51). The reappearance of a "linen cloth" is suggestive of a restoration. The wrapping of Jesus here in a linen cloth reverses that moment of fear and flight. There is also an echo here of the transformed demoniac, who, after his cure by Jesus, is seen "sitting there clothed and in his right mind" (5:15). That man had "lived among the tombs" (5:5) until his encounter with Jesus changed him. The echo of his story, just as Jesus is being laid in a tomb (15:46), is thus something that gives hope.

Further hope appears in the final detail of the two Marys "watching" where Jesus was laid (15:47). Just as Mark speaks of women "watching" or "seeing"* Jesus' crucifixion, so here he describes women again "watching" where Jesus was buried. Watchful women enclose Mark's narrative of Jesus' burial. Mark says that Joseph "rolled a stone" against the "entrance" or "gate"* to the tomb (15:47). The details together recall Jesus' parable of the man who leaves home and "orders the gatekeeper to be on the watch" (13:34). The two Marys here function as gatekeepers, keeping watch for the lord's return.

Summary of the passion narrative, Part III (15:6-47)

Mark's narrative of Jesus' death is carefully crafted. First of all, Mark weaves his narrative out of echoes and patterns of the Hebrew Bible, telling Jesus' story in the light of them. Second, he picks up earlier themes within his own Gospel, repeating them and making their significance more clear. Third and most important, he constructs a structure of dramatic irony, so that what seems to be leading to Jesus' total doom is in fact moving toward his resurrection.

Mark's use of the Hebrew Bible. The details of Mark's narrative are woven out of numerous images in the Hebrew Bible of "the just one" who is persecuted by powerful and obtuse figures of the world because they do not grasp his identity as God's servant. The primary sources here are Isaiah's "Suffering Servant," sent "like a lamb to the slaughter" by the obtuse kings of the world; the "just one "in the Wisdom of Solomon put to death by "the wicked" because he "boasts that God is his Father"; and the persecuted just one in Psalm 22 who is brought to the point of death and despair before he cries out to God and is rescued. The first two sources provide some of the details for Mark's account of the trial by Pilate and the mockery of the Roman soldiers. Along with Psalm 22, they also provide background

Mark 15

for the taunts of Jesus on the cross. Psalm 69 adds the detail of the sour wine given to Jesus in his thirst. All of them offer a pattern or structure that Mark wants his readers to find relevant and illuminating. It is the pattern of God's servant, who appears by the world to be doomed but who in the end is exalted by God. It is this structure of dramatic irony that Mark adopts for his narrative.

Mark's repeating themes. Again and again Mark repeats words or images that recall an earlier place in his Gospel. In each case he uses the echo to give an extra dimension to the present scene, sometimes making it fuller and sometimes pointing up its irony.

When he describes Jesus being mocked by the Roman soldiers, for example, he shows them kneeling before Jesus (15:19). It is a detail that ironically summons up earlier moments in the Gospel when people knelt before Jesus in awe (1:40; 3:11; 5:33).

When Mark tells of someone who is forced to carry Jesus' cross, he notes that he was called "Simon," thus reminding his readers of Simon the leper, who welcomed Jesus into his home (14:3), and Simon Peter, who has just denied him (14:66-72). The echoes intensify the irony of Simon Peter's betrayal.

When Mark describes the crucifixion of Jesus, he notes that the Romans crucified two revolutionaries with him, "one on his right hand and one on his left" (15:27). By his phrasing he ironically recalls the request of James and John for just those positions (10:37).

When Mark quotes Jesus' final death cry, he notes that some thought he was calling Elijah (15:34-35), thus repeating earlier stories of how people were confused about Jesus' identity (6:15; 8:28). The repetition underscores Mark's theme of Jesus' mistaken identity.

When Mark describes Joseph of Arimathea "awaiting the kingdom of God" (15:43), he recalls six other mentions of the kingdom (1:15; 4:11, 26, 30; 12:34; 14:25). He thus hints that the kingdom may now be imminent.

When Mark speaks of Joseph wrapping Jesus in a "linen cloth" (15:46), he summons up the stories of the young man who fled (14:51) and the man who had lived "among the tombs" (5:5), whom Jesus transformed (5:15). The echoes provide hope for Jesus' own restoration and transformation.

When Mark uses the verb "release"* to describe Jesus' death (15:37), he chooses a word that he has associated again and again with Jesus' acts of freeing people from sin and from disease (1:31; 2:5; 7:34). He has also placed it as an ironic refrain in Pilate's mouth, in the context of whether or not he should set Jesus free (15:6, 9, 15). By using it as a description of Jesus' last breath, Mark signals that Jesus' death is a freeing act.

Similarly, by using the same words for "splitting open"* the sanctuary veil (15:38) that he has used to describe the "splitting open" of the heavens at Jesus' baptism (1:10), Mark suggests that Jesus' death is not an end but a beginning.

Mark's dramatic irony. Mark tells the story of Jesus' death and burial in such a way that he alerts the reader to the fact that the plot is really moving in the opposite direction than it appears. He does this both by his echoes of the patterns in the Hebrew Bible and by his use of repeating themes.

Mark also hints at a new beginning by the way he frames the narrative of Jesus' burial with descriptions of women who follow Jesus' instruction to "watch." They remind his readers of Jesus' story of the lord who returns to his house.

Summary of the passion narrative, Parts I, II, and III (14:1–15:47)

Part I of Mark's passion narrative focuses on preparations of various kinds. They are ambiguously for both death and life. Part II focuses on Jesus' identity and how he is sentenced because he is mistakenly identified in both his trials. Part III focuses on the dramatic irony of a plot that may seem to be leading to death but is in fact leading to new life.

A NEW BEGINNING:
THE RESURRECTION OF JESUS AND THE REVELATION OF WISDOM
Mark 16:1-8

16:1 The women

The same three women who watched Jesus' death (15:40) reappear. Like the anonymous woman at the beginning of chapter 14, they come to anoint the body of Jesus. Mark has shaped his narrative to show that at either end of the passion narrative, there are women coming to anoint Jesus. In Mark's account, their actions claim Jesus as "messiah"—that is, as God's anointed.

16:1-2 The time

Mark says the women came "when the Sabbath was over." In Jewish liturgy, a distinction is made between Sabbath time and "ordinary time." The Sabbath is a time set aside to celebrate God and to reflect his kingdom. The other days are time to journey towards this perfect state of being. The Sabbath liturgy concludes with spices to "hallow" and "sweeten" the ordinary days of the week. Mark may have had this concluding prayer in mind when he describes the women bringing spices at the end of the Sabbath. On the literal level, the spices are for burial; on the symbolic level, they may also signify the transition to "ordinary time."

Mark 16

Mark also says they came "very early, when the sun had risen, on the first day of the week." Each phrase emphasizes, in a different way, a new beginning.

16:3-4 The stone

The "stone" at "the entrance to the tomb" suggests the sealing off of death from life. When the women say to one another, "Who will roll back the stone for us?" Mark shows their willingness to accept their vulnerability along with their trust that God will provide.

16:5 The young man

The young man "clothed in a white robe" is an angelic figure. The whiteness of his clothing summons to mind the transfiguration of Jesus (9:3), an event that Mark clearly constructed as a foreshadowing of Jesus' resurrection. He also resembles the young man who fled the garden when Jesus was arrested, leaving his linen cloth behind him. The fact that this young man is seen "sitting" also recalls the transformed demoniac, whom the townsfolk found "sitting there clothed and in his right mind" (5:35). Mark's detail about his being "on the right side" further recalls Jesus' proclamation to the high priest that he would "see the son of man seated at the right hand of the Power" (14:62). By means of all these echoes, Mark suggests that this young man represents a transformed life.

16:6 The young man's news

The words that Mark quotes the young man as saying form the heart of his Gospel: "You seek Jesus of Nazareth, the crucified. He has been raised; he is not here." The key words are "crucified" and "raised." Throughout his Gospel, Mark has stressed the necessary connection between Jesus and the cross, and between Jesus and resurrection. In Mark's narrative, it is the paradoxical union of those two seemingly contradictory elements that form his identity. Mark shows that both the high priest and Pilate mistake his being called "messiah" as a sign that he sought power. Mark also shows that both mistook his death as the ending of his power. The phrasing here suggests a paradoxical balance: Jesus is both the suffering, crucified one and the one whom God's power has raised up.

16:7a The commissioning of the women

Mark says that the young man told the women to "go forth."* (The verb is stronger than merely "go.") Mark has shown the women acting all along as disciples. By this act of commissioning, Mark suggests that the women

Mark 16

are also sent forth as apostles. They are, moreover, sent forth to the male disciples, even to the head disciple, Peter. The women are sent forth to witness to the men.

What are the implications of the role of men and women in Mark's Gospel? Many readers have observed that Mark shows Jesus' male disciples to be obtuse and foolish. Few seem to have noticed that Mark simultaneously shows that Jesus has female disciples who are insightful and wise. If the Gospel is read on a literal, historical level, it is difficult to know what to make of this. But if the Gospel is read on a symbolic level and in the light of the Wisdom traditions, Mark's purpose becomes clear. We have suggested before the extent to which Mark presents Jesus as God's Wisdom made flesh. In the light of the Wisdom writings, Mark characterizes Jesus as a nurturing, healing, compassionate, and maternal figure, always intent on giving and restoring life. Following the same traditions, Mark sets up a typical contrast in his Gospel between the wise and the foolish. There is a creative logic in his choosing women to be like Woman Wisdom, while their male counterparts act out the part of the foolish. Mark also makes the women's raised status and new ministry a symbol of the new creation that Jesus brings into being.

16:7b The message

Mark indicates that the message the women are sent forth to repeat is not about Jesus' glory but about his ministry. It repeats exactly what Mark has shown Jesus saying on the eve of his crucifixion: "But after I have been raised up, I shall go before you to Galilee" (14:28). It confirms his ongoing life: "there you will see him, as he told you." It sends the disciples back to where the Gospel first began. It suggests a new beginning.

16:8 The revelation to the women

The translation given above is conventional, but unfortunately it is badly misleading. The word translated "bewilderment" is *ekstasis* in Greek. Even someone who has never read Greek can see that its English counterpart is "ecstasy."*

The word "ecstasy" literally means "out of [a normal] state [of being]." In the Septuagint (the Greek translation of the Hebrew Bible that the evangelists followed), the word appears at two key moments in the book of Genesis. When God casts Adam into a "deep sleep" or "trance" while he is creating both man and woman (2:21), the word for "trance" is *ekstasis*. Similarly, when God casts Abraham into a "deep sleep" or "trance" while he is making the covenant with him (Gen 15:12), the word for "trance" is *ekstasis*. In both instances, the word conveys the action of God creating something new. It also implies a human being undergoing some shock of transition, a human being experiencing a transformation of consciousness.

Mark uses the word "ecstasy" more than once in his Gospel. When he wants to describe the state of the crowd that witnessed the rising up of the paralytic, he says, "They were all ecstatic and glorified God, saying, 'We have never seen anything like this'" (2:12b). When he wants to describe the changed condition of those who have witnessed Jesus' raising up of Jairus's daughter, he says that "They were out of their minds with ecstasy*" (5:42).

Mark also uses a related word to describe Jesus himself. When he wants to describe how "those close to" Jesus thought he was crazy for mingling so closely with the crowds, he says that they thought he was "out of [his] mind" (3:21).

All these earlier uses of the word support its meaning here. The women are, like Jesus, out of their minds at what they have learned from the angel. And like those who witnessed a paralytic rise up from his mat and a child brought back to life, they are in a state of ecstasy at the realization of Jesus' resurrection. The word conveys that they are undergoing some shock of transition. They are experiencing a transformation of consciousness.

It is a sign of this transformed consciousness that "they went out and fled from the tomb." The foolish (male) disciples fled from Jesus. The wise women follow the example of Jesus and flee from the tomb.

"They said nothing to anyone" because they were in a "trance"—like Adam, like Abraham. By his choice of words, Mark suggests that they were in a state of shock, undergoing a transforming experience. Their silence is more, not less, than words.

They are not silent because "they were afraid." This translation is again conventional but unfortunate. Again, Mark has used the word given here twice before in his Gospel—first, to describe the disciples' reaction to Jesus' stilling the storm (4:41), and second, to describe their response to the transfiguration of Jesus (9:6). The New American Bible (which is the translation given above) translates the first instance as "filled with great awe" and the second as "terrified." There is no justification for "terrified" because the context is Peter's exclamation that "It is good that we are here!" (9:5). Both contexts suggest the meaning of awe. The context here of "ecstasy" also supports a translation of "awe."

If we put all these pieces together, we would translate Mark's ending as follows:

And going out, they fled the tomb, for trembling and ecstasy* possessed them, and they said nothing to anyone because they were filled with awe.*

Such a translation would be a fitting conclusion to a Gospel that presents Jesus as Wisdom and the women as faithful disciples of Wisdom/Jesus. Throughout his Gospel, Mark has shown that the women disciples of Jesus not only follow after him but follow his example in serving others. Mark has also shown them to be "watchful," which is the way of Wisdom. He thus prepares his readers for an ending in which they begin to comprehend the revelation that Jesus/Wisdom cannot die but is still alive and in their midst. By showing them overcome by awe, Mark is dramatizing the theme of all the Wisdom writings that "Fear of the LORD is the beginning of Wisdom" (Prov 1:7; 9:10; Sir 1:12, 16; Ps 111:10). That fear is not fright but overwhelmed reverence before the divine mystery.

SUMMARY OF THE DESIGN OF MARK'S GOSPEL

Doublets

We suggested earlier that the two-stage healing of the blind man in 8:22-26 is a key to the theological design of Mark's Gospel. That is to say, Mark seems to have designed his Gospel in two parts, with the Transfiguration in the middle. In the first part (chs. 1–8), the reader is like the blind man who at first only sees "people looking like trees" (8:24). In the second part (chs. 9–16), Mark repeats many of the same images, events, and themes, and the reader now sees them more plainly.

The Transfiguration is pivotal because it reveals Jesus' inner glory. We have noted before that Peter's desire to "make three tents" or "booths"* (9:5) suggests the feast of Booths or Succoth, a harvest feast celebrating the end time of God's kingdom. The Markan text says that Jesus "metamorphosed"* before his disciples (9:2), that is, he changed form entirely. Jesus' "dazzling white" garments (9:3) suggest his relationship to other significant figures (for example, Moses and Elijah) who, in popular non-biblical writing of the time, are imagined ascending to the heavens clothed like angels. In this literary imagination, resurrection and ascension are similar and intertwined events. Thus to a Jewish audience of the time, this scene of Jesus' total transformation and gleaming garments in an end-time setting would have signified his ascension or resurrection from death to a heavenly state. Mark has not placed the scene of Jesus' resurrection at the end of his Gospel but here in the middle, where it illuminates both halves of his Gospel.

Mark 16

The most crucial difference between the two halves lies in Mark's presentation of the identity of Jesus. In the first part, Jesus reflects God's power in miracles of exorcism and healing, stilling the sea and walking on water, and the multiplication of bread. In the second part, Jesus appears vulnerable to the various plottings against him, and he speaks of dispossession, poverty, and death. In the first part, Jesus calls his disciples to be "fishers" on a grand scale (1:17), to preach and cast out demons (3:14-15; 6:12-13a), and to cure the sick (6:13b). But his instructions to them begin to shift radically at the end of chapter 8 when he says, "Whoever wishes to come after me must deny himself, take up his cross, and follow me" (8:34).

The second part of Mark's Gospel leads inexorably to Jesus' taking up his own cross. And Mark's Gospel is often referred to as the one in which "the cross" is key. But by placing the Transfiguration at the very center of his narrative, Mark signals that the cross is only one part of the story. The whole story involves *cross plus Transfiguration*. In fact, Mark shows that Jesus, in his key statements about the cross, indicates that the cross is *the way* to Transfiguration: "For whoever wishes to save his life will lose it, but whoever loses his life for my sake and that of the gospel will save it" (8:35). The cross is not about suffering in itself or suffering for its own sake. The cross symbolizes how God will transform our suffering. God's creative power to transform or transfigure us from suffering humanity into persons of radiant joy is the key to Mark's theology.

In the first part of his Gospel, Mark shows Jesus reaching out to the most alienated and suffering members of his community—those known to be sinners; those possessed by unclean spirits that deprive them of God's holy spirit; those alienated by leprosy or withered limbs; those who are paralyzed; and women of all kinds and ages who, for various reasons, are kept on the fringes of worship. He reaches out in order to "raise them up," to transform their lives. In the second part of his Gospel, Mark shows Jesus himself to be the one who is alienated and suffering, and then Mark tells us Jesus is also "raised up," transfigured (as he has already shown us) by the will of God.

In the first part of his Gospel, Mark shows Jesus as a teacher of Wisdom, speaking in aphorisms and parables or riddles. Yet at the end of chapter 4, as we have seen, Mark indicates that Jesus himself is a living parable or riddle, pointing to what God is like. In the second part of his Gospel, Mark develops this idea, showing that Jesus in suffering, even more than in power, reveals what God is like. Mark indicates this through the image of the split veil of the sanctuary (15:38), suggesting that Jesus, in his dying, has opened up access to God's dwelling. He confirms it in the cry of the centurion, "Truly this was the son of God" (15:39). In that cry Mark suggests how, in the dying Jesus, even a Roman soldier came to perceive God's image. Through that perception, Mark challenges his readers to understand how God is reflected even in suffering and dying humanity. Jesus as "son of man" represents us all; Jesus as "son of God" represents us all as made in God's image.

There is a mystery here not easily articulated. The first part of Mark's Gospel is filled with the miraculous; the second part is filled with mystery. Having miraculous powers is what we more readily associate with being God's image. It is difficult to see God's image in suffering and death. But throughout the second part of his Gospel, Mark indicates how Jesus shows and teaches that God reverses our natural expectations and gives us a "second sight," as it were, by which conventional human wisdom is turned upside down.

For example, Jesus surprises those who think that entering God's kingdom requires sophisticated learning, by saying that "whoever does not accept the kingdom of God like a child will not enter it" (10:15). He confounds the normal prizing of wealth by instructing the good, rich man to "Go sell what you have" (10:21). He overturns the normal ambitions for power by instructing his disciples clearly that they are not to "lord it over" others (10:42), but rather, "whoever wishes to be great among you will be your servant; whoever wishes to be first among you will be the slave of all" (10:43-44).

Above all, Jesus rebukes those who think that God's anointed ("messiah") should be immune from suffering and death. In chapter 8, he tells Peter explicitly that this way of thinking is "human-minded" and not "God-minded" (8:33). Then in chapters 14–15, Mark shows Jesus undergoing human suffering and death and somehow revealing God in that very process.

Mark shows that Jesus reveals God even in the process of dying because, at the same time that he shows Jesus being betrayed to his death, he indicates how God will transform that death. In chapter 14, Mark hints at this transformation by the way he describes the anointing of Jesus and by the way he links it to Jesus' last meal, which in turn foreshadows the meal of the Eucharist, itself a meal of transformation.

In chapter 16, Mark indicates the transformation of death through the whole episode of the women coming to the tomb. Through the repeated images of a new day (16:2), he projects a new beginning. Through the images of the stone rolled away (16:4) and the women fleeing from the tomb (16:8), he suggests an escape from death. Through the message of the young man in white (16:6-7), he confirms Jesus' own prediction (14:28) that he would be raised up and return to Galilee. Through his description of the women's silent, awed, ecstatic trance (16:8), he indicates their confrontation with the unexpected, overwhelming power of God to transform death itself into ongoing life.

Mark 16

Triad

Another way of seeing Mark's design is to see the whole Gospel arranged as a triad. First of all, the reader should take note that there are three beginnings. The first is the "beginning" of verse 1, suggesting the very opening of Genesis and the idea of God creating "in Wisdom." The second is the return to "the beginning of Creation" in Mark 10:6, which follows upon the transfiguration and introduces Jesus' radical teachings on poverty, powerlessness, and childlikeness. The third is in chapter 16 with its images of a new day and its message of Jesus' return, at what looks like the end, to the beginning of his ministry in Galilee.

From another perspective, there are three sections that each end in a scene of resurrection. The first section, chapters 1–5, concludes with the raising up of the daughter of the synagogue leader Jairus and the image of the witnesses "beside themselves with ecstasy" (5:42). The second section, chapters 6–9:8, concludes with the scene in which Jesus appears before his disciples transfigured in glory. Here Jesus is pictured in conversation with the great prophets Moses and Elijah, who are also portrayed in a transfigured state. In this scene, the three chief disciples are briefly transfigured too, as Peter seeks to build three harvest "tents" or booths to celebrate the end time, and all three are overcome with awe (9:6). The final section runs from 9:9, when Jesus and his disciples descend the mountain, to 16:8. In 16:6 the three women who have been watching learn that Jesus "has been raised," and transfigured by their new understanding, they are overcome with ecstasy and awe.

In all of these configurations, doublet and triad, the re-creative, transfiguring power of God's Wisdom is at the center.

OTHER ENDINGS BY OTHER AUTHORS

Some time after Mark completed his Gospel, three anonymous authors offered other endings to it. The modern reader may well wonder how anyone had capacity, the desire, or the audacity to do such a thing. They had the capacity because texts were not guarded by copyright laws until fairly recent times. They had the desire because the conventional translation of the last verse of Mark's Gospel made it appear to end in failure. They had the audacity because they regarded themselves as guardians of God's word.

Over the centuries, most commentaries have accepted the idea that the women disobeyed the angel's message because they were shaking with fright. Such a conclusion ignores, of course, the linguistic evidence that Mark uses some form of the word *ekstasis* three times in his Gospel, each time to convey the elevated feelings of those who have witnessed a miracle. It ignores as well the significant use of the word *ekstasis* in the Septuagint to indicate a trance or shift in consciousness induced by God.

It also ignores the linguistic evidence of Mark's use of "awe" to indicate key moments of change in Jesus' disciples—first, to describe their response to Jesus' power to still a violent sea (4:41) and then to describe their response to his transfigured glory (9:6). Its use here forms a typical Markan triad, and its meaning here is illumined by its function in the Transfiguration.

Such a conclusion also ignores the role of women throughout the Gospel of Mark: how they are repeatedly "raised up" by Jesus in the first part of the Gospel and how, in the second part, they fulfill the role of true disciples by following, ministering, and "watching," as Jesus has asked. It ignores Mark's use of the Wisdom traditions, where wise people are always contrasted with foolish ones and where Wisdom is portrayed as a woman. Above all, such a conclusion ignores the overall structure of the Gospel, in which God reverses the expected and re-creates all things. If one grasps such a structure, one is open to an ending in which those thought least likely are the ones transformed into witnesses.

It is possible (although not provable) that over the centuries, male leaders in the church have been alarmed at the idea of how a translation using the language of "ecstasy" and "awe" might elevate the role of women. It is possible that male commentators have had a mental block against seeing that while the male disciples in Mark's Gospel are made to look foolish, the female disciples are shown to be wise and faithful witnesses to Jesus' resurrection.

Whatever the cause, the three alternative endings to Mark's Gospel appear in manuscripts known to be faulty. Their dates suggest a limited use by the church. The "Shorter Ending" is dated somewhere between the seventh and ninth centuries. The third ending (called "The Freer Ending" because it is preserved in the Freer Gallery in Washington, D.C.) is not mentioned before Jerome in the fourth century.

The "Longer Ending" is dated from the second century because it was incorporated into a work of the time (Tatian's *Diatessaron*), but it is not mentioned by either Clement or Origen, significant church fathers of the third and fourth centuries. Tatian's *Diatessaron* was deemed heretical because of its attempt to harmonize all four Gospels. The "Longer Ending" was not made part of the official biblical canon until the Council of Trent in the sixteenth century. It is strange that it was canonized, even though it once formed part of a heretical work, particularly since the ending itself is guilty of trying to blend together different Gospel passages. Even stranger is the fact that although modern scholarship agrees it was not authored by Mark, it is still being printed in most Christian Bibles and used by the Catholic Church as the gospel on the Feast of Saint Mark!

Again the question arises as to why the Council made its decision and why the church has continued to honor it. Again the answer seems to lie in the way Mark's original ending has been translated and understood as signifying the women's failure to witness. Were the ending grasped as a description of the women's stunned awe at the realization of Jesus' resurrection, another ending would not be sought.

The Council perhaps justified its choice of this "Longer Ending" because it makes use of passages from Luke and Matthew. It does not seem to have considered, however, whether these borrowings do justice to the Gospels they are taken from or to the rest of the Gospel of Mark. It is important to look at the "Longer Ending" in detail.

THE LONGER ENDING

16:9-11 The appearance to Mary Magdalene

Some commentators have suggested that this verse rehabilitates Mary Magdalene as a witness because she is described here as giving the angel's message to Jesus' "companions." But the description of her as one who had been possessed by "seven demons" (a reference to Luke 8:2) is denigrating. Her speech here, moreover, is ineffective because "they did not believe" her. In the original Markan ending, as we have read it, Mary Magdalene is a witness to the resurrection and an apostle to the apostles. Here she is a former sinner whose words are not given credibility.

16:12-13 The appearance to two disciples

This is a vague reference to Luke's narrative of two disciples encountering the risen Jesus on the road to Emmaus (Luke 24:13-35). Omitted is Luke's development of this narrative into a eucharistic story in which the disciples recognize Jesus "in the breaking of the bread" (Luke 24:35). As it stands, the narrative here goes nowhere.

16:14-16 The commissioning of the Eleven

Jesus' injunction to "Go into the whole world and proclaim the gospel to every creature" comes from the ending of Matthew's Gospel (28:19). The insistence on baptism as the guarantee of salvation, however, is not in Matthew. And such a rigid distinction between the "saved" and the "condemned" is nowhere to be found in Mark.

16:17-18 "Signs will accompany those who believe"

The only two "signs" in the list that appear in the Gospels are the driving out of demons and the laying of hands on the sick. These are mentioned, however, not as "signs" but as ministries. The speaking "in new languages" is not in any of the Gospels, but in Acts and First Corinthians. The power to "tread on serpents" is mentioned in Luke (10:19), but not the power to pick them up. The power to "drink any deadly thing" without harm is nowhere in the New Testament. (And when these words have been taken literally, they have caused death.) In no Gospel does Jesus advocate the seeking of "signs." In fact, there are several places where Jesus rebukes the Pharisees for "seeking a sign" (Mark 8:11-12; Matt 12:38-39; Matt 16:1-4; Luke 11:16).

16:19-20 The ascension of Jesus

The description of Jesus "taken up into heaven" echoes the ending of Luke (24:51). In Luke, it is part of his way of ending the Gospel on a note of expectation. In the same passage, Luke shows Jesus telling his disciples to go to Jerusalem to await "power from on high" (24:49). In the "Longer Ending" there is no such waiting or expectation of the Spirit. Instead, the author tidies things up by saying that the disciples "went forth and preached everywhere while the Lord worked with them."

Summary of the "Longer Ending"

The "Longer Ending" pieces together phrases from other Gospels without doing justice to the way they function in their original contexts. In respect to Mark, if one perceives Mark's Gospel in the terms of this commentary, then the "Longer Ending" appears not only unnecessary but offensive because it clashes with the rest of Mark's Gospel.

As a final reflection, you might want to consider all the ways in which this "Longer Ending" undermines Mark's theological point of view:

—How does it undermine the role of women in Mark's Gospel?

—How does the insistence that "whoever does not believe will be condemned" undermine Mark's focus on Jesus' outreach to sinners, his emphasis on forgiveness, his saying that "Whoever is not against us is for us" (9:40), and his emphasis on God's will and power to transform rather than to condemn?

—How does the emphasis here on "signs" undermine Mark's repeated suggestion that God's kingdom is accessible in ordinary ways?

—How does ending with Jesus' ascension into heaven conflict with Mark's emphasis on Jesus' return to Galilee?

Mark 16

—This ending seems to close off discipleship as a thing of the past instead of opening it up to the future. What effect does that have on you as a reader and potential disciple?

The Gospel According to Luke
Michael F. Patella, O.S.B.

INTRODUCTION

The Gospel of Luke, the third Gospel in the New Testament canon, has a remarkable place in the study of Sacred Scripture, and this unique position does not stem solely from the fact that it is the only Gospel to have a second volume associated with it, namely, the Acts of the Apostles. Luke engenders a great deal of discussion on the level of New Testament formation, sensitivity to historical data, literary technique, and theological development. This commentary deals with these areas to a greater or lesser degree.

The Gospel message

Each Gospel relates a particular evangelist's theological interpretation of the kerygma, that is, the passion, death, and resurrection of Jesus. To do this, the Gospel writer takes events from Jesus' life as passed down from traditions and sources and composes a Gospel account. Under the inspiration of the Holy Spirit, an evangelist uses his composition to present his particular theology of redemption mediated through Christ's life. Details may or may not be accurate, but the truth of the Gospel goes beyond details. The central focus of this study, therefore, is the theological picture that Luke's Gospel paints of Jesus, his earthly ministry, and the early church.

Matthew, Mark, Luke, and John

Anyone reading the Gospels notices that there are stories within them that overlap, parallel, and seemingly copy each other. The reason for, and explanation of, this problem have been part of the church since the beginning. Scholars such as Origen and Augustine were among the first to develop theories on the formation of the Gospels. In the modern era, new theories have arisen that have continued the dialogue and discussion on the development of the New Testament.

The brevity of this commentary prevents any lengthy discussion of the sources Luke used in writing his Gospel; this question has an involved and complicated history. For simplicity's sake, our commentary notes the names of commonly held sources as well as the familiar vocabulary of biblical scholarship. Knowing the following terms will be most helpful:

- *Canon:* the official collection of books comprising the Bible.
- *Codex Sinaiticus* and *Codex Vaticanus:* two of the most dependable, extant New Testament manuscripts.
- Eschaton: the final times bringing God's eternal plan to fulfillment. The study and interpretation of the eschaton is called eschatology.
- *Evangelist:* the name given to the four Gospel writers: Matthew, Mark, Luke, and John.
- *Kerygma:* the proclamation of the passion, death, and resurrection of Christ that also describes how salvation comes through participation in the same passion, death, and resurrection.
- *Parallel:* a term used to describe a passage in one Gospel that has a like passage in another Gospel.
- *Q:* a hypothetical, oral source that contains material common to Matthew and Luke but not Mark.
- *Synoptics:* the Gospels of Matthew, Mark, and Luke, so named because they share so much of the same narrative line as well as the same material.
- *Textual witness:* early written documents containing all or part of the biblical canon.

Luke the evangelist

Not much is known about the evangelist Luke. The tradition says that he was both a physician and an artist from Syria who completed his Gospel between A.D. 80 and 90. Using Acts 20–28 as a guide, along with Colossians 4:14 and Philemon 1:24, many feel that he may have known Paul. Although it is impossible to prove these claims, the texts that Luke wrote indicate that he was a highly educated person, influential in the early church, aware of geography (outside Palestine anyway) and history, and very much attuned to the dynamic, direction, and development of Christianity.

Sensitivity to historical data

In addition to being considered a doctor and an artist, many have thought of Luke as a historian, because he gives greater attention to historical details than any other evangelist. For example, passages describing the birth of Jesus and the ministry of John the Baptist contain information on emperors, governors, and kings, and a good deal of it is close to accurate. Much of our information about Pontius Pilate comes from Luke. In large part, his information about the Herodian dynasty matches well with the writings of the ancient Jewish historian Flavius Josephus.

Literary technique

Luke is an economical writer. This evangelist avoids repetitions and superfluous information. He tells a story well, with attention given to rising action, climax, and denouement. His use of Greek is among the finest in the New Testament, and he is well-versed in Greco-Roman literary style. His prose has a nobility that has made this Gospel a favorite of many.

Theological development

Luke views the passion, death, and resurrection of Christ as the great salvific act that has affected the whole cosmos. The evangelist expresses this theology by presenting Jesus' earthly ministry as a battle between Christ and Satan. Christ's victory over evil comes with his death and resurrection. In Lukan theology, the death on the cross is actually a transfiguration into glory. Furthermore, by virtue of that death, the same transformative glory is promised to humanity, a concept that came to be known as *theosis*.

In this presentation, Luke relies on literary motifs to relay these key concepts. First, there is the motif of the diabolical force. Every good story needs an antagonist, and Luke elevates Satan to this position. Consequently, Christ's miracles and cures are more than kind deeds; they are attacks against the Evil One and his diabolical force. In other words, Christ is in a relentless pursuit of redeeming the world from Satan's clutches.

Second is the idea of the great reversal, a term used to describe the turn in fortune that will befall all between now and the *eschaton,* that is, the end times: the hungry now will have a banquet, while the rich go hungry; the humble will be exalted, and the exalted will be humbled.

Next, there is the schism motif. Christ will come to all, but some will heed his call to discipleship while others will not.

Finally, there is joy. The word appears more times in the Third Gospel than in any other New Testament work. In Lukan theology, for a world redeemed and transfigured by the blood of Christ, there can be no other Christian response than joy.

Luke 1

COMMENTARY

THE PROLOGUE

Luke 1:1-4

1:1-4 Address to Theophilus

The Gospel opens with a short prologue of a single periodic sentence, a style typical of ancient literature that often sets the tone and purpose of biographies and histories. Josephus and Polybius, for example, show similar introductions. Luke's use of this style often raises the question of whether he sees himself as writing a biography or a history. Opinions favoring one or the other abound. Perhaps the most we can say is that Luke is simply following the literary convention of the day as he writes his two-volume work. The Gospel, neither a biography nor a history, is an evangelical proclamation. A Gentile audience would expect such a prologue, and Luke is simply supplying it.

The identity of Theophilus is unknown. Possibilities range from his being a benefactor of the community, a church leader, or even a civil authority. Perhaps Theophilus is all three. On the other hand, using the name Theophilus (literally, "Beloved of God") universalizes the identity and allows every reader to be the addressee.

The prologue provides hints at the formation of the New Testament as well as the development of the early Christian community. What are the "events that have been fulfilled"? Who are the "eyewitnesses" and "ministers of the word"? Luke describes some of these events and personages within his two-volume work, particularly in the Acts of the Apostles, but how much of it is recoverable is difficult to answer. Of fascinating interest for source critics is Luke's explanation that he has investigated "everything accurately anew, to write it down in an orderly sequence." How many and varied were the initial documents before they saw their final editing at Luke's hand? Extant papyri, lectionaries, and targums certainly bespeak a Christian movement very much in ferment and development. Luke's project replaced the diverse gospel fragments floating around the Greco-Roman world. That this Gospel eventually became part of the New Testament canon attests to its nearly universal use over the course of the first two centuries.

THE INFANCY NARRATIVE

Luke 1:5–2:52

Only Matthew and Luke feature stories of the birth of Christ, although from two different perspectives. Luke centers his account on Mary, while

Matthew focuses on Joseph. It is obvious that Matthew and Luke were not copying each other in forming their respective infancy narratives. Nonetheless, they do share some details. Both have an angel relaying the divine plan to the human participants—Joseph in Matthew, Mary in Luke. Both state that this child will be born of the house of David in Bethlehem, that his name will be Jesus, and that these events will occur while Herod the Great is king of Judea (37 B.C.–4 B.C.). Most importantly, despite the many variations in the two different accounts, the two agree on the essential point that Mary is pregnant, and there is no human father.

Luke's purpose for including the infancy narratives is to situate the whole Gospel within the story of God's divine plan. Luke also uses references and allusions to the Old Testament, especially prophetic figures. Furthermore, he has passages dealing with John the Baptist precede those of Jesus. This structure prepares the reader for an account that aims to show Jesus as the one long-promised to deliver humankind from sin and death. Luke's infancy narratives grab the attention of his Gentile audience, catechize them, and graft them to the community of Israel by setting the many references to political events and leaders of the day within the context of the Old Testament. As Simeon proclaims in his canticle (2:29-32), Jesus is "a light for revelation to the Gentiles, / and glory for [the] people Israel" (2:32). Furthermore, this glory will not come easily, for even Jesus' mother, Mary, will be pierced by a sword. Thus, the infancy narratives serve as an abbreviated version of the Gospel and Acts. In the Acts of the Apostles, Luke recounts how Peter, Paul, and the Gentiles receive the light of revelation, but only after hardship and pain. On the final page of Acts, Paul is living, preaching, and teaching in that most Gentile of cities, Rome.

1:5-25 Announcement of the birth of John the Baptist

Luke provides a broad context for Jesus' birth, employing both Old Testament prophecies and typologies. Zechariah and Elizabeth are described as being "advanced in years," and thus past the age of childbearing. The announcement of the Baptist's birth, therefore, is similar to the miraculous birth genre found with Abraham and Sarah (Gen 18:1-15), Manoah and his wife (Judg 13:2-25), and Elkanah and Hannah (1 Sam 1:1-23). In addition, both Zechariah and Elizabeth are of priestly stock, which means that their son John would one day be serving in the temple at Jerusalem. None of the evangelists, however, imply that John the Baptist ever took on this role.

As a priest, Zechariah would take his turn serving in the temple twice a year for a week at a time. This detail no doubt led to the tradition, dating

Luke 1

from at least the sixth century, that Ein Karem, with its close proximity to Jerusalem, is the village of John's birth.

Angels are God's messengers and agents, and Luke mentions them twenty-five times in the Gospel. More than half of these occurrences fall within the first two chapters. The presence of an angel at the altar of incense (v. 11) underscores God's role in the events to follow. While in Matthew's Gospel the angel who appears to Joseph (1:20) remains unnamed, Luke specifies the identity of the heavenly messenger who comes to both Zechariah and Mary. The name Gabriel itself is a combination of two Hebrew terms, *Gabur* ("strong man," "warrior"), and *El* ("God"), therefore "Warrior of God." Gabriel has a role in the Old Testament. In the book of Daniel, this angel explains a vision to Daniel (8:17-26) while simultaneously giving Daniel understanding (9:22).

1:26-45 Announcement of the birth of Jesus and Mary's pregnancy

In Luke's chronology, Gabriel's announcement to Zechariah (1:8-20) precedes the one to Mary (1:26-38). Luke is setting the proper sequence of salvation history. If John is the precursor of Jesus in the ministry, he must also come first in the order of birth. In the sixth month of Elizabeth's pregnancy, Gabriel comes to Nazareth to deliver the news to Mary. Of course, Mary is extremely puzzled by this information, and when she expresses her doubt (v. 29), Gabriel encourages her. When Zechariah doubts, however, he is made mute (vv. 18, 20).

Whatever point Luke is trying to make by this comparison of the two personages, it is not too clear. Perhaps it is another way to indicate the Baptist's subservience to Christ, a point reiterated by the baby's leaping in Elizabeth's womb upon hearing Mary's greeting. Or since the recovery of Zechariah's voice excites wonder in the people (vv. 60-64), Zechariah's muteness reflects Luke's attention to the details of storytelling; it advances the theme and the plot.

1:46-55 The Canticle of Mary

Traditionally called the *Magnificat* in the Western church where it is sung at Evening Prayer, the canticle has all the markings of an early hymn. There are four hymns in these opening narratives, of which this is the first. Grounded in a reference to Abraham and referencing other forebears, this song has a decidedly Jewish-Christian cast. The piece contains the reversal theme found in 1 Samuel 2:1-10, but it is modified. Those who oppress now will be overthrown, and the lowly will be exalted; those who are hungry now will have their fill, but those who are satiated now will be sent away.

1:57-80 The birth of John and the Canticle of Zechariah

Zechariah regains his speech upon acknowledging the divinely given name of his son. The hymn Zechariah sings, also known by its Latin name, the *Benedictus,* the Morning Prayer canticle in the Roman Office, clarifies John the Baptist's role in the sweep of salvation history. He is to "go before the Lord to prepare his ways" (v. 76). The beautiful, poetic images "daybreak from on high will visit us" (v. 78) and "to shine on those who sit in darkness and death's shadow" (v. 79) have their foundation in Isaiah 8:23–9:2. Luke concludes this section on John the Baptist with a brief note placing John in the desert, where the reader will encounter him again at the beginning of chapter 3. The evangelist now moves on to the birth of Christ.

2:1-7 The birth of Jesus

Scholars have often considered Luke's attention to historical detail as one indication of the evangelist's high level of education—not only for the fact that he includes such information but more for the way in which he uses it. Greco-Roman historians wrote their accounts to favor their patrons or the party in power, much the same way as a local chamber of commerce writes about its particular locale today. Thucydides, Tacitus, and Josephus all had a certain editorial slant to their works that supported those who supported them. Luke stands within this tradition, but with an important difference: his bias is toward showing the hand of the holy Spirit at work in both Jewish and Gentile events of the day. Jesus Christ is to be considered the fulfillment of both cultural worlds. We have observed an example of Jewish fulfillment in the stories of Zechariah, Elizabeth, and Mary. In these opening verses of chapter 2, we see the events in the pagan world also cooperating and foretelling the birth of the Messiah in Jesus Christ.

A difficulty enters into this section with the names and dates of the people mentioned. Although the Roman historian Suetonius states that there were registrations of Roman citizens in 28 B.C., 8 B.C., and A.D. 14 (*Divus Augustus* 27.5), there is no record, outside the New Testament, which states that Caesar Augustus (27 B.C.–A.D. 14) decreed the enrollment of the whole empire, that is, non-citizens, for taxation or any other purposes. There were local registrations within various provinces from time to time, and once such census occurred under the Roman legate Quirinius, but he was not made governor of Syria until A.D. 6, when he also took control of Judea at the banishment of Herod's son Archelaus. Since Luke attests that both John the Baptist and Jesus were born under Herod the Great (37 B.C.– 4 B.C.), most scholars concur that it would be impossible for these events to have occurred at a time when Caesar Augustus, Herod the Great, and Quirinius were all simultaneously in power.

For Luke's theological intention, however, the important point is that during the *Pax Romana*, when the Gentile world looked to Augustus Caesar as the prince of peace, Jesus comes into the world as the true Prince of Peace. In fulfillment of the Old Testament prophecies, which establish the messianic line through the house of David, Jesus, a descendant of David, is born in Bethlehem, the city of David. In order to make this point, Luke takes historical facts, such as the census, and reworks them to fit his theological purpose, just as ancient historians altered details to suit the purposes of their patrons. For contemporary readers, such remolding of details may seem spurious or dishonest, but in the religious tradition, the truth that Jesus is the Savior of the world lies beyond the accuracy of some facts dealing with the reigns of various rulers.

The Greek term *phatnē* is translated as "manger" (v. 7) but can also mean "stable." The Greek *kataluma*, represented here as "inn," specifically means "lodging" or "guestroom," with space for a dining area (*kataluma* is the word employed in Luke 22:11). Reading together both *phatnē* and *kataluma*, we can see that Luke is probably describing the typical house of the day. These homes, built for extended families, had a living space on the upper floors with a stable at ground level. Both Matthew and Luke emphasize Jesus' Davidic lineage through his foster father, Joseph, as well as the fact that Jesus is born in Bethlehem, the city of David. It is reasonable to conclude that Joseph had family in Bethlehem and that he and Mary stayed with them. With all the relatives of the extended family eating and sleeping in the upper *kataluma*, the one private place for Mary to give birth would be in the *phatnē* or stable.

According to Roman, Greek, Coptic, Armenian, and other ancient traditions, the phrase "firstborn son" (v. 7) represents a title of honor. It does not imply that Mary had other children after Jesus.

2:8-20 Angels and shepherds

Once again Luke uses an angel to announce a birth, this time to the shepherds. Shepherds, although not social outcasts, were among the poorest people in the society. A group composed mostly of women and young children, they did not own land or sheep, and they worked for hire. Luke underscores Jesus' salvific role especially for the poor with this annunciation story; the shepherds are the first to hear the good news. With the angelic choir (v. 14) we have the third song in the infancy narratives, the *Gloria*. In Western liturgies this text serves as the foundation for the "Glory to God."

2:21-38 Circumcision, naming, and presentation in the temple

The parallel between John the Baptist and Jesus continues in verse 21. John is circumcised and named eight days after his birth (1:59-60), and now so too with Jesus.

In portraying this section, Luke relies on some elements of the Mosaic Law as well as stories about the prophet Samuel (1 Sam 1:24-28). God commands Abraham to circumcise male descendants and slaves as a sign of the covenant (Gen 17:12), a point the book of Leviticus stipulates (12:3). Although Luke states that both parents must undergo the rites of purification (v. 22), the Levitical prescriptions apply only to the mother (Lev 12:2-5). A Gentile Christian himself, Luke is not always accurate in his explanation of Jewish cultic and legal codes. Luke rightly notes that the firstborn must be consecrated to the Lord (Exod 13:2), but this redemption is accomplished by paying five shekels to a priest (Num 3:47-48). The sacrifice of turtledoves Luke describes is part of a woman's purification rite. These verses serve to emphasize Mary and Joseph as faithful, law-abiding Jews, and with them, Luke underscores the Jewish context of Jesus' birth and mission.

Nothing else is known about the identities of Simeon and Anna other than what this section tells us. Both represent the faithful Israelite who waits and does not lose hope in the coming redemption. Simeon's canticle, or *Nunc dimitiis* (2:29-32), is the fourth and final hymn from the Lukan infancy narratives and has traditionally been part of Compline or night office in the Liturgy of the Hours.

Simeon's words to Mary, ominous though they are, are also highly theological. With verse 34 we see the first instance of the schism motif, which runs throughout Luke's Gospel. Often in Luke's portrayal of Jesus' mission, one party or person will follow him, while another will turn away. One group will be saved, another will fall into perdition. In each case individuals choose their own fate by deciding for or against following Jesus. Simeon states that a sword will pierce Mary's heart as well. The discipleship that Jesus demands extends even to his mother. Not only does Luke indicate through Simeon that discipleship will not be easy, but he also elevates Mary to the role of the model disciple. To love Jesus is to suffer with him.

The widowed state of the prophetess Anna, daughter of Phanuel (vv. 36-38), has made her utterly dependent on God's goodness. Luke tells us that she "spoke about the child to all who were awaiting the redemption of Jerusalem" (v. 38), and thus she is the first evangelist. By starting out with the "redemption of Jerusalem," Luke sets his literary project in order. After the resurrection, the message goes from "Jerusalem, throughout Judea and Samaria, and to the ends of the earth" (Acts 1:8).

Luke 2

2:39-40 Nazareth and Bethlehem

According to the accounts of both Luke and Matthew, Jesus is born in Bethlehem but spends his youth and young adulthood in Nazareth. Mention of these two locales in this manner forms an enigmatic knot that is difficult to unravel. If there are serious questions surrounding the census (see 2:1-7 above), why do Mary and Joseph go to Bethlehem, when we know that Mary is from Nazareth (1:26)? The four Gospels and the Acts of the Apostles refer to "Jesus of Nazareth" but never "Jesus of Bethlehem." Is the whole narrative of the birth at Bethlehem a literary construction serving to demonstrate that Jesus, through his foster father Joseph, is the Son of David who is born in the city of David?

Scripture, history, and archaeology all show that there was a strong Jewish presence in various parts of Galilee, so it would not be a strange place for Jesus to have his upbringing. The most we can say about this puzzlement is that the two sources that mention Jesus' birth, Luke and Matthew, both specifically state that it occurs in Bethlehem. There are no texts that cite Nazareth as Jesus' birthplace. Basing their respective accounts on the oral tradition, the evangelists composed stories that get Mary and Joseph to Bethlehem and then back up to Nazareth. The importance of this Lukan narrative is that Jesus stands in line of the Davidic Messiah, and about that, Luke wants the reader to know, there can be no doubt.

2:41-52 The boy Jesus in the temple

Only Luke contains this story of how Jesus is lost while on the return trip from Jerusalem. Passover was one of the pilgrimage feasts, when devout Jews would go to Jerusalem to celebrate the occasion.

The story itself reflects a theological point that Luke makes explicit in recounting Jesus' earthly ministry: true discipleship goes beyond familial relationships (8:19-21 and 11:27-29). In addition, that this conversation takes place in the temple reflects Luke's ambivalent attitude toward the temple's existence, if not his positive disposition toward it. Luke frequently shows Jesus teaching in the temple up to the final days before his crucifixion. In the Acts of the Apostles, Peter and Paul also preach and teach in the temple.

Jesus returns with his parents to Nazareth, and nothing more is heard about him until he is an adult and begins his ministry. The next time we read of Jesus in Jerusalem will be at his triumphal entry (19:28-39), which leads to his death.

THE PREPARATION FOR THE PUBLIC MINISTRY

Luke 3:1–4:13

John the Baptist is the precursor of Jesus, and Luke shifts the focus from one ministry to the other. This transition entails Jesus' baptism and desert temptation.

3:1-20 The ministry of John the Baptist

Chapter 3, like chapter 1, opens with a periodic sentence, a strong indication that this section is a major literary unit.

As with the birth of Jesus (Luke 2:1-3), Luke situates John the Baptist within a geopolitical framework involving the Roman emperor and his Palestinian-Jewish client states. Tiberius Caesar succeeds Augustus. According to Luke's dating, the word of God comes to the desert-dwelling John the Baptist in A.D. 29.

The nominally Jewish king, Herod the Great, died in 4 B.C. and divided his kingdom among his three sons: Herod Antipas, the tetrarch, or ruler, of Galilee and Perea; Herod Archelaus, ethnarch over Judea, Idumea, and Samaria; and Herod Philip, the tetrarch in charge of Gaulanitis, Trachonitis, and Batanaea. Archelaus's misrule led the emperor Augustus to banish him in A.D. 6, at which time a Roman procurator was appointed to govern his territory. One such procurator was Pontius Pilate, who ruled the area from A.D. 26 to 36, the period Luke is writing about here.

Lysanias is difficult to identify. There is scant information about a person of that name ruling the area of Abilene at this time. Many have speculated on the reason why Luke includes this information. Was he addressing a Christian community based in Abilene (northwest of Damascus), or was he from Abilene himself? We may never know, but we have here a typical example of the manner in which Luke uses historical data—truth is more important than mere fact.

With the mention of high priests, Annas and Caiaphas, Luke grounds the Baptist's ministry within the history of Jewish Palestine. From John's Gospel (11:49; 18:13), we read that Caiaphas is the priest at the time of Jesus' death. Although only one high priest ruled at a time, Luke may include the reference to Annas simply because Annas was still alive while his son Caiaphas was in charge.

John the Baptist begins the public ministry in the parallel accounts of the other three Gospels as well, but just where John preaches is a question. Mark simply says "in the desert" (1:4). Matthew states "in the desert of Judea" (3:1),

Luke 3

which would place him under the jurisdiction of Pontius Pilate. Further on, both Matthew and Mark add that crowds come from Judea and Jerusalem, a region accessible to Perea and Herod Antipas's territory. Luke writes "in the desert . . . [the] whole region of the Jordan" (vv. 2-3), a reading that suggests along the Jordan River, including the Judean side of the river (Roman territory), but in any case, in that area east of Jerusalem as far as the mountains on the east bank. Since Galilee is also under Herod Antipas, Luke seems to introduce the idea that both Jesus and John, each in his proper time, face the same political ruler (see 3:19ff. and 23:6-12).

Luke firmly establishes John as the precursor. Not only does John preach a baptism of repentance for the forgiveness of sins, but the evangelist (vv. 4-6) also interprets the Baptist's role as the fulfillment of Isaiah's prophecy (40:3-5).

Judaism, with its whole tradition of the *mikvah*, or ritual bath, was well acquainted with the water ablutions that John mentions (v. 16). The reference to a baptism "with the holy Spirit and fire" further on in the verse emphasizes that Jesus' action goes beyond religious ritual; it will have an efficacy that will transform the whole created order, just as fire alters the material state of matter. Early Christian mosaics depict this point by presenting Jesus standing in the Jordan River with smiling fish surrounding his feet as the Baptist pours water over Jesus' head.

3:21-22 The baptism of Jesus

John clarifies his subservient role to Christ with his preaching in 3:15-18. From the beginning of Luke's Gospel, information about John the Baptist has come before the accounts dealing with Jesus. In keeping with this thematic development of the Baptist as precursor, Luke skillfully provides the account of John's arrest (3:19-20) before the narrative surrounding Jesus' baptism (3:21-22).

Luke shows Jesus praying at critical points in his life. To underscore the point that John is lesser than Jesus, Luke recounts the baptism itself in the passive voice. There is no conversation between the two individuals. Jesus is baptized as one among the crowd, the voice from heaven is directed only to him, and it is understood that the others do not hear it. Later, when the Baptist sends messengers to Jesus (7:18-23), there is no indication of his being aware of having baptized Jesus.

To interpret the baptism, Luke relies on a conflation of two Old Testament passages. The first half of the voice from heaven (v. 22) is a paraphrase of Psalm 2:7, while the second half is part of Isaiah 42:1. It should be noted, however, that the textual witnesses for this section display a wide variety of readings. One manuscript, for example, quotes Psalm 2:7 in its entirety: "You are my Son, this day I have begotten you." The version that we have here reflects the evidence from Codices Vaticanus and Sinaiticus, two of the most dependable of the extant Gospel manuscripts. A similar, although not an exact, quotation is found at the transfiguration of Jesus (9:35).

According to the science of the ancients, doves were considered not to have any bile and thus were symbolic of virtue. Not only were they worthy for sacrifice to God, but, as seen here, they also symbolized the divine presence.

3:23-38 The genealogy of Jesus

By setting Jesus' genealogy after the baptism, Luke fashions a twofold theological statement. First, after having seen Jesus' divine sonship pronounced in the voice from heaven (3:22), he now reiterates that point by stating it in verse 38. Second, Luke writes Jesus' ancestral line going all the way back to Adam, and by so doing connects Jesus to all humanity, unlike Matthew, who shows Jesus as descended from Abraham to stress his Jewish background and role (Matt 1:1-17). Luke also underscores Jesus' virginal conception by the use of the parenthetical expression "as was thought" (v. 23).

One theory of the formation of Luke's Gospel holds that the infancy narratives (Luke 1–2) were later additions to a primitive version of the current text (see above). If so, an earlier stage of the Third Gospel began with Jesus' baptism and genealogy. Supporting this possibility is a lack of similar introductory material in the other Gospels (Matthew notwithstanding), as well as use of Luke's Gospel by early Christians and heretics, particularly Marcion, who denied Christ's relationship with anyone in the Old Testament. In any case, in this final redaction Luke does a fine job linking the first two chapters to the third both literarily and theologically.

4:1-13 The temptation in the desert

The Spirit who descended upon Jesus at his baptism now leads him into the desert for forty days.

The desert brings life right to the edge. In the Jewish tradition, it can be a place of divine encounter, such as with Moses and the burning bush (Exod 3:1-14), or it can be the place of death (see Gen 21:14-16). Of course, the forty-year wandering of the Israelites, a communal experience that formed them into the people of God, takes place in the desert. Just so, Jesus' sojourn in the wilderness brings into clearer focus for him what his mission on earth will be.

Luke 4

The Synoptic Gospels all include the desert temptation, but there are differences among them in the telling. Mark's account is the shortest (1:12-13), and Luke's is most similar to Matthew's (4:1-11), but the similarities break down in the respective nuances of each account. In Matthew, the setting of the three temptations goes from the desert, to Jerusalem, to the kingdoms of the world, while in Luke we read desert, kingdoms of the world, Jerusalem. Luke's account has greater internal consistency, for Jesus' ministry will culminate in Jerusalem, and it will be in that city that he meets his greatest temptation as well as his greatest triumph (see below, Luke 22:39-46; 23:44-49; 24). As it stands in this passage, the three temptations are to riches, glory, and power, represented by bread, rule, and defiance of nature respectively. Jesus' reply to each of the temptations, all from the book of Deuteronomy (8:3; 6:13, 16), connects his experience in the desert with that of the wandering Israelites.

For Luke, the devil is a force in the yet unredeemed world of Jesus' ministry. In the Lukan narrative, this encounter in the desert is Jesus' first meeting with the devil, but certainly not the last (v. 13). Jesus will be in hard combat with the devil or Satan from here until his death.

THE MINISTRY IN GALILEE
Luke 4:14–9:50

The Spirit now leads Jesus to Galilee, the area north of Jerusalem and Samaria. This was the district of his upbringing, and he begins his earthly ministry there.

4:14-30 Jesus arrives in Nazareth

From the preceding section we know that Jesus was away from the region and his hometown. What is unclear, however, is how long he was away and why he departed. That he was baptized with all the people somewhere along the Jordan (3:3, 21) has led many to conclude that Jesus was associated with John the Baptist for some time before setting out on his own way.

Jesus reads from Isaiah 61:1-2, a messianic text. Although by the fourth century A.D. the rabbis had adopted a particular order of scriptural pericopes to be read throughout the year, it is uncertain whether such a system was in place in first-century Judaism. If it was, then Jesus demonstrates his authority in bypassing the accepted practice and choosing a passage of his own. His concluding comment (v. 21) allows the listeners to draw their own conclusions.

Luke 4

The reaction of the people in Nazareth reflects the schism motif, which Luke develops from the beginning (see 2:34). Some speak highly of Jesus, while others are filled with resentment at having one of their own preach to them, and Jesus calls them on this point by providing examples from their history when the people acted in like manner. The references to Elijah and Elisha serve to describe the kind of prophet people see in Jesus and, indeed, how he perhaps sees himself. Unlike the prophets of the south, such as Isaiah and Jeremiah, Elijah and Elisha lived in the north, and they, too, made the rounds raising the dead, feeding the poor, and healing the sick (1 Kgs 17:1–2 Kgs 13). Since Galilee is in the north, where much of Jesus' ministry is situated, both the actions and words of Jesus would have special resonance with the people. Jesus' comments draw the obvious conclusion. By their resistance to him, the townspeople are no better than their forebears who did not heed earlier prophets; therefore, they come under the same judgment. Jesus' insinuation enrages the people to the point where they try to kill him.

Nazareth is located on a hill overlooking the Esdraelon Plain. A rocky precipice encircles the southeast section of the town.

4:31-44 Exorcisms, cures, and healings at Capernaum

The central focus of Jesus' ministry is the reclamation of this world for the reign of God, and now the battle begins.

Capernaum lies along the northern shore of the Sea of Galilee, where archaeological evidence points to its being a busy fishing village. Much of Jesus' ministry takes place in this locale.

Unlike the temptation scene in Luke 4:1-13, here Jesus encounters not the devil but an unclean demon. For Luke, both the demon and the devil may represent the same evil force, but they are not one and the same entities. The devil, Satan, and Beelzebul (see 10:18; 11:14-23) are synonymous terms for the Evil One holding creation captive. Demons, on the other hand, play a lesser role and are subject to the devil. That this exorcism as well as the following cure takes place on the sabbath is significant: the reign of God is made manifest on the literal day of the Lord, which, metaphorically speaking, is the *Day of the Lord,* the moment when the end times arrive culminating in the Lord's decisive battle with evil. When the Gospels were written, apocalyptic thought filled the thoughts of Jew and Gentile alike, and this Lukan scene reflects such a mindset. The Gospels are in a large way responsible for the fact that judgment of good and evil is an important part of the Christian theological tradition.

The cure of Simon's mother-in-law follows. The world between sickness, disease, and demonic possession was not so well defined in ancient times.

Luke 4

None of it was good, and all of it was evil. Curing a person, therefore, would evoke the same reaction as an exorcism, a point made by the fact that Jesus "rebukes" the fever. Again, the event takes place on the sabbath, leading to the same conclusions as above. From earliest Christianity, a house located in the center of Capernaum has been held as the place of veneration commemorating this miracle, and churches have stood on the spot ever since to accommodate the thousands of pilgrims who continue to visit it.

The sabbath ends at sunset, yet people still come to Jesus for cures and exorcisms. The day of the Lord cannot be confined to the temporal cycle. The passage shows the melding of time with the *eschaton*. The demons always know Jesus' identity, even though the people do not, and these unclean spirits nearly always declare him the Messiah or state his divinity. Jesus prohibits them from speaking in order to demonstrate his power over them and their ruler, the devil.

Jesus leaves Capernaum at daybreak and goes to a deserted place. Tradition has often located this spot along the northeast shore of the Sea of Galilee, a place of volcanic rock and little vegetation. Luke, not known for his accuracy in Palestinian geography, ends the section by saying that Jesus goes to preach in the synagogues of Judea. This point of information is problematic. Judea is in the south. Luke's whole schema has Jesus making only one trip there, and it ends with his passion, death, and resurrection. The earliest manuscripts, Codices Sinaiticus and Vaticanus read "Judea," but another important codex has "Galilee," the district in the north, probably written thus to resolve the narrative contradiction. Most likely Jesus made more than one journey to Judea in his lifetime. Indeed, John's Gospel indicates that Jesus went to Jerusalem at least seven times. This verse (v. 44) reflects such a tradition.

5:1-11 The miraculous draft of fish and the call of Peter

Luke is the only Synoptic writer to include the story of the miraculous catch of fish within the call of Simon, although John's Gospel shows a similar miracle in a resurrection narrative (John 21:1-11).

Lake of Gennesaret is another name for Sea of Galilee (v. 1). Fishing in the Sea of Galilee is done only at night. If the men caught nothing at that time, there was nothing to be had. That they listened to Jesus at all is indicative that they respected Jesus' opinion even when it came to their own profession. There is a tinge of doubt in Simon's reply (v. 5), and his reaction only confirms his initial skepticism (v. 8).

Jesus speaks only to Simon, and Simon is the only one to reply. Luke is preparing the reader for the leadership role that Simon (Peter) will play throughout the Lukan corpus. We get the impression that the crowd must have been so large that the only way Jesus could be seen and heard without being overwhelmed by the throng was to sit in Simon's boat just off the beach, the same boat that sails out for the catch at the Lord's command. The emphasis on Simon's boat is Luke's way of underscoring the disciple's importance on the symbolic level. Early Christian iconography often used a boat filled with people to depict the church, just as the church has long been called the "bark of Peter."

The miracle excites awe and wonder. Moreover, it represents the multitudinous followers this disciple will "catch" once he becomes a fisher of people in Christ's name. In verse 8 Luke uses the name "Simon Peter" for the only time and shows the disciple moved to repentance. Jesus then speaks directly to Simon in listening distance of the others. Jesus' call results in these fishermen responding immediately. They leave everything and follow, thereby becoming models of the perfect disciples.

5:12-16 The cleansing of a leper

In the Old and New Testaments, the term "leprosy" is used to describe a variety of skin diseases, including leprosy itself. Any skin abnormalities, particularly those ulcerating or scabbing, made ritual purity impossible. Whether or not the disease was contagious, the affliction was considered a sign of sinfulness, and so people so afflicted were separated from the community to prevent physical as well as cultic contamination. After viewing the symptoms of the disease, the priests made the determination on purity or impurity (see Lev 13–14).

The man prostrates himself and acknowledges Jesus' authority both by the title "Lord" and by the supplication "if you wish" (v. 12). His action shows his faith, which Jesus recognizes. Jesus' commanding the cleansing is an affirmation of his lordship. The injunction not to tell anyone echoes the messianic secret found in much of the Gospel of Mark. Of course, it would be impossible to keep. It shows, however, that Jesus prefers that his actions rather than his words speak of his reign. Indeed, Jesus relies on such actions as proof of his being the Messiah (Luke 7:22). As a means of evangelization, the cure has the desired affect of bringing others to Jesus. Rather than portraying Jesus as being another miracle worker among many, Luke notes that the crowds assembled first "to listen to him." Only then were they "cured of their ailments" (v. 15).

Luke, more than any other evangelist, frequently shows Jesus alone at prayer, an activity hinted at in Luke 4:42. Often Jesus retreats to a deserted place or wilderness after an intense period of preaching, healing, and exorcising, as he does here.

Luke 5

5:17-26 The healing of a paralytic

Although all three Synoptic Gospels have the healing of a paralytic, only Mark and Luke feature the bearers of the stretcher letting the person down through the roof. This story provides a number of details that describe the effect Jesus was having in his ministry.

The crowds he was able to draw must have been exceedingly large. The fact that Jesus teaches from a boat in Luke 5:3 gives us a hint of their size. In this passage the stretcher-bearers cannot possibly make their way through the people gathered in front of the door and must resort to unconventional methods.

Luke shows his Syrian origins here. The Markan parallel to this story says, "After they had broken through" (Mark 2:4), a statement describing better the roofs of Jewish homes in Palestine, which were flat and made of a mud-and-sod mixture resting on wooden beams or stone arches. These roofs often served as terraces on warm summer evenings. To maintain their impermeability during the rainy season, they would be rolled with a large rounded stone to compact the grasses. Burrowing a hole to let down a pallet would have been relatively easy. On the other hand, Luke states "through the tiles" (v. 19), a detail reflecting the domestic architecture stretching from the Golan Heights up into most of Syria, where a series of stone arches commonly support a roof made of shingles.

Although many see this passage as the first of several "conflict stories," there is no reason to conclude that the Pharisees and teachers of the Law are present with bad intentions, for there are no harsh words between them and Jesus until he forgives the paralytic's sins. The Pharisees are correct in their criticism—only God can forgive sins—but they do not know the full meaning of what they say. Jesus, referring to himself as the "Son of Man" for the first time in Luke (v. 24), proves his divinity with the cure, and everyone, including the Pharisees and teachers, is awestruck. Their attitude may change as Jesus progresses in his ministry, but at this point the tension is not evident. In line with the schism motif that Luke has developed (see Luke 2:34), this scene gives reason to believe that this group of Pharisees and scribes are convinced that Jesus does have such authority.

As an Aramaic phrase, the title "Son of Man" can be loosely translated by the pronoun "someone." It is used frequently in the Old Testament, especially in Ezekiel and Daniel. It gains specific import, however, in the latter book, which reads, "As the visions during the night continued, I saw One like a son of man coming, on the clouds of heaven; When he reached the Ancient One and was presented before him, He received dominion, glory, and kinship; nations and peoples of every language serve him. His dominion is an everlasting dominion that shall not be taken away, his kingship shall not be destroyed" (7:13-14). This quotation from Daniel is seminal for formation of the Christian understanding of Jesus' identity, and it is this reference, combined with the cure, which causes the crowd and the Pharisees to be awestruck. They are able to make the connection between the miracle and the person performing it.

The event itself is a good example of the incarnational character of Jesus' mission. Forgiveness of sins and spiritual well-being are not separated from physical wholeness and restoration. The Son of Man does not ignore the material world or the suffering of those living in it. By the double action of forgiving sins and curing the paralysis, Jesus shows that God's beloved creatures are redeemed in this life as well as the next.

5:27-32 The call of Levi, the tax collector

The Jewish people detested tax collectors for good reason. On the religious level, tax collectors made themselves idolaters by cooperating with the Romans; thus they at least tacitly acclaimed Caesar's lordship. Dealing with Roman coinage, which featured an engraving of the emperor, would support such an accusation. On the nationalistic plane, by working for the Romans, Jewish tax collectors betrayed their people. They received their positions by bidding themselves out as agents to the Roman State. The Romans assessed the sum a district should provide to the emperor; the Roman officials demanded a surcharge for themselves, and the collectors were bound to bring in both while taking any extra as their remuneration. They could and would sell whole families into slavery in order to meet their demands. This position made them extortionists, both symbolically and literally.

All three Synoptic Gospels contain this story. Levi sits at the "customs post" (*telōnion* in Greek). This detail tells us that Levi taxed goods going from one political jurisdiction to another. Since nearly eighty percent of Jesus' ministry occurs along the northern shore of the Sea of Galilee, this customs post was most likely located at the mouth of the Jordan River, which formed the border between Galilee, under Herod Antipas, and Gaulanitis, under his brother Philip. The alacrity with which Levi leaves his post at the customs house indicates that his heart was predisposed to conversion before his encounter with Christ; Jesus' call is the catalyst causing the move toward repentance.

Levi's great banquet (*dochē* in Greek) with a large number of invitees underscores his wealth (v. 29). Luke's version differs from the Matthean (9:9-13) and Markan (2:13-17) accounts in several ways. Whereas the other two Synoptics specify that the Pharisees and scribes see Jesus in attendance

Luke 5

and then speak to his disciples, Luke simply states that the Pharisees "complained" to his disciples, which leads one to believe that they were at the celebration. Were the Pharisees invited and only saw the rest of the company when they arrived? Would they have gone to a tax collector's banquet in the first place? Whatever the answer, Luke wants the reader to know that the Pharisees were in close proximity to Jesus. Unlike the preceding passage of the paralytic, where friction is not necessarily evident between Jesus and the Pharisees, here Luke describes the encounter between the two with the use of the Greek verb *gongyzō*, "to grumble against someone" or "complain," indicating that some visible tension has arisen between them (v. 30).

The parallel accounts in the other two Synoptics show "Matthew" and "Levi, son of Alphaeus" as the names of the tax collector, but Luke reads "Levi," a name suggesting that he comes from a Levitical family and therefore would have some kind of priestly function (see Deut 31:9; Josh 13:14). Certainly Luke could have shortened Mark's reading by dropping the identifier "son of Alphaeus." The name "Levi" itself, however, contains overtones of the impending messianic age.

In Malachi 3:3 we read, "and he will purify the sons of Levi, / Refining them like gold or like silver / that they may offer due sacrifice to the LORD." This prophet emphasizes the impending Day of the Lord as well as the point that a messenger will come to prepare the way (Mal 3:1). Luke gives attention to John the Baptist as well as to the Day of the Lord. That Levi leaves his functions at the customs post is a sign that this remarkable day has arrived. Hence the feast, which the now repentant Levi holds, prefigures the heavenly banquet. By calling this former tax collector to a new life, the Lord Jesus has purified the sons of Levi. Note as well that with this passage Luke has blended the ministries of the Baptist and Jesus.

5:33-39 Feasting and fasting, new and old

Comparing the three Synoptic versions of this story, we see that Matthew has the disciples of John the Baptist asking Jesus why his disciples do not fast (Matt 9:14). Mark has "people" inquiring, but with a reference to both John's disciples and the Pharisees (Mark 2:18). Luke is obviously editing material that has come through Mark. The antecedent of the pronoun "they" (Luke 5:33) is difficult to identify. Since further on in the verse there is mention of the Pharisees in the third person, "the disciples of the Pharisees do the same," it would seem that the scribes are asking the question. As a professional class of writers who knew the written law, they would not necessarily be as prone to follow the oral traditions promulgated by the Pharisees, even though they may have very well been aware of them.

In addition, the thematic content supports the scribes as the ones interrogating Jesus. This question about eating habits follows within the context of Levi's great banquet (Luke 5:27-32). A similar controversy over feasting and fasting arises further on in Jesus' ministry (Luke 7:31-35). It seems obvious that Jesus has developed a reputation for being one who enjoys good food and wine, and according to the Gospel account, this accusation is not without basis. Not only does he use banquet imagery in much of his preaching, but he is frequently seen at dinner feasts with Pharisees, tax collectors, and sinners. Indeed, Jesus refers to himself as a bridegroom in this passage, thus making his ministry on earth a wedding banquet filled with the joy and the promise of new life. It is the Day of the Lord.

This passage reflects the tensions existing between the Christian movement and Pharisaic Judaism. Although Luke goes to great lengths to demonstrate Christianity's roots in Jewish tradition, particularly in the prophets (see Luke 1–2), the religious practices of the early Pharisees and Christians were incompatible. This irreconcilability stands as the background to the passage.

The parable about new and old patches, cloaks, and wineskins has a twist. The lesson about cloth and wineskins is easy to follow, and the conclusions are based on common sense. One uses old cloth to patch new, not vice versa; the fermentation of new wine needs the elasticity of new skins, not the brittleness of old ones. The summarizing statement, a verse that only Luke shows, however, is ironic: "[And] no one who has been drinking old wine desires new, for he says, 'The old is good'" (v. 39). After a discourse on the desirability of leaving the old for the new, Jesus concludes by admitting that we often prefer the comfort of the old to the challenges of the new, particularly when we see nothing wrong or bad with the old. On the other hand, the examination of the metaphor shows that, in this case, there is something wrong and bad about the old. Threadbare clothing is of little use to anyone, and wineskins can be used only once. We must not let comfort and security blind us to the blessings of the kingdom.

Jesus' point is that the life of a disciple is not a dour regimen of religious protocol, but a life of joy. We should not let self-complacency blind us to the banquet the Bridegroom has ushered in, a banquet that begins now even as we wait to see its fullness in the yet-to-come.

6:1-11 Debates about the sabbath

The Mosaic prohibition against work on the sabbath recurs in many places throughout the Pentateuch. The legislation first surfaces in Exodus 16:23-29, where Moses directs the Israelites on how to collect the manna the Lord has given them. They are to gather enough for the day at hand

and leave none for the next day. This instruction is in force until the sixth day, when they are to gather twice as much for the following sabbath. Interestingly, when some disobey Moses by keeping some manna longer than they are supposed to, the cache becomes rotten and wormy. When the leftovers are saved for the sabbath, however, the manna remains edible. This Exodus account gives rise to further legislation and consequent debates on what constitutes work on the sabbath.

The controversy revolves around sabbath regulation. If the disciples performed a similar action on any other day of the week, they would have been within their rights (Deut 23:25). Here, however, not only are the disciples in Luke 6:1-5 violating prohibitions against harvesting fields and threshing grain, but by carrying goods, they are also guilty of breaking a sabbath law (see Num 15:32). Jesus' reply to the Pharisees is nearly the same in the other two Synoptic parallels (see Matt 12:1-8; Mark 2:23-28).

The incident to which Luke refers is found in 1 Samuel 21:1-7. Jesus' point is that Pharisees overlook David's infractions, who, with his men, is guilty of breaking more laws than the disciples are. Yet the Pharisees become indignant at Jesus for a less serious offense, and he is the Lord of the sabbath. This moment is one of messianic revelation, but the Pharisees' legalism blinds them to it. The passage ends with "The Son of Man is lord of the sabbath" (v. 5), a verse that introduces another story on violating the sabbath.

The issue at hand is not that Jesus cures but that he cures on the sabbath, something that is considered work. As with the exorcism of the demoniac (Luke 4:31-37), the sabbath or Lord's Day here is also considered the eschatological Day of the Lord, when suffering will cease and wholeness will be restored. Jesus tries to make that point when he addresses the assembly (v. 9), and he proves his lordship in restoring the man's withered hand (v. 10). Seeing that Jesus' argument and actions are unassailable, the scribes and Pharisees become incensed.

It is important to note that Jesus' conflicts with the Pharisees reflect more the tension within the early Christian community concerning Jews and Jewish practice than they do between Jesus and the Jews. Both Jews and Gentiles saw themselves as followers of Christ, and passages such as these show the points of contention both inside and outside the Christian community. Thus, when Jesus castigates the Pharisees in this passage, we see and hear the early debates within the Jewish-Christian community.

6:12-16 The mission of the Twelve

There is a noticeable shift of direction in this scene. Away from the synagogues, towns, and people, Jesus goes "to the mountain to pray" (v. 12) in an all-night vigil. The exact mountain is unknown, though the use of the definite article indicates that Lukan tradition must have had some specific mountain in mind. Galilee has many high places that could qualify as quiet retreats for prayer, but two are the most likely promontories: Mount Hermon, rising from the northeast corner of the Sea of Galilee, and Mount Tabor, south of the sea, visible from Nazareth and on the Jezreel Plain. They both have been traditional places of prayer from earliest antiquity (see Ps 89:13), although Tabor is the more accessible of the two.

Jesus selects from all his disciples twelve men who will have a share in his ministry. The names of the Twelve do not match the lists of the other Gospels, nor do they correspond with what Luke writes in his second volume (see Acts 1:13). In fact, none of the lists in the Synoptics are in exact agreement with each other. How do we account for the fact that the apostles (and only Luke and Matthew call these men apostles) differ, especially when the early church placed so much emphasis on apostolic foundation in determining whether a community was orthodox or that its writings should be included in the canon? One suggestion for the variety of names is that each Gospel writer is recalling the representative figures peculiar to the community for which he is writing. These figures may have known or worked with one or more of what came to be called "the Twelve." All four Gospels agree that Judas Iscariot betrays Jesus, however.

After the night in prayer, Jesus returns to his ministry, except now the people come to him.

6:17-19 Ministering to a great multitude

The crowd's various lands of origin give the reader insight into Luke's geographical understanding as well as his theological agenda. The commission described in Acts 1:8 reads: "you will be my witnesses in Jerusalem, throughout Judea and Samaria, and to the ends of the earth." In the Acts of the Apostles, the apostolic mission follows that trajectory. Here in this passage, however, "Samaria" and the "ends of the earth" are not included. The explanation can be found in Luke 9:52-53, where Jesus and his disciples are not welcomed in the Samaritan village. Samaria's time will come, and so will the proclamation to the ends of the earth. For now, Tyre and Sidon, as seaports and in pagan territory, represent for Luke the future direction of the Christian movement. In this passage Luke paints a picture of a mission at the threshold.

6:20-49 Sermon on the Plain

The Sermon on the Plain evidences four sections: the Beatitudes, the exhortations, the analogy of trees and fruit, and the parable of the two houses.

Luke 6

Beatitudes. Jesus descends the mountain before preaching. The Moses typology, so much a part of Matthew's Gospel, does not exist in Luke. He raises his eyes towards his disciples, and addresses the people (v. 20), a simple gesture that calls forth discipleship on the part of the crowd. Because Luke has his Gentile audience in mind, he does not include the *lex talionis* found in Matthew 5:38. Certainly not as quoted or well known as Matthew's Beatitudes, the Lukan redaction is also shorter. Most critics believe that both Matthew and Luke use Q as the source material for their respective versions.

The great reversal theme, first outlined in the *Magnificat* (Luke 1:46-55), recurs here: the poor will inherit the kingdom, the hungry will be satisfied, those weeping will laugh. Luke addresses the people in the second person, whereas Matthew uses the third person. For this reason, some maintain that Luke foresees an immediate resolution to the suffering of the outcast while holding that Matthew pushes justice into the *eschaton*. The interpretation of the Lukan Beatitudes is not that simple, however. Because the Lukan eschatological vision surfaces through the juxtaposition of the Woes in verses 24-26, there is no reason to assume that Luke sees the resolution of the tension between the blessed and the woebegone occurring only within this lifetime. Likewise, Matthew's Beatitudes challenge people to address social injustices in this world.

Luke, like Matthew, places suffering and reward within the context of the Old Testament, in which true prophets faced torture and death, while the false ones found worldly grace and favor. As the Gospel narrative continues, the reader sees Jesus encountering a similar fate. The heart of the message is that we do God's will on earth to relieve suffering and oppression, realizing all along that ultimate mercy and justice will come only with the *eschaton*.

Exhortations. Luke goes to great lengths in explaining love of enemies (vv. 27-38). Human love should match divine love, a love that is "kind to the ungrateful and the wicked" (v. 35). This call to be "merciful, just as [also] your Father is merciful" (v. 36) is a particular Lukan characteristic. Because Luke defines so well the boundless quality of divine mercy, Dante refers to the evangelist as the *Scritsa mansuetudinis Christi,* the "narrator of the sweet gentleness of Christ."

The lesson on judging others is connected to love of enemies. The context surrounding the admonition not to judge others does not refer to assessing the rightness or wrongness of an action or of its moral content; obviously, the whole of the Beatitudes contains elements of judgment. Rather, Luke is addressing those who would play the part of God by judging the salvation or damnation of others, something only God can do. For those who would assume to take on that role, Luke offers a stern warning: they may end up condemning themselves. Similarly, those who extend the benefit of the doubt will have manifold blessings extended to them (v. 38).

Analogy. This comparison of a tree and its fruit is Q material. Matthew contains a nearly identical passage (Matt 7:16-20), but it is not as concise as the one we read here. The image of good and bad fruit and its association with prophecy echo several Old Testament prophetic utterances. Jeremiah performs an action of the good and bad figs (Jer 24:1-10), and a central metaphor for Isaiah (5:1-7) is the vine and grapes. Ezekiel has something similar (Ezek 19:10-14). Thus this short section functions as a reprise for Luke's reference to true and false prophets (vv. 23 and 26).

Parable. The comparison of the two houses (vv. 46-49; Matt 7:21-27) yields readings that reflect the geography of the two different communities. In Syria one would have to dig to reach the bedrock upon which to build; in Palestine and Israel, the bedrock is exposed. Syria has permanent rivers and streams running through it. Indeed, Antioch is situated on the Orontes, just one of several rivers in Syria. On the other hand, the country about which Matthew writes has only the Jordan, and no real city stands on its banks. The house for Matthew, therefore, is destroyed by wind and rain. The point in both readings, however, is the same: for one to follow Jesus, there must be care, determination, and full intention. The halfhearted who would try to be a disciple will simply wash away.

7:1-10 Healing the centurion's slave at Capernaum

Although Luke shares this story with Matthew, Luke's difference is most notable in that the evangelist includes the Jewish emissaries who are very supportive of the centurion. Several features draw our attention.

The centurion, as the name implies, was in charge of one hundred men. At this time in history, Romans ruled the country through their clients, with Galilee and Perea under the jurisdiction of Herod Antipas. Hence the centurion need not have been a Roman, even though he was a Gentile. That he was a Gentile, however, would have entailed difficulties enough, for a Jew could not enter a Gentile home without becoming ritually impure.

There are two words in Greek used for the term "slave." One is *doulos*, and the other is *pais*. In verses 2, 3, 8, and 10, Luke uses *doulos*, and in verse 7 we read *pais*. Of the two words, the latter, which literally means, "boy" or "youth," describes a more personal, endearing relationship. On the other hand, *doulos* expresses the servility associated with such a state. The translation here, with its use of "slave" and "servant" in the respective verses, shows the nuance between the two words. Luke contrasts the two terms in

Luke 7

the narrative. When using indirect address, as in verses 2, 3, and 10, or when the centurion speaks in the abstract, as in verse 8, the text shows *doulos*. When Luke quotes the centurion, however, he employs the term *pais*. From this juxtaposition we can see that Luke is emphasizing the kinship the centurion feels for his servant.

The interplay between the Jewish elders and the centurion is notable. Although the centurion is in service to the nominally Jewish tetrarch, Herod Antipas, he is still a Gentile. Herod Antipas, as a Roman client, has to pay tribute to the Romans, and he passes on this expense by levying heavy taxes upon the population. Nonetheless, the picture we have here shows some semblance of mutual respect between the two parties. The Jewish elders say that the centurion "loves our nation and he built the synagogue for us" (v. 5). Furthermore, the centurion exhibits all the signs of faith in the Lord God that the religious Jew shows. It seems that Luke has described a "God-fearer," a Gentile who found the monotheistic God of the Jews and their moral code appealing, but who was unable or unwilling to separate himself from his own family and ethnic group by dietary laws or circumcision (see Acts 10:22). Thus the Jewish elders in verse 4 can speak highly of the centurion. In addition, knowing that a religious Jew could not enter a Gentile house, the centurion obviates a potentially embarrassing situation by sending a second band of emissaries, this time "friends," with the advice that Jesus perform his deed from afar. Luke probably included this passage to support the place of Gentiles within the Jewish-Christian movement. As Jesus comes to the Gentile centurion, so, too, does he come to Gentiles in the Mediterranean world.

Finally, we see a positive exchange between the Jewish elders and Jesus. Although Luke often describes a great deal of tension between Pharisaical parties and Jesus, the relationship between Jesus and the Jews is not always hostile, as we see here. The elders may not be Pharisees specifically but may have some position of authority in the community, indicating some degree of formal adherence to the Mosaic Law.

The ruins of the second-century synagogue in Capernaum rest on a foundation of an earlier one, which according to one tradition is the synagogue in question here.

7:11-17 The son of the widow of Nain

This story is found only in Luke, and it is the first occurrence of restoring the dead to life found in this Gospel.

Tradition locates Nain on the southwest side of the Carmel mountain range in Galilee. That the prophet Elisha performed a similar miracle in

Luke 7

Shunem, on the northeast side of the same mountain range, no doubt influences the response of the crowd here (see 2 Kgs 4:8-37); they exclaim, "A great prophet has arisen in our midst" (v. 16). Some commentators also see an allusion to Elijah's raising the son of the widow of Zarephath, near Sidon in present-day Lebanon (1 Kgs 17:8-24).

In both these accounts the respective prophet resuscitates the dead by lying on top of them several times, and this point highlights the difference they have with the story involving Jesus at Nain. Here Jesus simply commands the young man to rise. The action reflects Jesus' authority, and the crowd recognizes this fact.

7:18-23 The messengers from John the Baptist

This passage is the first formal encounter between John the Baptist and Jesus. Though John baptizes Jesus in 3:21-22, he does so unknowingly. The infancy narratives show the accounts dealing with the Baptist preceding those of Jesus; for example, the annunciation to Zechariah and John's birth come before the annunciation to Mary and Jesus' birth in Bethlehem. This pattern emphasizes that John the Baptist is not the Messiah, but the precursor to the Messiah. Such an understanding is underscored at the baptism and is further clarified here. John the Baptist has seen himself as the forerunner (see 3:16-17). In sending disciples to ask such a question of Jesus now, he seeks confirmation that Jesus is the Messiah for whom he has prepared the way.

The Baptist's disciples in this narrative also play a role for the early church. At this time (A.D. 80–90) and even later, there was tension between the followers of John and those of Jesus. Luke's construction of having John's disciples asking Jesus if they "should . . . look for another" (vv. 19-20) serves as the Christian community's invitation to the Baptist's disciples to join the ranks of Jesus' followers.

Jesus' answer to the Baptist's messengers is based on his ministry thus far, including the raising of the dead, as seen at Nain, which Luke places immediately before this passage. Jesus' response draws on Old Testament prophecy, especially the sayings of the prophet Isaiah (29:18-19; 35:5-6; 61:1), whose preaching is echoed in the synagogue at Nazareth (see Luke 4:18-21). In framing his words by citations from Isaiah, we see how Judaism forms the crucial context for understanding the Gospels and the New Testament.

7:24-35 Jesus and John

Jesus' testimony about John lessens the tensions between their respective disciples as it extends a welcoming embrace to the Baptist's followers.

Jesus, the true Messiah, has tremendous regard and respect for John the Baptist: "A prophet? Yes, I tell you, and more than a prophet" (7:26).

The schism motif resurfaces at verses 29-30. Some who had chosen John's baptism see the plan of God fulfilled in Jesus, and others who had rejected John's baptism also reject Jesus and his message. In this latter group, Jesus mentions specifically Pharisees and scholars of the Law. The analogy of the children in the marketplace (vv. 31-32) is apt for them. No matter what the message or the deed, many people will find fault with God's design, because accepting the will of God necessitates a change in one's behavior. It would be wrong to assume that no Pharisees or scribes were disciples either of John or of Jesus; the reign of God split that group as well (see 7:1-10, 36-50; 13:31-33; 14:1-6). The hardness of heart they exhibit here crosses all class divisions.

Lest we tend to overlook the joy Jesus had in his earthly life, it would be good to note that he seems to have had the reputation of relishing good food and drink, as verses 33-34 suggest (see also 5:30; 7:36-50; 10:38-42). In addition, many of his parables and allusions are based on feasting metaphors (see 14:7-14, 15-24). As seen throughout Luke's Gospel, attention to conversion, concern for the poor, and enjoyment of all God's gifts go hand in hand. A dour disciple does not further the reign of God.

7:36-50 The woman of loving gratitude

It is often assumed that the woman is guilty of some kind of sexual sin, yet there is nothing in the text to suggest such a conclusion. The material concerning John the Baptist ("the poor have the good news proclaimed to them"—7:22) forms a good context for this passage. In the tradition this story becomes entangled with Matthew 26:6-13; Mark 14:3-9; John 12:1-8, all recording the anointing at Bethany on the journey to Jerusalem. In Luke, Jesus does not turn toward Jerusalem until 9:51, so this occasion, in the Lukan literary outline at least, is set in Galilee.

Simon the Pharisee's lack of attention to the details of hospitality notwithstanding, such an incident would be shocking in any case. Guests would have been reclining around the outside rim of a *triclinium*, a horseshoe-shaped table. While the left side of their torsos rested on elevated cushions to allow them to take food and drink with their right hand, their feet would be exposed to the wall's perimeter. Before the second century, the Roman custom was to have the *triclinium* open or near the *atrium*. Such an arrangement would explain how the woman gained access to the house. Nonetheless, she would have had to crawl around the outside rim of the table until she found the right set of feet before she could start the anointing. Even with the broadest, most accepting, and opened mind and heart, and even within the public culture of the Mideast, her actions would have been seen as suspicious or at least bizarre. Simon's consternation is understandable, if not permissible.

The text does not mention what kind of ointment the woman uses, but if it is contained in an alabaster jar, it would have been very expensive. The juxtaposition of using this ointment on the feet when the guest should have been anointed on the head accentuates the great release of guilt and shame this woman feels from having encountered Jesus somewhere along the way.

Jesus does not defend the woman by saying that she is sinless; rather, he acknowledges her sins and forgives them. The parable forms the interpretation of the event. Everyone is a sinner and everyone needs forgiveness. Only when we realize that we need the grace of Christ, do we see what a great gift the forgiveness is. This woman becomes the model of the proper response of limitless gratitude all people should show in light of the salvation Christ offers.

Simon's inner thoughts (v. 39) have an ironic twist. Jesus *is* a prophet, and he *does* know what kind of woman this is. That is why he responds in such a manner.

8:1-3 Women disciples from Galilee

Jesus' ministry is sustained and supported by the resources of several wealthy women disciples; three are named here: Mary Magdalene, Joanna, and Susanna. Joanna's marriage to Herod's steward, Chuza, certainly raises speculation on how much Herod and his court would have known about Jesus.

Luke refers to Mary Magdalene as one "from whom seven demons had gone out" (v. 2). The longer ending of Mark is the only other place in the Gospel tradition that describes her similarly (Mark 16:9). Exactly what is meant by the "seven demons" is unclear. If Jesus performed an exorcism over Mary Magdalene, there is no record of it, save for these verses from Luke and Mark; "seven demons" heightens the severity of her earlier possession.

The other evangelists do not name the women disciples until the death account (see Matt 27:56; Mark 15:40; John 19:25). Because he names the women here, Luke, who avoids repetitions, does not identify them at the crucifixion scene. He does name Mary Magdalene and Joanna as witnesses to the resurrection, however (24:10).

This group of men and women will follow Jesus to Jerusalem and remain there through the resurrection, but only the women and some of the men will stand at the cross (23:49).

Luke 8

8:4-18 Parables and response

The parable of the sower and its explanation appear in all three Synoptics. Luke's rendition, as usual, is a more compact version of this familiar story, leaving out the detail about the scorching sun, the shallow depth of rocky soil, and the trampled path. While Matthew 13:2 and Mark 4:1 state that the large crowd forces Jesus to preach from a boat, Luke has Jesus standing in the boat earlier in the Gospel narrative (see 5:1-11). Luke also underscores that the people come to him "from one town after another" (v. 4); Jesus' reputation has spread.

In verses 9-10 Jesus offers an explanation for parables. The "mysteries of the kingdom" (v. 10) are most probably the intuitive knowledge that comes with the intimacy the disciples have with Jesus. Paradoxically, Jesus must still explain the parable to them. This explanation can also be a reference to Isaiah 6:9-10: "Listen carefully, but you shall not understand! / Look intently, but you shall know nothing!"

That this parable is one of the clearest makes Jesus' commenting on it a puzzlement. Surely there are more difficult parables than this one that demand explanations. This dialogue, however, is the logical follow-up to the preceding one concerning the purpose of parables and an example of that intimacy the disciples have with the Lord. Its presence in the text most probably reflects the redaction of the early church in trying to underline the qualities of good disciples.

The term "seed" occurs six times in Matthew and Mark and four times in Luke. Most of the instances are in this parable and its explanation in all three Synoptics. Its use here and elsewhere shows that the word "seed" represents either the word of God or faith.

Naturally, among farmers the image is apt, and particularly so for Luke, who is writing for a community that tradition locates in Syria, one of the ancient world's breadbaskets. The farmers at this time would not plant the seed in rows as is done today; rather, they would walk along broadcasting the seed in front of them.

Any interpretation of this parable should allow for the fact that there is no limit given to the number of times the sower casts the seed. Just as a sower will go out at least once a year to plant, so will the word continue to fall on the soil. The emphasis in the parable is on the soil and the soil's response, not on the seed or the sower.

The connection that the parable of the lamp has with the explanation of the sower and the seed flows smoothly from Luke's hand. In a mixing of metaphors, the seed that has taken root in good soil now becomes a lamp. The knowledge of the mysteries of the kingdom, which we meet in verse

10, is catalyzed by the interpretation in verse 18: "To anyone who has, more will be given, and from the one who has not, even what he seems to have will be taken away." This verse is not describing the moral order; rather, it expresses growth in the word of God. Love and devotion to God build upon themselves and increase within a person to the point that others are drawn to God and the kingdom by the life of those who have let their seed flourish and their light shine. Jesus reiterates this theme when talking about the mustard seed (see Luke 13:19; 17:6).

8:19-21 Jesus and his family

Luke is less harsh in recording this event than either of the other two synoptic writers. Jesus' mother and brothers are unable to reach him "because of the crowd." In the parallel accounts in Matthew and Mark, his mother and brothers come calling for him as if he were a family embarrassment.

The question of Jesus' brothers often arises, especially in the Catholic tradition, which holds that Jesus was the only child of Mary. Explanations that the Greek word for "brother," *adelphos,* can also mean "cousin" are not at all convincing. A better basis for the claim is also founded on tradition, which sees Joseph as a man older than the young woman Mary. This tradition holds that Joseph lost his first wife to childbirth, a death common for women throughout history. Jesus' brothers, then, are really Jesus' half-brothers from Joseph's first marriage. It is impossible to prove or disprove the details of Mary's perpetual virginity. Of course, the virginal conception of Jesus is not the issue under discussion here. Luke is explicit, as is Matthew, that when Mary was pregnant with Jesus, no human father was involved (see above, Luke 1:26-38).

This short passage redefines human relationships under Christ. At this time and place, the extended family was one's first and only locus of identification. To lose or be ostracized from the family was equivalent to losing all personhood. Jesus redefines the lines of association and kinship by broadening the family boundary. Now, the evangelist seems to say, disciples form a new family, which is all-inclusive of those who hear and do the word of God. These new bonds of relationship are developed in Luke's second volume, the Acts of the Apostles.

8:22-25 The calming of the storm

With the phrase "One day" Luke shifts from Jesus' preaching to his performing miracles. The Lake of Galilee, below sea level and surrounded by hills and mountains, is well situated for sudden summer storms to arise without warning. As the hot, humid air rises, the colder air comes rushing

Luke 8

in, causing large swells in a very small lake. Recent archaeological finds suggest that the boat would most likely have been between eight to nine meters in length (twenty-six to thirty feet), two to three meters wide (seven to nine feet), and about one to two meters high (four to six feet), certainly enough space for Jesus and a large group of disciples.

Although natural phenomena could explain the miracle—these storms subside almost as quickly as they arise—the miraculous lies at the juncture of human experience and divine intervention. People today still speak of a sudden prayer as saving them from a nearly fatal collision. There is no way to prove whether this event of calming the storm occurred or not. The believer would not be wrong to follow the tradition, which says that it did.

The importance of this story, however, is theological. Up until this point, Jesus has been ministering in the Jewish areas on the western and northern shores of the Sea of Galilee. When he says to his disciples, "Let us cross to the other side of the lake" (8:22), he means the eastern shore, which at that time was in the pagan district of the Decapolis, meaning "Ten Cities." Encountering a storm on the lake while heading toward pagan territory shows Jesus in a battle. He is taking on the cosmic forces arrayed against his ministry, and he will not be cowed by them. Here a storm, which in the pagan culture of the surrounding region would have been associated with the god Baal (see 1 Kgs 18), obeys Jesus' command and everyone is saved. He is the Lord of the cosmos.

The story ends with a question, "Who then is this . . ." (v. 25). Luke has been prompting us all along throughout this narrative with questions or statements concerning Jesus' identity (see 4:22, 34, 41; 5:21; 7:16, 49), and the evangelist will continue to do so (see 9:9) before Peter finally declares him to be the Messiah (9:20).

8:26-39 Exorcising the Gerasene demoniac

Having safely crossed the lake, Jesus and the disciples land on the eastern shore, in pagan territory. Immediately demonic forces again challenge Jesus' lordship, but this time from outside the Jewish districts.

All three Synoptics include this account of the Gerasene demoniac. The name of the locale has its textual problems. In the manuscript tradition, an alternate name for "Gerasene" is "Gadarene," a confusion stemming from the attempts of various scribes to harmonize all three accounts. This attempt at harmonization was further complicated by the fact that Matthew 8:28 reads "Gadarene." The names "Gerasene" and "Gadarene" are based on two separate cities in the Decapolis, Gerasa (or Jerash) and Gadara, respectively. Neither is located on the Sea of Galilee, although Gadara is closer to the lake than Gerasa. Most likely each city's name was used interchangeably as the generic term for the area on the eastern shore, and exacting scribes, trying to address the discrepancies in the text, actually caused more confusion. The tradition locates the site at Kursi, in the northeast quadrant of the Sea of Galilee, which sits on a steep hill above the shoreline.

Not only is the man a demoniac but also, since he lives in tombs, he would be ritually impure to the religious Jews. He calls out to Jesus in a "loud voice" (v. 28), a signal of impending judgment. Unlike Matthew or Mark, Luke notes that Jesus had commanded the spirit to depart from the man even before the demoniac speaks.

Jesus demands the demons' name in order to show his authority over them, although he uses the singular of the noun. To know a name is to exercise control, and the demons freely give it, recognizing that they must be obedient to him. Luke alone states that the demons beg not to be sent to the abyss (v. 31). The swine, impure animals to the Jews, represent the demons' own uncleanness. In biblical Jewish thought, large bodies of water symbolized the entrance to the abyss, or Sheol. In his exorcism, Jesus sends the demons back to where they come from, the dwelling of the dead. On the one hand, he countermands their wish, and on the other, he proves to all that the demons had actually left the individual.

The pagan man, now free of demons, but bereft of friends and family due to his former state, wants to follow Jesus (v. 38). Jesus turns him into a Gentile missionary going through the city (Gadara? Gerasa?). Thus Luke prepares the reader for the mission to the Gentiles, a major theme in the Acts of the Apostles.

In Luke's narrative of Jesus' earthly ministry, Jesus has been battling the diabolical forces in the world ever since his temptation in the desert. The victory he has with this demoniac functions simultaneously as a realization and as an anticipation of the *eschaton*. In the former, all witness the flight of a legion of evil spirits. Yet the decisive showdown with Satan has yet to occur, and it will not come until Jesus dies and rises in Jerusalem.

8:40-56 Jairus's daughter and the woman with a hemorrhage

Luke follows Mark's order of having one miracle, the hemorrhaging woman, surrounded by another, the raising of Jairus's daughter.

Verse 40 informs us that Jesus has returned to the Jewish districts on the western shore of the Sea of Galilee. Luke, always the evangelist to find joy in the Gospel, specifies that the crowd "welcomed" Jesus. At this point the story of Jairus's daughter is introduced. Verse 42 prepares us for the

Luke 8

resolution of the story, when the hemorrhaging woman enters the picture in the next verse and turns our attention.

The woman touches the tassel on Jesus' cloak (v. 44). The term "tassel" most likely refers to the fringes religious Jewish men were commanded to wear on the corners of their outer garment in Numbers 15:38. The Greek Old Testament, or Septuagint, calls these tassels *kraspedon,* the same word Luke employs here. The woman is not merely grabbing at Jesus; she wants to clutch the holiest part of his clothing, a sign of her faith. Fearing rebuke, she falls at Jesus' feet. She bears witness to Jesus' miraculous act in front of all (v. 47), while Jesus commends and blesses her. Her faith opened her to Jesus' cure (v. 48).

Luke keeps the narrative flowing by having a messenger arrive from Jairus's house with the news that the young girl is dead (v. 49) even as Jesus is still speaking. When Jesus states that Jairus' daughter is only sleeping, this crowd, different from the one that initially welcomed Jesus, ridicules him. The comparison between the people in the two groups is noteworthy. The first, not enveloped by the fear and dread of losing a child, are in better straits to receive Jesus and his message with happiness and joy. The second, however, watching the passing of the girl and seeing the suffering of the parents, are too preoccupied to concern themselves with Jesus' visit. The Lord's visitation, however, comes to them, too, with the resuscitation of the daughter. Once again, faith is the operative condition for this miracle (v. 50).

Jesus allows only Peter, John, and James to enter the house with him. These three are selected out from the other members of the Twelve at the transfiguration as well (9:28). Peter occupies a central role in the Acts of the Apostles and the early church. John and James are the sons of Zebedee (5:10); the latter was martyred by Herod Agrippa (Acts 12:2), but what of John? There is a tradition that he is the beloved disciple, the author of the Fourth Gospel (John 13:23; 19:26; 20:2; 21:7, 20-24), but this conclusion cannot be substantiated with absolute certainty. Nonetheless, Paul refers to James, John, and Peter (Kephas) as "pillars" of the church in Jerusalem (Gal 2:9).

9:1-6 The mission of the Twelve

The ninth chapter of Luke introduces a shift in focus. Whereas Luke treats the Galilean ministry in chapters 4 through 8, chapter 9 turns the narrative's attention to the disciples and the beginning of the journey to Jerusalem.

By giving the Twelve authority over the demons, and linking that with the kingdom of God and curing, Luke heightens the eschatological tone of

Jesus' ministry. Jesus empowers his followers to join the cosmic battle with Satan. This warfare begins in the temptation scene (Luke 4:1-13) and surfaces throughout the Gospel, coming to a head at the crucifixion.

The injunction to take nothing for the journey ensures complete trust in God. That the Twelve are successful in their curing demonstrates that the kingdom of God has arrived. While this passage is most likely describing the missionary activity of the early church, it does not discount the probability that Jesus had at least the Twelve performing similar deeds in his life on earth. The parallels in the other Synoptics support such an assertion.

The Twelve are commissioned and sent (*apostellō*, 6:2), from which we get the word "apostle." On their names, see Luke 6:12-16.

9:7-9 Herod's thoughts

Herod Antipas was tetrarch of Galilee and Perea. His query in verse 9 echoes that of the disciples in the storm-tossed boat in Luke 8:25 and gives the reader an idea of the questions circulating during Christianity's infancy: Who is Jesus, and, in this case, what is his relationship to John the Baptist? In the Jewish tradition, Elijah is supposed to return to usher in the messianic age. See also 23:6-12.

Herod's wily and suspicious nature comes through in this passage. Unlike Matthew and Mark, Luke does not report Herod's infamous birthday celebration, which leads to the beheading of the Baptist, although earlier in his Gospel the third evangelist notifies the reader that Herod has had John imprisoned (3:19-20). From the Jewish historian Josephus, (*Ant.* 18.5.2) we obtain the information that Herod put John to death at his fortress-palace of Machaerus in the Transjordan.

In this description, Josephus also mentions the important detail that Herod feared John because the Baptist drew large crowds. Crowds could always fall into rioting and insurrection. Eventually both Roman and Jewish authorities will have similar fear of Jesus and will form an alliance to execute him as well.

9:10-17 Return of the Twelve and the feeding of the five thousand

Luke, as well as Mark, juxtaposes the return of the apostles with Herod's questioning about Jesus' identity. Herod tries to suppress the movement even as the movement continues to grow despite his efforts. Bethsaida, a town east of the Jordan River but on the northern shore of the Sea of Galilee, is part of the "Gospel Triangle," that segment of the land about which nearly eighty percent of Jesus' ministry takes place. Just south of the town lies a volcanic

Luke 9

deposit of basalt rock and rubble making farming or habitation impossible. Most likely this locale is the "private" area mentioned in verse 10.

The account of the feeding of the five thousand occurs in all four Gospels, though Matthew 15:32-39 and Mark 8:1-10 also feature a feeding of four thousand. The action of first blessing and then breaking the bread has strong eucharistic overtones, and as such, provides eschatological imagery.

Other details play into this imagery as well. Fish, because of their abundance, often symbolize the eschatological banquet. They can also refer to *garum*, a relish made of putrefying fish that was in heavy demand throughout the ancient Mediterranean world. The Greek verb *kataklinō* in verse 14 means to sit or recline at dinner, another reference to the eschatological banquet.

Luke has the crowd gather specifically in groups of fifty, which divides into five thousand evenly. Such a refinement allows Pentecost to function as an interpretive backdrop. In the Jewish tradition at this time, Pentecost was a celebration of the grain harvest and took place fifty days or seven weeks after Passover. In time the feast came to celebrate the giving of the Law to Moses, but whether it commemorated the Sinai covenant at this period is difficult to determine. In any case, the abundance of grain at harvest time symbolizes the abundant blessing of the end times. That five loaves of bread plus two fish equal the number seven underscores the emphasis on Pentecost. Of course, Luke writes about Pentecost in Acts 2, and that feast has prime importance in his work. The feeding of the five thousand, therefore, is one of Luke's ways to foreshadow the *eschaton*.

9:18-27 Peter's confession and the cost of discipleship

Luke is the only evangelist to open Peter's confession scene with Jesus at prayer. Although Matthew has the most elaborate version of Peter's confession, the other synoptic writers recount it. In all three Gospels, Jesus poses the question to the disciples, but Peter is the only one who answers. Their comments about John the Baptist and Elijah recapitulate Herod's thoughts in trying to identify Jesus. Elijah was the prophet whose return would usher in the coming of the Messiah. John the Baptist, as precursor, fits into this category as well, and mention of his name here reflects the early Christian community's appeal to the Baptist's disciples, who still feel that the Baptist is the Messiah.

All Synoptics display a set of three passion predictions. This one is Luke's first (see 9:44; 18:31-33). The context colors the moment. The eschatological overtones in both the feeding of the five thousand and Peter's confession take on a stark reality in the passion prediction. Yes, Jesus is the

Messiah ushering in a new age in which all can participate, but that new age comes with a price.

An aphorism encapsulates one of the great paradoxes of Christian life: gain is really loss and loss is really gain (v. 24). In the Lukan narrative, these words prepare the disciples for what lies ahead as it encourages the Lukan community. The eschatological term "Son of Man," along with one of Luke's favorite phrases, "kingdom of God," reaffirms the eschatological dimension that must be a part of any disciple of Christ.

9:28-36 The transfiguration of Jesus

Chapter 9 continues to focus on the small group of disciples, and once again we see Jesus at prayer. The interplay between the mission, eschatological feeding, confession, passion prediction, conditions of discipleship, and now transfiguration form a synthesis of Christian life.

What is the purpose of following Jesus, and where will it all lead? Luke as well as Matthew and Mark answers the question with the transfiguration. Many consider this event to be an account of a post-resurrection appearance. That all three Synoptics situate it within the ministry, however, militates against such an interpretation. It is better to view it as a foreshadowing of the glorification of the resurrection. Placed within this context of passion predictions and discipleship, the transfigured Christ shows the disciples, through Peter, James, and John, the promise that discipleship can bring both to this life and the life to come.

Moses and Elijah, representing the Law and the Prophets, respectively, give their approbation to what the disciples are seeing. Elijah's presence also has an element of foreshadowing; according to Jewish tradition, he is to usher in the messianic age. Both these worthies speak to Jesus of the "exodus" he is about to accomplish in Jerusalem (v. 31). "Exodus" has a double meaning. Naturally, the reader draws on the account of the Israelites' deliverance from death and slavery in Egypt to freedom and new life in the Promised Land. "Exodus," however, can also refer to death. On this basis, Jesus' death is a deliverance from slavery to new life, and his exodus is completed at the resurrection and ascension. Because so much of the material in this chapter deals with discipleship, the meaning death has for Jesus is the same for those who follow him.

The voice from the cloud resonates with the voice at the baptism (3:21-22), but with two differences. At the baptism, Luke writes, the voice comes from heaven and says, "You are my beloved Son; with you I am well pleased"; but here at the transfiguration, the voice comes from the cloud and says, "This is my chosen Son, listen to him" (v. 35). Because the voice from heaven at the baptism is in the second person, only Jesus hears it. At the transfiguration, the voice is in the third person, allowing the three disciples to hear it as well. The reference to the cloud is an echo from Exodus, where the glory of God's presence (Shekinah) is depicted as a cloud (Exod 13:21). God is present at the transfiguration too.

In Matthew's and Mark's version of the transfiguration, Jesus commands the three disciples not to say anything about what they had seen. Luke simply writes, however, that the three kept silent about the whole event "at that time" (v. 36). Although noting that the place of the transfiguration was of no importance to Luke, the tradition, based on Matthew 17:1 and Mark 9:2, locates it on Mount Tabor.

Placed in the context of the mission, eschatology, passion, and discipleship, the transfiguration becomes part of the promise to those who follow Jesus. As he is transfigured into glory by following the Father's will, so too will each Christian disciple be transfigured.

9:37-50 Exorcism and lessons on the kingdom

This case of demonic possession balances the eschatological tone of transfigured glorification by interjecting an attack from the realm of evil. Though the boy's symptoms seem like a case of epilepsy, and may very well have been, sickness was often attributed to the machinations of the devil. In the sense that goodness is from God and illness is not a good, the ancient interpretation hits the mark. Jesus, the one whom Peter confesses as the Messiah and the one whose glory is seen in the transfiguration, reclaims creation for God in the cure of the possessed boy. Only Luke concludes this story by saying that all were "astonished by the majesty of God" (v. 43). Not only does this bit of editing direct attention to the true source and goal of the exorcism, but it also enables the evangelist to omit verses that underscore the disciples' poor performance (see Matt 17:19-20; Mark 9:28-29). In his harsh words, Jesus shows his frustration in getting the message across to those closest to him (v. 41).

While all are marveling at God's greatness, Jesus predicts his passion for the second time (vv. 45-46). The redemption of creation will not be easy and will not be without suffering and death, a sober reminder after the transfiguration and the exorcism. The Lukan Jesus is emphatic about the suffering he must undergo (v. 44). Matthew and Mark do not include this heightened urgency in their parallel accounts. All three Synoptics, however, show the disciples afraid to ask for clarification about the upcoming passion. Luke states that the meaning was "hidden" from them (v. 45), a comment that ties into Jesus' frustration at verse 41 and leads into the instruction on greatness.

The disciples have difficulty comprehending the meaning behind the life and work of Jesus, as the argument about greatness demonstrates (vv. 46-48). With all they have seen in the ministry, all they have experienced by way of miracles, healings, and for at least three of them, the transfiguration, they still measure success according to the world's standards. The child whom Jesus placed at his side was most probably part of a group of children who would beg, pester, and tag along with these strangers for part of the distance through a town. Receiving a child like this is not always easy to do, yet that is the point of Jesus' action. Furthermore, in the society of that time, children were obligated to show respect to adults, not vice versa. The placement of this pericope after the second passion prediction for a lesson on greatness is particularly apropos.

The account about another exorcist (vv. 49-50) highlights the dispute about prestige and the rivalry the disciples have among themselves. The jealousies of the petty despots who ruled all of Palestine often prevented them from working toward mutual self-interest. For the Christian, the horizon line must be higher.

THE JOURNEY TO JERUSALEM

Luke 9:51–19:27

In all three Synoptic accounts, Jesus makes only one trip to Jerusalem, and that journey ends in his passion, death, and resurrection. Luke is the only evangelist, however, to magnify Jerusalem's theological purpose; it is the crucible into which Jesus' whole earthly ministry is funneled. Jerusalem becomes the city of destiny.

This point also marks the beginning of what some scholars call the "Big Interpolation," a large section of material that cannot be linked to Mark and, with few exceptions, has no parallel in Q. The interpolation extends to 18:14.

9:51-56 Departure for Jerusalem and Samaritan inhospitality

Luke describes the shift toward the holy city most dramatically (v. 51). The phrase "When the days for being taken up were fulfilled" signals the end of his Galilean ministry according to a divine plan. "He resolutely determined to journey to Jerusalem" shows an intensity of purpose in completing that divine plan. Luke's vocabulary in verse 51 breathes with metaphor. The Greek for "being taken up, received up" is the word *analēmpsis*, which means both "ascension" and "death." When combined with the "exodus" referred to in the transfiguration (v. 31), there develops the composite picture of death and glorification.

Luke 9

Jesus is going up, both literally and figuratively. Jerusalem is over 900 meters (2700 feet) above sea level, while the Sea of Galilee is nearly 100 meters (300 feet) below; he and his disciples must climb the Judean mountains to reach the city. Metaphorically, after the passion, death, and resurrection, Jesus will ascend to the Father, an ascension that also is his glorification. These events begin and, in a large way, take place within the time frame of Passover, the Jewish commemoration of the Exodus.

Luke's detail about passing through the Samaritan villages raises some questions. Jews in Galilee would avoid passing through Samaria as they made their way south to Jerusalem. The usual route was to walk along the Jordan Valley and begin the ascent at Jericho. It appears that Luke might be relying on some ancient tradition that Jesus passed through, if not ministered in, Samaria. John's story of the Samaritan woman at the well (4:4-41) corroborates Jesus' presence in that territory. Moreover, according to Acts, Samaria was the first non-Jewish region to be converted to Christianity. This short foray into Samaria functions as a foreshadowing of the missionary activity that the Acts of the Apostles will detail. Jesus' rebuke constitutes his stand against vengeance and violence, as well as reflecting his attitude toward missionary activity (see 9:5).

9:57-62 Would-be followers of Jesus

Whereas the disciples have already heard the discourse on the cost of discipleship (see 9:23-27), others joining Jesus have not. Jesus relates the proper comportment in three situations: one to a person who is ready to give all for the kingdom, another to a person who is asked to give all for the kingdom, and still another to one who wants to hold back from giving all to the kingdom. Jesus challenges them by using imagery and hyperbole. The curt answers he gives show the rhythm of someone hurrying with a direct purpose in mind, and the vacillation Jesus encounters with these three would deflect from that purpose.

To the first individual, Jesus underscores that personal comfort will often have to give way to the demands of discipleship. His response to the second may seem harsh, but in no way is it to be understood as negating one's obligations to one's parents or family. Rather, Jesus is seeing through what constitutes a lame excuse while speaking on a symbolic level. To follow Jesus is to enter into a life-giving relationship. There are plenty of people who refuse this relationship, and in this sense they are dead; they can bury the physically dead. The reply to the third individual likewise shows the immediacy of the call. In the Jewish and Hellenistic societies, family bonds were very tight and could hold one back from being

Luke 10

a disciple. Jesus first addresses this situation in 8:19-21, and his answer here is similar.

10:1-16 The mission of the seventy-two

The ancient manuscripts are evenly divided over whether the mission involves seventy or seventy-two disciples. Both numbers have a basis in the Old Testament. Seventy-two is a multiple of twelve, the number of the tribes of Israel; thus, by their going forth, a like number of disciples could represent the universalism of Jesus' mission. Alternatively, the narrative in Exodus 24 includes seventy elders who ascend the mountain with Moses, thereby making the disciples representatives of the Mosaic tradition.

Luke is the only evangelist to have a commissioning of a second group. In comparing the directives to the seventy-two disciples with the commissioning of the Twelve (9:1-6), we can see some differences as well as some points of contact. The Twelve are given authority over demons and the ability to cure diseases. Furthermore, they are charged with proclaiming the good news. The seventy-two disciples, on the other hand, travel in pairs as they bring the good news to households and towns. They are told to cure the sick, but Jesus says nothing about exorcizing demons; yet, they also do so (see v. 17).

Both the Twelve and the seventy-two are to travel light and perform with a singularity of purpose. In this section Jesus calls attention to attributes of Middle Eastern hospitality: there will always be someone to invite them into his or her home. The seventy-two are also told not to abuse the hospitality shown them (v. 8). Both groups are to shake the dust from the street of those towns that do not accept them (v. 11). An important difference, however, is that the seventy-two are to go ahead of Jesus and prepare towns for Jesus' eventual visit.

There is much debate on who constitutes the seventy-two. Were the Twelve selected from the seventy-two, or did they stand independent of them? Were there only seventy-two disciples, or were these seventy-two chosen from a much larger group? Were women in the line of Deborah, Hulda, Esther, Miriam, and Ruth involved, or was the mission restricted to men? These questions are difficult to answer. The important point is that Jesus commissions others to do his work on earth, and as such, the church does that work in him and in his name. Indeed, like the seventy-two, the church prepares the world for Jesus' visitation.

Jesus' comment about Sodom places the Christian message in context. To refuse the redemption he offers is a more heinous sin than any transgressions of sexual morality or proper hospitality. Even the Gentile cities

Luke 10

of Tyre and Sidon will fare better, since they can read the signs of the times (v. 13).

10:17-20 Return of the seventy-two

The joy of the seventy-two disciples arises from the power they have over demons, a power given them by Jesus and only in his name. Jesus' response in verse 18 seems awkward to many. Some scholars have suggested that the proper translation should be "They have observed Satan fall like lightning from the sky," with the subject of the imperfect verb, *theōreō* ("observe"), being "demons" in verse 17. Greek grammar can support such a construction. A conclusion can be that since the demons see Satan fall from the sky, they easily submit to the disciples. The disciples, empowered by Jesus, become agents with him in furthering the realm of God.

The section closes with Jesus reaffirming the purpose and direction of the disciples' new power. They are not self-serving magicians or sorcerers; they are participants in Jesus' ministry. The disciples, like Jesus and those whom they help, find their reward in God, a point that gains in importance as they follow him to the cross in Jerusalem.

10:21-24 The prayer of Jesus and blessing of the disciples

Luke frequently shows Jesus at prayer. Reflecting the joy the disciples display in their return, Jesus offers praise and thanksgiving to the Father. Luke connects this joy to the Spirit, who, in the Acts of the Apostles, takes on a greater role of consoling and fructifying (see Acts 2:1-36). Luke's reversal theme is evident in verse 21, with revelation coming to the childlike but not to the wise and learned. The whole monologue appears to come from Q (see Matt 11:25-27; 13:16-17) and is one of the few places in the synoptic tradition that shows Jesus explaining his relationship to the Father in a pattern that seems very Johannine.

The disciples, who went out on the mission without money bag, sack, or sandals, receive a great reward in their experience of life in the Lord. The prophets and kings did not see or hear the Messiah of God (Luke 9:20), but the disciples have seen and heard not only the Messiah but also the works done in his name. These works consist in redeeming the world from Satan's clutches.

10:25-29 The greatest commandment

Jesus answers the "scholar of the law" or lawyer with a question. This tack precludes any trap or misunderstanding by unveiling the true motivation on the lawyer's part. The verb "test" in verse 25 is also applied to the

Luke 10

devil in the temptation scene (Luke 4:12), thereby emphasizing the sinister quality of the lawyer's question.

Jesus turns the encounter to his advantage. The law that the lawyer quotes is the Jewish Shema, the prayer a devout Jew would recite everyday (Deut 6:4-5). The second half is found in Leviticus 19:18. By endorsing the lawyer's reply, Jesus proves to him and to all listeners that he and his message are not contrary to the Jewish tradition; rather, Jesus forces the audience to see his teaching as an elaboration or refinement of that tradition.

The scholar of the law, however, presses the point with his next question: "And who is my neighbor?" (v. 29). In this verse Luke states that the lawyer wishes to "justify himself," that is, to prove to Jesus in front of the people that he, the legal scholar, is in good stead in the eyes of God. Jesus challenges the lawyer further by responding with the parable of the Good Samaritan.

10:30-37 The parable of the Good Samaritan

Upon the death of King Solomon, Samaria, the region north of Judea, became the center of the northern kingdom at the division of the united monarchy. The Assyrians conquered it in 722 B.C., carted away most of the Israelite inhabitants, and replaced them with conquered peoples from other parts of their empire. These newcomers married into those Israelites left behind, resulting in a population too mixed for the religious Jews in the south to consider part of the covenant. In addition, these northerners, holding only to the books of Genesis through Deuteronomy, maintained their religious cult on Mount Gerizim in Shechem, whereas the Jews in the south saw true worship as taking place only in Jerusalem. The animosity was mutual, as we see in Luke 9:52-54. Samaritans still live and worship on Mount Gerizim today.

This parable exists only in Luke and reflects the theological direction set out in the Gospel and the Acts of the Apostles. The shock value of using a Samaritan as the protagonist in this parable is twofold. The road from Jerusalem to Jericho is solidly in Judea; thus the Samaritan is an unwelcome foreigner in an unfriendly country. The mention of this road also forces the audience to consider the possibility that he has worshiped in Jerusalem. Secondly, for any Samaritans who might hear this parable, this protagonist, by virtue of his journey to Jerusalem, would be a national traitor. On all fronts, then, he can claim no ethnic allegiance, and no people will claim him.

First the priest and then the Levite happen upon the half-dead victim. As officials in the Jerusalem temple, from which they are most probably returning, their prime concern is maintaining ritual purity. There has been shedding of blood, and if the man is dead, they would disqualify themselves from any temple service until undergoing the proper ritual purification, a time-consuming practice. They both avoid the problem by crossing to the other side of the road. The only one to respond mercifully is the outsider of two closed societies.

The searing lesson of this parable comes in verses 36-37. The lawyer would know from Leviticus 19:18 that a neighbor is defined as one's countryman and is limited by ethnic background. The parable, however, breaks through such an interpretation. The neighbor is the one who acts compassionately toward another, ethnic divisions notwithstanding.

Although the parable is prompted by an antagonistic question from a Jewish scholar, it would be wrong to think that this parable is addressed only to the ancient Jewish audience. In the Acts of the Apostles, Luke has an evangelizing mission to Samaria. This parable would have been as difficult for Samaritans to listen to as it would have been for the Jews. After all, the Samaritan is in Jewish territory returning from a Jewish holy city, and, depending on how one would want to view the tale, he aids a Jewish unfortunate.

The lesson for the Lukan community is the same for today's reader. To be a neighbor forces a Christian to go beyond friend and family and extend welcome and mercy to the outcast and even to one's enemy.

10:38-42 The discipleship of Martha and Mary

Traditionally, many have seen this story, which appears only in Luke, as a comparison between the Christian active life, symbolized by Martha, and the contemplative life, represented by Mary. Some exegetes interpret it as Luke's subtle way of silencing and sidelining women in the Christian ministry. The Lukan context, as others have pointed out, challenges both these assumptions.

Mary and Martha share a common ministry in the church. They are models for both men and women of a partnership in service to the reign of God. In this service the love of God is the source and end of all human endeavor, which Mary remembers but Martha seems to have forgotten. The gentle correction that Jesus offers Martha is a reminder to her that work is nothing without its connection to God. For this reason Martha needs Mary as much as Mary needs Martha.

11:1-13 Teachings on prayer

The Our Father or Lord's Prayer (11:1-4) has a revered place within the Christian tradition. With its references to the "name" (v. 2), "bread" (v. 3), and "sins" (v. 4), this prayer underscores a Jewish background. The differences between the Matthean and the Lukan accounts reflect a different theological nuance. While Luke, for example, does not highlight the separation between heaven and earth, Matthew does so by use of such phrases as "Our Father in heaven" (6:9) and "your will be done, / on earth as in heaven" (6:10). This discrepancy led many ancient scribes to try to harmonize Luke's address with Matthew's by adding the phrase "Our . . . in heaven" to "Father" in their versions of Luke's text. Luke's address here, however, matches all the other instances where the Lukan Jesus prays: "I give you praise, Father, Lord of heaven and earth" (10:21); "Father, if you are willing, take this cup away from me" (22:42); "Father, forgive them, they know not what they do" (23:34); and "Father, into your hands I commend my spirit" (23:46).

The structure is the same in the Lukan and Matthean accounts, subtle differences between the two notwithstanding. They both open by hallowing God's name, thereby affirming the divine majesty. They then move to Christ's intermediary role and conclude with a human petition.

Many see Luke's use of "sins" as his way of demonstrating Christ's efficacy. With his merciful forgiveness manifested in his passion, death, and resurrection, Jesus defeats Satan by breaking the vicious circle of suffering, fear, hate, and revenge the devil uses to hold humankind in thrall. The person at prayer asks Christ to forgive, and Christ has done so; therefore the person must also forgive.

Matthew's version of the Our Father (see Matt 6:9-13) is better known; indeed, this title for the prayer comes from the Matthew's account and not from Luke's. It is Matthew's rendition that also appears to be the basis for the Our Father found in the early Christian work called the *Didache* (8:2). The *Didache*'s version of the prayer became the form used throughout the centuries and includes the doxology that many Christian churches use in their worship. With the Lord's Prayer as a background, Luke continues the teaching on prayer with the parable of the importunate friend, a reading found only in Luke. Luke's wry comparison between divine response and human reaction—"if he does not get up to give him the loaves because of their friendship, he will get up to give him whatever he needs because of his persistence"—is echoed in the Lukan parable of the persistent widow (18:1-8). The point is that if humans will act on behalf of the petitioner solely from self-serving interest, how much more will God act from love. According to the Palestinian-Jewish custom of the day, the whole family slept on floor bedding in a single room, above the animals. To open the door would not only rouse the family but would also cause a fuss with the livestock, and all in the dark.

Luke 11

Luke tells us how prayers are answered (11:9-13). In his schema they have a natural, thematic, and visual flow from the parable. Someone coming at night would have to *seek* the house and door of a friend. Once found, he or she would have to *knock* at the door persistently to rouse the inhabitant to *open* it. The references to a snake and a scorpion provide insight into human response to an answered prayer. The listener or hearer would answer the rhetorical questions in verses 11-12 with a firm "None!" Such imagery, however, calls a person to faith. What might appear to be a snake or a scorpion at first glance might actually be the granted request. Again, the reader encounters Luke's analogical style based on divine response and human reaction (11:13).

11:14-23 The Beelzebul controversy

Each Gospel shows some version of the Beelzebul controversy. Although much of this section is from Q, there is evidence of what is called a "Marcan-Q Overlap"; that is, Q material is intricately tied up with Marcan narrative. A comparison between Matthew 12:29, Luke 11:20-21, and Mark 3:27 is such an example. To be sure, there are no Johannine parallels to the synoptic readings here, but there are certainly traces of such accusations against Jesus at several points in the Fourth Gospel: John 7:20; 8:48-52; 10:20-21. This multiple attestation makes certain the conclusion that Jesus was accused of being in league with the devil during his ministry.

Luke uses this pericope as one of the defining moments in his two-volume narrative. Whereas Matthew and Mark both state that someone must first tie up the strong man, Luke states that someone must overcome or be victorious over the strong man (11:22). There has been evidence of victory all along in the Lukan text.

11:24-26 The return of the evil spirit

Luke sees the contest with Satan as a real battle, and the enemy does not relinquish control easily. The house to which the seven other evil spirits return is the same good one from which the unclean spirit had previously departed. Their roaming through "arid regions searching for rest" stands as a metaphor for those people who do not fill their lives with the goodness of God. Nature abhors a vacuum, and thus seven other wicked spirits find a home within the now empty individual (v. 26). This understanding can be applied to Judas, about whom Luke states that Satan "enter[s]" (22:3). Judas never allowed into his heart the grace that Jesus brings, and thus the wicked spirits take up residence there.

In Luke's Gospel, the battle between Christ and Satan, announced at the birth (1:78-79), begins at the temptation (4:1-13). Jesus has been waging and winning battles against the devil demons all along, but Christ's ultimate victory over Satan, a victory of light over darkness, will come at the cross. This theme continues in the Acts of the Apostles.

11:27-28 True blessedness

The narrative flow forms a juxtaposition of seeming opposites. After the long deliberation about Beelzebul, the strong man, and unclean spirits, a woman in the crowd turns the subject to blessedness, and does so by making a reference to Jesus' mother. Jesus' response, however, demonstrates that his call goes beyond natural kinship; indeed, natural kinship might even be an impediment (see 8:19-21).

11:29-32 The demand for a sign

Luke avoids redundancy. The narrative sequence has already informed the reader that people are testing and arguing with Jesus (see Luke 11:15), so, unlike Matthew and Mark (12:38; 8:11-12), Luke does not mention Pharisees or scribes badgering Jesus. Jesus simply continues with his teaching.

The book of Jonah forms the necessary background for any interpretation of this passage. The Lukan text in verse 30 is helpful in this regard by supplying the central element of that particular Old Testament work. That Nineveh was the ancient capital of the Assyrians, the people who ravaged the Israelite kingdom under Shalmaneser V in 722 B.C., sharpens the drama of the Jonah story. Jonah is the son of Amittai. Amittai is also the name of one of the prophets from the time of King Jeroboam II (786–746 B.C.). If the name Amittai refers to one and the same person, then it would have been understood that Jonah came from the Israelite kingdom just as the Assyrian Empire was menacing it.

Jonah is sent on a mission, therefore, into absolutely alien and hostile territory, to a land feared and despised by all his compatriots. After fits and starts, including a sojourn in the belly of a great fish (Jonah 2:1), Jonah reaches his destination and preaches judgment, with the result that the whole city of Nineveh, from the king to the lowliest beast, repents. This repentance is the sign of Jonah to which Luke refers in verses 29-30. The explanation continues.

In verse 31 Luke also has a reference to "the queen of the south," or the Queen of Sheba (see 1 Kgs 10:1ff.; 2 Chr 9:1ff.; Matt 12:42). With this allusion the lesson works in reverse: the pagan makes the journey to the land of the true God. In both cases nonbelievers make acts of repentance or faith. Jesus

Luke 11

draws a comparison and contrast between those within and those outside the pale of revelation, and in so doing, proclaims the wide invitation of God's love and salvation as well as the breadth of human response to it. In the end Jonah, with his example of the Ninevites, and the queen of the south, with her pilgrimage to Solomon, will stand in judgment of those who reject Jesus.

11:33-36 The visibility of light

These verses are a reprise of the lamp motif seen in 8:16ff. Luke elaborates the analogy here. The discourses about Jonah and the queen of the south in verses 30-31 above provide the example of how "lights" and "lamps" can further evangelization. Matthew uses this Q material as well but places it at two different locations within the Sermon on the Mount (5:13-16 and 6:22-23). Luke, on the other hand, finishes this section with a wonderful simile for a true disciple. The Christian life involves the whole body and all human action. The way people conduct themselves determines the persons they will become. Filled with faith, these people, by their brightness will lead others from darkness into the light of faith. The light and darkness dichotomy in this Q material is reminiscent of John's Gospel.

11:37-54 Denunciation of the legal experts

This section, called the "Woes," has a parallel in Matthew 23:1-38. Differences between the two can be seen in Matthew's concern for and knowledge of the Law, something that Luke, in writing for a Gentile audience, has no need to address.

The Pharisee literally invites Jesus to breakfast, indicated by the Greek verb *aristáō*. If Palestinian social customs of ancient times are in any way similar to those today, the breakfast would be quite substantial and would be taken around ten o'clock in the morning, but it would not be the main meal of the day, which is taken in the evening. The fact that Pharisees and scholars take issue with Jesus in the manner that they do exposes an ulterior motive: they wish to observe his behavior with hopes of gaining evidence against him. If they had really wished to honor him, they would have invited him for the evening repast. Jesus recognizes this plot and responds by revealing their true motives in front of all. He also exhibits the shallowness and hypocrisy of their deeds. Jesus' denunciation at verses 47-51 foreshadows his own death. The system that killed the prophets will also, by implication, kill him, as verses 53-54 substantiate.

It is difficult to identify which Zechariah (v. 51) Luke is referring to. Many see him as Zechariah the priest, son of Jehoiadah (see 2 Chr 24:20-22).

Luke 12

Others have seen him as Zechariah the priest, the father of John the Baptist.

12:1-12 In face of persecution

We last read of the crowds in 11:29. Mention of them here returns our focus to Jesus' preaching. The reference to the "leaven . . . of the Pharisees" (v. 1) thematically connects this scene with the meal at the Pharisee's house (11:27-54).

In verse 4 Jesus calls his disciples, and possibly by extension the rest of the people, "friends." This is the only occurrence in all three Synoptic Gospels in which we see this form of address applied to Jesus' followers, and it is another example of a tradition Luke seems to share with John (see John 15:14-15).

In a time of persecution, people generally go into hiding and maintain a secret existence. Jesus' admonition describes a situation in which no hiding will be possible, even if it were desirable. True fear should be reserved for the One who can cast a believer into Gehenna after the body is dead (v. 5). This phrase serves as a circumlocution emphasizing that we need fear only God.

"Gehenna" is a Greek transliteration of the Hebrew *Hinnom*, the name of the valley on the western side of Jerusalem. Often cursed by the Jewish prophets for the child sacrifice that the Jerusalemites practiced there, it is also called Topheth (see 2 Kgs 23:10; Jer 7:31-32; 19:6, 11-14). In time, the Valley of Hinnom functioned as the city garbage dump, thereby making it ritually unclean. In both Jewish and Christian canonical and deuterocanonical texts, Gehenna is the metaphor for hell. As Jesus makes plain in other parts of his ministry, we have a hand in determining our salvation by opting to participate in God's grace. He emphasizes that our salvation lies beyond the reach of any persecutor.

Not even denying Christ in the face of danger and threat will bring eternal condemnation; only a sin against the holy Spirit has that power. The sin against the holy Spirit is the refusal of God's mercy and forgiveness when it is offered. Here, too, by having the choice to accept or reject the love of Christ, we have a role in determining our salvation.

God will not abandon those facing the sword. The holy Spirit will not only be present in fortifying the witnesses to Jesus but will also direct them in their actions and speak on their behalf, as Luke demonstrates in the Acts of the Apostles.

12:13-21 Greed and riches

This section consists of a dialogue followed by a parable. The first half, prompted by someone in the crowd calling out to Jesus, succinctly presents

Luke 12

Jesus' true role and ministry while offering an ethical and eschatological lesson.

The person who calls out from the crowd misunderstands Jesus' mission. The person errs by viewing Jesus as an arbiter whose judgment rests on interpreting the intricacies of a legal code. Jesus refuses to be cast in such a position, and he turns the table on the questioner as well as the brother. The issue, Jesus implies, is not who is right or wrong about the inheritance; it is about greed and avarice. If both exhibited less covetousness, one would be inclined to share with the other, and the other would not suspect that he was being cheated. Jesus' ministry is to the lost, and both brothers are sinners. His action allows the two to receive his message. No one loses, and both have the opportunity to enter the kingdom. The parable of the rich fool, which follows (vv. 16-21), illustrates the lesson.

At no point in his discourse does the rich fool credit God for the harvest. Furthermore, he never acknowledges that the bounty should have some purpose other than satisfying his own desires. Because he is so selfish and self-centered, he dies without benefit of both his wealth and God's love. With this parable, Jesus warns the two brothers to guard against ending up like the rich fool—a total loser. An example of how bad it will be for someone like this individual is found in the parable of the rich man and Lazarus (16:19-31).

12:22-34 Trust and faith in God

Matthew places this discourse within the Sermon on the Mount (see Matt 6:25-34), while Luke situates it on the journey to Jerusalem. Nonetheless, the lesson is the same: God's love is so abundant that he looks after every human need. In Luke, this passage provides the proper frame of mind and heart that stands in contrast to the focus of the rich fool seen above (vv. 16-21).

The Greek *korax*, translated here as "ravens" (v. 24), can also mean "crow"; in any case, it refers to a scavenger. Not only was such a creature forbidden as food to Jews, but it was considered a disgusting bird also among Gentile Greeks. Its repulsive character, therefore, makes the comparison all the more striking. Using the rhetorical form of the comparison of the greater, the listener or reader understands that if God tends to the needs of a repugnant carrion-eater, how much more will he care for his beloved people (see also Ps 147:9 and Job 38:41).

This same type of comparison is employed further on in the passage with the flowers, called *krinon* in Greek. Most probably it is the crocus, referred to in other parts of the Bible as the "rose of Sharon" (Song 2:1).

Against the green Galilean hillsides in rainy times of the year, these blossoms give a dazzling appearance. Yet the spectacular color of the grass and flowers is short-lived. As soon as the weather turns warm, both the herbage and the blooms shrivel up. In a land with little wood, dried grass is often used for fuel. Once again we hear the comparison of the greater. If God shows so much attention to what ends up in the fire, how much more does he care for his people.

Luke introduces a social justice theme not paralleled in Matthew's version. The "inexhaustible treasure in heaven" (v. 33) comes from almsgiving. Luke underscores the lesson of the discourse with verse 34. If we make ourselves rich in the eyes of God, our hearts and motivation will lead to union with God both in this life and the life to come. Furthermore, by becoming rich in heaven, we relieve ourselves of earthly anxiety.

12:35-48 The need for vigilance

The metaphors for vigilance all make the same point: the Lord's coming, or parousia, will happen when we least expect it. Each of the examples, however, gives a variety of views of what one can expect.

A master returning from a wedding would come with his bride (vv. 35-38). There would be feasting and celebration associated with the homecoming, which the servants should be ready to facilitate. In a role reversal, this master serves the servants. So too will it be at the eschatological banquet, when Jesus will be the host. The Lord's coming will arrive with the shock and surprise of a nighttime thief breaking into a house.

The notion of preparation introduces a paradox: this passage seems to contradict the parable of the rich fool (12:16-21). There readers are told not to worry about the morrow, food, or clothing, but here they are admonished not to take anything for granted, but to be ready for the unexpected. The paradox lies in the fact that adequate preparation is the result of letting go of worldly concerns and values. The prepared person will not be attached to the concerns of this life, even though she may be immersed in the midst of them.

The parable of the wise and just servant likewise has a strain of irony running through it (vv. 42-48). A good foreman will not take advantage of those under him, and if he does, the master will depose him upon his return. Such a punishment, however, is reserved only for the servant who knew his master's will and acted shamefully. The servant who does not know the master's will and commits the same actions will get off with a lighter punishment. The parable is a lesson in discipleship that parallels Luke 19:11-27. Followers of Christ will be held to a higher standard than nonbelievers.

Luke 12

12:49-59 Division, signs, conduct

Although this section appears to come from Q, verses 49-50 are found only in Luke's Gospel. The evangelist wishes to underscore that discipleship is not without its price, and the world will not gladly welcome the kingdom of God. Fire and water are both elements of destruction and cleansing, and as harsh as the imagery may seem, Luke uses them here to show the immediacy and totality of the impending *eschaton*. The more specific examples of how Christ's message will be received (vv. 51-53) depict a situation in the early church, most probably within the Jewish-Christian synagogues from which the Christians were eventually expelled.

In Israel and Palestine, rain can only come from the Mediterranean and only in the winter, hence the reference to the west wind (v. 54). Similarly, the Sahara, Sinai, and Arabian deserts lie in the south and are the source of the hot, desiccating breeze (v. 55). The signs of the times should be just as obvious.

This discourse works on several levels. The historical signs are the political precariousness of the Jewish state during the intertestamental epoch: Roman occupation, political dissension, and corrupt administration threatened the society to the point of anarchy. On the religious front, the signs of the times were Jesus' ministry (see Luke 4:16-21). These signs are the same no matter what the period in history. Issues of social justice coupled with the religious and spiritual emptiness are signs pointing to the eschatological reign. The Christian is called to respond to them.

The section ends with instruction to the early Christian community itself (vv. 57-59). As a people baptized in Christ's name, they should settle differences within the community and not resort to the pagan law courts. Christians have a new standard of behavior that encompasses personal behavior as well as ways of resolving injustices. These standards extend beyond restitution and include mercy, redemption, and forgiveness. Such an interpretation does not mean covering up shameful or wrongful behavior behind a cloak of secrecy; rather, it means making the community a living symbol of justice and reconciliation (see Matt 5:25-26).

13:1-9 Sin and repentance

The incident involving Pilate referred to here is one of the few places where he is mentioned outside the passion narratives, and it is very telling.

Many see Pontius Pilate as a weak, vacillating governor who feels overwhelmed by the vagaries of the mob, and, against his better judgment, he hands Jesus over to be crucified (see Matt 27:26; Mark 15:15; Luke 23:25;

Luke 13

John 19:16). Luke's narrative counters such an assessment by relating this slaughter, for which there is no other record in the Bible or any other extant work. Josephus refers to an uprising of Jews when Pilate uses temple money to build a Jerusalem aqueduct (*Ant.* 18.3.2 and *J.W.* 2.9.4). Pilate ruthlessly suppresses the tumult by having disguised, weapon-bearing Roman soldiers mixed among the Jews. At a given signal, they begin to hack away at the civilian population.

It is quite plausible that both Josephus and Jesus are referring to the same calamity. Likewise, along the southeastern wall of ancient Jerusalem are visible ruins from a collapsed tower (v. 4) dating to the intertestamental period, that is, the two centuries between the composition of the last book of the Old Testament and the first book of the New Testament.

The lesson that Jesus draws from these events releases human suffering from the capricious judgment of wrathful gods, where many of then contemporary pagan cults had placed it, or even from known or unknown sinful behavior, as many in the Jewish religious establishment then taught. Instead, Jesus is saying that suffering comes to good and bad alike, and that all humankind stands in need of repentance and redemption. Someone's misfortune is not an indicator of moral culpability. John's Gospel (9:2) features a similar lesson in the healing of the person born blind (see also Ps 7:12-13).

With the parable of the fig tree (vv. 6-9), Luke employs a graceful thematic continuity from the stress on repentance to the value of the sinner. The fig tree is highly prized for the luscious texture and sweetness of its fruit (see Judg 9:10-11; 1 Kgs 5:5; 2 Kgs 18:31). Furthermore, the fruit can be dried and preserved for years on end.

The inedible variety of figs looks exactly like the edible kind. Moreover, edible figs can only be pollinated by the female fig wasp *(Blastophaga psenes)*, which carries the pollen from the inedible fig and burrows into the buds of the edible one. Hence, for proper cultivation both types of fig trees are necessary. This delicate operation can confuse even the best gardeners, and patience is necessary to ensure a good harvest of the precious fruit. The lesson is that God will not give up on those who struggle with turning toward him. In addition, the great value placed on the fig tree characterizes the value of the sinner in God's eyes—not a reprobate or an outcast, but a prized possession, despite the possibility that the sinner may never "bear fruit."

13:10-17 The cure of the crippled woman on the sabbath

If Jesus was teaching in the synagogue, he must have originally met with respect from the synagogue leader. In fact, the leader reprimands not

Luke 13

Jesus but the crowd of people who seemingly have come on the sabbath to be cured. The cause of the leader's discomfort, therefore, is not that Jesus cured but that this curing occurred on the Lord's Day. Healing was seen as work and therefore prohibited. Jesus uses this opportunity to make several points about his identity, his reign, and the world.

The Jewish sabbath, since it commemorates the seventh day on which God rested from all his labors, is literally the Lord's Day. Because of the holy character of the sabbath, the regulations against work were intended to give everyone access to this life in the Lord. Judging from Jesus' response, it appears that in this situation, the sabbath regulations had ceased to provide the spiritual renewal that originally had been associated with them. Jesus' challenge to the custom is successful only because of his authority. He thus gives the sabbath an eschatological dimension. Access to life in the Lord now becomes a foretaste of the heavenly realm, where sin and suffering are put to rout. This interpretation is evident in Jesus' reply (v. 16).

The reference to Satan in verse 16, combined with the setting of the cure on the sabbath, characterizes a central aspect of Lukan eschatology. Sickness and malady are viewed as a part of Satan's malevolent realm, which has made inroads into God's creation. Jesus' role is to redeem creation, to win it back for God. Jesus overpowers the evil forces and ushers in the eschatological reign. No longer dominated by Satan, the crippled woman now has her sabbath rest.

13:18-19 The parable of the mustard seed

All three Synoptics show this parable. The mustard seed was considered the smallest of all possible seeds. The tree itself, the *brassica nigra,* grows wild throughout Palestine and Israel, but farmers also cultivate it. With small, bright yellow flowers and slender, dark green leaves, it can grow to a large, many-branched shrub or tree. As such, it is a metaphor for the small early Christian community, which has an influence on the world going far beyond its size and number to the point that others (symbolized by birds) make their home in it.

13:20-21 The measure of yeast

This parable appears only in Matthew and Luke. The bread of the time would have been sourdough, as most bread was until the development of dry yeast. Once the dough was kneaded, pieces were pulled away, flattened, and laid over a hot metal dome called a *tamboun*. The result was a large, circular crêpe or pita.

Not much yeast was needed to cause a batch of dough to rise, so, like the parable of the mustard seed, the leaven stands as a measure for the Christian community. In this parable the woman who adds the yeast to the flour is the Christ figure.

13:22-30 The narrow door, salvation, and rejection

With this parable Jesus indirectly answers the question put to him. Restrictions to entering the kingdom do not lie with God but with the human response to the divine invitation. Because Luke recapitulates the point that Jesus is on his way to Jerusalem (v. 22), many consider this section as the beginning of the second half of the journey narrative leading to the city of his death and resurrection.

The conventional city gate during this period had one wide, high central arch flanked by two lower, narrower portals. The main arch permitted camels, carts, and goods to pass. Those who wished to enter and who had no baggage trains could avoid the traffic by walking through either one of the narrow gates.

Applying this daily occurrence to the parable, the lesson seems to be directed to those who drag along their religious or social status, their material possessions, or their own ambitions in seeking easy access to salvation. Jesus counters this attitude by extracting a lesson from a familiar scene. Just as today those who travel light reach their destination more easily than those with much luggage, so too will those who keep their eyes and actions on salvation find the swifter path through the smaller doors. Any attempt to interpret these verses as showing that Gentiles are saved at the expense of the Jews is based on a faulty reading. The setting of the story is Jesus' trip to Jerusalem accompanied by his Jewish disciples, but the Lukan community to whom this story is told is composed mostly of Gentiles. All are instructed, therefore, to enter by the narrow gate, a passage that is difficult but not impossible.

The introduction of mixed metaphors in verses 25-30 is a result of various strands of tradition redacted into one parable. The second lesson is similar to the first: one should not rely on status to enter the kingdom. To use a modern parallel, ticket holders who arrive for a concert at the last minute may still not get in if there is a long line at the gate; their reliance on their ticket stubs proves to be no guarantee of entry. If they had been earnest in their desire, they would have arrived early and waited in line to be sure of getting a seat.

13:31-33 The Pharisees warn about Herod

Do the Pharisees come to Jesus as friends and allies, or are they simply trying to frighten Jesus into submission? In either case, Jesus does not alter

Luke 13

his intention to head to Jerusalem. Indeed, he uses the occasion to affirm it—he must go to Jerusalem (v. 33).

Lukan eschatology once again surfaces with the blending of three statements in verse 32. As in the parable of the crippled woman (13:10-17), curing the sick is seen as a successful assault on demonic forces. Furthermore, contained in this statement is a reference to Jesus' passion, death, and resurrection: "On the third day I accomplish my purpose" (v. 32). Jesus predicts his own death with his emphatic resolution to continue to Jerusalem, though, ironically, by traveling to Jerusalem he leaves Herod's jurisdiction.

13:34-35 The lament over Jerusalem

This passage, a rhetorical apostrophe, flows from the scene with the Pharisees immediately above and is a fine example of Luke's narrative finesse. Matthew's Gospel contains a parallel account, but in that Gospel Jesus utters these words after the triumphant entry into Jerusalem (see Matt 23:37-39).

In 13:33 Jesus says that a prophet should not die outside Jerusalem. His words over the city have him identifying with that destiny, and he does so by using a lament, a prophetic genre seen most clearly in Jeremiah and Lamentations. To be sure, prophets were also slain outside Jerusalem, but given the presence of the temple within the city and the city's history with the prophets, Jeremiah and Isaiah make Jerusalem the major symbol of a prophet's destiny (see 1 Kgs 9:7-8; 2 Kgs 21:16; Ps 118:2; Jer 22:5).

In verse 34 the reader should note the feminine imagery inherent in Jesus' self-referential term "hen" (see also Deut 32:11). Contained also is the allusion to his entering the city in 19:28-40.

14:1-6 Healing a man with dropsy on the sabbath

Dropsy, or edema, is characterized by a buildup of fluids, often in the extremities. It is usually symptomatic of a variety of diseases.

There are several similarities between this story and the account of the crippled woman (13:10-17). They are solely Lukan material, and in both cases the miracle occurs on the sabbath. The woman is cured in front of the synagogue leaders, and the man here is restored to health in the presence of leading Pharisees. Furthermore, neither the woman nor the man asks Jesus to be healed; rather, in both instances Jesus, moved by pity, takes the initiative to cure the individual. He explains his action using the rhetorical device of the comparison of the greater: if the Law makes allowances for saving livestock on the sabbath, how much more should one help a fellow human being on the holy day.

Unlike the passage about the woman, however, there is nothing in this story to indicate that the leaders were angry or that they had duplicitous intentions in "observing him carefully" (v. 1). It seems that the Pharisees here are indeed curious about how Jesus would handle such a case, and, he engages them with his question (v. 3). Because they, too, know the Law and its provisions, they remain silent. Once again, the sabbath setting connects physical well-being with eternal salvation, thereby giving the Lord's Day an eschatological dimension (see also Luke 6:1-11; 11:37-54).

14:7-14 Proper comportment of guests and hosts

With the man now cured of his dropsy, Luke continues to describe the action surrounding the dinner. Jesus observes the customs of courtesy and etiquette and ties these issues of daily protocol to a lesson about the kingdom. Luke calls this lesson a "parable" (v. 7), but its genre is closer to a wisdom saying. Only Luke contains this passage, although a parallel to verse 11 appears in Matthew 23:12, making this aphorism most probably a Q saying. It is also found in Luke 18:14.

The dining room would have been a *triclinium* (see 7:36-50). The host would recline on his left side at the top of the right extension of the table; the opening to the horseshoe-shaped construction would have been to his back. The place of honor would have been at the crossbar, making the position of the honored guest directly perpendicular to the host so that they could talk directly to each other. Succeeding places of honor continued along the crossbar and down the left side, with the lowest place situated at the end of the left extension; the guest would have to constantly readjust his position in order to converse with those in the lowest places. What Jesus notices, therefore, is a stream of guests jockeying for the spot perpendicular to the host while avoiding anything along the left extension, especially the last place.

In the Mediterranean world, an honor-shame based culture, the social gaffe of overstepping one's station, such as Jesus describes, would have been a mortifying experience. On the other hand, being asked to come higher would have been particularly enviable. The lesson goes beyond calculating a social standing among one's peers, however, and points to the proper disposition toward God and how we define our need for God's salvation in our lives. Social self-inflation is equated with spiritual self-righteousness. Those who assume that they are righteous enough to let themselves into the kingdom without any regard for the divine initiative will have to give way to those who know their unworthiness and depend on God's love and grace for everything.

Luke 14

Jesus then turns the lesson to the host. The Roman world ran on the patronage system, in which the rich and influential would curry favor among their constituencies in return for support, respect, and fulfilled obligations. In such a society, a family holding a lavish banquet for notable dignitaries and lesser functionaries would be renowned for their generosity and would thereby garner a great deal of influence in their local area. Such would be their payback.

The true act of generosity in the eyes of God, however, lies in bestowing respect and dignity on those who would not only be unable to repay in kind but whose very social standing carries no prestige whatsoever. The reward one gains in the resurrection of the righteous (Greek: *dikaios*) ties this lesson to the one Jesus teaches to the guests (v. 14). In both instances, then, humility before God becomes the proper comportment for entering the kingdom.

14:15-24 The parable of the great banquet

This parable originates in Q and has a parallel in Matthew (22:1-14).

Banquets in the Gospel tradition always contain a strong eschatological element. Luke's creativity shines in this passage as he situates the banquet parable within the setting of a large dinner and gracefully folds the parable into the scene with the guest's remark in verse 15. The excuses that the original invitees give for not going to the dinner are legitimate. A wedding feast would last for several days, and one who has purchased land or cattle would have a strong desire to examine the sources of his livelihood. But these mitigating circumstances arise after they have presumably already accepted the invitation; it is the summons to enter the feast that they refuse. In a society in which a patronage system governs many areas of life, their refusals are a disrespectful insult to the host's generosity.

Moreover, the last excuses introduce an eschatological dimension. According to Deuteronomic law, those who have built a house, planted a vineyard, or married a woman did not have to go on a military expedition or engage in any public duty for a period of one year (Deut 20:5-6; 24:5). By using these exemptions to explain why they cannot attend, they call attention to the dinner. The *eschaton* will not arrive without struggle. In order to sit at the banquet table in the kingdom of heaven, one must value it above any other facet of life, and acting on this value will be a struggle of warlike proportions. The banquet therefore becomes a metaphor for victory in the battle on behalf of the kingdom of God. Those refusing to come to the dinner demonstrate that they recognize this point. They simply do not hold the kingdom in as high regard as their daily affairs, as noble as those affairs may be.

The metaphor continues. The rich and wealthy have no need to participate in a banquet. The poor in the nearby city and district, who need the protection and favor of a rich lord, jump at the chance to go. There is still room at the table, so the invitation goes out to those who have no relationship to the host, and thus neither the host nor these guests have anything to gain from each other. The invitation is a purely gracious act.

The lesson of the parable places Jesus' mission in a microcosm. The self-satisfied, self-sufficient, and self-righteous are welcomed into the kingdom, but their self-inflated importance will block their will to enter. Those knowing their spiritual destitution will enter the kingdom willingly, and the Gentiles, who have no legal claim or right to come and dine, will also be invited to fill the dining hall.

14:25-35 The cost of discipleship

The Gospel of Matthew (10:37-38) shows a shortened parallel of verses 25-27. At the core of both accounts is Q source material, which Luke expands. The expansion continues into verses 28-33, a section that has no parallels. Luke concludes with a form of the saying about salt (vv. 34-35), which appears in all three Synoptics.

The language in verse 26 is harsh. In a reflection of the Semitic convention to employ hyperbole in order to make a point, Luke uses the Greek verb *miseō*, a term meaning "detest" or "abhor." The lesson teaches that no earthly attachment to a person, place, or thing should keep us from following God. Discipleship requires singleness of purpose, and this purpose is to go beyond natural ties and allegiances for the sake of the kingdom. Doing so will not be easy (v. 27).

The image seems to switch in verses 28-33, but the purpose of this scene is closely aligned to the preceding material and, in fact, explains it. Constructing a major building or preparing for a military expedition requires a great deal of planning. An architect or a general must calculate losses and the gains and make a decision accordingly. Being a disciple demands at least as much time and consideration. Disciples must acknowledge what they must sacrifice in order to take up the cross (v. 33).

References to building a tower and marching into battle may have been drawn from the life experience of the day. Herod the Great launched major construction in Caesarea Maritima, Jericho, Jerusalem, and even in the desert. Each of these projects involved a tremendous amount of planning to organize both human and material resources. Likewise, there was a major dispute between Herod Antipas and King Aretas of Nabatea, based on the former's divorce of his first wife, who was a Nabatean princess, in order

Luke 14

to marry Herod Philip's wife, Herodias. Ultimately, this dispute turned into a war, which ended when Rome intervened and forced King Aretas to give up his plans.

The whole lesson ends with the salt metaphor (vv. 34-35). In order for salt to lose its taste, it would have to cease being sodium chloride. Analogously, disciples who shrug off the cross cease being disciples of Christ.

15:1-32 Parables of the lost

At this point in the journey to Jerusalem, Luke has constructed a series of parables and lessons dealing with sinners and their chance for salvation.

Luke groups together three parables dealing with valuables lost and found. These parables form a unit in which the central personage in each story line is the Christ figure, and the person or object lost is then seen as the sinner. Two of the parables, those of the lost coin and the prodigal son, are found only in Luke's Gospel.

15:1-7 The parable of the lost sheep

Although this parable is Q material, Luke's introduction to it is different from Matthew 18:12-14. In Luke, Pharisees and scribes are grumbling about the tax collectors and sinners who gravitate toward Jesus. Their complaining leads into the parable of the lost sheep. The rhetorical question "What man among you . . . ?" (v. 4) relies on the common sense of the listener to conclude that no one would leave a whole flock to go after one lost sheep. The ridiculousness of leaving ninety-nine sheep in the desert to find a stray defies the imagination, but such ridiculousness is the point of the parable. Nearly equally ridiculous is inviting neighbors and friends to celebrate the return of the stray.

God's love for his creatures is so strong that it includes even the sinners, something that self-righteous individuals have a hard time appreciating. The joy that spreads through heaven also strikes our human ears as overmuch, but it emphasizes the divine welcome given to the repentant sinner.

The Greek uses *anthrōpos* for "man" (v. 4) and thus is a gender-inclusive term. Often in the Holy Land, both in antiquity and now, shepherds are boys, girls, and women, an interesting perspective for the story considering that the shepherd is the Christ figure.

15:8-10 The parable of the lost coin

The Greek for "coin," *drachma,* was of the approximate value of a *denarius* and was worth about one day's wage for a laborer; the woman's diligent search, therefore, is certainly justified. When the object of the search, in this case a coin, is compared to the lost sheep in the previous parable, we can see an increase in the stakes. No matter how valuable one sheep is in earthly terms, it is not worth risking ninety-nine other sheep to find it. In this parable, however, the other nine coins are not placed in jeopardy as the woman seeks out the lost coin.

As with the parable of the yeast (13:20-21), the woman is the Christ figure, and her intense desire to find the lost coin is analogous to God's desire to find the lost sinner. Moreover, the parable says something about the value of the lost sinner in God's eyes. Here the mention of the rejoicing among the angels (v. 10) echoes the heavenly rejoicing found in the parable of the lost sheep (15:7). In both cases, such a conclusion keeps the eschatological focus of the message.

We read that a woman lights a lamp to sweep the house, a detail that gives evidence of the Syrian origins of Luke's Gospel. Unlike houses in the Judean Hills or even the semi-arid desert fringes of the south, which were constructed of comparatively lightweight limestone or sandstone, allowing for use of windows and other openings, houses on the Syrian plains and heights had a different building material and style altogether. In these areas the common building block was the very heavy, volcanic, black basalt stone. To support upper stories, the walls of these buildings had to be of solid construction and could not contain many, if any, windows. Consequently, interior living spaces were dark, and lighting a lamp would have been necessary, even in broad daylight.

15:11-32 The parable of the prodigal son

This parable has had a great influence on Western art, being depicted in drama, music, ballet, and painting.

The story opens with the younger son asking his father for his share of the inheritance. Of course, it is for the father to decide whether his son deserves it, not the son himself. By his action the younger son communicates that he does not view the inheritance as a gift bequeathed to him because of his father's good graces; rather, he sees it as his due.

According to ancient Jewish custom (Num 27:8-11; 36:7-9), an inheritance is the father's property, which, according to the custom of the day, the father gave to his sons, although he was not bound by any means to do so. When the younger son demands his share of the inheritance, therefore, he is asking the father for a part of the father's life. It is as if the son is requesting the father's very soul, an understanding emphasized by the Greek term for "property," *bios*, the same word used for "life" or "living" (v. 12). By his request, the son is indirectly demanding the father's own death. The father, however, instead of taking insult with his son's effrontery, gives him the inheritance.

The young son squanders the inheritance on "a life of dissipation" (v. 13). The idea is that the son's living is so extravagant, profligate, wasteful, and glitzy, that there is nothing of merit in any of it. Not only is the son jeopardizing his physical life by dangerous living, but the return of enjoyment on his investment is so meager that it makes the whole venture worthless.

To feed a pig, which represents everything reprehensible to every Jewish sensibility, would be a curse indeed. God-fearing Gentiles in the Lukan community would have been familiar enough with Jewish customs to know how low the young son descended. The son is absolutely alienated from the community. The pods (Greek: *kerátion*) were probably from the carob tree and would be fit for human consumption (v. 16).

With verse 17 the audience is prepared for the next part, where the son acknowledges his sinfulness: "Father, I have sinned against heaven and against you; I no longer deserve to be called your son" (vv. 18b-19). Despite his egregiously bad behavior, he plans to ask for the status of a hired hand, which actually is how his father should have and could have treated him when he asked for the inheritance in the first place.

Father and son meet in verse 20, and the son begins his rehearsed speech, but he does not get to finish it. The father, so moved and filled with emotion at his son's return, does not hear a word he says. He cuts the son off in mid-sentence and tells the servants to prepare for a party, and he explains, "because this son of mine was dead, and has come to life again; he was lost and has been found" (v. 24). Because the son never has the opportunity to call himself a "hired hand," one cannot say that the father is refuting his son's assessment. Rather, we the audience can see that the father has always held this son in high regard and has never stopped loving him. The father's love and generosity toward his lost, now found son so border on the ridiculous that his actions preclude his wayward son's expression of shame and guilt. We have here a loving father whose love exceeds all bounds.

This parable then switches focus to the elder brother (v. 25). By external measure, the elder brother has been obedient and respectful of the father, whom his younger brother has both insulted and grieved. The dialogue between the son and the father, however, challenges such an assumption of his filial relationship.

The elder brother, after citing off his own virtues, explodes in front of his father (vv. 29-30). The father, defending his own act of forgiveness, corrects the elder brother (v. 32). The father insists that the prodigal son is both a son to him and a brother to his other son. The one who has been alienated is now restored to the family.

The elder son is blind to his father's magnanimity. As an elder son, he has a duty to support the father in his decisions, a duty that he obviously shirks. The positions are reversed. Now it is the elder brother who insults and acts disrespectfully, while the younger son, by humbling himself, shows respect. In spite of this, the father still goes on loving, this time toward the elder son (v. 31). The father's forgiveness and charity maintain the ties of a loving relationship toward both his sons. As with all parables, this one turns to the listener, asking us to identify with either the younger son, the elder brother, or the father.

In each of the successive parables of the lost, that which is lost increases in value, from stray lamb, to a drachma, to a son. With such a progression, the worth of the sinner also increases in God's eyes, and the listener is left with the conclusion that God loves all as parents love their children. Furthermore, in the first two parables the shepherd and the woman are the Christ figure, respectively. In the parable of the prodigal son, however, it is not absolutely clear whether the father is Christ or God the Father, and this ambiguity, no doubt, is intentional.

16:1-13 The parable of the dishonest steward

This parable appears only in Luke's Gospel. That the steward is clever to the point of being crafty makes the fact that Jesus commends him difficult for us to appreciate.

Stewards made a living by collecting rents and debts for their masters and charging the debtors interest on the amount owed, which would then go to the stewards' coffers. Here the steward is shameless in the lengths he will go to maintain his position. He is not trying to hide anything from the rich man; indeed, he may even want his employer to find out about his altering the books. His hope is that his cleverness may win back the rich man's favor, and barring that outcome, he will at least have made some grateful constituents to take him in. The steward's audaciousness in achieving his ends calls attention to Jesus' lesson. Anyone of us would go to the greatest lengths, no matter how unsavory, to ensure a secure place in this world; how much more should we devote our attention to the world to come (v. 8).

Jesus names the problem in verse 9. The term "dishonest wealth" reflects the danger that inheres in worldly goods. Jesus warns the listener to use the wealth, but not to place any trust in it. Only trusting in God will lead to an eternal dwelling; everything else is counterfeit.

The narrative then discusses the conclusions one can draw from the parable by indirectly referring to the description of the steward (vv. 10-13). In verse 1 the steward is accused of "squandering" the master's property. The steward has mismanaged, perhaps through incompetence, the "very small matters" of this world, so there is no reason to trust him in the larger matters of the next one (v. 10). That lesson is turned toward the audience in verse 12. Trust is earned, it is not assumed. Those who deal loosely and unethically with others should not expect others to honor and trust them.

Verse 13 is a Q saying that also appears in Matthew 6:24. "Mammon" (v. 13), a Greek transliteration of the Aramaic word, means more than wealth and riches; it can signify anything of this world that one relies on: titles, positions, privileges, and honors. To be sure, wealth is tied up with many of these perquisites, but mammon is anything which takes our attention away from God, the true source of life.

16:14-15 Encounter with the Pharisees

Luke alone features this reproof, which, with the notice that this particular group of Pharisees "loved money" (v. 14), is tied to the warning about wealth above. Jesus directs the criticism at the human desire for self-justification and public praise. The performance of good deeds, then, goes only as far as human acclaim. In such a case, people will never do an act that may be good but unpopular.

16:16-18 Sayings on the Law and divorce

The "law" in this passage refers to the Mosaic Law, the Jewish religious and cultic legislation, and reflects the context from which the Christian movement emerged. The evangelists and other New Testament writers interpreted the Old Testament, comprised of books both in Hebrew and Greek, as the precursor to the revelation of Christ. Now the "kingdom of God is proclaimed," but the ability to move into a new way of viewing one's relationship with God is not easy; hence "everyone who enters does so with violence" (v. 16). Jewish Christians found that the change from the Mosaic Law to Christ required a major shift in focus, and Gentile Christians, at first not welcome unless they had undergone conversion to Judaism (see Acts 10; 15), put themselves at risk with their pagan neighbors. Luke's Gospel stresses Christ as the ultimate arbiter of any interpretation of the Law (v. 17); in that sense, the law will not pass away, as the next saying demonstrates (v. 18).

Luke and Mark agree against Matthew in their readings on the prohibition of divorce. While Matthew sees unchastity as a mitigating circumstance for dissolving the marriage (see Matt 19:9; Mark 10:11-12), Luke's version of divorce legislation (v. 18) serves as an example of how the Law has lost its validity. According to the Mosaic teaching, a man could divorce his wife by simply signing a statement of dismissal; the woman had no similar option (Deut 24:1-4). Consequently, the woman and her children would be left to fend for themselves by begging and prostitution. Jesus nullifies this legislation by declaring that no one can divorce, and thereby demonstrates that the law and the prophets ended with John (v. 16).

16:19-31 The rich man and Lazarus

This parable appears only in Luke and reflects the evangelist's overriding concern for the poor and for social justice. In the tradition this is also known as the story of Dives and Lazarus, the former name stemming from the Latin *dives,* meaning "rich person." It is one of the best known of all Gospel stories, even prompting Ralph Vaughan Williams to compose a musical score based on this story. The name "Lazarus" itself is the Greek transliteration of the Hebrew abbreviation "Eleazar," a name that means "God has helped." Thematically, it is tied to the saying about God and mammon in 16:13.

The information concerning the rich man's clothing (v. 19) indicates that he is not simply well off—he is excessively wealthy. Purple dye was a costly commodity that very few people even among the rich could afford. These details heighten the contrast between the rich man and Lazarus, who not only has sores that dogs would lick but who even lacks the simplest garment to cover those sores. That Lazarus keeps company with dogs accentuates his dismal state, since dogs were considered filthy, undesirable animals.

Luke illustrates the theme of the great reversal in this parable, first outlined in the *Magnificat* (see Luke 1:46-55). In the parable the hungry are literally "filled with good things," while the rich are "sent away empty" (1:53). The dialogue between Abraham and the rich man amply describes the new state of things. We know that the rich man cannot claim ignorance of the fact that someone hungry is outside his door, for he refers to Lazarus by name (v. 24). There is even an arrogant tone in his request: he does not ask Abraham for the favor but requests that Abraham command Lazarus to come down and refresh him. Most likely he treated Lazarus in a similar fashion when they both were alive.

Abraham, in his reply, ensures that the rich man knows exactly why he is where he is so that neither the rich man, now suffering the flames of the netherworld, nor the audience can conclude that he is a victim of a great misfortune. No, the rich man's lack of charity and responsibility put him there; indeed, the rich man's great sin of omission fashioned the chasm between the two. We are forced to wonder why the chasm cannot be crossed. The answer says a great deal about salvation and damnation.

The lesson is not that God is a God of damnation and punishment, inasmuch as it gives us an example of how much of a role we play in our salvation. The rich man was oblivious to the needs of those around him while he was alive, and now that he is dead, he is still oblivious, as his call for Lazarus's services suggests. Herein lies the danger of wealth that Jesus always preaches: power and wealth blind us to the kingdom of God in this life and in the next. If we are not wide-eyed to the kingdom and its demands now, as Moses and the prophets tell us to be (v. 31), we will not be sensitive to seeing the kingdom after we die. The great irony in the story is that the rich man needs Lazarus in order to be saved. Had he paid attention to Lazarus begging for table scraps at the door of his house, the rich man would not be in the predicament he is in now.

The last verse of the parable, of course, is a reference to Jesus' own resurrection.

17:1-4 Temptations to sin

The journey to Jerusalem continues with further instruction along the way.

Each Synoptic Gospel has a variation of the warning against giving offense. Verses 3-4 parallel Matthew 18:15, thereby making them Q material. Luke injects a note of reality in verse 1b: as long as there is a believing community, there will be scandals. As great a sin as it is to lead one into temptation, it is far greater to do so to a "little one" (v. 2). Millstones, even one for household use, were heavy and expensive. The punishment suggested is severe indeed.

Where there is sin, there must be forgiveness, and Luke gracefully connects the two. We have another example of the mercy and tenderness that are so much a part of the Third Gospel. This mercy and tenderness, however, are not to be regarded as permission for further injury. Those who sin are to be rebuked, and if sinners repent, they are to be forgiven. The Gospel sees rebuke and forgiveness as a means of achieving both personal salvation and social justice. On the other hand, lest repentance and forgiveness be exercised on a quid pro quo basis, the saying continues with the proviso that because sins or even the same sin will occur numerous times, it must be forgiven each time the sinner repents. We are to imitate divine forgiveness in its limitlessness.

This passage addresses only how to deal with sinful behavior within the church community, but for Luke, mercy extends to those outside the community as well (see Luke 6:27-36).

17:5-6 Saying on faith

Once again, faith is compared to a mustard seed (see Luke 13:19), but the example switches to a sycamine tree (*morus nigra*; read "mulberry" in the text), a large tree with clustered berries. Both Matthew and Luke use the hyperbole from Q to make their point that nothing is impossible to the person who has faith. Matthew's phrase, however, refers to moving a mountain, which most scholars believe to be the original version.

17:7-10 The attitude of a servant

This piece on servants occurs only in Luke.

The social world of the Gospel is particularly evident in this passage dealing with masters and slaves. The lesson is that Christians should not expect praise and honor for performing those duties that they are obligated to perform. Moreover, the saying counters the thought that salvation can be gained on human merit alone and without God's grace. If our own deeds render us unprofitable servants, we have no other recourse for salvation than to depend on the divine initiative.

17:11-19 The cleansing of ten lepers

The prescription to the lepers to show themselves to the priests is found in Leviticus 14:2-9.

The most common route for Jews in Galilee to go to Jerusalem was through the Jordan Valley. Although cutting down through Samaria was not impossible, most Jews preferred to avoid Samaritan territory (see Luke 9:52). Did Jesus ever set foot in Samaria? Verse 11 can be translated "through the region between Samaria and Galilee." This passage is solely Lukan material and shows Luke's proclivity to highlight the faith of the social outcast over that of the established insider. Both Jews (Galileans) and Samaritans compose this group of lepers; both are society's outcasts, and therefore they associate with each other.

Luke's eschatological vision comes into focus with the emphasis on faith in verse 19. Jesus instructs the Samaritan leper, not that his faith has cured him, but that his faith has "saved" him. The leper is not only saved from his leprosy but gains eternal salvation—all from faith. The connection of faith with salvation occurs throughout Luke's Gospel, as we have seen with the woman in the house of Simon the Pharisee (7:50), the cure of the hemorrhaging woman (8:48), and even at the cross (23:43).

Luke 17

17:20-37 The coming of the kingdom and the Son of Man

In verses 20-21 Luke expresses a realized eschatology that supports the vision displayed in the dialogue with the Samaritan leper above. Indeed, the last phrase in verse 21 seems Johannine in its language as it underscores an *eschaton* already present.

The tone and theme switch suddenly to a future-oriented eschatology in verse 22. The opening words of this verse in Greek, which the English translation expresses, indicate a reversal of thought. In this first encounter with Lukan apocalyptic writing, the reading draws a parallel between sudden acts of destruction in the Old Testament and the Son of Man's impending arrival on the earth. Although found far more often in Ezekiel than in Daniel, the latter's use of "Son of Man" has greater bearing on the synoptic understanding of this term, an understanding that Luke shares. The heavily apocalyptic material in Daniel (see Dan 7:13; 8:15-17) is reflected in verse 22 and also figures prominently in the book of Revelation.

Luke includes a warning about following false prophets (as do the parallels in Mark and Matthew), but he also connects the coming of the *eschaton* with the fate awaiting Jesus in Jerusalem (v. 25). Furthermore, Luke builds a sense of urgency by relating Lot's escape from the explosive conflagration that destroyed Sodom; people should be vigilant and anxious. This sense of urgency also has a social justice theme, for injustice and oppression were the reasons for Sodom's obliteration (see Isa 1:9-16; Ezek 16:49-52). Any desire to hold on to the present is discouraged, and Lot's wife stands as an example of what might happen to the one who tarries. Those who make no permanent claims to this life will always be ready for the *eschaton* (v. 31).

To separate Jesus' words from the Gospel writer's is always extremely difficult. In this passage it is impossible. Verse 31 appears to be a prediction after the fact. Josephus describes the sudden arrival of the Romans at the gates of Jerusalem during the First Jewish Revolt (A.D. 66–70; *J.W.* 5.2.3]. Few if any were able to escape the destruction and massacre. The early Christians most likely interpreted the Jewish rebellion and the destruction of Jerusalem with its splendid temple as the fulfillment of Jesus' words, even as those words were mixed into their experiences of the catastrophe. What we have here is an amalgam of Q material, oral tradition, memory, and Lukan editing. (See Luke 21:20-24.)

One cannot take every passage of Scripture literally and apart from a larger theological context. Nowhere is this truer than in apocalyptic literature. Readers should be on guard against determining the saved, the damned, and the rapture by reading this material. Verse 37, in encouraging us to read the signs of the times, advises us to keep the whole Christian tradition in focus as we interpret those signs. And what are the signs? Jesus does not say, and this point is the essential part of the apocalyptic message.

Christians are to concern themselves with doing the will of God, for which Jesus has given his disciples abundant examples: taking care of the poor, trusting in God alone, and forgiving enemies. We are not to waste time trying to predict the future. The paradoxical presentation of the kingdom as already present (v. 21) and not yet here (v. 30) expresses its true reality. The kingdom will be manifested in living the life of Christ.

18:1-8 The parable of the persistent widow

Situating this pericope after the apocalyptic passage regarding the Son of Man offers the believer the proper way to maintain vigilance for the parousia, or second coming. With prayer and praying mentioned over thirty times in Luke's Gospel and the Acts of the Apostles, the parable of the persistent widow highlights this central feature of Luke's Gospel by emphasizing the necessity and efficacy of constant prayer. Moreover, because widows and orphans were to be special recipients of charity according to Jewish law (Deut 24:17-22), the early Christians would have been particularly attentive to the teaching.

The story appears only in Luke, and there are at least two ways to read it. The first is to see the unjust judge as the protagonist bearing the lesson for the reader. Similar to the literary style found in the parable of the dishonest steward (16:1-8), the intent of the teaching comes through the comparison of the greater: As an unjust judge grants a petition solely for self-serving purposes, how much more will a loving God grant the desires of his beloved petitioner.

A second, feminist interpretation, on the other hand, sees the widow as the protagonist and thus the vehicle for the lesson. In this case, she, in her weakness, becomes the Christ figure who combats evil and injustice on behalf of the poor and neglected. She is unstinting in her efforts, and the unjust judge, the symbol of oppression, is clearly afraid of her, as seen from the Greek verb *hypōpiazō* for "strike" (v. 5), which means to "treat roughly, maltreat, strike under the eye." Here, too, the intent of the teaching surfaces through analogy: As persistent as a widow is to secure her rights, so is God in securing the rights of those petitioning him.

The reference to the Son of Man (v. 8) brings the parable in line with the teaching on the last days (17:22-37): Pray constantly while living and working for the kingdom of God.

18:9-14 The parable of the Pharisee and the tax collector

This parable, also found only in Luke, continues the theme on prayer. Whereas the parable of the persistent widow (18:1-8) shows the necessity of constant prayer, the parable of the Pharisee and the tax collector displays the proper comportment for prayer.

No doubt the Pharisee does everything he says he does. Fasting and tithing are not only good things to do, but the former is also proclaimed by the prophets while the latter is required by the Law (see Deut 14:22-29). The purpose of the parable is not to discourage religious and pious practice; rather, its function is to call into question the reasons why people take on devotional works. The Pharisee gives the reasons for deeds: they are to justify himself in the world's eyes as well as in the eyes of God. Luke underscores this point in verse 9.

In contrast, the tax collector does nothing pious that we know of. In fact, as a tax collector, it would be most surprising if he ever did anything good for anyone. During the Roman occupation, tax collectors were not only traitors to their own people but also extortionists feeding off their compatriots. Furthermore, their dealing with the pagan Romans made them ritually impure, thereby excommunicating themselves from their fellow Jews. Compared with the dedicated, devoted Pharisee, a tax collector would never be considered honest, pious, or holy. Unlike the Pharisee, however, the tax collector knows his sinfulness. He pleads for mercy and demonstrates his need for God. The Pharisee, on the other hand, in singing his own praises, makes God his beneficiary. That the tax collector leaves justified was as shocking to the first-century audience as it is to us. So important is this parable that it sets the tone for those participating in the passion and crucifixion (see 23:48).

18:15-17 Access to the kingdom

This passage stresses that the people brought infants to Jesus, whereas the parallels in Mark and Matthew read only that children came. The mention of infants gives a glimpse of the sociological structure in the ancient world. Conversions were never individualistic or isolated events. If the master or mistress of the household became a follower of Christ, everyone in the extended family and even the slaves did as well. In the Acts of the Apostles we read similar accounts regarding baptism (Acts 16:15, 33; 18:8). Luke's reading could very well reflect and suggest the practice of infant baptism in the early church.

Society today often presents Christianity as a childish, trivial, or trite matter and will use passages like this one to justify doing so. To "accept the kingdom of God like a child," however, means to receive the kingdom of God with an open guilelessness to the gift that God offers, something that requires a healthy maturity. In this case, the tax collector in the preceding passage (18:9-14) is the perfect example of open guilelessness.

18:18-23 The rich official

Although in their respective versions of the story, both Matthew and Mark simply state that a man comes up to Jesus, Luke specifies that the one asking the question is a ruler. Thus Luke informs the reader that the individual is not only rich but also powerful, an important point for the story.

The ruler's fault is one of complacency, and in this regard he is similar to the Pharisee in 18:9-14. When he calls Jesus "Good teacher" (v. 18), Jesus responds in a sharp tone, because he can see through the unctuous language. The ruler hopes that by flattery he can increase in stature to gain eternal life. Jesus continues with listing the prescriptions of the Decalogue. These statutes should recall the whole Exodus experience, in which the people struggle between their ever present faithlessness and their eventual trust in God. The ruler's answer that he has observed all the commandments from his youth demonstrates that he has completely forgotten that covenantal relationship expressed by trust in God.

Jesus concludes by entering the ruler's mind-set. The first half of the answer would catch the man's attention, "There is still one thing left for you . . ." (v. 22a). The ruler can handle the challenge; by his wits he has already accumulated wealth and power. Then comes the surprise: "sell all that you have and distribute it to the poor . . . come follow me" (v. 22b). The man's sadness results from a double realization. The first is that he must surrender everything of worth in his life, and the second follows, namely, that everything he thought was of great value both in this life and the next is actually worthless. His life from his youth has been an act of faithlessness. To inherit eternal life, he must stop trusting in what he has trusted and place his trust in God.

18:24-30 On entering the kingdom of God

The dialogue with the rich official prompts Jesus' comment on the ease of a camel going through the eye of a needle, one of the most challenging verses in the Gospel (v. 25). The response from the crowd is certainly understandable: "Then who can be saved?" (v. 26).

A long-standing interpretation of this passage is that there was in Jerusalem a gate called the "Eye of the Needle," which required a cargo-laden camel to rest on all four legs and crawl through the door in order to enter the city. There is no evidence anywhere in the Mideast, however, of any gate called the "Eye of the Needle." In addition, camels are unable to crawl. Jesus is using a form of hyperbole that is a natural part of Semitic speech.

The lesson that arises from this encounter with the ruler is similar to the one taught in the parable of the dishonest steward (16:1-13), where trusting in one's own wealth and accomplishments instead of in God makes salvation difficult if not impossible. In both cases the responsibility for accepting salvation falls on us. Those who place all hope in their own accomplishments will never be open to God's mercy, simply because they have let worldly values blind themselves to it. Since power and wealth are idols, and seductive ones at that, the ruler in the story and others like him cannot even see the way into the kingdom, let alone enter it. In this sense, it is easier for a camel to pass through a needle's eye.

Peter, sensing the meaning of Jesus' hyperbolic example, responds in verse 28. His statement implies that he is looking for an answer as to whether he and the other disciples are saved or not. Jesus does not answer directly; rather, his reply is addressed in the third person (vv. 29-30). Jesus' statement reflects a realized eschatology as well as a future one. Forsaking worldly comfort has a present reward, yet the reward is not fully realized until one reaches eternal life. Unlike the Markan parallel, which speaks of persecutions along with the rewards (Mark 10:30), Luke does not mention such hardships. Because the next passage contains the third prediction of the passion, Luke avoids the redundancy by not including the sobering fact here.

This passage has been used over the centuries as a rationale for religious life.

18:31-34 The third prediction of the passion

Being a disciple has its rewards, but it also has difficulties, as Jesus reminds his band of followers with this third, final, and most vivid prediction of his passion (see 9:22, 44-45; but also 17:25).

Although both Matthew and Mark feature parallels to this passage, only Luke contains information about the prophets (v. 31) and the Twelve's inability to understand what Jesus is saying (v. 34).

18:35-43 The blind beggar of Jericho

Jesus is relentlessly pursuing his intent as described in 9:51. In going from Galilee to Jerusalem through the Jordan Valley, one would turn west at Jericho in order to take the Wadi Qelt road up into the Judean mountains. Jericho, an oasis and a prosperous city in Judea, was also the locale of Herod the Great's winter palace. These facts serve to accentuate the beggar's lowly social position.

All three synoptic accounts contain this story, but only Mark gives the blind man a name (Bartimaeus; see Mark 10:46). Comparisons are very important here. This blind man can "see" Jesus is the Messiah, whereas the Twelve cannot understand what he is saying (v. 34). This paradox fits well within the Gospel tradition, where the blind usually "see," while those who "see" are actually blind.

The beggar uses one of the earliest Christian titles applied to Christ, "Son of David" (v. 38), a title that rarely appears in Luke (see 3:31; 20:41). Jesus hears the distressful cry despite the commotion of the crowd and their efforts to silence the man. Jesus could have walked to the man, but he commands that the beggar be brought to him (v. 40). Among religious people of the time, physical disability was linked to sinfulness. By having the crowd lead the blind man to him, Jesus induces them to take responsibility for healing him, thereby redefining both suffering and sin. Jesus does not assume that the beggar wants to see; rather, he asks him to explicitly state his need (v. 41). Of course, the beggar requests sight, because he knows that Jesus can grant it, and by this action he demonstrates his faith. Hence Jesus can say, "Your faith has saved you" (v. 42). In true Lukan fashion, in the end everyone—beggar and crowd—glorifies God.

19:1-10 Zacchaeus the tax collector

This passage appears only in Luke and concludes what many scholars have called the "Lukan Gospel of the Outcast" (15:1–19:10). Its singular character lies in the fact that Luke, who devotes the whole tone of his Gospel toward embracing the poor and lowly, includes this passage, which focuses on the salvation of the rich and powerful. Unlike the rich official in 18:18-23, Zacchaeus does not depend on his wealth and status but on God's loving mercy to gain entry into the kingdom.

Tax collecting was a lucrative business. Romans used to sell the office to the highest bidder. For his part, the tax collector would then have to pay his contracted amount to the Romans as well as collect the fiscal revenues for them. Anything over and beyond those sums was his to keep. Failing to meet his payments would mean the Romans could confiscate his property and sell him and his family into slavery. Zacchaeus's position as the chief tax collector meant that lesser officials would have bidden for their offices from him, and if they did not produce the payment, Zacchaeus would have applied the appropriate penalties. In a word, Zacchaeus was very wealthy, and the resentment against him would have been very strong.

Despite his occupation, Zacchaeus is determined to see Jesus, even if it means looking foolish in doing so. Scholars are divided on whether to read the verbs "give" and "repay," which grammatically are in the present tense in Greek (v. 8), as present or future. In other words, is Zacchaeus boasting of present practices or making a statement of repentance to guide his future action? His hasty explanation to Jesus is heartfelt, for it would be of no

Luke 19

advantage to him, an extortionist, to heed a wandering prophet or wonder-worker. Furthermore, the fact that he does show knowledge of wrongdoing manifests the salvation that is visiting him. If Jesus comes "to seek and to save what was lost" (v. 10), Zacchaeus must be a sinner. Zacchaeus the sinner can make a claim of being a descendant of Abraham, and his earnest desire to get a glimpse of Jesus is proof enough that that is what he desires.

19:11-27 The parable of the ten gold coins

Matthew and Luke differ in the telling of this parable, which, in large part, comes from Q overlapping slightly with Mark 13:34. A major difference between the two is that Luke also has a subtext discussing servants who do not want this particular nobleman to rule over them. This subtext may have as its origin Rome's choice of placing Archelaus, son of Herod the Great, on the throne at the death of his father. Because of his tyrannical and nearly sadistic behavior, the Jews petitioned Rome to have him removed. Rome responded by giving him only one-third of Herod's kingdom and eventually banishing him completely because of his excessive cruelty and incompetence.

Of lesser importance is Matthew's use of *talaton* (25:15) and Luke's *mna* as the denomination of the currency involved, which is translated here as "gold coins" (v. 13). A *mna* ("mina") would be worth about one hundred days' wages, and a *talanton* ("talent") sixty times as much.

Luke introduces the passage by noting that the traveling party was near Jerusalem and that some were supposing that the kingdom of God was about to appear. The parable addresses some of these points. The absentee nobleman returns without notice and thus surprises his servants. The first two servants are prepared for his sudden reappearance and are able to produce interest on the money given them; the third is not so concerned and has only a handkerchief with the original amount. It should be emphasized that the servants are commanded to use the money in such a manner as to earn more; thus the third servant was not only foolish but also disobedient.

As a story that follows the passage about the rich Zacchaeus, this parable gives an example on the proper way to use riches. The metaphor demonstrates that goods are to be employed for the upbuilding of the kingdom, and goods that are not used for this purpose will be taken away, as we see done with the third servant's *mna*.

The Lukan subtext plays a role in this passage by representing absolute refusal on the part of some to acknowledge the kingdom of God at all, whether in Jesus' first coming or in his second. Luke concludes this subtext within the same passage by having the nobleman slay the opposition. Many often cite this passage as an example of Lukan anti-Semitism. There is nothing in it, however, to suggest that those who receive the nobleman/Christ are Gentiles or that those who do not are Jews.

With this parable Jesus' journey to Jerusalem, which begins at 9:51, has reached its destination.

THE TEACHING MINISTRY IN JERUSALEM
Luke 19:28–21:38

Jesus has taught in Galilee, along the road to Judea, and now he will teach in the holy city. He arrives in Jerusalem, the city where he will meet his passion, death, and resurrection. With this background, his teaching takes on urgency.

19:28-40 The entry into Jerusalem

All four Gospels contain the account of Jesus' triumphal entry into Jerusalem. The respective narratives share a great deal of information, and any differences among them are seen in some minor details.

For all three Synoptic writers, this triumphal entry is Jesus' first and only trip to Jerusalem, but John's Gospel, along with some details among the Synoptics, shows evidence that he may have gone to Jerusalem several times during his earthly ministry. The possibility of other sojourns to Jerusalem notwithstanding, what distinguishes this visit from all the others is the reception Jesus receives.

Bethphage and Bethany are both on the Roman road from Jericho to Jerusalem. We know from John 11:17-18 that Jesus has friends at the latter. This detail would explain how he could have made arrangements for the colt beforehand (Luke 19:29-31). All four Gospels show a heavy reliance on the prophecy in Zechariah 9:9 in their depictions of the scene.

In his descent from the Mount of Olives, Jesus encounters a rejoicing crowd. Matthew and Mark mention that the crowd also set garments and branches on the way; John specifies "palm branches" (12:13) but says nothing of garments, while Luke reads "cloaks" but does not include branches (v. 36). That three of the evangelists specify branches is used as evidence by some that the scene of the entry into Jerusalem described here actually refers to an earlier one at the time of the feast of Booths, or Sukkoth, a pilgrimage celebration falling in mid-September. Either Luke's source did not include branches, or Luke saw the reference as a superfluous detail. Whether or not the entry arises from the community's memory of a fall celebration at Sukkoth or a spring feast at Passover, the pertinent detail is that Jesus arrives in Jerusalem with throngs welcoming him.

Luke 19

The other evangelists have the crowd shouting "Hosanna," an Aramaic expression meaning "Save! I pray," a phrase unfamiliar to Luke's Gentile audience. Whereas the other Gospels have *"Blessed is he* who comes in the name of the Lord," Luke reads *"Blessed is the king"* (19:38, emphasis added). Luke's phrasing links Jesus' arrival in Jerusalem to the instruction on the imminent manifestation of the kingdom of God (see 13:35; 16:16; 18:15-17).

As an echo of the angels' hymn at the birth of Jesus (Luke 2:14), the crowd shouts out, "Peace in heaven and glory in the highest" (v. 38). What angels sang at Jesus' birth people now acclaim at his arrival.

Luke's depiction of the Pharisees in the crowd is less harsh than that of Matthew, who locates them in the temple after Jesus has cleansed it (Matt 21:16). Luke situates the Pharisees along the road leading into Jerusalem, and they seem more alarmed than hostile (19:39). Jesus' answer, a hyperbolic statement of fact, also serves as a challenge (19:40).

19:41-44 The lament over Jerusalem

The first lament over the city occurs in Luke 13:34-35 and is a Q saying (see Matt 23:37-39). Here, however, the reading appears only in Luke; both in theme and in imagery it is connected to the third and final reference to Jerusalem's destruction in Luke 21:21-24. Moreover, references to the siege (v. 43) are found in Jeremiah 6:6 and Ezekiel 4:2.

From the slopes of the Mount of Olives, Jesus would have seen the whole city spread out before him on the next hill. The temple with the doors to the holy of holies would have faced him. Tradition commemorates this scene at the Church of Dominus Flevit on the Mount of Olives. Archaeological evidence indicates that the most probable gate of Jesus' entry into the city rests underneath today's Golden Gate, which has been blocked since the eighth century. Today the Palm Sunday procession enters through St. Stephen's Gate, to the north of the Golden Gate along the eastern wall of the city.

19:45-48 The cleansing of the temple

Unlike Matthew or Mark, Luke concludes the entry into Jerusalem with the cleansing of the temple. Luke offers the most economic description of the event by not specifying the money changers, the animals, or even the "whip out of cords" (John 2:15). The phrase "My house shall be a house of prayer, but you have made it a den of thieves" is a blending of Isaiah 56:7 and Jeremiah 7:11.

The business transactions would have taken place in the Court of the Gentiles, surrounded by the Royal Portico, which was constructed for this very purpose. The merchants are not out of place in conducting their affairs in this area. In fact, the temple court served as the ground where worshipers proceeded from secular to sacred space by changing their pagan money to Jewish coins and purchasing ritually pure sacrificial victims. Jesus' anger, therefore, is not so much directed at those who have profaned a sacred zone with their mercantile greed; rather, he seems to be upset that any business should be associated with the temple at all. With incense, animals, oil, grain, and everything else needed for the sacrifices, the temple was a source of great income to the priests who had shares in most of the shops.

The glorious entry into Jerusalem ends on an ominous tone as the "chief priests, the scribes, and the leaders of the people" (v. 47), but not the Pharisees (19:39), plot to put Jesus to death.

20:1-8 Questioning Jesus' authority

It is natural that after such a dramatic action as cleansing the temple, the priests, scribes, and elders would question Jesus' authority. All three Synoptic Gospels feature this account within the same narrative sequence. The authority of Jesus' teaching was a major question throughout his ministry, as the earlier Beelzebul controversy substantiates (Luke 11:14-23).

The temple leaders named here comprise the Sanhedrin, the highest Jewish council. It was composed of three groups: the priests (the high priest as well as the former high priests and family representatives); the scribes (legal scholars); and the elders (the chief members of the leading families and clans). Totaling seventy-one members, this group was the official Jewish court. In Jesus' time it had jurisdiction in religious and secular affairs only in Judea, but capital cases had to be recommended to the Roman governor for approval. It met in Jerusalem within the temple complex.

Jesus' reply is structured to avoid falling into the trap the officials have fashioned. If he were to say that his authority comes from the Lord God, as indeed it does, they could accuse him of blasphemy. As it is, Jesus' response insinuates such a conclusion without providing any incriminating evidence. By referring to John the Baptist, Jesus also draws from the prophetic tradition to make his defense. The comments of the temple leaders indicate the great regard for the Baptist that many of the people held. This devotion to John has implications for the development of Christianity.

20:9-19 The wicked tenant farmers

This parable strikes a note of recognition with both the people (v. 16) and the scribes and chief priests (v. 19). The whole piece is an analogy of the prophetic tradition. The one who plants the vineyard represents God;

the tenant farmers, the people; the series of servants, the various prophets; the son, Jesus. The vineyard, as a fundamental symbol of Israel, and indeed the parable itself echo Isaiah (5:1-7), but it also surfaces as such in Psalm 80. Matthew (21:39) and Luke (20:15) reflect a literal understanding of the analogy by having the tenants cast the son from the vineyard before killing him (see Mark 12:8). Many think that a redactor tried to align the story with Jesus' crucifixion outside the walls of Jerusalem.

The context of this passage is, of course, the altercation Jesus has with the Sanhedrin in Luke 20:1-8. They refuse to recognize the hand of God in John the Baptist, whom Herod had put to death, and they continue in their refusal to see the hand of God in Jesus. Jesus ties his claim to divine authority by quoting from Psalm 118:22-23 (Luke 20:17), a verse that also resonates with Isaiah 8:14-15.

The schism motif enters here once again (see Luke 2:34). The leaders reject Jesus, but the people do not. God's promise takes root in the vineyard Israel, represented by the people's response, but this vineyard will also be shared with the Gentiles (v. 16).

Luke uses the parable's imagery and interpretation in Acts (18:6; 28:28). It also resurfaces in other New Testament writings, such as Romans 11:17-18 and 1 Peter 2:6-7.

20:20-26 Paying taxes to Caesar

The scribes and the chief priests are relentless in their attempts to trap Jesus by catching him off guard. After being shamed by the parable of the tenant farmers (20:9-19), they now send spies or agents to Jesus with hopes that he might incriminate himself by speaking against the empire. Jesus, however, sees through the ruse (20:23).

Roman coinage was highly symbolic for Jews concerned about paying taxes to the emperor. Engraved on the face of the denarius was the image of Tiberius Caesar—at the very least an offense against Jewish sensibilities, since it would go against the prohibition of graven idols. As a subject people, the Jews were required to use this currency for paying taxes and tribute to their occupiers. The question about the legality of paying taxes, therefore, involves the legality of handling idols to do so; the religious Jew should not be in contact with such pagan objects. Combined with these religious principles was the humiliation of paying the conqueror in the coin that transgressed their law code, thus forcing the Jews to participate in Roman paganism. Jesus' response not only avoids the trap the leaders set for him but also calls into question the meaning of true, righteous behavior.

Jesus gains the upper hand against his adversaries by not pitting allegiance to Rome against fidelity to the Torah (the holy writings of the Jewish religion, especially the first five books of the Old Testament). The lesson is that one is not defiled by paying taxes to Rome. Being righteous before God is an issue deeper than paying taxes to a pagan power.

The idea of rendering to Caesar the things that are Caesar's and to God the things that are God's has often been mistakenly used as an injunction for keeping religious and ethical questions separate from political or secular policies. Correctly read through an eschatological lens, Jesus' aphorism states that the things of this world have an impact on the next, while standards of the age to come should have an influence on this present life.

20:27-40 Sadducees and the resurrection

The Sadducees, opponents of the Pharisees, particularly over the teachings on the resurrection, are the next group to question Jesus with an eye toward tripping him up. Not much is known about them except that they were aristocratic conservatives tied to the temple cult (unlike the Pharisees, who promoted the synagogue movement). The circumstance they describe is based on levirate marriage (Deut 25:5-6), whereby a widow's brother-in-law marries her to ensure that the lands stay in the first husband's family and that his name is carried on. Jesus responds by discussing first the nature of a resurrected life and then the basis of the resurrection in the Jewish tradition.

The resurrected life goes beyond the dimensions of earthly existence. Thus expectations and practices in this world do not hold in the next. Moreover, the resurrected life transcends this one (vv. 35, 36, 38). By citing Moses, Jesus taps the source of Jewish faith as well as the sole component of the Sadducees' teaching, for their belief extended no further than the first five books of Moses, often called the Torah or the Pentateuch.

Jesus' argument is impeccable. The scribes, who along with the Pharisees believe in the resurrection, affirm Jesus' answer; the Sadducees who brought up the matter, on the other hand, are silent (vv. 39-40).

Unlike the parallel accounts in Matthew 22:23-33 or Mark 12:18-27, Luke's version contains a teaching that supports celibate life (v. 35; see also Matt 19:12).

20:41-44 David's Son

Jesus' opponents would want to make sure that there is nothing about him which would suggest that he is the Messiah. At the same time, they have to acknowledge that the people see him as a great man, and therefore he could quite possibly be the one long promised by the prophets. At that time the tradition existed of a Messiah arising from David's line, a belief to which the infancy narratives attest. The narrative here draws on this tradition.

In verse 42 Jesus cites Psalm 110:1, a coronation psalm, which in the Greek Septuagint is reflected in this translation. In Psalm 110 the psalmist is speaking, and "Lord" (uppercase here) refers to Yahweh. The "lord" (lowercase here) is the king whom Yahweh is placing on the throne. In its New Testament interpretation, "Lord" still refers to Yahweh, but David the king is speaking. Consequently, "lord" represents a messianic figure who is greater than David. In these verses Jesus states that the term "lord" refers to himself.

The early church drew on this tradition of a Davidic Messiah both here and elsewhere, and this psalm was used as one of the Old Testament writings prefiguring Christ. The other Synoptics contain passages parallel to this one.

20:45-47 Denunciation of the scribes

Jesus, after defending himself before both the Pharisees and Sadducees, takes the offensive. Scribes, as ones who could read, write, and interpret texts, are synonymous with the Pharisees. As a scholarly religious class who knew the Torah and the oral tradition with all the astuteness of master lawyers, they expected honor and deference as their due. As with all professions, there were good and bad members among them. Even Jesus was considered by his disciples to be a teacher.

The condemnation Jesus levels here (vv. 46-47) is directed toward those who are a part of the temple power structure and use their status and expertise for personal advantage at the expense of the poor and unprivileged. This short passage also reflects the debates between church and synagogue in the early days of the Christian movement. It sets the context for what follows in Luke 21:1-4.

21:1-4 The poor widow's contribution

Luke shares this story with Mark (see Mark 12:41-44). Each coin is a *lepton*, which is worth slightly more than one-hundredth of a denarius. Since a denarius is a day's wage, the widow places about one-fiftieth of a day's living into the treasury, and, as Jesus remarks, this is her whole livelihood.

Many hold that this story shows the widow's pious devotion, and she has become a model of religious dedication in that all should give from their sustenance and not their superfluity. The context, however, suggests another interpretation.

Jesus' first order of business upon entering Jerusalem is to go to the temple and drive out those "selling things" (19:45). His violent response to revenues generated by temple worship in that section of the Lukan narrative would be indicative of anger here. In addition, in the preceding passage Jesus has denounced the scribes for "devour[ing] the houses of widows" (Luke 20:47). Jesus is upset at seeing a poor woman think that God's will demanded making herself destitute so that others could become rich.

21:5-6 The destruction of the temple foretold

All three Synoptics contain the prediction of the temple's destruction. The building of Herod's temple, the edifice under discussion in this passage, began in 19 B.C. and was still under construction during Jesus' lifetime (see John 2:20). The whole complex was completed in A.D. 64, only to be totally razed six years later during the First Jewish Revolt. When it was completed, it was considered one of the most beautiful buildings in the whole Roman Empire. The people's awe and wonder at the stones were totally justified. As the house of God, its destruction would seem like the end of the world in the minds of the people (see Josephus, *Ant.* 15.11.1-7 and *J.W.* 4-5).

Is the prediction of the destruction a *vaticinium ex eventu*, that is, a foretelling after the event? If so, then the writer, Luke, is theologizing about the temple's destruction by placing a prediction of it on the lips of Jesus. On the other hand, anyone sensitive to the political climate of the day would know that the tensions would someday explode, resulting in catastrophic disaster for the nation.

This account forms a bridge between the story of the poor widow (21:1-4) and Luke's apocalyptic section (21:7-36).

21:7-11 The signs of the end

Luke 21:7-36 forms the Lukan apocalypse, but it is not the only place in the Third Gospel where apocalyptic imagery occurs (see Luke 17:22-37). Matthew 24 and Mark 13 have parallel passages.

The great part of the language and metaphor used here is characteristic of apocalyptic writing: signs, natural upheavals, disasters, wars, persecution, and a call to vigilance. Apocalyptic language is often, but not exclusively, associated with eschatological teaching, and in this sense this section is more rightly called the Lukan eschatological discourse. By definition, *eschatology* deals with the interpretation of the end times, the fulfillment of history, and culmination of human destiny. In general, we can say that this section shows eschatological concerns in apocalyptic language.

Rarely has anyone been able to identify conclusively the particular historical references to the events mentioned in verses 7-11. There has never been a time in human history when wars, earthquakes, famines, and plagues have not been a part of the picture. Since any one of these events and phenomena can occur without warning or notice, it is better to be prepared, and preparation consists in always looking for Christ in every person and circumstance.

21:12-19 The coming persecution

The early Christian community faced persecution from the home as well as from rulers of both synagogue and state. These Gospel verses, in non-apocalyptic vocabulary, are meant to console and strengthen the believers facing their tribulation.

Verses 14-15 form a doublet with Luke 12:11-12.

21:20-24 The great tribulation

The words that Jesus speaks in this passage ring true to the history of the destruction of Jerusalem.

The Roman general Titus arrived at Jerusalem and set up his main camp about one mile north of the Mount of Olives at Mount Scopus in the spring of A.D. 70. By July his men set to constructing a siege wall around the city to prevent the people of Jerusalem from escaping while protecting the Roman soldiers from Jewish raiding parties. Since such procedures were standard Roman military operations, the description in these verses need not be considered peculiar to the Roman siege in A.D. 70. Nonetheless, the arrival of the Romans came with unexpected suddenness, and internecine fighting among various Jewish sects had reduced the food stores, so that starvation became a major problem within the city (see Josephus, *J.W.* 5.2-3i). On August 28 (Ninth of Ab, by coincidence the same day the Babylonians breached the city some six hundred years earlier), Jerusalem fell to the Romans. Any Jewish survivors were taken captive, and the city, including the temple, was razed to the ground.

Old Testament prophecies are employed in the description: Hosea 9:7 in Luke 21:22; Sirach 28:18; Deuteronomy 28:64; and Zechariah 12:3 in Luke 21:24. Tradition has it that the Christians in the city fled to the city of Pella in present-day Jordan at the outbreak of hostilities. The "time of the Gentiles" (v. 24) foreshadows the great missionary ventures outlined in the Acts of the Apostles.

21:25-28 The coming of the Son of Man

The scene shifts from Jerusalem to the whole world. The language returns to apocalyptic terminology, drawing on Isaiah, Joel, Zephaniah, and Daniel. What has happened to Jerusalem may be a harbinger of the Son of Man's visitation upon the earth, but it is not an immediate warning signal. The scene is not bleak, however. The astral signs and natural calamities serve to notify that redemption is at hand. Just as the people of Jerusalem were mixed in their reception of Jesus, so too will the world be at his second coming.

21:29-33 The lesson of the fig tree

If people can read the signs in nature, they should be willing and able to read the signs of their deliverance.

The reference to "this generation" (v. 32) is ambiguous. In one sense, there is every reason to believe that many in the then contemporary generation would not pass away until after the First Jewish Revolt. On the other hand, if "all these things" refers to upheavals in nature ushering in the Son of Man, "this generation" is a timeless reference to the world; the *eschaton*, or end time, is always imminent.

21:34-36 Exhortation to be vigilant

One must stand with apocalyptic vigilance. The note of surprise resurfaces here (v. 34). Under an imminent understanding of the *eschaton*, the coming of the Son of Man will always be sudden. The directive to pray (v. 36) is a particularly Lukan concern. Jesus prays in the Garden of Gethsemane (22:39-46), and his note of "tribulations" (v. 36) looks toward his own passion.

21:37-38 Conclusion to the ministry in Jerusalem

During the pilgrimage feasts most people, particularly those without relatives in Jerusalem proper, camped on the fields and hills surrounding the city. The Mount of Olives appears to have been one such place.

Despite the discourse on the temple and Jerusalem, Luke is ambiguous toward both. Jesus teaches in the temple even as he speaks against it. Furthermore, in the Acts of the Apostles the temple becomes the site of many events in the ministry of Peter, Paul, and the other disciples. Jesus' public ministry ends with these verses.

THE PASSION

Luke 22:1–23:56

The passion narrative, the nucleus of the kerygma, forms the oldest part of the Gospel tradition. The accounts of the four evangelists show the greatest similarity with each other in this section. Nonetheless, each evangelist shapes the information to fit the theological architecture of his respective Gospel. In Luke, the themes found all along reach their climax. The schism motif, the great reversal, and the victory over evil all manifest Jesus' reclamation of the cosmos from Satan's clutches as Christ brings the promise of future glory to all.

22:1-6 The conspiracy against Jesus

The diabolical force that has been mounting challenge against Jesus from the very beginning (Luke 4:1-13) increases in intensity here when Satan "enter[s] into Judas" (v. 3). In Luke's narrative, now is the "time" (4:13) for which the devil has been waiting.

Both priests and scribes are at the center of the conspiracy, but by making Judas his agent, Satan fashions a more serious inroad against Jesus. Hence the passion is not merely a human drama; rather, it is an event that involves the whole cosmos. Luke's account of Jesus' passion, with its collusion between Satan and Judas, departs from the synoptic presentation and aligns itself more closely with the Johannine text, and in so doing respects the cosmological nature of the drama.

One of the major pilgrimage feasts that brought thousands to Jerusalem, the feast of Unleavened Bread was originally an agrarian festival celebrated in the spring during the grain harvest. Passover began as a nomadic feast, also held in the spring, when people took their flocks of sheep and goats from the winter to summer feeding grounds. The Jewish practice at the time of Jesus had joined these two feasts into one commemorating the Exodus from Egypt.

For the Romans, this annual spring holiday posed a major security risk. The throngs of people, coupled with the nationalistic overtones inherent in the Exodus event, set the stage for riots and insurrection. The temple leaders, functioning as colonial lackeys of Rome, were well aware that Jesus was a popular figure who fulfilled the messianic expectations of a great many. A conspiracy between Judas, the chief priests, and the guards that tries to find an opportunity to arrest Jesus away from the crowd is indicative of the volatility of the situation (v. 6).

22:7-38 The Passover meal

According to the synoptic dating, the meal takes place on Passover (v. 7); in John's Gospel (13:1) it is on the day before. Jesus must have had disciples and acquaintances in Jerusalem for him to give such specific instructions to Peter and John (vv. 10-12). For this reason, many scholars believe that Jesus went to Jerusalem on several occasions and not just this once, as Luke and the other Synoptics portray. Since women alone generally carried water jars, a man walking with one would attract attention. Jesus leaves the exact location for the meal unspecified to maintain secrecy in the face of impending danger. The Greek for "guest room" (v. 11) is *kataluma* (see 2:7).

It is nearly impossible to determine with absolute accuracy the Jewish Seder, that is, the Passover meal, at this period of history. Nonetheless, all indications are that it involved a total of three blessings of the cup. Luke mentions two of them—one at the beginning of the meal and one at the end (vv. 17, 20). Paul's version of what has come to be called the "institution narrative" is remarkably similar to that of Luke here (see 1 Cor 11:23-26). The elements of the Exodus sacrifice, such as blood, are reinterpreted in the light of Christ's life. He sheds his blood to ensure the life of God's people (see Exod 12:12-16; 24:5-8).

The mention of the betrayer's hand (v. 21), whom the reader knows to be Judas Iscariot (22:3), sparks an argument at the table. Jesus intervenes with a lesson that continues the reversal theme introduced in the *Magnificat* (Luke 1:46-55). Here at the Last Supper, Jesus gives a more positive rendition of the theme: disciples should reverse the roles themselves in order to further the kingdom. Doing so leads to true greatness (22:24-30).

Just as Jesus predicts the role of Judas, though unnamed (vv. 21-23), so too does he predict Peter's denial (vv. 31-34). The devil has already claimed Judas, and now he is attempting to take the rest of the Twelve, Peter included, as Jesus is well aware. Jesus needs Peter to support the others (v. 32), but Peter will falter, as Jesus predicts. Luke alone acknowledges in this manner the cosmic battle Jesus' life and death entail.

In a crisis one should be sure to prepare for the worst, a worry not present in easier times (vv. 35-37). The Twelve still have difficulty understanding Jesus' teaching and mission. They take his metaphors literally, and he loses patience (v. 38).

22:39-53 The agony and arrest

Jesus goes to the Mount of Olives, as is his custom (21:37-38). Prayer is a key element in the makeup of Luke's Gospel, and at this moment Jesus prays. The disciples, however, oblivious to the seriousness of events, fall asleep.

Many reliable ancient manuscripts do not include verses 43-44, but many other ones, just as reliable, do. Whether these verses belong in the Lukan text is a debated issue, but the balance tips for their inclusion. In Luke's temptation scene (4:1-13), the devil "depart[s] for a time," and because he does, Luke has no need of including the ministering angels found

Luke 22

in Matthew 4:11 and Mark 1:13. In Luke's narrative, Satan's time comes at the passion (22:3, 31). With Luke, therefore, the angel comes to minister to Jesus during his agony, the time and place where Satan exhibits his fury; it is Satan's "hour, the time for the power of darkness" (v. 53), an "hour" that will last through the crucifixion (see 23:44).

Jesus' emotional state is fragile, and he prays. The road from Jerusalem to the Judean desert passes up and over the Mount of Olives. He agonizes over a decision on whether to stay or to flee, and the tension brings him to the verge of a nervous breakdown (v. 44). A rare medical condition called "hematidrosis," a bloody sweat, sometimes occurs in people under extreme duress. For this reason some speculate that Jesus actually sweat blood. The text reads, however, that his "sweat became like drops of blood," that is, heavy and thick.

Judas finds his opportunity to hand Jesus over as he had planned with the temple authorities. It is unclear from Luke whether he actually kisses Jesus, although Matthew and Mark say so. Luke, the evangelist of "sweet mercy," is the only Synoptic to have Jesus heal the ear of the high priest's slave, while John's is the only Gospel to state the slave's name (John 18:10). Jesus' followers are ready to fight, but Jesus forbids them (v. 51).

22:54-65 Peter's denial

Peter's denial is recounted in all four Gospels.

Peter, always impetuous, follows as Jesus is led to the house of the high priest. Presumably the other disciples are hiding or at least keeping their distance from Jerusalemites. Fear overpowers Peter's usually forward manner, and he denies any contact or involvement with Jesus. Luke mentions that Jesus looks at Peter once the crowing has stopped. The glance acts as an acknowledgement of the action; Peter cannot hide from Jesus or himself, so he goes off weeping bitterly. His denial, followed by his remorse, displays Satan's near capture of him as well as the power of Jesus' prayer, for Peter, unlike Judas, will return (22:32).

Jesus spends the night in the house of the high priest, located, according to tradition and some scholars, on the southwestern slope of the city at a site currently called St. Peter in Gallicantu. Other archaeologists place the high priest's house on top of the western hill. Luke mentions only the priests and temple guards as ridiculing and demeaning Jesus here (vv. 64-65); the Romans will have their turn (23:36-37).

22:66-71 Jesus before the Sanhedrin

The Sanhedrin heard all cases dealing with Jewish law but could not inflict capital punishment, the penalty for blasphemy. Thus Jesus also has to undergo proceedings in a Roman court. The Sanhedrin uses this opportunity, therefore, to build their case before presenting him to Pilate, where they supplement the charge against Jesus with treasonable offenses (23:2).

The interrogation scene echoes details from the annunciation of Jesus' birth (1:32, 35). Jesus responds to the questions by quoting from Daniel 7:13, a text that asserts the divinity of the Messiah and thereby places the Sanhedrin under Jesus' judgment. They recognize his ploy immediately and hasten him to Pontius Pilate.

23:1-5 Jesus before Pilate

Like every colonial power in history, the Romans made friends with a certain class of the native population. This enabled them to impose foreign rule by wearing a domestic mask. In Palestine the temple priests were the class whom the Romans supported and who supported the Romans. They received revenues from performing the sacrifices of the people. In addition, they had shares in many of the shops and food providers of Jerusalem, and during the great pilgrimage feasts like Passover, this provided them with a healthy income. Roman stability secured the priests' status.

The Romans, on the other hand, needed the priests to guarantee their legitimacy. The priests enabled the Romans to appear as supporters of the Jewish faith. They acted as mediators between the emperor and the Jewish people, and as such they made Roman tax collection easier. In sum, there was an elite ruling class composed of Romans and Jews, both of whom had a vested interest in keeping the peace and suppressing any insurrection. Jesus, whose very presence garners crowds and who often questions the abuse by the authorities, presents a major threat to both parties.

Pontius Pilate's official residence was in the cosmopolitan seaport of Caesarea Maritima, Herod the Great's magnificent construction project. Within the amphitheater at the northern end was found a stone tablet incised with Pilate's name. From the Gospel accounts and Josephus, we know that Pilate went to Jerusalem only to strengthen the Roman presence among the crowds of pilgrims visiting the city during the Passover feast.

Pontius Pilate was not the weak, misinformed, and vacillating leader many think he was, and Luke notes his barbarity (13:1). The emphasis in this passage on Jesus' innocence is Luke's way of stressing that Jesus was not crucified for being a common insurrectionist (although that is the accusation), as many early Christian detractors at that time were saying.

In all of ancient literature, the only extant record of a Roman criminal court proceeding is the New Testament account of Jesus' trial before Pilate.

Luke 23

Despite the variations of the trial among the four evangelists, their narrative lines are all quite similar: questioning by Pilate along with hesitancy on his part over Jesus' guilt; release of a criminal named Barabbas in Jesus' place; and a handing over of Jesus for crucifixion.

23:6-12 Jesus before Herod

Luke alone features this account. Herod Antipas, the son of Herod the Great, is the Jewish client-king of Galilee and Perea, and he is probably in Jerusalem for the Passover feast. Because Jesus is originally from Galilee, Pilate sends him to Herod as a diplomatic courtesy. The two leaders had been at enmity with each other, probably because of Pilate's slaughter of Galileans (13:1), but Pilate's action here reconciles the two.

Herod has an interest in Jesus (9:9), and it appears that he wishes to see some spectacle (23:8). Jesus never indulges in such displays. Consequently, Herod and his soldiers mock Jesus, as the Roman soldiers will do in 23:36. Jesus is returned to Pilate, where he is condemned. The Christian tradition sees this episode as a prophetic fulfillment of Psalm 2:1-2. See Acts 4:25-28.

23:13-25 The sentence of death

The Gospel presentation of a vacillating Pilate is most apparent in this scene. Any information about releasing a prisoner in honor of the holiday we have from Matthew, Mark, and John, but not Luke (ancient and dependable manuscripts omit v. 17, which appears to have been an added gloss prompted by the readings in Matthew 27:15 and Mark 15:6). Luke simply mentions that Pilate releases Barabbas (v. 25). The Gospels are the only source we have that mentions this custom; ancient Roman historians never refer to such a policy. Is Luke, or the other evangelists for that matter, relating a historical fact? Scholars are divided on the issue. In any case, the guilty Barabbas serves as a point of comparison with the innocent Jesus.

23:26-32 The way of the cross

Crucifixion was a feared form of execution that the Romans reserved for slaves, subject populations, and the lowest criminals. The vertical shaft of the cross usually remained standing at the place of execution for successive use and to serve as a grim warning to the resident population. To add to their shame, the condemned were stripped naked and made to carry their own crossbeam amidst the jeers, taunts, and jabs of the crowd.

The Romans press Simon the Cyrenian into service, not because they pitied Jesus, but because they wanted to ensure that he lived long enough to undergo the ignominious death. By following behind Jesus, Simon becomes a model disciple, a point that would be important for the Cyrenians who formed part of the early Christian community (Acts 11:20; 13:1). The Gnostics, who denied the humanity of Jesus, will claim that Jesus was swept into heaven at the crucifixion and that Simon was mistakenly nailed to the cross, an interpretation that early Christian writers effectively counter.

People are following Jesus on the way (v. 27), and Luke's schism motif again surfaces; some are disciples, others are not. Luke often shows people divided along lines of discipleship, and this episode provides an example of that theme. The words to the "daughters of Jerusalem" (vv. 28-30), who bear a strong resemblance to a Greek chorus, reflect the scene described in the Lukan apocalyptic material (21:6-28). Here the context is one of forgiveness.

23:33-43 The crucifixion

Luke does not use the term "Golgatha"; he simply calls the area of crucifixion the "place called the Skull" (v. 33), which at the time of Christ was located outside the walls of Jerusalem. The spot of both the crucifixion and burial have been venerated as such since the second century, and the Basilica of the Holy Sepulchre has covered the place since the time of Empress Helena. The biblical, historical, and archaeological records confirm the area marked by the basilica as the true spot of Jesus' death, burial, and resurrection.

In this section there is another bracketed verse: "Father, forgive them, they know not what they do" (23:34), probably one of the most gentle verses in the whole Bible. Nearly the same manuscripts that do not include 22:43-44 are the ones that also exclude this one. Although scholars are also divided on whether this verse should be part of the original text, a strong case can be made for its inclusion. In addition to its presence in dependable manuscripts, the verse certainly fits with the theme of forgiveness that runs through Luke's whole Gospel, including the passion (22:49-51).

While Luke has Herod's men alone ridiculing Jesus in 23:11, the evangelist situates the mocking by the Roman soldiers here at verses 36-37. Matthew and Mark mention that the two criminals revile Jesus, but only Luke provides a dialogue in which one criminal reprimands the other. At this point Jesus again utters words of mercy, and again we see the schism motif, with one criminal acknowledging Jesus and the other cursing him.

Throughout the crucifixion and death, there are intentional echoes from Psalm 22, Isaiah 53, Wisdom 2–3. These Old Testament works become the lens through which the kerygma is interpreted.

Luke 23

23:44-49 The death of Jesus

Luke's portrayal of the death of Jesus has important differences from the other two Synoptics. As the scene opens, we read of the description of the three hours of darkness. Luke adds the detail about the eclipse of the sun (v. 45). An eclipse is impossible during a full moon, which would have been the case during Passover. This verse should be read, therefore, as a circumstantial phrase well translated as "while the sun's light failed." If there is any historical background to three hours of darkness, it is most likely attributable to a dust storm coming from the desert, which is a common occurrence in this area during the spring of the year. The important point, however, is to see this passage as an echo of the many apocalyptic prophecies and writings that describe the Day of the Lord as one in which the sun will not shine (see Isa 13:10; Amos 8:9).

The tearing of the temple veil in Luke comes before the death of Jesus and not after it, as it does in Matthew and Mark. Luke is a fine literary artist, and by such a placement of the verse, he constructs the ripping of the curtain as a part of the buildup to the death of Jesus, the climax of the passage. The tearing of the veil itself is laden with a great deal of Old Testament symbolism. We really have no way of knowing to which of the several veils in the temple Luke (or the other evangelists) is referring. The bigger question is whether Luke sees the tearing as a means to let the divine presence out or the means to allow humans in. Since this Lukan version occurs before the death of Jesus, letting the divine presence out is the better conclusion. This is the day of the Lord, and God's presence, his judgment, now centers on the cross.

Among the four Gospels, there are three versions of Jesus' last words from the cross. In each case Christ's final utterance is an expression of each evangelist's theology, which for Luke is trust in God. Jesus shows absolute confidence in the Father during this last moment, a mood quite different from his prayer on the Mount of Olives (22:39-46). With the word "Father," Luke connects this last prayer with the two other prayers Jesus has spoken throughout his passion: the agony (22:42) and the prayer for forgiveness (23:34). See also the prayer for the disciples (10:21) and the Lord's Prayer (11:2).

The centurion offers the first reaction and therefore the first interpretation of Jesus' death in verse 47. The statement that Jesus is innocent (or righteous, just) recalls the deliberations of the Sanhedrin, Pilate, and Herod. On another level, the use of "innocent/righteous/just" harks back to the passage from Wisdom 3:1-3: "But the souls of the just are in the hand of God, / and no torment shall touch them. / They seemed, in the view of the foolish, to be dead; / and their passing away was thought an affliction / and their going forth from us, utter destruction. / But they are in peace." Luke sees the centurion's statement as an act of glorification of God. Jesus has accomplished his "exodus," which he set out to do in 9:31. The "hour . . . of darkness" (22:53) has passed; it is now the hour of the Lord's glorification, ushered in by Jesus' loud cry from the cross (v. 46), a paraphrase of Psalm 31:6.

In the last two verses of the death scene, Luke portrays another dichotomy among several people; he separates the disciples and acquaintances from onlookers and mockers. The emphasis on the eyewitnesses will become an important point for the early church and will be used against those Gnostic detractors who would deny Jesus' actual death by crucifixion.

The Lukan proclivity to emphasize God's mercy becomes evident with the breast-beating onlookers as they return to their homes. The only other occurrence in Luke of breast-beating is in the parable of the Pharisee and the tax collector (18:9-14). In that parable the tax collector knows his sinfulness and asks for forgiveness. The onlookers, like the tax collector, know their sinfulness and depart asking for forgiveness. From Jesus' prayer from the cross, "Father, forgive them, they know not what they do" (23:34), we know that forgiveness is already there.

In Christian piety, verses 34, 43, and 46 are counted among the seven last words of Christ (see also Matt 27:46/Mark 15:34; John 19:26, 28, 30).

23:50-56 The burial of Jesus

The inclusion of the detail "a rock-hewn tomb in which no one had yet been buried," mentioned in some fashion in all four Gospels, underscores that Jesus' body is not laid in a tomb as part of a multiple burial. The evangelists stress that the tomb is new and unused. This detail later becomes important for the early church in countering Gnostic and Jewish charges that Jesus' body was confused among the corpses. All the activity has to be completed before the sabbath begins at sundown.

Joseph of Arimathea, like Simeon and Anna in the infancy narrative (2:25-38), awaits the "kingdom of God" (v. 51). With him, Jesus' universal message penetrates the Sanhedrin and, ironically, has a positive effect there. Joseph's concern for extending the legal prescriptions regarding burial of the dead ensures that Jesus is not totally excommunicated from his own nation. The women disciples from Galilee (8:1-3) are faithful throughout Jesus' ministry, are present at the crucifixion, and for the burial (v. 56).

Luke 24

THE RESURRECTION

Luke 24:1-53

Discrepancies among the four Gospel accounts reflect the oral transmission of the stories. Each Gospel account relates the respective evangelist's theological interpretation of the fact that Jesus bodily rose on the first day of the week.

Resurrection accounts among the four Gospels can be arranged in several categories. First, there are those dealing with the empty tomb on the first day of the week. Second, there are Jesus' appearances in Jerusalem and environs. And third, there are his appearances in Galilee. All four Gospels feature accounts of the empty tomb, and, to a greater or lesser extent, they all recount appearances in Jerusalem. Luke's is the only one, however, that does not contain any narratives of the Galilean appearances. On the other hand, the most protracted Jerusalem story (24:13-35) is found only in the Third Gospel. Because the second volume to the Lukan corpus, the Acts of the Apostles, relates the whole missionary venture of the church as starting in Jerusalem and from there "throughout Judea and Samaria, to the ends of the earth" (Acts 1:8), Christ's presence in Galilee is simply folded into the broader picture with references to the spice-bearing women (23:55-56) and the "men of Galilee" (Acts 1:11).

24:1-12 The resurrection of Jesus

Tombs were often sealed with a large, wheel-like stone that was rolled in a carved trench in front of a rectangular doorway. Several strong men were needed to move it. The lowly status of women in ancient society not only kept them from politics, but it also meant that they were not to be taken seriously. Paradoxically, this condition gave them some power, since they could come and go in the most volatile areas without raising suspicion, as their standing at the crucifixion and their visit to the tomb attest. Mary Magdalene is the only woman witness common to all four Gospels. For this reason, she has been called *apostola apostolorum*, the "apostle of the apostles."

That the stone has been rolled away when the women arrive is the first sign of something out of the ordinary. Luke has men, described in angel-like terms, stilling the women's fear and placing the resurrection in the context of Jesus' teaching and ministry. The men do not command the women to tell the others, but the women do so out of their own joy and enthusiasm, a truly Lukan ideal of the faithful disciple, and these women have not yet seen the risen Lord. Unfortunately, the men remain incredulous of the women's story, although Peter finds it sufficiently convincing to see for himself.

24:13-35 The road to Emmaus

The spice-bearing women have spread the word concerning the empty tomb, so the disciples in town know about it (24:9). One of the disciples along the road is called Cleopas (v. 18), a name similar to Klopas, the husband of one of the women at the cross, according to John's Gospel (19:25). Many have speculated with good reason that the two mentioned here are married to each other.

Luke is the only Gospel to present this passage, and there may be historical accuracy associated with it. At least three towns lay claim to being the Emmaus of this pericope. The text says that it is situated sixty stadia from Jerusalem, which is the distance for the round trip between the city and Emmaus, a walk one could make at that hour of the day, especially if as excited and enthusiastic as these two disciples. The Emmaus matching most of the criteria lies opposite present-day Moza, whose ruins from the 1948 war are still visible.

The reply to Jesus' questions summarizes the ministry as disciples would have seen and understood it (vv. 17-24). Jesus' explanation places all the events within the context of Old Testament prophecies and Jewish experience (vv. 25-27). They recognize him in the breaking of the bread, a detail reiterated when they relate the story to the Eleven and the others. They can fully *see* who Jesus is, however, and therefore *believe* in him only once the "traveling companion" explains the Law and the prophets. None of this information is new to these disciples; they are merely hearing it again as though for the first time, and the little hope they may have had has blossomed into faith: "Were not our hearts burning [within us] while he spoke to us on the way and opened the scriptures to us?" (v. 32). This passage presents a balance between the word (vv. 25-27) and sacrament (vv. 30-32), and as such, it is highly eucharistic and liturgical. See also Mark 16:12-13.

By specifically using "eleven" (v. 33) instead of "apostles," Luke highlights Judas's betrayal and prepares the narrative for the election of his replacement in Acts 1:15-26.

24:36-49 The appearance in Jerusalem

Maintaining that the resurrected Jesus is a ghost is more comprehensible to the disciples than believing that he is risen. With this Jerusalem appearance, paralleled in John 19:19-29, Luke presents an apology for those who deny the reality of the resurrection. He does so by having Jesus call the question on the nature of his current existence (v. 39a). Jesus then allows the disciples to feel his flesh and bone while he presents the marks of the crucifixion (vv. 39b-40). Finally, he expresses hunger, and they give him fish to eat. Because it symbolizes overabundance, fish is a sign of the eschatological age, which Jesus' resurrection has indeed ushered in.

As he does with the disciples on the road to Emmaus, Jesus here explains his life, ministry, and resurrection in light of the Old Testament prophecies and experience. The role of the disciples as witnesses to these events is emphasized. They are to start in Jerusalem before heading to the nations. This geographical plan is restated in Acts 1:8. The "power from on high" (v. 49) is the Holy Spirit, who descends upon them in Jerusalem (Acts 2:1-13).

This passage introduces the nature of the glorified body, a reality that goes to the heart of Christian belief. The resurrected life that Christ initiates goes beyond spiritual existence in eternity. It is a new life involving the glorified body that is not immediately recognizable to friends and loved ones, and therefore different from the mortal body, yet this glorified body has continuity with the mortal one. The glorified body transcends the limits of time and space, and yet it is physical. Wounds and blemishes are apparent, yet they do not scar or cause pain. Not much more can be said on the nature of the resurrected body than what Luke describes here. Luke wants faithful believers to know that the same destiny awaits them (see Acts 2:14-41).

24:50-53 The ascension

Luke recapitulates the ascension in the Acts of the Apostles (1:6-12), with some additions. The two ascension stories serve as a bridge connecting the two-volume work. Here it occurs on the same day as the resurrection; in Acts, it begins the apostolic ministry. This ascension account completes the journey to Jerusalem (9:51), while it also ends the Gospel. Jesus' exodus, first voiced in 9:31, is completed with the glorious ascension.

The road to Bethany passes over the Mount of Olives. Jesus was last on the mount during his agony and arrest, when the hour of the "power of darkness" held sway (22:53). His presence on the Mount of Olives now is the triumph over the dark power of Satan.

In Scripture, the Mount of Olives is considered the hill of God's judgment and glorification, and it takes on that role here. Jesus raises his hands in the Old Testament priestly blessing, he ascends gloriously into heaven, and the disciples are filled with joy. Although the Spirit does not come until they are gathered together at Pentecost (Acts 2:1-4), they participate even now in Christ's glorification by praising God in the temple (v. 53). They are the models for all Christians who await the fullness of Christ's reign.

The Gospel According to John

Scott M. Lewis, S.J.

INTRODUCTION

At first glance the Gospel of John seems deceptively simple and straightforward. As we read and study the text carefully, however, it becomes obvious that there is more to the text than we thought. John is a master of irony, and as the privileged readers we are in a position to appreciate the irony-laden words and actions of the Gospel's characters. John's Jesus uses ordinary words in a manner charged with different layers of meaning, which his listeners usually misunderstand. Water is not just water, nor is bread only bread. Finally, many concepts with which we are familiar are used in a unique way. The word "truth" in verse 14 of the prologue will be unfolded along with the narrative of the Gospel. We are familiar with the word "life," which is used fifty times in the Gospel of John. Its Johannine meaning, however, dances tantalizingly beyond our immediate comprehension. It is wise not to approach the text with preconceived ideas, but as if we are reading it for the first time. Let the text provoke, challenge, and enlighten you. Don't be afraid to question the text or argue with it.

One of the most striking features of the Gospel of John is its different portrayal of Jesus. In the Synoptic Gospels (Matthew, Mark, and Luke), we see much more of the humanity of Jesus. In John, Jesus is a majestic, serene figure, omniscient and totally in control of his destiny at all times. One scholar described John's Jesus as "God striding across the face of the earth." There are no exorcisms in John, and only seven miracles are described. Important miracles such as the raising of Lazarus in John 11 are absent in the other Gospels.

It is likely that John represents a parallel but independent tradition and is not dependent on the Gospel of Mark, as in the Synoptic tradition. Although the name "John" is ascribed to the Gospel, the actual author is unknown, the text referring to him merely as the "disciple whom Jesus loved" (see 13:23; 19:26; 21:7, 20). The text as we have it went through at least three stages of development and represented the tradition and teaching of the Johannine community rather than just one individual.

The Gospel According to John

The Gospel of John reflects the tensions, pressures, and influences of the time and place in which it was written. John has a very black-and-white view of the world: good and evil, light and darkness, spirit and flesh. His narrative is not given to the sort of nuance that we would normally expect and can seem unduly harsh and abrasive at times. Scholars tell us that the Gospel was written around A.D. 90, while the community was involved in acrimonious polemics with fellow Jews. The term "the Jews" (*hoi ioudaioi*) is often used in a very pejorative way, usually to describe the enemies of Jesus. It is important to remember that the author and his community were also Jews. We should not assume that the historical Jesus vilified or rejected his people.

Likewise, John reserves his strongest vitriol for fellow Christians who differ with him in matters of theology, especially those that relate to Jesus (christology). This is especially evident in the First Letter of John. Reading the text in a superficial and unquestioning manner often leads to sectarian or anti-Judaic misuses of the Gospel. Tragically, this has occurred often in our history. As we study the text, it is helpful to put ourselves in the shoes of the "enemies" of Jesus. What does the world look like through their eyes? Why did they respond as they did? Would we respond differently if we were in their place?

The famous prologue (1:1-18) is often described in terms of the overture to an opera, giving the reader a foretaste of the themes that will be developed at length through the rest of the Gospel. It contains John's theology in a compact form and introduces us to the plot of the Gospel narrative. Matthew and Luke narrate the earthly birth of Jesus, but John develops the theme of preexistence and takes us back to the very beginning, before the world was ever created. We as readers know where Jesus is really from, while most of the characters of the Gospel of John do not. John's Jesus is not the product of human societies; he is a stranger and alien in the world, even though it was created at his hands. The prologue introduces the theme of the descent and ascent of the emissary of God, as well as the opposition arrayed to thwart the mission of the Word made flesh, an opposition that is represented by the "world" and the "Jews." Finally, it contains the promise that the revelation and perfection of God's gifts brought by the eternal Word will make it possible to become children of God.

John 1

COMMENTARY

PROLOGUE

John 1:1-18

1:1-3 In the beginning

The phrase "In the beginning" in verse 1 echoes Genesis 1:1 and alerts the reader to the new creation motif present in the Gospel. The "Word" (*Logos*) is present in the Old Testament as the creative energy of God, as in Genesis 1 and Isaiah 55. The Greek term *logos*, a widely used philosophical term meaning "order," "reason," or "harmony," was chosen to express this aspect of God. The role of the *Logos* is parallel to that of divine Wisdom in the late Old Testament, as in Psalm 33:6; Wisdom 7:25; 8:5; 9:1; 9:9-11; and Proverbs 8:22-31. These passages describe a feminine Wisdom figure who is the divine artisan and co-creator and who was with God before creation. The *Logos* in John is the one through whom all things were created and who was with God and turned toward God even before creation. This is not a simple identification of God and the *Logos*, but a statement that what God was, the *Logos* also was.

1:4-5, 9 Life, light, and darkness

In verse 4 the theme of "life" (*zōē*) is introduced. Jesus has the power of life in him and is able to impart it to whomever he chooses (5:24; 11:25; 14:6). John sees the world in a stark contrast of light and darkness (vv. 4 and 9). The light comes from above, while darkness is from below (3:19; 8:12; 9:5; 12:46). The contrasting themes of light and darkness would have been readily understood by people in a variety of religious and philosophical traditions.

1:6-8, 15 John the Baptist

Verses 1:6-8 and 15 represent an "intrusion," meaning that they break the flow of the poem and possibly represent a later insertion. They emphasize the subordinate status and supporting role of John the Baptist. There was some rivalry between the disciples of Jesus and John the Baptist (see 3:22-36 and 4:1-2). His role was not completely clear in the first century, and many continued to follow him (Acts 19:1-7).

1:10-11 Opposition to the light

Rejection by both the world and "his own"—presumably the "Jews"—is introduced in verses 10 and 11. Opposition will intensify as Jesus approaches

John 1

the climax of his mission. This resistance will be present in almost every encounter that Jesus has with people and represents John's stark contrast between the world above and the world below.

1:12-13 Divine empowerment

Believing in the one from above is the key to empowerment, the power to become children *(tekna)* of God (vv. 12-13). This will be expressed in extended form in chapters 14–17. People are not children of God by nature; it is what they become when they are born from above (3:3), and it is by divine initiative, not human. For John, this is a status to be experienced in this life. It is not necessary to wait until the end times or death, as in traditional eschatology. This is similar to the principle of adoption and empowerment by the Spirit found in Romans 7–8.

1:14 The incarnation

This verse contains the most theologically provocative statement in the Gospel. The one who is the object of faith is described: the Word became flesh and dwelt among us. The Greek word that describes the dwelling of the Word literally means "to pitch one's tent" and possibly alludes to the instances in the Old Testament where Yahweh is said to dwell in the tent or tabernacle (Exod 25:8; 29:46; Zech 2:14; Sir 24:8).

The notion of the divine becoming flesh was a scandal to Greeks, who devalued the flesh and exalted the spirit or the mind, as well as to Jews, who safeguarded the oneness and transcendence of God. It is the concept of the incarnation that separates Christianity from both Judaism and Islam. Its vigorous assertion by John's community resulted in its marginalization from other groups of followers of Jesus. In addition to the notion of a physical body, flesh also means the limits of time and space, as well as mortality. With the incarnation, Jesus becomes the point of unity between the world above and the world below.

In the Old Testament, God's glory *(kabod)* is divine power perceptible on a human level (Exod 33:22; 40:34-35), and is all that human beings can bear. Verse 14 insists that they have seen his glory *(doxa)*, signifying that God's power has become visible in and through a human being. "Grace and truth" is an attribute of God found in Exodus 34:6 *(hesed w-emet)*. Grace is both a sign of God's favor and a description of God's goodness and kindness. John's definition of truth will unfold, as in 4:24; 8:32; 18:37-38. Truth is part of John's high christology, which unmasks the world and its pretensions.

1:16-17 God's gifts

This fullness of grace and truth has bestowed grace (or gift) in place of (or upon) grace (v. 16). This does not imply an inferior status of the previous gift, but its perfection or completion in the new. In verse 17 law is juxtaposed with grace and truth in a way that suggests the theme of fulfillment and perfection of Judaism in Jesus present in nearly every scene of the Gospel.

1:18 The unknown God

No one has ever seen God, who cannot be known through normal human means. All human claims about God are erroneous or incomplete. Human limitations are such that God is unknowable unless the doors of perception are cleansed, which can only be accomplished by the Spirit given through Jesus. In every scene Jesus reveals a God whom we have never known, and this will be reflected in the use of language that emphasizes the sharp dichotomy between above and below, spirit and flesh, light and darkness. There are similar ideas present in Gnostic literature and the Odes of Solomon (late first or early second century A.D.). They share the notion of a redeemer/revealer who reveals the unknown God and awakens humanity to its true origin and destiny. Gnostic groups who shared these ideas made liberal use of the Gospel of John, and it is for this reason that this Gospel was viewed with suspicion by many communities in the early church.

THE BOOK OF SIGNS
John 1:19–12:50

Many scholars believe that this section of the Gospel draws on a preexistent collection of miracles or signs. The evangelist selected and refined only seven of the miracles of Jesus. In the Synoptic Gospels, they are deeds of power *(dynamis)* and reveal the arrival of the reign of God. In John, however, they are called signs *(semeia)* and are a revelation of the identity of Jesus as the one sent from the Father above. Verses 1:29, 35, and 43 begin with "the next day," which is clearly an artificial literary device. Some are able to discern a pattern of seven days, which, coupled with 1:1, seem to signify the seven days of creation. This pattern is rather strained in some places, and there are other possibilities. Others see a three-day preparation patterned after Exodus 19, with God's glory being revealed on the fourth day (2:1-12). We will assume this pattern.

John 1

1:19-28 Day One

This interrogation of John at the hands of the Jerusalem delegation is unique to John. In verse 20 the Baptist himself denies a messianic status and admits a secondary status with regard to Jesus (cf. vv. 6-8, 15). He denies that he is Elijah (v. 21), but it is interesting to note that in Mark 9:11-12, Jesus reveals that John the Baptist was indeed Elijah. Elijah was the prophet who was expected to reappear in the last days to prepare the way for the Messiah (Mal 4:5-6; Sir 48:9). His replies "I am not" *(ouk eimi)* parallel the many "I AM" *(ego eimi)* statements of Jesus throughout the Gospel. The "prophet" referred to in verse 25 is one promised in Deuteronomy 18:15, 18 and amplified in the Dead Sea Scrolls from Qumran (1QS 9:11; 4Q Flor). The self-declaration from Isaiah 40:3 (vv. 23-27) and John's assertion of his baptism of water are paralleled in the Synoptic Gospels (Mark, Matthew, and Luke).

1:29-34 Day Two

John the Baptist witnesses to Jesus, beginning with a proclamation that he is the Lamb of God (v. 29) who takes away the sin of the world. John portrays Jesus as the paschal lamb (19:36) described in Exodus 12, although the paschal lamb of Exodus did not take away sin but was a sign of reconciliation. The paschal lamb imagery is also used in Revelation 5 and 1 Corinthians 5:7. Jesus came after John but ranks ahead of him because he existed before him (v. 30). This refers to the preexistence of the *Logos* in 1:1-3 and alludes to his divine status. The Spirit descending on Jesus is witnessed by John the Baptist rather than Jesus or the crowds, as in the Synoptic accounts (Mark 1:10; Matt 3:16; Luke 3:22). In verse 34 the Baptist acclaims Jesus the Son of God, the second in what will become a string of titles.

1:35-42 Day Three

Again John the Baptist recognizes the role of Jesus as the Lamb of God. Two of his disciples follow Jesus. In the Synoptic Gospels it is Jesus who seeks out and calls his disciples, while in John it is the disciples who search for Jesus. When Jesus asks them what they want, they ask, "Where are you staying *(menein)*?" The word is identical to that used in chapter 15 with the parable of the vine, when Jesus promises that the believer who remains or abides in him *(menein)* will enjoy the indwelling of Jesus and the Father.

The question has levels of meaning, and that is confirmed when Jesus invites the disciples to "come and . . . see." Verbs of perception in John have a deeper meaning than the mere physical. Here they are an invitation to the two disciples as well as John's readers to experience and comprehend

John 2

where Jesus truly abides—with God. Andrew, one of the two disciples, proclaims to his brother Simon that they have found the Messiah. When he brings his brother Simon to Jesus, he immediately receives the nickname Cephas (Peter, meaning "rock"). In Mark 8:27-30, this occurs after Peter's confession that Jesus is the Messiah and occurs halfway through his ministry.

1:43-51 Day Four

In verse 43 Philip is the only disciple directly called by Jesus, and the command "Follow me" is the formulaic call to discipleship present in all four Gospels. Philip proclaims to Nathanael that they have found the one prophesied by Moses and the prophets and that he is the son of Joseph from Nazareth (v. 45). His insistence is met with a contemptuous retort, "Can anything good come from Nazareth?" (v. 46), reflecting the unimportance of Nazareth in the first century. In the ancient Mediterranean world, it was sufficient to know one's village of origin and the name of one's father to place one in society. The irony is that Jesus as the Word made flesh is not from Nazareth, and his Father is God, which we already know as privileged readers.

Jesus addresses Nathanael as a true Israelite, with no duplicity or guile in him (v. 47). This is unlike Jacob (Gen 27:35) and is in line with a similar description in Psalm 32:2: "in whose spirit is no deceit." When Nathanael asks Jesus how he knows him, Jesus replies that he saw him under the fig tree even before Phillip called him, clearly an instance of supernatural sight (vv. 48-49). In amazement, Nathanael proclaims him Son of God and King of Israel (v. 50). All these titles—Lamb of God, Son of God, King of Israel—are true only to a certain point, but they are human categories and therefore inadequate. Jesus will transcend even these, and in a solemn pronouncement Jesus declares that they will see even greater things—the sky opened and the angels of God ascending and descending on the Son of Man (v. 51). This is a variation on Jacob's dream in Genesis 28:12-13, an important theme in rabbinic literature. Rents in the veil separating the physical and spiritual worlds are a favored aspect of apocalyptic theology, as in the baptism of Jesus in Mark 1:10, where the "heavens [were] torn open." Jesus is the bridge between heaven and earth, as well as the gateway.

2:1-3 A wedding banquet

It is the third day after the four-day preparation. This is the first of seven signs that the evangelist presents to disclose the divine identity of Jesus and is present only in John's Gospel. The wedding celebration would have lasted for several days, and the family honor would have depended on providing an adequate feast for the guests. The mother of Jesus is never referred to by name in the Fourth Gospel, nor is the Beloved Disciple, for it is discipleship rather than individual personalities that is important.

2:4-5 A request and a strange answer

When Jesus' mother brings to his attention the fact that the hosts have no more wine, he replies in what seems to us a very brusque manner. The address "Woman" in verse 4 sounds rude to modern ears, but it is actually an Aramaic form that is not disrespectful, although rather formal. "How does your concern affect me?" (*Ti emoi kai soi:* literally, "What do you have to do with me?") is an idiom found in both Aramaic and Greek and expresses defensiveness in the face of attack, as with the demons in Mark 1:24; 5:7, or a concern that someone is forcing an issue or intruding into one's private business.

There is a bit of tension in the story, for Jesus remains slightly aloof from the situation. It is clear that he is defined by his relationship with God the Father and not earthly family ties. His insistence that his hour has not yet come is an indication that he must adhere to the divine timetable. His hour is defined throughout the Gospel as the glorification or crucifixion (12:23), although in this context it probably also alludes to the first public manifestation of his power—he does not feel that the time is right to manifest himself. His mother does not doubt at all that Jesus will respond, and her order to the waiters to do whatever he says displays the absolute trust that is taken as an exemplar of discipleship.

2:6-12 The stone jars

Verse 6 describes six stone jars, each holding approximately twenty-four gallons. Stone jars were often used because, unlike pottery, they did not transmit impurity or defilement. The water that is drawn out of the jars has become wine (vv. 8-9). The steward's statement about the good wine being saved until now (v. 10) suggests John's theme of fulfillment and perfection (1:17), bolstered by the fact that six jars were used in Jewish rituals, one short of the number of perfection and fulfillment. The miracle seems unimportant and even trivial in itself, but it is symbolic of a change of the eon, a new world, and the advent of the Messiah. In Amos 9:11, 13; Joel 3:18; Isaiah 25:6, the advent of the messianic age is signified by an abundance of rich and sweet wine. Through this sign Jesus reveals his glory (v. 11) or divine power (*doxa;* 1:14; 5:41-44; 7:18; 11:4, 40; 12:43; 17:5, 22-24), and his disciples begin to believe in him.

2:13-17 The cleansing of the temple

In the Synoptic Gospels the cleansing of the temple is almost the last public act of Jesus and occurs after his triumphal entrance into Jerusalem, preceding his arrest (Mark 11:15-17; Matt 21:12-13; Luke 19:45-46). In John's Gospel it is one of the first public acts and takes place at the beginning of Jesus' ministry, during one of his three trips to Jerusalem. There is no way to reconcile this discrepancy other than to acknowledge that John's Gospel is an independent witness to the life of Jesus and orders the events in accordance with its own theological concerns and literary structure.

This is the first instance of opposition on the part of the "Jews." Jesus drives out the sellers of oxen, sheep, and doves, along with the moneychangers. In a rather violent Johannine twist, he uses a whip of cords and overturns tables and coins in the process. The quotations in verses 16-17 are from Zechariah 14:21 and Psalm 69:9 instead of Jeremiah, as in Mark 11:17 and contain no references to thieves. The offense is turning his Father's house into a marketplace.

2:18-22 A new temple

Jesus is asked for some sort of sign to authenticate his prophetic behavior (v. 18), which is consistent with an Old Testament prophet such as Jeremiah. His reply (v. 19) is "Destroy this temple and in three days I will raise it up." Thinking that he is referring to the Jerusalem temple (v. 20), they object that the temple has been under construction for forty-six years, and his claim must have seemed ludicrous. The rebuilding of the temple began in 20–19 B.C. and was completed and finished in the sixties of the first century. Forty-six years would have placed this event in A.D. 28.

This is one of many instances in which Jesus speaks on a symbolic higher plane but is misunderstood by people who interpret his words in literal and mundane ways. He is speaking of the temple of his body (v. 21), and of course the three days becomes a prediction of his resurrection. Two words for "temple" are used. The first, *hieros,* possibly refers to the entire temple precincts. The temple of Jesus' body is described with the Greek word *naos,* usually referring to the inner sanctuary, where the image of the god is to be found. This is written after the destruction of the temple, and Jesus is seen by John's community as the new temple *(naos)* or place of encounter with God. The final verse (v. 22) is a perfect illustration of how the Gospels were written. The words and deeds of Jesus are remembered after the resurrection and interpreted in light of that experience.

John 2

2:23-25 Imperfect faith

Although it appears that many begin to believe in Jesus because of the signs, Jesus is not convinced, as he is all too cognizant of the vagaries of human nature. The dangers of superficial or incomplete belief will be a recurrent theme in the rest of the Gospel.

3:1-2 Nicodemus by night

The introduction of Nicodemus in verses 1-2 is linked with the description of people with imperfect faith in 2:23-25. Nicodemus, a Pharisee and leader of the Jews, plays a symbolic role. He represents those who possess a natural human understanding of reality, as well as those who are sympathetic to Jesus but lack the conviction to make a full and unequivocal stand in faith. He appears again in 7:50 and 19:39 as a well-intentioned but rather timid figure.

In John's uncompromising polemic, Nicodemus is used to challenge followers to make a public commitment and face the cost; he cannot straddle two different worlds. Nicodemus comes by night (v. 2), which here accentuates his limited human understanding and his attraction to the light represented by Jesus. He acknowledges that Jesus is a teacher come from God, for the common expectation is that the ability to perform signs is proof of the presence and approval of God.

3:3-6 Second birth

The reply of Jesus is almost a non-sequitur (v. 3). He makes a solemn pronouncement that no one can "see" the kingdom of God (cf. 1:12-13) without being born from above *(anothēn)*. To "see" means to experience and understand, and the "kingdom of God" is not a place but a state of being. The word *anothēn* has two meanings—"again" and "from above." The theme of spiritual rebirth is widespread in ancient mystery religions and esoteric philosophies. Nicodemus takes it in the first sense (v. 4), which leads him to an absurdity, for Jesus is speaking on a spiritual plane but is understood in the physical or natural sense, a consequence of the natural barrier to knowing God described in 1:18.

Jesus rephrases the need for rebirth (v. 5) and insists that one enters rather than sees the kingdom of God, but only after being born both of water and Spirit. Does water mean normal human birth or baptism? Although the latter is likely, the first meaning is not thereby excluded. Additionally, the kingdom of God is also represented by the community of believers, and one receives the new life promised by Jesus by entrance into the group by means of baptism. The chasm between the earthly and human and the heavenly and divine is stated emphatically (v. 6). Those who are of the flesh judge according to the senses (7:24; 8:25). The Spirit, however, provides believers with a new mode of perception and understanding.

3:7-8 Wind and Spirit

Jesus explains this necessity in terms of wind and Spirit—the Greek word for both is *pneuma*. The Spirit, like the wind, is mysterious and cannot be controlled by human beings (Eccl 11:5; Sir 16:21), since it does not originate from them. Nicodemus's puzzled question is met with a rebuke from Jesus (vv. 9-12). Nicodemus represents the best of a religious tradition, but he does not have a deep understanding of the "earthly things," which were part of his own tradition, so Jesus questions whether he can comprehend the "heavenly things" that he will reveal. The status of Jesus is unique, for as the divine emissary (v. 13), he is the only one to have been in God's presence (see 1:18). Even the great spiritual figures who had ecstatic or revelatory experiences (Moses, Abraham, Enoch, etc.) are unqualified to reveal what Jesus can, because he has descended from above.

3:14-15 Lifted up

In his portrayal of the salvific nature of Jesus' death, John uses the story of Moses and the fiery serpents from Numbers 21:8-9. The Greek word *(hypsōsen)* means both "lifted up" and "exalted," representing a Johannine double meaning. The crucifixion is referred to in this Gospel as the exaltation or glorification of Jesus. The serpent's venom is human death, and Jesus follows with a discussion of the cure, which is eternal life through belief in the one sent from above.

3:16-17 God's love

Verse 16 is one of the most famous passages in the New Testament. Despite the many negative references to the "world" *(kosmos)*, here it is an object of God's love. It is unclear whether "perish" means through death or apocalyptic judgment, as in 5:28-29; both eschatologies are present in John. The incarnation is for salvation rather than condemnation (v. 17).

3:18-21 The mystery of belief and unbelief

One's salvation or condemnation depends on belief in the name of the Son of God. Belief is not intellectual assent to doctrine, but total surrender and openness to the object of belief. Verses 19-21 reflect the prologue, especially verses 10-11. Rejection of Jesus and a refusal to believe reflect the inner state of the individual. Those who are evil in orientation will not come to the light, while those who live the truth welcome it. Our modern awareness of human psychology and the dynamics of faith and doubt are more subtle and sophisticated, but John has a dualistic, either-or worldview.

3:22-36 Rivalry

Clumsiness in wording and transition indicates that verses 22-36 probably comprise several traditions. Verse 22 is evidence that Jesus is associated with John the Baptist, possibly as a disciple, and that they have gone their separate but harmonious ways. Both Jesus and John work in concert and appear to make a deep impression on many people. It is clear that Jesus is baptizing, but contrast this statement with 4:2. The locations of Aenon and Salim (v. 23) are unknown, although several sites have been proposed.

The dispute that arises between the disciples of John and a Jew is over ceremonial washings (v. 25). In the Synoptic Gospels, the disciples of Jesus are criticized for not washing their hands. A similar criticism is perhaps at the core of the disagreement, because in verse 26 the disciples of John complain to him that Jesus is baptizing independently and is gathering a following of his own. John replies that any power or influence can only be that which is granted by God (v. 27), similar to Jesus' reply to Pilate in 19:11. This reflects a strong current of divine predetermination throughout the Gospel of John, one also present in the sectarian writings of Qumran. John reconfirms his testimony from 1:19-34 (v. 28); his only role is to witness to Jesus (1:6-8, 15).

Verse 29 is similar in nature to an incident from Mark 2:18-20, which was also in the context of a controversy between disciples, although over the issue of fasting. Here the parable is interpreted in a manner that stresses the secondary and supportive role of John the Baptist. Recognizing the power granted to Jesus from above, John begins his fading exit from the scene (v. 30). He clearly is totally open to the Word of God, and he proves this by insisting to his own disciples that both he and Jesus are part of the same mission, which should eliminate any reason for resentment or competition.

3:31-36 The one from above

Verses 31 and 32 place Jesus in a completely different category. He has come from above and is above all, and he reveals what is from above and out of the reach of ordinary earthly people and will be rejected by many for precisely that reason (cf. 1:11). Jesus speaks for God (vv. 33-36), who has given over everything to him, and to accept the words of Jesus is to accept

John 4

the God who sent him (cf. Luke 10:22). The promise of eternal life is again given for those who believe in the one who has been sent (v. 36). There is an ominous note: those who reject Jesus will not receive eternal life, and the wrath of God remains on them (cf. Rom 2:5), which presumably includes judgment and punishment.

4:1-6 The new spiritual order

The story of the encounter of Jesus with the Samaritan woman expands on the dawn of the messianic age revealed in 2:1-12. Verses 1-3 explain why Jesus leaves Judea and heads to Galilee. The Pharisees have heard that Jesus appears to be outstripping John the Baptist in baptisms, although the evangelist (or someone much later) adds that Jesus himself did not do any baptizing, leaving that to his disciples. The number of disciples who are baptizing indicates the birth and spread of a new movement, and this is disquieting to the Pharisees. Jesus must pass through Samaria (v. 4), the region in central Israel and the habitation of the Samaritans. They enter Sychar (v. 5), near the ancient city of Shechem and site of Jacob's well (Gen 33:19 and 48:22). At noon Jesus sits down to rest by the well.

4:7-9 The woman at the well

When the Samaritan woman comes to draw water, Jesus asks her to give him a drink (v. 7). By entering a Samaritan village and speaking with this woman, Jesus has crossed ethnic, religious, and gender boundaries. The Samaritans were seen as ethnically impure, having intermarried with colonizers after the Assyrian invasion in 722 B.C. They were religiously suspect, worshiping in a different manner and having their own version of the Torah. And it would have been considered scandalous for him to speak directly to a woman, especially alone. Verse 8 underscores the fact that his disciples are not present, and he is alone with the woman. Her response is rather surly and aggressive (v. 9), emphasizing that Jesus is a Jew and she is a woman and a Samaritan. "Jews use nothing in common with Samaritans" is an understatement, for there was strong animosity between the two groups. The Greek wording is stronger: "Jews do not associate with Samaritans."

4:10-15 Living water

The preliminaries over, Jesus begins probing by stating that if she recognized who he is and understood the transcendental nature of the water he is offering, she would be asking *him* for a drink (v. 10). He promises "living water," which in a technical sense is any water that is flowing and not stored in cisterns or stagnant. As in other scenes, Jesus is using an ordinary word in a spiritual and transcendental sense, and at first the woman understands only on a mundane and human level (v. 11). She assumes that Jesus means some sort of water from the well in front of them. Her question in verse 12 is ironic: "Are you greater than our father Jacob?" John would answer in the affirmative, consonant with 1:17.

The symbolic use of the well becomes apparent in verse 13, as Jesus states that the water from the well will leave one thirsty again, representing the received religious tradition. The water that Jesus will give, on the other hand, will satisfy fully and abolish thirst forever. It will be a spring of water welling up to eternal life (cf. 1:4). In the Jewish tradition, the Torah was likened to living water. "The words of Torah are received into the heart till the Torah becomes a flowing spring" (*Yalkut Shimoni* 2, 480).

Water is used as the symbol of life in countless instances in the Old Testament, but it is used in an eschatological sense in the prophets (Zech 14:8; Ezek 47:1-12; Isa 44:3-4; Jer 2:13; 17:13f.) to symbolize the outpouring of the Spirit of God. That this is the meaning intended is clarified in 7:37-39, where Jesus makes an identical proclamation in the temple, with a parenthetical comment from the narrator that he was speaking of the Spirit. It is clear that although she is intrigued, the woman has still not caught the deeper meaning of the words, thinking only of an inexhaustible supply of water (v. 15). She addresses him as "Sir," which is a progression from her rather rude initial response.

4:16-19 A prophet

When Jesus tells the Samaritan woman to call her husband and come back (v. 16), she replies that she does not have a husband (v. 17). Jesus affirms the truth of her words in an ironical sense (v. 18), for she has had five husbands and is living with a man to whom she is not married. His words are not condemning, but merely a statement of fact. Stunned, the woman replies that he is a prophet (v. 19), and she moves closer to her recognition of his identity. This provides a transition from the dialogue about the living water to the verses that follow, which discuss proper worship in the new age.

4:20-24 Burning religious questions

The woman seeks a definitive answer about the correct place of worship: the center of Jewish worship is in the temple of Jerusalem, while Samaritans worshiped on Mount Gerizim (v. 20). In reply, Jesus informs her that the hour is very close when both forms and places of worship will be transcended by a new and universal spiritual order (v. 21).

Verses 23-24 are the essence of this scene's revelation. "The hour is coming" represents the traditional eschatology: the final days and the new age are in the future on the horizon, but Jesus adds, "and is now here," meaning that in his person the new order is present. A true worshiper is one who worships the Father in Spirit and truth, and they are the particular focus of God's attention. "Truth" refers to Jesus himself, who is filled with truth, as in 1:14, 17. Jesus promises to impart the Spirit—the Living Water—4:13-14 and 7:37-39, as well as the Paraclete in 14:15-17, 25-26; 15:26-27; 16:7-11, 12-15. The locus of the encounter of God is being shifted from particular places such as the temple or Mount Gerizim to Jesus himself, who provides access to the Father. Since God is Spirit, God must be worshiped in Spirit (v. 24), which Jesus alone imparts to believers.

4:25-30 Messianic expectations

The woman voices a messianic expectation, possibly a Samaritan variation referred to as the *taheb,* or restorer, of the prophetic figure foretold by Moses in Deuteronomy 18:15-18 (v. 25). This messianic figure is to have a teaching function, as in 14:25; 16:13-15; and Qumran 1QS 9:1. Jesus affirms that he is in fact this messianic figure.

The disciples return from town and are not a little shocked and scandalized that Jesus is conversing with a woman, but no one has the courage to challenge him (v. 27). The woman leaves everything and relates the event to those in the town, and the foreknowledge of Jesus seems to have been the crucial element in her hesitant question about the possibility of his being the Messiah (vv. 28-29).

4:31-34 Divine sustenance

When the disciples urge Jesus to eat something in verse 31, he replies cryptically that he has food from another source unknown to them (v. 32). The disciples, of course, interpret this in a literal and physical way, assuming that someone has been providing him with food on the side (v. 33). Jesus has to be very explicit as he insists that doing the will of the One who sent him is in itself sustaining, for the mission on which he has been sent is the work of God and is all-consuming (v. 34).

4:35-43 The harvest

This rendition of the proverb found in Matthew 9:37-38 is meant to heighten the sense of urgency concerning the mission. The eschatological harvest is ready now, not in the future, as the openness of the Samaritans to the Word of God proves. In verse 38, Jesus says that the way has already

John 4

been prepared by others, probably alluding to John the Baptist and Jesus himself. Non-Jews—Samaritans—have responded to the words of Jesus in faith and are being welcomed, and the followers of Jesus are invited to take part in the harvest. The new universal order described in verses 21-24 is making its appearance.

It is possible that these verses are addressing a situation in John's community around A.D. 90, namely, a number of Samaritan converts who might not have been welcomed enthusiastically by everyone. The message is clear: the Samaritans are the first to receive the words of Jesus and believe. The woman's testimony about Jesus' knowledge of the details of her life is convincing for her and apparently for many others (v. 39). Jesus accepts an offer of hospitality from the Samaritans and stays with them for two days (v. 40). Many come to faith independent of the testimony of the woman, believing that Jesus is "the savior of the world" (v. 42). The coupling of "world" with "savior" is found only here and in 1 John 4:14. After two days Jesus departs for Galilee (v. 43).

4:44-45 Uncertain welcome

The proverb in verse 44 is present in the Synoptic tradition (Matt 13:57; Mark 6:4; Luke 4:24) but seems strangely out of place here, since Jesus has been welcomed in Samaria and the next few verses relate his welcome in Galilee. The people of Galilee welcome him (v. 45); many of them saw what he had done in Jerusalem (see 2:13-25). But Jesus did not trust the people in Jerusalem who were dazzled by his signs (2:23-25). He saw them as fickle and imperfect in faith, and this rather ominous note could refer to future trouble.

4:46-54 Healing of the royal official's son

Jesus returns to Cana for his second sign, completing a cycle that began in 2:1-12. This is a different rendition of the healing of the centurion's son reported in Matthew 8:5-13 and Luke 7:1-10. When a royal official asks Jesus to come and heal his son, Jesus responds with a rebuke of people requiring signs and wonders in order to believe (v. 48). The man persists; Jesus tells him to go and his son will live (v. 49). When the official returns home and discovers that his son has been healed, he and his entire household believe. He is most likely a Gentile, and he comes to an authentic faith when faced with the sign that Jesus has performed, unlike many others in a similar situation.

In the context of four Jewish feasts (5:1–10:42), opposition to Jesus increases in tempo and vehemence. Jesus will be portrayed as the perfection and fulfillment of four feasts: Sabbath (5:1-47); Passover (6:1-72); Tabernacles (7:1–10:21); and Dedication (10:22-42).

5:1-9 The healing

The feast is not specified; the sabbath is most likely (v. 1). There are three variations to the name—Beth Zatha, Bethesda, and Bethsaida, but most commentators accept Beth Zatha (v. 2). The pools were thought to have curative powers, even in Canaanite times. The remains of the pool and its structures have been excavated near St. Anne's Church in Jerusalem. Some later manuscripts, none dating before the fifth century, describe an angel who stirs up the water periodically, providing healing for the first person to enter the agitated waters (v. 4). It was most likely a later explanation of the rather cryptic response in verse 7, and the verse is omitted in modern translations. Jesus seeks out the man who has been ill for thirty-eight years rather than the usual supplication from the sufferer (v. 6). Asking if he wants to be well is likely an attempt to evoke some sort of response on the man's part. The man seems to dodge Jesus' question and does not respond with any sort of faith or even a request (v. 7). His reply is more of a complaint. Jesus orders the man to rise, take up his mat, and walk in a manner reminiscent of Mark 2:9-12 (v. 8), and the man complies. The statement that it was a sabbath is the transition to the next part of the narrative, the controversy and the descriptions by Jesus of his relationship to God the Father (v. 9).

5:9-18 Controversy over the sabbath

The focus shifts to the "Jews," who object because the healing took place on the sabbath. Work is forbidden on the sabbath, which is to be kept holy. This is one of the Ten Commandments and is central to Israel's religion (Exod 20:8-11 and Deut 5:12-15). Israelites have even died rather than violate the sabbath, as when they refused to fight on a sabbath during the Maccabean Revolt (1 Macc 2:29-41).

The man immediately shifts the responsibility to Jesus (v. 11). The Jews begin interrogating him to determine the identity of his benefactor (v. 12). The man does not know who it was, both in the ordinary and the deeper sense (v. 13); in fact, he does not seem to be affected at all by the physical healing. Unlike the Samaritan woman in chapter 4, his encounter with Jesus has not resulted in faith or even curiosity. Jesus warns him not to sin anymore, implying that there is a link between sin and illness, as in Mark 2:5-7 (v. 14). This link is denied in the case of the man born blind in chapter 9, suggesting that Jesus' warning is meant for this man in particular and is not to be taken as a universal statement.

John 5

In a striking instance of ingratitude, the man informs the authorities that it was Jesus who healed him and commanded him to walk (v. 15). The authorities then begin to harass Jesus for his sabbath activities (v. 16). This represents the core of the passage and is the key for its interpretation. Since his Father continues to work, so must he; as the Son, Jesus can only do what his Father does (v. 17). Jesus does not deny or denigrate the sabbath, but because of his status transcends it. Birth and death occur even on the sabbath; therefore a long Jewish tradition insists that God continues to sustain and give life and to judge. This incites the authorities to a murderous rage, for in addition to breaking the sabbath, Jesus appears to have uttered blasphemy by making himself equal to God (v. 18).

5:19-24 Jesus answers the charges

In this verse and those that follow, Jesus does not deny the charge but enhances and clarifies his relationship with God, which empowers him to give life and to judge (v. 19). It was widely believed that a true son behaves in a manner that mirrors his father. This issue of paternity is also at the center of the debate in 8:31-59. The relationship between the Father and the Son is described in terms of love, which is at the core of the new divine-human relationship described in 14:10-14 and 15:9-11 (v. 20). The powers and prerogatives of the Father are shared with the Son, which in turn are shared with believers who abide in the Son. Jesus also shares in the divine power of giving life, continuing the theme of 1:4 and culminating in 11:25-44 (v. 21). God the Father is the sole judge of humanity, but being the emissary of God, Jesus shares the divine prerogatives, standing in the place of the one who sent him. Rejection or acceptance of Jesus is at the same time rejection or acceptance of God (vv. 22-23).

The exalted rhetoric associated with the identity of Jesus is not meant for christological speculation or doctrinal definition but describes the mission of Jesus and his role as revealer and giver of eternal life. Those who hear the word and believe in Jesus thereby believe God and already have eternal life. By belief in Jesus, one passes into a new order or relationship with God even before death (v. 24). The reference to condemnation anticipates the verses that follow.

5:25-30 The *eschaton*

Coupled with verses 28-29, this formal pronouncement (v. 25) is a reinterpretation of the traditional eschatology. It combines the coming eschatological judgment with what is called a "realized eschatology" ("the hour is coming, and is now here"—see 4:23). The *eschaton* and judgment have arrived with Jesus. Those who hear his voice and believe will live, while those who reject it continue in the realm of death. Only God the Father has life within himself (v. 23), but this is shared with the Son (see 1:4; 5:21; 11:25-44). The power of judgment has been given to the Son of Man, but this should be compared with the description of judgment in 3:17-21 (v. 27). Verses 28-29 represent a traditional eschatology with its roots in Daniel 12:1-3. The resurrection is for both the good and the wicked—the first for reward, the second for punishment. The power of Jesus lies in his complete openness and transparency to God, as well as his total harmony with the divine will (v. 30).

5:31-47 Witnesses

Jesus continues his defense against the charge of blasphemy and violation of the sabbath. According to both the Old Testament (Num 35:30; Deut 17:6) and the later rabbinic tradition, at least two witnesses are required for testimony in capital cases. John the Baptist was a witness (vv. 33-35), but they were content to rejoice in his light, not realizing that Jesus bears the greater light. Jesus has performed works (v. 36) that testify that the Father has sent him. His primary witness is God the Father (vv. 37-38), but they have never heard his voice or seen his form (cf. 1:18), and they do not recognize that Jesus himself is the voice and word of God. Even though the Scriptures witness to Jesus, they fail in their studies to recognize him (v. 39).

Finally, their unbelief is the result of not having the love of God within them, and the reason is that they have opted for human glory *(doxa)*, which is only esteem and praise, rather than the divine glory revealed in Jesus (vv. 41-44). Moses will be their accuser, for if they had really believed and interiorized the law of Moses, they would recognize who Jesus really is. This alludes to 1:17: the gift of Moses and the gift of Jesus are not in conflict with each other, for belief in the former prepares one to receive the latter.

The miraculous feeding is followed by an interlude with Jesus walking on the sea (vv. 16-21) and concluded with the "bread of life" discourse (vv. 25-59) and a conversation between Jesus and his disciples, with a confession of faith by Peter (vv. 60-71). John does not have an institution narrative of the Eucharist at the Last Supper, so many see this chapter as eucharistic in intent. Although it was certainly fruitful in later reflections on the meaning of the Eucharist, its *primary* meaning concerns the identity and mission of Jesus.

6:1-15 The miraculous feeding (cf. Mark 6)

Jesus has just been in Jerusalem and now suddenly turns up in Galilee (vv. 1-3). In chapter 7 he will be back in Jerusalem, leading some scholars

John 6

to speculate that chapters 5 and 6 may have been transposed at some stage. Tiberias is mentioned only here in the New Testament and was a city founded by Herod Antipas in A.D. 20 in honor of Tiberius Caesar. The crowds follow Jesus because of the many signs he has been performing with the sick, evidence that his work extended far beyond the seven miracles presented in the Gospel.

The feeding of the multitude will evoke memories of God's providing manna for the Israelites during their desert journey, as well as the imagery in Psalm 23. In the Synoptic accounts, there is no mention of Passover, and the concern for food occurs at the end of a long day of teaching, the issue being raised by the disciples rather than Jesus (vv. 4-5). Jesus is testing the disciples, for he is always in complete control of the situation and omniscient (v. 6). Philip responds with the enormity and seeming hopelessness of the situation (v. 7).

After the boy produces the five barley loaves and two fish, Jesus takes the loaves and gives thanks *(eucharistein),* suggesting a connection with the Eucharist (v. 11). There is a striking parallel with the account of the prophet Elisha in 2 Kings 4:42-44:

> A man came from Baal-shalishah bringing the man of God twenty barley loaves made from the first-fruits, and fresh grain in the ear. "Give it to the people to eat," Elisha said. But his servant objected, "How can I set this before a hundred men?" "Give it to the people to eat," Elisha insisted. "For thus says the LORD, 'They shall eat and there shall be some left over.'" And when they had eaten, there was some left over, as the LORD had said.

The Elijah/Elisha cycle forms a thematic backdrop for the New Testament portrayal of Jesus. Gathering up the fragments so that nothing may be lost is subject to several interpretations (v. 12). "Gathering" and "fragments" are eucharistic terms found in early patristic literature. In the *Didache* 9:4, the Eucharistic Prayer echoes similar concerns: "As this broken bread was scattered upon the mountains, but was brought together and became one, so let thy Church be gathered together from the ends of the earth into thy kingdom." It can therefore also refer to believers, as Jesus is concerned that he might lose nothing of what has been given to him (see 6:39 and 18:9) "Twelve" usually symbolizes the twelve tribes of Israel, but the emphasis is on the abundance of the food provided by Jesus.

As a result of this sign, the people acclaim Jesus as the prophet like Moses foretold in Deuteronomy 18:15 (vv. 13-14). He is the fulfillment of prophetic expectation; there is no mention of a Messiah. The sign has dazzled the crowds, and their faith and understanding are defective and incomplete, as is often the case in John. This deficient understanding is borne out by their desire to make him a king (v. 15). Since Jesus is aware of their intentions, he withdraws to the mountain to be alone and to escape them.

6:16-21 Interlude: Encounter on the sea

Verses 16-21 represent an interlude and a transition to the discourse back in Capernaum. They parallel the encounter on the sea after the feeding of the multitude in Mark 6:45-52 and Matthew 14:22-23. The disciples leave by boat without Jesus and soon find themselves in the midst of a storm (vv. 17-18). The appearance of Jesus walking toward them on the sea arouses fear (v. 19). His reply of "It is I" *(ego eimi)* can be construed as a simple identification of self or as a divine predicate, as in 6:35; 8:12, 58; 11:25; Exod 3:14; Isa 41:10 and 43:10 (v. 20). In Isaiah 41:10, *ego eimi* is even coupled with the injunction "Fear not." Given the importance of "I AM" statements in John, it is more likely a divine predicate, indicating that the presence of Jesus is also the presence of God. The crowd notices that Jesus did not leave with his disciples in the boat, and when they can't find him, they converge on Capernaum looking for him (vv. 22-25).

6:25-29 The bread from heaven

Jesus accuses the crowd of lacking comprehension of the signs and pursuing him only because of their satisfaction with the miraculous food (v. 26). He exhorts them to raise their sights higher and to seek lasting spiritual sustenance that only he can give (v. 27). God has set his seal on the Son of Man, signifying his authentic and unique status as an emissary from God. The crowd's question is a perennial one: what must we do to please God? Here it is phrased rather strangely as the "works of God" (v. 28). The "work of God" is singular in nature, namely, to believe in the one sent by God. Belief in the one sent by God is not mere intellectual assent but a complete reorientation of one's life and a personal relationship with him (v. 29).

6:30-33 Request for a sign

Since Jesus has challenged the Mosaic tradition, the crowd asks for an authenticating sign (v. 30) to justify his actions. Signs were supposed to lead one to faith (Gen 9:12-17; Exod 4:8-9; Isa 7:11-14). The crowd refers to the archetypal feeding miracle, the gift of manna in the desert (v. 31). The

John 6

phrase "He gave them bread from heaven to eat" is not found in the Old Testament but probably echoes Exodus 16:4, 15; Nehemiah 9:15; and Psalm 78:24. The rest of the chapter is an exegesis (what the Jews would call a "midrash") of that passage. The true bread is that which only God can give, giving life to the entire world, not just Israel. The manna in the desert cannot even approach this (vv. 32-33), as it is temporary and perishable.

6:34-40 The bread from heaven

The crowd understands in a literal and physical way, as did the Samaritan woman in the case of the living water (4:15), so they ask that Jesus give them this bread always (v. 34). In a solemn pronouncement, Jesus declares that *he* is the bread of life (v. 35), providing food and drink that will never leave one hungry or thirsty (4:14; 7:37). In the Old Testament tradition, Wisdom is depicted as providing nourishment (Sir 24:21; Isa 49:10), but as sustainer and life-giver, Jesus perfects and surpasses both Wisdom and the Torah. He is aware that some do not believe or have incomplete faith (v. 36). The universal nature of God's gift of life is emphasized by words such as "anyone," "everyone," and all (vv. 37, 40). God's will is that all people who believe in Jesus receive eternal life and be raised up on the last day (vv. 36-40).

6:41-51 Murmuring and rebellion

The bystanders begin "murmur[ing]," which calls to mind the rebellious behavior of the Israelites in the desert (Exod 16:2-12; Num 14:2-29). Interpreting Jesus' words literally as Nicodemus did, they marvel at the impossibility of his coming down from heaven. Their familiarity with the family of Jesus and his earthly origins becomes an issue as in Mark 6:3; Matthew 13:53-57; and Luke 4:16-30 (vv. 41-42), although the privileged reader knows that his descent is from the Father. The universal thread is taken up again from Isaiah 54:13. "They shall all be taught by God" (v. 45) signifies that anyone who has really understood or listened to God will believe in Jesus. As the living bread that came down from heaven, Jesus grants eternal life to those who eat this bread. This bread given for the life of the world is his flesh (v. 51), which alludes to his impending death.

6:52-59 Eat my flesh and drink my blood

Drinking blood would have been unthinkable for a Jew, especially in view of the strong prohibition in Leviticus 17:10-14. Likewise with eating flesh; the image is made even more graphic by the use of a different verb for eating that describes munching or chewing. This invitation to ingest eternal life through the flesh and blood of Jesus is explained further in verse 57: Jesus has life in him from the Father; the one consuming his flesh and blood will therefore have that same life.

The primary focus is on the broken body and spilled blood of Jesus that is given over in order to give life to and nourish the world. But the language is also eucharistic in nature, evoking Mark 14:22-25 and 1 Corinthians 11:23-28. The discourses in chapters 13–17 suggest that being nourished and sustained by Jesus, while including the Eucharist, does not exclude many other aspects of the Christian life (vv. 53-57). One must assimilate Jesus as one would food, allowing his life-giving presence to become the very fiber of one's being. In the context of the Passover, in which Jews celebrate God's gift of the manna in the desert, Jesus claims to transcend and perfect even this gift.

6:60-71 The first defections

In verses 60-66, many of the disciples take offense at the words of Jesus and his claim to be the source of life. The insistence that the spirit gives life but the flesh is of no avail signifies the limitations of human understanding. The words of Jesus are of a different order and represent both spirit and life, but many of his disciples leave because they cannot go beyond human categories and receive his words. Jesus asks the Twelve, the inner circle, whether they also want to leave, but Peter affirms their faith (v. 67). His confession of faith in verses 68-69 makes it very clear that there are no other possibilities; Jesus alone has the words of eternal life. It is not that they completely understand his teachings, but they trust him enough to know that their understanding will grow during their journey with him. The Twelve not only have come to believe, but they now know that Jesus is the Holy One of God—the One from above. Even this is open to question, for Jesus knows that Judas is going to betray him (vv. 70-71).

7:1-9 Jesus and his brothers

In chapters 7 and 8, Jesus goes to Jerusalem during the feast of Tabernacles, and his visit to the temple provokes threats, accusations, and attempted arrests. In several places Jesus states that the "Jews" were trying to kill him (5:18; 7:19). This prevents him from moving freely about, and Judea appears to be a place of danger (see 11:7-8). This is the feast of Tabernacles or Booths (Sukkoth), a popular annual harvest festival that celebrated God's care and guidance while the Israelites were in the wilderness (v. 2). The feast takes place on the fifteenth day of the seventh month, Tishri (September–October), and is described in Exodus 23:16; 34:22; Deut 16:13-15;

John 7

Lev 23:39-43. The feast became increasingly eschatological in orientation, pointing toward God's redemptive action at the end time.

Jesus' brothers advise him to go to Judea to show his works to his disciples. But this would be garnering human rather than divine glory. This attempt on their part to goad Jesus into making a public splash by performing miracles is evidence of their lack of understanding and true faith, and the narrator states tersely that they did not believe in him (vv. 3-5). That there may have been tensions and misunderstandings among Jesus' family members is probably more accurate than later piety would admit, for this is corroborated by Mark 3:21, 31-35, and 6:1-6, where his family is depicted in rather negative terms.

Jesus refuses, stating that his hour has not yet come, as in 2:4 (v. 6). The time is always right for his brothers; the world does not hate them because they have given it no reason to do so. Jesus, however, is hated because he is from above, and his presence shows the works of the world for what they are. Refusing to go, Jesus insists that they go on their own, stating that his time has not yet been fulfilled (v. 8). This initial reluctance to accede to the requests of others is also found in 2:4-7 and 4:48-50, which is indicative of the fact that his mission is totally defined by his relationship with the Father and obedience to the divine will.

7:10-36 Jesus goes to the feast

Jesus asserts his complete autonomy in verse 10 by his decision to go to Jerusalem alone. There is an air of expectancy surrounding his arrival, and a division has already occurred among the people. Some are open to his message, while others think that he is a deceiver (vv. 11-13). As Jesus begins to teach in the temple, his knowledge of the Scriptures evokes amazement from the crowd (vv. 14-15), questioning the origin and legitimacy of his teaching. Although the literacy and education of Jesus are debated by scholars, he is presented in John and in Luke (4:16-30) as being literate and conversant with the written tradition. Jesus insists that his teaching is not his own or a matter of learning but is of God, and this is obvious to anyone who seeks to do God's will (vv. 16-18).

The controversy in verses 19-36 centers on the origins of the Messiah. The argument Jesus has with the crowd concerns his healing in 5:9-10, which he defends on the basis of law and practice with respect to circumcision. Just as the sabbath is technically violated in order to do the will of God, Jesus does so in order to give life. He challenges the crowd to judge justly rather than by appearances; that is, sense data and rationality (vv. 19-24). They engage in speculation about the identity and possible messianic status of Jesus, but militating against this is their assertion that they know his origins, whereas the origins of the Messiah will be unknown. This is Johannine irony, for they don't really know where he is from; his origins and identity are not defined by earthly categories (1:1-3) but by God. There is also an extrabiblical tradition of the Messiah's hidden nature in *1 Enoch* 48:6 and *4 Ezra* 13:51-52.

Their failure to discover and accept his origins prevents them from believing in him. Again they try to arrest him, but his fate is determined by a divine timetable rather than a human one (vv. 25-31). Some of the crowd appears to be swayed by his signs, causing the chief priests and the Pharisees to send guards to arrest him. Jesus' enigmatic words about his departure and the inability of others to come will be repeated in 13:33. They of course misunderstand, believing that he is going to the Greeks (Gentiles) in the Diaspora, when in fact he is returning to the Father (vv. 32-36).

7:37-39 Last day of the feast

Jesus' solemn revelatory statement in verses 37-39 is an amplification of 4:13-14 and occurs in the context of the celebration of the feast of Sukkoth in the temple. Twigs of myrtle, palm, willow, and a citron are bound up in what is called a *lulab*, which is waved during processions around the altar while Psalms 113–118 are sung. A ceremonial water libation for abundant rain is celebrated on the eighth day. A procession to the Pool of Siloam brings back water in a golden vessel through the Water Gate to the temple for pouring onto the altar (*m. Sukkah* 4:9; Josephus, *Ant.* 3:245, 247). This was a ritualization of the prophecies in Zechariah 14:6 and Ezekiel 47:1-11, which spoke of water pouring out from the temple, the center of the world, and giving life wherever it flowed.

By naming himself as the source of living water, Jesus claims to be the fulfillment and embodiment of what is symbolized in the Sukkoth ritual, and the origin of the life-giving water is shifted from the temple to him. There is an ambiguity in the Greek in verse 38 that allows for a translation that describes the rivers of living water flowing from either Jesus or the believer. In either case, Jesus is the ultimate source, and he shares this with those who believe. A parenthetical comment explains that the living water is the spirit and that it was only given after the glorification (crucifixion) of Jesus (cf. 19:34).

7:40-52 A division in the crowd

Some in the crowd respond to Jesus' words with a proclamation of him as "the Prophet" (see 1:21; Deut 18:15), while others proclaim him Messiah.

John 7

But many reject Jesus because he is from Galilee, and the Messiah is supposed to come from Bethlehem. John does not tie Jesus in any way to Bethlehem, but the tradition in Matthew and Luke must have been widely known. Either way the statement is ironical: in one tradition Jesus was born in Bethlehem, while in John he is from above (vv. 40-43).

The guards sent to arrest Jesus are impressed by his words, earning the contempt of the Pharisees and an accusation that they, too, have been deceived by him. They also show a common contempt for the people of the land as being ignorant and accursed. Nicodemus reappears and seeks a fair hearing for Jesus in accordance with the law. The authorities chide him for being sympathetic to what is perceived as a Galilean movement, and they again assert that no prophet arises from Galilee (vv. 44-52).

7:53–8:11 The story of the woman taken in adultery

This incident is not included in the earliest handwritten manuscripts of John's Gospel, and in some later manuscripts it is placed either in other locations within John's Gospel or in the Gospel of Luke. It is probably an independent, free-floating tradition about Jesus.

The story focuses on the murderous impulses of the crowd and their projection of their own darkness on a helpless victim or scapegoat. A woman has been taken in adultery and is liable to stoning according to Leviticus 24:1-16; Deuteronomy 13:10; 17:2-7. She is being used by the Pharisees as a means of trapping Jesus into denying the law of Moses. He has been aware of their murderous impulses for some time, and hatred is equated with murder itself.

Jesus refuses to take the bait and merely writes in the sand and invites those who are sinless to cast the first stone. We cannot know what he wrote, and it does not matter, for it was sufficient to trigger a remembrance of sin on the part of the bystanders. Those present have been brought to an awareness of their own inner darkness. This story is more about non-condemnation than forgiveness, for Jesus only admonishes her not to sin again.

8:12-30 The light of the world

Verses 12-59 relate a long polemical encounter between Jesus and "the Jews," some of whom are initially open to his words. In the course of the encounter, Jesus echoes the "I AM" epiphany in Exodus 3:14 four times. The first three instances provoke controversy, the last an attempted stoning for blasphemy.

In verse 12, Jesus proclaims that he is "the light of the world," an image usually ascribed to God, as in Psalm 27:1. The light of life that his followers will have resonates with a passage in one of the Dead Sea Scrolls from Qumran (1QS 3:7) concerning God, as well as their self-description as "the sons of light." This proclamation is in the context of the Sukkoth ceremony of light (*m. Sukkah* 5:1-4). Four huge menorah or candlesticks were placed in the Court of the Women, and it was said that the light was sufficient to illuminate all Jerusalem, calling to mind Zechariah 14:6. The Torah was described in terms of light for the world in Wisdom 18:4; Proverbs 6:23; Psalm 119:105; and Baruch 4:2, as well as in the rabbinic tradition.

John is portraying Jesus as the embodiment and fulfillment of these passages and as an expression of the light coming into the world in 1:4-5. People bring judgment on themselves by their acceptance or rejection of this light (3:19-21). The Pharisees question the validity of his testimony, to which Jesus claims the Father as a corroborating witness (vv. 13-18), necessary under a tradition in which two or more witnesses are required (Num 35:30; Deut 17:6; 19:15) and no one can testify on his or her own behalf (*m. Ketub* 2:9). Jesus insists that the root problem is that the crowd does not know him or the Father (cf. 1:18; 14:7); indeed, they do not do so because they are from "below," with all the accompanying ignorance and limitation, while Jesus is from "above" (vv. 19-24). Verses 24 and 28 link the "I AM" assertion with life-giving power to overcome sin and Jesus' revelation of the Father. The final instance (v. 58) refers to the preexistence of Jesus, as revealed in 1:1-3.

8:31-59 Son of Abraham, Son of God

The sharp exchange between Jesus and a group of halfway believers has for centuries provided fuel for anti-Semitic theological attitudes. It is important to place it in the context of the struggle of John's community with Jewish authorities toward the end of the first century. The negative images and statements should be understood as the rhetorical devices of the author and not a condemnation of the Jewish people by Jesus.

Addressing those who had begun to believe in him (v. 30), Jesus exhorts them to remain or stand fast (Greek: *menein*; cf. 15:10) in his word in order to be truly liberated, for their incipient faith still has a long way to go. The truth that they will then know will make them free (v. 32). This truth consists in knowing God through Jesus (1:14; 4:23-24; 14:6) and has nothing to do with human or conceptual knowledge. Taking his statement literally, they retort that they have never been enslaved, conveniently forgetting the sojourn in Egypt and their current occupation by the Romans.

But sin itself is slavery (Rom 6), and in order to be truly free, they need to be liberated by a son who abides or remains in God's household (Rom 7).

John 8

The crowd first claims to be offspring of Abraham, then of God. By denying that they are illegitimate in verse 41, they are possibly impugning the parentage of Jesus. Jesus rejects both of their paternal claims, for parentage is revealed in the behavior and attitudes of offspring. Abraham was noted for his faith and openness to God; if they were his offspring, they would believe in Jesus, since he was sent from God. If God were their Father, they would love Jesus as the one sent from God. Since they reject Jesus and want to kill him, they are displaying deceitful and murderous behavior, proving that the devil rather than God or Abraham is their father (vv. 41-44). Those who reject Jesus do not belong to God (v. 47).

Amid accusations of being a Samaritan or possessed (v. 48), Jesus insists that he honors his Father and is in turn glorified by him. When Jesus proclaims that whoever keeps his word will never die (v. 51), derision and an accusation that he is trying to make himself greater than Abraham (vv. 49-55) are the response (cf. the ironical question concerning Jacob in 4:12). His statement that Abraham rejoiced to see his day and that he existed even before Abraham (1:1) results in an attempt on his life, leading Jesus to flee (vv. 56-59).

9:1-7 The healing of the man born blind

The healing is the mere prelude to the extended controversy between the blind man and the Pharisees in verses 8-34. The blind man and the Pharisees move in opposite directions—the man toward the sight of faith, and the latter deeper into the sightless darkness of willful ignorance. The disciples ask the perennial question concerning the blind man: Whose fault is it? "Who sinned, this man or his parents?" (v. 2). It was traditionally held that physical infirmity was the result of sin on the part of the individual or his parents (Exod 20:5; Luke 13:1-5). Jesus rejects this explanation (vv. 3-4); the man was born blind in order to play a role in revelation of the works of God.

With a reference to 8:12 and an allusion to his approaching death, Jesus declares that he is the light of the world as long as he is in the world and so must act accordingly (vv. 3-4). After anointing the man's eyes with a paste of saliva and mud, he tells him to wash in the Pool of Siloam (vv. 6-7), which, according to a loose etymology, means "sent." Jesus, of course, is the one who is "sent," indicating that it is by means of an encounter of faith with him that human eyes are opened to the truth.

9:8-23 Controversy

People first question whether the man who now has his sight is in fact the same one who used to sit and beg, then whether he was actually blind or not (vv. 8-13). The healing, performed on a sabbath, sparks a tremendous controversy with the Pharisees. They question the man's parents concerning his blindness, but they refuse to answer (vv. 18-23). Their fear that they will be expelled from the synagogue reflects the situation in the eighties and nineties rather than during the lifetime of Jesus. The main objection on the part of the Pharisees is that Jesus sinned by healing on the sabbath, so God cannot be with him (vv. 16, 24).

9:24-34 Second interrogation

The Pharisees' insistence that they do not know where Jesus is from (v. 29) is ironic, for that is the crux of the problem. Had they recognized his divine origin, they would have been open to his message. The man grows bolder as the interrogation continues: in verse 17 he proclaims that Jesus is a prophet, while in verses 30-32 he insists that God must be with Jesus for him to be able to restore his sight. He has read the meaning of the sign correctly and his conclusion is self-evident. But he is ridiculed, called one born in sin, and expelled from their presence.

9:35-38 Coming to faith

Jesus finds the man and asks him if he believes in the Son of Man. Strangely, there is no mention of the Messiah. "Son of Man" refers to Jesus and describes his human revelatory role (1:51; 3:13-14; 5:27; 6:27, 53, 62). When the man asks who the Son of Man is so that he might worship him, Jesus reveals himself, and the man does reverence. His journey has been from blindness to sight in many respects, and from unbelief to faith. Throughout the controversy the man repeatedly admitted his ignorance on many matters, but he was spiritually open and astute enough to read the meaning of the sign that Jesus performed, while the others plunged deeper into darkness and ignorance.

9:39-41 Blindness

The proclamation in verse 39 is the core of the story: Jesus came for judgment, in the sense that those who are blind but open to God's word might see, while those who claim to have sight will be shown to be completely blind. When some of the Pharisees take umbrage at the suggestion that they are blind, Jesus responds that blindness is not a sin; the greatest sin is to claim to see (and understand) when one does not. The presence of Jesus as the light provokes judgment in the acceptance or rejection of others (1:9-11; 5:27; 8:12; 12:46-48). The story is the antidote for dogmatism of any sort and can be understood on one level as a metaphor for humanity, for

John 9

only by admitting "blind[ness]" can humanity receive the sight that Jesus offers.

10:1-16 Good and bad shepherds

The extended metaphor in verses 1-16 is opaque and puzzling, even for the immediate audience (v. 6). Who are the ones referred to in the metaphor? Are the thieves, robbers, and hirelings messianic prophets and pretenders, the current Jewish leadership, or members of other Christian communities? The images from the Old Testament are clear enough: bad shepherds, representing the compromised leadership of Israel, are portrayed in Jeremiah 23:1-8; Ezekiel 22:27; Zephaniah 3:3; Zechariah 10:2-3, 11:4-17. Numbers 27:16-17 speaks of the need for a leader to lead the people in and out, ensuring that they are not like sheep without a shepherd. There is an extended tirade against bad shepherds in Ezekiel 34:1-11, but God promises to seek out his sheep and place a Davidic shepherd over them (Ezek 34:23-24).

In the New Testament the followers of Jesus are sheep (John 21:16-17). In the Synoptic tradition a number of instances refer to the lost sheep of the house of Israel or sheep without a shepherd (Mark 14:27; Matt 9:36/ Mark 6:34; and Mark 15:24). Although the metaphor could be directed at other Christian groups, the most likely targets are the Pharisees and Jewish leaders, especially since chapter 9 ended with their condemnation by Jesus. They have already been shown to be blind; now John will portray them as deaf to the word of God. Using the "I AM" proclamation (vv. 7, 11), Jesus establishes that he is both the shepherd and the gate for the sheep. Those sheep that truly belong to God and to Jesus will hear his voice and follow, and will not listen to those who are not from God and do not have the well-being of the people in mind. This is understood more clearly in the context of the intracommunal struggle depicted in 1 John. Jesus provides access to God by being the gate (Ps 118:20), the mediator between God and humanity. Those who enter through the gate will have life in abundance (1:4; 3:16; 5:21; 11:25-44). The other sheep that do not belong to the fold (v. 16) possibly represent the Gentiles (17:20-23) but can also refer to other Christian groups. The motif of one shepherd drawing others into the fold of the one God is found in Micah 5:3-5; Jeremiah 3:15; 23:4-6; Ezekiel 34:23-24.

10:17-21 Laying down one's life

Jesus is loved by the Father because he willingly lays down his life and takes it up again in fulfillment of the Father's command. He is not a victim; his death is a deliberate act of self-giving love. The claims of Jesus provoke another controversy (vv. 19-21).

10:22-42 A Hanukkah encounter

The feast of Hanukkah (vv. 22-23) probably occurred in December, and the encounter takes place in the Portico of Solomon (Acts 3:11). Hanukkah celebrates the rededication of the Temple in 164 B.C., as recounted in 1 Maccabees 4:52-59. A long argument erupts over whether Jesus is truly the Messiah, to which he offers as evidence the works he has performed. The sheep that hear his voice follow, and he will give them eternal life, so that they will never perish. No one can take them away, because they have been given to Jesus by the Father, who is greater than all (vv. 24-29). He follows that with an assertion that he is one with the Father (v. 30), but in 14:28 he states that the Father is greater than he. The assertion of unity refers to the mutual indwelling and relationship of the Father and the Son and should not be seen as a metaphysical statement concerning the divine nature.

The bystanders attempt to stone Jesus for blasphemy (vv. 31-33), because as a man he has tried to make himself God. In reply, Jesus quotes Psalm 82:6, in which heavenly beings *(elohim)* are addressed as gods. If those to whom the word of God came could be addressed as gods, he reasons, then it is not outrageous to do so for one consecrated and sent into the world as the Son of God. The crowd is not impressed with his exegesis and tries to arrest Jesus, but he escapes across the Jordan. Many begin to believe in him, noticing that John the Baptist performed no signs, but that what he said about Jesus is true.

11:1-16 A delayed mission of mercy

The raising of Lazarus is found only in John's Gospel, although Jesus restores life to the son of the widow of Nain in Luke 7:11-17. In the Synoptic tradition it is the incident in the temple that pushes the authorities to move against Jesus, whereas John represents this as the last sign and defining act of the public ministry of Jesus. This is the first mention of Mary and Martha in John (cf. Luke 10:38-42), and the anointing of Jesus by Mary is mentioned, although it will not appear until chapter 12.

When Jesus receives word from the sisters that his friend Lazarus is ill, he echoes the reason for the illness given in the case of the blind man in 9:3: the glory of God and his Son. Jesus loved Lazarus and his sisters, so his intentional two-day delay upon hearing of Lazarus's illness is shocking and baffling from the human point of view. His disciples are appalled at his intention to return to Judea (v. 8), for his life has been in danger there.

Jesus continues with the symbolism of light as in 8:12 and implies urgency in his intention. The disciples still do not understand, and when Jesus states that Lazarus is asleep, they take his words literally. Jesus has

John 11

to tell them bluntly that Lazarus is dead (vv. 11-15). Thomas expresses a resigned willingness to return with Jesus and die with him, ironical in light of later events (v. 16). The prelude in verses 1-16 makes it clear that the situation that greets them on their arrival in Bethany is the result of a deliberate decision by Jesus.

11:17-33 Jesus encounters Martha and Mary

Jesus will encounter Martha in verses 17-27 and Mary in verses 28-37. Upon arrival, they are greeted with the news that Lazarus is dead and has been in the tomb for four days (v. 17). This underscores the fact that he is definitively dead, for according to rabbinic tradition the spirit of the departed hovered around the body for three days. The "Jews" who have come to mourn with the sisters are here portrayed in a positive manner. Martha's pointed greeting in verse 21 expresses disappointment and perhaps even a bit of reproach, but she is still hopeful in verse 22. In reply to Jesus' reassurance that her brother will rise, Martha acknowledges the conventional Jewish (Dan 12:2) and early Christian (Mark 12:18-27; 1 Thess 4:13-18; John 5:28-29) view of the resurrection as occurring in the future on the last day (vv. 23-24).

Jesus' "I AM" statement in verse 25 is unequivocal: as the one who is the resurrection and the life, he has the power of life within him (1:4; 5:24-26). Life *(zōē)* is used thirty-six times in John, seventeen of these with the modifying word "eternal." This is the life not of the world to come but of the world above and does not apply only to the afterlife. The promise of life to the believer in verses 25-26 seems nonsensical if it is taken to refer to biological life and death. But spiritual and biological life and death are contrasted in a manner to convey the promise to the believer that he or she will never be separated from God, even by death. Eternal life, which is direct knowledge of God, begins in the present rather than in some distant future.

Martha responds in faith to Jesus by acknowledging him as the Messiah, Son of God, and the "one . . . coming into the world," which is probably a prophetic figure as in Deuteronomy 18. Mary confronts Jesus with the same words as Martha did in verses 21-22, but she kneels at his feet in reverence.

11:33-37 A puzzling grief

Jesus is moved and upset by the weeping of Mary and the Jewish mourners with her, and he begins to weep (v. 35), which is puzzling considering the deliberate nature of his delay, his intention to restore the life of Lazarus, and his complete foreknowledge. Although some remark at how much

Jesus loved Lazarus, others comment that given what he had done for the blind man, he should have been able to help his friend.

11:38-44 Roll away the stone

Jesus orders the stone to be removed from the tomb despite Martha's protestations that there will be a stench after four days in the tomb (vv. 38-39). The prayer of Jesus in verses 41-42 is for the benefit of the crowd so that they might believe. After his command to Lazarus to come out, the man appears still bound hand and foot with his face wrapped in a cloth. This is not a resurrection but the resuscitation or reanimation of a corpse. Lazarus will have to die a second time. The resurrection involves a qualitative change in the nature of the body. When Jesus rises from death, the face-covering is rolled up and placed to one side in a definitive gesture (20:7), while Lazarus is still bound.

11:45-54 Panic in high places

The raising of Lazarus brings many to faith (v. 45). When the news is related to the Pharisees, the lights burn late in the Sanhedrin as the Pharisees and chief priests meet to decide what to do about Jesus. Verses 47-48 are both poignant and ironic: the chief priests and Pharisees are afraid that Jesus, left unchecked, would attract many followers, causing the Romans to deprive them of their land and nation. This, of course, is written after that had become a fact.

Caiaphas, high priest from A.D. 18–36, makes his first appearance in verses 49-50. His comment is meant as a solution for ridding themselves of a meddlesome prophet. With Johannine irony, he unwittingly prophesies in his office as high priest that Jesus would die on behalf of the people and the whole nation. John adds that his death is also to gather into one the dispersed children of God, possibly referring to the Jews in the Diaspora, although Gentiles may also be included (v. 52).

From that day on, there is a plot to kill Jesus (vv. 53-54), causing Jesus to hide in a town called Ephraim. He in effect becomes a hunted man. The crowd heading for Jerusalem for Passover asks aloud whether he will make an appearance or not, and the chief priests seek to arrest him. The tension builds for the transition to entrance into Jerusalem and the passion in chapter 12.

12:1-9 The anointing at Bethany

There are parallels to this anointing (vv. 1-8) in Mark 14:3-9; Matthew 26:6-13; and Luke 7:36-50, although they vary in form. John's version is unique in many respects: the one raising objections is named as Judas, the woman performing the anointing as Mary, and the location of the dinner as the home of Lazarus and his sisters rather than Simon the Leper or Simon the Pharisee.

Anticipating the impending death of Jesus, Mary anoints him as an act of love and devotion, as well as a proleptic preparation for burial. Judas cannot comprehend this act of love and objects to the expense and the possibility of giving the money to the poor. But the poor are not at the heart of his concern, only his own lack of love and the gathering momentum of evil in his life (v. 6).

12:12-16 The entrance into Jerusalem

Jesus' messianic entrance is essentially identical in all four Gospels, but in John it represents his third trip to Jerusalem (2:13; 7:10), and there is no cleansing of the temple. The crowd cries "Hosanna," meaning "Save," which is taken from Psalm 118:25-26. A royal messianic acclamation is indicated, but Zechariah 9:9 is the prophetic passage used to modify the description of the entrance, depicting Jesus seated upon an ass's colt rather than mounted or riding a chariot. This can signify the distinctively non-political nature of his messianic status or emphasize the universal elements found in Zechariah. This reinterpretation is a post-resurrection theological insight by the disciples (cf. 2:22).

12:9-11, 17-19 The whole world goes after Jesus

The presence of Lazarus causes a sensation and attracts many to faith in Jesus (vv. 9-11; 17-19). The fear of the Pharisees in verse 19 that the "whole world" is going after Jesus is well-founded and fulfills the fears voiced in 11:50-52. If this is accurate, it is hard to understand why there is no mention of Lazarus in the other Gospels.

12:20-33 The hour of the Son of Man

The "whole world" is indeed going after Jesus, which is indicative of his universal mission and the ingathering of the scattered children of God (11:52). This is confirmed by a request via Philip and Andrew (vv. 20-22) from a group of visiting Greeks (Hellenes) to "see" Jesus. The Greeks were likely "God-fearers"—Gentiles attracted to Judaism and its practices but not full members. This is the trip wire that signals that the hour for the Son of Man to be glorified has arrived (v. 23). His hour was always associated with his future glorification (2:4; 4:23; 7:30; 8:20).

The image of the grain of wheat (vv. 24-25) dying and bearing fruit is also found in some Greek mystery religions but is also similar to the seed analogy used by Paul in 1 Corinthians 15:36. This grain of wheat expresses the principle of death and life and the necessity of the earthly to give way to the heavenly. It is coupled with the pronouncement about loving one's life and losing it, hating it and preserving it for eternal life (v. 25), which counsels a "letting go" of one's life rather than a fearful grasping. This principle is a fundamental and well-attested element in early Christian tradition: Mark 8:35; Matthew 16:25; Luke 9:24, as well as a parallel tradition in Matthew 10:39 and Luke 17:33.

Likewise, verse 26 is similar in some ways to the command to take up one's cross found in Mark 8:34; Matthew 16:24; and Luke 9:23. John does not portray Jesus as the Man of Sorrows but the Lord of Glory. Jesus admits to being troubled in verse 27, but his request for the cup to pass from him in Mark 14:36 is here only a brief rhetorical question, followed by an assertion that this hour is his sole reason for being there.

Jesus' request to the Father to glorify him (v. 28) is answered by an affirmative voice from heaven. Some of the crowd hear thunder, others an angel; not all are attuned to heavenly realities. There is some similarity to a *bat qol* ("daughter of a voice"), which Jewish tradition believed to be a heavenly voice that declares God's will, teachings, or commandments to individuals or groups. Jesus' death is a judgment on the world (v. 31), which will be one of the dimensions of his trial. Being "lifted up" (3:14; 8:28) from the earth is clearly his impending crucifixion. As a result, he will draw all people to himself, which, coupled with 3:16, implies a more universal mission than Israel alone.

12:34-36 The light will soon depart

Puzzlement is the reaction of the crowd in verses 34-36. Tradition depicts the Davidic Messiah as remaining forever, but Jesus insists that the Son of Man will be lifted up, which contrasts popular expectations with the early Christian reinterpretation of the messianic tradition. There is a warning: the light (Jesus) will not be around much longer, so his listeners are encouraged to believe while they can, lest they walk in darkness. Believing in the light will enable them to become children of the light, which is echoed in Luke 16:8; 1 Thess 5:5; and especially in the literature of the Qumran community (1QS 1:10; 1QM 1:1).

12:37-50 Human praise and the glory of God

In spite of Jesus' signs, most have not believed, and Isaiah 53:1 (v. 38) and 6:1-10 (v. 40) are invoked to explain their unbelief. This is repeated elsewhere in the New Testament: Rom 10:16; Mark 4:11-12; Acts 28:26-27.

John 12

The revelation of God's glory is a thread running throughout Isaiah (6:1-10; 40:5; 42:8; 48:11; 60:1), so John is able to assert that Isaiah saw the preexistent glory of Jesus (v. 41). Among those who have come to believe in Jesus are many authorities, but with a fear reminiscent of 9:22, they refuse to do so openly for fear of expulsion from the synagogue, as in the case of Nicodemus and Joseph of Arimathea (3:2; 19:38).

John's accusation that they preferred human praise to the glory of God depicts a conflict in the Gospel between the transcendent and earthly, the human and the divine, and those who are open to God's revelation and those who cling to human traditions and perceptions. Such examples can be found in every age and in every religion. The gauntlet is thrown down in verses 44-50: since Jesus represents the Father who sent him, rejection of him is rejection of the Father. Those who refuse to believe are not condemned by Jesus, who did not come for that purpose (3:18-21), but will be judged by the word revealed by him on the last day. Today we would have a much more nuanced explanation of conversion and the dynamics of faith and doubt, and it is hoped that we do not condemn those who do not share our views. These words conclude the section of the Gospel designated by scholars as "The Book of Signs."

THE BOOK OF GLORY

John 13:1–20:31

Scholars designate chapters 13:1–20:31 as "The Book of Glory" because they describe the glorification of Jesus and his return to the Father. The farewell discourse that follows the meal is in the ancient tradition of testaments of famous men (see Gen 49; Josh 22–24; Deut; Socrates in Plato's *Phaedo; Testaments of the Twelve Patriarchs*). These testaments usually consisted of exhortations, prayers, consolation of followers, predictions of the course of future events, and the appointment of a successor. Chapters 13–17 are a composite work, woven together artistically from collections of teachings. This is reflected in their repetitious quality and by "seams" in the discourse. For instance, at the end of 14:31, Jesus says, "Get up, let us go!" but the discourse continues for three more chapters. The discourses describe the impending departure of Jesus and the change of mind, heart, and behavior necessary to overcome the world as he has. The union of Jesus with the Father is dying to the world; the union of the believer with Jesus is the same, and these teachings provide the means. Love is the path to God, but John's depiction of love is very specific: laying down one's life for others.

John 13

John's version of the Last Supper is comparable to those of the Synoptic tradition (Matt 27:17-29; Mark 14:19-25; Luke 22:7-38), but with some significant variations. John does not describe the preparations for the meal, and it is not a Passover meal, for Jesus dies on the day of preparation for Passover (19:31, 42). Jesus himself is the Paschal Lamb (1:29; 19:36), although the paschal lamb for Passover does not have an expiatory function. The account of the foot-washing takes the place of the Synoptic institution of the Eucharist. The practice of the Eucharist by the Johannine community is assumed (6:55-58), so the foot-washing becomes an interpretation of the Eucharist's significance.

13:1-5 Fully aware and deliberate

In keeping with the theme of the omniscience and foreknowledge of Jesus (6:6; 12:30), he is fully conscious of his heavenly origin and destiny. Throughout the Gospel Jesus moved about with an awareness that his hour had not yet come (2:4; 7:30; 8:20), but now he fully realizes that it has arrived. His love for his own in the world has been to the end or utmost *(telos)*, and the end is his self-giving death (v. 1), which Jesus demonstrates with the foot-washing. Judas, as the tool of Satan and the forces opposed to God, has already decided on his treacherous mission (v. 2). Speculation concerning the motives of Judas is futile, for the four Gospels give different reasons. For Matthew, money is the reason, while John ascribes the instigation to Satan.

13:5-11 The foot-washing

Foot-washing was a job considered too menial for a Jewish slave to perform, and it was usually reserved for the lowliest slaves of the household. It is similar to the pattern of the descent and humiliation of the Son as he assumes the condition of a slave that is described in Philippians 2:1-11. For John, however, it is a pattern of self-giving love. Peter objects to being washed (vv. 6-8) because he does not understand the meaning of Jesus' death. One of the things that he does not understand is that Jesus' action bears witness to a rejection of worldly honor and shame values of domination and subservience. He replaces it with a new model for human relationships: loving and humble service and laying down one's life for others (15:13; 16:2; 21:19; 1 John 3:16). The egalitarian nature of the early Johannine community reflects this model. It is later that he and the others will understand, as is often the case (2:17, 22; 7:39; 12:16; 14:29).

The foot-washing symbolizes the salvific death of Jesus, so when Jesus tells Peter that unless he is washed he will have no part in him, the laying down of one's life for others comes to mind (15:13), as well as the kind of death Peter himself will later experience (21:19). The insistence on being washed (vv. 8, 10) likely evokes the baptism that is the rite of passage into the community and a sharing in Jesus' death.

13:12-17 A model of discipleship

As teacher and lord, Jesus was willing to wash their feet; how much more they should be willing to do the same for one another. The foot-washing is given as a model or paradigm not only of humble and loving service, but of self-sacrificing love. He is not proposing an anemic Holy Thursday ritual, but a pattern or model to be imitated in every aspect of life, from small acts of kindness to sacrificial death. It only has the power to bless when it is understood and put into practice (v. 17).

13:18-30 A traitor in their midst

Jesus is again troubled, as in 12:27, but this time it is because of his knowledge that there is a traitor in their midst (cf. Matt 16:21; Mark 14:18). When the disciples want the identity of the traitor, they must go through an intermediary—the Beloved Disciple (vv. 23-25). This disciple reclines with his head on Jesus' chest, but the word used is *kolpos*, which means "bosom." The same word describes the close relationship that exists between Jesus and the Father (1:18), suggesting that the Beloved Disciple was believed by his community to enjoy an analogous relationship with the Lord, endowing him with more authority and respect.

Jesus reveals the identity of the traitor by giving him a morsel to eat (v. 26). The significance of the morsel is open to interpretation: some see it as a sign of the unfailing love of Jesus even to the one who betrays him (see Ps 41:9-10), while others detect hints of early eucharistic practices. After Judas accepts the morsel, Satan enters him (v. 27). Jesus orders him to do quickly what he has planned to do, making Jesus fully in control of his fate. Even at this stage, none of the disciples have any understanding of these words or actions (v. 28); awareness will come after the fact. After Judas leaves, the narrative states tersely that it was night, for on a deeper level the darkness has the upper hand (v. 30).

13:31-35 Something new, something old

In verses 31-33 Jesus enigmatically refers to his departure and the inability of others to find him or follow him (7:33-36; 8:21-22), underscoring his divine and otherworldly origin. He gives his "new" commandment (vv. 34-35) as a parting legacy that is in effect a summation of the foot-washing and his impending death. The love commandment is not new, for Jesus quotes Deuteronomy 6:5 and Leviticus 19:18 in Mark 12:28-34. The author of the Johannine letters admits as much (1 John 2:7; 3:11); it has been told from the beginning. Its newness here is its eschatological nature and its radical definition: laying down one's life for others. This is the guiding principle for the dawning messianic age.

Love in John is not emotion, sentiment, or personal attraction, but very practical, dynamic, and demanding. Jesus himself is the revelation of God's love (3:16; 1 John 3:16) in his ministry and in his death (15:12-13). Love will now be the distinguishing mark of disciples of Jesus (v. 35) rather than dress, diet, rituals, or observance of the law, as Christians are always in need of calling to mind.

13:36-38 Peter's boast

Simon Peter wants to follow Jesus and can't understand why he cannot. The cross is where Jesus is going, and Peter will follow later (21:19). Peter's brash promise that he will lay down his life for Jesus reveals just how little he understands the meaning of the foot-washing and the new commandment, and it is met with the prediction of his threefold denial before the cock crows (vv. 37-38).

14:1-4 The departure of Jesus

Jesus gives words of consolation and encouragement to his disciples, who are still captives of their ignorance and lack of comprehension. They continually ask where he is going and why they are unable to go. At this stage it is a solitary journey; Jesus has descended from the Father and is now returning to him. Jesus reassures them that there are many dwelling places in his Father's house and that after preparing a place for them, he will return and take his followers with him (vv. 2-4).

14:5-7 The way

Jesus' assertion that the disciples know the way is met with puzzlement by Thomas, which provides Jesus with the opportunity to declare, "I am the way and the truth and the life" (v. 6). The "Way" is the self-designation of the early Christian movement in Acts 9:2; 19:9, 23; 22:4; and 24:14, 22. Additionally, the term was used in the Qumran community (1QS 9:16-21) and in a stream of Jewish writings known as "two-way" spirituality, for example, the *Didache* (chs. 1 and 5). Jesus is a manifestation of the truth (1:14, 17), and knowing him sets one free (8:32), but not all are able to accept it (18:38). "Life" has been a constant thread throughout the Gospel, and the granting of eternal life is the root mission of Jesus (1:4; 3:16; 5:24-26; 11:25-26).

The association of all three terms—"the way and the truth and the life"—with the person of Jesus is a christological proclamation that asserts the utter uniqueness of Jesus and the inability of anyone to come to the Father except through him. This exclusive and sectarian statement was probably generated in the Johannine community's struggle with the synagogue and with other Christian groups. From our own historical vantage point, it is possible to broaden our understanding. Jesus can also be defined as "the way and the truth and the life" with respect to his example of complete self-giving, love, and service to humanity. Although Jesus is the gate to the Father, it is in the living out of this spiritual path or pattern that one has access to God, regardless of who one is.

14:8-14 The indwelling and empowerment

Knowing Jesus is the same as knowing the Father, since Jesus manifests him perfectly in his own person (v. 8). This is not understood by Philip, whom Jesus chides for his inability to get it despite his long association with him. In verses 10-12 Jesus elaborates on his words, insisting that he dwells in the Father and the Father dwells in him, the evidence being the works that the Father performs in him. But this divine empowerment is also available for those who believe in him (v. 12); in fact, believers will be able to do even greater things.

This stunning promise is given scant attention in modern church settings, much to our spiritual detriment. Even though Jesus is returning to the Father, his disciples are expected to continue his work. This will be developed in chapters 15–17. Jesus will also do anything that is asked in his name (vv. 13-14). To pray in the name of Jesus has nothing to do with a quasi-magical power in pronouncing a name; it means to ask for something with the same mind and heart as Jesus and presupposes abiding in him through the Spirit, as commanded in chapter 15.

14:15-24 The love commandment revisited

Loving Jesus is only accomplished by keeping his commandments (vv. 15, 21, 23, 24). Although Jesus gave his disciples only one commandment—to love one another—it is clear from other passages and the letters of John that the other commandment is to believe that Jesus is the one sent from God. Love is a mode of knowing God as well as an empowering principle, for both Jesus and the Father will love and reveal themselves to those who love Jesus. All these things are possible through the sending of the "Advocate" (Paraclete),

John 15

which is a fulfillment of the requirement for rebirth in the Spirit in 3:1-8 (cf. 20:22). It will be the alter ego of Jesus and his continuing and permanent presence in the community (14:15-17, 25-26; 15:26-27; 16:7-11, 12-15).

"Paraclete" was originally a legal term meaning advocate, counselor, or stand-in. It fulfills a variety of functions: teaching, 14:17 and 15:4; prophecy, 14:2-3 and 16:13-15; witness, 8:17-18 and 15:26. Its origin is God (15:26 and 16:28), and the world cannot receive it (14:17). It is clear that John's community is a Spirit-filled community in which teaching and revelation are continuous.

14:25-30 Jesus' gift of peace

Jesus bestows his peace on the disciples, signaling his departure. He makes it clear that it is not an earthly peace, which is merely the temporary absence of violence. This is God's peace—wholeness or *shalom*—given through the Spirit to abolish fear and the sense of distance or separation from God. Because of this gift of peace, Jesus is able to repeat the opening line of the chapter: "Do not let your hearts be troubled or afraid" (v. 27). All other forms of peace depend on this transcendent peace. He assures them that he will come back (v. 28) and observes that they should rejoice that he is going to the Father, "for the Father is greater than I," which contradicts 10:30. The ruler of this world—Satan—is now coming in the context of the impending passion, but he has no power whatsoever over Jesus, who goes to the cross to prove to the world that he loves the Father and is totally obedient to his will (v. 30).

15:1-11 Abiding in Jesus, the true vine

Jesus promised that he would always be present in the community. Now he relates how the members of this community will continue to be sustained and nourished with life and power. In describing the nature of the union of the disciples with Jesus and the Father (vv. 1-11), Jesus utilizes the metaphor of the vine, which was a well-known Old Testament symbol for Israel (Ps 80:8-19; Isa 5:1-7; Jer 2:21; Ezek 17:6-8; 19:10-14; Hos 10:1; Eccl 24:27). Since Jesus declares in an "I AM" statement that he is the true vine (v. 1), it is probable that the followers of Jesus are being depicted as the true Israel. The image of vine is similar to that of Body of Christ used in 1 Corinthians 12:12-27; Col 1:18; Eph 1:22-23, although these instances stress the element of interdependence and equality more than the image of the vine does.

In verses 1-11 the word "remain," or as it is often translated, "abide" *(menein)* appears ten times, illustrating the mutual indwelling and continuous union with Jesus, not just at key moments in one's life. Those who

John 15

remain connected to the vine are sustained and nourished, while those who do not remain on the vine wither and die and are useless (vv. 4-6). In the metaphor of the vine, branches, and vine grower, it is clear that they refer to Jesus, his believers, and the Father, but the meaning of the pruning and burning is unclear. Jesus' disciples have already been cleansed by his words (13:10), but the pruning can also refer to those with imperfect faith, such as those the author of the epistles rails against.

The branches are judged according to the fruit produced, which is similar to the means of discerning false prophets in Matthew 7:15-20; Luke 6:17-44; and 1 John. The fruit would be the good works done in obedience to the commandments of Jesus. By remaining in Jesus, his words remain in believers, and anything they ask will be done for them (v. 7). It is in this indwelling and the bearing of its fruit that God the Father is glorified (v. 8). To "remain" assumes fulfilling the love commandment of Jesus (vv. 12-14). Love is the golden thread that binds Jesus, his followers, and the Father (vv. 9-10), who is love itself (1 John 4:8, 16).

15:12-17 Love and the new relationship

All this changes radically the relationship between believers and Jesus. No longer are they servants or slaves but friends (vv. 13-15). This friendship is epitomized by the personal experiential knowledge of the activity and purpose of Jesus, as well as cognizance of everything that Jesus has heard from the Father (vv. 14-15). Nothing is to be hidden; nor is there any sense of the vertical or hierarchical, which is also the model of John's community. This is dependent on obedience to the commandments of Jesus (v. 14). It was Jesus who chose his followers, although chapter 1 depicts them as seeking him out. But now they are appointed to go and bear lasting fruit (20:21), receiving from the Father whatever they ask in Jesus' name (v. 16). Repeating verse 12, they are commanded to love one another, for this is what makes the indwelling possible (v. 17).

15:17-27 The world's hatred

Since the disciples and Jesus abide in one another, the world will hate the disciples just as it hated Jesus (v. 18). Recalling 13:16, Jesus reminds the disciples that they are not greater than the master, so they can expect the same treatment (v. 20). Those who reject Jesus have no excuse, for he has spoken his words to them and performed signs in their midst (vv. 21-24). Hatred of Jesus is equal to hatred of the Father (v. 23) and is the fulfillment of Psalms 35:19 and 69:4 (v. 25). These verses reflect the alienation and sense of being under siege that was felt by John's community. The Advocate (Spirit) that Jesus will send will continue his work and will give testimony through his followers, presumably in the form of good works and signs (v. 26).

16:1-3 Dubious favors for God

Jesus continues in this vein by giving his disciples ample warning of the world's hostility (v. 1). Expulsion from the synagogue (cf. 9:22; 12:42) reflects the experience of the Johannine community after the Jewish self-definition at Jamnia following the destruction of the temple in A.D. 70. Although the *birkath ha-minim* recited in synagogues toward the end of the first century contains a prayer for the destruction of the *minim* (heretics) and the Nazarenes (Christians), there is little documented evidence outside the New Testament of actual killing. The stoning of Stephen in Acts 7:58–8:1 is immediately linked with the zealous persecution of Paul (9:1-9), who admits to having been a violent persecutor of the church of God (Gal 1:13; 1 Cor 15:9). He warns that there will be a time when those who kill them will think that they are offering worship to God (v. 2).

Killing out of a warped sense of devotion or piety has been an unhappy reality in all ages and in all religions, and our own age is certainly no different. The reason, according to Jesus, is that the perpetrators have never known him or the Father (15:21; v. 3). Their murderous hatred is proof of their unbelief, for those who truly know and love God are not captive to murderous impulses. Throughout the controversies Jesus has repeatedly accused his tormentors of plotting to kill him, and it is clear that his disciples can expect the same treatment.

16:4-20 The departure of Jesus

The departure of Jesus has been mentioned in 13:36; 14:5; and 16:5, always accompanied by incomprehension on the part of the disciples. Jesus assures them that it is advantageous for them that he go away (vv. 5-7), for this is necessary for the Advocate to come (cf. 7:39). The Advocate or Spirit of truth (vv. 12-15) will act as an intermediary between Jesus and John's community, declaring all that Jesus has received from the Father. It will remind them of the words that Jesus spoke during his ministry, and it is implied that in leading them to all truth, it will also declare things that have not yet been spoken.

But most of all, the Spirit of truth (cf. Qumran texts 1QS 3:19) will prove the world wrong about sin, righteousness, and judgment, all three of which are aspects of the world's rejection of Jesus. For John, unbelief is synonymous with sin, while righteousness is the vindication of Jesus by his being raised from the dead and returning to the Father. The world judges incorrectly by refusing to recognize Jesus as being sent from the Father and by its inability to penetrate beyond external appearances.

Jesus toys with the phrase "a little while" (vv. 16-19) to refer to his impending death and the time before his reappearance after the resurrection, which causes puzzlement and consternation among the disciples. By way of explanation, the grief that they will feel upon his death is contrasted with the joy (15:11; 16:20, 22; 17:13) they will experience "on that day" (14:20; 16:23, 26) when they will see him again. Although most scholars take "on that day" to refer to the resurrection, a reference to a second coming is not excluded, for the traditional eschatology (cf. 21:22-23) and John's realized eschatology coexist in the same Gospel.

The alternating joy and sorrow on the part of the world and the disciples over the death of Jesus is a perfect example of the vast chasm that separates worldly and divine perceptions (v. 20). At that time they will have no more questions, for all will be clear, and whatever they ask the Father in Jesus' name will be given to them (vv. 23-26). The "complete . . . joy" signals the access to God that they will enjoy and the mutual indwelling that they will experience.

16:21-24 Messianic birth pangs

The image of the woman giving birth in verses 20-22 has a long biblical tradition and is used to denote the travail of messianic struggle (Isa 26:16-19; 66:7-11; Mark 13:19, 24; Matt 24:9, 21, 29; Acts 14:22; 1 Cor 7:26; 10:11; 2 Cor 4:17; Rom 8:22; Rev 12; Mic 4:10). John uses the image of new birth twice (1:13 and 3:38) to signify the new stage in the soul's journey. Here it refers to the birth of the new age, which is accomplished in Jesus and the accompanying suffering and tribulation.

The disciples think that they now understand (vv. 29-30); they see that Jesus knows everything, so they now believe that he came from God. Jesus is not impressed, and in a parallel to his response at Peter's confident boast in 13:38, he informs them that they will desert him and leave him alone. Verse 33 acts as an *inclusio* with verse 1, that is, creating a frame or bracket by placing similar material in both verses. Jesus has informed them beforehand of all the troubles they will have, but they should have courage because he has conquered the world, which is an anticipatory reference to his approaching death. As followers of Jesus encounter struggles, this should be kept in mind so that they do not lose heart.

Chapter 17, sometimes called a "prayer of ascent" or the "priestly prayer of Jesus," brings together the elements introduced in the prologue and unfolded during the account of the ministry of Jesus. The scope of Jesus' prayer encompasses the time before the foundation of the world, when he was in God's presence, and the accomplishment of his earthly ministry. His prayer also stretches toward the future and those who will come to faith.

Compared with the Gospel of Luke, Jesus does not appear to pray as often, for John only depicts Jesus doing so here and at the tomb of Lazarus. But John's Jesus enjoys an intimacy with God that is so close and immediate that prayer, which supposes a distance or absence, becomes secondary. Verses 1-26 are more in the form of a blessing than a personal prayer, for Jesus is mostly concerned with the disciples he is leaving behind, who have reached a stage of reception of his words and belief that he came from God. It is the prayer of one who is supremely confident, in complete control of his destiny, and aware that he has completed his mission satisfactorily.

17:1-8 Glorification

The mutual glorification of the Father and the Son is the focus of verses 1-5. Aware that the hour has come, Jesus lifts his eyes heavenward, as in 11:41, and asks for God's glory so that he may in turn glorify the Father. Although Jesus has been given authority over all people, he gives eternal life to those whom the Father has given him—in other words, those who believe that he has come from God (1:4, 9-13; 3:14-21, 31-36; 4:13-14; 5:24-25; 6:35; 7:37-38; 8:12; 10:27-29; 11:25-26; 12:47; 14:6-7). He is crystal clear in defining eternal life: to know the Father, who is the only true God, and the one sent by God, Jesus the Christ. A core element of John's Gospel is the insistence that Jesus Christ is the only means of access to God (see 10:25-29; 14:6) and to eternal life. He asks again (v. 5) for the glory he had before the world began (1:1-3), thereby returning to his divine origins after the completion of his mission. The disciples have received and accepted all God's words that Jesus passed on to them, as well as his divine origin (vv. 7-8).

17:9-19 Prayer for his disciples

Jesus' concern for his disciples is the central focus of verses 9-19. He prays for their protection (vv. 9-10) rather than for the world. Since he is returning to the Father and in one sense already has departed this world, they will be his presence and instruments in the world (v. 11). He prays that they continue to be protected in the name of God which Jesus has received (vv. 11-12) and which he revealed (v. 26). Revealing God's name is better understood as disclosing the essence, nature, and quality of God rather than repetition of a proper name. The complete joy (v. 13) that the disciples share is the result of knowing God directly and continually (15:11; 1 John 1:4; 2 John 12) through the Spirit. The presence of unaffected joy authenticates spiritual and religious claims, which should cause all Christian communities to pause and reflect.

Jesus addresses the Father as "holy" (v. 11), which is the characteristic of God in the Old Testament and sets him apart (Isa 5:16; 6:3). Those who worship God are commanded to be holy as God is (Lev 11:44; 19:2; 20:7; 1 Pet 1:15-16). He therefore prays that since they are in the world, they be kept one as Jesus and the Father are (v. 11) in a unity of holiness. To this end, he prays that they be "consecrate[d]" (which can also be translated as "sanctified") in the truth, which is God's word (v. 17) embodied in Jesus (1:9, 17; 8:31-32). They must be protected in the divine name (v. 12) and from the Evil One (v. 15), who is the negative ruler of this world (12:31; 14:30; 16:11).

The disciples do not belong to the world; in fact, the world hates them because of the presence of the light within their community (v. 14) and because they have received God's words from Jesus (vv. 14-17). He therefore prays that they be consecrated or set apart in the truth that is God's word, for they are being sent into the world with the same message as Jesus (v. 18; 20:21). The glorification of Jesus is his death and resurrection, for it is in this that he reveals God and fulfills God's will. The disciples glorify Jesus when they continue his mission of divine revelation, and that indeed is their mission (v. 18; 20:21).

17:20-26 That they may be one

The prayer in verses 20-26 is directed toward those who will be brought to faith by the witness of the disciples. Jesus' prayer for unity signifies far more than institutional solidarity; he prays that they may all be one, but it is a special sort of unity, a mysticism of love. Jesus shares the glory given to him by the Father with the disciples and invites them to experience God's love in the same way that he does (vv. 22-24). This perfection of unity and love is the palpable presence of God that reveals God to the world and continues the mission of Jesus. It is this visible manifestation of God's love in the community and its members that both reveals God and draws others to faith. Jesus closes his prayer (vv. 25-26) by again insisting that the world does not know God, but he does. He has revealed the name of God, and the same love with which the Father loved the Son will be present among his followers.

THE PASSION NARRATIVE

John 18:1–19:42

The long-predicted hour of Jesus has arrived (3:14; 8:28; 12:32-33) when he will be "lifted up" for the sake of all humanity. While the other Gospels portray the crucifixion as terrible and tragic, for John it is the glorification of Jesus. Jesus scarcely seems to suffer—he is not a helpless victim (10:18), for this is not Mark's man of sorrows. Although John's account of the passion of Jesus parallels the Synoptic accounts in many respects, there are some important variations. Comparing John's account with the others is interesting and enlightening, and a "Parallel Gospel" book is very useful for this purpose.

For instance, the trial before Pilate is structured and long, with Jesus interacting with Pilate in a manner very different from his laconic responses in Mark. Objections have been raised by some that the passion narratives, especially John's, have little basis in fact and are nothing more than an attempt to give historical expression to prophetic texts from the Old Testament. That represents an extreme position, for mainstream scholarship recognizes that while the passion narrative should not be considered a court record or a narration of brute facts, it does rest on a solid framework of tradition. It is a theological interpretation of the death of Jesus; the passion is therefore refracted through the prism of John's theological concerns.

This is a very important issue, as the Johannine passion narrative plays a prominent part in the spiritual and liturgical life of the Church. John uses strident language and negative imagery in his depiction of "the Jews," and this has helped fuel hateful and sometimes violent behavior and attitudes toward Jewish people and their faith. We must remember that in John's narrative, the term "the Jews" denotes those who were actively opposed to Jesus. The narrative cannot be taken at face value: Pilate was not a benign, well-intentioned man led astray by a violent crowd, and any Jewish complicity is limited to a particular handful of individuals who desired Jesus' death.

18:1-12 The arrest

Crossing the Kidron valley is associated with death (cf. 1 Kgs 2:37), made more so by the darkness and the presence of tombs. Gethsemane means "oil press"; John is alone in referring to it as a garden. The prayer for the cup passing from Jesus (but cf. 12:27) and its associated anguish over his impending death are lacking. Soon Judas arrives with a cohort of troops, along with the temple guards and the Pharisees. Since a cohort consisted of six hundred men, it is likely that it was a small detachment of soldiers. Interestingly, John alone reports that the Pharisees took an active role in the arrest. No kiss from Judas betrays Jesus in John's story, for Jesus is majestic and in total control of the situation and has complete knowledge of the events that are going to unfold (v. 4).

John 18

When Jesus asks the arresting party whom they are seeking, they reply, "Jesus the Nazorean." To this he replies, "I AM" (Exod 3:14), and the force of the divine name knocks them to the ground. This should be understood as a theological rather than a historical statement. Clearly Jesus is in full possession of his divine status even at the point of his arrest. In the scuffle with the sword, John identifies the attacker as Simon Peter and the victim as Malchus, slave of the high priest. In Matthew, Jesus rebukes them with the admonition that those who take up the sword will die by it (Matt 26:52), while in Luke he simply heals the slave's severed ear. For John, Peter's action interferes with the divine plan, and Jesus has to insist that he is to drink of the cup the Father has given him. Jesus tells his arresters to let the others go, fulfilling his own words (6:39; 10:28; 17:12) about not losing any of those given to him by the Father.

18:13-27 Interrogation before the high priest

Jesus is taken to Annas, the high priest from A.D. 6 to 15 and father-in-law of Caiaphas, the current high priest. Reference is made to Caiaphas's unwitting prophecy in 11:49-50. Mark depicts Jesus as being dragged before a nocturnal plenary session of the Sanhedrin, but the summary session before a handful of officials described in John is probably closer to the truth.

During the drama of Peter's threefold denial, the scene shifts from the courtyard to the interrogation room, then back to the courtyard for the remainder of his denials. The identity of the "other disciple" in verses 15-16 who gains access to the proceedings because of his acquaintance with the high priest is unclear, but in all probability it is the Beloved Disciple, also not named in the Gospel. While Jesus is being interrogated, Peter undergoes one of his own interrogations (vv. 17-18). His reply to the maid's question about whether he is a disciple of Jesus is "I am not," sharply contrasting with the "I AM" of Jesus in the garden.

Jesus was questioned about his disciples and his teaching, but not about any messianic claims or alleged threats against the temple. His reply is sharp and rather combative: he has taught openly, saying nothing in secret. Since he has openly proclaimed God's word to the world, they have no excuse. He also invites the high priest to ask those who heard him, meaning his followers and disciples, who are now bearers of his words (vv. 20-21). His boldness earns him a blow and a rebuke from one of the temple guards (v. 22) for showing disrespect (Exod 22:7; Lev 19:14; 20:9; Isa 8:21).

Jesus is then transferred to Pilate for further questioning (v. 24), but no formal charges have been brought, nor is there any condemnation for blasphemy or any other charge, although he has been accused of this throughout the Gospel, beginning in 5:18. The scene shifts again to the courtyard, where Peter is asked twice about being a disciple of Jesus and being seen with him in the garden (vv. 25-27). Again he mirrors the "I AM" of Jesus with "I am not." The last question was from a relative of Malchus, making Peter's denial even more ridiculous and mendacious. As the cock crows, Jesus' predictions of denial and flight in 13:38 and 16:32 come to mind.

18:28–19:15 The trial before Pilate

In the dramatic trial before Pilate, two trials are taking place. The first is the apparent trial of Jesus, while on another level, "the Jews," Pilate, and all humanity are on trial, being given the opportunity to choose either God's kingdom as revealed in Jesus or the world, which is opposed to God. The structure of the trial is carefully crafted and highly symbolic. In seven brief scenes (18:29-32, 33-38a, 38b-40; 19:1-3, 4-7, 8-11), Pilate shuttles back and forth between the inside of the praetorium, where Jesus is being held, and the crowd in the outer courtyard. These symbolize respectively the spiritual realm that Jesus represents and the world that rejects his revelation. Pilate is caught between these two worlds, feeling the pull of both, but in the end he opts for the world of Caesar rather than that of God.

18:28-32 Before Pilate

As they arrive at the praetorium, it is morning (v. 28), the beginning of the new day of redemption, and in sharp contrast to the "night" that fell when Judas departed the upper room to betray Jesus. With a touch of Johannine irony, the Jewish authorities refuse to enter the praetorium, for Passover is approaching and they do not want to defile themselves. They are worried about committing sacrilege but are ignorantly preparing to perform the greatest sacrilege of all, the killing of the Lamb of God. Pilate asks them what the charges are (v. 29), but they answer evasively (v. 30), insisting that the fact that he is here is proof enough that he is a criminal.

Pilate is massively uninterested in judging the case and demands that they judge him themselves (v. 31), but they correctly point out that under Roman occupation they do not have the right to judge capital crimes. The stoning of Stephen in Acts 7:54–8:1 can be seen as an extra-judicial murder or mob violence rather than an execution. The Romans were indifferent to the variety of religious beliefs in their empire, and subject people were permitted to continue their worship unhindered. In Acts 18:12-17 the Roman proconsul Gallio deems religious questions outside his jurisdiction and tosses Paul's case out of court. To the question "Why was Jesus put to death?" we might look to 11:47-53, where the Jewish authorities are fearful

18:33-38a The kingdom of Jesus

Entering the praetorium, Pilate begins a private interrogation of Jesus (vv. 33-38). He asks Jesus whether he is King of the Jews. This is the first mention of this charge, although there is a basis for it (1:49; 12:13), and it hints at the religious and political nature of the accusations against Jesus. His reply is a question (v. 34): Did you figure this out on your own, or did others tell you this? The contemptuous retort of Pilate places the onus for the charges back on the Jewish authorities, and he asks Jesus what he has done (v. 35).

By explaining that his rule or kingdom is not of this world, Jesus means that its origin, values, and methods are from God rather than the world (v. 36), evidenced by the refusal of the use of force and violence to defend himself. He is not referring to a place or calling for a turning away from the concerns of life in this world. Pilate's uncomprehending conclusion that Jesus is indeed a king is met by refusal on the part of Jesus, and an insistence that his sole reason for coming into the world was to testify to the truth (v. 37), and anyone belonging to the truth listens to him—even Pilate himself if he so chooses. Pilate shows himself to be far from the truth with his famous query in verse 38: "What is truth?" The irony is that "truth" is literally staring him in the face!

18:38b-40 Barabbas or Jesus

Pilate declares Jesus innocent (cf. Luke 23:4, 14, 22) and offers to release a prisoner in honor of the Passover (cf. Mark 15:6-14; Matt 27:15-23), asking the crowd if they want him to release the King of the Jews. There is no historical record of any such Passover custom. The crowd makes its choice: Barabbas (v. 40), who is a revolutionary, a man of violence representing the kingdom of the world. The crowd has made its first choice.

19:1-7 The scourging

Pilate has Jesus scourged (v. 1), as in Matthew 27:26-31 and Mark 15:15-20, while Barabbas disappears from the scene. As the soldiers parody royal trappings and hail Jesus as King of the Jews, they are unwittingly doing obeisance to a real king (v. 3). In Luke's Gospel it is not until Jesus is before Herod Antipas (23:6-12) that he is dressed in royal garb. The Son of God is contrasted with the humanity of Jesus as Pilate proclaims, "Behold, the man!" Judging by external appearances, Pilate and the others do not see anything divine, but the Johannine claim of the incarnation is clear (v. 5).

Three times Pilate declares that he finds no evidence of wrongdoing in Jesus (18:38; 19:4, 6), as in Luke 23:4, 14, 22. This heightens the sense of guilt on the part of the "Jews," as John takes great pains to shift the bulk of the responsibility onto them. Pilate is portrayed as a tragic and vacillating figure who is the victim of circumstance. He was even venerated as a saint in the early Coptic church. We know from Philo and Josephus that Pilate was in fact a venal and ruthless individual, who ruled with an iron fist and was not reluctant to spill blood. The "Jews" declare that Jesus has to die for violating the law by making himself the Son of God (v. 7). This alludes to the punishment for blasphemy set forth in Leviticus 24:16 and repeated in the rabbinical tradition. Jesus' claim to a filial relationship with God represents the core of John's Gospel and almost resulted in stoning on numerous occasions.

19:8-12 Where are you from?

But when Pilate hears the statement that Jesus ought to die (v. 8), it strikes fear into him, for "Son of God" could mean many things in the Greco-Roman world, including a divine or semi-divine being. Pilate does not want to run afoul of the gods and their many powers. Hastening back into the praetorium, he asks Jesus where he is from, probably indicating a desire to know if he is of human or divine origins (vv. 8-9). The readers of the Gospel, of course, are fully aware of Jesus' origins, for this has been a point of contention throughout the Gospel.

Jesus refuses to answer, for Pilate has already had his chance to receive the revelation of God through Jesus and showed himself to be closed to that reality (18:37-38). Pilate impatiently reminds Jesus that he has absolute power of life and death over him (v. 10), and so Jesus would do well to answer his questions. But his earthly power is illusory, Jesus claims, for he can only do what is permitted by God (vv. 11-12). Similar views were expressed by John the Baptist in 3:27, reflecting the current of predetermination that runs throughout this Gospel. Jesus makes an ambiguous comment about the one who handed him over being guilty of the greater sin. This has traditionally been thought to refer to Judas, but Caiaphas and the Jewish authorities are also strong candidates.

19:13-16 Whose friend?

Pilate tries all the harder to release Jesus, and the crowd resorts to a form of blackmail, claiming that if he does, then he is no friend of Caesar. Anyone making himself king opposes Caesar (v. 12). They are speaking the language of power, which the Romans understand and respect well. "Friend of Caesar" is an honorific title given by the emperor as a sign of special favor, and to lose that status can only mean that one is an enemy of Caesar, not a healthy thing to be. Jesus calls his followers friends, too, but Pilate chooses to be the friend of an earthly king, preferring human power and glory. The fear factor is decisive, and the possibility of lost prestige and security pushes him over the edge. He seats himself on the judge's bench and in a mocking (but ironically true) fashion presents Jesus to the crowd as a king (vv. 13-14). They make their choice of kingdoms by calling for the crucifixion of Jesus, at the time of the preparation day for the Passover, clearly underscoring the role Jesus plays as the Lamb of God.

When an incredulous Pilate asks if he should crucify their king, the chief priests (not the crowd) answer, "We have no king but Caesar!" These are shocking words, implying a preference for an earthly and pagan king to the king sent by God and can be interpreted as a definitive rejection of the kingdom of God. Although it calls to mind 1 Samuel 8:7, where the Israelites are said to have rejected God by demanding a king like the pagan nations, it is hard to envision the chief priests publicly repudiating their God and traditions in such a manner.

19:17-30 The crucifixion of Jesus

John's theological hand is evident in his version of the crucifixion account. Pilate hands Jesus over to be crucified (v. 16), but in Johannine fashion, Jesus carries his own cross—he is in command of his destiny—and Simon of Cyrene (Mark 15:21) does not make an appearance. As in the Synoptics, the two others are crucified on either side of him, but they do not revile him (v. 18), and they are not called bandits or thieves. The inscription placed on the cross in three languages—Hebrew, Latin, and Greek—is most likely intended to convey a universal sense of God's revelation to the world through the crucified Jesus (vv. 19-22), for he has been "lifted up" and is drawing all people to himself (12:32). But the chief priests are outraged and protest vehemently to Pilate that it should not state that Jesus was the King of the Jews but merely a claimant to the title. Pilate stands his ground, and his adamant "What I have written, I have written" gives a definitive and unalterable sense to the crucifixion. Again Pilate is portrayed as at least ambiguous about his condemnation of Jesus, and here he appears to have the final word in the matter.

The soldiers cast lots for the garments of Jesus (vv. 23-25) in fulfillment of Psalm 22:19. John informs us that the garment was seamless, perhaps suggesting the garment of the high priest, which, according to Josephus, is seamless (*Ant.* 3:161). Jesus would then be a priestly mediatory figure between God and humanity, fitting well with John's theology. Jesus' relationship with the Father was expressed in terms of oneness, and Jesus prayed for the oneness and unity of his disciples (17:11, 22-24). This suggests that the seamless robe can also symbolize the community of disciples, an interpretation favored by the church fathers.

The Synoptic accounts merely relate that a group of women looked on from a distance, but here the mother of Jesus and the Beloved Disciple stand at the foot of the cross, along with several women. The mother of Jesus, unnamed in the Gospel, appears at the beginning (2:1-11) and the end of the mission of Jesus. The Beloved Disciple plays a prominent role in the passion narratives (13:23; 21:24-25) and is claimed to be the source of the Gospel witness. His appearance at the foot of the cross underscores his special relationship to Jesus and his uncommon loyalty in the hour of his death; in fact, he is portrayed as the model disciple. His identity is illusive, and it is not even certain that he was one of the Twelve. The dying Jesus commends his mother to the care of the Beloved Disciple, asking that their relationship be that of mother and son (vv. 26-27). The community of disciples, the mother of Jesus, the Beloved Disciple, and all who come to faith are joined together in the new family of believers whom Jesus leaves behind.

Fully aware and in command to the very end (v. 28), Jesus exclaims, "I thirst," in order to fulfill Psalm 69:22. Common wine is given to him on a sprig of hyssop (v. 29), which is used to smear the blood over the lintels before Passover (Exod 12:21-23). After receiving the wine, he declares, "It is finished," denoting that he has accomplished everything that the Father has sent him to do (17:4), and his mission is complete (v. 30). He has truly "loved them to the end" (13:1). After bowing his head, he hands over the spirit, signifying both his death and the release of the Spirit promised in 7:39 and 14:16-17. The absence of a cry of divine abandonment, darkness at noon, the rending of the temple veil, earthquakes, a loud cry at the moment of death, or a declaration by a centurion (Mark 15:33, 34, 37, 38, 39) is striking.

19:31-37 The piercing of the side of Jesus

In John's idiosyncratic chronology of the events of the passion, the death of Jesus occurs on the day of preparation. This is before the start of the sabbath and Passover, which in that year coincided, making it a particularly solemn occasion. An exposed corpse would be particularly defiling (Deut 21:23), so the "Jews" ask Pilate to authorize the coup de grâce in the form of the breaking of the legs, which causes suffocation, and the taking down of the bodies. This is done to the other two who were crucified with Jesus, but it was unnecessary in the case of Jesus, since he is already dead (vv.

32-33). A soldier pierces the side of Jesus and blood and water flow out (v. 34). It is seen as the fulfillment of Scripture (Exod 12:10, 46; Num 9:12; Ps 34:20-21), which prohibits broken bones in the lamb sacrificed for Passover, which is an amplification of John's portrayal of Jesus as the Paschal Lamb. The piercing of the side is an expression of the messianic text Zechariah 12:9-13.

This incident, unique to John, is layered with meaning. In Christian tradition this has been seen as the release of the Spirit and divine life for the church. The blood and water have been associated with the Eucharist (cf. Mark 14:24) and baptism. The solemn witness offering testimony in verse 35 is probably none other than the Beloved Disciple himself. He is testifying to three things: it was Jesus on the cross; he was human; he really died. These things may seem self-evident to us, but all three have been denied then as well as today, as a visit to the religion section of any modern bookstore will show. Some groups denied that Jesus was really a human being; he just appeared to have a body. Others denied that Jesus died on the cross, claiming that someone died in his place. John insists on the incarnation (1:14; 1 John 4:2-3) as well as the witness of blood and water (1 John 5:6-7).

19:38-42 The burial of Jesus

Joseph of Arimathea is mentioned in all four Gospels, but John adds that he was a secret follower for fear of the Jews (v. 38). In John's eyes, this is a particularly egregious failing, and to drive the point home, Nicodemus is the next person to appear in the narrative. He came to Jesus by night in 3:2 and did not fare well in his encounter with him; in 7:50-52 he offers hesitant support of Jesus before his fellow Pharisees. John insists that public and unequivocal profession of belief in Jesus is necessary, ruling out any sort of fence-sitting. By their bold and public actions, both men seem to be moving toward full and explicit faith. Joseph has obtained the body of Jesus from Pilate, and Nicodemus brings one hundred pounds of myrrh and aloes. They bind the body of Jesus along with the spices according to custom. It is an unhurried and well-prepared burial. The other Gospels have Jesus placed hastily in a tomb, so that the women head for the tomb on Sunday morning to anoint the body with the spices. A new tomb in which no one has ever been buried is in a garden very close to the place of crucifixion, and that is where Jesus is laid.

20:1-10 The empty tomb

Mary Magdalene is present in all four Gospels, but here she is alone, before sunrise. In Mark 16:1 and Luke 24:1 the women are heading for the tomb to anoint the body of Jesus with spices; in John, it has already been done (19:40). When Mary Magdalene saw that the stone has been removed, she runs to tell Simon Peter and the Beloved Disciple, assuming that someone has taken the body from the tomb, as was the case in Matthew 27:64; 28:13-15. Both disciples run to the tomb (vv. 3-5). The Beloved Disciple arrives first but, possibly out of deference, does not enter, although he looks in and sees the burial cloths. There is a bit of tension between the two disciples, and it is clear that in this Gospel the Beloved Disciple is the star and is highly esteemed and beloved by Jesus. But in this chapter and in chapter 21, Peter's leadership is recognized.

As Simon Peter enters the tomb (vv. 6-7), he sees the burial cloths, and the cloth covering the face of Jesus is carefully rolled up and placed to one side in a separate place. Such a detail likely illustrates that the resurrection is a very deliberate and definitive conquest of death, for we remember that in 11:44 Lazarus exited the tomb still bound in the burial cloths. Additionally, the Greek grammatical construction points to God as the source of the action. When the Beloved Disciple enters the tomb, he sees and believes, implying that Peter has somehow failed to comprehend the significance of the burial cloths.

There is a strange statement (v. 9) that they did not yet understand the Scripture that Jesus had to rise from the dead. The early Christian tradition claims that the resurrection was foretold in the Scriptures (Acts 2:24-27; 1 Cor 15:4), but it is not clear to which passages they refer. In John's Gospel many things in the life of Jesus and in Scripture are clarified only after the sending of the Spirit (2:27; 12:16). Obviously, the Beloved Disciple believes in Jesus and that he is somehow alive. But there were many theological currents in the first century concerning the afterlife, which is illustrated in Mark 9:10, as the disciples discuss what rising from the dead might mean.

20:11-18 Jesus and Mary Magdalene

This resurrection encounter (vv. 11-18) between Jesus and Mary Magdalene is unique to John. Mary Magdalene remains alone outside the tomb weeping (v. 11). She looks into the tomb and sees two angels in white on either end of where the body had been (v. 12). They were not present when the two disciples were there; it is possible that the Mary story was a separate account joined to the race to the tomb by the evangelist. All the Gospels report figures in the tomb, but with variation in details.

The angels ask Mary a pointed question (v. 13): "Woman, why are you weeping?" Implied in the question is the assumption that if she really believed and understood the significance of what had transpired, she would not weep (16:20-22). She merely repeats her fears that the body has been stolen.

Jesus appears and asks her exactly the same question but adds, "Whom are you looking for?" recalling 1:38; 6:24, 26; 7:34, 36; 12:21; and 18:4. Still uncomprehending and unable to recognize Jesus, thinking him to be the gardener, she asks about the location of the body (v. 15). It is only when Jesus speaks her name (v. 16), recalling the Good Shepherd in 10:3-5, that she recognizes him with the exclamation "Rabbouni!" Jesus' admonition not to hold on to him has puzzled people for centuries (other translations say "Don't touch me," implying that she has not yet done so). After all, he invites Thomas to touch his wounds in 20:27. But it is clear that at this point the mission lacks one final step: ascension to the Father, and it is for this reason that he asks her to let go of him (v. 17). This is not like the raising of Lazarus, for Jesus does not just resume his life as it was three days ago. After his return to the Father, he will appear to his disciples (vv. 19-31; 1 Cor 15:3-8; Acts 9:3-6). It is not a rebuke, and she is granted the singular honor, earning her recognition as the apostle to the apostles, of carrying an electrifying message to the others.

Through the Gospel the relationship of Jesus to God the Father has been exclusive (see 1:18). Those from below are incapable of knowing or comprehending God. But now, with the impending completion of the mission, that relationship has been radically altered, for he refers to "my Father and your Father, my God and your God," implying that they are now his brothers and sisters. Those who believe in Jesus (and potentially all humanity) can experience the same relationship with God as Jesus does (14:18-24; 16:16-24; 17:6-19). Seeing Jesus is of supreme importance in post-resurrection faith, and it means far more than mere sense perception. It implies understanding and believing. Mary's proclamation in verse 18, "I have seen the Lord," speaks of a life-transforming experience.

20:19-23 The upper room

The disciples have not been transformed, for they have not seen Jesus. They are behind locked doors for fear of the Jews (7:13; 9:22; 19:38) when Jesus stands in their midst, presumably without the use of the door (v. 19). He greets them with a traditional greeting of "Peace" *(Shalom)*, but in view of the peace promised in 14:27 and 16:33, it is God's peace that he brings. Showing them his hands and feet (v. 26) parallels Luke 24:36-43 and serves to confirm his humanity and identity, as in 19:34 and 1 John 4. Uttering the peace blessing again, he gives them the same mission that the Father gave him for the sake of the world (3:16; 17:18). They will be the instruments by which others come to saving faith, for as bearers of the Spirit, they will make God present to the world for generations to come.

The opening words of both the book of Genesis and John's Gospel speak of a beginning, and as Jesus breathes the holy Spirit into the community of believers, it is clear that God is creating them anew. The Hebrew word *ruah* means "breath," "wind," or "spirit." The Spirit was promised in 14:16-17, 26; 15:26; 16:7-15, and it will provide the powers needed to continue Jesus' ministry, as well as interpreting the meaning of his ministry to his followers. Matthew's Jesus gives the power of the binding and loosing of sins to Peter (16:19) and the community (18:18). John confers this authority on the entire community of disciples, for it is the consequence of the divine Spirit dwelling within the community.

20:24-29 Doubting Thomas

Thomas was not present when Jesus came, and when the transformed community exclaims, "We have seen the Lord!" he refuses to believe unless he can actually see and touch the nail marks and the wound in the side of Jesus (vv. 25-26). A week later, when Thomas was present, Jesus repeats his appearance and greeting of peace, then invites Thomas to place his finger within his wounds and to cease his lack of faith and believe. It is not clear whether Thomas actually does so, but he eloquently confesses faith in Jesus as Lord and God—a more exalted profession than anyone else in the Gospel made.

Thomas is known to history as "doubting Thomas," but this obscures the fact that alone in the Gospel of John he is given a significant role (11:16; 14:5; 21:2), and in early Christian tradition he carried the gospel to India. He was of sufficient stature that some Christians even attached his name to a collection of sayings known to us as the Gospel of Thomas. In verse 29 Jesus seems to chide Thomas a bit for believing on the basis of proofs and declares blessed those who have not seen but believe, a statement clearly aimed at the second- or third-generation Christians in the time of the Gospel's composition. Temporal proximity to Jesus is of no particular advantage; in fact, our own faith is in many ways a greater witness, since we have not been given the visual proofs available to the original disciples.

20:30-31 First ending

The primitive form of the Gospel likely ended with verses 30-31, in which John declares that there were many other signs that Jesus performed that are not written in this book. The few presented in the book serve but

John 20

one purpose: to bring others to faith (or to help those already believing to continue) that Jesus is the Messiah and Son of God, and through this belief receive life in his name.

We have seen how the original Gospel seems to end with 20:30-31, complete with the purpose of its composition. Chapter 21 is likely an epilogue, although some scholars maintain its unity with the entire Gospel. Several independent elements have been woven together to form the chapter. Unresolved issues are dealt with, most notably Peter's estrangement from Jesus following his threefold denial as well as some tension between Peter and the Beloved Disciple and their respective supporters. Readers will of course recognize the story of the miraculous catch from the story of Jesus' calling of the disciples in Luke 5:1-11, but this is probably a parallel tradition rather than a direct literary dependence.

EPILOGUE:
THE RESURRECTION APPEARANCE IN GALILEE
John 21:1-25

21:1-14 Appearance at the Sea of Tiberias

The story opens on the Sea of Galilee (here called Tiberias, after the city). In Mark 14:28 and 16:7, Jesus has promised that they will see him in Galilee, so from the standpoint of coherence, this story fits better with Mark. All the appearances of the risen Christ have been in Jerusalem. Simon Peter and six other disciples have fished all night, catching nothing. At dawn Jesus stands on the shore, but the disciples fail to recognize him, in a manner similar to the appearance to the disciples on the road to Emmaus (Luke 24:13-35) and the appearance to Mary Magdalene (20:15). Addressing them as "Children," Jesus quizzes them and then directs them where to put down their nets, resulting in a huge haul of fish.

It is no surprise that the Beloved Disciple is the first to recognize Jesus and exclaims, "It is the Lord!" Peter impetuously jumps into the water and arrives at the shore before the heavily laden boat. They discover that Jesus has prepared a fire, along with fish and bread. At the direction of Jesus, Peter drags the net to shore, and the narrator reports that it held 153 fish. This obsessive attention to detail has excited the curiosity of exegetes for two thousand years. Many have searched for symbolic or esoteric meaning. Augustine points out that the sum of the numbers from 1 to 17 equals 153, while for Jerome 153 equals the number of types of fish known to ancient natural science. The Hebrew numerological system for finding hidden meanings and truths within words *(gematria)* has yielded inconclusive results. Those wishing to follow the arguments can consult a detailed commentary.

The full meaning is perhaps inaccessible in our age. For us, the most likely and useful answer is that it is a symbol of universality and completeness and involves the quest to bring souls to God. In Mark 1:17 and Luke 5:10, Jesus promises to make the disciples "fishers of men," and the metaphor was widely used in an eschatological sense to mean the ingathering at the end of time. In fact, verse 11 states that although there were so many fish, the net was not torn, implying a seamlessness and limitless capacity.

Jesus invites the disciples to have breakfast (vv. 12-13) and distributes bread and fish, suggesting both 6:1-15 and the eucharistic practices of the early community. It is supposedly the third post-resurrection appearance to the disciples (v. 14) but should be the fourth if Mary Magdalene is counted as a disciple. We wonder why they returned to their former occupations after the appearance in the upper room and the gift of the Spirit, and indeed they act as if the risen Jesus is unfamiliar to them. This would seem to indicate an independent tradition that has been incorporated into the Gospel.

21:15-19 The rehabilitation of Peter

Peter denied Jesus three times, as foretold in 13:38 (18:17, 25-27). After the breakfast Jesus puts Peter on the spot with a rigorous and uncomfortable examination. He addresses him formally as "Simon, son of John" rather than "Cephas," for his fidelity and performance have not lived up to his appellation of Peter (meaning "rock"). Jesus asks him if he loves him "more than these." This last phrase is ambiguous; it can mean "more than you love these other disciples" or "more than these others love me." Most exegetes favor the latter meaning, for it would be more in keeping with the context of the story.

Peter's painful grilling continues; three times he must respond affirmatively to the poignant question Jesus addresses to him, matching his threefold denial. His affirmations are met only with the command "Feed my lambs" and "tend my sheep." It is clear that humble service is the leadership model in the Johannine community. The third time that Jesus fires the question at him, Peter is hurt and responds that Jesus knows everything, including the fact that he loves him, for Jesus is omniscient throughout the Gospel. Jesus then uses the occasion to tell Peter that his life will no longer be his own and that he will be led where he does not want to go, referring to Peter's eventual martyrdom in Rome, the way in which he will glorify God, as did Jesus.

This didactic story draws on the Good Shepherd (10:1-6, 11-18) and the love commandments (13:14-15, 34; 14:15, 21, 23-24; 15:12-14), all of which

John 21

portray the full expression of love as laying down one's life for others. Peter is now rehabilitated, and the story ends with Jesus uttering the invitation and command of discipleship found in Mark 1:17 and 2:17: "Come, follow me!"

21:20-23 Rivalry and misunderstanding

Packed into verses 20-23 are two problems facing the community. The first is the rivalry between Peter and the Beloved Disciple. Peter turns and sees the Beloved Disciple following them, and the narrator refers back to the Last Supper to remind the reader of who he is. Peter's plaintive, very human question is "What about him?" Peter wants to know if the Beloved Disciple is going to suffer martyrdom too!

Jesus is rather brusque in his response, basically telling Peter that it's none of his business, and that if Jesus wants the Beloved Disciple to remain until his return, it is no concern of Peter's. He should worry about his own discipleship, and Jesus repeats the command (v. 22): "*You* follow me!" (emphasis added). But this gives rise to a misunderstanding that is soon widespread, namely, that the Beloved Disciple would not die. It is obvious that the recent death of the Beloved Disciple, whoever he might have been, has caused consternation within Johannine communities. The author of this story takes pains to set the record straight: Jesus did not say that the disciple would not die, only "What if I want him to remain until I come?"

Both Paul and Mark expected the imminent return of Jesus, the parousia, and their eschatology and ethics reflected that expectation (1 Thess 4:13-18; 1 Cor 15; Mark 13). The passage of time and the delay of the return of Jesus generated theological tensions and difficulties of faith within early Christian communities (1 Thess 4:13-18; 2 Pet 3:3-10). In the Gospel of John two eschatologies are allowed to coexist—the traditional one oriented toward the future and the "realized eschatology" of John, depicting the presence of the end-time realities in the person of Jesus (5:24-27; 11:23-25; 14:22-24). This passage may reflect a Johannine eschatological reinterpretation more in harmony with the rest of the New Testament, necessitated by the delay of the parousia.

21:24-25 Second and final ending

The final ending refers to the many other things that Jesus did and, in a possible allusion to the other Gospels, speculates that the whole world would not be sufficient to contain the books that would be required. But we wish that the author had not been so reticent.

The Acts of the Apostles

Dennis Hamm, S.J.

INTRODUCTION

Welcome to a sequel. If the Acts of the Apostles were a contemporary film rather than an ancient document, they might call it "The Gospel of Luke: Part Two," for this book of the New Testament is clearly a sequel to the Third Gospel. The easiest way to recognize that fact is to read the first four verses of Luke's Gospel, where the author addresses one Theophilus (likely a new convert and possibly the sponsor of the publication—the one who paid the copyists) and then to flip forward to the opening phrase of Acts: "In the first book, Theophilus . . ." That should be enough to indicate that we are dealing with a two-volume work. Those who study and write about Luke's work are so conscious that his contribution to the New Testament canon—that is, the collection of books accepted by the church as inspired by God—is a two-volume project, deserving to be treated as a single masterpiece, that they commonly refer to it simply as Luke-Acts, as we shall do in this commentary.

This obvious fact of the unity of Luke-Acts has long escaped most readers because the conventional ordering of printed editions of the New Testament separates Luke's Gospel from its sequel by placing the Gospel of John between them. Those who chose that sequence had a perfectly good reason: the arrangement keeps the four canonical stories of Jesus together as a bundle. That way, Acts makes an appropriate bridge from the stories about Jesus to the letters of Paul. But this arrangement also has a downside: it has accidentally distracted readers from recognizing the continuity between the two parts of Luke's work.

During the last third of the twentieth century, biblical scholars have focused less on the study of discrete segments of texts and more on the form and meaning of entire documents. That focus has produced a fresh appreciation of the integrity and artistry of the work now commonly called Luke-Acts.

How does Luke himself understand his project? Luke expresses his intentions regarding the whole of Luke-Acts in the four-verse introduction at the head of his Gospel.

The Acts of the Apostles

> ¹Since many have undertaken to compile a narrative of the events that have been fulfilled among us, ²just as those who were eyewitnesses from the beginning and ministers of the word have handed them down to us, ³I too have decided, after investigating everything accurately anew, to write it down in an orderly sequence for you, most excellent Theophilus, ⁴so that you may realize the certainty of the teachings you have received.

Notice that the subject of his work is "the events that have been fulfilled among us." The phrase "events fulfilled" suggests that those events were not simply happenings but truly fulfillments of the Scriptures of Israel. The "us" in question is the Christian community of Luke's own time, a group far enough removed in time (at least by forty or fifty years) from the life, death, and resurrection of Jesus that they needed the testimony of eyewitnesses and preachers of the word to learn about those events. And yet the "us" was in such continuity with that first generation of Christians (the eyewitnesses) that those events could be understood as fulfilled among *us*. In other words, Luke's audience could still think of the past events as having been fulfilled among *them*. This also applies to subsequent readers, including us.

Did Luke think that such "fulfillment" events were still occurring in his own time? Yes. Other parts of Luke-Acts indicate this awareness quite clearly. Consider Jesus' final words at the close of Luke's Gospel: "Thus it is written that the Messiah would suffer and rise from the dead on the third day, *and that repentance, for the forgiveness of sins, would be preached in his name to all the nations, beginning from Jerusalem*" (Luke 24:46-47, emphasis added). Notice that what is said to fulfill the Scriptures here is not only the death and resurrection of the Messiah but also the preaching of repentance in the name of Jesus to all the nations, which is precisely what Acts is all about. So "the events that have been fulfilled among us" include not only the story of Jesus (told in the Third Gospel) but also the story of the church (the subject of Acts) as it continues to unfold in Luke's own generation. By the extension implied in his vision, our generation is included as well. This awareness of the end-time fulfillment occurring in the time of the church comes through strongly in an assertion in Peter's speech in Acts 3:24: "Moreover, all the prophets who spoke, from Samuel and those afterwards, also announced these days."

Are there other clues to the unity of Luke-Acts? There are many. Take, for example, the words that Gabriel speaks to Mary at the annunciation.

> "He will be great and will be called Son of the Most High, and the Lord God will give him the throne of David his father, and he will rule over the house of Jacob forever . . ." (Luke 1:32-33).

It is instructive to see what happens to those predictions throughout the remainder of Luke-Acts. In the world of first-century Judaism, the word about Jesus' inheriting David's throne meant becoming the Messiah, the end-time political and religious leader of a restored people of Israel. When does Luke show Jesus taking up that role? Certainly not in the Gospel. Nowhere in Luke's narrative of Jesus's life, death, and resurrection does Jesus become king in that conventional sense. Indeed, talk of kingship occurs only ironically—in the accusations of the Sanhedrin, in the mockery of the leaders and soldiers under the cross, and in the inscription on the cross: "This is the king of the Jews." But the implication of these ironic references is that Jesus has failed to inherit the throne of David in the conventional sense. His kingship turns out to be far grander than that.

The reader has to begin reading the second volume, the Acts of the Apostles, to learn Luke's understanding of how Jesus inherits David's throne. In Peter's speech at Pentecost, we hear Peter recite a psalm of David, Psalm 16, in which the speaker of the prayer expresses the hope that his flesh will not "see corruption." Peter then asserts that these words of David were not spoken about himself but about the Messiah. Psalm 16, Peter says, must be interpreted in the light of 2 Samuel 7:12 and Psalm 132:11 in a way that points only to Jesus. Jesus now reigns over end-time Israel, not from an earthly throne in Jerusalem but as risen Lord of the Christian community. That is just one example of the careful continuity between the Gospel of Luke and the Acts of the Apostles. This commentary will highlight many more such links between the first and second parts of Luke's two-volume work.

Why did Luke's readers need a sequel? These preliminary observations may begin to suggest some of the reasons why Luke added a sequel to his new edition of the story of Jesus.

A church increasingly composed of non-Jews (Gentiles) needed help in understanding how Gentiles could claim the heritage of Israel. Luke tells the story of the church to demonstrate that their experience is the fruition of "the light to the nations" (Isa 49:6) that the People of God was always meant to be.

People living after the generation of the original eyewitnesses needed a way of understanding how the life of Jesus still had relevance in their own lives. Luke shows how the life of Christians, individually and communally, is always some kind of replay of the life of Jesus. Thus Stephen's death parallels Jesus' death, and the travels and trials of Paul mirror the travels and trials of Jesus.

As a community spreading throughout the Roman Empire, the church needed an account of itself that demonstrated honorable roots (origins in

The Acts of the Apostles

the ancient people of Israel) and posed no political threat to Roman law and order. And so Luke stresses biblical fulfillment and underscores the innocence of Jesus and his followers in the courts of Roman officials.

A growing church needed models for interacting with the worlds it was encountering. And so Luke told its early history not simply as reminiscences of "the way we were" but in the form of episodes that could model "the way we *are*." Indeed, that is why the Acts of the Apostles has been of permanent value to the church. While we can never succeed in simply replicating the early days of the church, we can always find reminders of what has been permanently important to the life of the church in Luke's portrayal of those early days.

What are we to make of all those short speeches? A good third of the content of the Acts of the Apostles consists of brief speeches. Often readers have taken these to be something like "tapes" of the apostolic preaching. Intense study of the Greek-writing historians of the first century has, however, led scholars to another conclusion. One of the tools of history writing in the Mediterranean world of those days was the composition of speeches put on the lips of key figures to interpret the meaning of the events narrated. In other words, even when Hellenistic (Greek) historians had verbatim records of what an important person said on a particular occasion, they would consider it part of good history writing to use the benefit of hindsight, along with the sources at their disposal, and compose a speech that captured the essential truth of what was happening. Most Lukan scholars judge that the speeches in Acts represent that kind of history writing, that is, Luke, drawing upon the tradition handed down from the apostles, composes speeches and puts them on the lips of Peter, Paul, and Stephen to explain to his readers the meaning of the history he is telling.

To those of us who thought we were hearing in those speeches the very words of Peter and Paul, this way of understanding the speeches was, at first, disappointing. But in the end, taking Luke to be writing speeches in the manner of his peer historians makes better sense of the material. For each of those speeches makes more sense as addressed to Luke's readers rather than as addressed to the audience within the plot line of the narrative. Indeed, the speeches build on one another and presume an audience that has read the Third Gospel and the rest of the Acts of the Apostles.

What we have in those cameo speeches, then, is not a set of tapes that we have to sort out for ourselves (like editors working with Richard Nixon's White House tapes); rather, what we have are Luke's authoritative interpretations of the early history of the church. Because of their content, they also give us examples of the early church's use of Scripture in proclaiming the good news. At the end of the day, this is a more satisfying and instructive way of reading those speeches. This commentary aims to make that apparent.

Outline. Many commentators have observed that Jesus' words to the disciples before his ascension contain a kind of outline of Acts: "You will be my witnesses in Jerusalem, throughout Judea and Samaria, and to the ends of the earth" (Acts 1:8). That observation is illustrated in the following outline:

I. The Risen Christ and the Restoration of Israel in Jerusalem (1:1–8:3).
II. The Mission in Judea and Samaria (8:4–9:43).
III. The Inauguration of the Gentile Mission (10:1–15:35).
IV. The Mission of Paul to the Ends of the Earth (15:36–28:31).

This way of outlining the major movements of Luke's history also reflects one of the main texts from the Scriptures that he uses to interpret what is going on in the early history of the church:

> For now the Lord has spoken
>   who formed me as his servant from the womb,
> That Jacob may be brought back to him
>   and Israel gathered to him;
> And I am made glorious in the sight of the Lord,
>   and my God is now my strength!
> It is too little, he says, for you to be my servant,
>   to raise up the tribes of Jacob,
>   and restore the survivors of Israel;
> I will make you a light to the nations,
>   that my salvation may reach to the ends of the
>   earth. (Isa 49:5-6)

Notice that this prophecy about Servant/Israel entails two stages: first, the restoration of Israel (the twelve tribes of Jacob); second, becoming a "light to the nations." In the Acts of the Apostles, Luke shows how this prophecy is fulfilled.

Isaiah's first stage, the end-time restoration of Israel, unfolds in the first two movements in Acts—first in the formation of the Jerusalem community out of Jews from all nations (1:1–8:3), then in their outreach to Jews in the surrounding area and to Samaritans (8:4–9:43).

Isaiah's second stage, becoming a "light to the nations," unfolds in two further movements—first in the inauguration of the mission to the

The Acts of the Apostles

Gentiles (10:1–15:35), then in Paul's mission to "the ends of the earth" (15:36–28:31).

This commentary will highlight the two continuities sketched in this introduction: (1) the continuity between the story of Jesus and the story of the church, and (2) the continuity between the Christian story as a whole and the longer story of Israel's life with God, as told in the Greek version of the Hebrew Scriptures. The importance of this approach was underscored by the recent document of the Pontifical Biblical Commission, "The Jewish People and Their Sacred Scriptures in the Christian Bible" (Vatican City: Libreria Editrice Vaticana, 2002; available at http://www.libreriaeditricevaticana.com).

Although the format of this commentary does not allow for footnotes, the author's dependence on prior commentators will be obvious to those familiar with Lukan scholarship. Readers who wish to pursue their study of Luke-Acts more deeply should consult the following: Luke Timothy Johnson, *The Acts of the Apostles* (Collegeville, Minn.: Liturgical Press, 1992); James D. G. Dunn, *The Acts of the Apostles* (Valley Forge, Pa.: Trinity Press, 1996); Joseph A. Fitzmyer, S.J., *The Acts of the Apostles,* Anchor Bible 31 (New York: Doubleday, 1998); and Ben Witherington, III, *The Acts of the Apostles* (Grand Rapids, Mich.: William B. Eerdmans, 1998).

Now let us begin to read Luke's sequel.

COMMENTARY

THE RISEN CHRIST AND THE RESTORATION OF ISRAEL IN JERUSALEM

Acts 1:1–8:3

Luke shows how Jesus' mission to initiate the end-time restoration of Israel finds expression in the emergent, Spirit-filled Christian community in Jerusalem.

1:1-5 Introduction: "As I was saying, Theophilus . . ."

Luke introduces this sequel to his Gospel by addressing Theophilus, as he did in the prologue to his Gospel (Luke 1:1-4), indicating that this is a continuation of the same project described there. Literally, the Greek of verse 1 says, "I dealt with all that Jesus *began* to do and teach," implying that Acts will treat what Jesus *continues* to do and teach through the apostolic church. And the phrase "through the holy Spirit" more naturally modifies "chosen"—that is, "after giving instructions to the apostles whom he had chosen through the holy Spirit." For Luke, alone among the Synoptic writers, notes that Jesus chose the Twelve after spending the night in prayer (Luke 6:12-13), which for Luke often precedes a special empowerment by the Spirit (see Luke 3:21, leading to 4:18; Acts 1:14, leading to 2:1-4; and Acts 4:23-31).

As in the Gospel, the centerpiece of Jesus' teaching remains the kingdom of God. Jesus' reference to "the promise of the Father" alludes to at least three passages in the Third Gospel: (1) Luke 11:13: "If you then, who are wicked, know how to give good gifts to your children, how much more will the Father in heaven give the holy Spirit to those who ask him?"; (2) Luke 12:32: "Do not be afraid any longer, little flock, for your Father is pleased to give you the kingdom"; (3) Luke 24:49: "And [behold] I am sending the promise of my Father upon you; but stay in the city until you are clothed with power from on high." The gift of the Spirit at Pentecost will also signal a further manifestation of the kingdom of God already inaugurated in the ministry of Jesus (see Luke 11:20 and 17:21).

Linking this blessing with John the Baptist's prophecy about being "baptiz[ed in] the holy Spirit" (Luke 3:16) also ties this promise to Ezekiel's promise of a cleansing restoration of the people of Israel that will accompany the gift of the divine Spirit (Ezek 36:24-27).

1:6-12 The ascension of Jesus

Since the disciples are Jews who have identified Jesus as their long-awaited Messiah, it is reasonable for them to ask if Jesus will now restore the kingdom to Israel (v. 6). After all, he has been speaking to them for forty days about the kingdom of God, which, in the common expectation of the day, is supposed to be a restoration of the nation to what it was when David reigned a millennium before. Jesus does not deny the appropriateness of the question; he simply refuses to reveal to them the divinely decreed schedule (v. 7). Jesus also reinterprets their implied notion of the kingdom; it is not going to be a matter of nationalism but a new kind of unity empowered by the holy Spirit, as foreshadowed by the new "family" portrayed in Luke 8:1-21.

In this, Jesus echoes what he had said to them on Easter Sunday (Luke 24:49). When he tells them that the Spirit's power will enable them to be his witnesses from Jerusalem "to the ends of the earth" (v. 8), he alludes to Isaiah 49:6, where the Lord tells his Servant that he will not only restore the tribes of Jacob but will also be a light to the nations, "that my salvation will reach to the ends of the earth."

Although the traditional word for the withdrawal of Jesus' physical presence from the apostles is "the ascension," it might be more accurate to

Acts 1

describe Luke's description of this event as an "assumption," since the author portrays it as an act of the Father. To describe this departure, Luke draws upon the biblical traditions about the assumptions of Enoch (Gen 5:23-24; Sir 49:14b) and Elijah (2 Kgs 2:9-11; Sir 48:9). To interpret the event, he adds what have been called "apocalyptic stage props"—the movement upward into the heavens, a cloud as vehicle, and the interpreting angels.

This is Luke's second account of the ascension. The first account, given at the end of Luke's Gospel (24:50-51), sets the event on Easter Sunday and describes Jesus in details that recall the description of the high priest Simon II in Sirach 50:1-24. Like Simon, Jesus' presence occasions worship (Sir 50:17, 22); he raises his hands and pronounces a blessing (Sir 50:20), and this is followed by references to the community's blessing God and rejoicing in the temple (Sir 50:22-23). In so doing, Jesus is acting like the temple priest at the end of the daily Whole-Offering (also called the Tamid, or "regular," service; Exod 29:38-42; Num 2:1-10). And within the Gospel narrative, Jesus is doing what the priest Zechariah was unable to do at the end of the Tamid service, whose incense ritual is the scenario briefly portrayed at the beginning of Luke's Gospel. By alluding in this manner to Sirach 50, Luke was celebrating Jesus the way Ben Sira celebrated Simon II as the climax of his Praise of the Ancestors (Sirach 44–50). For Luke, it is Jesus, not Simon II, who is the climax of Israel's history; and so Luke chooses to end his first volume by portraying Jesus' departure on Easter Sunday with those overtones.

Why, then, does Luke take the liberty to narrate this event so differently as he begins his second volume? Some scholars suggest that in Acts Luke has expanded the time frame of Luke 24 to the round (and biblically symbolic) number forty, in order to associate the ascension closely with the outpouring of the Spirit on the fiftieth day, Pentecost (the Jewish feast of the giving of the Law on Mount Sinai). The apocalyptic stage props serve four purposes: (1) to recall the transfiguration (Luke 9:18-36, another mountain episode, when the disciples could not pray, as now they can); (2) to look forward to the outpouring of the Spirit and the mission that follows; (3) to recount the departure of Jesus in a way that recalls 2 Kings 2:9-12 (another narrative about the transmission of spirit for prophetic succession); and (4) to point toward the final coming (described already in Luke 21:27 as coming "in a cloud," alluding to the cloud imagery of Daniel 7:13, but in the singular, to prepare for Acts 1:9). Thus Luke is able to speak of one reality, the final departure of Jesus from his assembled followers, from two interpretive points of view. Luke 24 alludes to the ascension as a fitting ending of the story of Jesus; Acts 1 narrates the same event as the beginning of the story of the mission of the Church, initiated by the risen Lord and empowered by the gift of the Spirit.

1:13-26 The community gathers to restore "the Twelve" by electing Matthias

The apostles (minus Judas Iscariot) whom Luke had carefully called "the eleven" at Luke 24:33 gather with the "women, and Mary the mother of Jesus, and his brothers" (v. 14). This group, numbered at 120 in verse 15 (notice the multiple of 12), comprises the nucleus of the church that will become the heart of restored Israel in chapter 2.

"The women" no doubt included Mary Magdalene, Joanna, Susanna, and Mary the mother of James, and the many other women who had accompanied Jesus and the Twelve and had "provided for them out of their resources" (Luke 8:3). They are the ones "who had come from Galilee with him" (Luke 23:55) and, coming to anoint the body of Jesus in the tomb, discovered it empty and became the first witnesses to the resurrection (Luke 24:10, 22-23).

His "brothers" are the very ones who, together with Jesus' mother, were last seen in Luke 8:19-21, standing at the edge of a crowd around Jesus when he said, "My mother and my brothers are those who hear the word of God and act on it" (v. 21). Whatever the ambiguity of their status then, now they are at the center of the believing community. Like Jesus after the water immersion by John and before his special anointing by the Spirit (Luke 3:21), the community is immersed in prayer.

Jesus' prayer that Simon Peter, even after denying Jesus, will turn back and strengthen his brothers (Luke 22:32) begins to be fulfilled, as Peter now asserts his leadership (Acts 1:15).

The first agenda item to be addressed by the community is the replacement of Judas Iscariot, who had been "numbered" among the core group (v. 17). Because of the symbolic meaning of Jesus' choice of twelve, indicating the restoration of the twelve tribes of the people of God, "the eleven" (Luke 24:33) must again become the Twelve.

The importance of the number twelve becomes clear when one recalls the words of Jesus at the Last Supper: "And I confer a kingdom on you, just as my Father has conferred one on me, that you may eat and drink at my table in my kingdom; and you will sit on thrones judging the twelve tribes of Israel" (Luke 22:29-30). Whatever Matthew's parallel saying may mean in the context of his Gospel (Matt 19:28), for Luke this is a reference to the leadership of the Twelve in the Jerusalem church after Pentecost. "Judging" here has the sense it has in the book of Judges, which features twelve charismatic leaders who led the tribes of Israel before the time of the monarchy. The reconstituted Twelve will similarly "judge" (that is, exert Spirit-filled leadership among) the reconstituted people of Israel after Pentecost.

The way the words of Peter (1:16-20) and the prayer of the community (1:24-25) speak of Judas's death is full of irony. Abandoning a community that will soon express its unity and detachment from material possessions by selling fields, with no one calling anything his own, Judas invested his blood money in a field ("turned away . . . to his own place," v. 25) and died there in a horrible, isolated death. Whereas Matthew's account of Judas's death (Matt 27:5) parallels the suicide-by-hanging of David's betrayer Ahithophel (2 Sam 17:23), Luke's version reflects the punitive death-by-falling that was Antiochus IV's end (2 Macc 9:12-14).

The community makes sure that Judas's replacement will be a qualified witness to the resurrection by choosing two candidates who were present with Jesus from the baptism of John through the ascension. Then, having done their human best, they put the final choice out of their hands, leaving it up to God through the device of casting lots. Thus Matthias is chosen to restore the Twelve.

2:1-13 The coming of the Spirit

Pentēcostēs (literally "fiftieth") is the Greek name for the Israelite feast of Weeks (*Shavuʿot* in Hebrew). The second of the three classical pilgrim feasts of Israel—Unleavened Bread/Passover, Weeks, and Booths (see Exod 23:14-17; 34:22; Deut 16:16)—the feast of Weeks was called "Fiftieth" in Greek because it occurred seven weeks, or fifty days, after the feast of Unleavened Bread/Passover. Originally an agricultural feast celebrating the end of the grain harvest, Pentecost eventually came to be associated with the giving of the Law at Sinai.

Luke narrates the Pentecost events in words and images that evoke the revelation at Mount Sinai. The reconstituted Twelve (among the 120) are gathered like the twelve tribes at Sinai. The sounds from heaven, the filling of the *whole* house (like the shaking of the *whole* mountain in Exodus 19:18), and the fire recall the theophany (appearance of God) at Sinai. The tongues of fire symbolize the reality that the powerful presence of God (like fire) will find expression in human words, the prophetic ministry of the disciples. The appearance of fire also corresponds to John the Baptist's prediction that Jesus would baptize "with the holy Spirit and fire" (Luke 3:16). In the fuller sweep of the narrative, the parallel between Jesus and Moses is evident in that Jesus ascends with a cloud (1:9) and then mediates the gift of the prophetic word of God to the people (2:4, 11, 18, 33). Thus Luke underscores the fact that on the feast of the giving of the Law (the privileged communication of God's word) comes the end-time gift of the holy Spirit to empower a fresh expression of the divine word in the ministry of the apostles.

The list of nations from which the Jewish pilgrims and converts come symbolizes the future implications of what is happening here. By highlighting this inclusive gathering, Luke proclaims that this is in fact the fulfillment of the expected end-time ingathering of Israel. The Pentecostal gift is destined for Jews first, but then also for the "ends of the earth" (Acts 1:8), "those far off" (2:39; see Isa 57:19).

When Luke says that they "were *confused* because each one heard them speaking in his own language" (v. 6, emphasis added), he appears to be alluding to the story of the tower of Babel (in its Septuagint version, that is, the Greek translation of the Hebrew Old Testament). Whereas Genesis 11 tells of a sinful people who wish to make a name for themselves and are scattered in confusion and lose their ability to communicate (literally "to *hear* one another"), Acts 2 tells of a people of many languages who gather, are "confused" by a new ability to "hear," and are empowered to become a new community as they repent of their sins and call upon the name of the Lord. The likelihood of the allusion becomes even stronger when one notes that the name Babel is rendered *Sygchysis* ("Confusion") in the Septuagint.

2:14-36 Peter explains: the Spirit of God is restoring end-time Israel, and the crucified Jesus is its risen Messiah and Lord!

In this speech of Peter to the festival crowd, Luke employs a kind of biblical interpretation that the Dead Sea Scrolls have taught us to call a *pesher*. The word *pesher* is simply Aramaic for "interpretation." But in the hands of the Essenes, an ascetical community that lived at Qumran, a *pesher* meant understanding a biblical passage as fulfilled in the present or recent history of their own community. Luke now has Peter explain the significance of the Pentecost events in a series of such *peshers*.

After a deft and humorous remark about the enthusiastic behavior of the community (they are not drunk; it's only nine in the morning, v. 15), Peter quotes Joel 3:1-5, joining it with a crucial phrase from the Greek version of Isaiah 2:2 ("in the last days"). He says, in effect, that what has been happening in Jerusalem is the fulfillment of these end-time prophecies. Whereas Israel had experienced a special infusion of God's spirit on an occasional king or prophet, now "in the last days" the gift of the prophetic

Acts 2

spirit has been made available in a surprisingly inclusive way, transcending gender ("your sons and daughters," "my servants and my handmaids") and age ("young," "old," v. 17).

In true *pesher* fashion, Peter proceeds to apply specific phrases to recent and current events. He interprets the phrase "wonders . . . and signs" of verse 19 as the wondrous deeds God had done through Jesus. As his story continues to unfold, it will become clear that Joel's reference to those "who calls on the name of the Lord" will be applied to those who call upon the name of the Lord *Jesus* in Christian faith (see 9:14, 21; 22:16). And so the quotation from Joel 3, fortified by Isaiah 2:2, interprets *what time it is:* it is the inauguration of the long-awaited end-time, begun by God in Jesus and continued by God through the church.

But this outpouring of the Spirit on the community of believers is more than a sign of the end times; it is also a sign of the resurrection and enthronement of Jesus. To make this point, Luke (through Peter) enlists the last third of Psalm 16, which contains the clause ". . . you will not abandon my soul to the nether world, / nor will you suffer your holy one to undergo corruption" (1970 version). With the traditional understanding that all the psalms come from David, Peter argues that since David himself died and therefore *his* flesh obviously "saw corruption," the words must apply to someone else. Add to this the prophecy of Psalm 132:11 that God would set one of David's descendants on his throne, and these texts turn out to apply to the Messiah *in his resurrection*. It is in this sense, as risen king of restored Israel, that Jesus can be called "the Anointed One" ("Messiah" in Hebrew, "Christ" in Greek).

Then, to show how the risen Jesus is entitled also to the name "Lord" (used in the quotation from Joel 3 in Acts 2:21), Peter enlists the first verse of Psalm 110: "The Lord said to my Lord, 'Sit at my right hand / till I make your enemies your footstool'" (1970 version). The final verse of the speech (2:36) summarizes the whole speech succinctly.

2:37-41 The response to the proclamation

When the people ask Peter what they should do, he invites them to repent and be baptized in the name of the Lord Jesus (which, in the light of the preceding speech, means belief in the resurrection of Jesus). And when Peter promises that they will receive the "gift of the holy Spirit," we now understand that the events of Acts 2 are the fulfillment of John the Baptist's promise that one mightier than he would baptize "in the holy Spirit and fire" (Luke 3:16; see also Acts 1:5). Mission to the Gentiles is already glimpsed when Peter joins "you and . . . your children" with "and to all *those far off*" (Isaiah's phrase for

Gentiles in Isaiah 57:19, emphasis added). Jewish and Gentile Christians alike will qualify as those ". . . whom the LORD shall call" (Joel 3:5).

2:42-47 The first Christian community

Although the portrait of the *koinōnia*, or communal life, of the Jerusalem Christian community (vv. 42-47) has often been used to illustrate the ideals of vowed religious life, Luke clearly means it to portray the Christian community of Jerusalem as restored Israel. Each of the details is powerfully suggestive, describing who they are and what they are about.

The "teaching of the apostles" to which they devote themselves no doubt refers to the teaching of Jesus and the kind of biblical interpretation regarding Jesus just displayed in Peter's Pentecost speech. Since "the breaking of the bread" (v. 42) refers to the practice of the Lord's Supper, "the prayers" are likely the traditional prayers of Jewish life, such as the *Shema* (Deut 6:4-9; note the reference to the Christians regularly gathering in the temple area in verse 46, presumably for prayer, as in 3:1). That the apostles are said to perform "wonders and signs" (v. 43) reinforces the continuity between their ministry and that of Jesus, just described as commended by God with "wonders and signs" in verse 22. Their sense of mutual service (see Luke 22:25-27) leads them spontaneously to share their possessions, even to sell property to meet one another's needs (v. 45). That they continue to meet in the temple area is consistent with the description, at the end of Luke's Gospel, that "they were continually [or regularly] in the temple praising God" (Luke 24:53). The Jewish Christians' allegiance to Jesus as Lord and Messiah has not meant severance from the life of the temple.

Finally, notice that verse 47b describes this Christian communal life as "being saved"—an explication of a phrase from Joel quoted in verse 21 ("everyone *shall be saved* who calls on the name of the Lord"; emphasis added). The awe (*phobos*, literally "fear") that comes upon everyone is reminiscent of the fear that God sent upon the nations as they witnessed the progress of the Exodus and Conquest (Exod 15:16; 23:27; Deut 2:25; 11:25; 32:25; Josh 2:9). This awe is a continuation of the people's response to the new Exodus already begun in the story of Jesus (see Luke 1:12, 65; 2:9; 5:26; 7:16; 8:37; 21:26).

This cameo picture of the life of the Jerusalem Christian community reflects the fulfillment of the jubilee theme struck in the quotation of Isaiah 61:2 at Luke 4:19.

3:1-26 The healing of the man born lame and Peter's explanation

Having referred to "many wonders and signs worked through the apostles" (2:43), Luke now describes in detail one such sign—the healing of the lame man at the temple gate. As in the case of the Pentecost events, he also provides a speech that interprets the significance of that sign.

Consistent with the statements that the disciples, after the resurrection, were regularly in the temple (Luke 24:53) and that they continued to meet in the temple precincts (Acts 2:46), Luke shows Peter and John going up to the temple "at the ninth hour, the hour of prayer," that is, at the time of the regular afternoon Tamid service (see Luke 1:10 and Acts 10:30), what we call 3 P.M.

Why Luke foregrounds this particular healing becomes evident when we attend to the details. What unfolds here interrupts routine. The friends of the beggar carry the immobile man and prop him up at the gate, a daily drill for them. And Peter and John are entering the temple precincts for their customary participation in the mid-afternoon liturgy (see Luke 24:53). When the beggar, apparently without looking, begs for alms (*eleēmosynē*), Peter commands him to look at them. Gaining his attention, he commands him to walk, using language that contrasts the power of silver and gold with the power of the name of Jesus. Something astoundingly new breaks the routine of daily begging.

In the Greek Bible (the Septuagint, whose conventional sign is LXX), *eleēmosynē* sometimes means "alms," but more often it means "the mercy of God" (as in LXX Isa 1:27 and LXX Ps 23:5). The original readers of Luke's Greek would have been aware of a kind of pun here: the beggar was expecting *eleēmosynē* in the sense of mere alms; what he receives is a surprising *eleēmosynē*, the mercy of God in the form of liberation from lameness.

Luke emphasizes the fact that the man not only stands and walks—he *leaps*, a detail mentioned *twice* in verse 8. This stress on leaping recalls the only other place where the Bible mentions the lame leaping, Isaiah 35:6: "Then will the lame leap like a stag." Now it becomes clear why Luke chooses precisely this healing as the one to highlight in the context of his description of the birth of the church. Isaiah 35:5-6 is a prophetic description of the restoration of Israel, now understood as fulfilled in the Jerusalem messianic community.

Just as the Fourth Gospel, where faith in Jesus is the deepest kind of seeing and thus we are *all* born blind in that sense, highlights the healing of a man born *blind*, so Luke highlights this healing of a man born *lame*.

What the healing account itself began, with its allusion to Isaiah 35 in the language of leaping, the speech continues in its further interpretation of the healing, using still more references to the Scriptures.

First, who did it? When the crowds attribute the healing to the apostles, Peter announces that this was the work of "the God of Abraham, of Isaac, and of Jacob," who has "glorified his servant Jesus." Since this way of referring to God echoes the call of Moses in Exodus 3:6, Peter may be implying that this healing is a sign that God is working a new Exodus through the long-awaited prophet-like-Moses, who is Jesus (recall the "wonders and signs" language of 2:19, 22).

This identification of Jesus is further underscored by the *pesher* citation of Deuteronomy 18:15, 18-19 at verses 22-23. Regarding the person who fails to respond to ("hear") God's words spoken by that prophet, Luke replaces Deuteronomy's vague warning ("I myself will make him answer for it") by substituting Leviticus's stiffer sanction for failing to participate in the liturgy of the Day of Atonement (Lev 23:29): "[that person] shall be cut off from his people." Notice that, as Luke understands it, Jews who accept Jesus as the Messiah do not divorce themselves from the people of Israel; rather, they constitute the true Israel, and those who fail to accept Jesus are, in effect, excommunicated.

This healing is also a sign of the end times: "*All* the prophets who spoke, from Samuel and those afterwards, also announced *these days*" (v. 24, emphasis added). Further, this healing is a sign that what is unfolding here in Jerusalem is a fulfillment of God's ancient promise to Abraham: "In your offspring all the families of the earth shall be blessed" (v. 25, alluding to Gen 22:18; and see 12:3; 26:4). In the final verse of the speech, Luke makes a clever play on the words "raise up" that were just heard in the quotation from Deuteronomy 18:15: God has indeed "raised up" his servant Jesus, not simply in the sense of commissioning him but also in the new sense of resurrection from the dead. Now the risen Lord is working through the likes of Peter and John, offering new opportunities for conversion to the life of the Spirit.

4:1-22 The temple authorities confront the apostles on the question of authority

The spectacle of Jesus' followers teaching crowds in the temple precincts ("Solomon's Portico," 3:11) alarms the temple authorities. Not only are these Galileans usurping their teaching authority with the people, they are proclaiming in Jesus "the resurrection of the dead," which, for the Sadducees, was one of the false doctrines of the Pharisees. The Sadducees held as true only what could be found in a strict reading of the Pentateuch (the first five books of the Old Testament), and they found no teaching about immortality or resurrection in those five scrolls (see Luke 20:27-40).

When the rulers and elders gather to meet as the Sanhedrin, they raise the same question they had earlier raised with Jesus after he had driven out the sellers and continued teaching daily in the temple area (Luke 20:1-8), namely, the question of authority. This time their question is about the power that healed the lame man: "By what power or by what name have you done this?" (v. 7). It is the same issue raised by the healing and addressed by Peter in the previous speech (3:12-13). And the answer is the same here. The healing was an act of God done in the name of Jesus; the healing showed that the Sanhedrin's judgment (Jesus was an offender deserving death) has been overruled by the "higher court" of God, as confirmed by the resurrection of Jesus.

Peter's empowerment by the holy Spirit fulfills Jesus' promise to his disciples in Luke 12:11-12. To drive home that this victory of God's power and authority is greater than any earthly authority, Peter cites a favorite psalm used by the church to celebrate God's action in the death and resurrection of Jesus (see Luke 20:17 and 1 Pet 2:7). Paraphrasing Psalm 118:22, Peter says to the assembly, "He is 'the stone rejected by you, the builders, which has become the cornerstone.'" In the context of Psalm 118, the rejected stone refers to Israel, cast aside by imperial power yet rescued by God, who will use it as a cornerstone. This verse serves wonderfully as a Christian *pesher* because it is not only an apt celebration of the death and resurrection of Jesus, but it also evokes the image of the end-time temple interpreted as the Christian community.

What is more, the theme of the psalm—that God's power to *save* is greater than imperial power—provides the background for Peter's wordplay on the theme of healing/saving. The Greek word for "heal" and "save" in verses 9 and 12 is *sōzō*, which can mean any aspect of the whole range of rescuing, from physical healing to eschatological salvation. In verse 9 it denotes the physical healing of the paralytic, whereas in verse 12 it apparently refers to ultimate salvation. Thus the physical cure of the man born lame becomes not only a sign of the restoration of Israel but also of the full salvation of all who believe: "There is no *salvation* through anyone else, nor is there any other name under heaven given to the human race by which we are to be *saved*" (v. 12, emphasis added).

Although that verse is sometimes applied to the uniqueness of Jesus within the context of religious pluralism, a different context may be operating here. For an audience familiar with the claim of Roman emperors to the title of *sōtēr* ("Savior"), the mention of *sōtēria* ("salvation") suggests a contrast between the imperial power that controls the temple officials and the divine power working through Jesus. As in Psalm 118, true power and authority come not from worldly empire but from God's power, here exercised in the name of the risen Lord Jesus.

When the Sanhedrin orders the apostles "never again to speak to anyone in this name" (v. 17), Peter and John say, "Whether it is right in the sight of God for us to obey you rather than God, you be the judges." It is a clear assertion that these religious officials have lost whatever religious authority they had. The behavior of the Sanhedrin has shown that these men are more interested in preserving their own control than in serving the authority of God. That the healing of the beggar at the temple gate is "a remarkable sign" they readily admit, but they choose to ignore its significance. Luke underscores the public nature of this event in the closing statement in the episode: "For the man on whom this sign of healing had been done was over forty years old" (and therefore well known to frequenters of the Temple Mount).

4:23-31 The prayer of the community and God's response

Luke portrays Peter and John returning and reporting to "their own" (Luke could mean anything from the Twelve, to the 120 of Acts 1:15, to the 5000 "men" [*andres*] mentioned at 4:4) what the chief priests and elders had told them. What follows is either (a) a miracle of choral speaking, in which this large group improvises a *pesher* interpretation in unison or (b) a prayer-speech that historian Luke composes (in *pesher* style) to convey how the early community understood persecution and responded to it in their prayer and action. The latter seems more likely.

This episode presents us with one of the most striking examples of *pesher* interpretation in the entire New Testament. Luke introduces it by having the group invoke God as creator (v. 24b: "Sovereign Lord, maker of heaven and earth and the sea and all that is in them"). Then they quote the first two verses of Psalm 2. The community then proceeds to apply the references to persons and actions of the initial verses in Psalm 2 to the actors and happenings of their recent experience in Jerusalem. "The Gentiles" are of course the Romans. "The peoples"—in the context of the psalm, a parallel expression for the Gentiles—now becomes "the peoples of Israel" (note that Luke retains the plural, "peoples," to echo the wording of the psalm). As for "the kings of the earth," Herod Antipas was the king before whom Jesus was arraigned (see Luke 23:6-12), and Pilate was the representative of the "king" of the Roman Empire. The "rulers" are the Sanhedrin leaders (see vv. 5 and 8) who had also just forbidden them to speak any more about Jesus. And they had indeed "gathered in this city against your holy servant Jesus whom God had *anointed*" ("christed" catches the overtones of the Greek).

When we hear "And now, Lord, take note of their threats" (v. 29), knowing the thrust of the rest of Psalm 2, we might expect something like "shatter

Acts 4

them like an earthen dish" (Ps 2:9b). Instead, we hear quite the opposite: "Enable your servants to speak your word with all boldness, as you stretch forth [your] hand to heal, and signs and wonders are done through the name of your holy servant Jesus" (vv. 29-30). In response to the official crucifixion of Jesus and the present resistance of the rulers, they pray for empowerment to continue the mission of Jesus in word and work, especially preaching and healing. The divine response to their prayer (v. 31) is the "mini-Pentecost" that follows.

4:32–5:11 Life in the Christian community

Acts 4:32-35 provides another cameo picture of the Jerusalem Christian community. With Acts 2:42-47, it makes a frame around the intervening episodes, which exemplify how God has worked through the leadership of the apostles (Peter and John) to continue Jesus' preaching and healing ministry. The description of the community as being "of one heart and mind" and holding everything in common embodies the Greek ideal of friendship. And the statement that "there was no needy person among them" alludes to the Hebrew ideal of covenant justice expressed in Deuteronomy 15:4. The jubilee note struck here echoes the jubilee theme of the passage from Isaiah 61 that Jesus read at his debut in the Nazareth synagogue (Luke 4:18-19). This spontaneous "faith sharing" of material goods to meet the needs of all is mediated through the leadership, a fact that is signified by their laying the proceeds of real estate sales "at the feet of the apostles" (v. 37).

To show that even from the beginning it was a struggle to live out the ideals of Christian community life, Luke now presents examples. First he offers a good example in Joseph Barnabas, who did it right (4:36-37). Then comes a dramatic account of a bad example, the deceptive behavior of Ananias and Sapphira (5:1-11).

The reference to Barnabas introduces one who will emerge as a key player in the Jerusalem Christian community and its mission. (So important does this coworker of Paul become that the second-century *Epistle of Barnabas* was attributed to him.)

The sin of Ananias and Sapphira lies not so much in possessiveness as in their deception. As Peter himself grants, the property was theirs to keep or sell as they wished. But pretending that they were donating the whole proceeds, when in fact they were holding back part—this was nothing less than lying to the holy Spirit! Ironically, Luke notes that Sapphira falls dead "at the feet" of Peter as punishment for deceptively laying "at the feet of the apostles" only part of the property proceeds from the sale of their property. What is done to the community is done to the Spirit of God. The whole episode echoes another famous holding back, that of Achan, who, after the battle of Jericho, kept for himself some of the banned goods (Josh 7).

5:12-16 Another summary

The Jesus group continues to assemble in the temple precincts (see 3:11). And the "signs and wonders" that God had done through Jesus (2:22), for the continuation of which they had prayed (4:30), continue to happen through the apostles. As contact with the mere tassel of Jesus' garment was enough to occasion healing in his ministry (Luke 8:43-44), now people seek even Peter's passing shadow as a medium of healing and deliverance from evil spirits.

5:17-42 Testing the mission: the work of God or human beings?

With divine help, the apostles move from prison to preaching. Strikingly, when the angel of the Lord opens the prison gates for them, he instructs them to go and take their stand in the temple and tell the people all about "this life." Like their Master, who entered the temple not simply to expel the vendors but also to take his stand there and teach the people daily (Luke 19:45–21:38; and see Luke 2:46, where the twelve-year-old Jesus teaches in the temple), the apostles, too, continue the mission in what remains for them their sacred center, the temple area. Like Jesus, they *occupy* the temple precincts as the right place to do God's will by teaching the people (5:21, 42; see Luke 20:1).

This miraculous "jail break" strikes the theme of the unhindered word that will be reprised in the great escape of Acts 12. Indeed, the final word of the book is *akōlytōs* ("without hindrance"), describing Paul's preaching the kingdom of God and the Lord Jesus Christ even while under house arrest (28:31).

When they are accused of disobeying orders, Peter and the apostles repeat what Peter and John had said once before to the Sanhedrin, namely, that when divine and human orders collide, they must obey God rather than human beings (v. 29; see 4:19-20). To justify this response, they cite the ruling of a "higher court." Drawing upon what will become a traditional Christian application of Scripture, they announce that in the resurrection God has overruled the curse of crucifixion (death by "hanging . . . on a tree"; see Deut 21:23 and Gal 3:13) by exalting Jesus to his "right hand" (Ps 110:1). And the purpose of this is to renew the people of God, Israel.

Then comes the famous intervention of Rabbi Gamaliel, whom Paul will name as his mentor in Acts 22:3. Citing the short-lived movements of other would-be messiahs—Theudas and Judas the Galilean—Gamaliel argues that obedience to false prophets comes to nothing; so let (divinely guided) history show whether this Jesus movement is of God or not. The implication is that Jesus will be shown to be another false prophet. The Sanhedrin chooses to listen to a man, Gamaliel, rather than to the evidence of God demonstrated in the signs and wonders done through the apostles. At the same time, Gamaliel's wait-and-see approach exemplifies the kind of openness that led to others of the house of Israel eventually accepting Jesus as their Messiah.

Acts 6:1-7 Crisis and solution: choosing the Seven

No sooner had the Jerusalem church dealt with challenges from the outside than it had to deal with an internal conflict—a quarrel between "Hellenists" and "Hebrews" regarding an alleged neglect of the widows among the Hellenists. The "Hellenists" are best understood as Greek-speaking Jews, probably people who grew up in the Diaspora (Jewish communities scattered outside Palestine beginning after the Babylonian Exile) and later immigrated to Judea. "Hebrews," then, would be indigenous, Aramaic-speaking Jews. We have evidence, even as far back as the Maccabees (ca. 170 B.C.), that there had long been tension between the Jews who had taken on the language and even some of the customs of the Hellenistic world, on the one hand, and the more traditional Jews who preferred to speak Aramaic and avoid Hellenistic ways, on the other. This passage lets us know that the infant Christian community of Jerusalem included Jews from both subgroups and that becoming Christian did not automatically remove the "liberal" or "conservative" baggage that they brought with them.

Luke informs us that the community had set up a daily dole (of food, presumably) to take care of the needy among them, especially widows. But the widows of the Greek-speaking group were somehow being neglected. Luke does not mention the cause of the neglect. (Was it a combination of scarcity and prejudice—the ["Hebrew"] Twelve favoring their own kind? Or were they too busy to oversee the distribution properly?) Whatever the source of the problem, the Twelve apply a familiar practical solution: they increase the staff. Too busy with the service (*diakonia*) of the word to tie up their time with serving at table, they call the entire community together (here called "disciples" for the first time in Acts) and charge them to select seven good men to carry out this other *diakonia*. That the seven chosen all have Greek names suggests a kind of affirmative action on the part of the community: they choose members of the Greek-speaking group, thereby assuring that the neglect of the Hellenists' widows would be remedied.

Although the word for the service (of both word and table) is *diakonia*, the Seven are not called *diakonoi* (from which comes the English word "deacons"). Moreover, the service performed by Martha (Luke 10:40), the Twelve (Acts 1:12, 25), and Peter and Silas (12:25) is also termed *diakonia*, indicating that the term has not yet acquired its technical sense. Still, although Luke is probably not describing the creation of the office of deacon here, this episode points toward the later three-tier structure of bishop-priests-deacons reflected in the writing of Ignatius of Antioch. For that reason, this passage has traditionally been associated with the church office of deacon.

This freeing up of the Twelve leads to a continuing rapid growth of the church, even attracting some of the temple priests to the fold.

6:8-15 Stephen accused

Curiously, after Stephen has been commissioned as one of the Seven to "serve at table," thereby freeing the apostles for the service of the word, Luke proceeds to show Stephen engaged in precisely that apostolic work. Like the Twelve (2:43; 4:30; 5:12) and like Jesus before them (2:22), he is filled with power to do "wonders and signs" (6:8). What Luke describes is more a matter of prophetic succession than delegation: Jesus to the Twelve, then the Twelve to the Seven, exemplified by Stephen. Luke will indicate in Stephen's speech that the line of succession reaches back to Moses and the patriarchs, even as it reaches forward to the church of Luke's day (and ours). The same Spirit that empowered Jesus and the Twelve to preach and heal empowers Stephen to do the same.

As in the case of Jesus and the Twelve, the exercise of that prophetic ministry meets opposition, arrest, and a hasty "trial." Whereas Luke had omitted any mention of false witnesses in his very brief account of the Sanhedrin's investigation of Jesus (Luke 22:66-71), as he also omits in his presentation of the crucifixion Mark's taunt of the head-wagging passers-by about destroying and building the temple, he does introduce here some false witness against Stephen. Like the witnesses at the trial of Jesus in Mark and Matthew, they accuse their adversary of threatening the holy place (the temple). They also make him out to be an enemy of the Law of Moses. The discourse that follows in the next chapter will do much more than simply rebut those charges. It will show how the Law and the temple reach fulfillment in Christian life and worship.

7:1-53 Stephen addresses the Sanhedrin

In Luke's Gospel the risen Jesus spoke to his disciples about the fulfillment of things written about him in the Law of Moses, the prophets, and the psalms (Luke 24:27, 44). Our author has already shown us how the events of Jesus' life, especially his death and resurrection (Luke 24:46), fulfill the Law of Moses (the Torah, or first five books of the Bible). Peter's speech in Acts 3:22 gave one example: Jesus is the prophet-like-Moses whom God would "raise up," alluding to Deuteronomy 18:15.

Now, in the first half of Stephen's speech, the longest speech in Acts (more than twice as long as Peter's Pentecost speech), we hear Torah narrative applied to Jesus at length. Without explicitly mentioning the name of Jesus Messiah—"the righteous one" at verse 52 being as close as he comes—Stephen retells the stories of Abraham, Joseph, and Moses in ways that point to Jesus' death and resurrection and to the post-Easter church.

Just as the canticles of Mary and Zechariah celebrated the conception of Jesus and the birth of John the Baptist as leading to the fulfillment of God's promises to Abraham (Luke 2:55 and 73), Stephen tells of God's promise to Abraham that he would give the land to his descendents through a process that would entail rescue from slavery "in a land not their own" (v. 6) to freedom to "worship me in this place" (v. 7). In that last phrase Luke alludes to God's promise to *Moses* regarding worship at *Sinai* (Exod 3:12) and makes *this place* refer to *Jerusalem*. The remainder of Acts will portray true worship centered on the risen Jesus (recall that the disciples had worshiped the risen Lord on Easter Sunday near Bethany, Luke 24:52).

The brief account of the Joseph story then serves to illustrate how God begins to fulfill the promises to Abraham by rescuing his descendants from famine by means of a person who was first rejected and later emerges as their savior. The brother they had sold to slave traders eventually rose to become a prime minister whose grain reserve program saved their lives.

This pattern of God working through a rejected-one-become-savior is elaborated more fully in the rendition of the story of Moses that follows. And here Luke chooses words even more carefully to highlight the parallels between Moses and Jesus. The young Moses was "powerful in his words and deeds" (v. 22; see Luke 24:19 regarding Jesus). Like Jesus, Moses was misunderstood by his kin (v. 25). As Moses was asked, "Who appointed you ruler and judge over us?" (v. 27), so too was Jesus (Luke 12:14). Luke then becomes more richly specific in verses 35-36: "This Moses whom they had rejected . . . God sent as [both] ruler and deliverer. . . . This man led them out, performing *wonders and signs* in the land of Egypt, at the Red Sea, and in the desert for forty years" (emphasis added). Note how Acts uses the phrase "wonders and signs," first found in the quotation of Joel in Acts 2:19, both for what God did through Jesus (Acts 2:22) and for what God now does through the apostles (2:43; 4:30).

If readers have not grasped the connection with Jesus by this time, our author makes it crystal-clear with the reference to Deuteronomy 18:15 at verse 37: "God will raise up for you, from among your own kinsfolk, a prophet like me." That this applies to Jesus was already established in Peter's speech (Acts 3:22).

Thus far Stephen has dealt with the charge that he speaks against the Law; indeed, he has shown how the message about Jesus fulfills the thrust of the narratives about the ancestors and Moses. Now the speech takes up the matter of the temple, which this discourse takes to be really a question of what makes for true worship. If God promised Abraham that Israel would come to "worship . . . in this place" (v. 7), how has that promise been fulfilled? Stephen says that the people have been disobedient in the matter of worship from the beginning. First there was the idolatry of the golden calf (vv. 39-41). Then God gave them over to worship of the gods of the nations, as exemplified in the Greek version of Amos 5:25, which Luke applies to the whole period before their exile in Babylon by changing Amos's reference to exile beyond Damascus to exile beyond Babylon. The speech makes the case that the move beyond the divinely mandated portable tent of testimony (the desert tabernacle, the place of the divine presence) to the fixed and solid temple built by Solomon was misunderstood by some in Israel as a way of magically confining God to that space. That misunderstanding was a step in the direction of idolatry and an attempt to box God, who "does not *dwell* in houses made by human hands," as illustrated by the quotation from Isaiah 66:1-2 (emphasis added).

By this time in the speech, Stephen has moved from a story about "*our* ancestors" (v. 39) to one about "*your* ancestors" (v. 52, emphasis added). His climactic word to those who have accused him of speaking against the Law is to accuse them of not observing it themselves.

7:54-60 The martyrdom of Stephen

If the charges brought against Stephen had suggested a parallel with the synoptic tradition of the trial of Jesus, the death of Stephen clearly and powerfully mirrors the death of Jesus—and also responds to the question of true worship. When Stephen announces a vision of the heavens opening and the Son of Man standing at the right hand of God (v. 56), his adversaries take him outside of the city to kill him, just as they did to his Master. And just as Jesus commended his spirit to the Father, Stephen can pray, "Lord Jesus, receive my spirit" (v. 59; see Luke 23:46). As Jesus prayed to God to forgive his crucifiers, so Stephen prays to *Jesus*, "Lord, do not hold this sin against them" (v. 60).

Acts 7

Two themes shine through this narrative: (1) the follower of Jesus relives the story of Jesus, sometimes quite literally; (2) Stephen answers the question about true worship with his prayer to Jesus as Lord and with the giving up of his life.

8:1-3 Saul (Paul) spearheads the persecution of the church

Saul, first mentioned as minding the cloaks of Stephen's stoners at 7:58, is said to approve this extra-judicial execution (8:1), which triggers a persecution of the church in Jerusalem. Thus begins a scattering of "Jews for Jesus" throughout Judea and Samaria. The note that the apostles were exempt from the persecution suggests that it was the Hellenists who are scattered.

THE MISSION IN JUDEA AND SAMARIA
Acts 8:4–9:43

In the remainder of chapter 8 and all of chapter 9, Luke presents Philip evangelizing the margins of Israel among the Samaritans and with the Ethiopian eunuch. Then comes the conversion/call of Saul on the road to Damascus and, finally, Peter's work among his fellow Jews, just before his dramatic experience with Cornelius's household draws him into mission to the Gentiles. In germ, these two chapters describe the major transitions announced in Acts 1:8: "You will be my witnesses in Jerusalem, throughout Judea and Samaria, and to the ends of the earth." Philip, Saul (Paul), and Peter take the last three steps.

8:4-25 Philip the evangelist versus Simon the magician

We saw that Stephen was a mouthpiece for Lukan Christology (the doctrines of the person and works of Christ) and also an example of the imitation of Christ. Now another member of the Seven, Philip, enters the scene as another kind of example. The first episode featuring Philip demonstrates how the Christian mission extends beyond Judea into the realm of the "heretical" (from the Jewish point of view) Samaritans and how that mission trumps the pagan magic typified by Simon Magus.

To describe the outreach of the mission beyond Jerusalem to the margins of the people of Israel, Luke five times uses his favorite word for that—*euangelizomai*, from which we get our word "evangelize." Luke found it in his Greek Bible, especially in Isaiah (40:9; 52:7; 60:6; 61:1), where the prophet speaks of announcing the coming saving power of God. Luke employs the word to describe the preaching of angels (Luke 1:19; 2:10), of John the Baptist (3:18), of Jesus (4:18 [Isa 61:1]; 4:43; 7:22; 8:1; 9:6; 16:16; 20:1), of the apostles

(Acts 5:42); and in the present episode, the word describes the mission of the whole dispersed church (8:4), of Philip (vv. 12, 35, 40), and of Peter and John (v. 25). It is all a matter of telling what God is doing.

After describing the preaching and healing of Philip in words that recall the work of Jesus and the apostles (8:7), Luke speaks of the conversion of one Simon. Though he had gained an enthusiastic following as a magician before Philip's arrival, even he is converted by Philip's evangelizing (vv. 9-13). (Our word "simony," denoting the purchase or sale of spiritual things, derives from Simon Magus, alluding to his misguided attempt to buy the power to mediate the holy Spirit [vv. 18-19].)

Curiously, only when the apostles Peter and John come down from Jerusalem to pray for and lay hands on the Samaritan converts do they receive the holy Spirit (vv. 14-17). Luke here distinguishes between baptism "in the name of the Lord Jesus" and this infusion of the Spirit. A similar distinction will be made later—but in reversed order (Spirit baptism, then baptism in the name of Jesus)—in the conversion of Cornelius and his household (10:44-49).

Though some Christian groups have turned this narrative distinction into a doctrine of two baptisms (water baptism and Spirit baptism), Luke, followed by the Catholic tradition, presents as normative Peter's description of baptism and reception of the holy Spirit as one unified event (2:38). Where Luke narratively separates Spirit and baptism, he seems to be making a special point in each case. Here the point is to underscore the privileged role the apostles have in affirming the mission to the Samaritans through their mediation of the Spirit.

8:26-40 Philip and the Ethiopian eunuch

In this episode Philip is drawn, by both an angel of the Lord and the Spirit of the Lord, even further toward the margins of the house of Israel. The fact that the next candidate for conversion and baptism is a eunuch has important prophetic resonances. For example, Isaiah 56:3-5, part of a vision of the restoration of Israel that Jesus quoted in his takeover of the temple (Luke 19:46), speaks of eunuchs finding a home and an imperishable name in the coming restoration. Since Luke will treat the later conversion of the centurion and his family as the breakthrough to the Gentiles, our author would have us understand the eunuch as a convert to Judaism. Yet his ethnicity as an Ethiopian is important to Luke's theme of the universality of the church's mission.

The text that the eunuch is reading aloud (v. 28) is Isaiah 53:7-8, from the famous fourth Servant Song, which Luke quotes only here in his two

Acts 8

volumes. It is important to note that this is the Septuagint version, whose wording here differs significantly from the Hebrew. The wording of the Old Greek is peculiarly open to being understood as applicable to the death and resurrection of Jesus. The rendering of Luke Timothy Johnson, in his *Acts of the Apostles* (Collegeville, Minn.: Liturgical Press, 1992), illustrates this well: "As a sheep led to the slaughter, and as silent as a lamb before its shearer, so he does not open his mouth. In his lowliness his judgment was taken away. Who will recite his generation? For his life is taken away from the earth." The application of this text to the childless Jesus would have a special appeal for the eunuch. Jesus' "generation" after he was "taken away" in resurrection is his growing band of post-Easter disciples, now including this eunuch.

Though he went to Jerusalem "to worship" (v. 27), as a eunuch he was explicitly prevented from entering beyond the Court of the Gentiles (see Deuteronomy 23:2, where eunuchs are banned from "the community of the Lord"). How different here, where his reception of the gospel of Jesus leads him to ask, "What is to prevent my being baptized?" Thus the one banned will indeed become a member of the community of the Lord.

Along with illustrating the spread of the word (1:8), this episode demonstrates the process of interpreting the Scriptures that Luke surely had in mind when he spoke of Jesus explaining to the disciples at Emmaus what referred to him in all the Scriptures "beginning with Moses and all the prophets" (Luke 24:27).

9:1-19 The conversion and commissioning of Saul

Although this key episode in the history of the church is traditionally called the "conversion" of Paul, it is not a conversion in the sense of changing from one religion to another, for Saul/Paul does not cease to be a Jew; he moves from being a Jew who persecutes the growing "Jews for Jesus" group to being a Jew for Jesus himself.

Is this a conversion in another sense, namely, turning from an immoral life to a moral one? Even in his persecution of the church, Paul is zealously pursuing what he understands to be the will of God. Yet Luke describes Saul as "breathing murderous threats," which is at odds with the commandment against murder. And Luke's description of the martyrdom of Stephen (7:54–8:1) showed Saul minding the cloaks of those performing the "extralegal" stoning and "consenting to this execution."

Further, the change from persecutor to promoter is surely some kind of transformation and reorientation. This has led some to call what happens to Paul a prophetic commissioning, for he is stopped in his tracks to be sent on a mission. Maybe it is best to say that this is both a conversion and a commissioning.

Luke describes the event as a theophany. It parallels the encounter of Moses with the divine Presence in Exodus 3. Like Moses, Saul is startled with a manifestation of brightness, hears his name called twice, hears the voice identify itself, and receives a commission.

The revelation that he receives, "I am Jesus, whom you are persecuting," is a striking summation of a major theme of Paul's letters: the identification of the risen Lord with his church, which Paul elaborates in his treatment of the Christian community as the body of Christ, especially in Romans and 1 Corinthians.

When Paul addresses the voice in the vision as *Kyrie*, it most likely means "Lord" in the full sense of the appellation. The identification of that Lord as Jesus, then, parallels Stephen's calling Jesus "Lord" (7:59). That this title recurs twelve more times in this chapter suggests that Luke would have us understand this beginning of the mission to the Gentiles as a special manifestation of the lordship of the risen Jesus. For references to this experience in Paul's own words, see 1 Corinthians 9:1 ("Have I not seen Jesus our Lord?"); 2 Cor 4:4:6; Gal 1:12.

To this paradox of the enemy of the Christian movement becoming its greatest promoter, Luke adds another: when his eyes were opened, he could see nothing (v. 8). Though he became temporarily blind, he really did have, in a deeper sense, an "eye-opening" experience. The cure from that physical blindness that accompanies his baptism underscores his spiritual enlightenment. Luke will elaborate on this imagery in the later retellings of this episode in chapters 22 and 26.

Notice that our author has four different and suggestive ways of naming the growing church in this passage: "the disciples of the Lord" (v. 1); "the Way" (v. 2); "all who call upon your name" (v. 14, echoing Joel 2:32 quoted in Acts 2:21; and see Romans 10:13); and "the holy ones" (v. 13, a Jewish term for Israel set apart for the Lord's service, here appropriated by Christian Jews, as Paul will do in his letters).

9:19b-31 Saul preaches in Damascus and visits Jerusalem

The adversary turned promoter begins his apostolic life right there in Damascus by preaching in the local synagogues that Jesus is the long-awaited Christ (Greek for the Hebrew term *Messiah*, or "Anointed One"). When Luke says that Saul proclaimed Jesus as the Son of God, he probably means this title in the same sense, that is, as Messiah (see Psalm 2:7). Later theology will apply it in the full sense of divinity, as in John 1:1, 18.

Acts 9

How Saul "will have to suffer" for the name of Jesus (v. 16) is soon demonstrated in the plot by the Jews of Damascus against his life (v. 23) and then in the similar efforts of the Roman Hellenists (v. 29). In Rome, it takes Barnabas's testimony to render him credible and acceptable to the local disciples. As in the case of Philip (8:14-17), the mission of the one whom later tradition will call "the Apostle" needs the seal of approval from the Jerusalem leadership. This Roman sojourn is possibly the visit to which Paul refers, with a different emphasis, in Galatians 1:18-20.

In contrast to the cloak-and-dagger escapades that characterized Paul's debut as an apostle, the one-line summary at verse 31 describes the growth of the church throughout the entire area as peaceful and abundant.

9:32-43 Peter heals at Lydda and Joppa

Just how that growth mentioned in the summary of verse 31 occurred is illustrated by two episodes from Peter's healing ministry. Visiting a Christian community ("the holy ones") in the plains town of Lydda, he heals a long-term paralytic named Aeneas. The sight of old Aeneas healed moves "all the inhabitants" to "turn to the Lord" (now shorthand for coming to Christian faith). Another exemplary disciple, Tabitha, falls sick and dies, apparently prematurely. Her resuscitation at Peter's command occasions the conversion of many in Joppa.

Commentators have noticed that the language Luke uses to describe these healings is reminiscent of the Deuteronomic historian's description of the wonder-working of Elijah and Elisha (1 Kgs 17:17-24; 2 Kgs 4:31-37). This further underscores Luke's presentation of the disciples as prophetic successors of Jesus, just as he is the prophet-like-Moses. They are not, however, successors in the sense of replacing Jesus; their ministry is an expression of the risen Lord Jesus working through them.

THE INAUGURATION OF THE GENTILE MISSION
Acts 10:1–15:35

Although Luke knows of others who brought the gospel to Gentiles (see the reference to Cypriot and Cyrenean Christians who evangelized Greeks in Antioch at 11:20), he chooses to focus on the experience of Peter, who was divinely led in this direction in dramatic ways. The accounts of Herod Agrippa's persecution of Christians, followed by his own punitive death, then the first mission of Paul (Acts 13–14), all lead naturally to the Council of Jerusalem (Acts 15), which resolves an important policy question raised by this unexpected success among the nations.

Acts 10

10:1-33 Visions and revisions: the mission of Peter to Cornelius

To describe the change that Peter undergoes in chapter 10 as a "conversion" might seem strange to our way of thinking, but Luke clearly sees this transformation of Peter as parallel to Paul's "conversion" in importance. Paul changed from seeing the Jesus movement as a threat to the will of God to seeing it as the very fulfillment of God's plan. Similarly, Peter is moved from perceiving the messianic movement as a Jews-only affair to understanding it as God's blessing for Gentiles as well. Although this vision is implied in Peter's second speech (see 3:25), it takes the divine interventions portrayed in the present chapter to enable Peter to see the practical consequences of the promise to Abraham that his descendants would be a blessing for "all the nations of the earth" (Gen 18:18; 22:18). Thus, as in the case of Paul's transformation, Luke will tell the story of Peter's change three times. In both transformations, the initiative is not human but divine.

Cornelius is a "God fear[er]." This is not a formal social classification but a description of a Gentile who, without formally joining the people of Israel (entailing circumcision for males), has taken on Jewish beliefs and pious practices such as almsgiving and prayer at the hour of temple worship.

Luke underscores the fact that the actions of both Cornelius and Peter are divinely prompted by linking their actions to interlocking visions. The angel of God makes it clear to Cornelius that the intervention is a response to his prayer and tells him to send for Peter at Simon the tanner's place. Peter's vision confronts him (three times!) with a powerful puzzlement: shown a sheet full of clean and unclean animals, he is instructed to kill and eat. In effect, this is a command to ignore a primary Jewish identity marker. (It also evokes the cosmic covenant God made with Noah in Genesis 9, where Noah and family, representing all humanity, were given "every creature that is alive" to eat, Gen 9:3.)

When the messengers from Cornelius, presumably Gentiles, arrive at Simon's place with the account of their master's visions, Peter's readiness to offer them hospitality indicates that he has begun to learn the lesson of the animal vision: if all animals are clean, the major social barrier between Gentile and Jew has been eliminated. Peter himself states at verse 28 that he has learned this lesson.

Several elements suggest that, though he is only a "God-fear[er]" (a Gentile worshiper of YHWH, but not a full-fledged convert), Cornelius's piety has achieved a kind of temple intimacy with God. The angelic vision happens "about three o'clock" (vv. 3 and 30; literally "the ninth hour," the time of the afternoon sacrifice, in the spirit of Psalm 141:2, Judith 9:1, and Daniel 9:21). His prayers and almsgiving have reached God "as a memorial offering before

397

Acts 10

God" (v. 4; and see v. 31), and he can refer to his own "non-kosher" home as "here in the presence of God" (v. 33, a phrase whose Old Testament connotation is the temple presence of God, as in Leviticus 4:4, 18, 24). Sacred space now extends to wherever people respond to the will of God.

10:34-48 Peter evangelizes Cornelius and his household

Peter's speech to the household of Cornelius is a rich résumé of Lukan theology. God shows no partiality, but whoever fears him and acts uprightly is acceptable to God (*dektos*, "acceptable," or "accepted," like a valid temple sacrifice). This principle does not address the contemporary question of religious pluralism but rather the first-century question of who is a candidate for God's messianic blessing. The reference is to persons like Cornelius and company: no matter what their ethnic identity, as long as they are receptive to God's revelation through the people Israel and do what is right, they are acceptable to God.

Peter can speak of the whole life of Jesus as God proclaiming "peace through Jesus Christ" (v. 36, alluding to Isa 52:7). When he refers to "how God *anointed* Jesus of Nazareth with . . . Spirit and power" (v. 38, emphasis added), he is rooting Jesus' title of "Christ" in the prophetic anointing for mission interpreted by Isaiah 61:1 at Luke 4:18. Fittingly for this context, he calls Jesus "Lord of *all*" and "the one appointed by God as judge of the living and the dead" (emphasis added).

The action of the Spirit is said to interrupt Peter's speech, but in fact Luke has communicated fully to his readers. The *shalom* ("peace") that God has proclaimed to Israel through Jesus is meant for all. And God presently demonstrates that thesis by way of the endowment of the Holy Spirit upon Cornelius's receptive household. Pointedly, Luke notes that "the circumcised believers who had accompanied Peter were astounded that the *gift of the holy Spirit* should have been *poured out* on the Gentiles also, for they could hear them *speaking in tongues* and glorifying God" (v. 45, emphasis added). The language is carefully chosen to recall the Pentecostal outpouring of the holy Spirit in chapter 2 (see 2:17, 18, 33, 38). That the gift of the Spirit should precede baptism in the name of Jesus demonstrates, again, that the mission to the Gentiles is God's will. It also shows that circumcision is not required for entry into the messianic people of God.

Christian tradition will honor another person, Paul, as the Apostle to the Gentiles par excellence (indeed, Paul identifies himself that way in Galatians 2:7), but Luke has made it clear that that mission was authenticated by no less a person than the chief of the apostles, Peter. And Peter was simply responding to the initiative of God.

Acts 11

In the broader framework of the narrative in Acts, Peter's journey from Jewish Joppa to Roman Caesarea (10:23-24) is a miniature of the word journey from Jerusalem to Rome.

11:1-18 Peter explains God's actions to the Jerusalem authorities

As Simon Peter needed three similar visions to begin to fathom God's intentions regarding Jewish-Christian relations to the Gentiles, so Luke himself deems it necessary that this turn to the Gentiles be told three times. As in the case of Saul's conversion/call, our author first narrates the events directly (Acts 10) and then provides two interpretations of those events in subsequent speeches (chs. 11 and 15).

Since Peter's acceptance of Gentile hospitality is a violation of Jewish law, and his extension of the messianic renewal to the Gentiles was done without authorization from the Jerusalem church authorities, the apostles rightly demand an explanation. The recital of Peter's rooftop visions of the menagerie in the linen sheet, the embassy from Cornelius's house, the visit, the account of Cornelius's vision—all this is familiar enough to us who have read chapter 11. But what follows presents five fresh elements of interpretation.

First, the experience of Cornelius's household in their response in faith to the preaching of Peter is described as being "saved" (v. 14; compare with Acts 2:47). Second, Peter equates their experience of the holy Spirit with the apostles' own experience on Pentecost, pointedly referred to as "the beginning" (v. 15). Third, these endowments of the Spirit are, for the first time, described as what John the Baptist and Jesus meant by being "baptized with the holy Spirit" (v. 16; see Luke 3:16 for John's word and Acts 1:5 for Jesus'). Fourth, Peter refers to the Pentecost experience as the moment when he and the rest of the Twelve "came to believe in the Lord Jesus Christ" (v. 17); this implies that their initial discipleship during Jesus' earthly ministry had not yet constituted full Christian faith. Full Christian faith requires acceptance of Jesus as risen Lord and the gift of the holy Spirit. Finally, the Jerusalem leaders view the Cornelius episode not simply as a singular episode but as a paradigm of what God wills: "God has then granted life-giving repentance to the Gentiles too" (v. 18).

11:19-30 The Antioch mission

Although Luke has highlighted Peter's encounter with Cornelius as the paradigmatic and authoritative breakthrough, this passage makes it clear that the word has been reaching the Gentiles through other agents as well. In the wake of the persecution that followed the martyrdom of Stephen,

Jerusalem messianists (Christians) brought the word to Greek-speaking Jews from Cyprus and Cyrene, and these in turn evangelized Greeks (Gentiles) up in Antioch of Syria.

As in the case of Peter and Cornelius, this outreach to Gentiles in Antioch is ratified by Jerusalem authorization: the elders send Barnabas, who in turn enlists the help of Saul of Tarsus. When Luke says Barnabas "encouraged" the people to remain faithful (v. 23), he may be hinting at the meaning of his nickname (Barnabas = "son of consolation"), which he said the apostles applied to this Levite from Cyprus (see 4:36).

In Paul's letter to the Galatians, he refers to himself as "entrusted with the gospel to the uncircumcised, just as Peter to the circumcised" (Gal 2:7). If this seems to be at odds with Luke's portrayal of Peter's evangelization of the household of Cornelius, it should be noted that Paul nowhere claims to be the *first* missioner to the Gentiles. And Luke does give us significant episodes about Peter's evangelizing the circumcised (Acts 2–5; 9:32-43). Nor do we hear of Peter spending much more time among the uncircumcised.

Having described the developments of a mixed (Jewish-Gentile) church in Antioch, which is emerging as an entity distinct enough to warrant a special name, *hoi Christianoi* ("Christians," the first use of the name), Luke illustrates their solidarity with the Jewish-Christian brothers and sisters in Judea. Responding to Agabus's prophecy about imminent widespread famine, the Antiochenes send relief to the Jerusalem elders.

12:1-25 Great reversals: Peter's escape and Herod's death

This book called the Acts of the Apostles turns out to be mainly about the acts of *two* apostles, Peter and Paul. Up to this point, Peter has dominated the stage. In the present chapter, Luke rounds off the story of Peter before taking up in earnest the missions of Paul.

Using as his centerpiece a favorite genre of Hellenistic entertainment, the "great escape" story, Luke vividly illustrates divine power at work through accounts of vivid reversals and transitions.

First there is the transition from James to James. The third of four Herods mentioned in Luke-Acts, Herod Agrippa I, the grandson of Herod the Great, has James of Zebedee, one of the Twelve, killed by the sword. No motive is given. Before the chapter closes (v. 17), it is clear that the key Jerusalem leader is not one of the Twelve but another James, the brother of the Lord. To underscore the fact that the followers of Jesus relive his story (recall especially the martyrdom of Stephen in chapters 6 and 7), Luke notes that this persecution by Herod occurs during Passover time.

Divine power and justice are displayed in the dramatic reversal experienced by Herod. The chapter begins with the king's arrogant and violent exercise of power in arbitrary persecution, execution, and arrest; it ends with Herod's being hailed as a god, only to suffer an ignominious death. Notice that this idolatry occurs in the secular capital, Caesarea (Maritima), and the idolaters are a pagan embassy from Tyre and Sidon. This is one of a series of examples in Acts showing how Gentiles can be idolatrous in their theism. And Tyre was famous for its propensity to treat a man as a god (see Ezek 28).

Another subtle transition that Luke signals here is the growing division between the minority group called "the church" (vv. 1 and 5) and the Jewish majority. At the end of his Gospel and the beginning of Acts, Luke was careful to stress that the first Christians were, and remained, practicing Jews. Then, describing the plot of the Jewish community in Damascus against Paul, Luke could state simply, "the Jews conspired to kill him" (9:23). Now here in chapter 12 Luke can refer to Agrippa's persecution of the church as "pleasing to the Jews" (v. 3), and Peter can speak of his rescue "from the hand of Herod and from all that the Jewish people had been expecting" (v. 11). While Jews will continue to join the growing church, the hostility between this minority and the majority begins to deepen.

These transitions and reversals frame the marvelous escape of Peter. Luke's interest in paralleling God's work in the mission of Jesus and the church with the divine liberating action of the Exodus continues here. As in Exodus (3:2; 4:24 LXX; 14:19; 23:20, 23; 32:34), an angel of the Lord is instrumental in leading the action (vv. 7-11, 15, 23). The biblical word for smiting (*patassō*) is used playfully here to point up the contrast between the gentle smiting that the angel uses to awaken Peter (v. 7) and the fatal smiting of Herod at the end (v. 23), reminiscent of the smiting of Sennacherib's troops by the angel of the Lord in 2 Kings 19. As in the story of God's dealings with Israel in the Hebrew Bible (Old Testament), the same divine power continues to bring both liberation and reprisal. Luke's dwelling with such zest on these events fits well the spirit of a book whose final word, describing Paul's unstoppable preaching while under house arrest, is *akōlytōs* ("unhindered").

The return of Barnabas and Saul to Antioch after completing their "relief mission" (*diakonia*) to the poor of Jerusalem (v. 25) completes the excursion begun at 11:30. This is likely the visit to which Paul refers in Galatians 2:1-10, when "the pillars" (James, Cephas, and John) urged Paul to continue being "mindful of the poor."

Acts 13

Acts 13:1-3 From five leaders, two missioners: the sending of Barnabas and Saul

Having rounded off the story of Peter's leadership of the early church, Luke now picks up the story of Paul, which will dominate the remainder of the book. Indeed, this second half of the history could well be called "The Acts of Paul." An illustrious quintet of church prophets and teachers—including one Simeon called *the black* (Niger), an African (Lucius from Cyrene), and a childhood companion of Herod Antipas—are pictured here fasting and praying. Barnabas and Saul are chosen by the holy Spirit (in prophecy, presumably) and sent off to do what the Spirit calls "the work." The work, of course, is what the quotation from Habakkuk at verse 41 calls what God is doing and something that the scoffers will never believe.

13:4-13 Barnabas, Saul, and John Mark evangelize Cyprus

This first outreach of the person that Christian tradition will call "the Apostle to the Gentiles" is a reprise of elements that characterized the first outreach of Philip to the Samaritans and then that of Peter to the Gentile household of Cornelius. As Philip met, in the person of Simon Magus, the power of evil present in the pagan world of magic and overcame that power with the Spirit of God, here the three Antiochene missioners encounter that same dark power in the person of a magician who happens to be an apostate Jew, Elymas bar-Jesus. Note that the Apostle, first introduced with his Jewish name, Saul, at the stoning of Stephen (Acts 7:58), is now called by his Latin name, Paul (v. 9; possibly a nickname, since *paulus* means "little"), probably because his mission will mainly address Gentiles from now on.

Paul taunts the magician, accusing him of reversing the plan of God, "twisting the straight paths of [the] Lord" (compare Luke 3:5, quoting Isaiah 40:3-5, "winding roads shall be made straight"). And Elymas's punishment of blindness parallels Paul's temporary fate when he was stopped in his tracks bent on resisting the plan of God in the community of the Way in Damascus (see Acts 9:6-11, where Paul, temporarily blinded, is sent to Straight Street!). Luke says that they evangelize the island from stem to stern (from Salamis in the east to Paphos in the west), but he details only the conversion of the island's governor, Sergius Paulus, Paul's first Gentile disciple. Sergius is for Paul what Cornelius was for Peter.

13:14-52 Paul preaches in a synagogue in Pisidian Antioch

Although the name Galatia does not appear during this first missionary journey, Paul and Barnabas's ministry in Antioch of Pisidia (to be distinguished from Antioch of Syria, some three hundred miles to the east), and then in Iconium, Lystra, and Derbe, takes them into the southern part of that Roman province. Since we have no evidence that Paul evangelized farther north in Galatia, these are likely the "churches of Galatia" that Paul addressed in his famous letter by that name (Gal 1:2 and see 1 Cor 16:1).

As Peter began his post-Easter apostolic career with a speech proclaiming the life, death, and resurrection of Jesus in the light of the Hebrew Scriptures (Acts 2), Paul now does the same. Like Peter, Paul first addresses his message to his fellow Jews and to Gentile "God fear[ers]." As in the case of Peter's Pentecost speech, we can detect the hand of historian Luke employing the *pesher* technique, that is, using ancient texts to interpret recent events in the life of the community in the light of Easter faith.

The scene is reminiscent of Jesus' speech in the synagogue at Nazareth (Luke 4:14-30). The local Jewish community is gathered for readings from Scripture followed by interpretive preaching. In broad strokes Paul rehearses the familiar highlights of God's special relationship with Israel: the exodus from Egypt, the desert period, the conquest, and the kingship (Saul and David). Then he "fast forwards" to the coming of Jesus as savior of Israel, heralded by John. The phrase "according to his promise" (v. 23), in this context referring to Jesus as descendant of David, seems to have Nathan's prophecy to David especially in view (2 Sam 7:12-14).

The second half of the speech, concerning the death and resurrection of Jesus and the mission of the church, draws even more heavily on biblical references to interpret the Christian experience.

As we have come to expect from Luke, blame for the death of Jesus is assigned to both Jewish and Roman leaders. Yet the death is interpreted as the fulfillment of "the oracles of the prophets" and "all that was written about him" (vv. 27, 29). Earlier parts of Luke-Acts have taught us some of the Scripture passages to which such statements refer—for example, Isaiah 53:7-8 (Acts 8:32-33); Psalm 31:6 (Luke 23:46); and the stories of Joseph and Moses in the Torah exemplifying the pattern of the rejected leader who becomes a savior (Acts 7:9-38).

When it comes to the resurrection, the Old Testament references become more abundant and explicit. Reference to "raising up" the son of David (v. 33), also to be known as Son of God, gives new meaning to 2 Samuel 7:12-14 ("I will raise up your heir after you. . . . I will be a father to him, and he shall be a son to me"). The quotation of Psalm 2:7 in verse 33 ("You are my son; this day I have begotten you") interprets the resurrection as a moment of accession to the throne as king of Israel. Thus the same verse that we first heard at the scene by the Jordan ("You are my beloved Son," Luke 3:22), referring there to divine sonship and introducing a genealogy extending back to "Adam, son of God," here takes on a further dimension—the messianic one.

The quotation of Isaiah 55:3 ("I shall give you the benefits assured to David") becomes even more meaningful when we discover that the immediate context of that verse in Isaiah includes reference to an everlasting covenant (v. 2) and a mission to the Gentiles (v. 4). As in Luke 24:46-47, all three realities—the death and resurrection of the Messiah and the mission of the church—are grounded in Scripture. The use of Psalm 16:7 ("You will not suffer your holy one to see corruption"), fulfilled not in David but in the resurrection of Jesus, echoes the interpretation that Peter made at the heart of his Pentecost speech (Acts 2:25-31).

The language about justification through faith in verses 38-39 shows Paul using language that is characteristic of his letters, especially Romans and Galatians.

Although this speech gets a positive response and "many" in that synagogue congregation follow Paul and Barnabas, when "almost the whole city" (v. 44) turns out, no doubt including a majority of Gentiles, the (unpersuaded) Jews begin to contradict Paul. This prompts a final invocation of Scripture, announcing both continuity and novelty. The passage from Isaiah that Simeon alluded to in his canticle at the presentation of Jesus in the temple (Luke 2:29-32) Paul quotes in full (v. 47): "I have made you a light to the Gentiles, that you may be an instrument of salvation to the ends of the earth" (Isa 49:6b). What Simeon applied to Jesus, Paul now applies to himself and Barnabas as exponents of the Christian mission. Indeed, Paul had just declared, ". . . through him [Jesus] forgiveness of sins is being proclaimed to you" (v. 38). That is, the risen Lord Jesus is now working through the likes of Paul and Barnabas. The novelty is that Jewish rejection of the good news triggers a turn to the Gentiles (v. 46).

With painful irony Luke shows that what was originally understood as the Jewish mission to be a "light to the Gentiles" now leaves many Jews behind. That Paul and Barnabas can later return to Pisidian Antioch to strengthen the disciples there and appoint elders (14:21-23) indicates that they left behind a community of believers (presumably composed of the Jews and converted Gentiles mentioned in 13:43) when they first left this town.

Does the strong language of Paul in verses 46-47 mean that God has abandoned the chosen people because of their unbelief? That interpretation has been the first step of Christian anti-Semitism. Luke's point is rather that which is reflected in Paul's own letters: the gospel is meant for Jews first, then Gentiles (see Rom 1:16; 9:24; 10:12). Another purpose is to present a paradigm of early Christian mission experience: the message will be accepted by some Jews and Gentiles and rejected by others, but God will use this rejection as an occasion for the advance of the mission (which is also Paul's interpretation in Romans 11). Paul will continue to address Jews first as his mode of operating, for example, in Iconium (14:1), Thessalonica (17:1), Beroea (17:10), Athens (17:17), Corinth (18:4), and Ephesus (18:19).

In shaking the dust off their feet (v. 51), Paul and Barnabas act on the advice Jesus gave to the Twelve (Luke 9:5) and the Seventy-two (Luke 10:10-11). And the rejoicing of the disciples in the midst of rejection and persecution acts out the fourth Beatitude of the Sermon on the Plain (Luke 6:23).

14:1-28 Paul and Barnabas, from Antioch to Antioch

Before zooming in on the marvelous details of the healing of the lame man at Lystra, Luke sketches the experiences of Paul and Barnabas in Iconium to highlight what is characteristic of their mission. (Uniquely in Acts, they are called "apostles," at verse 4 and again at verse 14, probably more to acknowledge their being on a mission [13:2] than to indicate special status.) Here they draw a positive response from "a great number of Jews and Greeks [Gentiles]." As in the work of the Twelve in Jerusalem, the Lord confirms the word through signs and wonders. As in Pisidian Antioch, the response of the larger population is divided and evokes persecution from Gentiles and Jews alike.

When we come to the dramatic events at Lystra, there can be no doubt that Luke has chosen to foreground this healing by highlighting parallels with the healing done through Peter and John in Acts 3. As in the case of that first major healing in the life of the Jerusalem church, here we have a healing of a man born lame sitting outside a temple, done with a verbal command, and resulting not only in standing and walking but even in leaping. Both healings are interpreted as a sign of the salvation that comes through faith (3:16; 14:9). Thus the first Gentile healing matches the first Jewish healing. The work of the second great leader (Paul) is inaugurated by a healing that parallels the dramatic healing of the first great leader of the Church (Peter). And the responses are similar. As Peter and John had to deflect the adulation of the crowd in the Jerusalem Temple, so Paul and Barnabas, taken by the pagans for Zeus and Hermes, are compelled to dodge the blasphemy of having sacrifice offered to them!

The brief speech attributed to both Barnabas and Paul invokes a strategy of evangelization that has typified missionary work at its best. Instead of moving directly to the fulfillment of messianic expectations (non-existent for the pagans of Lystra), the apostles proclaim the "living God," the creator revealed in the good gifts of nature that they celebrate in their own

Acts 14

sacrifices—the rains and the fruitful seasons. This acknowledgment of God as creator and sustainer of all life is, of course, at the heart of Jewish monotheism; now Christianity makes it a necessary foundation of its proclamation of the gospel. Appreciation of Jesus requires knowledge and acceptance of God the creator.

The would-be stoners from Iconium, joined by adversaries from Pisidian Antioch, finally catch up with the apostles in Lystra (v. 19) and manage to carry out their intentions on Paul, leaving him for dead. Supported by the disciples, he is able to return to town and to continue his mission the next day. It is a sign of their courage that they are able to act in the spirit of the motto expressed in verse 22 and circle back through the very towns from which their persecutors came. In Lystra, Iconium, and Antioch they find Christian communities large and stable enough to require the appointment of elders (presbyters) for their governance. Luke has no trouble portraying a church that is at once charismatic and prophetic, and, at the same time, requiring the structure of appointed officers (recall the conjunction of teachers and prophets among the five named at 13:1 and the appointment of *diakonoi* in chapter 6; and see the discussion of 20:17 and 28 regarding *episcopoi*, *presbyteroi*, and *diakonoi*).

We sense a kind of symmetry in the narrative as the apostles return to the community that commissioned them in Syrian Antioch. This first mission commenced at the beginning of chapter 13 with mention of offices (prophets and teachers), prayer and fasting, and designation of chosen persons for "the work" with a laying on of hands and a send-off. Now that mission comes to a close with mention of officers (elders) appointed and commissioned with prayer and fasting and a reference to "the work" Paul and Barnabas have now accomplished (14:22-26). Luke has been careful to show that this first mission was not so much what Paul and Barnabas had done but "what God had done with them and how he had opened the door of faith to the Gentiles" (v. 27).

15:1-35 The "Council" of Jerusalem. The early church resolves its first big crisis: must Gentile converts become Jews?

This account of the early church responding to and resolving its first major crisis displays at its best Luke's genius as a historian. If you have ever been a part of a leadership committee, recall a time when that group met to resolve a major policy issue. No doubt that process entailed more than one meeting, and those meetings took hours before all sides of the issue were voiced. Full resolution and implementation likely required more hours of meeting, debate, and work.

By analogy with that contemporary experience, consider what the fledgling church was facing at this point and how Luke describes its response. Becoming disciples of Jesus as the Christ had been largely a Jewish matter. It was natural, then, for the Jewish Christians to expect Gentile converts to do what Gentile converts had always done, namely, undergo circumcision (for males) and keep the full 613 laws of Moses. Obviously, those who had specialized in teaching and living the Torah, like the converts who belonged to the party of the Pharisees, would be inclined to see it this way. Others, however, such as Paul and Barnabas, who were more broadly experienced in what God had been doing among the Gentiles, were convinced that a Gentile should not have to become a Jew to become a Christian.

Remarkably, Luke manages to present the resolution of this crisis in a passage that takes only five minutes to read! In thirty-five verses, our author cuts to the essence of the matter and, in the telling of it, provides a paradigm of ecclesial decision-making that has subsequently characterized the church at its best.

Verses 1-2 present the "state of the question": visitors from the Jerusalem headquarters challenge the lenient practice of the Antioch community (not requiring circumcision of male Gentile converts), and Paul and Barnabas promptly oppose the Jerusalem people. (Although Luke does not mention Peter at this point, this confrontation could well be the altercation that Paul himself describes, for another purpose than Luke's, in Galatians 2:11-14. This is one way of reconciling the accounts of Acts 15 and Galatians 2.)

Recognizing that this is an issue that needs to be resolved at a higher level, the local church sends Paul, Barnabas, and some other representatives to Jerusalem. Their trip up to Jerusalem ("up" because topographically one always goes *up* to Jerusalem even when the trip is a north-south journey) is punctuated by their regaling the disciples with stories of the conversion of the Gentiles. Though the Antiochene party is graciously received, the Pharisee Christians firmly restate their position: Gentile converts must get circumcised and observe the Mosaic Law.

Since the Antioch delegation is meeting with "the apostles and presbyters [elders]," this is not a plenary session of the whole church but a leadership meeting. As any recorder of minutes will recognize, the phrase "after much debate had taken place" saves Luke an enormous amount of ink and parchment. Then Luke has Peter get up and retell what we who have read Acts 10 and 11 recognize as the story of Cornelius and his household. This time the words of Peter highlight new dimensions of that experience. He says that God purified their hearts by faith, alluding to Ezekiel 36:25-26. He argues that God's endowment of the holy Spirit upon those Gentiles shows that salvation comes by "the grace of the Lord Jesus" (v. 11). The argument against the Jerusalem policy is clinched with Paul and Barnabas describing the "signs and wonders God had worked among the Gentiles through them," which we readers recognize as a reference to the events narrated in Acts 13–14.

The clincher comes, surprisingly, from the mouth of James, the leader of the Jerusalem church, that is, the one we would most expect to support the "conservative" policy of circumcising Gentile converts. His argument turns out to be a *pesher*, that is, an application of Scripture to current events, such as we have met in the speeches of Peter and the one of Paul in Pisidian Antioch. James finds confirmation of the position represented by Paul and Barnabas in the Greek version of Amos 9:11-12.

As in the case of the other *peshers*, the interpretation here requires the Greek version (Septuagint) of the prophet. This part of Amos 9 is about the restoration of Israel. But where the Hebrew text has *edom* (Edom), the Septuagint translator has read *'adam* (humanity), so that a statement about the conquest of a remnant of Edom becomes one about "the rest of humanity" seeking the Lord. How does James (or Luke) find in this passage from the Greek Bible an affirmation of an unhindered mission to the Gentiles? It reflects the same two-stage mission that the early community found in Isaiah 49:5-6, namely, (1) restoration of the tribes of Israel ("the fallen hut of David") and (2) the reception of the Gentiles ("the rest of humanity").

James's solution is to acknowledge that the mission to the Gentiles is God's will but also to maintain some continuity with the past by insisting that they should require from Gentile converts what Israel had always required of resident aliens, as spelled out in Leviticus 17–18. As a sign that they are joining a community with Israelite roots, Gentile converts should follow the usual rules for resident aliens and "abstain from meat sacrificed to idols, from blood, from meats of strangled animals, and from unlawful marriage" (v. 29). (Alternatively, a convincing case can also be made that the issue here was not so much menu as venue, that the four items of the apostolic decree referred simply to the behavior involved in participating in pagan temple feasts, and that Gentile believers were hereby warned to make a clean break from such places.)

Notice that Luke's crisp account of what must have been a more extended process provides a paradigm for problem solving and decision-making in the church. It comes down to three movements:

1. Conduct a full hearing of the community's experience of what they understand God to be doing among them (here, the accounts of Peter, Paul, and Barnabas).

2. Try to understand that experience against the faith-community's tradition as currently understood (here, James's citation of Greek Amos 9).

3. Make a practical policy decision that affirms the values evoked in steps 1 and 2 (here, the decision to free Gentile converts from unnecessary obligations, but requiring them at least to keep the Levitical rules for resident aliens—or, on the alternative interpretation, to cease frequenting pagan temple feasts).

This very human problem-solving process is something that the community can boldly describe with the words "It is the decision of the holy Spirit and of us . . ." (v. 28).

THE MISSION OF PAUL TO THE ENDS OF THE EARTH
Acts 15:36–28:31

The travels described in Acts 16–20 cover two more distinct journeys, the second and third missionary journeys of Paul (and companions). And each journey has a distinct geographical center of gravity: as the first addressed communities in southern Galatia, the second concentrates on major cities in Macedonia and Achaia, and the third centers in, and radiates from, the great Ephesus.

Like the first journey described in chapters 13–14, the second and third also begin and return to Syrian Antioch and include one major speech by Paul—the only address to a Gentile audience (in Athens, 17:22-31) and the farewell address at Miletus to the Ephesian elders (20:18-35). Yet because these two journeys are separated by what is only a brief return to Syrian Antioch (18:22), it may be helpful (and even more faithful to Luke's narrative) to think of the activities recounted in these five chapters as the Aegean mission. Together, these travels form a whole, moving from what Paul himself refers to as "the beginning of the gospel" at Philippi (Phil 4:15) to Paul's "last will and testament" addressed to the Ephesian elders at Miletus (Act 20:17-38). The remainder of the book (Acts 21–28) is a distinct segment devoted to journeys related to Paul's Jewish and Roman imprisonment and "trials" (really hearings) in Jerusalem and Caesarea Maritima, and finally house arrest in Rome.

15:36-41 Paul and Barnabas separate

Luke's delicate treatment of the interplay between the human intentions and divine will continues to unfold dramatically. What will eventually become Paul's greatest missionary expansion begins simply with the intention

Acts 15

of revisiting and strengthening the churches he had founded in the first mission (Acts 13–14). That God can work with the results of human frailty is implied in Luke's notice that Paul and Barnabas had a "disagreement" (whose depth is suggested by the Greek word here, *paroxysmos*, v. 38, from which the English "paroxysm" derives) about whether Mark, who had deserted the previous mission at Pamphylia, should be allowed to accompany them. Thus the breakup of the first team leads to the formation of a powerful new team—Paul and Silas. First introduced in verses 22-32 as a leader in the Jerusalem community and a prophet, Silas is usually taken to be the same person as the Silvanus mentioned in the New Testament epistles.

16:1-5 Timothy joins Paul and Silas

This brief passage shows Paul's nuanced approach to Jewish/Gentile relations in the Christian mission. Even as he continues to promulgate the apostolic decree of the Council of Jerusalem (15:23-29), which frees Gentile converts from having to become Jews, he can still insist that Timothy undergo adult circumcision. Apparently Timothy was raised Jewish by his mother (named Eunice, we learn in 2 Timothy 1:5) but had never been circumcised (prevented by his Greek father?). That Paul convinced him to get circumcised, even though he was now a Christian, suggests that Paul still considered mission to Jews important enough to take this surprising step to make Timothy more acceptable to his fellow Jews.

16:6-10 The call to Macedonia

The movement of this team of three into fresh mission territory presents again the delicate interface of the divine and human in their decision-making. As they move westward, they are prevented from moving south by the holy Spirit and from moving north by "the Spirit of Jesus." When Paul receives a dream vision of a Macedonian calling for help, that call still requires ratification by human decision (v. 10).

A note on the "we" passages

The introduction of the first person plural ("we") in verse 10 signals the first of the famous four "we" sections in Acts (16:10-17; 20:5-15; 21:1-18; 27:1–28:16). To account for this phenomenon, commentators have noted that the first person plural was sometimes used in ancient travel narratives as a literary device to evoke immediacy. However, this does not appear to be the case with Acts, a work of history. The abruptness of the shifts from third-person narrative to first-person (and back again) is more easily accounted for as deriving from the actual involvement of the author (or his sources).

Moreover, ancient historians were eager to indicate their presence at the events they described when they had grounds to make such a claim. We have no evidence of their making such claims groundlessly.

16:11-15 The conversion of Lydia and her household

Seeking a Jewish house of prayer, Paul, Silas, Timothy (and Luke, if we understand "we" historically) encounter a group of women gathered by the riverside. With marvelous economy of words, Luke describes one Lydia. She is a businesswoman, a dealer in the luxury item of purple cloth, a God fearer, and wealthy enough to be mistress of a household. Such is her openness and response to Paul's sharing of the word that Luke describes it in language reminiscent of the conversion of the Emmaus pair in Luke 24:31-32: "The Lord opened her heart." Conversion and baptism lead immediately to generous hospitality. Since the missioners later return to "Lydia's house" (v. 40) after their release from prison, she may well have emerged as the leader of the first house church of Philippi (and thus the first in what will later be known as Europe).

16:16-40 Further adventures in Philippi: deliverance, imprisonment, and further deliverance

On his way to the house of prayer, Paul encounters some unsolicited and annoying advertising. A slave girl with a mantic spirit goes around shouting what is in fact the truth: "These people are slaves of the Most High God, who proclaim to you a way of salvation" (v. 17). Though true enough in a Christian context, the ambiguous language would have been heard by pagans as announcing Paul and Silas as promoting a new cure in the name of the god that they promote as the top god of the pagan pantheon. When Paul puts a stop to this with a command in the name of Jesus and the woman is delivered of the oracular spirit, her exploiters, distressed by the loss of business, bring the missioners before the Roman magistrates. The charge: illegal (anti-imperial) proselytizing.

The foursome are stripped, beaten, and imprisoned. During the night an earthquake opens the jail doors and unchains the prisoners. When the jailer finds the missioners freed but still present, he responds to these portents by falling on his knees and asking, "What must I do to be saved?" And they say, "Believe in the Lord Jesus and you and your household will be saved." As in the case of Lydia, openness leads to conversion of a household, hospitality, and baptism.

When the Roman authorities realize their mistake and try to dismiss Paul and friends discreetly, Paul confronts the police. He and his men are

Roman citizens, and he insists that their beating and imprisonment without trial are a miscarriage of justice that ought to be reversed, not secretly but officially. This elicits a sheepish apology from the magistrates, who come to apologize and to ask them to leave town. This they do, but not without stopping at Lydia's place to encourage the budding Philippian community.

17:1-15 From Thessalonica to Beroea, with mixed reviews

Although Luke treats Paul's mission in Thessalonica (some hundred miles west of Philippi) as a brief, three-week encounter, the community he founded there was significant enough to receive the earliest letter we have from the Apostle's hand, 1 Thessalonians.

The events here are described in language that resonates with the Third Gospel. When Luke notes that Paul joined the local synagogue community according to "his usual custom," he could be referring to Paul's usual missionary strategy. He could as well mean that Paul attended synagogue as his Jewish practice, much as Jesus attended the Nazareth synagogue "according to his custom" (Luke 4:16). His teaching in that house of prayer and study is summarized in words that reflect the message of Jesus to the disciples on Easter Sunday ("The Messiah had to suffer and rise from the dead," v. 3; see Luke 24:26, 46-47). And when those in the Jewish community who find Paul's message a threat drag to the magistrates some of the small Christian community growing in Jason's place, their accusations echo those leveled against Jesus: "They all act in opposition to the decrees of Caesar and claim instead that there is another king, Jesus" (v. 7; see Luke 23:2).

Some sixty miles to the southwest, Paul and Silas find a much more receptive synagogue in Beroea, where people engage the missioners in biblical study, not just on the Sabbath but "daily" (v. 11). But the zealous Thessalonian adversaries soon arrive to stir up the crowds against them, much as the pre-Christian Paul (Saul) traveled distances to block the spread of what he had determined was a dangerous Jewish heresy, "the Way" (Acts 9:2).

17:16-34 Paul in Athens

In this episode Luke presents Paul giving the only fully developed speech to a Gentile audience. He describes that audience with care when he highlights the Stoics and Epicureans in verse 18 (both named only here in the New Testament). The mere mention of the names evokes stereotyped philosophical positions regarding humanity, nature, and the gods. Stoics perceived reality as a unified, organic cosmos in which the divinity inhered pantheistically as a kind of "law." Humanity was part of that cosmos and found happiness by harmonizing with that essentially benevolent law of the cosmos.

Epicureans, on the other hand, had a more mechanistic notion of the world, in which the divine was conceived in a "deistic" way at best (the divinity causing the cosmos but remaining uninvolved with it). Epicureans expected mere dissolution after death and, meanwhile, sought happiness by prudently doing what was most sensibly pleasant. It makes sense, then, for Luke to describe the crowd reactions as divided. On the one hand, there were those who heckled Paul, dismissing him as a "seed-pecker," a reaction that fits the Epicureans, who would have found Paul's teaching radically incompatible with their own. On the other hand, there were those who were initially confused (thinking Paul to be speaking of new gods, *Iēsous* and *Anastasis* ["Resurrection," mis-heard as the name of the divine consort of *Iēsous*?]) yet remained open to the preacher and wanted to hear more. And this reaction fits the Stoics, who would have found some tantalizing convergences with their worldview and lifestyle and would have been drawn to further inquiry.

The notion that the deity is not captured in sanctuaries and does not need human worship (see 7:48) would have been congenial to Stoics and Epicureans alike. But against Stoic pantheism, Paul asserts the biblical notion of a transcendent creator who *made* everything and, moreover, sustains everything. Paul reminds them of the common origin of the human family ("made from one"—compatible with the biblical account of origin from Adam and also the fresh beginning with Noah). Echoing his brief proclamation to the Lycaonians at Lystra, Paul remodels LXX Isaiah 42:5 and calls them to contemplate the earth with its seasons as a habitat for humanity and a revelation of the Creator's care.

Where he might have cited Scripture for a synagogue audience, here Paul enlists instead an ancient Stoic poet from his region, Aratus ("for we too are his offspring"), and he also quotes a sixth-century B.C. author, Epimenides of Knosses: "In him we live and move and have our being." Thus Luke appropriates Hellenistic language to assert against Stoic pantheism what we might call a biblical pan*en*theism. Against the Stoic notion of endless cycles of cosmic rebirth and death, he announces the biblical doomsday. Against the coldness of Epicurean "deism," he asserts the biblical notion of God's intimate involvement with creatures. If Luke has said in verse 24 that human handicraft cannot *house* God, in verse 29 he argues that human skill and wit cannot *image* the divinity. The unexpressed element of the argument is the biblical idea that the only adequate image of the living God is living human beings, who are images of the King of the universe insofar as they are stewards of the earth.

Acts 17

If Jesus is going to be the ultimate judge of the human family, it would follow that the criteria are what we have heard him teach in the Third Gospel, especially in the Sermon on the Plain (Luke 6:20-49).

Commentators have noted that Paul is portrayed using this philosophical "natural theology" approach just this once in Acts. And in his first letter to the Corinthians, he makes a point of not coming to them with the wisdom of philosophers but simply with the "foolishness" of a crucified Messiah. Was the approach of Paul in Athens simply a failed strategy, never to be repeated? It would seem, rather, that the church has seen in this episode a model of how Jerusalem can speak to Athens. Thomas Aquinas, for example, used the philosophical categories of a rediscovered Aristotle to speak to his European culture. And theology has always been an effort to recast the givens of revelation in the language of one's own time and place. One can even see in this brief masterpiece hints of the basis for the interreligious dialogue that challenges us today.

18:1-17 Paul in Corinth

Because the New Testament contains two of the letters that Paul later wrote to the Christian community in Corinth, we know more about this community than any of the other churches that Paul founded. The correspondence that we call 1 and 2 Corinthians gives us a privileged window on the texture and tensions of this vibrant community in the middle fifties of the first century. In the first half of Acts 18, Luke, apparently working from sources other than Paul's letters, sketches the beginnings of that fascinating church. Some of the strokes of that sketch provide precious contact with historical data; other strokes limn Luke's inspired interpretation of those events, showing what God is doing through human failures and successes in that busy crossroads of the ancient world.

Acts 18 offers two important links with secular history. The Roman historian Suetonius tells us that the emperor Claudius expelled members of the Jewish community of Rome because of an "uproar" caused by one "Chrestus" in A.D. 49. Scholars have taken that to be a garbled reference to *Christos*. It would seem to refer to a stir caused by Jewish Christians from Jerusalem preaching Jesus as the Messiah. Priscilla and Aquila, then, seem to be part of that group expelled from Rome. They are "Jews for Jesus" who host Christian meetings at their house (1 Cor 16:19), as they will later do in Rome, when Nero allows Jews to return five years later (see Rom 16:5). This enterprising couple takes in as houseguest Paul, their fellow tentmaker and messianic missioner. An inscription found at Delphi dates the proconsul of Achaia, Gallio, to A.D. 51–52, thus providing another link to secular history.

But it is sacred history that most interests Luke. He shows that the whim of an emperor and the adjudication of a proconsul can play into the divine project. Aquila and Prisca (Priscilla) become two of Paul's principal co-workers, and their hospitality enables the Apostle to settle into what was (next to his twenty-seven-month stay in Ephesus; see 19:10) his second most extended sojourn in a single town, lasting some eighteen months.

Paul's extended sessions at the local Jewish house of study, with Gentile God-fearers as well as Jews in attendance, issue in the usual mixed results. Most Jews reject the novelty of a crucified craftsman proclaimed as the Messiah and "the Lord." But there are notable exceptions: Crispus, the synagogue leader, and one Titus Justus, the God-fearer who owned the house next door to the synagogue. Paul's work is affirmed by a night vision of Jesus assuring him in language that recalls the divine promise of support to the prophets Isaiah and Jeremiah ("I am with you").

Tellingly, the mixed Christian community is called the Lord's "people" (*laos*, the biblical word for the people of the covenant; source of our word "laity"). When Paul's Jewish adversaries bring him before the bench of the proconsul Gallio, he unwittingly affirms that "covenantal peoplehood" of the Christians by dismissing their charges against Paul as a matter of Jewish doctrine, titles, and law (v. 15).

18:18-28 Further mission notes and the integration of Apollos

Luke's intent in the remainder of chapter 18 seems mainly to give a summary of activity occurring between Paul's work in Corinth and his work in another major urban center, Ephesus (to be treated in Acts 19). The résumé highlights features that are key to Luke's interpretation. (1) Paul continues to operate as a Jew (see the reference to the Nazirite haircut, v. 18; for background, see Num 6:1-21). (2) He continues his mission to fellow Jews (he dialogues with the Ephesian synagogue congregation). (3) He stays in touch with church officials at the Jerusalem headquarters (v. 22). (4) The Christian mission continues in an orderly way. For example, Paul revisits and affirms communities established in Phrygia and Galatia. And when Apollos, a skilled rhetorician from the Hellenistic Christian/Jewish community of Alexandria, arrives in Ephesus and begins to preach the "Way of the Lord" with enthusiasm, but incompletely, Paul's co-workers, Priscilla and Aquila, explain the Way to him more fully. Apollos's move from Ephesus to Achaia is done with the recommendation of the Ephesian Christians.

(The power of Apollos's ministry was such that some of those he trains will form a kind of "I had the great Apollos as my personal trainer" faction,

Acts 18

and Paul will have to address this issue in 1 Corinthians 1–3. See especially 1 Corinthians 3:6: "I planted, Apollos watered, but *God* caused the growth," emphasis added).

19:1-40 Paul in Ephesus: the Way of the Lord Jesus versus magic and idolatry; evangelizing from the Asian capital (19:1-12)

Paul's encounter with twelve Ephesian "disciples" who had not received the holy Spirit provides an instructive parallel with the previous episode—Priscilla and Aquila's instruction of Apollos. Both involve the instruction of disciples who are somehow incomplete. Apollos's incompleteness was subtle: although he had been instructed in the Way of the Lord (vv. 25-26; see 9:2; 14:16; 16:17) and taught accurately about Jesus and was ardent in spirit, he knew only the baptism of John, was not described as filled with the Spirit, and needed to be taught *more* accurately about the Way. Similarly, these twelve Ephesians, who seem to have missed the training of Aquila, Priscilla, and the reformed Apollos, also knew only John's baptism and had not even heard that there was a holy Spirit.

As in the case of the conversion of Cornelius's household (10:44-46), a "mini-Pentecost" follows. These two descriptions of "regularizing" disciples tell us two interesting things about the emergent church: (a) that the influence of John the Baptist was more powerful than we usually give him credit for, and (b) unity of belief and practice within the church had been a struggle from the beginning.

The summary description in verses 8-12 portrays the shape of the next twenty-seven months of Paul's evangelization. Despite past rejections, his serious effort to bring the Good News to his fellow Jews first continues with a three-month colloquium in the Ephesian synagogue. That this effort was not entirely without success is hinted at in the reference to the *disciples* whom Paul took with him after a nasty confrontation compelled him to change his venue to the hall of Tyrannus.

During the next two years Ephesus becomes a mission center from which the whole province of Asia is evangelized, "Jews and Greeks alike." The description of healings occasioned even by cloth or aprons touched to Paul's skin demonstrates that the healing ministry begun in Jesus (Luke 8:44-47, the woman with the flow of blood) and continued through Peter (Acts 5:15-16) persists in the Apostle to the Gentiles. See Paul's own reference to his work as "what Christ has accomplished through me to lead the Gentiles to obedience by word and deed, by the power of signs and wonders . . ." (Rom 15:18-19; see also 2 Cor 12:12).

19:13-20 The power of Jesus' name versus demons and magic

The power of the risen Lord Jesus over the competing powers of this world is now illustrated by two vivid and entertaining anecdotes regarding demons, magic, and idolatry.

When the seven sons of the high priest Sceva attempt to deliver a man from demonic oppression by using Jesus' name in a magical way, they themselves are rebuked, overpowered, and sent packing, naked and wounded. The spiritual power of the name of the Lord Jesus, properly used, is dramatized by the immense commercial value of books burned by those converted from their magical practices (v. 19).

19:21-40 A confused assembly confronted

The Way of the Lord Jesus continues to have practical consequences. The silversmiths of Ephesus riot when their livelihood (selling silver models of the world-famous temple of the goddess Artemis) appears to be threatened by the Christian preaching against idolatry. (Archaeology helps us to picture the structures involved here. One of the "seven wonders of the ancient world," the temple of Artemis, the Artemision, was four times the size of the Parthenon, with 127 sixty-foot pillars. The dimensions alone help us understand why silver models of the place were such hot items in the religious tourism trade. And the "theater" was not like your local movie house but a magnificent amphitheater carved into a mountainside, 495 feet in diameter.) Two important points emerge from Luke's account of this disruption. First, the intervention of the town clerk models the way for Roman officials to work out tensions with Christians: ("let the matter be settled in the lawful assembly," v. 39).

Second, some of Luke's word choices hint that he is making a subtle contrast between pagan chaos and Christian order. Describing the riot, Luke says that the city was filled with *synchysis* ("confusion"—v. 29). Used only once in the New Testament, this is a deftly chosen word, for it is the word used in the Septuagint at Genesis 11:9 (the sole occurrence in the Greek version of the Torah) to translate the name "Babel." And Luke has already used the verbal form of the word to describe the Pentecost experience as a reversal of Babel's confusion (Acts 2:6), Pentecost being the occasion when people are confused by their ability to understand!

The contrast is further enhanced by Luke's using *ekklēsia* to describe the confused assembly in verses 32, 39, and 41. Apart from Acts 7:38, where the word refers to the assembly of the Hebrews at Sinai, *ekklēsia* elsewhere in Acts always means the community of the church. Only in this passage is the word used for a non-ecclesial assembly. For the original readers of

Acts 19

Acts, this word choice could only have pointed up the contrast between the two kinds of "assembly"—the confused riot of the silversmiths versus the orderly growth of the church (vv. 10-17, 20). The final two occurrences of *ekklēsia* in Acts turn up in the very next chapter, in verses 17 and 28, where they describe the Ephesian church as an assembly driven by motives quite other than idolatry, greed, and anxiety.

20:1-16 Journeying toward Jerusalem (and the resuscitation of "Lucky")

In a note between the episodes of the triumph over the exorcists and the riot of the silversmiths (19:21), Luke had already referred to Paul's decision to travel to Jerusalem (and then move on to Rome). Although Paul later (24:17) refers to the purpose of this journey as the bringing of alms to Jerusalem (the collection referred to in his letters to Corinth and Rome—for instance, Romans 15:25-28), there is no mention of the collection here in chapter 20. Perhaps the delivery of the Jerusalem relief fund was not the public-relations success Paul had hoped for.

After a farewell tour of churches in Macedonia and three months in "Greece" (Achaia, centering, no doubt, around unnamed Corinth), Paul, intending to join what was apparently a pilgrim group of Jews sailing for Syria, learns of a plot against him and decides to take a more indirect route, looping back around the Aegean basin. The seven names listed (plus the author or his source, since the second "we" section begins in verse 5) comprise a delegation representing most of the sectors of Paul's mission. This delegation fits the notion that this is indeed the "Jerusalem relief fund" trip (see Rom 15:25-27).

The colorful anecdote about the resuscitation of Eutychus (aptly named "Lucky," the meaning of his name in Greek) may well be included here simply for its entertainment value and its parallel with the account of Peter's raising of Tabitha (9:36-43). But given Luke's careful choice of words and phrases—"on the first day of the week" (v. 1; see Luke 24:1); "upstairs room" (v. 8; see 1:13; 9:37, 39); "break[ing] bread" (vv. 7, 11; see Luke 22:19; 24:30; Acts 2:46); a fallen youth taken up "dead" (v. 9) and revived by Paul imitating the gestures of Elijah and Elisha and taken away as a *pais zōnta* ("living lad"), it is hard to dismiss the possibility that the author intends the reader to reflect on the story's symbolic resonances, especially when one notices that the event sits between references to Passover ("the feast of Unleavened Bread," v. 6) and Pentecost (v. 16). For the Christian practice of the breaking of the bread on the first day of the week (Sunday) is always a celebration of death and restoration to new life, precisely as these things are interpreted in the light of the Jewish feasts of Passover and Pentecost.

As for the detailed itinerary surrounding this anecdote, the listing of places could simply be explained as evidence of an eyewitness's passion for detail. It could also reflect Luke's intention to show how Jesus' heroic follower Paul imitates his master even in his making an extended final journey to Jerusalem, where he too will be interrogated by Jewish and Gentile officials.

20:17-38 Paul's testament to the Ephesian elders

Paul makes a point of bypassing Ephesus (to avoid those plotting against him?), but he is eager to summon the elders of that community to Miletus, some forty miles to the south, so that he can bid them farewell. What follows is the only speech in Acts that Paul addresses to a Christian audience.

The speech follows the conventions of other biblical testaments, touching on the topics of a review of the speaker's life, commissioning of successors, encouragement and warnings regarding the future, farewell and blessing. Like other classic farewell addresses, it serves both to present the speaker as a model for the readers/auditors and also to address the historical aftermath of the speaker and interpret what is going forward historically.

In the context of Luke-Acts, the speech is a privileged moment in Paul's own imitation of Christ. Like Jesus, he makes his own "passion prediction" on the way to Jerusalem. And his farewell address to the Ephesian elders has much in common with Jesus' own farewell address to the apostles at the Last Supper (Luke 22:25-38). Like Jesus at the supper, Paul characterizes authority in the messianic community as one of humble service, focuses on the kingdom, encourages his listeners to care for those left in their charge (Jesus: "Strengthen your brothers"; Paul: "Help the weak"), and warns of future challenges. That Paul can serve as model to the extent that he himself has imitated Jesus is suggested by explicit reference to Jesus in the beatitude that climaxes the speech: "It is more blessed to give than to receive" (v. 35).

Several things about the language of this speech are worth noting. Along with Luke's calling the group "presbyters" (*presbyteroi,* or "elders," v. 17), the usual term in Acts for leaders other than the apostles in the churches, Paul calls them "overseers" (v. 28, translating *episkopoi,* the word rendered "bishops" in later Christian writings). This reflects the apparent equivalence of those terms as found, for example, in Titus 1:5-7. In the ordinary Greek of the day, *episkopos* meant "superintendent" or "guardian" in any of a variety of social settings. In first-century Christian writings it serves as a Hellenistic equivalent of the more Judean term "elder," which Luke uses for both Jewish and Christian leaders throughout Luke-Acts. In the second century these terms will be used to designate distinct roles in the evolving three-tier hierarchical structure of a single local bishop (*episkopos*), directing a number of elders (*presbyteroi*, from which the English words "priest" and "presbyterate" derive), supported by a further group of *diakonoi*, or deacons.

One remarkable verse (v. 28) deserves special attention: "Keep watch over yourselves and over the whole flock of which the holy Spirit has appointed you overseers, in which you tend the church of God that he acquired with his own blood." This translation, which renders straightforwardly what scholars generally agree is the best reading of the Greek text, raises the question of what it can mean to speak of God's blood. An early response to this problem was the introduction of the variant reading "church of the Lord" for "church of God," which was open to the understanding that "his blood" referred to the blood of the Lord Jesus. But the more difficult reading, "church of God," does appear to be the more authentic one. A possible solution of this crux is to translate the final phrase, "the blood of his Own" (referring to the Son, Jesus). In any case, with the references to "holy Spirit," "God," and "blood," we have in this verse a rare New Testament adumbration of the later, more developed doctrine of the Trinity. Using phrases that catch important aspects of Paul's theology as it is expressed in the Pauline letters (conversion to God, faith in the Lord Jesus, the power of the Spirit to form community, the gospel of God's grace, the plan of God, the importance of perseverance), this speech is a fitting conclusion to Luke's narrative of Paul's intra-Christian ministry.

21:1-14 Paul and the delegation continue the journey to Jerusalem

After departing from Ephesus, Paul and companions continue the journey to Jerusalem. This stage of the journey comprises the third "we" section in Acts (vv. 1-18), implying the author's presence during this part of the journey. The summary gives us a glimpse of how people got about the Mediterranean in those days: they hung around a port until they found a cargo ship going in the general direction of their intended destination.

The fact that Paul and his entourage find communities of Christians in Tyre and Ptolemais indicates that the evangelization of Phoenicia, to which Luke referred in 11:19, took root and flourished. Indeed, the intensity of communion with the disciples at Ptolemais is enough to warrant the same kind of prayerful seaside send-off they received at Ephesus (20:36-38).

These episodes illustrate that hearing and following the Spirit are not a simple matter. Although the Tyrian Christians keep telling Paul "through the Spirit" not to embark for Jerusalem, he continues. Obviously, he feels they have misinterpreted the Spirit in this case. And when Agabus, who prophesied accurately the famine during the reign of Claudius (Acts 11:28), acts out symbolically what he perceives to be the Spirit's message regarding Paul's fate in Jerusalem, he gets it only partly right: Paul will indeed be bound in Jerusalem, but by Romans, not by Jews. Faced with Paul's determination to go to Jerusalem even if it means death, it is the companions, not Paul, who imitate Jesus' struggle in facing the prospect of death (Luke 22:39-42), first with resistance, then acceptance.

21:15-26 Paul has his Jewish fidelity challenged

When Paul and company arrive in Jerusalem, James and a plenary session of the Jerusalem elders hear Paul's report about what God has been doing through his ministry among the Gentiles. The Jerusalem Christian authorities are happy enough with that good news, but they inform Paul that the success among the Gentiles has raised concerns among the "many thousands" (v. 20) of Jewish Christians in the area who have gotten the idea that he is urging all the Jews in the Diaspora to abandon the Mosaic practices. Although nothing we have read in Acts supports this charge, Paul's own letter to the Romans shows that the notion that he was denigrating the Mosaic Law was prevalent enough to warrant the full-scale defense that he makes in that major letter.

James's strategy for damage control in this regard—having Paul accompany four men to the temple and sponsor the ceremonies fulfilling their nazirite vows (see Num 6:3-20 for the nazirite ritual)—seems promising. Twentieth-century digs to the south of the Temple Mount have revealed the *mikvaot* (immersion baths), where pilgrims ritually purified themselves before climbing the stairs leading up into the temple precincts. The public nature of this purification, along with Paul's sponsoring of the sacrifices (twelve animals, three apiece for four men) would offer a clear rebuttal to the accusations that Paul was discouraging observance of the Torah.

The reference in verse 25 to the policy regarding Gentile converts expressed in the apostolic decree of the Jerusalem Council (Acts 15:23-29) strikes an odd note here. Paul, after all, played a major part in that meeting and, indeed, helped promulgate its policy regarding Gentile converts (16:4). But the notice serves to remind the reader that the present issue, Paul's attitude toward Jewish observance of the Torah, is something other than what is expected of Gentile Christians.

Given Paul's own language about "[dying] to the law" (Gal 2:19), some commentators find Luke's portrayal here of Paul's "compromise" implausible. Yet it can be argued that Paul is acting in a way wholly consistent

Acts 21

with the policy he articulates in 1 Corinthians 9:19-21: "Although I am free in regard to all, I have made myself a slave to all so as to win over as many as possible. To the Jews I became like a Jew to win over Jews; to those under the law I became like one under the law—though I myself am not under the law—to win over those under the law. To those outside the law I became like one outside the law—though I am not outside God's law but within the law of Christ—to win over those outside the law."

Sadly, in the end the strategy fails, for in the events that follow, nothing indicates that Paul's Jerusalem relief fund was accepted, and no one in the Jerusalem Christian community comes to his rescue in the confrontation that continues to unfold. The Jerusalem church, so robustly present in the early chapters of Acts and now grown to "many thousands," disappears from view during the final seven chapters.

21:27-36 Romans rescue Paul from an attempted lynching

In addition to the local members of the sect of the Nazarene, other Jews, pilgrims from the province of Asia, mount an attack against Paul. Having recognized their fellow provincial, the Gentile Trophimus, some had jumped to the conclusion that Paul had taken this man into the court of Israel on the Temple Mount, thereby breaching the barrier separating Gentiles from the space reserved for Israelites. Signs posted on the balustrade forbade Gentiles to pass this point on pain of death. The rioting crowd falls upon Paul, haul him out of the sacred space, and try to kill him on the spot.

At this point the cohort commander intervenes with centurions and soldiers, who bring him to "the compound," a reference to the Antonia fortress, the military headquarters and barracks contiguous with the northwest corner of the temple platform. The shout of the crowd—"Away with him!"—echoes the cry at the trial of Jesus before Pilate (Luke 23:18).

21:37-40 Paul identifies himself

When Paul identifies himself as a Jew and a Roman citizen to the cohort commander, the latter is relieved that he is not "the Egyptian"—the last rabble-rouser the Romans had to deal with. The reference fits Josephus's account of an "Egyptian false prophet" who, a few years earlier, had led thirty thousand (Josephus's number) to the Mount of Olives to wait for Jerusalem to fall like Jericho in the days of Joshua. Paul and his purpose are something else entirely, as his ensuing speech will reveal. Having spoken to the commander in Greek, the *lingua franca* of that part of the empire, he now proceeds to address the crowd in what Luke calls "Hebrew"—almost certainly a reference to Aramaic, the mother tongue of Jesus and the common language of Judea.

22:1-21 Paul's first defense speech

Paul's exchange with the cohort commander had raised questions of ethnicity and status. Paul is a Jew, not "the Egyptian." He speaks Greek as well as Aramaic. And he is a Roman citizen. Now as he begins his speech, he makes it clear that he speaks as a Jew to Jews ("My brothers and fathers"). The clause "what I am about to say in my defense" renders the word *apologia*, the classical term for a legal defense, thereby setting the agenda for the final seven chapters of Acts. Facing a crowd driven by the zeal for the Mosaic Law—who are attacking Paul because they think he has violated that Law—he makes the perfect move to win their good will. He displays his Jewish pedigree, citing his Jewish upbringing, his training in the Law, even describing his own past persecution of "this Way" as stemming from precisely the "zeal . . . for God" that they are presently demonstrating in their persecution of him.

Just as Luke repeated twice the story of Peter's first mission to Gentiles in his encounter with Cornelius's household (in Acts 10, 11, and 15), so he retells the story of Paul's conversion/commission here, for the second in what will be another series of three accounts. No clumsy redundancy, these repetitions are the author's way of underscoring the importance of these pivotal events. As in the case of Peter's encounter with Cornelius, each retelling comes with variations and developments that fit the immediate context and help the reader fathom the significance more deeply.

In this version of Paul's encounter with the risen Jesus, the brightness is enhanced: at the most brilliant time of day, *noon*, Paul experiences a brightness that outshines the noontime sunlight! His visual impairment is not called blindness here but is simply ascribed to the brightness of the light. Whereas in the account of Acts 9 the companions heard the voice but see no one, here they see the light but hear no voice.

These are not the discrepancies of a negligent author but variations of an artist in full control of his material. Saying that "the Lord" answered Paul enhances the nature of the vision as a theophany, that is, a manifestation of God. (It is not impossible that Luke's emphasis on blindness in the midst of brightness is prompted by his perception that Paul here experiences the noontime blindness that Deuteronomy 28:28 promises Israel if it does not hearken to the voice of the Lord.)

The Jewishness of Ananias is enhanced. He is a "devout observer of the law" (v. 12). And he announces that their ancestral God has designated Paul to witness (what he had seen and heard) "before *all*" (emphasis added) about "the Righteous One," an eminently Jewish title for Jesus, denoting fidelity to the covenant and echoing Luke's unique version of the confession of the centurion under the cross (Luke 23:47: "This man was *dikaios*" ["innocent," "righteous"]). Here there is less emphasis on the physical cure from blindness; restored vision simply follows upon Ananias's word.

If Paul's adversaries are challenging his mission to Gentiles, the final part of the speech claims that the outreach to the nations was far from the action of an apostate. Like the great prophet Isaiah, Paul "saw the Lord" in the temple, protested his unworthiness, and received his mandate there, at the liturgical heart of Israel (v. 18; see Isa 6:1). In response, the crowd repeats the rejection of 21:36.

22:22-29 Paul imprisoned

Just as the tribune was caught in a false assumption about Paul earlier (that he was "the Egyptian," 21:38), now he is caught in another mistake about the Apostle's identity—assuming that this Jew is not a Roman citizen. Wrong again. This vivid drama, with Paul stretched out for interrogation under the lash and then rescued at the last minute, is more than good storytelling. It also demonstrates for Luke's readership that Paul, as a Roman citizen, is eminently qualified to mediate the gospel to the Roman world as well as to the Diaspora.

22:30–23:11 The investigation continues: Paul before the Sanhedrin

Having learned of Paul's Roman citizenship, the commander (Claudius Lysias, we learn in verse 26) tries a gentler mode of getting to the facts of the charges against Paul. He orders the chief priests and the full Sanhedrin to convene for a hearing. Notice that these people are not necessarily gathered as adversaries of Paul; they comprise the official Jewish body that the commander now looks to in order to discover whether Paul is a danger to Roman law and order. Thus we are not yet dealing with a trial; Lysias is still conducting a Roman investigation to see if Paul has done something that warrants a Roman trial.

Paul's declaration that he has always conducted himself with a clear conscience before God surely applies to his whole life and supports the notion that his experience on the road to Damascus is better understood as a prophetic call rather than a conversion, at least in the moral or religious sense.

The exchange between Paul and the high priest Ananias is loaded with irony. Paul comes across as a better exponent of the Law than does its official guardian. His assertion that he did not realize Ananias was the high priest implies that the latter's behavior, punishing an unconvicted person, was hardly the deportment expected of a person in that office.

Before any formal inquest begins, Paul asserts that he is a Pharisee (v. 6) and makes a simple proclamation of the gospel: "I am on trial for the hope in the resurrection of the dead." Commentators note Paul's shrewdness in playing the afterlife card, a key point of division between the two parties. As Jesus' controversy with the Sadducees in Luke 20:27-40 demonstrated, Sadducees denied the resurrection. And as Luke notes here in a rare aside, neither did they believe in postmortem survival as "angel" or "spirit." For the Sadducees, if you could not find it in the Torah, it didn't count. This, of course, splits the Sanhedrin, with the Pharisees refusing to condemn Brother Paul.

But more is going on here than clever forensic strategy. By the time of Luke's writing of Acts, the high priest Ananias has indeed been "struck," assassinated in A.D. 66, according to Josephus. The Sadducees have ceased to exist as authorities, having lost their power base with the destruction of the temple by the Romans in A.D. 70. This leaves the Pharisees, the current leaders of formative Judaism, as the most important figures for Luke's readers. They emerge in this episode not so much as defenders of Paul but rather as men acting in bad will. Though they accept "the resurrection of the dead" as a hope, they resist Paul's testimony that the hoped-for resurrection has already begun concretely in Jesus of Nazareth.

It is this, rather than Paul's legal guilt or innocence, that will remain the issue for the remainder of the book. It is really the gospel that is on trial. In the context of the narrative, Paul's focus on the resurrection makes it clear to the Roman tribune (the most important auditor of this hearing) that the charges against Paul are Jewish matters, nothing of concern to imperial governance.

23:12-35 A plot to assassinate Paul and a Roman rescue

A group of more than forty of Paul's co-religionists make a pact not to eat or drink until they have killed him. Luke offers no motive for such fanaticism. One can only surmise that these men exhibit the kind of rebellious zealotry that will come to expression some ten years later in the Zealot revolt against Rome in A.D. 67–70. They may have perceived in Paul's messianic mission to the Gentiles (and his rumored "watering down" of Jewish practices) a vitiation of Judean nationalism.

Tipped off by Paul's nephew regarding the plot to ambush his prisoner (v. 16), Lysias moves to place him in the protective custody of an armed cavalry, who are to escort him safely to the governor Felix (in office A.D. 52–59, the sixth prefect after Pontius Pilate).

Luke gives us the gist of the report Lysias sends to Felix. Given that our author has already provided his version of the events reported in the message, Luke no doubt expects the reader to smile at the way this Roman official tweaks the truth to put the best possible face on his conduct. We know from 21:27-40 that Lysias first quelled the riot, arrested Paul, and eventually ordered him interrogated under the lash. Only *then*, when Paul announced his citizenship, did the tribune first learn of it. As Lysias tells it in his report, his action with Paul was from the beginning a bold rescue of a known Roman citizen. In his favor, his present "protective custody" action has in fact become such a rescue.

We may wonder why Felix, when he learns that Paul is from Cilicia, does not send him there for trial. In fact, Syria-Cilicia is a double province at this time (Vespasian will split it later), and Felix governs the area in which the charges have been brought against the accused. So he is responsible for the trial.

24:1-27 Paul is heard before Felix, in public and privately

Finally, with the arrival from Jerusalem of Ananias and some elders with their attorney, Paul faces a formal trial before the procurator Felix. After paying unctuous compliments to the governor, Tertullus, the prosecuting attorney, levels a set of broad and, as we readers know, unfounded charges against Paul: (a) he sows dissension among Jews all over the world [empire] (*oikoumenē*) and (b) he tried to profane the temple. Tertullus even tries to dignify with the term "arrest" (v. 6) what we know to have been an attempt at mob lynching.

As in his speech on the Antonia barracks steps to the crowd of would-be lynchers (Acts 22), Paul answers these false charges by rehearsing the facts that establish his exemplary and eminently traditional Jewish behavior. Far from desecrating the temple, he went there to worship their ancestral God. He is still a Torah-keeping Jew who worships the God he has always served in good conscience, except that now it is according to "the Way" that his adversaries dismiss as a "sect." Their charges are hearsay and therefore without merit. The original plaintiffs were the "Jews from . . . Asia" (21:27), but they are not present to testify. And the only thing that the present plaintiffs have witnessed was his proclamation that he is on trial "for the resurrection of the dead" (v. 21; see 23:6).

Paul's claim to have come "to bring alms for my nation and offerings" (v. 17) is the sole reference in Acts to his transmission of the Jerusalem relief fund (see Rom 15:25-26) as the main motive for his presence in Jerusalem. By calling the collection "alms for my nation" and linking it with his sponsoring of sacrifices for the nazirites fulfilling their vows, he casts those actions in language that associates them with the essence of Jewish piety.

Felix's knowledge that Paul, as bearer of these funds, controls a substantial amount of money may well be what generated the governor's hope for a bribe (v. 26).

Since Felix is informed about "the Way" (through his Jewish wife Drusilla?), and since he has perhaps decided that the Way is no threat to Roman social order, he postpones judgment, pending further (unnecessary) consultation with Lysias. Felix allows two years to elapse without coming to judgment. Like most of the leaders in Luke-Acts, Jewish or Roman, Felix wants chiefly to look after his own interests. (Regarding Felix's administration, the Roman historian Tacitus observes, "He exercised the power of a king with the spirit of the slave.")

25:1-12 Paul appeals to Caesar and comes before Agrippa

This chapter of Acts functions mainly as a transition. Luke is setting the scene for Paul's climactic speech before Agrippa in chapter 26. As he does so, he strengthens two themes important to his history: (a) the controversy regarding Paul and the Christian Way is a thoroughly Jewish matter, and (b) the legal structure and personnel of the Roman Empire are functioning at this time as instruments of divine Providence.

When Jewish leaders present their (now two-year-old) case against Paul and request that he be sent to them in Jerusalem (to be ambushed and killed along the way), Festus asserts his imperial authority. If they have charges to bring against a man in Roman custody, let them do it on the procurator's turf, before his tribunal in Caesarea (v. 5). Luke reflects Paul's adversaries' charges in Paul's response: he has done nothing against the Torah or against the temple *or against Caesar*. "Against Caesar" is a new note, paralleling the charges of the Sanhedrin against Jesus before Pilate (Luke 23:2). When Festus offers Paul the option of facing a formal trial before the Sanhedrin in Jerusalem, he appeals to Caesar. This allows Festus to unburden himself of this case, and he decides to send Paul to Rome.

25:13-27 Paul before Agrippa

Enter King Agrippa and his twice-widowed sister Bernice. Agrippa—Herod Agrippa II—is the fourth Herod to appear in Luke's work. Herod the Great, the famous builder of Caesarea and Masada and spectacular renovator of the second temple, reigned at the time of the infancies of John the Baptist and Jesus (Luke 1:5). Herod the Tetrarch (Antipas), son of Herod the Great, ruled Galilee and Perea during the rest of Jesus' life. Herod Agrippa I (ruled A.D. 41–44), grandson of Herod the Great, appeared (and died) in Acts 12. Now we meet the great-grandson, Herod Agrippa II (who

Acts 25

ruled after A.D. 50). We learn nothing new in Festus's report to Agrippa, but the way the report is expressed is telling. Festus characterizes the elders' charges as entirely a Jewish affair—"some issues . . . about their own religion"—much as Gallio spoke when he dismissed the Corinthian Jews' quarrel with Paul in Acts 18:15 and as Lysias wrote in his report to Felix (23:29). There is a nice irony in the title used for the emperor in v. 26. The Greek word that our New American Bible version translates (accurately, in this context) as "our sovereign" is *ho kyrios* (literally, "the lord"). Given that the last instance of that word was a title for the risen Jesus (23:11) and the next instance, a few verses later, again refers to Jesus (26:15), the use of the title here (for Nero!) highlights the irony that the true lord of this history is not the emperor but Jesus—an irony that the book of Revelation will exploit richly.

When Festus invites Agrippa to interrogate Paul, it is not as a formal trial but rather as a hearing in the service of the Roman process; Festus hopes the Jewish king will come up with something substantive to report to Rome. This move also gives Luke the opportunity to underscore another parallel between the experience of the Apostle and his Master: as Procurator Pilate sent Jesus to the then current Jewish king (Herod Antipas) for a kind of hearing, so Procurator Festus presents Paul to another Jewish king. In Jesus' case, of course, Pilate was attempting to shunt the accused off to another jurisdiction. Festus, however, does not intend to let his charge slip out of Roman custody.

Verses 23-27 set the stage for Paul's final extended apologia in chapter 26. Luke packs the audience hall with an entourage that includes "cohort commanders and the prominent men of the city" (v. 23). Thus Paul will be addressing, along with Festus, Agrippa, and Bernice, powerful members of Caesarea's Gentile community.

26:1-23 The inquest before Governor Festus and King Agrippa

The speech that Paul gives to these powerful representatives of the Jewish and Gentile communities is, like the speeches in Acts 2, 3, 13, and 17, one of Luke's theological masterpieces. Much of what we denote by the post-biblical terms "ecclesiology" (theology of church), "Christology" (how Jesus is the Messiah), and "soteriology" (theory of salvation) Luke communicates through this speech.

First, Luke highlights Paul speaking as an expert Jew (a Pharisee, and therefore one highly trained in Israelite tradition) to a well-informed Jewish leader (Agrippa was completing the project of his great-grandfather, the renovation of the Second Temple). Moreover, Paul had demonstrated his

Acts 26

zeal for his people's tradition in his efforts against what he had at first perceived as a threat to those traditions, the Way of the Jesus people. To top it off, the centerpiece of his teaching and preaching is the essence of Jewish hope—resurrection from the dead. The unmentioned novelty, of course, is that Paul and the rest of the people of the Way have been announcing that the expected end-time general resurrection has been stunningly anticipated by the resurrection of a single person, Jesus of Nazareth (see the reference to "the first to rise from the dead" at verse 23).

Paul then recounts for the second time the experience on the road to Damascus, making it the third time for us readers (who first heard of it in the original narrative of Acts 9 and then in the speech of Acts 22). The variations in the details and language in this third telling are far more than an effort at literary variety. The language about light, darkness, and seeing participates in a consistent symbolic theme carrying powerful implications.

This time the light from the sky *is brighter than the noonday sun*, flattening *everyone* to the ground. And the language about blindness—which was quite literally physical in the Acts 9 account, then muted in the Acts 22 version—is not even applied to Paul here. That imagery now describes the experience of Gentile converts. Here the emphasis is on the fact that Paul will witness to what he *has seen* and that he is being missioned to *open the eyes of the Gentiles* so that *they* may *turn from darkness to light*. Thus what Paul first experienced literally in his physical blindness in the first account becomes a metaphor for the Christian mission to the nations in this third account. This metaphor is developed further at the climax of the speech: Paul is saying "nothing different from what the prophets and Moses foretold, that the Messiah must suffer and that, as the first to rise from the dead, he would *proclaim light both to our people and to the Gentiles*" (vv. 22-23, emphasis added).

And how, precisely, does Luke understand that the risen Messiah "proclaims light" after the resurrection? The whole of Luke-Acts answers that question, especially in its use of quotations of Isaiah. At Luke 2:30-32, during the presentation in the temple, when Simeon takes the child Jesus into his arms and sings his famous *Nunc Dimittis*, he draws upon Isaiah's imagery of vision and light: "for my eyes have seen your salvation [LXX Isa 40:5] / which you prepared in sight of all the peoples, / a light for revelation to the Gentiles [Isa 42:6; 49:6], / and glory for your people Israel."

At his debut in Nazareth, Jesus employs LXX Isaiah 61:1-2 to characterize his mission, and the center of that quotation is "He has sent me to proclaim . . . recovery of sight to the blind" (Luke 4:18). Jesus does indeed give sight to the blind in the physical cure of the blind in his pre-Easter activity (Luke

7:21; 18:35-43), but it takes the post-Easter activity of the church in Acts to fulfill the promise of the Servant functioning as a light to the Gentiles. Luke makes that quite explicit when, at the synagogue in Pisidian Antioch, he has Paul and Barnabas (both!) say, "We now turn to the Gentiles. For so the Lord has commanded us, 'I have made you a light to the Gentiles, that you may be an instrument of salvation to the ends of the earth'" (Acts 13:46-47; see Isa 49:6). Strikingly, language describing the Servant of Yahweh in Isaiah, earlier applied to Jesus by Simeon, is now applied to the post-Easter continuation of Jesus' mission by his followers. Thus when we hear the reference to the risen Christ proclaiming "light to the Gentiles" at the climax of Paul's speech in Acts 26, we know that what Paul and the rest of the church are doing is not only in continuity with Jesus' mission but their work is somehow the work of the risen Lord himself.

This was the import of Paul's vision on the road to Damascus ("Saul, Saul, why are you persecuting me?"—v. 14b). The risen Lord is identified with the believing community, and through them he opens the eyes of the nations and brings them from darkness to light. At the end of the book, Luke will have Paul use Isaiah 6:9-10 ("They have closed their eyes, / so that they may not see with their eyes") to characterize those of Israel who, like Saul before his conversion, fail to respond to the mission.

Whereas Festus responds to the defense simply with amazement ("You are mad, Paul") and Agrippa with cynicism, Festus, Bernice, and the rest comment that Paul is doing nothing that deserves death or imprisonment (v. 31). Thus, like Jesus (see Luke 23:4, 14, and 22), Paul is declared innocent three times by Roman officials and a Jewish king (Lysias, 23:29; Festus, 25:25; and Agrippa, 26:31-32). And also like (and with) Jesus, he is fulfilling Servant Israel's vocation to be a light to the nations.

27:1-44 To Rome: storm, shipwreck, and survival

As he nears the end of his history, Luke gives us a whopping good sea adventure. Some recent commentators have wondered why Luke, who can be so sparse in his treatment of such momentous events as, for example, the early spread of the Christian mission into the Hellenistic world (11:20-21), decides at this point to spend so much parchment on the details of Paul's voyage to Rome. Some scholars, subscribing to the theory that the "we" sections are a literary convention and noting resonances with other ancient accounts of shipwreck, have suggested that Luke has imaginatively embellished some minimal facts available to him regarding Paul's voyage. Others, noting the abundance of nautical technical terms, posit that Luke took over an available voyage account and applied it to Paul.

It is, however, simpler and more reasonable to presume that Luke is sparse when his sources are sparse and that he willingly shares details when he has access to them, especially when he was an eyewitness to the events he describes. The first-person plural of this final "we" section (27:1–28:16) supports such an interpretation. Moreover, we have no evidence of the "we" form used as a literary convention in ancient history writing by authors who are not describing their own experience.

That Paul himself was richly experienced in sea travel and its dangers is clear from his remark in 2 Corinthians 11:25: "Three times I was shipwrecked, I passed a night and a day on the deep. . . ." And the tradition that Luke was a close companion of Paul is firm (Phlm 24; Col 4:14; and 2 Tim 4:11). There is no reason to presume that he was inexperienced in sea travel or lacked the vocabulary to describe it. Of course, master storyteller that he is, he knows he has a "good yarn" here. He tells it with relish and in a way that serves his history of what God has accomplished in and through these events, which could be called the passion and vindication of the Apostle Paul.

As a Roman citizen, Paul, accompanied by his faithful companion Aristarchus (see 19:29; 20:4; Col 4:10; and Phlm 24) and the narrator (presumably Luke), is placed under the protective custody of a centurion, one Julius. There being no commercial passenger ships in antiquity, Julius books passage on a ship returning to the Aegean area. The "philanthropic" (*philanthropos*) Julius allows Paul to visit friends, probably Christians, during a stop at Sidon. Because of the late fall weather, the ship hugs the coast, passing behind the shelter of Cyprus. At Myra they transfer to an Alexandrian grain ship headed for Italy. When they put in at Fair Havens, in the mid-south side of the island of Crete, Paul advises wintering there, since continuing now would entail loss of cargo and lives—reasonable advice that will turn out, in the end, to be only partly accurate.

When the voyage continues and a hurricane wind (a "northeaster") forces them dangerously off course, Paul provides quite a different sort of message. A dream vision enables him to urge courage and to predict (more accurately than his earlier commonsense prediction) safety to all aboard. The God he belongs to and serves would save them. It is significant that he says "God" rather than "the Lord Jesus" here; it is language that a pagan audience would more easily understand, and Luke is emphasizing that it is the maker of heaven and earth who is managing what is going forward in the midst of this chaos of nature.

Speaking of Luke's use of language, one cannot help noting that the description of Paul, acting in the manner of the host presiding at a Jewish

Acts 27

meal (taking bread, thanking God, breaking the bread), evokes the language of the Last Supper and Christian Eucharist. Most commentators rightly insist that Luke surely does *not* mean to say that Paul, attended by his two Christian companions, is presiding at a Christian celebration of the Lord's Supper before a "congregation" of 273 pagans! At the same time, Luke the savvy wordsmith surely knows that his Christian readers (or hearers) would catch the resonance with the Christian liturgy (and with Luke 5:16 and 22:19).

Indeed, once that resonance is heard in verse 35, further resonances abound. For example:

1) Immediately before this mealtime blessing, Paul had said, "Not a hair of the head of anyone of you will be lost." This, of course, repeats what Jesus had said in his end-time discourse (Luke 21:18), which also speaks of "signs in the *sun, the moon, and the stars*," and asserts that "on earth nations will be in dismay, *perplexed by the roaring of the sea and the waves*" (Luke 21:25, emphasis added). In this literal experience of such a sea, Luke has made a point of noting that "neither the sun nor the stars were visible for many days" (Acts 27:20).

2) In a way that is more obvious in Greek than in English translation, Luke uses "salvation" language suggestively. The words used to describe physical survival of storm and shipwreck in this account (*sōzō* in vv. 20, 31; *sōtēria* in v. 34) are, to be sure, the usual words for describing rescue and survival; but in Luke's work, they are also used for salvation in the ultimate (eschatological) sense (e.g., *sōtēria*, "salvation," at Luke 1:77 [forgiveness of sins]; at 19:9 [Zacchaeus's conversion]; and at Acts 4:12; 13:26, 47; *sōtērion*, "salvation," at Luke 2:20 and 3:6 [Isa 40:5]; *sōzō*, the verbal form of "save," at Luke 7:50; 8:12; 13:23; 17:19; 18:26; 19:10; Acts 2:21 [Joel 3:5]; 2:47; 4:12; and 15:1, 11). That diction makes it easy, even inevitable, that readers will hear salvation overtones in the storm and shipwreck account of Acts 27.

3) Finally, in an extended work that has thematized the importance of detachment from material goods on the Christian journey of following Jesus, all the literally realistic details of dumping cargo, jettisoning gear, cutting off the dinghy, and abandoning anchors point to the need for traveling light to achieve salvation. (See Luke 10:4; 14:33; 18:25-27: "'For it is easier for a camel to pass through the eye of a needle than for a rich person to enter the kingdom of God.' Those who heard this said, 'Then who can be saved?' And he said, 'What is impossible for human beings is possible for God.'")

This is not to say that Luke has composed an allegory of Christian life in Acts 27. Rather, he has reported this tale of God's care of Paul and his mission in such a way that the historical account of nautical disaster and survival resonates with and alludes to the end-time situation of the church and the world. (We are "all in the same boat," and God is our only hope.) A further clue that Luke has this resonance in mind may be the fact that only his version of the synoptic tradition of the stilling of the storm pictures Jesus and the disciples as *sailing* (*pleontōn*, Luke 8:23).

28:1-10 Malta: hospitality, vindication, and healing

The story of the sea travel, including the "we" section that tells it, continues through the arrival in Rome (in verse 16, where the New American Bible translates "he entered," the Greek has "*we* entered"). The safe arrival of all 276 on the shore of Malta leads to a supreme irony. Everything has been building, we readers have been led to believe, to a trial and judgment by the highest authority of the secular world, Caesar. But Luke will end his second volume without any mention of that Roman trial (which, tradition tells us, resulted in Paul's death). Instead, we are told of judgment by a lower, more spontaneous "court," reflecting the higher, divine judgment.

In Mediterranean antiquity, survival of disaster demonstrated divine favor. Luke calls the hospitable Maltese natives *barbaroi* (that is, non-Greek-speakers), but he speaks of their uncommon *philanthropia*. When they see Paul attacked by a snake, they interpret that as a sign of divine disfavor—indeed, proof that Paul is a murderer (v. 5). However, when he fails to swell up and drop dead, they call him a god! An overreaction, to be sure, but a powerful point has been made. As God had vindicated Jesus through resurrection, so he vindicates Paul through rescue from storm and snakebite. Further affirmation comes by way of Paul's ability to extend Jesus' healing ministry to the father of Governor Publius and other sick of the island who come to him.

28:11-31 Arrival in Rome and testimony to Jews

How a work ends is a matter of great importance to any careful author, especially in antiquity (recall Aristotle's stress on the importance of a beginning, middle, and end of a work). Luke chooses to end his two-volume work, not, as we already observed, with the expected Roman trial, but with several encounters between Paul and local Jewish leaders. Because these dialogues issue in "mixed reviews" at best and end with Paul quoting Isaiah 6:9-10 and turning once again to Gentiles, some commentators have read this as a declaration that God has, at this point, severed his covenant relationship with the Jews. Since this kind of interpretation has supported Christian anti-Judaism, it is important to read Luke's narrative ending carefully, on its own terms.

Acts 28

The first contact that Paul and his two companions make on Italian soil is with people in Puteoli, whom Luke calls "brothers." Since it is the Gentile Luke who refers to them as brothers, the presumption is that they are fellow Christians. After a week of enjoying their hospitality (the Roman guard himself apparently glad for the break), they move on to the Forum of Appius and then to the rest stop called Three Taverns. At both places brothers come down from Rome to meet them. Paul's response to the brothers ("Paul gave thanks to God and took courage," v. 15) confirms the likelihood that these are also Christians. (The Christian community in Rome had been founded by others than Paul or Peter, possibly by the "travelers from Rome" [2:10] who had witnessed the birth of the church at Pentecost.)

The author James D. G. Dunn makes a charming interpretive conjecture regarding Luke's inclusion of the name of the Alexandrian ship that takes Paul's party to Rome, the *Dioscuri* ("Zeus's Boys," that is, Caster and Pollux, twin sons of the god Zeus). Noting that Luke uses "brothers" four times in the next few verses, first of Christians then of Jews, this author suggests that Luke calls attention to the name of the ship because for him the Christian and Jewish "brothers" that Paul is about to encounter are "indeed twin children of the one God, brothers of Paul, and so of one another."

Once established in Rome, apparently under house arrest in his own rented lodgings (v. 28), Paul calls together (non-Christian) Jewish leaders, who are also called "brothers" (vv. 17 and 21). His purpose is a kind of preemptive defense. Since the plaintiffs in his case are the Jerusalem Jews, he presents his apologia to their Roman counterparts. For us readers, the defense is familiar: the Roman authorities in Caesarea have not found him guilty of anything warranting the death penalty, and his behavior is perfectly Jewish: he preaches "the hope of Israel." What is new is his hinting at the possibility (not pursued) of a countersuit (v. 19). They reply that they have heard nothing bad about him, by letter or hearsay. But they have heard about this controversial "sect" that he promotes, and they do want to learn more about that.

To this end, Paul holds an all-day conference with an even greater number of Jewish leaders, focusing on the heart of the matter: the kingdom of God and Jesus as fulfillment of the Scriptures. Some are convinced, others are not, and they leave without agreeing among themselves. As commentary on this divided response, Paul invokes Isaiah 6:9-10, implying that those who have failed to accept Jesus as the hope of Israel have fulfilled that prophecy. He adds, alluding to LXX Isa 40:5 (quoted earlier at Luke 3:6), that "this salvation of God has been sent to the Gentiles; they will listen."

Does this final word of Paul mean that the door is closed to further mission to Israel? No more than the presence of Isaiah 6:9-10 in the original commission of Isaiah of Jerusalem indicated that he had no mission to his people (belied by the sixty chapters that follow in the scroll of Isaiah). The rejection of the gospel by the majority of historical Israel is, for Luke, a fact to be faced. But this fact, and the turn to the Gentiles, is no more a definitive dismissal of the Jews than are the parallel moments in the synagogues of Pisidian Antioch (13:46-47) or Corinth (18:6). In ending with this episode, Paul has helped his (largely Gentile) readers understand (a) their relationship to historical Israel, (b) the majority of Israel's rejection of its Messiah, and (c) how the Gentiles have become beneficiaries of Israel's vocation to be a "light to the nations" (Isa 49:6).

Meanwhile, in the spirit of the parables of the barren fig tree (Luke 13:6-9) and two lost sons (Luke 15:11-32), the door remains open. In Paul's continued ministry during his house arrest, he receives "*all* who came to him" (emphasis added). He models the community's ongoing mission as "he proclaimed the kingdom of God and taught about the Lord Jesus Christ with boldness of speech [*meta parrēsias*], without hindrance [*akōlytōs*]" (v. 31, my translation). Note that the last two words powerfully affirm the theme of freedom running through the whole of Acts; *parrēsia* is that same freedom and boldness of speech for which the community prayed in Acts 4:29 and which the leaders exhibit throughout Acts (2:29; 4:13, 31; 9:27-28; 13:46; 14:3; 18:26; 19:8; and 26:25). And the final word, *akōlytōs* ("without hindrance") reminds us that neither the one who was sent to proclaim release to prisoners (Luke 4:18) nor his Spirit-led followers were hindered by imprisonment or even death.

Luke's two-volume work, which began in the Jerusalem temple, ends with the mission continuing unabated in a rented Roman apartment. In the end, Luke's history is not so much about Peter or Paul as about the fidelity of God and the continuing prophetic mission of the followers of Jesus. If the ending of Acts surprises us by failing to include the martyrdom of Paul (which was surely known to Luke), that very inconclusiveness serves to remind us that we are invited to continue the story with our lives.

The Pauline Letters

Vincent M. Smiles

INTRODUCTION

On his own admission, Paul once tried to destroy the church, but because of "a revelation of Jesus Christ" (Gal 1:11-16) he became in many respects the greatest of the apostles (1 Cor 15:8-10) and the most important witness of early Christianity. His conversion to become "an apostle of Christ Jesus" (1 Cor 1:1) happened about three years after Jesus' death (c. A.D. 33); he then worked as an apostle for about thirty years, until his own death in Rome during the persecutions of Nero (c. A.D. 64).

By far the most important source for knowledge of Paul is his own letters. The Acts of the Apostles, written by the same author as the Gospel of Luke, also provides an important history, but "history" in the modern sense of the term, that is, having a strong focus on factual information, was not Luke's primary purpose. As in the Gospel, Luke's *primary* concerns were theological, to provide "assurance" about Jesus' life, death, and resurrection (Luke 1:4; Acts 2:36).

Neither Luke nor Paul knew Jesus personally. It is *possible* that Luke knew Paul personally, as the famous "we" passages in Acts suggest (Acts 16:10-17; 20:5-8, 13-15; 21:1-18; 27:1–28:16). However, those passages may be stylistic devices rather than proof of eyewitness participation in Paul's ministry, and in various ways Luke seems *not* to have known Paul well: his letters are never mentioned or quoted, his attitude to the law and his Pharisaic past (Gal 3:1-29; Phil 3:2-6) are not understood (e.g., Acts 23:6; 26:5), and Luke has Paul in Jerusalem more frequently than Paul's own report allows (Acts 9:23-26; 11:27-30; 12:25; 15:1; cf. Gal 1–2). Therefore, though Acts is valuable, Paul's own letters remain the decisive source for knowledge of his ministry.

There are thirteen letters that bear Paul's name, and the letter to the Hebrews has also been attributed to Paul, but that was doubted as early as Origen (about A.D. 200), and today there is virtual consensus that Paul had no role in its composition. Of the thirteen, there is general agreement that Paul wrote Romans, 1 and 2 Corinthians, Galatians, Philippians, 1 Thes-

The Pauline Letters

salonians, and Philemon. The other six letters divide into two groups: Ephesians, Colossians, and 2 Thessalonians, which in the view of *most* scholars Paul probably did not write, and 1 and 2 Timothy and Titus (the Pastoral Letters), which *nearly all* scholars believe Paul did not write. Reasons for doubting Paul's authorship of Ephesians, Colossians, and 2 Thessalonians will be given in the introductions to those letters. Authorship, however, is a complex matter. Paul wrote in the name of his co-workers (e.g., Timothy and Silvanus), indicating their support for the letter. When others wrote in his name, they did so because of some connection, however remote, with his authority and tradition.

Paul's original seven letters (epistles) were written between the late forties and early sixties A.D., *before* any of the four Gospels (A.D. 65 to 90). The letters are very *circumstantial,* meaning that Paul composed them to respond to particular situations that he and his churches faced. That is why his letters are such valuable witnesses of early Christianity. Interpretation of the letters must always take these circumstances into account. This is also true, for the most part, of the letters that Paul probably did not write. Ephesians is the exception in that it appears to be a general treatise on the church, written with a broad audience in mind rather than a particular community. Colossians and 2 Thessalonians, however, were composed in light of real problems facing churches that looked to Paul as *"the* apostle," as he was known to later generations. The authors wrote in Paul's name because it evoked great authority and trust.

The most important circumstance of Paul's time that we must bear in mind was his presumption that the end of human history (the *eschaton*) was at hand (see 1 Cor 7:29-31). Although later he was not so sure (Phil 1:20-24), early in his ministry Paul was convinced that he would be alive at "the coming of the Lord" (1 Thess 4:15). When "with the voice of an archangel and with the trumpet of God" the Lord Jesus himself would "descend from heaven," Paul expected that he would be among those "still alive," who would be "caught up together" with the dead "to meet the Lord in the air" (1 Thess 4:15-17). From such texts (e.g., also Mark 13:26-27; Matt 24:40-41), some modern Christians have developed the notion of "the rapture," and have combined it with the presumption that Paul and the evangelists were not talking about expectations of the first century but about the end of the world in the twentieth, and now twenty-first, century.

This is naïve, not to say shallow and self-serving, interpretation. How can we presume that Paul wrote primarily for us today? What about the people to whom he actually wrote, not to mention all the centuries in between? A full reading of the letters shows that Paul and his later disciples wrote entirely for the people and circumstances of their own time. The Scriptures are relevant today because the theologies, principles, and values they enunciate are foundational for the church in every age. Taking texts out of context and isolating chosen ideas for literal fulfillment today (what about the dragon of Revelation 12:3-4?) does no justice to the intentions of the biblical authors. That Paul and others were wrong about the near end of the world is only another indication that the Scriptures, like Jesus, have to do with "the weak flesh of humanity" as well as with the divine Spirit of inspiration (see Vatican II, Dogmatic Constitution on Divine Revelation, art. 13).

The value of Paul's letters for the church today is as great as the challenges the church faces. For questions of doctrine and morality, in debates about the nature of the church and of ministry, and facing questions about evangelization and mission, the church now, as always, has to turn to Jesus and to the church's original foundation and inspiration. Paul is particularly important as the witness of how the earliest churches first enfleshed the gospel of Jesus. His descriptions of the church, particularly as "the body of Christ" (1 Cor 12:27); his instructions about the Eucharist (1 Cor 10–11) and inclusion of women among church leaders (e.g., Rom 16:1-7); his recounting of major incidents (Gal 1:13–2:14); and his christological understanding (e.g., Phil 2:6-11)—these and many other aspects of his letters, and of the letters written in his name, are primary texts for the church today. The best approach to the letters requires prayer, an open mind, and careful study both of their individuality and of the conversation, and sometimes vigorous debate, that together they represent.

The Letter to the Romans

Robert J. Karris, O.F.M.

INTRODUCTION

Dr. Karris recommends a pronoun-rich reading of Romans

How should you approach Romans? Nibble on it piecemeal as the Lectionary does? Or meet it head on? I recommend the courageous second approach. Begin reading chapter 1 and go straight through to chapter 16. Along the way make a detailed list of the personal pronouns Paul uses. How often does he use "I" or "we" or "you" or the third person? Why, for example, does the personal pronoun "we" dominate Romans 5:1-11 and 8:31-39? Who is the "I" of Romans 7:7-25? Why does "I" occur so poignantly and so frequently in Romans 9–11? Who is the "you" of Romans 6:12-23? Why are there so many imperatives in Romans 12:1–15:13?

Further, as you mosey through the text, take a close look at the way Paul begins (1:1-16) and ends (15:14-33) his letter proper and how he insists on his role as the apostle to the Gentiles (1:5, 13; 15:16, 18, 27). In your reading you can't but notice how often Paul buttresses his presentation with quotations from the Greek or Septuagint translation of Scripture, for example, Romans 3:11-17, and you may be envious of the scriptural literacy of the first hearers of his letter.

Be sure not to miss the numerous questions with which Paul energizes his text. For example, Romans 4:1: "What then can we say that Abraham found, our ancestor according to the flesh?" and Romans 11:1: "I ask, then, has God rejected his people? Of course not!" Do you have the feeling that Romans 8:31-39 or Romans 11:33-36 forms a grand conclusion or peroration and are puzzled why Paul soldiers on after these two magnificent confessions of faith?

Although you're tired, struggle through the Roman directory of Romans 16. From a careful reading of 16:1-16, scholars have discerned that there were some five house churches in Rome and that women played a major role in earliest Christianity. If you're not too weary, you may ask why Paul ends his letter with a doxology (16:25-27) rather than a simple wish, as in 1 Corinthians 16:24: "My love to all of you in Christ Jesus." From this

The Letter to the Romans

courageous and careful hands-on approach you will be in a very good position to ask and test the answers to such questions as the literary form, addressees, purpose, and messages of Romans.

Check the background you bring to your reading of Romans

Against what background should I read Romans? Various church traditions have provided us with backgrounds. For example, there is the Lutheran background of underscoring human dependence upon God's grace and faith over against legalism in all its forms. Unfortunately, most Roman Catholics bring little informed background to Romans, for Paul's letters, especially Romans, are rarely preached upon during Sunday Mass. Contemporary scholars successfully interpret Romans as a story of God's dealings with humankind going back to Adam, Abraham, the giving of the law, the death and resurrection of the Lord Jesus Christ, and final glory. Others make some good sense of Romans as the gospel of God's love and peace over against the Roman imperial gospel of peace and prosperity.

In this commentary I follow Stanley K. Stowers in reading Romans against the background of the Jewish view of Gentiles. Paul states this Jewish viewpoint very clearly in Galatians 2:15: "We, who are Jews by nature and not sinners from among the Gentiles." This Jewish view of Gentiles is manifest in a passage from the religious romance *Joseph and Aseneth,* which dramatically portrays Joseph's abhorrence of kissing the pagan Aseneth: "It is not fitting for a man who worships God, who will bless with his mouth the living God and eat blessed bread of life . . . to kiss a strange woman who will bless with her mouth dead and dumb idols and eat from their table bread of strangulation and drink from their libation a cup of insidiousness" (8.5-7 in C. Burchard's translation).

The Jewish philosopher Philo of Alexandria champions the view that the law of Moses frees Gentiles from their desires, so that they can achieve their goal of self-mastery over their passions. In Book IV.55 of his *Special Laws,* Philo comments: "The law thinks that all those who adhere to the sacred constitution, established by Moses, ought to be free from all unreasonable passions, and from all wickedness" (C. D. Yonge translation). 4 Maccabees 1:16-19 maintains that wisdom derived from the law is the master of human passions:

> Reason, I suggest, is the mind making a deliberate choice of the life of wisdom. Wisdom, I submit, is knowledge of things divine and human, and of their causes. And this wisdom, I assume, is the culture we acquire from the law, through which we learn the things of God reverently and

the things of men to our worldly advantage. The forms of wisdom consist of prudence, justice, courage, and temperance. Of all these prudence is the most authoritative, for it is through it that reason controls the passions (NRSV).

With the above background in mind, we will be able to glimpse how Paul maintains that the Gentile believers' new life in Christ, not works of the law, has given them control over their passions (see 6:12-23). We will better appreciate Paul's indictment of the Gentiles in Romans 1:18-32, his dramatization of the Gentile "I" in 7:7-25, and his exhortations in 12:1–15:13, for example, 12:2: "Do not conform yourself to this age but be transformed by the renewal of your mind, that you may discern what is the will of God, what is good and pleasing and perfect." In brief, we will be better able to understand all of Romans, which reveals the gospel of the Apostle to the Gentiles.

The literary form and purposes of Romans

Scholars have called Romans a letter essay or an ambassadorial letter. I treat Romans as a letter of persuasion, technically a protreptic letter. Its main purpose is to persuade the Gentile Christians in Rome about the truth of Paul's gospel for/to the Gentiles. If they accept Paul's gospel to the Gentiles, they may also be willing to help support Paul's mission to the Gentiles in Spain (15:22-24) with personnel and money.

In writing an account of his gospel to the Gentiles, Paul has one eye on Jerusalem. He is anxious that the saints in Jerusalem accept the money that he has collected from Gentile converts and its symbolism of the unity of his law-free gospel with the gospel preached by Jerusalem. Perhaps this aspect of Paul's purposes accounts for the many quotations from Scripture in Romans, for the Judean Christians could be persuaded by arguments from Sacred Scripture. While it seems clear to me that Paul knew something about the situation in Rome, I am not fully persuaded that a purpose of Romans was to settle the so-called controversy between "the weak" and "the strong" in Romans 14:1–15:13. Why would Paul write the weighty first thirteen chapters of Romans to handle such a relatively small problem? We usually don't eliminate a mosquito with a blunderbuss.

What makes Romans tick?

Those who have taken my earlier recommendation and persevered through a pronoun-rich reading of Romans have gone beyond the spoon-fed selections of Romans from the Sunday Lectionary and are ready for the strong food of rhetorical criticism. The cement that holds the various sections of

The Letter to the Romans

Romans together is formed from the three ingredients of Paul's rhetoric. Although it is clear that the Roman Christians know who Paul is and that he knows something about them and their circumstances, Paul has to establish his position as a person of integrity, trust, authority, and goodwill, especially in the light of possible slurs about the truth of the gospel he preaches (see Rom 3:7-8). This ingredient of Paul's rhetoric is called *ethos* and is especially prominent in his use of "I" in his introduction to and conclusion of Romans, and I would venture to suggest that Romans 9–11, which uses "I" twenty-seven times, contains much *ethos* (besides considerable *pathos*).

As a superb letter writer, Paul makes his points according to *the logic* of his time. Our preliminary reading has repeatedly discovered one component of Paul's logic, namely, his reliance of the authority of Sacred Scripture. As a matter of fact, it has been calculated that fifty-one of the eighty-nine quotations of Scripture found in Paul's letters occur in Romans, and thirty-nine percent of Romans 9–11 consists of citations from Sacred Writ. Paul normally uses the third person for these quotations.

Sometimes the reason for Paul's use of Scripture is relatively clear to us moderns. For example, the chain of quotations in Romans 3:10-18 refers to the entirety of the thinking, willing, articulate, and acting human being: throats, tongues, lips, mouths, feet, eyes. In Romans 15:9-12 Paul makes his case about the Gentiles by quoting the entirety of Scripture, that is, its three major portions: Law, Prophets, Writings. It goes without saying that Paul expects his hearers to know their Bible.

In our preliminary reading of Romans, we have frequently stumbled across another major component of Paul's logic when we encountered questions such as "What are we to say?" (Rom 4:1; 6:1; 7:7; 8:31; 9:14, 30), or exclamations such as "Of course not" (Rom 3:4, 6, 31; 6:1, 15; 7:7, 13; 9:14; 11:1, 11), or second-person addresses to an imaginary conversation partner, such as Romans 9:19-21:

> You will say to me then: "Why does he still find fault? For who can oppose his will?" But who indeed are you, a human being, to talk back to God? Will what is made say to its maker: "Why have you created me so?" Or does not the potter have a right over the clay, to make out of the same lump one vessel for a noble purpose and another for an ignoble one? (trans. H. Anderson, p. 545; other examples in Rom 2:1-5, 17-29; 8:2; 11:17-24; 14:4, 10).

Technically speaking, this component of Paul's logic bears the name of diatribe, which unfortunately for our understanding has the meaning in contemporary English of "a bitter verbal or written criticism." Stanley Stowers defines ancient diatribe in this way: "A term for teaching activity in the schools, literary imitations of that activity, or for writings which employ the rhetorical and pedagogical style typical of diatribes in the schools." Typical of the diatribe in the schools were intense dialogues, questions, and answers.

Those familiar with teaching in the Middle Ages recognize a cousin of the diatribe in the "sic et non" and "quaestiones" traditions of the scholastics, as they raised questions and provided answers for and against an interpretation. Contemporary classrooms provide a distant cousin of the diatribe when they feature questions and answers. Finally, it should be noted that the goal of the diatribe modality is pedagogical and hortatory, not polemical, that is, it is motivated by a concern that students learn; it does not arise from Romans' contempt of false opinions. Finally, as Stowers maintains: "It is also a misunderstanding to read dialogical features (e.g., objections) as references to actual groups in the Roman church." I invite advanced students to explore the diatribe style manifested in Epictetus's "Concerning Anxiety" in Book II.13 of his *Discourses.*

Surely the vast majority of us readers are not trained in reading a text that contains a heavy component of the teaching style called diatribe. So we will have to take our time and exercise great patience. To me, this component of Paul's logic shows how carefully he constructed Romans and how he endeavored to engage his hearers and to win them over to full acceptance of his gospel to the Gentiles. Further, just think of how skilled a reader Phoebe was to proclaim Paul's complex letter intelligently and persuasively (Rom 16:1-2).

Lastly, Paul uses *pathos* to influence the minds of his hearers through engaging their hearts and emotions. Who can miss the *pathos* that floods through Romans 9:1-5; 10:1; 11:1-2; for example, Romans 9:3: "For I could wish that I myself were accursed and separated from Christ for the sake of my brothers, my kin according to the flesh"?

Further, Leander E. Keck has pointed to another dimension of *pathos:* The speaker or author should experience in himself the same emotions he wants to inspire in his hearers. In Book II.47.195 of his *Concerning the Orator,* Cicero writes of how he defended Manius Aquilius in court:

> For here was a man whom I remembered as having been consul, commander-in-chief, honored by the Senate, and mounting in procession to the Capitol. On seeing him cast down, crippled, sorrowing and brought to the risk of all he held dear, *I was myself overcome by compassion before I tried to excite it in others* (Loeb translation modified).

It seems that this characteristic of *pathos* may stand behind Paul's frequent use of "we," for example, in Romans 5:1-11; 7:5-6; 8:31-39, and the exhortatory materials in 12:4; 13:11-12; 14:7-8, 10, 12, 13, 19; 15:1-2, as Paul demonstrates that he shares the same emotions that he wants to evoke in his hearers.

Finally, I invite my readers to take another glance at Romans 15:30-33. Paul is not looking forward to his confrontation with the Judean believers and wants the Romans to join him in the struggle by their prayers on his behalf. In this passage Paul's *ethos* and *pathos* embrace and invite the hearers to storm heaven for his deliverance.

The messages of Romans

In the exposition of individual passages, I will have an opportunity to describe the various messages of Romans. According to my count, there are 146 references to "God" in the sixteen chapters of Romans. This overwhelming number tells me that Romans is about God. In particular, it explains God's actions in the face of apparent injustice. Or as Luke Timothy Johnson says so well: "The argument of Romans is, at root, simple. God is one and God is fair."

A simple outline of Romans

I wholeheartedly encourage my readers to engage in a serious, continuous, and pronoun-rich reading of Romans, and I have composed my commentary to aid such a reading. The following outline presents a basic road map through this long, intricate, and richly rewarding letter that Paul wrote from Corinth about A.D. 57.

Romans 1:1-15 Beginning

Romans 1:16-17 Theme

Romans 1:18–11:36 Body

Romans 12:1–15:13 Exhortations

Romans 15:14-33 Conclusion

Romans 16:1-27 Greetings, a warning, final doxology

COMMENTARY

ADDRESS

Romans 1:1-15

1:1-7 The apostle to the Gentiles introduces himself and his gospel

In these compact verses Paul introduces himself, his gospel, and the gist of his message. He did not take it upon himself to speak for God and God's Son as their apostle. God called him, a zealous persecutor of the church, to be an apostle to the Gentiles (see Gal 1:11-24). I pause here and urge my readers to go back to my Introduction (p. 439) to see what I have to say about the Jewish view of Gentiles: They are sinners. Yet God has called the Jew Paul to preach the gospel to these sinners.

The good news or gospel that Paul preaches is not totally new but has antecedents in the Scriptures (1:2). We will be frustrated if we look exclusively for individual verses in the Old Testament. Paul is looking more to the broad sweep of God's purpose of giving life to women and men. Paul will refer again to God's salvific purpose when he considers Abraham (Rom 4), Adam (Rom 5:12-21), the gift of the law (Rom 7:1–8:30), those powers that try to separate us from God (Rom 8:31-39), and God's election of Israel (Rom 9–11).

The gospel is about God's Son, born a Jew from a royal house, and "established as Son of God in power according to the spirit of holiness through resurrection from the dead, Jesus Christ our Lord" (1:4). Paul makes no mention here that this royal figure was crucified by Roman power. Instead, he uses the eschatological category of resurrection from the dead to indicate that God has done something new and final in Jesus. Death has not conquered Jesus. God has exalted him to be Lord.

Richard A. Horsley has been reminding us that Paul's gospel stands in radical contrast to the imperial gospel, inaugurated by Caesar Augustus, whose victories and rule were considered good news. Augustus was hailed by an inscription at Priene as "[a Savior] who has made war to cease and who shall put everything [in peaceful] order" (F. W. Danker). It is not happenstance that Paul will follow his introduction with an indictment of Gentile idolatry and vices (1:18-32). Jesus, Son of David, Son of God, is Savior and Lord, not Caesar.

It is also significant that Paul exhorts his hearers in Romans 5:1: "Let us have peace with God through our Lord Jesus Christ" (author's translation). Americans who think that emperor worship, bread, and circuses are beyond their ken should take a closer look at American Civil Religion and the

Romans 1

United States' multiple shrines dedicated to pleasure, consumerism, and the fountain of youth.

God has called Paul "to bring about the obedience of faith" (1:5). Paul announces here a major theme of Romans, which he will develop at great length with the example of Abraham, who was a Gentile, an ungodly person, but who believed (4:5). Already we hear the briefest of hints about theodicy: Should we Gentiles believe in a God who seems not to have been faithful to the people God first called? If God were not faithful to them, how can we Gentiles have confidence that God will be faithful to us? See Romans 9–11.

1:8-15 Paul gives thanks and states that he worships God through preaching

My sole comment here is on Romans 1:9: "God is my witness, whom I worship with my spirit in proclaiming the gospel of his Son" (author's translation). Paul uses the Greek verb *latreuein*, "to worship." His worship of God is through his missionary activity of proclaiming the gospel of the Lord Jesus, not through emperor worship. In Romans 12:1 Paul tells the Romans how to worship: "I urge you therefore, brothers, by the mercies of God, to offer your bodies as a living sacrifice, holy and pleasing to God, your spiritual worship."

In Romans 15:16 Paul again uses worship terminology to describe his preaching of the gospel: "to be a minister of Christ Jesus to the Gentiles in performing the priestly service of the gospel of God, so that the offering up of the Gentiles may be acceptable, sanctified by the holy Spirit." It does not seem to me that Paul is merely using worship language in a figurative way.

HUMANITY LOST WITHOUT THE GOSPEL
Romans 1:16–3:20

1:16-17 Paul states the theme of his letter

My readers can peruse all thirteen of Paul's letters and not find another instance where Paul announces the theme of his letter as he does here, for Romans alone is modeled after a scholastic diatribe or instruction (see Introduction, pp. 442–43). Paul will explicate this theme in the rest of Romans, often by using the questions of scholastic diatribe. While the gospel is God's power for the salvation of all people, it is meant first for God's elect people.

I borrow from two renowned commentators to define "God's righteousness." Joseph A. Fitzmyer accentuates it as an attribute of God who is judge for God's people: "It is a quality whereby God actively acquits his sinful people, manifesting towards them his power and gracious activity in a just judgment. . . ." Ernst Käsemann underscores God's dominion over the world: "God's sovereignty over the world revealing itself eschatologically in Jesus . . . the rightful power with which God makes his cause to triumph in the world which has fallen away from him and which yet, as creation, is his inviolable possession."

I believe that we can capture some of the nuances of "from faith to faith" if we look at Paul's quotation from Habakkuk. I translate the Septuagint of Habakkuk 2:4: "The righteous person will live because of my faithfulness." The reference behind "my" is God, who is faithful to the person who has kept right relationship with God. Although Paul has dropped "my," it seems that the background of Habbakuk is still in his mind. The Greek word *pistis*, which is regularly translated by "faith," also means "faithfulness" and "trust." God's righteousness reveals God's faithfulness to God's chosen people and to creation and leads to a faithful response. Would that sermons were preached on the gospel of God's righteous fidelity to God's elect and God's creation!

1:18-32 The plight of the Gentiles

I ask you to skip ahead to Romans 3:21-24. Read that passage carefully: "But now the righteousness of God has been manifested . . . the righteousness of God through faith in Jesus Christ for all who believe. For there is no distinction; all have sinned. . . . They are justified freely by his grace through the redemption in Christ Jesus." It would seem that Romans 3:21-24 is the "logical" next paragraph after Paul's theme sentence in Romans 1:16-17. But before Paul could arrive at this "solution," he had to state the "problem": All have sinned. Put another way, in the style of a scholastic diatribe Paul develops his theme of "God's righteousness unto salvation" by contrasting it with its antithesis: sin's domination over humans (see 3:9) and the law's inability to cope with sin (3:20).

The dominant Jewish view of Gentiles pulses through this passage. Later on, in Romans 6:17, Paul will remind his Gentile hearers that they were formerly in the same boat of lacking mastery over self, because they "were once slaves of sin." From the key sin of idolatry all other sins cascade forth. As Wisdom 14:12 states:

> For the source of wantonness is the devising of idols;
> and their invention was a corruption of life.

And Wisdom 14:25-27 continues:

Romans 1

> And all is confusion—blood and murder, theft and guile,
>   corruption, faithlessness, turmoil, perjury,
> Disturbance of good men, neglect of gratitude,
>   besmirching of souls, unnatural lust,
>   disorder in marriage, adultery and shamelessness.
> For the worship of infamous idols
>   is the reason and source and extremity of all evil.

There is no excuse for such behavior: "For although they knew God they did not accord him glory as God or give him thanks" (1:21; see 1:32).

Contemporary society almost forces us to bypass the capital sins and even murder in Romans 1:29-31 and to focus on what Paul says about same-sex love in 1:24-28. As Richard B. Hays and others have shown, there is no doubt that Paul condemns these actions that are willingly chosen. Luke Timothy Johnson formulates the question for contemporary application: "Or is it [same-sex love], as some studies and many people claim, the 'natural' mode of sexual expression for a small portion of the world's population?"

2:1-5 The Gentile who boasts

In the very beginning of my Introduction (p. 439), I asked my readers to make their way through all of Romans by asking questions such as: What personal pronouns does Paul use? Romans 2:1-5 is a very important case in point, for Paul changes from the third person pronouns of 1:18-32 to "you" singular. The NAB's translation of Romans 2:1 and 3 masks Paul's use of the Greek *ō anthrōpe*, which is used in scholastic diatribe and means "fellow" or, in our parlance, "guy." I render Romans 2:1, which continues Paul's discussion of how passions rule Gentiles: "Therefore, you are without an excuse, guy, like anyone who judges." Paul's diatribal address picks up "the insolent, haughty, and boastful" Gentiles of Romans 1:30 and skewers them. For they, too, are sinners. Romans 2:4 finds a parallel in Wisdom 11:23:

> But you [God] have mercy on all, because you can do all things;
>   and you overlook the sins of men that they may repent.

2:6-16 Three key teachings

Gentiles are still very much in Paul's eyes as he refers to two fundamental beliefs about God that are based in the Scriptures. God "will repay everyone according to his works" (2:6). Proverbs 24:12 states: God "will repay each one according to his deeds." Romans 2:11 confesses: "There is no partiality with God." Sirach 35:12 professes: "For he is a God of justice, /

who knows no favorites." The Gentile is judged by deeds, but so too is the member of God's chosen people, for God is impartial.

A further fundamental belief is imbedded in Romans 2:16: "according to my gospel, God will judge people's hidden works through Christ Jesus." The gospel, for which Paul fought so uncompromisingly in Galatians, is that Gentiles do not have to become Jews and observe the law in order to be justified in God's sight. In turn, Christ Jesus will not judge them on the basis of their observance of Jewish covenantal law but on the observance of the law in their hearts. As Charles H. Talbert comments, "A pervasive belief existed among ancient Jews as well as pagans that all people had some elemental knowledge of morality for which they were responsible."

2:17-29 A pretentious teacher, who is a Jew and would teach Gentiles

Again, note the change of personal pronoun, as third person gives way to "you" singular. Stanley Stowers has helped me to see this passage as a diatribal attack on the pretentious teacher, who happens to be a Jew and is not the "typical Jew." I recall many of J. F. Powers's short stories that featured Roman Catholic clergy. Clergy who read these stories were up in arms, for they mistakenly thought that Powers was attacking them, whereas he was pointing his literary finger at people, lay or clergy, who were greedy, self-centered, and lazy.

A compelling parallel to what Paul is doing in this passage occurs in what Epictetus writes in his discourse: "To those who take up the teachings of the philosophers only to talk about them." Epictetus addresses the would-be teacher, whose deeds are evil: "For your own evils are enough for you: your baseness, your cowardice, the bragging that you indulged in when you were sitting in the lecture room. Why did you pride yourself on things that were not your own?" (*Discourses* 2.19.19, in Loeb translation). Instead of teaching Gentiles the true way to God, this vain teacher leads them away from God. Indeed, Isaiah 52:5 is verified here, for the Gentiles revile God's name because of what the Jewish teacher has done or failed to do.

3:1-9 God's chosen people, although sinners, are still advantaged

Paul continues his scholastic diatribe with a series of five objections or questions. Each objection is twofold. See 3:1, 3, 5, 7-8a, 9a for these questions and 3:2, 4, 6, 8b, and 9b for Paul's responses. Although this series of questions and answers functions very well here, it is a foretaste of Paul's extensive discussion in Romans 9–11 about God's fidelity in the face of the nonbelief in Jesus the Christ on the part of most of the chosen people.

Romans 3

I focus on Paul's responses in 3:4 and 3:6 and then on both question and answer in 3:9. Romans 3:4 reads: "God must be true." God's truthfulness refers to God's covenant fidelity to the chosen people. See Psalm 89:2: "The promises of the LORD I will sing forever, / proclaim your loyalty [truthfulness] through all ages." Romans 3:6 proclaims that God is judge of the world. Psalm 94:2 pleads with God: "Rise up, judge of the earth; / give the proud what they deserve." Romans 3:9a is surely a difficult sentence, especially since the antecedent "we" of 3:8 is ambiguous. If the "we" includes both Paul and his imaginary Jewish interlocutor, then the translation is: "What then? Are we [Jews] disadvantaged? Not at all." If the "we" refers solely to Paul, then F. W. Danker's translation makes sense: "What then? Am I protecting myself? Am I making excuses? Not at all."

Readers should not miss the occurrence of the noun "sin" for the first time in Romans 3:9b. Through the use of personification, Paul paints sin as a master who dominates Jew and Gentile. What irony for those who believed they had achieved self-mastery.

3:10-20 Observance of the law does not lead to justification

If my readers have an image of Paul rapidly dictating this letter to his scribe Tertius (see 16:22), this passage should cause a drastic revision of that image. For nowhere in Scripture are these ten quotations found together in the same book. They seem to have been composed beforehand. Take 3:13, for example. "Their throats are open graves; / they deceive with their tongues" (author's translation) is found in the Septuagint of Psalm 5:10. The next line of 3:13, however, comes from the Septuagint of Psalm 139:4: "The venom of asps is on their lips." The motif of "no one, not one" surges through 3:10-12, and the full involvement of the human person (from head to toe) seems to be the ordering principle for 3:13-18.

Paul's long chain of Scripture quotations should not distract us from the conclusion he draws in 3:20: "No human being will be justified in his [God's] sight by observing the law." That is, neither the chosen people nor the Gentiles find justification in the law. Romans 3:21-26 will state where justification may now be found.

JUSTIFICATION THROUGH FAITH IN CHRIST

Romans 3:21–5:21

3:21-26 The soteriological heart of Romans

Having argued his thesis by means of its antithesis in 1:18–3:20, Paul now formulates it positively in a section that is soteriologically and christologically significant but dense. I highlight five key points and leave to advanced students an investigation of the likelihood that Paul adapted earlier tradition in 3:24-26. First, the law does not bring about justification, although it testifies to it (3:21). Paul will address the role of the law in Romans 4 and 7–11, for "the law is holy, and the commandment is holy and righteous and good" (7:12).

Second, "[all sinners] are justified freely" (3:24), that is, God has declared them to be acquitted of their sin.

Third, Christ's death on the cross is front and center stage in the words "by his blood" (3:25). Christ's shedding of his blood has brought about redemption, an image that denotes being ransomed from the slavery and domination of sin (see 3:9).

Fourth, 3:25 employs another image—that of expiation. God has set forth Jesus Christ on the cross as the new expiatory sacrifice that takes away sin through the shedding of his blood. The Old Testament background seems to be Exodus 25:17 ("You shall then make an expiating cover") and Leviticus 16:15-16: "Then he (Aaron) shall slaughter the people's sin-offering goat, and bringing its blood inside the veil, he shall do with it as he did with the bullock's blood, sprinkling it on the expiatory and before it. Thus he shall make atonement for the sanctuary because of all the sinful defilements and faults of the Israelites" (author's translations).

Fifth, four times in this passage "faith" or "to believe" occurs (3:22). Justification, redemption, expiation are not forced upon men and women. They have to respond in faith to God who has done these things for them through Jesus Christ.

3:27–4:2a A person is justified by faith

This section is yet another dialogue in diatribe modality. In it Paul leads his readers to appreciate the centrality of faith for both Jew and Gentile. God who is one does not require two ways but only one—that of faith. The section begins with "boasting," ends with "boasting," and leads to the example of Abraham (4:2b-25), whose faith was credited to him as righteousness (4:9).

I lay out this dialogue, modifying the NAB translation above and indicating the interlocutor by "I" and Paul by "P." Paul formulates the interlocutor's questions in such a way as to lead to his key theological teachings.

I: Is there reason to boast?

P: It is ruled out.

Romans 3–4

I: By what principle? That of the law?

P: No, rather by the principle of faith. For we consider that a person is justified by faith apart from works of the law. Does God belong only to Jews? Does he not belong also to Gentiles?

I: Yes, also to Gentiles.

P: For God is one and will justify the circumcised on the basis of faith and the uncircumcised through faith.

I: Are we then annulling the law by faith?

P: Of course not. On the contrary, we are supporting the law.

I: What then are we to say? Have we found Abraham, to be our forebear by his own efforts? For if Abraham was justified on the basis of his works, he has reason to boast.

All of Romans 4:2b-25 will give Paul's response: Faithful Abraham has no reason to boast.

4:2b-25 Abraham's faith and the God who justifies the ungodly

Romans 4:2b-25 provides Paul's reasons why Abraham has no reason to boast: he did nothing to earn justification. Put positively and compactly, Abraham, a Gentile, believed God despite all evidence to the contrary. In fashioning his final answer to the diatribal dialogue that commenced in 3:27, Paul utilizes another feature of the scholastic diatribe: teaching by means of examples. For instance, Epictetus draws upon luminaries of the philosophical tradition such as Plato, Diogenes, and Epicurus to paint positive and negative examples. Paul reaches back into the Jewish tradition to forebear Abraham. It is very important to note what characteristics of Abraham are of theological interest to Paul and what Abraham's example says about God.

Recall what Paul says about the sins of the Gentiles in 1:18-32. Abraham was a Gentile, an idolater, an ungodly person when God called him out of Ur of Chaldea. Drawing upon Genesis 15:16, Paul notes: "Abraham believed God, and it was credited to him as righteousness" (Rom 4:3). Abraham hadn't undergone the rite of circumcision when he believed (Gen 17). Nor was he being rewarded for having offered gracious and generous hospitality to strangers (Gen 18). He had not yet been obedient to God in his willingness to sacrifice his only son, Isaac, the carrier of God's praises (Gen 22). Abraham was the recipient of a gift (Rom 4:4). Why did God do this? The reason is found in God's nature: God justifies the ungodly (4:5). Earlier, in 3:10-18,

Paul displayed one of his ways of interpreting Scripture as he strung together quotations from various parts of Scripture in a chain. In 4:7-8 Paul follows another method, namely, citing a Scripture passage that contains the same key word. Both of these passages, then, interpret each other. In this instance Paul quotes Psalm 31:1-2 in the Septuagint because it contains the same key verb "to credit." The NAB's "does not record" (4:8) masks this point. Through God's act of justification, God forgives iniquities. In 4:9-12 Paul draws yet another point from Abraham's faith: Through his faith Abraham is the father of both the uncircumcised and the circumcised.

In Romans 7–8 Paul will pay close attention to, and argue extensively about, the role of the law. In 4:13-16 Paul whets his hearers' appetites with apodictic statements, the key of which is: "If those who adhere to the law are the heirs, faith is null and the promise is void" (4:14).

In 4:17-22 Paul moves away from his earlier, more abstract consideration of Abraham as a model of faith and gets specific. Again Paul confesses a cardinal point of his and our faith: God "who gives life to the dead and calls into being what does not exist" (4:17). Through this faith Abraham was empowered to trust God's word and promise. Abraham's God has given life to his almost dead body and to the dead womb of his wife, Sarah. In 4:23-25 Paul moves from Abraham's faith in the God who justifies the ungodly and gives life to the dead and draws himself and his hearers into the story. Notice the change of personal pronouns in 4:24-25: "It was also for *us* . . . *our* Lord . . . for *our* transgressions . . . for *our* justification" (emphasis added).

Scholars who interpret Romans from a story perspective have hit pay dirt in Romans 4. The story of Abraham and Sarah captivates believers, who are led to see in these forebears their stories of hoping against hope (4:18), believing that God draws life out of death and trusting that God justifies ungodly people such as us who may have been overcome by sin.

5:1-11 God's many gifts through Jesus Christ our Lord

This is an exceedingly rich passage. I offer six considerations. First, I urge my readers to note Paul's use of "we." I count seventeen uses of "we/our." I would venture to say that Paul is including himself with his Gentile hearers, and his main purpose is *pathos*. In my Introduction (p. 443) I stated that the author experiences the emotion that he wants his listeners to experience. In this passage the "emotions" are the entire gambit of God's gifts: peace, love, boasting, hope, reconciliation, the Holy Spirit.

Second, in this passage Paul often makes reference to teachings he presented earlier. Boasting (5:2, 3, 11), which Paul and his society considered good as long as it was done decently, stands in stark contrast with the illegitimate boasting of 3:17 and 4:2 and ties this passage to what preceded it. Because of God's many gifts, the Gentiles can toot their own horn, and do so to God's honor. The peace (5:1) that the Gentiles are experiencing is not that created by Caesar Augustus but by Jesus Christ our Lord (see 1:7). In 1:16 Paul proudly proclaimed that he was not ashamed of the gospel of Jesus Christ, crucified as a criminal but raised by God from the dead. Romans 5:5 contains the same verb "to shame": Hope does not shame because of the reality of God's gift of absolutely gratuitous love (see 5:5).

Third, in 5:3-5, Paul displays his literary prowess as he fashions a *sorites* (literally: "a heap"), as he moves from affliction to endurance to proven character to hope.

Four, notice how many times Paul refers to Jesus Christ (5:1, 2, 6, 8, 9, 10, 11). Jesus Christ is God's Son (5:10). Through the shedding of his blood we have reconciliation with God, that is, enemies have turned their tanks into plows. In Jewish tradition there is the story of a mother and seven sons who resisted the tyrant Antiochus and preserved their faith and ancestral customs, even though they were mercilessly tortured and killed for their fidelity. Their deaths were of great benefit to the entire nation. 4 Maccabees 17:22 reads: "Through the blood of these devout ones and their death as an atoning sacrifice, divine Providence preserved Israel which had previously been mistreated" (NRSV modified). Jesus' death is of even greater benefit to humanity.

Fifth, the multiple gifts that Gentile believers experience do not come from their own inner strength but through God's Spirit, who is other and holy (5:5).

Finally, Paul's "how much more" argument in 5:10 prepares his hearers for his argument in 5:12-21. See, for example, 5:15. God's gifts through Jesus Christ enable people to attain the self-mastery that they and their culture have been longing for.

5:12-21 The wondrous consequences of the obedience of Jesus Christ

In Romans 5:12 the "we" style vanishes (except for the use of "our" in the formulaic ending of 5:21: "through Jesus Christ *our* Lord"; emphasis added), and Paul adopts the discursive third person style. If you ask how 5:12-21 connects with what has preceded, I give two answers. It gives an analysis of sin that is more profound than that given in 1:18–3:20. Further, it praises the wondrous gifts that have come about through the faithful obedience of Jesus Christ and thus continues the general thematic of 5:1-11. Paul may have composed this passage on another occasion and saw how fitting it was for this letter.

It is important to quote two Scripture passages as background to Romans 5:12-14. Genesis 2:16-17 states: "The LORD God gave man this order: 'You are free to eat from any of the trees of the garden except the tree of knowledge of good and bad. From that tree you shall not eat; the moment you eat from it you are surely doomed to die'" (NAB). Adam's sin of disobedience brings about death. Wisdom 2:23-24 speaks of the reign of death: "For God formed man to be imperishable; / the image of his own nature he made him. / But by the envy of the devil, death entered the world, / and they who are in his possession experience it" (NAB). As Luke Timothy Johnson writes: "Everyone has sinned the way Adam did, so that the effect of Adam's sin continues, and continues to be symbolized by the death experienced by all humans."

But as Paul teaches through the extensive comparisons of 5:15-21, Adam's disobedience is not the end of the story. Paul makes his point much more succinctly in 1 Corinthians 15:45: "So, too, it is written, 'The first man, Adam, became a living being,' the last Adam a life-giving spirit." The risen Lord Jesus stands at the beginning of the new creation. While on the side of Adam are disobedience, transgression, and death, on the side of the New Adam there are obedience, acquittal, life, and grace. "In conclusion, just as through one transgression condemnation came upon all, so through one righteous act acquittal and life came to all" (5:18). In Romans 6–8 Paul will spell out the meaning of incorporation into the life of the New Adam through baptism (Rom 6), the role of the law (Rom 7), and the driving force of God's Spirit (Rom 8).

Advocates of the story approach to Romans are happy that Paul has finally shown the narrative that lies below the surface of his discursive soteriology and christology. Jesus, God's Son, has redeemed believers not from one single sin but from the power of sin and death. Those who experienced the power of Osama bin Ladin on 9/11/01 have no doubt that the transgression of one single individual has a negative effect on millions. Even the musical *Beauty and the Beast* teaches us that the selfish, heartless action of one individual has consequences for an entire household. On the positive side, the narrative of the life of Francis of Assisi (d. 1226) continues to breathe fresh life into countless people of all faiths.

JUSTIFICATION AND THE CHRISTIAN LIFE

Romans 6:1–8:39

6:1-14 Baptism and the newness of life

Paul develops the points he has been making in Romans 5:12-21 by means of an objection by an imaginary interlocutor in 6:1-2. Throughout

6:2-14, Paul will be answering the absurd question of 6:1: "Shall we persist in sin that grace may abound?" The attentive reader will note Paul's use of "we" in 6:1-9 and his use of "you" plural in 6:11-14. What the Gentile believers in Romans experienced in baptism Paul also experienced. Thus Paul engages in *pathos* or exhorting his hearers on the basis of common experience. Finally, from his description of baptism (6:2-5), Paul will draw upon some common principles (6:6-10) and then apply them (6:11-14).

The ritual of infant baptism and especially the baptism of adults at the Easter Vigil give us some inkling of Paul's view of baptism. The immersion of the baptizand is likened to Christ's death and burial; the lifting up out of the water is likened to Christ's resurrection. The change of clothing points to the newly baptized's change of status.

Although I have been trying to interpret Romans without explicit reference to Galatians, I believe that some verses from this earlier letter help us to appreciate what Paul means here by baptism. Galatians 3:1-5 very clearly points to the explosive nature of the Christian experience of baptism. See especially Galatians 3:5: "Does, then, the one who supplies the Spirit to you and works mighty deeds among you do so from works of the law or from faith in what you heard?" Baptism may very well have been the occasion for the display of the multiple gifts of the Spirit (see 1 Cor 12–14), the time when the love of God was manifestly "poured out into our hearts through the holy Spirit" (Rom 5:5) and the time when the newly baptized cried out "Abba, Father!" (Gal 4:6; Rom 8:15) as a profession of their new status as children of God.

Romans 6:6-10 largely consists of "principles." Paul's use of "for" in 6:5, 7 announces principles. For example, 6:7 states that the person who has died has lost the very means of sinning, namely, "our sinful body" (6:6). The "if" sentences of 6:5, 8 formulate principles. The "we know" sentences of 6:6, 9 remind listeners of principles.

Romans 6:11-14 applies these principles to Paul's Gentile listeners, who were quite aware of the vices that dominated their society (see Rom 1:18-32). "Therefore, sin must not reign over your mortal bodies so that you obey their desires" (6:12). In Romans 8 Paul will spend considerable time on the role of the Holy Spirit in believers' everyday lives of living out the newness of baptismal life.

6:15-23 Be addicted to the Lord Jesus Christ

Paul develops his teaching some more by means of another rhetorical question in the first person: "What then? Shall we sin because we are not under the law but under grace? Of course not!" (6:15). With the exception of 6:19, where Paul uses "I," this entire section is in the second person and is addressed to Gentile believers who once engaged in sins of which they are now ashamed (6:21; see 1:24-28).

To me, the best contemporary analogy to the master-slave relationship that Paul utilizes in this section is addiction. We all know of individuals who are addicted to gambling or alcohol or drugs and will do just about anything to get their daily "fix." These individuals are in thralldom, in slavery to their addiction. Even though they realize in their sober moments that they are destroying their lives and those of the people they love, they cannot help themselves. They are very clever at hiding their addiction and at making excuses for their conduct.

If we apply this analogy to 6:16-23, we realize that because of all that God has done for us in Jesus Christ—justification, redemption, gift of the Holy Spirit, baptism—we are now to be addicted to righteousness, sanctification, and life. We are to be "obedient from the heart to the pattern of teaching to which [we] were entrusted" (6:17). The reference here is most likely to the core of teaching given at the time of baptism in the midst of one's brothers and sisters. In 6:19, 22 Paul introduces a new term, "sanctification." Just as their God is holy or "other," the lives of believers are to be "other." How "other"? Paul's reference back to the sins of Romans 1:18-32 gives a glimpse of what has to be left behind in believers' new addiction to Jesus Christ.

This section ends with a rousing summary: "The wages of sin is death, but the gift of God is eternal life in Christ Jesus our Lord" (6:23). I conclude by accentuating the plural number of the "you" that Paul employs in this section. Individuals do not come out of addiction by themselves. They need outside help, community, loved ones. In this instance, they need the Christian community or local house church.

7:1-6 The role of the law: Part I

As Paul has been making his case that new life in Christ has freed believers from the power of sin and death, he has often dropped hints about the role of the Mosaic law. I mention some of Paul's earlier pronouncements about the law. See 3:20: "no human being will be justified in his sight by observing the law; for through the law comes consciousness of sin." In Romans 4:14-15 Paul states: "For if those who adhere to the law are the heirs, faith is null and the promise is void. For the law produces wrath; but where there is no law, neither is there violation." After mentioning the law in 5:13, Paul says in 5:20: "The law entered in so that transgression might increase but, where sin increased, grace overflowed all the more." Finally,

Romans 6:14-15 reads: "For sin is not to have any power over you, since you are not under the law but under grace. What then? Shall we sin because we are not under the law but under grace?" These hints have whetted our appetites. Now Paul sets the table for a full course on the law.

Again, I invite my readers to check Paul's personal pronouns. Romans 7:2-3 is an illustration in the third person. Romans 7:1 and 4 have "you" plural and the fictive kinship term "brothers [and sisters]." Romans 7:4c-6 employs "we" pronouns as Paul identifies himself with his Gentile hearers.

The illustration is pretty straightforward, as it talks about the binding force of law for a married couple while both partners are alive. It presupposes that this married union will result in the bearing of fruit (children; see 7:4-5). Once the husband has died, the law of marriage for the wife ceases. She is free to marry another.

Paul introduces the application of this illustration by the words "in the same way" in 7:4, but note the ways in which he transfers the terms of the illustration. See, for example, 7:4: "You also were put to death to the law through the [crucified] body of Christ, so that you might belong to another, to the one who was raised from the dead in order that we might bear fruit for God." It is clear that believers now belong to another, namely, Jesus Christ. It is also clear that the death of Jesus Christ has destroyed the power of law over believers. When we were without the Spirit, that is, in the flesh (see Romans 8 for more detail), the law awakened sinful passions by forbidding certain actions. Like people caught in a bad marriage, we were held captive to destructive forces. But now that the law is dead, we may serve "in the newness of the spirit" (7:6).

7:7–8:2 The role of the law: Part II

Paul develops his thought here about the relationship between law and sin by means of two diatribal objections and answers in 7:7a and 7:13a. Each answer is developed further in what follows. I am indebted to Stanley Stowers for the interpretation that the "I" that occurs in virtually every verse of 7:7-25 is an instance of what the Greeks called *prosopopoiia*, or "speech in character." Finally, 7:25a and 8:1-2 are Paul's remarks to the "I."

Speech in character "is a rhetorical and literary technique in which the speaker or writer produces speech that represents not himself or herself but another person or type of character." Thus the "I" is not Paul nor a Jew nor a Christian; rather the "I" is the Gentile striving to attain self-mastery by means of observance of the Mosaic law. In his own way, Joseph A.

Fitzmyer is on the same wavelength as Stowers when he comments that the "I" is: "unregenerate humanity faced with the Mosaic law—but as seen by a Christian."

Key verses in this interpretation are 7:15 and 7:19, which are paralleled in Greek literature and philosophy. Romans 7:15 reads: "What I do, I do not understand. For I do not do what I want, but I do what I hate." Romans 7:19 states: "For I do not do the good I want, but I do the evil I do not want." Such was the situation of Medea in Greek tragedy, who, overcome by anger and the desire for revenge, killed her own children. In Euripides' *Medea* the main character wails: "I am overcome by evil. Now, now, I learn what horrors I intend, but passion overpowers sober thought, and this is the cause of the direst evils for men and women" (1077–1080; Loeb modified). Medea, a pagan, is the model for lack of self-mastery.

There is a heart-rending version of Medea in Samuel Barber's "Medea's Dance of Vengeance." See also the Roman poet Ovid, who in his *Metamorphoses* comments: "I see the better and approve it, but I follow the worse" (7.20-21; Loeb). In his *Discourses* the Stoic philosopher Epictetus writes: "What he wants to do he doesn't do, and what he doesn't want he does" (2, 26.4; Loeb modified).

Into this pagan situation of being mastered by the passions, Jewish apologists such as Philo of Alexandria proclaimed that the Jewish Mosaic law made Jews more self-controlled, better able to control their passions. In Book IV.55 of his *Special Laws*, Philo praises the Mosaic law: "The law thinks that all those who adhere to the sacred constitution, established by Moses, ought to be free from all unreasonable passions, and from all wickedness" (C. D. Yonge translation).

Paul agrees that "the law is holy, and the commandment is holy and righteous and good" (7:12). But he also realizes that sin has overwhelmed the law: "For sin, seizing an opportunity in the commandment, deceived me and through it put me to death" (7:11). If Gentiles cannot turn to the Mosaic law for liberation from the powers of sin, death, and flesh, they must turn and have turned to Jesus Christ. Before the "I" of the "speech in character" has a chance to complete its tale of woe and misery, Paul, the author of this letter, interrupts and exclaims: "Thanks be to God through Jesus Christ our Lord" (7:25a).

In Romans 8:1-2 the author Paul again returns from using "speech in character" and in 8:2 addresses the "I," now turned to "you" singular: "For the law of the spirit of life in Christ Jesus has freed *you* from the law of sin and death" (emphasis added). That is, Paul does not immediately turn to the hearers of his letter by using "you" plural. He is completing his theological thought and captivating his hearers by using the artistry of "speech in character."

8:3-13 The life of God's Spirit in the believer

All of Romans 8 addresses the question: If the law is unable to give life, then whence comes life? In this section Paul answers this question by pointing to the Gentile believers' experience of the Spirit. I invite my readers to once again look carefully at the pronouns in this section. Although "us" occurs in 8:4, I would suggest that 8:12 contains the key "we" statement: "Consequently, brothers [and sisters], we are not debtors to the flesh, to live according to the flesh." Paul expresses his teaching about the flesh and the Spirit in the third person in 8:5-8. Romans 8:9-11, 13 captures the attention of Paul's Gentile listeners at Rome, as Paul uses "you" plural. Self-mastery does not come from the law but from the Spirit. Romans 8:13b reads: "If by the spirit you put to death the deeds of the body, you will live."

For the rest I focus on two points. Romans 8:3 contains a lapidary statement about Paul's view of God, who has given life to believers by "sending his own Son in the likeness of sinful flesh and for the sake of sin." God's own Son has become human and through his death has taken away humanity's sin. My second point deals with Paul's contrast between flesh and Spirit. For Paul "the flesh" is not to be confused or equated with sexual sins. "The flesh" is the entire human person, turned away from God and turned toward self. Paul's discussion of the flesh and the Spirit in Galatians 5:19-23 is very illuminative. In Galatians 5:19-21 Paul lists among "the works of the flesh" such human intellectual and willful actions as "idolatry, sorcery, . . . envy, . . . acts of selfishness." For Paul, "the Spirit" comprises God's actions toward the world, God's presence in the world, for God's people, in a creative way. Galatians 5:22-23 is very enlightening, for Paul lists among "the fruit of the Spirit" such creative actions as "love, . . . generosity, . . . self-control."

8:14-30 The future of believers is now

I formulate the theme that courses through this long section in this way: What believers experience now is the foretaste, the firstfruits, the down payment of what is to come. In more technical terminology, Paul is talking about eschatology in the process of realization. Scholars who pursue a story approach to Romans rightly note that Paul seems to momentarily draw the curtain back from the end time to show believers what it will be like. At the same time, Paul stresses that believers are already experiencing in the Spirit, in hope, what God's gracious purpose has in store for them. They have been saved—in hope (8:24). I also invite my readers to see how often Paul joins hands with the experience of the Gentile believers in Romans by frequently using "we." I refer to 8:16, 17, 18, 22, 23, 24, 25, 26, 28.

Here are the believers' present experiences that point to the future. They are "children of God," sons and daughters of God, brothers and sisters of Jesus. Romans 8:15 says pointedly: "*You* received a spirit of adoption, through which *we* cry, *Abba*, 'Father'" (emphasis added to "you" and "we"). The Holy Spirit has brought about this experience of adoption into God's family (see 8:16). Amidst present sufferings, glory awaits believers. That is their hope, for they are not like the pagans, "who have no hope" (1 Thess 4:13). They await what Revelation 21:1 refers to as " a new heaven and a new earth," that is, a time when God's curse upon humanity and the earth is lifted. See Genesis 3:17-19: "Cursed be the ground because of you! / In toil shall you eat its yield / all the days of your life. / Thorns and thistles shall it bring forth to you. . . . / By the sweat of your face / shall you get bread to eat." Believers await in groaning the fulfillment of the firstfruits of the Spirit, namely, the redemption of their entire selves (8:23).

Among the vicissitudes of human life and the life of faith, the Spirit comes to believers' aid and intercedes with God for them. As James D. G. Dunn says so well: "The Spirit is seen here as typically active not so much in the heights of spiritual rapture as in the depths of human inability to cope." In 8:28-30 Paul captures the final experience believers have: It is the confidence born of their faith "that all things work for good for those who love God" (8:28). Glorification is the ultimate destiny of all who have faith in Jesus Christ as their Lord (8:30). Paul speaks of it as already present.

8:31-39 A hymn to the God who is for us

I have counted a dozen occurrences of "we/our/us" in the Greek of this relatively short passage. Paul again engages in *pathos* and identifies himself with his listeners. To what does "this" in 8:31 refer? Is it a reference to the sufferings Paul mentions in 8:18-25? I would suggest that it's a reference to the various battles which believers wage against the powers of sin, death, and the flesh and which Paul has treated in Romans 5:11–8:30.

Paul once again adopts the style of a scholastic diatribe and raises questions in 8:31, 32, 33, 34, 35. The scene is the courtroom of the Last Judgment. Paul's answers seem like an early creed and reveal deep faith in what God has done for believers: God is for us; God lovingly handed his Son over for our salvation; God acquits the ungodly; Christ Jesus died, was raised, is at the right hand of the Father, and intercedes for us; we conquer overwhelmingly through the God who loves us; God loves us in Christ Jesus our Lord.

Romans 8

The trials that Paul experienced as a missionary and apostle do not have the power to separate him from the love of Christ (8:35). It is for God's sake that Paul endures all this, as he demonstrates from Psalm 43:23 in the Septuagint. No creature whatsoever, no matter how fearsome, is able to separate believers from God's love, manifested in Christ Jesus our Lord (8:38-39).

This hymn has provided courage to believers after national, community, and personal disasters. People battling cancer have drawn tremendous strength by looking at God through the lens of this hymn. Believers of all stripes rejoice that Paul shared his experience of God, which forms the basis for our experience of God.

JEWS AND GENTILES IN GOD'S PLAN
Romans 9:1–11:36

9:1-5 Paul's *ethos*, *pathos*, and logic on dress parade in the service of theodicy

I make four opening remarks for all of Romans 9–11. The rousing hymn in praise of God that Paul created in Romans 8:31-39 almost seems to defy any new thoughts. Shouldn't Paul conclude his letter, send greetings, and call it quits? If Paul were only dealing with the salvation of humankind, he might very well stop with 8:39. But in Romans Paul is concerned with God and how justification by faith for both Gentiles and Jews accords with God's earlier choice of Israel as God's special people. Remember that the theme sentence of Romans goes: The gospel "is the power of God for the salvation of everyone who believes: for *Jew first*, and then Greek" (1:16; emphasis added).

Second, Paul, a fervent Jew, the apostle to the Gentiles, bares his heart (*pathos* and *ethos*) on the question: Has the word of God failed? (9:6). Twenty-seven times, compared with eight in Romans 1:18–8:39, Paul uses "I." Stanley Stowers captures Paul's *pathos* and *ethos* well: "Even his mission to the Gentiles turns out to be an episode in the self-story of an Israelite acting for the sake of his people."

Third, the *logic* of Paul's argument in these three chapters is thoroughly scriptural—almost 40 percent of these ninety verses. James W. Aageson has well said: "The reliability of *God's word* to Israel was at stake; and it was to *God's word*, the Scriptures, that Paul turned to argue that it had not failed." In my commentary I will be tracking Paul's use of Scripture and implore my readers to be patient as they gradually discern how Paul is joining Scripture texts via themes. At the same time I advise my readers that Paul, even in Romans 9–11, does not neglect scholastic diatribe, for example, Romans 11:17-24.

Finally, although Paul is truly a religious genius, it is difficult to imagine him composing Romans 9–11 off the top of his head. Paul has frequently wrestled with and anguished over the issues of these chapters and may have preached a sermon or two about them.

In 9:1-5 Paul engages in deep and sincere *pathos* ("great sorrow and constant anguish") over his fellow Jews, the majority of whom have not believed in the gospel of Jesus as Messiah and Lord. God has gifted them so generously. While nothing can separate believers from the love of Christ (8:35), Paul, similar to Moses in Exodus 32:32, is willing to be "separated from Christ for the sake of" his brothers and sisters, his kin according to the flesh.

9:6-13 Paul's thesis and scriptural arguments from the patriarchs

In 9:6 Paul states the proposition that he will be defending from God's word throughout Romans 9–11: The word of God has not failed. The word of God's promise (9:9) and God's call (9:7, 12) are determinative of who God's children are. For example, "This means that it is not the children of the flesh who are the children of God, but the children of the promise are counted as descendants" (9:8). Paul's Scripture quotations come from Genesis 21:12; 18:10, 14; 25:23, the earliest narratives of God's people. Even the citation from a prophetic text (Mal 1:2-3 in Rom 9:13) refers back to the very beginnings of Israel. In this first section of Scripture argumentation, Paul has introduced in 9:7b and 12 a theme that he will pick up in Romans 9:24-26, namely, the theme of "call." The citation from Genesis 21:12 in Romans 9:7b should be translated: "In Isaac your offspring will be called."

9:14-18 God is not unjust; God is sovereign

After using elements of scholastic diatribe throughout Romans 1–8, Paul does not think it time to put it to bed. It has been so useful in helping him engage his listeners. Although God has chosen one and not another, God surely is not unjust. In Romans 9:15 Paul proves God's sovereignty by quoting Exodus 33:19 exactly as it is in the Septuagint: "I will show mercy to whom I will. I will take pity on whom I will" (author's translation).

In 9:16 Paul draws his conclusion by picking up the theme of God's mercy: "So it depends not upon a person's will or exertion, but upon God, who shows mercy." Paul's quotation from Exodus 9:16 is almost verbatim as it describes God's power over Pharaoh. Using the same inferential words he did in 9:16 *(ara oun)*, Paul draws his conclusion in 9:18, again emphasizing God's mercy: "Consequently, he has mercy upon whom he wills, and

Romans 9

he hardens whom he wills." Having employed the theme of God's call in 9:6-13, Paul now joins it to the theme of God's mercy: God is the one who calls in God's mercy. The astute reader will notice that Paul is joining Scripture quotations together by means of identical words and themes.

9:19-29 God's mercy, call, and ultimate fidelity

The questions/objections of scholastic diatribe hold 9:19-22 together. Paul combines citations from Isaiah 29:16 and Job 9:12 to answer these objections. How dare a human being even raise such objections! In 9:23 Paul resumes his theme of "mercy" and in 9:25-26 his theme of "call" to show that not only Jews but also Gentiles receive mercy and are called. But God has foreseen through Isaiah that not all is lost for Israel, which has not responded positively to the gospel. Quoting Isaiah 10:22, Paul says: "'Although the number of the Israelites were like the sand of the sea, a remnant will be saved'" (author's translation). The theme of "remnant," introduced here, will reappear in Romans 11:5. Key, too, are words from Isaiah 1:9 in Romans 9:29: The Lord has left us descendants (literally: "a seed").

9:30-33 Surprisingly pagans have faith; unfortunately Israel has not

Paul moves his considerations along by two more questions in 9:30 and 32 and by adding in 9:31-32 the way God has chosen both Jews and Gentiles, that is, through faith and not by works. Paul buttresses his considerations with a combined citation from two passages in Isaiah where he finds the same words. The words "whoever *believes* in him shall not be put to shame" come from Isaiah 28:16, which also contains the word "stone" (emphasis added). Isaiah 8:14 in the Septuagint also contains the word "stone" as well as "stumble" and "rock." Paul's interpretation of these two passages is daring and christological, for the stone laid by God in Zion as a sure foundation has become the stumbling stone, Jesus Christ. See 1 Peter 2:6-8 for a similar use of Isaiah 28:16 and 8:14.

10:1-13 Righteousness through faith

Romans 10:1-4 continues Paul's discussion of righteousness, and 10:5-13 provides scriptural support. Paul's concern for his fellow Jews is palpable (10:1). He does not slander them, for they manifest zeal for worshiping God and obeying God's law that is genuine (10:2). See, for example, 1 Maccabees 2:27: "Then Mattathias went through the city shouting, 'Let everyone who is zealous for the law and who stands by the covenant follow after me.'" But they have not submitted to the righteousness of God that has been revealed in Christ Jesus and in the gospel. Through Jesus Christ God has acquitted believers. What the law tried to accomplish, God has accomplished in Jesus Christ. Thus he is the end and goal of the law.

The Scripture citation of Leviticus 18:5 in Romans 10:5 is verbatim and supports the view that righteousness comes from the law. Paul's Scripture citations in Romans 10:6-8 stem from Deuteronomy 9:4; 30:12-14, and Psalm 106:26 in the Septuagint. Although the passages from Deuteronomy talk about God's gift of the law, Paul has interpreted them christologically via his "that is" clauses in 10:6-8.

Paul's main point about the righteousness that comes from faith is evidenced in his explicit quotation of Deuteronomy 30:14 in Romans 10:8: "'The word is near you, / in your mouth and in your heart' / (that is, the word of faith that we preach)." In Romans 10:9 Paul interprets "mouth" from Deuteronomy 30:14, and in 10:10 he explains "heart" from Deuteronomy 30:14 and does so by relying upon early confessions of faith: Jesus is Lord; God raised Jesus from the dead. In 10:11 Paul recycles and universalizes the quotation from Isaiah 28:16 he quoted earlier in 9:33. Paul's final citation in this section is verbatim from Joel 3:5. It is God who is described as calling in Romans 9:7, 12, 24, 25, 26. Now Gentile and Jewish believers do the calling.

10:14-21 God's chosen people have been disobedient while the senseless Gentiles have believed

This section shows that God's chosen people have no excuse for not believing the gospel. As is his custom, Paul makes his case by means of the questions of scholastic diatribe and his responses, which are largely taken from Scripture, especially Isaiah. One theme that joins this passage to the previous section is that of *word*. See 10:8: "'The word is near you, / in your mouth and in your heart' / (that is, the word of faith that we preach)." See also 10:17: "and what is heard comes through the word of Christ," and 10:18: "and their words to the end of the world." While Paul underscores the belief of the foolish Gentiles (10:19-20) and chastises Israel's disobedience (10:21), he announces in advance his "solution" to the nonbelief of God's chosen people. Quoting Deuteronomy 32:21, Paul says: "I will make you jealous of those who are not a nation" (Rom 10:19). See Romans 11:11-15 for Paul's treatment of this theme of jealousy.

11:1-10 Israel's rejection is partial

By means of diatribal questions and quotations from Scripture, Paul continues to present his resolution of the place in God's plan of Israel's failure to believe in Jesus Christ. Paul's own experience as a Jew who is a

Christian (11:2) answers the first question (11:1). Paul cites the example of the seven thousand who remained faithful during Elijah's time as further proof. Just above the verbs "I alone *am left*" (11:3) and "I *have left* for myself" (11:4) hovers the theme that Paul introduced earlier in Romans 9:27—the remnant (emphasis added). In 11:5 Paul makes the connection explicit: "So also at the present time there is a remnant, chosen by grace."

Paul concludes this section by referring to the Law (Deut 29:3), the Prophets (Isa 29:10), and the Writings (Ps 68:24 in the Septuagint) and links all three by the catchword "eyes." James D. G. Dunn helpfully maintains that the adverbial phrase *dia pantos,* with which Paul concludes this section, "is better translated 'continually' than 'for ever.'" The very existence of a remnant indicates that the rejection is only partial.

11:11-24 Paul censures Gentile Christian arrogance

Paul's main point about the destiny of God's chosen people comes across loud and clear: God has not abandoned them. See, for example, 11:24: "how much more will they who belong to it by nature be grafted back into their own olive tree." In making this point, Paul addresses his Gentile listeners and censures them for possible arrogance against unbelieving Israel.

Readers who have been diligently tracking Paul's use of Scripture quotations in Romans 9–11 may have had the same experience I did, that is, the realization that Paul does not cite a single word of Scripture in this section. Rather, elements from scholastic diatribe dominate this passage, for example, 11:11 and 11:17-24. In 11:13-16 Paul addressed the Gentile Christians in the second person plural. In 11:17 he begins to use the second person singular in his personification of the wild olive shoot and in doing so hones in on possible boasting and arrogant taunting on the part of Gentile Christians. Note how Paul singles out the imaginary person in 11:17 by using "you." Romans 11:18 continues to address the imaginary person with imperatives. Verses 19-24 formulate a dialogue between Paul and his imaginary person. Of course, Paul's responses and imperatives carry the day.

11:25-32 God has mercy on all

Paul's Scripture citation in Romans 11:26-27 is a combination of Isaiah 59:20-21 and Isaiah 27:9. Most important is Paul's modification of Isaiah 59:20, where the Greek of the Septuagint reads *heneken* ("for the sake of"), that is, "The deliverer will come for the sake of Zion" (author's translation). By exchanging *ek* ("out of") for *heneken,* Paul makes a potent christological statement: Christ is the deliverer and has come from Zion (and indeed for Zion's sake).

Throughout this section, which has Gentile believers in mind, there is an ebb and flow between universality and particularity. Three statements point to universality: "the full number of the Gentiles" (11:25), "thus all Israel will be saved" (11:26), and "that he might have mercy upon all" (11:32). Romans 11:29 breathes particularity: "For the gifts and the call of God are irrevocable." How God holds together universality and particularity is being revealed now as God lets men and women in on his mystery, and we frail human beings struggle mightily and sometimes sin grievously in our attempts to fathom and live by this mystery.

11:33-36 Praise to God

Paul's Scripture citation in Romans 11:34 is verbatim from Isaiah 40:13. Scholars are unsure to what extent Paul cites Scripture and what Scripture he cites in Romans 11:35. Job 41:3 has been proposed. These verses are justifiably called hymnic. In Greek the rhyme of 11:33 sounds forth: *ploutou, theou, autou, autou, anex-, anex-*. The rhythmic driving force of 11:36 even roars through the English: "From him and through him and for him are all things." Paul's use of quotations from Scripture and rhyme and rhythm serve one purpose: the praise of God, whose ways he has been describing since Romans 1:16. Human beings stand in awe and in worship of this gracious and merciful God.

THE DUTIES OF CHRISTIANS

Romans 12:1–15:13

12:1-3 The overture to Paul's exhortations

I offer three preliminary considerations for all of Romans 12:1–15:13. First, those of us who have been paying close attention to Paul's use of pronouns will notice how frequently he employs imperatives in Romans 12:1–15:13. For example, 12:2: "Do not conform yourself to this age," and 15:2: "Let each of us please our neighbor for the good, for building up."

Second, I supply some background material so that we may be better able to recognize the similarities and differences between the block of exhortations in 12:1–15:13 and those in other writings. The exhortations that Paul artistically presents in 12:9-21 have some parallels in Jesus' Sermon on the Mount. Compare Matthew 5:44: "Love your enemies, and pray for those who persecute you," and Romans 12:14: "Bless those who persecute [you], bless and do not curse them."

An example of a very common "two ways teaching" is found in a section of the *Didache*, which dates to the same time as Romans. The *Didache* reads:

Romans 12

> There are two ways, one of life and one of death, and the difference between the two ways is great. This then is the way of life. First, love the God who made you, and second, your neighbor as yourself. And whatever you do not want to happen to you, do not do to another. . . . And now the second commandment of the teaching. Do not murder, do not commit adultery, do not engage in pederasty, do not engage in sexual immorality. Do not steal, do not practice magic, do not use enchanted potions, do not abort a fetus or kill a child that is born (1:1-2 and 2:1-2; Loeb translation modified).

The *Didache* continues:

> And the way of death is this. First of all it is evil and filled with a curse: murders, adulteries, passions, sexual immoralities, robberies . . . deceit, arrogance, malice, insolence. . . . It is filled with persecutors of the good, haters of the truth. . . . Murderers of children and corruptors of what God has fashioned, who turn their backs on the needy, oppress the afflicted, and support the wealthy (5:1-2; Loeb modified).

Although Paul has some items in common with the "two ways teaching," he did not see fit to adopt this very popular "ethical" schema.

Third, one of the reasons Paul does not adopt such traditional materials as the "two ways teaching" is that he is spelling out the practical implications of his theology of love (12:9-21; 13:8-10; 14:1–15:13) and the Spirit (12:4-8) and of faith (12:3, 6; 14:1, 22-23). In brief, he is telling the Romans in 12:1–15:13 what Romans 5:5 means: "the love of God has been poured out into our hearts through the holy Spirit that has been given to us."

I make three points about Romans 12:1-3. First, 12:1-3 and what follows are not independent of what has gone before in the previous eleven chapters. Paul uses his authority (his *ethos*) and draws inferences ("therefore") from what he has previously stated and now summarizes in the phrase "by the mercies of God."

Second, there is a very close connection between what Paul says in 12:1 ("offer your bodies as a living sacrifice") and what he had said earlier, for instance, in 1:24: "Therefore, God handed them over to impurity through the lusts of their hearts for the mutual degradation of their bodies." Paul's Gentile listeners are now worshiping God (12:1) rather than creatures (1:25).

Third, behind the command "Do not conform yourself to this age" (12:2) stands the eschatological perspective that has dominated Romans 1–11; for example, 3:21: "But *now* the righteousness of God has been manifested" (emphasis added). The eschatological dimension of 12:2 also points ahead to 13:11-14, which deals with the perspective of the end time and rounds off this section of exhortations. Technically, 12:2 and 13:11-14 form a thematic *inclusio*, that is, the placement of similar material at the beginning and end of a section.

12:4-8 One body with many gifts

In 1 Corinthians 12–14 Paul wrote a far more extensive treatment of the one body with many parts and of the gifts *(charismata)* of the Holy Spirit. Although here in Romans 12:4-8 Paul does not say that the "gifts" (12:6) come from the Holy Spirit, expressions such as "according to the grace given us" seem to presuppose the Holy Spirit (12:6). "Prophecy in proportion to the faith" (12:6) invites special comment. Prophecy is not so much foretelling the future but forthtelling, and could very well blend with the gift of exhortation (12:8).

"In proportion to the faith" is a phrase that resonates in Christian communities across the ages. One believer looking at a text of Scripture may see a valid but surface meaning, whereas the prophet may see far deeper and speak more challengingly about the same Scripture text. The development of Paul's thought in 1 Corinthians 12–14 may also give us a clue as to why Paul in Romans 12:9-21 gives exhortations about love. Paul's hymn to love in 1 Corinthians 13 occurs after a detailed discussion of the body of Christ and the gifts of the Spirit. The Corinthians are to pursue love in exercising their gifts (1 Cor 14:1).

12:9-21 The path of love

It is certainly easier to delve into the literary structure and theology of this passage than to abide by its thirty injunctions. Yes, thirty. That's what Philip F. Esler maintains. I just counted them, and he's right. For example, 12:11 has three: "Do not grow slack in zeal, be fervent in spirit, serve the Lord"; 12:16 has four: "Have the same regard for one another; do not be haughty but associate with the lowly; do not be wise in your own estimation."

With its flowing translation, the NAB translation of 12:16 hides some of its artistry. Here Paul uses the same Greek verb *(phronein)* three times ("have the same regard; do not be haughty; do not be wise"). Paul's artistry also shines forth in the connection between 12:13-14, where the same Greek verb *(diokein)* occurs and stands behind *"exercise* hospitality" and "bless those who *persecute"* (emphasis added). Paul's sprinkling of similar mnemonic devices throughout 12:9-16 has led Esler to suggest that we have here "a

Romans 12

precious fragment of Paul's oral proclamation on the subject of the love that must characterize the life and identity of Christ-followers."

The injunctions of Romans 12:17-21 deal with peace, forgiveness, and non-retaliation. They are different, too, in that they contain the only explicit citations of Scripture in this section: Deuteronomy 32:35 in Romans 12:19 and Proverbs 25:21-22 in Romans 12:20. Giving food and drink to an enemy (12:19) has the result of heaping "burning coals upon his head" (12:20). Obviously, we are not to take "heaping burning coals upon" someone's head literally. I rely on Frederick W. Danker's interpretation of this obscure action: to "cause a person to blush with shame and remorse." In our language, especially in certain regions, there are expressions that are opaque to outsiders. For example, the first time I heard "The pastor threw a ram," I had little idea what it meant and tried to visualize an elderly pastor throwing cattle around. I was told that the pastor was very angry. I had to convert "ram" into an expression for "anger." Similarly, we have to convert "heaping burning coals upon" into an expression for "shaming a person."

Some years ago my work took me to a diocese where the Scripture adopted for reflection and implementation for the entire year was Romans 12:9-21. What a whale of an agenda for any church, local or diocesan!

13:1-7 Civil authority and the believer

Why does Paul say what he does in this passage and why now? The answer to "why now" is easier to provide. In this section Paul is tidying up some loose ends from what he has just said in 12:17-21. If Christians are not to exact revenge for evil done them (12:19), who is? They are to leave "room for the wrath" (12:19), which God will exercise through legitimate civil authority. See how "wrath" recurs in 13:4-5, for example, 13:4: "It is the servant of God to inflict wrath on the evildoer." Paul is also providing some extra specificity to what he said in 12:9: "Hold on to what is good." Notice that the word "good" occurs three times in 13:3-4 in verses couched in the diatribal "you" singular style. For instance, 13:3: "Then do what is good and you will receive approval from it."

Paul was raised in a hierarchical and patriarchal society and was heir to views of the role of government in God's created order. In its address to kings and magistrates, Wisdom 6:3 expresses something very similar to what Paul says in Romans 13:1: "Because authority was given you by the LORD and sovereignty by the Most High." But Wisdom 6:3 immediately characterizes God as the One "who shall probe your works and scrutinize your counsels!"

Paul does not give absolute authority to the Roman emperors who ruled the roost in his day. Such rulers are "servant[s] of God" (13:4), not gods to be worshiped. Luke Timothy Johnson has expressed well the hermeneutical implications of 13:1-7: "If all civil authority is from God and ordered under God, then it equally follows that a civil authority that does not respond to God's will can be considered disqualified as a true authority, and so could be resisted 'for conscience's sake.'"

13:8-10 Love your neighbor as yourself

Paul continues what has been called his "general exhortations" by double linking Romans 13:8-10 to what has gone before. The immediate connection is between 13:7 and 13:8, where the same Greek root *(opheil)* appears. In 13:7 the NAB translates it by "due[s]"; in 13:8 by "owe." Variations of "love one another" (13:8) occur in 12:5: "So we, though many, are one body in Christ and individually parts of one another"; 12:10: "Love one another with mutual affection; anticipate one another in showing honor"; and 12:16: "Have the same regard for one another." Further, Paul introduced the thirty injunctions of Romans 12:9-21 with "Let love be sincere."

In listing specific commandments of the Decalogue in Romans 13:9, Paul follows the order of Deuteronomy 5:17-21. Leviticus 19:18 supplies Paul with the commandment of love of neighbor. After much discussion of the role of the law earlier in Romans 1–11, Paul sums it up. What people tried to accomplish by living the Mosaic law Christian believers now accomplish by their faith-filled lives of loving their neighbors as themselves.

13:11-14 A passage that led to St. Augustine's conversion

This passage connects with the earlier eschatological passage of Romans 12:2: "Do not conform yourself to this age but be transformed by the renewal of your mind." Thus 13:11-14 forms an *inclusio* (see p. 469) with the opening gambits of Paul's general exhortations. Romans 13:13-14 echoes with earlier passages in Romans. Romans 6:13 reads: "And do not present the parts of your bodies to sin as weapons for wickedness, but present yourselves to God as raised from the dead to life and the parts of your bodies to God as weapons for righteousness." See also Romans 8:12-13. In an earlier letter Paul also used the contrast between night/darkness/evil deeds and day/light/good deeds (1 Thess 5:4-11). Believers are to put on the Kevlar body armor of light (13:12) and the attitude of the Lord Jesus (13:14; see Phil 2:5-11).

In Book 8.12 of his *Confessions*, St. Augustine tells the story of hearing a young child's sing-song of "Take and read, take and read." He went back to the place where he had put Paul's text. He writes: "I snatched it up, opened it and in silence read the passage upon which my eyes first fell." The passage was Romans 13:13-14. St. Augustine continues: "I had no wish to read further, and no need. For in that instant, with the very ending of the sentence, it was as though a light of utter confidence shone in all my heart, and all the darkness of uncertainty vanished away" (F. J. Sheed translation). Augustine was on the threshold of casting off the desires of the flesh and giving himself over to the fruit of the Spirit.

14:1–15:13 Principles that govern conduct with regard to indifferent matters

Scholars are divided on the question of whether in Romans 14:1–15:13 Paul is addressing a concrete situation in the Roman house churches. I, for one, do not think so. Nor do I think that Paul is specifically addressing a situation where "the weak" are Jewish Christians and "the strong" are Gentile Christians. After making two methodological points, I treat the principles that Paul enunciates in this section.

A number of my readers may have already perused my commentary on Galatians in this booklet. In that letter it was fairly clear that Paul was engaged with teachers/influencers who were championing circumcision and observance of the Mosaic law. See, for example, Galatians 6:15: "For neither does circumcision mean anything, nor does uncircumcision, but only a new creation." In 1 Corinthians 8:7 the situation is clear and deals with meat sacrificed to idols: "But not all have this knowledge. There are some who have been so used to idolatry up until now that, when they eat meat sacrificed to idols, their conscience, which is *weak,* is defiled" (emphasis added).

However, when we take a close look at Romans 14:1–15:13, it is very difficult to ascertain what was going on. Eating and drinking (14:2, 21), special days (14:5-6), and clean and unclean food (14:14) are vague and insufficient evidence on which to depict a battle over indifferent matters that was actually raging in or among the Roman house churches.

Moreover, I challenge my readers to find multiple references to "the weak" and "the strong" and to their positions in this passage. Romans 14:1 and 15:1 are the only two verses that refer to "the weak," while Romans 15:1 is the only verse that addresses "the strong." In our quest for finding or making order out of what Paul says, we are the ones who create the camp of "the weak" and the camp of "the strong."

As J. Paul Sampley has shown, this is indeed Paul's goal in writing so obliquely rather than directly, as he did in Galatians and 1 Corinthians.

Sampley writes: "Direct speech is argumentative and confrontational while figured speech is allusive and evocative; direct speech needs proofs, while figured speech invites the hearer to establish its veracity by self-application." I might add that Paul's two diatribal questions in 14:4, 10 help him get his listeners to apply his teaching to themselves.

If this lengthy passage doesn't deal with specific questions in the Roman house churches, then what's it all about? It's about the principles to be applied in those multiple situations that involve indifferent matters, that is, not questions of faith and morals, but which nonetheless can create ugly stains on the fabric of community life. Paul has arrived at these principles from previous experiences with communities, especially in Corinth. N. T. Wright's comment about 14:1–15:13 is helpful: "This is what justification by faith looks like when it sits down at table in Christian fellowship."

I give a few of the principles that course through this section and invite my readers to discover others as they explore Paul's interchange of the personal pronouns "you" and "we" and engage in their own self-application of Paul's teaching. "We shall all stand before the judgment seat of God" (14:10). "Nothing is unclean in itself" (14:14). "The kingdom of God is not a matter of food and drink, but of righteousness, peace, and joy in the holy Spirit" (14:17). Paul appeals not only to principles but also to the example of Jesus Christ: "For Christ did not please himself" (15:3); "Welcome one another, then, as Christ welcomed you" (15:7). Finally, in 15:9-12 he appeals to all of Sacred Writ—the Law, the Prophets, and the Writings—to show the universality of God's welcome.

During the course of my work, I have traveled to different cultures and experienced firsthand the struggle involved in realizing that what I thought was "universal law" was an indifferent matter. St. Peter's in Rome doesn't have kneelers, yet I thought that such a practice was de rigueur. I was pleasantly surprised when I was served pea soup with ham in a German friary on a day of abstinence: "Ach, what is pea soup without ham?"

CONCLUSION

Romans 15:14–16:27

15:14-24 Paul needs the assistance of the Roman believers in spreading his gospel to Spain

I make three observations. As Paul concludes his rich letter to the Romans, he repeats three times that his gospel is for the Gentiles (15:16, 18). It is the gospel he has been preaching throughout this very letter.

Second, Paul's description of having preached the gospel of Christ "from Jerusalem all the way around to Illyricum" (15:19) should be taken in a global sense, for Paul has not preached to every individual or in every town.

Finally, 15:24 should not be read as if Paul were alerting the Roman house churches that he planned to visit them during a whistle stop. The Greek behind "to be sent on my way" really means to supply food, money, companions, means of travel, and such. The Roman believers could not make all these arrangements overnight. Also, according to Joseph A. Fitzmyer, "there is thus far no evidence of Jewish habitation in Spain prior to the third century A.D." So Paul could not follow a procedure of preaching first in a Jewish synagogue. Moreover, as Robert Jewett surmises, Paul had to have the Scriptures translated "into the Celt-Iberian dialects still employed by most of the population in Spain." The nice things that Paul says about the Roman believers in 15:14, 22-24 (technically: *captatio benevolentiae*) are in service of winning them over to the task of preaching his gospel.

15:25-33 Paul's anxiety about his reception in Jerusalem

In Romans 12:8 Paul mentions the gift of generosity: "if one contributes, in generosity." Romans 12:13 exhorts: "Contribute to the needs of the holy ones." Paul is taking the collection he gathered from Gentile Christians to fulfill the pledge he made in Galatians 2:10 to help the poor among the Jerusalem Christians. This money, however, is not just alms. It is a symbol of the unity of the churches: The Gentile Christians "decided to do it, and in fact they are indebted to them, for if the Gentiles have come to share in their spiritual blessings, they ought also to serve them in material blessings" (15:27).

Paul's words in 15:30-31 reveal the apprehension he has about his upcoming journey to and meeting in Jerusalem: "Join me in the struggle by your prayers to God on my behalf, that I may be delivered from the disobedient in Judea." Jews may well consider Paul, a former zealot, to be a turncoat. Jewish Christians, who are zealous for the Mosaic law, may view Paul's law-free gospel for the Gentiles as repugnant. Would the Jerusalem Christians actually reject the collection and its symbolism?

16:1-16 Five house churches and leadership roles for women

To some, Romans 16:1-16 may appear to be as inspiring as reading a church directory. To others it has become a window into Romans and the early church. Behind 16:5, 10, 11, 14, 15 there is evidence of at least five house churches in Rome, or more probably tenement house churches. See, for example, 16:5: "Greet also the church at their house," that is, the house of Prisca and Aquila.

There are eight women mentioned as active in promoting the gospel: Phoebe, Prisca, Mary, Junia, Tryphaena, Tryphosa, Persis, and Rufus's mother. I single out Phoebe and Junia for further comment. Phoebe is a wealthy woman who is a *diakonos* and *prostatis* (16:1-2). The first term may be translated as "minister" and indicates a position of responsibility in the church. Archbishop Rabanus Maurus (d. 856) commented: "This passage teaches by apostolic authority that women are also constituted in the ministry of the church" (PL 111:1605D). The second term may be translated as "benefactor," if one understands that this term indicates a person of enormous prestige and influence.

It is highly likely that Phoebe not only carried Paul's letter to the Romans to the house churches but also read it to them. You see, Phoebe was likely among the five percent of the population who could read. Further, in reading Romans, she surely had to know what it was about. Ancient letters (and manuscripts) did not have spacing, chapters and verses, and subheadings. I give a simple example. Suppose I put a recent headline in capital letters without spacing: FLORIDAKEYDEERREBOUNDS. Without too much effort you read: Florida key deer rebounds. But is "key" an adjective meaning "principal"? Does "key" refer to the Florida Keys? Is "key deer" a technical name for a special species of deer? The reader would have to know answers to these questions in order to read this simple sentence out loud meaningfully. Just think of the skill Phoebe must have if she is to navigate successfully through all the elements of scholastic diatribe that Paul used in composing his letter!

I make three points about Junia (16:7). First, she is a woman. St. John Chrysostom (d. 407), who was proficient in Greek and was a misogynist, commented: "To be an apostle is something great. But to be outstanding among the apostles, just think of what a wondrous song of praise that is. . . . Truly, how great the wisdom of this woman must have been that she was even deemed worthy of the title of apostle." Second, the fathers of the church and Greek grammar indicate that Junia is an apostle and outstanding among the apostles and not merely held in high regard by male apostles.

Third, Junia was not an apostle of a church, for nowhere in 16:7 does Paul refer to her as such. Contrast 2 Corinthians 8:23 and Philippians 2:25. I am of the opinion that Junia is an apostle in the same sense as Paul, who had seen the risen Lord (1 Cor 9:1) but was not one of the Twelve. She may have been among the five hundred who saw the risen Lord (1 Cor 15:6).

16:17-27 Final goodbye with warning and doxology

There are three strange elements in Romans 16. In the previous passage we encountered the first one. Nowhere else in his letters does Paul extend greetings to twenty-four people. He desperately wants to establish a home base among the Roman Christians for his evangelical mission to Spain.

In 16:17-20 we run into the second extraordinary element in the farewell section of a Pauline letter. Paul now warns the Romans of people who "do not serve our Lord Christ but their own appetites" (16:18). One is reminded of Philippians 3:19, where Paul warns of false teachers, whose "God is their stomach."

Words we hear or speak during a farewell provide a contemporary analogy to Paul's seemingly unmotivated warning in these verses. Sometimes farewell words do not seem motivated by the event. After the magnificently glorious celebrations that surrounded my First Mass in my parish church, I was leaving home. My father kissed me and said, "Don't forget where you've come from." To this day I remember and abide by this unmotivated farewell reminder not to overly honor myself and thereby dishonor my parents. In this warning Paul is indeed speaking "rather boldly" (15:15).

Paul ends Galatians with: "The grace of our Lord Jesus Christ be with your spirit, brothers. Amen" (6:18). He concludes his other letters in a similar fashion. But once again, Romans is strange. Paul finishes with a doxology. It is fitting that Paul concludes by praising and honoring God, for God has been the theme of this very long letter. It is fitting that at the conclusion of a letter whose main purpose is to reveal God's plan for the Gentiles Paul praises God for revealing this very plan. I. Howard Marshall rightly contends that doxologies also have a hortatory purpose. Romans 16:25 asks for strengthening and perseverance and repeats some of the themes of Romans 8:25-27.

In my final comment I persevere to the end with my reading program for Romans and invite my readers to check the pronouns of this doxology: "you" and "I." Paul has the Romans ("you") at heart. At the same time, this is his doxology. He is the one who is praising and honoring God, revealing his *ethos,* showing his true colors.

BIBLIOGRAPHY

James W. Aageson, "Scripture and Structure in the Development of the Argument in Romans 9–11," *Catholic Biblical Quarterly* 48 (1986) 265–289.

Frederick W. Danker, *Benefactor: An Epigraphic Study of a Graeco-Roman and New Testament Semantic Field*. St. Louis: Clayton Publishing Co., 1982.

James D. G. Dunn, *Romans 1–8, 9–16*. Word Biblical Commentary 38AB. Dallas: Word Books, 1988.

Philip F. Esler, *Conflict and Identity in Romans: The Social Setting of Paul's Letter*. Minneapolis: Fortress, 2003.

Joseph A. Fitzmyer, *Romans*. Anchor Bible 33. New York: Doubleday, 1993.

A Greek-English Lexicon of the New Testament and other Early Christian Literature. Third edition (BDAG). Revised and edited by Frederick W. Danker. Chicago: University of Chicago Press, 2000.

Robert Jewett, "Romans," in *The Cambridge Companion to St. Paul*. Edited by James D. G. Dunn. Cambridge: Cambridge University Press, 2003, pp. 91–104.

Luke Timothy Johnson, *Reading Romans: A Literary and Theological Commentary*. Macon, GA: Smyth & Helwys, 2001.

"Joseph and Aseneth," A new translation and introduction by C. Burchard in *The Old Testament Pseudepigrapha II*. Edited by James H. Charlesworth. Garden City, NY: Doubleday, 1985, pp. 177–247.

Ernst Käsemann, "'The Righteousness of God' in Paul," in *New Testament Questions of Today*. Philadelphia: Fortress, 1969, pp. 168–182.

Leander E. Keck, "*Pathos* in Romans? Mostly Preliminary Remarks," in *Paul and Pathos*. Edited by Thomas H. Olbricht and Jerry L. Sumney. Atlanta: Society of Biblical Literature, 2001, pp. 71–96.

I. Howard Marshall, "Romans 16:25-27—An Apt Conclusion," in *Romans and the People of God: Essays in Honor of Gordon D. Fee on the Occasion of His 65th Birthday*. Edited by Sven K. Soderlund and N. T. Wright. Grand Rapids: Eerdmans, 1999, pp. 170–184.

Paul and Empire: Religion and Power in Roman Imperial Society. Edited by Richard A. Horsley. Harrisburg: Trinity Press International, 1997, pp. 1–8.

Romans

J. Paul Sampley, "The Weak and the Strong: Paul's Careful and Crafty Rhetorical Strategy in Romans 14:1–15:13," in *The Social World of the First Christians: Essays in Honor of Wayne A. Meeks*. Edited by L. Michael White and O. Larry Yarbrough. Minneapolis: Fortress, 1995, pp. 40–52.

Stanley K. Stowers, "The Diatribe," in *Greco-Roman Literature and the New Testament: Selected Forms and Genres*. Edited by David E. Aune. Atlanta: Scholars Press, 1988, pp. 71–83.

———. *A Rereading of Romans: Justice, Jews, and Gentiles*. New Haven: Yale University Press, 1994.

Charles H. Talbert, *Romans*. Smyth & Helwys Bible Commentary. Macon, GA: Smyth & Helwys, 2002.

N. T. Wright, "The Letter to the Romans," in *The New Interpreter's Bible*. Volume X. Nashville: Abingdon Press, 2002, pp. 393–770.

The Letters to the Corinthians
Maria A. Pascuzzi

INTRODUCTION

First and Second Corinthians are literary windows affording readers a "Paul's-eye" view into the life and development of one very dynamic Christian community. As we peer through them, what we see can quickly challenge idealized notions about the cohesiveness and harmony of the earliest communities of believers (cf. Acts 4:32). The way Paul tells it, the community at Corinth was characterized by rivalry (1 Cor 1:12); obsession with status and superior wisdom leading to arrogance (1 Cor 1–4); disregard for the less spiritually enlightened and gifted (1 Cor 8:1-13; 12–14) as well as for the economic have-nots (1 Cor 11:17-22); sexual immorality (1 Cor 5:1-13; 6:12-20); assertiveness with regard to individual rights (1 Cor 6:12-13); and, as time went on, a suspicious and disdainful attitude toward Paul himself (2 Cor 1:12–2:12; 10–12).

Such behavior serves to remind the reader that conversion did not produce an immediate social and moral transformation to a new way of life rooted in gospel values. Paul had to deal with this reality, and in his correspondence he commands, exhorts, persuades, threatens, does everything possible to refocus the community on the gospel and bring about transformed gospel living.

While these letters serve as windows on the past, they also reflect back to us much that still characterizes Christian living today. As we attempt now to understand the conflicting impulses, values, and behavior that gave rise to what Paul perceived as inauthentic Christian living at Corinth, perhaps we can better understand what contributes to inauthentic Christian living in our own day. We may also find in Paul's exigent call to the Corinthians to transform their lives the impetus for our own continued transformation in light of the gospel. Before examining each letter, some preliminary information about Corinth, Paul's work there, and the nature and purpose of the letters is needed to establish a context in which these letters can be more adequately understood.

The city of Corinth and its citizens

Corinth was strategically located on a narrow isthmus that linked mainland Greece to its north with the Peloponnesus to its south. The city was also an important east-west axis, located within a few miles of two great harbors: Cenchreae, which handled commerce to and from points east, and Lechaeum, which handled commerce to and from points west. This Greek city flourished from the fifth century B.C. until it was left in near ruin by the Romans in 146 B.C. A century passed before Corinth was refounded as a Roman colony in 44 B.C. The city was rebuilt according to Roman architectural patterns, reorganized politically in line with Roman government structures, and repopulated with Rome's urban poor, freedmen (former slaves), and slaves from among its conquered populations, as well as immigrants from the east, including Jews. Greek descendants of those who had survived Corinth's assault continued to live amidst its ruins. However, in this new Roman Corinth, they were regarded as resident aliens.

Within a few decades of its refounding, Corinth became the capital of the new Roman province Achaia. By the time Paul arrived, about A.D. 50/51, Corinth was emerging as Greece's premier city and the commercial, manufacturing, and cultural megacenter of the entire eastern Mediterranean. The stamp of Imperial Rome, as well as the influx of tradespersons, merchants, and tourists who came to visit Corinth's numerous shrines or to attend the Isthmian games, philosophers, and orators were all factors that contributed to the variety of ideas, mores, and perspectives that gave Corinth its vitality and appeal.

Paul's move to Corinth was probably calculated. The city's pluralistic and cosmopolitan character was clearly advantageous to him. He would no doubt get a hearing, and even a modestly successful mission among such sophisticated city-dwellers could lend credibility to his gospel of a crucified Messiah and validate his Gentile mission.

However, pluralism and sophistication were only two aspects of the social and the cultural ethos that dominated Corinth. The Corinthians were known to be fiercely competitive, driven by the desire for status, wealth, honor, and power. The route to these involved navigating the Roman patronage system, a network of hierarchically ordered patron-client relations. In return for the benefactions and enhanced social status gained through access to a rich patron's circle of influence, clients supported and promoted the patron, bolstering his status and ultimately widening his sphere of power.

Judging from Paul's description of the situation in the community, as noted above, it appears that these ingrained primary social and cultural values were carried over into the Christian community by the newly converted, with negative consequences. Their behavior, still conditioned by Corinth's secular values and aspirations, was destroying God's *ekklēsia*, a microsociety whose unity and holiness were to distinguish it from the macrosociety from which the converts came.

In these letters Paul negotiates the problems arising from this clash of values and deals with their negative impact on the life of the community. However, his greater concern is to further the process of resocialization by inculcating a perspective rooted in the gospel and the values and behavior consonant with that. This was no easy task, since Paul needed to remove Corinth's ethos from the Corinthians without removing the Corinthians from pagan Corinth (see 1 Cor 5:9-10)!

Paul's mission in Corinth and the Corinthian church

The Acts of the Apostles, a key secondary source for Paul's life and work after his own letters, provides scant information about Paul's founding mission in Corinth. He came to Corinth after a short and largely unsuccessful stay in Athens (Acts 17:15-34). He found lodging and work as a tentmaker with Priscilla and Aquila, a Jewish-Christian couple, and was soon joined by his co-workers Silas and Timothy (Acts 18:1-5). According to Luke, Paul began evangelizing in the synagogue, but as Jewish opposition increased, he refocused his efforts on the Gentiles and moved his ministry base to the home of a Gentile believer, Titus Justus (Acts 18:5-8). Luke reports that Paul ministered at Corinth for a year and a half (Acts 18:11), but without specifying dates for this sojourn. The mention of Paul's arraignment before Gallio (Acts 18:12-17), proconsul of Achaia from either A.D. 50 to 51 or 51 to 52, has figured significantly in attempts to date Paul's ministry in Corinth, which many scholars place sometime between A.D. 50 and 52.

More insight about Paul's life and ministry at Corinth and the composition of the community is gained from the Corinthian correspondence itself. Paul declares that he had come to preach, not baptize, though he admits baptizing a few, perhaps in the earliest days of his ministry (1 Cor 1:14-17). By deliberate choice, he preached his gospel without eloquence (1 Cor 1:17; 2:1-5). Just how rhetorically unimpressive Paul was is hard to say. However, he may have been outclassed in the eyes of the community by a certain Apollos, famed for eloquence, who preached at Corinth after Paul's departure (Acts 18:24; 19:1; 1 Cor 3:6). Paul testifies that he worked to support himself so that he could preach his gospel to all free of charge (1 Corinthians 9). This may reflect his deliberate choice to avoid entanglement in the patronage system with its obligation. Both Paul's choice to forego financial support as well as his alleged lack of rhetorical prowess are issues that will surface again in 2 Corinthians 10–12.

With regard to the community, composed of Jews and Gentiles, the latter apparently predominated, judging by the decidedly pagan aspect of the issues Paul treated, for example, food sacrificed to idols and attendance at pagan temple feasts (1 Cor 8–10), as well as references to their former idolatrous way of life (1 Cor 6:10; 8:7; 12:2). Past assumptions that community members were drawn from Corinth's lower classes, largely based on remarks about their insignificant origins and status (1 Cor 1:26-31), have been modified in view of recent research into the social composition of urban Christian communities. It is now acknowledged that along with the economically poor, the Corinthian community included others disadvantaged because of ethnicity, class, or gender biases, and still others considered to be persons of some means and social stature who are mentioned in the text (e.g., 1 Cor 1:14; 16:17, 19; see further Rom 16:1, 21-23).

Given the diversity of this community, estimated to number anywhere from fifty to two hundred persons, scholars prefer to speak of it as "socially stratified." This socioeconomic diversity probably accounts for community tensions at the Lord's Supper, where the poor were disregarded (1 Cor 11:17-22), and other situations where some members may have used their means or status to the detriment of others (e.g., 1 Cor 6:1-11) or to exempt themselves from certain moral dictates (e.g., 1 Cor 5:1-13).

The nature and purpose of Paul's Letters to the Corinthians

Paul wrote 1 Corinthians from Ephesus about A.D. 55/56. Second Corinthians was written a year or so later from Macedonia after Paul received Titus's update on the situation at Corinth. Evidence in these letters indicates that Paul had actually written more than two letters to this community. In 1 Corinthians 5:9, Paul states that he had written a previous letter, no longer extant, containing information relevant to an issue he was now writing about in 1 Corinthians 5. Then, in 2 Corinthians 2:1-4, he speaks of a "tearful letter," obviously predating 2 Corinthians. Attempts have been made to identify this "tearful letter" with 1 Corinthians or with 2 Corinthians 10–13. However, both identifications have been seriously questioned, and the possibility that the "tearful letter" is also lost cannot be excluded.

Many scholars have argued that 2 Corinthians is a combination of at least two letters: 2 Corinthians 1–9 plus 2 Corinthians 10–13. Others have suggested five or six. What is important to recognize here is that 1 and 2 Corinthians are only part of a continuous dialogue between Paul and this community. Fortunately, they are preserved in the canon of the New Testament, where they are designated "first" and "second" in view of their respective lengths. However, they were not necessarily letters one and two in Paul's ongoing correspondence with the community, which included at least four letters.

First and Second Corinthians are true letters reflecting contemporary Greco-Roman conventions of letter writing. Each letter has an opening section with its requisite features, a body, the main part of the letter, where key matters are taken up, and a conclusion. These and other formal and stylistic features will be noted in the course of the commentary. Here it is important to underscore that in Paul's day the letter functioned as a substitute for personal presence when this was not possible (1 Cor 5:3) or, in some cases, not desirable (2 Cor 2:1-2). In 1 and 2 Corinthians, we read what Paul wanted to say about issues and developments in the community articulated from his point of view. In other words, we read only one-half of a dialogue between partners involved in an ongoing relationship. Many details and facts already known to Paul and the Corinthians are omitted. At times Paul quotes the Corinthians (e.g., 1 Cor 6:12; 7:1) and offers clues about the evolving situation there (e.g., 2 Cor 11:4-15). These do illumine some Corinthian views and some of the content and contours of Paul's own remarks. However, a fuller picture of the situation depends, to a large extent, on the piecing together of textual and extratextual clues.

It is a commonplace in Pauline studies to refer to Paul's writings as "occasional letters." What is recognized in the use of this term is that his letters were prompted, or occasioned, by particular circumstances, questions, or behavior arising in the daily life of the communities Paul had founded that necessitated a response from him. They are not sustained and systematic expositions of Paul's accumulated theological insights. Even Romans, the one letter written by Paul to a community he had not founded, is now considered to have more of an occasional character than previously assumed.

Thus, what we find in 1 and 2 Corinthians are *ad hoc* responses intended primarily for a particular community and its peculiar needs. This is not to suggest that Paul lacked any theological framework within which he formulated his responses. Rather, it is to caution against assuming that what we read is Paul's coherently articulated and exhaustive last word on all issues. It is more likely we are reading Paul's first word on a variety of issues, most of which arose only after he had moved on to evangelize elsewhere.

Though a letter and a speech were not identical, the letter substituted for speech, as noted above. In Paul's day, speech was of utmost importance.

Political leaders, as well as those who claimed to teach religious and philosophical truths, were expected to speak eloquently and persuasively. Rhetoric, the study of how to argue persuasively in a given situation, was a main component of Greco-Roman education. Though it was primarily concerned with techniques for researching, constructing, and ultimately delivering a winning speech, its aims and conventions also affected how people wrote. Given this overlap between speech and letter and the fact that Paul designed his letters to be read aloud (Phlm 2; 1 Thess 5:27), it is reasonable to expect that Paul employed contemporary techniques of argumentation to make as persuasive a case as possible for his own points.

Speeches, or arguments, were classified according to three types, each ordered to a distinct purpose and appropriate to a different setting. The forensic or judicial speech, proper to the courtroom, was used to defend or accuse someone in view of a past action. The deliberative speech, for use in the assembly, sought to persuade or dissuade about future courses of action. Finally, epideictic speech, appropriate for a variety of public occasions, employed praise or blame to affirm important values and reinforce the audience's current adherence to them. Speeches normally began with an introduction and concluded with a recapitulation of key points. In between, other standardized components were incorporated depending on the type of argument. However, every argument had two indispensable parts: a statement of the thesis/point to be proved, followed by the proofs. Persuasion, regardless of the speech type, ultimately depended on three factors: the moral character of the speaker, or proof based on *ethos*; the ability to evoke the proper emotional response from the audience, or proof based on *pathos*; and finally logical arguments, or proof based on *logos*.

With regard to the Corinthian correspondence, the deliberative type of argument is dominant in 1 Corinthians, where Paul frequently attempts to persuade or dissuade the community about possible courses of action in view of what is advantageous to the community (e.g., 1 Cor 7; 8–10; 12–14). At certain points, he also introduces forensic and epideictic rhetoric as the situation demands (e.g., 1 Cor 5; 9; 13).

In 2 Corinthians we come across a changed situation. A wedge has been driven between Paul and the community by outsiders. Speaking in his own defense, Paul employs forensic rhetoric at 2 Corinthians 1:1–7:6 and again at 2 Corinthians 10–13. In 2 Corinthians 8–9, Paul deliberates with the community, urging it to go forward with a planned collection that will benefit both the impoverished community at Jerusalem and the Corinthians themselves, who will be distinguished for their generosity.

Throughout these two letters Paul's appeals to his own character and to the emotions of the community are deftly interwoven with logical arguments, evidencing both Paul's rhetorical sophistication and his intention to persuade rather than simply impose his will. Recognition of the rhetorical nature of 1 and 2 Corinthians contributes to a more informed and profitable reading of these letters, which are composed of discreet argumentative units where Paul is engaged in persuasion.

The First Letter to the Corinthians

Maria A. Pascuzzi

INTRODUCTION

The occasion and structure of I Corinthians

Sometime after Paul had left Corinth and was settled into his ministry at Ephesus, oral and written reports about a number of developments in the community at Corinth reached him. Through "Chloe's people," that is, members of her household, Paul was orally apprised of rivalries within the community (1 Cor 1:11). He says that he had also heard about a case of sexual immorality (1 Cor 5:2) and divisions at the Eucharist (1 Cor 11:18). Chloe's people or others could have been the source of this information. Other information, whose source is unspecified, concerning lawsuits (6:1-11), fornication (6:12-20), inappropriate attire at the liturgy (11:2-16), and disagreement over the resurrection (1 Cor 15) may have also been referred to Paul orally.

Paul's second source of information was a letter written by the Corinthians asking his advice on various issues (1 Cor 7:1). Their questions related to matters ranging from sex within marriage, which, apparently, some wanted to renounce (1 Cor 7:2-6), to the advisability of marriage (7:7-40), to whether one could eat food offered to idols (1 Cor 8), to the use of spiritual gifts (1 Cor 12–14). This letter was brought to Paul by community delegates, presumably the persons Paul mentions at 1 Corinthians 16:17. In addition to Chloe's people, this delegation may also have supplied some of the oral information. As a response to the information that had reached him, Paul composed 1 Corinthians.

To explain the ideological basis that influenced the thought and motivated the behavior reflected in 1 Corinthians, some scholars have hypothesized that some group (e.g., Gnostics or Judaizers) or person (e.g., Apollos) from outside the community introduced ideas at variance with what Paul had preached. Others explain the problems as deriving from "overrealized eschatology," that is, the Corinthians misinterpreted Paul's message, incorrectly assuming that they were already fully transformed and free of all moral constraints. Another explanation holds that the Corinthians understood Paul, lived according to what he had preached, but that Paul, for political reasons, changed his mind about things and now saw their behavior as a problem.

Each theory has been subjected to scrutiny and found to be inadequate. What seems apparent from 1 Corinthians is that here we encounter real flesh-and-blood people working out the implications of their new faith. In light of more recent investigations into the social and cultural ethos of the Corinthians, it is possible to understand the Corinthian situation as testimony to the difficulties that accompanied the planting of the Christian gospel in a pagan environment such as Corinth, where environmental influences were still strong. The difficulties Paul addresses in this letter are not between the community and himself, but rather within this nascent community struggling with its own identity, ethos, and behavior.

In 1 Corinthians, Paul deals with a larger number of disparate issues than in any other of his letters. The variety of issues, along with what scholars perceived as multiple literary and logical incongruities (e.g., contradictory responses on idol meat at chs. 8 and 10), led to speculation that 1 Corinthians was a compilation of letters. This hypothesis has proved to be unwarranted, especially in view of more recent insights about how Paul unfolds his arguments. Most scholars now affirm the literary unity of first Corinthians.

Nonetheless, it is still not easy to fathom the letter's logic as Paul shifts from topic to topic. A variety of ways of understanding the letter's structural organization have been proposed. Many understand 1 Corinthians to consist of an introduction (1:1-9) and conclusion (16:1-21) enclosing the body of the letter, which is envisioned according to a two-part structure: responses to matters referred orally to Paul (1:10–6:20), followed by responses to the Corinthians' letter (7:1–15:58). The phrase "now in regard . . . " (e.g., 7:1, 25; 12:1) is usually taken to signal the beginning of Paul's response to a question or issue raised in the letter.

Currently, there is a growing tendency to understand the structure of 1 Corinthians along the lines of a deliberative speech. Paul's exhortation "that there be no divisions . . . that you be united in the same mind and in the same purpose" (1:10) is construed as his major thesis. The body of the letter consists of a series of rhetorical proofs or demonstrations in support of the thesis (1:11–15:58). The thesis plus demonstrations are encompassed by the exordium at 1:1-9 (the rhetorical equivalent of the literary introduction) and the recapitulation at 16:13-18 (the argument's conclusion).

Understood from the vantage point of rhetoric, 1 Corinthians is a sustained argument on the single theme of unity, cast in the form of a deliberative speech.

The two-part literary schema and the rhetorical schema are both useful for understanding the letter's structure, provided we recognize that neither accounts perfectly for its structure and we do not adhere too rigidly to either one. In the case of the two-part schema, an "oral matter" intrudes on the written responses at 11:18. Additionally, there is no indication that the discussion on hairstyles at 11:2-16 or on the resurrection at chapter 15 is actually a response to a written inquiry. In the case of the rhetorical schema, while chapters 1–4 clearly relate to the problem of factionalism and support Paul's call for unity, not every piece of advice or resolution of a problem found throughout 1 Corinthians 5–16 is constructed in view of resolving the problem of factionalism (e.g., ch. 7). In fact, in 1 Corinthians 5–16, Paul is not always deliberating (e.g., chs. 5, 9, and 13). Thus, rather than insisting on either structural schema, it may be more useful to focus on the discrete units or blocks of argumentation contained in 1 Corinthians. Careful examination of their content, as well as Paul's persuasive strategy, should allow us to apprehend Paul's major concerns in this letter.

A final point of consideration regarding the structure of 1 Corinthians concerns a compositional pattern Paul uses to arrange his thought, which is especially recurrent in this letter. The pattern is evidenced when Paul introduces a topic, (A), shifts to another topic, (B), then returns to his original topic, (A'); hence the designation ABA', or concentric pattern. 1 Corinthians 8–10 is a good example. Paul discusses idol meat in chapter 8, (A), shifts to discuss his apostolic rights in chapter 9, (B), then returns to idol meat in chapter 10, (A'). As scholars now recognize, the B section, once perceived to rupture the flow of Paul's thought, actually reinforces the point being made in the adjacent A and A' sections. The B section is an example of the rhetorical technique "digression," an insertion into an argument to amplify or support the main point. This way of unfolding an argument clearly contrasts with a linear arrangement of ideas to which modern readers are accustomed. However, it accorded with the accustomed literary and rhetorical methods of Paul's day. Once we understand Paul's method of unfolding an argument, both its coherence and its point become more readily apparent.

Paul's theological perspective in I Corinthians

Paul's responses to the Corinthians were shaped by the dialogue between himself and them, but they were rooted in Jewish tradition, enriched by Paul's understanding of what God had done in Christ. Paul shared with other Jews an apocalyptic view centered on the hope that God would intervene to overthrow the evil order now reigning in the world, after which a new order under God's sovereignty would be ushered in. According to Paul, God had powerfully intervened as hoped, but in an unexpected and paradoxical way through the mystery of Christ crucified (1:18). Christians were therefore living at a crucial juncture point: the world in its present form was passing away (7:31; 10:11), the new order was beginning (2 Cor 5:17b). For Paul, this entire transition hinged on Christ's death and resurrection, the eschatological (end-time) salvation event through which humanity gained the renewed existence that Jewish tradition associated with the end-time. The inauguration of the end-time would be signaled by the outpouring of the Spirit (1:7; 2:12; 3:16). Coincident with this salvation event, God was now calling into Christ's fellowship the new, end-time community (1:9).

Since Paul believed that all this had been accomplished through Christ, to whom the Corinthian community owed its existence, he brings his christological insights to bear on his responses to this community. Their human wisdom is revalued in light of God's wisdom and power shown forth in Christ crucified (1:18). Their boasting is shown to have no foundation, since everything comes from God in Christ (3:21-23; 4:7). Through Christ's death they have been washed, redeemed, sanctified (1:30; 5:7; 6:11) and brought back for God (6:19-20; 7:23). They are now the "church of God" (1:2), "God's temple" (3:17).

As a result, how the Corinthians behave can never be independent of God, under whose sovereignty they stand and by whose will they are called and empowered by the Spirit to live lives of holiness (1:2). In Christ, believers formed one body (12:12), a unity effected through baptism and manifested and reinforced by the Eucharist (10:16-17). Immorality that threatened the community's holiness had to be avoided (5:13; 6:18; 10:14). Likewise, unity-destroying distinctions and behavior, whether based on status (11:17-24), knowledge (ch. 8), or spiritual endowment (chs. 12 and 14), had to be abandoned. The well-being of the whole church would form the context for discernment and behavior (6:12b; 8:3; 10:24, 31-33; 14:12), motivated by love (ch. 13).

Paul stresses throughout 1 Corinthians that this eschatological existence is not yet complete (1:7-8). That would come in the future, when death would be conquered, physical bodies would be transformed into glorious resurrection bodies, and all things would be subjected to God through Christ (ch. 15). In the meantime, the Corinthians were to use the freedom wrought by Christ to preserve their holiness and unity, the twin hallmarks of God's

The First Letter to the Corinthians

eschatological community (see, e.g., Ezek 37:15-28). The extent to which Paul's commands and exhortations throughout 1 Corinthians are concerned with the true nature of the community underscores the centrality of ecclesiology in this letter. How should this community, poised between the event of Christ's death and resurrection and the promise of future glory, live in the present? Paul's concern in 1 Corinthians is to help the community with this perennially difficult question.

OUTLINE OF FIRST CORINTHIANS

1:1-9	**Introduction**
1:1-3	Greeting
1:4-9	Thanksgiving
1:10–4:21	**Argument for Unity in the Community**
1:10-17	Divisions in the community
1:18–2:5	The wisdom of the cross
2:6–3:4	The wisdom of the mature
3:5-23	The community and its leaders
4:1-21	Cross-wisdom: the ultimate critique
5:1–6:20	**Arguments Concerning Immorality within the Community and Relationships with Those Outside the Community**
5:1-13	Argument against sexual immorality
6:1-11	Argument against recourse to pagan courts
6:12-20	Argument against sexual immorality
7:1-40	**Concerning Marriage and Sexual Relations**
7:1-16	Advice to the married, unmarried, and widows
7:17-24	Advice on one's social status
7:25-40	Advice to virgins/engaged couples, married women, and widows
8:1–11:1	**Argument Concerning Food Offered to Idols**
8:1-13	Concern for others trumps knowledge as a criterion for action
9:1-27	Renunciation of rights: an illustration based on Paul's praxis
10:1-13	Complacency and God's wrath: an example based on Israel's past
10:14-22	Against communion with idols: judge for yourselves
10:23–11:1	Summary: seek the good of others

11:2–14:40 Arguments Concerning Aspects of Community Worship
11:2-16   Argument concerning hairstyles
11:17-34   Argument concerning division and abuses at the Lord's Supper
12:1–14:40 Argument concerning spiritual gifts

15:1-58   Argument for the Resurrection
15:1-11   The resurrection of Christ: rehearsing the facts
15:12-34   The reality of the resurrection of the dead
15:35-49   The resurrection body
15:50-58   The resurrection event

16:1-24   Conclusion
16:1-12   The collection, Paul's travel plans, Apollos
16:13-24   Concluding exhortations and greetings

COMMENTARY

INTRODUCTION

1 Corinthians 1:1-9

1:1-3 Greeting

The opening section of an ancient letter consisted of three parts: the name of the sender, the name of the recipients, and a greeting. Paul follows this convention, naming himself and Sosthenes as the letter's co-senders. Co-sender need not imply that Sosthenes was co-author of this letter. Throughout 1 Corinthians, the first person "I" dominates. This suggests that a single author, Paul, was responsible for the composition and content of the letter. Moreover, even when the plural is used, what is usually intended is the whole community of Christians, for example, "are we provoking the Lord?" (10:22).

Paul adds a description of himself that is brief but dense with insight into his self-understanding. He is first of all an "apostle," a term that is both a title and a description of a function. It derives from the Greek verb *apostellō*, which means "to send." Used in conjunction with the phrase "of Jesus Christ," here the term "apostle" denotes Paul's function as one sent out on behalf of, or as an envoy of, Jesus Christ. Paul does not appropriate this function for himself; rather, it is enjoined on him as one "called" to be Christ's envoy "by the will of God" (see further Gal 1:15). By underscoring the divine initiative, Paul reminds the Corinthians that he is an authorized

1 Corinthians 1

envoy of Christ, in whose name and by whose authority he worked among them and now writes to them. Stated from the perspective of rhetoric, Paul has established his *ethos* here. This will serve as an important argument throughout the letter.

Unless the Sosthenes mentioned in 1:1 is the same Sosthenes named in the Acts of the Apostles, we have no information concerning his identity. In Acts 18:17, Sosthenes, a synagogue official at Corinth, is mentioned in the context of Paul's arraignment before Gallio, the proconsul. After Gallio had refused to hear the case against Paul brought by the Jews and had ejected them from the tribunal (Acts 18:15-16), the Jews seized Sosthenes and beat him. Whether Sosthenes was beaten because he was sympathetic to Paul is not known. Nor is it ever recounted in Acts or elsewhere that this particular Sosthenes converted to Christianity. Thus there are no compelling reasons to identify the Sosthenes of Acts 18:17 with the person mentioned at 1:1 who is also called by this commonly used name. The most we can deduce from 1:1 is that this Sosthenes was in Ephesus with Paul. Given the fact that Paul adds no other information about him, either here or in the rest of 1 Corinthians, it is also reasonable to deduce that the Corinthian community was familiar with this Sosthenes, called "our brother," a term used for fellow believers and co-workers.

Paul identifies the recipients of this letter as the "church of God that is in Corinth" (1:2). The term *ekklēsia*, which can be translated "church," "assembly," or "congregation," was used in secular Greek to refer to a political assembly. Paul distinguishes his addressees as the *ekklēsia* "of God," which exists not by self-determination or in view of common political concerns, but because God has called it into being.

This theological qualification of the community is augmented by three others. First, the community is sanctified, that is, made holy or set apart for God in Christ Jesus, through whom they have received this new identity. Second, they are called to be holy. This is not a mere rephrasing of the previous qualification; rather, it defines how the community must live in view of the fact that it has been sanctified. Finally, the community at Corinth does not exist independently but is part of a universal fellowship of believers who call upon the name of the Lord and are subject to his authority. These theological, christological, and ecclesiological qualifications ascribed to the community at the outset of the letter influence all that follows.

Paul concludes this opening section with his characteristic grace and peace greeting. Rather than the usual Greek *chair* ("to rejoice"), Paul substitutes *charis* ("grace") and adds the Jewish greeting *shalom* ("peace"). *Charis* expresses Paul's understanding of how God acts toward humanity, in infinite generosity. *Shalom* expresses the result of God's generous activity, humanity's entire well-being that comes from God through Christ.

1:4-9 Thanksgiving

Paul's thanksgiving section adheres to the ancient letter form in which some type of thanksgiving followed the opening formula. Paul's thanks are directed to God, the source and bestower of the grace the Corinthians have received. This grace has taken the form of enrichment in every spiritual gift, especially in "discourse" (speech) and "knowledge." Paul, who is himself spiritually enriched (14:18), is genuinely grateful to God that the Corinthians enjoy such blessing. Indeed, these gifts confirm Paul's testimony to Christ and verify that the gospel has taken root among the Corinthians (1:6). Yet Paul knows that the full outworking of God's purposes lies beyond the present and the Corinthians' current state of spiritual endowment. The Corinthians must still await the final revelation of Jesus Christ and continually rely on the work of Christ to keep them irreproachable until that day of judgment (1:7-8). Paul's thanksgiving ends on a note of confidence, because "God is faithful" and called the Corinthians into fellowship *(koinōnia)* with Jesus Christ.

Within this section Paul introduces some key theological points that anticipate issues to be addressed in this letter. His thanksgiving to God for the bestowal of grace contrasts with the Corinthians' boastful attitude, for which Paul will repeatedly chide the community, reminding them that everything they have is a gift from God through Christ (4:7). The very gifts for which Paul expresses thanks will unfortunately turn out to be a source of division in the community. Paul will have to address this and remind the Corinthians that every gift comes from the same Spirit (12:4), is set at the service of the same Lord (12:5), and is ordered to the welfare of the whole body of believers (12:12-26).

Likewise, the eschatological perspective that circumscribes the thanksgiving will be brought forward in Paul's attempts to redress the problems that derive from the Corinthians' over satisfaction with their current spiritual status. Paul will repeatedly remind the community that the future eschatological event impinges on how they live and behave in the present (4:5; 6:13-14; 7:29-35). Finally, of overriding importance in the rest of 1 Corinthians is the fact that the Corinthians are divinely created in fellowship with Christ. This fellowship with, or participation in, the life of the risen Jesus is the basis for their hope of future glory (15:20). However, participation also enjoins upon each believer the ongoing task of realizing this fellowship. In some way or another, the reality of this fellowship will pervade Paul's responses throughout the letter.

1 Corinthians 1

ARGUMENT FOR UNITY IN THE COMMUNITY
1 Corinthians 1:10–4:21

This first major section of the letter body forms a coherent unit revolving around Paul's call for unity in the face of reported divisions within the community. Apparently, multiple factors are behind the divisiveness: attachment to particular teachers, pursuit of wisdom apart from the wisdom of the crucified Christ that Paul has preached, and boasting in status. In his effort to move the Corinthians to restore unity, Paul will have to clear up two misconceptions—one relating to the nature of the gospel, the other to the role of ministers.

Divisions in the community (1:10-17)

1:10-17 Report of rivalries

Paul begins with an urgent plea in the name of the Lord Jesus, under whose authority the Corinthians stand, that they let go of their divisions and be united. "United" translates a Greek verb that literally means "restore." Thus Paul is not urging the Corinthians to do something new but to restore the unity of mind and purpose proper to those called into fellowship with Christ. The source of Paul's information about the community situation is disclosed immediately—"Chloe's people." These associates of Chloe were likely traveling on her behalf from Ephesus to Corinth, where they observed the situation.

Returning to Ephesus, they reported to Paul, informing him of rivalries stemming from allegiances to particular persons. Some were identifying themselves with Paul, others with Apollos, others with Cephas, and some even claimed allegiance to Christ alone. The phrases "I belong to Paul . . . Cephas," etc., have been taken as the slogans of actual parties at Corinth, and great effort has been exerted to reconstruct the particular ideological bias of each group. However, Paul's use of these phrases may simply be his way of putting into his own words his understanding or interpretation of the situation. In fact, Paul's use of the introductory words "I mean that . . ." (v. 12) just before the mention of the so-called parties seems to indicate that we are hearing Paul's rearticulation of the report about rivalries which he construes in relation to four figures.

Clearly there were divisions in the community that may have revolved around the favoring of some person over another (vv. 11-13), which may have been linked to who baptized whom (vv. 13-16). Additionally, Paul's contrast between the cross of Christ and the wisdom of human eloquence (v. 17) suggests that this, too, was at the root of the divisions. However, that the community was actually divided into four clearly delineated groups does not seem to have been the case. In fact, Paul never refers to them again in the letter. Paul's characterization of the situation in this way allows him to set the stage for his handling of the problem of disunity.

For Paul, it is simply inconceivable that Christians be divided at all, let alone on account of allegiance stemming from baptism, the sacrament that unites all believers to Christ and to one another. The series of rhetorical questions in 1:13 underscores the absurdity of partisanship. Christ is not divided, and neither can those baptized into Christ be divided! In an aside (vv. 14-16), Paul dissociates himself from baptism-based partisanship by disclaiming any extensive personal role in baptizing. This disclaimer introduces an opening for Paul to highlight what he is called and sent to do as an apostle: preach the gospel, and "not with the wisdom of human eloquence" (v. 17). With this negation, Paul rejects persuasive wisdom as antithetical to the wisdom of the cross that he preaches. This opposition seems to be at the root of divisions in the community that Paul deals with in the next step of his argument, where he will set out the essence of his gospel.

The wisdom of the cross (1:18–2:5)

In the foreground of this section of Paul's argument is the paradoxical message of the cross, God's wisdom and power (1:18-25). The Corinthians themselves are testimony to this message (1:26-31); its very essence accounts for Paul's preaching without persuasive words (2:1-5). Divisions, though not directly mentioned in this subsection, are in the background, since vain pursuit of human wisdom and boasting about those who make the best case for it are fundamental to the divisiveness.

1:18-25 The paradox of the cross

The gospel Paul preaches is Christ crucified, God's wisdom and power. God's cross-revealed wisdom defies human wisdom and divides humanity into two groups: the perishing, who reject this message as foolishness, and those being saved, for whom it is the power of God. The divine overthrow of human wisdom foretold by Isaiah (Isa 29:14) was taking place in the cross. Even the wise man, scholar, and philosopher, representatives of the sharpest thinkers of this age, are incapable of fathoming God's wisdom and power revealed in Christ crucified because theirs is human wisdom, originating in this age, which God has made foolish (1:21). According to human categories, crucifixion, epitomizing weakness and suffering, simply cannot cash out as any kind of wisdom or power, let alone divine wisdom and power!

Humankind's objections to this message are ethnically and historically particularized in the reactions of Jews and Greeks. Jews want signs. Accustomed to a God who had worked wonderfully and powerfully to deliver and save Israel in the past, Jews simply cannot see in a crucified Messiah the power and wisdom of God. For them, the cross is an affront, a stumbling block (see Rom 9:32-33; 11:11). Greeks, on the other hand, want wisdom, that is, the insights and strategies that lead to power, success, and honor. In Greco-Roman society in general, and in Corinth in particular, these were considered the manifestations of the truly wise person. For such as these, the cross signified everything that was counter to wisdom; cross-wisdom was an oxymoron, sheer foolishness. Despite the fact that Jews and Greeks differed with regard to how divine wisdom and power should be authenticated, they were in agreement that it would have to be authenticated by something other than the mind-boggling paradox of the cross.

Yet, it is precisely through what both reject that both Jews and Greeks are saved. Therefore, despite their expectations, Paul insists, "we" preach Christ crucified, a message that disregards humanly established ways of knowing God's power and wisdom, which are known in the cross or not at all. Humans must either give up their categories and accept the crucified Christ as the means of salvation or keep to their own standards, rejecting the message of the cross and perishing. In summarizing his reflections, Paul restates the paradox of the cross. Its very weakness is God's power, more powerful than human strength. Its very absurdity is God's wisdom, wiser than human wisdom. This is the gospel. It runs counter to the world's wisdom. It is fathomed by those willing to see differently and able to live in the tension of this paradox.

1:26-31 The experience of the Corinthians

This paradox is now considered in light of the Corinthians' own experience. Before their call, many were the world's nobodies. So little is there to recommend them that Paul can describe them only by what they were not: not wise, not powerful, not of noble birth. But now they, too, are signs of God's power, with Christ the crucified one as the source of their power. God did not choose them according to the standards of the world. God's wisdom does not correlate, nor has it ever correlated (see Deut 7:7), with the social hierarchy established by humans. It defies human categories, demolishes human standards, and inverts human hierarchies. Now the wise are shamed. The nobodies are chosen by God to undo the somebodies, to reduce to nothing the world's standards, which are incapable of comprehending God's wisdom.

In God's choice of the Corinthians, God reveals an authority to act in a way that is independent of the world and what it thinks or how it judges things ought to be. As a result, no human being has any grounds for boasting. Self-satisfaction and arrogance are eliminated, because everyone obtains grace and salvation in the exact same way. No one has an upper hand, a more superior way or insight into God's wisdom, a higher status meriting a more privileged place within God's plan of salvation. There is only one way to know God and God's salvation: the paradox of the cross, which is God's wisdom and power. Thus competition and boasting and the resultant divisions in the community are excluded.

Paul appropriates words from Jeremiah 9:23 to conclude this subsection. Within the context of this letter, these words constitute a radical challenge to the Corinthians to let go of their boasting in human words of wisdom and human categories and begin to live out their dependence on God's grace, the source of their salvation.

2:1-5 The preaching of Paul

Since the content of the gospel message is Jesus Christ and him crucified, when Paul came to Corinth he deliberately put aside grandiose speech and the use of powerful rhetorical strategies to persuade the Corinthians of this mystery. Considering that the idea of Christ crucified, source of salvation and the very revelation of God's wisdom and power, was (and still is!) such a hard sell, one would think that Paul would have pulled out all his rhetorical stops to convince the Corinthians of the truth of this message. Instead he comes in "weakness and fear and much trembling" (v. 3) and speaks his message and proclamation without persuasive words of wisdom. Paul's emphatic "my" message and "my" proclamation" (v. 4) is apparently intended to distinguish himself from skilled orators and their message.

Why Paul voluntarily puts himself at such apparent rhetorical disadvantage becomes clear in verses 4-5. True understanding of God's wisdom can never come through human wisdom, which it transcends, nor through mere human articulation, which it eludes. It comes only through the power of the Spirit. Ironically, despite his apparent rhetorical disadvantage, Paul is the most advantaged because his proclamation is powered by the Spirit (v. 4), who brings about faith that rests, appropriately, on God's power.

Paul's lack of rhetorical prowess, like the Corinthians' lack of social status, illustrates again the paradoxical nature of God's wisdom, which defies human reason and subverts human standards of judgment. As God's grace does not take account of social standing, neither does it rely on the persuasive ability of the messenger and words of human wisdom for its actualization in the life of the believer. The implications for the Corinthians are clear: attachment to rhetorically skilled ministers and captivation with their hollow human wisdom leads only to vain boasting and division.

The wisdom of the mature (2:6–3:4)

Paul clears up misconceptions about wisdom, its attainment, and what constitutes true spiritual maturity (2:6-16). Unfortunately, the Corinthians who have received the Spirit persist in their immaturity, running after wisdom that sounds reasonable and is persuasively presented. As long as they persist on this course, they cannot benefit from the spiritual instruction and true wisdom that Paul is capable of imparting (3:1-4).

2:6-16 True wisdom

In an apparent reversal of what he has just stated, Paul announces that he actually does speak a wisdom to the mature. Paul's about-face has so baffled interpreters that some regarded this subunit as originally not part of the letter. Others read it as an indication of Paul's inconsistency and insincerity. Many now read Paul's about-face as intentional irony, to wit: You want wisdom! I have wisdom for the mature. Then, having set up the spiritual snobs in the community for his esoteric message, Paul dismisses them as total infants, too stupid and immature to attain to such wisdom! Whether Paul's intention was to humiliate, as suggested by this view, is not altogether certain.

What we learn from the text is that here Paul deals with wisdom and spiritual maturity. These were of great importance not only to this community but also to Paul. However, Paul meant something radically different by these terms. Here he reconsiders both terms in light of the gospel in order to instruct the community concerning true wisdom and how it is attained, to deal with divisions caused by the spiritually enlightened, and ultimately to advance his argument for unity.

Paul begins by affirming that he does preach a wisdom, something that he has overtly claimed from the outset of this letter (1:17-18). However, this wisdom differs from that to which the Corinthians aspire. A variety of religious and philosophical currents had made their way to Corinth, but Paul does not specify the type or content of the wisdom being pursued by some in the community. He simply associates it with the "wisdom of this age" (2:6), which is opposed to God's secret and hidden wisdom. The rulers of this age, operating with its wisdom, are incapable of penetrating God's wisdom; otherwise they could never have crucified the Lord of glory. The fact that they did simply illustrates that the pursuit of human wisdom leads to utter ignorance, not spiritual insight. Corinthian Christians who pursue the wisdom of this age through human reason are likewise incapable of penetrating God's wisdom, remain unenlightened, and are spiritually immature, despite their claims to the contrary.

The true wisdom to be pursued, which brings knowledge and enlightenment, is beyond what the human mind and heart can conceive and hence unattainable through human reason. It is knowable, as Paul already stated at 2:4, only through the agency of the Spirit. Paul supports his point by a commonsense argument based on human experience. The Corinthians would no doubt agree with him that one's inner workings are really scrutinized and known only by one's self. Arguing by analogy, Paul says, so it is with God. God's own Spirit scrutinizes the depths of God. Whoever would apprehend God's wisdom must be in touch with the Spirit of God and equipped with the categories and language of spiritual realities, because this is what the Spirit reveals. Paul and the Corinthians have received the Spirit of God. They are spiritual and equipped to speak of and understand God's wisdom in Spirit-taught language. Once this wisdom, summed up in the message of the cross, is understood, the criteria by which humans judge are radically changed.

3:1-4 Continued Corinthian immaturity

Paul now explains that he could not impart to the Corinthians the spiritual knowledge and insight they so desired. This was not due to any inability on his part or to any innate lack on the Corinthians' part. They had received the Spirit. They should have been able to handle Spirit-taught words, understand spiritual realities, and live as mature persons, that is, spiritual persons. But they were acting in a "fleshly" way, that is, contrary to the Spirit who unifies, still judging according to human criteria, as demonstrated by their unity-destroying behavior. While they persisted in jealousy and rivalries, they were showing themselves to be all too human. Viewed from a spiritual angle, they were still spiritual infants, unable to absorb the mysterious wisdom of the cross, the solid food reserved for spiritual adults. They had not been ready for solid food in the past, and their current wrangling over wisdom and wisdom teachers and superior status proves that they are still not ready!

The community and its leaders (3:5-23)

Paul's next step in his argument for unity deals with misunderstandings revolving around the role of community leaders. Their distinctive tasks are complementary (3:5-9); indeed, every member of the community whose foundation is Christ must contribute to its unity and holiness, in view of

1 Corinthians 3

which one will be judged (3:10-17). Since all belongs to God in Christ, only God's wisdom revealed in Christ counts (3:18-23).

3:5-9 Paul and Apollos: co-workers in God's field

The opening rhetorical question underscores the absurdity of the partisanship that has grown up around certain ministers. Paul and Apollos are mere farm hands, working at different but equal tasks in God's field, the community, whose growth depends on God alone. The insignificance of ministers, implied in the rhetorical question, is reinforced through this metaphor and serves to warn the Corinthians against attaching too much importance to any one minister. Moreover, since, as the metaphor implies, ministers work for the same boss and undertake complementary tasks directed to the same goal, to oppose one minister to the other is to undermine God's own work.

3:10-17 Everyone's work will be fire-tested

At the end of 3:9, Paul changes metaphors, describing the community as God's building, and now advances his argument employing construction imagery (3:10-15). Paul, the wise master builder, laid the foundation for God's building, Jesus Christ. As a foundation determines the contours and shape of the concrete structure arising from it, so must the community of believers, whose oneness is underscored by the term "building," be determined by its foundation, Christ. Each member builds up from this one foundation and must take care that the contribution made is consistent with it and ordered to the building's unity. Paul directs this warning not to Apollos and himself but to the Corinthians. They can build on the foundation with precious stones, or with perishable materials such as wood or hay, by which Paul means the fleeting and fatuous stuff of human wisdom. The latter will not stand the fire test, that is, the day of judgment, when retribution or salvation will be awarded in light of one's work.

Indeed, if anyone destroys this building, now further qualified as God's temple (3:16-17), God will destroy that person. Paul uses the Greek term *naos*, translated "temple," which actually referred to a particular place within the temple—the inner sanctuary where God's holiness dwelt. Thus the Corinthian community, *corporately as a community*, indwelt by God's own Spirit, is now the living locus of God's holiness. As a result, each member's behavior must be oriented from and toward the community's holiness.

3:18-23 All belong to God in Christ

In concluding this subunit of argumentation, Paul once again takes up the themes of wisdom and folly and very bluntly addresses the Corinthians. The world's wisdom is mere craftiness, a human construct of hollow notions, two facts attested by the Scriptures Paul cites (Job 5:13 and Ps 94:11).

If you think yourself wise in view of that standard, your self-perception is actually self-deception! Give up that standard! Accept and submit to the inverted order that is paradoxically God's wisdom, epitomized in the cross, and then, though the world considers you a fool, paradoxically, you will be truly wise!

Within this paradoxical perspective, the futility of exalting any one minister over another and divisive boasting over human wisdom becomes apparent. Every minister plays an equal and complementary part in unfolding God's plan, and all ministers are at the service of the Corinthians, who together have "everything" (3:21). Here Paul cites a popular maxim of his day summarizing all the privileges believed to accrue to the ideal wise person, a completely self-sufficient person of superior status who was beyond the petty rules and regulations that applied to the less enlightened.

In contradistinction to this privilege and autonomy, Paul reminds the Corinthians that together, as a community, they are co-sharers and co-inheritors of all things in and with Christ. As such, no one can use his or her freedom and privilege for individual self-promotion and boasting, or toward whatever destroys the unity of the community in Christ through which these privileges exist. Moreover, the Corinthian community ultimately stands in and through Christ in direct and subordinate relationship *to God* (3:23). The Corinthians must ultimately live in faithful obedience to God and answer to God, not Paul or Apollos or Cephas, not even Christ, but God who holds all together and judges all according to the wisdom made manifest in the cross.

Cross-wisdom: the ultimate critique (4:1-21)

In this final step of his argument, Paul returns to the role of ministers and appropriates another set of metaphors that stress the subordinate role of ministers and the singular character upon which they are to be judged—trustworthiness (4:1-5). This is followed by a stinging critique of the Corinthian community in light of cross-wisdom. Judged by the criterion of the cross, their lives are shown to be a repudiation of God's counter-order wisdom (4:6-13). Paul's highlighting of their failure to live lives transformed by the gospel of the cross is intended to restore a sense of realism to the situation so that the Corinthians can go forward to restore the unity of the community.

4:1-5 Ministers are required to be trustworthy

Changing metaphors, Paul now describes ministers as "servants" and "stewards," persons who work under the authority of a master and are accountable to the master's standards. The singular requirement to which they are held is trustworthiness, that is, they must be faithful to the proclamation of Christ crucified, God's wisdom. In context, this statement should probably be understood as an implicit critique of the standard of judgment applied to ministers by the Corinthians. They were impressed by parcels of wisdom and grandiose speech, the wrong criteria applied by some Corinthians, who had wrongly arrogated to themselves the right to judge ministers. It was not that ministers were beyond judgment. But they were accountable to God, not the Corinthians.

Even the fact that Paul is the founding apostle of this community in no way invests the Corinthians with any particular right to judge him or any other minister of God. The right to judge and the criterion for judgment are God's alone. So much so is this the exclusive prerogative of God that Paul, who is spiritually mature, does not even bother to judge himself. (How much less should the spiritually immature judge others?) Besides, Paul knew that even were he to find himself beyond reproach by the light of his own conscience, it was not one's conscience but only God who is the ultimate arbiter of truth and under whose eschatological judgment everyone must pass. God's future judgment is the only thing that counts, and God's verdict depends not only on what one does in the present but also on one's hidden motivations!

4:6-13 Cross-wisdom: the ultimate critique

Paul now explains that he has discussed these things by way of reference to Apollos and himself in order to teach the Corinthians a beneficial lesson about how they are to act among themselves. Through the example of Apollos and himself, Paul was able to underscore the cooperative and complementary character of ministry. Neither he nor Apollos does anything that is self-serving; rather, both work toward the same common purpose. Neither is a Hellenistic wise man to be made a rallying point for partisan allegiance; rather, both are servants and stewards whose allegiance is directed to God.

The Corinthians are to learn from this "not to go beyond what is written" (4:6). The meaning of "what is written" is a matter of speculation. It could refer to the Scriptures in general, to the gospel of the cross, to all Paul has thus far written in this letter, or to the specific sections of Scripture he has so far cited. The whole phrase, "not to go beyond what is written," could also be Paul's adaptation of an adage connoting something like "stick to the guidelines."

Whatever the case, Paul's clear intention is stated in the rest of verse 6, namely, that they desist from the divisive behavior caused by their pitting one leader against another. This is accompanied by prideful boasting ("inflated with pride," literally being "puffed up"). As the image suggests, they are "puffed up" by empty wind, mere pretentiousness but no substance.

Paul's three questions in verse 7 serve as a reality check. There is nothing different or special about the Corinthians. Anything they have is a gift, made possible by the cross of Christ. Yet, rather than living an existence consonant with that reality, characterized by the paradoxical wisdom of the cross, the Corinthians live another triumphant existence guided and evaluated in view of other standards. They claim to have it all, to be rich in spiritual-intellectual assets, and to have been already empowered to reign. In philosophical circles, especially among the Stoics, to be rich and to reign were applied to intellectual-spiritual status and represented the prerogatives of the ideal wise person. Apparently, the Corinthians were still aspiring to the values of their world, mixing up the goals of gospel living with society's goals and using the standard of judgment applied by society to measure their own wisdom and spiritual maturity.

In his critique of the Corinthians, Paul transposes the whole problem to a theological key. In that key the problem is presented as rooted in a premature arrogating of the full privileges of end-time living and the status of the spiritually perfect by the community. Paul goes on to contrast the Corinthians' grandstanding with the lot of apostles with purposeful irony aimed at Corinthian pretentiousness. Apostles are weak and considered fools; their lives are characterized by hardship and deprivation. So low is their social status that Paul likens apostles to "the world's rubbish, the scum of all" (4:13)! All this is in contradistinction to the lot of the Corinthians, who, Paul mockingly observes, are wise, strong, and esteemed. Judged by the world's standards, apostles are nothing and the Corinthians are everything! But when each stands under the critique of the cross, all such judgments are reversed. By their vain boasting and glorying in their own achievements, the Corinthians repudiate God's wisdom and the suffering and crucified Christ in whom this wisdom was revealed. In the starkest possible terms, Paul makes it clear that true ministers, indeed every true follower of Christ, must be co-sharers not only in Christ's glory but in his sufferings and status as one rejected by the world.

4:14-21 Concluding admonition

Having just taken the Corinthians down a few pegs, Paul now explains that his harsh rhetoric was not intended to shame but to admonish and refocus the perspective of the Corinthians, whom he genuinely loves. Whereas in 3:1-5 Paul referred to his relationship with the community using the maternal imagery of nourishing, here he refers to himself metaphorically as their "father" (4:15), giving expression to the intimate relationship between himself and this community engendered through his preaching of the gospel. Paul's paternal intervention and call for the community to be imitators of him (4:16) could be read as the ultimate expression of patriarchal arrogance. However, read in context, Paul's call for imitation is contingent upon his own imitation of Christ and refers to the pattern of renunciation, suffering, and servant-model type of leadership that he undertakes for the sake of the gospel. Here Paul's own *ethos* becomes a powerful appeal to the Corinthians to transform their own lives. In Paul's absence, he sends Timothy as one who will model this life pattern ("my ways in Christ Jesus," 4:17) for the community. This manner of life is not a distinct imposition on the Corinthians, but the pattern of life required of all Christians everywhere. Here again Paul reminds the Corinthians that they are no maverick community of elite spiritualists, but part of a universal fellowship.

Despite the arguments that Paul has set out in this first major unit of the letter, he is concerned that some will persist in the behavior that has been a source of division in the community. He has already made it eminently clear that God's wisdom and power are not compatible with human words, no matter how elegant and persuasive the articulation. Here he contrasts empty words and true power again, and if need be, Paul will come and reveal the impotence of the empty talkers.

With this final warning, Paul concludes the first major argument of this letter. Throughout this argument for unity, he has applied the scandalous and paradoxical lens of the cross to the situation of this community. Through that lens, it becomes clear that the Corinthians are still dominated by the values and presuppositions of their culture. They are still searching for the human wisdom that will unlock the door to power and status, still judging people by the secular categories of prestige and success. They remain impressed by elegant words and controlled by the desire for enhanced status afforded by attachment to the best purveyor of human wisdom. The Corinthians' culturally conditioned living of the gospel had emptied the cross of Christ of its power and value and resulted in the problems that were threatening to destroy Christianity at Corinth. The restoration of the community's unity, as Paul has demonstrated, would require nothing less than the entire realigning of its values with God's countercultural cross-wisdom.

ARGUMENTS CONCERNING IMMORALITY WITHIN THE COMMUNITY AND RELATIONSHIPS WITH THOSE OUTSIDE THE COMMUNITY

1 Corinthians 5:1–6:20

Paul now takes up three ethical issues, beginning with a case of sexual immorality at 1 Corinthians 5. The logical disjuncture between the previous discussion in chapters 1–4 and its themes and this new one, focused on an individual case of sexual immorality, has contributed to the speculation that 1 Corinthians is not one unified literary composition. However, this is too radical an assessment since there are word links—for example, to boast, to judge—between 1 Corinthians 5 and the chapters that precede it. Nonetheless, it is clear that chapters 5–6 do form a distinct macro-unit, structured according to the ABA' pattern. Sexual immorality is introduced in 5:1-13 (A). Then Paul discusses Christian recourse to pagan courts in 6:1-11 (B), before again dealing with sexual immorality in 6:12-20 (A').

Why Paul introduces these three topics here can perhaps be best explained in view of their rhetorical-pedagogic function in the letter. As 1 Corinthians progresses, Paul takes up a variety of questions for which there are no black-and-white answers. Instead, the community has to consider not only the good but also the better courses of action that they as Christians must adopt in view of the well-being of the whole community. Multiple criteria have to be considered, and keen powers of discernment are needed to weigh the options.

A closer look at 1 Corinthians 5–6 reveals the community's incompetence to handle matters where clear-cut decisions are called for. In the face of this, here in chapters 5–6, Paul first reorders the Corinthians' focus within the fundamental boundaries of absolute good and evil as a prelude to assisting them with decisions on issues that admit of shades of gray. If the community cannot judge black-and-white cases of community-destroying behavior, how can Paul expect them to be able to discern what is best for the community?

Argument against sexual immorality (5:1-13)

In this subunit of argumentation, Paul deals with a blatant case of sexual immorality within the community. It was apparently tolerated rather than dealt with and stopped. Paul's unequivocal judgment is that the offender needs to be expelled from the community to protect its holiness. The decision to excommunicate, however, ultimately remains with the community. In this compact unit, Paul argues to persuade the Corinthians to take the prescribed action.

1 Corinthians 5

5:1-5 The community's failed judgment

Whatever the exact contents of the report Paul heard, he states the problem this way: "there is immorality *(porneia)* among you (plural)." This manner of articulating the problem indicates that Paul's overriding concern is with the community, which has allowed the situation to go unchecked. The Greek term *porneia* is a comprehensive term covering all forms of sexual immorality. By adding the phrase "a man living with his father's wife," Paul qualifies the immorality as incest. "Father's wife" was used to distinguish one's stepmother from one's biological mother (Lev 18:7-8).

What Paul says, literally, is that the man "is having" his stepmother, a verb normally used to indicate a sexual relationship, which, in view of the present tense, should be considered ongoing. Such a relationship, proscribed by both Jewish and Roman law, is simply wrong, even if the offender's father is dead. Thus there is no need to argue for the man's guilt. Yet, the community has failed to judge the situation for what it is—a case of rank evil in its midst—and has allowed the brother to carry on unimpugned. Not only that, they are inflated with pride either because of the relationship or perhaps despite it. Whatever the case, their haughty attitude is the real cause of Paul's consternation and the bigger issue circumscribing the problem addressed in this chapter.

Since the Corinthians have failed to judge correctly and do the obvious, Paul, who has judged correctly, outlines the action that ought to be taken. The exact punishment envisioned by him is unclear. He could be intending physical death, or physical punishment coupled with expulsion, or simply expulsion from the community. When all the data is assessed, it seems more likely that Paul intends the latter. Banished from the community, presumably the offender will come to his senses and repent. Whatever the punishment, one thing is clear: it is ultimately ordered to the benefit of the offender so that "his spirit may be saved on the day of the Lord" (v. 5). Here Paul is not deliberating with the community among possible courses of action. This is the only course possible, and it is imperative that the community carry it out.

Paul obviously realizes that commanding alone will not move the community to take action, and so he couches his call for expulsion in three distinct arguments. The first argument is introduced with his remark that such behavior is not found even among the pagans! This statement is no doubt an exaggeration. However, the exaggerated comparison between the pagans and the Corinthians functions as an appeal to their emotions (argument based on *pathos*). The community should be ashamed of itself for disregarding a common standard of decency that even pagans are capable of observing. Appeals to the emotions, especially shame, were considered among the most powerful arguments to induce a person or group to change judgments, if for no nobler reason than simply to avoid being disgraced. To the Corinthians, who lived in an honor/shame culture, saving face was of utmost importance.

5:6-8 "you are unleavened"

After dismissing the Corinthian boasting as not good, Paul proceeds to appeal to the Corinthians' reason. Using a commonsense maxim, he takes up the metaphoric language of dough and yeast and argues on analogy that the evil one's presence is corrupting and compromising the entire community's true character of sinlessness. Since the community is sinless, it cannot at the same time have sin in its midst. This incompatibility demands that the sinner be expelled, metaphorically expressed in the command to "clear out the old yeast" (v. 7). Paul explains why sinlessness is the character of Christian existence and necessitates this cleansing in one brief phrase: "for our paschal lamb, Christ, has been sacrificed." The mention of the paschal lamb and unleavened bread recalls the rites of the Jewish Passover, which Paul symbolically interprets and transposes to a moral key. Through Christ's blood, Christians are morally cleansed, constituted holy, a condition willed by God (see 1 Thess 4:2). This is the core of Paul's reasoning and the ultimate ground of the specific command to expel the sinner. Paul concludes this section by exhorting the community to live in a manner consistent with its own sinless/holy character.

5:9-13 The community's failed judgment

Paul returns to the community's failed judgment by referring to his previous letter to the Corinthians. They had missed Paul's point. He was not prohibiting social interaction with the immoral of the society at large but, as he now clarifies, with anyone calling himself a brother who perpetrated any of the vices Paul now lists in verse 11. The introduction of the list of vices allows Paul to class the offending brother with egregious sinners. By doing so, he again appeals to the community's emotions, to elicit a sense of abhorrence for and alienation from "such a person," which should move them to judge and expel him. The vice-list makes clear that there is no double-standard. A vice-doer who is a brother is not a brother but a sinner. Here Paul draws the line not between Christians and pagans but between Christians and pseudo-Christians. There can be no social contact with the latter!

In conclusion, Paul disclaims any obligation to judge those outside the community. As outsiders, they cannot corrupt the community's holiness.

But those within can, and so he reminds the community of its obligation to judge the sinners within the community and, as this case warrants, "purge the evil person from your midst" (v. 13). This paraphrase of a formula repeated in Deuteronomy (e.g., Deut 17:7; 19:19; 21:21; 22:21, 22, 24) echoes the punishment prescribed in the Torah for egregious sins and evokes Jewish abhorrence for sexual sin, especially incest, considered the characteristic practice of pagans (Lev 18:1-3).

Thus, by Jewish lights and by the standards of common decency of society at large, incest is intolerable. Christians cannot ignore these standards as a baseline for their own behavior. However, what ultimately must guide Christian behavior is the person of Christ and the event of his death, on account of which the community's corporate identity as sanctified is established. This ecclesial identity is linked to ethical behavior, which must be ordered to safeguarding the sanctified life of the community.

Since Paul does not discuss the reasons why the offending brother undertook this relationship or why the community tolerated his presence, speculation abounds concerning their motives. In view of the discussion in 1 Corinthians 1–4, where it appears that some had arrogated to themselves the status and prerogatives of the ideal wise person, perhaps their complacent disregard for this violation of the standards of common decency, or even boasting about it, was intended to demonstrate that they had arrived at a state of perfection that allowed them to transcend all the conventions to which the unenlightened were obligated. If so, then here again some community members confused the standard of human wisdom and the exercise of privileges reserved for the world's wise with the standards that must guide Christians and the privilege of sanctified life in Christ, which enjoins on each member the obligation to live as a sanctified member of a sanctified community.

Argument against recourse to pagan courts (6:1-11)

Having brought up the need for the community to exercise jurisdiction for internal matters, Paul leaves aside the issue of sexual immorality and excoriates the community for abdicating this responsibility and allowing the adjudication of internal community issues to take place before pagan courts. Paul does not say how he learned about this situation. However, he argues against such recourse on two grounds. First, Christians are competent to adjudicate their own disputes (6:1-6), and second, Christians ought not to have such disputes requiring litigation in the first place (6:7-8). In concluding, Paul reminds the community that certain forms of behavior are simply incompatible with its new corporate ecclesial identity (6:9-11).

1 Corinthians 6

6:1-6 Competence to judge

Paul first expresses his shock in a rhetorical question, one of the nine such questions that he will use in this subunit to bring his argument forward. Explicit in this first question is the community's failure to carry out its responsibility by going before the "unjust" (v. 1). Although the Roman court system was known for its corruption and favoring of the well-to-do in its exploitation of the poor, in context "unjust" is probably to be taken less as a moral evaluation and more as a term to distinguish those outside from those inside the communion of the holy ones.

In the next two rhetorical questions Paul reminds the community of its judicial prerogatives. The belief that the holy ones would judge the world was rooted in Jewish apocalyptic eschatology, which envisioned the role of judgment as one of the prerogatives of God's elect (Dan 7:21-22). Many later Jewish writings also anticipate the participation of the holy ones in the final judgment (e.g., Wis 3:7-8; Sir 4:11).

Paul goes further in his next question to suggest that they will even judge the angels (v. 3), presumably the fallen ones, who were expected to undergo judgment (2 Pet 2:4). By reminding them of their prerogatives as holy ones, Paul builds an argument from greater to lesser to point up both the absurdity and inappropriateness of recourse to pagan courts. If in their glorious eschatological future they will sit in judgment on the world (including, obviously, the ones to whom they now hand over their judgments) and even angels, how much more so should they be capable of handling minor and ordinary everyday cases in the present! Paul does not specify what type of cases, but his choice of words underscores their inconsequential nature.

Why, then, Paul continues, do you elevate to the role of judges "people of no standing in the church"? (v. 4). It would be bad enough had the community simply failed to perform its duty, but it has actually ceded its privilege to a secular system and its standards of judgment. This act of submission to that system indicates that the community is still tied to the social conventions of the world and has yet to redirect its total allegiance to the community of faith. Paul's explicit intent to shame the community should at least awaken their concern to save face, and indeed they have much to be ashamed about. The need to take inconsequential cases before unbelievers seems to point up the community's deficiency when it comes to judiciousness, despite all the claims to be truly wise!

6:7-8 Renouncing litigation

With two more questions Paul advances his argument in another direction. Community members should renounce their right to litigate to the

1 Corinthians 6

detriment of other community members and, instead, endure injustice and defrauding. This idea had great currency among philosophers who held that a truly wise person was above injury or insult. Seeking redress would simply negate this claim, and the wise one would show himself or herself to be no better than anyone else! Paul may be playing off Corinthian arrogance at this point.

Beyond that, it is important to recognize that what Paul says here is quite consistent with what he says elsewhere about how Christians must comport themselves (Rom 12:17) and, though unstated, is obviously rooted in the example of Christ, who endured injustice without seeking redress. But not only have the Corinthians paraded their problems before the unjust, but in the very act of doing this they have become perpetrators of injustice and cheating against their own family. The distinction between the world and the family of faith has been blurred.

6:9-11 Final warning

Paul's final rhetorical question insinuates that the glorious eschatological destiny that awaits the Corinthians will not be had simply by waiting. In fact, if they do wrong they risk sharing the lot of those who will not inherit the kingdom. Paul again cautions them against self-deception (v. 9; cf. 3:18) and lists the vices that characterized some of their former lives as pagans. They have to continuously renounce all such behavior and live as those who are washed, sanctified, and justified. Together these three terms express the fullness of the transformation that has taken place in the lives of believers, who are now in Christ and made one and holy by the indwelling of the Spirit of God. In this one family of believers, brothers cannot go against brothers, nor can the holy ones mix with the unjust.

Argument against sexual immorality (6:12-20)

Paul now returns to the topic of sexual immorality. However, here there is no indication that the type of *porneia* under discussion, that is, extramarital sexual unions, perhaps with prostitutes, represents the actual behavior of some community members or simply behavior that could hypothetically result from the exercise of freedom understood apart from a theological context. In the form of a dialogue between himself and an imaginary dialogue partner, Paul engages and corrects the Corinthians' errant thinking and then, through a series of rhetorical questions, moves his argument against fornication forward. He frames this entire discussion within two important parameters: Christians are free (6:12), but they belong to God (6:19).

6:12-14 Everything is lawful for me

The phrase "Everything is lawful for me," marked off in the biblical text with quotation marks, is a Corinthian principle or slogan cited by Paul. Paul had indeed preached freedom from sin as one of the hallmarks of new Christian existence (1 Cor 6:11; Gal 5:1). However, once again it appears that the Corinthians had interpreted Paul's freedom teaching apart from its theological and ethical significance and in accord with societal ideas and categories. According to the philosophers, freedom was the authority to act on one's own, the quintessential right and privilege of the ideal wise person. Especially among the Stoics, it was believed that this freedom was manifested in one's acting according to nature.

After qualifying the use of freedom in view of what is beneficial, presumably for the whole community, and the need for self-control, Paul moves closer to the heart of the matter in verse 13, where he quotes another Corinthian slogan: "Food for the stomach and the stomach for food." In other words, as the Corinthians saw it, the sating of the stomach was considered a natural biological necessity. Moreover, they obviously held that no moral value could be attached to acts of natural biological necessity, because the body was meant ultimately for destruction, which proved its moral insignificance.

The Corinthians presumably transferred this way of thinking to sex to argue that it was merely another natural biological necessity, no more than the functioning of morally insignificant parts of a morally insignificant body. The blatant disregard for the body manifested in such thinking accorded very well with the view of the body expressed by the philosophers, especially the Stoics, who looked forward to death as the release of the soul from one's paltry body.

Here Paul's concern is that the inferior status accorded to the body could lead to fornication, and so he insists that the body is not meant for immorality but for the Lord! Moreover, against nature which destroys, Paul establishes the power and purpose of God, who raised Jesus and who will raise us. That future glorious eschatological destiny imbues the body with moral value and impinges on what one does in the body in the present. The reality of the resurrection, which grounds Paul's argument here, anticipates his fuller argument for the resurrection in chapter 15.

6:15-20 You are not your own

Through a series of rhetorical questions, Paul now adds to this argument, rooted in the resurrection destiny of the body, an argument rooted in the believers' union with Christ and another rooted in a consideration of the body as the temple of the holy Spirit. Picking up on his statement that the body is for the Lord, Paul now reminds the Corinthians of their union with

Christ, a union so intimate that Paul uses the imagery of sexual union to describe it. As unthinkable as it would be for a man or woman to take his or her body, which is one with his or her spouse, and unite it sexually to another, so also is it unthinkable for a Christian who is one with Christ ("one spirit with him," v. 17) to form another union. This union of believers with Christ in one holy body precludes immoral unions between a believer and a prostitute, which constitute a defilement of the whole Christian community. Thus Paul commands believers to flee immorality!

Before discussing the sanctifying role of the Spirit, Paul counters another Corinthian argument to the effect that the physical body has nothing to do with sin. This squares well with the Corinthian argument that bodily actions were deemed to have no moral significance, which Paul has already countered. It may also underscore how much the Corinthians' thinking was influenced by the philosophers of the day, since the argument that the body has nothing to do with sin fits very well with the Stoic idea that sin is not in the performance of any particular external act but is a matter of interior intention. Paul does not recognize this dichotomy between act and intention. His reaction is clear: a fornicator defiles not only the community but himself or herself, who is indwelt by the Spirit.

Here Paul returns to the image of the temple of God. At 3:16-17 Paul spoke of the Spirit who indwells the community as a whole, and now he applies this metaphor to every member individually. As the entire community must safeguard its holiness, so must each individual believer, whose body is no longer his or her own to use at will but is the sacred place of God's dwelling. Thus the Corinthians, corporately and individually, are free, but they are not totally autonomous. God has a claim on them. They have been bought at the price of Christ's death.

For Corinthians, exposed to the buying and selling of slaves in the marketplace, the implications of this metaphoric language would have been clear. They now belong to God and stand under God's authority and will. To accept the offer of freedom that comes through Christ is to stand in a new relationship, to accept a new bondage with ethical implications. Therefore the freedom exercised by those in Christ is never absolute freedom but freedom exercised within the parameters of belonging to God in Christ and ordered to God's glory. It was this relationally circumscribed and theologically inflected understanding of freedom that the wise ones at Corinth apparently failed to perceive.

In both 1 Corinthians 5 and here in 6:12-20, Paul does not treat sexual morality as a purely individual matter of choice, with only individual consequences. Since the community forms one sanctified whole, the immorality of one member can damage the sanctified life of the whole body. The community as a whole must be vigilant about this holiness and take responsibility to cleanse itself from whatever mars that holiness (5:1-13). The individual, too, must be vigilant for the life of the whole and avoid through his or her own exercise of freedom any defilement of the community's sanctified life (6:12-20). By the holiness of its life, manifested at the level of moral existence, the community of believers must glorify God and distinguish itself from the world. To bring community issues before outsiders blurs the distinction between this holy community and the world, dishonors God, and shows the community to be incapable of the reconciling love demanded by the cross-wisdom that must guide this community (6:1-11).

CONCERNING MARRIAGE AND SEXUAL RELATIONS
I Corinthians 7:1-40

Having just discussed immoral sexual relations outside marriage, Paul now turns to discuss the question of sexual relations within marriage, offering advice to the married as well as to the unmarried and widows (7:1-16). This is followed by an apparent digression relating to social status (7:17-24). Then Paul redirects himself to virgins, widows, and married women.

It is important to remember when reading 1 Corinthians 7 that Paul is not writing a systematic treatise on marriage but is responding to questions posed by the community (see 7:1). His answers are conditioned by his belief that the community is living in the last days of the end-time and that the Lord's second coming is quickly approaching. Unfortunately, Paul's advice here has been mistakenly read as a devaluation of marriage and human sexuality and expressive of an overall contempt of women. Once one recognizes the occasional nature of Paul's responses and the eschatological urgency that conditioned them, it is quite clear that this presentation of Paul and his teaching is a distortion in service of a negative agenda about marriage, sexuality, and women that was not Paul's.

To appreciate Paul's discussion, some information about currents of discussion in Paul's day will be helpful. Among the philosophers, the relative merits of marriage were a regular topic of discussion, and written record reveals their ambivalence about it. While it was conceded that marriage was good for the ordinary citizen and promoted the well-being of society, some argued that marriage, with all its obligations and strains, was ill-suited to the ideal wise one and hindered the pursuit of wisdom. For such a one, it was argued, to remain unmarried, which did not imply sexually chaste, was a better option.

1 Corinthians 7

Some of the Corinthians who fancied themselves as spiritually enlightened seem to have taken up the lines of this debate with regard to their own situation. Some may have thought that sexual asceticism would further their pursuit of wisdom and establish their superior status as those dedicated to spiritual matters rather than the mundane preoccupations of the less enlightened. In any event, the community directs the matter to Paul, who does not have black-and-white answers to these issues. Rather, he considers with the community what is preferable, balancing his answers between what is practically doable in the particular situation in which members find themselves and the urgency of the present eschatological situation.

7:1-16 Advice to the married, unmarried, and widows

Paul begins by citing another Corinthian slogan. This one is concerned with "touch[ing] a woman," a euphemism for sexual intercourse. Apparently some proposed the renunciation of sexual relations within marriage in view of their new spiritual status or even the renunciation of marriage and sex altogether in preference for celibacy. While Paul clearly prefers the latter, he clarifies that within the married state, one cannot renounce sexual activity in order to be more spiritual, because this misplaced asceticism could wind up leading to immorality! Far from denouncing erotic pleasure within marriage, Paul urges married people to do what is proper to married people. Marriage enjoins on both man and woman equal obligation and equal rights over their sexual relationship. Neither can unilaterally withdraw from these obligations except for prayer, an option afforded by Jewish law, which Paul seems to have in mind here. But even this must be by mutual agreement. It is possible that some at Corinth were appealing to Paul's own celibacy to justify sexual asceticism. However, he makes it clear that celibacy is a gift from God. Since celibacy cannot be self-imposed or externally imposed, for Paul it follows that not marrying is possible and preferable only if one is gifted with celibacy by God.

To the unmarried and widows, Paul does cite his own celibacy as a model to be followed, although he is well aware that the sexual drive may prove to be too much for some, in which case he counsels marriage. To the married, Paul specifies that he repeats the Lord's own instruction, that is, the prohibition of divorce. Though Paul cautions both men and women against divorce, his remark, addressed specifically to women (v. 11), seems to take for granted that some women are divorcing or are intending to do so. Whether women are contemplating divorce as a way to free themselves for spiritual pursuits or to free themselves from husbands whose spiritual pursuits preclude sexual relations is not certain. Paul's reminder to women that they should not attempt to remarry (to avoid adultery) seems to support the latter scenario.

Paul's next set of counsels concerns believers who are married to unbelievers. There is no reason for one who has become a believer to divorce an unbelieving spouse unless the unbeliever finds the believing partner's faith to be a problem and chooses to initiate the divorce. Then the believer is not bound. Otherwise, such marriages can be occasions of grace and holiness even for the non-believer and the couple's children.

7:17-24 Advice on one's social status

Although Paul may appear to digress in this subsection with the introduction of contrasting religious/ethnic statuses (circumcised-uncircumcised/Jew-Gentile) and social statuses (slave-free), this shift in focus allows Paul to continue to address the Corinthian situation from another angle. Apparently, some at Corinth are operating with the conviction that to really pursue the spiritual concerns proper to one's new Christian identity, one needs to change one's life circumstances or status, as if there were only one right or true life context or status appropriate to an authentic Christian life. By underscoring the insignificance of ritual identity markers/ethnicity and social status as a gauge for one's faithful obedience to God, Paul is able to illustrate the general principle he announces both at the beginning and the end of this subsection. This principle challenges the Corinthian assumption by establishing the fact that one's particular life context or social status in no way jeopardizes one's Christian freedom or ability to lead an authentic Christian existence. Thus there is no need for married people or any others to divest themselves of their particular set of circumstances.

7:25-40 Advice to virgins/engaged couples, married women, and widows

In the remaining verses, Paul's advice is directed alternately to virgins/engaged couples (7:25-28 and 36-38), married women and widows (7:39-40), with a brief interlude (7:29-35) in which he offers an explanation for his consistent counsel to celibacy.

The question concerning virgins probably relates to whether an engaged but not yet married girl should proceed with marriage or remain unmarried. Paul advises celibacy but in the end leaves the decision up to the engaged couple, who do well whether they marry or not. Paul's insertion of the remark that the choice to marry is not a sin may have been necessitated by a contrary claim that marriage was sinful, an idea not unknown among early Christians (see 1 Tim 4:1-5). Paul's second reminder against divorce, now exclusively addressed to married women, may underscore the reality of wife-initiated divorce within the community. It is Paul's opinion that it is better for widowed women to remain unmarried.

Paul explains his preference for celibacy in view of the unfolding eschatological plan, an event of cosmic proportion. The world in its present form is passing away; human existence, with its characteristic forms, institutions, and priorities, is now relativized. Time is growing short, and the pressures will be intense in this brief interval before the unfolding begins. It is in light of this exigent situation that Paul counsels those who are unmarried to remain as they are, contrasting what he envisions as their total devotion to the Lord with the divided attention that characterizes the married. Indeed, Paul prefers that all persons be free from the legitimate distractions of daily life in anticipation of the imminent coming of the Lord. Since Paul was not gifted with the charism of marriage, it is important to keep in mind that he speaks from the biased vantage point of a celibate. Clearly, stress, strain, and distraction are not the exclusive domain of the married. Thus we have to keep in mind that by Paul's best lights and in view of the eschatological exigency, he counsels celibacy as the better choice.

ARGUMENT CONCERNING FOOD OFFERED TO IDOLS

1 Corinthians 8:1–11:1

In pagan cities such as Corinth, a good part of social life involved participation in cultic banquets at the temple, where meat sacrificed to idols was consumed, or at private dinner parties, where hosts served their guests sacrificed meat that went from the temple to local butcher shops, where it was purchased for consumption in private settings. Did the Corinthians, now converted from their former pagan ways, need to refrain from eating this meat? The community was divided in its response to this question, with its complicated theological and social implications, and apparently referred the issue to Paul, who responds from the angle of Christian knowledge and the exercise of rights and responsibility. In terms of literary composition, this unit is arranged according to the A (ch. 8) B (ch. 9) A' (ch. 10) pattern. In terms of rhetoric, there are four movements plus a summary which need to be considered.

8:1-13 Concern for others trumps knowledge as a criterion for action

Paul begins by citing another Corinthian slogan but notes that knowledge is not an unqualified good. It can puff up with pride, whereas love builds up. Paul even registers doubt that the enlightened ones' knowledge is as complete as they claim. Apparently some Corinthians, presumably those whom Paul had already chastised for their arrogance, argued in view of their superior knowledge that there was no reason to forego eating meat sacrificed to idols. An idol had no existence; therefore, so-called idol meat was just meat.

Judging from Paul's remark at verse 10 about reclining at table in the temple, it appears that the enlightened were arguing in view of their knowledge that they could continue to participate in the cultic banquets at the temple. However, "the weak" (in context, the less intellectually sophisticated) understood such eating to be charged with religious significance. They were apparently shocked that others would continue this practice. Perhaps they were even shocked at the continued social intermingling with pagans that this practice would presumably entail.

In principle, Paul agrees with the intellectuals. They are operating with sound theological principles. Idols do not exist. There is only one God. Objectively speaking, Paul could even agree that a decision to continue eating idol meat followed logically from what they and he knew to be true. Thus Paul is not questioning the legitimacy of their right in regard to idol meat. However, he makes it clear that knowledge, even when rooted in sound theological principle, is not the exclusive criterion for determining praxis. Concern for other members of the community must take precedence over the exercise of a legitimate individual right.

Earlier Paul reminded the enlightened that their exercise of freedom was circumscribed by their belonging to God in Christ (6:19). Here he explicitly adds the other dimension that circumscribes the Christian exercise of freedom—the community. To scandalize any member of the community by the arrogant and complacent exercise of a right, which in the case of eating idol meat brings no benefit to anyone (v. 9) and scandal to some, simply because it can be justified in principle, amounts to a sin against the weaker brother, indeed against Christ. The phrase "against Christ" refers to the whole communion of believers, who together are later identified as the body of Christ (12:12). Thus Paul firmly warns against exercising rights, no matter how legitimate, to the detriment of one member, which is to say, to the detriment of all. He concludes this subunit of argumentation in the first person, injecting the course of action he would follow, which clearly depends on renouncing one's right out of love and concern for the entire community.

9:1-27 Renunciation of rights: an illustration based on Paul's praxis

Chapter 9 appears to be a departure from Paul's discussion of the right to eat idol meat. A closer look at this subunit reveals that it is an integral part of his argument. Here Paul problematizes his apostolic freedom in order to stress his renunciation of this freedom and thus provide a model of Christian praxis for the community. With regard to the right to eat idol meat, Paul has just argued that Christians must consider not only their freedom to exercise this right but also the possibility of freely renouncing that right when it negatively impacts others in the community. Indeed, this is what Paul said he would do (8:13).

Now, in chapter 9, Paul provides a model of renunciation in view of his own apostolic lifestyle and practice. He begins by building a strong case for his apostolic right to financial support. He is free. He is an apostle, and he has all the rights of every other apostle.

Paul first establishes these rights by reference to apostolic practice in verses 4-6, followed by simple examples based on the soldier, the vine planter, and the shepherd in verse 7. All these are supported by their trade. Paul supplements his argument by reference to a Mosaic law that prescribes recompense in the form of food even for oxen (vv. 8-9)! In verses 10-11, Paul further establishes his rights in view of the extent and the quality of his relationship with the Corinthians. Paul has shared spiritual blessing with them and is entitled to material recompense, even more so than other ministers.

After interjecting that he has renounced all these rights for the sake of the gospel (v. 12), Paul resumes the case for his own rights in view of a tradition associated with both Jewish and pagan practice, namely, the recompense of temple personnel who carried out the sacrifices at the altar. They were entitled to a portion of the sacrifice.

The final argument Paul calls upon to establish his right to support is the command of the Lord (see Luke 10:7) concerning recompense for the preachers of the gospel.

With his rights firmly established, Paul again affirms that he has freely given up the exercise of these rights (v. 15) and makes it clear that his purpose in writing about this is not to oblige the community to recompense him. He then proceeds in a roundabout way to explain his motives for setting aside his rights. In effect, he says that he did not undertake the work of preaching the gospel of his own volition; instead, it was an obligation imposed on him by God. Paul will do this, whether willingly or unwillingly, because he is compelled by God. Thus there is no cause for boasting in this. But he is quite proud of the fact that he has not taken advantage of the right to support that comes with this commission. On the contrary, he says that the only recompense he desires is no recompense at all! In offering the gospel free of charge, Paul renounces his right to support and presents himself as an exemplar of renunciation of rights.

Paul's argument becomes clearer in verses 19-23. In a series of rhetorical statements, he describes his missionary strategy of adaptability in order to accomplish his goal of winning as many as possible to the gospel. He presents himself as willingly living by the cultural, ethnic, and intellectual constraints of others in the service of the gospel; hence his reference to having become a "slave." To the intellectually sophisticated at Corinth, for whom freedom and the exercise of rights go hand in hand, the idea of renouncing one's rights can only appear to be weakness and foolishness. But Paul's slavish freedom is, paradoxically, true freedom manifested in the ability to adapt one's self to the needs of others. While the intellectuals at Corinth exercise their rights to the scandal and destruction of the weak, Paul's renunciation of rights, a true act of freedom, is ordered to the opposite end, namely, to save.

After using his own apostolic lifestyle as a model of freedom for the renunciation of rights, Paul now concludes this subunit of argumentation by exhorting the community to a life of discipline and self-control that supersedes the immediate concern of idol meat and its renunciation (vv. 24-27). The sports imagery employed by Paul makes perfect sense to anyone aware of the rigors of an athlete's life and would not be lost on the competitive Corinthians, whose city was home to the famous Isthmian games. Calling to mind the extent to which athletes train and discipline themselves in order to win a crown woven of perishable leaves, Paul exhorts the Corinthians to exercise and discipline themselves all the more, since they aspire to an imperishable crown. The Corinthians cannot be complacent as if they were running without a purpose or simply punching at air; rather, they must train and drive themselves to win this crown. In context, the self-discipline that Paul exhorts is aimed, above all, at the Corinthian intellectuals. Rather than complacently exercising their rights to the detriment of others, they need to practice restraint for the sake of the whole community.

10:1-13 Complacency and God's wrath: an example based on Israel's past

Paul's account of his own apostolic practice was intended as an exemplary lesson on the exercise of Christian freedom and served to develop and illustrate the point made in 8:13. Now Paul directs his attention to the complacent attitude of the Corinthian intellectuals, whose self-satisfaction with their own knowledge and exercise of rights is bringing them to flirt with idolatry. In addition to the problem of scandal, Paul is concerned that the Corinthian intellectuals are courting disaster by frequenting pagan temples, believing that they are beyond polytheistic superstitions and practices. Paul considers their actions a preamble to their own undoing. To

1 Corinthians 10

illustrate and warn against such an outcome, he cites the example of Israel, whose complacency incurred the wrath of God.

In 1 Corinthians 10:1-4, Paul showcases the spiritual endowments of Israel. These verses contain allusions to select episodes from Israel's exodus (see Exod 13–14) and wilderness experience (see Exod 16–17; Num 20–21). Paul retells the stories, stressing the fact that all the Israelites enjoyed God's deliverance and protection, and all were sustained on the wilderness journey by God's providence. In his retelling of these episodes, Paul uses language that is clearly anachronistic, referring to Israel's exodus as a "baptism," specifically a baptism into Moses (v. 2), and their nourishment as a type of unifying spiritual communion underscored by the repetition of "all" and "the same" (v. 3). Paul even metaphorically identifies Christ with the water-giving rock which, according to Jewish legend, followed Israel in the desert.

Paul's point here is not to suggest that the Israelites had Christian sacraments; rather, he is attempting to create an analogy between the experience of Israel and that of the Corinthians. Though seemingly complicated in its presentation, the point is simple. As one people, Israel experienced powerful spiritual signs of God's favor and all the spiritual nourishment necessary to sustain them. Yet, despite such spiritual endowments, they still incurred God's wrath and were destroyed (v. 5). Israel took God's gifts for granted as signs of immunity from God's wrath and continued in idolatrous and immoral ways.

In a series of examples underscoring Israel's self-destructive behavior (vv. 6-10), Paul warns the Corinthians to avoid this kind of presumptuous conduct. The reference to Israel's sitting down to eat and drink (v. 7) recalls the erection of an altar of sacrifice to the golden calf (Exod 32) and Israel's subsequent feasting and rising up to revel (i.e., worship) this idol. This is a particularly apt reference for the Corinthians, who think they are secure in their knowledge and immune from idolatry. However, by going off to apparently innocuous feasting with their pagan friends in the venues associated with their former pagan lives, they are not above becoming entangled in idol worship. Moreover, as no amount of spiritual security saved the Israelites, who persisted in sexual immorality (v. 8), so likewise, if the Corinthians persist in sexual immorality, neither will they be saved. In case the self-styled intellectuals at Corinth could possibly miss the point of this storytelling, Paul makes it clear: If you think you stand secure in your knowledge, watch out! Others who believed themselves just as secure fell (v. 12).

Though Paul's concluding words of reassurance appear to, they do not negate the stern warning. On the contrary, the reassurance makes the warning all the more urgent. God is faithful and will assist the Corinthians with the testing and trials that they are bound to encounter. However, when through their arrogant reliance on their own power and knowledge rather than on God's power and wisdom they bring upon themselves testing and trials, then they are certain to fall as Israel did! Hence, rather than boasting in the exercise of this right to eat idol meat, which is intended to showcase their superior knowledge and unconstrained freedom, they ought to shun the practice.

10:14-22 Against communion with idols: judge for yourselves

As chapter 9 looked back to the discussion of chapter 8 and served to illumine and illustrate the need for renunciation of rights, 1 Corinthians 10:1-13, with its warning rooted in the example of Israel, looks forward to 1 Corinthians 10:14-22, where Paul now argues against participation at temple banquets. After the command to flee idolatry, Paul appeals to the Corinthians as "sensible people," a phrase that may be laced with sarcasm. Whatever the case, in view of the analogical argument he is about to set forth, Paul expects them to judge for themselves whether frequenting temple banquets is an innocuous practice.

Paul begins with what he and the Corinthians would agree on: participation in the Lord's Supper is an actual sharing in the blood and body of Christ, which effects a solidarity or bonding among believers and with Christ. The emphasis here is on the "sharing" and the oneness or solidarity effected (v. 18). Thus one cannot participate and intend non-solidarity, since the very act of participation produces it. It is clear that Paul does not recognize any dichotomy between the act of participation and the participant's intention.

As a second example of the bonding and solidarity effected through meal participation, Paul cites the historical example of the Jews ("Israel according to the flesh," v. 18). Their participation in the "altar" is Paul's way of saying they joined themselves to God. Both examples illustrate that eating a meal in the presence of God effects a solidarity between the community and God whom it worships.

Now Paul can go forward to draw a conclusion based on analogy: if eating a meal sacrificed to God effects solidarity with God, then eating a meal sacrificed to idols effects communion with idols. But Paul cannot draw this conclusion without contradicting what he had said previously (8:1-6). Aware of this (v. 19), he restates the conviction that an idol is nothing, and moves the analogy forward by substituting the term "demons" (v. 20). In referring to demons, Paul probably has in mind Deuteronomy 32:16-17. Based on this text, a Jewish tradition evolved which, while discounting the

1 Corinthians 10

existence and divinity of anyone or thing but God alone, acknowledged the existence of demonic powers, variously referred to as gods or "idols," that actively opposed the purposes of God in the world. Apparently picking up on this tradition, Paul denies the existence of actual pagan idols but acknowledges the existence of supernatural powers. Since the absolute exclusiveness of the solidarity with God in Christ precludes any other union, the enlightened ones have to make a choice: participation at the table of demons or the table of the Lord. The Corinthians cannot have it both ways.

Paul concludes this section with two rhetorical questions. The first reverts back to the example of Israel set out in 10:1-13 and recalls the destruction that accompanied their complacency. Lest any of the enlightened ones doubt a similar outcome if they continue at cultic banquets, Paul leaves them with a final question that puts their presumed knowledge and power in perspective. Perhaps they are intellectually stronger than the weak. But are they stronger than the Lord? The answer is clear.

10:23–11:1 Summary: seek the good of others

In his argument so far, Paul gives a single response, in light of two separate criteria, to the question of participation in temple banquets. First, the practice should be renounced out of love and concern for the other members of the community (8:1-13 argument plus 9:1-27 example). Second, the practice should be renounced because participants in temple banquets implicate themselves in idolatrous worship and risk incurring God's wrath (10:1-13 example plus 10:14-22 argument).

Now, in the final subsection of this extended argument concerning food offered to idols, Paul considers whether meat sacrificed to idols can be consumed in non-cultic, private settings. Paul's discussion is framed by two concerns: that freedom is exercised in view of what is upbuilding for the community (v. 24) and that whatever activity is undertaken should be directed to the glory of God (v. 31). Within this framework, Paul considers the eating of previously sacrificed meat purchased at the market and eaten in a believer's own home or at a dinner party in the home of an unbeliever to be a legitimate practice, which, of itself, does not contravene either of the two concerns. Presumably, the enlightened at Corinth already know this. It is the weak who need to understand that eating sacrificed meat in private venues is a legitimate exercise of freedom. Thus informed, the weak need to overcome their scruples and cease to create problems where they do not exist.

In verses 28-29 Paul adds a proviso enjoining renunciation if "someone" in any private setting calls attention to the meat's origin. Paul does not identify the informer as a believer. Regardless, this proviso is part of the ethic of concern for others that Paul is attempting to instill in the community. Modeled on Christ's example of selfless love, Christian freedom seeks the good of others and the glory of God. It is neither constrained by unwarranted scrupulosity nor simply ordered to self-satisfaction. As one whose praxis is rooted in imitation of Jesus, who sought the salvation of many, Paul's call to the Corinthians to imitate him is ultimately a call to live Christlike lives.

ARGUMENTS CONCERNING ASPECTS OF COMMUNITY WORSHIP

1 Corinthians 11:2–14:40

In this next major section of 1 Corinthians, Paul sets out three separate arguments that are linked by the fact that each concerns problematic behavior affecting the community's worship. Without mentioning the source of his information, he first deals with a problem relating to the hairstyles of some community members praying and prophesying at the liturgical assembly (11:2-16). A more serious problem, which Paul has learned of through oral sources, concerns abuses and divisions at the Eucharist, the very sign and source of the community's unity, which is being negated by their behavior (11:17-34). Finally, in a lengthy argument concerning spiritual gifts (12:1–14:40), a topic presumably raised by the Corinthians in their letter, Paul deals with the problems created by the misguided desire of some to show their superior spiritual status by flaunting certain spiritual gifts and deprecating others.

Argument concerning hairstyles (11:2-16)

11:2-16 Liturgy and hair etiquette

The logical sequel to Paul's remark at 11:2, concerning traditions, seems to be the discussion at 11:17-34. Though the community is faithful to the traditions, which earns Paul's praise (11:2), their behavior at the Eucharist, not their hairdos, is an exception to this fidelity to tradition, which earns Paul's censure (11:17). Thus 11:3-16 appears to be out of place in its current literary context. Not surprisingly, some commentators argue that verses 3-16 were a later insertion into the text. However, this need not be the case. If the Corinthians had raised this issue, Paul may have felt compelled to give a response, which, however awkwardly, he locates here along with other responses about issues affecting community worship. In addition to the awkward fit, the exact nature of the problem is somewhat obscure, as is Paul's argumentation.

What can be inferred from 11:3-16 is that in the context of the liturgical assembly some women *and* men, as is clear from 11:4, were transgressing

1 Corinthians 11

codes relating to hair etiquette, which apparently upset others in the community. Contrary to custom, some women were praying and prophesying with their hair unbound, while some men, likewise engaged, wore their hair long. The mention of having one's hair cut off (vv. 6-7) and the later references to long hair (vv. 15-17) suggest that hairstyles, not head coverings or veils, are under discussion. Why some in the community felt free to abandon this custom is a matter of speculation. Some hypothesize that the transgressors were attempting to concretely express the extinction of ethnic, status, and gender distinctions presumed to be the intent of Paul's baptism/new creation preaching (see, e.g., Gal 3:27-28; 2 Cor 5:16-17). Regardless of their motivation, Paul rejects the abandonment of the custom relating to hairstyles.

To make his case, Paul begins his argument by establishing a schema of relationships (vv. 3-4). Obviously, Paul does not intend the word "head" in the literal sense. As a metaphor, it is most often understood to stand for "authority over" or "source of," although other renderings are possible. Whatever the case, in Paul's schematic formulation, the point is that one member of the pair is precedent and preeminent with regard to the other. Within this logic Paul insists that how one acts either honors or dishonors one's figurative head/source. Men who transgress the hair etiquette dishonor Christ, while women dishonor the men of the community (vv. 4-6).

Paul does not explain why a particular hairstyle is an occasion of dishonor to one's figurative head/source. However, it requires no stretch of the imagination to get the connection. Even in our own day, clothing, hairstyles, tattoos, body piercing, and the like are often construed as positive or negative reflectors of parents, schools, or other institutions thought to have some investment in the person under scrutiny. In the Mediterranean culture of Paul's day, unbound hair on a woman was associated with sexual permissiveness, and short-cropped hair was associated with lesbianism and prostitution, while men with long hair were thought to be effeminate.

With regard to the presence of a woman with unbound hair at the assembly, Paul would be objecting to her appearance as a sexually loose or available woman. In reference to men praying and prophesying with long hair and women with cropped hair, if the latter was an actual case (which is not clear from the text), Paul would be objecting to the blurring of gender distinctions caused by the adoption of inappropriate hairstyles.

A second argument is unfolded in verses 7-12. The contrast stated in verse 7 is explicated in verses 8-9, where, in reference to the account of creation in Genesis 2, Paul explains his claim that woman is the reflected glory of man in view of her having been made from him. Consequently, a woman is expected to avoid anything that dishonors a man. Thus she must keep her hair bound.

What Paul intends in verse 10 is an enigma. It is not certain whether he is expressing an additional claim that a woman needs her hair bound because of "the angels" or whether verse 10 is an implication deriving from verses 8-9. Paul could be alluding to the belief that angels, considered the protectors of the order of creation, were present as the custodians of the liturgy. The enigmatic expression "have authority over her head" may mean that the woman should take charge of her own head and keep her hair bound in view of the order and decorum of the liturgy, over which the angels stood guard.

Paul's statements stressing the reciprocity between man and woman (vv. 11-12) need not be taken as a contradiction of what he has previously argued; rather, Paul makes two equally valid observations. Men and women are equal and interdependent. As such, they have an equal right to pray and prophesy in the church, and hence to assume roles of liturgical leadership. This equality, however, does not allow for the abandonment of social norms or for the abolition of gender differences, which Paul believes are to be maintained through external markers, namely, long, bound hair for women and short hair for men. Paul's assertion of the equality and interdependence of men and women, notwithstanding gender difference, is usually overlooked by those who view this entire passage as a statement of the absolute subordination of women.

In the concluding verses, Paul adds a third and fourth argument, neither of which is developed. The third argument appeals to what nature teaches, by which Paul must mean that long hair is inappropriate for men and appropriate for women (vv. 14-15). The fourth and final argument appeals to the custom of the churches of God (v. 16). In case the Corinthians are not persuaded by his three preceding arguments, Paul adds this last appeal to remind the Corinthians that, in any case, they ought to conform their practice to that of all believers.

Argument concerning division and abuses at the Lord's Supper (11:17-34)

11:17-22 Your meetings do more harm than good

Paul's commendation of the Corinthians at 11:2 was perhaps part of his rhetorical strategy to prepare the community for the rebuke with which he begins his discussion of their behavior at the Eucharist (v. 17). Paul's next statement, namely, that he has heard about divisions within the community (v. 18)—as if he were unaware of such divisions—has led many to conclude that 1 Corinthians must be a composite of at least two letters. However, the additional remark "and to a degree I believe it" is a bit of mocking sarcasm. Paul knows well the extent of the divisiveness in the community. Since it has invaded even their Eucharist assembly, Paul now observes that more harm than good results from this coming together. Verse 19 should probably be taken as a continuation of Paul's mocking. What else can be expected but divisions when some community members are still concerned only about their own individual status, well-being, and self-satisfaction!

To understand Paul's comments, it is helpful to recall that in earliest Christianity the Lord's Supper was not the highly ritualized, one-hour event in a church to which we are accustomed. Smaller assemblies of believers at Corinth would gather at the home of the head of one such assembly, whose house would have been large enough to accommodate the entire community. There all believers gathered as one to eat an actual meal, during which they shared the bread and cup of the Lord's Supper, the sign and source of their unity. But Paul says even though they are assembled for this purpose, each comes to eat "his own supper," not to eat the "Lord's supper" (v. 20), with the result that some are sated while others go without and are even made to feel ashamed (v. 22).

Sometimes Paul's rhetoric is taken as a description of the economic disparity within the community that is thought to underlie the problem discussed here. However, economic disparity is only one aspect of a much larger picture. Established social convention dictated that rank and status be acknowledged by one's place at table and the amount and quality of food and drink one was apportioned. When this larger picture is considered, it appears that Paul's overriding concern is that societal norms are being used as the standard of comportment at the Eucharist. These norms encourage divisions and self-aggrandizement and promote self-serving behavior, all of which undermine the unity of the community and negate the whole purpose of the Eucharist. If members' only purpose in coming is to serve their own needs and eat to their own satisfaction, then they ought to stay in their own homes (v. 22). Whatever the Corinthians think of themselves, Paul makes it clear that he cannot praise them.

11:23-26 The tradition of the institution

To call the Corinthians back to their senses, Paul reminds them of the tradition concerning the founding of this communal meal (vv. 23-26). Since Paul's letter antedates Mark, the first Gospel, by almost fifteen years, we have here the earliest preserved account of the institution of the Eucharist. Paul employs the technical terms "received" and "handed on" used in Jewish culture for the transmission of important traditions. This tradition is "from the Lord," meaning that the origin of this tradition of sharing the cup and bread is with the Lord himself. The community gathers in the *present* to observe *the Lord's* last supper, to recall the *past* historical event of Jesus' betrayal and self-sacrificing love symbolized in the bread and cup, and to proclaim this death until his *future* coming.

For Paul, the whole point of this coming together is to remember (vv. 25-26) the death of Christ and to allow the reality and meaning of that death to take form in their own lives. What matters to Paul is not the words of the tradition per se, but that the Corinthians live as one saved community rooted in the self-sacrificing love of Christ! Their self-serving behavior betrays Christ's self-sacrificing love and destroys the reality effected through his death. As such, they are not eating the "Lord's supper" (v. 20) but continuing in their own community-destroying ways.

11:27-32 The tradition and the situation in the Corinthian community

Paul now applies the tradition to the specific situation of abuse and division at the Lord's Supper. In context, verses 27-28 refer neither to a person's moral condition nor to the discernment of the Real Presence. Rather, to eat unworthily means to behave in a way that promotes divisions that are antithetical to the whole purpose of the Eucharist. Unworthy participants are responsible for the body and blood of the Lord, in the sense that they are held responsible for offending the community of believers who are the body of Christ. To eat and drink without "discerning the body" refers to the self-serving behavior that disregards the well-being and unity of the whole body of believers. Such blatant disregard is an act of self-incrimination (v. 29) through which those who eat unworthily bring God's judgment on themselves.

Exactly what Paul means in verse 30 remains an enigma. It seems, however, that he takes the illness and death of some members of the community as a sign that God's judgment has already befallen the community. Apparently Paul expects this to be taken as a warning by the Corinthians to discontinue their abusive behavior in order to avoid future condemnation (v. 32).

11:33-34 Practical advice

Paul concludes his discussion with pragmatic instructions in which he prescribes the behavior appropriate to Christians gathered to celebrate the source and sign of their unity. Above all, each one's behavior is to be characterized by consideration for the other. Temporal waiting is obviously a first step in showing consideration. However, beyond mere waiting, Paul

1 Corinthians 11

probably also has in mind a true openness to and receptivity of the other born of the selfless love and desire for unity that the Eucharist is meant to symbolize and engender. Paul's notice in verse 34 that he defers the treatment of other unspecified matters to a future visit underscores the importance of this discussion about behavior at the Eucharist.

Argument concerning spiritual gifts (12:1–14:40)

The expression "Now in regard to" at 12:1 indicates that Paul is about to begin a new argument, which extends from 12:1 through 14:40. This is Paul's final and lengthiest argument relating to a matter affecting community worship. In this particular argument, concerned with "spiritual gifts" (Greek: *pneumatika*), Paul addresses a problematic situation involving the use and abuse of spiritual gifts (Greek: *charismata*). Though Paul does not say, it is likely that he became aware of this situation from the Corinthians' letter to him.

What can be inferred from the argument is that competitiveness in the community revolving around the possession and manifestation of spiritual gifts deemed to be more superior, especially the much-vaunted gift of tongues, was threatening the unity of the community (ch. 12) and creating disorder and chaos at the community's prayer assembly (ch. 14). In response, Paul unfolds an argument in three segments, forming an ABA' pattern. Section A (= 12:4-31a) contains a general discussion that stresses both the need for unity in diversity and diversity in unity, while the A' section (= 14:1-40) is more specifically focused on the advantage of prophecy over speaking in tongues and the order that must obtain within the prayer assembly. In the middle B section (= 12:31b—13:13), a rhetorical digression, Paul develops and discloses the key motive that must inform the exercise of spiritual gifts, namely, Christian charity.

The whole issue under discussion in chapters 12–14 presumes a situation in the community at Corinth in which extraordinary spiritual gifts and their manifestation were an everyday reality in the life of the community. It is important to remember when reading the argument here that Paul is grateful for and acknowledges the inherent goodness of each spiritual gift with which the community has been endowed, including the gift of speaking in tongues (see 1:5). Unfortunately, some viewed their gifts, especially speaking in tongues, as tokens of superior spiritual status, exercised for self-aggrandizement. It is this skewed view and abusive use of the gifts that Paul rejects and seeks to correct by his discussion of the relative significance of each gift, whose exercise must be ordered to the upbuilding and unity of the whole community.

A variety of gifts from the same Spirit for the common good (12:1-31a)

In this first subunit of argumentation, Paul introduces the new topic (vv. 1-3) and then locates the origin of all spiritual gifts in the same divine source (vv. 4-11). A body analogy, commonly used in Greco-Roman speech to illustrate the relationship of the one and the many, is employed by Paul in verses 12-26 to stress the diversity and interdependence of community members. In conclusion, Paul applies this analogy directly to the situation at Corinth and ranks members in view of gifts and roles (vv. 27-31a).

12:1-3 Introduction

Paul's desire that the Corinthians not "be unaware" implies a certain ignorance about spiritual realities, despite the fact that some in the community are apparently posing as authorities on the subject, believing that the mere manifestation of certain spiritual gifts, especially ecstatic utterances, somehow makes them authentic spiritual persons. Paul corrects this assumption in the next two verses. In their former lives as pagans, the Corinthians may have been caught up in the thrill of ecstasy, but it was all futile, since they were swept off to dumb idols (v. 2). Thus their own experience underscores the fact that ecstatic experience and accompanying utterances, of themselves, cannot be the measure of what it means to be an authentically spiritual person.

The true test of whether one is guided by the Spirit of God is that one is able to confess that "Jesus is Lord" (v. 3). Paul contrasts this confession with the statement "Jesus be accursed." Rather than an actual utterance heard in the Corinthian prayer assembly, the latter statement should probably be taken as a rhetorical counterpoint introduced by Paul to dramatize the antithesis between what is authentically Spirit-empowered and what is not. For Paul, the acknowledgment of the Lordship of Jesus alone is the criterion by which one judges who lives in the realm of the Spirit and is authentically Spirit-inspired.

12:4-11 Manifestations of the Spirit

Up until this point in his argument, Paul has spoken of spiritual realities *(pneumatika)*. Here in verse 4 he introduces the word "gifts" *(charismata)* for the first time. By redefining authentic spiritual realities as "gifts," Paul indirectly undermines Corinthian arrogance. No one has merited such gifts, and since each community member's gift derives from the same source, none is inherently inferior to another. Along with the diversity of gifts inspired by the Spirit, there are also various forms of service and workings that are also divinely ordained. All these gifts in all their diversity ultimately derive from God and are given through the agency of the Spirit. To each member of the

529

1 Corinthians 12

community is given some manifestation of the Spirit (v. 7). Since the Spirit is manifest in the manifold gifts, services, and workings, any claim that any one particular gift, service, or working is a fuller manifestation of the Spirit is simply unwarranted. Moreover, to devalue any gift is to devalue the work of the Spirit. Thus, as arrogance is undermined by virtue of the fact that any manifestation of the Spirit is a gift, so also is the competitiveness that derives from the false assumption that certain manifestations are superior to others.

In the second half of verse 7, Paul now adds a second criterion for determining who is authentically spiritual and what is authentically Spirit-inspired. That which is an authentic manifestation of the Spirit must in some way benefit others. The manifestations are given neither for self-glorification nor for advancing one's own status but for the common good. When the latter is not the end toward which the public manifestation of the Spirit is ordered, it cannot be an authentic Spirit-inspired manifestation, nor can the person be authentically spiritual.

With these two criteria established, Paul proceeds to give a representative listing (compare with the list at 12:28 and Rom 12:6-8) of the manifestations of the Spirit in verses 8-11. In all, Paul mentions nine examples of the Spirit's manifestations in these three verses, portraying them as common occurrences in the community at Corinth. "Faith" (v. 9) is apparently a reference to a particular endowment for a special service (although Paul does not specify), and not the saving faith common to all believers.

Judging by Paul's discussion in chapter 14, it was the gift of tongues that was apparently creating most of the disturbance in the community. Paul's careful listing of these distinct yet all Spirit-inspired gifts at work in the community is probably intended to put this particular gift of tongues in its proper context. It is only one among many. The repetition of "to one/to another" and the "same/one Spirit" underscores both the activity of the Spirit, the source of each gift, and the importance of each individual member of the community whose gift, though different from that of another, contributes to and is necessary for the common good.

In verse 11, Paul concludes this subsection on gifts and succinctly restates the key points he has made so far: every distinct gift is the work of the Spirit. It is a gift freely given to individual believers through God's generous grace, to be exercised in the service of the church for the promotion of the common good.

12:12-26 Diversity in unity, unity in diversity

Paul now carries his points forward by means of an analogy between the church and the body. The body analogy was a common figure of speech in political discourse in antiquity. Human societies were compared to a body, whose well-being depended on each member of society knowing his or her place. Usually the analogy was employed to conserve the status quo, especially as a means to keep the lower classes in their place and dissuade them from dissent or rebellion that could upset the balance of power. Paul uses the analogy not to subordinate but to stress the diversity, interdependence, and importance of all the members of the community, who together form one body.

The analogy is introduced in 12:12, which concludes with the phrase "so also Christ," not with "so also the community/church" as one might expect. For Paul, the body of believers is Christ, or the body of Christ, a metaphoric expression he employs to express what he believes to be the reality of Christian existence. Believers are bound in a living unity with the risen Lord, which is effected through the unifying activity and presence of the Spirit in baptism (v. 13). Hence, though many, they form one body, the body of Christ.

Having established the analogy, Paul now stresses the need for diversity within this unity by means of an absurd staging of talking body parts announcing their liberation from the body (vv. 14-16)! The result of the withdrawal of any part, either in view of its superiority or inferiority to the other parts, would be a distorted entity, but not a body which, of its very nature, requires the diversity of parts (vv. 19-20). Paul's lesson is clear. A human body cannot be a body without the diversity of parts. Likewise, the body of Christ cannot be a body without each distinct believer, whose place and function in the body depend on God (v. 18). Hence the diversity within the community is not a reality to be obliterated, nor even merely tolerated. It is essential.

Whereas in verses 14-20 Paul's stress is on the necessity of diversity in unity, in verses 21-26 the accent falls on the need to maintain unity amidst the diversity. No member of the community can afford to scorn any other member or set up divisive distinctions. The "weaker" and "less honorable" parts probably allude to community members who were looked down on either because of social status or lack of intellectual and spiritual sophistication or both. Paul reminds the arrogant of the community, who likely associate themselves with the more "presentable" or "honorable" parts, that those they scorn need to be honored and cared for. God has not differentiated among members as a basis for division, for there can be no division in the body, which relies on the interdependence of its parts for its functioning. Moreover, not only are the weakest links indispensable to the life of the community, but it is to these that God has given greater honor (v. 24).

1 Corinthians 12

Thus if there is division and discord, the whole body suffers, because no member is independent of the other in the body of Christ.

12:27-30a Application to the church

The analogy is now directly applied to the community of believers, who are Christ's body. Within this body, God has gifted members with diverse gifts and functions. As with the preceding list (vv. 8-10), here, too, in verse 28, Paul seems to provide a representative rather than exhaustive list. He numerically ranks the first three. There is no way of knowing if the enumeration is intended to suggest a hierarchy of authority among these three. Minimally speaking, the enumeration suggests that Paul considered these three very important ministries.

The other gifts or functions, introduced by "then," parallel each other's importance, though they are probably of lesser importance than those enumerated. Once again Paul lists varieties of tongues last (see 12:10), apparently to reinforce the fact that tongues are only one among many gifts bestowed for the common good. Each of the concluding rhetorical questions begins with the Greek negative *(mē)*, which always expects the answer no! No, all cannot have the same gift or perform the same function, and no one person can have all the gifts and perform all the functions. Here again Paul emphasizes the necessity for diversity in unity. Against the arrogant in Corinth, who apparently measure a member's spiritual endowment and worth in view of *one* gift, speaking in tongues, Paul asserts that diversity is not only good but necessary! Some of the Corinthians have unfortunately mistaken uniformity for unity. Paul wants the latter, which is only truly achieved when each member's distinct contribution is valued and incorporated with all others to build up the whole body.

Love, the more excellent way (13:1-13)

This poetic encomium (speech) in praise of love is often taken as an abstract meditation on love, with little connection to the discussion of spiritual gifts. However, in context this encomium is actually an integral part of Paul's argument in chapters 12–14, through which he presents love as the quality of Christian life par excellence and the absolute norm that must govern the exercise of the gifts of the Spirit. Verse 31 of chapter 12 introduces this poetic interlude, which begins at 13:1.

13:1-3 Gifts without love are of no account

Using himself as a hypothetical example, Paul asserts that without love the exercise of gifts is futile and empty. The first gift Paul mentions is tongues.

Exercised apart from love, the tongues-speaker produces only a strident noise, like brass instruments struck without purpose. Though Paul begins with the Corinthians' prized gift, we must not hastily assume that his sole purpose here is to deflate the arrogant Corinthians by devaluing what is most important to them. This becomes apparent in verses 2-3, where Paul considers other gifts and practices. Even if one should prophesy, a gift Paul considers superior to tongues (see 14:5), or have extraordinary faith, without love this person is nothing. Likewise, should one choose a life of self-abnegation and hardship, as Paul himself did (see ch. 9), without love such practices are of no account. In sum, all gifts and religious practices are equally of no account unless motivated and informed by love.

13:4-7 In praise of love

Paul's praise of love personified begins with two positive statements in the first half of verse 4 and ends with one long verse extolling four of love's positive features (v. 7). From the second half of verse 4 through verse 6, Paul focuses on what love is not or does not do. In all, there are eight negative statements. Most of the negatives correspond directly or indirectly to actual behavior of the Corinthians already criticized by Paul. For example, "jealous" and "inflated" (v. 4b) recall behavior and attitudes that Paul castigated in chapters 1–4 and 5. To "rejoice over wrongdoing" (v. 6) probably alludes to behavior censured in chapters 5 and 6. "Does not seek its own interest" (v. 5) evokes Paul's discussion of meat offered to idols and the renunciation of one's rights in the interest of others (chs. 8–10).

Thus Paul's list of negatives is not merely a poetic extolling of the abstract notion of love but a rather pointed indictment of the Corinthians' behavior. By all counts, Corinthian behavior is devoid of Christian love. In view of the assertions of verses 1-3, the Corinthians should realize that their exercise of gifts and other religious practices is entirely void. They have gained nothing by their displays. They are nothing, despite their own exalted self-perception.

In verse 7, Paul summarizes positively the character of love. Belief and hope are focused on the future. Strengthened by them, Christians are enabled to bear and endure in the present. Especially in view of the repeated "all things," Paul's statement in verse 7 can unfortunately be read as an exhortation to suffer any kind of abuse, believe anything, or maintain hope at all costs, even when unrealistic. Far from promoting abusive, self-destructive, or self-deceptive behavior, here Paul advocates behavior governed by love that transcends the self-interest, jealousy, and competitiveness leading to strife and division and promotes reconciliation and unity.

1 Corinthians 13

13:8-13 The abiding nature of love

Paul now advances his argument for the preeminence of love in view of its enduring character in contrast to gifts, all of which are temporal. Paul singles out prophecy, tongues, and knowledge, underscoring their transitory, incomplete, and imperfect nature (vv. 8-9). Given this, these revelatory gifts allow the Corinthians only a partial understanding of the mysteries of God in the present. Unfortunately, the Corinthians pride themselves on their possession of such gifts and assume that they offer complete access to divine mysteries. However, complete access and understanding are a future reality associated with the end-time. When the *eschaton* arrives, these limited gifts will lose whatever partial significance they now have, since the perfect will replace and fulfill the partial (v. 10).

To illustrate his point, Paul uses an analogy (v. 11). As childhood values, behavior, and ways of thinking are abandoned as one matures into adulthood, so are the lesser or partial spiritual gifts abandoned at the *eschaton*. Prizing and boasting in partial spiritual gifts, just like prizing and boasting in certain ministers (see 3:1-4), again shows that the Corinthians are spiritually immature, despite their claims to the contrary.

In verse 12, Paul reinforces his point with one more analogical argument. Like indistinct mirror images, the insights acquired through temporal spiritual gifts are useful now but nothing at all compared with the perfect (face-to-face) vision promised at the *eschaton*. Faith, hope, and love are all hallmarks of Christian life in the present. Love is the greatest both because it is the supreme motive that allows Christians to use all the Spirit's gifts for the end toward which God has ordained them and because it alone endures eternal.

The use of spiritual gifts in the context of worship (14:1-40)

Having discussed the necessity of diverse gifts (ch. 12) and established love as the absolute criterion for evaluating the use of gifts (ch. 13), Paul now focuses specifically on the problems occurring at community worship deriving from the exercise of spiritual gifts. Apparently, those in the community fixated on speaking in tongues as a demonstration of spiritual superiority are causing chaos in the community. In chapter 14, Paul first unfolds a sustained argument for the desirability of prophecy over speaking in tongues (vv. 1-25) and then lays down instructions regulating community worship (vv. 26-40).

14:1-25 Argument in favor of prophecy

Paul's preference for prophecy is predicated on two main arguments enunciated in verses 2-5 and developed in verses 6-25. First, what is articulated through prophecy is directed to human beings and is intelligible to the entire assembly, whereas tongues are directed to God and are not intelligible to all (vv. 2-3). Second, prophecy builds up the community, whereas tongues is an exercise in self-edification (v. 4). In verse 5, Paul restates his points, insisting that prophecy is the greater gift, although he acknowledges that tongues could have edifying value if they are interpreted.

Paul develops his argument that tongues are unintelligible in verses 6-12. With the exception of verse 6, where Paul offers an autobiographical reflection, perhaps hypothetical or perhaps an actual comment on his strategy at Corinth (see 2:1), this subsection is constructed around three analogies (vv. 7-11). In the first, tongues are likened to isolated notes sounded by a flute or harp. Unless the notes form a coherent pattern, no intelligible melody is produced and listeners are at a loss. Likewise, if a bugle is made to emit a series of random sounds, troops would not know they are being called to assemble for battle. In this second case, the lack of intelligibility is not merely benign. Paul's third analogy turns on the variety of languages. When no common language exists to unite two people, they remain estranged, an unfortunate outcome. For Paul, speaking in tongues amounts to unintelligibility (v. 9), on a par with the three examples cited. Paul concludes by positively acknowledging the zeal of the Corinthians. It is good, but it needs to be directed toward acquiring the gifts that build up the whole community (v. 12).

The lack of intelligibility and its consequences are now considered in view of the community's worship assembly (vv. 13-19). Without the complementary gift of "interpretation," for which speakers in tongues should pray, tongues do not edify. The Corinthians may feel that truly genuine spiritual experience transcends the human mind. However, Paul suggests that in some way their experience in the Spirit must be translated into what is intelligible with the mind, because only in this way is the community built up (vv. 14-15). Additionally, when intelligibility is lacking, community members cannot authentically participate in community prayer. They can say "Amen," but since they have no idea what they affirm, their prayer and praise are rendered inauthentic. In concluding, Paul claims that he could outdo any of the Corinthians when it comes to speaking in tongues (v. 18). However, he again sets an example of renunciation for the benefit of others, consistent with what he had recommended in chapters 8–10.

Paul now turns to his second concern: the effect of tongues and prophecy on outsiders/unbelievers. In verse 21, Paul cites Isaiah 28:11-12. An interpretation of this text then follows in verse 22, which states, in effect, that tongues are for unbelievers, while prophecy is for believers. In all probability,

1 Corinthians 14

verse 22 represents the view of some Corinthians who claim that their dazzling displays of ecstatic speech would win over unbelievers. Paul challenges and corrects this view in verses 23-25, insisting that tongues negatively impact unbelievers, while prophecy brings them to recognize the presence of God. However we construe these verses, Paul's view is clear in verses 24-25: prophecy is also better for unbelievers.

14:26-40 Regulating community worship

The varieties of gifts spoken of in chapter 12 are evident when the Corinthians congregate for worship, which Paul here describes as a lively, Spirit-filled assembly of believers, each bringing some spiritual gift. To ensure that every gift, including tongues, is directed to its proper end, that is, the upbuilding of the community (v. 26), Paul proposes some rules of order. He first regulates the use of tongues, which some apparently exercised in an uncontrolled manner, monopolizing the community's assembly time and creating disorder. As a gift, tongues cannot be excluded, but Paul sets three controls on their use. He limits the number of contributions from those gifted with tongues, prohibits simultaneous speaking in tongues, and enjoins the speaker of tongues to exercise this gift in silence if there is no interpreter (vv. 27-28).

With regard to prophecy, Paul also limits the number of contributions to two or three. However, Paul allows that as many as have a revelation may speak, as long as no two speak simultaneously, so that each may listen to and learn from the other (vv. 29-31). These controls may sound reasonable to modern readers accustomed to ordered and decorous worship assemblies, in which everyone's place and time to speak are predetermined. However, some of the Corinthians who like to show off their spiritual gifts may perceive these controls as contrary to the free flow and spontaneous activity of the Spirit. Who is Paul to constrain the Spirit? Paul seems to anticipate and eliminate this type of objection by reminding the community that God's Spirit cannot inspire any disorder or chaos, since God is a God of peace (v. 33).

At 1 Corinthians 11:5, Paul indisputably takes for granted that women pray and prophesy in the assembly. Is he now contradicting himself in verses 34-35 by enjoining silence on women, commanding their subordination to their husbands, to whom they are instructed to direct inquiries? Some commentators suggest that verses 34-35 are an interpolation (later insertion) dating from the late first century, more akin to the view expressed by the author of 1 Timothy as found, for example, at 1 Timothy 2:11-12. Others who take these verses as original offer a variety of suggestions. Some argue that male elitists in the Corinthian community, not Paul, held the view expressed in verses 34-35, which Paul actually challenges here, although no text evidence supports this suggestion. Moreover, it depends on an interpretation of verse 36 as a sarcastic rejoinder by Paul to the elitists. Some claim that Paul addresses only married women, though this distinction is not evident from the text. Still others argue that verses 34-35 contain Paul's real position, while 11:2-6 represent his concession to some women whom he allows to speak, but with restrictions.

Given the limited evidence, it may remain impossible to determine which suggestion accurately accounts for verses 34-35. In the end, the greater problem presented by these verses is not whether Paul did or did not write them, but how they are interpreted and applied. Responsible interpretation requires that these verses be considered in view of Paul's larger vision of church as the union of all men and women using their gifts and talents to advance the gospel of Jesus Christ.

As Paul concludes, he backs the Corinthian spiritualists into a corner (v. 37). Either they recognize what he has written (ch. 14 and maybe chs. 12–13) as a commandment of the Lord, or they are not the genuine prophets and spiritual people they claim to be. Then, without singling anyone out, Paul announces the consequence for non-compliance (v. 38) before succinctly reiterating in verses 39-40 what he has argued in chapter 14.

ARGUMENT FOR THE RESURRECTION

I Corinthians 15:1-58

Paul's last major argument of 1 Corinthians is a lengthy defense of the resurrection of the dead. As we have seen throughout this letter, exclusive concern for the spiritual and disregard for the physical underlie many of the behavioral problems Paul has addressed. In this particular argument, the focus is on errant thought not problematic behavior as Paul now considers the Corinthians' spirit-body dualism vis à vis the question of the resurrection. In line with their dualistic beliefs, it appears that some Corinthians consider eternal life an entirely spiritual existence, experienced apart from the body left behind at death. The paltry body has no place in this exclusively spiritual dimension of future existence (see above at 6:12-20), hence the denial of the resurrection of the dead (v. 12).

Against this view, Paul develops a three-stage argument. He first rehearses the tradition concerning Christ's resurrection (vv. 1-11). Next he argues for the resurrection in view of three factors (vv. 12-34). In the third subsection, Paul discusses the manner in which the dead are raised (vv.

1 Corinthians 15

35-49). He concludes this argument by affirming that the resurrection is a mystery apprehended through faith (vv. 50-58).

15:1-11 The resurrection of Christ: rehearsing the facts

Paul begins by reminding the Corinthians that what he preached to them was nothing other than the central gospel tradition concerning Jesus' death and resurrection, a tradition he himself had "received" and "handed on" (see 11:23). This tradition was articulated in an ancient Christian creed, which Paul now cites in verses 3b-5. The central faith conviction professed in this creed by the earliest Christians was fourfold: Christ died, he was buried, he was raised, he appeared.

Paul's recitation of the tradition serves two purposes here. First, it serves to remind the Corinthians that they cannot simply reject, alter, or hold a belief contrary to any of the foundational elements of the Christian faith. It is on this complete profession of faith, not just one or two elements of it, that they presumably took their stand. Moreover, it is through this faith that they and all believers are saved. If any aspect of this central faith conviction is altered or rejected, their faith would be in vain, a possibility Paul hopes to avert.

Second, the recitation provides Paul with the opportunity to introduce historical testimony to Christ's resurrection (vv. 5-8). This testimony is essential to his argument for the resurrection of the dead. It is important to observe that Paul insists that Jesus "appeared to" the witnesses, not that they saw Jesus. This is intended to underscore the fact that the risen Jesus was not a construct of the witnesses' imagination. Peter is listed as the first to whom Jesus appeared, a privilege that contributed to his status in the early church; then come the "Twelve," Jesus' inner circle of disciples, who exercised an authoritative and foundational role in earliest Christianity. The circle of witnesses widens as Paul mentions more than five hundred brethren, then Jesus' brother James, a prominent leader in the Jerusalem community (see Acts 15), then "all the apostles"(v. 7), obviously a reference to a group larger than the Twelve. Paul finally lists himself as the last and least of those to whom Jesus appeared (see 1 Cor 9:1; Gal 1:16; Acts 9:3-5). The autobiographical aside "as to one born abnormally" (v. 8; literally "born of an abortion") is a strange expression, probably inserted to emphasize Paul's exceptional route to apostleship.

Notably absent from Paul's list of witnesses are women, who according to all four Gospels (see Mark 16:1-8; Matt 28:1-10; Luke 24:1-9; John 20:1-18) were the first to witness to the resurrection. Whatever the reason for the omission, which is a matter of speculation, Paul has compiled what he considers to be a list of witnesses sufficient to verify that Jesus who died and was buried was indeed raised from the dead!

15:12-34 The reality of the resurrection of the dead

Paul now moves to the specific controversy in the Corinthian community, which becomes explicit in verse 12: some deny the resurrection of the dead. To counter this claim, Paul advances three arguments in verses 12-34. First, he exposes both the logical inconsistency of their claim in view of the testimony to the resurrection and the chain of absurd conclusions one would have to draw if one were to reason based on the Corinthians' premise (vv. 13-19). In verses 13-14, Paul lists each of these conclusions. To reinforce his point, he restates the same chain of conclusions in verses 15-17 but in the reverse order, adding that the Corinthians would still be in their sin (v. 17)! Moreover, the dead in Christ would simply have perished (v. 18). With this first argument Paul sets out the devastating consequences of the Corinthians' claim and, as a final reinforcement, notes how utterly sham is their hope and how pitiable they indeed are if there is no future resurrection (v. 19).

Paul's second argument (vv. 20-28) begins with the attested reality of Christ's resurrection (v. 20), based on which he draws out the key consequence of this central gospel conviction for believers: they, too, will be raised through Christ. Paul illustrates this fact in two ways. First, Christ is the "firstfruits." The ripening of the firstfruits signaled that the rest of the fruit would also ripen and would soon be ready for harvest. Paul metaphorically applies this idea to illustrate that Christ's own resurrection guarantees and heralds the resurrection of all believers (v. 20). Second, Christ is the antitype of Adam. Whereas through Adam death became the destiny of all, through Christ all believers are destined to life (vv. 21-22). Then, in language rooted in Jewish apocalyptic, Paul describes the events that will transpire at the Lord's second coming (vv. 23-28).

The resurrection of believers is a future event coinciding with Christ's second coming, not before. When the resurrection is completed, then comes the "end," that is, the fulfillment of God's salvific plan in Christ, which entails the subduing and destruction of all powers hostile to God and the establishment of God's reign. This work begun through Christ's death and resurrection will come to completion at his second coming. Every sovereignty, authority, and power (v. 24)—terms referring to hostile cosmic powers and perhaps more pointedly to the political leaders and corrupt structures of Roman Corinth—will be destroyed. Death is personified as the last enemy, the quintessential symbol of all resistance to God, since it is the lot of all those under the reign of sin (v. 26).

1 Corinthians 15

Christ must reign until he has subdued all these enemies and they are subjected to him. This idea is expressed in verses 25 and 27, where Paul alludes to and christologically reinterprets Psalm 8:7 and Psalm 110:1 to confirm the necessity of Christ's reign and his ultimate victory over all things, including death. While it is difficult to know whether by "him" in verse 27 Paul means Christ or God, the psalm allusions suggest that Paul intends that all is made subject to Christ through God, who is the One exempt from subjugation. Indeed, in the end Christ himself will be subjected to the One so that God may be all in all (v. 28).

In phases one and two of his argument against the Corinthian denial of the resurrection, Paul first showed the absurdity of their denial and then established the certainty of the future resurrection of all believers, which is guaranteed through Christ's own resurrection. In this third step (vv. 29-34), Paul marshals two *ad hominem* arguments to complete his case against the Corinthian position. Paul first alludes to a practice apparently common among the Corinthians, namely, vicarious baptism on behalf of the dead. Though such a practice is not attested elsewhere in the New Testament, Paul's reference here indicates that it was a practice in Corinth. He does not opine about the value of vicarious baptism or inform us about the extent of this practice at Corinth. In view of his overall argument, he simply insinuates that the practice is useless if there is no future resurrection of the dead. By practicing vicarious baptism while simultaneously denying the resurrection, the Corinthians simply demonstrate their own logical inconsistency.

Paul's second argument concerns suffering. He continuously puts his own life in jeopardy and suffers for the sake of the gospel (see, e.g., 2 Cor 4:8-11; 6:3-10; Acts 18:23-40). Why would he do this if there were no hope of future resurrection? But Paul does suffer hardship, and this attests to the truth of the resurrection. Otherwise, he says, with a dash of sarcasm, the only wisdom to live by is that of self-fulfillment, which characterizes life without hope. This wisdom is encapsulated in the maxim Paul cites in verse 32, which was associated with the Epicurean school of philosophy. For Paul, this is no wisdom, because it fails to reflect the central Christian conviction that believers are destined to life through Christ. Paul concludes with sharp commands to the Corinthians to come to their senses. Citing a popular maxim attributed to the Greek poet Menander (v. 33), Paul warns the whole Corinthian community to stay away from those who deny the resurrection of the body. Since Paul has just cited the useless wisdom of Greek philosophy in verse 32, it may be that he is warning the Corinthians against dangerous dabbling in Greek philosophical ideas that subvert the gospel. If the Corinthians do this, they are not unlike those who are ignorant of

God, that is, the pagans. Paul's concluding remark (v. 34c) sets recourse to pagan ideas on a par with recourse to pagan courts (see 6:5). Both are shameful!

15:35-49 The resurrection body

The two questions posed in verse 35 expose the basis of the Corinthians' qualms about the resurrection. They cannot understand how the dead are raised, nor can they imagine what a resurrected body will be like. In verses 35-49, Paul deals with the second question and leaves the other until verses 50-58. In his response to the question about the form the resurrection body will take, he employs a variety of analogies to argue that the resurrected body is a transformed spiritual body. Since a sown seed must die in order to become a full-grown plant, a fact that Paul presents as perfectly obvious to anyone capable of observing nature, the Corinthians are just plain fools to assume, as Paul implies they do, that a resurrected body is just a reanimated dead body (v. 36)!

Paul develops the seed analogy and through it establishes the crucial point that the sowing/fruition process is one that includes both transformation and continuity. The sown seed that must die does not come forth at harvest time as a reanimated seed; rather, it undergoes a radical transformation and continues its existence in a new and distinct body. Yet this body is necessarily organically linked to the seed because each seed transforms into a body peculiar to that seed (vv. 37-38). The mention of different kinds of seeds with different bodies leads to a new analogy in view of distinctions concerning flesh (v. 39), and finally to another analogy based on distinctions between terrestrial and celestial bodies, each with its own peculiar manifestation (vv. 40-41).

The application of the analogies set out in verses 36-41 now begins with Paul's statement, "So also is the resurrection of the dead" (v. 42). The contrast/continuity between sown seed and full-grown plant is still at the basis of the four new sets of contrasting pairs now introduced: corruptible/incorruptible (v. 42), dishonorable/glorious (v. 43), weak/powerful (v. 43b), natural body/spiritual body (v. 44). The human person will continue in embodied existence, but as the contrasts make clear, the new body will be incorruptible, glorious, constituted in power, and above all a spiritual body, which does not imply some vague, ethereal existence but rather a body animated by the Spirit of God.

A new analogy built on an Adam/Christ contrast is introduced in verses 45-49 to further the natural/spiritual body contrast set out in verses 42-44. Paul begins with the observation that the first man was gifted only with

1 Corinthians 15

physical, natural life (see Gen 2:7), whereas Christ was a life-giving spirit (v. 45). The one kind of body and existence that humans inherit from Adam precedes the other, spiritually animated existence that comes through Christ (v. 46). In and through Christ, the Corinthians will attain and live this completely transformed spiritual existence, but it is a future eschatological reality that must be awaited.

In view of the context, the contrast between "earthly" Adam and "heavenly" Christ (v. 47) should probably be understood as a restatement and reinforcement of the contrast already made between the natural life inherited through Adam versus the spiritual life inherited through Christ. Paul makes it clear in verse 48 that Christians are indebted to both the first and the last Adam. During their earthly existence, their likeness is to the earthly Adam; however, in their future eschatological existence in their resurrected bodies, believers will bear the likeness of Christ, whose resurrection is the guarantee of their own future resurrection. How will this happen? This first of the two questions with which Paul began this subsection at verse 35 is now taken up in the concluding section of chapter 15.

15:50-58 The resurrection event

Paul's last section begins with a bold declaration that, at first, seems to play right into the hands of the Corinthians. Part of their problem with the resurrection is that they cannot fathom how anything corruptible and corporeal squares with future spiritual existence. However, Paul is not sustaining their argument. Rather, by underscoring the incompatibility of future eschatological existence with present existence, Paul actually argues for the absolute necessity of the resurrection. Without it, one cannot participate in future eschatological existence! But how will it take place?

The answer is a mystery, an insight about God's preordained plans hidden from the world (see 2:7) that Paul now unfolds in charged apocalyptic language and imagery. As Paul writes, he considers the second coming of Christ imminent. He and others ("we") who will not have died at the second coming, along with all those who are already dead in Christ, will be changed and resurrected into God-given spiritual bodies. Paul uses typical apocalyptic motifs and images (e.g., suddenness, the sound of the trumpet, awakening of the dead) to describe the end-time resurrection scenario. With the exception of the description of the Lord's arrival, Paul's revelation here is comparable to that found in 1 Thessalonians 4:13-18, the only other place in his writings where a revelation of this kind is unfolded.

In verses 53-54, Paul introduces a new metaphor to ensure that the Corinthians understand that the body will not be discarded or annihilated at death to give way to the eternal existence of the soul alone. He insists that the corruptible/mortal body will clothe itself in incorruptibility/immortality. Hence resurrected life will still be an embodied existence, but our flawed natural bodies will undergo a total transformation. When this occurs, the promise of victory over sin and death will have been fulfilled, not because of any human merit but because of what God has done in Christ (vv. 55-57).

Paul's concluding exhortation sounds rather general and disconnected from the whole preceding argument. However, it actually follows from the argument. The reality of the resurrection, which Paul has just argued in fifty-seven verses, is, in the final analysis, that which sustains Christians in their faith and their work of living and spreading the gospel. With this surety, neither their hope, faith, or labor is in vain!

Paul's argument in chapter 15 is not a self-contained theological treatise on the reality of the resurrection but rather the culmination of all the preceding arguments in 1 Corinthians. Throughout this letter Paul has challenged the community to eschew behavior motivated by the ideas, values, and structures of pagan Corinth. As he now makes eminently clear in chapter 15, it is the reality of Christ's resurrection and the prospect of their own that constitute the moral compass that must guide and shape the Corinthians' lives. Their behavior must be compatible with the new moral order whose inauguration begins in the mystery of Jesus' death and resurrection and culminates in the mystery of their own resurrection, when God's purposes in history will be fully realized. The fact of the resurrection requires a radical reorientation of the lives of all believers, in the body, in the present, in anticipation of the future resurrection.

CONCLUSION

1 Corinthians 16:1-24

With the major problems and issues of the Corinthian community now addressed, culminating in the extended discussion of the resurrection, Paul now brings up three final matters: the collection for the saints, his travel plans, and Apollos. Each is briefly treated in the first half of this chapter (vv. 1-12). In the second half of chapter 16, following the ancient letter form, Paul formally concludes this letter with a few exhortations and greetings typical of his own letter closings (13:23). In both verses 1 and 12, Paul begins with the formula "Now in regard to," first used at 7:1, which may indicate that his comments on the collection (vv. 1-4) and Apollos (v. 12) are responses to questions posed by the Corinthians in their letter to Paul.

1 Corinthians 16

16:1-12 The collection, Paul's travel plans, Apollos

Background information about this collection and the reason for it are not provided here. Paul assumes that the Corinthians know about this collection for the saints, meaning the Jerusalem community, as is clear from verse 3. Elsewhere, at Galatians 2:1-10, Paul recounts a visit to Jerusalem and his meeting with the church's leaders. After sanctioning his mission to the Gentiles, the leaders asked Paul to remember the poor, presumably of the Jerusalem community, which he said he was eager to do (v. 10). Thus the contribution for Jerusalem's poor, which Paul urged on all his Gentile communities, was apparently Paul's way of honoring that request. Writing a few years later in his letter to the Romans, he explains why the Gentile Christians ought to make this contribution. It is a debt owed by them to Jewish Christians, through whom they have become beneficiaries of Israel's spiritual blessings. Hence Jewish Christians should share in and benefit from the material blessings of Gentile believers (see Rom 15:27).

In addition to this express purpose, Paul may have viewed the collection as a way to foster unity between Gentile and Jewish Christians and to develop within the communities he founded a sense of benevolent regard for all believers everywhere. Paul's instructions, in line with those given in Galatia and presumably in Macedonia (see 2 Cor 8), underscore the fact that the collection was a part of Paul's missionary practice and not an imposition on this one community. At this time there was obviously no centralized system of collection in Corinth. However, no one was exempt from putting money aside privately and on a regular weekly basis, as clear from verse 2. Paul expects all collecting to be completed before his arrival, at which point the funds would be entrusted to the community's own appointees, whom Paul would provide with letters of recommendation, a common practice at the time to ensure the status of the envoys (see 2 Cor 8:16-24). Paul's final remark reveals his hesitancy to go to Jerusalem, although he apparently did go, bringing funds from Macedonia and the province of Achaia, of which Corinth was capital (see Rom 15:26).

In verse 5 Paul switches to a discussion of his travel plans. He assures the Corinthians that he will return to them, but not right away. He intends to stay in Ephesus, whence he writes this letter, to capitalize on evangelizing opportunities, notwithstanding opposition (vv. 8-9). The mention of Pentecost, a Jewish feast celebrated in late spring, places Paul's departure from Ephesus for the region of Macedonia in early summer. Only after visiting the communities of Macedonia, presumably at Philippi and Thessalonica, would Paul come down to Corinth to stay with them at some length, perhaps the entire winter (vv. 5-6).

1 Corinthians 16

After mentioning his own plans, Paul speaks of Timothy, who is apparently being dispatched by Paul to Corinth (see 4:17). Timothy's youth (see 1 Tim 4:12) and perhaps inexperience probably explain Paul's reminders to the community about how Timothy should be treated.

Paul concludes this first half of chapter 16 with the mention of Apollos, whom the Corinthians hoped would return to Corinth (v. 12). Some claim that verse 12 belies a real rivalry between Apollos and Paul and interpret Paul's comments as an attempt to dispel suspicions that he was obstructing Apollos's return out of jealousy. However, in view of Paul's description of the collaborative character of his relationship with Apollos at 3:5-9, it seems reasonable to take verse 12 at face value as an indication that there was no rivalry between the two co-workers. Whether Apollos ever did return to Corinth is not known.

16:13-23 Concluding exhortations and greetings

With five terse exhortations, Paul begins the formal conclusion to 1 Corinthians. As he does elsewhere (e.g., 1 Thess 5:6; Rom 13:11-14), he exhorts the Corinthians to "be on guard," a phrase freighted with eschatological significance. The day of judgment is imminent, and eschatological urgency is the framework of believers' lives. Therefore, believers must be on guard for the arrival of the day of judgment and vigilant over their conduct as they await the second coming. "Be courageous" and "be strong" are rather general appeals, while the remaining two exhortations appear to be directed specifically to the Corinthian situation. By denying the resurrection, some were straying from the faith, in which, Paul now exhorts them to stand firm. The final exhortation that every "act should be done with love" recalls not only chapter 13 but the whole ethic of love and concern for others, rooted in the example of Christ, which Paul has sought to inculcate through his responses in 1 Corinthians.

After these brief exhortations, Paul singles out for praise some model members of the community who have used their gifts to serve the other members of the community (v. 15). He then exhorts the community to be "subordinate" to them (v. 16). This deference is not owed in view of any hierarchical office those praised occupy within the community. Rather, it is the witness of their lives spent in service to others that calls forth the community's respect and recognition (v. 18).

The passing on of greetings (vv. 19-20) is part of Paul's strategy to maintain communication between the churches and to reinforce the sense that all believers everywhere are joined in one new family of faith. Prisca and Aquila, who had arrived in Corinth shortly before Paul and offered him work (see Acts 18:1-3), are now living in Ephesus and are apparently leaders within the local church there. The greetings include a kiss, a public sign of the unity and reconciliation that existed among community members. The addition of the word "holy" (v. 20) need not imply that Paul has in mind here some type of greeting reserved for the liturgy.

Paul adds a postscript in his own handwriting, unusual with regard to ancient letter writing conventions and something Paul did only occasionally (see Gal 6:11-18), presumably to ensure his personal concern. Even more unusual in these final verses is the inclusion of a conditional curse (v. 22), which serves to reinforce the series of strict warnings Paul has already enunciated in this letter. The curse is followed by a prayer, *Marana tha*, "Come, our Lord," and then a typical grace benediction. Paul concludes with an assertion of personal love for the community, which is unique to this letter. This expression of love allows Paul to recall one of the letter's major themes and reinforce his own *ethos* as a loving, caring father, a powerful argument indeed for why the community should heed his advice, admonitions, and appeals.

The Second Letter to the Corinthians

Maria A. Pascuzzi

INTRODUCTION

Occasion and purpose

When we turn to 2 Corinthians, it is evident that the solid relationship between Paul and the Corinthian community, presupposed in 1 Corinthians, is no longer intact. Rather, the community's trust in Paul has eroded, and their relationship is seriously strained. Paul now finds himself in a defensive position, reflected in the letter's rhetoric, which is largely apologetic, struggling to win back the trust and esteem of the community.

Since there is no independent account of what precipitated this crisis and elicited 2 Corinthians, the situation must be reconstructed. A likely scenario based on the text evidence runs as follows: Paul had promised to return to Corinth for a lengthy visit after concluding his ministry in Ephesus and then visiting Macedonia (1 Cor 16:5-7) but did not do as promised. Rather, sometime after sending 1 Corinthians, he apparently changed his mind, deciding to stop at Corinth once on his way to Macedonia and again on his return from Macedonia, after which he would bring the Corinthians' collection for the poor to Jerusalem (2 Cor 1:15).

Paul did not follow through on these plans either. Evidently, he learned that the troubles in the Corinthian community had escalated, even though he had sent Timothy (1 Cor 4:17) and dispatched 1 Corinthians to deal with key problems. This troublesome situation was further exacerbated when rival missionaries arrived in Corinth. They discredited Paul and instigated a crisis between the community and him (2 Cor 11:4). To remedy the situation, Paul made an unscheduled, "pain[ful]" visit to Corinth, where he was publicly humiliated (2:5). Once back in Ephesus, he wrote the now lost tearful letter (2:4) and sent it to the community via Titus. Anxious to hear the community's reaction to this severe letter, Paul left Troas and met up with Titus in Macedonia (2:12-13). Titus reported that many in the community had realigned themselves with Paul (7:5-16), although doubts lingered about his trustworthiness, since he had changed plans and failed to make the promised visit (1:12–2:4). Apparently, others remained under the influence of the intruders, allied with them against Paul. In response to this situation, Paul composed 2 Corinthians.

Second Corinthians is our only source of information about the intruders. Paul's counter brag at 11:22, that he is as much a Hebrew and Israelite as the intruders, indicates that he regards them as Jewish Christians. Apart from this, Paul says only that they are "false apostles" (11:13) who preach a gospel different from his (11:4-5). They have "letters of recommendation" (3:1) and are supported by the community (11:7-12). They evidently boast about their rhetorical skills and knowledge (10:10; 11:6), appealing to their supernatural power (12:12) and visions (12:1) as proof of the superiority of their gospel and ministry.

Unfortunately, this information is too general, and probably too biased, to allow for a definite identification of the intruders. Though scholarly speculation abounds, perhaps the most that can be safely stated is that the intruders were Jewish Christians. Paul considers them adversaries and holds them responsible for having driven a wedge between himself and the community. As he tells it, they alleged that he was a frail and gutless preacher, forceful only on paper (10:1-18), deficient in speech (11:6), and without "letters of recommendation" (3:1-3). They apparently cited Paul's refusal of Corinthian financial support as testimony that he was no true apostle (11:7) and raised the suspicion that he was deceitfully intending to profit from the collection he promoted (12:12-16). Paul's failure to demonstrate the power of his message with miracles and signs and his lack of ecstatic visions (12:1-10) were also apparently evinced as confirmation of his inferior status.

The intruders were clearly attempting to dismantle Paul's apostolic authority and invalidate his ministry. They probably found a receptive audience among the spiritual elitists in the community, whose captivation with eloquent speech and boasting in ecstatic gifts and knowledge had already been a source of discord at Corinth (see 1 Cor 8–14). Although Paul reserves his most direct and vehement attack on the intruders until chapters 10–13, they are in the background of his argument throughout the letter.

The unity of 2 Corinthians

Scholars who claim that 2 Corinthians is a composite of letters or letter portions usually cite three blocks of text as evidence to support this claim: (1) 6:14–7:1; (2) chapters 8–9; and (3) chapters 10–13. They argue that these text blocks differ so significantly from their immediate literary context in either content or tone that they must have been once-independent letters

The Second Letter to the Corinthians

or pieces of letters occasioned by separate circumstances. Some would even argue that chapters 8 and 9 were each originally separate letters. Additionally, some maintain that at 2:13 Paul unexpectedly breaks his narrative, resuming it at 7:5. They point to the intervening material, that is, 2:14–7:4, as further evidence that 2 Corinthians is a composite. In view of these arguments, 2 Corinthians could be a combination of anywhere from two (chs. 1–9 and 10–13) to six letters or letter fragments.

However, the case for the composite nature of 2 Corinthians may not be as strong as it seems. First of all, the manuscript evidence supports the letter's compositional integrity. Second, as our study of 1 Corinthians has shown, digressions are not always signs of later insertions, nor does change of tone or topic necessarily signal a new letter or letter fragment. Third, when Paul's rhetorical strategy is considered, 2 Corinthians appears less disjointed and incoherent than is insisted by those who divide it.

Beyond these three observations, the fact that there is no scholarly agreement on the number of separate letters allegedly contained within 2 Corinthians is itself telling. Moreover, those who insist on dividing the letter are obliged to answer two crucial questions: What circumstances occasioned the writing of each presumably independent letter, and why were they stitched together to form canonical 2 Corinthians? So far the answers have not been compelling enough to warrant abandoning attempts to understand this letter as a coherent whole.

In its final canonical form, 2 Corinthians displays the typical features of an ancient letter. It has an opening section complete with name of sender, addressees and a greeting (1:1-2), and a blessing of God in place of the usual thanksgiving (1:3-11). The body of the letter extends from 1:12 through 13:10, after which there is a formal conclusion (13:11-13), with exhortations, greetings, and a benediction typical of Paul's endings of his letters.

From a rhetorical perspective, 2 Corinthians can be considered a defense speech (forensic rhetoric) within which Paul includes one hortatory unit concerning the collection (chs. 8–9). After the opening (1:1-11), Paul attempts to dispel doubts about his sincerity by clarifying the motives behind his change in travel plans and to showcase his good character in order to gain the community's good will (1:12–2:16). Then he goes to the heart of the matter—the defense of his ministry, which has come under attack. After dissociating himself from charlatans who peddle God's word (2:17), Paul follows with a series of arguments that underscore the validity of his ministry and his apostolic authenticity (3:1–7:16). Having worked to win back the community's support and esteem, he feels confident enough to solicit the community with regard to the collection for the saints, a matter of great concern to him (chs. 8–9). Then he directly confronts those whom he holds responsible for exacerbating matters and instigating the crisis at Corinth. In four stinging chapters, Paul attacks the intruders, unfavorably comparing their ministry and motives to his own to show that they, not he, are the real charlatans (2 Cor 10–13:10). After this climactic counterattack, there follows a standard epistolary conclusion (13:11-13).

Key theological ideas

The First Letter to the Corinthians focused on various colorful problems pertaining to life in the community and community life in relation to the world outside. In contrast, 2 Corinthians focuses almost exclusively on the issue of legitimate Christian apostleship and the true character of ministry in the service of the gospel. Paul's understanding of apostleship is rooted in his theology of the gospel, specifically in the dialectic between weakness and power (see 1 Cor 1:18-31), which he applies to his own life and ministry. In his abundant suffering, Paul shares in the sufferings of Christ (2 Cor 1:5), and in his own afflicted body he carries about the dying of Jesus (4:10-11). These sufferings do not undermine his apostolic legitimacy but authenticate it, since it is precisely through weakness and suffering that God's divine power to save is made manifest (4:7). That is why Paul never attempts to overcome his weakness or shrink from suffering; rather, he boasts in it (see 11:30; 12:5), since it indisputably distinguishes him as a true minister of the glorious new covenant in Christ (2:14) through whom God has reconciled the world, inaugurating the new creation (5:11-21). In addition to his suffering, Paul also points to his sincerity (2:17), his willingness to forgive (2:10), his selfless concern for the Corinthians (12:11-18), and his moral integrity (8:20-21). All are a piece of the cruciform existence that characterizes the apostle's life and distinguishes and authenticates Paul as a true minister of the gospel.

This same cruciform existence must be the hallmark of every Christian life. Paul does not recommend weakness, suffering, death, or poverty to the Corinthians as ends in themselves (see 1:3-6; 4:10-12; 8:8-15). Rather, he insists that receptivity to the gospel message, the story of God's power and glory paradoxically manifested in Christ crucified, is demonstrated in one's acceptance of suffering, one's glorying in weakness, and one's selfless service to others for the sake of Christ, whose love constrains us to live no longer for ourselves (2 Cor 5:14-15).

OUTLINE OF SECOND CORINTHIANS

1:1-1	***Introduction***
1:1-2	Greeting
1:3-11	Blessing
1:12–2:16	***Paul's True Motives and Character***
1:12-14	Paul is sincere and reliable
1:15–2:4	The motives for Paul's change in travel plans
2:5-11	The fate of the offender
2:12-16	A positive outcome
2:17–7:16	***Paul Defends His Ministry***
2:17–4:6	Ministers of a new covenant
4:7–5:10	A ministry of affliction
5:11–6:10	A ministry of reconciliation
6:11-13	A personal appeal to the Corinthians
6:14–7:1	A call to holiness
7:2-4	Paul resumes his appeal
7:5-16	Paul's complete confidence in the Corinthians
8:1–9:15	***The Collection for Jerusalem***
8:1-8	The example of the Macedonians
8:9-15	Motives for giving
8:16–9:5	Titus, his collaborators, and the collection drive at Corinth
9:6-15	The rewards of giving
10:1–13:10	***Paul's Counterattack on the Intruders***
10:1-18	Paul refutes his opponents' accusations
10:1-11	Spiritual weapons
10:12-18	Paul boasts in his own labors
11:1–12:10	The "fool's speech"
11:1-21a	A "little foolishness"
11:21b–12:10	Paul's foolish boasting
12:11-21	Epilogue and transition
13:1-10	Final warnings
13:11-13	***Epistolary Conclusion***

2 Corinthians 1

COMMENTARY

INTRODUCTION

2 Corinthians 1:1-11

1:1-2 Greeting

Paul's self-identification as an apostle of Christ Jesus by God's will underscores the authoritative basis of his ministry, which is the result of God's initiative. Timothy, who had evangelized with Paul at Corinth (1:19), is mentioned as co-sender of this letter. Whether this implies co-author is not certain. The letter is addressed to the "church of God . . . in Corinth." The addition of "with all the holy ones throughout Achaia" allows Paul to accent universality, as he did at 1 Corinthians 1:2. Given the Corinthians' behavior, the designation "holy ones" seems ill-fit. However, this is their vocation (1 Cor 1:2), of which Paul again reminds them. The salutation, where Paul typically combines Greek *charis* (grace) and Hebrew *shalom* (peace), expresses his understanding of God's generous gifting of humanity with and through Christ and the well being or *shalom* that results.

1:3-11 Blessing

Paul begins with a typical Jewish benediction (vv. 3-4), blessing God who graciously comforts him in all his afflictions. Paul turns this experience into an opportunity to comfort others, becoming the conduit of God's comfort for those in need. Though the blessing proper does not extend beyond these two verses, two key terms, "affliction" and "encouragement" (Greek: *paraklēsis*, also rendered "encouragement" or "consolation") are repeated in verses 5-7. Here the focus is on Paul's relationship with the community, and the general notion of affliction is now subsumed under Christ's sufferings. As co-participants in Christ's sufferings, Paul and the community are bound to each other. Although Paul's share of Christ's suffering is "overflowing" (v. 5), he accepts this in view of its positive benefit for other Christians who must also endure suffering.

In verses 8-11, Paul concludes by appealing to the Corinthians for their prayers, reminding them of sufferings he endured in Asia, which left him so despairing that he had resigned himself to death. Beyond speculation that Paul here alludes to some experience in Ephesus (see, e.g., 1 Cor 15:32; Acts 19:23-40), it is impossible to know, based on the scant text information, to what traumatic experience he refers. Nonetheless, Paul makes clear that the experience did not nullify his faith. Rather, it resulted in his complete reliance on God and a more profound faith that, in the future, God would rescue him from death through the resurrection.

Why Paul begins with this blessing of God and emphasis on his suffering needs to be considered within the context of the whole argument he unfolds in this letter. As noted, the rival apostles had apparently cited Paul's suffering and weakness as evidence of his inferiority. Rather than deny his suffering, Paul subverts this criticism by identifying his suffering as a participation in the sufferings of Christ. Paul is not incapacitated by it; on the contrary, his suffering enables him to act as an agent of comfort to community members in their time of affliction. Suffering, the common lot of Paul and the community, cannot be a source of alienation between them, since their co-participation in Christ's suffering bonds them further to each other. Moreover, suffering has brought Paul to a more complete reliance on God and has increased his hope in God. What could be wrong with the apostle's suffering? Clearly, nothing!

It is important to underscore that Paul does not promote suffering as an absolute good but values his suffering insofar as it serves his ministry. Indeed, it is in Paul's "overflowing" suffering, identified with Christ's suffering, that God's saving grace overflows and not, as the rivals would have the Corinthians believe, in demonstrations of power! Thus suffering cannot be discounted as a mere sign of weakness, and the Corinthians, far from taking offense at Paul's suffering, should bless God too! They should see in it the degree to which God is at work in Paul and find in his suffering both a source of comfort and union between themselves and their apostle, whose ministry they are called to share and support through prayer (v. 11).

PAUL'S TRUE MOTIVES AND CHARACTER

2 Corinthians 1:12–2:16

Circumscribed within the accusations brought against Paul by the outsiders and the larger controversy they have instigated is the community's own questioning of Paul's sincerity in view of his apparent failure to keep his word and visit them. If not addressed, this issue risks being magnified by the larger controversy. Therefore, before Paul tackles the major bone of contention raised by the intruders, that is, the legitimacy of his apostleship (v. 17), he first deals with this issue to make sure he has the community on his side. Paul begins by boasting of his sincerity especially toward the community (1:12-14). After showing that he has legitimate motives for foregoing his promised visit (1:15–2:4), Paul returns to the fate of the offender (2:5-11) before giving thanks for the positive outcome to this particular crisis and

2 Corinthians 1

posing a final question that provides the opening for Paul to defend his ministry before the Corinthian community (2:12-16).

1:12-14 Paul is sincere and reliable

In verses 12-14 Paul transitions from the opening blessing but keeps the focus on the mutually beneficial relationship between himself and the community, boasting of his candid and sincere conduct "especially toward you"(v. 12). Paul is certain of this because what he says and writes he does by the "grace of God," that is, as one divinely commissioned to reveal God's wisdom in a completely intelligible way (v. 13). Not only can the Corinthians put away their doubts, but they can enjoy with Paul a relationship of mutual understanding and pride that will grow until "the day of [our] Lord Jesus" (v. 14). The benefit to the community accruing from Paul's sincere and candid preaching of the gospel justifies Paul's boasting and the community's boasting in him. This clearly distinguishes Paul from the false preachers, whose ministry is a vehicle for self-promotion.

1:15–2:4 The motives for Paul's change in travel plans

At issue here is Paul's failure to go forward with his planned double visit to Corinth (v. 16). He had not followed through on previously announced travel plans (1 Cor 16:5) nor on his new modified plans. The Corinthians are understandably irked and have begun to wonder whether Paul can be trusted.

In response, Paul offers two reasons for his change of plans. The first is unfolded in verses 15-22, where Paul begins with the positive statement that the purpose of the visit was to be of benefit (a double favor) to the community (v. 15), something with which the Corinthians presumably agree. Then in verse 17 Paul poses two questions, to which some Corinthians were likely to respond yes! Yes, you did act lightly! Yes, you are a vacillator, saying yes one day and no the next day! But Paul insists on his trustworthiness, which is guaranteed in view of two certainties: God's faithfulness (v. 18) and the constancy of Jesus (vv. 19-20). If Paul is commissioned by God who is faithful to preach the gospel of the Son of God who is ever constant, then Paul, too, must be trustworthy. Thus, the source of Paul's commission and the very commission with which he is entrusted both demand and attest to his own constancy and not simply with regard to his travel plans. The Corinthians should have no problem agreeing with this, since, as Paul reminds them, when they say "Amen," a reference to a liturgical formula, they put their faith in Christ in whom all the promises of God are fulfilled and thereby ultimately express their faith in the constancy of God.

Paul presents the second motive for his change of travel plans in 1:23–2:4. Not only is Paul constant, he is also pastorally concerned for the community with which he is bound in Christ through his apostolic commissioning (v. 21). Since his work is to advance the community's joy (1:24), and they his, the Corinthians should realize that Paul had their best interests at heart when he decided to forego another potentially painful visit (2:1). Instead, Paul substituted the planned visit with a letter, (the now lost "painful" or "tearful" letter), the purpose of which was to express his "abundant love" for the community (2:4).

2:5-11 The fate of the offender

The disclosure of the second motive brings Paul back to the painful visit and the fate of the one offending him (2:5-11). Most scholars assume that when Paul made his unscheduled visit to Corinth to address the crisis, some community member publicly challenged his authority. The fact that Paul reminds the Corinthians that this act of effrontery was not simply a cause of personal pain but an offense against the whole body of believers at Corinth (v. 5) may indicate that some in the community did not see it this way at all. However, "the majority" apparently did and acted to discipline the offender (v. 6).

Although no details about the disciplinary action are disclosed, Paul interprets the action as a demonstration that the community is "obedient in everything" (v. 9) and now asks that they forgive the offender (vv. 7-8). Neither the offender's identity nor the exact nature of the offense is mentioned. Attempts to identify the offender here with the community member censured for immorality (see 1 Cor 5:1-13) have failed to convince for a number of reasons. For example, Paul's approach to the offender here is quite lenient in comparison with his severe posture toward the offender of 1 Corinthians 5. Moreover, the roles attributed to Satan in each situation are substantially different. At 1 Corinthians 5:5, Satan was to destroy the offender's flesh. Here at 2:11, Satan is a potential threat to the community if the offender is not forgiven. Since Paul elsewhere associates the false apostles with Satan (11:13-14), his concern here may be that the intruders/Satan will seize upon this situation to sow further discord within the community and between the community and Paul; hence Paul's recommendation to forgive and restore the offender to fellowship.

2:12-16 A positive outcome

Paul now recalls how he had come to hear that the majority of Corinthians did the right thing and disciplined the offender (vv. 12-13). Having

2 Corinthians 2

decided to send Titus to Corinth with the tearful letter, Paul went on to Troas to evangelize. While there, he was so distracted by his concern over the unfolding of events in Corinth that he aborted his evangelizing mission and went to Macedonia to catch Titus as he was returning from Corinth. Paul's relief at the positive outcome and his joy that the gospel was being advanced led him to express words of thanks to God (v. 14).

The metaphoric language introduced here touches on Paul's apostolic self-understanding, his role and his adequacy to perform that role, which he will defend at length beginning in 2:17. The first metaphor is drawn from the practice of triumphal processions in which conquering generals paraded their captives (v. 14). Here Paul's apostolic self-understanding emerges as he metaphorically presents himself as a captive paraded about by the victor, God. Paul, the itinerant missionary, is not at liberty to be self-directing (see 1 Cor 9:16-17). Rather, as a captive, dragged about by God, he exudes "the odor of the knowledge" of God in every place (2:14). The imagery of "odor" may derive from Sirach 24:15, where God's wisdom is referred to as a scent or fragrance. If so, then Paul presents himself as the shamed and afflicted apostle/captive who emanates God's odor/wisdom. Since Christ is the wisdom and, therefore, the true aroma of God, the apostles who proclaim Christ are indeed the "aroma of Christ" (v. 15) exuding the message of Christ crucified, God's wisdom. As one bound to fulfill this role, Paul acknowledges its serious implications. To some, through faith, what the apostle secretes will be the scent of salvation leading to life; to others, it is the odor of death leading to destruction (see 1 Cor 1:18). Paul's concluding question, "Who is qualified for this?" underscores how crucial the ministry of the gospel is. The question remains unanswered here, but the implication is clear. No one is fit for the task, save whomever God captures and equips to execute it.

PAUL DEFENDS HIS MINISTRY

2 Corinthians 2:17– 7:16

So far Paul has attempted to allay doubts about his reliability, reestablish his good character, and regain the community's good will. All this paves the way for his engagement with the major point of controversy: the validity and authenticity of his ministry. Though the controversy is ostensibly between Paul and the community, lurking in the background of his comments are the intruders. Their arrival and style of ministry have precipitated the crisis, since Paul is being unfavorably compared with them.

Paul begins by refuting a double charge and launches the first step of his defense, which is built around the contrast between his and Moses' ministry (2:17– 4:6). Having established the superiority of the ministry of glory with which he is entrusted, Paul argues that this ministry is characterized by afflictions that, paradoxically, constitute the credentials of a true apostle (4:7–5:10). He continues the characterization of his ministry as one of reconciliation (5:11–6:10), which climaxes with a personal appeal to the Corinthians (6:11-13). At this point Paul introduces a brief digression (6:14–7:1) before resuming his appeal (7:2-4), after which he expresses his complete confidence in the community (7:5-16).

2:17–4:6 Ministers of a new covenant

Based on his opening statements, it appears that two charges were laid against Paul, both relating to the validity of his ministry: one concerned his refusal of financial support (2:17); the other, letters of recommendation (3:1). As already discussed, the financing of teachers and preachers by well-to-do patrons was customary in Paul's day. Though Paul accepted financial patronage from some congregations (see Phil 4:16; 2 Cor 11:9), his refusal of Corinthian support (1 Cor 9:1-18) galled this community. Besides suspecting Paul of hypocrisy, the Corinthians were evidently not convinced by his argument that the nature of the gospel demanded that it be preached gratis (1 Cor 9:15-18). They operated with the notion that only paid ministers were quality ministers who could be expected to give their all (see 12:13 and 11:7-12). To make matters worse, Paul lacked "letters of recommendation." In antiquity, great value was placed on the testimony of authoritative figures who vouched for others' credentials through letters. Paul knew the importance of this social convention and, when necessary, could invoke his own authority to recommend others (see Rom 16:1 and 1 Cor 16:3).

In response to the first charge, Paul berates financed ministers as hucksters who "trade on the word of God" (2:17). He dissociates from them, contrasting their profit-driven ministry with his own, which is carried on in sincerity, to which God witnesses. For Paul, this is sufficient. As for letters of recommendation, here, too, Paul distinguishes himself from "others." That he would need to provide such credentials "again" is preposterous, as his question underscores (3:1), precisely because his relationship with this community, metaphorically referred to as a letter that Paul carries about in his heart for all to read, testifies to the authenticity of his ministry. This letter/relationship owes its origin to Christ and pertains to the new covenant, powered by the Spirit and written on hearts of flesh (see Jer 31:33; Ezek 11:19; 36:26), of which Paul is a minister. He would not be adequate to the task except that God has qualified him for it; hence he takes no credit—perhaps in contrast to "some others"—for the success of his ministry, which is "not of letter but of spirit" (3:6).

The contrast introduced here is not between a spiritual reading of the Old Testament versus a literal one, as often assumed, but between two possible principles by which the new covenant is to be animated: the Mosaic law, which drove the old covenant but brought death, or the Spirit who gives life (v. 6b). This contrast, in which the law is deprecated and by extension the entire old covenant, raises questions about God's purposes in giving the law, which Paul does not pursue here. Instead, he goes forward with the old/new antithesis by contrasting his ministry with that of Moses. The contrast builds on Paul's interpretation of Exodus 34:1-4, 29-35, the account of Moses' ascent to Sinai to receive the stone tablets on which the law was engraved. A key element in this account, taken up by Paul in verses 7-11, is the glory of the Lord reflected on the face of Moses, which became so resplendent as a result of his encounter with the Lord that the Israelites could not stare at Moses unless his face was veiled. In light of this, Paul reasons that if the Mosaic covenant, pejoratively termed the "ministry of death," was attended by such glory, albeit a glory destined to fade, then the ministry of the Spirit, a ministry of righteousness destined to endure, must be all the more glorious. Paul further insists that the greater glory of the new covenant has nullified whatever glory once attended the old covenant.

Confirmed in this hope, Paul contrasts his ministry, characterized by openness, with that of Moses, characterized by covertness, as symbolized by the veil. Paul claims that Moses donned this veil to keep the Israelites from acknowledging the abrogation of this whole old covenant, whose vanishing glory was visible on his face (vv. 12-13). Paul's aim here is not to charge Moses with deception but, as is clear from verse 14, where the veil becomes a metaphor for Israel's blindness, to impugn the Israelites for their hardened minds. Paul then transfers his remarks about historical Israel to his Jewish contemporaries, hardened still. Though Paul condemns them for failing to acknowledge that the old covenant is abrogated through Christ, he also appeals to them to "turn to" (convert to) the Lord, identified with the eschatological Spirit of freedom, which all believers experience (cf. Rom 8:2). Conversion removes the veil.

In verse 18, Paul reprises the key elements that have been part of his argument so far: veil, face, glory. Implicit in this verse is the contrast between the superior experience of all believers who pass "from glory to glory" and are progressively transformed into the image of God and the vanishing glory of Moses and the Mosaic covenant. In short, Paul has argued that what the Spirit accomplishes in believers through the ministry of the Spirit, of which he is a qualified minister, eclipses the ministry of Moses, a ministry of law carved in stone, which was impotent to save. Though harsh in his denigration of the law and law-based ministry, Paul's views here are consistent with those he expresses elsewhere, especially in Galatians and Romans. It has been suggested that Paul's rivals in Corinth were Jewish Christians who insisted on the continuing validity of the law. Whether they in fact espoused this position is not certain. What is certain is that here Paul seems to refute such a view.

Paul wraps up this first phase of his argument by reaffirming that his ministry has its origin in God's mercy (4:1-6). Though the stakes attached to this ministry of glory are high (see 2:15-16), he is not discouraged. On the contrary, commissioned and qualified by God, he is a confident minister of the gospel. He has no need to resort to deception and cunning, practices he renounces as contrary to the gospel; rather, he ministers in openness and honesty, not compromising the truth of the word of God. This truthful manner of ministry, configured to the truth of the gospel, validates Paul's ministry and justifies his self-commendation.

Paul's admission that his gospel appears veiled to some (4:3) raises the possibility that his detractors accused him of being less transparent and sincere than he claimed. However, Paul denies that his preaching style leads to incomprehension. If some fail to perceive the light of the gospel, it is because the "god of this age" (Satan; 4:4) has blinded them. Paul knows himself to be above reproach in this matter because he preaches only Jesus Christ, in whom the light of the knowledge of the glory of God is revealed.

4:7–5:10 A ministry of affliction

In this second phase of his defense, Paul reflects on the paradoxical nature of authentic Christian ministry. Logically, the treasure, that is, this great ministry of glory, ought to be entrusted to a robust and resilient minister equal to the task. But it has been entrusted to Paul, weak and fragile as a common clay jar with a short shelf life. This paradoxical arrangement is not accidental but essential. Paul's weakness attests that apostolic ministry is powered by God and not the apostle, a fact borne out in the four antitheses set out in verses 8-9. In the course of his ministry, Paul survived potentially devastating adversities, not by the dint of his own inner resources but by the power of God. Paul's sufferings and weakness also attest to his union with Christ, whose suffering and death, Paul firmly believes, are being replicated in his own life of suffering and always with the paradoxical result that life triumphs.

This is evidenced among the Corinthians themselves. Life is at work in them, while, and precisely because, death is at work in Paul (vv. 10-12). However much Paul's suffering demonstrates God's power, affirms his union with Christ, and is the source of life for others—all good things—what ultimately makes his suffering bearable is the knowledge that he and all believers will be raised and brought into the presence of God and Christ. This certainty is rooted in the belief Paul shares with the Corinthians that God who raised Jesus will also raise them (vv. 13-14). Verse 15 expands the thought of verse 12. Everything Paul suffers is for the community, so that the life that more and more of them come to experience will occasion praise and thanks to God.

Paul's firm hope in the resurrection and his present lived experience of inner renewal, even while his body is consumed by the rigors of ministry, bring him to affirm again, "we are not discouraged" (4:16; see also 4:1). In verse 17, Paul introduces a present/future contrast as he considers his sufferings in the context of the coming glory. By comparison with that future glory, eternal and weighty, Paul's suffering is light and momentary, further qualified in verse 18, as visible and transitory. Hence his focus must not be on his present suffering but on what is invisible and everlasting.

The mention of eternal glory leads Paul to reflect on his future destiny beginning at 5:1. This destiny concerns all believers, who are included in the "we." Paul's greatest desire is to be with the Lord permanently, which he speaks of as being at "home" (5:8). At present, he says, our "earthly dwelling," that is, the physical body, is a tent, a temporary home. When death destroys it "we have" (v. 1), Paul declares with certainty, a more permanent building, a spiritual or resurrection body awaiting us in heaven.

But how do believers exist between death and resurrection? For Paul, a disembodied existence, here negatively represented in the terms "naked" and "unclothed" (vv. 3, 4) was unthinkable. Though he considers the physical body/tent a weight (v. 4), Paul does not want the disembodied, "unclothed" state that death effects, which can reasonably be taken to mean he does not want to die. Instead, he prefers that his body be "further clothed" (v. 4), in other words, progressively transformed until the mortal is swallowed up by life (see also 1 Cor 15:53-54). The Spirit is already enabling this progressive transformation from death to life (see 3:15; 4:16), guaranteeing (see 1:21-22) God's future and complete transformation of what is mortal. Until then, Paul acknowledges that the body is an obstacle to complete and permanent union with the Lord, who is known now through faith and not by sight in that direct face-to-face way that Paul desires (see 3:18 and 1 Cor 13:13).

This yearning for the Lord apparently outweighs Paul's misgivings about death as he now declares his preference to leave the body to be at home with the Lord. Paul's discussion of the impermanent, burdensome, and limiting character of the physical body could reinforce the view of some Corinthians, earlier refuted by Paul, that the body has no moral value (see 1 Cor 6:12-20). Here Paul concludes by pointedly reminding them that the Lord will judge each of them in view of the good or evil done "in the body," the only place where ethical behavior and moral purpose are manifested.

In this second phase of his defense, Paul has provided the Corinthians with a new framework for evaluating valid ministry and authentic apostleship. Within this framework, weakness and suffering necessarily, even though paradoxically, constitute the hallmarks of a genuine minister because the gospel is paradox. In Christ, God manifests power in weakness, glory through apparent shame, and brings life from death (see 1 Cor 1:18-30). In Paul, an apostle of Jesus Christ, God's glory and power are again made manifest in the apostle's weakness, sufferings, and death. The Corinthians are not only joined to Paul in suffering (1:7), but through his ministry of hardship they are already experiencing life.

5:11–6:10 A ministry of reconciliation

At the end of the previous argument, Paul's focus shifted to the future of all Christians. Now at verse 11 he returns to his self-defense, beginning a third phase in this long argument for the legitimacy and authenticity of his apostolic ministry. He addresses the community from beginning to end ("you," v. 12 and v. 20), though clearly with an eye to his rivals. Paul admits that his task is "to persuade" others (v. 11), yet he implicitly distinguishes himself from his rivals by emphasizing his transparency before God, which he hopes the Corinthians will also recognize. Despite his claim to the contrary, Paul is, in fact, commending himself, but not for selfish reasons. His purpose is to give the Corinthians reason to take pride in him, a man of substance (heart) and to rebut those who are all show, able to boast only in externals, perhaps even in ecstatic experiences (see 12:1) and miracle-working (see 12:12). Besides, as Paul makes clear, ecstatic experiences are private matters between an individual and God (see further 1 Cor 14:2). They are irrelevant to ministry, which is "for you" (v. 13). Paul provides this information to enable the Corinthians to make an informed choice between himself and his opponents.

Paul continues by appealing to the community's identification with the death of Christ and then draws out the implications of this event (5:14-17), whose universal significance is underscored in Paul's statement "one died for all" (v. 14b). How Christ's death benefits all humanity is assumed but not explained here. Rather, Paul is concerned to draw out the implications of Christ's death for all believers, about which the Corinthians obviously need to be reminded. First, all believers owe their new life to Christ and so must pattern their lives after his. Second, as a result of Christ's death, believers no longer belong to the realm of the flesh, that old existence of corruption and death that heretofore characterized human existence. Thus it follows that as those now "in Christ" (v. 17), the Corinthians can no longer know or judge Christ or anyone else "according to the flesh" (v. 16), that is, according to their old criteria.

Paul cites his own example to show how standards and values once considered important are now invalid (v. 16). Christ's self-emptying love is the basis of reconciliation and unity. This love has made possible the existence of this community, and Christ's love must be what compels the community to act and to judge. Since the Corinthians and Paul now know from the same perspective in Christ and are expected to judge based on the same criterion, namely, Christ, it is clear that the community's negative assessment of Paul according to the old standards of power and prestige obviously needs to be reconsidered!

Believers belong to a "new creation" (v. 17), an entirely new order in which cosmic brokenness is now being reversed by the cosmic reconciliation willed and set in motion by God, who has "reconciled us to himself through Christ" (v. 18). Reconciliation is what God alone accomplishes through the agency of Christ. God, through Christ, rights the relationship between all creation and God's-self and all creation with itself, no longer counting believers' trespasses against them (v. 19). Paul is tasked with making known God's reconciling activity in Christ. However, he is no mere bearer of a message about a past event. Through his own ministry it is "as if God were appealing" (v. 20). Paul clearly understands himself as an agent of God's ongoing reconciling work, mediated in the present through his apostolic life and ministry. Thus he appeals to the Corinthians to be reconciled to God, which implies reconciliation among themselves and with Paul, God's minister of reconciliation.

Paul again directs the Corinthians' attention to what God has done in Christ, this time focusing on God's intention that believers "might *become* the righteousness of God" (v. 21, emphasis added). "Becoming" God's righteousness suggests that while God's salvific purposes are made known in Christ, believers are called to respond to God's offer by choosing to live out this righteousness. If so, a certain moral connotation seems to be attached to the notion of righteousness and needs to be manifested in holy living.

Knowing well the Corinthians' practical lapses both with regard to unity/reconciliation (see 1 Cor 1–4) and holiness (see 1 Cor 5–6; 8–10), Paul justifiably fears that the community has received the grace of God in vain (6:1). He therefore appeals to them to turn and respond to that grace. Though Isaiah, cited here in support of this appeal (6:2a; see Isa 49:8), envisioned the day of salvation as a future event, Paul believed that with the advent of the Messiah, that day had come. Salvation was a present offer, a grace to which the Corinthians needed to respond.

Paul brings the discussion of his ministry of reconciliation to a close by underscoring his own *ethos*. Neither he nor his co-workers has done anything to impede the Corinthians from responding to God's grace and fully partaking of this reconciliation. To reinforce his point, Paul briefly recaps how he has lived and worked among them. He has demonstrated endurance in the face of numerous difficulties (see also 4:8-10; 11:23-29; 12:10). Some hardships were inflicted by others (e.g., beatings, imprisonments); some were self-imposed (labors, vigils, and fasts). But Paul has not simply endured the hardships. He has acted with "purity," a reference to his selfless motives, and has demonstrated many other virtues (vv. 6-7a) that attest to his authenticity as an apostle.

That Paul is able to withstand whatever befalls him is due to God who equips Paul "with weapons of righteousness at the right and at the left" (v. 7). The mention of the right and left could simply mean that Paul is fully prepared. In the context of the military metaphor, we should probably understand that Paul is prepared for both the offense and the defense, since the right hand wielded the sword and the left held the shield. Responses to Paul's ministry have alternated between extremes from glory to dishonor, from insult to praise (v. 8a). Whatever the response, Paul is prepared to fight whatever battles he must to spread the gospel.

Having once again demonstrated the authenticity of his ministry, Paul now introduces a final set of seven contrasts (vv. 8b-10), through which he deals with the negative assessments that have plagued his ministry. The first statement of each pair contains a negative evaluation of Paul, most likely reflecting the views of some in the Corinthian community. Paul simply counters each one by offering his own positive view of himself without adding any criticism of the Corinthians. The latter is unnecessary. In the end, the Corinthians' negative appraisal of their apostle shows that many are still attached to their former way of knowing and to judging "according to the flesh" (see 5:16). This again confirms their spiritual immaturity (see 1 Cor 3). If they were truly spiritual people, they would understand God's wisdom manifested in Christ crucified (1 Cor 1:18-31). With Christ as their

2 Corinthians 5–6

standard of judgment, they would share Paul's positive assessment of his life and ministry, recognizing God's paradoxical wisdom at work in him.

6:11-13 A personal appeal

In a spirit of reconciliation, Paul now makes a personal and emotionally charged appeal to the Corinthians, in which he stresses his openness and affection for them and asks that they reciprocate by making room in their hearts for him. Rather than chastise the community, Paul speaks as a parent and guide to the Corinthians, whom he considers his beloved children in Christ (see 1 Cor 4:15).

6:14–7:1 A call to holiness

Having focused so far on his own ministry and relationship to the community, Paul now turns to the community's relation to the world outside. This shift in focus, coupled with the presence of some ideas and vocabulary not typical of Paul, have led many scholars to conclude that 6:14–7:1 is a non-Pauline fragment inserted by an editor. However, no manuscript evidence indicates an insertion here, and as many scholars now recognize, the passage is sufficiently Pauline in vocabulary and construction to be reasonably considered authentic. In fact, as with other Pauline digressions, closer examination often reveals logical links to the surrounding context. For example, at 6:1 Paul had already expressed concern that the Corinthians had received the grace of God in vain; hence this brief section in which Paul exhorts the community to recall its true identity and reaffirm its exclusive allegiance to God and Christ is entirely consonant with that concern.

Additionally, having just underscored his pedagogical relationship to the community in 6:13, Paul now assumes a teaching role at 6:14. He instructs and warns about alliances still maintained by some in the community that contravene allegiance to Christ and undermine the reconciliation achieved through Christ. This is especially evident in their strained relationship with Paul, God's minister of reconciliation.

Paul begins with a command that echoes the Old Testament prohibition (see Lev 19:19; Deut 22:9-11) against mismatching or, in the case of animals, misyoking pairs that do not naturally go together. The command is followed by six rhetorical questions containing six antithetical pairings: righteousness/lawlessness, light/darkness, Christ/Beliar, (an alternate term for Satan), believer/unbeliever, and the temple of God/idols (6:14b-16a). Through this series of questions, Paul again stresses the exclusive character of Christian existence (see 1 Cor 10:21). Implicitly, he exhorts the Corinthians to dissociate themselves from all that is pagan and to ally themselves exclusively with God, Christ, righteousness, light, etc.

Paul was quite aware that Christians would necessarily maintain contacts with unbelievers (see 1 Cor 5:9-10) and, in some cases, be married to them without necessarily compromising their relationship with Christ (1 Cor 7:12-14). Thus he cannot have intended here an absolute prohibition of all contact with non-believers. The point, rather, is that the believer's exclusive aligning of self to God in Christ necessitates the renunciation of all activity involving alliances which compromise the believer's relationship with God and Christ and which defile the community, now identified as "the temple of the living God" (v. 16b). For Paul, the community constituted the spiritual temple of God in virtue of its being indwelt by the Spirit of God (1 Cor 3:16-17).

In verses 16b-18, Paul links a series of Old Testament references (Lev 26:12; Ezek 37:27; Jer 31:33c; Isa 52:11; Ps 2:7; Jer 31:9c) that underscore the reciprocal and exclusive relationship between God and the community. This radically exclusive relationship with God marks off true believers from unbelievers, whether within or outside the community, whose allegiance is divided. Moreover, it enjoins on each member of the community the obligation to be cleansed of all defilement in order to maintain the holiness of the community (7:1).

The function of this brief digression is to remind those in the community, probably the same spiritual elitists Paul criticizes in 1 Corinthians, that their continued courting of danger in pagan temples and their rabid pursuit of superficial, transient realities are at the heart of the problems in Corinth. They are responsible for compromising their relationship with Christ through the *koinonia* they establish with pagan idols in pagan temples. In their pursuit of external manifestations of wisdom and power, they show themselves attached to the conventions of the world and thus misjudge true ministers and misinterpret true ministry.

7:2-4 Paul resumes his appeal

Having implicitly inculpated the Corinthians for their tenuous relationship with Christ and near-ruptured relationship with himself, Paul resumes the plea begun above at 6:11-13, exhorting the community to make room for him. Once again he underscores his good faith toward them. He has not wronged, ruined, or taken advantage of anyone, in contrast, perhaps, to those who, in Paul's estimate, were taking financial advantage of the community (see 2:17; 11:19-20).

Though the Corinthians misjudge and malign Paul, he assures them that his intention is not to condemn them (v. 3a). On the contrary, as he has

2 Corinthians 7

"already said" (v. 3b; obviously a reference to 6:11) and now repeats, he holds them in his heart, and his affection for them is so deep that he desires to die and live with them. Here Paul adopts, but inverts, a classic expression, "to live together and die together" (see 2 Sam 15:21) to articulate his own deepest desire to be fully reconciled with the community and share with them full partnership in the gospel. Despite the strained relationship with the community and the affliction Paul experiences, he expresses optimism that the Corinthians will reciprocate and that their relationship with Paul will be fully restored.

7:5-16 Paul's complete confidence in the Corinthians

Since Paul now picks up on points previously narrated at 2:5-13, many scholars assume that 7:5-16 originally followed on 2:13. Grammatically speaking, this position is difficult to sustain. Paul speaks in the first person singular ("I") at 2:13 and the first person plural ("we") at 7:5. If 7:5 had originally followed 2:13, why the switch from "I" to "we"? Additionally, certain vocabulary employed from 6:11 through 7:4 (e.g., affection, boasting, consolation, joy, distress), recurs in 7:5-16, suggesting more continuity between this unit and what immediately precedes it than is usually admitted.

Moreover, the claim that 7:5 is the direct continuation of 2:13 requires assuming either (a) that Paul abruptly broke off the story at 2:13 to focus on his own ministry until 7:5, at which point he just as abruptly returned to the thought of 2:13, or (b) that 2:14–7:4 is another original Pauline letter or letter fragment inserted here by a later, albeit inept, editor unconcerned about coherency! Assumption (a) implies that Paul was an erratic thinker/writer; assumption (b) implies that the letter lacks literary integrity. Both are drastic and, from the perspective of Paul's rhetorical goals and strategy, unnecessary.

It is important to bear in mind that at 7:5 Paul has reached a new point in his argument. So far he has carefully unfolded a defense of his ministry, which began at 2:14. At 8:1 he will begin his appeal to the Corinthians for money. The success of his collection drive clearly depends on the degree to which the Corinthians are well disposed to him. If they are not, Paul has little reason to hope that they will entrust their money to him, especially given the misgivings they had about his sincerity (see 1:15-24).

To ensure that there were no residual hard feelings over the painful letter that could compromise his collection appeal and the continuation of his defense, Paul again focuses on the painful letter and his anxiety over it, which he only briefly mentioned at 2:1-13. Here, however, he speaks about the letter and its purpose, as well as his encounter with Titus, much more extensively and with new emphases. This elaboration of previously but briefly narrated points in the service of advancing one's argument at a later stage is an example of the rhetorical technique known as *amplificatio* ("amplification"). In its present position in the letter, this amplification functions as a hinge text. Through it, Paul continues and intensifies the optimistic line introduced at 7:4 and paves the way for his collection appeal in chapters 8–9.

Three smaller units comprise 7:5-16. In the first unit, vv. 5-7, Paul describes the terrible state he was in at Macedonia before Titus came. The "fear" Paul experienced (v. 5) was probably due to his uncertainty about how the Corinthians would react to his "tearful letter" sent via Titus. Having written a stinging letter rebuking the community over the offense he suffered during his unexpected visit to Corinth, Paul knew that his letter had as much potential to alienate the community as it had to elicit their support and action on his behalf. Titus's arrival brings Paul a triple dose of encouragement (vv. 6-7). Beyond the joy of Titus's company, Paul is further encouraged to learn that Titus has not been rebuffed but edified by the Corinthians. The source of Titus's edification, the Corinthians' heartfelt concern for their apostle and remorse over the offensive incident, is the good news that relieves Paul of his anxiety and moves him to rejoice. As delighted as Paul is at this outcome, he is not insensitive to the pain he caused the community.

In the next unit (vv. 8-13a), Paul apologizes, but not without first distinguishing between "worldly sorrow" and "godly sorrow" (7:10). Paul truly regrets the former, by which he means whatever momentary indignation the Corinthians experienced. But he does not regret the latter, because "godly sorrow" induces repentance, which is ultimately beneficial to the Corinthians (v. 10). It has awakened their sense of earnestness and an appropriate sense of indignation against the one who offended Paul, as well as their yearning to patch things up with Paul (v. 11). From Paul's perspective, the severe letter accomplished what he had intended, namely, that the Corinthians would show themselves truly Christian in the sight of God by their concern for his minister, Paul (v. 12). Thus Paul has good reason to be encouraged (v. 13a).

In the final subunit, vv. 13b-16, Paul again speaks of Titus. His success among the Corinthians was a source of joy to Paul, who had not lost face! The Corinthians had come through for him, having more than vindicated his boasting about them. All this joy and encouragement move Paul to express his complete confidence in the community (v. 16).

In this unit Paul has amplified the bare facts narrated earlier at 2:5-13, stressing every positive outcome of a situation that could have ended badly

2 Corinthians 7

but, fortunately, did not. The Corinthians have shown themselves to be spiritually mature and have benefited from their repentance. Titus accomplished his task unscathed, returning to Macedonia impressed by the Corinthians' obedience and concern for Paul. Paul is encouraged and optimistic about his relationship with the Corinthians.

THE COLLECTION FOR JERUSALEM
2 Corinthians 8:1–9:15

Having praised and flattered the Corinthians to the point of declaring his full confidence in them, Paul now banks on the hope, engendered by Titus's report, that mutual trust has been restored to press his case for the collection. The collection, for reasons already discussed (see 1 Cor 16:1-4), was of singular importance to Paul's gospel. If he has overestimated the Corinthians' good will, he could railroad his own cause. If, however, his optimistic assessment is correct, then this is the time to launch his appeal!

8:1-8 The example of the Macedonians

These first six verses constitute an introduction to Paul's argument. He is about to ask the community for money. This is never an easy task, and though Paul is hopeful that his reconciliation with the community is solid, he has to be cautious and avoid awakening any suspicions or hostile feelings. Thus he wisely begins by focusing on God, the Macedonians, and Titus. In this way Paul keeps himself out of the spotlight and lets the story of the Macedonian Christians rouse the Corinthians' emotions.

Despite their utter poverty, the Macedonians did not view the collection as an imposition but as a privilege through which they could express their fellowship with the "holy ones" (v. 4). They not only insisted on participating, but given the opportunity, they contributed "beyond their means" (v. 3) in a spirit of joy and generosity (v. 2). Paul attributes this abundant generosity not merely to the Macedonians' own goodness or sense of justice nor to anything he himself did or said, but to the grace *(charis)* of God (v. 1). In responding to this gift of grace, the Macedonians have shown their devotion to the Lord (v. 5). Their good example prompts Paul to urge Titus to go to Corinth (v. 6).

Whether Titus had been initially responsible for the collection drive among the Corinthians is unclear. There is no mention of him in conjunction with the collection instructions at 1 Corinthians 16:4. What we do know is that Titus had success among the Corinthians over other delicate issues, is purportedly well disposed toward them (see 7:7, 13b, 15), and is obviously equal to the task. By putting Titus in charge of the collection, Paul minimizes his own role and keeps himself in the background.

This story of the Macedonians' heroic generosity is quite moving and should have accomplished the desired effect of rousing the Corinthians' feelings of admiration or even envy, given their proud and competitive spirit. In either case, Paul has captured their attention and takes the occasion to exhort them not merely to participate in the collection but to excel in this gracious act *(charis)* of giving (v. 7). *Charis* can mean both "grace" and "gift" and is Paul's preferred term for the "collection." At verse 1 he used *charis* to refer to God's gift of grace given to the Macedonians, which enabled their own giving. Since, as Paul understands it, giving flows from being gifted, the Corinthians, who have been abundantly gifted by God, as underscored in verse 7, should naturally give freely and abundantly without being prodded. In fact, Paul refuses to mandate giving (v. 8), not because he fears their disobedience but because the gracious act/collection *(charis)* flows from the graces/gifts *(charismata)* received.

8:9-15 Motives for giving

Paul first relies on the example of Christ's own self-emptying gift *(charis)* to support his exhortation. His unique interpretation of Christ's self-emptying in terms of rich/poor is probably influenced by the current discussion and should not be taken as an indication of the historical Jesus' economic situation. At Philippians 2:6-11, we learn that Christ's self-emptying love demonstrated itself not only in the fact of incarnation but in the taking on the form of a "slave" and the subsequent total impoverishment that resulted from death on a cross. As a result of Jesus' self-emptying love, the Corinthians have been rescued from the poverty of alienation from God and restored to God's friendship (see 5:7-19). They are rich now. Paul proposes that they emulate Christ by manifesting their own love in their own self-emptying for the sake of enriching others. On a practical level, Paul would like to see this love be manifest in their participation in the collection. Thus he encourages them to complete what they had already begun, assuring them that whatever they contribute, if properly motivated, will be deemed acceptable (vv. 11-12).

In addition to the example of Christ's love, which should be the Corinthians' primary motivation, Paul invokes the principle of equality as another motive for giving. Relatively speaking, the Corinthians are better off than the members of the Jerusalem community. Paul clarifies that he is not suggesting that the Corinthians disadvantage themselves (v. 13). Rather, by

2 Corinthians 8

giving of their current surplus, they would be supplying what the poor lack. It is important to note that Paul does not advocate self-impoverishment as an end in itself but in view of fostering an equitable balance of goods necessary for living. He apparently intends that this principle of equality will be an ever-present motivating factor in all Christian communities, since he assures the Corinthians that if they were to fall on hard times, their needs would likewise be met in view of this same principle (v. 14). The citation from Exodus 16:18 recalls the distribution of manna in the desert according to need and serves to illustrate and support Paul's point (v. 15).

8:16–9:5 Titus, his collaborators, and the collection drive at Corinth

Paul now discloses the practical steps that will be taken to ensure that the Corinthians will heed his exhortation and come through on the collection. Paul renounces a direct role in the collection to avoid eliciting criticism that could undermine the collection (vv. 20-21). Instead, a delegation of three will be sent to Corinth to oversee the project. Paul delegates Titus, who has already had success among the community and is apparently anxious to go back and undertake this task. The identity of the second and third delegates is a matter of speculation. The second is simply referred to as "the brother," someone well known to all the churches and famed for his preaching (v. 18). He has been appointed "by the churches" (v. 19), though Paul does not say which churches. The third delegate, referred to as "our brother," that is, a member of Paul's entourage, is recommended for his earnestness (v. 22).

Paul returns in verse 23 to underscore Titus's status as his co-worker and to qualify the other two delegates as representatives of the churches. If the Corinthians respond enthusiastically with regard to the collection, it will stand as a testimony to their love and be known to all the churches. Moreover, their cooperation will further vindicate Paul's boast, which can only serve to advance and strengthen the reconciliation between Paul and them (v. 24).

At 9:1 Paul now protests that it is superfluous to write to the Corinthians about the collection for the saints. It is not necessary to assume that this statement signals the start of a new, once originally independent letter. On further consideration, it becomes apparent that the mention of the collection allows Paul to reintroduce the topic of the Macedonians, but in such a way as to instigate the Corinthians to get onboard with the collection and cooperate with the delegates. Paul says that he has boasted to the Macedonians of the Corinthians' year-old eagerness to participate in the collection. He also reports that the Corinthians' example stirred the Macedonians' zeal for the collection and prompted them to contribute (v. 3). In fact, both Paul and the Corinthians know that they had done next to nothing about the collection since the previous year. Thus Paul gives the Corinthians fair warning that with the arrival of the advance delegation in Corinth, they had better expedite the project and be ready for Paul's arrival in the event that any Macedonians accompany Paul (vv. 3-4). Failure on the Corinthians' part would bring shame not only on themselves for being less generous than the poorer Macedonians, but on Paul too (v. 4). Yet Paul is hopeful that motives other than the desire to avoid shame will induce the proud Corinthians to attend earnestly to the collection. This is why he has sent an advance delegation. Their purpose is to encourage and help the Corinthians arrange for their "promised gift" so that it will be ready as a "bountiful gift" and not a last-minute act of begrudging giving (exaction) in order to save face (9:5).

9:6-15 The rewards of giving

Paul now offers a theological foundation, supported by scriptural citations, for his collection project. Picking up on the term "bountiful," he begins with a commonsense statement about sowing and harvesting (v. 6). Applied metaphorically to the topic of giving, what Paul suggests is that bountiful giving will produce bountiful rewards. But if generosity has its own rewards, the Corinthians need to realize that generous giving is made possible by God, who first provides the abundance, so that with their own needs met, the Corinthians can give from their abundance (v. 8). This statement reinforces the theological idea already present at 8:1-7, namely, that God is the one who graces/gifts and whose grace enables our gracious giving. That God is the source of all good works is reinforced at verse 9 with a citation from Psalm 111:9 and further reinforced in verse 10a, where the influence of Isaiah 55:10-11 is discernible. Here God is described as not only supplying the seed (grace), that is, creating the possibility of giving, but sustaining this good work of giving by continually multiplying the seed and increasing the "harvest of your righteousness" (v. 10; see Hos 12:10).

At verse 11, Paul reminds the Corinthians that they have already been richly endowed precisely for the sake of being generous "through us," that is, Paul and his collection project. Once the collection is distributed and the poor are assisted, they will give thanks to God for the generosity of the Corinthians, which God has enabled (v. 12), and ultimately God will be glorified (v. 13). Thus the Corinthians are again exhorted to contribute to the collection, not only for their own advantage but because in doing so they demonstrate their obedience to the gospel (v. 13). This authentic

2 Corinthians 9

expression of Christianity, manifested in generous giving, will bring forth thanks to God for "his indescribable gift" (v. 15).

PAUL'S COUNTERATTACK ON THE INTRUDERS
2 Corinthians 10:1–13:10

Apart from some indirect gibes and insinuations apparently aimed at the rival apostles (see, e.g., 2:17; 3:1; 4:2; 7:2), Paul's primary focus up to this point in the letter has been his conflicted relationship with the community. His goal has been to overcome their differences and restore trust; in consequence, Paul was able to renew his appeal to the Corinthians concerning the collection. Now he turns to confront the intruders, who were attempting to upstage him and capitalize on the strained relationship to promote themselves.

This final unit serves as a kind of rhetorical knockout punch, packed with invective and sarcasm. Paul refutes accusations leveled against him (10:1-18) and positively contrasts himself with his rivals, who are exposed as charlatans (11:1–12:10). Paul then recaps his major points and brings up the subject of his imminent third visit to Corinth (12:11-21). With the mention of the visit, Paul transitions to the final chapter, where he issues a series of warnings to the community (13:1-10), which are followed by the epistolary conclusion (13:11-13). Throughout this unit Paul takes on his rivals, but his remarks are addressed to the Corinthians. Ultimately, his concern is to safeguard this community and bring about their obedience to the gospel so that when he returns to Corinth, he and they may again enjoy full partnership.

Paul refutes his opponents' accusations (10:1-18)

Two subunits are distinguishable in this opening segment of Paul's argument. The first, verses 1-11, begins and ends with the intruders' criticism of Paul in regard to rhetorical competence. In the second subunit, verses 12-18, Paul is concerned about territorial jurisdiction, around which he develops the theme of boasting in preparation for chapters 11–12.

10:1-11 Spiritual weapons

Paul begins with an exhortation, pointing to the gentleness and clemency of Christ (v. 1a), but quickly alludes to a criticism brought forth by his opponents (v. 1b). Paul denies that he lacks boldness. If he is meek and humble, it is in imitation of Christ. But he is quite prepared to deal boldly with his opponents, who claim that he walks "according to the flesh" (v. 2). In Paul, this phrase usually means to live a sinful life. However, beginning in verse 3, the context requires that the phrase be taken to mean according to human arguments/persuasive strategies. Paul renounces such cunning (see 4:2) and battles with spiritual weapons (literally "weapons powerful to God"), which will be so effective against the slick but vacuous arguments of his opponents that Paul will take every thought captive in obedience to Christ (vv. 4-5). In this battle Paul expects to overpower his smooth-talking opponents and win back the Corinthians to complete obedience to Christ, which also means full fellowship with Paul. When this occurs, Paul will punish his opponents, who subvert the gospel (v. 6).

As Paul continues, he commands the Corinthians to face the facts (v. 7a). It is doubtful that someone has accused him of not being Christian; rather, Paul's opponents probably alleged that he was not a true apostle and hence without authority. This seems to be supported by verse 8, where Paul boasts of the authority given him by the Lord. If the opponents were connected to the Jerusalem church, they may have claimed that they were possibly commissioned by Jesus himself (see 5:16) during his earthly ministry or by his immediate disciples. Since Paul cannot claim to have received his apostolic commission in this way, his opponents may have used this fact to discredit his apostolic legitimacy. Yet Paul insists that his claim to be "of Christ" is valid, and his exercise of apostolic authority is genuine, since it is ordered to building up the community (v. 8).

In verses 9-11, Paul returns to allegations concerning his weak personal presence and lack of rhetorical competence and assures the Corinthians that when he arrives, the allegations will be shown to be baseless.

10:12-18 Paul boasts in his own labors

After his ironic jab at his self-commending opponents (v. 12a), who use only one another as a basis of comparison and risk deluding themselves (v. 12b), Paul criticizes his opponents for overstepping boundaries by coming to Corinth to minister. This is not just a matter of guarding his own turf for selfish reasons. Corinth, a Gentile city, was part of Paul's ministerial jurisdiction to the Gentiles, apportioned to him and his co-workers by God (v. 13) and confirmed by the apostles at the Jerusalem council (see Gal 2:6-10).

Apparently, in Paul's mind the two broad ministerial jurisdictions established at this council along ethnic lines of demarcation—one for the circumcised/Jews, the other for the Gentiles—also implied geographical lines of demarcation. Unlike his opponents, who did not honor these boundaries, Paul did not overreach his territorial limits (v. 14) or build on anyone else's labors (v. 15). Thus Paul, who is approved by the Lord and whose work has

2 Corinthians 10

been done within the limits established by God, is the one with the legitimate right to boast in what has been accomplished at Corinth (vv. 17-18).

The "fool's speech" (11:1–12:10)

In view of the recurrence of the words "fool," "foolishness," and "foolish," this segment of Paul's argument is usually referred to as the "fool's speech." Paul first explains why it is necessary that he engage in a little foolishness (11:1-21a) and then indulges in his own foolish boasting (11:16–12:10). Throughout this speech Paul deftly uses the rhetorical skill he was said to lack to deride his opponents and their claims.

11:1-21a A "little foolishness"

Though Paul considers boasting foolishness, he finds it necessary to engage in a "little foolishness" (v. 1) of his own, since the Corinthians not only tolerate the boasting of his opponents but also are swayed by them to accept a different gospel to their own peril (v. 4). Like the father of a bride, responsible for safeguarding the virginity of his daughter until she wed her betrothed, Paul's apostolic task is to preserve the community incorrupt for Christ alone. However, he fears that like Eve, seduced and deceived by Satan disguised as a serpent, the community was allowing itself to be seduced and corrupted by these superapostles. In comparison with these, Paul is in no way inferior (v. 5). Though he concedes that he lacks training in the art of oratory, he denies lacking knowledge, which he has abundantly demonstrated (v. 6).

In bringing up his practice of preaching the gospel free of charge (v. 7), Paul seems to have abruptly changed topics. However, this issue is closely linked to the charge of inferiority, since in Paul's day it was assumed that preachers without financial backing were second-rate. Paul now appears to be second-guessing himself, questioning whether his choice was a mistake, since it could be cited as further proof of his inferiority. If he were a true apostle, he should have taken the support due to him. He had already explained why he renounced his apostolic right to financial support (1 Cor 9) and does not repeat those reasons here. Here he simply asserts that he has not and will not burden the Corinthians (v. 9).

That the Corinthians continue to find grounds in this for despising Paul as inferior is not his problem. He will not allow his preaching of the gospel to be compromised by the patronage system and intends to boast of his independence from such social conventions. And he will continue to operate this way! This is not because he disdains the Corinthians, whom he assures of his love (v. 11). Rather, his goal is to stop the superapostles from using the Corinthians' financial support to feign friendship and manipulate allegiance when their real intention is to supplant Paul and boast of the successful mission at Corinth as if it were the result of their work and not his (v. 12). Paul's verbal assault on these predators is vehement. He rejects them as false apostles and deceivers. Masquerading as apostles of Christ, they are actually ministers of Satan. According to Jewish tradition, Satan disguised himself as an angel of light (see *Apocalypse of Moses* 17:1-2). Thus, like Satan, so his followers. Paul concludes this tirade with a short eschatological statement obviously intended as a threat. In the end, they will be unmasked, and their judgment will correspond to their deeds.

After ten verses of defense and attack, Paul reminds his readers that he is going to begin his "fool's speech," even though it goes against his own better judgment (v. 16). The circumstances require that he take on the role of a boaster. By doing this, he risks being considered foolish, but he fears far greater risks to the community if he does not. The Corinthians should be able to deal with him in this assumed role, since they gladly put up with *real* fools (v. 19)! This stinging sarcasm continues as Paul describes the excessive tolerance of the "wise" Corinthians, who put up with the worst abuses at the hands of their ministers (v. 20)! Paul's mocking depiction of the Corinthians as gullible pawns is intended to force them to realize how foolish is their attachment to his opponents, who actually victimize the community. Paul concludes with an admission of weakness, but this is probably intended ironically, since he is about to boast quite boldly.

11:21b–12:10 Paul's foolish boasting

The fool's speech proper begins here. The agenda for this bragging contest is set by the opponents. Whatever they dare boast of, Paul will too (v. 21b). The contest begins with a focus on titles. On the first point, Paul can equally claim the three titles Hebrew, Israelite, descendant of Abraham, which are claimed with boastful pride by his opponents (v. 22). Ethnically, culturally, and religiously, there is simply no disparity between himself and the rivals.

When it comes to the next title, "ministers of Christ," Paul ironically stakes his claim to this title, not on powerful deeds or notable accomplishments, as his rivals did, but on suffering—and Paul's were unparalleled (v. 23b)! He lists them in spades, bragging about all the dangers, hardships, beatings, deprivation, and humiliation he has endured throughout his ministry (vv. 24-28). All this suffering, which had been cited by his opponents to discredit his apostolic authority and ministry, Paul now shamelessly showcases as that which legitimates his claim to the title "minister of Christ." Paul is clearly the supersufferer! Since suffering and affliction, paradoxically, constitute the credentials of a true apostle and authentic minister (see 4:7– 5:10), the Corinthians should recognize Paul's apostolic legitimacy.

In this clever and ironic twist, Paul has pulled the rug out from under his opponents, who consider demonstrations of power authenticators of apostolic ministry. Paul knows very well that his opponents would never admit of, let alone boast of, weakness, even if they had suffered! Thus the irony of his question, "Who is weak, and I am not weak?" (v. 29)!

Since Paul must boast, he boasts of another episode of weakness and indignity—his escape from Damascus (vv. 30-33; see also Acts 9:23-25). His purpose in adding this particular example to the catalogue of hardships already recited is illumined by the contemporary Roman military practice of awarding the "wall crown" to the first soldier to scale the enemy's wall. By contrast, Paul is but a weakling, an anti-hero being shuttled down the wall in a basket! Paul's intentional spoof on the practice of recognizing and rewarding displays of power is a perfect lead-in to the last item of comparison in the fool's speech (12:1-10).

Apparently the superapostles had impressed the Corinthians with displays of spiritual power and descriptions of ecstatic experiences. Paul knows that comparing such experiences serves no purpose (v. 1), since weakness, rather than displays of power, authenticates ministry. However, having been forced into this boasting contest, Paul has no choice but to recount a revelatory experience of his own. His reluctance is evident in the fact that he speaks in the third person. This is a rhetorical device that allows him to distance himself from this visionary episode, which, though extraordinary, has little to do with the authenticity of his daily ministry. Only God knows how "this person" was transported to Paradise, the highest of heavens, where he was granted special revelations meant to be kept secret (vv. 3-4). About "this person" Paul has reason to boast (v. 5), since he has been granted access to a place few have been permitted to enter and has been privy to ineffable revelations.

But at this point Paul again subverts the boasting contest by introducing his own terms: "about myself I will not boast, except about my weaknesses" (v. 5b). Were he to boast about his experience to impress the Corinthians, he would be telling the truth, since he has had an "abundance of the revelations" (vv. 6-7a). But he will not boast, because he has been given a "thorn in the flesh." Though the exact nature of this affliction is not certain, its purpose is. Paul twice emphasizes that this "thorn" was given to him precisely to prevent his being "too elated" (v. 7). Paul's thrice-repeated plea that he be relieved of this suffering is reminiscent of Jesus' supplication in the garden (see Matt 26:39-44). The Lord's answer (v. 9), presented as authoritative divine revelation, reminds Paul that the only thing that counts is God's grace—not mystical experiences or human displays of power, but God's grace.

Moreover, God's "power" (v. 9; here a synonym for grace) is brought to perfection in weakness. Thus Paul need not seek to overcome weakness and avoid suffering. When he is weakest, as measured by human standards, he is strongest, not by the dint of his own resources but by the grace/power of God paradoxically manifested in weakness. Rather than despising Paul, the Corinthians ought to recognize that his weakness is powerful testimony that God is at work in their apostle's life and ministry. In light of this revelation, Paul's conclusion makes perfect sense: he will boast of his weakness and be content with his hardships (vv. 10-11).

In the end, even though Paul's revelatory experience ironically turned out to be another affirmation of his weakness, he has won this boasting contest. He has won not on his opponents' terms nor even on his own, but ultimately on God's terms. God manifested his power and wisdom in the weakness and folly of the cross (see 1 Cor 1:18-31), and God continues to do so in the weakness and suffering of his ministers, whose lives are conformed to the life of Jesus (see 4:10-11).

12:11-21 Epilogue and transition

The fool's speech is over, and as if embarrassed by his own peacock performance, Paul reminds the Corinthians that their failure to support him forced him into foolish self-commendation (v. 11). Having excused himself, Paul now recaps major points made in the two preceding sections. He is not inferior. Opponents may call him a "nothing," but no number of insults can change the fact that he is a true apostle (v. 11c). Though Paul refrains from saying that he accomplished signs among the Corinthians, he insists that they "were performed among you" (v. 12). The use of the passive may be intended to underscore the power of God at work through the apostle's weakness. Paul then restates his motive for refusing their support (v. 13). His request that they forgive him for this "wrong" is pure sarcasm.

Paul is ready to go back to the community and announces an imminent visit (v. 14a). His founding visit to Corinth was followed by a second, "painful" visit (chs. 1–2). This will be his third (v. 14). His refusal to accept their financial support remains a delicate issue. Paul tries to dispel the rancor about his praxis by showing that his motives, unlike those of his opponents, who are indirectly impugned here, are selfless. First he stresses that his interest is in them and not their possessions (v. 14b). Then he points to the customary financial setup between children and parents. In view of this, it is clear that Paul alone behaves as a true parent to the Corinthians, while his opponents subvert this natural order of things by taking. While they live off Paul's spiritual children, he is impelled by his profound love for the Corinthians "to spend" himself and be "spent" for them (vv. 14c-15).

The comparison between Paul and his opponents is implicit in his emotionally charged question, "If I love you more, am I to be loved less?" (v. 15c). If the Corinthians are honest, they will have to admit that they have been shortchanging Paul when it comes to love and support. They will also have to grant that Paul has truly never burdened them (v. 16a). However, Paul knows that his opponents have planted the suspicion that he is deceitfully living off the Corinthians by covertly siphoning money from what they had put aside for the collection (v. 16b). Paul denies doing this. In fact, he has opted out of direct involvement in the collection and is sending Titus (see 8:16-24). On a previous mission to Corinth, Titus had been positively impressed by the Corinthians, who apparently felt comfortable and confident enough with him to admit their error (see 7:5-15). If the community has confidence in Titus, who shares with Paul the "same" values and approach to ministry, to suspect Paul of dishonesty is not only unfounded but also illogical.

Paul knows that what he has said sounds like a defense, and in many ways it has been, but he hastens to add that his testimony before God in Christ (see 2:17) is part of his apostolic service to upbuild the community (see 10:8). Paul's apprehension about this trip derives from concerns about what he may discover upon his return to Corinth. His fear is that the unity and holiness of the community are still being compromised by the same litigious and immoral behavior (vv. 21-22) that he had already addressed in 1 Corinthians. If so, Paul also fears that he may be in for another humiliating experience, comparable to what occurred on his second visit. His announcement of an imminent visit, his expressed fear that the Corinthians had still not conformed their lives to the gospel, and his mention of unrepentant sinners provide the transition to the concluding chapter.

13:1-10 Final warnings

The juridical significance of the qualifier "third" (v. 1a) is made clear in v. 1b, where Paul cites a legal prescription which states that the testimony of at least two or three witnesses is required to convict an alleged wrongdoer (see Deut 19:15). Paul had witnessed wrongdoing and served warning on his second visit, which he now repeats in absentia (v. 2a). Should he again find anyone persisting in wrongdoing on this third visit, Paul's case against the wrongdoers would be conclusively established (v. 2b). Paul will not be lenient in dealing with unrepentant sinners and offers this as proof to the community that Christ is speaking through him (vv. 2c-3a). As Paul's weakness testified to his conformity to Christ, so also does his power. Paul will come in the power of Christ and deal boldly with the Corinthians (v. 4).

In the next series of admonitions (vv. 5-9), Paul, who has been under intense scrutiny with regard to his apostolic authenticity, turns the tables and admonishes the Corinthians to scrutinize themselves about their own authenticity. Examine and test yourselves, Paul cautions. Are you living in the faith, that is, do your lives conform to the gospel? Would your lives show that Christ is in you?

Though Paul expresses himself in a somewhat convoluted way in verses 6-9, the import of these statements is this: what the Corinthians think of Paul is less important than whether they advance in their life in Christ and commitment to the gospel. If this occurs, it does not matter to Paul whether or not he is judged an authentic apostle by their criteria. He has acted according to the truth and rejoices when the Corinthians are strong even if he is weak. Paul can and does pray for the community. However, in the end it is up to the Corinthians to renew their commitment to Christ and to live as true Christians. Paul's hope is that this severe written warning will be effective. Otherwise, despite claims to the contrary (see 10:10), Paul will be severe when he is again present among them and will exercise his apostolic authority to build up this community, which risks destroying itself.

EPISTOLARY CONCLUSION

2 Corinthians 13:11-13

After bidding the Corinthians to rejoice, Paul exhorts them to mend their ways, encourage one another, agree with one another, and live in peace (v. 11). These exhortations recall the situation of 1 Corinthians, where Paul had to deal with immoral lives in need of reform (1 Cor 5–6); disedifying rather than mutually upbuilding behavior (1 Cor 8–10); disagreement (1 Cor 1–4); and discord (1 Cor 12–14). The reader who gets the impression that the situation at Corinth has not significantly improved is probably right. Paul has tirelessly preached the gospel and labored to create a community of believers at Corinth. In the end, though, it is the responsibility of each believer to make Christian community a reality at Corinth. Whether Paul is absent or present, the Corinthians, who are Paul's partners in the work of the gospel, are responsible for the continual renewal of their lives and

2 Corinthians 13

the work of reconciliation (see 5:17-20). Once they are a community of love and peace, then the God of love and peace will dwell among them.

After hearing this letter read to them, the Corinthians were to exchange a "holy kiss," a symbol of each member's willingness to heed Paul's exhortation and to work toward unity and reconciliation. Paul typically closes his letters with a blessing, but this is the only time he invokes the blessings of the Lord Jesus Christ, God, and the holy Spirit (v. 14). While the prayer is Trinitarian in structure, it does not necessarily express all that is understood about the nature of God as enunciated in the doctrine of the Trinity. In the context of this letter, what the prayer does express is Paul's sincere desire that through the outpouring of Christ's grace, through which the community has come to know the love of God, they may live in the fellowship of the holy Spirit, who indwells each of them and is the source and sustainer of their unity in Christ.

The Letter to the Galatians
Robert J. Karris, O.F.M.

INTRODUCTION

I write this commentary for beginners and those who want a quick refresher course for preaching. But this is not a "commentary for dummies," for I envision my beginning readers as people who want clear but not simplistic exposition. I stand on the shoulders of other commentators and will acknowledge them, especially the premier commentator of our era, J. Louis Martyn.

To get us thinking about the complex thought world behind the letter to the Galatians, I tell the story of the poor friars who planned to raise money for a new bell tower by selling flowers from the friary garden. Their business became so popular that it adversely affected the trade of the local florist, who tried by various means to get the friars to sell honey or bread instead. Finally, he hired the local thug, Hugh McNails, who beat up the friars and persuaded them to close their flower shop. The moral of the story is: Only Hugh can prevent florist friars.

Readers from the United States might groan over the moral of this story, but they would get the pun. But readers from Europe would have a hard time understanding what was going on. You see, for some sixty years the Ad Council, along with the federal and state governments, has been so successful in promoting a slogan that 95 percent of U.S. adults and 77 percent of children recognize Smokey Bear and his slogan: "Only you can prevent forest fires." So it is understandable that Americans would recognize the pun.

In reading Galatians, we Americans are often like people from Europe who have not been exposed to Smokey Bear's slogan. When Paul talks about "the elemental powers" in Galatians 4:9, people of his time would know what he is referring to, whereas we scratch our heads in wonderment. The Jews of Paul's day would have little difficulty picking up on Paul's references to Abraham in Galatians 3–4, whereas Gentiles at that time and we today might be left in the dark.

The Letter to the Galatians

Let me take the Smokey Bear slogan a step further. Behind that slogan stand an entire governmental structure and a view of society. Who has the power to influence 280 million people to hold such name recognition if not the federal government, which promotes freedom of speech and which has power across state lines? The appeal to "you," an individual, and not to communities is quintessentially American. In a similar way, behind the phrase "the elemental powers" stands a view of reality in which the four powers of water, air, earth, and fire are the elementary building blocks of the world. Behind the name "Abraham" stands the entire story of God's dealings with the chosen people. In brief, this commentary aims to see what stories are at work in Galatians.

What makes Galatians tick?

Galatians is so short that readers sometimes think that it will be a breeze to read and comprehend. But after Paul's relatively simple narrative account in chapters 1 and 2, readers may stumble through the rest of the letter. Let me isolate the building blocks of Galatians and point to the cement that holds these blocks together.

The master plan of Galatians is that of an R&R letter: rebuke, which commences at 1:6, and request, which begins at 4:12. The most evident building blocks of this master plan are its beginning in 1:1-5 and its conclusion in 6:11-18. As we will see in the commentary proper, astute readers can pretty well discover the main thrust of Galatians from these two blocks of material. Paul tells the Galatians what he wants to say, then says his piece, and summarizes what he has said.

The largest building blocks are twofold: situational and preformed. What I call the preformed materials comprise the vast majority of Galatians: Paul's apologetic autobiography in 1:11–2:21, his argument from Scripture in 3:5–4:7, his scriptural allegory in 4:21-31, and his exhortations in 5:1–6:10. While these materials are not exactly cookie-cutter pieces, they give the impression that Paul has used them before. On the other hand, the situational building blocks are the means by which Paul makes Galatians and its preformed materials distinct, much as exterior and interior designs make "seen-one-seen-them-all" houses distinct in large subdivisions. Also, it is from these situational sections that we glimpse what is going on behind the scenes in Galatians 1:1-5; 1:6-10; 3:1-5; 4:8-11; 4:12-20; 5:2-12; 6:11-18.

The cement that holds these building blocks together consists of the three components of Paul's rhetoric. Like any good speaker or writer, Paul has to establish or reinforce his position as a person of trust, integrity, and goodwill. The Greeks called this *ethos*, from which our word "ethics" derives. Paul consumes almost all of Galatians 1–2 reestablishing his trustworthiness: his gospel is from God, not from human beings.

As a good speaker, Paul argues his case according to the *logic* of the time. He uses the argument of examples. He himself and Abraham are examples in Galatians 1–3. Paul also argues from accepted principles of faith. I give two examples. In 5:1 Paul first states the premise and then draws the conclusion, introducing it with the inferential adverb "so" (*oun* in Greek): "For freedom Christ set us free; *so* stand firm and do not submit again to the yoke of slavery." Sometimes Paul states his conclusion first and then enunciates his premise. A good example occurs in 5:4-6. In 5:4 Paul gives his conclusion from the two principles of faith he first articulates in 5:5-6. I put in italics the inferential particle "for" (*gar* in Greek):

> 5:4. You are separated from Christ, you who are trying to be justified by law; you have fallen from grace. 5. *For* through the Spirit, by faith, we await the hope of righteousness. 6. *For* in Christ Jesus, neither circumcision nor uncircumcision counts for anything, but only faith working through love.

Finally, Paul uses *pathos* to engage the hearts of his listeners. I give two quick examples. Who can read Galatians 4:13-20 and not realize that Paul is smuggling himself into the hearts of his beloved Galatian brothers and sisters: "So now have I become your enemy by telling you the truth?" (4:16). Galatians 1:6 is a wake-up slap in the face: "I am amazed that you are so quickly forsaking the one who called you!!" I recall in this context a cartoon that shows Paul with a startled look on his face as he reads a letter: "You have time to write to the Corinthians, the Thessalonians, the Philippians, but I'm amazed that you're too busy to sit down and write a simple letter to your mother!"

These three ingredients of Paul's rhetoric are operative today. Analyze any president's State of the Union address, and you'll see ethos, logic, and pathos on dress parade. This example also prepares us for reading Galatians, for not everyone on both sides of the aisle will be giving a standing ovation for every argument the president makes. Did all Galatians applaud Paul's letter to them? Were the teachers/influencers won over by Paul's argumentation?

The teachers or influencers from outside

I agree with contemporary scholars who avoid the labels "Judaizers" or "opponents" to talk about the people behind the scenes who occasioned

Galatians. I will follow J. Louis Martyn and Mark D. Nanos, who call these outsiders "the teachers" and "the influencers" respectively. The scholarly community mainly uses the method of mirror reading to ascertain what these teachers/influencers were advocating. That is, scholars accentuate the situational building blocks and from them try to discern why Paul is using the preformed materials he selects. Finally, they reconstruct through these mirrors what was happening in the Galatian churches.

For example, in the situational materials on Galatians 1:1-5, Paul underscores his call to be an apostle from Jesus Christ and not from human beings. So the inference is made that the teachers/influencers were saying that the gospel Paul preaches to the Gentiles is of human origin. The pre-formed materials of Galatians 1–2 seem to corroborate that inference, for Paul argues mightily that his gospel came from divine revelation and not from the earlier apostles, who, indeed, did not force him to alter his gospel.

Another example occurs in Galatians 3:1-5, where Paul argues that the Galatians' faith came from Paul's preaching and the Spirit and not from works of the law (including circumcision). The remainder of chapter 3 will deal with the case of Abraham, to whom the promise was made before the mandate of circumcision. In brief, we infer from these indications that the teachers/influencers asserted that the Galatian Christian males had to be circumcised and that all Galatian Christians had to observe the Jewish law to be true Christians.

Date and destination

I date Galatians between A.D. 50 and 55, and thus before Romans. I tend to agree with J. Louis Martyn that Paul wrote it to his converts in North Galatia, or the territory of Galatia, and not to his converts in South Galatia, or the Roman province of Galatia.

COMMENTARY

ADDRESS

Galatians 1:1-5

1:1-5 Salutation and anticipation of the letter's theme

If you compare this salutation with the salutations of the other genuine Pauline letters, except the letter to the Romans, you will note that Paul has expanded his normal greeting. Take, for example, the salutation in 1 Thessalonians 1:1: "Paul, Silvanus, and Timothy to the church of the Thessalonians in God the Father and the Lord Jesus Christ: grace to you and peace." Galatians 1:1-5 retains the skeleton of the typical Pauline greeting: "Paul to . . ., grace to you and peace," but has much more.

Galatians 1:1 makes two key points. First, Paul underlines the fact that he is the one sent, the apostle of Jesus Christ and God the Father, and not the emissary of some human being, no matter how exalted. Paul will focus on this factor in even greater detail in 1:11–2:21. The second point that Paul makes in Galatians 1:1 is that God the Father raised Jesus from the dead. What had been expected to occur at the end of time in Jewish eschatological expectation, namely, the resurrection of the dead, has broken into time and space now in the resurrection of the Jewish Messiah, Christ Jesus. In the light of this event, can business in the Jewish and Christian communities be conducted as usual?

The second notable expansion of Paul's normal greeting is found in Galatians 1:4, where he probably quotes an early confession that uses sacrificial terminology and then modifies it with one that employs apocalyptic terms. The confession reads: The Lord Jesus has given himself to take away our sins, that is, to eliminate the death-bearing effects of our sins. Implied is the fact that Jesus the Lord did this through the sacrifice of himself on the cross and not through obedience to the law. Using apocalyptic expressions, Paul states that the result and purpose of Jesus' death are our rescue from the present evil age.

Further, Jesus' death has end-of-the-world implications, for it has rescued believers, both Gentiles and Jews, from the present evil age, where sin and death roam about and take captive for their purposes even such a good thing as the law, God's gift to Israel. In brief, Paul anticipates his theme. With the death and resurrection of Jesus, the end of time has come forward and the new creation has begun (see Gal 6:15).

LOYALTY TO THE GOSPEL

Galatians 1:6-10

1:6-10 The beginning of the rebuke part of Galatians

While other letters in antiquity and Paul's letters follow the greeting with a thanksgiving period, Galatians does not. Was Paul so angry with the Galatians that he shot right past the normal courtesy of a thanksgiving? No, he adapted the rebuke statement that was also common in letter writing after the greeting. I paraphrase a pertinent example: "I am amazed that after all my instruction, you have botched the job, etc." The rebuke presupposes some close relationship between the sender and the recipient of the

Galatians 1

letter. Paul will be spelling out the reasons for his rebuke right up to 4:12, where he makes his request.

In Galatians 1:6 Paul makes it very clear that some of the Galatians are in the process, not of forsaking him and his preaching, but of forsaking God and the new creation they are enjoying. In the situational verse, Galatians 1:7, he also provides another hint of what is happening among the Galatians, for "some . . . are disturbing" them. The "disturbance" in question is not a telemarketer calling at dinnertime or someone playing loud music at two in the morning. Rather the disturbance is moral, on the level of conscience.

I find a wonderful parallel in 1 Thessalonians 1:9-10, where Paul reminds his Gentile converts that they "turned to God from idols to serve the living and true God and to await his Son from heaven, whom he raised from [the] dead, Jesus, who *delivers us from the coming wrath*" (emphasis added). It seems that the teachers/influencers are telling the Galatians that Paul's gospel will not deliver them from God's wrath. In our terms, unless the Galatians supplement Paul's teaching with theirs, they're going to hell.

PAUL'S DEFENSE OF HIS GOSPEL AND HIS AUTHORITY
Galatians 1:11–2:21

1:11-24 Paul, zealot for ancestral traditions, becomes apostle to Gentiles

Among the major points in Galatians 1:11–2:21 is Paul's example. Paul insists: Even though I was a zealot for Judaism and its ancestral traditions, I gave it all up. Thus this section prepares for Paul's plea in 4:12: "Be as I am, because I have also become as you are." Paul is saying: "You Galatians are trying to go back to where I was before Christ's revelation of a new creation to me. Don't do it." Parallels to Paul's call are best found in Philippians 3:4-16, where Paul accentuates his zeal for observance of the law: "In righteousness based on the law I was blameless" (Phil 3:6).

Another major point in this section is Paul's insistence that his gospel for and to the Gentiles did not come to him from human agency or human tradition, even that of Cephas (Peter), but from revelation. It was God who called Paul as God earlier had called prophets such as Jeremiah and revealed his Son to Paul (1:15-16). From Galatians 1:4 we know that the word "Son" is shorthand for the Son's significance in the story of humankind: The Son, who died for our sins and was raised from the dead, rescues Jews and Gentiles from this evil age.

2:1-14 Paul fights for inclusive table fellowship

As Paul continues his apology for his apostolic ministry and gospel to the Gentiles, we should keep in mind the wise counsel of George Lyons: "Ancient autobiographies were more concerned with ethical characterization and edification than with chronology and exactitude" (p. 60). So Luke's account in Acts 15 and Paul's account here of what happened at the Council of Jerusalem may both be true, since they are told from two different perspectives.

Paul's main points are threefold. The first point concerns the rite of circumcision, by which males entered into the chosen people and committed themselves to observe God's gift of the law. The leaders of the Jerusalem church did not compel Paul to circumcise Titus (2:3) or add the ritual of circumcision to his apostolic ministry (2:6).

The second point occurs twice, in 2:5 and 2:14: "the truth of the gospel." While the good news or gospel at Paul's time might refer to a military victory or the birth of an emperor who would change the world and effect lasting peace, for Paul the gospel of Jesus Christ has the power to save through the gift of the Spirit and effects a new creation amidst the old structures of the world. The new creation effected by the gospel has replaced any distinction based on circumcision and uncircumcision: "For neither does circumcision mean anything, nor does uncircumcision, but only a new creation" (Gal 6:15). This is the truth of the gospel; this is "our freedom that we have in Christ Jesus" (2:4). In Paul's view, the teachers/influencers want to liberate the Galatians from this freedom and enslave them by means of circumcision and observance of the law (2:4).

A question introduces the third point: Why the big fuss over who eats what with whom? I answer that food and drink are languages. Do you eat hot dogs on Christmas? Do you toast the bride and groom with water at a wedding? Indeed, not all days are equal; some should be celebrated with better-quality food and drink. Religion also enters into the area of food and drink, as Christians quickly realize when they reflect on the eucharistic bread and wine and Roman Catholics recall their obligation to fast and abstain on Good Friday.

As is the case today, during Paul's time the quality and quantity of food and drink were also social markers. Even at the same symposium, which consisted of eating, a libation to the gods, and drinking with conversation, the patron may have received better food, while his clients were given inferior fare. Jews may have sat in the same room with Gentiles but dined at their own table on specially prepared kosher food and drink. It seems to me that Philip Esler has provided a very helpful way to view what was happening during table fellowship in Antioch. As Jewish and Gentile

Christians shared one loaf and one cup, some Jewish Christians were overwhelmed with the fear that a Gentile Christian, not having completely forgotten idolatrous ways, may have secretively offered a drop of eucharistic wine to a god. How could a person put oneself in the position of participating in such idolatry?

2:15-21 Righteousness, the works of the law, and faith

There are three issues in Galatians 2:16. The meaning of righteousness or justification is the first one. The image seems to stem from the criminal law court system, where a person (or a people) is acquitted, vindicated, judged in the right. Helpful background is Psalm 143:1-2:

> LORD, hear my prayer;
>   in your faithfulness listen to my pleading;
>   answer me in your justice.
> Do not enter into judgment with your servant;
>   before you no living being can be just.

When sinful human beings as God's elect appear before God's law court, God in gracious mercy acquits them; they do not justify or acquit themselves. Modern computer technology has come to our interpretive aid in this matter by supplying the example of word-processing programs that justify margins, that is, they make them straight. Without word processing, the words on this page would not have straight left and right margins but would be out of order, in chaos.

The second issue concerns the meaning of "the works of the law." From the immediate context of Galatians 1–2, it seems that the phrase "the works of the law" refers to those things that distinguish Jews from Gentiles, namely, circumcision, dietary laws, and festivals. But from Galatians 3–4 it seems better to take "the works of the law" in a more comprehensive sense to refer to observance of the law.

In the third issue, grammar and christology hold hands: Is the Greek genitive *Iesou Christou* objective, subjective, or authorial? For years scholars have taken it to be objective, that is, "faith in Jesus Christ." A more appealing interpretation is to take this genitive to be subjective, that is, "the faithfulness that Jesus Christ manifested in his death on the cross for us." If the genitive is authorial, then Jesus Christ is the author of both his and the Christians' faith.

From these three considerations I draw some conclusions. Paul is not attacking the Jews as an arrogant people who are trying to earn heaven by their meritorious deeds. Paul gives himself as an example of how a Jewish zealot became the preacher of a law-free gospel to Gentiles. Through Christ's death and resurrection for us, God has shown a new way of being righteous with God's people. Men do not need to be circumcised, people do not need to observe dietary laws and the sabbath to become members of God's people in Christ. As we will soon see in chapter 3, Paul deals with the big picture—the story of how God fashions a community of faith by liberating people from the powers of the old age and inaugurating a new creation.

FAITH AND LIBERTY

Galatians 3:1–4:31

3:1-5 The Spirit's role in Christian life

Galatians 3:1-5 begins another long section of rebuke and personal example. In a culture that cherished wisdom, Paul's rebuke of the foolishness of the Galatians is harsh. The example that follows throughout chapter 3 is that of Abraham, who was justified without circumcision. Galatians 3:1-5, along with 3:6-29, allows us to glimpse the preaching of the teachers/influencers, who are championing "the works of the law," especially circumcision. Paul reminds the Galatians that in a very graphic way he had preached Jesus Christ crucified to them and that they listened to this message, which elicited faith. Their faith did not come from "the works of the law," about which they had not yet heard. The gifts of God's powerful Spirit did not come to them from their performance of "the works of the law," about which they were blissfully ignorant.

Paul draws the logical conclusion from his argument based on the Galatians' actual experience: Are you so stupid that you don't recognize that you have already received God's eschatological gift of the Spirit and don't need to complete your faith or membership in God's people with "the works of the law"? With a telling play on two meanings of the word "flesh," that is, flesh as circumcision of the foreskin and flesh as the realm of human weakness, Paul further castigates the Galatians for their stupidity of beginning in the ways of God's powerful Spirit and ending with the flesh. In 5:13–6:10 Paul will return to this contrast of flesh and Spirit when he gives guidance about Christian conduct.

3:6-29 The story of Abraham, the law, Abraham's seed, and us

There are many starting points for the story of St. Francis of Assisi. Some authors start with Christ's command to Francis: "Repair my house." Others commence with Francis's overcoming of his dread of lepers, pariahs of his society. Still others underscore Francis's profound experience of God, who to Francis was "My God and my All." The stories told from these starting points will have many things in common, for example, the economic situation of the time, the importance of Lateran Council IV, the crusades against another pariah of that society, the Muslim. Each story, however, will end up with its singular view of Francis of Assisi and what his life meant then and might mean now.

In 3:6-29 Paul is telling the story of Abraham, the law, Abraham's Seed, which is Christ Jesus, and us. His telling of this story seems very different from the way the teachers/influencers were telling it. Yet both they and Paul were using the same common materials, that is, Israel's Scriptures in their Greek version, the Septuagint. Whereas Paul's starting point is Christ Jesus and his faithfulness, the starting point of the teachers/influencers seems to have been God's covenant made with Abraham, which was sealed by circumcision and in which believers remained by faithfully observing the law.

Notice how often Paul refers in this passage to Jesus Christ, who is Paul's real starting point and the goal of the story of Abraham. See, for example, Galatians 3:16, where Paul interprets God's promise to Abraham and his seed to refer to Christ. Galatians 3:23-29 is permeated with references to Christ Jesus. For example, 3:23 reads: "Before faith came, we were held in custody under law, confined for the faith that was to be revealed." As Sam K. Williams says so well, the word "faith" here is best translated as "Jesus-Christ-faith."

From his starting point of Jesus Christ, Paul returns to the story of Abraham. It seems that the teachers/influencers commenced their story with Genesis 17:10-11, where God instructs Abraham: "And this is the covenant that you shall keep between me and you and your seed after you for their generations. Every male among you will be circumcised . . . this circumcision will be a sign of the covenant between me and you" (author's translation). Paul, however, commences his story of Abraham by quoting Genesis 15:6: "Abraham believed God, and it was credited to him as righteousness" (3:6; author's translation). By selecting Genesis 15:6 as his key text, Paul scores the big point that Abraham is the father of faith, not of circumcision, for he believed and was declared righteous before he or his descendant was even circumcised.

Having made his point that God justified Abraham by faith, Paul then turns back to the promise God made to Abraham in Genesis 12:3: "All the nations will be blessed through you" (author's translation). By means of his citations of Genesis 15:6 and 12:3, Paul can conclude against the teachers/

influencers: "Consequently, those who have faith [the Gentiles] are blessed along with Abraham who had faith" (Gal 3:9).

In Galatians 3:10-25 Paul uses Scripture and human analogies to deal with the role of God's gift of the law. In 3:10-14 Paul uses four Scripture texts to attack the teachers'/influencers' reading of Deuteronomy that God's blessings descend upon those who obey the law. Against their reading Paul quotes Deuteronomy 27:26: "Cursed be everyone who does not persevere in doing all the things written in the book of the law" (author's translation). Implied is that no one can fully obey the law and therefore falls under the curse. Paul supports his case in 3:11 by quoting Habakkuk 2:4 about the centrality of faith, not the law: "The one who is righteous by faith will live" (author's translation).

Then, in 3:12 Paul summons the Pentateuch to ground his position, as he cites Leviticus 18:5: "The one who does these things [the matters of the law] will live by them" and not find true life. Finally, in a daring soteriological move Paul returns to Deuteronomy 27:26 to pick up the theme of "cursed be everyone" and to integrate it with another passage in Deuteronomy that speaks of "cursed be everyone": "Cursed be everyone who hangs on a tree" (Deut 21:23; author's translation). Paul then professes his faith: "Christ ransomed us from the curse of the law by becoming a curse for us" (3:13).

In Galatians 3:15-18 Paul builds his argument about the deficiency of the law by using an analogy and Scripture. Paul's analogy of a human will and testament employs the same Greek word behind "covenant" *(diatheke)* and depends upon the legality that no one can annul or amend the will once it has been ratified. Reading the Septuagint of Genesis 13:15, 17:8, 24:7, Paul states that God's promise was to Abraham and to his "descendant" in the singular. Of course, in Paul's eyes that singular descendant is Christ (3:16). Calculating the time between Abraham and the Sinai covenant, Paul makes his case that the law, which came 430 years later (see Exod 12:40), cannot annul God's promises made to Abraham and through him to the Gentiles.

In Galatians 3:19-25 Paul gives two answers to his question: "Why, then, the law?" (3:19). Galatians 3:19-22, especially 3:19, provides the first answer: "It was added for transgressions." The context indicates that the law was added to restrain transgressions. In this sense it was the disciplinarian of which Paul talks in 3:24-25. In 3:19 Paul masks God's action in giving the law: "It was promulgated by angels at the hand of a mediator." As Leviticus 26:46 clearly indicates, the mediator was Moses. The role of the angels in the giving of the law finds a parallel in the Septuagint of Deuteronomy 33:2

at the giving of the law: "the angels were with God at God's right hand" (author's translation). See also Acts 7:53.

In a mini-summary of the points he has been making from verse 10 onward, Paul writes: "For if a law had been given that could bring life, then righteousness would in reality come from the law. But scripture confined all things under the power of sin, that through the faithfulness of Jesus Christ the promise might be given to those who believe" (3:21-22; author's translation). Paul will have more to say about the law in Romans 7:12: "So then the law is holy, and the commandment is holy and righteous and good."

In Galatians 3:23-25 Paul gives a second answer to the question "Why the law?" He uses two images: imprisonment (confined in custody) and that of a disciplinarian. Both of these images are severe but point to a temporary reality, until Jesus-Christ-faith has come onto the scene.

Paul concludes his argument with the teachers/influencers by calling the Galatians' attention to baptism, by which they become one in Christ Jesus, who is Abraham's descendant. Galatians 3:28 is most likely a liturgical formula that describes the new eschatological reality of Christian community effected by Christ's death and resurrection and the gift of the promised Spirit. For Paul's purposes, the first line is most important: "There is neither Jew nor Greek"/Gentile. Christian communities are still wrestling with the implementation of the vision of this confessional statement of the new reality in Christ Jesus: "There is neither slave nor free person, there is not male and female; for you are all one in Christ Jesus."

If we go back to my opening example of stories about Francis of Assisi, I would say that one major criterion by which we can judge the truth of each story is this: Does it give life? Using this criterion, I would have to say that Paul's story is true, because it has already given life to the Galatians, who had received the Spirit through Paul's preaching of this story as gospel. The question remains: Will the Galatians reaffirm Paul's story or accept that of the teachers/influencers?

4:1-11 Elemental powers of the world, heirs, and the Spirit's cry of "Abba, Father"

I treat three points. While Galatians 3:23-29 and 4:1-11 repeat certain themes, for example, both refer to baptism (3:27-28; 4:4-8), what is surely different between them is Paul's reference to "the elemental powers of the world" (4:3; see 4:9). In my Introduction (pp. 581–82) I mentioned that when we are faced with this type of jargon, we are like foreigners coming to the United States and trying to figure out the meaning of the pun "Only Hugh can prevent florist friars." I provide the following three parallels. Wisdom 13:1-5 is invective against people who worship the four elements of fire, water, earth, and air and do not infer from these good things the God who made them. Wisdom 13:1 states: "For all people . . . were in ignorance of God, and who from the good things seen did not succeed in coming to the knowledge of the one who is" (author's translation).

In their stories of Abraham, both Philo of Alexandria and Josephus, contemporaries of Paul, depict Abraham as overcoming the pagan worship of the elements as gods and coming to the worship of the true God. In Book I.155–156 of his *Jewish Antiquities,* Josephus writes:

> Abraham determined to renew and to change the opinion all people had then concerning God. For he was the first . . . to publish . . . that there was but one God, the Creator of the universe. . . . This opinion was derived from the irregular phenomena that were visible both at land and sea, as well as those that happen to the sun, and moon, and all the heavenly bodies (modified translation of William Whiston).

With the above background in mind, we begin to glimpse what was going on behind the scenes in Galatia. The teachers/influencers congratulated the Galatians on giving up their worship of the elements and the festivals associated with their worship and invited them to imitate Abraham, who explored the heavenly bodies to ascertain "days, months, seasons, and years" (4:10). What Abraham discovered is contained now in the Jewish sacred times. Paul's attack on the teachers/influencers and the Galatians is radically christocentric. As he says in 4:3: "In the same way we [Paul the Jew included] also, when we were not of age [and before God sent his Son], were enslaved to the elemental powers of the world." If the Galatians return to observing sacred days, after having received Paul's law-free gospel, they are turning back again to "the weak and destitute elemental powers" (4:9).

The figure of Abraham, the first Gentile believer, is one link between Galatians 4:1-11 and 3:6-29. Another is "heir" (Gal 3:29 and 4:1-2). The law's time to be guardian is over, for God has sent God's Son, born as a human being, born as a Jew, to ransom those under the law, so that both Jews and Gentiles might receive full legal rights as heirs (4:5).

Galatians 4:6 is vitally important: "As proof that you are sons, God sent the Spirit of God's Son into our hearts, crying out, 'Abba, Father'" (author's translation). Here Paul is using the same argument he used so powerfully in 3:1-5: the experience of the Galatians. Paul seems to be making another point by his interchange of pronouns "*you* are sons" and "into *our* hearts."

Galatians 4

Both Gentile Christians and Jewish Christians (Paul included) are heirs together. Both have the same Father, whose name is given in both Aramaic ("Abba") and Greek.

It is fitting that Paul concludes the "rebuke" part of his letter with a sarcastic rebuke: "Do you want to be slaves to them [the elemental powers] all over again?" (4:9). Paul now turns to his "request."

4:12-20 Paul begins his request and appeals to the affections of his friends

G. Walter Hansen and Richard N. Longenecker make a good case that Paul commences the request section of his letter with Galatians 4:12, which contains the first imperative of the entire letter. Hansen notes that a rebuke letter often concluded with a request for renewal of friendship and a change of conduct. These components are obvious in the short papyrus letter contemporaneous with Paul. I adapt Hansen's text:

> I am amazed (rebuke; see Gal 1:6) that you did not see your way to let me have what I asked you to send by Corbolon, esp. when I desired it for a festival. I beg you (request) to buy (imperative) me a silver seal and to send (imperative) it to me posthaste.

In the midst of expending much energy on showing his integrity *(ethos)* and arguing from Scripture and from the Galatians' experience (logic), Paul now wears his emotions on his sleeve *(pathos)*. He is tender as he addresses his converts as "brothers and sisters" (4:12) and "my children" (4:19). Like the good wisdom and evangelical teacher that he is, Paul's first exhortation is: "Be as I am" (4:12). In other words, Paul is not telling the Galatians to do something that he doesn't do himself. In the context of this letter, the focus of this appeal is on Paul's self-sacrificing relinquishment of Jewish conduct that separated Jews from Gentiles (circumcision, dietary laws, sabbath) and his adaptation of Gentile ways.

Paul further appeals to the generous and gracious acceptance he received from the Galatians when he appeared on their doorsteps with a weakness of the flesh. Might this weakness of the flesh be the wounds Paul received for preaching the gospel? See 2 Corinthians 11:24-25: "Five times at the hands of the Jews I received forty lashes minus one. Three times I was beaten with rods, once I was stoned." The Galatians did not spit on Paul and reject him, but would have spent an arm and a leg to assist him.

Galatians 4:17 provides a hazy snapshot of the teachers/influencers: "They show interest in you, but not in a good way; they want to isolate you, so that you may show interest in them." It seems that the teachers/influencers are courting the Galatians, so that they might separate them from their fellow Gentile Christians and include them in the exclusive club of the Jewish Christians who observe the law. Paul is the champion of inclusivity, not exclusivity. He wants both Jewish and Gentile Christians around the same table.

I recall an experience I had some time ago when I went to a restaurant with an African-American confrere. The owner stopped us near the entrance, looked me in the eye, and addressed me: "This is an exclusive club. You can get a membership card immediately and be seated." I was being courted to leave my confrere behind and enjoy exclusive table fellowship. My confrere and I walked out of the restaurant together and sought an inclusive table. Will the Galatians leave their friend Paul standing at the door as they rush to fill a table in an exclusive club?

4:21-31 You are children of the promise and of the Spirit

There are four keys to unlock the meaning of this troublesome passage. The first key is the supposition that Paul is swept into his interpretation of Sarah, Hagar, and their sons because the teachers/influencers were using these figures to instruct the Galatians to follow the path of Sarah's son, Isaac, whom Abraham circumcised and who inherited the promise. Paul turns the exegetical tables on these teachers/influencers and uses Sarah's son for his purposes of proclaiming that the Gentiles, like Isaac, are heirs of the promise (4:28).

The second key is the meaning of "allegory" (4:24). The Greek verb Paul uses here has the generic meaning "to use analogy or likeness to express something." Like any good preacher, Paul is finding an analogy between the historical events of Genesis 21 and the historical events of his own time. As R.P.C. Hanson says: "He (Paul) is doing what he is doing in his scriptural expositions of I Cor. 9 and 10 and II Cor. 3. . . . He is envisaging a critical situation which took place under the Old Covenant . . . as forecasting and repeated by a situation under the New Covenant" (p. 82).

The third key is the Greek verb that stands behind Galatians 4:25: "It *corresponds*" (emphasis added). Literally the Greek verb *systoichei* means "stands in line with." The reader is to imagine two lines over against each other: the troops of General X are arrayed against the troops of General Y. Or the lines may be drawn according to radical contrasts: flesh on one side, Spirit/promise on the other side; slavery on one side, freedom on the opposite side; Hagar on one side, and Sarah on the other. So standing in line with "slave" are Hagar, Ishmael (although never named), flesh, Mount

Sinai, the present Jerusalem. Standing in line with "free" are Sarah (although never named), Isaac, promise/Spirit, the Jerusalem above.

The fourth key is Paul's quotation of Isaiah 54:1 in 4:27. As Richard B. Hays says: "Paul's major purpose for citing Isa 54:1 is to evoke Deutero-Isaiah's central theme of God's gracious eschatological restoration of Israel and a universal embrace of the nations" (p. 304). Put briefly, the New Jerusalem, which apocalyptic texts such as Revelation 21 expected at the end of time, has appeared because of the boundary-breaking death and resurrection of Christ Jesus. In it are Gentiles who live without the law.

Now that we have used these four keys to gain entrance to Paul's extended analogy, we are somewhat prepared to appreciate the three conclusions he draws for the Galatian Gentiles. The first is that the Galatians are like Isaac and are children of the promise (4:28). The second depends upon acquaintance with a Targumic tradition that Ishmael harassed Isaac because he was circumcised willingly at age thirteen and therefore was more righteous than Isaac, who was circumcised after a mere eight days (see 4:29). The third is found in the one and only quotation from the law in this passage (see 4:21): "'Drive out the slave woman and her son. / For the son of the slave woman shall not share the inheritance with the son' / of the freeborn." Paul uses Scripture to convince his Galatian converts to do something they should have done at the very beginning: Throw the teachers/influencers out of your community!

EXHORTATION TO CHRISTIAN LIVING

Galatians 5:1–6:10

5:1-12 Paul's authoritative appeal that the Galatians stand firm in freedom

Paul's appeals in this section tell us much about Christian freedom, Christian community, and the message of the teachers/influencers. If we go back to my introductory gambit about the slogan "Only you can prevent florist friars (forest fires)," we realize that this makes sense in our American culture of rampant individualism. For the "you" that Smokey Bear is pointing to is an individual, not a community. Paul's view of freedom should be seen from the way Paul uses this term in Galatians. Christians are free to form an inclusive community (3:26-28). They have freedom from the power of sin (3:22), from the power of the law (3:23), from the elemental powers of the world (4:3). As Sam K. Williams says: Christians are free "from the religious and cultural prisons whose darkness breeds prejudice, suspicion, and resentment" (3:26-28).

If the Galatians are circumcised, they will join an exclusive club and be obligated to fulfill all its regulations (5:3). Being circumcised or not being circumcised is no longer a way of joining community, but rather "faith working through love" (5:6). Those who are inspired by Christ's Spirit through faith manifest Christ's self-sacrificing love for one another in community (see Gal 2:20). If one tries to supplement Christian faith with the ethnic marker of circumcision and tries to be justified by observance of the law, that person has fallen from grace (5:4). "A person is not justified by works of the law but through the faithfulness of Jesus Christ" (2:16; author's translation).

From this passage it is very clear that the teachers/influencers were trying to persuade the Galatians to fully join the Christian community by being circumcised (5:2). They are "a little yeast" that is negatively influencing "the whole batch of dough" (5:9). They are causing headaches and heartaches of faith for the Galatians (5:10).

Paul displays angry humor in 5:12. Deuteronomy 23:2 provides the best interpretive parallel: "No one whose testicles have been crushed or whose penis has been cut off, may be admitted into the community of the Lord." Paul says: Those who are cutting off foreskins so that others may gain definitive entry into the community should have their own penises cut off and thus be banned from belonging to the community. Is there any doubt that community is a dominant theme of this passage?

5:13-26 Part One of Paul's ethical appeal: The apocalyptic battle between Flesh and Spirit

Behind this passage another aspect of Paul's confrontation with the teachers/influencers seems to be raging. These teachers/influencers are saying to the Galatians that once they have been circumcised and become members of the Israel of God, they will have the law to guide them in their moral lives and the community of the law to support them when the evil spirit has led them into sin. To Paul this approach to the ethical life is eschatologically outdated and christologically deficient. I call my readers' attention to Galatians 1:4: The Lord Jesus Christ "gave himself for our sins that he might rescue us from *the present evil age*" (emphasis added). Rescue from the present evil age is not by means of the law but by means of God's Spirit (4:6, 29; 5:16-24). I make three explanatory remarks.

First, J. Louis Martyn is indeed correct to see that Paul is using apocalyptic language here to describe what the results in the moral sphere are of Christ's incursion into "the present evil age." He writes:

Galatians 5

> The Spirit's war against the Flesh . . . was declared by God when he sent his Son and the Spirit of this Son into the territory of the Flesh. This war is, then, the new-creational struggle, the apocalyptic war of the end-time, the war in which God's forces are the ones on the march. . . ." (pp. 530–531).

Paul's apocalyptic imagery of warfare is clear in Galatians 5:13, for the Greek word behind "opportunity" literally means "a staging area for an army." Galatians 5:17 describes the warfare between flesh and Spirit, which "are opposed to each other." Just as in a real war one's options are curtailed in this war, so that "you may not do what you want." The stakes in this warfare are very high, for "inherit[ance of] the kingdom of God" is the goal and prize. We do a disservice to Paul's thought when we take flesh in either its capitalized or noncapitalized form to refer to sins of the flesh. Flesh is the entire world turned against God; flesh refers to human beings turned in upon themselves and away from God.

Although Paul does not invoke the entire law for moral guidance, he is not antimonian. Through the eschatological experience hoped for in Jeremiah 31:33-34, the Galatians have knowledge of what God wants written on their hearts. As James D. G. Dunn says, they depend "more on inward apprehension of what is the appropriate conduct than on rule book or tradition" (p. 296). Further, "the whole law is fulfilled in one statement, namely, 'You shall love your neighbor as yourself'" (5:14). The Galatian Christians are to be slaves to "one another through love" (5:13), as Paul turns the slave/free dichotomy on its head and says in effect: Sure, you are free, free to be in bondage by love to one another. The first fruit of the Spirit is "love" (5:22). People do not need the law to discern the works of the flesh, for they are "obvious" (5:19). Against the fruit of the Spirit "there is no law" (5:23), as if a generous grocer who is feeding the poor were responding to her complaining neighbors: "Is there a law against helping the poor?"

Finally, the flesh destroys community. See the "vices" in the middle of the "works of the flesh": "hatreds, rivalry, jealousy, outbursts of fury, acts of selfishness, dissensions, factions, occasions of envy" (5:20-21). See also the anti-community behavior Paul rebukes in Galatians 5:13 and 5:26. But the fruit of the Spirit fosters community: "peace, patience, kindness, generosity, faithfulness, gentleness, self-control" (5:22).

Throughout the centuries Christians have been heirs to the battle Paul is waging in Galatians 5:13-26. One side says: They need detailed laws and regulations to prevent them from sinning. Another side states: They need to be genuinely attentive to the Spirit. For those old enough to remember the immediate post-Vatican II days, I invoke the battles between those who cherished the detailed instructions given in the moral manuals and those who championed works such as Bernard Haring's *The Law of Christ*, which stressed the role of the Spirit in moral life.

6:1-10 Part Two of Paul's ethical appeal: The serious consequences of behavior within the household of faith

I take Galatians 6:10, which Hans Dieter Betz has called the summary and conclusion of Galatians 5:1–6:9, as my starting point. Paul's ethical appeal ends with a universal dimension "do good to all," and with a particular dimension, "especially to those who belong to the family of the faith." This is not a natural family or household, but one formed by faith. In this household there are people who teach and lead their fellow members into a deeper understanding of Christian life (6:6). In it there is fraternal correction, done in a spirit of gentleness and love, as members are socialized into appropriate Spirit-led conduct (6:1). In imitation of Christ's self-sacrificing love manifested in his death on the cross for us (Gal 2:20), members of the faith community bear one another's burdens and thus fulfill the only true law, the law of Christ (6:2).

As a modern example of what Paul is saying, I think of my own religious community of Friars Minor, who are white, African American, Hispanic, and Asian, and who are socialized into what it means to be a community of brothers not so much by rules and regulations, but by the example of fellow friars who have faithfully and creatively followed the guidance of the Spirit.

In Galatians 6:7-9, Paul again reveals the apocalyptic bent of his theology. There are ultimate consequences from deeds sown in the flesh and in the Spirit. But Paul ends his serious reminder with a note of encouragement: "Let us not grow tired of doing good, for in due time we shall reap our harvest, if we do not give up" (6:9).

CONCLUSION

Galatians 6:11-18

6:11-18 Postscript and summary of the letter

As Paul summarizes his message, there are pathos and ethos in his description of himself: I bear in my body the brand marks of Jesus Christ (6:17). Paul's scars are signs of his love for Christ Jesus and the Galatians. Paul continues to attack the teachers/influencers who champion circumcision as the saving supplement to Paul's gospel (6:11-13). In my tradition, it's as if someone were to accost a regular church member and say that he will only be saved if he recites the Novena to St. Anthony of Padua every Tuesday. It is not circumcision that is foundational but the cross. What God has done to Sin and Flesh and Law by the death and resurrection of his Son has changed the world and transformed Paul (6:14).

In Galatians 6:15 Paul introduces the term "new creation." I find a compelling parallel to "new creation" in one of my favorite books from New Testament times. *Joseph and Aseneth* tells the story of the conversion of the Gentile Aseneth so that she could marry Joseph (see Gen 41:45). In Joseph's prayer over Aseneth, I have italicized the "new creation" words: "Lord God of my father Israel, the Most High, the Powerful One of Jacob, who gave life to all things, and called them from darkness to light, and from error to truth, and from death to life, you, Lord, bless this virgin and *renew* her by your spirit, and *form her anew* by your hidden hand, and *make her alive again* by your life" (8.9; modified translation of C. Burchard).

The death and resurrection of the Lord Jesus and the sending of his creative Spirit have brought about the new creation. This new creation, however, is not just revealed in individuals but also and especially in the household of faith, where Jew and Gentile, male and female, slave and freeborn are sitting at the same table, enjoying their freedom in the Spirit, in the midst of the present evil age, and awaiting God's righteousness in hope.

BIBLIOGRAPHY

Hans Dieter Betz, *Galatians*. Hermeneia. Philadelphia: Fortress, 1979.

James D. G. Dunn, *The Epistle to the Galatians*. Black's New Testament Commentary. Peabody, MA: Hendrickson, 1993.

G. Walter Hansen, *Galatians*. The IVP New Testament Commentary Series. Downers Grove, IL: InterVarsity Press, 1994.

R.P.C. Hanson, *Allegory and Event*. Louisville: Westminster John Knox Press, 2002.

Richard N. Longenecker, *Galatians*. Word Bible Commentary 41. Dallas: Word Books, 1990.

George Lyons, *Pauline Autobiography: Toward a New Understanding.* Atlanta: Scholars Press, 1985.

J. Louis Martyn, *Galatians.* Anchor Bible 33A. New York: Doubleday, 1998.

Mark D. Nanos, *The Irony of Galatians: Paul's Letter in First-Century Context.* Minneapolis: Fortress, 2002.

Sam K. Williams, *Galatians.* Abingdon New Testament Commentaries. Nashville: Abingdon, 1997.

The Letter to the Ephesians

Vincent M. Smiles

INTRODUCTION

Authorship and destination

Ephesus, on the west coast of Asia Minor (Turkey), was in Paul's day a large seaport city. Paul stayed there for about three years (Acts 20:31) and undoubtedly wrote some of his letters from there, but whether he wrote the letter to the Ephesians is a matter of some doubt.

Ever since the sixteenth century, scholars reading Ephesians in Greek have wondered whether Paul could be its author. Even reading the text in English, those familiar with Paul's letters find reasons to wonder: its ornate, elevated style (especially in chapters 1–3), its purely universal view of "the church," the focus on Christ's cosmic victory over "the powers" with little stress on Christ's death, the comparative lack of apocalyptic expectation combined with a view of salvation already accomplished, the absence of "brothers" as a form of address and of any personal expressions of affection, and the obvious dependence on Colossians—all give reason to question whether Paul is the author. The evidence against Paul as the author is so strong that today about 75 percent of scholars regard Ephesians as pseudonymous.

As with Colossians, however, the issue of authorship may be more complicated. Some, who accept that Paul did not write Colossians, think nevertheless that he may have had some input into that letter. Similarly, with respect to Ephesians, it is possible that the author knew Paul personally—he or she certainly knew Paul's letters (not only Colossians)—or may have written Ephesians expanding on a text written by Paul himself. That text might simply have been Colossians, but a further theory is that Ephesians is an enlarged version of the letter to Laodicea (see Col 4:16). On balance, however, the evidence favors more distance between Paul and Ephesians than these latter theories allow, especially given that Colossians also was probably not composed by the apostle himself.

This commentary will presuppose that Ephesians was written by an admirer of Paul, about twenty or thirty years after his death (i.e., A.D. 80–90). The writer knew Colossians very well, but was also well acquainted with Paul's other letters. Whether Ephesians was originally addressed to Ephesus is doubtful, since first, the words "in Ephesus" (1:1) are missing from the best and earliest manuscripts of the letter, and second, both 1:15 and 3:2 suggest that Paul and the readers had only "heard" of one another, as though Paul had never been there. Whereas Paul's letters always speak to the *particular* circumstances of individual churches, providing specific instructions, Ephesians envisions Paul writing from prison (3:1; 4:1) in *general* terms about challenges for "the church" at large. Ephesians, therefore, is often viewed as a kind of encyclical letter to Paul's churches in general, in Ephesus and elsewhere.

The relationship with Colossians and the purposes of Ephesians

The closeness between Colossians and Ephesians is far more obvious than is the similarity between any other two Pauline letters. This is not to say that they were written by the same author; they probably were not. More probably, the writer of Ephesians composed freely, with major ideas and phrases of Colossians making their presence felt naturally. Some obvious similarities are noted in the commentary on 4:17–5:20. Other passages where similarities are easily detected include:

Ephesians	*Colossians*	*Topic*
1:7	1:14	redemption—forgiveness
1:21-23	1:16-19	Christ's victory as head—fullness of God
2:5	2:13	dead made alive
3:2-3	1:25-26	hidden mystery revealed to Paul
5:22–6:9	3:18–4:1	Wives, husbands, children, slaves
4:15-16	2:19	Christ the head—body bound together
6:21-22	4:7-8	Tychicus, the news-bearer

Major themes of Ephesians, most notably the cosmic Christ as head of the universal church, were evidently largely inspired by Colossians; the connection is beyond dispute.

On the other hand, Ephesians is quite different from Colossians in what it says about Judaism. Colossians contests "the philosophy" (Col 2:8), evidently deriving mainly from Judaism, that required obedience to certain laws (2:16-23). Such laws, says Colossians, are mere "human tradition" (2:8, 22), having to do with "the elements of the world" (2:8, 20), which Christ has defeated (2:14-15, 20). Judaism is not specifically mentioned in Colossians, but these warnings portray the Jewish law in a rather negative light; only 3:11 ("no longer Greek and Jew") suggests the possibility of Jewish and Gentile believers living peacefully within the one body.

Ephesians 2:11-18, on the other hand, presumes a very high estimation of Judaism; theirs are "the covenants," to which Gentiles are joined by faith in Christ. The language of "those far off" being brought "near" is Jewish terminology for conversion to Judaism. Most significant is the triple mention of Christ's achieving "peace" (2:14, 15, 17), reconciling Jews and Gentiles "in one body" (2:15-16). It has, therefore, been suggested that Ephesians was written, in part, to reach out to Jewish Christians and present to them a friendly understanding of Paul, softening some of his harshness (e.g., Gal 3:1-21). At the same time, it appeals to Gentile believers to be welcoming of Jewish Christians. In any event, it is clear that Ephesians has a keen concern for the unity of all believers under "one faith" (4:1-6). The primary purpose for its composition, therefore, was to provide a vision of Christ and of "the church" that would make unity among "the churches" and their various believers possible.

The value of Ephesians today

The author of Ephesians lived in a time of transition. The foundational "apostles and prophets" (2:20) had all died. The church, therefore, or better "the churches," had to adjust. Ephesians represents a second/third generation voice that reminds the various churches that they are God's "handiwork, created in Christ Jesus" (2:10) and that they must "live worthily" of their "calling" (4:1). As Paul himself had done, so also the Ephesians writer reminds believers of the fundamentals: they belong together as one body in Christ.

The Catholic Church of the twenty-first century has its own transitions and tensions: What and who is "the church"? How is it to fulfill its mission? Who is to be included in deciding such questions? For all its emphasis on the universal church, Ephesians agrees with the rest of the New Testament that "the church" is the community of the baptized, whether a local congregation (e.g., Col 4:15), "the churches" of a particular region (e.g., Gal 1:2), or the church in general (as in Ephesians). In each manifestation the church is "the body of Christ" (1 Cor 12:27; Eph 1:23), both a physical and a spiritual reality. But in the minds of far too many Catholics, "the church" really only comprises the pope, bishops, and priests; they do not see themselves as truly "the church." Ephesians and the entire New Testament are a corrective to this distortion. Similarly, Ephesians' view of ministry, that it is the task of *all* the baptized (4:11-12), needs to be reaffirmed, as it was by the Second Vatican Council.

Ephesians was written by one of the baptized, a man or woman, perhaps a "teacher," some decades after Paul's death. It represents the voice of the faithful struggling under new and difficult circumstances to recall and remain faithful to the original inspiration of the gospel. The unfathomable "love of Christ" (3:19) is still with the church; Ephesians invites a continuing rediscovery of the ancient tradition so that that love can be more vibrant in the church and so that the church can reach out more effectively to the world.

COMMENTARY

1:1-2 Greeting

The opening is very similar to that of 1 Corinthians and nearly identical with that of Colossians. Except for Galatians, Paul's letters always describe believers as "holy," but Ephesians refers to believers as "holy" nine times (e.g., 1:4, 18; 3:8, cf. 2:21; 4:24), proportionally more frequently than any other letter; this accords with the letter's strong ethical emphasis (4:1–6:9). The greeting (1:2) is identical with the longer greeting of Paul's own letters (e.g., Rom 1:7), "grace" being an especially important theological term (see 2:5-8).

1:3-14 A blessing prayer

After the opening, most of Paul's letters have a "thanksgiving," but Ephesians (also 2 Cor 1:3) first has a traditional opening of Jewish prayer, "Blessed be God . . ." (1:3), and then also, quite uniquely, a "thanksgiving" (1:16). Both give thanks by recalling the actions and gifts of God. This "blessing" uses liturgical language; much of its phrasing is hymn-like. There are lots of repetitions: "in Christ" ("in him") occurs nine times, ten times if we include "in the beloved" (1:6); the phrase "for the praise of his glory" occurs three times (1:6, 12, 14). The section comprises a single sentence in Greek and features the sort of effusive language that is also found in Colossians (e.g., Col 1:9-20) but is even more prominent here. Phrases like "blessed us with every spiritual blessing" (1:3), "favor of his will" (1:5), "intention of his will" (1:11), and synonymous verbs (e.g., "chose," 1:4; "destined" 1:5, 11) combine to emphasize the abundance of God's favors.

The theological perspective, taking off from Colossians, emphasizes the initiative of God (2:5-10) which in Christ and beyond human calculation "chose" believers "before the foundation of the world" for holiness (1:4; 2:21), "adoption" (1:5), and "redemption" (1:7, 14; Col 1:14). God had always planned for "the gospel of salvation" (1:13); "the mystery of God's will"

Ephesians 1

was "made known" to the faithful (cf. 3:5; Col 1:26), and it was "set forth" (accomplished) in Christ (1:9). God's "plan" and "purpose" were "to sum up all things in Christ" (1:10-11), that is, "to bring all things under Christ as head" (cf. 1:20-22; 4:15), a further key theme taken from Colossians (1:20-22; 4:15, cf. Col 1:18; 2:10).

God's purpose that believers be "holy and blameless" (1:4) consumes the entire second half of the letter (4:1–6:17). But, in a sense, God's purpose has *already* been fulfilled; believers "*have* redemption [and] the forgiveness of sins" (1:7; Col 1:14). And yet, for all the emphasis on the *present fulfillment* of blessings, there remains an echo of Paul's point (Rom 8:23; 2 Cor 1:22; 5:5) that the "the holy Spirit" is "the first installment" of coming redemption, not yet its completion (1:14; cf. 4:30).

1:15-23 A thanksgiving prayer

Whereas the "blessing" focuses on what God has accomplished in Christ, this "thanksgiving" is more a prayer that believers will appropriate the gifts they have received. If the letter was addressed to Ephesus, then Paul himself could hardly be the author of the opening sentence ("*hearing* of your faith"; also 3:2), since he spent about three years in the city (Acts 20:31). The prayerful thanks, however, are no less sincere, as also the prayer that God will grant them "a spirit of wisdom and revelation by knowledge" of God (1:17). As in Colossians 1:9-10, this prayer highlights the importance of sound knowledge, but here also it is not intellectual knowledge that is primary, but rather deep spiritual recognition, with "the eyes of the heart" (1:18, cf. 3:18-19).

Among the prophets, "knowing God" was the key to the covenant (e.g., Hos 6:6; Isa 11:2; Jer 31:31-34). Here "knowledge" of God involves knowing all the blessings which God has granted in Christ and which this writer delights in listing in heaps of words: "hope," "call," "riches of glory," "inheritance," "the surpassing greatness of God's power" (1:19-20). Believers "know" God's "power," which is at work *now* (in every generation), as it also "worked in Christ," not only "raising him from the dead" but also "seating him" above all powers in the universe (1:20-21). This develops the theme taken over from Colossians (Col 2:15), namely, that Christ's victory, which for Paul would be complete only at the second coming (1 Cor 15:24, cf. Rom 8:38), is complete *now*; God "put all things beneath [Christ's] feet." Dramatic though that is, even more so is the statement that "God gave Christ as head over all things to *the church*" (1:22).

This is the first of nine times that "the church" is mentioned (also 3:10, 21; 5:23-32), and in every instance it refers to the *universal* church, as opposed to a local congregation (e.g., Rom 16:1, 5; Col 4:15). As in Colossians

(Col 1:18), the church is a cosmic entity, but this writer expands this idea: as Christ is "head" of the church, so he is the head of all creation (1:10). By virtue of Christ, the church has an extraordinary status and role; according to God's eternal purpose, it is the means by which "God's wisdom is made known" to all the powers of the universe (3:10-11). The church also is "seated with [Christ] in the heavens" (2:5-6). To be sure, the writer recognizes that for believers themselves, the victory is not complete (6:10-17). Nevertheless, the vision of a present realization of salvation is extraordinary; Paul's expectation of Christ's imminent return (e.g., 1 Thess 4:13-17) has faded, and suffering is virtually unmentioned (only 3:13; cf. Rom 5:3; Phil 1:29-30). Rather, the church is Christ's (glorified) "body" and his "fullness" within history (1:23; 4:10).

The Greek phrasing of 1:23 is very difficult. The New American Bible translation is possible (see 4:10), but more natural, given the form of the verb, is: "the fullness of the one who *is filled* with respect to all things in every way." As Christ was "raised" and "seated" in heaven (1:20), so also Christ "is filled" with "all the fullness of God" (Col 1:19; 2:9) and will in turn fill believers (3:19; 4:10, 13; Col 2:10). Either way, the vision of the church is breathtaking. Though Christ is head of the universe, only the *church* is Christ's body and fullness. The church, therefore, is the destiny of the universe! Though this is a beautiful spiritual vision, once the church gained power in history, the vision became susceptible to distortion, particularly the notion that all peoples and beliefs must surrender to the church. The church today must be far more humble!

2:1-10 From death to life

The opening phrase (also 2:5) is strongly reminiscent of Colossians 2:13. "The age of this world" and "the ruler of the power of the air" (2:2) presuppose (as does Colossians) that "this world" is dominated by spiritual forces which are beyond human control but which Christ has defeated (Col 2:15). Those evil powers account for the "disobedience" of non-believers (2:2), and "all of *us*"—strongly emphasized in the Greek—were once like them and were destined for "wrath" (2:3, cf. 1 Thess 1:10). But God's "great love" seized the initiative and "brought us to life with Christ" (2:4-5) and "seated us with him in the heavens" (2:6). God's cosmic victory in Christ means that "the coming ages"—perhaps spiritual forces, not just time periods—will see "the richness of [God's] grace" to believers (2:7), who have their home in the heavens (cf. Col 3:3-4).

The writer is at pains to emphasize that God's action was a matter of grace, not of human deserving (cf. Rom 3:27; 4:4-5; Gal 2:16-19). What Paul

Ephesians 2

had said in the context of a debate over Jewish law, this writer applies to "works" in general, so that there will be no "boasting." Paul would agree with the sentiment (e.g., Rom 3:27–4:5); faith itself and the living of it have to do with God's power (Gal 3:23-25; Phil 1:29; 2:13). The point is *not* that humans have no responsibility (Phil 2:12; Gal 5:13–6:10), but simply that neither law nor human action defines the relationship with God (Gal 3:1-14; Eph 2:15; Col 2:14). Believers, as believers, are God's "handiwork." God even "prepared" our "good deeds" in advance! What could emphasize the point more?

2:11-22 The one people of God

As believers had once been "dead in sins," so also they had once been "distant" from the chosen people. There is a switch in this section from God to Christ as the primary actor. The writer displays a high regard for Israel and seems oblivious to any hostility with Jews or the problem of Jews rejecting the gospel. All of this contrasts markedly with Paul's own situation (cf. 1 Thess 2:14-16; 2 Cor 11:24; Rom 9:1-3; 10:1). But this writer says simply that God has "made the two into one new humanity, creating peace" (2:15), as though there was no division between "circumcision" and "uncircumcision" (2:11).

In being "without Christ" Gentiles, as Gentiles, had also been "alienated" from Israel and its "covenants of promise" and therefore were "without hope" (2:12). The writer shares with Paul that, by God's design, Israel, Christ, and the church are intimately connected (cf. Rom 9:1-4; 11:21-31). "But now," "by the blood of Christ" Gentiles have the blessings of Israel. This passage (2:13-16; cf. 1:7) is the closest this letter comes to sustained reflection on the sacrificial death of Jesus; for Paul himself, "Christ crucified" was always the starting-point (e.g., Rom 3:24-26; 1 Cor 1:17–2:2; Gal 3:1-3).

In any event, Christ remains the key. The blessings of Israel are the prize, but the means is Christ, not the law (2:14-15). This is the point of division from Judaism, which believers must recognize while retaining the deepest respect for Judaism and the law, as Paul did (Rom 7:12). Ephesians is implicitly appealing for unity between Jewish and Gentile Christians.

The text again becomes reminiscent of Colossians in seeing Christ's death as destroying "the dividing wall" (2:14), "the law with its . . . legal claims" (2:15; cf. Col 2:14). It is *different*, however, in that here there is no debate with some "philosophy" insisting on laws (cf. Col 2:16-23). This writer sees "the two," Jews and Gentiles, reconciled "to God in one body" (2:16). "In one body" is best understood, in the context, as a reference to the church and perhaps reflects the thought of Colossians, and of Paul himself, that in Christ "there is no longer Greek [Gentile] and Jew" (Col 3:11; Gal 3:28). In other words, the writer is dwelling on the reality of Jews and Gentiles within the church, not on the external relationship of the church with Judaism. Christ "destroyed enmity" and "preached peace" to both Jews and Gentiles (2:17), and "through Christ" all have "access" to God (2:18).

The conclusion is that enmity has been destroyed, at least within the church. All believers, whether Jews or Gentiles, belong to God's household (2:19); reconciliation with God means reconciliation with one another. The writer images the church as an organic, not a static, building; the whole is "jointed together" and "is growing" into a "holy temple" (2:21). This latter phrase would have a particular poignancy, especially for Jews, in light of the destruction of the Jerusalem temple by the Romans in A.D. 70.

The image of the "apostles and prophets" (2:20) as the church's foundation contrasts with Paul's image of "Jesus Christ" as the church's sole foundation (1 Cor 3:11). Ephesians seems deliberately to recall and to nuance Paul's idea. The church is in a new situation: the foundational generation has died, and the church, no longer expecting Christ's imminent return, must look to how it will endure through history. Christ remains "the capstone" (or "keystone") of the building (2:21). In remaining faithful to the "apostles and prophets," the church remains "apostolic" (and prophetic), as it is also "one, holy, and catholic" (universal). All the baptized together are God's "one building in the Spirit" (2:22).

3:1-13 Remembering Paul's ministry

Though not a member of the Twelve, Paul was by far the most important of the apostles within the New Testament (Acts 13–28), but there were many other "apostles and prophets," men and women alike, who had "labored together in the gospel" (Phil 4:2-3; cf. Rom 16:1-15). But the writer now remembers Paul as the apostle par excellence "for you the Gentiles" (3:1); he had been a prisoner and suffered many times "on your behalf" (also 3:13; 2 Cor 11:21-33). Paul was God's reliable instrument; he had received "God's grace" (3:2, 7; Rom 15:15; Gal 2:9) "for your benefit" (3:2), and "the mystery of Christ" "by revelation" (3:3-4, cf. Gal 1:11-12). The writer knew Paul's letters (not only Colossians), and believers could "read" them (not only Ephesians) "to understand [Paul's] insight" (3:4) for themselves.

This passage (3:2-7) recalls and develops Colossians 1:25-27. It presupposes, in the manner of apocalyptic literature (e.g., Dan 8:17-19), that God's

Ephesians 3

plan of salvation is ancient, but "in other generations" (3:5) had been kept secret until the appointed time (cf. 3:9). In Colossians the recipients of "the mystery" are all the baptized (Col 1:26), but here, consistent with their founding role, the primary recipients are "the holy apostles and prophets" (3:5), that is, Paul himself and those who worked with him. The content of "the mystery" recalls 2:11-18: "the Gentiles," "through the gospel," share in the fulfilled "promise" to Israel. It was this gospel—the inclusion of the Gentiles—for which Paul was commissioned by God's "power" (3:7; cf. Gal 1:16).

For a third time Paul's apostolate is referred to as "the grace given" by God (3:8; cf. 3:2, 7), and again it is emphasized that Paul received this apostolate "to preach to the Gentiles." Why such emphatic repetition was thought necessary is impossible to know. During his ministry Paul had not been accepted by all as an "apostle" (1 Cor 9:1-2; Gal 1:1–2:9) and had conceded that he was "the last of the apostles" (1 Cor 15:9). Here he is referred to as "the least of all the saints" (3:8), which brings into sharp relief how great was God's grace. Paul had highlighted the same contrast in his autobiographical accounts (1 Cor 15:8-10; Gal 1:13-16). He knew from personal experience that God often chooses the most unlikely instrument to advance the gospel (1 Cor 1:27-29).

It is a unique thought that the purpose of Paul's apostolate was so that "God's manifold wisdom might be made known to the heavenly principalities and authorities," those powers that Christ had defeated (1:20-22). Indeed, this had happened "through the church," which means that now the church participates with Christ in the continuing mop-up campaign against "the devil" (6:11-12). "By God's eternal purpose, made effective in Christ" (3:11), the church can be "bold" in this endeavor (3:12) and should not be discouraged at the thought of Paul's "afflictions" (3:13).

3:14-21 A prayer

The intensity of already intense language is now increased as the writer breaks into prayer that God will enable believers to have greater and greater power in the Spirit "to know" the unknowable "love of Christ" (3:19). The prayer has two parts: a petition (3:16-19) and a doxology (3:20-21).

"For this reason" recalls 3:1 and that this is "Paul" at prayer, on his "knees" before "the Father" of the universe. The heart of Christian spirituality is caught in the petition; the "power" derives purely from "the Spirit," but it is not a power for doing (cf. 2:8-9) so much as for *surrendering* "by faith," so that "Christ may well in your hearts" (2:16-17). This is reminiscent of Paul's great claim, "I no longer live, rather Christ lives within me" (Gal

2:20), which he claimed for believers generally, not just himself (cf. Rom 6:8-11). All believers are to "be rooted and founded in love" (cf. Col 1:23; 2:7). This means primarily "the love" that Christ has shown (2:4; cf. Gal 2:20; 1 John 4:10), as the next part of the petition indicates, but believers' love for others (4:2, 15; 5:2) and for "the Lord" (6:24) is also envisioned. Believers do "know" that love, but the prayer asks for their (ongoing) "strengthening" to plumb the unfathomable "love of Christ" in all its dimensions (3:18-19). The end of the journey is "to be filled" by Christ (1:23) "with all the fullness of God" (cf. 4:10-13; Col 1:19; 2:9-10).

As the petition hints at the cosmic reach of Christ's love, so the doxology praises God, who, as "Father" of the universe (3:15), can (and will) "accomplish far more than all we ask or imagine" and whose "glory" both "in the church" and "in Christ Jesus" exceeds the universe and all the powers within it (3:20-21).

4:1-16 Growing to maturity in Christ

"The church" is not explicitly mentioned in this section, but the focus on "unity" (4:3-6, 13) and "ministry" (4:11-12) as the means for "the whole body" (4:16) to grow to maturity in Christ shows that the church and how it functions are the main concerns. But this is not mere description; rather, the writer proclaims that the church must "live" by these ideals if it is to be true to its "calling" (4:1, 4). Though there is now emphasis on human responsibility, the priority of "grace" (as in 2:8) remains prominent (4:7-11).

The reminder of Paul's being "a prisoner" adds deep feeling to the "appeal" (cf. Rom 12:1) that believers "live in a manner worthy" of their "call" (4:1). The narrative of God's "call" filled the first part of the letter and now leads to the imperative of believers' existence. And the first imperative is to be "humble," "gentle," "patient," and "loving" toward one another; only so will true "unity" be maintained. "Unity" is a gift of "the Spirit," but it can be destroyed; "the bond of peace" is a way of summarizing all the qualities needed to preserve it. Thus "the spirit" in "the unity of the spirit" is both human and divine; even God's gifts sometimes need human cooperation. Unity here and now ("one body") is to mirror "the one hope" (redemption, 1:14) to which believers "were called" (4:4).

The early churches were inevitably quite diverse in many respects. There was, for instance, more than one baptismal formula. Matthew's (Matt 28:19) finally became standard, but it is not the same as Paul's (Gal 3:28; cf. 1 Cor 12:13), which itself was not fixed (cf. Col 3:11). Ephesians (4:4-6) reflects a further formula or, at least, additional liturgical language of baptism. The insistence here that there must be "one faith, one baptism" (4:5) bespeaks attempts of the early churches, no matter how diverse or scattered, to be "one body." The emphasis here on God as the "one God" of the entire universe (4:6) furthered these efforts considerably. For the New Testament (e.g., John 17:20-23), Christians being divided among themselves is unthinkable.

The writer now picks up a theme well known in Paul's own writing, namely, that "to each one" in the church God has given some "measure of Christ's gift" (4:7; cf. Rom 12:3-8; 1 Cor 12:4-11). This is reinforced by reference to Psalm 68:19, which, in the context of recounting God's saving deeds for Israel, actually speaks of God's *"receiving* gifts" from Israel's, and God's, enemies. Jewish tradition applied the psalm to Moses "ascending" Mount Sinai and receiving gifts from God. Ephesians seems to reflect that idea but switches the text to speak of *Christ's* "ascending" and *"giving* gifts" to the church. As the writer sees it, it was Christ who "ascended on high and took captivity captive," the same victory that was earlier described as *God's* action (1:20-22). Having despoiled the powers, Christ distributed the enemy's wealth, so to speak, to the church (cf. Mark 3:27).

The writer pauses to dwell further on the psalm in relation to Christ: he who "ascended" and "filled" the universe with his presence (4:10) first "descended to the lower regions of the earth" (4:9). This is sometimes interpreted to refer to Christ "descending to the dead" (as in the Apostles' Creed; cf. 1 Pet 3:19), but far more likely, it refers to the incarnation (as in John 3:13).

Christ's gift of "apostles" and "prophets" and other primary ministers (4:11) was bestowed so that the church might be the fully functioning "body of Christ" (4:12, 16). It is perhaps important to emphasize that women, as well as men, were such primary ministers (e.g., Rom 16:1-12; Phil 4:2-3; Acts 2:17-18; 21:9). Paul had taught that "God designated some in the church to be, first, apostles; second, prophets; third, teachers" (1 Cor 12:28), but that listing followed on his insistence that *every* member of the church had some "spiritual gift" or "ministry" "for the common good" (12:4-7) and that no one's contribution was to be neglected or despised (12:14-27). Both Paul and Ephesians agree that the primary ministers are not to be the only ministers, but are rather "to equip the *holy ones for the work of ministry*" (4:11-12), an emphasis taken up vigorously by the Second Vatican Council, but sometimes, even today, forgotten. The writer adds "the evangelists [and] the pastors" (4:11) to Paul's list, which reflects the new situation of ministry toward the end of the first century. Later "bishop," "presbyter," and "deacon" became established titles (e.g., 1 Tim

3:1-13; Titus 1:5), and, sadly, women were increasingly excluded from leadership (1 Tim 2:11-15).

All gifts and ministries have the same aims (4:13), which, in various ways, have already been named: "building of the body" (2:21-22), "unity of faith" (4:5), maturity and "the fullness of Christ" (1:23; cf. 3:19). The purpose of leadership is then stated in negative terms so that the church will not be tossed about "by every wind of teaching" arising from "human trickery" (4:14). To the contrary, the church is to be characterized by "speaking the truth in love" so as "to grow into Christ, the head, in every way" (4:15; cf. 1:22).

Paul himself had not extended the image of "the body of Christ" (1 Cor 12:27) to Christ being its "head." Later on this notion, especially in combination with 5:23 ("wives subordinate to their husbands"), contributed to a very patriarchal view of the church. As used here, however, it is a beautiful, dynamic notion of the church organically growing toward Christ and his "fullness." The church not only grows into Christ, it also grows from him, as well as from the functioning of all its members, and so "builds itself up in love" (4:16). The key to the whole is the unity of believers with one another and with Christ (4:3-6, 13, 16).

4:17–5:20 Once darkness, not light

This very long section of ethical exhortation is, in part, dependent on Colossians but also has some unique concerns and images. The dependence on Colossians is apparent in a long list of words, phrases, and concepts that are sometimes almost identical with the earlier letter. Examples include: "old self"—"new self" (4:22-24; Col 3:9-10); "forgive as God forgave you" (4:32; Col 3:13); "greed" as "idolatry" (5:5; Col 3:5); "wrath" for the "disobedient" (5:6; Col 3:6); "psalms, hymns and songs" (5:19; Col 3:16), and so on. Ephesians is unique, however, in its much stronger use of the imagery of "light" versus "darkness" (4:18; 5:8-9, 11-14, cf. Col 1:12-13), its concern for "anger" and proper speech among believers (e.g., 4:31), and a stronger emphasis on separation from outsiders (5:6-7; cf. Col 4:5-6).

The writer solemnly warns believers ("I testify in the Lord") that they must be different from "the Gentiles." Most readers, though not all, were "Gentiles," in the sense that their natural heritage was not in Judaism (3:1; 2:11); but "Gentiles," even in Paul's time (e.g., 1 Cor 5:1), was used to refer to non-believers, who, unlike Jews and Christians, did not acknowledge the one God (1 Thess 4:5). As the imminent expectation of Christ's return receded and the church, though still a small minority, became a *part of* society, as opposed to watching and waiting for its destruction (see 1 Cor

1:18; 7:29-31), it became increasingly necessary for Christians to distinguish themselves from the dominant culture, although living within it. Baptism and other rituals, as well as "the faith," were essential boundary markers, but on a day-to-day basis even more important was (and is) "living" by the highest ethical ideals.

The writer vividly portrays "Gentile" behavior as "futile" ("foolish"), having no understanding of "the life of God" (the life that God enables) because of "the hardness of their hearts" and their consequent surrender of themselves to "every kind of impurity" (4:17-19). Such negative evaluations of "outsiders" by "insiders" inevitably arise among emerging religious groups; they change, however, if a group—as happened with Christianity—itself becomes dominant. Power changes perspectives. Believers today have to be humble in their evaluations of "outsiders" and have to apply to *themselves* Scripture's many warnings about "ignorance" and "excess" (4:18-19).

When believers "learned Christ" (a completely unique expression), the learning had nothing to do with being either "callous" or "impure" (4:19-20), and therefore the transformation from "the old self" to "the new" must mean putting aside "deceitful desires" and turning to "holiness" (4:22-24). The dependence on Colossians 3:8-11 shows that baptism is in mind here. The "new self, created by God's design" (4:24), transforms the relationship with God and with others.

The next paragraph (4:25-32) follows a pattern of mentioning, first, the vice to be avoided and then the good to be espoused. There is clear encouragement for truthful and loving words, as there is also, throughout the letter, a deep concern about "falsehood" (4:14, 22, 25; 5:6) and about the misguided "impulses" (2:3) and "futile thinking" (4:17-18), which impede true knowledge and understanding (e.g., 4:13-14; 5:17-18). The writer quotes Zechariah 8:16 to urge believers to "speak the truth" and adds as motivation, "For we are members of one another" (4:25, cf. Rom 12:5). Psalm 4:5 is quoted to make the point that "anger" (though inevitable) must not become "sin"; "Do not let the sun set on your anger" was proverbial even then. "Anger" here denotes the "fury" that leads to "bitterness" and "shouting" (4:31) and provides "an opportunity for the devil" (4:27; cf. 6:11; 2 Cor 2:11). Far from "stealing," all must "work with their own hands" (cf. 1 Thess 4:11) and be prepared "to share with anyone in need" (4:28).

"Foul speech" ought to have no place among believers (5:3-4), but speech must rather be "good" for "building" the church and "imparting grace" (4:29). The injunction not to "grieve the holy Spirit" reflects Isaiah 63:10, which recalls Israel's "provoking God's holy Spirit" by disobedience. The rest of that verse (4:30) repeats the thought of 1:13-14, namely, that by faith believers were "sealed with the holy Spirit" as a "pledge" of the coming "redemption." Meanwhile, destructive anger and the bitter words that accompany it must be "removed" (4:31); in their place belong kindness, compassion, and "forgiving one another" as God has forgiven us (4:32, cf. Col 3:13; Matt 6:14).

To forgive as God forgives leads naturally to the thought that believers become "imitators of God" (cf. Matt 5:48), living like God's "beloved children" (5:1) and like Christ who "loved us" to the point of "surrendering himself for us" as a "sacrifice to God" (5:2). Paul urged his churches to "imitate" himself (e.g., 1 Cor 11:1; Phil 3:17); the exhortation to imitate God is unique to this letter. The following warnings focus especially on sexual morality (actions and speech) and on "greed," which is equated with "idolatry" (5:5; Col 3:5). The repeated warning against "obscenity . . . or suggestive talk" (5:4; cf. 4:29) perhaps indicates that the writer had witnessed or at least heard of such inappropriate speech among the churches. "Thanksgiving" should better characterize their conversation, as well as the awareness that immorality forfeits salvation (5:5).

Perhaps a particular person or teaching is in mind with the warning against "empty arguments." That warning and the explanation that such things bring "the wrath of God on the disobedient" (5:6) closely imitate Colossians (Col 2:8; 3:6), where a particular problem was in view. In any event, the writer wishes for there to be a clear boundary between the church and, at least, the "immoral" ones in society who were alluded to in the previous warnings—"do not be associated with them" (5:7; cf. 5:11). This compares interestingly with Paul's words to the Corinthians, distinguishing between the "immoral of this world," with whom association was unavoidable, and the "immoral" within the church (1 Cor 5:9-13). For Paul, it was the latter that were the real threat.

The contrast this writer draws between the church and the larger society is abundantly apparent in the following verses (5:8-14) with their imagery of "light" and "darkness." Prior to "learning Christ" (4:20), believers were "darkness," but now "in the Lord" they *are* light" and must "live as children of light," which recalls 5:1: "Be imitators of God." "Light" as a metaphor for God and the realm of God is very common in Scripture (e.g., Ps 27:1; 44:4; Isa 9:2; 60:1, 19-20; Mic 7:8; John 1:4-9; 8:12). The darkness is not beyond God's realm, but it resists God's invitation (cf. John 3:20-21). Light, on the other hand, produces every kind of goodness (5:9), discerns "what is pleasing to the Lord," and "exposes" the "hidden, shameful" deeds of darkness as evil (5:10-12).

Ephesians 4–5

The next verses (5:13-14) are difficult, and interpretation has to squeeze out of the text what it does not precisely say. To "be exposed by the light" and thus to "become visible" means to "come into the light," which presumably has something to do with conversion. Indeed, perhaps the writer is suggesting that believers have an obligation so to "expose" and indict as evil "the fruitless works of darkness" (5:11) that evildoers will come to the light of Christ. It is perhaps in that sense that "what [or whoever] becomes visible *is* [or 'becomes'?] light" (5:14) and is identified with Christ. The quotation supports this interpretation, since it is almost certainly a baptism hymn (cf. Rom 6:3-4) and addresses the newly baptized: "Awake, O sleeper, and arise from the dead, and Christ will shine on you" (cf. Isa 60:1). Ephesians, of course, intends the reminder for more than just the newly baptized. Ultimately, believers, like Jesus (John 8:12), are to be "the light of the world" (Matt 5:16).

The whole congregation is to see that they "walk" as "wise ones" (5:15), "making the best of the opportunity" (Col 4:5) in the midst of the present "evil days" (5:16; cf. 6:13). Neither being "ignorant" ("foolish") nor "getting drunk" will enable the proper "understanding" that is so essential (4:17-18, cf. 3:18-19; 4:13-14). This long section comes to an end by again borrowing from Colossians (Col 3:16), exhorting believers, "filled with the Spirit" (5:18), to share "psalms and hymns" with one another (such as 5:14) and constantly to "give thanks . . . to God the Father" (5:19-20).

5:21–6:9 Household rules

This section obviously corresponds to, and is a development of, Colossians 3:18–4:1. The development is noteworthy. Ephesians dwells at far greater length on men's obligation to love their wives and, in comparing that love to Christ's love for the church, produces an impressive meditation on the relationship between Christ and the church. Nevertheless, the same enormous problems regarding the "subordination" of wives and the "obedience" of slaves exist for Ephesians as for Colossians. Both presuppose the unquestioned patriarchal structure of first-century society.

Whereas, in other respects, Ephesians wants the church to be different from the rest of society (5:7, 11) and probably sees these instructions also as furthering that purpose, society's template with regard to marriage and slavery remains unchanged. For Ephesians, the "difference" is a greater measure of "love" for wives (5:25) and less "bullying" ("threatening") for slaves (6:9). It has taken until modern times for the *structures* of society and for the church itself to change, and the process is not even yet complete. We cannot, therefore, judge them; we have to turn the eye of discernment onto ourselves, and how we interpret and apply these verses is a test for that discernment.

Verse 21, grammatically, could as well be included with the previous section as with this one, but its verb ("be subordinate") is intended to be applied in a special way to "wives" (5:22). The author assumes that wives ought to "subordinate" themselves to their husbands (cf. 1 Pet 3:1-6) and, going beyond Colossians, strengthens this idea by weaving it into the theme of Christ as "the head of the church" (5:23). The *distortion* of this text that sometimes leads women to think they must stay with an abusive husband or men to think they have a right to hit their wives (!) has been criticized strongly by the American Catholic bishops. It intends, in fact, to make Christian marriage into a model of the love Christ has for the church and probably also into a demonstration of the goodness of Christian faith. We can certainly affirm that intention and that spouses should subordinate themselves to *one another* (5:21; 1 Cor 7:4).

The idea that Christ's death was, specifically, "for the sake of" the *church* (5:25) is unique to this letter. Paul's emphasis—the two thoughts are not contradictory—was that Christ died "for the ungodly" (Rom 3:23-26; 5:6-8), outsiders being more clearly included. That sacrifice is to be a model, for wives and husbands alike, of how they are to love one another. Christ "sanctified" the church, "cleansing" it both by his death and by baptism (5:26). The church is imaged here as Christ's bride (cf. Ezek 16:8-9), whom he will espouse to himself at the final judgment "in splendor," "holy and blameless" (5:27).

To love one's spouse is also to "love oneself" (5:28), one's own "body" and "flesh" (5:29). That, says the writer, was how "Christ loved the church, since we are members of his body" (5:29-30; cf. 1 Cor 12:27). Mention of "flesh" prepares for the quotation from Genesis 2:24, which is the climax of the second creation story (the first = Gen 1:1–2:4). That story focuses primarily on humans and the creation of sex and marriage (Gen 2:20-24). Ephesians takes that text—most notably, "the two shall become one flesh"—and applies it, as "a great mystery . . . to Christ and to the church" (5:31-32) and the "marriage" between them. How ironic and tragic that such a beautiful image has sometimes been a device for violence, including the violence of the subordination of women to men. The writer returns to the theme of marriage in the church and emphasizes that "each man should love his wife as himself" and, as ancient society would expect, that "the wife should respect [literally 'fear'] her husband" (5:33). *Mutual love* and respect would properly be our modern emphasis.

The command that children should "obey" their parents (6:1) is nearly identical with Colossians 3:20 but adds motivation by quoting Deuteronomy 5:16 (cf. Exod 20:12). Different words (from Colossians) are used to instruct "fathers"—we would say "parents"—not to "provoke children to anger" (6:3). The command to "raise children in the instruction of the Lord" (6:4) is unique to Ephesians. The lengthy instructions to "slaves" (6:5-8), as in Colossians 3:22-25, probably indicate both the presence of slaves among the readers and the need to make slavery compatible with faith. "There is no longer slave nor free" (Gal 3:28) is being compromised. As the husband is likened to Christ (5:23), so also is the slave master (6:5), with terrible effects in later history. We can apply to ourselves the exhortations to serve "in sincerity of heart," rather than for "currying favor" (6:5-6), and fruitfully be aware that there is one God "in heaven" over all, no matter status or identity (6:8-9).

6:10-20 Final exhortations

In this final section the writer envisions Christian life as a great battle against "the evil spiritual powers" (6:12) that Christ has defeated (1:20-22). The battle continues because believers *are* "flesh and blood," but the evil they battle is not (6:12). Ultimately, in spite of 2:4-8, even Ephesians knows that the process of salvation is not yet complete. Therefore, especially through prayer (6:18-20), believers need *God's* "strength" and "armor" to withstand "the tactics of the devil" (6:11-13). "The evil day" (6:13) is the time of "temptation" ("testing") and "evil," from which we also pray to be delivered in the Lord's Prayer (Matt 6:13).

Drawing on Old Testament texts listing the weaponry of God (Isa 11:5; 59:16-17; Wis 5:16-23), the writer describes the (primarily defensive) armor that will see believers through the fight: "the girdle of truth," "the breastplate of righteousness," and so on (6:14-17). "The gospel of peace" (6:15) might better be translated "the *proclamation* of peace," meaning that believers must be "ready" to witness to the "peace" that God gives and thereby to "extinguish the flaming arrows" aimed at them (6:16). This passage, in other words (cf. 5:11-14), might be a hint of some concern for defense of the gospel among non-believers. The only *offensive* weapon in the believer's armor is "the sword of the Spirit, which is the word of God" (6:17); evangelization, that is, sharing the gospel, is part of the believer's task. "The word" is not to be identified with the Bible or any part of it; "the word" is "alive and active" (Heb 4:12) in and among believers. The Bible enables us to recognize "the word," but it does not define it.

It is for continued, vigorous sharing of "the mystery of the gospel" (6:19) that the writer asks the recipients to pray, as they also pray for themselves and "for all the holy ones" (6:18), that is, the church. The final reminder of Paul's "imprisonment" keeps the great apostle's memory present as the letter draws to a close (6:20).

6:21-24 Conclusion

The note about Tychicus's bringing "news" of Paul and "that he may encourage your hearts" (6:21-22) is nearly word-for-word identical with Colossians 4:7-8. The letter concludes, wishing "peace to believers." "Love with faith" (6:23) is unique to Ephesians, as is the final blessing. On the other hand, "grace" was a key term in Paul's theology (e.g., Rom 3:24; 11:6, cf. Eph 2:8) and in all his final blessings. Paul and Ephesians agree: "grace" is the beginning and the end of Christian existence, and our only hope for "immortality" (6:24). Many manuscripts add "Amen."

The Letter to the Philippians
Vincent M. Smiles

INTRODUCTION

The importance of Philippi

Philippi was located about 110 miles northeast of Thessalonica in Macedonia. It got its name in 360 B.C. from Philip II of Macedon, father of Alexander the Great. In 42 B.C. it was the scene of a great battle to decide the successor of Julius Caesar; Caesar Augustus, the emperor at the time of Jesus' birth, was the victor. In 31 B.C. he made Philippi a Roman colony, permitting army veterans to settle there. Philippi, therefore, enjoyed special status; it came under Italian law and was exempt from various taxes. Paul was aware of its prestige (see 3:20; 4:22).

According to Acts 16:9, a vision summoned Paul to preach the gospel in Macedonia. From the very beginning Paul's relations with Philippi were warm and affectionate; it was the one church that consistently supported him in his apostolic work (4:15-16, cf. 1:5). Its founding members and leaders included a number of women (4:2-3; Acts 16:13-15), but unlike other cities of Paul's mission, Philippi seems not to have included a synagogue or any large Jewish population. The issue of when and where Paul wrote his letter to the Philippians takes us into its particular difficulties.

Challenges for interpretation

Scholars are agreed that Paul wrote Philippians, but most also believe that the letter we have was originally two or three separate letters. The most obvious seam is between 3:1 and 3:2; the switch of mood is so abrupt that even those who defend the unity of the letter struggle to explain the transition. Another difficulty is the delayed thank-you (4:10-20), which interrupts what looks like a standard ending of a letter (4:8-9, 21-23).

These and other observations have given rise to numerous theories about the original *letters* to Philippi and, of course, such theories affect the question of when and where Paul wrote. A common theory of multiple letters regards 4:10-20 as *letter A*, written from prison in Ephesus, about A.D. 55. *Letter B,* from prison a few weeks later, comprises 1:1–3:1a, 4:4-7,

21-23, and *letter C* includes the polemical 3:1b–4:3, 8-9 after Paul's release and was written perhaps from another city (Corinth?). A more simple theory would be: *letter A* = 1:1–3:1; 4:1-7, 10-23 (from Ephesus, about 55), and *letter B* = 3:2-21; 4:8-9 (from Corinth, about 56). All such theories presuppose that an editor, for some reason, conflated the original two or three letters and in doing so chopped off the openings and endings of one or more letters to avoid needless repetition.

Those who reject such theories insist that, in spite of difficulties, the letter is coherent and should be read as a unity, and certainly it *can* be read as a unity. The commentary to follow will do so, without denying that the theories of division are, at least from a historical perspective, very valuable. Assuming its unity, where was Paul when he wrote Philippians? The traditional view is that he wrote from Rome in the early sixties while under house arrest (Acts 28:16-31). Philippians, however (see 1:12-20; 2:17), envisions more than house arrest, and travel between Rome and Philippi was more difficult than the ease of communication that is presumed in the letter (2:19-30). Some scholars think Ephesus was the more likely place of writing, some time in the mid-fifties. There is no explicit record of Paul being imprisoned in Ephesus, but that is not an insurmountable problem (see 2 Cor 1:8; 11:23; 1 Cor 15:32). The best guess, therefore, is that Philippians comprises one or more letters written from prison in Ephesus in the mid-fifties and perhaps also from Corinth a year or so later.

COMMENTARY

1:1-2 Greeting

The opening is brief and simple but includes interesting details. Timothy is named as co-sender, but he probably had little to do with the actual composition of the letter. From 1:3 Paul speaks in terms of his particular experience (e.g., 1:12-17); this letter, like the others that are original to Paul (Romans, 1 and 2 Corinthians, Galatians, Philippians, 1 Thessalonians, Philemon), bears the imprint of one very strong personality. It is unusual that Paul here does not claim the title "apostle." It was sometimes important for him to do so (e.g., Rom 1:1; Gal 1:1-12), but in the warm relationship he shared with Philippi, there was no such need. "Slaves" recalls Jesus' instruction about leadership (Mark 10:44).

Even more interesting, but also strange, is Paul's special mention of "the overseers and ministers." The Greek terms *(episkopos* and *diakonos)* are sometimes translated "bishop" and "deacon" (e.g., 1 Tim 3:2, 8), but in his list of primary church functions (1 Cor 12:28), these titles have no place, and in fact "overseers" are never mentioned again in the original letters. He uses "minister" *(diakonos)* to describe, among others, himself and other leading "ministers" of the gospel (1 Cor 3:5; 2 Cor 3:6), but only in the case of Phoebe (Rom 16:1) does it have an official ring to it. These titles are so unusual that some scholars think the phrase was inserted by an editor, but this is doubtful. They must have been leaders of various house-churches—people like Euodia, Syntyche, and Clement (4:2-3).

The letter is addressed to *"all* the holy ones" (the baptized); he greets them with the standard but significant formula he employs in all his letters: "Grace to you and peace . . ." Though Paul addresses the community six times as "brothers" (e.g., 1:12), it is important to note that he is addressing women and men alike (note 4:2-3). *Adelphoi* ("brothers") in this context is best translated "believers."

1:3-11 The thanksgiving

The warmth of Paul's relationship with the Philippians is evident here: "I thank my God at *every* remembrance of you, praying *always* with joy at my *every* prayer for *all* of you." In Greek the italicized words all begin with the letter "p," increasing the emotional and rhetorical effect. "My God" (also 4:19; Rom 1:8) denotes a personal relationship and is quite common in the psalms (e.g., Ps 22). "Joy" characterizes this letter throughout (1:18; 2:2, 17; 3:1; 4:1, 4, 10).

As a "thanksgiving," the passage is a standard feature of letter writing (cf. Rom 1:8-15; 1 Cor 1:4-9, etc.), but there is nothing standard or merely formal about Paul's "joyful" remembrance of the Philippians and of their "partnership in the gospel from the first day until now" (1:5). "Partnership" (or "participation"—see 2:1; 3:10; 4:15) refers both to their spiritual and their material sharing in the task of the gospel (see 4:15). They "defend and confirm" (1:7) the gospel by living it and by "struggling together" for its progress (1:27). They have also generously enabled Paul's missionary endeavors by their gifts to him (4:16); the phrase "until now" may refer to Paul's having just received their latest contribution.

The beginning of the "good work" that God "will continue" in them was that "first day," when Paul came to Philippi and was received, according to Acts 16:11-15, by Lydia and the other women at the "place of prayer." Lydia herself is not mentioned in Philippians, but the leadership of women seems to have remained important (4:2-3) in the intervening years. Lydia was from Thyatira (northwest Asia Minor), says Luke (Acts 16:14), so she may no longer have been in Philippi.

Philippians 1

The "day of Christ" is the first of several references to the expected return of Jesus (see 1:10; 2:16; 3:20-21). Some years earlier Paul had fully expected to be alive for Jesus' return (1 Thess 4:15-17), but now he realizes that he may die first (1:20-23). Nevertheless, the end will come soon, and Paul's confident prayer (1:9) is that, at the judgment, the believers of Philippi will be "pure and blameless" (1:10). In the meantime, he says, he "longs for them with the affection of Christ Jesus" (1:8); Paul's love for his churches was unmistakable (1 Thess 2:7-8; 2 Cor 11:11). His final prayer is that they "will be filled with the fruit of righteousness" (1:11). Paul will resume this theme of "righteousness through Christ" in the fiery words of 3:2-9.

Although he was in prison (1:7, 13-17), the apostle was joyful and confident. Epaphroditus, who has delivered the Philippians' gift (4:18), remains with Paul, recovering, we will discover later, from a near brush with death (2:25-30). Also with Paul is Timothy, of whom Paul will speak affectionately (2:22).

1:12-26 The irresistible progress of the gospel

The first paragraph here (1:12-18) is remarkable, speaking as it does of the effect of Paul's imprisonment, first among "the praetorium and all the rest" (1:13), probably denoting non-believers, and second, among believers also (1:14-18). "The praetorium" (palace guard) refers not to a place but to the soldiers and others of "Caesar's household" (4:22). Paul wants the Philippians to know that his imprisonment, although on the surface a disadvantage, "served to advance the gospel." This goes along with Paul's optimistic tone, in spite of the most difficult circumstances. Even among non-believers it has become known that Paul's imprisonment is "in Christ," meaning that they see Paul, not as a common criminal, but as a witness of Christ. And "most of the believers," far from being intimidated by his imprisonment, have gained greater confidence "to speak the word fearlessly" (1:14).

It is amazing that Paul has such equanimity in the circumstances he describes next. "Some," he says, "proclaim Christ because of envy and rivalry" (1:15), "thinking to cause me trouble in my imprisonment" (1:17). We know, then, that these opponents were Christians, but it is impossible to know much else about them or what sort of "trouble" (or "affliction") they might cause for Paul. Because he was a champion of the freedom of Gentile believers from the Jewish law, Paul ran into opposition many times, including in Antioch, Jerusalem (Gal 2:1-14; Acts 15:1-5), Galatia (Gal 1:6-9; 6:12-16), and Philippi (Phil 3:2-9; cf. Rom 3:8; 6:1-15).

The "trouble" these people sought to cause was perhaps simply distress in Paul's own mind. Their intention, however, may have been even more sinister, hoping to make his imprisonment worse and more protracted. Whatever the case, Paul refused to see it as a defeat. There was no trouble that could subdue his joy and confidence in Christ! Especially encouraging for him are those believers who preach Christ "for the sake of God's will" (1:15, not merely human "good will") and "out of love," aware that Paul was in prison "in defense of the gospel" (1:16). All that matters for Paul, whether to his advantage or not, is that "Christ is proclaimed; in that," he says, "I rejoice"!

"And I will continue to rejoice," he insists, "because I know that 'this will result in deliverance for me.'" These last words are from the book of Job (13:16). Whether or not the Philippians would recognize the reference—Philippians is almost devoid of Old Testament quotations—it seems clear that Paul sees in Job's words a reason for confidence. In the text in question, Job rebukes his friends because they have presumed to speak for God. Job, however, is convinced that they do not understand God's ways and that God, somehow, will vindicate him and bring him "deliverance" (or "salvation"). In applying this text to himself, Paul appears to be saying that he "knows" what will happen to him. In reality, however, he does not even know whether the outcome will be "life or death" (1:20). Either alternative will be "deliverance"!

"The prayer" of his friends in Philippi and the "support of the Spirit of Jesus Christ" (1:19) are further reasons that Paul is confident. In fact, his confidence extends to "eager expectation and hope" (1:20). "Hope" here denotes the biblical virtue that "waits with eager longing" (Rom 8:19); it is not to be understood, as so often in modern speech, as a vague and anxious desire ("I hope the weather will be nice"). Paul fully "expects" his hope to be fulfilled. "I shall not be put to shame," he says, "in any way," meaning that there is nothing his enemies can do to defeat him. That is true for the simple reason that Paul has let go of any personal gain or advantage; all that matters is that "Christ is glorified," and whether that happens by Paul's "life or death" (1:20), it is all he desires.

Indifference to death is difficult to understand. We associate such indifference with the depths of despair and pain, but here it arises in a letter which, more than any other, exudes hope and joy. This gives a glimpse into Paul's spirit and into what motivated his long and difficult ministry. For Paul, "life" itself is nothing other than "Christ," and therefore "to die is gain" (1:21). To the Galatians he had said, "I have been crucified with Christ. I no longer live, rather, Christ lives within me" (Gal 2:19-20; cf. Rom 8:10-11). His entire life and identity are enfolded in his allegiance to Jesus. He is, therefore, content "to live in the flesh" for the sake of "fruitful labor" (1:22) for the gospel. On the other hand, he has a great desire "to depart this life and be with Christ—which is far better" (1:23). Nevertheless, he knows that it may be "more necessary for [their] benefit" to remain (1:24) and, for some reason, he seems convinced that this is the more likely outcome.

In fact, Paul is sure that he will "remain and abide with" them for their "progress and joy in the faith" (1:25), "so that" the Philippians "may boast in Christ Jesus" when Paul comes to them again. "Boasting" is closely related to the joyful hope that so fills this letter. Paradoxically, there is no such thing for Paul as "boasting" (Rom 3:27; 4:2; 1 Cor 1:29), as though humans could somehow be independent of God. On the other hand, within the relationship of faith, Paul often speaks of the joyful boast that believers can have because of what God enables within them (e.g., Rom 5:2-3; 2 Cor 1:12-14; Phil 2:16; 1 Thess 2:19).

1:27–2:18 Encouragement and instructions

Paul now changes his tone. In a long, complex sentence (vv. 27-30), he turns emphatically to instruction: "Only [one thing]—conduct yourselves worthily . . ." "Conduct yourselves" could be translated "be citizens" (cf. 3:20) and would be relevant in Philippi, which, as a Roman colony, was proud of its full citizenship rights. Believers, however, now are citizens under "Christ's gospel," and Paul's wish is that whether he can "come and see" them or not (2:12), he should "hear about" them that they "stand in one spirit" (1:27). "Spirit" might include reference to the Holy Spirit, but the parallel phrase "one mind" shows that Paul is primarily thinking of the spiritual unity of believers. "The faith of the gospel" (1:27) is a unique phrase; it probably means "the faith that arises from the gospel." Though the Philippians are being persecuted, they are not to "be startled in any way by the opponents" (1:28), the latter referring probably to unbelievers, the probable source of the trouble Paul himself experienced in Philippi (1 Thess 2:2).

The next part of this complex sentence gets even more difficult. "This," he says, "is proof to them of destruction, but of your salvation" (1:28). "This" must refer to the whole situation of belief opposed by unbelief. The next two phrases ("proof to them of destruction, but of your salvation") could mean (1) that unbelievers think that the outcome will be "destruction" for the church, with Paul, however, assuring believers that in reality it will be their "salvation." Alternatively, (2) Paul assures the church that the present situation shows that unbelievers are bound for destruction (cf. 1 Cor 1:18; 2 Cor 4:3), but believers for salvation (1:28; cf. Rom 8:28). "And this," he concludes, "is from God," meaning not only salvation but also the mysterious outworking of things that, on either interpretation, unbelief cannot fathom.

The next two verses (1:29-30) assert that *everything* derives from God, both the capacity "to believe"—faith is a gift (cf. Gal 3:23-25)—and "to suffer" for Christ. The Philippians share "the same struggle" which they saw in Paul when he was persecuted in Philippi (1 Thess 2:2; Acts 16:20-24) and which they now hear about as he languishes in prison. For Paul, to suffer for Christ is a privilege (Rom 5:3) and an opportunity to experience grace (2 Cor 12:8-10).

Paul's rhetoric rises to a higher pitch as he reminds the Philippians of the fundamental qualities of life "in Christ" and appeals to them to live these out in full. "If there is . . ." is purely rhetorical; there is no question of whether these qualities are present (cf. 4:8). The passage is carefully and artistically phrased, so that commentary might obscure rather than clarify. Verses 1-4 prepare for the exhortation of verse 5 and the uniquely beautiful, but also deeply theological hymn of verses 6-11. Because of its unusual wording and rhythm, some scholars believe that Paul *quotes* a hymn that he did not himself compose. In any event, he found it deeply meaningful.

The crucial phrases parallel and reinforce one another, but not merely for rhetorical effect. Paul may have in mind emerging tensions within the Philippian churches (4:2-3), which he wishes to forestall. "Encouragement in Christ" and "comfort of love" (2:1) are synonymous; "love" refers both to the love Christ has for believers and to the love he inspires in them for one another (Gal 2:20; Phil 1:9). "Participation (or 'fellowship') in the spirit" recalls Paul's blessing that has been adopted into the liturgy (2 Cor 13:13) and, more clearly than 1:27 ('in one spirit'), alludes to the Spirit of God that believers share. The words "compassion (or 'affection') and mercy" reflect Paul's insistence elsewhere on the primacy of the love-command (Rom 13:8-10; Gal 5:14).

"Complete my joy" (2:2) finishes the thought begun with all those "ifs" and recalls the great joy Paul felt with regard to the Philippians (1:4; 4:1). Being "in Christ," believers can be of "the same mind" and have "the same love," that is, mutual love for one another. The next phrases—"united in heart (or 'mind'), thinking one thing"—repeat and reinforce the same notion. The words "Do nothing" (2:3) are actually not in the Greek text, though it is reasonable to supply them. Paul simply says, "Nothing out of selfishness nor from vainglory ('conceit'), but with humility regard others as more important . . ." "Others" here refers to believers; elsewhere Paul extends this love to outsiders (4:5; Gal 6:10; 1 Thess 3:12; 5:15). "Humility"

Philippians 1–2

and making others' interests more important than one's own (2:4, cf. 1 Cor 10:24, 33; 13:5) are not to be understood as groveling subservience; being humble has nothing to do with being a doormat (John 18:22-23). The humility Paul describes is self-sacrifice for others born out of unity in Christ. The basis for such humility is what Paul turns to in the Christ-hymn that follows.

Paul introduces the hymn with a third use of the verb *phronein* ("think") in this immediate passage (2:1-5; see 3:15); the related noun is part of the word "humility" ("lowly thinking"—2:3). It denotes an attitude or mindset more than "thought." The New American Bible translation may be correct, but more probably Paul is simply pointing to "the attitude that is also in Christ Jesus" himself (2:5), as the opening lines of the hymn suggest. Paul presents Christ's loving and humble attitude as the model for Christian morality. The hymn itself is almost impossible to interpret in a short space; we will confine ourselves to a few essentials.

Whether the hymn is poetry as such or simply rhythmic, exalted prose, it is constructed around balanced, pregnant phrases that tell and celebrate the stages of Christ's redemptive acts for the world. It can be divided into six stanzas of three lines each, dealing with: beginning—emptying—dying—being exalted—being named—being glorified. The first half comprises Christ's actions, the second half God's. The central point is the little phrase "death on a cross." The hymn evokes and may, in some respects, be modeled on the great Servant Song of the Good Friday liturgy (Isa 52:13–53:12).

The major problem of the first three lines (2:6) is whether they envisage Christ in divine preexistence ("in the form of God"), analogous to John 1:1, or as the antitype to Adam, who also was "in God's image" (Gen 1:26-27), but who, unlike Christ, "grasped at" equality with God and was disobedient (Gen 3:1-19). There are strong arguments on both sides. It is also possible—and an easy way out—that Paul might have entertained aspects of both interpretations. Other texts (notably 2 Cor 8:9; Gal 4:4; Col 1:15-17) show that the preexistence of Christ was not foreign to Paul, but Christ as the antitype of disobedient Adam is even more clearly attested (Rom 5:12-21; 1 Cor 15:22). A great deal depends on how individual phrases are translated and interpreted. "Equality with God" as "something to be *grasped at*" suggests the Adamic interpretation, but the crucial Greek word *(harpagmon)* could also be rendered "something to *be held on to*" or *"be taken advantage of."* Overall, the Adamic interpretation is more likely, but certainty is impossible.

The next stanza ("emptying") has three phrases describing Christ's entrance into the human condition (2:7). The preexistence interpretation sees here the description of the incarnation, as in John 1:14 ("the Word became flesh") and can properly say that it was precisely in being a "slave" (not in spite of it) that Jesus revealed who God is. "Emptied himself" evokes 2 Corinthians 8:9 ("though he was rich, Christ became poor for your sake"). The Adamic view focuses on the contrast between human arrogance ("You will be like gods"—Gen 3:5) and Christ's humility.

The final stanza of the hymn's first part describes Christ's self-sacrificial death (2:7-8). All can agree that Christ's "obedience to death" is, for Paul, the heart of the gospel, and, as here, he sometimes focuses on Jesus' death without explicit mention of the resurrection (e.g., 1 Cor 2:2; Gal 2:19-20). In the immediate context, Christ's self-emptying death provides the basis for the self-sacrifice that Paul wants the Philippians to practice toward one another (2:3-4). The nadir of the hymn is the little phrase "death on a cross," which many interpreters understand to be Paul's addition to the hymn he is quoting. That view may be correct; the phrase breaks the rhythm. On the other hand, standing at the center, it may be intended to stand alone as the turning point. Paul was not bound by rules as he either quoted or composed. However understood, it is a stark but powerful image: Christ crucified, the one on whom human redemption turns, seemingly abandoned (Mark 15:34; Gal 3:13).

"Because of this" (2:9) recalls the similar turning point in the hymn of the Suffering Servant (Isa 53:11-12) and does not primarily envisage reward for suffering but points to the *ways* of God, victory *through* suffering. God reveals in Jesus the *reversal* of human expectations by highly exalting the Crucified and bestowing on him "the name above every other name." This may refer to the exalting of the name "Jesus" itself (2:10), but probably it envisages God conferring on Jesus the name "Lord." Throughout the Old Testament, "Lord" *(kyrios)* is the translation for the sacred name YHWH, the sacred name for God (Exod 3:14; 20:7). The preexistence view of the hymn sees Jesus being raised again to his previous exalted status (cf. John 17:5). The Adamic view takes at face value that God "highly exalted" Jesus and "gave him a name" he did not previously have (cf. Acts 2:36; Rom 1:3-4). The latter view is not, of course, a denial of Jesus' divine nature but simply says that it was *not yet so fully* articulated. That Paul saw Jesus as "the Son of God" is quite clear (e.g., Rom 8:2, 32; Gal 4:4), but in Paul's time the formulations of the Nicene Creed were far in the future.

Be that as it may, the present text provides clear precedent for later formulations. Isaiah 45:23, clearly quoted in 2:10-11 ("every knee shall bend . . . every tongue confess") applies to Jesus words that the text from Isaiah uses of God; all creation and all parts of creation will own and confess that

"Jesus is Lord" (Rom 10:9; 1 Cor 12:3) and in glorifying Jesus will glorify "God the Father." So concludes this remarkable hymn. Its second half is not as relevant to Paul's point that believers are to imitate the humility of Jesus. Nevertheless, in depicting also the final stage of Christ's self-sacrifice, it enables believers to have a greater vision of the path of faith.

In the next paragraph (2:12-18) Paul uses the example of Christ to exhort the Philippians to both greater effort and a deeper vision. Of great interest is the command "Work out your own salvation." It arises from mention of Paul's "absence." When present, *he* worked for their salvation; now "all the more" he throws the responsibility on them. It is a remarkable command, however, because usually salvation, for Paul, is exclusively *God's* work (e.g., 1 Thess 5:9) and, in fact, he hastens to correct any misunderstanding by emphasizing that "*God* is the one who . . . works in you both to desire and to work" for salvation (2:13; cf. 1:29). Nevertheless, Paul also knows that humans have a part in the salvation of themselves and of those close to them (Rom 11:14; 1 Cor 7:16; 9:22); believers' conduct does matter.

The difference, therefore, between believers and the world ought to be apparent. Believers "shine like stars in the cosmos" (2:15), but not if "quarrels and disputes" (2:14) mark their behavior. The world, says Paul, is "crooked and perverse"; believers are to be "innocent." This can come across as an idyllic, unrealistic vision, but Paul presupposes a community where *every* member "works for salvation." There is here no handing over of responsibility to a class of "ministers and overseers" (1:1); all together "hold on to the word of life" and will prove the value of Paul's "labor" on "the day of Christ" (2:16). Meanwhile, for all his apparent optimism (1:25; 2:24), Paul acknowledges that he may be "poured out as a libation," almost certainly a reference to martyrdom (2 Tim 4:6). "Sacrifice and service" is the language of temple worship and is used elsewhere both of Paul (Rom 15:16) and of believers generally (Rom 12:1; 15:27; Phil 2:30; 4:18). Paul would find death a reason for "rejoicing" (1:23; cf. 3:10), and if it happens, he asks that the Philippians "rejoice with" him (2:18)!

2:19–3:1 Travel plans

Paul often includes, usually toward the end of his letters (see Rom 15:14-32; 1 Cor 16:5-12), some indication of the travel plans for himself and others. He hopes "to send Timothy soon" (2:19) so that he will be able to bring back good news. Paul takes this occasion to speak very warmly of Timothy (1:1; Acts 16:1), who was like a devoted child to the apostle (1:22). Paul also hopes that he himself will soon be able to come to Philippi (1:24).

Philippians 2–3

He thinks it even more urgent "to send Epaphroditus," who came as "an apostle" of the Philippians (2:25), bearing their gift (4:18). The next verses suggest regular communications between Paul in prison and the Philippians. They have heard that Epaphroditus fell seriously ill ("close to death"—2:27, 30), and word has come back of their concern, so that now Epaphroditus is concerned for *them* (2:26, 28). Though he figures nowhere else in the New Testament, he was a "co-worker" with Paul for a while (2:25). Paul regarded it as a mercy of God that Epaphroditus recovered from his illness (2:27) and is concerned that the Philippians should receive him warmly and "hold such people in high regard" (2:29; cf. 1 Thess 5:13). He "risked his life" both "for the work of Christ" and for the "service" the Philippians wished to render to Paul (2:30).

The word "finally" (3:1) can signal the near conclusion of a letter (2 Cor 13:11; cf. Eph 6:10; 2 Thess 3:1) or the conclusion of one topic and transition to another (1 Cor 7:29; 1 Thess 4:1). Here, following "travel plans," the letter should be drawing to a close, but it does not, and it is unusual that there is a second "finally" (4:8). Further, the natural sequence of "Rejoice in the Lord" (3:1) is either 4:1 or 4:4, certainly not 3:2! These observations have convinced scholars either that Philippians comprises more than one letter (the majority view) or that something has caused Paul to create a very awkward transition after 3:1. In any event, 3:1 or at least the command to "rejoice in the Lord" concludes the first (half of the) letter, recalling one of its major themes. It is "no burden" to him to repeat himself (about joy), but it is rather a "safeguard" for them (cf. Neh 8:10; Pss 81:1; 21:1).

3:2-11 An urgent warning against false faith

This paragraph shows how Paul's feelings of affection can burst into anger at those who would threaten the direction of believers' faith in Christ. The threat probably comes from conservative Jewish Christians, similar to those he contended with in Galatians. In that case the opponents were already present (Gal 1:6-7; 6:12). In this case Paul seems simply to be afraid of their imminent arrival in Philippi, and he uses harsh invectives to emphasize that such persons are not to be trusted. In calling them "dogs," he turns on them a common Jewish epithet directed at Gentiles (Mark 7:27); "evildoers" may be an ironic twist on their claim to be "law-doers," and "mutilation" *(katatome)* is a sarcastic reference to their insistence on "circumcision" *(peritome*—3:2; cf. Gal 6:12). *They* are not the true "circumcision," says Paul; *"we are,"* we "who worship through the Spirit of God" (3:3).

The opponents claim that with their adherence to the traditions and laws of Israel, *they* represent the true "Israel" ("descendants of Abraham"

—Gal 3:6-9, 29). Paul insists that they are nothing of the kind and sees this as an urgent issue, because it has to do with whether believers have "confidence" in Christ—note the repetition of this word (3:3-4)—or implicitly regard Christ's death as worthless (cf. Gal 2:20-21). By his conversion Paul was convinced that the covenant, from Abraham on, was founded simply on grace and faith (Rom 4:1-5; 9:6-16); the law was secondary (Rom 4:13-17; Gal 3:15-17).

Paul's critique of these Jewish-Christian opponents must *not* be taken as a critique of Judaism, as has too often been the case. Paul's love of his heritage (e.g., Rom 9:1-5) and his confidence that God would be faithful to the covenant with them (Rom 11:1-2, 29) are well attested. The enduring value of God's covenant with the Jews was also strongly affirmed at the Second Vatican Council. This polemic has to do with particular circumstances in Philippi, not with Judaism as such.

Paul presents himself as the model to follow. If circumcision or law-obedience were crucial, Paul would have "even more" reason for "confidence" than the opponents (3:4). There follows in verses 5-6 his recounting of the privileges he enjoyed by birth and his chosen way of life as a "Pharisee," all of which attest to his unique pedigree as a devoted member of the chosen people. His "zeal" for the law, in which he had been "blameless" (3:6), had even extended to persecution of the church (cf. 1 Cor 15:9; Gal 1:13-14; Acts 7:58–8:3; 9:1-2). But what he had once thought of as "gains," now "because of Christ" he reckons as "loss" (3:7). No human privilege or achievement "counts" for anything when compared with "the supreme good of knowing Christ Jesus my Lord" (3:8).

The key issue for Paul in all his letters is the nature of the divine-human relationship—specifically, by what is it characterized? As here, he rejects law and tradition as its foundation; elsewhere he rejects human wisdom or any kind of superior status, whether religious or social (Rom 2:17-29; 1 Cor 1:18-31). All such "gains" are simply "so much rubbish"; what matters is to "know Christ" (3:8), which means to have "faith in" him (3:9), in the sense of joyful trust. To "be found in him" looks forward to the judgment, when those who are "in Christ" will have no reason for fear (2:16).

Verses 9-11 describe the purpose of letting go of former privileges and status: it is "to know him and the power of his resurrection" (3:10). "Resurrection," however, is not merely in the future; it is a *present* experience, even in the midst of suffering (2 Cor 4:7-18; 5:17). To be "in Christ" is already to "walk in newness of life" (Rom 6:4; cf. 7:6). None of this, however, is a human accomplishment. The relationship ("righteousness") believers enjoy with God derives from a "righteousness" gained by Christ that is conferred as a gift; it is not essentially dependent on law or tradition (3:9). Even "faith" (3:9) is not the *condition* of "righteousness" but simply the *way it is lived*.

3:12-21 The ongoing journey toward Christ

Having stressed again *God's* initiative (cf. 1:29; 2:13), Paul turns emphatically to the theme of human responsibility, though even here Christ's action is prominent. He uses a series of verbs ("received," "made perfect," "pursue") to describe the *process* of "straining forward" toward "perfection" in Christ. He is at pains to say that, to be sure, he is not totally "perfected," but that, as he wishes them to do, he makes maximum effort to "possess" that for which he is already "possessed by Christ" (3:12). Therefore, he lets go of "the past" and sets his sights only on "the prize of God's upward calling" (3:13-14). Paul may again have death in mind (cf. 1:23; 2:17), but "calling" is an important word in his letters to denote both the event of conversion and the life of faith to which it leads (e.g., Rom 4:17; 8:30; 1 Cor 1:9, 26; 7:15-24). Paul considers himself and others as, in a sense, "perfect" (3:15, cf. 1 Cor 2:6; Matt 5:48), but this perfection consists in the "attitude," which he wants the Philippians to have, of *striving* for perfection! If some are inclined to disagree (cf. 1 Cor 11:16), Paul is sure that he is right and that "God will reveal this also" to them. Meanwhile they should remain constant in the progress already attained (3:16) and join together in being "imitators" of Paul and of those whose behavior is a true model.

Paul's confidence in himself, that he is a proper guide and "model" for believers, should not be seen as arrogance. The ultimate example he has in mind is Christ in his self-emptying death (2:6-8), to which all believers are to seek to be "conformed" (3:10). Paul's self-assurance derives from long years of having lived in imitation of the self-sacrificial example of Jesus. On the other hand, "there are many" whose behavior makes them "the enemies of the cross" (3:18). Paul had "often" told the Philippians of such people; they, therefore, must have known who they were. We, however, can only plead ignorance. Perhaps they are the opponents Paul inveighs against in 3:2, but that is not clear. The criticisms of them are very vague, but they may indicate moral laxity of some kind. A warning against laxity also appears in Galatians (Gal 5:13-26) following that letter's stern teaching against being overly concerned with law. The pattern here is similar.

By contrast with such people, whose "minds are set on earthly things" (3:19), "*our* citizenship is in heaven, from where we await a *savior*, the *Lord*." "Citizenship" (cf. 1:27) and "savior" are never found again in Paul's own letters; they are suited very specifically for this city with its "Roman" citizenry, which acknowledged the *emperor* (probably Nero) as "Lord" and

"Savior." The contrasting of the emperor with Jesus is undoubtedly deliberate, though Paul is not preaching political rebellion (cf. Rom 13:1-7). His point is precisely that believers' hope is *not* in politics. Believers' hope is in Christ, who will, at his coming, "change our lowly body to conform with his glorified body" (3:21), a theme that Paul develops at length elsewhere (1 Cor 15:35-57). The *present* experience of *gradually* "being transformed" into the image of the Lord (2 Cor 3:18) anticipates that future "change" at the resurrection. Gradual transformation is what Paul has largely had in mind since 3:10.

4:1-9 Final appeals and exhortations

The opening demonstrates once again Paul's deep affection for, and joy in, the Philippians. We never hear elsewhere of Euodia and Syntyche. The appeal to them to "have the same mind" is the same plea of 2:2 (Rom 15:5). Paul asks his "true yokemate" (*Syzygos*—perhaps a proper name) to "assist them," probably meaning to act as an arbitrator. They were important leaders of the church in Philippi, having been foundational, along with Lydia (Acts 16:13-15), in establishing the church there. We cannot know what their dispute was, and in any case it was not overly serious; Paul has confidence that they will work it out. We also do not know anything more about "Syzygos." The word (name?) is masculine; this is not a reference, as is sometimes supposed, to Paul's wife.

Paul exhorts them all yet again to "rejoice." In that joy their "kindness" (or "gentleness") can and should "be known to all" (4:5). "The Lord is near" refers to the soon-expected "day of Christ" (2:16; cf. 3:20). In the meantime they must not "worry"; that would be the opposite of joy. They must simply make their prayers and requests known to God (4:6), and "the peace of God" (cf. John 14:27), which has to do with far more than the absence of conflict or suffering (1:29), "will guard their hearts and minds" (4:7). "Peace" is the gift that flows from "grace" (1:2; Rom 5:1-11). "Finally" Paul exhorts them simply to hold fast to all that is good and repeats again the theme of learning from and imitating his manner of following Christ. The "peace" blessing is also found elsewhere (Rom 15:33; 2 Cor 13:11).

4:10-20 Thanks for the Philippians' generosity

Many commentators regard this section as "letter A," sent before the other letter(s) as a thank-you note. That could be correct, but this is not the first time Paul has received a gift from the Philippians (4:16; cf. 2 Cor 11:9); this is the "revival" of their generosity—not that their concern had flagged, but they "lacked the opportunity" to show it (4:10). Now, however,

Philippians 4

Epaphroditus has delivered their gift (4:18), and Paul rejoices at their concern and, as is typical, not only gives thanks for the material blessing but also reflects on the spiritual riches he has in Christ (4:13). As elsewhere, Paul can appear slightly arrogant as he assures them that he has "learned" to be "self-sufficient" (4:11-12). He just barely says "thanks" (4:14), but his tone is not so much arrogant as embarrassed.

Elsewhere, especially in the Corinthian letters (1 Cor 9:3-18; 2 Cor 12:13-16), Paul refused to exercise his "right" to be paid for his apostolic work, "working night and day" rather than be a burden on anyone (1 Thess 2:9). For some reason, however, he had long ago entered into a financial arrangement with the Philippians (4:15) but was hesitant to accept their money. It might appear that he wanted their *possessions* rather than *themselves* (2 Cor 12:14) and be no better than other "peddlers of the word of God" (2 Cor 2:17). Further, his enemies might say that he appropriated for himself (2 Cor 8:20-21) money he had promised to collect for Jerusalem (Gal 2:10; Rom 15:25-26). So he assures the Philippians that he is "not eager for the gift" but for "the profit that accrues to *their* account" (4:17). The money is fully adequate to his needs, but, more important, it is "an acceptable sacrifice, pleasing to God" (4:18). And God will also fill their every need "according to his wealth in glory" (4:19). Paul concludes his thank-you in the manner of a prayer, giving glory to God (4:20).

4:21-23 Final greetings and blessing

The sending of greetings is common enough (see 1 Cor 16:19-20; 2 Cor 13:12), but particular here is the mention of greetings from some in "Caesar's household" (4:22), which to many suggests that Paul was in Rome. This is possible, but Caesar's officials and servants were in major cities throughout the empire, including Philippi. The mention of Caesar (only here in Paul's letters; cf. Rom 13:1-7) would be meaningful for this Roman colony. Paul ends the letter with his standard blessing (1 Cor 16:23; Gal 6:18); it echoes his opening greeting (1:2). "Grace" is the beginning and end of Christian existence.

The Letter to the Colossians
Vincent M. Smiles

INTRODUCTION

Colossians among Paul's letters

Among the thirteen letters that bear Paul's name, Colossians has a unique place. Seven letters are universally accepted as written by Paul (Romans, 1 and 2 Corinthians, Galatians, Philippians, 1 Thessalonians, Philemon). A large majority think that Paul did not write the Pastoral Letters (1 and 2 Timothy, Titus) or Ephesians, and a growing majority think the same regarding 2 Thessalonians. That leaves Colossians. A small majority favor the conclusion that Paul himself is not the author, but a number of them think that Paul was still alive and may have had some say in the letter's composition. In this case, someone like Timothy was the main author, with Paul providing input. Just about all would agree with one author's description of Colossians as a "bridge" between Paul himself and those who continued his ministry and wrote further letters in his name.

Colossians certainly bears many striking similarities to Paul's letters, but with regard to style and theology and the absence of some key Pauline terms (e.g., "righteousness," "law," addressing the readers as "brothers"), its distinctiveness is very apparent. The image of Christ and the church as cosmic entities is particularly distinctive, as also is the style of lengthy sentences overflowing with synonymous expressions. Whoever wrote Colossians knew Paul's letters, and perhaps Paul himself, quite well but also had developed a unique style and theological view. Paul sometimes wrote in the name of his co-workers; here one of them or someone associated with them has written in Paul's name.

The close connections between Colossians and Ephesians is discussed in the commentary on Ephesians (see p. 603).

When and why was Colossians written?

A reasonable hypothesis is that the letter was written from Ephesus, perhaps while Paul was in prison in Rome or shortly after his death (i.e., early to late sixties A.D.). It has two main purposes: first, to respond to the challenge presented by "the philosophy" (2:8), and second, to provide some support for Epaphras (1:7; 4:12-13) and others in their furthering of Paul's ministry. "The philosophy" probably had its home in Judaism (note 2:11, 16, 21) and invoked ideas from popular philosophy, such as "the elements of the world" (2:8), which were identified with spiritual "powers" (2:10, 15, 18). Colossians has none of the polemic of Galatians, but as in that case, the law was being introduced as a necessary factor between believers and God, as though the divine-human relationship required a legal code (see 2:13-15). Like Paul in Galatians, this writer insists that believers live "in Christ" (2:7) and indeed "in God" (3:3) and have no need of any such intervening power (cf. Gal 2:19-21).

The value of Colossians for today is in that teaching. Believers in every generation need to remember that nothing is to displace the primacy of a direct relationship with God "in Christ."

COMMENTARY

1:1-2 Opening greeting

The opening verse is identical to the opening words of 2 Corinthians 1:1. In Corinth (1 Cor 9:1-5; 2 Cor 11:5-33) and in Galatia (Gal 1:1–2:14), Paul had to defend his apostolate. In Colossae his apostolate seems to have been unchallenged, but the words "apostle of Christ Jesus by the will of God" might have been necessary because the Colossian churches did not know him by sight (2:1) and also he wanted to make more effective the commendation of those who would continue his ministry (1:7; 4:7-14). Timothy had long been a major partner in Paul's mission (1 Thess 1:1; 3:2; Acts 16:1-3). Although the addressees are "the believers in Colossae" (1:2), the letter is intended also for other churches (4:13-15). The greeting here is shorter than usual (cf. Rom 1:7; 1 Cor 1:3).

1:3-8 Thanksgiving

In Greek this thanksgiving comprises just one sentence. Generally, it echoes Paul's thought and language well; "giving thanks," "praying," and recalling of the recipients' coming to faith are all characteristic of Paul's thanksgivings (e.g., Phil 1:3-5; 1 Thess 1:2-5). Further, faith, love, and hope are featured here, as in 1 Thessalonians, but whereas, for Paul, hope is a quality that enables "eager expectation" for the coming reward (Rom 8:18-25; Phil 1:20), here it suggests not expectation but the reward itself "reserved for you in heaven" (1:5).

The Colossians "heard" the gospel from Epaphras and recognized in it "the grace of God." Epaphras had established the church in Colossae (1:7-8; 4:12-13) and had been imprisoned with Paul (Phlm 23); he also provided the news of the Colossians' faith (their "love in the Spirit") and (probably) of the competing "philosophy" (2:8). The strong commendation ("our beloved fellow slave . . .") unites Epaphras closely with Paul, confirming his fidelity to Christ *on your behalf* (cf. 1:24; 2:1); the latter phrase is otherwise used most often of *Christ's* sacrifice (e.g., Rom 5:8; 8:32; 1 Cor 11:24). The gospel, says the writer, "has come to you" and indeed to "the whole world," something of an exaggeration in the first century (1:23)! In any event, the gospel is "bearing fruit" among the Colossians (1:6); the writer is not fearful for them (2:5), as Paul was for the Galatians (Gal 4:11).

1:9-14 Prayer for the Colossians

This section also comprises one long sentence. It describes an enthusiastic prayer for the Colossians' growth in faith. "From the day" Paul and his companions "heard" about it, they have been praying (the verbs express continuous action) that the Colossians "might be filled" with all necessary spiritual gifts (1:9-11). There is a strong emphasis on gifts of "knowledge" and "wisdom" (1:9-10), which goes along with this letter's contesting of "a philosophy" (2:8) and with the description of Paul and his companions as those who "teach with all wisdom" (1:28). Faith has everything to do with commitment and right action, another strong emphasis of this letter (1:10, 21-22; 3:1–4:6), but faith must also be intelligent both to direct behavior (2:16-23) and for the sake of witness to outsiders (4:5-6). Behavior and knowledge are virtually inseparable (1:10).

The second half of the prayer shows that *what* believers "know" goes far beyond mere intellectual knowledge; it has to do with knowing the dignity that God bestows on believers, already granting them "a share with the saints in light" and transferring them "to the kingdom of his beloved Son" (1:12-13). Such language of future blessings realized *now* contrasts with Paul's own theology (2:12; 3:1, cf. Rom 6:5), but it reminds the Colossians that "the reality" is already theirs (2:17).

The prayer witnesses to the charismatic enthusiasm that also characterized Paul's experience of church prayer (e.g., 1 Cor 14:1-19). It conveys the thankful "joy" (1:11-12) of being in Christ; "in him" they "have redemption, the forgiveness of sins" (1:14). "Forgiveness" is virtually unmentioned in Paul's own letters (only Rom 4:7). Paul's theology deals more with God's *gifts* in Christ (Spirit, freedom, adoption) than with sins removed. Here the

Colossians 1

prayer, which has become a celebratory recounting of God's action (1:12-14), prepares for a glorious hymn in praise of the cosmic Christ.

1:15-20 The cosmic Christ

These verses encapsulate a hymn or spiritual song (3:16, cf. John 1:1-18; Phil 2:6-11), older than the letter itself, that was incorporated here, with a few editorial touches, by the letter's author. As it stands, it has two main parts: describing Christ's role in creation (1:15-17) and in reconciliation (1:18-20). Its editing is not easily distinguished from the original. Still, scholars have ventured some educated guesses, which can illustrate the kind of development that may account for this difficult but profound text.

1. "Of the church" (1:18a) breaks the established rhythm and restricts "all things" to "the church." Probably "the head of the body" originally envisaged "the body" of *creation,* applying to Christ language that, in the wider Greco-Roman culture, was sometimes used of Zeus. "Of the church" was added to prepare for subsequent teaching (2:19).

2. In 1:16b the "powers" listed correspond precisely to the "powers" which are a part of the competing teaching and which God "stripped away" and defeated (2:8-10, 15). They may have been added to 1:16 to emphasize their subordination to Christ.

3. Probably the hymn originally spoke of God ("the fullness," cf. 2:9), by means of Christ's *resurrection* ("the firstborn from the dead," 1:18), "reconciling all things through him" (1:20; cf. 2 Cor 5:18-19). The reference to Christ's death ("the blood of his cross") *after* the resurrection is awkward and looks like an editorial addition.

It is reasonable to think that the original hymn might have looked something like the following. If the bracketed lines are omitted, we end up with two stanzas of four lines each (italicized text); one theory does just that and *could* be correct.

> 1:15 *He is the image of the invisible God* (2 Cor 4:4),
> *firstborn of all creation* (Prov 8:22-31; Rev 3:14),
> [16] *for in him all things were created* (1 Cor 8:6; John 1:3)
> (in the heavens and upon the earth) (Phil 2:10)
> *all things were created through him and for him* (cf. Rom 11:36)
> [17] (and he is before all things
> and all things hold together in him

¹⁸ᵃ and he is the head of the body). (Eph 4:15)
¹⁸ᵇ *He is the beginning,*
firstborn from the dead (1 Cor 15:20),
(that he might be the first among all)
¹⁹ *for in him all the fullness was pleased to dwell* (2:9-10)
²⁰ *and through him to reconcile all things* (2 Cor 5:18-19),
(whether things on earth or things in heaven).

As edited by the letter writer, this was a Christian hymn, but several scholars maintain, with good reason, that it was either modeled on an earlier Jewish hymn in praise of Wisdom (cf. Prov 8:22-31) or was inspired by applying Wisdom traditions to Christ (e.g., Wis 7:22-30), as in John 1:1-18.

The hymn was adapted to provide a theological base from which to fight "the philosophy" (2:8). If we could know this (probably Jewish) "philosophy" as the Colossians did, we would, undoubtedly, recognize some measure of sincerity and goodness in its teachers. Paul had described even Peter as "clearly wrong" and a "hypocrite" (Gal 2:12-14); so here, these teachers are described in negative terms (2:8, 18) but were not necessarily evil. Nevertheless, their teaching compromises the gospel. It seems to have involved "the elements of the world" (2:8, 20), "the principalities and powers" (2:10, 15), which humans were to obey by certain ascetic practices (2:21-23). However, the fault was not asceticism (note Matt 6:16-18; 1 Cor 7:29-35), but requiring trust to be placed in "principalities," as though they could produce what Christ had *already* accomplished. The "powers" were, in effect, becoming rivals of Christ.

The hymn, therefore, makes clear that Christ is the ruler of the *cosmos*; all powers, including angels (2:18), are subject to him. He is "the image of the invisible God, the firstborn of all creation" (1:15). The hymn has a very high view of the divinity of Christ, but it is a step in the development of doctrine, not its completion; it has not reached the level of the Nicene Creed. And yet, in both parts of the hymn (1:15, 18), Christ is supreme over creation, both its agent and its goal (1:16), the one in whom "all things hold together" (1:17). What elsewhere is said of God (Rom 11:36) is ascribed here to Christ (1:16d), who is clearly understood as preexistent before the rest of creation (1:17-18).

It is very important in this letter that Christ is "the head" not only of creation but also "of the church" (1:18). "The church" here, like Christ, is a cosmic entity, since it is "his body" (1:24). The major focus, however, remains on Christ; "in him all the fullness was pleased to dwell and, through him [Christ] to reconcile all things to him" (i.e., "to God," 2 Cor 5:19, but

Colossians 1

see 1:22). "The fullness" evidently refers to God (cf. 2:9), or at least that's the way the writer of the letter sees it. In the original it might simply have referred to "the fullness" of spiritual reality (cf. John 1:14, 16). "Fullness" is an important concept in both Colossians and Ephesians (Eph 1:23). As Christ bears "the fullness" of God, so believers are to "be filled with all the fullness of God" and "of Christ" (Col 2:9; Eph 3:19; 4:13).

"Reconciliation," though using a slightly different Greek word, was also important in Paul's own letters (Rom 5:10-11; 2 Cor 5:18-20). There, as here, it denotes God's action in and through Christ, but whereas "the world," for Paul (2 Cor 5:19), meant simply human beings, estranged by sin from God (e.g., Rom 5:12; cf. Col 1:22), here "all things" includes the universe itself, which the ancient world sometimes saw as out of balance. They admired its beauty and order, but natural and moral evils suggested that the "body" of the *cosmos* needed the *logos* of God—reconciliation. Once again, this answers "the philosophy"; believers do not need lesser authorities ("the principalities and powers"). In Christ "the head," God has "reconciled all things" (1:20), including by "the blood of his cross" (cf. 2:14-15!).

1:21-23 The meaning of the hymn for Colossae

The amended hymn is immediately applied to the Colossians; they once were "alienated" (from God) and "hostile in mind." "Mind" has more to do with attitude than with intellect; proper "understanding" in that broader and deeper sense is crucial (e.g. 1:9-10). "Evil deeds" (1:21) are both the cause and the demonstration of minds out of tune with God (cf. Rom 1:18-32). "But now" (cf. Rom 3:21; 6:22) Christ has "reconciled" them "in his fleshly body through death" (1:22). "Fleshly body" (cf. 2:11) is a strange phrase; both terms were important for Paul (e.g., Rom 6:6, 12; 7:4; 1 Cor 12:13, 27; Rom 7:5; 8:3), but he never combined them as here. In the present context "body" recalls, and contrasts with, 1:18. The cosmic Christ is "head" of both the universe and the church, but Jesus, in his own "*fleshly* body through death," achieved reconciliation. In baptism believers "strip off" the "fleshly body" (2:11).

Christ's purpose is to "present" the reconciled before God (cf. 1:28) like a "holy, unblemished" sacrifice (cf. Rom 12:1), "irreproachable" at the judgment (1:22) in spite of their sinful past. They, of course, must "persevere in the faith"; all is not yet complete. They must remain "firmly grounded, not shifting from the hope" that the gospel produced. The gospel of the cosmic Christ has been "proclaimed in all creation under heaven," a considerable exaggeration (as in 1:6), but aiming to demonstrate that the gospel, contrary to "the philosophy," is in accordance with God's plan for the universe "from all eternity" (1:25-26). This exaltation of the gospel, and of Paul as its "minister" (*diakonos*—cf. 1:25), goes beyond anything that Paul himself said (cf. Rom 1:16-17; 15:19), but it furthers the Colossians' idea of Christ and the church as cosmic entities. It also prepares for the next section.

1:24–2:5 Paul, his co-workers, and God's eternal plan

If Colossians was written, in part, to establish the authority of those who continued Paul's ministry, this purpose is largely accomplished here. To "rejoice in sufferings" echoes Paul's tendency to see suffering, and even death, as nothing in comparison with the joy of being in Christ (e.g., Rom 8:18; Phil 1:19-23). The following claim for Paul's sufferings, as "completing what is lacking [!] in the afflictions of Christ" (1:24), is surprising and, on the face of it, shocking. The notion that somehow Christ's death might be inadequate was anathema to Paul (Gal 2:21); it is inconceivable that such a claim is intended here. Rather, dwelling on Paul's thoughts about his sufferings as an apostle (especially 2 Cor 4:7-10), the writer sees them as having a role "for your sake . . . on behalf of [Christ's] body, the church," which, like all creation, continues to "groan" as it awaits "the redemption of our bodies" (Rom 8:18-25). It might be, as one author has suggested, that the crucial phrase should be hyphenated: "I am completing what is lacking in *Christ's-afflictions-in-my-flesh* for the sake of his body." In this case, it is not Christ's own sufferings that might be lacking, but rather the sufferings of Paul for the sake of Christ and the church.

This emotional recalling of Paul's sufferings "for your sake" and the reminder that he was the church's "minister according to God's stewardship" (1:25) shed a favorable light also on Paul's co-workers, "we" who aid him in "proclaiming" and "instructing" (1:28). "We," strongly emphasized in the Greek, includes Timothy, Epaphras, and Tychicus (1:1, 7-8; 4:7-14). Paul had "fulfilled for you the word of God," the word that was an ancient and "hidden mystery, but now is manifested to God's holy ones" (1:26). "Holy ones" (cf. 1:2) denotes *all* the baptized, but here there is some emphasis on the preachers.

"Hidden mystery" is apocalyptic language. "Apocalypse" is the Greek word for "revelation," and in apocalyptic literature (especially Daniel and Revelation; cf. Mark 13; Matt 24), God's ancient plan for the world is "revealed" to a seer (Daniel, Enoch, John, the apostles), who then imparts it to others through speech or writing (e.g., Dan 2:19-28; cf. 7:1-28; Rev 1:1, 9-11). The plan ultimately always has to do with the *eschaton*, the end of the world ("the hope of glory," 1:27). However, here the expectation of the end is not as imminent as for Paul himself (e.g., 1 Cor 7:29-31; 1 Thess 4:13-17), though it has not disappeared, as it mostly has today.

Colossians strikes a wonderful balance: the "mystery" is "Christ in you," an experience here and now that anticipates "the glory" hoped for. The apostles proclaim the gospel "so that," at the judgment, they will be able to "present everyone perfect in Christ" (cf. 1:22; Phil 2:16). That was the reason for Paul's "labor and struggle," and that, indeed, was the purpose of Christ's "power working within me" (1:29).

As there is a strong emphasis on the "power" of Christ at work within Paul (1:29), so there is also emphasis on his "struggle for your sake (cf. 1:24) and for those in Laodicea" (2:1). Epaphras (1:7-8) had acted as Paul's emissary, but Paul remained the key authority. Paul's concern for his churches (see 2 Cor 11:28) was important to emphasize, especially for those who had never known him personally (2:1). His struggle had been for their encouragement, their "unity in love," and, returning to a prominent theme, their "understanding" (cf. 1:9-10). Neither Paul nor his co-workers own and control the gospel; their purpose is that believers attain "all the richness of fully assured understanding and knowledge" (2:2). It is the entire community that is to understand "the mystery of God, Christ."

"Mystery" recalls 1:27 (above). The phrase "God, Christ" is confusing; the ancient manuscript copiers produced fifteen variations on this phrase in their attempts to explain it (e.g., "God the Father," "God, the Father of Christ")! It is not impossible that Christ is called "God" here, but "the God of Christ" (cf. 1:3; 2 Cor 1:3) is also possible, or perhaps the thought is that "Christ" is the content of "God's mystery." This goes along well with "the mystery, which is Christ in you" (1:27) and is perhaps the best we can do. In any event, it is "in him" that "all the treasures of wisdom and knowledge are hidden" (2:3), and therefore for believers they are not hidden at all (cf. 2 Cor 4:1-6).

The writer hints for the first time at the presence of some threatening ideas. Their "knowledge" of Christ should keep them safe from seemingly persuasive but actually "specious arguments" (2:4). Though Paul cannot be with them "in the flesh," he is with them "in the spirit" (cf. 1 Cor 5:3). If he were with them, he would rejoice at "the strength" of their "faith in Christ" (2:5). The writer's confidence, in spite of the threat, is notable.

2:6–3:4 Hold to "the faith"; no further "philosophy" is needed

The writer now turns to countering the threat of alternative ideas, doing so first by general encouragement that sets the theme for the major sections to come. Just as they "received Christ" and were "rooted and established in him," so they must "walk" (2:6-7). There is first a constant reminder of what believers *already have* in Christ and why no further teachings or dictates (2:14, 20) are required. "The faith" here denotes *what* "you were taught," the message as preached by Epaphras (1:7), but faith as *trust* and *relationship* (2:5) is by no means separate from the message (cf. Rom 10:9), an important point for the church today. Faith in its fullness leads naturally to fullness of "thanksgiving" (*eucharistia*, 2:7).

Whether the writer has a specific "someone" in mind is difficult to say (see 2:16-18). Certainly there is no one in Colossae comparable to the opponents in Galatia (Gal 1:7). Nevertheless, there is the seductive power of some "philosophy," which the writer regards as based in "human tradition," having to do with "the elementary powers of the world" (2:8, 10, 15; cf. 1:21). The "elements" (earth, air, fire, water) were widely thought to be the foundational components of the universe and were sometimes regarded as personal forces (e.g., Wis 13:2; Gal 4:3; 2 Pet 3:10-12); in Judaism they could be associated with angels and the giving of the law (Acts 7:53; Gal 3:19; 4:9-10).

The attraction of such teaching is that it takes seriously the invisible and unpredictable "powers" that affect human existence. Further, it prescribes practices (2:21), in the manner of the sacred laws of Judaism, for dealing with those forces. In this regard there is a link between the problem envisioned here and that in Galatia. And, as in Galatia, the solution is to recall the status already attained in Christ (e.g., Gal 4:1-7). Thus whatever is "not according to Christ" is to be rejected (2:8; cf. Gal 5:2-4).

"In him"—the tenth occurrence of this idea so far—"dwells the whole fullness of the deity bodily" (2:9), a very strong statement of Christ's identity with God (cf. 1:19; John 1:1, 14). The present tense is important; this was not merely something that happened in the past, when Christ was on earth. It is true now, and believers, who are "in Christ," already "share in this fullness" of divinity (2:10; cf. John 17:20-23). There can be no improvement, says Colossians, on Christ as the means of access to God. Christ is "the head of every principality"; the "elements" have nothing to add.

The next paragraph employs a series of metaphors, focused largely around baptism, to bring out the meaning of being "in him." Jewish writers sometimes spoke of "circumcision" as the "stripping away" of vice; circumcision ultimately had to involve the "circumcision of the heart" (Deut 30:6, cf. Rom 2:29). Such circumcision "was not administered by hand." The "stripping off of the fleshly body" (cf. 1:22) could be achieved only "by the circumcision of Christ," that is "by baptism." In baptism believers were "buried with" Christ and even "raised with" him "by faith in the power of

God." (2:12). That believers are *already* "raised" goes notably beyond what Paul himself said (cf. Rom 6:5; 8:11; 2 Cor 4:14), but it makes the point about what believers have in Christ.

The baptismal imagery continues, employing perhaps language of the liturgy and highlighting the transformation from a life "dead in transgressions" (Eph 2:1) to one in which God "brought you to life with him" (cf. Rom 6:4), "forgiving us all our transgressions" (2:13; cf. 1:14). These are already vivid metaphors, but now they pile up even further, going beyond the language of baptism. Verses 14-15 contain six verbs ("obliterating," "removed," "nailing," "despoiling," "made a spectacle" and "leading in triumph"). Presumably their subject, following the sequence from 1:13, is God rather than Christ. It is also possible that the writer is content to be ambiguous, permitting the imagery to have its effect regardless. Probably at least 1:14 describes God's action.

God "obliterated the bond" that, with its "legal claims," held sinful humans in debt. "The bond" is the legal document listing human failures. The image is like the slave with the impossible debt in Jesus' parable (Matt 18:21-35). When human behavior is stacked beside the demands of the law, then humans deserve condemnation. In freeing humans, God did not obliterate the law—the law is "holy" (Rom 7:12)—but rather the condemnation that it produces (cf. Rom 8:1-4). God "removed [the bond] from our midst, nailing it to the cross" (2:14), a powerful way to speak of God in Christ making peace with the world (1:20, 22; 2 Cor 5:18). If God is the subject, then "in him" (not "by it") God "despoiled," more literally *"stripped away,* the principalities and powers, made a public spectacle of them, and paraded them" in a victorious procession, like a general with prisoners of war (2:15).

It would, therefore, be nonsense for believers to revert to a position from which God has set them free (cf. Gal 4:8-10) and permit anyone to "pass judgment" on them with regard to religious rules and regulations (2:16). Such things are "a shadow" in comparison with "the substance," literally "the *body* of Christ" (2:17; cf. 1:24). The word "disqualify" is related to the word for "prize" in Philippians 3:14, but here the thought is that someone might "deny [believers] the prize" of being "in God" (3:3).

There is further difficult use of multiple images with no agreement on precisely what the writer means. In discussion with the competing philosophy, some advantage seems to have been claimed for ascetic practices (cf. 1:23) that enable "self-abasement" ("humility," cf. 3:12) not only by obeying regulations but also by "the worship of angels," meaning probably by being able to *join in with* "the worship of angels" (cf. Isa 6:2-3; Dan 7:10;

Rev 4:9-10; 7:11-12). This is what the "visions" were probably about as the person was "entering into" worship (not "taking his stand"). The claims made were probably impressive and attractive.

The writer, however, is quite scathing in evaluating these claims, whatever they are. Such a person is "inflated [conceited] without reason," not genuinely "humble" at all (cf. Phil 2:1-5). This is not true spiritual understanding but suggests only "a fleshly mind" (2:18). Such a person—a believer is envisaged—ought rather to "hold on to the head" (1:18; 2:10), who alone guarantees the proper "support" and "growth" of the body (2:19). The main point is repeated and emphasized: if believers "died with Christ" (cf. 2:11-12; Rom 6:2, 8), being liberated "from the elements," it is nonsense to return to "regulations." Far from taking believers into heavenly worship, that only projects them back into the insecurities of "living in [this] world" (2:20, cf. 3:1); they are back again to being dictated to, and "the glorious freedom of the children of God" (Rom 8:21) is lost!

The divine-human relationship does not rest on law but on God's love and compassion (Rom 5:6-8; 9:16; Gal 2:11-21). Regulations have a place; this writer will soon provide more than enough (3:18–4:1)! But such rules ("Don't touch, don't eat"), like the things they deal with, "are bound for destruction"; ultimately they are only "human precepts" (2:22; cf. Mark 7:7). They have "a semblance of wisdom," a passing usefulness (2:23), but Jesus did not come with a system of law—"the sabbath is for people, not people for the sabbath" (Mark 2:27). In any context, ancient or modern, this is quite a radical stance and by no means easily maintained. It nevertheless reflects well both Jesus and Paul.

In conclusion, believers "were raised with Christ" (3:1; cf. 2:12), who is "seated at God's right hand" (3:1; cf. Ps 110; Matt 22:44; Acts 2:34; 1 Cor 15:25). Their focus is not to be on "things of earth" (3:2), religion and rules that skew the relationship with God. Having "died" with Christ (cf. Gal 2:19-20), the "life" of the baptized is now "hidden with Christ in God" (3:3). "Hidden" evokes God's ancient "mystery" and "wisdom" (2:3) manifested to believers (1:26-27), but now believers are themselves a *part of the mystery*, so that at the end, "when Christ, your life, appears," they also "will appear with him in glory" (3:4). Why bother with "angels" when you already commune with God?

3:5-17 Reject evil, do good

Having reminded believers that they "died and were raised with Christ" (2:12, 20; 3:1), the author now tells them to "put to death the parts of you that are earthly" (3:5). Now the rubber, so to speak, hits the road: believers do in fact "live in the world" (2:20) and indeed "in the flesh" (cf. 2:23)! Paul himself had faced the same irony (e.g., Gal 5:1, 13-17). Though believers have "stripped off the old self . . . and put on the new" (3:9-10), they remain "in the flesh" (Gal 2:20), and its temptations are always at hand (see Rom 8:3-8). God's reconciling of humans does not eliminate their freedom or their capacity to reject goodness.

The first list of vices (3:5) centers mostly on sexual sins (cf. 1 Thess 4:3-4) but culminates with "greed," which some ancient writers regarded as among the worst evils (cf. Luke 12:15). Here it is equated with "idolatry." Such things earn "the wrath of God" (cf. Rom 1:18). The Colossians are again reminded (cf. 2:13) that their own lives were once characterized by such vices, but now "they must put them all away"; there follows a further list centering on vices that disrupt friendship and community, culminating with the command to "stop lying."

The language next recalls baptism (cf. 2:11-12) and, as earlier, uses the metaphor of "stripping off." Baptism involved disrobing before entering into the baptismal pool and then "putting on" a new garment to symbolize "putting on Christ" (Gal 3:27; Rom 13:14). The "new self," says the writer, "is *being* renewed [an *ongoing* process!] for knowledge (cf. 2:3), according to the image of its creator" (3:10; cf. 1:15; Gen 1:26-27). It is not just a matter of virtues but of an entirely "new self," "new creation" (2 Cor 5:17). As the perversion of "knowledge" had distorted humanity (Rom 1:18-23), so genuine knowledge will characterize the new humanity.

Baptismal language continues. Apparently, in Paul's churches the baptismal formula included something like "In Christ there is no longer Greek and Jew" (3:11; cf. 1 Cor 12:13; Gal 3:28). This expressed succinctly the new reality created in baptism and experienced within the church, where all races, classes, and genders were able to be together as "one body" (3:15; 1 Cor 12:12-27). The formula predated Paul, but he used it because it suited so well his desire to break down the barrier in the church between the Jews ("circumcision," Gen 17:9-14), the original chosen people, and all the rest (see Eph 2:11-18). That also means that all other barriers of privilege and status are abolished in Christ; *all* who have faith—even the barbarous "Scythians"—"are clothed with Christ," are members of the same body.

But, of course, there is tremendous tension here, both for the ancient churches and today. Slavery, for example, continued to be practiced even within the church (3:22-25; Eph 6:5-9; 1 Tim 6:1-2; Titus 2:9-10; 1 Pet 2:18-20)! It took Christianity many more centuries to recognize fully the social implications of the gospel. And, truth be told—not least in relation to the full equality of women—the church continues to struggle even today. In any age, what ultimately matters is "Christ," who "is all and *is in all*" (3:11).

As "God's chosen ones," believers must "clothe themselves" with virtues (3:12); this list features qualities of compassion and gentleness, stresses the obligation to forgive "as the Lord forgave you" (3:13; cf. Matt 6:12; 18:21-22), and culminates with "love, the bond of perfection" (3:14). "The peace of Christ" (cf. Phil 4:7) is to "reign in your hearts," and indeed it was into peace "in one body" that believers "were called" (3:15). There is emphasis again on "wisdom" (cf. 2:3) and mutual instruction, but not only in an intellectual sense; "psalms, hymns and spiritual songs" are also to flavor their conversation (3:16). They are to do everything "in the name of the Lord Jesus, giving thanks . . . through him" (3:17).

3:18–4:6 Household rules

Having put "human precepts" in their place (2:22), the writer now provides several precepts as a guide for Christian households. The difference is that these are not offered as essential in themselves; they also, as history has shown, are "shadows" rather than "reality" itself (2:17). This is particularly clear with respect to the instructions to slaves and slave owners. All of these commands presuppose a patriarchal society in which "the master" had legal rights of control and possession with respect to his wife, children, and slaves.

Such "household codes" were quite well known in the ancient world generally and had a considerable impact on the later writings of the New Testament (Eph 5:21–6:9; 1 Pet 2:18–3:7). Particular effort was made to enforce the submission of wives to husbands (Titus 2:5; 1 Cor 14:34-35) and to stop women from being leaders of house-churches (1 Tim 2:11-15). That women were such leaders is beyond question (e.g., Rom 16:1-15: note Phoebe, Prisca, and Junia; Phil 4:2-3).

The first command here is specifically to "wives" (3:18), not women in general. Single women and widows, particularly if they were wealthy (e.g., Lydia, Acts 16:14), could operate reasonably independently and themselves be heads of households (e.g., Nympha, 4:15). Nowadays husbands and wives properly are "subject to one another" (Eph 5:21, cf. 1 Cor 7:2-5), should "love" and "not be bitter" toward one another, and mothers as well as "fathers" should not "provoke" or "embitter" their children. The command to "obey parents" (3:20) derives from Exodus 20:12 (cf. Mark 10:19).

Most problematic is the command to "slaves" to "obey your human masters in everything" (3:22). Slave owners made full use of such texts to insist that slavery was a divinely ordained institution. Needless to say, this is a "human command" that has thankfully been destroyed (cf. 2:22). The instructions for slaves are lengthier, probably because there were slaves among the letter's recipients—Onesimus, one of those who delivered the letter (4:9), was a slave (Phlm 10-16). Further, Christian faith was already beginning to expose slavery as morally questionable (3:11!) and provided some opportunity for slaves to attain freedom (1 Cor 7:21); 1 Timothy 6:1-2 shows that bitterness could arise between slaves and their Christian masters. The church, however, had no power (yet!) to alter the economic structure of the Roman Empire; it had to conform in order to be accepted (4:5; cf. 1 Tim 6:1; Titus 2:5). The command to "masters" to treat their slaves "justly and fairly" (4:1) was intended to eliminate cruelty, at least among Christian "masters" (cf. 1 Pet 2:18-20).

The remaining exhortations turn first to the theme of constant, thank-filled prayer (4:2; cf. 1 Thess 5:17-18) and include the request that the Colossians should "pray also for us." Once again (as in 1:24-29) Paul and his co-workers are closely associated in the task of proclaiming "the mystery of Christ," for which Paul suffered imprisonment (4:3) and for which he had primary responsibility (4:4; cf. Eph 3:1-7). The command "Conduct yourselves wisely toward outsiders" shows that the church was already becoming a sufficiently public entity that its reputation was important. "Making the most of the opportunity" (or "time") has in mind that time is short before the end (1 Cor 7:29-31). The relationship with outsiders is especially in mind in the final words of instruction; "gracious speech, seasoned with salt" means conversation with others that is wise, good-humored, and interesting. Believers are not to be insipid and boring and certainly not closed off from the world. They must be able rather "to respond to each one," particularly with respect to faith (1 Pet 3:15).

4:7-18 Commendation of co-workers and final greetings

This section seems to require accepting the letter to the Colossians as Paul's own composition, since it is so detailed and personal. Most of the names here also appear in Philemon 23-24. But if such details were enough to make a text original to Paul, then 2 Timothy and Titus would also be his compositions, but very few scholars think that they are. These greetings and commendations make sense when we remember that Paul's mission had always been a team effort. The persons named were part of that team, at least for a short time. If the team—what scholars call "the Pauline school"—and individuals within it were to continue Paul's ministry, they had to assume the authority he exercised and continue the mission in his name. This section says what the writer believes Paul would have said if he could personally greet the Colossians and commend his co-workers to them. The more personal notes regarding Mark (4:10) and Archippus (4:17) deal with real people in real circumstances but do not require Paul himself as author.

Tychicus seems to have joined the team late (Acts 20:4; 2 Tim 4:12; Titus 3:12). He not only brought news of Paul but was also "to encourage [the Colossians'] hearts" (4:8), corresponding exactly to a description of Paul's ministry (2:2). Tychicus carried the letter and would also read it to the gathered community. Onesimus (Phlm 10) was to accompany him; he was from Colossae or thereabouts (4:9). If Colossians was written while Paul was alive, as some think, then it was delivered when Onesimus returned to Philemon.

Aristarchus was from Thessalonica, had traveled with Paul, and had been in prison with him (Acts 19:29; 20:4). "Mark, cousin of Barnabas," accompanied Paul and his cousin during early missions (Acts 12:12; 13:5, 13) and was the cause of a disagreement between Paul and Barnabas (Acts 15:37-39). Barnabas (Acts 4:36-37) was the one who brought Paul into the circle of the apostles (Acts 9:26-27) and was Paul's major companion in the early days (11:29-30; 13:1–15:38), but they had a serious disagreement when Barnabas sided with Peter in Antioch (Gal 2:11-14), and they went their separate ways. This verse (4:10) suggests reconciliation with Mark. "Jesus [a common Jewish name in those days], known as Justus," along with Mark, was "of the circumcision" (i.e., were Jews); they—Mark and Justus—were the "only" Jews who worked with Paul "for the kingdom of God." They were "a comfort" (4:11) in that Paul suffered great distress at the resistance to the gospel among Jews generally (see Rom 9:1-4; 10:1). Other "Jews" had worked with Paul (e.g., Prisca and Aquila, Acts 18:2; Rom 16:3-5); the writer must mean that these were the Jews presently in "the Pauline school." Mention of them supports the letter's point that the Colossians need add no Jewish observances to their life in Christ.

Epaphras was a key figure for the Colossians (1:7). Like Onesimus, he was from Colossae. The description of him as "a slave of Christ" (cf. Rom 1:1; Phil 1:1), "striving for you in his prayers" (4:12) and bearing "much labor" (the word also denotes "distress") amounts to a very strong commendation (4:13). "Luke, the beloved physician" (2 Tim 4:11; Phlm 24) and "Demas" round off the group sending greetings. There is a later tradition that "Demas deserted" Paul (2 Tim 4:10). Finally, greetings are also sent to "the believers in Laodicea" and to "Nympha and the church in her house" (4:15). Later copiers of the letter changed the text to read "Nymphas and the church in *his* house," since they could not accept that a woman was apparently named as the leader of a church. She probably functioned in a manner similar to Phoebe (Rom 16:1), Stephanas, and others (1 Cor 16:15-18; 1 Thess 5:12-13), that is, as leader of a house-church. "Church" here denotes a small congregation (twenty to forty people?), whereas in 1:18 it means "the church universal."

There is a final command that there must be a sharing of letters. The letter to the Colossians is to be read in Laodicea, the Laodicean letter (presumably from Paul) in Colossae (4:16). The letter to the Laodiceans, of course, is unknown, though there is an apocryphal letter of that name (easily found on the Web). Some think that the letter to the Laodiceans is actually Ephesians or the text on which Ephesians is based. Archippus (4:17) was perhaps Philemon's son (Phlm 2) or, at any rate, was a member of that house-church. In Philemon 2 he is described as Paul's "fellow soldier," but he may have shown some unwillingness to "fulfill the ministry which he received" (4:17).

The greeting in "my [Paul's] own hand" (cf. 1 Cor 16:21; Gal 6:11) assures the readers that the letter is genuinely "from Paul," at least in the sense that it represents well what he would say in these circumstances. The reminder of his imprisonment secures an emotional bond with the recipients. The closing blessing is extremely brief; later copiers added "Amen."

The First Letter to the Thessalonians

Vincent M. Smiles

INTRODUCTION

The importance of I Thessalonians, and its place and date of writing

The First Letter to the Thessalonians is the earliest of all the New Testament writings. It was probably composed in Corinth—perhaps Athens—in A.D. 49 or maybe even earlier (41–44?). Thirteen letters bear Paul's name; of them, scholars agree that Paul wrote at least seven (Romans, 1–2 Corinthians, Galatians, Philippians, 1 Thessalonians, Philemon); the authenticity of each of the others (Ephesians, Colossians, 2 Thessalonians, 1–2 Timothy, Titus) is disputed. Paul was martyred (probably) in Rome in the early sixties; he wrote all his letters, therefore, before any of the Gospels were written (Mark—c. 70—being the first Gospel). This makes Paul the earliest witness of Christianity, and 1 Thessalonians the earliest part of Paul's testimony.

Thessalonica (modern-day Thessaloniki or Salonika) is located at the far northwestern end of the Aegean Sea. In Paul's time it was the principal city of the Roman province of Macedonia. According to the more traditional reconstruction of his apostolic journeys (following the outline of the Acts of the Apostles), Paul ventured into Macedonia and Achaia (Greece) in the late forties, after a long ministry in Syria and Asia Minor that was based in Antioch (c. 34–48). It is possible, however—some think probable—that he began his westward journeys earlier, reaching Greece as early as 41. Whatever the date, he arrived there from Philippi (1 Thess 2:2; Acts 16:11–17:1) and subsequently traveled south to Beroea (Veria), Athens, and Corinth (1 Thess 3:1; Acts 17:10–18:1).

The evidence of Acts

As indicated, Acts also recounts these travels, but there is not always complete consistency between Acts and Paul's own letters. Acts was written about twenty years after Paul's death (about 85) and is primarily a *theological* narrative about the early church. It contains some valuable historical

The First Letter to the Thessalonians

information, but exact history is not its primary purpose. In the case of Paul's mission in Thessalonica, there are some clear contrasts between Acts and 1 Thessalonians: Acts 17 (a) has Paul in Thessalonica only three weeks; (b) envisions mostly Jewish converts; and (c) does not mention Timothy being in Thessalonica. The letter, however, (a) implies a more substantial stay than three sabbath sermons (2:9; see also Phil 4:16); (b) envisions a mostly Gentile community (1:9, "turned from idols"); and (c) makes clear that Timothy was a primary missionary (1:1; 3:2-6). In all cases the letter to the Thessalonians, written by an eyewitness, is to be preferred over Acts, which is an important but secondary source. Acts, therefore, is not a major help either in reconstructing this part of Paul's history or in understanding the letter. While not dismissing Acts, interpreters of Paul must focus *primarily* on the texts of his letters.

The occasion and purpose of I Thessalonians

Fortunately, 1 Thessalonians provides valuable clues to its context, and its purpose is substantially clear. Paul, Silvanus, and Timothy had labored long and hard in Thessalonica (2:9) and had successfully established house-churches there (5:27), which yet were sufficiently united that Paul could refer to them as "the church of the Thessalonians" (1:1). The letter does not say why the "apostles" (2:7) left Thessalonica, but given the letter's focus on "affliction" (1:6; 3:3-7), it probably had to do with local opposition (2:14); in this regard Acts 17:5-9 may well be correct. In other words, the missionaries probably left before they wanted to. Paul, then, was anxious about this fledgling church; would they be able to persevere?

In Athens the apostles decided that Timothy must return "to find out about [their] faith" (3:5). The news he brought back elated Paul, and he set about writing this letter of thanksgiving and encouragement. Timothy also seems to have relayed to Paul some questions and concerns, both from the Thessalonians themselves and, perhaps, from his own observations. Most notably, they seem to have asked about whether believers who had died would be included in the resurrection of the dead (4:13-18). There may also have been questions about marriage (sex?—4:3-7), and some members of the community may have been faltering in their commitment to Christ (5:14). It must be said, however, that detecting real problems behind Paul's advice is extremely difficult; not every exhortation from Paul necessarily corresponds to some issue among the readers.

Does I Thessalonians comprise one letter or two?

Such reconstructions of what was going on in Thessalonica become all the more tenuous when we take into account the views of some experts that 1 Thessalonians actually comprises more than one letter. The theory goes that 1 Thessalonians 2:13–4:2 was originally a separate (earlier) letter, written shortly after Paul had left Thessalonica, and that when Paul's letters were gathered together, this shorter letter was incorporated into the "second letter," comprising 1:1–2:12 and 4:3–5:28. The strongest argument in favor of this theory is the second "thanksgiving," which begins in 2:13. This is unique among the letters certainly written by Paul (cf. 2 Thess 2:13). There is also some tension between 2:6-7, which suggests some lapse of time since Paul's founding visit, and 2:17, which speaks of being absent from Thessalonica "for a short time."

These arguments cannot lightly be dismissed, but they have not convinced most scholars who continue to take the letter *mostly* as it is. "Mostly" signals a problem, and the problem is 2:13-16, particularly 2:14-16. The latter three verses, which feature very harsh language against "the Jews who killed the Lord Jesus," have been debated vigorously for many years. As the commentary will show, there are substantial reasons for thinking that they (along with 2:13?) may have been added to the letter in the late first century.

Again, however, most scholars are not convinced of this. The policy adopted here is to acknowledge the weight of these important questions about the letter's integrity, but nevertheless to interpret the text as it has come to us from ancient tradition. The minority view may yet prove to be correct, but for now the weight of the evidence is that 1 Thessalonians has come to us essentially as Paul wrote it.

The importance of I Thessalonians for the church today

For the life of the church, this is by far the most important question. The letter's history is essential for a basic understanding of what the letter *meant* to its first audience, but it is because of what the letter *means* today that believers still read it. Historical study is essential to a modern reading, but it is not the whole of it. Present meaning, however, is largely determined by present questions and concerns; every generation will hear somewhat differently based on its circumstances. The following are some obvious themes that are important for the church today.

1. *The church as a local community:* In spite of the Second Vatican Council (e.g., the Dogmatic Constitution on the Church), "the church" today still connotes, for a large number of believers, the institutional church and the hierarchy. For Paul and the New Testament as a whole, there was no such connotation. In those days "the church" meant everything

from a house-church (e.g., Rom 16:5; Gal 1:2) to that whole collection of "the churches" that had been established in various cities of the Roman Empire (see 2 Cor 8:24; Col 1:24). Paul's authentic letters are all addressed to the men and women of the community, whether Thessalonica, Corinth, or elsewhere. This was true whether the community was to be praised for its faith (e.g., 1 Thessalonians, Philippians) or corrected for its abuse of the Eucharist (1 Cor 11:17-34) or some other fault. "The church of the Thessalonians" had its leaders (see 5:12-13), but Paul's primary concern was "the church," from which its leadership and ministry arose.

2. *Leadership in the church:* Male, ordained clergy have dominated leadership in the church for so many centuries that modern readers inevitably read the New Testament as though it presupposed the same structure. This, however, is not the case. We know nothing specific about the leaders whom Paul mentions in 1 Thessalonians 5:12-13, but from Paul's other letters we know that women were included among the primary leaders of the churches (see Rom 16:1-7; Phil 4:2-3; Col 4:15). And though Acts (14:23) says that Paul "appointed presbyters in each church," in the authentic letters "presbyters" are never mentioned. Ministry in Paul's churches did not primarily depend on "appointment" (ordination) but on the charisms of the Spirit (1 Cor 12). This means that structures of ministry, even today, are susceptible to change.

3. *The ongoing power of the gospel:* Finally, it should be noted that Paul was vividly aware of the *presence* of God's action in believers' lives and of the ongoing power of the gospel. After so many centuries of history, believers have a tendency to look to the past as the source of inspiration and revelation. This, of course, is correct as far as it goes, but it misses Paul's emphasis that the word of God *"is now* at work" among believers (1 Thess 2:13), that *"now* is the day of salvation" (2 Cor 6:2). The inspiration of the Bible is to be found not only in its writers but also in its readers.

COMMENTARY

1:1 Greeting

Paul associates Silvanus and Timothy (Acts 16:1-3) with himself in the writing of the letter. Silvanus ("Silas" in Acts) was from Jerusalem; Paul met him there at the conference (about A.D. 48) when the status of Gentiles in the church was discussed (Acts 15:1-27). Subsequently, he replaced Barnabas as Paul's traveling companion after Paul and Barnabas had a disagreement (15:36-40). He then traveled with Paul through Asia Minor and assisted in establishing churches in Galatia (16:6), Philippi (16:11-29), Thessalonica (17:1-4), and Corinth (18:5; 2 Cor 1:19). After Corinth he is no longer mentioned in association with Paul, but 1 Peter 5:12 associates him with Peter and the writing of that letter.

Timothy was extremely important to Paul (see Phil 2:19-23). It was Timothy whom Paul sent back to Thessalonica to find out how the church was doing (1 Thess 3:2, 5); that "sending" confirms that Paul was the leader of the team. Timothy joined Paul's mission shortly after Silas (Acts 16:1-3) and then remained throughout Paul's apostolate (Rom 16:21; Acts 20:4), probably until the imprisonment that ended with Paul's death in Rome. Though the letter speaks throughout in terms of "we" (except 3:5; 5:27), there is no reason to doubt that Paul is the primary and perhaps the sole author of the letter. Nevertheless, the collaborative nature of his leadership is important to note, and it may, in part, help to explain why his companions and successors felt free, after his death, to write letters in his name (e.g., Ephesians, Colossians, 2 Thessalonians).

The addressee is "the church of the Thessalonians." We should envisage a house-church or several of them (5:27), a fairly small community by modern standards. "Church" in the New Testament always designates a community of people, whether a house-church (e.g., Rom 16:3-5; Acts 2:46), the believers of a city (1 Cor 1:2), or the church as a worldwide community (Eph 1:22-23); it never designates an abstract institution, nor is it ever identified simply with its leadership. The church exists "*in* God the Father and the Lord Jesus Christ." The greeting is brief (cf. Rom 1:7; 1 Cor 1:3), with "grace" *(charis)* being an especially important term for Paul—a near one-word summary of his gospel (Rom 5:15-21; 11:6; 1 Cor 15:10; Gal 1:6; 5:4). Paul inserts *charis* ("grace") where standard Greek letters had *chairein* ("greetings"), and he adds "peace" (Hebrew *shalom*), perhaps reflecting a greeting found in Jewish letters.

1:2-10 Thankful remembrance of preaching in Thessalonica

This is similar to the "thanksgiving" sections of Paul's other letters (e.g., Rom 1:8-15; 1 Cor 1:4-9; Phil 1:3-11), but here he is particularly enthusiastic and joyful, because in spite of persecution (1:6; 2:14; 3:6-8), they have persevered in the "work of faith, the labor of love, and the endurance of hope" (1:3). This triad (faith, love, hope) is recalled later (5:8: "the breastplate of faith and love, helmet of hope"). In fact, a major reason for the letter is Paul's desire to encourage them in faith and love, but most especially in hope, in the face of persecution and the death of loved ones (4:13-18). Paul recalls here their positive reception of "the gospel" (1:5) and reminds them of their "election" and that they are "loved by God" (1:4).

Election, more commonly referred to as God's "call," is a key idea in Paul's letters (see Rom 9:7-26; 11:26; 1 Cor 7:18-24), this one in particular (2:12; 4:7; 5:24). It is the starting point for much of Paul's theology, pointing as it does to God's initiative of love and grace. The election takes place apart from human expectation or calculation (see Rom 5:6-8: "while we were sinners"), and indeed, even "apart from the law" (Rom 3:21). The Thessalonians "knew *that*" (rather than *how*) they "were chosen" in "the gospel" that Paul and his companions preached (1:5).

"Gospel" in the New Testament never refers to a book, nor does it refer to any particular doctrines. It refers simply to the *act* of proclamation, which was not "in word alone" but was a matter of "power" and "the holy Spirit" and "conviction" (1:5). For Paul, the gospel always has about it immediacy and living power; it happens "today" (2 Cor 6:2: "*now* is the day of salvation") and has powerful effects. In other words, *God enables* faith (Phil 1:29) and the "knowing of election" (1:4); behind true preaching there is always the loving action of God.

The effect among the Thessalonians was that they "became imitators of [the apostles] and of the Lord" both in "affliction" and in "joy" (1:6). More than that, they became "a model" for believers throughout the region. Their gracious "reception" of the apostles became legendary, so that others reported how the Thessalonians "turned from idols to serve the living and true God" (1:8-9). The abandonment of traditional religions was one of the most difficult and amazing acts of ancient believers. In the context of modern freedoms, it is difficult to appreciate that such "turning" required great courage, since it inevitably caused social disruptions, even in families (1 Cor 7:12-15; Luke 12:51-53: "father against son, son against father") and was the source of persecution both from locals (2:14; Acts 17:5-9) and, ultimately, from the Romans.

Verse 10 explains their motivation. It is an important verse, since it is the earliest summary of what believers preached and believed. "Awaiting [God's] Son from heaven" points to the very apocalyptic atmosphere of early Christian experience. Paul and others expected to be "alive" at "the coming of the Lord" (4:15), which is also described as "the coming wrath" (1:10). But for believers this will not mean "condemnation" (Rom 8:1), but rather "rescue" at the hands of God's resurrected "Son." How and when

Jesus will come again is an important issue in 1 Thessalonians (2:19; 3:13; 4:13–5:11; 5:23), but later it recedes in importance (e.g., in Ephesians).

Such expectation, however—a vibrant awareness of the nearness of God—holds rich vitality for spiritual life and should not simply be dismissed as outdated. Investments in this world (marriage, business) have their own goodness, but their value is better seen in the light of the world to come, "for the framework of this world [and all our investments] is passing away" (1 Cor 7:31).

2:1-12 Paul's defense of the apostles' preaching in Thessalonica

As already in 1:4 Paul addresses the community as "brothers," but this does not mean he intends the letter only for men; the term *adelphoi* is best translated "believers." Paul presupposed the patriarchal culture of his world (e.g., 4:4; 1 Cor 11:2-16: "husband, the head of his wife," 11:3), but he also knew that "in Christ" such patriarchy has no place (Gal 3:26-28: "no longer male and female" in Christ), and, to some extent, working with women in leadership, he did overcome patriarchal biases. It is inaccurate, therefore, to portray Paul as a misogynist; the evidence that women worked with him in his apostolic labors is unmistakable (e.g., Rom 16:1-7, 12-15: Phoebe, Prisca, Junia; Phil 4:2-3: Euodia, Syntyche).

Paul turns to a defense of the apostles' behavior while in Thessalonica. "Defense" suggests there had been accusations, but there is no direct evidence of this. Elsewhere Paul, when attacked, was not shy about directly rebuffing his detractors (2 Cor 10–13; Gal 2:11-14). In Thessalonians, for some reason, Paul fears being thought of as one of those preachers of his time who represented themselves as experts in some religion and traveled around making money from their converts. He acknowledged that apostles had the right to material support (1 Cor 9:3-7), but he also knew of Christian preachers who, in his view, were greedy "peddlers of the word of God" (2 Cor 2:17) and whom he contrasted with himself in his preaching of the gospel "without charge" (2 Cor 11:7; 1 Cor 9:12).

Paul had come to Thessalonica by way of Philippi, where he also had encountered opposition (2:2). In reminding the Thessalonians of his conduct, he says five times what it did *not* involve: deception, people-pleasing, flattery, greed, and being a (financial) burden (2:5-9). It's a veritable catalog of what preachers should avoid. It was rather a matter, "through our God" (2:2), of great "struggle," of "toil and drudgery, working night and day, in order not to burden any of you" (2:9). "As apostles of Christ, we could," he says, "have imposed our weight, but we were gentle [or 'infants'] among you, like a nursing mother cherishing her children" (2:7). It is interesting

1 Thessalonians 2

here to recall Jesus' words: "Among the nations those who are seen as rulers over the Gentiles lord it over them. . . . But it shall not be so among you. Rather, whoever wishes to be great among you will be your servant" (Mark 10:42-43). Paul's actual conduct accords with Jesus' instruction.

In 2:11 Paul changes the image, comparing Silvanus, Timothy, and himself to a "father, exhorting and encouraging each one as his own children." Against any possible detractors, Paul insists that their conduct was devout, just, and blameless (2:10) as they taught the community that their conduct also must be "worthy of the God who [even now] calls [them] into his kingdom" (2:12). It is important to note the *present* tense—the gospel is not a thing of the past.

2:13-16 Four problematic verses

This paragraph, especially verses 14-16, is much disputed in modern scholarship, the dispute being whether this generalizing and harsh condemnation of "the Jews" is authentic or was added later in light of persecution by Jews (e.g., John 16:2) and the destruction of Jerusalem by the Romans in A.D. 70. Paul's letters were indeed collected and edited. Second Corinthians, for instance, may be a conflation of at least two letters to Corinth (2 Cor 1–9 and 10–13), and 1 Corinthians 14:33b-36 may be an editorial addition to that letter. However, here, as also in those cases, the ancient manuscripts are as they are, and scholars, no matter what their convictions, cannot cut and paste the Bible as they choose.

The evidence that 2:(13?)14-16 is a later addition has some weight:

1. It does not fit well into the flow of the letter, much less into the sequence of Paul's ministry. "God's wrath has come upon them" (2:16) does not fit well into this early period; it might fit better after Jerusalem was destroyed in A.D. 70.

2. It contains some (for Paul) unusual ideas (e.g., that Jews were responsible for Jesus' death; cf. 1 Cor 2:8, where "rulers of this world" does *not* designate Jews).

3. It seems harshly anti-Jewish, especially in light of Paul's affection for his heritage (e.g., Rom 9:1-5: "I could wish that I myself were accursed for the sake of my people"; 11:1-2).

On the other hand, the arguments in favor of its authenticity are also persuasive:

1. All ancient manuscripts contain the passage.

2. Its unusual features may derive from the use of traditional language by Paul (cf. Luke 11:47-51).

3. The critique is not *anti*-Jewish so much as *intra*-Jewish, not unlike the harsh words of the prophets (e.g., Jer 7:33-34) or Jesus (Matt 23:29-33).

4. Though he loved his heritage, Paul was quite capable of harsh critique of Jews with whom he disagreed (see Rom 2:17-24). In the presence of such uncertainty, it is foolish to be dogmatic one way or the other, though the case for authenticity does seem slightly stronger.

As the letter stands, 2:13 accords well with the theme of 1:5, namely, that the gospel, though proclaimed by human agency, ultimately derives its power from the "word of God, which is now at work in you who believe." "Word of God" here does not mean words *about* God, but rather the word that *God speaks* now, in every generation, the word that "is active and alive" (Heb 4:12). Paul's angry language in 2:14-16 gives no warrant whatsoever to anti-Semitism and, in some respects, is rather questionable. The primary responsibility for the death of Jesus lay with the Roman authorities, crucifixion being a Roman punishment. And the accusations that Jews "do not please God and are opposed to everyone" (2:15) are more reflective of the anti-Jewish propaganda of ancient authors than of the esteem for Jews that Paul elsewhere demonstrates.

The horror of Christians using Scripture to justify unspeakable cruelty toward innocent people must be forever rejected. If Paul did indeed write these words, he intended to assure the Thessalonians that they were suffering just like "the churches of God in Judea" (2:14), and his anger no doubt derived, in part, from the harsh treatment that he received in some synagogues (2 Cor 11:24: "five times I received thirty-nine lashes from the Jews"). But his very accepting of that punishment witnesses that he remained connected to Judaism. He longed for Jews to accept the gospel (Rom 9:1-3; 10:1), and he lived out his belief that "the gifts and call of God" to Israel "are irrevocable" (Rom 11:29).

2:17–3:13 The difficulty and the joy of recent events

Paul now resumes his expressions of affection and longing for the Thessalonians. Such emotional outpouring may seem strange today. His language, in part, is conventional—he also tells believers in Rome that he "long[s] to see" them (Rom 1:11), though he had never even met them; he calls the Philippians also his "joy and crown" (Phil 4:1), and he tells the

Corinthians (2 Cor 1:14) and Philippians (Phil 2:16) as well as the Thessalonians that they will be his "boast at the coming of the Lord" (2:19).

But convention alone does not explain his language. The range of strong emotions in Paul's letters is considerable—joy, gratitude (Phil 4:10-14); rage (Gal 3:1; 5:12!); outrage (2 Cor 11:13-15); sorrow (2 Cor 2:1-4); and exhilaration (Phil 4:4-7). The list could go on. But for all his churches, even when he was angry at them (Gal 4:19-20), he clearly held a sincere affection (2 Cor 11:11: ". . . because I do not love you? God knows that I do!").

That affection is nowhere more evident than here. Away from Thessalonica, the apostles felt "orphaned" (2:17). Paul himself had tried twice to return to them, "but Satan prevented us" (2:18). Satan is mentioned again in 3:5 as "the tempter" who might do harm to the community's faith. In both cases Paul may have seen "Satan" in the political opposition which he himself had encountered in Thessalonica (see Acts 17:6-7) and which now harassed the believers and prevented Paul's return. This forced separation, whatever its cause, became completely unbearable for Paul, and while in Athens they determined that Timothy must return to find out whether the Thessalonians' faith was holding up under the pressure (3:1, 5). Why Timothy could make the journey and Paul could not is impossible to answer. Timothy's mission was "to strengthen and encourage" and especially to see to it that "no one was disturbed" by the persecutions and other "afflictions" they were enduring (3:2-3). Paul had warned them that suffering is inevitable in the life of faith, and now they have experienced it for themselves (3:4).

"Just now," however—as though he had just walked through the door!—Timothy has brought "the good news of [their] faith and love," and Paul, suffering some distress of his own (whether in Athens or, more likely, Corinth), is "consoled by [their] faith" (3:6-7). Indeed, for him this good news of their "standing in the Lord" is "life" itself (3:8). It may be significant that though Timothy recounted their "faith and love," he could not speak of their "hope" (1:3; 5:8). It has been suggested that "hope" was the one thing that was "lacking in [their] faith" (3:10), and that may well have been. Harassment from other citizens and the death of loved ones (4:13) must have been a heavy burden. Whatever the circumstances, the Thessalonians were enduring well, and Paul now simply breaks into prayer, wondering what "thanksgiving" he can possibly render for the joy he feels on their account (3:9).

What he comes up with are two petitions. Predictably, he prays first that "God and our Lord Jesus" will make it possible for himself, Silvanus, and Timothy to visit Thessalonica soon (3:10-11). His second prayer is addressed

1 Thessalonians 4

to "the Lord" (Jesus) alone, a telling indication of how closely, even in the earliest theological reflection, Jesus was identified with God. He prays that Jesus will "increase [their] love" and "strengthen [their] hearts" to be "blameless" at his "coming with all his holy ones" (3:12).

What Paul means by "holy ones" is not immediately obvious. We naturally think of angels (Matt 16:27), and that may well be correct, but elsewhere Paul never mentions angels or "holy ones" (saints) at the Lord's coming. For Paul, "holy ones" always refers to *believers* (e.g., Rom 1:7; 12:13; 15:25-26); he regularly addresses his letters (this one being the exception) "to the saints" of Rome, Corinth, and so on. But the language Paul uses here is traditional; he quotes from Zechariah 14:5, which speaks of God's coming "and all his holy ones with him." The tradition Paul employs, therefore, certainly envisions angels, as also most probably Paul himself does. It would be nice to think that Paul has in mind the believers of Thessalonica who have died (4:13; note 4:14b), but 4:16 says "they will rise" when the Lord "will descend from heaven." The whole picture is a further reminder of the deeply apocalyptic character of this letter and of early Christian experience in general.

4:1-12 Exhortation to holiness

Just as the thanksgiving in this letter is inordinately extended, so also are the exhortations to good behavior, this being the first such section, 5:12-22 the second. Extended exhortation, however, is not unusual for Paul (Rom 12:1–13:14; Gal 5:13–6:10) and makes sense, given his aim of "strengthening" in this letter.

There are several difficulties for interpreters, most especially in verses 3-6. The biggest problem is the interpretation of verse 4, which very literally reads: ". . . that each of you know how to obtain (control?) his vessel in holiness." All agree that this metaphor ("vessel") has to do with proper sexual conduct, but does Paul mean (a) to obtain a *wife* or (b) generally to control *sexual behavior*? The first option (as in the New American Bible) is not popular these days, but that, of course, is not a reason to reject it. It is also *possible* that Paul is referring to, and forbidding, consanguineous marriages (Lev 18:6-18), which Greek society permitted in order to keep the woman's inheritance in the family. If this is the case, then the injunction "not to exploit a brother in this matter" (4:6) refers to the business contract involved in transferring the woman's property to her husband. In any event, 4:3-7 almost certainly intends to warn the Thessalonians against sexual "impurity"; the latter word, in Paul, regularly refers to sexual misconduct (e.g., Rom 1:24; Gal 5:19).

1 Thessalonians 4

The alternative is that both men and women are being told to "control [their] sexual behavior" and that 4:6 either reinforces this by forbidding any sexual irregularities or, perhaps (but less likely), introduces the different issue of justice in business practices ("do not defraud"). Overall the first option ("obtain a wife"), whether we like it or not, seems more likely. If this is correct, then this is one of those texts where Paul's, and his society's, patriarchal biases show (cf. 1 Cor 11:2-16), and modern believers are not bound to first-century cultural standards. In any event, believers are not called to "uncleanness," a general term for various types of immorality (2:3), but to "holiness" (3:13).

Paul speaks here—and 4:8 strongly confirms this—as one who represents Christ ("in the Lord"), so that to ignore him is tantamount to "ignoring God" (cf. Luke 10:16). Paul was always adamant that his apostolic authority derived from God (Gal 1:6-12); it was not, he acknowledged, from official channels and was not always recognized by others (1 Cor 9:2); it was nevertheless real and effective (1 Cor 15:10). "The will of God" for the Thessalonians is their "holiness" (4:3-4), by which he means that they are to live by "the holy Spirit that God gives [them]" (4:8; again, note the present tense). "Holiness" (4:7) is not primarily something to be attained, as though they did not have it, but is a gift they are to practice. Already, he says, they know his instructions—they are "God-taught"—and he has no need to tell them about love, which they practice "toward all the believers" (4:9-10). He concludes the section by urging them to "live quietly, mind [their] own business, and work with [their] own hands" so as to provide for their needs and be on good terms with outsiders (4:11-12).

4:13-18 The hope of faith in the face of death

This is one of the most fascinating apocalyptic texts in the entire New Testament and, for study purposes, should be compared with similar texts (e.g., Mark 13; Matt 24; Rev 21). We learn here that Paul and his contemporaries expected Jesus' second coming in the very near future, and, indeed, Paul expected to be "alive" for the event (4:15). By the time he wrote Philippians 1:21-24 (six to ten years later), he could anticipate that he might be dead before the end, but a vivid expectation of Jesus' return never left him.

Occasionally, believers are disconcerted at the early church's "mistake" in expecting Jesus to return "soon" (Rev 1:1-3), and critics sometimes make it a basis for discrediting Christian faith. Imminent expectation was not, however, foundational to faith. The delay of the end did, understandably, disturb some early believers (2 Pet 3:3-10), but then as now faith's primary focus was on being "God's children" and on living out that reality in the here and now.

The pressing circumstance in Thessalonica, about which the Thessalonians had probably questioned Timothy, was the death of some of their loved ones; would they also "be with the Lord" at his coming (4:14, 17)? Paul is interestingly inconsistent in his answer: 4:14b ("God *will bring* [them] *with* Jesus") does not quite jibe with 4:16 ("the dead in Christ *will arise*" at *his descent* "from heaven"). This slight confusion reminds us not to be too caught up in the details of what will happen at the end; there are many differing descriptions in the New Testament.

The point Paul makes is that believers' grief should be tempered by the hope of the resurrection and the awareness that God is very near. The basis of this hope is the power of Jesus' death and resurrection (see 1 Cor 15:12-19). That power reaches beyond death, so that those "who are left alive at the Lord's coming" will have no advantage over "the dead in Christ" (4:15). God will "take up" the living and "raise up" the dead, and "thus we shall always be with the Lord" (4:16-17).

Modern readers of 4:17 ("we will be caught up with them in the clouds") need to beware of fundamentalist interpretations which insist that this text foretells a very literal "rapture" (snatching up) of Christians into heaven at the end of the world. Those who interpret the text this way often also insist that "these are the last days," as though they had some knowledge denied to everyone else. Mark 13:32 insists to the contrary that "no one—not the angels, not even the Son—knows that day or hour." Paul, like Jesus (Matt 24:40-41), used the imagery of apocalyptic literature in accordance with the culture of his time; but believers are bound by faith, not by particular cultural ideas, whether of marriage (4:4; Col 3:18, "wives, be subordinate"), slavery (Col 3:22, "slaves, obey your masters"), or apocalypticism. Bumper stickers that claim, "When the Rapture comes, you take the wheel!" are cute at best; at worst, they are a serious misreading of Scripture, not to say arrogant. Paul's major point, speaking to believers grieving at the death of loved ones, is that God is very close to the living and the dead, both now and in eternity.

5:1-11 Further instructions about the coming end

The apocalyptic atmosphere continues unabated in this next section, with Paul suggesting (as in 4:1-2, 9) that the Thessalonians know everything he might tell them about "times and seasons." Evidently this was already discussed at some length when he, Silvanus, and Timothy were with them. The imagery Paul uses ("thief in the night," "birth pangs") is also found in other apocalyptic texts, both Christian (Matt 25:43; Mark 13:8) and Jewish (1 Enoch 62:4), and "the day of the Lord" recalls prophetic texts of God's coming judgment (Joel 2:1; Amos 5:18-20). Paul's point here is that believers have nothing to fear; they are "children of light and the day" and so live by a different code than "the rest" of the world that are "in darkness" (5:4-6).

We encounter here the dualism of apocalyptic thinking, namely, the idea that "we, who are being saved" stand over against "them, who are perishing" (1 Cor 1:18; 2 Thess 2:10). The division of time into "this age" and "the age to come," and of humanity into the "saved" and the "lost," was a regular feature of apocalypticism long before the time of Jesus (e.g., Dan 12:1-3). To this day, such language convinces some Christians that outside of Christian faith there is no salvation, but the question of whether unbelievers can be saved is answered both in Scripture (Matt 25:31-46) and in church teaching (Dogmatic Constitution on the Church, art. 16) with a clear yes. Paul, to be sure, thought that unbelievers were headed for "the coming wrath" (1:10), but in this, as in other things, believers must exercise discernment, relying not only on Scripture but also on God-given intelligence, on the guidance of the Spirit, church tradition, and, as Vatican II reminds us, "the secular sciences" (The Church in the Modern World, art. 62).

The strength of Scripture is in the great principles it enunciates of love and justice and its revelation that all people are created "in God's image" and are God's children. A strict application of the Bible's laws and its pronouncements of judgment has never served the church well. Paul's knowledge of the world and history was far more restricted than ours, as also therefore was his context. It is essential that we keep these things in view as we evaluate Paul's text.

For their part, believers are to avoid idle carousing; they are to be clothed with faith, love, and hope as they await the fullness of salvation (5:8-9). Paul recalls again Jesus' "dying for us," which is the basis of Christian hope (5:10; see 4:14). Paul, in fact, recalls the power of that death over and over in his letters (e.g., Rom 3:25; 4:25; 14:9; 1 Cor 1:18-25; Gal 2:19-21). It binds us to God, so that "whether we live or die," there is no separation (5:10).

5:12-22 Final instructions and exhortations

The exhortations here are universal in scope, applicable to any church in any age. And yet they witness to essential, fundamental truths of faith about both church order and Christian morality. In 5:12-13 we have the earliest text ever on church leadership. Paul addresses the entire community, asking them to "acknowledge those who labor among you." These were the women and men who functioned as primary leaders by virtue of their spiritual gifts and faith-commitment. The presumption of some that women were not church leaders has to do with our patriarchal history and bias, not with historical accuracy. The Pontifical Biblical Commission acknowledged already in 1976 that "some women collaborated in *the properly apostolic work*" and named Prisca (Rom 16:5), Euodia and Syntyche (Phil 4:2-3), Phoebe and Junia (Rom 16:1-2, 7) as examples. Paul urges the church to hold such people in high esteem and to show them love. And that is all; leaders are essential, but the task of ministry belongs fundamentally to the church as the body of Christ (1 Cor 12:7, "to each is given the manifestation of the Spirit for the common good").

Having described the leaders as "those who admonish (instruct) you," Paul goes on to tell the whole community to "admonish the disorderly" (not "the idle," though note 2 Thess 3:6-12). He may have a specific problem in mind here, but what that was we cannot know. The same is true regarding the commands to "encourage the fainthearted [and] support the weak" (5:14). Perhaps these are believers who are timid in the face of persecution. Whatever the case, it is the task of the church to support them. It is also everyone's responsibility to "ensure that no one repays evil for evil"; they are rather to seek the good of all, including outsiders (5:15; cf. 4:12).

The series of rapid-fire commands that follows in 5:16-22 reads like poetry; only the added sentence in 5:18 ("this is God's will for you in Christ Jesus") disturbs the rhythm and rhyme of the Greek text. Theology and spirituality can be much enriched by meditation on these exhortations. In spite of all the hardships that so preoccupy this letter, Paul insists that believers "rejoice always, pray unceasingly, in every circumstance give thanks." The charismatic character of early Christianity is apparent in the command not to "extinguish the Spirit," the Spirit being envisaged as a flaming fire (cf. Acts 2:3, "tongues as of fire"). A primary gift of the Spirit was prophecy, which, though much valued by Paul (1 Cor 14:1-5, 29-33), was subject to abuse and therefore required discernment (5:21). Paul's concern for the church's public image is again apparent in the final command, "Avoid every appearance of evil" (5:22).

5:23-28 Final greeting and blessing

Finally, Paul once again breaks into prayer (cf. 4:11-13) and, once again, the "holiness" and "blamelessness" of the Thessalonians are what he requests (5:23). Their sanctification to the point of being "perfect" is not something they can accomplish of themselves, and thus Paul asks God to accomplish this in them. "Holiness" is not primarily a human endeavor (cf.

4:3). The prayer looks forward to "the coming of our Lord Jesus Christ," when their divinely gifted integrity of "body, mind and spirit" will be apparent. The "God who calls [them] is faithful and will accomplish this" (5:24).

Paul asks for their prayers and, as elsewhere, he instructs them to greet one another "with a holy kiss" (5:26; Rom 16:16; 1 Cor 16:20; cf. 1 Pet 5:14). He then solemnly puts them on oath to "make sure the letter is read to all the believers" (5:27), meaning probably that there were several house-churches within the church of Thessalonica, as was also true in other places (Gal 1:2; Col 4:15). His final blessing is the same as at the end of all his letters. Its fullest form, which we still use today at the beginning of our liturgies, is found in 2 Corinthians 13:13, and as was the case at the beginning, he wishes them "the grace of our Lord Jesus Christ." So ends the very earliest piece of Christian literature—a powerful witness of what the church was and is always to be, a *community* of "faith, love and hope" (1:3; 5:8).

The Second Letter to the Thessalonians

Vincent M. Smiles

INTRODUCTION

The challenges of 2 Thessalonians

For being such a short letter, 2 Thessalonians presents a surprising number of challenges for modern interpreters. A primary issue is whether or not the letter was written by Paul himself, with most scholars these days believing that it was not. A second major issue is the letter's situation: when was it written, who were its intended recipients, what were their problems, and where were they located? Those problems are difficult enough and also have to be answered for a few other New Testament books, but they pale in comparison with the difficulty of understanding what the author says in the central part of the letter. What is meant by "the restrainer" in 2:6-7? Is this a good or an evil power? In fact, is "restrainer" even the correct translation of the Greek term? And who is "the rebel" (or "the lawless one") in 2:3-9, whose coming "springs from the power of Satan"? These problems of 2:3-9 will be dealt with in the commentary itself; the other problems need to be clarified, as far as possible, immediately.

Who wrote 2 Thessalonians?

There are several New Testament letters which the ancient church accepted as written by Paul but which modern scholarship, for good reasons, believes he did not write. Almost all scholars have long regarded the Pastoral Epistles (1 and 2 Timothy and Titus) as not written by Paul; Ephesians, Colossians, and 2 Thessalonians comprise a middle group, whose authenticity has been doubted. Complete certainty is impossible, but in recent years *most*, though not all, scholars have come to accept that 2 Thessalonians was not written by Paul.

Although, superficially, the letter appears to be authentic, closer examination shows that it uses Paul's style and vocabulary in a strange way. It imitates and even, at points, copies from the earlier letter, using it as a model. For example, 2 Thessalonians 1:1 repeats the opening of 1 Thessalonians almost word for word, a practice otherwise unknown among Paul's letters. Even 2 Corinthians 1:1-2, initially almost identical to 1 Corinthians 1:1-3, ultimately differs substantially. The second letter (2 Thess 2:13) has a second thanksgiving, imitating a unique feature of 1 Thessalonians, and the prayers in 2:16 and 3:16 appear to be modeled on prayers in the earlier letter (1 Thess 3:11; 5:23). Furthermore, 2 Thessalonians 3:8 largely repeats 1 Thessalonians 2:9. Such similarities might ordinarily be expected to indicate the same author, but actually copying and imitating his own writing is not a feature of Paul's certainly authentic letters.

In addition to such unexpected imitation, there are also some unexpected stylistic differences. In 2 Thessalonians there is a strange predominance of long, complex sentences (e.g., 2 Thess 1:3-10—one sentence in Greek!) and of long noun-phrases (e.g., 2:8-10). To be sure, such features also appear in the certainly authentic letters, but not to this extent. In a detailed examination of such stylistic peculiarities, one author has shown that 2 Thessalonians resembles Colossians and Ephesians, whose authenticity is also doubted.

In addition to these stylistic observations, the theology of 2 Thessalonians does not appear authentic; most notably, its central section (2:1-12) clashes strangely with Paul's eschatological teaching in 1 Thessalonians 4–5. The latter presupposes that the end is very close (e.g., 4:15, "we who are *alive,* who *remain* at the coming of the Lord") but envisages no way to calculate the time of the end (5:1-3). This is consistent with Paul's views elsewhere (e.g., Rom 13:11-12; 1 Cor 7:29) and with Mark 13:32 ("About that day or hour no one knows, not the angels in heaven nor even the Son"). However, 2 Thessalonians 2:1-6 presupposes that such calculation is possible and even claims that Paul had instructed the readers about it (2:5).

Furthermore, for being such a short letter, 2 Thessalonians has an unusual number of appeals to the letters and tradition of Paul and his companions (2:2, 15; 3:6, 14, 17) and an unusual number of reminders of when Paul was with them (2:5; 3:10, cf. 2:14). The impression is that the writer of 2 Thessalonians had to go to unusual lengths to "authenticate" this letter as being from "Paul." This is consistent with the situation at the end of the first century, twenty to thirty years after Paul's death, when the apostle had become a revered figure and it was important to appeal to his authority to settle difficult questions.

In this regard, one author has noted that Paul himself, when giving information about "the end," did so not only on his own authority but also by appeal to "a mystery" or "a word of the Lord" (note 1 Cor 15:51; 1 Thess

4:15), which is in line with apocalyptic writing in general (e.g., Dan 7:15-16; Rev 1:2; 22:16). In 2 Thessalonians 2:3-12, however, the only source is "Paul" himself. For this writer, Paul has become the higher authority, and thus a letter in his name will suffice to settle the present crisis about an apocalyptic question.

Further, though pretending to derive from Paul, 2 Thessalonians is unusually lacking in expressions of love. In the authentic letters Paul is effusively affectionate (e.g., Phil 1:8; 2:12; 4:1), and, in fact, nowhere is this more evident than in 1 Thessalonians (e.g., 1 Thess 2:7-8, 17). Even when angry, Paul expresses affection (1 Cor 4:14-15; 10:14; 2 Cor 11:11; Gal 4:19-20). That Paul would write to the Thessalonians at a time when they were suffering greatly and would not express personal affection is unthinkable.

In modern culture, to write a text and place someone else's name on it comes across as fraudulent, but in the ancient Greco-Roman world it was not so unusual, and, in fact, the character of Paul's ministry makes such letters unsurprising. First, like many others, Paul *dictated* his letters to secretaries, people like Tertius (Rom 16:22, "I, Tertius, who wrote this letter greet you in the Lord"). Such secretaries could sometimes have an influence on the way things were expressed.

Second, and more important, Paul included others, named and unnamed (1 Thess 1:1, "Timothy, Silvanus"; Gal 1:2, "all the believers with me"), among the senders of his letters, though he himself seems to have been the only real author in most cases. This reflects the collaborative nature of Paul's missionary endeavors. Therefore, just as it was natural for Paul to write in their names, so it was natural, when Paul was not around, for them to write in his name, even after his death.

And third, both Jewish and Greco-Roman societies knew of many examples of texts being written in the name of famous dead people (e.g., Psalms of Solomon, Letters of Plato). As in many of those cases, so in the case of Paul's co-workers and successors, the purpose was not fraud for profit, but simply to appeal to the apostle's authority to help those who stood in the tradition of his teaching.

It is, of course, impossible to prove in any definitive way whether or not Paul wrote this letter. People of good faith can reasonably disagree on this matter, as is also the case with other disputed books. Modern believers properly focus, not on such historical questions, but on the theology and spirituality of the texts. However, in our attempts to understand Paul, it is perhaps important to realize that not everything that goes under his name necessarily conveys an accurate portrait of him and his theology.

The Second Letter to the Thessalonians

The situation of the letter

Who, then, did write 2 Thessalonians and, more important, when and under what circumstances? Evidently the letter intends to guide believers "about the coming of our Lord Jesus" (2:1) in the context of persecution (1:4) and particularly to warn them against those who claim that "the day of the Lord is [already] here" (2:2). After the destruction of Jerusalem by the Romans (A.D. 70), confusion and speculation about the time of the end were rife (e.g., Mark 13:5-7; 2 Pet 3:3-10). The book of Revelation suggests (e.g., 13:7) that in the nineties (under the emperor Domitian) persecution of believers in Asia Minor was a major problem. Many scholars think that this may be the context also of 2 Thessalonians. If so, then the letter was written to a real situation, but not to a specific community. It is meant to remind believers in various churches (see Rev 2–3) of established apostolic tradition (2:15) so that they are not "shaken out of [their] minds" by the claims of more recent teachers (2:2).

This need to appeal to authoritative tradition explains why the author used 1 Thessalonians as a model and insisted that what he wrote truly came from the apostle's hand (2 Thess 3:17). Such appeals to older authority are found elsewhere in Scripture (e.g., Daniel, Pastoral Epistles).

Interpreting 2 Thessalonians in the church today

The debate about authorship and the uncertainties of it remind us to be humble in the face of questions we cannot definitively settle and to maintain a careful balance in interpreting Scripture. Reason, as well as faith, is a gift of God, and reason, along with tradition and doctrine, is to guide interpretation of the Bible. Regardless of authorship, 2 Thessalonians is sacred Scripture that can still speak to the heart of the church.

"Literal" interpretations, which imagine that biblical texts were written with the early twenty-first century in mind, only introduce the sorts of confusions that 2 Thessalonians warns against. A true "literal" interpretation never forgets the letter's first-century context and what the author wanted to accomplish in that time among those believers. It also does not forget the limited perspective and knowledge of the ancient writer, who, like Paul himself, expected the end to come very soon. It is not a disparagement of the ancient texts when we admit that such expectations were mistaken. The texts have remained valuable in every generation for their spiritual wisdom and their witness to the faith-experience of first-century believers; their value does not reside either in exact recall of historical events or in precise delineations of God's future plans. The Scriptures, though inspired, have their limitations, just as we, in the midst of our limitations, are not without divine inspiration.

The church today is not, for the most part, persecuted, as was the church to which this letter was addressed. But the church today has its own sufferings and perplexities and can gain much from contemplating the courage and perseverance of ancient believers. We cannot identify with everything this letter has to say, but if we look carefully beneath the surface, we can discover that the same divine Spirit that urged and consoled believers then is still with us in the modern world.

COMMENTARY

1:1-2 Prescript and greeting

The prescript (1:1), which, in accordance with ancient style, includes the sender's and recipient's names, is an exact copy of 1 Thessalonians 1:1, adding only the word "our." If Paul is not the real author, it is *possible* that either Silvanus or Timothy might be. The greeting (1:2) is identical to the longer greeting of Paul's authentic letters and, in that regard, differs slightly from 1 Thessalonians. This may indicate that the author knew the other letters; the model for this one, however, is certainly 1 Thessalonians. "Grace and peace" (2:16; 3:16) were primary theological terms, being respectively the foundation and the fruit of the gospel (e.g., Rom 5:1-2).

1:3-12 The (first) thanksgiving

Proportional to the length of the letter, this is an amazingly long thanksgiving (cf. Rom 1:8-15), and, even more remarkable, 1:3-10 comprises in Greek one long, very complex sentence. This is one of the reasons for thinking that Paul did not write it. Nevertheless, it contains a number of challenging ideas, which in part reflect 1 Thessalonians and in part are somewhat unique. "We *ought* to give thanks" (also 2:13) is awkward phrasing, never used by Paul himself, but the reasons for thanks are very much in Paul's tradition, in that fidelity to the gospel (Phil 1:5) and the fruitfulness of God's gifts among believers (1 Cor 1:4) were always important for the apostle. In this case the writer especially commends believers for their growth in faith and love, even in the midst of "persecutions and afflictions." The themes of faith and love (1:3), of the Thessalonians as model believers (1:4), and of looking forward to Christ's coming judgment (1:7, 9) are all reminiscent of the initial thanksgiving in 1 Thessalonians and were important ideas for Paul himself.

Not typical of Paul is the lengthy dwelling here on the theme of divine retribution for "those who are afflicting you" (1:6). Presumably the latter are identical with those who "do not acknowledge God and do not obey the gospel" (1:8), though it is possible the writer has different groups in mind. The idea of severe retribution appears again in 2:10-12, making this letter far harsher and more vengeful in its tone than any other letter under Paul's name. Such passages are usually, and understandably, not popular, and care is indeed needed in their interpretation.

Harsh, condemnatory warnings, however, are found throughout Scripture, including sayings from Jesus (e.g., Luke 13:1-9); they are not confined, as is sometimes imagined, to the Old Testament. They express God's rejection of evil and bias for justice, but also the human authors' anger, especially in the face of persecution. They are, it must be emphasized, more than outweighed by expressions of God's love and mercy (e.g., Exod 34:6-7; Luke 15:11-32) and by the demand that believers must love their enemies (e.g., Lev 19:33-34; Matt 5:31-38). The harshness of this letter undoubtedly reflects the bitter experience of religious persecution.

The consolation for believers is that God's judgment is just (1:5), as is shown in their being "considered worthy of the kingdom of God" for which they suffer (cf. 1:11, praying "that our God make you worthy of the call"). Behind this is the idea, important for Paul himself, that salvation derives "not from human desiring or striving, but from God who has mercy" (Rom 9:16; cf. Eph 2:8-9). "The revelation of the Lord Jesus from heaven with his mighty angels" (1:7) recalls 1 Thessalonians 3:13 and various other apocalyptic texts (e.g., Matt 24:31). Also typical of apocalypticism is the expectation of "blazing fire" at the end (e.g., 1 Cor 3:13-15; Isa 66:15-16), delivering punishment for the "disobedient," who will be "separated from the presence of the Lord." On the other hand, "on that day" of judgment the Lord will "be glorified among his holy ones" and "be marveled at by all who have believed" (1:10).

The writer personalizes this general description by saying that the reason for the "glorifying" and "marveling" was that "our testimony to *you* was believed" (1:10); believers will be a cause for celebration on judgment day. "Holy ones" here, as in 1 Thessalonians 3:13, probably refers to "his mighty angels" who will accompany him (1:7), so that the writer envisages the earthly believers joining the heavenly host in triumphant praise of the Lord (see Phil 2:10-11; Rev 7:9-17).

The thanksgiving concludes with a prayer that is somewhat reminiscent of 1 Thessalonians 1:2-3. The prayer asks that God "might make believers worthy" and "complete" their "every good purpose and work of faith." The latter phrase is also found in 1 Thessalonians 1:3 but otherwise is slightly unusual for Paul (cf. Rom 3:27-28; 9:32).

2:1-12 The central problem:
Is this the end of the world?

After that long thanksgiving, finally the heart of the matter: "the coming *(parousia)* of our Lord Jesus Christ and our being gathered to him" (not "with him"). The readers have been radically "shaken out of [their] minds" by the claim that "the day of the Lord is here" (not merely "at hand"). The writer does not know whether it is some spirit-filled utterance that has disturbed them or a "word" of prophecy or even a "letter" claiming to be from Paul. Whatever it is, it is deceitful. This imprecision, with the writer covering all bases, suggests that the letter is not written to a specific, known situation but is intended to respond to some end-of-the-century situation(s) in which persecutions had convinced believers that history was all but over.

Verse 2 provides glimpses into early church worship that enable us to see how ecstatic speech and prophecies, while deeply valued, also had to be regulated and subjected to discernment (cf. 1 Cor 14:29-32). First Thessalonians 5:19-21 also advises, "Do not extinguish the spirit, do not despise prophecies, but *test everything*"! The human condition is such that "spirit" and prophecy are inevitably ambiguous; not everything that claims to be from God necessarily is so. The readers are envisioned as profoundly shaken by some communication, possibly even "a letter pretending to be from Paul," that has them convinced that the end of the world is already here! In 3:11 it appears that some have even ceased working because of this conviction.

The writer urges the Thessalonians not to be deceived "in any way" and then begins an explanation (vv. 3-8) of why they should realize that "the day of the Lord" has not yet come (cf. Mark 13:5-7, "Beware, lest anyone deceive you . . . the end is not yet!"). This explanation is very difficult to interpret. It begins with, "For unless the apostasy comes first, and the rebel (lit. 'the lawless one') is revealed," but then the sentence becomes simply an extended description of "the rebel" and remains unfinished. It should probably be understood as meaning, "For *the end is not here,* unless the apostasy . . ." "Apostasy" refers to the defection of believers. Since some inevitably faltered in the face of persecution, it was commonly accepted that the great "temptation" (testing) at the end would produce considerable apostasy (1 Tim 4:1, cf. Mark 13:13, 20); thus the prayer "Lead us not into [the] temptation [of the last days]" (Matt 6:13).

The long description of "the rebel, the one doomed to destruction" is reminiscent of various Old Testament texts, most notably Daniel 11:36-37 ("He shall exalt himself, making himself greater than any god"), describing the arrogant King Antiochus, who in 167 B.C. had desecrated the temple sanctuary and viciously persecuted the Jewish people (1 Macc 1:41-63). The whole passage (2 Thess 2:3-9) is full of elements commonly found in apocalyptic texts about the signs of the end of the world: the rebel "seat[ing] himself in the sanctuary" is reminiscent of "the abominating desolation" in Daniel 9:27 (a further reference to King Antiochus) and Mark 13:14, and the theme of deception and apostasy recalls Mark 13:22 (see 1 Tim 4:1 and 2 Tim 4:4). In other words, the writer knows the apocalyptic traditions well and employs them here in full measure to demonstrate, by expert knowledge, that the readers have been deceived. This is not the end of the world! Not yet!

The most difficult problem in this very complex passage is "the restrainer." In verse 6 "what is restraining" *(to katechon)* is an impersonal (neuter) power, but in verse 7 "it" becomes "he" *(ho katechon)* who is active "until he *passes from* the scene" (not "is removed"). The New American Bible, along with the majority of scholars, ancient and modern, takes "the restrainer" to be a benevolent power that holds back "the rebel" until the latter is finally "revealed." What or who "the restrainer" is supposed to be is impossible to know; suggestions include the Roman Empire, angelic powers, or the gospel that must be preached to all nations before the end (Matt 24:14). Until that time "the mystery of rebellion is already at work, but only until the restrainer passes away," and then, simultaneously it would seem, "the rebel will [both] be revealed" and will be killed by "the Lord Jesus, with the breath (or Spirit) of his mouth." This "coming" *(parousia)* of the Lord is the true end for which the readers should wait. This interpretation may be correct, but its major weakness is that "restrainer" may not be the best translation of the Greek term.

An alternative interpretation, found in the notes of the New American Bible, is very different. The Greek word for "the restrainer" *(katechon)* is ambiguous; elsewhere it usually means "possess" or "seize." If that is the meaning here, then "the possessing power" *(katechon)* is probably not benevolent but is some evil force (person) that anticipates the coming of the final, more terrible evil one. In this case verses 5-7 read:

> Do you not recall that while I was still with you, I told you these things; and now you know the "possessing power," so that the rebel might be revealed in his own time, for the mystery of rebellion is already at work, but let the "possessor" be for the moment, until he passes away.

Believers here are told to wait; "the rebel" will soon enough be revealed and destroyed after the "possessing power passes from the scene." Both interpretations agree that believers are told to wait and hold on to the instruction given long ago. Though now is the *beginning* of the end (see 1 Thess 1:10; 4:13-18), the *end* of the end will be the "coming" *(parousia)* of "the Lord Jesus" and not before. It is impossible to know for sure which interpretation is correct, but overall evidence favors the first.

The passage continues, in tones reminiscent of the harsh words of 1:6 and 8-9, to talk not only of "the lawless one," whose "coming" *(parousia)* "springs from the power of Satan," but also of those who "are perishing, because they have not accepted the love of truth." Though they were deceived by Satan's displays of "power and signs and false wonders" (2:9), the writer insists that they themselves bear responsibility for not accepting the truth. In its reasoning the passage is similar to Romans 1:18-32, which condemns human refusal to "glorify or give thanks" to God, even though knowledge of God was easily available, so that God "gave them up to their passions" and permitted their sins to be their punishment. Here God is envisaged as sending "a deceiving power so that unbelievers might believe the falsehood" and be condemned (2:11-12). Such judgmental, apocalyptic language needs careful evaluation and application. Its rather narrow context is not to be forgotten; certainly a fundamentalist interpretation, which would view all "unbelievers" as necessarily "condemned," would be a misuse of this text. "Love of truth" is a universal value, but complete clarity about "the truth" remains beyond our grasp.

2:13-17 A second thanksgiving and prayer

In contrast to the harsh condemnation of unbelievers in 2:10-12, the writer turns to a prayer of thanksgiving for salvation and does so with precisely the same phrase as in 1:3 ("We ought to give thanks to God"). The "choosing" of believers here is a near synonym of God's making them "worthy of the kingdom" (1:5) and "calling" them (1:11). Once again, fully consistent with Paul's own theology, there is a strong emphasis on God's initiative in preparing believers for salvation. "First fruits" (1:13), for Paul himself (e.g., Rom 8:23; 11:16; 1 Cor 15:23), usually suggests the early harvest of something that promises more to come; the meaning here is less clear. It is possible, however, that instead of "first fruits" *(aparchen)*, the text should actually read "from the beginning" *(ap'arches)*, which would emphasize the foresight of God's plan.

In any event, God prepared believers "through sanctification by the Spirit" (God's work) and "belief in truth" (human response). One of the things that distinguishes this letter from 1 Thessalonians is a strong concern with the acceptance of "the truth" (2:10, 12, 13) and the danger of "deceit" (2:9, 11). Neither word is found in 1 Thessalonians. This writer sees "the truth" as coming "through the gospel" (preaching) of Paul and his companions. It is belief in this truth that will lead to possessing "the glory of our Lord Jesus Christ," and therefore believers must "stand firm and hold fast to the [apostolic] traditions" they have received "whether through oral statement or letter" (2:15; cf. 2:2).

The further prayer in 2:16-17 is curiously similar, in a couple of phrases, to that in 1 Thessalonians 3:11-13. The content, however, is different, with this prayer once again emphasizing God's initiative in "loving us [in Christ] and giving eternal consolation and good hope through grace" (2:16). Paul's idea that God enables "every good deed" in believers (2 Cor 8:9) is one that later writers especially liked to repeat (2:17; cf. Eph 2:10; Col 1:10; 2 Tim 3:17).

3:1-16 Final instructions and prayers

In a letter filled with prayers, the writer now asks believers to "pray for us, that the word of the Lord might speed forward (literally 'run') and be glorified" (3:1). There is no way of knowing who "the perverse and wicked persons" (3:2) might be who are envisioned as harassing Paul and his companions. Paul suffered a great deal in his ministry (2 Cor 11:23-33), including in Thessalonica (1 Thess 1:6; Acts 17:5-10), and this writer effectively reminds readers of that fact. That "not all have faith" helps explain this suffering, but "the Lord is faithful who will strengthen you and guard you from the evil one" (3:3). Similarly the writer expresses confidence that the believers are, and will remain, true to the instructions Paul provided, and once again breaks into prayer that "the Lord may direct their hearts" to the greatness of God's love and Christ's endurance in his suffering (3:5).

There follows a lengthy paragraph of instructions that appear to respond to a real situation of Paul's ministry, and some see this as evidence that Paul did indeed write this letter. However, the writer knew 1 Thessalonians and easily reproduces the situation of Paul's letter in order to invoke Paul's authority for the sake of his troubled readers at the end of the first century. Furthermore, though the letter is only fictively addressed to Thessalonica, it is by no means impossible that the very real situation addressed included the kinds of problems identified here. Expectation of the world's imminent end must indeed be a very disruptive experience.

The writer warns the community to avoid any persons who are disruptive and not obedient to "the tradition they received from us" (3:6), once again a focus on apostolic tradition! Believers are to recall Paul's own behavior; he and his companions were models to be imitated. In pursuit of this portrayal, 3:8 borrows both verbally and conceptually from 1 Thessalonians 2:9, that Paul and his co-workers "labored night and day so as to be a burden to no one," in spite of their considerable "authority" (3:9, cf. 1 Thess 2:7). Paul lived out the servant-leadership of Jesus (Mark 10:42-45; John 13:12-14) and is thus a model to be imitated (3:9).

The injunction that "if anyone is unwilling to work, neither should that one eat," (3:10) is quite believable as a tradition that might have come from Paul, given his own self-reliance. It is probably also an allusion to sharing all things in common (Acts 2:44). What the writer is primarily concerned about is the "disorderly" conduct of those who are not doing productive work (3:11) but are being busybodies, perhaps fomenting speculation about the end of the world. Such people are solemnly warned that they are to "work quietly and eat their own food" (3:12). The community as a whole is to persevere in doing good (3:13).

There follows a solemn instruction to the community that "if anyone does not obey our word through this letter, [they are to] take note of, and not associate with, such a person" (3:14). This harsh treatment, however, does not mean they are to excommunicate the person permanently. The language here recalls Paul's instruction in 1 Corinthians 5:9 regarding believers who were guilty of serious immorality. The instruction "Do not regard the offender as an enemy, but warn as speaking to a brother or sister" (3:15) also recalls Matthew 18:15-18, where a process is established for dealing with offenses and reconciliation within church communities. It is instructive to recall that these are the origins of the sacrament of reconciliation, with private confessionals not originating until many centuries later. The paragraph closes with yet another prayer that "the Lord of peace give you peace always and in every way."

3:17-18 Further "proof" of Paul's authority and final blessing

In conclusion the writer tries very hard—one might say, too hard—to convince the readers that this letter indeed derives from Paul himself (3:17). His purpose, of course, is to appeal to Paul's authority in order to reassure churches that are suffering in very difficult persecutions and need encouragement and instruction. Paul himself did authenticate his letters with his own handwriting (2 Cor 16:21; Gal 6:11; Phlm 19), but never three times over! The text, however, is Sacred Scripture, regardless of its author, as is also true of other biblical texts. The Scriptures arise from the church and from the faith of believers, and the church did not disappear with the deaths of the apostles. This letter arises from a church that is suffering and witnesses that, even in the absence of Paul, believers held onto faith and enabled the church to grow.

The final blessing (3:18, "The grace of our Lord Jesus Christ be with you all") corresponds with Paul's standard final words in his letters (e.g., 1 Thess 5:28; 1 Cor 16:23; Gal 6:18) and is now used in the liturgy.

The First Letter to Timothy

Terence J. Keegan, O.P.

INTRODUCTION

The First Letter to Timothy is the first of three letters usually referred to as the Pastoral Letters because they deal with matters concerning the leadership and organization of the Christian community. While some think that Paul may have composed 2 Timothy and possibly the others as well, most scholars believe that they come from a period after the death of Paul, probably composed by followers of Paul who were concerned that his legacy be handed on to the next generation of Christians. The practice of ascribing later writings to an earlier major figure was common in the ancient world; it can be found in the writings of the Old Testament and other ancient Jewish writings, as well as in the literature of ancient Greece and Rome.

Regardless of who wrote them, all agree that these letters are presented as having the authority of Paul and that they are generally consistent with themes that appear in other Pauline letters. Ultimately, however, the question of authorship does not affect their authoritative status, for, whoever wrote them, they are part of the inspired scriptural conversation between God and God's people.

Similarities among all three Pastoral Letters have led many scholars to consider them together when dealing with questions of authorship as well as interpretation. While there are striking similarities between 1 Timothy and Titus, there are striking differences between these two and 2 Timothy. 1 Timothy and Titus were written in an ancient letter form known as "commandments of a ruler," a letter from a ruler to a delegate and his community. Both of these letters deal with leadership roles in the community, the responsibilities of various groups within the community, and the threat of some kind of Jewish Christian false teaching. 2 Timothy deals with none of these matters but instead is a personal letter exhorting Timothy, by imitating Paul, to be the person through whom authentic Pauline teaching is to be transmitted to future generations. It makes no mention of offices within the community or the responsibilities of community members. Timothy is charged to combat false teaching, but the false teachings are nowhere described as Jewish.

The First Letter to Timothy

While 2 Timothy may not have been written by Paul during his life, it was composed in the style of a distinctively Pauline letter and contains passages and biographical material that many feel are authentically Pauline. 1 Timothy and Titus depart in significant ways from the Pauline letter form, and their similarities indicate that they were composed probably subsequent to 2 Timothy and possibly by a different person or persons.

These three letters, like Philemon but unlike the other Pauline letters, are each addressed to a single person. The intended audience, however, is not just Timothy or Titus (the ones to whom these letters are addressed) but the larger Christian community (the implied reader). Paul had preached in all the communities to which he wrote letters, with the exception of the Roman community, and even there he was known to many members of the community and would shortly be visiting that community. Unlike these letters, the Pastoral Letters are addressed to church leaders and members of a later generation that may not have known Paul personally. Addressing these letters to Timothy and Titus not only suited the content and purpose of these letters (orderly succession of leaders and correctness of teaching) but also extended the authority of Paul, through persons known to him in his lifetime, to communities of a later generation.

Interestingly, Timothy and Titus are both presented as young men and are instructed to serve as models of behavior for young men in their communities (1 Tim 4:12; Titus 2:7). The historical figures were indeed young men when Paul first encountered them early in his ministry. They would have been much older toward the end of Paul's ministry, where some scholars attempt to locate the Pastoral Letters.

Timothy appears in all of Paul's undisputed letters except Galatians and frequently appears in the Acts of the Apostles. He is listed as Paul's coauthor in most of the letters that include a coauthor (2 Cor 1:1; Phil 1:1; Col 1:1; 1 Thess 1:1; 2 Thess 1:1; Phlm 1). Titus appears only in 2 Corinthians and Galatians. They both appear as trusted companions of Paul, true to his teachings. "For this reason I am sending you Timothy, who is my beloved and faithful son in the Lord; he will remind you of my ways in Christ [Jesus], just as I teach them everywhere in every church" (1 Cor 4:17). "As for Titus, he is my partner and co-worker for you . . ." (2 Cor 8:23).

According to the narrative of 1 Timothy, Paul had gone to Macedonia, leaving Timothy temporarily in charge of the community at Ephesus. At some later date, whether in Macedonia or elsewhere, he wrote to Timothy, charging him to fulfill his responsibilities until he, Paul, returned. In detailing Timothy's responsibilities, the letter deals with the organization of the community, the roles of its leaders and all the other members of the community. It also explains how to handle the problem of false teachers, including those who, in their asceticism and renunciation of marriage, claimed Paul as their champion. While both 1 Timothy and Titus deal with false teachings and church order, in 1 Timothy the false teachings are more complex and the church organization further developed.

One of the reasons so many scholars are convinced that 1 Timothy was written long after the death of Paul is that it, like Titus, seems to address a period in the development of the early church when concern is for settled order and correct transmission of doctrine. The great Pauline themes of faith, righteousness, and grace, in dynamic development in Paul's early letters, appear here in fixed formulas. The apostolic and charismatic leadership of the early church is past, and the present need is for order, discipline, and virtue in a stable church structure. These letters shift away from Paul's perspective on believers living in a world that is in tension with the coming age. They appropriate the Pauline tradition for a new situation to refute false teachers and to establish the church as the kind of community that can carry the Pauline tradition forward into future generations. The shift apparent in these letters is somewhat comparable to that called for in the document The Church in the Modern World issued by the Second Vatican Council, calling on the church to become more fully engaged with contemporary secular society.

The emphasis of 1 Timothy on God's universal saving intention (2:4-6; see also Titus 2:11-14), as well as its positive view of creation (4:3-4), served to bring the Pauline gospel into the mainstream of contemporary society. While its moral vision of the compatibility of the ethics of church with that of society is somewhat at odds with the perspective of social alienation found in the book of Revelation, both of these parts of the New Testament, each in its own way, challenge the contemporary reader to find ways in which to engage society without betraying the integrity of the gospel message.

COMMENTARY

1:1-2 The opening

Ancient letters usually began with an identification of the sender and the recipient, followed by a short greeting. This letter begins by identifying its sender, "Paul"; his position, "apostle of Christ Jesus"; and the source of his authority, "God our savior and Christ Jesus our hope." This way of identifying the sender also focuses on an important theme both of this letter and of the letter to Titus—the theme of hope. In this letter and especially in Titus, God is the ground and object of hope, which is fulfilled in the gift of eternal life (1 Tim 4:10). God is the source of hope insofar as he saves us by being faithful to the divine promises, sending Christ Jesus to redeem us and form us into a chosen people (Titus 2:14).

The recipient is identified as "Timothy, my true child in faith." This expression illustrates an understanding of the church as a genuinely new family that needs to be nurtured and protected as it grows and matures, as well as designating Timothy as the legitimate representative authorized to minister in Paul's name. The expression "true child" is also used of Titus in the letter addressed to him (Titus 1:4), but in 2 Timothy, Timothy is addressed as "dear child" (2 Tim 1:2). The language in 1 Timothy and Titus emphasizes the authentication of Timothy and Titus. They are teachers in whom communities can put their trust. The greeting expands the typical Pauline greeting, "grace and peace," by the addition of "mercy," perhaps in anticipation of the stress on mercy in the thanksgiving at 1:13.

SETTING THE CONTEXT
1 Tim 1:3-11

1:3-7 Defend against false teaching

As Paul goes off to Macedonia, Timothy is left behind in Ephesus and given responsibility to exercise leadership in Paul's absence. While in 2 Timothy Paul entrusts his gospel to Timothy (2 Tim 1:14; 2:2), in 1 Timothy it is Paul to whom the gospel has been entrusted (1:11; 2:7). Paul remains in control and continues to exercise his responsibilities (3:14; 4:13). Timothy, as his representative, is charged to counter with correct instruction the false teaching that has arisen at Ephesus. The purpose of the instruction, however, is not simply to negate the false teaching but to "love from a pure heart, a good conscience, and a sincere faith" (1:5). Here, as elsewhere in 1 Timothy and Titus, there is a clear connection made between correct doctrine and a morally and religiously integrated life.

The "myths and endless genealogies" (1:4) that are being taught by these "teachers of the law" (1:7) are probably the same as what the letter to Titus calls "Jewish myths and regulations of people" (Titus 1:14). Some think that "genealogies" (1:4; see Titus 3:9) in the false teachings indicate some kind of gnostic speculation. More likely, however, they concern speculations on the lineage of the patriarchs. Here and in Titus there is lack of specificity on these false teachings, both because there is no need to provide a hearing for dangerous opinions and because the real point of the letters is to promote a well-integrated life for members of well-ordered communities.

1:8-11 The value and function of the law

The law referred to in these verses is the Jewish Law, concerning which Paul had said, "a person is not justified by works of the law but through faith in Jesus Christ" (Gal 2:16). Nevertheless, he also maintained that "the law is holy, and the commandment is holy and righteous and good" (Rom 7:12). The law was able to point out sinfulness, although it lacked the power to save. 1 Timothy 1:8-11 is saying essentially what Paul had said. A concern of this letter is with those who continue to oppose Paul by imposing Jewish legal obligations or who misrepresent Paul by teaching a kind of libertinism that gives free rein to all kinds of behavior.

These verses employ a common feature of popular moral preaching, namely, a listing of typical vices. The list here is based on the core of the Old Testament law, the Ten Commandments. The vices listed are said to be opposed to "sound teaching" (1:10; 4:6), which, like "sound words" (6:3), refers in 1 Timothy and Titus to the kind of teaching that leads to correct moral behavior (see Titus 1:9, 13; 2:1, 2, 8).

OPENING BRACKET

1 Tim 1:12-20

This passage and another similar passage near the end of the letter (6:11-16, 20-21a) bracket the body of the letter (2:1–6:10, 17-19). These bracketing passages focus on the overall purpose of the letter: the entrusting of Paul's gospel to Timothy for the purpose of protecting it from false teachers. In the opening bracket more emphasis is placed on Christ Jesus appointing Paul to his ministry (1:12), while the closing bracket emphasizes Timothy's responsibility to guard what has been entrusted to him (6:20) "until the appearance of our Lord Jesus Christ" (6:14). Both, however, focus on the charge entrusted to Timothy (1:18; 6:20), both times using the Greek vocative case (indicating the person addressed, "Timothy"), a case rarely used in the New Testament and used only these two times in this letter, a clear indication of their parallel and bracketing function.

In both passages Timothy's responsibilities are set in the context of community attestation: "prophetic words" (1:18) and "many witnesses" (6:12). In both Timothy is encouraged with metaphors of competition: to "fight a good fight" (1:18) and to "compete well for the faith" (6:12). In both Timothy is warned about the dangerous opposition that threatens the faith (1:19-20; 6:21). The special bracketing function of these passages is further highlighted by the fact that both include a doxology, an act of praise (1:17; 6:15-16). Both doxologies emphasize the uniqueness of God: "the only God" (1:17) and "the only ruler" (6:15), which provides the basis for the letter's emphasis on universal salvation (2:3-6). God's desire that all be saved is the reason why Paul was appointed an apostle (2:7) and the reason why Timothy is being charged to defend Paul's gospel in the face of opposition.

1:12-17 Prayer of thanksgiving

Pauline letters typically have a passage immediately after the opening in which Paul gives thanks to God for what God has done for the community or person to whom the letter is addressed. While 2 Timothy has the characteristic Pauline thanksgiving (2 Tim 1:3-5), it is lacking in both 1 Timothy and Titus. The belated thanksgiving in the present passage is addressed to Christ rather than to God, and the thanksgiving is for what Christ has done for Paul, not for what God has done for the letter's recipient. The present passage is actually more like the interjected thanksgivings in Paul's letters in which Paul thanks God for favors to himself (Rom 7:25; 1 Cor 15:57).

This thanksgiving, as part of the opening bracket, does serve as a foundation for the main themes of the letter and is appropriately placed after the passages that deal with false teaching and immorality. Paul himself was "once a blasphemer and a persecutor and an arrogant man" (1:13). Subsequently, by grace and faith, he became a Christian leader and "an example for those who would come to believe in [Christ]" (1:16). Paul serves as an example for readers up to the present day of how "the grace of our Lord" (1:14) can transform even the most arrogant person into a servant of Christ. The remainder of the letter will continue these themes, that is, upright living that follows from correct understanding of Christian doctrine as well as the proper exercise of leadership and authority in the Christian community.

The Christian doctrine at the heart of this passage, "Christ Jesus came into the world to save sinners" (1:15), is introduced by "this saying is trustworthy," a phrase regularly used in the Pastoral Letters to identify a basic truth of early Christian faith (1 Tim 3:1; 4:9; 2 Tim 2:11; Titus 3:8). The passage concludes with a doxology which, like the doxology found at the end of the letter (6:15-16), includes all four elements usually found in New Testament doxologies: the object of praise, "the king of ages, incorruptible, invisible, the only God"; an expression of praise, "honor and glory"; an indication of time, "forever and ever"; and a response, "Amen." Interestingly, while the thanksgiving is addressed to Christ Jesus (1:12), the doxology is addressed to God.

1:18-20 Timothy's responsibilities

The mention of Timothy's name in verse 18 is a departure from the style of letter writing in the Hellenistic world. Names of recipients would normally appear only in the opening and closing of the letter. Mention of his name at this point serves the bracketing function of this passage and refocuses the letter on Timothy (the recipient) after the thanksgiving has been focused on Paul, highlighting the seriousness of the challenge Timothy is facing in opposing error in the church. He is to take up this challenge "in accordance with the prophetic words once spoken about you" (1:18). Prophecy—words uttered by God's spokesperson—is the only charism that appears in all of Paul's lists of spiritual gifts (Rom 12:6; 1 Cor 12:10, 28, 29; see 1 Cor 13:2; 14:6, 22). Here and at 4:14 prophecy is associated with the charismatic authorization of Timothy's ministry, a ministry here described as fighting a good fight with the weapons of faith and a good conscience.

While the opponents Timothy is to deal with are never identified and their teaching is only vaguely described, two individuals are cited with whom Paul presumably had to deal. They are cited here as examples of the kinds of persons Timothy is to beware. Both names appear in 2 Timothy. Hymenaeus said that the resurrection has already taken place, (2 Tim 2:17-18), and Alexander the coppersmith did Paul a great deal of harm (2 Tim 4:14). Their use here may be an indication that 2 Timothy preceded and influenced 1 Timothy. Both men have been "handed over to Satan" (1:20), the procedure indicated for the incestuous man in 1 Corinthians 5:1-5. In both places the procedure—what today would be called excommunication—is not punitive but educative and should lead to conversion. A similar procedure appears in Titus 3:10-11. Support for this procedure emphasizes the overall concern of 1 Timothy and Titus with correct teaching and good order in the community.

THE HOUSEHOLD OF GOD

1 Tim 2:1–3:15

2:1-7 Universal salvation and good citizenship

After the opening bracket, the four main sections of the letter deal with good order in the community, true devotion as opposed to false teaching, the responsibilities of Timothy as a community leader, and dealing with false teachers. False teaching threatens the stability of the community both in itself and with respect to the surrounding secular world. Praying for everyone, from kings on down, serves a dual purpose and is rooted in the fundamental doctrinal truth that "there is also one mediator between God and the human race, / Christ Jesus, himself human, / who gave himself as ransom for all" (2:5-6). First, it furthers God's purpose, for which Paul is appointed preacher and apostle, that everyone be saved and come to a knowledge of the truth. Emphasis on God's desire to save all people is as important for the contemporary reader of this letter as it was for the original readers in their situation. Nowhere in the New Testament is this desire more explicit than in 1 Timothy 2:4.

Second, it furthers the desire of the developing Christian community to have its members accepted as good citizens in civil society. The quiet, tranquil lives desired is described using a technical term, "devotion" (2:2), sometimes translated "religion." It is the word used in the Roman world for reverence for the gods and respect for traditional values and practices, a combination of piety and correct behavior. This much esteemed virtue receives little notice in the rest of the New Testament but is prominent in 1 Timothy and Titus (2:2; 3:16; 4:7, 8; 6:3, 5, 6, 11; Titus 1:1; 2:12). It is a virtue that pertains to the special concern of 1 Timothy and Titus that Christians lead lives worthy of their calling, lives that can be held in high esteem by the surrounding world. This passage illustrates a developing understanding of the church, not as an isolated and dangerous sect but as a community that is open to all, and of Christian life as fully compatible with good citizenship.

2:8-15, 3:1a How men and women are to pray and live

In the introduction to this letter, Paul spoke of Timothy as "my true child in faith" (1:2), indicating an understanding of the church as a genuinely new family. Here and later in the letter (6:1-2, 17-19) there is a list of duties, often called a "household code." Such lists in other writings (Eph 5:22–6:9; Col 3:18–4:1; 1 Pet 2:13–3:8) focused on members of a familial household; here, however, the whole church, the household of God, is addressed.

The concern of these verses is with community worship that is filled with factions and quarreling. Men are addressed in 2:8 and simply told to pray "without anger or argument." The remainder of the chapter concerns women's behavior in the assembled community. Women are not only admonished about appropriate dress and conduct, but they are also forbidden "to teach or to have authority over a man" (2:12). It is not clear why women are singled out for such extensive treatment, but all three Pastoral Letters seem to accept the widespread belief at that time that women were notoriously unable to control their sexual passions (1 Tim 5:11-15; 2 Tim 3:6-7; Titus 2:4-5). The belief that women were weak-willed and easy prey to false teachers probably influenced the prohibition on public teaching and the requirement that they remain completely silent in the Christian assembly

(2:11-12; 1 Cor 14:34-35). While some have suggested that the injunction to "be quiet" (2:12) refers not to prayer but to aggressive confrontations, this passage has provoked more discussion than any other in the Pastoral Letters in recent years. It must be acknowledged that great harm has come upon women throughout the history of the church because of understandings of this passage.

While women are in some ways subordinate to men in Paul's letters, one does find there women prophets (1 Cor 11:1-13) and a degree of equality among men and women (Gal 3:28). The unusual interpretation of the Adam and Eve story (Gen 2) used to support the subordination of women is likewise contrary to Paul's teaching, for Paul clearly speaks of Adam's sin, not Eve's (Rom 5:12-19). 1 Timothy's inventive interpretation of Genesis 2 (2:13-14) is, interestingly, a clear example of scriptural warrant for interpretive strategies that go beyond the original meaning of the text. One needs to go beyond the original meaning of 2:11-12 by reading this passage with a hermeneutic of suspicion. Hermeneutics involves the methods used to interpret a text. The apparent meaning of a text is often colored by cultural presuppositions that are now known to have been mistaken. A hermeneutics of suspicion is a method that questions the validity of these cultural presuppositions and seeks a deeper meaning in the text. This method enables contemporary readers to arrive at fresh meanings of the text that are free from the cultural assumptions of the past.

At the same time, one must recognize that just as past assumptions about family structures and power relationships were not absolute but rather culturally conditioned, the same can be said for what contemporary society regards as appropriate about family structures and power relationships. Reading the Pastoral Letters with a hermeneutic of suspicion can help contemporary readers go beyond the culturally conditioned values of both past and present centuries.

The message of this passage for the church of the first century as well as for the church today is that good order based on sound doctrine needs to be maintained in the church. Women throughout history have spoken powerfully for the kind of sound doctrine promoted by 1 Timothy. The church was blessed because St. Catherine of Sienna did not take the injunction to silence literally when she persuaded Pope Gregory XI to return from Avignon to Rome in 1376. She was clearly more interested in what is a primary concern of 1 Timothy, the preservation of authentic Christian tradition.

The final verse in the passage on women emphasizes the role of motherhood in the salvation of women (2:15). Childbearing, however, fits in with God's plan for salvation only when it is accompanied by faith and love, the

1 Timothy 3

hallmarks of Christian existence; by holiness, the condition of belonging to the Lord; and self-control, a quality valued in Hellenistic society and a continuing motif in 1 Timothy and Titus (2:9, 15; 3:2; Titus 1:8; 2:2, 5); qualities equally expected of women as well as of men. "This saying is trustworthy" (3:1a) pertains to what precedes rather than to what follows. This is the second use of this phrase in the Pastoral Letters, a phrase which usually signals a basic truth of early Christian faith (1 Tim 1:15; 4:9; 2 Tim 2:11; Titus 3:8). Like every other use of this phrase in the Pastoral Letters, it is connected with a statement on salvation. In this case it is used to ratify the previously expressed teaching on the salvation of Christian women and more broadly the teaching on salvation which began in 2:3-4 affirming that God "wills everyone to be saved and to come to knowledge of the truth" (2:4).

3:1b-7 Qualifications for bishops

After spelling out the duties of men and women in the community, the letter continues with listings of the qualifications for leadership positions in the community. The purpose of this passage is to provide a stable structure for the community in the face of forces that have the potential to cause its disintegration. The qualifications listed here, like the previous treatment of the role of women, are culturally conditioned and concerned with public respectability in the context of a particular culture. The only uniquely Christian features in these lists are the requirements that the bishop "not be a recent convert" (3:6) and that deacons hold "fast to the mystery of the faith with a clear conscience" (3:9).

The list contains no specification of the actual roles of bishops and deacons in the community, and apart from the two items mentioned above, the qualifications listed are typical of what would be expected of pagan and Jewish officials. All these qualifications, however, are in keeping with two major concerns of 1 Timothy and Titus, namely, that the community be well ordered under reliable leadership and that the Christian community, by reason of its integrity, be respected by the surrounding world (3:7). One qualification that appears in the lists for both bishop and deacon is that they not be lovers of money (3:3) or greedy for sordid gain (3:8). Leaders who are mercenary would clearly detract both from good order within the community as well as from the reputation of the community in the surrounding world. This characteristic is specifically attributed to false teachers who are harming the community (6:5; see Titus 1:11).

It is tempting to see in the offices of bishop and deacon their well-defined positions as they appear in the developed church of the second century. Nevertheless, it is far from clear just how well defined these positions had

1 Timothy 3

become in the context of 1 Timothy and Titus. Another group that appears in these letters are the presbyters, who seem to be synonymous with bishops (5:17, 19; Titus 1:5-6). Timothy and Titus have significant administrative and teaching authority, and Titus himself is given the authority to appoint presbyters (Titus 1:5), but nowhere are Timothy and Titus called bishops. Whether bishops have the kind of authority described for Timothy and Titus is not clear.

3:8-13 Qualifications for deacons

How the office of deacon differs from that of bishop/presbyter is similarly unclear. The qualifications are similar, and the functions are not mentioned. The fact that they are listed second might indicate that here, just as in the later church, their role is subordinate to that of bishop. Even more problematic is the reference to women in verse 11. Some hold that this passage refers to deaconesses like Phoebe (Rom 16:1), but what her role was or what the role of these women were is not clear. It is possible that this verse refers not to deaconesses but to the wives of deacons, who, like their husbands, must have qualities that contribute to the good order of the community and its reputation in the surrounding world.

3:14-15 Conclusion on the household of God

These verses bring to conclusion the first main section of the letter on the household of God (2:1–3:15) and serve as a transition to what follows. "These matters" (3:14) refers to all that has preceded in this section in the same way that "these things" (4:11) refers to all that precedes in each of the next two main sections of the letter. In this first main part of the letter Paul detailed Timothy's responsibilities for the household of God. While Timothy is temporarily in charge, Paul continues to be responsible for the community (1:11; 2:7) and plans to return (3:14). Paul's plans to visit his communities are often noted in his letters (Rom 15:24; 1 Cor 4:19; Phlm 22). Mention of these plans gives added importance to the letter, which is to take the place of Paul's authoritative presence, supporting 1 Timothy's intention of serving as a kind of church constitution for a developing Christian community. The good order that precedes and the opposition to false teaching that will follow are what Paul intends for the Christian community.

The Christian community is then described using two images, "the household of God" and "the church of the living God, the pillar and foundation of truth" (3:15). The first image treats the church as a well-ordered structure exhibiting proper behavior, the main concern of the passages that preceded. The second image focuses on the church as a living faith-community whose organization and moral life are based on the solid foundation of sound doctrine, the concern of the second main section of the letter.

SOUND DOCTRINE OF DEVOTION/RELIGION
I Tim 3:16–4:11

3:16 Mystery of devotion

The second main section of the letter begins by providing the theological basis for this solid foundation of truth by using what appears to be a passage from a liturgical hymn. The letter speaks of this solid foundation as "the mystery of devotion" (3:16), the second use of this technical term in this letter (see 2:2). The hymn sums up the content of Christian faith on which Christian living is based. The use of passages from hymns or confessions is common in New Testament letters and serves to remind readers of the fundamental truths that they believe and express in their community worship. A similar passage from a hymn is used in 1 Peter 3:18-19, 22.

An indication that the passage in 1 Timothy is taken from a hymn is the fact that it consists of three balanced couplets: flesh-spirit (contrast), seen-proclaimed (complementary), world-glory (contrast). This passage summarizes the church's authentic faith in the paschal mystery: Jesus died on the cross (his manifestation in the flesh) and rose from the dead. He was first seen by angels then proclaimed by apostles to the Gentiles. People all over the world have come to believe in Jesus, who is now enthroned as Lord of the church and will come again to judge the living and the dead.

4:1-5 Problems in later times, apostasy

The letter here turns attention to the fundamental problem mentioned at the start of the letter—people teaching false doctrines (1:3), doctrines opposed to the fundamental truths of Christian faith just summarized in the hymn (3:16). False teachers, upsetting the lives of the faithful and dividing communities, had been a problem from the earliest days of Christianity. Paul dealt with false teachings in his early letters and communities. False teachers became especially troublesome as the church attempted to settle into a structured and sustainable existence.

So important is the matter of correct teaching that the author has raised the stakes from a simple contrast between truth and falsehood to an end-time contrast between the forces of good and the forces of evil (cf. 2 Tim 3:1-9). He appeals to the prophetic Spirit to set the stage for the end-time conflict, clearly the same Spirit who had vindicated the crucified Jesus in the preceding hymn (3:16). References to the Spirit are rare in the Pastoral

1 Timothy 4

Letters, with each reference emphasizing a different aspect of the Spirit (see 2 Tim 1:14; Titus 3:5). Here the prophetic Spirit foretells the end-time conflict with "deceitful spirits and demonic instructions" (4:1).

The notion that deceit is characteristic of the end times was common in the New Testament era. It is found in the Marcan apocalypse (Mark 13:5-6, 22) as well as in parallel passages in Matthew and Luke. False teachings are referred to elsewhere in the Pastoral Letters, but only here are specific issues identified, which are then refuted with an explicit argument. These two issues—"they forbid marriage and require abstinence from foods" (4:3)—are similar to problems Paul encountered at Corinth about marriage (1 Cor 7:1-3) and food (1 Cor 8:4-13; 10:23-33). The problem here might also be related to the claim by Hymenaeus (see 1 Tim 1:20) that the "resurrection has already taken place" (2 Tim 2:18). This claim is consistent with the teachings of a later heretical group, the Gnostics, who viewed the material world as evil. If those transformed by the saving grace of Jesus were already "resurrected," already living full spiritual lives, abstinence from physical pursuits such as sex, marriage, and food would be consistent with their denigration of the material world.

These errors are refuted by appealing, as Paul did (1 Cor 8:6; 10:26), to the one God who created all that is. "Everything created by God is good" (4:4) echoes the words of Genesis 1:31: "God looked at everything he had made, and he found it very good." The goodness of God's creation was tainted by sin, but the redemption won by Jesus has overcome all the evil caused by sin. Nevertheless, powerful sects preaching that the material world is evil have arisen throughout the history of the church. These included the Gnostics of the early church; the Manichees, among whom St. Augustine once was numbered; and the thirteenth-century Albigensians, against whom St. Dominic preached, to name but a few. According to 1 Timothy, everything created by God is not only good, but "it is made holy by the invocation of God in prayer" (4:5). This powerful assertion about the goodness of all that God creates is as important today as it has been throughout the history of Christianity. Receiving God's good creation in prayer pertains clearly to the common Christian practice of thanking God in prayer before meals, but it can pertain equally to the use of sex within marriage or to any other good thing.

4:6-10 Training for devotion, false versus true teachers

After reflecting on the conflicts of the end times (4:1-5), Paul addresses a charge to Timothy that involves a contrast between the true teacher exemplified in the person of Timothy and the false teachers discussed in 4:1-3. "These instructions" (4:6) probably refers to the previous instructions on the goodness of creation. False teachers are concerned with "profane and silly myths" (4:7; see 1:4), while true teachers are concerned with "the words of the faith and of the sound teaching" (4:6). False teachers require unwarranted asceticism based on a false understanding of resurrection and the spiritual life (4:3). True teachers train for devotion (4:7), knowing that future life is still a promise (4:8, 10). Christians trained in devotion would lead lives that could be held in high esteem by the surrounding world. Training for devotion is somewhat like, but far more important than, physical training. "Devotion is valuable in every respect, since it holds a promise of life both for the present and for the future" (4:8).

This statement on the importance of devotion is the third of the trustworthy sayings to appear in the letter (see 1:15; 3:1). This saying is unique among the trustworthy sayings in the Pastoral Letters, since only here are specific implications of the saying spelled out. The first implication is "toil and struggle" (4:10). God has promised the life to come, but the path to that life will involve effort. There is, however, no suggestion here or elsewhere in this letter that the author is thinking of the kind of hardship and persecution that is discussed in 2 Timothy (2 Tim 3:10-12; 4:5). The second implication concerns Christian hope, an important theme in both this letter and in Titus (1 Tim 1:1; 4:10; 5:5; Titus 1:2; 2:13; 3:7). God is the ground and object of hope, which is fulfilled in the gift of eternal life. The final implication is God's gift of salvation. Every time a trustworthy saying appears in the Pastoral Letters it refers to some aspect of salvation. God wills that all people be saved, but God also wills that they come to a full knowledge of the truth (2:4). Those who do so are the faithful, whom God particularly wills to be saved. These are the ones who toil and struggle for devotion.

4:11 Conclusion

This second main section of the letter concludes with an instruction to "command and teach these things" (4:11; see 3:14; 6:2), a reference to all that has preceded in this section. Timothy is charged to command and teach about training for devotion and the rejection of teaching that is opposed to the fundamentals of Christian faith.

INSTRUCTIONS ABOUT LEADERSHIP
I Tim 4:12–6:2

4:12-16 Timothy's duties

After a discussion of true and false teachings, the third main section of the letter focuses on the duties of the leader of the community. In the

1 Timothy 4

previous verses Timothy was encouraged to "give these instructions" (4:6) and to "train yourself for devotion" (4:7). This section further expands on these two fundamental duties of a community leader. He is the church's authorized teacher and guardian of its faith, and he is to witness to that faith in the way he lives and performs his duties.

The overall concern of 1 Timothy and Titus for a stable Christian community with an authorized leadership is here manifest in the solemn description of Timothy's authorization for ministry: "through the prophetic word with the imposition of hands of the presbyterate" (4:14). This is the only passage in 1 Timothy dealing with how leaders assume their positions. It differs significantly from 2 Timothy, where Paul imposes hands on Timothy (2 Tim 1:6), transmitting his own authority. It differs as well from Titus, where Titus appoints presbyters (Titus 1:5). The intent of the present passages is to establish both the charismatic and the transmitted authority of the church leader. The charge "let no one have contempt for your youth" (4:12) is reminiscent of what Paul wrote about Timothy to the Corinthians: "no one should disdain him" (1 Cor 16:11). The narrative of the letter presumes that he is still a young man who has been raised up by the presbyterate to a position of leadership and enabled by the gift of the Spirit to "attend to the reading, exhortation, and teaching" (4:13).

The list of five qualities that Timothy is to model (4:12) are noteworthy, since they significantly differ from the list of six qualities in 2 Timothy that are observed in Paul (2 Tim 3:10-11). Common to both lists are faith and love, the hallmarks of Christian existence (see 1:14; 2:15; 6:11). 2 Timothy also lists patience, endurance, persecutions, and sufferings, qualities important for the character and purpose of that letter. Instead of these, 1 Timothy lists speech, conduct, and purity, qualities more specific to the nature and purpose of 1 Timothy.

The passage concludes with a series of imperatives directed at Timothy: "be diligent . . . be absorbed . . . attend . . . persevere " (4:15-16), which emphasize the importance of his position and the seriousness of his responsibilities. He is to do these things for two reasons: first "so that your progress may be evident to everyone" (4:15). "Progress" is a technical term employed by Stoics and other philosophers, but appearing elsewhere in the New Testament only in Philippians 1:12, 25 (interestingly, the only book in the New Testament besides 1 Timothy that speaks of both bishops and deacons). "Progress" refers to a person's moral and spiritual evolution. For Plutarch, progress comes between natural dispositions and perfection. Virtues important in the surrounding world are important as well for 1 Timothy and Titus. Timothy's moral and religious development should not only inspire

1 Timothy 5

the Christian community but also bring credit to the community in the eyes of others. The second reason he is to do these things is to "save both yourself and those who listen to you" (4:16). God is the savior of all, but Timothy has been brought into this plan by reason of his authorization and spiritual gifts.

5:1-2 Respect for men and women, old and young

The instructions to Timothy continue, but the focus shifts from how he is to deal with false teaching to how he is to deal with the members of the household of God. The present section differs from earlier sections dealing with household members (2:8–3:13). There a household code (2:8-15) dealt with the behavior of various members of the community, followed by a section (3:1-13) dealing with qualifications and responsibilities for positions of leadership. The present section deals with how Timothy and others are to treat various members of the community, first considered in terms of age and sex. Greater attention is paid to older men, continuing an Old Testament concern for men in their old age (Sir 3:12-14), but all are to be treated with respect and kindness. Within the household of God, obligations toward one's immediate family are to be extended to all members of the community.

5:3-16 Rules regarding widows

This long section addresses the place of widows in the community, obviously a matter of concern in the church at the time the letter was written. As with all members of the community, widows are to be treated with the respect that is owed them (5:3). There are, however, different categories of widows. First and foremost is "the real widow, who is all alone, has set her hope on God and continues in supplications and prayers night and day" (5:5). Christians have an obligation to provide for family members who become widows (5:4, 8, 16), but those left with no one to provide for them become the responsibility of the community. These real widows are to be "enrolled," a term which probably indicates not only that they are being provided for but also that they have some official role in the community. The qualifications laid down for being enrolled (5:9-10) are similar to qualifications listed for bishops and deacons (3:2-3, 8-9).

Besides these "real widows," there are the widows who have families that can provide for them, widows of any age who are self-indulgent (5:6), and younger widows, "less than sixty years old" (5:9), who might not be self-indulgent but might become so. The advice given about younger widows manifests concerns raised elsewhere in the Pastoral Letters. Women are especially prey to false teachers disturbing the church (2 Tim 3:6-7). Rather than risk succumbing either to the desire for marriage or to the wiles of false teachings (see Titus 1:11), it would be better for them to marry and manage a home and children (5:14). The recommendation to remarry should also be seen in connection with the false teachers' attack on marriage in 4:3. An additional concern of these letters is the repute of the community in the surrounding world. Young widows should marry lest they fall into kinds of behavior that bring disrepute on the community (5:14).

5:17-22 Rules regarding presbyters

After dealing with those older widows who serve a special function within the community, the letter now deals with older men, presbyters, who have a special function in the community. It is not clear how the presbyters dealt with here are any different from the bishops of chapter 3. Titus 1:5-9 uses "bishop" and "presbyter" almost interchangeably, the term "presbyter" referring to the person's status within the community, a respected member of the community, and the term "bishop" referring to his function, exercising oversight and leadership in the community. Like Timothy, presbyters have a responsibility for teaching and preaching, what the qualifications for bishops state they must be able to do (3:2; Titus 1:9). Like widows, they are to be provided for by the community. In fact, presbyters "deserve double honor" (5:17). The scriptural basis provided in the next verse appears in two parts. The first is clearly from Deuteronomy 25:4 (see 1 Cor 9:9), but the second is a saying of Jesus (Matt 10:10; Luke 10:7). While some believe that only the first is referred to as Scripture, others feel that this passage may be early evidence for the conferral of scriptural status on New Testament literature or sources.

Just as there was a concern with widows who stray and bring disrepute on the community, there is an even greater concern with presbyters who sin. When accusations are brought against presbyters, they are entitled to what today would be called "due process." Those who indeed do sin, however, are to be reprimanded publicly, "so that the rest will also be afraid" (5:20). The need for harsh treatment of errant church leaders is all too evident in the contemporary church.

The admonition that care should be taken not to "lay hands too readily on anyone" (5:22) could refer to the ordination of presbyters (see 4:14), but in the present context it more likely refers to the laying on of hands involved in the reconciliation of sinners. Timothy is exhorted not to play favorites but to reconcile to the community only those who have fully repented of their sins. The bottom line is a word of advice to Timothy, which applies, through him, to all with positions of leadership: "keep yourself pure" (5:22).

5:23-25 Timothy's duties

The final comment in verse 22, "keep yourself pure," connects as well to the verse that follows. Timothy bears a heavy responsibility for the church at Ephesus and must be both spiritually and physically fit for the task at hand. The rejection of a false dietary asceticism (4:3-4) is here reinforced by the recommendation to make proper use of the good things, like wine, created by God for one's physical well being (5:23). This advice to Timothy parallels the advice given earlier to young widows about remarriage (5:14), rejecting false teaching and extolling God's good creation. The emphasis on the public character of both sin and good deeds relates to the overall concern of 1 Timothy and Titus for the public perception of the Christian community. The behavior of Christian leaders, good or bad, will affect the public perception of the community. Whether or not their deeds are public, they will not long remain hidden.

6:1-2 Conclusion on slaves

In chapters 2 and 3 the letter had addressed the responsibilities and qualifications of various members of the community in the "household of God"—husbands and wives, bishops, and deacons. The previous chapter shifted the focus and looked at the way the community and its leaders should deal with certain members—older men, widows, and presbyters. Here the focus seems to shift back to the responsibilities of certain members within the community. Just as bishops and deacons are to conduct themselves in ways that bring honor to the Christian community, slaves are charged with a similar responsibility.

There is no suggestion here, nor generally in the New Testament, that the Christian community was to overthrow the social structures of society. In 1 Timothy and Titus especially, Christians are charged to behave as good citizens in what was considered a well-ordered society. Slaves are encouraged to fulfill their responsibilities to their masters, even to their Christian masters, "so that the name of God and our teaching may not suffer abuse" (6:1). The motive for similar advice to slaves in Titus is expressed positively: "so as to adorn the doctrine of God our savior in every way" (Titus 2:10).

Dealing with slaves at this point in the letter, shifting back to responsibilities of certain members of the community, is not really out of place. This third main section of the letter is concerned with the responsibilities of leaders in the community. Timothy is, as Paul describes himself in Titus 1:1, a slave of God, as are all those who exercise leadership roles. Timothy, above all, as a slave, must fulfill his responsibilities to his master. The final words of verse 2, "teach and urge these things" (cf. 3:14; 4:11), conclude this third main section

1 Timothy 6

of the letter. These words, which are unfortunately and inexplicably missing from many editions of the New American Bible, refer not just to the advice to slaves but to all the responsibilities that Timothy and other leaders, slaves of God, have been charged with in this section of the letter.

FALSE TEACHING AND TRUE WEALTH

I Tim 6:3-10, 17-19

6:3-10 The evils of false teaching exposed

The focus of the letter now shifts from the responsibilities of true teachers to a criticism of false teachers in this fourth and final main section of the letter. As in chapter 4, Timothy is advised to beware of false teachers and to be strong in adhering to correct doctrine, the doctrine that leads to religion/devotion (6:3; see 2:2; 3:16; 4:7, 8; 5:4; 6:5, 6, 11). In this chapter the correct understanding of religion is contrasted with the understanding of those who think that religion can be a source of material gain (6:5; cf. Titus 1:11). These are the people who fall into erroneous beliefs and end up experiencing a host of vices—"envy, rivalry, insults, evil suspicions, and mutual friction" (6:4-5). They are the ones referred to earlier in the letter who have "turned to meaningless talk" (1:6) and are "paying attention to deceitful spirits and demonic instructions through the hypocrisy of liars with branded consciences" (4:1-2). "Religion with contentment" (6:6) expressed the Stoic ideal of being content in any situation, but here it expresses a perspective on life restored by the saving mission of Christ. Religion is indeed a source of great gain if it leads to a Christian appreciation for moderation and sufficiency. Those, however, who use religion to achieve material wealth will stray into error and encounter an array of evils, for "the love of money is the root of all evils" (6:10).

6:17-19 Conclusion on the wealthy

While this passage appears after the first part of the closing bracket (6:11-16), it serves to conclude the fourth and final section of the body of the letter on false teachers. This passage deals with a final group within the household of God not yet treated in the letter—the rich. They are fittingly dealt with here and told not to be proud (6:17), after the emphasis on the overarching power of God in the final doxology (6:15-16). While it is wrong to use religion to pursue wealth, it is admirable to use wealth in the service of religion, recognizing that the ultimate source of security is not transient wealth but the eternal God. As with the earlier section on slaves, this passage dealing with the wealthy is really not out of place, since it concludes

1 Timothy 6

the previous section, which dealt with the connection of false teaching and the inappropriate pursuit of wealth (6:5).

In a broader perspective, wealth is viewed in the same light as were marriage and food. "Everything created by God is good, and nothing is to be rejected when received with thanksgiving" (4:4). Just as Timothy and all Christian leaders are slaves of God, they are to rely on God for all the good things they need to fulfill their ministries. The reason for the proper use of riches, like the reason for all the moral exhortations in this letter, is "to win the life that is true life" (6:19).

CLOSING BRACKET

1 Tim 6:11-16, 20-21a

6:11-16 Timothy's responsibility and accountability

While the false teacher's misuse of religion leads to ruin, the true teacher's correct pursuit of religion leads to eternal life. This passage, together with 6:20-21a, closely parallels the opening bracket of the letter (1:12-20). That bracket appeared after the formal opening (1:1-2) and an expression of concern for the problem of false teachings (1:3-11). It began with a thanksgiving for the mercy and promise of eternal life extended to Paul, the true teacher (1:12-17).

In this final bracket Timothy is encouraged to follow the example of Paul, to "compete well for the faith" (6:12; see 1:18) and "to keep the commandment without stain or reproach" (6:14). His role of being a faithful witness parallels not only Paul's but also that of Jesus before Pilate (6:13). In the opening of the letter Timothy was addressed by Paul as "my true child in the faith" (1:2); here he is addressed as "man of God" (6:11), an expression used in the Old Testament for a person with a prophetic function (1 Sam 2:27; 1 Kgs 13:1). Its use recalls the prophetic charge to Timothy in the opening bracket (1:18).

Timothy is charged to keep "the commandment" (6:14), a term that appears nowhere else in the Pastoral Letters. In this context, however, it likely refers to the tasks entrusted to Timothy at the laying on of hands (4:14). It would involve both his teaching responsibilities as well as his responsibility to provide moral leadership by his own good example. He is to keep this commandment "until the appearance of our Lord Jesus Christ" (6:14), a reference to the eschatological parousia (second coming) of the risen Lord, similar to 1 Thessalonians 3:13; 5:23, but without suggesting that the appearance will occur during Timothy's lifetime.

This final charge to Timothy concludes with a doxology (6:15-16) that is strikingly similar to the doxology that concludes the thanksgiving in the

1 Timothy 6

opening bracket (1:17). Like that earlier doxology, it includes all four elements usually found in New Testament doxologies: the object of praise, "the King of kings and Lord of lords, who alone has immortality, who dwells in unapproachable light, and whom no human being has seen or can see"; an expression of praise, "honor and eternal power"; an indication of time, "eternal"; and a response, "Amen."

Unlike the doxology at 1:16 and unlike all the other New Testament passages that are commonly identified as doxologies, this one in chapter 6 is the only one that does not use the Greek word for "glory," *doxa*. Instead, this final doxology uses the word "power." While 1 Timothy and Titus respect the power of earthly rulers, their power is subject to God's, and only his is an "eternal power" (6:16).

6:20-21a Final recommendation

The final words of Hellenistic letters usually recapitulate and emphasize the main themes of the letter. The final words here complete the closing bracket by summarizing the advice given to Timothy throughout the letter, addressing Timothy directly, as in the opening bracket (1:18). They renew the warning about the dangerous opposition that threatens the faith (6:21; see 1:19-20). Timothy is to "guard what has been entrusted" (cf. 1:18) and "avoid profane babbling" (cf. 4:7).

BLESSING

1 Tim 6:21b

This letter's closing is, curiously, the shortest of all such closings in the New Testament. Both 2 Timothy and Titus, like Paul's authentic letters, include second- and third-person greetings as well as references to travel plans prior to the final blessing. These omissions serve only to reinforce the focus of this letter on the singular responsibility of Timothy, the community leader, to overcome opposition by adhering to sound doctrine in promoting the internal life of the community as well as in securing its good reputation in the surrounding world. The blessing itself, "grace be with all of you," is identical to that found at the end of 2 Timothy. Titus and most of Paul's letters have longer blessings, but all, except Romans, use the identical words found in 1 Timothy. In all these letters, including Philemon, the blessing is addressed to "you" in the plural, an indication that even those letters addressed to individuals were intended to be heard by the larger community.

The Second Letter to Timothy

Terence J. Keegan, O.P.

INTRODUCTION

Of the three Pastoral Letters, 2 Timothy contains by far the greatest amount of biographical material about Paul. Most agree that it contains material dating from Paul, and some feel that it was written by Paul himself. It was probably the first of the Pastoral Letters to be written, possibly by someone other than the author of 1 Timothy and Titus. One of the most noticeable differences between 2 Timothy and the other Pastoral Letters is the large number of references to persons and places, but there are other, more significant differences. Unlike these other letters, 2 Timothy has no codes of behavior for community members, no discussion of qualifications for various ministries, and no element of anti-Jewish polemic.

2 Timothy is essentially a reflection on the ministry of Paul and on how that ministry is to be continued after his death. Timothy is the person closely associated with Paul's ministry and has become his designated successor. The two focuses of this letter, Paul and Timothy, highlight the succession of the latter in the ministry of the former. Though there is mention of Timothy's responsibility to instruct others who will in turn become teachers (2:2), the letter is mainly concerned with Timothy's own vocation and ministry. Fidelity to his vocation demands that he follow the sound teaching he learned from Paul. Timothy is to be loyal to his faith and not ashamed of bearing witness either to the Lord or to Paul. The letter's emphasis on suffering contrasts with the goal in 1 Timothy and Titus of leading quiet and peaceable lives in society.

In 2 Timothy Paul is presented as imprisoned and in chains, deserted by others because of the shame brought on by his chains. Paul is nonetheless confident of the salvific effects of his prolonged imprisonment and proclaims Christ as sovereign judge over all. Paul's fearlessness in the face of evil is the basis of the advice to Timothy to protect his community from the impact of false teaching (2:14–3:9) without fearing the personal attacks that may result (3:10-12). Paul is presented as the model for Timothy in both word (1:13; 2:2; 3:14) and deed (3:10-11). There is no suggestion, however, that Timothy should be a model, as in the other Pastoral Letters, where Timothy and Titus are to serve as models for the communities they lead (see 1 Tim 4:12-15; Titus 2:7-8). The advice in 2 Timothy focuses primarily on Timothy. Not only are there no specific directions concerning the community, but there is no indication of where Timothy is presumably located. While 1:18 might be read as a hint that the community he is leading is Ephesus, 4:12 indicates that although he may once have been there, he no longer is.

While 1 Timothy and Titus are concerned with the organization of the church in the post-Pauline era and were probably written later than 2 Timothy, both presume that Paul is still active and free to travel. Since 2 Timothy is chronologically located near the end of Paul's life, its position after 1 Timothy seems natural. This letter reads like Paul's last will and testament, containing the parting advice of one convinced that his present imprisonment will end with his death. While addressed to Timothy, it speaks powerfully to a modern culture that needs to regain its focus on the value of loyalty, fidelity, and suffering for the sake of the gospel.

COMMENTARY

1:1-2 The opening

The letter opens, as is typical of Hellenistic letters, with the identification of both the sender and the receiver, followed by a greeting. The sender, Paul, is identified as "an apostle of Christ Jesus by the will of God for the promise of life in Christ Jesus." The first part, "an apostle of Christ Jesus by the will of God," is identical to the identification at 2 Corinthians 1:1 (cf. 1 Cor 1:1). This identification echoes Paul's conviction that the will of God determined the shape of his life and his work as an apostle. The identification in this letter, however, continues by focusing on "the promise of life" as the purpose of Paul's apostolate. The phrase "promise of life" is an expression used only in the Pastoral Letters (cf. 1 Tim 4:8). God has promised and guarantees the gift of eternal life. Just as the hope of eternal life motivated the apostolate of Paul, this hope should motivate Timothy and the readers of this letter.

Timothy, the receiver of the letter, is identified as "my dear child." In 1 Timothy he is called "my true child in faith" (1 Tim 1:2), similar to what Titus is called, "my true child in our common faith" (Titus 1:4). "True child" suits the purpose of these letters as mandates to Timothy and Titus to minister in Paul's name. "Dear child" in 2 Timothy uses the language denoting deep friendship that Paul had used of Timothy (1 Cor 4:17). Its use in

2 Timothy suits the purpose of the letter as a reflection on Paul's ministry in the context of a personal farewell and a designation of Timothy as the legitimate and faithful heir who will carry on the Pauline legacy. The opening concludes with the greeting typical of all Paul's letters, but with the addition of "mercy" to the typical Pauline "grace and peace." Both 1 and 2 Timothy add this word to the greeting, but not Titus.

1:3-5 Thanksgiving

Pauline letters typically have a passage immediately after the opening in which Paul gives thanks to God for what God has done for the community or person to whom the letter is addressed. These thanksgivings also serve to summarize the main themes of the letter. 2 Timothy, alone among the Pastoral Letters, has this characteristic Pauline thanksgiving. While 1 Timothy has a kind of belated thanksgiving (1 Tim 1:12-17), it is different in form and function from the typical Pauline thanksgiving. The thanksgiving in 2 Timothy is more typical, although the words used, *echō charin* (cf. 1 Tim 1:12), are different from the Pauline *eucharistō* (Rom 1:8; 1 Cor 1:4; Phil 1:3; 1 Thess 1:2; Phlm 4).

This thanksgiving stresses the double focus of the letter, Paul and Timothy, by thanking God for Timothy's faith (1:5) and expressing Paul's desire to see Timothy once more (1:4). Paul's desire to see Timothy actually frames and colors the entire letter. In the final chapter Timothy is urged to come quickly and to bring Mark (4:9, 11, 21). Timothy, the other focus of the letter, is presented as one in whom the true faith lives on, though the emphasis on faith and the desire for the visit suggests that Timothy's faith may have been a matter of concern.

TIMOTHY'S VOCATION AND PAUL'S SUFFERING

2 Tim 1:6-18

1:6-14 Pauline model of vocation

The dual focus of this letter is evident in the sequencing of four exhortations to Timothy to carry on Paul's ministry (1:6-14; 2:1-7; 2:14-26; 3:10-17). These exhortations are separated by doctrinal material and sections dealing with Paul's life and imminent departure. This first exhortation deals with Timothy's vocation, which flows from and is modeled on Paul's. An interesting feature of this exhortation is the frequent use of the first person plural pronoun. Paul and Timothy are viewed together, especially in the center of this chiastically arranged exhortation (1:9-10) as saved and called to their vocations by the saving grace of Christ's death and resurrection.

2 Timothy 1

The exhortation begins and ends by speaking of their common vocation as based on the gift of the Spirit, a gift that is transmitted from Paul to Timothy (1:6-7, 13-14). Just before the center Paul encourages Timothy to bear the hardships of his ministry, not being ashamed either of his testimony to his crucified Lord or of Paul, now a chained prisoner (1:8). Right after the center Paul notes how he has suffered for his ministry, not being ashamed either of his sufferings or of his Lord (1:11-12). In 2 Timothy and in the undisputed letters, but not in 1 Timothy or Titus, suffering is integral to Paul's self-understanding (Rom 8:35-39; 1 Cor 4:9-13; 2 Cor 4:7-11; Gal 6:14-17; Phil 3:8-11; 1 Thess 2:2).

The exhortation opens with a reference to the transmission of office from Paul to Timothy "through the imposition of my hands" (1:6), a transmission that involved the gift of the Spirit. The term used here, *charisma,* was coined by Paul to distinguish real gifts of the Spirit from ecstatic phenomena, *pneumatika* (see 1 Cor 12:1, 4). It is a term used in the New Testament only in the letters of Paul and in the literature dependent on him, a term that highlights the gratuitous nature of the gifts and points to their ecclesial function. Everywhere in Paul and in the Pastoral Letters the gift of the Spirit is for building up the church as the body of Christ.

A similar passage in 1 Timothy speaks of Timothy's gift being conferred through the imposition of hands of the presbyterate (1 Tim 4:14). In 2 Timothy it is Paul alone who imposes hands. Both passages refer to the practice attested to elsewhere in the New Testament and the early church of using the imposition of hands for the transference of power, the appointment to office, and the conferral of the gift of the Spirit.

The differences between the passages illustrate the differences between these two letters. 1 Timothy is concerned with the community as a whole and shows Timothy being brought into the ministry by a group of elders to share in their responsibility for leading an orderly Christian community. 2 Timothy is concerned with the specific role of the departing Paul in designating Timothy as his successor, who, like him, will be expected to accept his share of hardship for the gospel. The advice in verse 8 flows from the previous verses. Because of the strength that comes from God's gift of the Spirit transmitted by Paul, Timothy can endure the hardships involved in testifying to the Lord, not being ashamed either of the Lord or of Paul.

The hymn-like central section of this exhortation (1:9-10) attributes three qualities to God's saving purpose. First, it is gratuitous. Like Paul in the letter to the Romans, this letter establishes a clear contrast between human works and divine grace. Second, it is accomplished in Christ Jesus, and third, the initiative derives from all eternity. Even though this salvation was made manifest in the saving work of Jesus Christ, it was willed by God from all eternity. This brief passage is an interesting condensation of the theology, Christology, and eschatology of the Pastoral Letters. The one God establishes his purpose for salvation from all eternity. That salvation is made manifest by Christ's "appearance," which here refers to the past appearance of the Savior Christ Jesus, who destroyed death and brought life and immortality. Later in the letter the eschatological picture will be completed when the same term "appearance" is used to refer to a future appearance of Christ Jesus, who is to judge the living and the dead (4:8; cf. 1 Tim 6:14; Titus 2:13). Christian life, for the Pastoral Letters, lies between these two appearances of Christ Jesus.

This life is now available through the gospel for which Paul "was appointed preacher and apostle and teacher" (1:11). As he hands on his ministry to Timothy, Paul expresses confidence that Christ Jesus is able to guard what has been entrusted to Paul "until that day" (1:12), a clear reference to the final day when Christ will be revealed as God's eschatological agent (cf. 1:18; 4:8). The exhortation concludes with the mandate to Timothy to "guard this rich trust with the help of the holy Spirit" (1:14). The confidence that Christ will guard this trust between his two appearances is based on the belief that Timothy and those who follow him will be aided by the holy Spirit in transmitting the true gospel of Jesus Christ. Here 2 Timothy expresses the distinctively Pauline idea of the indwelling of the holy Spirit (1 Cor 3:16; 6:19) more clearly than do the isolated references to the Spirit in the other Pastoral Letters (1 Tim 4:1; Titus 3:5).

1:15-18 False and faithful friends

This passage is the first of several biographical passages in this letter. Together with the last such passage, 4:16-18, it speaks of Paul's being without human contact, a lonely prisoner about to die. These two passages, just after the beginning and just before the end, share in the framing function of the appeals for Timothy to visit Paul (1:4; 4:9, 11, 21) and help define the letter as a testamentary farewell. The mention of Onesiphorus in both passages contributes to their framing function. Ephesus (1:18) in Asia (1:15) was where Paul exercised much of his apostolate and where he left a thriving Christian community. Ephesus was also where almost everyone abandoned him on his arrest. Now in Rome he draws on this experience to encourage Timothy, who once was in Ephesus but probably no longer is there (see 4:12). Onesiphorus, who alone was not ashamed of Paul's chains, can serve as a model for Timothy not to be ashamed either of Paul or of his "testimony to our Lord" (1:8).

This passage contains two prayers for mercy—one for the family of Onesiphorus (1:16), the other for Onesiphorus himself (1:18). These prayers for mercy recall the note in Philippians that God had shown mercy to Epaphroditus because of his service to Paul (Phil 2:25-27). They also relate to the addition of "mercy" to the greeting at 1:2. The first prayer was for mercy in the present, but the second is for mercy in the eschatological future, "that day," which Paul had spoken about in reference to himself (1:12). The second prayer might imply that Onesiphorus is already dead, in which case it would be one of the earliest examples of Christian prayer for the dead.

EXHORTATION TO BE STRONG AND ENDURE SUFFERING

2 Tim 2:1-13

2:1-7 The hardships of faithful ministry

Like the first exhortation, this second exhortation begins and ends with a reference to what the Lord has given to Timothy (1:6, 14; 2:1, 7). However, while the first exhortation focused on the gift of God through the holy Spirit, this exhortation emphasizes the task that has been entrusted to Timothy. Timothy, with "the grace that is in Christ Jesus" (2:1), is to entrust to others what he has learned from Paul. These others, in turn, will be able to continue the chain of faithful transmission.

Significantly, 2 Timothy uses a technical term for "entrust" that in ancient times was used to refer to some kind of treasure, such as a valuable item or a sacred story, that was entrusted to another. This sacred trust, the gospel of salvation, is referred to three times in this letter as that with which Paul has been entrusted (1:12), that which Timothy is to guard with the help of the holy Spirit (1:14), and finally that which Timothy is to hand on to others who will continue its transmission (2:2). This term is used only once in the other Pastoral Letters, in the conclusion to 1 Timothy, where Timothy is urged to "guard what has been entrusted to you" (1 Tim 6:20).

These other letters use different language to speak of that with which Paul has been entrusted (1 Tim 1:11; Titus 1:3) and what Paul entrusts to Timothy (1 Tim 1:18), but they never speak of Timothy or Titus entrusting it to others. While Titus is to appoint leaders for orderly community life (Titus 1:5), the transmission of Paul's gospel to future evangelists is a concern only of 2 Timothy. Timothy is not alone in passing on Paul's teaching. There were "many witnesses" (2:2), but clearly not all of them remained faithful witnesses. Timothy's task is to establish a chain of transmission involving faithful witnesses, a task that will involve hardships like those Paul is enduring (cf. 1:12).

The hardships to be endured are compared to the hard work associated with soldiers, athletes, and farmers. Athletes compete to achieve "the winner's crown" (2:5). If Timothy bears the hardships of his ministry "like a good soldier of Christ Jesus" (2:3), he is assured that the Lord will give him the understanding needed to fulfill the task of faithful transmission (2:7). While 1 Timothy uses the athletic image in discussing training for devotion (1 Tim 4:7-8) and metaphors of competition (1 Tim 1:18; 6:12), neither 1 Timothy nor Titus suggests that Christian life will involve suffering. In both these letters advice is given to be under the control of authorities (Titus 3:1) and to pray for kings that "we may lead a quiet and tranquil life" (1 Tim 2:2). 2 Timothy alone among the Pastorals links fidelity to the gospel to a life that will involve hardship and suffering. Here Paul's suffering is presented as the model for Timothy (2:3, 8-9; cf. 3:12).

2:8-13 The gospel and its reward

The letter next identifies the message to be transmitted: the gospel for which Paul is suffering, "Jesus Christ, raised from the dead, a descendant of David" (2:8). Being introduced with "remember," these words are clearly an early creedal formulation that uses terminology employed in Paul's letters. "Raised from the dead" is language Paul commonly uses to refer to the resurrection. In Romans 1:3 Paul uses the phrase "descended from David" to identify Jesus as the Messiah, the expected ideal king of Israel. These expressions are not used elsewhere in the Pastoral Letters. They are used here to recall the traditional faith of the church with which Timothy has been entrusted. Paul is suffering in chains for these words, but the words are not chained. Timothy's task is to continue the transmission of these words so that others may "obtain the salvation that is in Christ Jesus."

This passage concludes with another selection of traditional material, probably a section of a hymn, assuring Timothy and the readers of the letter that fidelity with Christ means victory with the Lord (2:11-13). It is introduced by "this saying is trustworthy," a phrase regularly used in the Pastoral Letters to introduce a basic truth of early Christian faith (1 Tim 1:15; 3:1; 4:9; Titus 3:8). The four-line selection opens with the Pauline notion that Christian life can be spoken of as dying with Christ (cf. Rom 6:3; Gal 2:19-20). The four lines from this hymn have a recurring pattern that would lead one to expect the final phrase to be "he will be unfaithful." Surprisingly, it is instead "he remains faithful, / for he cannot deny himself" (2:13).

2 Timothy 2

Paul often affirms the absolute fidelity of God (see 1 Cor 1:9). Here the absolute fidelity of God is attributed to Christ Jesus. This section, whose purpose is to exhort Timothy to be strong and endure hardships for the gospel, concludes with an assurance of the absolute fidelity of Christ. While the immediate concern of this passage is with the responsibilities of a first-century evangelist, its message applies equally well to people living out their Christian vocation in any way in any age. Jesus, the Savior and Judge, remains true to his people regardless of how faithful they may or may not be.

DANGER OF FALSE TEACHING

2 Tim 2:14–3:9

2:14-26 Dealing with false teachers

The first exhortation to Timothy focused on the gift of God through the holy Spirit (1:6-14), and the second on the task entrusted to Timothy (2:1-7). This third exhortation deals with how he is to fulfill the charge to entrust to faithful people what he has heard from Paul in light of the ever-present danger of false teaching. The danger arises because people dispute about words (2:14), quarrel because of foolish and ignorant debates (2:23), and become more and more godless as a result of profane and idle talk (2:16).

Paul's advice to Timothy for dealing with this problem is twofold. First, he must be pure in himself. "Turn from youthful desires and pursue righteousness, faith, love, and peace, along with those who call on the Lord with purity of heart" (2:22). If he can present himself "as acceptable to God, a workman who causes no disgrace" (2:15), he will be able to impart "the word of truth without deviation" (2:15). Second, he must himself "avoid foolish and ignorant debates" (2:23) and then be able to charge others to stop engaging in useless disputes.

The basis for this advice is found in the center of this passage, where Old Testament texts are cited as "God's solid foundation" (2:19). "The Lord knows those who are his" is quoted from Numbers 16:5, where it dealt with a revolt against Moses. God will protect and empower those who are doing his work, not the false teachers. The second quote is even more important. "Let everyone who calls upon the name of the Lord avoid evil" (2:19) is a combination of allusions to Isaiah 26:13 and Sirach 17:21. God calls whom he wills, but humans must accept the call by themselves calling "on the Lord with purity of heart" (2:22) and avoiding the kind of behavior that is harmful to the gospel. The next chapter has the familiar verse on the inspiration and usefulness of Scripture (3:16-17), but the passage in 2:19 is the only Old Testament passage actually cited in this letter. The following two verses (2:20-21) clearly anticipate the passage in 3:16-17. Timothy and others entrusted with Paul's gospel are compared to various kinds of vessels that, when cleansed, become vessels "for lofty use, dedicated, beneficial to the master of the house, ready for every good work" (2:21).

The next verse encapsulates an aspect of this letter that has timeless significance for Christians—the essential link between Christian faith and the life of virtue. Timothy and all Christians can and should lead lives of exemplary virtue precisely because they have called "on the Lord with purity of heart" (2:22). For Christians, their pattern of behavior is an expression of their deepest convictions.

While this exhortation is primarily concerned with Timothy and others entrusted with Paul's gospel, it does shed some light on the false teachers. Just before the center of this passage, two of them, Hymenaeus and Philetus, are identified, as well as their false teaching "that [the] resurrection has already taken place" (2:18). While specific moral issues appear elsewhere (see 1 Tim 4:3), this is the only precise false doctrine identified in any of the Pastoral Letters. Hymenaeus and Alexander (cf. 4:14) were identified as enemies of Paul in 1 Timothy 1:20, although their errors were not mentioned there.

Paul had taught that in baptism we die and rise with Christ (Rom 6:8; cf. 2 Cor 6:14-15). Some in Corinth had distorted Paul's teaching by denying the future resurrection of the dead (1 Cor 15:12), probably maintaining what was being taught by Hymenaeus and Philetus, that is, that Christians already enjoyed the fullness of resurrected life. Paul, as well as the Pastoral Letters, clearly teaches that although we have died with Christ and now live with him, there will be a future resurrection when all will be judged on the life they have led (Rom 14:10, 12; 1 Tim 6:12-16; 2 Tim 4:1, 8).

The exhortation concludes with advice on dealing with false teachers, correcting them with kindness so that "they may return to their senses out of the devil's snare" (2:26), advice that sounds less harsh than what Paul is said to have done in 1 Timothy, handing them "over to Satan to be taught not to blaspheme" (1 Tim 1:20; cf. Titus 3:10-11).

3:1-9 False teaching in the last days

In the previous exhortation Timothy was urged to "pursue righteousness, faith, love, and peace, along with those who call on the Lord with purity of heart" (2:22), in contrast to false teachers who taught that the resurrection had already occurred. Here the contrast is intensified by advancing the context to the last days (cf. 1 Tim 4:1-5). The last days are distinguished from "that day" (1:18; 4:8), the day when the Lord will appear

2 Timothy 3

as just judge. The last days precede "that day." They will be dangerous times; the church will be beset by people who will harm the faithful with cruelty, violence, and aggressiveness. Here, as elsewhere in the Pastoral Letters, false teaching leads to base morality, just as good teaching leads to good morality. False teaching can be easily recognized as such by the results it produces.

The virtue of religion/devotion, prominently treated in 1 Timothy (1 Tim 2:2; 3:16; 4:7, 8; 6:3, 5, 6, 11), is here mentioned in terms of its false understanding: "they make a pretense of religion but deny its power" (3:5). In 1 Timothy it was observed that some think religion can be a source of material gain. These are people who fall into erroneous beliefs and end up experiencing a host of vices: "envy, rivalry, insults, evil suspicions, and mutual friction" (1 Tim 6:4-5). In 2 Timothy the list is longer and the evils more intense (3:2-4).

The danger posed by false teachers is further illustrated by the evil influence they are able to exert on impressionable women. These women, eager to learn but lacking the erudition to distinguish true from false teaching, are led by their passions to accept appealing but perverse teachings (3:6-7). All three Pastoral Letters seem to accept the widespread belief at that time that women were notoriously unable to control their sexual passions (1 Tim 5:11-15; Titus 2:4-5). The false teachers who impress women are compared to the Egyptian magicians who were clever enough to impress Pharaoh but opposed the truth that came from God (3:8-9). They turned their staffs into snakes, as had Aaron, but Aaron's staff swallowed their staffs (Exod 7:11-12).

PAUL'S EXAMPLE AND TIMOTHY'S COMMISSION
2 Tim 3:10–4:8

3:10-17 Imitation of Paul and the role of Scripture

The previous description of intensified evil in the end times sets the stage for this fourth and final exhortation to Timothy. With the approach of the end times, wicked people will become even more so (3:13) and good people will be persecuted (3:12). Interestingly, the term used to describe the good people who will be persecuted is the same term, "religion/devotion," which in 1 Timothy and Titus is that all-important virtue that will secure respect for the Christian community in the surrounding world.

Timothy is reminded about what he knows of Paul and is encouraged to remain faithful in following him (3:14). Timothy is reminded of nine important aspects of Paul's heritage that he is to follow (3:10-11). First among these is his teaching, the subject of much of this letter (1:13-14; 2:2, 8-9). Timothy is also aware of Paul's way of life and purpose. Timothy is aware as well of the six qualities that characterized Paul's life: the Christian virtues of faith, patience, love, and endurance (3:10), which were the basis of his teaching, life, and purpose, and the persecutions and suffering (3:11) that were the inevitable result. Just as Paul had responded to God's call to work as an apostle, so too should Timothy. In the Acts of the Apostles Paul is said to have visited the three cities mentioned here—Antioch, Iconium, and Lystra (Acts 13:1–14:23)—and to have commented, "It is necessary for us to undergo many hardships to enter the kingdom of God" (Acts 14:22). It is interesting to note that Timothy came from one of these cities, Lystra, born of a Jewish mother who became a believer, and a Greek father (Acts 16:1).

Timothy's faith, a faith that he received from his mother and grandmother, was mentioned in the first chapter (1:5). Presumably it was from them that he first learned the Sacred Scriptures, the Scriptures of Judaism. It was clearly from Paul, however, that Timothy learned how the Sacred Scriptures could give "wisdom for salvation through faith in Christ Jesus" (3:15). How Timothy is to use the Sacred Scriptures is spelled out in the final two verses, beginning with the observation that "all scripture is inspired by God" (3:16). The more than one hundred citations of these verses in the writings of the patristic period show that they were generally understood to mean that each and every part of Scripture comes from God. At the same time, however, these writings emphasize the usefulness of Scripture far more than its inspiration and the variety of interpretive techniques used by the Fathers indicates that they had a far broader understanding of inspiration than the narrow literalism of contemporary fundamentalism.

Timothy is instructed to use the Scriptures, as Paul had, creatively guided by the Spirit, to fulfill the ministry with which he has been charged thus far in this letter. He is to use the Scriptures in teaching the sound doctrine he has received from Paul, handing it on to other faithful ministers (2:2). He is to use the Scriptures to refute the false teachers who have already become active (2:14) and whose activity will intensify in the final days (3:5). He is to use the Scriptures to correct his "opponents with kindness" when it is possible to lead them "to knowledge of the truth" (2:25). Finally, he is to use the Scriptures for training in righteousness. In order to accomplish his ministry, Timothy must himself be pure (2:22). He will then belong to God, be able to impart "the word of truth without deviation" (2:15), "be competent, equipped for every good work" (3:16; cf. 2:21).

2 Timothy 4

4:1-8 Timothy's solemn commission

After the preceding sequence of instructions and exhortations, the main body of the letter comes to a close with a solemn commissioning in which Paul hands over his ministry to Timothy. The solemnity of the commissioning is emphasized by the charge being given "in the presence of God and of Christ Jesus" (4:1; cf. 1 Tim 5:21). This commissioning begins and ends with a reference to the final appearance of Christ Jesus as judge (4:1, 8), providing an eschatological context for the seriousness of Timothy's ministry.

Here, as earlier in the letter, the end time, "that day," is distinguished from the "last days," the dangerous times for which Timothy is now being prepared. These are the times, mentioned earlier, when "people will not tolerate sound doctrine . . . will accumulate teachers . . . and will be diverted to myths" (4:3-4; cf. 2:18; 3:6-7). Sound doctrine is a major concern throughout the Pastoral Letters, but its meaning varies. In 2 Timothy it is the words of Paul that serve as the basis for the missionary activity charged to Timothy and others (1:13; 4:3). In 1 Timothy and Titus, sound doctrine has become the moral content of Paul's gospel, involving both accuracy in teaching and the proper morality to which it leads (1 Tim 1:10; 4:6; 6:3; Titus 1:9, 13; 2:1, 2, 8).

The solemn commissioning begins with the charge "proclaim the word" (4:2). The ministry of the word is a ministry without which a Christian community cannot exist. In Acts, Paul's ministry is summarized as "preach[ing] the kingdom" (Acts 20:25; 28:31). Except for Philemon, Paul wrote about his preaching in all his letters, most eloquently in Romans 10:14-15. The charge continues with four more imperatives, all of which entail Timothy's emulating Paul and carrying on his ministry.

After a digression in which Timothy is warned about the threat of people succumbing to false teachers in the times to come (4:3-4), there is another series of four imperatives exhorting Timothy to follow Paul's example. These imperatives are introduced by "but you" (4:5), contrasting what is expected of Timothy with the expected failures of others. Timothy is to be "self-possessed in all circumstances" (4:5), a quality expected of a bishop in 1 Timothy (1 Tim 3:2). He is to "put up with hardship" (4:5), just as he had known Paul to endure persecutions and suffering (3:11). According to 1 Timothy, Christ Jesus had appointed Paul to the ministry (1 Tim 1:12). Now that Paul is about to depart, it is Timothy's turn to "perform the work of an evangelist" (4:5), a dominant theme in 2 Timothy that is all but absent in 1 Timothy and Titus. The final imperative sums up all those that have gone before and sums up the entire message of this letter: "fulfill your ministry" (4:5).

The message of this letter is clearly intended for all Christians of all times. The challenge to Timothy to fulfill his ministry challenges all Christians to consider the demands of their Christian vocations. For him as for all, fulfilling one's ministry involves fidelity much more than success. It involves being willing to suffer for the gospel, recognizing that the reward for fidelity is sharing in the life of the resurrection. Timothy is not urged to settle into a secure and comfortable life; rather, he and all are urged to witness, in word and deed, to the truth that is Christ in the midst of a world that prefers to follow its own desires (4:3).

The final three verses complete this final exhortation by providing the reason for the exhortation and for the letter: Paul is about to die (4:6). Just as Paul used the metaphor of athletic competition (2:5) when he urged Timothy to "bear your share of hardship" (2:3), he here applies the athletic metaphor to himself (4:7). Paul has competed well. He has kept the faith, both in the sense that he has been faithful in his office as preacher and teacher and also in the sense that he has carefully handed on the gospel and its solid doctrine to his successor. Interestingly, denial of belief in a future resurrection was the only doctrinal matter explicitly attributed to the false teachers (2:18). This autobiographical reflection fittingly ends by affirming Paul's expectation of his vindication in the future resurrection of the dead for himself as well as for all who long for the Lord's appearance (4:8).

PERSONAL POSTSCRIPT

2 Tim 4:9-18

After the conclusion of the main body of the letter, Timothy is urged four times to visit Paul (4:9, 11, 13, 21). The alleged reason is Paul's loneliness in the final days of his imprisonment before his impending death. The appeal in this section of the letter, however, provides additional biographical information about Paul, information that further supports the overall purpose of the present letter. An overarching concern of the letter is that Paul's legacy be continued (1:6; 4:1-2).

The geographical places named in this section provide a summary of the areas evangelized by Paul that now are to be cared for by his successors. Most of the persons named are associates of Paul who will be responsible for carrying on his ministry in these various regions. It is not known where Timothy presently is, but he must be somewhere other than Ephesus, otherwise he would already know that Tychicus (Titus 3:12) had been sent there (4:12).

Two of those named are cast in a negative light in ways that are significant for the letter as a whole. Demas, who was "enamored of the present world" (4:10), deserted Paul. In Acts, Demas was once a companion of Paul (Col 4:14; Phlm 24), but in the apocryphal Acts of Paul he is said to have rejected Paul's teaching on the future resurrection, saying that "it has already taken place in the children whom we have, and that we are risen again in that we have come to know the true God" (Acts of Paul 3:14). This false teaching is what led Demas to be enamored of the present world and to have deserted Paul, who is in prison and about to die. The whole thrust of 2 Timothy is toward the future resurrection which motivates the steadfastness in ministry and endurance of hardships that Paul exemplifies and which he encourages in his successors.

The other person treated negatively is Alexander the coppersmith (4:14). Just as Paul expects the Lord, the just judge, to award the crown of righteousness to himself and to "all who have longed for his appearance" (4:8), others, like Alexander, will be repaid according to their deeds. He is probably the same Alexander mentioned in 1 Timothy as an opponent of Paul (1 Tim 1:20). He is here described as having "resisted our preaching" (4:14). Timothy is warned to be on guard against him as he takes on responsibility for the ministry of preaching.

An interesting feature of this passage is Paul's request that Timothy bring the cloak, papyrus rolls, and parchments from Troas (4:13). The importance of the Scriptures for Timothy's ministry has already been noted (3:14-17). The cloak may be related to Elisha's succession to Elijah, which was symbolized by the assumption of his mantle (2 Kgs 2:11-14). Paul's request for his cloak and Scriptures might indicate his desire to transfer to Timothy the symbols of his ministry.

As this section draws to a close, Paul recalls his earlier trial, when everyone deserted him. He was lonely then as he is now, but then as now his strength was from the Lord. It is in this strength that he is able to say "may it not be held against them" (4:16), recalling the words of Jesus on the cross (Luke 23:34). In that earlier trial the Lord had rescued Paul (4:17), just as the Lord had rescued him in previous difficulties (3:11). This time he expects to die, but he can use the same language to describe what is to come: "the Lord will rescue me from every evil threat and will bring me safe to his heavenly kingdom" (4:18). The doxology concluding this section, like the doxologies in 1 Timothy (1 Tim 1:17; 6:15-16), contains the four elements of the classic New Testament doxology: the object of praise, "to him"; an expression of praise, "be glory"; an indication of time, "forever and ever"; and a confirmatory response, "Amen" (4:18).

THE CLOSING

2 Tim 4:19-22

As is typical in New Testament letters, the conclusion of this letter begins with a series of greetings, naming both those to be greeted, "Prisca and Aquila and the family of Onesiphorus" (4:19), as well as those in Rome sending greetings, "Eubulus, Pudens, Linus, Claudia, and all the brothers" (4:21). The closing greeting is interrupted by additional personal and place names, continuing the thoughts expressed in 4:9-13 and adding a final plea for Timothy to come to Rome (4:20-21). Prisca and Aquila were frequent coworkers with Paul (Acts 18:2; Rom 16:3; 1 Cor 16:19). Onesiphorus had served Paul both in Ephesus and Rome (1:16-18). However, none of the four sending greetings from Rome appear elsewhere in the New Testament, and their mention here is surprising, since, according to 4:11, only Luke was with Paul in his imprisonment, and Paul is pleading for Timothy to join him. Possibly they are Christians in Rome who, while not ministering to Paul in prison, will provide leadership to the Roman community after his death. Linus appears in early church traditions as the successor to Peter as leader of the church in Rome.

The letter ends with a blessing, as do all Paul's letters. Unlike the blessings at the end of 1 Timothy and Titus, this blessing is in two parts. "The Lord be with your spirit" (4:22) is in the singular, addressing Timothy, the recipient of this letter, and emphasizing the intensely personal nature of this letter. "Grace be with you all" (4:22), the blessing found at the end of 1 Timothy, is in the plural. Only these stylized closing words interrupt the letter's consistent focus on Timothy as an individual. Nevertheless, they indicate that this highly personal letter, addressed to Paul's designated successor, is intended to be read by a larger community.

The Letter to Titus

Terence J. Keegan, O.P.

INTRODUCTION

The letter to Titus is similar to 1 Timothy in content and purpose. While it is addressed to a different person, Titus, who has responsibility for a different community, Crete, it is concerned, like 1 Timothy, with pastoring the communities in the post-Pauline era. Like 1 Timothy, but unlike 2 Timothy, it provides qualifications for community leaders, codes for members of the community, and directives on ensuring that the community maintain a good reputation in the surrounding secular world. Its similarity to 1 Timothy in both language and content indicates some kind of relationship between these two letters. They may have been written by the same person or, at the very least, one was influenced by the other.

While Titus and 1 Timothy are quite similar in content and purpose, Titus addresses a situation less developed and complex than that addressed in 1 Timothy. Unlike the situation in 1 Timothy, where bishops/ presbyters and deacons were already in place, in this letter Titus is charged to appoint the bishops/presbyters for the communities on Crete, a place, according to Acts, that Paul had stopped at only briefly as a prisoner on his way to Rome (Acts 27:7-15). This letter deals with a newly founded form of Christianity, unlike the situation in 1 Timothy, where it could be said that a bishop should not be a recent convert (1 Tim 3:6).

While the opponents referred to in 1 Timothy included some with Judaizing tendencies, that is, Jewish Christians who believed that Gentile converts should be made to observe Jewish religious laws and customs, in Titus the treatment of opponents is almost entirely focused on those with Judaizing tendencies (1:10, 14; 3:5, 9). The more clearly delineated threat of opponents is also more decisively dealt with. The letter to Titus links the reason for appointing leaders to the threat of Judaizing false teachers. But because the opponents threaten the good order of the community, greater emphasis is placed on behavior within the community than on the responsibilities of the newly appointed leaders. Church structures in Titus are fewer and simpler than those described in 1 Timothy, but Titus is richer in theological elaboration and the household codes are more fully developed. In this theological elaboration, Titus provides an explanation for the basis of Christian behavior, namely, the gift of God given in Christ through the power of the holy Spirit.

While Titus is the shortest of the Pastoral Letters, its opening is by far the longest. In fact, apart from that found in Romans (Rom 1:1-6), Titus's description of the sender (1:1-3) is the longest of any New Testament letter. Furthermore, this description of Paul, the sender, contains the most comprehensive description of the apostolate in the New Testament. For this reason, some suggest that Titus may have preceded 1 Timothy, introducing Paul and his apostolate and explaining how that apostolate is to be carried on by others in a particular local church setting. The present order of the Pastoral Letters in the New Testament is due to the ordering principle used at the time the scrolls of the various books were gathered together and bound into a single volume. At that time the supposed Pauline corpus was organized with the letters to churches preceding letters to individuals, and letters within these two groups organized according to length. Hence Titus was placed between 2 Timothy and Philemon.

COMMENTARY

1:1-4 The opening

Like most ancient letters, this letter begins with an identification of the sender and the recipient followed by a short greeting. This letter begins by identifying its sender, "Paul"; his position, "a slave of God and apostle of Christ Jesus"; and the purpose of his apostolate (1:1-3). The purpose of Paul's apostolate here, as elsewhere, involves faith in Jesus Christ. This letter and 1 Timothy, however, are concerned not only with faith but with the proper appreciation of that faith, that is, "religious truth" (1:1), which involves both correct belief and appropriate behavior. The term used here for "religious," elsewhere translated as "devoutly" (2:12), is the word used in the Roman world for reverence for the gods and respect for traditional values and practices. This much esteemed virtue receives little notice in the rest of the New Treatment but is important in Titus and especially in 1 Timothy (1 Tim 2:2; 3:16; 4:7, 8; 6:3, 5, 6, 11).

An important element in that correct belief and the motivation for appropriate behavior is the hope for a future resurrection. The letter's restrained eschatology (1:2; 2:13; 3:7) implies that the letter was written for a Christian community that no longer lived in imminent expectation of the parousia. In its more settled state, the community needed proper instruction in the fine points of Christian faith. The "hope of eternal life that God, who does not lie, promised before time began" (1:2) is what is proclaimed in the word with which Paul has been entrusted. God our savior, "who wills everyone to be saved and to come to knowledge of the truth" (1 Tim 2:4), has entrusted this proclamation to Paul. As God's slave (1:1), Paul is bound—to fulfill his appointed task. That task involves the salvation of God's people.

The recipient is identified as "Titus, my true child in our common faith." This expression illustrates an understanding of the church as a genuinely new family that needs to be nurtured and protected as it grows and matures, as well as designating Titus as the legitimate representative authorized to minister in Paul's name. The greeting begins with the typical Pauline greeting, "grace and peace" but continues with "from God the Father and Christ Jesus our savior" (1:4).

THE NEED FOR CAPABLE, AUTHORIZED LEADERSHIP

Titus 1:5-16

1:5-9 Appointment of presbyters/bishops

Omitting the thanksgiving that is common at this point in letters (cf. 2 Tim 1:3-5), the letter identifies its purpose as charging Titus with the good order of the church at Crete. Titus's charge is twofold: to "set right what remains to be done" and to "appoint presbyters in every town" (1:5). This section dealing with "presbyters" (1:5) and a "bishop" (1:7) is the only section in the entire letter dealing with church leaders. Unlike 1 Timothy, this letter says nothing about deacons (cf. 1 Tim 3:8-13) or widows (cf. 1 Tim 5:3-10). In Titus the presbyters and bishops are clearly identical. The presbyter appointed in each town (1:5) is the bishop of that town. The term "presbyter" refers to the person's status within the community, a respected member of the community, while the term "bishop" refers to his function, exercising oversight and leadership in the community.

The list of qualifications for the presbyter/bishop in 1:6-8 is almost identical to the list of qualifications for the bishop in 1 Timothy 3:2-4. For 1 Timothy and Titus, he must be an effective leader whose personal character is a credit to the community he leads. While the qualifications are similar to what would be expected of any reputable official in the secular world, the duties of such a leader are specific to the needs of the community, "holding fast to the true message as taught so that he will be able both to exhort with sound doctrine and to refute opponents" (1:9). These duties overlap those ascribed to presbyters in 1 Timothy, "preaching and teaching" (1 Tim 5:17), but the specific charges to exhort (1 Tim 4:13; Titus 2:15) and to refute opponents (2 Tim 2:25; Titus 2:15) are elsewhere ascribed only to Timothy and Titus.

Charging newly appointed presbyters with these responsibilities is an indication of the critical threat facing the community addressed by this letter. Throughout 1 Timothy and Titus there is a concern for sound doctrine or teaching (1 Tim 1:10; 4:6; 6:3; Titus 1:9, 13; 2:1, 2, 8), a concern related to the need for stability and order as the church faces an immediate doctrinal and moral threat. This concern should not be read, however, as a prohibition of innovative thinking, but only of erroneous teaching that harms the community. In 1 Timothy and Titus sound doctrine means the kind of well-grounded, correct doctrine that results in correct moral behavior.

1:10-16 Silencing false teachers

The first part of the charge to Titus, to "set right what remains to be done" (1:5), is what is of concern in most of the rest of this letter. Titus is here charged to do what the presbyter/bishops he appoints will be expected to do—"to refute opponents" (1:9). The immediate problem is the false teaching of the Jewish Christians, which is upsetting whole families (1:10-11). The church in Crete, which included a large number of Jewish Christians, likely encountered a problem similar to one Paul had to deal with—Gentile converts being required to observe elements of the Jewish Law like circumcision and dietary restrictions (cf. Gal 5:1-2; Phil 3:1-4). A similar problem is dealt with in 1 Timothy (1 Tim 1:7; 4:3-4). There the concern about dietary restrictions is dealt with by affirming the goodness of all of God's creation, including foods and sex (1 Tim 4:4). The response in Titus, "to the clean all things are clean" (1:15) echoes the response of Paul in his letter to the Romans: "nothing is unclean in itself" (Rom 14:14).

What specifically was being taught in Crete is not clear other than that it involved "Jewish myths and regulations" (1:14) that had to do with some things being declared unclean. The false teachers are characterized as failing in one of the qualities just ascribed to a bishop, "teaching for sordid gain" (1:11; cf. 1:7; 1 Tim 3:8). In this regard they are like the false teachers dealt with in 1 Timothy, "supposing religion to be a means of gain" (1 Tim 6:5). As in 1 Timothy, the false teachers are further described as failing not only in their teaching but also in their lives (1 Tim 6:3-5). False beliefs lead to immoral behavior. "They are vile and disobedient and unqualified for any good deed" (1:16). The rhetorical device of ascribing a list of vices to the false teachers discredits these opponents. Those who had been influential insiders are now treated as outsiders.

Titus 1

An indication of the critical nature of the problem confronted is the harshness with which the false teachers are to be dealt. Titus and the newly appointed presbyters are to "silence them" (1:11) and "admonish them sharply" (1:13). As his mandate for dealing with issues in the community is being summed up, Titus is told to "let no one look down on you" (2:15). A similar authoritarian stance is recommended for Timothy in 1 Timothy, but it is more concerned with dealing with behavior within the community (1 Tim 4:12; 5:20) than with the threat of opponents. The harsh, authoritarian stance in both these letters contrasts with the kind and gentle approach recommended in 2 Timothy (2 Tim 2:24-26).

PROPER BEHAVIOR IN THE CHRISTIAN COMMUNITY

Titus 2:1–3:8

2:1-10 The church and social structures

Setting right what remains to be done (1:5) involves not only correct doctrine but also good order in the community that is "consistent with sound doctrine" (2:1). These verses (2:2-10) are the first part of the "household code" for the church at Crete, a code that continues at 2:15–3:3. The reason given for this code is twofold: "so that the opponent will be put to shame without anything bad to say about us" (2:8) and "so as to adorn the doctrine of God our savior in every way" (2:10). Behavior consistent with sound doctrine will adorn that doctrine, enhancing the reputation of the Christian community in the surrounding world. A radically new religious community might be suspected of being a threat to civil order. Christians behaving in accord with sound teaching will lay to rest any such concerns.

Like the household codes in 1 Timothy (2:8-15; 6:1-2, 17-19), this code pertains to the entire community as the household of God, unlike the codes in other letters that focus on the family group (Eph 5:22–6:9; Col 3:18–4:1; 1 Pet 2:13–3:8). Titus, however, goes beyond 1 Timothy in that all members of the community are not only expected to exhibit certain qualities but are also expected to play important roles in the furtherance of the community. Older men, like the bishop in 1 Timothy (1 Tim 3:2; cf. Titus 1:8), are expected to exhibit social qualities found in leading citizens; they are to be "temperate, dignified, self-controlled" (2:2). They are also to possess specific Christian virtues by being "sound in faith, love, and endurance" (2:2). Paul had identified these three virtues as the qualities in the Thessalonians for which he thanked God: "your work of faith and labor of love and endurance in hope" (1 Thess 1:3). While Paul will later place love in the final, emphatic position (1 Cor 13:13), putting "endurance in hope" last expressed his concern in his letter to the Thessalonians about life beyond the grave and the future coming of Christ. The letter to Titus is also concerned with the future coming of Christ (2:13), but here the quality in the final position is simply "endurance."

A concern for future generations is evident in the rest of this section. The qualities expected of older women are specifically intended to enable them to "train younger women" (2:4) to be good wives and mothers so that Christianity might be perceived as contributing to the stability of society (2:5). Just as Timothy is urged to "set an example for those who believe" (1 Tim 4:12), Titus himself is to serve as a model for younger men, teaching them by word and deed to live in such a way that no one will be able to speak ill of the Christian community (2:6-8). This letter's concern that young people become respectable members of society is not found elsewhere in the New Testament but is consistent with the overall concern of 1 Timothy and Titus for the continuing life of the community.

Slaves deserve special mention (2:9-10; cf. 1 Tim 6:1-2), because in those days the vast majority of the population in urban areas were slaves. While many were well educated and some even held powerful positions, their civil status was that of slaves. Here, as elsewhere, the concern of 1 Timothy and Titus is that Christian faith should enable members of the community to become even better members of society, adhering to accepted norms of behavior, "to adorn the doctrine of God our savior in every way" (2:10).

2:11-14 Salvation

The reason for the previous household code stressing good Christian and civil behavior among all members of the community is that "the grace of God has appeared, saving all" (2:11). The verses that follow summarize Christian belief in the twofold appearance of Christ. Just as Paul is described in the identification at the start of this letter as being between the past revelation of the word and the future hope of eternal life (1:2-3), so the later Christian community lives between the two appearances of Christ. In his first appearance he saved us by his redemptive death; he "gave himself for us" (2:14). By baptism and the holy Spirit Christians are cleansed and empowered to live lives worthy of their faith as they await the future coming of Christ.

This theologically dense passage on the appearances of Christ Jesus is the most thorough treatment of the basic Christian kerygma in the Pastoral Letters. Unlike 1 Timothy, which speaks only of the end-time appearance

Titus 2

of Christ Jesus, Titus stresses both Christ's future appearance (1:13) and the salvific nature of his past appearance (2:11; 3:4). Unlike 1 Timothy, where only God is called "savior" (1 Tim 1:1; 2:3; 4:10), in Titus the term is used both for God (1:3; 2:10; 3:4) and Christ (1:4; 2:13; 3:6), although the two are clearly differentiated in 1:3-4 and 3:4-6. God is the source of hope insofar as he saves us by being faithful to his promises, sending Christ Jesus to redeem us and form us into his chosen people (2:14). We are saved by the past appearance of Christ, but it is the future appearance that is the source of the hope (2:13) that is the basis for the household code. While future hope is more prominent in Titus (1:2; 2:13; 3:7), this same theological foundation is found in 1 Timothy, though it is not as fully expressed in that letter (1 Tim 2:3-6).

2:15–3:3 Exhortation to good citizenship

The household code (2:1-10), interrupted by providing its theological foundation (2:11-14), is here concluded by explicitly charging Titus to exhort the community to good citizenship. "These things" (2:15) that Titus is to say are the things he is told to say in 2:1-10. He is further charged to "exhort and correct" (2:15), doing what the presbyter/bishop he will appoint will be expected to do (1:9). Furthermore, he is told to "let no one look down on you" (2:15), just as Timothy was told to "let no one have contempt for your youth" (1 Tim 4:12). Both Timothy and Titus are presented in these letters as younger companions of Paul who are placed in positions of authority in their respective communities.

After the personal charge to Titus, the preceding household code is then summarized in terms that make explicit that, as a whole, it is to be understood as a charge to good citizenship. The "them" in 3:1 refers to all those whose behavior was commented on in chapter 2. In 1 Timothy, Christians were urged to pray "for kings and for all in authority" (1 Tim 2:2). Here they are to be "under the control of magistrates and authorities" (3:1). The charge to obey civil authority is found elsewhere in the New Testament (Rom 13:1-7; 1 Pet 2:13-17), but in 1 Timothy and Titus it is integral to the moral exhortations throughout the letters. These letters urge Christians to participate fully in civic life through gainful employment, respect for neighbors, and obedience to civil authority.

3:4-8 Baptismal hymn

These verses contain language used nowhere else in the Pastoral Letters, most likely because they are part of a preexisting hymn. The previous passage on salvation (2:11-14) offered a kind of commentary on this hymn and provided the theological basis for the exhortation in the household code. Now the letter presents the hymn itself, labeling it as a trustworthy saying (3:8; cf. 1 Tim 1:15; 3:1; 4:9; 2 Tim 2:11), a phrase regularly used in the Pastoral Letters to identify a basic truth of early Christian faith.

The present passage provides a brief synthesis of Pauline theology. Apart from Romans 6:3-11, it contains the most important statement on baptism in the New Testament. Through baptism Christians are no longer slaves to sin but are reborn by the holy Spirit as heirs in hope of eternal life. This hymn situates its teaching on baptism in the context of the two appearances of Christ, the context for all the exhortations of Titus. It further presents the Pauline teaching on justification as the basis for the baptismal lives now led in hope. The use of this hymn allows the letter to Titus to connect its treatment of the Jewish Christian problem to that confronted by Paul. In Galatians and again in Romans, Paul confronted those who felt that people could be saved by their own righteous deeds. For Paul as well as for the letter to Titus, people are "justified by his grace" (3:7) and not by "any righteous deeds" (3:5).

The previous passage on salvation (2:11-14) explained what is involved in living lives based on baptismal conversion, denying impiety and worldly passions while living modestly, justly and piously and waiting in hope for the appearance of Christ. This hymn makes explicit the early Christian teaching that baptismal lives are led by the power of the holy Spirit. Only here and in 2 Timothy 1:14 is the role of the holy Spirit in Christian living explicitly mentioned in the Pastoral Letters. While teachings about the holy Spirit are not emphasized in these letters, the theological concerns of these letters are firmly grounded in the early traditions about the holy Spirit.

FINAL DIRECTIVES TO TITUS

Titus 3:8-11

As the letter draws to a close, the main points of the letter are summarized. What Titus was told to say in chapter 2 (2:1, 15) he is here told to insist on, that is, that people do good and avoid evil (3:8-9). Avoiding evil involves specifically the kinds of evil promoted by the Judaizing opponents at Crete (1:10-16), like arguing about genealogies. The tasks assigned to bishops and to Titus as well, to exhort and refute opponents (1:9; 2:15), are here given further specification, consistent with what Paul is said to have done in 1 Timothy (1 Tim 1:20). Excommunication is to be used as a last resort in dealing with one who upsets the community. Calling the person a "heretic" and further pointing out that the person is "perverted and sinful and stands

Titus 3

self-condemned" (3:10-11) gives expression to the overall perspective of 1 Timothy and Titus, linking belief, true or false, with behavior, good or bad.

FINAL REMARKS AND FAREWELL
Titus 3:12-15

Mention of travel plans is a common feature at the end of Paul's letters. Here the mention of travel plans, those of Paul and of others, are presented in a way that illustrates authorization for ministry, one of the overarching concerns of 1 Timothy and Titus. Paul is now about to send either Artemis or Tychicus to Crete to replace Titus while Titus visits Paul at Nicopolis (3:12). In 2 Timothy 4:12, Paul had sent Tychicus to Ephesus. Just as Paul has sent Titus, Timothy, and others to administer churches, Titus is now charged to send others, Zenas and Apollos, to exercise their ministries in other places (3:13). They, like Titus and Timothy, are to devote themselves to their ministries (3:14; cf. 1 Tim 4:6, 16; 2 Tim 2:15; 4:2; Titus 1:5). While verse 14 continues the instruction on the two missionaries, the phrase "our people" can be understood as applying to the entire community.

The letter concludes with a greeting and a final blessing, both typical of the way Paul concludes his letters. While the greeting is addressed to Titus ("you" in the singular), who is then to extend Paul's greeting to others, the blessing is addressed to "all of you," an indication that the blessing and indeed the entire letter is intended not for a single person, Titus, but for the whole church.

The Letter to Philemon

Terence J. Keegan, O.P.

INTRODUCTION

The letter to Philemon is the shortest but one of the most intriguing letters in the New Testament. Almost all scholars agree that it was written by Paul himself during one of his imprisonments. It provides one piece of an extended conversation involving Paul, Onesimus, Philemon, and others. The information the other parts of the conversation would provide remain a mystery and have been the subject of much conjecture. Fortunately most of this missing information, while interesting, is not crucial for appreciating the ongoing significance of this short and beautiful letter.

Paul is clearly in prison at the time of the letter, but the where and when of the imprisonment are not known. Discussions on these questions are usually linked to discussion about his imprisonment at the time he wrote his letter to the Philippians, and answers vary widely. Were both letters written from Rome and hence later than the letter to the Romans? Were one or both written from Ephesus or some other location? Was one written from an earlier or later imprisonment than the other? It seems most likely but hardly certain that Philemon was written during an earlier imprisonment, possibly at Ephesus, from which Paul expected to be released, and hence be able to visit Philemon and continue his ministry. Travel for both Onesimus and Paul from Ephesus to Colossae, the usually assumed location of Philemon's home, would be relatively easy, since they are only about a hundred miles apart.

Onesimus is a slave belonging to Philemon and is, at the time of the letter, with Paul. Why he has left his owner and is with Paul is also the subject of much speculation. He has done something to offend his owner, which could have been some inappropriate act while he was in his service or which may simply have been his running away. While he may have been a runaway slave, the prevailing opinion is that he was visiting Paul to appeal to him for advice and assistance in his difficulty with his owner. Some have even suggested that Philemon sent his pagan slave to minister to Paul in prison. It is also not certain what Paul expects Philemon to do. He is clearly asking him to receive Onesimus back as a brother in the Lord and to charge Paul for whatever debt Onesimus owes. Paul, however, also says that he would like Onesimus to be able to serve him and seems to be suggesting that Philemon do even more than he is explicitly asked to do, perhaps even give Onesimus to Paul as his slave.

This letter, like others in the New Testament, simply accepts slavery as an institution without discussing its morality. This letter does, however, recognize the tension that exists between the liberating message of the gospel (cf. Gal 3:26-28; 1 Cor 12:13) and the slavery that society accepted. In its treatment of Christian brotherly love, it provides a basis for later Christian understanding of the slavery issue. It calls for a reordering of relationships on a higher plane than those possible within secular society. While many questions will remain unanswered, the letter to Philemon can be read by Christians of all ages as an exposition on the new relationship that exists among people as a result of their incorporation into Christ. This relationship, which transcends all other relationships, including that of master and slave, is based on the new life that all Christians share by reason of the grace that comes from Christ. This new life involves both mutual love and partnership in promoting the gospel.

COMMENTARY

THE OPENING

Phlm 1-3

1-2 Senders and recipients

Like all Paul's letters, the letter to Philemon opens by identifying both the senders and the recipients. The senders are Paul and Timothy. Elsewhere Paul calls himself "an apostle of Christ Jesus" (1 Cor 1:1) or "a slave of Christ Jesus" (Rom 1:1), but here he identifies himself a "a prisoner for Christ Jesus" (1). This identification refers not only to his actual status as a prisoner but even more to the reason for his being a prisoner—his preaching of the gospel of Christ—and most especially, in the context of the purpose of this letter, to Christ's total, authoritative claim on Paul and Paul's dedication to that claim. Timothy's being called a "brother" establishes his close relationship with Paul and also prepares for Paul's addressing Philemon as "brother" (7, 20) and his appealing to Philemon to accept Onesimus as a "brother" (16).

The main recipient of the letter is Philemon, but the letter is also addressed to other key individuals in his community, Appia and Archippus, and to the whole community. In the early church, communities were usually small enough to gather for worship in a private home, often that of a leading citizen like Philemon. While the immediate purpose of the letter is to persuade Philemon to do a good deed, the argument of the letter involves Philemon's understanding of his and Onesimus's relationship within the whole community. Using the terms "brother" and "sister" as well as "co-worker" sets the stage for the new relationship Paul seeks to bring about between Philemon and Onesimus. Addressing the letter to the whole community provides greater incentive for Philemon to comply with the letter's request. It also gives the letter applicability, beyond Philemon himself, to the whole community as well as to Christian communities of future generations.

3 Greeting

The formal greeting is similar to those used in Paul's other letters and has the same wording as the greeting in Paul's other letter from prison (Phil 1:2). While formal, this greeting, together with the formal blessing at the end (25), frames the body of the letter within the context of God's grace. Paul's theology of grace is nowhere developed in this letter, nor are other aspects of his theology. It is reasonable to assume, however, that Philemon and his community, having been converted by Paul, are familiar with the main aspects of Paul's teaching. God's graciousness toward Philemon and his community should inspire their graciousness toward one another.

THANKSGIVING

Phlm 4-7

4-5 Philemon's love and faith

The thanksgiving, which follows the opening greeting in all Paul's letters except Galatians, usually involves thanking God for some quality in the letter's recipient and serves to introduce the main themes of the letter. Here Paul thanks God for Philemon's love and faith, qualities that will be the basis of Paul's appeal in the body of the letter. Paul sees in Philemon's faith not just his assent to the gospel but the way his vital faith has been operative in his life—"faith working through love" (Gal 5:6). Philemon's love "for all the holy ones" (5) includes those in "the church at your house" (2), Paul himself (7), and will shortly be extended to include Onesimus (16).

6-7 Effects of Philemon's love and faith

In the opening of the letter, Paul referred to Philemon as "our co-worker" (1). He now strengthens that designation by referring to him as "brother"

Philemon 6-7

(7), associating him more closely with himself and with "Timothy our brother" (1), the co-author of the letter. Paul suggests that he and Philemon together can now do even more good for the holy ones than what Paul has already seen Philemon doing. Thus far, Paul has drawn an extremely positive picture of Philemon. As the letter develops, Philemon will be expected to live up to this positive picture. The themes of prayer (4), love (5, 7), partnership (6), good (6), and refreshing the heart (7) will all be used as Paul develops his argument.

APPEAL ON BEHALF OF ONESIMUS

Phlm 8-21

8-12 Paul appeals out of love

Paul claims the right to order Philemon to do the good he is about to propose, but refrains from exercising this right. This right probably derives from Paul's apostolic authority, although Paul called himself a prisoner rather than an apostle in the introduction to the letter. Because of the encouragement he has felt on the basis of the good that has come from Philemon's love, rather than order him to do what is proper, Paul urges him "out of love" (9). The love here referred to is both Philemon's love for all the holy ones (5) and Paul's and Timothy's love for Philemon (1). Paul refers to himself as an old man and as a prisoner (9) as motivation for Philemon to extend to Paul the love he has for the holy ones.

Having established the basis of his appeal as the love relationship that exists between himself and Philemon and their mutual love for the holy ones, Paul now identifies the object of his appeal. Whatever he may have been, Onesimus has become Paul's child in prison. By bringing him into Christianity, Paul has become his "father." Paul will describe him as "my own heart" (12). Onesimus has become one of the holy ones mutually loved by Paul and Philemon. Significantly, the term "child," which Paul uses to refer to Onesimus and often to Christians in general, is used in his letters for only one other individual, namely, Timothy (1 Cor 4:17; Phil 2:22), Paul's partner in spreading the gospel and a co-author of this letter.

The extensive use of family language in this letter indicates that a new model of mutual relationships has already been established within the Christian community, a model of relationships that is in tension with the master/slave relationship accepted in Roman society. Paul does not advocate the overthrow of the institution of slavery, but he does advocate overcoming the tension by fully incorporating the Christian slave into the familial relationships within the Christian community. In at least two ways

Paul has described a new household in tension with the structured household of Philemon. First, in this new household Paul, not Philemon, is the head; both Philemon and Onesimus are his children. Second, Paul's father/child relationship with Onesimus has priority over Philemon's master/slave relationship with Onesimus.

The name Onesimus, a common name for slaves, means "the useful one," enabling the play on words in verse 11. Away from Philemon, Onesimus was useless to him. Now a Christian devoted to Paul, he has become useful both to Paul and to Philemon. He will become useful to Philemon when Paul sends him back, but his real usefulness to both Philemon and Paul will become clear later in the letter.

13-14 Philemon's voluntary good deed

Paul never explicitly states what it is that he expects Philemon to do. He had said that he had a right "to order you to do what is proper" (8), but here says he wants the good Philemon will do to be voluntary (14), a good deed on the part of Philemon in response to the grace of God. He says he would have liked Onesimus to remain with him, serving him in prison for the gospel, an indication that Onesimus, like many slaves at that time, was well educated and hence equipped to be of service to Paul and the gospel. However, he sends him back to Philemon and apparently expects Onesimus to be with Philemon when he is released from prison and visits Philemon (22).

15-18 Paul's request

Paul appears to be asking Philemon to receive his slave back, charging Paul for anything that Onesimus might owe as a result of previous misdeeds or his temporary absence. Paul, however, is asking for much more. He is asking that Philemon receive Onesimus back not only as a slave but also as a brother in the Lord. He is asking that he receive Onesimus both as a man, that is, as a fellow Christian who is his slave, and in the Lord, that is, as a co-worker in the gospel. Most of all, Paul is asking that Philemon receive Onesimus back just as warmly as he would welcome Paul. Onesimus has become Paul's "own heart" (12). Just as Philemon is Paul's co-worker in the gospel (1), so too Philemon should regard Onesimus as a co-worker, like Paul, in the gospel. Verse 17 implies that Paul's primary concern was to effect a reconciliation between Philemon and Onesimus.

Modern readers are often disappointed that Paul does not ask Philemon to grant freedom to his slave. While some scholars think that there are passages (16, 21) that can be read as hinting that Paul desires Onesimus's freedom, most do not, and all agree that the letter falls far short of reconsidering the practice of slavery. In fact, recent studies in cultural anthropology have shown that Philemon's simply freeing his slave would not have fundamentally altered his relationships within the household. Paul wants to alter these relationships. The letter offers a model for transforming the way Christians view one another, now seeing other human beings with eyes reconditioned by faith in Jesus Christ. The transforming power of God's grace, personally experienced by Paul, led to his conviction about God's ability to make all things new (2 Cor 5:17). Paul was actually asking Philemon for something far more radical than freeing his slave. Paul's declaration that Onesimus is Philemon's brother both "as a man and in the Lord" (16) indicates not merely a spiritual reevaluation in the sight of the Lord but a real change in the social relationship between slave and owner.

As the father of Onesimus (10), Paul now accepts responsibility for the debts of his son. In so accepting this responsibility, however, Paul is emphasizing the intensity of his relationship with Onesimus and setting the stage for the implied request at the end of the letter. Martin Luther saw in Paul's letter to Philemon a parallel to the kenotic hymn Paul quotes in Philippians (Phil 2:6-11), his other letter from prison. Christ emptied himself of his right with the Father and instead died to bring us into favor with God. As Christ pleads our cause and takes our part, so too Paul has emptied himself of his rights and takes the place of Onesimus in order to get Philemon to waive his right to punish Onesimus and instead welcome him as a brother.

19-21 Personal appeal

Paul's letters were dictated by him and written by a scribe, but he would sometimes add a note at the end in his "own hand" (19; cf. 1 Cor 16:21; Gal 6:11). By writing in his own hand he is concluding his appeal by making his request intensely personal. He now not only restates his agreement to pay Onesimus's debt but also reminds Philemon of the debt he owes to Paul. The new life in Christ that Philemon now lives he owes to Paul, that is, he owes Paul his "very self" (19). With this comment Paul draws Philemon into the creditor-debtor relationship as a debtor as well as a creditor. The sphere of mutual relationships is expanded. Philemon, in fact, has the same relationship to Paul as does Onesimus. For both, Paul is their father in faith. For both, Paul is their partner in the gospel (1; 13).

Paul is expecting Philemon to reflect on the significance of these relationships when Paul asks to "profit from you in the Lord" (20), followed by his appeal to Philemon to "refresh my heart in Christ" (20). Paul is expecting Philemon to reflect on his love for Paul and his partnership with him in the gospel and to consider what he can do to further support him in his ministry. Near the beginning of the letter Paul thanked God for Philemon's love, faith, and partnership, noting that "the hearts of the holy ones have been refreshed by you" (7). He identified Onesimus as "my own heart" (12) and now asks Philemon to "refresh my heart" (20). Paul concludes this personal appeal by expressing his confidence that Philemon will not only do what Paul has explicitly asked, that is, receive Onesimus back as a brother in the Lord, but will do even more (21).

Paul is certainly expecting that Philemon will accept Onesimus not only as a returned slave and a brother in the Lord but also as a beloved co-worker in the gospel, a partner with Paul and Philemon. He may also be expecting that Philemon will refresh his heart by granting the wish Paul had earlier expressed: "that he might serve me on your behalf" (13). Philemon indeed may have Onesimus back forever by giving him to Paul as their mutual partner in the gospel.

This letter calls not only Philemon but all Christians to adopt new patterns of mutual respect, mutual responsibility, and mutual concern. This letter can help Christian communities today to reflect on the roles and concerns of minorities and others who might be marginalized. Accepting the transforming power of God's grace will not only alter relationships but can offer new possibilities for living out Christian faith in freedom and joy.

CONCLUSION

Phlm 22-25

22 Travel plans

Travel plans are a common feature of Paul's letters, appearing just before the final greetings and blessing. Here Paul indicates his hope to be able to visit Philemon. There must have been a realistic prospect of his being released from prison, a development for which he asks the prayers of Philemon and his community. His arrival at the home of Philemon would be an appropriate occasion for Philemon to refresh his heart by granting him Onesimus. To this point in the letter, "you" has been in the singular, referring to Philemon alone. The request for prayers, however, uses "your" in the plural, indicating not only that Paul is asking for the prayers of the community but also that this personal letter to Philemon is intended to be read to the entire community.

Philemon 23-25

23-25 Greeting and blessing

Greetings are another common feature of Paul's letters, appearing just before the final blessing. The greetings from Paul's fellow prisoner, Epaphras, and four fellow workers are addressed to "you" in the singular, that is, to Philemon alone, possibly because they were personally known by Philemon. The final blessing, however, is addressed to the entire community, using the blessing formula similar to those found in Paul's other letters and identical to that in Paul's other letter from prison, the letter to the Philippians (Phil 4:23).

The Letter to the Hebrews

Daniel J. Harrington, S.J.

INTRODUCTION

Among the books of the New Testament, the Letter to the Hebrews stands out for its rhetorical and theological brilliance. It is arguably the greatest Christian sermon ever preached or written. Its author deserves to be revered as the patron saint of preachers. He has presented the essential claim of Christian faith that Christ died for our sins in a persuasive argument with a deep emotional appeal. One way to introduce this book is to describe Hebrews as a sermon in written form, of uncertain origin, intended to encourage perseverance in Christian faith.

A sermon in written form

The author describes his work as a "message of encouragement" (13:22), which most interpreters take to mean a speech or sermon in written form. The only literary features that might qualify Hebrews as a letter or epistle are the travel plans and personal greetings that appear in 13:23-24. These features may have been attached to the sermon as it was sent from one community to another. Or perhaps they were interpolated into the text to promote its association with the corpus of Pauline letters.

Hebrews is no ordinary sermon. Indeed, it is a highly literary and rhetorical sermon that is at once simple and subtle. The basic theological point is simple: Christ is both the perfect sacrifice for sins and the priest who offers himself as a sacrifice. The work's sophisticated use of the Greek language indicates a high level of education on the author's part. As a good preacher, the author interweaves expositions of biblical texts and exhortations to faith and good actions. While he sometimes appears to make a formal delineation between exposition and exhortation, he always joins the two. Exposition leads into exhortation, and exhortation leads to further exposition. He announces his main themes beforehand, repeats keywords, begins and ends units in similar ways (a technique called inclusion), and uses various rhetorical devices (alliteration, arguments "from the lesser to the greater," etc.).

The rhetorical handbooks of the Greco-Roman world distinguished three kinds of speeches: forensic or judicial (used in accusing or defending someone in a legal trial), deliberative (used in persuading a public assembly to take action), and epideictic (used at public memorial occasions to confirm a community's values by praise or blame).

Hebrews best fits the conventions of epideictic rhetoric. It celebrates the greatness of Jesus as the Son of God and as the great high priest and promotes the values that he stood for. It offers comparisons with the angels, Moses, the priests of the old covenant, and Melchizedek to extol the greatness of Jesus. It praises and blames those who are being addressed and seeks to confirm their positive beliefs in the hope of rousing them from spiritual sluggishness and of rescuing them from the danger of falling away from the Christian faith.

The basic outline of Hebrews is clear enough. The first main part (1:1–4:13) establishes Jesus' superiority as God's Son to the angels and to Moses and uses various biblical texts to explore Jesus' significance and the need for persevering in Christian life. The second main part (4:14–10:18) concerns the high priesthood of Christ and the perfect sacrifice of Christ. The third main part (10:19–13:25) reflects on the nature of Christian life and the need for perseverance and endurance in the face of suffering. There are many much more elaborate outlines. But even the simple tripartite outline is not entirely adequate, since the author is so skilled in making transitions, in anticipating themes to be developed later, and in integrating biblical expositions and exhortations.

Of uncertain origin

The authorship of Hebrews has always been controversial. The early church writer Origen said: "But who wrote the epistle, in truth God knows" (Eusebius, *Ecclesiastical History* 6.25.14). Although the reference to "our brother Timothy" in 13:23 might suggest Pauline authorship, the language, literary style and form, and theology are very different from those of Paul's genuine letters. The attributions to Barnabas (see Acts 4:36) and Apollos (see Acts 18:24) are at best guesses.

The sermon in written form is anonymous. The author never names himself, nor does he reveal much personal information. But some reliable statements can be made about his identity. The author had sophisticated knowledge of the Old Testament in its Greek translation and displays a good familiarity with the techniques of Jewish biblical interpretation. He must have been Jewish. Nevertheless, he was convinced that God had done something so dramatically new and significant through the life, death, resurrection, and exaltation of Jesus that the institutions of the old covenant with Israel through Moses on Mount Sinai were no longer effective. They were only types or shadows of the realities fulfilled in Christ. As he addresses his audience, the author seeks to serve as their teacher and pastoral guide. To respect the mixed genre of Hebrews as a sermon in written form, I refer in the commentary to the author, the writer, and the preacher alternatively, as well as to the readers, the congregation, the community, and the audience.

Those originally addressed in Hebrews seem to have been Jewish Christians who had embraced Christianity with enthusiasm but were wavering and in danger of giving into discouragement and falling away, especially in the face of suffering (see 12:3-11). It is very tempting to locate the community in Rome on the basis of 13:24 ("those from Italy send you greetings") and the earliest attestations of Hebrews in Clement of Rome's first letter to the Corinthians (1 Clement). But there is no certainty here. Neither is the date of composition certain, since practically anytime between A.D. 50 and 100 is possible. The absence of any reference to the destruction of the Jerusalem temple in A.D. 70 might suggest an early date (the fifties or sixties), though one must admit that the author is more interested in explaining Scripture than in commenting on contemporary events. With these cautions in mind, the hypothesis that Hebrews was addressed to a Jewish Christian community at Rome in the late fifties or early sixties of the first century A.D. remains nonetheless the most attractive setting.

Uncertainty also surrounds the history-of-religions background of Hebrews, so much so that this issue is often called "the mystery of Hebrews." Although some of the author's biblical expositions sound something like what one finds in the writings of Philo of Alexandria, he seems more interested in typology than in allegory. The portrayal of Melchizedek as a heavenly figure in some Dead Sea Scrolls was initially thought to illumine Hebrews 7. But it now appears that the author simply gives his own christological readings of the pertinent biblical texts. Concepts that developed in Gnosticism are sometimes read back into Hebrews, but again the results only highlight the author's theological originality. The New Testament document that is closest to Hebrews is 1 Peter. It is a sermon addressed to alienated and suffering Christians, who are urged to find encouragement and hope in the example of Christ the Suffering Servant. While those addressed in 1 Peter were mainly Gentile Christians, the main audience for Hebrews appears to have been Jewish Christians.

To encourage perseverance

Hebrews is a sustained theological reflection on the very early Christian confession of faith that Christ died for us and for our sins. This confession appears both in Paul's writings (see Gal 1:4; 3:13; 2 Cor 5:14, 21; Rom 5:6; 14:15) and in the pre-Pauline creedal formulas that Paul quotes (see 1 Cor 11:24; 15:3; Rom 3:25-26).

The author of Hebrews shares and develops the idea of the sacrificial nature of Christ's death and its atoning value. However, his most distinctive theological contribution is the concept of the high priesthood of Christ. According to early Christian tradition (see Mark 10:45; 14:24; and especially 14:36), Jesus willingly offered himself in death. Since the one who offers a sacrifice is a priest, the author endeavors to show that Christ can be called a priest despite the fact that he was not born into the Jewish priestly tribe of Levi. The basic theological claim of Hebrews is that Christ is both the perfect sacrifice for sins and the priest who offered himself as that sacrifice.

In developing this thesis, the author assumes that Christ is the key to the Old Testament Scriptures. Not content to leave behind the Old Testament, he argues that the words of Scripture only make sense when attributed to Christ or applied to him. His favorite texts are the messianic Psalms 2 and 110, and in his exhortations he calls upon Psalms 8 and 95 among others. The description of the Day of Atonement ritual in Leviticus 16 is the basic source for establishing Christ's sacrifice and priesthood.

The author insists on the superiority of Christ as the Son of God over the angels and over Moses. Because Christ is both the high priest and the perfect sacrifice, his saving action—his death, resurrection, and exaltation taken as a single event—has made possible the forgiveness of sins, confident access to God, and hope for eternal life with God.

The people addressed in Hebrews seem to be having a hard time in accepting the absolute sufficiency of Christ's perfect sacrifice on the cross. If they are to persevere in Christian faith, they need a spiritual renewal. At various points the author addresses their situation directly with stern warnings and words of encouragement. Most of all, he hopes that his biblical-theological presentation of Christ's sacrifice and priesthood will give them the appropriate theological framework to put aside their doubts and spiritual sluggishness and to revitalize their Christian faith and practice.

To that end the author portrays Christ as the pioneer (the one who has already gone before us) and the leader for those who follow him on the way to eternal life with God. The risen and exalted Christ remains a mediator on our behalf in the present (9:24) and will appear again to bring salvation in the future (9:28). His perfect sacrifice renders unnecessary the sacrifices and priests of the old covenant. In fact, these persons and institutions were at best types or signs that have received their full definition in Christ.

Two hard questions

Does Hebrews illumine the Christian priesthood? The work is mainly concerned with the priesthood of the Old Testament and the priesthood of Christ. It does not speak directly about the communal priesthood of all Christians (see 1 Pet 2:9; Rev 1:6; 5:10; 20:6) or about the Christian ministerial priesthood. However, many Christians have found in Christ's priesthood an apt metaphor for describing Christian life in general. It has also been traditional among Catholics and other Christians to find in Christ's priesthood the model and dynamism for the ministerial priesthood. But some Protestants regard Christ's priesthood to be the end of all claims to priesthood, since his perfect "once for all" sacrifice has rendered unnecessary all other sacrifices and priesthoods. The problem is that Hebrews is silent on this important question and can be (and has been) read as supporting or denying all the various positions about priesthood.

Is Hebrews anti-Jewish? Since both the author and his audience seem to have been Jews, such a charge seems unfair and anachronistic. In fact, Hebrews is an interpretation of Judaism in the light of Christ. Without the authoritative Scriptures of Israel and the great heroes and institutions of the biblical tradition, there would be little substance to Hebrews. And yet perhaps more than any other New Testament writer, the author of Hebrews insists that the old covenant, priesthood, and sacrificial system have been superseded through Christ. Modern Christian readers need to respect the historical (Jewish) setting of Hebrews and to be sensitive to the anti-Jewish potential of the text when it is taken out of its first-century Jewish Christian context.

Reading Hebrews

Hebrews is a sermon in written form. It presents a sustained theological argument, and so it may be helpful to read it straight through at one sitting. Its rhetoric and theology are highly sophisticated and difficult for modern readers, and therefore it deserves careful study, with the commentary that follows as a guide. It may be helpful to look up the Old Testament texts that the author quotes in order to appreciate how he handles these texts from his christological perspective. One must be aware, however, that the author used the ancient Greek version (Septuagint) of the Old Testament, which often differs from the Hebrew text on which our modern translations are based. A communal reading of this sermon in written form might serve as a final exercise. A well-prepared and reverent group reading of the whole text takes about fifty minutes. The exercise will help those who have worked through this difficult text to appreciate better the truth of the author's own comment: "The word of God is living and effective, sharper than any two-edged sword" (4:12).

COMMENTARY

GOD'S SON AND GOD'S WORD

Heb 1:1–4:13

1:1-4 Prologue: Jesus as the climax of divine revelation

The prologue serves as an introduction or overture to the entire sermon by calling attention to major themes and to the pivotal place of Jesus in the history of salvation. Using the device of alliteration, in which several words begin with the same letter ("past . . . partial . . . prophets"), the author begins in 1:1-2a by showing how Jesus continues the story of God's communication to Israel and brings it to a definitive point or climax. He develops the idea by four contrasts. (1) Whereas God spoke "in times past," now he has spoken "in these last days" (the new era ushered in by Jesus and issuing in the fullness of God's kingdom). (2) Whereas God spoke "to our ancestors" (historic Israel), now he has spoken "to us" (the Christian community). (3) Whereas God spoke "through the prophets" (including Moses, Joshua, and David, as well as those known traditionally as the prophets), now he has spoken through "a son" (Jesus). (4) Whereas God spoke "in partial and various ways," now he has spoken in a full and definitive way (through Jesus).

In describing the person and work of Jesus in 1:2b-3, the author highlights his identity as the Messiah and as Wisdom. Jesus' identity as the Messiah is developed with the help of two psalms (2 and 110) that serve as major texts throughout the sermon. Both psalms originated in the ritual associated with the coronation of kings in ancient Israel. The king was "anointed" as part of his coronation, and the word "Messiah" means "the anointed one." By declaring Jesus as "heir of all things" (see Ps 2:8) and as taking his seat at God's right hand (Ps 110:1), the author tells us right away that Jesus is the Messiah of Jewish expectations. What historic Israel hoped from its kings, Jesus has provided.

Jesus' identity as the Wisdom of God is established by evoking terms and motifs from various Old Testament passages in which Wisdom is portrayed as the agent of God in creation (see Proverbs 8, Sirach 24, and Wisdom 7). The author affirms that Jesus was God's agent in creating the universe ("through whom he created the universe," see Prov 8:30; Wis 7:22), that he reflects God's glory and represents God's being (see Wis 7:26), and that he carries on God's work of creation ("who sustains all things"). The motif of Jesus as the Wisdom of God is prominent in early Christian hymns preserved in other New Testament books, most notably Colossians 1:15-20 and John 1:1-18.

While identifying Jesus as God's Messiah and Wisdom, the author also introduces his major theme of Jesus' role in the "purification from sins," a work accomplished through his sacrificial death on the cross and his subsequent exaltation to the heavenly throne of God. Likewise, in 1:4 he announces the theme that will be developed in what follows immediately: the superiority of Jesus to the angels. This theme is related to the superior "name" that Jesus bears as the Son of God. The author's task will be to show why the Son should be regarded as superior to the angels.

1:5-14 Jesus as superior to the angels

Why the author felt compelled to take on this task is not certain. There is some evidence in the Dead Sea Scrolls and other early Jewish texts for veneration of angels. And some early Christians may have regarded Jesus as an angel. Or the issue may have been entirely theoretical.

The device that the author uses to establish Jesus' superiority to the angels is a chain (or *catena*) of biblical quotations. While the *catena* genre was used by Jewish writers of the times, the author of Hebrews makes it serve his christological purpose. For him, Christ is the key to the Scriptures, and so all the biblical texts that he quotes are assumed to speak to or about Christ. There are three pairs of quotations (1:5, 6-7, 8-12), along with a single quotation of Psalm 110 (109):1 (1:13).

The introduction to the *catena* in 1:5a ("to which of the angels did God ever say") establishes that the purpose is to prove the superiority of the Son. The concluding comment in 1:14 about the angels as servants is a case of "inclusion," in which an argument is begun and ended in similar ways.

In 1:5 the first pair of quotations—Psalm 2:7 and 2 Samuel 7:14—serve to identify Jesus as God's Son and Messiah: "You are my son . . . he shall be a son to me." The assumption is that God is the speaker and addresses Jesus as his Messiah/Son. Part of the ideology of kingship in ancient Israel was that the king became God's "son" at his accession to the throne. And so when applied to Jesus, the terms "Messiah" and "Son" are synonyms.

In 1:6-7 the second pair of quotations—Deuteronomy 32:43/Psalm 97(96):7 and Psalm 104 (103):4—establish the inferiority of the angels to the Son of God. The assumption is that God spoke these words when Jesus the Wisdom of God took on human flesh ("when he leads the first-born into the world") and that these words concern the Son of God. The first text says that the role of the angels is to worship the Son, and the second text presents the angels as instruments of God ("winds . . . a fiery flame").

In 1:8-12 the third pair of quotations—Psalm 45(44):7-8 and Psalm 102 (101):26-28—takes texts originally addressed to God and applies them to the Messiah/Son ("your throne, O God . . . O Lord, you established"). The emphasis is on the eternity of Jesus' reign as God's Messiah/Son ("forever and ever . . . God, your God, anointed you . . . your years will have no end"). While such things cannot be said of angels, applying these biblical affirmations about God to Christ suggests his own authority, eternity, and even divinity.

In 1:13 the final (single) quotation—Psalm 110(109):1—applies what was said by God to the king at his coronation ("sit at my right hand / until I make your enemies your footstool") to the resurrected and exalted Messiah/Son. Throughout Hebrews, the center of attention will be Jesus' death, resurrection, and exaltation understood as one great event. The *catena* concludes in 1:14 with a comment about the role of the angels as servants of God ("ministering spirits") on behalf of all those who seek salvation.

2:1-4 A call to commitment and responsibility

At many points in his sermon the author addresses his audience directly and challenges them to apply his message about Christ to their own situation. Even in his exhortations, however, he injects new theological considerations based on the Old Testament and on God's saving activity in Jesus.

As a good preacher, the author moves in 2:1 from the *catena* of biblical quotations to their significance for Christian life and includes himself among those being addressed ("therefore we must attend . . ."). The expression "what we have heard" may refer to the gospel message in general, to the biblical passages applied to Christ in 1:5-14, or to Jesus as the Word of God—or all three at once. The danger that the audience faces is expressed by the phrase "so that we may not be carried away," which evokes the image of a ship failing to reach its harbor safely. The author fears that his people may drift away from the gospel that they had once embraced.

The warning in 2:2-3a builds on the case developed about the Son's superiority to the angels. It employs the rhetorical device of arguing "from the lesser to the greater" and assumes that the law was given to Moses on Sinai through the mediation of angels (see Acts 7:53; Gal 3:19). If the Mosaic Law given through angels punishes each and every transgression, how much more will God punish neglect of the salvation given through Christ.

The logic is that the greater revelation (the gospel) given through the greater revealer (Christ) will exact greater punishment from those who fail to attend to it.

Having raised the threat of severe punishment, the author in 2:3b-4 reminds his audience about the nature of the salvation brought by Christ. It was announced by Jesus ("the Lord") and confirmed by the apostolic witnesses and by God through miracles ("signs, wonders, various acts of power") and through the gifts of the holy Spirit (not a major figure in Hebrews). Note the "trinitarian" dimension that serves as the framework for describing the saving work of Christ.

2:5-9 Jesus as the Son of Man

Having reflected on the significance of the salvation brought by Jesus for the community of faith, the author takes up again the theme of Jesus' superiority to the angels. According to a biblical tradition (see Deut 32:8; Dan 10:20-21; 12:1), God placed the world in the present age under the governance of angels. According to early Christian faith, however, the new age or "world to come" (2:5) has already been inaugurated in and through Christ. But the quotation of Psalm 110(109):1 in Hebrews 1:13 ("until I make your enemies your footstool") could give the impression that Christ's reign was still future. And so the author contends that Christ's reign is both present and future and that it began with Jesus' incarnation, death, and exaltation.

The biblical vehicle for the author's argument is Psalm 8:5-7(4-6), which is part of a meditation on the great dignity of human beings. The psalmist ("someone . . . somewhere") praises God ("you") for God's care and love for humankind ("man . . . the son of man") and observes that God has placed human beings a little lower than the angels and given them stewardship over the world (see Gen 1:26, 28).

True to his interpretive principle that Christ is the key to the Scriptures, the author assumes that Psalm 8 speaks about Christ as the "son of man." In his interpretation (2:8b-9), he affirms that God has already placed all creation under the governance of Christ as the Son of Man. The problem is that humans do not yet perceive Christ's sovereignty, though they surely will do so in the fullness of God's kingdom. What is now perceived through faith is the risen and exalted Christ ("crowned . . . with glory and honor"). His glorification followed from his suffering and death, when he was lower than the angels "for a little while" (the adverb is interpreted chronologically rather than qualitatively). The paradox is that Christ's humiliation in his passion became the occasion for the exaltation of us all. The idea that Christ's death was the perfect sacrifice for sins and opened up the possibility for the salvation of all humans is introduced by the concluding clause: "that by the grace of God he might taste death for everyone" (2:9).

2:10-18 Christ in solidarity with humans

The fundamental affirmation of Hebrews is expressed in 2:10: God ("for whom and through whom all things exist") made Jesus the pioneer or champion ("leader") to bring all humans to salvation, and the way by which this goal was achieved was through the cross, in which Christ was made "perfect through suffering." This statement captures the self-sacrifice involved in Jesus' death on the cross as well as the atoning value of his death for others. Thus Jesus can be understood (as we will see) as both the priest (because he offered himself willingly) and the sacrifice (because his death was for us and for our sins).

Jesus' solidarity with humans and his special relationship with God are established in 2:11-13 by a series of Old Testament quotations. Both Christ ("he who consecrates") and humans ("those who are being consecrated") share a common origin in God and in humanity. And so Christ can call other humans "brothers." The first biblical quotation is Psalm 22:22(23)—from the prayer of the righteous sufferer, which is also the source of Jesus' last words on the cross, according to Mark (15:34) and Matthew (27:46). In the author's christological framework, Jesus ("I") confesses and praises God ("you") among his fellow humans ("to my brothers"). In the second biblical quotation (Isa 8:17-18), Christ ("I") professes trust in God ("in him") and identifies himself with other humans ("I and the children God has given me"). Thus Christ is the link or mediator between God and humans.

The classic question, Why did Christ become human? is taken up in 2:14-18. By sharing our humanity, Christ was able to render inoperative the devil as the one who has power over death and to free us from the fear of death that makes us slaves (2:14-15). The object of Christ's saving work was the "descendants of Abraham," which includes not only Israel as the chosen people of God but also the many nations of which Abraham was the father (2:16). Only by being fully human could Christ be both our priest ("a merciful and faithful high priest") and our sacrifice ("to expiate the sins of the people"). Only by being tested through suffering could Christ help us as we are being tested. These ideas about the priesthood of Christ will be developed at great length in chapters 5–10.

3:1-6 Jesus as superior to Moses

The preacher returns in 3:1 to direct address. He reminds his congregation that as "brothers" of Christ and of one another, they share in the holiness that reflects God the holy one par excellence and in the call to eternal life with God. Identifying Jesus as "the apostle" (the one "sent" from God—the only New Testament application of this title to Christ) and "high priest" (a title already introduced in 2:17 and soon to become the center of attention), the author in 3:2 focuses on Jesus' fidelity to God as "the one who appointed him." He also introduces the figure of Moses and the characterization of Moses as "faithful in all his house."

This description of Moses comes from Numbers 12:7(8): "Not so with my servant Moses! / Throughout my house he bears my trust." In the Old Testament context, Moses appears as the instrument of God's revelation who is superior to Aaron, Miriam, and all other recipients of divine revelation. The "house" is Israel as the people of God, where Moses functioned as the "servant" of God.

In comparing Moses and Christ in 3:3-6, the author is more concerned to praise Christ than to denigrate Moses. He proceeds on two fronts: the house (3:3-4) and the servant (3:5-6). Just as the architect-builder of a house deserves more praise than the house itself, so God (and Christ as God's agent) deserves more praise than Moses in founding the people of God. Just as in a large household a son is more important than a servant, so Christ the Son is more important than Moses the servant in the people of God. Whereas Moses was a servant "in" God's house, Christ was a son placed "over" the house. Thus Jesus' faithfulness as God's Son was superior to the faithfulness of God's servant Moses.

The preacher concludes in 3:6b by identifying the Christian community as the "house" or people of God ("we are his house") and by warning the community to retain their confidence and pride in what God has done and continues to do for them through Christ the Son. Otherwise they may cease to be God's house.

3:7-19 The negative example of Israel in the wilderness

A good preacher frequently offers a congregation positive examples to be imitated and negative examples to be avoided. As a way of challenging the congregation to emulate the fidelity displayed by Christ, the author presents the negative example of ancient Israel wandering in the wilderness between the exodus from Egypt to the entrance into the land of Canaan.

The main biblical text is Psalm 95(94):7b-11 (which is read in light of Numbers 14). The text is introduced as having logical significance ("therefore") and as being from God ("as the holy Spirit says"). In Psalm 95 the admonition to be faithful follows an invitation to worship God, most obviously at the Jerusalem temple (Ps 95:1-7a). The admonition itself recalls the episode of Israel's rebellion in the wilderness (see Exod 17:1-17; Num 14:21-23). The place in which the rebellion took place was called in Hebrew "Massah" (meaning "testing") and "Meribah" (meaning "quarreling"). The text begins with a call to hear God's voice "today" (Heb 3:7b = Ps 95:7b). Then there is a warning to avoid the rebelliousness displayed by the Exodus generation in the wilderness for forty years (Heb 3:8-9 = Ps 95:8-9). Finally, God recalls his anger at that generation and his resolve that they would not find "rest" in the land of Canaan (Heb 3:10-11 = Ps 95:10-11).

Having quoted this biblical text at length, the author in 3:12-15 makes an application to the situation of his audience in the first century A.D. First, in 3:12 he warns them against falling away from the living God, as the Exodus generation did, through "an evil and unfaithful heart." Then, in 3:13 he encourages them to regard every day as "today" and not to allow their hearts to be hardened. Finally, in 3:14-15 he warns them again that their partnership with Christ depends on remaining faithful "until the end." The final warning and the application in general are underscored by a repetition of Psalm 95:7b-8 and by bringing back the key words ("today . . . hear his voice . . . harden not your hearts . . . rebellion").

The application is an example of the actualization of Scripture. Just as the psalmist used the negative example of the Exodus generation to motivate people in his own generation, so the author of Hebrews applies both the example and the biblical text to early Christians in his own day. This process of actualization is carried on whenever the letter to the Hebrews is proclaimed today, since "the word of God is living and effective" (4:12).

Still another rhetorical device in the preacher's repertoire is his use of rhetorical questions. From what had been said and from the way in which the questions are asked, it is clear what answers the preacher expects. The first two questions (3:16 and 3:17) are answered by two more questions, while the final question (3:18) receives a response by means of a declarative sentence (3:19).

The first pair of questions (3:16) establish that those who had rebelled were those Israelites who came out of Egypt with Moses. Their disobedience is the main topic in Psalm 95:7b-11. The second pair of questions (3:17) indicate that God was angry with those people because they sinned in putting God to the test and in rebelling against God. The punishment for that generation's rebelliousness was death in the wilderness before any could enter "rest" in the land of Canaan (see Num 14:29-30).

The third question (3:18) affirms that God swore an oath against the disobedient Israelites, so that they could not enter his rest. And the concluding comment (3:19) attributes their failure to "lack of faith." The author has made two important rhetorical moves here. He has linked disobedience to lack of faith as effect and cause (see Num 14:22-23). And he has repeated the word "rest" several times, thus preparing the listener to ask whether it may refer to something beyond life in the land of Canaan.

4:1-13 The abiding promise of sabbath rest

Having explained Psalm 95:7b-11 in terms of the disobedience and lack of faith shown by the Exodus generation, the preacher in 4:1-2 moves to the congregation that he addresses ("Therefore, let us . . .") and tells them that God's promise of entering "rest" remains a possibility in the present. He warns them to be on guard lest they fail to have that promise brought to fulfillment. Like the Exodus generation, they have received the "good news" (the same word as "gospel"). Like the Exodus generation, they run the risk of failure if they do not respond in faith. What they should learn from the negative example of the Exodus generation is the pivotal importance of faith issuing in obedience. Only then can they hope to enjoy the "rest" that God has promised.

What is this "rest"? It is not simply life in the land of Canaan after the Exodus from Egypt. Indeed, it remains a present possibility for the early Christians as God's people ("we who believed"). To clarify the meaning of "rest," the author in 4:3-5 uses the Jewish interpretive technique of explaining one verse in Scripture by another linked to the first by a common word. Part of the author's main text has been Psalm 95:11: "As I swore in my wrath, / 'They shall not enter into my rest.'" Genesis 2:2 is another text that mentions "rest": "And God rested on the seventh day from all his works." The second text, of course, is from the biblical account of creation and expresses God's plan for creation. The combination of the two texts suggests that "rest" really refers to eternal life with God. The "rest" denied the Exodus generation was but a shadow of the rest that God has enjoyed since the beginning of creation and that God makes available to all who believe.

In 4:6-8 the author makes clear that God's promise of rest remains valid, despite the failure of the Exodus generation to attain to it because of their disobedience. The key word in this section is "today," which suggests that God's promise of rest remains a possibility even after the Exodus generation. Here the author works with the traditional ascription of the psalms to David (see 4:7). Now David lived long after Joshua, the one who finally did lead God's people into the promised land of Canaan. If Joshua had given genuine rest to God's people, David would not have been able to speak about "today" as the time to hear God's voice and so enjoy rest with

Hebrews 4

God. In Greek the names Joshua and Jesus are the same. But the rest that God's people enjoyed under Joshua's leadership was but a shadow or type of the genuine rest that is now available to God's people through Jesus' leadership.

Finally, in 4:9-10 the author brings together what he has been saying about rest: "a sabbath rest still remains for the people of God" (4:9). This sabbath rest is God's own sabbath rest on the seventh day of creation (see Gen 2:2); it is not simply life in the land of Canaan or even observance of the sabbath day. Rather, it is sharing in God's sabbath rest, which began on the seventh day of creation and lasts forever. It is fullness of life with God.

And yet, as 4:11 makes clear, the enjoyment of God's own rest demands a deliberate choice ("let us strive to enter into that rest") to avoid the kind of disobedience displayed by the Exodus generation ("so that no one may fall").

The preacher ends the first main part of his sermon in 4:12-13 with reflections on the word of God and the omniscience of God. The word of God (4:12) is more than the book we call the Bible. Because it comes from the living God, the word of God is living and active. Throughout his sermon thus far, the preacher has been concerned to show that the Scriptures can speak effectively to people in his own time. They are not simply witnesses to the past but rather have significance for "today." So effective are the Scriptures in addressing the concerns of people today that they can be compared to a sharp ("two-edged") sword that can penetrate into a person's inmost self ("between soul and spirit, joints and marrow") and can distinguish among thoughts and intentions.

In 4:13 the subject changes from the word of God to God ("him"), or more precisely, to the omniscience of God. Nothing can remain hidden from God. And to God everyone must be ready to render an accounting as to a judge. Thus the author seeks to motivate his congregation to strive ever more vigorously for eternal life with God ("rest") by reminding them of the possible consequences of not doing so.

THE PRIESTHOOD AND SACRIFICE OF CHRIST
Heb 4:14–10:18

4:14–5:10 Jesus as the compassionate high priest

The author began his sermon by establishing Jesus' identity as the Son of God. In the central section of his sermon, he will show how the Son of God is also the great high priest. The material in 4:14-16 serves as the link between the first two main sections, and enables the preacher to advance his argument about the saving significance of Jesus' death and resurrection. The reuse of many of the same words and ideas in 10:19-23 will in turn enable him to round off (by the device of "inclusion") the second part and move to the third and final part.

True to his craft as a preacher, the author in 4:14-16 alternates between theological statements about Jesus' high priesthood (4:14a, 15) and exhortations ("let us . . . ," 4:14b, 16). The first theological statement (4:14a) must be understood against the background of the Jewish Day of Atonement ritual described in Leviticus 16. There the Jewish high priest is instructed to pass through the curtain in front of the Holy of Holies and to offer sacrifice on behalf of the sins of the people. But Jesus the Son of God "has passed through the heavens" in his resurrection and exaltation. Whereas the Jewish high priest entered only the earthly symbol of God's presence, Jesus has entered the real abode of God (heaven). More than anyone else, therefore, Jesus deserves the title of "great high priest." The first exhortation (4:14b) concerns perseverance in the confession of faith in the saving significance of Jesus' death "for us" and "for our sins."

The second theological statement (4:15) again takes as its premise an idea in Leviticus 16—that the high priest is a sinner and makes atonement for his own sins. Though Jesus was "without sin," he nonetheless experienced the moral and physical testing (see Mark 1:12-13; Matt 4:1-11; Luke 4:1-13) that is part of the human condition. As fully human, the Son of God can "sympathize with our weaknesses." The second exhortation (4:16) moves beyond "holding on" and urges the readers to approach God's throne with boldness. This confidence is based on the new relationship made possible through Jesus' activity as "our great high priest" in his sacrificial death and in his exaltation. While the motif of God's throne might imply judgment and condemnation, now through Christ it has become a "throne of grace" (a place of divine favor) from which one can expect mercy and grace from God. It is Christ who makes possible this access to God's throne and this confident attitude among those who approach God.

But how can Jesus of Nazareth be called a high priest at all? In ancient Israel only men from the tribe of Levi who could trace their heritage back to Aaron were qualified to serve as high priests. As the author freely admits in 7:14, Jesus was descended from Judah and so had no earthly claim to the Jewish priesthood. The answer to the question resides in the different qualifications for priesthood developed in 5:1-10 and in the different priesthood explained in 7:1-28. (Note the reuse of terms from 5:1-3 in 7:27-28.) The intervening exhortation in 5:11–6:20 spells out the consequences of Jesus' different high priesthood for Christian life.

The high priest is first of all (5:1) a mediator between God and humans. As a human himself, he represents other humans before God, especially in his task of offering sacrifices for sins. Secondly (5:2-3), the high priest stands in solidarity with other humans because he shares their weakness. Thus he can show compassion to "the ignorant and erring." And as he offers the atoning sacrifices, he does so both for his own sins and for the sins of others. Thirdly (5:4), the high priest is called by God as Aaron was (see Exod 28:1) and does not take up the office on his own. More important than Aaronic/levitical descent for establishing Jesus' right to priesthood are the criteria of mediatorship, solidarity with others, and divine appointment. According to these criteria, it is possible to call Jesus "our great high priest."

The author applies these criteria in reverse (or chiastic) order. The divine appointment of Christ as high priest is established in 5:5-6 by means of quotations from the author's favorite biblical passages—Psalms 2 and 110. The author assumes that the speaker is God and the one addressed is Christ. Both psalms were used in coronation rituals for kings in ancient Israel, and so can be called "messianic." Since for the author and other early Christians the key to the Scriptures is Christ, these two oracles are understood to concern Christ. The first oracle (Ps 2:7 = Heb 5:5) establishes that Christ is God's Son (see Heb 1:5), and the second oracle (Ps 110:4 = Heb 5:6) introduces the idea (to be developed at great length in Hebrews 7) of the eternal priesthood of Christ "according to the order of Melchizedek." The two quotations interpreted from a christological perspective are put forward as proof that God has called and appointed Christ to be the great high priest.

Christ's solidarity with other humans is established in 5:7-8 by reference to his suffering—a universal human experience: "he learned obedience from what he suffered." The description of Christ's suffering most vividly evokes the episode in Gethsemane (see Mark 14:32-42; Matt 26:36-46; Luke 22:39-46) but probably also takes in all of his passion and death and indeed his entire life "in the flesh." The reference to his "prayers and supplications with loud cries and tears" places Jesus in the context of the many Old Testament lament psalms (see Psalms 3, 5, etc., and especially Psalm 22). From the author's christological perspective on biblical interpretation, Christ has become the speaker par excellence of the lament psalms. And in his case "because of his reverence" his prayers were heard, and he was vindicated through his resurrection and exaltation.

Christ's mediatorship, according to 5:9-10, surpasses that of any other priest: "when he was made perfect, he became the source of eternal salvation for all who obey him." The reference to Christ's being made perfect alludes to his having reached his "goal" through his death and resurrection, which in turn has made possible "eternal salvation for all who obey him." No other priest could bring about eternal salvation. The best that the Old Testament priests could do was the annual Day of Atonement ritual with its hope that the people's sins of the past year would be wiped away. The final verse (5:10) anticipates the full treatment of the different priesthood of Christ "according to the order of Melchizedek" in chapter 7.

5:11–6:12 A call to Christian maturity

Hebrews is not simply a theological treatise. It is a sermon that interweaves biblical exposition and theology with reflections on the spiritual condition of the audience. Between his discussions of Christ's high priesthood in 4:14–5:10 and 7:1-28, the author issues a call to spiritual maturity (5:11–6:12) and offers an assurance about God's promises (6:13-20).

The call to Christian maturity in 5:11–6:12 consists of a reprimand (5:11–6:3), a stern warning (6:4-8), and a word of hope and encouragement (6:9-12). In the first part of the reprimand (5:11-14) the author admits that his topic of Christ's priesthood is "difficult to explain." But he locates the difficulty not so much in the material but rather in the audience ("you have become sluggish in hearing"). He goes on in 5:12 to scold them for failing to advance in Christian life. By this time they should have become teachers but in fact they stand in need of learning again the basic elements (the ABCs) of Christian faith. They remain in Christian infancy: "You need milk, [and] not solid food." In 5:13-14 he develops the contrast between the spiritually immature as lacking "experience of the word of righteousness" and the spiritually mature who can "discern good and evil." The Christian ideal is the integration of doctrine and practice.

The second part of the reprimand (6:1-3) challenges the congregation to move forward in their theological education and practice. The author urges them not to remain at the basic level, without of course neglecting the basics entirely—no more than one can neglect one's ABCs in writing or reading. The list of basics in 6:1b-2 is founded on "repentance from dead works and faith in God." Initiation into Christian life is covered by "baptisms and laying on of hands," while life-after-death is treated in "resurrection of the dead and eternal judgment." As they became Christians, the members of the congregation learned the distinctively Christian interpretations of Jewish beliefs and practices. Even though they seemed to be wavering about these matters, the author hopes that by moving them forward to "advanced" teaching about Christ's priesthood and sacrifice all these issues will fall into place again for them. As a good preacher, however, he acknowledges in 6:3 that their progress depends ultimately on God ("if only God permits").

The stern warning in 6:4-8 (see 10:26-31) is intended to shock the community into recognizing the seriousness of turning aside from Christian faith. The author declares that repentance after apostasy is impossible for those who have been "enlightened and tasted the heavenly gift and shared in the holy Spirit"—a general description of Christian initiation (which need not be broken down into the separate sacraments of baptism, Eucharist, and confirmation)—and "tasted the good word of God and the powers of the age to come"—a reference to God's word encountered in the Old Testament and in the preached gospel and to the signs and wonders that were part of early Christian experience. Those who fall away from Christian faith are said to be recrucifying the Son of God and holding him up to contempt. The theology of this stern warning seems to be that since Christ's death has made possible the forgiveness of sins, those who reject its saving significance have nowhere else to go for repentance and forgiveness. The rhetorical force of the warning seeks to awaken the community to recognize the seriousness of their situation.

The stark choice that is before the community is illustrated in 6:7-8 by the contrast between the good soil and the bad soil (see Mark 4:3-9; Matt 13:3-9; Luke 8:4-8). Whereas the good soil that produces useful crops receives a blessing from God (see Gen 1:11-12), the bad soil that produces only thorns and thistles is cursed (see Gen 3:17-18) and burned off. This dramatic contrast underscores how serious a decision lay before the wavering Christians. Will they produce good fruits and be blessed by God in Christ? Or will they produce thorns and thistles, and so share in the curse imposed upon Adam?

Having gotten the congregation's attention by his stern warning, the preacher in 6:9-12 offers some mitigating words of hope and encouragement. He first expresses in 6:9-10 confidence that his dear friends will enjoy the "better things related to salvation" because God will surely recognize their good works and the love that they have shown in serving their fellow Christians ("the holy ones"). Then in 6:11-12 he expresses his personal solicitude ("we earnestly desire") that they will persevere and so come to the fullness of what they can hope for in Christ. The stern warning of 6:4-8 has been replaced by the soothing talk of 6:9-12. But as the final comments in 6:12 indicate, the problem of spiritual sluggishness remains. If they are to enjoy what God has promised, they need to imitate the faith and patience shown by their spiritual forebears—a theme developed at length in Hebrews 11.

6:13-20 An assurance about God's promises

The reference to "inheriting the promises" in 6:12 provides the occasion for an assurance about God's promises in 6:13-20, which in turn prepares for the reflection in 7:1-28 about God's promise of a priest "according to the order of Melchizedek" in Psalm 110:4.

The key biblical text in the assurance is Genesis 22:16-17 in which God, impressed by Abraham's willingness to sacrifice his son Isaac, promises to Abraham many descendants. The two key points in the text for the author of Hebrews according to 6:13-15 are the content of the promise and the oath formula by which it is introduced ("he swore by himself"). The content of the promise is "'I will indeed bless you and multiply' you." The oath formula is distinctive precisely because God "swore by himself." And the result is that Abraham obtained the promise "after patient waiting"—mostly likely not through Isaac alone but superabundantly through Christ.

In 6:16-18 the preacher continues his reflection on the oath and the promise of Genesis 22:16-17. In 6:16 he sets forth two basic principles of law: We humans customarily swear an oath by someone greater ("so help me God"), and we use an oath to end an argument ("I swear to God"). Then in 6:17-18 he refers back to Genesis 22:16-17 to make the case that God's promise is based not only on the content of the promise itself but also on the oath that precedes it. We can trust God's promise to Abraham and his descendants (in Christ) because it is based on "two immutable things"— God's word and God's oath. The significance of these reflections will become clearer in the meditation on Psalm 110:4 in chapter 7.

The final two verses (6:19-20) bring the listeners back to the topic of the high priesthood of Christ, which will be treated at length in chapter 7. They also introduce two striking images. God's promise fulfilled in Christ is "an anchor of the soul" (6:19), and Jesus is the "forerunner"—the leader who has gone before us to eternal life with God (6:20). As the high priest of Leviticus 16 entered the Holy of Holies on the Day of Atonement, so Christ has gone before us to enter God's heavenly court.

7:1-28 Jesus as a priest according to the order of Melchizedek

After moving from the first reflection on Christ's priesthood in 4:14–5:10 to exhortation in 5:11–6:20, the author returns to his main theological topic: Jesus' priesthood according to the order of Melchizedek.

In the Old Testament Melchizedek appears only in Genesis 14:17-20 and Psalm 110:4. These two passages will serve as the biblical basis for the author's argument about the superiority and eternal character of the priesthood of Christ. Although there were some speculations about Melchizedek in early Jewish and Christian writings, here the author is concerned only with establishing his points on the basis of these two biblical texts. How he handles them reveals much about Jewish biblical interpretation in the first century A.D. and about the Christian conviction that Christ is the key to the Scriptures.

The reflection on Genesis 14:17-20 in Hebrews 7:1-10 seeks to show the superiority of Christ's priesthood to the Jewish levitical priesthood. In 7:1-2a the author introduces Melchizedek as "king of Salem and priest of God Most High" and focuses on the two matters of greatest importance to his argument: Melchizedek blessed Abraham as he returned from battle, and Abraham gave to Melchizedek a tithe or "tenth of everything."

In 7:2b-3 the author considers the person of Melchizedek. His name can be interpreted in Hebrew to mean "king of righteousness" or "righteous king." Likewise, the name of his city "Salem" (which was most likely Jerusalem) can be associated with the Hebrew word for "peace." As righteous king and king of peace, Melchizedek was a type of Christ. Moreover, in Genesis 14:17-20 Melchizedek comes out of nowhere. He is given no genealogy ("without father, mother, or ancestry"), and nothing is said about his birth or death ("without beginning of days or end of life"). This argument from silence contributes to the author's case that Melchizedek prefigures Jesus the Son of God. But the real focus of attention is the superior priesthood of Melchizedek and Christ.

The rest of the argument on the basis of Genesis 14:17-20 in 7:4-10 focuses on the acts of blessing and tithing. By Jewish custom the superior figure blesses the inferior figure. By Jewish custom all the other tribes pay a tithe or tax to support the priestly tribe of Levi (see Num 18:21-24). But according to Genesis 14:17-20 Abraham gave a tenth of all his spoils (a tithe) to Melchizedek, who had blessed Abraham. Both actions show the superiority of Melchizedek to Abraham. Since the patriarch Levi—from whom the Jewish levitical priests traced their lineage—was a descendant of Abraham, these two actions, according to the reasoning of the author of Hebrews, suggest the anteriority and superiority of Melchizedek's priesthood to that of Levi. It is as if Levi, before he was born, had already acknowledged the superiority of Melchizedek and so of Christ. The next step in the argument is to prove that Christ's priesthood is the priesthood of Melchizedek.

The reflection on Psalm 110:4 in Hebrews 7:11-28 seeks to establish the eternal character of Christ's priesthood. The text is quoted in 7:17: "You are a priest forever / according to the order of Melchizedek." The oracle is introduced by an oath formula, which is quoted in 7:21: "The Lord has sworn, and he will not repent: / 'You are a priest. . .'" The author contends that the promise (ratified by an oath) of an eternal priesthood in Psalm 110:4 has been fulfilled in Christ.

Having established the anteriority and superiority of Melchizedek's priesthood in 7:1-10, the author now argues that the priesthood of Melchizedek has found its fulfillment in Christ, and that Christ's priesthood has superseded that of Levi. Whereas the events described in Gen 14:17-20 preceded chronologically the law of Moses and the levitical priesthood, the oracle in Psalm 110:4 (whose origin in David's time is assumed) came later than the law of Moses and the levitical priesthood.

In 7:11 the author reasons that if the levitical priesthood brought "perfection" (see 7:28), there would have been no need for God to promise another priesthood in Psalm 110:4. He observes in 7:12 that a change of priesthood implies a change of law. This is part of his argument that Christ represents better promises and a better covenant.

There was, however, an obvious obstacle to calling Jesus a priest in a Jewish context. Jesus did not belong to the priestly tribe of Levi. Rather, he belonged to the royal tribe of Judah through King David. The author freely admits this fact in 7:13-14. How then could Jesus be called a priest? This was made possible through Jesus' resurrection from the dead. Jesus became a priest "by the power of a life that cannot be destroyed" (7:16), thus fulfilling the promise of an eternal priesthood ("forever") in Psalm 110:4. His priesthood replaced the weak and imperfect priesthood of Levi. Because Christ's priesthood has provided an access to God that was impossible under the old priesthood, it has introduced "a better hope" (7:18-19), which is eternal life with God.

The eternal priesthood of Christ is based according to 7:20-22 not only on the promise of God ("You are a priest forever") but also on the oath of God ("The Lord has sworn, and he will not repent"). At this point the author builds on his reflections about two immutable things—God's promise and God's oath—in 6:13-20. Just as Christ's priesthood means "a change of law" (7:12) and "a better hope" (7:19), so it is also "the guarantee of an [even] better covenant" (7:22). The levitical priesthood was not eternal, since the levitical priests died (7:23). But since the risen Christ lives forever, his priesthood is eternal (7:24) and so is "always" able to make intercession with God (which is what priests do) for "those who approach God through him" (7:25).

The concluding reflection in 7:26-28 highlights the heavenly character of Christ's priesthood. He is "holy, innocent, undefiled, separated from sinners, higher than the heavens" (7:26). His death on the cross represents the one, perfect sacrifice. And so he has no need to offer sacrifices every day for his own sins and the sins of others. In describing the perfect sacrifice of Christ in 7:27 the author summarizes the theology of his entire work: "he did that once for all when he offered himself." Christ is both the priest (the one who offers sacrifice) and the victim (what is offered), and his sacrifice has value "once for all." There is no need for other sacrifices or other priests in the light of Jesus' one, perfect sacrifice.

The final verse (7:28) argues for the superiority and eternal character of Christ's priesthood on three counts. Whereas the law merely "appoints" high priests, the oracle about Christ's priesthood in Psalm 110:4 is accompanied by a divine oath. Whereas the levitical high priests were subject to "weakness," the risen Christ is the Son of God "made perfect forever." Whereas the levitical priesthood was part of the law of Moses, Christ's priesthood which came later than the law not only with regard to Christ but also to Psalm 110:4 is the key to the better covenant—the primary topic of chapter 8.

8:1-6 Jesus' heavenly priesthood

Having established the eternal character of Christ's priesthood on the basis of Psalm 110:4, the author argues that the place of Christ's priesthood and sacrifice is heaven. As a good preacher, he offers in 8:1 both a recapitulation ("we have such a [great] high priest") and a transition to the next topic (heaven as the locus of Christ's priestly ministry). Here Psalm 110:1 ("The LORD said to my Lord: 'Sit at my right hand . . .'"), which was already cited in 1:13 (see also 1:3), serves as one starting point. The other starting point is the early Christian belief that Jesus, having really died, was raised from the dead and now lives with God in glory ("at the right hand of the throne of the Majesty in heaven").

The two main topics of 8:2-5 are the sanctuary and the sacrifices associated with Christ's priesthood. The sanctuary where Christ ministers has been established by God, not by human beings. It is therefore the "true tabernacle" in the sense that every earthly sanctuary is a copy and shadow of the heavenly sanctuary. This theme is developed in 8:5.

Before that, however, the author must treat in 8:3-4 the heavenly nature of Christ's sacrifices. If Christ were on earth, he would not be offering sacrifices since by the definition of the law of Moses he would not be a priest (because he was from the tribe of Judah, not of Levi). But of course, the sacrifice of Christ was his own self in his death on the cross. Those priests who function on earth do so at an earthly sanctuary and offer earthly gifts and sacrifices to God. Their sanctuary is only "a copy and shadow of the heavenly sanctuary" (8:5).

Such language is reminiscent of Plato's teaching that the visible world is but a copy and shadow of the ideal world. A more likely source, however, is God's instruction to Moses in Exodus 25:40 when Moses began to construct the tabernacle: "See that you make everything according to the pattern shown you on the mountain." The idea is that God gave Moses a "blueprint" or prototype of the tabernacle on Mount Sinai. The heavenly sanctuary of Christ's priesthood is "the real thing," and other sanctuaries are at best poor imitations. Since the author had already established the "better promises" and the "more excellent" character of Christ's ministry, 8:6 functions as another summary. It also serves as a transition, since it introduces the theme of a "better covenant."

8:7-13 The old and new covenants

This section contains the longest continuous Old Testament quotation in the New Testament. The text is the prophecy of God's new covenant with his people that appears in Jeremiah 31:31-34. The historical background is the prophet's recognition that soon Jerusalem and its temple would be captured and destroyed by the Babylonians in the early sixth century B.C. While often described as a prophet of doom, Jeremiah was also a prophet of hope. His hope was based on God's fidelity to his people and to his promises, not on the strength of Judah's armies and kings. His prophecy of a new covenant looks forward to a restored and superior relationship between God and Israel, one more perfect than anything that Israel had yet experienced.

The author in 8:7 introduces the quotation by observing that if the first covenant had been perfect and without blemish, there would have been no need for a second or new covenant. At this point and 8:13, his only explicit interest is with the word "new" in the promise of a new covenant. Nevertheless, there are other themes in Jeremiah 31:31-34 that are also important, especially the ideas of God's renewed relationship with Israel, the internal appropriation of the new covenant ("in their minds . . . upon their hearts"), and the forgiveness of sins.

The concluding comment in 8:13 explores the implications of the "new" covenant. Such language, according to the author, makes the first covenant "obsolete." He goes on to qualify that strong term by explaining that "what has become obsolete and has grown old is close to disappearing." That was the perspective of the prophet Jeremiah, for he recognized the catastrophe that would soon fall upon Judah in the early sixth century B.C. Is it also the perspective of the author of Hebrews? If so, to what does he refer? Could it be the Jerusalem temple (which was destroyed in A.D. 70), the institutions of the Old Testament (priesthood, sanctuary, sacrifices, etc.), or Judaism in general? Why are they said to be "close to disappearing," instead of already "disappeared"?

9:1-10 The earthly sanctuary

Having argued that the sanctuary of Christ's priesthood is in heaven, the author explains that the earthly sanctuary described in Exodus 25–26 was a shadow or "parable" of the real thing. He also prepares for the characterization of Christ's perfect sacrifice in 9:11–10:18 in terms of the rituals of the Day of Atonement (Leviticus 16).

The "earthly sanctuary" of the first covenant is described in 9:1-5 in terms of its "regulations" (which in 9:10 are called "regulations concerning the flesh"). Taking his information from Exodus 25–26, the author first in 9:2 mentions the outer tent or tabernacle, with its furnishings consisting of the lamp-stand, the table, and the bread of offering. The name of the outer tent is "the Holy Place." The inner tent is called "the Holy of Holies," the place where only the high priest could enter once a year on the Day of Atonement (9:3-5). Its furnishings—the gold altar of incense, the gilded ark of the covenant, a gold jar containing manna, Aaron's staff, and the tablets of God's covenant with Moses—are more exotic and elaborate than those of the Holy Place. The list is drawn from the book of Exodus and from popular traditions, not necessarily from the realities of the Second Temple. The most important feature of the inner tent, however, is "the place of expiation" (often translated as "the mercy seat"), the place in the Holy of Holies that was sprinkled with blood by the high priest on the Day of Atonement (see Lev 16:14-15; Rom 3:25). Recognizing that prolonging these descriptions might lead to distraction, the author in 9:5 abruptly breaks off his treatment ("now is not the time . . .").

To highlight further the importance of the rituals of the Day of Atonement, the preacher in 9:6-7 contrasts what happened in the outer tent and what happened in the inner tent. Whereas in the Holy Place many priests repeatedly performed their sacrifices for sins, only the high priest might enter the Holy of Holies once a year for the purpose of sprinkling blood there "for himself and for the sins of the people."

However important the rituals of the Day of Atonement might seem, they were inadequate when compared with the perfect sacrifice of Christ (9:8-10). These institutions of the old covenant were used by the holy Spirit to foreshadow the genuine "way into the sanctuary" that Christ the high priest would reveal (9:8). They belonged to "the present time" and could not perfect persons in the depth of their being ("in conscience"). They were "regulations concerning the flesh" that were in force "until the time of the new order" or "the age to come" that has been inaugurated by Christ's life, death, resurrection, and exaltation. They functioned as symbols or parables, dealt with earthly things (food, drink, ablutions, etc.), were open to only a select few (the priests), and were imperfect by nature. They pointed to the perfect sacrifice of Christ offered in his death on the cross for us and for our sins.

9:11-28 The efficacy of Christ's blood

The essence of the Day of Atonement ritual was the high priest's sprinkling of animal blood inside the Holy of Holies. Based on the idea of blood as a symbol of life and as an agent of purification, this action was believed to take away the past sins of the people (including those of the high priest himself) and to prepare them for renewed life before God in the new year. For the author of Hebrews, Christ is both the perfect high priest and the perfect sacrifice (in his death on the cross). His blood, shed only once, accomplished what the blood of animals shed annually could not achieve.

In 9:11-14 the author affirms that Christ the "high priest of the good things that have come to be" ("the age to come," which is already here) has entered the divinely constructed tent (heaven) with his own blood (not animal blood) as the perfect sacrifice offered once for all, with "eternal redemption" as its result. He celebrates the greater efficacy of Christ's sacrifice by arguing in 9:13-14 "from the lesser to the greater." If the animal blood used in earthly sacrifices had any efficacy with regard to the body, how much more has Christ's perfect sacrifice on the cross ("the blood of Christ") cleansed consciences from sins and made it possible to worship the living God. By entering the heavenly sanctuary with his blood, Christ provided an effective cleansing from sin and made possible right relationship with God (what Paul calls "justification").

In 9:15-22 the author contends that the blood of Christ has inaugurated the new covenant prophesied by Jeremiah. Christ is the mediator of that new covenant through his death on the cross (9:15). To explain this point in 9:16-17, he plays on the double meaning of "testament," which can refer to a "covenant" and to a "last will and testament." Just as a last will is activated only when the person dies, so the promise of the new covenant has been activated through the death of Christ. The result is redemption from sins under the old covenant and participation in the eternal inheritance. Just as the old covenant given to Moses on Sinai was ratified by the sprinkling of blood upon an altar (see Exod 24:3-8), so the new covenant has been ratified by the shedding of Christ's blood on the cross. In 9:22 the author describes blood as a means of purification and of forgiveness, and observes that "without the shedding of blood there is no forgiveness" (see Lev 17:11).

In 9:23-28 the author argues that by approaching God in the heavenly sanctuary with his own blood Christ brought about a complete purification

Hebrews 9

of sins. But Christ's work is not simply a past event ("once for all," see 9:12). Rather, Christ the high priest continues to exercise a priestly ministry in heaven: "that he might now appear before God on our behalf" (9:24). Moreover, Christ the high priest will exercise a priestly ministry at the last judgment when he "will appear a second time" (9:28). Since he has already taken away sins by his death on the cross, then his task will be "to bring salvation to those who eagerly await him." Thus there are three phases in the priestly work of Christ: cleansing from sin (past), ongoing mediation on our behalf (present), and final deliverance (future).

10:1-18 Christ as the effective priest and sacrifice

As he reaches the close of his reflections on the priesthood and sacrifice of Christ, the author in 10:1-4 insists that the repeated sacrifices under the law of Moses were ineffective. At best they were "a shadow of the good things to come" as opposed to the true form or image, and so they were incapable of making perfect those who offered them at the Day of Atonement (10:1). The very fact that these sacrifices were repeated every year shows their inability to bring about real atonement for sins (10:2-3). Finally the author asserts in 10:4 that the blood of bulls and goats cannot take away sins.

Next in 10:5-10 the author contends that the many sacrifices offered according to the law of Moses have been superseded by the one perfect sacrifice of Christ. To make this point he places the words of Psalm 40:5-7 in the mouth of Christ "when he came into the world" (the incarnation) as a statement of Christ's vocation and the superiority of his sacrifice. In 10:8 the author identifies the sacrifices of Psalm 40 with those offered according to the law of Moses. Then in 10:9-10 he goes on to contrast those sacrifices with the one perfect sacrifice of Christ's body offered on the cross. His sacrifice has superseded and even abolished the animal sacrifices. Only the one perfect sacrifice of Jesus Christ was able to make people holy ("consecrated"). That sacrifice was offered in a spirit of faithful obedience to God's will: "Behold I come to do your will."

Just as the many sacrifices under the law have been superseded by the one sacrifice of Christ, so according to 10:11-14 the many priests have been replaced by the one priest. Under the law of Moses there were many priests who offered the same sacrifices over and over without being able to take away sins (10:11). However, Christ the one great high priest "offered one sacrifice for sins" (in his death on the cross) and has been exalted to God's right hand (Jesus' resurrection and ascension, described in terms of Ps 110:1). The one perfect sacrifice of Christ is summarized as follows: "For by one offering he has made perfect forever those who are being consecrated."

Hebrews 10

Whereas the repeated sacrifices by the priests of the old covenant were ineffective, the one sacrifice of Christ the priest of the new covenant brings about the forgiveness of sins. The motif of the new covenant is introduced by quotations from Jeremiah 31:31-34 in 10:15-17. The new covenant that is inscribed on hearts and minds matches the total interior obedience of Christ ("I come to do your will"). The new covenant wipes away sins and allows God's people to make a new start. So effective is the one perfect sacrifice of Christ in forgiving sins that there is no need for any more sacrifices: "Where there is forgiveness of these, there is no longer offering for sin" (10:18). Thus the sacrificial system of the old covenant, which was at best a "shadow" of Christ's sacrifice, has been superseded. From now on the forgiveness of sins is necessarily linked to Jesus' sacrificial death for us and for our sins. Other sacrifices have been rendered unnecessary.

PERSEVERANCE IN CHRISTIAN LIFE

Heb 10:19–13:25

10:19-39 A call to persevere in faith

Following a pattern set in 5:11–6:12, this passage consists of an appeal (10:19-25), a stern warning (10:26-31), and a word of encouragement (10:32-39). It ends on a note of faith, which prepares for the catalogue of the heroes of faith in chapter 11.

Using language reminiscent of 4:14-16, the author in 10:19-21 provides a theological foundation for his appeal by affirmations about what has happened through Jesus' death, resurrection, and exaltation. Through the blood of Christ we have access to the heavenly sanctuary and have a great high priest who mediates with God on our behalf. The three appeals in 10:22-25 feature the virtues of faith, hope, and love. The call to approach God in faith ("with a sincere heart and in absolute trust") in 10:22 builds upon the conviction that Christ's perfect sacrifice has brought about the forgiveness of sins—an experience that is symbolized in baptism. The call to persevere in Christian hope in 10:23 builds on the trustworthiness of God and of God's promises. The call to live in love with fellow Christians in 10:24-25 builds upon the need for Christian community to be the place where Christians encourage one another to love and to do good works in preparation for the Day of the Lord (judgment). The passing observation that some were absenting themselves from the Christian assembly (10:25) is another symptom of the ecclesial situation of the community to which the author wrote.

The stern warning in 10:26-31 (see 6:4-8) again concerns a post-baptismal sin of the most serious kind—apostasy (see 10:29). If one rejects Christ after

Hebrews 10

having embraced Christian faith, there is no effective sacrifice for one's sins because the sacrifices of the old covenant have been superseded and the all-sufficient sacrifice of Christ has been rejected. All that remains for such persons is the "fearful prospect" of judgment and punishment. The seriousness of their sin is highlighted by another argument "from the lesser to the greater." If according to Deuteronomy 17:6 a person may be put to death for idolatry or blasphemy on the testimony of two or three human witnesses, how much greater will the punishment be for those who spurn the Son of God, profane the blood of God's covenant, and commit outrages against the holy Spirit. The fearsome character of God's judgment is reinforced by quotations from Deuteronomy 32:35-36: "Vengeance is mine; I will repay . . . The Lord will judge his people." This stern warning concludes with one of the most menacing sentences in Scripture: "It is a fearful thing to fall into the hands of the living God" (10:31).

As in 6:9-12, the stern warning is balanced by a word of hope and encouragement in 10:32-39. The author in 10:32-34 urges the community to recall what they suffered shortly after having become Christians ("after you had been enlightened"). The way in which these sufferings are described—public abuse, imprisonment, and confiscation of property—may reflect conditions that prevailed at Rome for some Christians in the late fifties or early sixties of the first century A.D. The preacher's point is that the new Christians endured these sufferings joyfully because they were convinced that they had "a better and lasting possession" (10:34). He goes on in 10:35-36 to exhort these people to confidence and endurance in the present situation out of the conviction that they will surely be rewarded by God ("great recompense . . . receive what he has promised"). Then in 10:37-38 he appeals to the second coming of Christ with a christological interpretation of Isaiah 26:20 ("he who is to come shall come") and urges perseverance in faith by quoting Habakkuk 2:4 ("my just one shall live by faith"). He ends in 10:39 by counting himself and his community "among those who have faith and will possess life," thus preparing for the catalogue of biblical exemplars of faith in chapter 11.

11:1-40 Examples of persevering faith

To explain what it means to be "among those who have faith and will possess life" (10:39), the author presents a catalogue of figures from the Old Testament who provide models of persevering faith in God's promises. Similar lists of biblical heroes can be found in Sirach 44–49 and Wisdom 10:1–11:4. What distinguishes the list in Hebrews 11 is the resolute emphasis on "by faith." For the author of Hebrews, faith involves the knowledge of unseen realities, a generous response to God's call, a hopeful trust in God's promises, and faithful endurance in the face of suffering and death.

What may appear to be an abstract definition of faith in 11:1-2 is more a programmatic statement to be illustrated by the examples that follow. That faith involves trust in God's promises ("what is hoped for . . . things not seen") is clear. The problem comes with the Greek words *hypostasis* ("realization") and *elenchos* ("evidence"), and whether they are to be taken as objectively as those translations suggest or in a more subjective way ("assurance . . . conviction"). Of course, faith involves both objective and subjective dimensions, as the following examples will show.

The first examples (11:3-7) correspond to events and figures in Genesis 1–11. The work of creation described in Genesis 1 (11:3) was carried out by the power of God's word, and we understand this to be so "by faith." The reason why God accepted the sacrifice of Abel rather than that of Cain (see Gen 4:1-7) is attributed in 11:4 to Abel's superior faith and righteousness. The reason why Enoch was taken up into heaven (see Gen 5:24) was his great faith, according to 11:5. The case of Enoch leads to a brief reflection in 11:6 on the life of faith as the only life that is pleasing to God and on the necessity for belief in God and in God's desire to reward those who seek him. In the cases of creation, Abel's sacrifice, and Enoch's assumption, the author has provided an interpretation ("by faith") that is not explicit in the biblical texts. In the case of Noah (11:7) he has a strong biblical example of faith. According to Genesis 6:8-22, Noah obeyed God's command to build an ark on the strength of his trust in God's promises "about what was not yet seen" and he was rewarded by "the salvation of his household." Noah's act of faith was both a witness against the corrupt world and a foreshadowing of Abraham's "righteousness that comes through faith."

A second set of biblical examples of faith is provided by Abraham and other patriarchs in 11:8-22. According to 11:8-10, faith is what motivated Abraham to leave his homeland and to enter the promised land of Canaan (see Gen 12:1-4), even though he did not know where he was going. And yet by "dwelling in tents" he acknowledged that the promised land of Canaan was not to be his perfect and final abode. Rather, it was a sign or shadow of the heavenly city of God, "the city with foundations, whose architect and maker is God." Faith, according to 11:11-12, is what enabled Abraham and Sarah to accept the promise (see Gen 17:15-22) that despite their advanced ages and her sterility they would have a son named Isaac, and that their descendants would be as many as "the stars in the sky" and "the sands on the seashore." Abraham's faith rested on the person of God: "for he thought that the one who made the promise was trustworthy" (11:11).

Hebrews 11

In 11:13-16 the author interrupts his list for a reflection on the as-yet-unfulfilled or eschatological nature of the faith displayed by Abraham and Sarah and indeed by all the great Old Testament exemplars of faith. Since "all these died in faith," they failed to enjoy during their lifetimes on earth the fullness of life with God—something that has been made possible through Jesus' death, resurrection, and exaltation. Rather, they remained "strangers and aliens on earth" (11:14; see Gen 23:4) in search of a homeland. However, they recognized that their true homeland was not the land from which they came (and to which they could return) but rather the city that God had prepared for them in heaven. What these heroes of faith hoped for has become a reality through Christ.

The theme of the as-yet-unfulfilled character of the patriarchs' faith is developed by further examples in 11:17-22. Faith moved Abraham to offer his son Isaac as a sacrifice to God, despite the fact that God's promise of many descendants was to be through Isaac (11:17-19). What made Abraham willing to obey God's command was, according to the author, a belief in God's power to raise the dead back to life, and so Isaac was a symbol foreshadowing the resurrection of Jesus. The blessings bestowed by Isaac and Jacob (11:20-21) were signs of their hopes for future generations. The observation that Jacob gave his blessing while "leaning on the top of his staff" (see Gen 47:31 in the Greek version) adds to the "pilgrim" motif of faith. The fact that Joseph gave instructions about the Exodus from Egypt and about moving his bones out of Egypt (11:22; see Gen 50:24-25) indicates the incomplete nature of what he experienced and his trust that there would be much more to the promises of God.

The faith displayed by the patriarchs was also at work in Moses and the Exodus generation according to 11:23-31. Faith led Moses' parents to conceal him in defiance of Pharaoh's decree to kill the male infants of the Hebrews (11:23; see Exod 2:1-10). Faith led Moses to identify himself not with the royal household of Egypt but rather with Israel as the people of God (11:24-27; see Exod 2:11-15), even though this meant suffering "the reproach of the Anointed" and so prefiguring the sufferings of Christ. Faith led Moses to command the elders of Israel in Egypt to sprinkle blood from the Passover lambs at the doors of the residences of the Hebrews (11:28; see Exod 12:21-23). He had no guarantee beyond his faith in God's promises that this action would protect the Israelites from "the Destroyer of the firstborn." Faith led Moses and others to cross the Red Sea with the conviction that they would emerge safely and that the Egyptians would not do so (11:29; see Exod 14:22-28). Faith led Joshua to trust that the walls of Jericho would fall (11:30; see Josh 6:12-21), and faith led the Gentile prostitute Rahab to ally herself with the people of God by protecting the Israelite spies (11:31; see Josh 2:1-21; 6:22-25).

A good preacher knows when to bring a topic to its conclusion ("What more shall I say?"), and so in 11:32-38 he summarizes the subsequent history of God's people. After a list of heroes (11:32), he gives examples of triumphant faith in 11:33-35a and still more examples of endurance in the face of suffering in 11:35b-38. These heroes bore their sufferings out of faith in the resurrection (see 11:35a), which was appropriate since this world "was not worthy of them" (11:38a).

However great was the faith that these heroes displayed, they nonetheless did not yet receive what had been promised (11:39-40). What God promised was forgiveness of sins and eternal life with God—something made possible through Jesus' death, resurrection, and exaltation. By contrasting the heroes of Old Testament faith and "us" (Christians), the author suggests that "we" have received what God promised and so are in a superior position to them.

12:1-17 A call to persevere in faith

The heroes of faith celebrated in chapter 11 constitute a "cloud of witnesses" for Christians (12:1). Nevertheless, the Christians addressed in this sermon are still engaged in a struggle or race that demands endurance and discipline. In this contest they have the good example of Jesus as "the leader and perfecter of faith" (12:2). What is especially significant for them is Jesus' own willingness to endure the suffering and shame of the cross in full expectation of his exaltation to God's throne (see Ps 110:1) and the perfect joy of life in heavenly glory. For Jesus, the cross was a trial to be endured in the hope of glory.

In 12:3-4 the preacher addresses the community's own situation in the light of Christ's example. His endurance of hostility from sinners should inspire them to "not grow weary and lose heart" (12:3). Moreover, their situation, however serious it may seem, in fact has not yet reached the point of "shedding blood" (12:4), which suggests that they have not yet faced martyrdom.

To help the community to understand its present sufferings and to encourage them to persevere in faith, the author offers a reflection on the theme of suffering as a discipline, with Proverbs 3:11-12 as his main text. His emphasis is on the educative or formative (rather than punitive) value of suffering. In the biblical passage quoted in 12:5-6 the sage directs his student ("my son") to accept the divine discipline as a sign of God's love and concern for him. In the biblical world a father had the ultimate responsibility for child rearing (especially in the case of sons). In his first application in 12:7-8 the preacher suggests that their present sufferings are proof that God regards the Christians as legitimate "sons" for whom he takes responsibility.

He goes on in 12:9-11 to compare the discipline applied by earthly fathers with the discipline applied by God. If earthly fathers win respect from the sons whom they discipline, how much more should we respect "the Father of spirits" in our sufferings (12:9). Moreover, the benefits from divine discipline—sharing in God's holiness, and "the peaceful fruit of righteousness"—in the present and the future far outweigh the benefits that may come from a human father's application of discipline. Divine discipline is superior to human discipline in forming children of God.

Rather than obsessing over their present sufferings, the addressees need to get back on the "way" of discipleship. Using language from Isaiah 35:3 and Proverbs 4:26, the preacher in 12:12-13 urges them to pull themselves together and walk along the straight path with renewed spiritual energy. They also need to remove whatever hinders their spiritual progress. Therefore, according to 12:14, they need to strive for the peace and holiness that come from God and that bears witness to God in the world. They need to guard against the "bitter root" (see Deut 29:18) of division that can harm the life of the whole community (12:15). And they need to learn from the negative example of Esau who because of his impatience and desire for momentary gratification (see Gen 25:29-34) sold his birthright to Jacob and could not get it back when he sought Isaac's blessing (see Gen 27:30-45). The case of Esau reiterates in a subtle way the author's previous stern warnings about the impossibility of repentance after apostasy (see 6:4-8 and 10:26-31).

12:18-29 A call to heavenly worship

Through Christ's priestly sacrifice on the cross, we have access to God. What the institutions and rituals of the old covenant were powerless to do, Christ has accomplished by making possible right relationship with God (justification) and participation in the heavenly worship of God.

This point is developed in 12:18-24 by contrasting the old worship symbolized by Mount Sinai (12:18-21) and the new worship symbolized by Mount Zion (12:22-24). The description of Mount Sinai is taken mainly from Exodus 19 (see also Exod 20:18-21 and Deut 4:10), though what appears to be awesome in Exodus 19 is interpreted negatively as terrifying in Hebrews. The Sinai experience was full of violent images of storms, fire, and trumpet blasts. It featured a command (Exod 19:12-13) to stone any animal that touched the sacred mountain. Even Moses the mediator of the Sinai covenant confessed that he was "terrified and trembling" (Deut 9:19). By contrast, the new heavenly worship symbolized by Mount Zion is peaceful and joyful. Here Mount Zion is not the earthly city of Jerusalem but rather the heavenly Jerusalem (see Revelation 21–22), "the city of the living God." It is inhabited by angels, "the firstborn enrolled in heaven" (perhaps the saints of the Old Testament, Christian martyrs, or Christians who had already died), God the judge of all, and Jesus the mediator of a new covenant. Whereas Abel's blood bore witness against Cain's guilt and cried out for vengeance (see Gen 4:10), Jesus' blood spoke more eloquently in that it won forgiveness of sins and brought about perfect reconciliation with God.

The contrast is followed by an admonition not to reject God's warning (12:25-29). In the new covenant of Mount Zion/heavenly Jerusalem it is God who speaks. If the people of the Sinai covenant refused to listen to Moses and were punished for their obduracy, how much more punishment can Christians expect if they fail to heed the heavenly voice of God and his Son (see 6:4-8; 10:26-31; 12:15-17).

While the author of Hebrews is generally concerned with realized eschatology (the present benefits of Christ's saving action) and spatial eschatology (heaven and earth), he does occasionally engage in temporal eschatology (as in 10:27-28). Here in 12:26-28 his biblical text is from Haggai 2:6: "I will once more shake not only earth but heaven." The earth shook at the giving of the old covenant at Mount Sinai (see Exod 19:18). But the sixth-century prophet Haggai spoke of a future shaking that would involve both earth and heaven. At God's future eschatological intervention both earth and heaven will shake. Nevertheless, the final shaking will be good news for those who have persevered in faith and in the worship of God. The result will be the removal of "shaken, created things" (12:27). Then the kingdom of God will be "the unshakable kingdom" in which the worship of God will be conducted "in reverence and awe." To those consoling and encouraging words, the preacher adds a concluding comment designed to bring his audience back to the serious challenge that faced them in the present: "For our God is a consuming fire" (12:29; see Deut 4:24; Isa 33:14).

13:1-6 General instructions

Under the heading "let mutual love continue" (13:1), the author encourages the cultivation of the human virtues of hospitality, compassion, chastity, and avoidance of greed. In each case he provides a theological motivation.

As Acts and the New Testament epistles show, there was an extensive network of communication among early Christians. The virtue of hospitality toward emissaries (apostles) and other travelers was essential to its smooth functioning. The theological motive about receiving angels attached to the admonition not to neglect hospitality (13:2) alludes to episodes involving Abraham and Lot in Genesis 18 and 19. The directive to be mindful of prisoners and victims of torture (13:3) is accompanied by an appeal to human solidarity. The call to respect marriage and to avoid adultery (13:4) invokes God's judgment against fornicators and adulterers (see 1 Cor 5:13; Eph 5:5). The rejection of greed (13:5) is balanced by contentment with what God gives. The theological motive for such an attitude is trust in God as expressed in God's own promise according to Deuteronomy 31:6, 8. The concluding confession in 13:6 quotes Psalm 118(117):6 to the effect that confidence in God casts out all fear. In this short instruction the motives are quite varied: biblical precedents, human solidarity, divine judgment, and trust in God. The absence of a direct appeal to Christ in these instructions is unusual in a work that is so directly centered on Christ as Hebrews is.

13:7-17 Community life and worship

This section begins and ends with instructions about "leaders" (13:7-9 and 13:17), and contains an intervening reflection on worship (13:10-16). The leaders "who spoke the word of God to you" may include not only those who actually evangelized the group addressed in this work but also the apostles and even the Old Testament heroes of faith celebrated in chapter 11. The statement in 13:8 that "Jesus Christ is the same yesterday, today, and forever" sounds like an early Christian confession of faith, and at the same time fits well with the emphasis in Hebrews on Christ as the eternal leader of God's people. This confession is followed by a warning in 13:9 not to be swayed by "strange teaching." The example of "foods, which do not benefit those who live by them" may refer to the Old Testament sacrifices or to the Jewish food laws. If, however, Hebrews was directed to a Jewish Christian community at Rome (as many scholars think likely), then there may be an allusion to the struggle between the "weak" and the "strong" treated by Paul in Romans 14–15. The author of Hebrews clearly takes the side of the "strong."

The intervening section on worship (13:10-16) begins in 13:10 by making a distinction in the worship of the old covenant and the new covenant. The "altar" refers more likely to the heavenly sanctuary at which Christ the high priest presides than to a church building or even to community celebrations of the Eucharist. Those who continue to "serve the tabernacle" (under the old covenant) have no right to the "altar" of Christ (under the new covenant). If (as seems likely) the original addressees were Jewish

Christians, this statement expresses a sharp distinction between "old covenant" Judaism and "new covenant" Jewish Christianity.

In 13:11-12 the author makes a final attempt to explain Jesus' death in terms of sacrifice. According to Leviticus 16:27, the carcasses of the animals whose blood was used in the Day of Atonement ritual were to be taken outside the camp and burned. In Jesus' time it was forbidden to hold an execution within the city walls of the holy city of Jerusalem. Therefore Jesus was crucified at Golgotha, a small hill which was outside the city walls. Thus according to 13:12 Jesus suffered "outside the gate" in accord with the type or pattern laid out in Leviticus 16. His death was the perfect atoning sacrifice. In light of this typology, the author invites the community to "go to him outside the camp" (13:13) and thus share in the shame that Jesus suffered in his crucifixion. Such action will confirm that their true city is the heavenly Jerusalem ("the one that is to come") and that they have "no lasting city" on earth.

What is true worship for these Jewish Christians? It is not to be found in the sacrifices of the old covenant. Rather, according to 13:15-16, Christian worship is preeminently the praise of God and good deeds. Only here does the author "spiritualize" the concept of sacrifice and relate it to acts of public worship ("a sacrifice of praise") and to good works done by Christians ("God is pleased by sacrifices of that kind," 13:16). Elsewhere, the focus has been on the material sacrifices of the old covenant and the death of Christ interpreted as the perfect sacrifice of the new covenant. The extent to which the "sacrifice of praise" might refer to the Eucharist remains uncertain.

The section ends in 13:17 by returning to the topic of "leaders." Here the leaders are clearly those who presently exercise oversight in the Christian community addressed in this work. The author urges respect for and cooperation with these leaders as being most beneficial for both the leaders and the community.

13:18-25 Final prayers and greetings

The author first in 13:18-19 requests prayers on his own behalf. He attests to the purity of his own intentions ("we have a clear conscience") and hopes to meet soon with the community in person. He clearly knows these people personally, and may well count himself among their leaders (see 13:17).

Then in 13:20-21 the author formulates a prayer on behalf of the community. He prays first (13:20-21a) that God may enable them to do God's will, and then (13:21b) he asks that God may carry out in them what is pleasing to God. God is the beginning and the end of all their good works.

Hebrews 13

The description of Jesus as "the great shepherd of the sheep" is unique in Hebrews (but see John 10:11 and 1 Pet 5:4), whereas the reference to Jesus' resurrection and to "the blood of the eternal covenant" are prominent themes throughout the work.

The request for a favorable reception in 13:22 consists of what is generally regarded as the author's own description of his sermon in written form ("this message of encouragement") and a somewhat disingenuous comment about his having written "rather briefly." The personal information in 13:23 provides a reference to Timothy that is the work's only real link to Paul. Assuming that this is Paul's co-worker, we may suppose that the author knew Timothy. Or perhaps the reference to Timothy was interpolated later to make a connection with Paul and his circle.

The greeting in 13:24a is directed to both the "leaders" (see 13:7, 17) and "all the holy ones" (a common way of referring to Christians). Many scholars find in 13:24b ("those from Italy send you greetings") grounds for supposing that the recipients are in Italy (most likely in Rome), and that the author is conveying greetings from Italians who are living where he is (outside Italy). The text, however, is ambiguous, and it could be read in the opposite way to indicate that the sermon in written form was sent from Italy to another place outside Italy.

The final blessing in 13:25 ("grace be with all of you") is both formulaic (see Titus 3:15) and at the same time expressive of the author's theology of Christ's priestly sacrifice as the ultimate and effective manifestation of God's favor toward humankind.

The General Letters

Patrick J. Hartin

The term "catholic letters" has traditionally been used to designate a group of seven New Testament writings: James, 1 and 2 Peter, 1, 2, and 3 John, and Jude as distinct from the writings of Paul. In the Eastern church the word "catholic" (used in the sense of "universal") was applied to these seven writings. This was an outgrowth of the theological understanding that they were writings addressed, not to any specific church, but to the church at large. This designation indicated the encyclical nature of the letter in that it was intended to be circulated among many churches. In the Western church the designation for these writings was "canonical epistles" (*epistolae canonicae*) indicating the idea that they were letters approved for reading in the liturgy throughout the Christian world.

When Bishop Athanasius of Alexandria issued his Easter letter containing the list of New Testament books in A.D. 367, the catholic letters were placed immediately after the Acts of the Apostles and before the letters of Paul. This same order can be found in many ancient lists of the New Testament canon. It seems that this was the traditional order. The Codex Sinaiticus and the Latin Vulgate adopted a different order, with Paul's letters following the Acts of the Apostles and the catholic letters placed after Paul's writings. The very influential role that the Latin Vulgate played ultimately established this sequence as the traditional one followed today.

The Letter of James

Patrick J. Hartin

INTRODUCTION

Author

The author identifies himself as "James" (Greek, *Iakōbos*), recalling the Hebrew name Jacob, father of the "twelve tribes of Israel." This name was very common in the biblical world. Three significant members of the early Christian community bore this name: James, son of Zebedee, apostle and brother of John (Mark 1:19), executed by Herod Agrippa about A.D. 44 (Acts 12:2); James, son of Alphaeus, also an apostle (Mark 3:18); and James, "brother of the Lord" (Gal 1:19).

Some information regarding the author can be deduced from the text: (a) *He is at home within the world of Judaism.* He makes great use of the Wisdom traditions of Israel. His thought betrays the concrete mentality of the Hebrew Scriptures rather than the abstract thinking of the Greek. (b) *He is also at home within the world of nascent Christianity.* He shows numerous relationships with the thought and traditions of the Gospels, particularly the Sermon on the Mount. (c) *He writes with the authority of a teacher* (3:1). (d) *He does not appear to be an apostle.* The letters of Paul and Peter carefully indicate their role as apostles in their opening greetings (1 Cor 1:1; 1 Pet 1:1). Instead, the author refers to himself as "a slave of God and of the Lord Jesus Christ" (1:1).

James, "the brother of the Lord" and head of the Jerusalem church, appears to fit best the picture of the author that emerges from the text. He was equally at home in the world of Judaism and the world of early Christianity. Paul indicates that this James was among those who were privileged to witness the risen Jesus (1 Cor 15:7). He exercised an important position within the early Christian community in Jerusalem (Acts 12:17). He was an influential figure at the Council of Jerusalem (A.D. 49). Paul refers to him as one of "the pillars" of the church (Gal 2:9). He remained leader of the Jerusalem church until his martyrdom in A.D. 62. The Jewish historian Josephus also mentions him.

One major difficulty with this suggestion is *the excellent quality of the Greek*—it is among the best in the entire New Testament. Stylistically, the writer shows great finesse at using literary devices to make his argument succinctly. This demands someone well educated in Greek rhetorical skills.

The best way to harmonize the evidence is to understand the reference to James (1:1) as demonstrating the writer's desire to invoke James as the authority behind this letter. He must be someone who was closely associated with James. The writer sends this letter in James's name ("the brother of the Lord") shortly after James's death to encourage Jewish-Christian communities in the Diaspora (particularly in the area of Syria or northern Palestine) to hold on to his traditions and teachings and to remind them of the importance they have as "the firstfruits of his [God's] creatures" (1:18).

The term "brother of the Lord" has been variously interpreted in the Christian tradition (see discussion in Patrick J. Hartin, *James*, Sacra Pagina Series 14 [Collegeville: The Liturgical Press, 2003] 16–25). However, it is best to see the word "brother" as referring to a broader understanding of kinship (rather than to a physical brother of Jesus). For two reasons: First, degrees of kinship were more loosely defined in the ancient world than they are today. (See, for example, John the Baptist's condemnation of Herod Antipas: "It is not lawful for you to have your *brother's* wife" [Mark 6:16; see also Luke 3:19]. Here, Herod Antipas was only the *step-brother* of Herod Philip.) Second, the above argument supports the Catholic tradition that Mary remained a virgin after giving birth to Jesus.

It is in this sense that this commentary refers to the author as "James, the brother of the Lord."

Hearers/readers

The text identifies the hearers/readers very graphically: "to the twelve tribes in the dispersion" (1:1). The best understanding of this phrase emerges from the hope for the restoration of the twelve-tribe kingdom of Israel. The Exile marked the beginning of the *dispersion* of the people of Israel, and the word "dispersion" (or *Diaspora*) became a technical term for those Israelites living outside Palestine. During the Exile the prophets proclaimed the restoration of this twelve-tribe kingdom. This became a central conviction in late Jewish eschatology and apocalyptic literature. It also lies behind Jesus' call to repentance (Matt 4:17). In Matthew 15:24 Jesus countered the appeal of the Syrophoenician woman with these words: "I was sent only to the lost sheep of the house of Israel." This passage conveys Jesus' mission as gathering in and reconstituting the twelve-tribe kingdom of Israel.

In addressing his hearers/readers in this way, James describes his task as similar to that of Jesus. They constitute the beginning of the restoration of the house of Israel. In line with 1:18, James sees that those who now belong to the new Israel are the "firstfruits" and represent a foretaste of the future, final restoration of God's people.

Genre and purpose

The letter of James belongs to the general class of Wisdom literature that proliferated throughout Israel and the ancient Near East in the first two centuries B.C. While Martin Dibelius classified James as *paraenesis* (a collection of moral exhortations), some modern scholars have proposed that it should be viewed more precisely as *protreptic discourse,* that is, a discourse containing sustained arguments that strive to develop a theme more thoroughly. Since the purpose of protreptic discourse is that of *social formation,* James aims at reminding his hearers/readers of those values that give them their identity as the twelve-tribe kingdom and separate them from the wider society.

Major themes

While the name of Jesus occurs only twice (1:1; 2:1), references to God are far more numerous. The concept of God is at home in the world and belief of Judaism in the first century A.D. In line with the Jewish profession of faith, God is one (2:19). God is merciful and compassionate (5:11); the Father of lights, the creator of the world (1:17); the champion of the poor (5:1-6); and the lawgiver and the judge (4:12; 5:9).

James's message calls believers to harmonize their faith and action. James's ethic was not meant to be read in an individualistic sense, but rather in a communitarian way. James lies squarely in the tradition of the prophets before him in giving expression to the voice of the poor and the marginalized in society. In line with Jesus' teaching, James promises the poor the inheritance of the kingdom (Jas 2:5; Luke 6:20) and challenges the conscience of every hearer/reader to respect the poor.

COMMENTARY

1:1 Greetings

This opening follows the usual structure of a first-century letter by mentioning the author, those to whom it is written, and concluding with greetings. The writer identifies himself simply as James. Since he does not identify himself further, the reader associates him with the most important James in the early church, the leader of the church in Jerusalem, "James, the brother of the Lord" (see Introduction, pp. 768–69). Rather than speak from above, the author chooses the term "slave of God," which recalls the long biblical tradition that identifies leaders of the people in this way, such as Moses (1 Kgs 8:53), David (1 Kgs 8:66), and the prophets (Jer 7:25). It is used in the sense of obedience to God's will and loyalty to God's service (see also Phil 2:7; 1 Pet 2:16).

The community to whom the author writes is identified as "the twelve tribes in the dispersion." By this term the readers are described as the fulfillment of Israel's hopes in the restoration of God's twelve-tribe kingdom in the eschatological age. The long-awaited hopes of the past are now being realized with these Christian communities that are emerging from the people of Israel. The word "dispersion" (literally, Diaspora) means "scattering" and refers to those areas outside Palestine where the people of Israel had been scattered (see Deut 30:4; Neh 1:9; see Introduction, p. 769). Undoubtedly, James is writing to Jewish Christians, who see their community as the beginning of these hopes, for they are the "firstfruits" (1:18). The author intends to outline the type of life this newly constituted Israel is called to embrace. This writing helps readers of every age to see themselves as true heirs of Israel's traditions. He uses the standard form of "greeting" that opens Greco-Roman letters *(chairein)*. He deliberately uses this brief greeting in order to connect with the word for "joy" *(charan)* in the next verse. This is part of James's style of using catchphrases to develop the letter.

1:2-11 Testing, wisdom and the lowly

In place of the traditional thanksgiving section that characterized a Pauline letter, the letter of James introduces two sections expressing joy (1:2-11) and blessing (1:12-27), which present the major themes that will unfold throughout the letter.

The first introductory section (1:2-11) begins with a call to the community to *"consider it all joy"* (1:2; emphasis added) when they experience *the testing of their faith* (1:2-4, *the first theme*). Faith is as important for James as it is for Paul, occurring some sixteen times in this short letter (1:3, 6; 2:1, 5, 14[twice], 17, 18[three times], 20, 22[twice], 24, 26; 5:15). Whenever believers, individually or as a group, are involved in the ordeal of suffering, they should accept it joyfully. As gold is tested and purified by fire, so believers will be purified by trials. Testing produces steadfastness, which in turn leads to wholeness or integrity *(perfection, 1:3-4)*. It reminds the reader of

Matthew's Jesus in the Sermon on the Mount exhorting his hearers: "So be perfect, just as your heavenly Father is perfect" (Matt 5:48).

A second theme emerges in 1:5-8 with the request for wisdom. In the biblical traditions God is the source of all wisdom: "The beginning of wisdom is the fear of the LORD" (Prov 9:10). The gift of wisdom enables people to act in the midst of trials so that their actions lead to wholeness (*perfection*). "Indeed, though one be perfect among the sons of men, / if Wisdom, who comes from you, be not with him, / he shall be held in no esteem" (Wis 9:6). Wisdom is that one gift needed for perfection understood as wholeness, completion, and integrity. James instructs his hearers/readers that if they lack wisdom, they are to ask God, for God is the only one who can grant it. This is similar to the command of Jesus, "Ask and it will be given to you" (Matt 7:7). The believer must pray to God for wisdom, for the knowledge of how to act correctly. For James the root cause of unanswered prayer is lack of faith in God. One is "of two minds" (1:8), having a divided loyalty, as Jesus indicates in Matthew's Sermon on the Mount: "No one can serve two masters. . . . You cannot serve God and mammon" (Matt 6:24). This is a central theme for James, who calls on his readers to make a choice between friendship with God and friendship with the world (4:4).

James introduces a third theme here that has importance throughout the letter, namely, *the contrast between rich and poor* (1:9-11). Both the poor and rich are called upon to "take pride" or to boast in what God does for them. The background for this concept of boasting lies in the Hebrew Scriptures, where God is the source of all blessings (see Jer 9:22-23). The lowly are to rejoice because God has given them an exalted status within the Christian community, where they experience equality with one another. The rich, on the other hand, are those who have lost their position within the wider community, only to discover a true status within the Christian community. True humility finds favor with God (see Sir 3:18). The rich recognize the fragility of life: those who place confidence in their own "pursuits" will waste away suddenly like a wild flower burnt up by the scorching heat (1:11).

1:12-27 Testing, hearers and doers of the word

A second introductory section, introduced with the word "Blessed," again announces major themes that will be taken up in the body of the letter. The first theme expressed here (*endurance under testing brings with it the crown of life*, 1:12-18) is parallel to the first theme of the previous section. Essentially James is saying: "Blessed is the person who withstands trial; that person is progressing toward salvation" (1:12). This is similar to the

Beatitudes described in Matthew 5:3-12. James wishes to emphasize that present trials will effect their reward ("the crown of life," 1:12), because such trials give believers the chance to show their love for God.

The trials that are experienced are not to be regarded as temptations sent by God (1:13). The Gospel tradition holds that temptations do not come from God but from the devil (e.g., Jesus' temptations in the Synoptic Gospels). James continues in the same tradition. The truth is that people are tempted by desires that entice them. The consequence of desiring is described in terms of the image of giving birth (1:14-15): when desire conceives, it gives birth to sin; and when it is fully mature, it gives birth to death in its turn.

James's image of God emerges clearly from this section. God is not the source of evil but the origin of everything that is good (1:16-17). James describes God as the "Father of lights" (1:17). Unlike the heavenly bodies, whose movements result in variations of the light they send out, their creator, God, is unchanging. God's love for humanity is always constant. God's greatest gifts to humanity have been those of creation and rebirth as "the firstfruits of his [God's] creatures" (1:18). This connects back to the opening of the letter to "the twelve tribes in the dispersion." God's gift of rebirth is meant to encompass all humanity: the first implies that others will follow.

A series of sayings brings this introductory section to a conclusion (1:19-27): be slow to anger (1:20-21); quick to hear (1:22-25); and slow to speak (1:26-27). They contain wisdom advice for the hearer/reader on how to lead life in order to be counted among those who are blessed. The hearers/readers are admonished first of all to be *"slow to wrath"* (1:19; emphasis added), because human anger does not conform to God's righteousness, the moral standards set by God. "The word that has been planted in you" (1:21) refers to the word of the gospel that was implanted in the hearts of the believers when they came to rebirth as God's creatures. They are to welcome this word by putting it into practice in their lives. For James salvation requires a response on the part of the believer that is demonstrated in action led according to the moral standards set by God.

Next, James takes up his call to "be quick to hear" (1:19; emphasis added), which focuses on putting faith into action: *"Be doers of the word and not hearers only"* (1:22; emphasis added). This phrase is a suitable summary of the whole letter, expressing the central call to the believer. The word is God's will expressed also in the biblical law (or Torah). The word of the gospel, the message of Jesus, the biblical law—these are all expressions for God's word, God's moral law for God's people. They are different stages of the same reality. Jesus' message captures the heart of the biblical law in the "royal law

James 1

. . . 'You shall love your neighbor as yourself'" (2:8). James illustrates his call to put faith into action by means of a brief parable. The point is captured in 1:24: those who do not follow God's word in their lives are like those who glance briefly at themselves in a mirror and immediately forget what they looked like.

Finally, the saying "be slow to speak" (1:19; emphasis added) is taken up in 1:26-27. In effect, James says: "If you think you are religious but you lack control of speech, you deceive yourselves and your religion is worthless." James is concerned with the inconsistency between belief and speech and returns to this theme elsewhere throughout this letter (2:14-17; 3:9-10; 4:3). This leads him to provide a definition of religion in terms of action (1:27). It is expressed first in terms of caring for widows and orphans. Believers are called upon to imitate God in their actions. The community shows its true relationship with God by reaching out to the least members of society. *Orphans and widows* were symbolic for the most unfortunate members and a reminder of God's care for their community in the past: "You shall not violate the rights of the alien or of the orphan, nor take the clothing of a widow as a pledge. For, remember, you were once slaves in Egypt, and the Lord, your God, ransomed you from there; that is why I command you to observe this rule" (Deut 24:17-18; see also Exod 22:20-23; Ps 94:1-23). The affliction of orphans and widows came from their lack of protection and legal status when the head of the family died. James adds a further identifying marker for his community: religious people should also keep themselves from the defilement of the world (1:27). The call is made not to be conformed to the standards of this world but to take one's values from the gospel message, which continues God's will as expressed in the biblical Torah.

Five themes from this introductory section will be explored throughout the letter: endurance through trial (1:2-4; 12-18; 5:7-11); asking for wisdom (1:5-8; 3:13-18; 4:1-10); the contrast of rich and poor (1:9-11; 2:1-13; 5:1-6); being doers of the word (1:22-25; 2:14-26; 4:13-17); and control of the tongue (1:26-27; 3:1-12; 4:11-12).

2:1-13 Do not show favoritism

James begins the body of the letter by taking up the theme of the contrast between rich and poor introduced before (1:9-11). He envisages a context in which the rich exploit their positions to oppress the powerless. Discrimination against people is incompatible with the faith of Jesus Christ. This is the second of only two explicit references to Jesus in the letter (1:1). The phrase "faith in our glorious Lord Jesus Christ" is difficult to translate. Literally it reads: "the faith of our Lord Jesus Christ of the glory." In referring to the "faith of our Lord Jesus Christ," James refers to Jesus' faithfulness to the Father's will through the obedience of his life. Jesus' faithfulness becomes an example for all believers. In the letter of James faith is directed toward the Father rather than toward Jesus (see 2:19, 23).

James goes on to paint a vivid picture of discrimination: favoritism shown to the rich at the expense of the poor (2:2-4). Even worse, this discrimination is within the assembly, where it ought not occur. James calls the gathering place of Christians an "assembly" (literally, "synagogue," 2:2). The choice of the word "synagogue" in preference to the more customary Christian designation of *ekklesia* is interesting. This is the only time in the New Testament where a Christian gathering is identified as a "synagogue," indicating the closeness of James's community to its roots within the world of Israel.

James provides an example of such atrocious behavior that every reader has to concur that this is not the way the community should behave as followers of Jesus (2:2-4). In a sense, James challenges the accepted values of his own world, in which honor is bestowed upon the rich and powerful. This example also challenges every succeeding generation to reevaluate its own treatment of people and to root out every form of discrimination. Indirectly, James reminds them of Jesus' teaching: the poor are promised the inheritance of the kingdom (2:5; see Matt 5:3).

James provides further support for his call not to discriminate in 2:5-13. He begins by providing an argument based upon God's actions: God has chosen "the poor in the world to be rich in faith and heirs of the kingdom" (2:5). Discrimination also transgresses the royal law, namely, "You shall love your neighbor as yourself" (2:8). James insists that those who belong to a community guided by "the royal law" of love cannot discriminate. The law of love is the true law guiding every aspect of life. Just as Jesus presented the law of love as the epitome of the law itself (see Matt 22:36-40), so James sees it fulfilling the same role. To discriminate breaks Jesus' command to love and makes one a transgressor of the law (2:9). One is called on to carry out the whole law (2:10-11).

Jesus' teaching in the Sermon on the Mount upholds the same vision of carrying out the whole law: "Do not think that I have come to abolish the law or the prophets. I have come not to abolish but to fulfill. Amen, I say to you, until heaven and earth pass away, not the smallest letter or the smallest part of a letter will pass from the law, until all things have taken place" (Matt 5:17-18). This is not casuistry, but rather an understanding of what the law (Torah) is all about. The law (Torah) is the expression of God's will for humanity. One's whole life must be orientated toward implementing God's will completely.

James 2

James's thought concludes with an expression of general principles of judgment and mercy (2:12-13). Mercy triumphs over judgment: for those who have practiced mercy, there is no need to fear judgment (see Jesus' parable on the judgment of the nations, Matt 25:31-46).

2:14-26 Doers of the word / faith and works

This passage continues the line of thought of the previous passage (2:1-13), in which James had stressed that an imitation of Jesus' faithfulness (2:1) excluded discrimination against others. Now, in 2:14-26, this same faith is examined more fully, especially insofar as it expresses itself in action. He presents the theme of the whole argument in 2:14. Faith that is alive needs to demonstrate itself in action—that is the type of faith that saves. In the style of a Greek diatribe, James uses an imaginary example to illustrate the type of faith that saves (2:15-17). On its own faith without works is dead.

James describes a situation in which a living faith will manifest itself in appropriate deeds. His illustration of a brother or sister lacking clothing or food is reminiscent of the parable of the judgment of the nations in Matthew 25:31-46. James concludes with a brief summary of what he had stated in the opening thesis (2:14): faith without works is dead (2:17). He repeats the same refrain again in 2:26. By way of offering proof for his argument, James invents an imaginary opponent to whom he issues the challenge: "Demonstrate your faith to me without works" (2:18). The implication in this challenge is that of course he cannot. Then James offers to show him his faith from his works (2:18). The very heart of the Jewish profession of faith in God as one (the *Shema Israel* expressed in Deuteronomy 6:4-5) required a response in active love. Jesus stressed the same concept that this profession of faith needed to be demonstrated in love of neighbor (Matt 22:36-40). James continues these traditions by showing that true faith needs a response of love (2:18-19); otherwise it is a dead faith, in the same category as the faith of the demons, who believe that God is one "and tremble" (2:19).

To support his perspective (2:20-25), James turns to the Scriptures. Abraham's exemplary behavior is used to support his thesis that good works are necessary. The choice of the example of Abraham is deliberate. As the forefather of Israel, he is also the father of James's community as heir of Israel's traditions. Abraham was justified not by faith alone but rather through his works, seen especially in his willingness to offer his beloved son Isaac on the altar. A conclusion is drawn from the scriptural reference. What was true in the case of Abraham is true universally (2:24): faith unaccompanied by works is not genuine. Abraham is characterized here as "the friend of God" (2:23).

This is significant because James wishes to draw a sharp distinction between those who seek friendship with God and those who find friendship with the world (see 4:4 and the comment on 1:8).

In addition to the holy patriarch, James gives a further example from the Scriptures of someone whose faith flowed forth into works, namely, the prostitute Rahab (2:25). Matthew's early Christian traditions held her in high regard, as can be seen through her incorporation into the genealogy in Matthew's Gospel as an ancestor of Jesus (Matt 1:5). Her hospitality to the messengers of God's people is held up for imitation. She exemplified what James said earlier about caring for widows and orphans (1:27). Christian congregations ought to receive representatives of the church in the same way. Rahab becomes a type of the Christian congregation. James finally clinches his basic thesis with a statement that harks back to the opening of this passage (2:14, as well as to 2:17): "just as a body without a spirit is dead, so also faith without works is dead" (2:26).

Most attention in the letter of James has been focused on this passage because of its seeming conflict with Paul's thought regarding the relationship between faith and works. However, James and Paul are considering two very different issues. James is speaking about *works of faith*, whereas Paul has in mind *works of the law* (Rom 3:28). James's focus is on living out faith in action: "Be doers of the word and not hearers only" (1:22). Faith needs to demonstrate through works that it is alive. Paul, on the other hand, was concerned with a different issue, namely, the question of how one arrives at faith: not through the Jewish law, but through God's free gift. Paul was contrasting *faith with the law*, while James was contrasting *an active faith with a dead faith*.

3:1-12 The tongue and speech

Chapter 3 turns attention to the teacher and the wise person. Once again James takes up themes mentioned in the introductory sections. In the spirit of the Wisdom literature, James gives advice on how to lead life in harmony with faith. An admonition on not becoming a teacher forms the introduction to the discussion on the tongue (3:1). This consideration is particularly appropriate for the role of a teacher within the community. Teaching was exercised chiefly through the oral word of instruction rather than through the written word. The teacher's role in the early church was vital for the development and growth of the community. It could be either positive (building up the community) or negative (undermining or destroying the community).

The role of teachers is often mentioned in the early church (see Acts 13:1; 1 Cor 12:28; Eph 4:11). Teachers focused attention on guiding the community to remain true to their traditions, while showing how these traditions could be newly interpreted and applied to the new situations of the Christian communities. In speaking of the teacher, James does not have an office in mind, but rather a function that is being exercised. James himself functions as a teacher for his community in that he endeavors to apply the Torah and Jesus' teachings to the situation of his own community. For James, the reason people should not become teachers is that "we all fall short in many respects"—in other words, "all of us make many mistakes" (3:2). This theme is common in Hellenistic writings and is also found in the Scriptures (Sir 19:15; Eccl 7:20; 1 John 1:8 and 10). Only "the perfect [person]" (3:2) is able to control speech.

Once again James introduces the theme of perfection or wholeness (see 1:4; 1:25; 2:22). The believer strives for wholeness or integrity in every dimension of life, including speech. James adds image to image, building up the picture of the evil perpetrated by the unguarded tongue (3:3-5a). Like the charioteer, who controls a horse through a small bit, or the pilot, who guides the ship by means of a tiny rudder, so the small tongue controls and guides the whole body, for good or evil. Using language derived from philosophy that had become part of popular culture, James speaks of the evil influence that the tongue exercises on human life at every stage of its development (3:6). James concludes pessimistically that "no human being can tame the tongue" (3:8).

The letter further develops the dangers of the tongue (3:5b-10) by using two frightening images: the tongue is a fire, and the tongue is a cosmic force (3:6). The tongue of the natural, unredeemed person cannot be tamed; it is a "restless evil, full of deadly poison" (3:8). James goes on to speak of the contradictory work of the tongue: we bless God and curse one another (3:9-12). To bless God is the greatest function of the human tongue: thrice daily the devout Jew praised God. But at the same time this tongue is used to curse one another. James emphasizes that the person who is the object of the curse "is made in the likeness of God" (3:9). Consequently, the curse is directed at God.

3:13–4:10 Call to friendship with God

A feature of ancient instruction was the use of what is termed a *topos*, that is, the systematic development of a theme or topic in a standard way. Two such *topoi* lie behind James's instruction: the *topos* of speech (in the previous passage, 3:1-12) and the *topos* of envy (in the present passage, 3:13–4:10). For this reason 3:13–4:10 is judged to be a single unit as it deals clearly and systematically with the topic of envy. Attention now shifts from

James 3–4

the teacher to the wise person. This section opens with the rhetorical question: "Who among you is wise and understanding?" (3:13) and introduces the argument that a believer's whole life must demonstrate works/deeds that are inspired by wisdom from above (3:13).

True disciples know that it is characteristic of truly righteous persons to be inspired by divine wisdom. In this way they show dependence on God. James illustrates a twofold lifestyle for his readers: the one is led without the wisdom from above and is characterized by a life full of "bitter jealousy and selfish ambition" (3:14), which is "earthly, unspiritual, demonic" (3:15). In contrast to this "non-wisdom," James sketches a lifestyle influenced by true wisdom from above (3:17): it is "pure, peaceable, gentle, compliant, full of mercy and good fruits, without inconstancy or insincerity" (3:17). Jesus taught in Matthew's Sermon on the Mount that "by their fruits you will know them" (Matt 7:16). Genuine believers will always exhibit wisdom by the kind of life they lead, which will bring them righteousness (3:18).

James continues to expand the argument by developing this *topos* of envy (jealousy) in 4:1-10. His reference to conflicts and wars (4:1) is characteristic of this *topos* of envy. James is not saying that wars and conflicts have occurred within his community. Instead, he is using a rhetorical device to draw attention to the consequences of envy. James 4:2 is a difficult verse to translate. The New Revised Standard Version (NRSV) offers a more logical option than the New American Bible (NAB): "You want something and do not have it; so you commit murder. And you covet something and cannot obtain it; so you engage in disputes and conflicts." The reason for preferring this translation to the NAB comes from the reference "You kill (murder)." In the NAB translation (see text above) this phrase stands on its own, whereas in the NRSV translation it is understood as a consequence of the inordinate desire of envy, which is the main theme of this whole section.

The heart of James's letter occurs in 4:4 with the contrast drawn between friendship with the world and friendship with God. A choice is given to the hearer/reader: you have to decide between friendship with God or with the world. This reaches back to the opening of the letter (1:8), where reference was made to the "man of two minds." Jesus offers the same choice in the Sermon on the Mount: "You cannot serve God and mammon" (Matt 6:24). The opening word of 4:4 ("Adulterers") underscores the seriousness of this choice, since it recalls breaking the covenant relationship between God and God's people. Throughout the Hebrew Scriptures the breaking of the covenant relationship is compared to the rupture of the marriage bond through adultery.

As he has done previously, James offers two scriptural quotations to support his argument. The first quotation (4:5) is difficult to identify: "The spirit that he has made to dwell in us tends toward jealousy." Probably James is quoting a text from memory, which makes identification difficult. James adds a second quotation: "God resists the proud, / but gives grace to the humble" (4:6, which comes from Proverbs 3:34).

From discussing the causes of strife, James turns attention to its remedies (4:7-10). One is asked to submit to God and to resist the devil (4:7). The call to "cleanse your hands . . . and purify your hearts" (4:8) symbolizes a call to pay attention to both actions ("hands") and thoughts ("hearts"). See Sirach 38:10: "Let your hands be just, / cleanse your heart of every sin." "You of two minds" (4:8) again refers to 1:8 and 4:4: you cannot vacillate in allegiance to God. James concludes his argument (4:10) with a saying that is reminiscent of the Jesus saying: "Whoever exalts himself will be humbled; but whoever humbles himself will be exalted" (Matt 23:12; see Luke 14:11; 18:14). Humility is not a social condition but a moral and spiritual one.

4:11-12 Speaking evil against another

For the third time James returns to the theme of speech (see 1:26; 3:1-12). Those who set themselves over against their brothers and sisters by criticizing and judging them also speak against the law and pass judgment on the law. Jesus utters similar instructions not to judge another in the Sermon on the Mount (Matt 7:1). Slander is a serious breach of the command to love one's neighbor (2:8; see also Lev 19:16-18). God is the lawgiver, and humanity is called to be a doer of the law. The concept of God as lawgiver and judge is fundamental to the Hebrew Scriptures. Humanity must be careful not to usurp God's role. James sums up the argument with a rhetorical question: "Who then are you to judge your neighbor?" (4:12). Paul asks a similar question in Romans 14:4: "Who are you to pass judgment on someone else's servant?"

4:13–5:6 Judgment on the rich because of friendship with the world

Here James reflects on a major theme in this letter: the choice between friendship with the world and friendship with God. Two examples (4:13-17; 5:1-6) show how a choice for the world leads to certain consequences. James returns to the theme of the rich for the final time (see 1:9-11; 2:1-13). Merchants are viewed as examples of those who seek friendship with the world (4:13-17). James condemns them for their presumption in laying plans without any reference to God or God's will (4:15). James concludes with a statement that implies responsibility for one's actions (4:17).

In 5:1-6 James changes focus from merchants to the rich, landowning class. When James calls upon the rich to "weep and wail over your impending miseries" (5:1), he is not addressing them (the rich) directly, but his own community. As with the prophets before him, this exhortation is intended to encourage the hearers/readers to remain faithful by showing what is about to befall those outside the community (namely the rich).

James's first attack is against the substance of the rich persons' wealth: it is valueless (5:2-3). In mentioning the coming misfortunes, the author presents them as having already occurred: their garments are damaged; their gold and silver have been destroyed. Matthew 6:19-20 (Luke 12:33-34) presents an interesting parallel to this text: "Do not store up for yourselves treasures on earth, where moth and decay destroy, and thieves break in and steal. But store up treasures in heaven, where neither moth nor decay destroys, nor thieves break in and steal. For where your treasure is, there also will your heart be."

James levels three accusations against the rich: they have defrauded the day-laborers out of their just wage (5:4); they have lived their lives in luxury and self-indulgence; and they have brought the innocent or "righteous one" into court for trial, so that he has been condemned (5:6). Once again the rejection of God's power forms the basic indictment James levels against the rich. They have made a choice for friendship with the world and have usurped everything to suit their own prosperity. The rich have yet to discover and experience the reality of God's power acting on behalf of the poor and oppressed (5:4). The oppressed do not resort to violence; instead they place their confidence in God's judgment at the end of time (5:5-6). This passage brings the body of James's letter to an end.

5:7-11 Call to patient endurance

In concluding the letter (5:7-20), James does not use the customary method of ending letters. Instead, he uses other approaches also evident in Hellenistic letters. In this passage the theme of eschatology is taken up. Many New Testament letters contain eschatological references in their conclusions (see 1 Cor 16:22; 2 Pet 3:12-14; and Jude 18-21).

At the same time James connects back to themes that appeared explicitly in the introductory section, namely, steadfastness and endurance during trial (1:2-4 and 1:12-18). He urges the readers to have patient endurance until "the coming of the Lord" (5:7). This reference speaks of an imminent expectation for Jesus' coming at the end of time: "Behold, the Judge is standing before the gates" (5:9). This would indicate an early date for the writing. James helps his readers to see themselves as belonging to that long line of witnesses, the prophets, who remained ever faithful and persevered in their allegiance to the Lord (5:10). They are a prophetic community with values different from those of the world.

A second example of faithful perseverance is offered, namely, that of Job (5:11). James shows a reliance on the way the traditions about Job had developed in the intertestamental period, that is, the period of two centuries between the composition of the last book of the Old Testament and the first book of the New Testament. In the biblical book bearing his name, Job is hardly a patient person. However, in the intertestamental period (see the *Testament of Job* 1:5; 4:6; 27:6-7) he is presented this way. James uses this popular image of Job to challenge his hearers/readers to a life of patience and perseverance when faced with their own suffering and trials.

5:12 Call to avoid taking oaths

In this single verse James condemns the taking of oaths and appeals once again to his readers to examine their speech (see 1:26; 3:5-12; 4:11-12). In the Christian community one's word should be one's bond. There should be no need for taking oaths, since one should be able to presume truthfulness. The words "either by heaven or by earth" are substitutes for the original form of the oath and are used intentionally to avoid the validity of the oath, and hence its binding force. Jesus in the Sermon on the Mount speaks similarly about avoiding the taking of oaths (Matt 5:33-37).

5:13-18 Prayer

This concentration on the theme of prayer forms a fitting end to the letter, creating an "inclusion" with the opening, that is, the repetition, at the end of a section, of a word or phrase used at its beginning—in this case, prayer. In 1:5 James spoke about asking God for wisdom; now he argues that the way to obtain wisdom is through prayer. Not only is prayer the major theme of this section, but the various words for prayer are the controlling structural elements in its development. In every situation and need the appropriate response is that of prayer. In both suffering and joy people should raise their voices to God in prayer (5:13). The response of the sick is to call in the presbyters (or elders) of the church (5:14-15), who will pray over them and anoint them with oil in the name of the Lord.

James must be reflecting here some ritual in use in his community. Anointing with oil reminds the hearer/reader of the disciples' anointing the sick and casting out demons with the use of oil (Mark 6:13). When ill, one turns to God and asks the support of the community in praying to God for healing. The power of prayer cannot be measured.

James 5

Finally, Elijah, the prophet, is portrayed as a man of prayer. The effectiveness of Elijah is not related to any superhuman gifts or qualities he possessed, but to the fact that he prayed with great intensity and sincerity (5:17-18).

5:19-20 The great commission

The letter concludes somewhat abruptly with an admonition to bring back those who err from the error of their ways. 1 John 5:16 and Jude 22-23 also call on the community to pray that those who sin will change their ways. These three writings (James, 1 John, and Jude) bear witness to the existence of other ways of concluding ancient letters. Once again the community dimension of the letter shines through. Every member of the community shares a responsibility for one another. The commission with which James entrusts his hearers/readers is one that is confined to his own community. James wishes to ensure that those who belong to his community continue to remain true to their commitment. The call to conversion brings together everything that has been said throughout the letter. The hearers/readers are to take the author's instructions and put them into practice. The letter ends on a high note of confidence and assurance in the work of God's salvation.

The First Letter of Peter

Patrick J. Hartin

INTRODUCTION

Author

The writer identifies himself as "Peter, an apostle of Jesus Christ" (1:1). He also says that he was a witness to Christ's sufferings (5:1) and shares "in the glory to be revealed" (5:1). Although he addresses fellow elders (literally "presbyters"; 5:1), he speaks with authority, showing that he holds a position in the early Christian church that makes his voice respected.

At first glance the identification of the author with Peter, leader of the Twelve and witness to Christ's sufferings, seems justified. His position of authority within the early Christian community, his knowledge and use of the Old Testament, his association with both Silvanus and Mark as well as with the city of Rome—all these agree with what is known about Peter.

However, two major difficulties call this identification into question: *(a) the outstanding quality of the Greek* makes it among the best in the New Testament; *(b) the letter's theology bears a resemblance to Paul's theological ideas,* for example, some typical Pauline phrases appear: *in Christ* (3:16; 5:10, 14); *to serve* (1:12; 4:10). Paul's underlying stress on the importance of Jesus' death and resurrection is also well reflected in the thought of First Peter.

The above arguments militate against the writing coming directly from Peter. As with the letter of James, the writer invokes Peter's authority to resolve issues that had arisen after the apostle's death (A.D. 64). The letter probably originated from a circle of Peter's disciples in Rome, using the help of Silvanus and Mark (5:12-13), who account for some themes that were at home in Paul's thought. The letter was probably written in the early seventies, shortly after the destruction of Jerusalem in A.D. 70. The reference to Rome in a symbolic way as "Babylon" (5:13) would be a veiled reference to the Roman destruction of the city of Jerusalem (just as Babylon some five centuries earlier had destroyed Jerusalem). The attitude toward the state that First Peter endorses is very similar to Paul's views as expressed in Romans 13:1-7: they both uphold the state's authority (see 1 Pet 2:13-17).

Hearers/readers

The first letter of Peter identifies the hearers/readers as "the chosen sojourners of the dispersion in Pontus, Galatia, Cappadocia, Asia, and Bithynia" (1:1). The letter uses the reference to the dispersion differently from the way it occurs in the letter of James, where it refers to the scattering of Jewish-Christians outside the land of Palestine. In First Peter the term is used metaphorically, referring to Gentile Christians, who, as God's own people (2:9), are scattered like strangers in this world. Their real homeland is not here but in heaven. The places mentioned (Pontus, Galatia, Cappadocia, Asia, and Bithynia) are names for Roman provinces situated in the northern, central, and western parts of Asia Minor north of the Taurus Mountains. This territory covered an area of some 128,000 square miles. The address (1:1) indicates that this letter was meant to be circulated throughout the provinces of this region. The sequence of names probably indicates the route along which this letter would be circulated.

Major themes

First Peter is a very pastoral letter. The writer aims at strengthening the faith of his hearers/readers. He begins by recalling the Christian hope and inheritance based upon Jesus' resurrection from the dead (1:3-7). Jesus' sufferings are presented as a model for the hearers/readers, who themselves are enduring hostilities and suffering. They can be certain that just as Jesus' sufferings led to glory, so will theirs (1:11). The letter uses some remarkable imagery to describe the dignity of Christian believers: they are true heirs of the inheritance of God's people, Israel: the community is "a living stone" (2:5); "a chosen race, a royal priesthood, a holy nation, a people of his [God's] own" (2:9). This vision of their identity helps them face the challenges of living in a hostile world. Drawing upon well-known household codes, the writer gives direction on how to lead faithful Christian lives within this context.

COMMENTARY

1:1-2 Greetings

The writer opens the letter using the traditional Greco-Roman formula for a letter that identifies the sender, mentions the recipients, and concludes with a form of greeting. Referring to himself as "Peter, an apostle of Jesus Christ," the writer identifies himself with the leader of the original apostles (Mark 3:16). While the apostle Peter is unlikely to have actually written this letter himself (see Introduction, p. 784), the writer invokes Peter's authority for this letter. It is in this sense that this commentary refers to the author as Peter.

The readers are identified as "the chosen sojourners of the dispersion." The "dispersion," or Diaspora, is a technical term referring to Jews living outside their homeland, Palestine. However, the implied readers are certainly not Jews, nor are they Jewish Christians; rather, they are Christians who have come from the Gentile world. As such, this designation should be understood metaphorically as referring to Gentile Christians, who are "sojourners" here on earth, exiles from their true homeland in heaven. The writer uses the term "dispersion" differently from its usage in James 1:1.

The location of the recipients is more specifically identified as "Pontus, Galatia, Cappadocia, Asia, and Bithynia," names of Roman provinces in Asia Minor. The concept of "sojourners" implies that the way of life of these followers of Jesus is different from that of the world around them. They are also called "chosen sojourners," indicating that their identity comes from God's choice of them to become part of God's people. The writer refers to this same concept later when he identifies them as "a chosen race, a royal priesthood, a holy nation, a people of his own" (2:9), using the words of the Exodus covenant (see Exod 19:6).

Finally, the writer mentions the role of the Father, the Spirit, and Jesus Christ in the work of salvation. In doing so, he shows the basis for their identity as God's chosen ones: their choice is founded upon the Father's "foreknowledge" (1:2), particularly the Father's will and intention, to make them into his new people. God's choice of them also involves their "sanctification by the Spirit" (1:2), whose power enables them to lead their lives according to their new dignity. God's choice also includes their "sprinkling with the blood of Jesus Christ" (1:2). Just as Moses ratified the covenant of Sinai with the blood that he sprinkled on the altar (symbolizing God) and the people (Exod 24:3-8), now the new covenant is ratified with Jesus' blood that is sprinkled upon these hearers/readers. This phrase also prepares the reader for one of the major themes that runs throughout this letter, namely, the redemptive work of Jesus and its significance for believers (see 1:18-21; 2:21, 24; 3:18; 4:1, 11). The writer concludes with a prayer that grace and peace be multiplied among the hearers/readers.

1:3-12 Praise for salvation given by the Father, through the Son, and by the Spirit

In place of the traditional thanksgiving section found in Paul's letters, the writer immediately moves to the body of the letter. In the first part of the body the author reflects on the theme of the believer's identity (1:3–2:10). He begins by praising God the Father for the great gift of salvation. This blessing bears notable similarities to the opening of the letter to the Ephesians: "Blessed be the God and Father of our Lord Jesus Christ, who has blessed us in Christ with every spiritual blessing in the heavens" (Eph 1:3). The hearers/readers are reminded that they have been born to a new life through Jesus' resurrection (1 Pet 1:3).

This metaphor of new birth (1:3) has led some commentators to see this as a reference to baptism and to postulate that this writing was based upon an original baptismal homily. While this reads too much into the metaphor, the theology of baptism certainly influences this writer's thought. This new birth gives rise to the hope in an imperishable inheritance in heaven (1:3-5), and for this God is protecting them (1:5). The future hope is contrasted with their present experiences of suffering (1:6), which reveals the genuineness of their faith (1:7). Like precious gold that is purified by fire, so their new faith experiences testing or purification in order to prepare them for the coming of Jesus Christ (1:7).

The writer reminds the hearers/readers, who have not seen Jesus, how they love him and believe in him (1:8). Long ago the prophets of the Hebrew Scriptures foretold this salvation for which the believers are now hoping (1:10). These prophets were led by the Spirit to announce the message of the sufferings of Christ and his subsequent glory (1:11). The prophets show that the path from suffering to glory is the center of Jesus' saving work and the heart of the Christian way of life. This message clearly speaks to Peter's present readers, who are experiencing sufferings and trials. It reminds them that their rebirth in faith is more precious than gold, that it was foretold in the past and looks forward to a future glory.

1:13–2:3 Call to lead a holy life

The hearers/readers need also to respond to the new life they have received through a life that is worthy of their faith (1:13-14). Holiness should dominate their lives. The imagery of the Passover seems to lie behind this section. At Sinai, the LORD God was identified as the Holy One, who called on the Israelites to be holy: "For I, the LORD, am your God; and you shall make and keep yourselves holy, because I am holy" (Lev 11:44; 19:2). First Peter quotes this text and addresses the same call to holiness to his hearers/readers: they are to imitate God in all their actions (1:16). To be holy means to be different, to be set apart. The Israelites were a nation set apart for the worship of God alone. The same is true of Christians: they are called to be different in that their way of life sets them apart from the nations around them (as the writer indicated in the opening of the letter when he referred to them as "sojourners" [1:1]). Their values do not come from the world, but have God as their source. Their new life of holiness enables them to address God as "Father," which inspires an attitude of "reverence" (1:17) for the mystery of God's love and rule over all.

The author goes on to remind the hearers/readers of certain truths they have accepted. Continuing with the Passover theme, he reminds them that just as the Israelites were ransomed from slavery, so have they been ransomed "with the precious blood of Christ" (1:19), not with precious metals "like silver or gold" (1:18). They have been ransomed from the futile way of life they inherited from their pagan ancestors (1:18). First Peter compares the work of Jesus to that of "a spotless unblemished lamb" (1:19): they have received their redemption through the blood of the spotless lamb (Isa 53:7-10). This is a further reminder of the Passover motif (Exod 12:1-30). Through his death, Jesus has ransomed Christians, enabling them to place their trust, their faith, and their hope in God (1:21).

The author repeats many of the themes introduced at the beginning of the letter (1:22–2:3). They are called to "love one another intensely" (1:22). This love is a response to Christ's work, which planted "the imperishable seed" in them (1:23). In support, the author quotes Isaiah 40:6-8, which contrasts the frailty and transitory nature of human life and its accomplishments with the word of the Lord, which remains forever (1:24-25). Their faith endures forever because God is trustworthy. Their growth in new life involves two dimensions: first of all, the stripping away of all vices (2:1) hindering that growth, and the nourishment and enjoyment of the new life they have received (2:2-3). The author concludes with an allusion to Psalm 34:9: "Taste and see how good the LORD is; / happy the man who takes refuge in him."

2:4-10 A holy people

Two metaphors dominate this passage: that of a living stone (2:4-8) and that of a people (2:9-10). The author uses numerous texts from the Hebrew Scriptures to illustrate his vision. The image of a living stone is applied to his hearers/readers. While humanity has rejected them, God has specially chosen them as "living stones" (2:5). They should allow God to build them into a spiritual household to become a holy priesthood able to offer acceptable sacrifices to God through Jesus Christ (2:4-5) who is a "living stone" (2:4).

Three quotations from the Hebrew Scriptures illustrate the meaning. Christ is the "cornerstone" or foundation stone (see Isa 28:16), and whoever places trust in him will be supported (2:6). Further, this living stone (which is Christ) was rejected (2:7) but has become the cornerstone (see Ps 118:22). Finally, he uses Isaiah 8:14 very freely to indicate how Jesus becomes an obstacle and a stumbling block for some (2:8). This metaphor of the living stone and its supportive Hebrew Scripture texts illustrates two things: it shows, first of all, how Jesus Christ is the model for the believing community: just like Jesus, believers are chosen by God but rejected by humanity, especially the world of the pagans. Secondly, since Christ is the cornerstone and foundation for faith, believers are being built in him into a spiritual house as a holy priesthood offering true spiritual worship to God (2:5).

The second metaphor of a holy people (2:9-10) expressing the true identity of Christian believers is revealed in four phrases: a chosen race, a royal priesthood, a holy nation, God's own people. These phrases are all derived from Exodus 19:5-6. Christians as God's possession give worship to God through the power of Jesus' death and resurrection. Their most important characteristic is that they have become "God's people," just as Israel of old was chosen as God's people (2:10). Reflecting on Hosea 1:6-9 and 2:25, the writer proclaims that the readers were originally separated far from God, but now they have been brought into God's household to become God's people (2:10).

2:11-12 Conduct in a pagan environment

The author now begins a second major theme of the letter, namely, the Christian life of witness in the context of a Gentile world (2:11–4:11). The readers are to consider themselves as "aliens and sojourners" in this present world (2:11). Since their true homeland is to be found in heaven (1:1), they are to conduct themselves in this world as though they are just passing through. Their way of life should bear witness to their beliefs among Gentiles (2:12). Even though Gentiles abuse them, Christians are called to respond in a manner worthy of their beliefs. This witness should bring the Gentiles to revise their view of Christians and ultimately to confess and praise their God at the end of time.

2:13-17 Respect for civil authorities

This passage considers the principles outlined above (2:11-12), which called believers to lead lives as "aliens and sojourners" in this world. This is not a call for believers to become a withdrawal sect such as the Qumran community; rather, Christians are called upon to honor civil authorities. Belief in the Lord Jesus should lead Christians to accept the authority of the emperor and governors, acknowledging their right to punish wrongdoers

1 Peter 2

and to reward those who act for good (2:13-14). This witness should silence those who are suspicious of Christians (2:15; see 2:12). The best answer to those hostile to the Christian community is the life-witness of obedient Christians (2:15). Baptism has set believers free from the stipulations of the Jewish Torah (as Paul indicates forcefully in Gal 3:23-27), as well as from slavery to the elemental powers of the world (in the context of a pagan world [Col 2:20-23]). This freedom is not a freedom for license, but a freedom to lead one's life under God's rule (2:16).

The first letter of Peter upholds a positive relationship between Christians and the state; Christians are urged to acknowledge and to give honor to all: the community, God, and the emperor as supreme ruler (2:17). The letter gives expression to a consciousness of the Christian's double obligation of fulfilling God's will as well as the demands of political authority. It is the same issue addressed in the saying of Jesus: "Repay to Caesar what belongs to Caesar and to God what belongs to God" (Mark 12:17). Clearly, First Peter reflects a situation very different from that of the book of Revelation, where Christians are being persecuted by the state for not participating in emperor worship, a context that First Peter does not envisage here. The thoughts of First Peter are very similar to those found in Romans 13:1-7, which may indicate evidence of a common tradition that both First Peter and Paul are using independently.

2:18–3:7 Household instructions

First Peter uses the literary form of "household codes" to express his instructions. A number of such codes or lists appear in the New Testament letters (for example, Col 3:18–4:1; Eph 5:21–6:9; 1 Tim 2:8-15; 5:1-2; 6:1-2; and here 1 Pet 2:18–3:7). These lists describe the ethical obligations members of a household have toward one another. Such lists embrace every possible relationship within society and were very popular among the philosophers of that time.

The developing Christian communities drew up similar ethical lists depicting the way their members should interact with one another as well as with every level of society. The need for such directions was felt most urgently in largely Gentile Christian communities. They wanted to witness to their faith in Jesus Christ in such a way that the wider society would see their faith influencing them to become valuable citizens within society. These lists are an illustration of how the Lordship of Jesus Christ transforms the lives of believers to affect every relationship and to attract others to make a similar confession in the Lord Jesus Christ. In this household list First Peter gives attention to the relationships of slaves, wives, and husbands. When interpreting these household codes, they must be read in the context of their own world and not simply transposed into a twenty-first-century society that would describe these relationships very differently.

2:18-25 Attitude of slaves toward their masters

According to First Peter, belief in God should lead slaves to accept their masters' authority and to endure suffering even when innocent (2:18-19). First Peter differs from the traditional advice to slaves by focusing on the difficult lot of slaves and by considering situations where they suffer unjustly. They are invited to view their unjust sufferings in the light of the unjust suffering of Christ. In such situations, they are called to unite with the sufferings of Christ by following the example that he set. The description of the suffering and death of Christ on our behalf (2:22-24) is presented in terms of the Suffering Servant of Isaiah 52:13–53:12. Christian slaves are called upon to live out their commitment to Christ in a concrete way by imitating his suffering. Christ obtained salvation through suffering for sinners, so Christian slaves can bring others to salvation through the witness of their sufferings. No mention is made here of the responsibilities of masters toward their slaves!

3:1-7 Attitude of wives and husbands

First Peter continues the household code with reference to wives and husbands. Again its thoughts are rooted in the social structure and attitudes of the first century A.D. Christian wives are instructed on how to relate to their husbands who are not believers (3:1). By the witness of their lives and through their belief in Christ, they hope ultimately to win over their husbands to the Christian faith (3:1-2). The wives' concern should not focus on extravagant externals, such as "braiding the hair, gold jewelry, or dressing in fine clothes" (3:3); instead, they should cultivate a gentle internal disposition at peace with God and one another (3:4). Reaching back into the tradition of the Hebrew Scriptures, First Peter holds up Sarah for imitation because of the way in which she respected Abraham by calling him "lord" or "master" (3:6; see Gen 18:12 LXX), a term that indicates respect and honor for the husband. Likewise the wives of pagan husbands should demonstrate respect and honor for their husbands, showing that they are daughters of Sarah (3:6). Abraham and Sarah were important figures in the world of early Christianity (Rom 4:19-25; 9:9; Gal 4:22-31).

Husbands are also instructed to examine their relationship with their wives (3:7). While the cultural view of women dominates this picture ("showing honor to the weaker female sex"), yet the equality of women with men

1 Peter 3

is acknowledged, since in the life of Christ "we are joint heirs of the gift of life" (3:7; see also Gal 3:28: "There is neither Jew nor Greek, there is neither slave nor free person, there is not male and female; for you are all one in Christ Jesus"). First Peter shows that proper relationships cannot be separated from a relationship with God that is expressed in prayer (3:7).

3:8-12 General advice to the whole community

This section brings the household instructions to an end. Generally, household codes would turn to consider the relationship of parents and children at this point. Instead, First Peter turns attention to relationships within the entire community and urges unity and love for one another so that their way of life will truly reflect a Christian community (3:8). Instead of returning evil for evil, they are called to react with a blessing (3:9). That is the way Jesus acted, and they are called to act in like manner (see 2:21-25). Their unity with Christ gives direction to the way they lead their lives. First Peter quotes Psalm 34:13-17 to remind the community that "whoever would love life . . . must turn from evil and do good" (3:10-11).

3:13-17 Christian attitude toward suffering

The Christian is exhorted to have confidence in the midst of suffering. The sufferings envisaged here do not necessarily point to some state persecution, as was the case with the book of Revelation. It seems that Gentiles living in the same society with Christians cannot understand their lifestyle and values. The Gentiles respond with abuse and ridicule, and ostracize them because of their commitment to the Lord Jesus, but this should not cause them to be afraid (3:14). When challenged, Christians should be ready to witness to their faith (3:15). First Peter calls on Christians to make their defense in gentleness and with respect, while being willing to accept suffering, if that is God's will (3:16-17).

3:18-22 Example of Christ

Jesus suffered as an innocent person for the guilty. His death is the reason the hearers/readers and indeed all Christians are now able to approach God (3:18). His suffering led to the ultimate experience of death. But death was not the end. He "was brought to life in the spirit" (3:18) and went "to preach to the spirits in prison" (3:19). It is not too clear who these spirits were. Possibly First Peter has in mind an interpretation of Genesis 6:1-4, where evil angels were held responsible for leading humanity astray into an ever greater wickedness that ultimately provoked God's righteous judgment in sending the flood. These evil angels were imprisoned in a pit after their sin with women. Jesus' proclamation to them by his death and resurrection is a way of demonstrating his victory over the forces of evil: these evil spirits no longer have power over humanity.

This example of Christ's suffering and consequent triumph in the resurrection gives hope to Christians who innocently endure suffering and persecution. Because Christ's triumph over evil is complete, Christians have nothing to fear. Christ has redeemed them from the powers of evil and death and has given them future hope through their new birth in Christ. Reference to Noah (3:20) is also significant. First Peter argues that just as God rescued the faithful Noah from the evil world by means of water, so too God liberates faithful Christians from the evils of their world by means of the waters of baptism (3:21). Jesus' resurrection makes the waters of baptism effective and brings salvation to those who accept it (3:21). Through his resurrection, Jesus Christ shares God's power, and all authority in the universe is subjected to him (3:22). Behind this beautiful description of the saving work of Christ lies a creedal formula in use in the early church. Not only does First Peter use the Hebrew Scriptures as a source to support his teaching, he also uses the language of the liturgy that permeates the Christian community:

> Put to death in the flesh, brought to life in the spirit, he went to preach to the spirits in prison, and having gone into heaven, he is at the right hand of God, making angels, authorities and powers subject to him (3:18, 19, 22; see also 1 Tim 3:16).

This passage has enormous importance for Christian believers. Just as Christ's death brings life, so too Christian suffering is considered life-generating. Christians participate in Christ's death and resurrection through baptism. As Christ "was put to death in the flesh" and "was brought to life in the spirit" (3:18), so Christians die to their sins and are made alive in the spirit through baptism. Christian believers are made aware that they share both in Christ's sufferings and in his resurrection.

4:1-6 Christians live according to God's will

First Peter connects back to the previous section by stressing that Christians who lead a life of suffering with Christ are also dedicated to avoiding a life of sin (4:1) and living according to God's will (4:2). Their lifestyle distances them from the way of life of their Gentile neighbors. First Peter presents a list of vices (4:3) similar to the lists that Paul used in his letters (see Rom 1:29-31; 1 Tim 1:9-10; 2 Tim 3:2-5). The vices described here reflect the type of feasts that pagans used to celebrate. Before becoming Christians, First Peter's hearers/readers used to participate in these celebrations, but now, having embraced Christ and become God's people, they distance themselves from such activities (4:4).

Further, First Peter envisages a preaching of the good news to those who have died (4:6). While Peter does not mention who does the preaching, it seems that he has 3:18-20 in mind, where Jesus preaches after his death. This time, however, the preaching is not to the powers of evil but to those who have died. While the exact reference of "the dead" is disputed, the best explanation is that "the dead" are Christians who had heard and accepted the gospel message but subsequently died before Christ's return.

For early Christians this was an enormous problem, since many believed that Christ would return during their own lifetime. Here First Peter assures his hearers/believers that while in the eyes of the world these Christians have ended up in death in the same way as those who have not believed ("condemned in the flesh in human estimation"), they now share in Christ's triumph over death through resurrection ("they might live in the spirit in the estimation of God," 4:6). First Peter assures his hearers/readers that as Christ triumphed over the powers of evil (3:18-22), so those who believed in him and his message would share with him in that triumph in the resurrection.

4:7-11 Living with the expectation of the end time

With this passage the author brings to an end the second major theme of the letter, namely, the Christian life of witness in the context of a Gentile world (2:11–4:11). First Peter reminds the hearers/readers that the eschatological hour is near (4:7). Consequently, the community must lead its life marked by prayer (4:7), love (4:8), hospitality (4:9), and service of one another (4:10). First Peter presents love as the central virtue "because love covers a multitude of sins" (4:8). This maxim appears in the Hebrew Scriptures (Prov 10:12; Ps 32:1), as well as elsewhere in the New Testament (Jas 5:20) and in early Christian literature (*1 Clem* 50:5).

First Peter's quotation of Proverbs 10:12 is closer to the Hebrew text, although he usually quotes from the Greek translation (LXX). This could indicate that he is relying upon the way in which it was being quoted in early Christian tradition. While the exact meaning of this proverb is somewhat vague, the general intent is clear: in loving others one fulfills the essence of the gospel call to love God and neighbor. Consequently, one experiences God's forgiveness for all sins. This passage culminates in a doxology to the praise of God (4:11).

4:12-19 Suffering as a Christian

The writer begins the third and final section of the letter (4:12–5:11) taking up themes that were introduced elsewhere in the letter. All the themes bear a strong eschatological emphasis. First Peter 4:12 returns to the theme of suffering that has dominated the letter. The readers are invited to see their sufferings as a purification (4:12) and as a sharing in Christ's sufferings (4:13). That should be cause for rejoicing, because those who have suffered are promised that they will share in Christ's glory (4:14). The present sufferings initiate the eschatological judgment within God's household (4:17). The prospect of suffering should not cause fear among Christians; rather, it should be seen to be "in accord with God's will" (4:19), and consequently they should place themselves in the care of their ever "faithful creator" (4:19).

5:1-5 Exhortation to the leaders of the community

The author identifies himself as a "fellow presbyter and witness to the sufferings of Christ" (5:1). The term "presbyter" or "elder" reflects the Jewish world, where the leaders of the community were identified by this term. It referred not simply to age but rather to the role exercised by leaders within a community. As such, First Peter exhorts his fellow elders (or leaders) to take care of the community that has been entrusted to them (5:1-2).

In offering advice to the elders, the writer uses traditional imagery. Earlier in the letter First Peter had referred to Christ as the "shepherd and guardian of your souls" (2:25). Now the leaders of the community are called to care for "the flock of God" that has been entrusted to them (5:2). First Peter defines the type of leadership they should exercise through a number of contrasts: they should carry out their leadership role "willingly" (not "by constraint") (5:2). They should not be inspired by greed, but by a desire for service (5:2). Finally, they should "not lord it over" those in their care, but should be examples to the community ("the flock," 5:3). Finally, First Peter uses the image of Christ the shepherd to encourage them to act like shepherds toward those entrusted to their care (4:4). This brings the author to address a universal appeal to the members of the community: "God opposes the proud, but bestows favor on the humble" (4:5; see Prov 3:34).

5:6-11 Final exhortations: trust God

This section draws the body of the letter to a conclusion. The readers are called to humble themselves (5:6); to cast all their anxiety upon God (5:7), to keep alert (5:8). The devil, like a roaring lion (see Ps 22:14), is inciting the Gentiles to persecute the Christians. What First Peter's readers are

1 Peter 5

experiencing is not unique, because Christians throughout the world are enduring similar sufferings and persecutions (5:9). A doxology concludes the body of the letter. The author promises that Christ will support and strengthen them in this struggle (5:10-11).

5:12-14 Final greeting

The letter concludes in the traditional way with personal greetings. Silvanus is identified either as the bearer of the letter or the one who acted as Peter's scribe in writing it (5:12). Greetings are sent from "the chosen one at Babylon" (5:13), referring to the church in Rome (see Introduction, p. 784; the book of Revelation also refers to Rome as Babylon in 14:8; 17:5; 18:2). Greetings also comes from "Mark, my son," referring probably to John Mark from Jerusalem (Acts 12:12-17) and indicating that Peter was responsible for his conversion to the Christian faith ("my son," 5:13). The Christian greeting "Peace to all of you who are in Christ" concludes the letter.

The Second Letter of Peter

Patrick J. Hartin

INTRODUCTION

Relationship between Second Peter and Jude

Virtually the whole of the letter of Jude is incorporated into Second Peter. Of Jude's twenty-five verses, no less than nineteen reappear in some form in Second Peter. A brief overview of this relationship can be seen from the following chart:

- 2 Peter 2:1-18 reproduce Jude 4-16
- 2 Peter 3:2-3 correspond to Jude 17-18
- 2 Peter 3:14 and 18 parallel Jude 24-25
- 2 Peter 1:1-2 echo Jude 1-2

That Second Peter used the letter of Jude appears evident from the above comparison. Second Peter is not an exact reproduction of Jude, but rather an adaptation and expansion. For example, the exclusion of the references to the apocryphal books of the *Assumption of Moses* and *1 Enoch* (Jude 9 and 14-15) is more easily understandable if we imagine the writer of Second Peter deliberately dropping Jude's references because they were not universally accepted as part of Scripture.

Author

This writing states that it is from "Symeon Peter, a slave and apostle of Jesus Christ" (1:1). The author is further acknowledged to be a witness to the transfiguration (1:16-18), implying that the author is Peter. There is also a reference to First Peter (3:1). Despite these indications, it is impossible to identify the author with the apostle Peter for the following reasons: (a) *The relationship between Second Peter and Jude:* Since Jude is a late writing and Second Peter has made use of Jude, Second Peter must be even later. (b) *There are also indications that the first generation of Christians had by now passed away:* "From the time when our ancestors fell asleep" (3:4). The writer belongs either to the second or third generation of Christians. (c) *The writings of the* apostle Paul have been made into a collection and are considered as Scripture: ". . . beloved brother Paul, according to the wisdom given to him, also wrote to you, speaking of these things as he does *in all his letters*. In them there are some things hard to understand that the ignorant and unstable distort to their own destruction, just as they do *the other scriptures*" (2 Pet 3:15-16; emphasis added). (d) *Concern for the time of the second coming:* In the early decades after Jesus' death and resurrection, the first followers expected his imminent return (see 1 Cor 7:29-31). When this did not happen, the question of his return became increasingly important. We seem to be at a late period in the early church when the teaching regarding the Second Coming was under major attack.

This writing breathes an atmosphere that is at home at the end of the first century A.D. Since Peter died around A.D. 64, the apostle Peter could not have written it. As with First Peter, the author of Second Peter was probably one of Peter's disciples. He invoked Peter's authority to stress the traditional belief of the Christian faith and to correct the inroads of false teachers in areas and communities where the apostle Peter had originally taught. By invoking Peter's authority, he reminds his hearers/readers of Peter's teaching and speaks in the way Peter would have spoken in order to solve the problems these new teachers were raising. It is in this sense that this commentary refers to the author as Peter. It is best to see this letter coming from around the close of the first century or the beginning of the second century A.D.

Hearers/readers

The address is very "catholic," that is, universal: "To those who have received a faith of equal value to ours" (1:1). Since 3:1 refers to First Peter, perhaps the author is addressing the same readers in Asia Minor who are referred to in 1 Peter 1:1. It also presumes an audience that is very familiar with the writings of Paul and upholds Paul's authority (3:15-16). This indicates areas of Asia Minor where both Paul and Peter were active. The actual place of origin does not greatly matter, but since the author wrote in the name of Peter, he must have been associated with the same sphere of influence as Peter, probably Rome.

Literary form

The external form appears to be that of a letter (1:1-2). Instead of personal greetings at the end, the writing concludes with a brief doxology (3:18). Indications of a personal relationship between the sender and the recipients, so characteristic of a letter, are also lacking.

The literary form seems to be better suited to *the form of a testament*, a type of writing very popular in Christian and Jewish circles. The setting for a testament depicts someone who bids farewell to his intimate associates. He speaks about his imminent death and offers admonitions and edifying words, preparing them for calamities that are about to come when he departs. Examples of such testamentary farewell speeches abound throughout the biblical writings. The most characteristic of these are the speeches of Jacob (Gen 47:29–49:33); Moses (Deut 29–31); Joshua (Josh 23–24); and the twelve patriarchs (in the apocryphal writing *Testaments of the Twelve Patriarchs*). In the Christian context there are the final farewell discourses of Jesus (John 13–17); and Paul (Acts 20:18-38). The writing of Second Timothy also falls into this category of a farewell testament. Since the characteristic features of a testament are all evident in this writing, it is justified in designating Second Peter as a "testament" or farewell speech that is sent (hence the letter form at the beginning) to encourage Christians to remain true to the teachings of the apostle Peter (and Paul) and to warn them against accepting the novel heresies that are currently being propagated.

COMMENTARY

1:1-2 Greetings

The writing opens with the usual epistolary features naming the author, the recipients, and extending greetings. However, these are the only specific features of the letter format. The writer identifies himself as "Symeon Peter" (1:1), using the Semitic form of his name Symeon to remind the hearers/readers that he was one of the original followers of Jesus. This form Symeon also occurs in Acts 15:14. He is further identified as "a slave and apostle of Jesus Christ" (1:1). This designation shows his relationship to Jesus as his "slave" (see commentary on Jas 1:1) as well as his relationship to the spread of Christianity as an apostle.

The readers to whom this writing is addressed are not clearly defined: "to those who have received a faith of equal value to ours" (1:2). However, the writer stresses the essential equality between the faith of the apostles and that of the second- and third-generation Christians.

Finally, greetings are sent, using the phraseology of 1 Peter 1:2 "May grace and peace be yours in abundance." (Note a similar phrase in Jude 2: "May mercy, peace, and love be yours in abundance.") To this Second Peter adds the phrase "through knowledge of God and of Jesus our Lord" (1:2). As this is an important theme that is developed throughout this letter, it is introduced here at the beginning to draw the attention of the hearers/readers to this theme. Paul was also accustomed to use the opening greetings as a way of introducing important themes to his hearers/readers (see Rom 1:1-7).

1:3-4 Main theme announced

In place of the thanksgiving found in Paul's letters as well as Greco-Roman letters, Second Peter introduces the main ideas of this writing. God's power is the source and foundation for the Christian life. This power has communicated to believers everything they need for "life and devotion" (1:3). God has also bestowed great promises on believers (1:4), promises that are challenged by the opponents, especially those relating to the parousia (3:3-4). The whole purpose of God's promises is for believers to come "to share in the divine nature" after escaping the corruption of the world (1:4).

Second Peter is using vocabulary that is at home in the Hellenistic world to give expression to the work of God and of Christ. This shows that the writer seeks to express his thoughts in language that the Greco-Roman world would understand. This concept of sharing in the divine nature would be developed later in the writings of the church fathers to extol the concept of human divinization through the work of God and of Christ. Essentially, Second Peter is stating his theme that one overcomes the corrupting influence of this world through God's gift in Christ to share in God's nature.

1:5-11 Exhortation to remain firm in their call

The way of life of the believers is expressed through a number of virtues that the writer lists: faith, virtue, knowledge, self-control, endurance, devotion, mutual affection, love (1:5-7). The list begins with the virtue of faith and ends with love. The enumeration of virtues (and vices) was a popular way of presenting moral teaching in the Greco-Roman world. Paul reflects this mode of teaching well in his ethical instructions (e.g., Phil 4:8; 1 Tim 3:1-12). The positive exhortation is interrupted with one negative note where the author warns that whoever does not strive to embrace these virtues is "blind and shortsighted" (1:9). This foreshadows one of the major concerns of this letter, namely, the false teachers who exemplify this spirit of blindness. For the writer, perseverance in remaining true to one's call is essential for the Christian (1:10-11).

1:12-15 Peter's testament

The writer speaks in the manner of the apostle Peter, who sees his death approaching (1:14). He wants to leave behind for his hearers/readers a reminder of what he had taught (1:15). This shows the nature of this present writing as a "testament," a very popular literary genre in the ancient world in which a famous person leaves behind a document that testifies to his enduring teaching (see Introduction, pp. 798–99). Perhaps, it would be best to identify Second Peter as a "testamentary letter." Here Peter, as the implied author, is aware that his death is imminent ("since I know that I will soon have to put it aside," 1:14). He refers to his human life as a "tent" (1:13), in the manner of Isaiah 38:12, which will be discarded in death. This letter, then, becomes a way in which Peter can remain with them after death: "I will always remind you of these things" (1:12); "to stir you up by a reminder" (1:13); "I shall also make every effort to enable you always to remember these things after my departure" (1:15).

1:16-21 Defense of prophecy concerning Jesus' second coming

In traditional testaments, reference to the leader's life would be given as an example for his hearers/readers. This section does exactly this by referring to events in Peter's life, such as being a witness to the transfiguration (1:17). This aspect of a testament will recur again in 3:1-3. This section gives attention to the major reason for this writing: to present Peter's defense against false teachers. The traditional faith of the community is under attack. The essence of the attack relates to belief in Jesus' second coming (*parousia*). Peter defends his (and his fellow apostles') proclamation against two charges by the opponents: the second coming of Christ is a myth (1:16-18), and the prophecy of the second coming is not a true prophecy (1:20-21).

Second Peter denies both charges. In the first instance, the second coming is not based on "cleverly devised myths" (1:16), but on preaching that was based upon eyewitness experiences of God's own revelation when God testified to Jesus as God's own Son at the transfiguration (1:17). The appeal to the authority of the transfiguration serves as a defense for the teaching on the parousia (second coming). The transfiguration foreshadows the second coming of Jesus.

The second defense (1:20-21) concerns the truth of prophecy. The writer presents a memorable definition of biblical prophecy: "*. . . there is no prophecy of scripture that is a matter of personal interpretation, for no prophecy ever came through human will; but rather human beings moved by the holy Spirit spoke under the influence of God*" (1:20-21; emphasis added). For Second Peter, the interpretation of prophecy must rest upon a communal understanding rather than simply an individual feeling. The divine inspiration of the Hebrew Scriptures is clearly attested. The Hebrew prophets were divinely inspired witnesses to the coming of the Lord (1:21).

2 Peter 2

2:1-10a Defense against the false teachers

A characteristic feature of the genre of a testament is that a leader makes prophecies about the future. Second Peter presents the apostle Peter looking into the future and foreseeing the emergence of false teachers (2:1). While the characteristic of a testament was to present the prophecy (in this instance, the coming of false teachers) as an event to come in the future, it becomes clear from the rest of this chapter that these false teachers are already a problem within the community. The writer compares the false teachers that have appeared in their midst to the false prophets in the Hebrew Scriptures (2:1). The writer offers a long illustration from the Hebrew Scriptures to show how the wicked are punished and the righteous vindicated (2:4-10a).

This lays the groundwork for the argument that the future parousia brings with it reward and punishment (3:3-10). All the illustrations are taken from the letter of Jude. In fact, nineteen of Jude's twenty-five verses are taken over by Second Peter either in their entirety or in part (see Introduction, p. 797). In this section Second Peter makes use of Jude 4-8 and changes it in a number of ways. He puts all the examples from the Hebrew Scriptures in their chronological order as they appear in the Bible: rebellious angels, the flood, and Sodom and Gomorrah. In addition, Second Peter adds the two positive examples of Noah and Lot (2:5, 7-8) so that the hearer/reader sees clearly that God rewards those who stand up against false teachers. Second Peter argues this quite strongly in 2:9: just as God rescued the two righteous men (Noah and Lot) in the past and punished those who did evil (the rebellious angels, the people of Sodom and Gomorrah), so God will act in a similar way in the future. God will rescue "the devout" and punish "the unrighteous" (2:9), namely, those who do evil, identified later as the false teachers.

2:10b-16 Denunciation of the false teachers

The writer points out how the false teaching gives rise to an evil way of life. Again, most of this material comes from the letter of Jude 8-16 and is adapted to suit Second Peter's context. The first example (2:10b-11) concerns reviling "glorious beings," that is, the angels. The false teachers deny that the angels have any influence on humanity. Second Peter leaves out Jude's example of Michael and Satan because it does not fit his context. According to the understanding of the time, one of the roles of angels was to report to God about the actions of human beings (see Job 1:6-12). The angels should by rights have brought accusations against the false teachers before God's throne, but they did not do so (2:11).

The second example (2:12-14) shows how the immoral lives of the false teachers reflect the lives of animals rather than human beings (2:12). Second

Peter seeks to warn his hearers/readers against any association with these false teachers, since they draw others into their evil ways (2:14).

The final example in this section is that of Balaam (2:15-16, taken from Jude 11). For Second Peter, the example of Balaam illustrates a false prophet who strayed from the true message. Even his donkey rebuked him (2:16; see Num 22:23-35). Balaam becomes a further example to the hearers/readers of the punishment of an evildoer.

2:17-22 Further denunciations

Second Peter accuses his opponents of being people who lack direction. They act like "waterless springs and mists driven by a gale" (2:17). In the first instance, Second Peter shows the harmful effects these false teachers have on others (2:17-19). Again the writer is relying upon Jude 12-13, 16. The effect of their teaching is to seduce Christians, especially those who have recently converted from paganism: "Those who have barely escaped from people who live in error" (2:18). Second Peter shows the consequences of what happens when belief in the second coming of Christ is denied together with belief in reward and punishment at the last day. Since there is no final judgment, they give themselves over to a life that knows no restrictions, as is seen in leading a life devoted to the "licentious desires of the flesh" (2:18).

Second Peter then considers how the teaching of the false teachers harms themselves (2:20-22). When they became Christians, they "escaped the defilements of the world through the knowledge of [our] Lord and savior Jesus Christ" (2:20). Now their teaching has drawn them back, and their situation is worse than it was previously (2:21).

Finally, the author uses two well-known parables to arouse revulsion in the minds of his hearers/readers: he compares these false teachers to a dog that returns to its own vomit and to a sow that returns to wallow in mud (2:22). The first proverb comes from Proverbs 26:11: "As the dog returns to his vomit, / so the fool repeats his folly." In the world of the first century, a dog was not the well-received, domesticated animal of today. A "dog" was generally a word used to insult someone. So the two animals (dog and sow) would evoke the same feelings of revulsion in the hearers/readers. The source of the second proverb is unknown; it was probably a traditional proverb found in their culture.

3:1-10 Defense regarding the delay of the parousia

The writer opens this passage in a formal way (3:1-2), reminding the faithful of Peter's authority. It is also a reminder of the genre of a testament. He deliberately associates this writing with First Peter by identifying it as his "second letter" (3:1). As with a testament, this letter serves to take the place of Peter's physical presence among them. A further dimension of the genre of a testament is found in the rest of this passage, where the writer, using the figure of Peter, looks into the future and speaks about these false teachers who are to come (3:3), a vision that has now been realized within the community.

This section considers the heart of the opponents' teaching. The writer begins with a call to remember the tradition, particularly the teachings both of the prophets and of Jesus, whose message his apostles handed on (3:2). Previously the false teachers had accused Peter of inventing myths (1:16). Second Peter again reiterates that his teaching is based upon the word of Christ passed on through the apostles (3:2). He spells out clearly the heart of the opponents' rejection: the return of Christ (3:4). The question "Where is the promise of his coming?" (3:4) is a typical biblical question, implying doubt and derision on the part of the one asking the question (see also Judg 6:13; Isa 36:19).

The basis for the opponents' objections rests on the perceived permanence of the world: "From the time when our ancestors fell asleep, everything has remained as it was from the beginning of creation" (3:4). They claim that God has not been actively involved in the world, so why should God begin now? To this Peter gives a number of responses taken from biblical history:

- By God's word, the creation occurred and earth was formed from water (3:5; see Gen 1:9-10). The concept that all things were derived from water as the original element was also a Greek philosophical understanding.
- By God's word, the world was destroyed by water (3:6; see Gen 7:4).
- By God's word, the earth and everything on it will be destroyed by fire (3:7; the biblical roots of this belief in the destruction of the world by fire are found in late Hebrew writings such as Isaiah 66:15-16 and Malachi 3:19. The source for this biblical view is probably to be traced back to the Persians.)
- The delay in the parousia only appears to be a delay from the human perspective. With God time does not matter: "With the Lord one day is like a thousand years and a thousand years like one day" (3:8; this saying finds its origin in Psalm 90:4).
- The delay is actually a sign of God's patience, making it possible for more people to repent (3:9). This statement is a deduction from the very definition of God as a God of mercy and compassion (Exod 34:6).

- Finally, as Jesus predicted in Mark 13:32-37, the day of the Lord will come unexpectedly, like a thief in the night (3:10).

Second Peter rests his argument on the understanding that since the world has already undergone change through the power of God's word (in the creation and in the flood), so too it is to experience change in the future with the return of Jesus and a final judgment. While the end of the world is a certainty, Second Peter (as with the rest of the New Testament) gives no speculation on when this will occur.

3:11-13 Consequences of this teaching

Because the world will end in such a cataclysmic way, the readers should lead lives that strive after "holiness and devotion" (3:11). This call is set within the context of apocalyptic language that sees the destruction of the world (3:12) and the emergence of "new heavens and a new earth" (3:13). This description of the destruction of the world by means of fire is found only here in the New Testament; nevertheless, it was a common cultural view of the first century A.D.

3:14-16 Even Paul agrees with this teaching

Second Peter appeals to Paul's letters for support, since Paul taught the same things that Second Peter is teaching. Paul taught that there would be a judgment of all at the end of time (Rom 14:10-12). Paul also envisaged the delay of judgment as a time for repentance (Rom 2:4-5). In appealing to Paul's support, Second Peter makes three important observations. He understands that Paul was inspired in the writing of his letters ("according to the wisdom given to him," 3:15). Secondly, he shows that there was a tendency within the early church to collect Paul's letters ("in all his letters," 3:16). Thirdly, Paul's letters are considered to have an authority equal to that of the Hebrew Scriptures ("the other scriptures," 3:16). Consequently, the hearers/readers can rely on this teaching concerning the parousia, since it is the traditional teaching of the church, and the two greatest apostles, Paul and Peter, also bear witness to this traditional belief.

3:17-18 Final exhortation and doxology

The writer makes a final appeal to his hearers/readers to be on guard against the deceptions of the false teachers (3:17). He addresses his hearers/readers as "beloved" (3:17), a term that he had used frequently throughout this final chapter (3:1, 8, 14). In a positive way, he returns to his opening statement (1:2), where he encouraged his readers to grow in the "knowledge of God and of Jesus our Lord." This final appeal reminds the reader of the importance of the traditional teaching and knowledge about Jesus and his preaching, especially as it relates to his second coming and the end of the world: You can be sure that Jesus Christ will return. Finally, Second Peter ends with a doxology in praise of the Lord Jesus Christ. This praise is meant to be addressed to Jesus from now until eternity (3:18).

The Letters of John
Scott M. Lewis, S.J.

INTRODUCTION

The First, Second, and Third Letters of John were written after the Gospel of John, possibly around A.D. 100–115. They were written by an anonymous Presbyter, or elder (2 John 1; 3 John 1) and intended for the various house churches comprising the Johannine communion. First John is not written in the style of an ancient letter. Its repetitious and circular nature suggest a homily, possibly intended to be read to the assembled community to which it is addressed. Second and Third John, on the other hand, are short and terse and follow the conventions of ancient letter writing.

The letters are examples of parenesis, or moral exhortation. The Presbyter wants not only to encourage and strengthen his fellow believers but also to ensure that they continue to believe and behave in a manner consistent with the faith in which they stand. The three letters were probably written by the same author, although he was not necessarily the author of the Gospel, since the letters differ on some theological points, such as the atoning and expiatory nature of Jesus' death (1 John 1:7; 2:2; 4:10).

Church communities were no different in the first century than they are in the twenty-first; there were problems, disagreements, and divisions. The much idealized view of Christian living presented in chapters 14–17 of the Gospel has given way to human realities, and now the elder who writes these letters must deal with a major crisis. A serious schism has arisen, and the unity of the communities has been broken (1 John 2:18-27; 4:16; 2 John 7-11). Those who deny Jesus the Christ in any way are antichrists, liars, and false prophets (1 John 2:18, 22; 4:1, 3).

Additionally, it is apparent that many of the discourses in the Gospel, especially chapters 14–17, are subject to misinterpretation, especially those dealing with sin, Christian living, and the ongoing role of the Spirit. It appears that some believed that the Spirit was leading them in new directions. The elder seeks to set the record straight. He reiterates forcefully the essential elements of the Gospel revelation, especially the importance of the incarnation, the love commandment, the Spirit, the nature of sin, and eschatological expectations. The stark contrast between light and darkness, truth and falsehood, love and hate characterizes the letters, reflecting the dualism of the Fourth Gospel and its community. One stands with light or darkness—there is no middle ground. Readers wishing to delve into the history of the Johannine community and its struggles will profit from Raymond Brown's *The Community of the Beloved Disciple*.

The First Letter of John

Scott M. Lewis, S.J.

COMMENTARY

PROLOGUE

1 John 1:1-4

1:1-4 The Word of Life

As in the Gospel (1:1), the opening line speaks of the "beginning," referring here primarily to the revelation of God in Jesus in which the Christian community has placed its faith. The Word of Life—the *Logos* (John 1:1)—is not some abstraction or concept but was made real and concrete for the world. It was seen (John 1:39; 14:9; 19:35; 20:18, 25) and touched (John 20:27), signifying that Christ truly came in the flesh (4:2; 2 John 7). Since the author's community has seen and touched the Word of life, his testimony carries weight, and he gives this testimony so that the readers may have fellowship or sharing *(koinonia)* with his community. Fellowship with his community includes the experience of the mutual indwelling of the Father and the Son (17:11, 21, and 23) and is the source of complete joy that he wishes for his readers (15:11; 17:13). Breaking the unity of the community is tantamount to breaking communion with God.

GOD AS LIGHT

1 John 1:5–3:10

1:5–2:2 Light and darkness

The core of the message is verse 5: God is light, and in him there is no darkness at all. Light must be understood in the ethical sense. Jesus revealed the God whom no one had ever seen (John 1:18). Hatred, violence, greed, selfishness, and so on are alien to God; when they are attributed to God, they are a human projection. This is connected to the statement that God is love (4:8-9), demonstrated by his revelation in Jesus and the expiation of our sins.

This entire section will consist of the logical consequences of that first principle. If God is light, then those who claim fellowship with him must be light; if there is no darkness in God, then those who claim fellowship with him must not have darkness within them. What is demanded is an imitation of God himself, which would be impossible without the transforming power of the Spirit.

Verses 6, 8, and 10 begin with the conditional "If," representing those things for which the author reproaches his opponents. They all involve denying sin in one's life and claiming fellowship with God while walking in darkness. Those who do this lie and do not act in truth (v. 6). Walking (a Jewish term for how one lives one's life) in the light and acting in truth, however, result in fellowship with one another (v. 7), as well as the washing away of all sins with the blood of Jesus. This affirms the importance of the death or exaltation of Jesus, and the blood of Christ is explicitly linked to the forgiveness of sins (1 John 2:2, 12; 3:5, 8; 4:10; 5:6-8).

Walking in the light does not mean that one is perfect, and it is only realistic to admit that even the best people will sin. Claiming to be sinless when one is not is self-deception and lying, which is characteristic of Satan in John 8:34, and in so doing we cut ourselves off from God. Acknowledgment of sins results in forgiveness and cleansing, because Jesus is our Advocate with the Father and expiation for both our sins and those of the whole world (1:8–2:3). The reference to the sins of the whole world is a universalistic element that probably draws on John 1:29 and 20:23 and is a welcome counterbalance to the usual Johannine sectarianism. In the Gospel of John the Advocate (Paraclete) refers to the Spirit, while here it is applied to Jesus.

2:3-11 Walking in the light

The litmus test for knowing Jesus is simple: anyone claiming to do so must keep his commandments (v. 3) and live just as Jesus lived (v. 6). Knowing God has nothing to do with intellectual or factual knowledge but is a deep and personal relationship. If God is love, then those claiming to know God must manifest this love in their lives. With a backward glance at the "new" commandment in John 13:34, the author admits that it is not new, but a very old commandment, whose origins stretch back to the creation and which has been proclaimed anew (v. 7) by Jesus. It is an eschatological commandment; the new age of light is dawning, and the darkness is passing away. The true light (see John 1:9)—Jesus and the community of believers—is already shining (v. 8). Walking in the light is equated with loving one's brother or sister; the one who does that is in the light and will not fall, while the one hating his brother truly walks in darkness (vv. 8-11).

2:12-14 Family of believers

The author addresses his words in a figurative fashion to the broad generational spectrum of the community, stretching back to its foundation: children, fathers, and young men (vv. 12-14). He reminds them of what they have received and encourages them to stand fast: their sins have been forgiven; they know both Jesus and the Father; they are strong and the word of God remains in them; and they have conquered the evil one (John 17:15).

2:15-17 Denunciation of the world

Verse 15 makes the startling statement that if anyone loves the world, "the love of the Father is not in him," which seems strange in view of John 3:16. There is a stern warning not to love the world or the things of the world; they are snares and allurements, ephemeral in nature, and tainted with sin (vv. 16-17). In John 3:16, however, the "world" is the created order and humanity, while here it describes all those things that are opposed to God. God is the only enduring reality; all else is fleeting and can be taken away. Therefore, those who do the will of God remain forever.

2:18-23 The last hour

Eschatology is suddenly center stage: it is "the last hour." This represents a more traditional apocalyptic eschatology, anticipating the return of Jesus. In the Gospel it is alluded to only in 5:26-29 and 14:1-3. Not only is the antichrist coming but now many antichrists have appeared (v. 18). These antichrists are, of course, those who have broken with the author's community, for he states that "they went out from us" (v. 19), but their desertion proves that they never really belonged anyway, for they were on the side of darkness.

The issue appears to be one of christology: the liar is one who denies that Jesus is the Christ (v. 22), and anyone denying the Son is also denying the Father. We have only one side of this controversy, so it is unclear in what sense they are denying the Son. John is not an example of theological moderation; for him, even those who adhered to a more moderate christology are counted among the unbelievers.

2:24-27 Anointed with the Spirit

The members of the community are well armored, being anointed by the holy one and possessing all knowledge (vv. 20, 27). This anointing of the Spirit will teach them to discern true and false and, in fact, will teach them everything. Since through the anointing they already know the truth, there is no danger as long as they stand fast in what they have heard from the beginning (v. 26).

2:28–3:10 Children of God

In John 1:12-13 those who believe in Jesus are promised the opportunity to become children of God. In John 3:3 Jesus insists that only those who have been born "from above" *(anothen)* can see the kingdom of God. The author of 1 John encourages the "children" (v. 28) of the community to stand fast, for those who are righteous are begotten by God. The fact that they are children of God is proof of the Father's great love for them (1 John 3:1). There is a tradition of adoption by God as sons and daughters (Gal 4:15; Rom 8:15), but the Johannine tradition posits an actual transformation as God's children now, but it will be complete only at the time of Jesus' return. The hope is that when what we are to become is revealed, we shall see God as he is; since he is pure, we must be pure (3:2-3).

The focus changes in verse 4 to the one who sins: he is lawless; he does not know God. The one who acts righteously and loves his brother belongs to God and is begotten by him, and whoever sins belongs to the devil (v. 8), for parentage is determined by one's visible life (cf. John 8:34). Continuing with the language of birth and generation, it is clear that no one begotten by God sins or can sin, because "God's seed remains in him" (v. 9). This is incomprehensible in light of 1 John 1:8-10, and there have been countless attempts to resolve the contradiction. Misunderstandings of verses such as this one can lead to questionable behavior. God's seed can be taken to mean the divine principle implanted in someone by the Spirit; one is in the process of transformation and cannot sin insofar as he or she is in God. One who is truly and completely in God cannot sin.

LOVE FOR ONE ANOTHER

1 John 3:11–5:12

3:11-18 The love commandment revisited

We return to the love commandment in verse 11 (John 13:34; 15:12), the fundamental principle of the community. But here love is contrasted with evil and murder, with Cain as an example (v. 12). The presence of hate within an individual renders him a murderer, and no murderer has eternal life (v. 15), a replay of the argument that Jesus had with some of the "Jews" in John 8:44. Hatred is equated with murder in Matthew 5:21-22; this explains why Jesus often accused his opponents in the Gospel of John of wanting to kill him despite the absence of overt violence. The world is likened to Cain, for its deeds are evil, and hatred is what the followers of Jesus can expect (John 3:19-21; 7:7; 15:18-20; 16:18-25; 17:14). Their belief in Jesus and their living of the love commandment expose the hidden hatred and negativity of the world.

In John 5:24 Jesus promises that those who believe in him have already passed from death to life; in 1 John 3:14, the fact that they love their brothers is proof that this has occurred. It was through the exemplar of Jesus laying down his life for them that they came to know love. To live one's life as Jesus did means to lay down one's life for one's brothers (v. 16), and this includes tending to the needs of others. In a question similar to that posed in James 2:15-17, the author asks how the love of God can remain in one who passes by someone in need and refuses compassion (v. 17), which is always concrete and practical. This is followed by the exhortation to love in deeds and in truth rather than mere words (v. 18). The poor and the needy are usually the losers when a community becomes elitist and self-absorbed in an overly interiorized and privatized spirituality. Love for the Johannine community is not sentiment or feeling, but practical and demanding living for others.

3:19-24 The heart as judge

How can one be sure of belonging to the truth and being right with God? Verses 19-22 propose the heart as the judge; if one is not condemned by the heart, then confidence in God is the result. This is rather vague, but is developed a bit in 4:18, which states that perfect love casts out fear. If one still fears God's judgment, that is evidence that one must still grow in love. If the heart is not afraid, that is an indication that one's heart is right with God. That God is greater than our hearts and knows everything is not intended to induce fear but a sense of freedom and peace for the believer. God is fully aware of our real intentions and our desire to do his will.

The central theme of the letter is hammered home again in verses 23-24: the commandments of God are to believe in the name of his Son, Jesus Christ (John 1:12; 3:16; 14:1; 20:31), and to love one another (13:34; 15:12). Those who obey these two inextricably linked commandments will continue to experience the mutual indwelling of Jesus, with the presence of the Spirit as confirmation. There is an echo of the great love commandment in Mark 12:18-34, but with the addition of the faith requirement.

4:1-6 Testing the spirits

In a Spirit-filled, charismatic community, the question of the discernment of spirits is extremely important. In our own time the failure to exercise discernment in cases of the claims of charismatic leaders has often resulted in tragedy. All sorts of things can be said under the seeming influence of the Spirit by many different people, a problem faced in 1 Corinthians 12:3, 1 Thessalonians 5:11-22, and Revelation 2:2. In John 14:26 and 16:13, a teaching function is ascribed to the Spirit, and many of the author's opponents appear to have taken that very seriously.

By what standard can their accuracy be measured? The author warns his audience to be wary and to test the spirits, since so many false prophets have gone out into the world, certainly referring to his opponents (v. 1). In Deuteronomy 13:1-5 and 18:20-22, the false prophet is one who speaks the names of unknown gods. In a similar vein, those spirits that acknowledge that Jesus Christ has come in the flesh belong to God, while those not doing so are the spirit of the antichrist (vv. 2-3). Fidelity to the primal revelation is crucial. The emphasis on "come in the flesh" (v. 2) might indicate that some were denying the salvific value of the humanity or "flesh" of Jesus. The full incarnation of the Word *(Logos)* is manifested in the human and social sphere in care for the poor and the weak and the needs of others—in other words, in concrete acts of love.

It is obvious to the author that those who do not acknowledge Jesus belong to the world, for the world eagerly accepts their teachings, while the truth concerning Jesus is a sign of contradiction and an occasion of opposition from the world (vv. 4-5). The writer claims that "we," meaning his community, belong to God, as does anyone who listens to them, while those who do not belong to God refuse to do so. This is a question of the correct interpretation of the Christian revelation and message, and the author takes the correctness of his community's proclamation as his point of departure. The spirit of truth he equates with the stance of his community, while the spirit of deceit describes his opponents. In an intriguing parallel, the Qumran community believed in the opposition of two spirits, truth and injustice (1QS 3:13-20), while deceit or falsehood was the characteristic of those opposed to God.

4:7-18 God is love

"Love" appears twenty-seven times in this short section. Verse 7 exhorts us to love one another because love is of God (v. 8). Everyone who loves is begotten by God and knows God; in fact, God is love. God took the initiative with love, and this was accomplished through the sending of his only Son into the world (cf. John 3:16) as expiation for our sins and so that we might have life through him (vv. 9-10). This is not a poetic flight of fancy or speculation, for God is known to be love by his actions, as in the faithful covenant loyalty of the Old Testament *(hesed)*. Love is not a noun or adjective but a verb and describes both God and the response of believers in Jesus. Since God has loved us in such a fashion, we must love one another (v. 11) in order to be of God.

The nature of the unseen God dominates the next portion, framed by verses 12 and 20: no one has ever seen God (v. 12), but if we love one another, we will know God, and his love will be brought to perfection in us, with the presence of the Spirit as proof (v. 13). This describes a transformative process, for the source of the love is God, not humans. The presence of this perfected love in us removes whatever fear of the day of judgment we might have had, for we have become the love that is God (v. 17). Perfect love (God) and fear cannot coexist; if we are not afraid of the judgment, it is proof that we are in God, while the presence of fear is evidence that our transformation is incomplete (v. 18). A reflection on this section should encourage Christian preaching and teaching that focus more on actualizing the transformative love of God than on morbid or fearful images of God and punishment and judgment.

4:19-21 The unseen God

We are able to love because God has first loved us—this is not a massive self-help project (v. 19). The unseen God is loved in other people; hating others while claiming to love God is an absurdity and a lie. The quality of the communal relationship with God is reflected in the interpersonal relationships of its members, a constant challenge to all church congregations.

5:1-5 Loving God

Almost like a refrain, the author repeats his belief that all who believe that Jesus is the Christ or who love the Father are begotten by him. Loving God and obeying his commandments empower one to love the children of God, presumably only members of the community. The love of God is synonymous with obeying his commandments, and his commandments are not burdensome, which finds agreement in the entire biblical tradition (Deut 30:11-14; Matt 11:28-30). Those begotten by God conquer the world (John 16:33) by means of faith in Jesus as the Son of God and share in his victory (vv. 4-5).

5:6-12 Testimony and witnesses

Jesus Christ has three impeccable witnesses that are in agreement: water, blood, and the Spirit (vv. 6-7), possibly to satisfy the requirement in Deuteronomy 19:15 for at least two witnesses. Testimony is also crucial throughout the Gospel of John. The witnesses of blood and water resonate with the witness from the foot of the cross (John 19:34-35) and address the objections of those opponents who deny that Jesus has come in the flesh. The blood and water also represent the baptism and death of Jesus, that is, his earthly and incarnate ministry. The Spirit is the third witness, and its presence within the community continues to testify to the blood and water, and it is the Spirit of truth. Older English translations of verse 7 add "in heaven: the Father, the Word, and the Holy Spirit; and these three are one." This phrase was added by copyists during the christological controversies of the fourth and fifth centuries and is not present in the oldest manuscripts that we possess.

EPILOGUE

1 John 5:13-21

5:13-21 Sin, prayer, and final reflections

The author of the Gospel of John writes so that his readers will come to believe in Jesus as the Messiah and Son of God and that through believing they might *have* life in his name (John 20:31). The elder writes this letter so that his readers might *know* that they have eternal life (v. 13), and all the exhortation and testimony are to affirm what they have already received. With this confidence, believers can ask for anything in accordance with the will of God and be assured of being heard (vv. 14-15).

One of the first things one should pray for is any brother or sister who is committing sin, and if this is done, God will grant life to the sinner. The fact that believers can sin has already been acknowledged in 1:5–2:2, although 2:28–3:10 seems to rule it out. In 2:1 Jesus is the one who intercedes on behalf of sinners, but here other Christians make intercessory prayers, presumably through Jesus. But the proviso is that the prayers should only be for those whose sins are not "deadly," for although all wrongdoing is sin, not all sin is deadly. This echoes the unforgivable blasphemy against the holy Spirit in Mark 3:28-30, as well as the Jewish tradition that placed the worship of other gods or the rejection of God in this category. It is not clear what constitutes a "deadly" sin, but given the repetitious warnings in these letters, the most likely candidate is a denial that Jesus is the Son of God or that he has come in the flesh. There is the rather shocking statement that one should not pray for one whose sin is deadly. It would seem that this is the person most in need of prayers, but the dualistic worldview of the Johannine community will not admit any middle ground or equivocation.

In John 17:9 Jesus states his intention not to pray for the world but only for those given to him by God. It is only in the context of his farewell prayer that his prayers are solely on behalf of his followers, but a literal or superficial understanding of this and similar passages can generate a narrow and overrigorous exclusivism. Fortunately, we also have passages like John 3:16 and 12:47, which assure us that God's action in Jesus is not to condemn the world but to save it. Verse 18 asserts that no one begotten by God sins, being protected by God from the clutches of the evil one (cf. John 17:15). Even though the members of the community belong to God, the whole world is under the power of the evil one, which is a disturbing statement in view of Jesus' claim that the ruler of this world will be driven out (John 12:31) and that believers have conquered the evil one (1 John 2:12-13). This stark dualism seems more in keeping with the Dead Sea community at Qumran or the later Gnostic groups. The action of Jesus Christ has given us the ability to discern the one who is true, and that one is Jesus himself, who is true God and eternal life (v. 20).

The letter ends with the incongruous admonition to be on guard against idols—this has not been mentioned in the Gospel or the other letters. In what sense is it a threat? For John's community, the true God has been revealed to them in Jesus Christ, and the refusal to believe in him is tantamount to idolatry. In both the Old and New Testaments, idolatry is the root human sin and by far the gravest.

The Second Letter of John
Scott M. Lewis, S.J.

COMMENTARY

The Second Letter of John is in the form of a conventional Hellenistic letter. The author—presumably the Presbyter (elder) of 2 and 3 John—is writing to one of the sister communities in order to warn them against his opponents, the "deceivers" and "antichrists," who are spreading what he deems to be false teachings.

1-3 Address and greeting

The Presbyter writes to the "chosen Lady" and "her children," whom he loves in the truth. Some have taken the "chosen Lady" to be an actual person, but most assign metaphorical value to the address. He is referring to one of the communities, which he holds in very high regard. Her "children" are those believers who are walking in truth and love.

4-11 Body of the letter

The Presbyter rejoices to find that "some" of her children are walking in truth, which eases in to the warning that he has for them. Addressing the Lady directly (v. 5), he exhorts her to live the fundamental commandment from the beginning (John 13:34; 1 John 2:7-8, 24), namely, to love one another. Love is walking according to his commandments, and as he made clear in the previous letter, this includes correct belief concerning Jesus Christ. The reason for his concern (v. 7) is that many "deceivers" have gone out into the world and do not acknowledge Jesus as "com[ing] in the flesh" (1 John 4:2). Some have suggested that this refusal refers to the return of Christ, but it is more likely that it involved a denial of the incarnation or full humanity of Christ (John 1:14), or a separation of the Christ from the human Jesus.

For the Johannine community, knowing and adhering to the truth received in the beginning (v. 5; 1 John 2:24) is synonymous with salvation and eternal life (John 6:27, 29; 20:31; 1 John 2:25). The writer warns them (vv. 8-9) that straying from the truth can cost them eternal life, for those who do not remain in the teaching of the Christ do not have God. The word translated as "progressive" in verse 9 is more correctly understood as "going too far" or "going beyond" what is proper or right. The author is uncompromising and asks the community not to receive or grant hospitality to anyone who arrives bearing these false teachings, in fact not even to greet them. Since those who were missionaries or itinerant teachers relied on hospitality, he hopes that these harsh measures will hinder the growth of his opponents' teachings.

The Johannine community's sectarian nature is quite evident in this form of excommunication or shunning. The false teachers are believed to belong to the realm of the world and darkness, and anyone who even greets them is tainted by their evil works (v. 11). It is distressing that dialogue and mutual respect are so lacking in these letters as well as in the Gospel. It seems that the love commandment in the Johannine tradition applies to fellow Christians, and more precisely, other Johannine Christians (1 John 2:9-11; 3:11, 23). Assigning those outside of our group to a lesser status is a form of tribalism that is the bane of all religious traditions, to which our own history bears painful and tragic witness.

12-13 Closing

Using a conventional ending, the author claims to have much more to tell the community members but will wait for an opportunity to visit in person so that "our joy may be complete," which is a Johannine expression indicating the joy resulting from a communion or fellowship in love and in truth. The "children," or members of his community, also send greetings.

The Third Letter of John

Scott M. Lewis, S.J.

COMMENTARY

The Third Letter of John was also written by the Presbyter, but this time to a named individual. Despite being the shortest letter in the New Testament—and one that fails to mention Jesus directly—it is intriguing in that it gives us a momentary and partial glimpse into the tensions of the Johannine communities. In this letter the author's opponent even has a name—Diotrephes.

More of a private and personal letter, it does not address the theological tensions of 1 and 2 John. Governance and authority in the community are its overriding concerns, and we can even detect elements of a power struggle between the Presbyter and Diotrephes.

1-4 Address and greeting

The Presbyter's addressee is an individual named Gaius, a common Roman name, which prevents an identification with others of the same name in the New Testament (Acts 19:29; 20:4; Rom 16:25; 1 Cor 1:14). That Gaius is esteemed by the Presbyter is clear: he is addressed as "beloved," he is loved "in truth," and his "soul is prospering." These are indications that he walks in the truth and in love, that is, he has remained faithful to the correct christology, and he extends loving hospitality to members of the Johannine communion, who also walk in the truth. Love is the nature of God, and this God has been revealed in Jesus. This is the "truth" in which believers are invited to participate.

5-12 Body of the letter

Hospitality is a privileged expression of love and walking in the truth (vv. 5-8). Gaius has been exemplary in this practice, and glowing reports from traveling brothers have been received by the Presbyter. He hints that these travelers are missionaries or teachers of a sort, for they are completely dependent on community members and receive nothing from outsiders.

This is for the sake of the Name, most likely an allusion to Jesus. He urges continuous support of them so that they all may be "co-workers in the truth" (v. 8), which in this context is the work of proclaiming the Johannine Gospel message.

The Presbyter names and describes his adversary, a man named Diotrephes (vv. 9-10), about whom we know nothing other than what is present in this letter. It appears that he exercises some authority or control in the community, although it is unclear whether he actually holds any sort of office. The "church" *(ekklesia)* to which the Presbyter writes (v. 9) signifies the congregation rather than an extended institution or structured community. Gaius appears to be a loyal member of that community, one whom the Presbyter can trust.

The Presbyter describes Diotrephes: he loves to dominate; he does not acknowledge the Presbyter's authority; he spreads "evil nonsense" about him; and most of all, he refuses to extend hospitality to emissaries from the Presbyter's community. On top of that, he prevents members of his community from doing so and expels those who do. Some scholars see this as reflecting the rise of the early episcopate, but this is unlikely. The early Johannine communities were egalitarian in nature, and house congregations were united in a communion of unity in Jesus Christ and the path of love.

This appears to be more of a personal power struggle. The Presbyter paints a negative portrait of Diotrephes, but we must remember that we are hearing only one side of the story; a letter from Diotrephes would probably present a very different point of view. Although the Presbyter rages at Diotrephes for refusing hospitality to his emissaries, in 2 John 10-11 the Presbyter commanded the "chosen Lady" to treat his theological opponents in exactly the same way! A standard exhortation to do good and avoid evil in order to be of God (v. 11) is followed by praise for Demetrius, although the nature of the good report concerning this person is not clear.

13-14 Closing

The author insists on waiting for a personal visit to relate other matters to Gaius. He closes with a peace salutation and a greeting from the friends of his community to those in Gaius's, each by name. It is interesting that the term "friends" is used rather than "children." "Friends" would be more in keeping with John 15:14, indicating that they are keeping the commandments of Jesus.

The Letter of Jude

Patrick J. Hartin

INTRODUCTION

The letter of Jude, one of the shortest New Testament writings, is also one of the most intriguing. It was taken up almost in its entirety into Second Peter. Its place in the canon has often been challenged, not least of all by the early church, which was concerned with its usage of the apocryphal books of *1 Enoch* and the *Assumption of Moses*.

Author

The writer of the letter identifies himself as: "Jude, a slave of Jesus Christ and brother of James" (v. 1). In the New Testament world the name Jude (or more accurately "Judas") was quite common. Matthew 13:55 notes that James, "the brother of the Lord" and leader of the Jerusalem church, had a brother named Judas: "Is not his mother named Mary and his brothers James, Joseph, Simon, and Judas?" The writer, then, identifies himself with this James, the leader of the Jerusalem church and "brother of the Lord."

However, the information we glean about the author from the text presents some difficulties in making this identification: (a) *The writer's vocabulary shows a good knowledge of Greek*—some twenty-two words occur only in this letter in the New Testament (excluding Second Peter's borrowing from Jude). (b) *The opening greetings,* "May mercy, peace, and love be yours in abundance" (v. 2), differ from the common Pauline greetings: "Grace . . . and peace" (e.g., Phil 1:2). However there are similarities with the opening of a number of other New Testament letters. For example, a threefold listing of "grace, mercy, and peace" occurs in 1 Timothy 1:2; 2 Timothy 1:2; and 2 John 3. The letters of Peter have the greetings as "May grace and peace be yours in abundance." The opening of Polycarp's letter to the Philippians (written before A.D. 155) also has a similar form: "Mercy and peace from God Almighty and Jesus Christ our Savior be multiplied to you." All this shows that a variation of the form used by Jude was common in the post-apostolic period. (c) *The writer comes from a period after the apostles:* In verses

17-18 the author does not include himself in the group of apostles but gives the impression that he belongs to a later generation.

All these arguments point to the letter coming from a second-generation Christian at the end of the first century. As with the letters of James and First Peter, the writer invokes the name of Jude because he wishes to endorse his authority in settling problems that have arisen in a certain area of the Christian church.

Hearers/readers

The letter is an immediate response to a sudden danger arising within certain Christian communities. Intruders entering the communities are undermining their traditional faith as well as their morals. It is addressed: "To those who are called, beloved in God the Father and kept safe for Jesus Christ" (v. 1). The writing does not provide a detailed description of the readers or of their opponents. From the letter some information can be deduced about the first hearers/readers of this letter. From its tone the letter seems to be directed to a definite church or group of churches. The use of the Hebrew Scriptures and apocryphal allusions indicate a Jewish-Christian community. The writer's identification of himself as "brother of James" must indicate a community in which James's authority was recognized. The cultural mixture of Jewish and Greek elements in this letter is similar to that of the letter of James and would perhaps argue for a similar destination. Given this information, the area of Syria or northern Palestine would seem to be the most likely destination.

Genre and main thoughts

While this writing commences with the traditional opening formula of a letter, it lacks final personal greetings and ends with a doxology praising God. A close reading reveals that the literary form of a letter suits it best. In verses 3-4 the writer shows his pastoral intent of writing to a group of Christians for whom he holds responsibility. He aims at helping them meet the new challenges arising from the inroads of intruding teachers within their community. Drawing upon their common heritage, the writer warns his hearers/readers about the dangers they face. It is a wonderful record of an early Christian church struggling to hold firm to the traditional faith, while at the same time opening up to the new culture around it.

Jude 1

COMMENTARY

Verses 1-2 Greetings

Using the customary format of a letter, the writer refers to himself as Jude, "a slave of Jesus Christ" (see Jas 1:1; Titus 1:1). This phrase "slave of Jesus Christ" recalls the biblical tradition that identifies figures like Moses (1 Kgs 8:53) and David (1 Kgs 8:66) as a "slave of God." As with the letters of James and First Peter, the writer invokes the authority of an apostolic figure, Jude, for this letter (see Introduction, pp. 822–23). It is in this sense that this commentary refers to the author as Jude. Since he is less well known, he identifies himself further as the "brother of James" (probably James "the brother of the Lord," Gal 1:19). This would imply that he is writing to Jewish Christians, since James was an important figure in their world. The writer identifies the readers in a general sense as "those who are called." Paul refers to his hearers/readers in Rome in a similar way (Rom 1:6). Finally, he extends greetings: "may mercy, peace, and love be yours in abundance" (v. 2; see 1 Tim 1:2; 2 Tim 1:2).

Verses 3-4 Occasion for the letter

The usual thanksgiving section is missing. The author intended to write to his readers about their common salvation, but a more urgent topic arose. Many false teachers have entered the community of his hearers/readers and are distorting their faith, especially their belief in Jesus Christ. The writer urges the hearers/readers "to contend for the faith" (v. 3). This image is taken from the world of athletic contests. Since only one person can win the prize, Jude exhorts his readers to be the ones who win in this struggle. He says two things about these intruders (v. 4): they "pervert the grace of our God into licentiousness," implying their moral degeneration into sexual immorality; and they "deny our only Master and Lord, Jesus Christ," implying doctrinal teaching that refuses to acknowledge the Lordship of Jesus and his teaching.

Verses 5-7 God punishes those who are unfaithful

The phrase "I wish to remind you" is a marker identifying the beginning of the argument based on past examples. Using three examples, Jude reminds his hearers/readers of figures who fell from positions of favor with God and were punished because of their sins.

His first reference is to God's chosen people, whom God liberated from slavery in Egypt. They complained against God in the desert and were destroyed because of their lack of faith (v. 5; see Num 14).

In the second example, angels of God came down to earth to seek out women (Gen 6:1-4). They were punished by God in chains and darkness until the judgment day (v. 6; see *1 Enoch* 10:4-6, 12-13).

Thirdly, Sodom and Gomorrah were punished in eternal fire because of their "sexual promiscuity" (v. 7).

Verses 8-9 Application

These verses consider the intruding teachers: they "defile the flesh" (like Sodom and Gomorrah, they practice sexual immorality); they "scorn lordship" (like the Israelites at the time of the Exodus, they reject God's covenant and authority); and they "revile glorious beings" (like the angels, they refuse to serve and obey God). The implication is that these false teachers will experience similar judgments and punishments.

In verse 9 Jude cites a story taken from an apocryphal Jewish writing, *The Assumption of Moses* (though many modern scholars prefer to name it more correctly *The Testament of Moses*). This work exists in only one Latin manuscript text, dated from the sixth century A.D. Unfortunately this manuscript ends before the description of the death of Moses. The story that Jude narrates here is presumed to refer to the lost ending of this manuscript.

The book of Deuteronomy says that Moses died and was buried in the land of Moab, "but to this day no one knows the place of his burial" (Deut 34:6). Jude's quotation fills in details surrounding Moses' death and envisages a struggle between Michael and Satan over the body of Moses. Satan argued that Moses did not deserve burial because he had once killed an Egyptian (see Exod 2:12). Michael did not condemn Satan but simply said: "May the Lord rebuke you!" leaving judgment to the Lord. The point of this story is that the archangel Michael did not take on himself the power of passing judgment but left judgment to the Lord. Likewise, Jude says that God is the final judge and God will pass judgment on these intruding teachers.

Verses 10-13 Further examples of God's punishment

Jude turns now to consider the intruding teachers, who act like irrational animals (v. 10). They despise what they do not understand. Jude sees that their irrational attitudes will eventually lead to their own destruction (v. 10). Three more examples of sinners are taken from the biblical tradition and applied to the intruders (v. 11): Cain, Balaam, and Korah.

These false teachers are walking in *"the way of Cain"* (emphasis added). Cain murdered his brother Abel (Gen 4:8), so these intruding teachers are committing spiritual murder against the community.

Jude 10-13

The intruders are also practicing *"Balaam's error"* (emphasis added). From references to Balaam in the book of Numbers (22–24; 25:1; 31:16-18), the implication emerges that Balaam led the Israelites into sin. In like manner these intruding teachers are leading the community that Jude addresses into sin.

Finally, *"the rebellion of Korah"* (emphasis added) refers to a revolt that Korah led against the authority of Moses and Aaron (Num 16). In like manner these intruding teachers are fomenting a rejection of Jude's authority and teaching. In the tradition these three examples symbolize those who lead the community into error and reject the duly appointed leaders of the community. These examples are certainly apt for the dangers these intruders pose to the community that Jude addresses.

Even the early Christian meals that remember the Lord's supper (called *agapai*, or "love feasts") have been infiltrated by these intruding teachers (v. 12). In graphic imagery, Jude uses four images drawn from nature (vv. 12-13) to describe these intruding teachers. Common to these images is the concept that they do not act according to their nature. Instead they create chaos: "waterless clouds"; "fruitless trees"; "wild waves of the sea" splashing foam everywhere; and "wandering stars" (vv. 12-13). The implication for Jude's hearers/readers is clear: they are to avoid all contact with the intruding teachers because these teachers do not act according to the ways set by God. Instead they cause chaos by leading people astray.

Verses 14-19 Further warnings of judgment

Jude shows that the rise of these intruding teachers had been foretold in the past by both the prophets and the apostles. Jude refers to the example of Enoch (Gen 5:21-24), who was taken up to be with God without dying. He became an important figure in Jewish tradition between the testaments, as is seen from the influential apocryphal writing *1 Enoch*. Jude quotes from this writing to assure his hearers/readers that God will execute judgment on these intruding teachers: "Behold, the Lord has come with his countless holy ones to execute judgment on all" (vv. 14-15; see *1 Enoch* 1:9). This quotation lies closer to the text of *1 Enoch* discovered in Qumran than to other extant texts. The quotation's purpose is to stress the traditional teaching of divine judgment (Matt 16:27; 25:31-46).

Jude adds further support from Christian tradition by quoting a saying from the apostles: "In [the] last time there will be scoffers who will live according to their own godless desires" (v. 18). Since no such quotation appears in the rest of the New Testament, its origin must belong to the wider world of Christian tradition. The point of these references to *1 Enoch* and the apostles is clear: the presence of these intruding teachers was foretold in the past, and one can be certain that God's punishment and judgment await them.

Verses 20-23 Build up your faith

These verses present the climax of the letter. Jude spells out clearly why he has written them. He wants to build up the community's faith (v. 20). The way to accomplish this is through prayer in the Spirit, remaining in God's love, and relying upon Christ's mercy as they await the coming of the Lord (v. 21). For this reason they are to guard against the evil teachings of the intruders. It is not sufficient for the community and individuals to protect themselves from these false teachers.

While verses 22-23 contain a number of very difficult textual problems, nevertheless the basic meaning is clear: Jude reminds the members of his community of their responsibility to reach out to those who are wavering (v. 22) and "to save others by snatching them out of the fire" (v. 23). This is somewhat similar to the conclusion to the letter of James, where the hearers/readers are instructed that "whoever brings back a sinner from the error of his way will save his soul from death and will cover a multitude of sins" (Jas 5:20).

Verses 24-25 Final doxology

The letter concludes without any personal greetings so characteristic of Paul's letters. Instead, it ends with a hymn of praise (a doxology) in honor of God through Jesus Christ. God keeps the community from harm and brings them morally blameless into God's presence. This community praises this one God, the Savior, for God's glory, majesty, power, and authority that was in the past, is now, and will continue to be "for ages to come."

The Book of Revelation
Catherine A. Cory

INTRODUCTION

More than any other part of the New Testament, the book of Revelation evokes greatly varying reactions among its readers. Some find it surreal and confusing or simply silly and therefore want to ignore it completely. Others find it endlessly fascinating because of its many colorful and sometimes grotesque images. Others, fearful about the future, view the book as an illustrated timeline that will help them better prepare for the events of the end of the world. Still others see it as a kind of "war manual," explaining how they should conduct themselves in the impending battle between the righteous ones and the forces of evil in the world.

But is there more to the book of Revelation? Does Revelation have anything to say to believers who are not fixated on determining the date of the end time and instead want to read the Scriptures to hear God's voice in the present time, to inspire faith, and challenge themselves and their faith communities to right behavior, now, in the midst of the activities of their everyday lives? To some people's surprise, the answer is yes, provided we seek to understand the book of Revelation from within the social and historical context in which it originated and as the type of literature it is—apocalyptic. The Second Vatican Council's *Dei Verbum* and the Roman Catholic Pontifical Biblical Commission's "Interpretation of the Bible in the Church" strongly encourage this approach to the study of Scripture, and nowhere is it more important than in our study of the book of Revelation.

As a first step to reading and interpreting any piece of literature, it is important to learn something about its author and the place and time in which the author wrote. This information helps us determine the author's point of view. We must also take into account any historical circumstances or cultural differences that may have affected his or her approach to the topic. Although Sacred Scripture is different from other literature in the sense that Christians believe it to be inspired of God, its human authors are true authors. Since the word of God is mediated through these human authors' historical and cultural circumstances, we need to ask similar questions about the identity of the biblical author and the place and time in which he lived. Therefore, we will begin this commentary by asking what we know about the author of the book of Revelation and the time and place in which he wrote.

Another thing we need to know when we sit down to read a piece of literature is its genre or literary form. Only then do we know what expectations to have about its meaning. For example, if we know that a particular story is a fable, we can expect to read about talking animals, and we know that we should look for its moral or central teaching. However, we would *not* expect a fable to give us a scientific study or a lesson in history. When we read the Gospels of the New Testament, we can expect to hear the story of Jesus. We know that the narratives will be realistic, having some of the features of a history or biography, but hopefully we also know that they were written for the primary purpose of proclaiming faith in Jesus as the messiah of God. The word "gospel" means "good news." To expect something different—for example, a documentary on the life of Jesus—is to seriously misunderstand the author's intention and, as a consequence, misinterpret the meaning of the biblical text. Therefore, before beginning our reading of the book of Revelation we also need to ask about its genre.

Authorship

The author of the book of Revelation does not tell us much about himself, except that his name was John and that he saw himself as God's servant (1:1). Two early church writers, Justin Martyr (c. A.D. 160) and Irenaeus (c. A.D. 180), associated the author of this book with the apostle John and with the writer of the Fourth Gospel, also known by that name (see *Dial.* 81 and *Adv. haer.* 3.11.1-3; 4.20.11). However, most biblical scholars today think that the author of the book of Revelation was neither an apostle of Jesus nor the author of the Gospel of John. The reasons for this view have to do with differences in the style of writing and the probable date of composition of this book. At most, we can say that the author of the book of Revelation was an early Jewish Christian prophet by the name of John, otherwise unknown in early Christian literature.

Date of composition and location of the work

John tells his readers that he received the visions about which he writes while residing on Patmos, a small island in the Aegean Sea. Further, he tells us that he was there because he "proclaimed God's word and gave testimony to Jesus" (1:9). Thus we can probably assume that his exile on Patmos came as a result of his preaching activity. He also incorporates letters to seven churches of Asia Minor (modern Turkey) into his work. Therefore, we can locate this work in the eastern Mediterranean.

Concerning the date of composition of the book of Revelation, the text itself provides few clues. The most important piece of evidence is the author's use of the term "Babylon" for Rome (18:2). In other Jewish literature written toward the end of the first century A.D., this term is used to describe Rome, but only after the Roman armies had destroyed Jerusalem and the temple in A.D. 70 (see *2 Esdr.* 3:1-2, 28-31; *2 Apoc. Bar.* 10:1-3; 11:1; 67:7; *Sib. Or.* 5:143, 159). Recall that the Babylonians had destroyed the Jerusalem temple in the sixth century B.C. and deported the people of Judea, throwing them into the darkest period of their history. Because the book of Revelation also makes this connection between Rome and Babylon, scholars generally agree that it had to have been written after A.D. 70. The early church writer Irenaeus (*Adv. haer.* 5.30.3) suggests that Revelation was written toward the end of Domitian's reign (A.D. 81–96), so, without other evidence to the contrary, a date of A.D. 95–96 is reasonable. This means that the book of Revelation is among the last books to be written in the New Testament. This book was commonly accepted as Sacred Scripture by the latter half of the second century.

The genre of the book of Revelation

What can we say about the genre of the book of Revelation? John describes his work as a prophecy, even though he never actually calls himself a prophet (1:3). A careful reader of this book will notice right away that we do not have a continuous story as we find in the Gospels. Instead, John records the visions (images) and auditions (voices) that came to him through a divine being, usually an angel. The subject matter of these visions and auditions are "heavenly things" and future events. This kind of work is generally described as an "apocalypse," from a Greek word that means "revelation." In fact, in some Bible translations the book of Revelation is given the title "Apocalypse."

Typical of this genre, the seer (that is, the recipient of the visions) receives revelations through mediation of some sort and then records them in writing. The revelations involve secrets of the *cosmos* (the workings of the heavenly bodies, the fixing of the calendar, names and activities of angelic beings, places of reward and punishment) and secrets about the future (political and historical events, the destiny of God's people, etc.). Sometimes the seer is allowed to journey to the heavenly locations. In those cases the apocalypse also describes the details of the heavenly journey. Most apocalypses also include a command to the seer to seal up the written account of the visions for some future time.

If we assume that the book of Revelation belongs to the genre "apocalypse," what then are we to understand about its interpretation? Some people read the book of Revelation to find out what will happen when this physical world is destroyed or to discover when it will come to an end—in other words, as a roadmap of the end time. However, we can be quite certain that the author of the book of Revelation did not write it for that purpose and that the original audience did not understand it in that way. Therefore, we would be seriously misled about its meaning if that is what we seek to learn from it today.

Perhaps the best way to understand apocalypses is to investigate the precursors or forerunners of the genre. In recent decades scholars have been debating whether apocalypses have their roots in the writings of the prophets or in Wisdom literature. This question arose out of the fact that one can see features of both genres in a wide variety of Jewish and Christian apocalypses and, in particular, in the book of Revelation.

As mentioned above, John himself describes his book as a prophecy (1:3; 22:7, 10, 18, 19). Nowhere in Revelation does he distinguish Jewish prophets of old from Christian prophets. Therefore, it is reasonable to assume that he understood his prophecy to function in the same way as the prophets before him. Whereas we tend to think of prophets primarily as predictors of the future, the prophets of the Old Testament were better known as spokespersons of God on behalf of the covenant. In that capacity the prophet brought accusations against Israel and Judah when they failed to keep the covenant and warned of God's punishment against wrongdoers. The prophet also brought a message of consolation when, in the midst of their suffering, they thought God had abandoned them or when they repented of their sin.

Thus the Old Testament prophets' message was principally a call to conversion and a divine consolation in times of trouble. The prophets also complained against the people, saying that God would punish them if they continued in their wicked ways, but the prophets did not engage in fortune-telling or what modern people understand as predicting the future.

Another important aspect of biblical prophecy is its grounding in a particular place and time. In other words, the prophetic author's original, intended meaning is closely connected to the historical circumstances out of which he wrote. For the book of Revelation this means that we ought to read it as a call to conversion and a message of consolation written first for the churches of Asia Minor, in *their* historical and cultural situation, and now reinterpreted for *our* historical and cultural situation. This is a process that requires prayerful reflection, but it is also in keeping with our understanding of the prophets' role as the conscience of the people.

Other scholars argue that the genre "apocalypse" has its roots in Wisdom literature. The Old Testament books included in this category are Proverbs, Job, and Ecclesiastes, along with Sirach (also known as Ecclesiasticus) and Wisdom of Solomon. While Wisdom literature covers a wide variety of topics, it is principally concerned with questions about universal truth, the meaning of life (and death), and what constitutes human good. As one might expect, then, it also addresses issues of theodicy (response to the problem of evil): Why do the righteous suffer without warrant? Why do the wicked appear to go unpunished? What is the meaning of human suffering, and where is God's justice? All of us can relate to these questions, especially when the difficulties of life become too much to bear.

How have these theodicy questions traditionally been addressed within Judaism and Christianity? Needless to say, answers have never come easily. The reason? Jewish and Christian respondents must come to terms with two interrelated and sometimes apparently contradictory assertions: God is sovereign (all-powerful and in control) and God is just. If we acknowledge the existence of evil in the world, we are forced to question whether or to what extent God has power over evil. On the other hand, if we assert the sovereignty of God, then we must wonder about God's justice, since experience shows us that evil does indeed go unpunished at times, and good people do suffer harm.

The sages (wise teachers) of the Old Testament Wisdom literature wrestled with similar questions. The book of Job is an excellent example. If we accept that the genre of the book of Revelation has roots in Wisdom literature, we can see how it treats questions of theodicy by repeatedly asserting that God is sovereign, reigning supreme not only over the heavenly realm but also over the earthly realm and even the underworld. In addition, it repeatedly asserts that God is just, promising reward to God's holy ones and punishment of the wicked. This message of hope and consolation is especially powerful if the audience for which it is intended is experiencing persecution for its faith.

Finally, as mentioned above, the apocalyptic genre does not presuppose a sustained story line that extends from the beginning to the end of the book. Likewise, the reader of the book of Revelation will observe that the book is not organized chronologically. Rather, its author describes a collection of visions, some of which are situated in the heavenly realm and others on earth; some pertaining to the believing community as it anticipates persecution, others relating to those who have endured the suffering and proved themselves faithful. Often the author will introduce a particular idea or image in an early vision and then return to it later in a series of expanded visions or auditions. For these reasons the reader must resist the temptation to impose a chronology on the book. Any attempt to see the book as a linear map of the events of the end time will necessarily lead to misunderstanding of its message.

Biblical scholars have not yet conclusively answered the question about the origins of the apocalyptic genre. However, its parallels with biblical prophecy and Wisdom literature give us a clearer sense of what to expect when we read apocalypses. To sum up, apocalypses do three things: (1) they console people in situations of persecution; (2) they present a particular interpretation of historical events that focuses on the justice and sovereignty of God and the triumph of good over evil; (3) they persuade their hearers to keep covenant with God, that is, to live in a way that assures that they will be among God's elect in the end time.

Outline of the book of Revelation

Anyone who has done any in-depth study of the Bible knows that there are almost as many outlines of a given book as there are scholars studying it. Unfortunately, the authors of these biblical books did not provide us with their outlines, so modern readers use whatever clues they can find in the text to uncover the author's intent and then construct an outline accordingly. In turn, the outline provides a map for studying the book in an organized way. The outline provided here is designed to highlight the patterns of the symbolic number seven in the book of Revelation.

I. Rev 1:1-8 Introductory materials
II. Rev 1:9–11:19 First cycle of visions
   A. Rev 1:9-20 Initial vision of one like the son of man
   B. Rev 2:1–3:22 The seven letters to the seven churches of Asia Minor
   C. Rev 4:1–5:14 The vision of God's throne and the Lamb
   D. Rev 6:1–7:17 The opening of the seven seals
   E. Rev 8:1–11:19 The seven trumpets
III. Rev 12:1–20:15 Second cycle of visions
   A. Rev 12:1-18 Vision of the woman and the dragon
   B. Rev 13:1-18 Vision of the beasts of the sea and the land
   C. Rev 14:1-20 Vision of the Lamb and imminent judgment
   D. Rev 15:1–16:21 Visions of the seven bowls

The Book of Revelation

    E. Rev 17:1–18:24 Fall of Babylon (interlude)
    F. Rev 19:1–20:15 Seven visions of the last things
IV. Rev 21:1–22:5 Vision of the New Jerusalem
V. Rev 22:6-21 Concluding materials

The commentary that follows is organized according to this outline, with additional subdivisions as needed. However, before beginning our analysis of the book of Revelation, a brief introduction to the symbolism of its colors and numbers is in order.

Symbolic numbers in the book of Revelation

Numbers are used liberally throughout the book of Revelation, and readers sometimes mistakenly take them literally rather than symbolically, as intended by the author. Here are the most commonly cited numbers and their symbolic meanings:

- Three = a number suggesting a few, a limited number, or a limited time.
- Four = fullness, especially as it relates to the breadth of the universe (e.g., four corners of the world); universality.
- Seven = perfection, fullness, perfect orderedness. In the book of Genesis it is the number of the completeness of creation.
- Ten = sometimes denoting a limited number, other times recalling the ten kings of Daniel 7:24, who oppress the holy ones of God in the period before God's reign is finally established.
- Twelve = fullness or completeness, especially bringing diversity into unity. Israel was made up of twelve tribes. The calendar year consists of twelve months, and the day has two sets of twelve hours.
- Thousand = a number signifying myriads, a number too large to count.

These numbers, as well as multiples, combinations, or fractions of these numbers, occur throughout the book of Revelation. In each case the context will help us understand their significance.

Symbolic colors in the book of Revelation

Like numbers, the colors in the book of Revelation are also symbolic. Again, the context will help us understand their significance, but this list of color symbols will help us get started.

- White = victory, triumph
- Red = bloodshed, violence

- Scarlet = royalty, bloodshed
- Purple = royalty
- Black = famine
- Pale green = death

The exalted Christ is frequently represented as wearing white, as are the martyrs who make up his heavenly army. The dragon that wreaks havoc on the earth is red, and the whore Babylon wears scarlet and purple. Thus the first thing the reader will observe is that the colors in the book of Revelation mark out the two sides in a great battle between good and evil.

COMMENTARY

INTRODUCTORY MATERIALS

Rev 1:1-8

The introductory section of this book consists of a prologue (1:1-3), from which the title of the book is derived, followed by what appears to be the "address" portion of a letter (1:4-8).

1:1-3 Prologue

The first word of the document, *apocalypsis,* means "revelation." Thus the book is known as Revelation or the Apocalypse. The author of the book, who is also the recipient of the revelation, identifies himself as John and describes his purpose in writing: to witness to "the word of God and to the testimony of Jesus Christ" (1:2). He also describes his work as prophecy (1:3). Notice the relationship of parties involved in the transmission of this revelation. The revelation belongs or pertains to Jesus Christ (1:1). It is given by God but is mediated through an angel to John, who in turn reported what he saw to others (the community of believers, 1:1-2). The prologue concludes with a beatitude (a saying that begins, "Blessed is the one . . . ") for those who hear the word and act upon what they hear (1:3). This is a prophet at work, acting as spokesperson for God and calling people to conversion.

1:4-8 The "address"

This subunit looks like the "address" portion of a letter, but it is somewhat misleading because the letter form is abandoned almost immediately. The author, again identified as John, says that he is writing to the seven churches of Asia. However, he may not have had exactly seven in mind, since seven is a symbolic number representing fullness or perfection. In fact, he may have been referring to *all* the churches of first-century Asia, now Turkey.

This opening of the letter contains an extended greeting, beginning with the words "grace to you and peace" (1:4). Notice John's use of patterns of three. This grace and peace has a threefold source: God, the seven spirits before God's throne, and Jesus. Further, God is identified with three tenses of the verb "to be"—"who is and who was and who is to come" (1:4)—an expansion of the divine name "I AM," revealed to Moses at the burning bush (Exod 3:14). Finally, Jesus is described in terms of three roles or functions: "faithful witness, the firstborn of the dead and ruler of the kings of the earth" (1:5). His activities on the community's behalf are also enumerated in a pattern of three: he loves us, freed us from sin, and made us a kingdom and priests of God (1:5-6). In these very succinct statements, John is asserting God's sovereignty, Jesus' triumph over evil and death, and the believers' reason for hope and consolation. As we shall see later, these are the primary elements of John's theodicy (response to the problem of evil).

Finally, the opening of the letter contains a prayerlike expression of confidence in Jesus' return (1:7). The text of the prayer is constructed of quotations from the Old Testament books of Daniel and Zechariah. Daniel 7:13 describes a vision of "one like a son of man" (a heavenly being who has the appearance of a human) who comes before God's throne in heaven to receive, from God, an everlasting dominion and kingship over all the earth. In the interpretation of Daniel's vision (Dan 7:15-27), this heavenly being is shown to be a symbol of the holy ones of God (Dan 7:18, 22). However, here, in the book of Revelation, the one who will come on the clouds is Jesus Christ.

In Zechariah 12:10 the prophet speaks on behalf of God, saying that God will pour out a spirit of compassion on Judah and Jerusalem, so that they will mourn over the one whom they have pierced. Here, in the book of Revelation, the message continues to be one of hope and consolation, but with an added emphasis on the revelation of Christ as the "pierced" one.

This section ends with a declaration of the sovereignty of God, who is almighty, the beginning and end of all things (1:8). Alpha is the first letter of the Greek alphabet, and Omega is the last.

FIRST CYCLE OF VISIONS

Rev 1:9–11:19

This first cycle of visions consists of an initial vision (1:9-20) followed by seven letters to the churches of Asia Minor (2:1–3:22), a vision of God's throne and the Lamb (4:1–5:14), the opening of seven seals (6:1–7:17), and the blowing of seven trumpets (8:1–11:19).

INITIAL VISION OF "ONE LIKE A SON OF MAN"

Rev 1:9-20

After the prologue and the opening, John recounts a vision of a heavenly being (1:9-20). He begins by affirming his relationship with his hearers in terms of what they share in Jesus. Again, notice the use of the pattern of three: "I John . . . who share with you the distress, the kingdom, and the endurance we have in Jesus" (1:9). Taken together, these three expressions speak to John's understanding of what it means to participate in the Christian life. The word translated here as "distress" can also mean "persecution" or "tribulation," referring to the end time. The word translated as "kingdom" can also mean "kingly reign" or "sovereignty" and should be taken to refer to the hope the hearers share in the full manifestation of God's power over evil in the end time. Finally, the word "endurance," also translated "patient endurance," is key to understanding John's message. The word appears seven times in Revelation (1:9; 2:2, 3, 19; 3:10; 13:10; 14:12), and in each case it describes how Christians ought to respond to the troubles they face *because* they are Christian. Later, in 3:10, John is quite explicit that he associates these troubles with the end time.

Next, John provides the temporal and spatial setting for the vision (1:10-11). The "Lord's day" or "the day (dedicated) to the Lord" is most likely a reference to Sunday, the first day of the week and the day on which early Christians gathered to celebrate Eucharist (see Acts 20:7; 1 Cor 16:2). On this day he was "caught up in spirit," that is, under the influence of the Spirit, perhaps in a trance of some sort, when he heard a great trumpetlike voice. In the first century A.D., the trumpet was used in cultic (worship) settings to signal different elements of the worship service or to announce the beginning of festivals or other public events.

Some biblical scholars have seen in John's description of the setting of his first vision some parallels with the call narratives of the Old Testament prophets (cf. Isa 6; Jer 1; Ezek 1–3). If Revelation 1:9-10 is the setting for John's call to prophesy, then the command to write down the words of the vision and distribute them to seven churches (1:11) describes his first task as prophet. All these churches were located in what is now Turkey.

The vision that follows consists of three parts: the account of the vision itself (1:12-16); John's response to the vision (1:17-18a); and an interpretation of the vision (1:18b-20). The imagery of the vision is highly symbolic, much of it coming from the writings of Daniel and Ezekiel. The "one like a son of man" (a heavenly being in human form) is an allusion to Daniel 7:13 (see comments on 1:7 above, p. 836). The mention of his snow-white hair parallels that of the Ancient of Days [God] in Daniel 7:9. Other details of John's description of the heavenly being—dressed in a long robe with a golden sash, with feet that gleamed like polished metal and eyes that blazed like fire (1:13-15)—have parallels with Daniel's vision of a heavenly being in human form who comes to deliver a message about the conflict of nations (Dan 10:5-6).

This description of "one like a son of man" is also reminiscent of Ezekiel's visions of God on the throne. In both cases, what would have been God's torso is said to gleam like amber, and what would have been God's feet has the appearance of fire (see Ezek 1:27; 8:2). Ancient peoples believed that one's power to act resided in the hands and feet and that one's will, intellect, and judgment resided in the eyes and heart. Thus John's heavenly being manifests full power, intellect, and judgment through his unusual feet and eyes (1:14-15).

Finally, the long robe and girdle with which the heavenly being is clothed (1:13) are reminiscent of the dress of the priests of the Jerusalem temple (see Exod 28:4; 39:29; Wis 18:24). Perhaps John is suggesting that this heavenly being has been set apart for some special function in the divine liturgy. This would be consistent with his mention of the trumpet in 1:10. In apocalyptic literature the two-edged sword is a symbol of eschatological (end-time) judgment. The fact that it comes from the heavenly being's mouth means that his *words* are judgment (1:16).

John's terrified response (1:17) and the consolation that follows (1:17-18) are typical of visions of this sort. See, for example, Daniel's response to the vision of the "man" dressed in linen (Dan 10:8-9) and the heavenly being's words of comfort given in response to his alarm (Dan 10:10-12). In the interpretation of John's vision (1:18-20), the heavenly being reveals himself as the resurrected Christ, the one who was dead but now lives (1:18). The resurrected Christ explains that the seven stars in his hand are the guardian spirits of the seven churches (ancient peoples believed that cities prospered because their guardian angels protected them), and the seven golden lamps are the seven churches (1:20).

The number seven is especially significant here. In Greco-Roman culture the rainbow was thought to consist of seven colors. In the second century A.D., some of the Roman emperors included seven stars on their minted coins as a symbol of world domination. Thus the message of this vision is ultimately one of hope and confidence in the One who possesses power over anything that might affect the churches. Just as the heavenly being in the vision walks among the lamps, the risen Christ continues to dwell among them, and just as he holds the stars in his hand, the risen Christ continues to be responsible for their guardianship.

LETTERS TO THE SEVEN CHURCHES
Rev 2:1–3:22

John goes on to record seven letters to the churches of Asia Minor (2:1–3:22). The letters follow a very strict literary pattern, with few variations.

Form of the letters to the seven churches:

- To the spirit of the church in _____
- write this: _____ says this:
- I know . . . _____ (message of consolation)
- yet I hold this against you: _____ (accusation)
- To the victor I will give _____
- Whoever has ears ought to hear what the Spirit says to the churches.

In the opening address of each letter, after the church is identified, the writer describes the source of his prophetic message, namely, the exalted Christ. Notice that almost all the descriptions of Christ are taken from the initial vision, suggesting that we ought to see the letters as part of a larger unit that begins with the vision of "one like a son of man" (1:9-20). In the body of each letter, the church is either consoled on account of the sufferings they endure, or scolded for their offenses against God. In most cases they are both consoled and scolded!

From these letters we can discover what the author thinks are the problems of the churches in his day. Pay careful attention to the section of each letter that begins "Yet I hold this against you . . . " As we read these letters, we might also want to think about whether these problems have any counterpart in the lives of today's faith communities.

The command to listen, which is found in the conclusion of each letter, is typical of prophetic literature. The phrase "to the victor," also in the conclusion of each letter, describes the rewards that faithful ones will receive on account of their devotion to Christ who has conquered; those who shed their blood for the ransom of the saints will be exalted by God (5:5, 9-10). At the conclusion of the book of Revelation, in the vision of the New Jerusalem, we learn that those who conquer (i.e., the victors) will inherit the fullness of covenant relationship with God (cf. 21:7).

What, then, is John doing by including these seven letters in the first major unit of the book of Revelation? On one level he is simply playing the part of a scribe, writing down the words dictated by the exalted Christ. However, we cannot neglect the fact that he is also acting as prophet or spokesperson of God, delivering messages of consolation and warning. In fact, this is the perspective from which the whole of the book of Revelation ought to be read. These are communities that were apparently well known to John and for which he felt responsibility, much as the prophets of the Old Testament felt responsible to call the Israelites to conversion.

2:1-7 Message to the church at Ephesus

Because of its location on the western coast of Asia Minor and at the mouth of the river Cayster, Ephesus was an important commercial center for the eastern part of the Roman Empire in the first century A.D. It was also considered to be among the largest cities of the province, with a population estimated at 250,000. The city played an important role in the life of first-century Judaism and Christianity. The Jewish historian Josephus, for example, notes that there was a substantial Jewish population in Ephesus. The Acts of the Apostles suggests that Paul used Ephesus as his base of operations for two years during his missionary activity (Acts 19:1-41). In addition, early traditions associate John, the author of the Fourth Gospel, with Ephesus. It is also said that Mary, the mother of Jesus, lived there for a time and died at Ephesus.

The city contained shrines in honor of a full range of Greek and Roman deities. Its most important religious site was the temple of Artemis, a Greek mother-goddess and goddess of fertility, which was considered to be one of the Seven Wonders of the World. There was also a 25,000-seat theater in Ephesus. The library of Celsus was located there, along with temples for the imperial cult and shrines of the Egyptian deities. The city had also gained a reputation as a place to study magic, so it was not uncommon to find exorcists there.

In this letter John praises the church at Ephesus for their faithful endurance in the face of deception by false apostles and their heresies (2:2-3). However, he warns them that their initial love (zeal?) has waned, and they are now in danger of losing their faith unless they reform their ways (2:4-5).

John's choice of description for the exalted Christ—holding the seven stars and walking among the seven lampstands (see the commentary on 2:1)—is especially appropriate for the church at Ephesus because it was a rich and powerful city, and many biblical scholars think that the church at Ephesus was the mother church of the area. However, John may also want to remind the faithful that the exalted Christ continues to be present among them and therefore knows their deeds, both good and bad.

The promise made to those who conquer (2:7) is reminiscent of the second creation story in Genesis, in which Adam and Eve were barred access to the tree of life after their sin (Gen 3:24). In this letter, those who will be allowed to eat of the tree of life are being restored to an intimate relationship with God such as Adam and Eve enjoyed in paradise. The "tree of life" imagery in Genesis may have been introduced here as a counterpoint to the sacred tree of the cult of Artemis.

2:8-11 Message to the church at Smyrna

The city of Smyrna was located on the western coast of Asia Minor, north of Ephesus. It had a good harbor, and its location at the end of a major east-west road made it an important commercial city in the first century A.D., though its origins date back to 1000 B.C. Along with Ephesus, Sardis, and Pergamum, it was one of four centers of the provincial assembly of Asia Minor and the first in the province to build a temple to the goddess Roma (Rome). In A.D. 26 the city built a temple to Tiberius, making it second only to Pergamum as a center for the emperor cult (worship of the emperor as a manifestation of the Roman deities). Although we know relatively little about life in Smyrna in the first century, evidence from the second century indicates that the city was suffering under many conflicts—between Christians and non-Christians, between rich and poor, and between local government authorities and Roman provincial authorities. Bishop Polycarp was martyred at Smyrna in A.D. 155.

This letter differs from the form outlined above in that there is no accusation of the community, presumably because the author has nothing with which to charge them. He acknowledges their economic poverty, calling them rich, presumably rich in faith (2:9). Further, he encourages them to stand firm in the face of persecution and not to fear the suffering that is about to befall them (2:10). They will be arrested, he says, and some will even be put to death, but those who are faithful to the end will survive the "test[ing]" and will be rewarded with eternal life. Thus the description of the exalted Christ as the one who "once died but came to life" (2:8) is consistent with John's expectations for the future of the community at Smyrna.

Revelation 2

The source of the Christian community's persecution appears to have been the Jewish synagogue ("assembly") in Smyrna (2:9), further suggesting an intra-family fight between Jews and Christian Jews, that is, Jews who accepted Jesus as the messiah. The ten days of tribulation (2:10) may be an allusion to the story of Daniel and his friends, who were tested for ten days when they refused to eat the king's food, which had been dedicated to idols (Dan 1:12-15; cf. 5:3-4). The promise that those who conquer will escape the "second death" (2:11) is a reference to final judgment (see 20:11-15).

2:12-17 Message to the church at Pergamum

Like many of the major cities in Asia Minor, Pergamum's history is very long. During the Hellenistic period, in the early third century B.C., it became famous as the capital of an independent kingdom in western Asia Minor. However, on the death of its last king, King Attalus III, in 133 B.C., the kingdom was bequeathed to the Romans, and shortly after that time Pergamum became the capital of the Roman province of Asia Minor. During the reign of the Roman emperor Augustus (31 B.C.–A.D. 14), the province was reconstituted, and perhaps at that time Ephesus became its capital, but Pergamum likely retained some of its special status for imperial authorities, being the first to build a temple to Augustus.

Throughout this period the city of Pergamum was known as an important center of learning, having one of the largest libraries in the world, and a center for the arts, including a famous school of sculpture. Pergamum also possessed a sanctuary of Asclepius, a Greek god of healing, where people could obtain medical care and where they studied rhetoric. The famous medical doctor Galen was from Pergamum. Temples to several other deities were located here, including a temple to Zeus, the highest deity in the Roman pantheon. The city was also known for its silver mines and for the making of textiles and parchment. Agricultural work flourished here as well.

In this letter the exalted Christ is described as having a sharp, two-edged sword, suggesting judgment, either of the Christian community or of the city itself (2:12; cf. Isa 11:4; 49:2). The author of the letter begins by acknowledging the difficult situation of the community: they live in the place where Satan has his throne (2:13). This is likely a reference to the position of esteem that Pergamum held in the emperor cult and in the worship of Roman deities. It is interesting to note that the previous letter calls the synagogue at Smyrna the "assembly of Satan" (2:9), suggesting some kind of collusion between the Roman authorities and the synagogue. Here, too, the Christian community is praised for standing firm in the face of persecution (2:13).

However, all is *not* well. John accuses the Christian community of harboring some who teach that it is permissible to compromise their faith and participate in idol worship (2:14). (For the story of Balak and Balaam, see Num 22:1–25:3.) They also tolerate the teachings of the Nicolaitans, who apparently hold a similar view on participating in pagan cults (2:15; 2:6). In other words, they have accommodated the practice of their faith to the demands of the wider culture to such an extent that they have compromised the integrity of their faith. Needless to say, the author of the letter considers this to be a very serious problem! Hence the description of the exalted Christ as having a sharp, two-edged sword, the symbol of judgment (2:12).

The promise made to the ones who conquer (2:17) has messianic and salvific overtones. Jewish apocalyptic literature describes an expectation that the manna of the Exodus will return in the messianic age. The meaning of the white stone (2:17) likely has something to do with victory, and the new name signals a new destiny or a new way of life.

2:18-29 Message to the church at Thyatira

The city of Thyatira was located in Lydia in the western part of Asia Minor. Although few artifacts remain today, the city is believed to have played an important role in the civic life of the area from the second century B.C. through the third century A.D. Apparently it was also an important center for the making and trading of wool. The Acts of the Apostles tells a story about a woman named Lydia, who was from Thyatira and was baptized by Paul after listening to his preaching (Acts 16:11-15). Lydia was a dealer in expensive purple dyes. Like several of its neighbors, Thyatira had religious sites associated with the emperor cult and shrines to the Greek and Roman deities.

In this letter the exalted Christ is described as the Son of God, with eyes of fire and shining feet (2:18), perhaps in contrast to the sun god Helius, whose devotees had a shrine in Thyatira. The members of the Christian community are praised for their love, above all, and for the fact that they continue to grow in holiness (2:19). However, they are scolded for enduring the influence of a prophetess who deceives people and lures them into idolatry (2:20). It is likely that she is a Nicolaitan (see 2:12-17). The name Jezebel is a reference to a Canaanite queen of King Ahab, who established the cult of Baal (worship of any of various local fertility or nature gods among Semitic peoples) in Israel and doomed Ahab's dynasty (2 Kgs 10:7). Fornication and adultery should be understood metaphorically to describe participation in idol worship.

Finally, a double promise is made to the victors (2:26-28). First, they will be given authority over the nations, an allusion to Psalm 2, which, already

Revelation 2

by the first century B.C., was thought to refer to the Jewish messiah. Second, they will be given the morning star. The meaning of the latter is uncertain.

3:1-6 Message to the church at Sardis

Sardis was located in Asia Minor, approximately sixty miles inland from Smyrna and Ephesus. Along with Ephesus, Smyrna, and Pergamum, it was one of four centers of the Roman provincial assembly of Asia and the regional capital of Lydia. The Jewish historian Josephus mentions the existence of a large Jewish community there in the first century A.D. However, we know little about the Christian community in Sardis until the second century, and then primarily through the writings of Melito, the bishop of Sardis. Apparently, persecutions of Christians were conducted in Sardis during that period. The city was founded in the third century B.C.

In this letter the description of the exalted Christ appears to build upon the mention of the morning star at the end of the previous letter, but like the other letters, it also includes details from the initial vision of "one like a son of man" (3:1; see 1:16, 20). Again, like the earlier letters, the author begins, "I know your works . . . " (3:1). However, he has nothing positive to say about this community. They may have a reputation of goodness, but they are in fact as good as dead! Thus he tells them that they better wake up and strengthen what still survives of their faith (3:2). If they do not, he will come when they least expect and inflict judgment on them (3:3).

The promise to the victors is a robe of victory (3:4-5; see "colors" in the introduction to this commentary, pp. 834–35) and assurance that their names will always be found in the book of life (3:5), an allusion to the book of names of the holy ones in 20:12.

3:7-13 Message to the church at Philadelphia

Philadelphia was located in western Asia Minor, along a route between Smyrna and Sardis. The city was founded in the second century B.C. by one of the kings of Pergamum, when the area was still an independent kingdom. Because of the fertile farmland around it, Philadelphia became a center of agriculture, as well as leather working and textile making. However, the area was also prone to earthquakes, and Philadelphia was hit especially hard in the early part of the first century, leaving significant damage to city buildings and walls. It suffered another setback when, in A.D. 92, during the reign of Domitian, the provinces were ordered to destroy half of their vineyards and were not allowed to plant new ones. This city's most important deity was Dionysius, the god of wine. Some from among the Christian community at Philadelphia were martyred along with Polycarp at Smyrna in A.D. 155.

Breaking with the pattern of the previous letters, the description of the exalted Christ in the letter to the Philadelphians does not go back to the initial vision of "one like a son of man," except for the mention of keys (3:7; cf. 1:18). Here the key is the key of David, suggesting authority that is granted them because of their faith in the messiah of the Jews. The open door is a metaphor for opportunity (3:8). The writer acknowledges that the community has little power right now, but he tells them that eventually their opponents—the "assembly (synagogue) of Satan" is a derogatory reference to the Jewish community at Philadelphia—will come to their way of thinking (3:9).

Although hinted at in other letters, here the theme of theodicy is made explicit: God will vindicate the righteous and make the wicked see the error of their ways. The promise given to this community is an anticipation of the final vision of the book of Revelation, the New Jerusalem (3:12). As we shall see later, the New Jerusalem will have no need of a temple because the whole city and its inhabitants will constitute the temple of God and the Lamb (see 21:2, 22-23).

3:14-22 Message to the church at Laodicea

Located southeast of Philadelphia, Laodicea was a major commercial city in the first century A.D. Because it was not far from Hierapolis, the waterfall that emptied out of the hot springs of that city apparently could be seen in Laodicea. It had been founded during the reign of the Greek king Antiochus II (261–246 B.C.) and, under Roman rule, had grown into a manufacturing center for clothing and carpets made from a special type of black wool produced in the area. Laodicea boasted a medical school known for the healing of eye diseases, and it served as a major banking center. The city itself was very wealthy, as evidenced by the fact that it rebuilt quickly and without aid from outside sources after a devastating earthquake in A.D. 60.

In the opening of this letter, the exalted Christ is given three attributions, none of which is connected to the initial vision of the "one like a son of man" (3:14; see 1:9-20). Here we find the only reference in the New Testament to Christ as the "Amen," meaning "So be it." This attribution suggests a position of great authority, much like the third attribution, "source of God's creation" (3:14). The Greek word *archē*, here translated as "source," can also mean "ruler" or "beginning." The second attribution, "faithful and true witness," recalls 1:5 and anticipates 19:11, where Christ is similarly described.

Unlike most of the other letters, the phrase "I know your works" (3:15) is not an introduction to praise or consolation, but rather an indictment. Using the imagery of water, perhaps the now tepid, sulfurous water descending from the hot springs at Hierapolis, the writer says he is about to spit them out of his mouth because, comfortable in their riches, they are disgustingly lukewarm in their faith (3:15-17). Worse yet, they have deluded themselves into thinking that they are among the spiritual elite, people of admirable faith (3:17). This letter, then, is intended as a rude awakening to the church at Laodicea!

With an ironic twist, the message quickly turns to consolation. Their spiritual poverty will be remedied by a gift of fire-refined gold (3:18), an Old Testament image for the purifying effects of suffering (Mal 3:2). They will be relieved of their nakedness with garments of victory, the reward of the martyrs, and they will be given new sight through the saving ointment that Jesus brings (3:18). Recall that these are the things for which this city is renowned: riches, fine clothing, and medicine for eyes. Again the author draws upon the image of an open door—opportunity—and promises that anyone who opens to Jesus will dine with him, a clear allusion to Eucharist (3:20). Finally, the victor is promised a seat on God's throne (3:21). We will return to both of these images—the open door and the throne of God—in the next section of this book.

THE VISION OF GOD'S THRONE AND THE LAMB
Rev 4:1–5:14

There are several types of visions in the book of Revelation. This vision is a theophany, that is, a revelation or manifestation of God. The Greek word *theos* means "God." Typically, theophanies have a mountain setting. The seer (i.e., the recipient of the vision) is taken to, or otherwise allowed to see, where God resides. The vision is accompanied by heavenly voices and cosmic manifestations of the power of God, like lightning, fire, and thunder. The seer usually describes himself as being in a trance, and time appears to stand still, at least momentarily. In this theophany John sees an open door and is told, "Come up here . . . " (4:1; see 3:20).

The throne that John is allowed to see derives its imagery from the Hellenistic royal court. Hence the description of the immense throne at the end of the throne room and the floor that looked like a sea of glass (4:2, 6). In ancient cultures the throne was the symbol of the king's authority. Therefore, the more intimidating it was, the more it said about the king's authority. Interestingly, in this vision the one seated on the throne (4:3) is described, not in anthropomorphic terms, as one might expect, but by analogy to precious stones, perhaps to suggest that God's kingly splendor surpasses that of any earthly king.

The identity of the twenty-four elders (4:4) is unknown, though scholars have suggested that they represent the sum of the twelve tribes of Israel and the twelve apostles. The same two groups appear together in the final vision of the New Jerusalem in Revelation 21–22. Twenty-four, being a multiple of twelve, represents fullness or perfection. They are dressed in white, symbolizing victory, and they wear crowns of gold, symbolizing their royal authority (4:4). The seven spirits of God are the angels of the presence, who stand before God's throne (4:5).

The "four living creatures" (4:6) are called watchers, or *merkabah* angels, in the Jewish hierarchy of angels. These watchers are sometimes portrayed as angels of fire who support God's throne or as heavenly beings covered with eyes, with which they constantly keep watch over the throne. The notion probably originated with the Jewish idea of the cherubim, who were part of the throne of the ark of the covenant in the holy of holies. In distinguishing these watchers as the four different animal creatures (4:7-8), John most likely was influenced by Ezekiel 1:5-14. In later Christian theology the symbols of the four living creatures become associated with the four Gospels: the lion (Mark), the ox (Luke), the man (Matthew), and the eagle (John).

The watchers' prayer of praise recalls the description of God in the opening of the book of Revelation: "The Lord God almighty, / who was, and who is, and who is to come" (4:8; cf. 1:8). Each time the watchers give glory to God, the twenty-four elders bow down in homage to God (4:10). The casting down of their crowns (4:10) is similar to Hellenistic oriental kingship rituals in which vassal kings cast their crowns at the emperor's feet to declare their allegiance and identify themselves as the emperor's vassals. The proclamation, "Worthy are you" (4:11), was the standard way that the Roman emperor was addressed as he entered the throne room. All this is to say that John's audience would have readily understood the message of this vision: God is, always was, and always will be all-powerful and king over all that exists.

John signals a new scene in his vision of the heavenly throne room when he says, "[Then] I saw . . . "(5:1). The first scene shows that God is sovereign; this second scene will address the question of God's justice. The description of the One on the throne holding a scroll (5:1) resembles depictions of the Roman emperor seated on his throne as judge and holding a *libellus*, a petition or letter in the form of an open scroll. The seer, John, first experiences extreme pain when he fears that no one is able to open the scroll and thereby dispense justice (5:4). However, when one of the elders tells him that the lion of the tribe of Judah and the root (i.e., descendant) of David will open the seals, we also learn about his qualifications to do so—he has triumphed

Revelation 4–5

(5:5)! The Greek word is *nikē*, meaning "to win," "to triumph," or "to win the right." But over what did he triumph?

Suddenly John sees a Lamb standing in the midst of (or as part of) the throne (5:6). This is no ordinary lamb! John says that it "seemed to have been slain" (5:6), meaning that it has the marks of having been slaughtered, but it is, in fact, alive! John observes that the Lamb has seven horns and seven eyes. Horns were thought to contain the power of an animal or an object: in this case the Lamb possesses the fullness of power (5:6). It also has seven eyes, symbolizing full knowledge or insight (5:6). Ancient people thought that an individual was able to see, not because of the light that came into the eye, but because of light that was *inside* the person. These eyes, John says, are the seven spirits of God. They are sent out into the world, bringing knowledge of all that is happening on earth (5:6).

When the Lamb steps up to receive the scroll (5:7), the four living creatures and the elders reveal in song how the Lamb won the right to open the scroll (5:8). Three actions are attributed to him: (1) he was slaughtered (i.e., crucified); (2) he ransomed the holy ones (i.e., the Christian believers); (3) he made them a kingdom and priests for God (5:9-10). Now he stands before God's throne, ready to dispense justice on God's behalf by vindicating the holy ones: they may be oppressed now, but they will reign on earth (5:10). God's holy ones are not present in heaven, but their prayers are represented before God by the four living creatures and the elders (5:8).

The scene concludes with everyone in the heavenly throne room singing in praise of the Lamb and the One seated on the throne (5:11-12). The heavenly choir numbers not in the thousands but *thousands* of thousands, suggesting a number too great to count. Everyone in the heavenly realm participates in this divine liturgy, creating a scene of perfect harmony, with no hint of suffering, pain, injustice, or evil. Finally, as if to crown this glorious moment, John observes that all created beings—those in heaven, on earth, and under the earth—join in the cosmic song of praise to God and the Lamb (5:13). The four living creatures confirm the event by saying, "Amen," meaning "So be it," and the elders worship their king (5:14).

THE SEVEN SEALS

Rev 6:1–7:17

The contents of the scroll, which the Lamb received in the previous vision, cannot be revealed until all of its seals are broken. Thus the cycle of the seven seals is closely connected to the vision of God's throne and the Lamb. Scrolls sent by kings or important dignitaries carried the seal of the sender to verify their authenticity. The seal also ensured that only the intended recipient would have access to the contents of the scroll. The four living creatures are the ones to announce the opening of the first four seals (6:1, 3, 5, 7). As each seal is broken, John receives yet another revelation. Although his vantage point for these visions is in the heavenly realm, all the activity associated with the opening of the seals takes place on earth.

6:2-8 The first four seal visions

The first four visions associated with the opening of the seals come in rapid succession. The first, the rider on the white horse, represents victory in war (6:2). Several scholars of the book of Revelation suggest that John has in mind the Parthians, whose equestrian armies were known for their skill with the bow and who were long-standing enemies of the Romans. John observes that he *was given* a crown (6:2). The passive verb form does not reveal the giver, but John's audience would have understood it to be God. That is, God allowed the war and God handed over the defeat of the Romans to the Parthians. However, we should not understand this to mean that God is responsible for evil. Rather, John is saying that nothing happens that is outside God's control; God is sovereign in all things!

The second horse, bright red, represents bloodshed (6:4). Its rider wields his sword *by permission* (6:4), suggesting again that God is firmly in control of these earthly events. The rider takes peace from the earth, in this case, Rome, and makes people slaughter one another (6:4), a reference to the civil strife that often follows war.

When the third seal is opened and the black horse appears, John observes that its rider carries a scale for buying and selling (6:5), thus revealing another consequence of war, namely, famine. Food shortages that require someone to pay a day's wages for a day's worth of bread are extreme, to be sure. The words that announce this famine come from the midst of the four living creatures (6:6), perhaps from God or the Lamb, suggesting that God is permitting the famine or at least knows of it. The command not to damage the oil and the wine (6:6) may simply mean that God will not allow this famine to end in total annihilation. However, some scholars have suggested that oil and wine were not principally food but objects for religious ritual, and were excluded from the famine for that reason.

The opening of the fourth seal brings another horse, sickly green, the color of death (6:7-8). Its rider and Hades, the place of the dead, are given power by God to unleash all the consequences of war—killing by sword, famine, pestilence, and wild animals—on one-fourth of the earth, suggesting that their effects are comprehensive and yet limited (6:8).

Revelation 6

John may have borrowed his imagery of four horses and their horsemen from the book of Zechariah. The prophet describes a vision of four horsemen sent by God to patrol the earth, that is, the nations that were complacent while Jerusalem suffered (Zech 1:8-17). At this point an angel appears and asks God how long Jerusalem must wait for God's mercy (Zech 1:12). The question is one of theodicy. The angel tells Zechariah to prophesy, declaring to the people that God is moved to compassion for Jerusalem and angry at the nations that did not come to its aid. The point of the prophecy of Zechariah is this: God is sovereign, but also just and merciful. So, too, in the book of Revelation: the horsemen are sent out, under God's authority, to take away the peace of Rome. In the next vision, the opening of the fifth seal, the faithful will ask how long it will be before God avenges their suffering. As he watches these visions unfold, one can imagine John being quietly gleeful, since, as we discover later, he perceives Rome to be the ultimate foe of the believing community.

6:9-11 The fifth seal vision

With the opening of the fifth seal, the scene shifts to the faithful martyrs residing under God's altar in the heavenly realm (6:9). The martyrs praise God's sovereignty and at the same time ask when God's justice will be manifest on their behalf (6:10). In response, they are given white robes, signifying victory, and told to enjoy their rest until the full number of martyrs has been reached (6:11). This is not to say that God is responsible for the martyrs' deaths, but rather that their deaths are somehow part of God's larger plan in the battle of good over evil.

6:12-16 The sixth seal vision

The opening of the sixth seal is accompanied by cosmic signs that are typical of apocalyptic literature: an earthquake, the sun turning black and the moon turning to blood, stars dropping from the heavens, and mountains falling down (6:12-14). Thus the action has shifted again to the earthly realm, though it appears that John is still in the heavens. John tells us that people of *every* social status responded to the cosmic signs with fright, begging for the earth to swallow them to protect them from God's wrath and the wrath of the Lamb (6:15-16). His point, of course, is that no one was unaffected by these phenomena. However, the intense cosmic activity (6:12-14) also suggests that all of creation is working on *God's* behalf, not theirs.

John also observes that these people are trying to avoid the *wrath* of the Lamb (6:16). A wrathful lamb is a strange paradox, because we tend to think of lambs as cute and cuddly, but already we know that it is no ordinary lamb, since earlier it was identified as the lion of the tribe of Judah and the root of David (5:5) and described as having seven horns and seven eyes (5:6). This sixth vision ends with the peoples exclaiming, "Who can withstand it?" (6:17), because it appears that *no one* will escape God's wrath.

7:1-17 Interlude between the sixth and seventh seal visions

The situation seems dire, but there is reason for hope. In a two-part interlude between the sixth and seventh seal visions—7:1-8 and 9-17—John witnesses God's protective action on behalf of the tribes of Israel, which represent the believing community. Like the previous vision, the setting is the earthly realm. First, John sees four angels holding back the forces of destruction, perhaps another reference to the four horsemen, so that they can do no harm to the universe (7:1; see 6:1-8). When the announcing angel orders them to hold back the forces of destruction a little longer, it becomes clear that this process of marking the servants of God with a seal (7:2-3) is for their protection. In the Greco-Roman world, people branded slaves on the forehead to indicate ownership. Likewise, in Ezekiel 9:1-3 the Lord tells Ezekiel to put a mark on the forehead of the people who grieve over the terrible things that were happening in Jerusalem. Thus the sealing of the servants of God sets them apart as belonging to God and, therefore, under God's protection. The number sealed—144,000, or 12,000 from each tribe—should be understood symbolically: perfection or fullness (12) multiplied by fullness (12), multiplied again by a number too great to count (1,000). In other words, John is not witnessing the sealing of a relatively small gathering of the elect, but an unbelievably massive crowd of people, a sea of humanity!

The second part of this interlude (7:9-17) is introduced by John's observation of a great multitude standing before the throne of God and the Lamb (7:9). The crowd that John sees is most likely the 144,000 who were sealed in the preceding scene (see 7:1-8). They are wearing robes of victory and crying out in praise and thanksgiving for the source of their salvation, namely, God and the Lamb (7:9-10). Their palm branches are symbols of victory in war (cf. 1 Macc 13:51; 2 Macc 10:7) but are also reminiscent of the feast of Tabernacles, when Jews gathered in Jerusalem to celebrate the harvest festival and build booths or tents in remembrance of God's loving care during the Exodus. This feast also anticipates the messianic age, when God's kingdom will be fully manifest and everyone will come to Jerusalem to worship God, and the whole city will be as holy as the temple (see Zech 14:16-21). In the concluding vision of the book of Revelation, the New Jerusalem (21:1–22:5), John will provide us with a fuller version of this Tabernacles motif.

Revelation 7

Again John is permitted to witness the heavenly liturgy, with all the angels surrounding the throne, the four living creatures, the elders, and now the crowd too big to count gathering to worship God in song (7:11-12; see 5:9-14). It should be noted that their prayer contains exactly seven words of honor, symbolizing the fullness of praise to God (7:12).

Almost as if interrupting the liturgy, one of the elders asks John the identity of the ones in white robes. John defers to the elder, who then provides interpretation for him: these are the ones who have come through the persecution as martyrs, joining their blood with Christ's (7:13-14). What follows is a prophecy of consolation: they will no longer need to build tabernacles (tents) for themselves because *God* will tabernacle (i.e., shelter) them (7:15). Echoing the prophet Isaiah, the elder further declares that the white-robed crowd will never again suffer hunger, thirst, heat, or grief and, instead, will be led to springs of life-giving water (7:15-17; see Isa 49:10; 25:8).

Imagine how the elder's prophecy must have sounded to John and those soon to be martyrs! It is a profoundly moving message of hope. In fact, this entire interlude (7:1-17) would have been seen as a defiantly faith-filled response to the problem of theodicy: despite appearances to the contrary, God is absolutely sovereign and just! God protects the holy ones and will surely rescue them from their sufferings, so that they can participate in this glorious liturgy of praise. John will return to these images once again in the vision of the New Jerusalem at the end of the book of Revelation (21:2–22:5).

THE SEVEN TRUMPETS

Rev 8:1–11:19

After the intense drama created by the opening of the previous six seals, finally the seventh and last seal is opened (8:1). The scroll could have been unrolled at this point. This is what one might have expected, especially after John's lament in Revelation 5:1-5 about finding no one worthy to open the scroll. However, surprisingly, there is no reading of its contents. Instead, there is silence in the heavens (8:1), perhaps the silence that one encounters in worship or in the presence of the divine. The rhetorical effect is to create an atmosphere of heightened anticipation. Thus the reader is forewarned that there is even greater drama to come!

Breaking the silence, John is given another vision (8:2-5), in which seven angels, probably the archangels of Jewish tradition, are given seven trumpets, a traditional symbol of the announcement of God's judgment (see Isa 27:13; Joel 2:1; Zeph 1:16). Is this the content of the scroll, revealed not in words but in visions? Perhaps, but the text does not tell us. John's vision continues when another angel is given incense with which to offer up the prayers of the believing community (8:3-4). These prayers, now rising up to God, were first voiced in Revelation 6:10—"How long will it be, holy and true master, before you sit in judgment and avenge our blood on the inhabitants of the earth?"

The angel then fills the censer with fire from the altar—God's holy fire—and throws it down to earth, where it manifests in imagery associated with apocalyptic judgment (8:5). Again the issue is theodicy. The author is asserting that nothing happens without God's permission and that God, who is sovereign, will ultimately vindicate the faithful ones.

8:6-12 The first four trumpet visions

The setting for John's visions has shifted again from the heavenly to the earthly realm (8:6), where, with the blowing of each trumpet, plagues are inflicted upon the earth. Scholars have observed that these plagues are similar in content to the plagues of the Exodus. For example, the first vision, which describes hail and fire mixed with blood being cast upon the earth, recalls the seventh plague of hail and fire in the Exodus story (8:7; see Exod 9:23-26). Likewise, the second vision describes the sea turning to blood, recalling the first plague of the Exodus story, in which the Nile River is turned to blood (8:9; see Exod 7:20). This recollection of the Exodus is interesting, especially in light of the last scene of the previous cycle of visions (7:9-17), in which the believing community and all the heavenly beings celebrate the fullness of the feast of Tabernacles, also recalling the Exodus.

The seven angels who stand closest to God's throne are the ones to announce the plagues (8:2, 7, 8, 10, 12), signaling that the plagues originate with God and descend upon the earth by God's permission. Recall that the plagues of the Exodus story were plagues only for the Egyptians; for the Hebrew peoples they were miracles, a central feature of God's liberating activity on their behalf. Likewise, by comparison, the plagues of the book of Revelation are miracles and part of God's larger plan for the salvation of the community of believers. This understanding of the plagues is confirmed by the scene that precedes the blowing of the trumpets: the offering of the prayers of the saints, who cry, "How long, O Lord?" (see 8:4).

Like the pattern established in the visions of the four horsemen, the first four visions of the trumpets are described very briefly and follow one another in rapid succession (8:6-13; cf. 6:1-8). However, in contrast to the visions

Revelation 8

of the four horsemen, the Roman Empire is no longer the object of destruction, but the earth itself. The destruction is substantial, and yet limited in scope, since one-third of the created world is affected by each plague (8:7, 8, 10, 11, 12). As yet, there is no mention of harm coming to the believing community or even to humanity in general. Rather, in systematic fashion, first the things of the earth are affected, then the things of the sea, followed by the things of the fresh waters, and finally the things of the heavens.

In the vision of the third trumpet, "Wormwood" is the name of the star that makes the fresh waters bitter. In the book of Jeremiah, wormwood is described as a bitter poison that God uses to punish wrongdoers (Jer 9:15; 23:15).

8:13 Interlude between the fourth and fifth trumpet visions

In a brief interlude between the fourth and fifth trumpets (8:13), John sees and hears a bird of prey flying in the sky. The Greek word *aetos* is sometimes translated as "eagle," but "vulture" is more accurate for its connotations of impending doom. The bird cries out "Woe" three times, anticipating the three trumpets still to come, much like the prophets who cried "Woe" when they announced God's judgment against the wrongdoers. See, for example, Isaiah 3:9, 11; 45:9-10; Jeremiah 13:27; 22:13; 23:1; 48:46; Ezekiel 13:18; 16:23; 24:9.

9:1-12 The fifth trumpet vision

When the fifth trumpet is blown (9:1), we quickly learn that the woes are directed at humanity itself. The fallen star is a traditional symbol for a fallen angel or Satan (9:1; see Isa 14:12-15; Luke 10:18; Jude 13). The abyss generally refers to Sheol, the place of the dead, also called Hades. However, in Revelation it is the place where the fallen angels are imprisoned until the end-time judgment (see 17:8; 20:1-3). The key that was given to the fallen angel (9:1) is a symbol of power over the abyss, and even though God is not named, the passive form of the verb "to give" indicates that God is the giver of the key.

When the fallen angel opens the abyss, smoke pours out (9:2)—later we will see that the source of the smoke is a pool of fire within the abyss (see 20:7-10)—followed by an army of locusts (9:3). These are not ordinary locusts, because they do not eat vegetation; rather, they sting their human prey like scorpions (9:5). No one escapes their sting, except those who had been marked with the seal of God on their foreheads (9:4; see 7:1-8). In the ancient world both insects were considered offensive to humans, much as some people today feel about snakes or rats (see Luke 10:19).

John's description of the locust-scorpions—looking and sounding like horses and chariots, having crowns on their heads, and military armor where their chests should be (9:7, 9)—is reminiscent of the imagery used in the vision of the first horseman, a symbol of the Parthians (cf. 6:1-2). The "hair like women's hair" (9:8) may also refer to the Parthians, whose men were known to wear their hair long. Their reign of terror is limited to five months—half of ten—meaning a short time (9:5, 10). The name of their king, in both Hebrew and Greek, is translated as "Destruction" (9:11).

Indeed, the state of affairs looks desperate for humanity; suffering and destruction are everywhere! And yet, the careful reader will observe that God is still in control of this situation. The angel who unlocked the abyss received the key from God (9:1). The passive verb forms used to describe the activity and limitations of the locust-scorpions—"were given" (9:3), "were told" (9:4), and "were not allowed" (9:5)—all suggest that God is the all-powerful One, permitting the locusts to inflict pain and suffering. However, this is not to say that God is the cause of suffering. Rather, John is saying that evil has a *human* face (9:7), and in its destructive rampage it inflicts suffering on the whole human race. The book of Joel describes a similar plague of locusts, which God allowed for the purpose of calling people to repent (Joel 1:6-7, 15; 2:1-11; cf. Exod 10:12-15). Remember, too, that God has arranged in advance for the protection of the holy ones; they have the seal of God on their forehead (see 9:4). Thus, even in this terrible scene of destruction, John asserts that God is sovereign and just, calling people to conversion and protecting the chosen ones.

9:13-21 The sixth trumpet vision

Immediately afterward, the sixth angel-trumpeter announces another vision: the release of the destructive forces associated with the four angels located at the four directions of the universe (9:13-21). Although John does not specifically mention it, this may be the vulture's second woe (8:13; see 11:14): The order for their release comes from a voice located among the four horns of God's altar (9:13). In ancient religions the power of the deity was thought to reside in the horns of its altar. Therefore, this order comes directly from God. The fact that the angels are held ready for the exact date and time (9:15) also indicates that what is about to happen is completely under God's control. Again, the object of God's wrath is humanity, and like the previous vision, its scope is limited (one-third means a limited number; see 9:15). However, unlike the earlier vision, the angels are released not simply to harm their victims but to *kill* them (9:15).

Suddenly a cavalry of immense proportions appears on the scene (9:16): as a symbolic number, 200 million is double the product of ten thousand times ten thousand, which signifies fullness on top of fullness, multiplied by num-

Revelation 9

bers too great to count. They come from the Euphrates River (9:14), which, in the late first-century A.D., was the eastern boundary of the Roman Empire. The horses are monstrous, with lionlike heads and serpent tails, complete with stinging mouths (9:17-19). What a nightmare! Their riders wear red, blue, and yellow armor, and the plagues they bring are fire (red), smoke (blue), and sulfur (yellow; 9:17-18). The symbolic meaning of these plagues is unclear, except that they probably represent the abyss and they kill. The purpose of the vision is revealed finally at its end. God allowed the destruction of one-third of wicked humanity in the hope that the rest would repent (9:20-21). However, they do not repent, and so we move to the next vision.

10:1–11:14 Interlude between the sixth and seventh trumpet visions

The next two visions form an interlude between the sixth and seventh trumpets, much like the interlude we saw between the opening of the sixth and seventh seals (7:1-17). The literary effect is to create a "pregnant" pause in the action, heightening the reader's anticipation for what is to come. We also have a change of setting here. In the previous six trumpet visions, John was in the heavenly realm observing what was taking place on earth. Now he is back on earth watching a mighty angel come down from heaven (10:1).

The first of these two visions (10:1-11) is reminiscent of the throne vision in Revelation 4, especially in the mention of the rainbow or halo and thunder (10:1, 3; see 4:3, 5). This angelic being also shares some features with the earlier "one like a son of man," namely, a face like the sun and legs like columns of fire (10:2; cf. 1:14-15). Apart from this angel, only two other angels in the book of Revelation are called "mighty": the angel who issued the challenge for a worthy one to come forward to open the scroll held by the One seated on the throne (5:2) and the angel who will throw a stone into the sea as a prophetic action against "Babylon" (18:21). Who is the mighty angel in 10:1? Most likely it is not "one like a son of man." However, it is reasonable to conclude that it is closely connected with God's glory, and that it comes with divine authority to deliver a message.

Unlike the scroll of the earlier throne vision, we are told that the scroll held by this angel is open, not closed (10:2; cf. 5:1). However, we are not told the content of the scroll. Although all the angels in the book of Revelation speak with a loud voice, this one reveals his high status through his lionlike voice and the response he receives from the seven (symbolizing fullness or perfection) thunders (10:3). When the thunders "speak" John's impulse is to write down what he hears, but he is told by another voice not to write but to "seal up" what was said (10:4). The significance of this command is unclear, except to say that humans will not be allowed access to this part of John's vision.

Then the mighty angel raises his right hand toward heaven—the traditional position of oath-taking—and swears by the eternal One that there will be no more delay (10:5-6). He swears on God who *created heaven, earth, and sea*, thus explaining why the angel stands as he does, with one foot on the sea and the other on the land, while pointing toward the heavens. In other words, the message he delivers pertains to the entire created order! When the seventh angel sounds his trumpet, the mystery of God will come to completion (10:7). The Greek word *mystērion* usually means *hidden purposes*, referring to something hidden from view.

Again John hears a heavenly voice; it is the angel who told him not to write what the seven thunders said (10:8). Now he is told to take and eat the scroll that the mighty angel is holding. The scene is reminiscent of Ezekiel, who is handed a scroll and told to eat it (Ezek 2:9–3:15). Ezekiel's scroll contains words of lament, mourning, and woe. When he first eats it, it is sweet in the mouth, but later he learns that it is directed against Israel and he goes off, in bitterness and anger, to do what God commands. For John, too, the prophecy he must deliver will at first taste sweet but in the end will bring him bitterness (10:9-10). Thus the eating of the scroll is accompanied by the command to prophesy (10:11).

Immediately John takes up his mandate, and so begins the second vision of this interlude (11:1-14). His first task is to measure the inner parts of the Jerusalem temple, excluding the outer court of the Gentiles and those who worship there (11:1-2). The prophetic act, also seen in Ezekiel 40–43 and Zechariah 2:1-5, symbolically marks out the space where God's glory resides on earth. It also identifies the boundaries of protection for God's people.

What follows then is a message of consolation for the believers. They are told that the holy city will be overrun, but for a limited time—three and a half years, half of seven, the number representing fullness or completion (11:2). The number *three and a half* is also an allusion to Daniel 7:25 and the cruel reign of King Antiochus IV, who persecuted Jews a little more than two centuries earlier for "a year, two years, and a half-year." In the concluding vision of the book of Revelation, the city will be measured again and established forever as the dwelling place of God and the Lamb (21:15-27).

John is now told about two unnamed witnesses (the Greek word is *martyria*), who will prophesy for forty-two lunar months, or three and a half years—the same amount of time that the city will be overrun—while wearing sackcloth, the coarse dress of prophets and a sign of repentance (11:3). The witnesses, who are further described as two olive trees and two lamps (11:4), recall Zechariah 4–6. The two images are related, of course, because lamps were fueled by the oil from pressed olives. In the book of Zechariah the olive trees represent Zerubbabel, the anointed king of Israel and the one who laid the foundations of the temple, and Joshua, the high priest who was responsible for building the temple. These two were anointed—*messiah* means "anointed"—"who stand by the Lord of all the earth" (Zech 4:14). Similarly, in Revelation the witnesses are said to "stand before the Lord of the earth" (11:4).

Although they are unnamed in the book of Revelation, these two witnesses appear to have connections to Elijah and Moses because of the things they are able to do to those who harm them (11:5-6). In the Old Testament stories Moses is identified with the plagues of the Exodus, especially changing water to blood (Exod 7:14-25). Elijah was said to have words like fire (Sir 48:1) and the ability to close up the heavens so that it would not rain (1 Kgs 17:1). According to the prophet Malachi, Elijah was expected to return to preach repentance before the end-time Day of Judgment (Mal 3:23-24). Deuteronomy 18:15-22 describes God's promise to raise up a prophet like Moses from among the people. Therefore the original readers of the book of Revelation would have readily recognized the connections that John was making between the witnesses in his vision and Moses and Elijah.

Without transition, the voice from heaven tells John that the witnesses, when they complete their testimony, will be attacked by the beast from the bottomless pit (11:7). We will learn more about the beast later in 13:1-8. For now, it is sufficient to say that it is the embodiment of evil. What follows is a story of the trial, unjust punishment, rescue, and vindication of the witnesses. The story follows the pattern of the Wisdom tale, which can be found throughout Jewish Wisdom literature. See, for example, the story of the vindicated righteous one in Wisdom 2:10–3:12 and some of the stories of Daniel in the book of Daniel. The Wisdom tale provides a fitting answer to the problem of the unwarranted suffering of God's holy ones, because it carries a message of consolation and hope for the persecuted: as God rescued and vindicated the righteous one in the story, so we can trust that God will rescue and vindicate us!

Here is how the Wisdom tale unfolds. As soon as the witnesses have completed their testimony, the beast conquers them and kills them (11:7). Their unburied corpses are left in the street of the "great city," probably Rome, to be viewed by passersby as a mockery and disgrace (11:8-9). The inhabitants of the earth, probably those who are in allegiance with Rome, celebrate and gloat over the destruction of the witnesses because their testimony was torment to them (11:10). Horrors! The witnesses could not have come to a worse end! But three and a half days later (symbolic of a limited time), the voice says, God comes to their rescue (11:11). God's own breath (*pneuma*, also translated "spirit") of life enters into them, and the inhabitants of the earth hear God's voice calling the witnesses, "Come up here." All the while their enemies are watching! (11:11-12). They respond with fear as they see the witnesses' restoration (11:11) because they realize the full extent of their wrongdoing, and they know that they are about to experience the full fury of God's punishment. We can almost hear their lament, "Oh, no! What did we do?" An enormous number of people (seven thousand, or a full number too great to count) fall victim to God's punishing wrath (11:13). But God's rage is also restrained—only a tenth of the population is killed. Those who remain repent and give glory to God. Thus the Wisdom tale teaches that God is sovereign and just; God will rescue the holy ones and punish the wicked. But God is also merciful and will not destroy creation forever.

A brief note on the city's symbolic names: "Sodom" and "Egypt" suggest that the city has a reputation for immorality (see Gen 18:22-32; Exod 1:11-14; and Isa 1:10). Also, the phrase "where . . . their Lord was crucified" does not refer to a place but to the forces that oppose the Christian believers (i.e., Rome; see 1 Cor 2:6-8). Parallels between the story of the two witnesses and the story of the death and resurrection of Jesus are unavoidable and probably intentional. The reader is reminded that Jesus Christ is "*the* faithful witness" (1:5; emphasis added) of whom they are disciples.

At this point the narrator of the book of Revelation announces that the second woe has passed and the third is about to come (11:14). However, we cannot be certain which is the second woe—perhaps the releasing of the four angels at the four corners of the universe (9:13-19) or the story about the vindication of the two witnesses (11:1-13). Likewise, as we shall see, John does not clearly identify the third woe. What follows is a scene of triumph, not woe.

11:15-19 The seventh trumpet vision

When the seventh angel blows his trumpet (11:15), a heavenly voice announces that God's kingdom has replaced the kingdom of the world (i.e., the Roman Empire). The setting has again shifted to the heavenly realm. The twenty-four elders, who were first introduced in the throne vision of Revelation 4, fall down in worship, praising and thanking God for asserting the fullness of power against evil and rescuing the righteous believers (11:16-18). John's mention of the destroyers of the world (11:18) is probably a reference back to the king of the locust-scorpions, identified as Abaddon

Revelation 11

or Apollyon (see 9:1-12). However, it may also be a reference forward to the dragon and its two beasts that will be revealed in Revelation 12 and 13.

Suddenly the heavenly temple, even the holy of holies, is opened so that all believers can see and enjoy God's unmediated presence (11:19). The ark of the covenant, which once contained the tablets of the Sinai covenant, was lost when Solomon's temple was destroyed in 587 B.C. but is now restored in the heavenly temple (11:19). This detail recalls a legend about Jeremiah hiding the ark of the covenant and other artifacts of the temple for the day when God "gathers his people together again and shows them mercy" (2 Macc 2:7). The thunder, flashes of lightning, and other cosmic happenings (11:19) confirm that John is experiencing a theophany, that is, a manifestation of God. Thus ends the first half of the book of Revelation.

SECOND CYCLE OF VISIONS
Rev 12:1–20:15

The second half of the book of Revelation begins with an intercalation, that is, a vision inserted within another vision. This literary technique suggests that the two visions are to be interpreted together as a single, interrelated unit. The outer vision (12:1-6 and 13-17) begins in the heavens and eventually shifts to the earthly realm. Likewise, the inner vision (12:7-12) begins in the heavens and ends with a transition to earth. The outer vision (12:1-6, 13-17) describes an immense dragon attacking an unnamed woman enthroned in the heavens. The inner vision describes a war in heaven in which the angel Michael throws the dragon down to earth (12:7-12). The two visions work together to explain, in symbolic imagery, how the forces of evil came down upon God's holy ones. We will examine each vision separately, and in their parts, and then look at them together.

VISION OF THE WOMAN AND THE DRAGON
Rev 12:1-18

12:1-6 Part one of the vision of the woman and the dragon

In the opening scene of this vision, John sees an unnamed woman with the sun as her raiment, the moon as her footstool, and twelve (symbolizing fullness or perfection) stars as her crown (12:1). Without warning, the beauty and serenity of this scene are shattered by the realization that the woman is in the throes of childbirth, a traditional image for the sudden and unexpected arrival of the end time (12:2). Adding to the drama, an enormous red dragon is waiting in earnest for the child to be born so that he can eat it as soon as it is born! (12:3-4). In Revelation, red is the color of violence and bloodshed.

The dragon's ten horns (12:3) recall the book of Daniel, in which a ten-horned, devouring beast symbolizes the kingdom of the Greeks, who persecuted the Israelites because they refused to give up their Jewish cultural and religious practices (see Dan 7:1-28). The seven diadems or crowns (12:3) on the dragon's seven heads also signal kingship. However, the identity of the kingdom that is associated with the dragon will not be revealed until 17:1-6, where she is described as Babylon.

The message of the vision is one of consolation in the face of persecution. The woman is in a truly difficult situation, but the child born to her is male (12:5); in a patriarchal culture a male child was considered to be a sign of God's blessing. We also learn that he is destined to rule with great strength (12:5). The Greek version of Isaiah (LXX Isa 66:7) and Psalm 2:7-9 both express hope in a king who would be God's son and rule with a rod of iron.

As the vision progresses, the message of hope continues to play out in dramatic fashion. The child is rescued from the jaws of the dragon, snatched up to God (12:5), while the woman escapes to the desert, where God had made a place for her (12:6). God harbors her for a period of 1,260 days (i.e., 42 months, or three and a half years), symbolizing a limited time (12:6; see 11:3-14). Thus, although the desert is often a place of danger, here it is a place of protection.

12:7-12 Vision of the war in heaven

John leaves us wondering about the woman in the desert and now turns our attention to the inner vision (12:7-12). Immediately, the reader learns that war is about to break out in heaven (12:7). The war is quick and decisive: the dragon and his angels are soundly defeated by the archangel Michael and his angels (12:7-8) and then tossed out of the heavenly realm (12:9)! The apocalyptic sections of the book of Daniel likewise describe the archangel Michael as a warrior prince who battles against the enemies of God's people and utterly destroys them (Dan 10:10-21; 12:1-4). Almost as a side note, we learn the dragon's names and the activity by which he is known: "the ancient serpent (referring to the snake who seduced Eve in Genesis 3:1-6), . . . the Devil (literally 'slanderer' or 'enemy') and Satan ('accuser' in Hebrew), who deceived the whole world" (12:9).

A heavenly voice confirms what John has just witnessed: the salvation, power, and sovereignty of God are now manifest (12:10a), and the accuser (i.e., prosecutor) of the woman's offspring—the persecuted believers—has been driven out of the heavens, conquered by the blood of the Lamb, Jesus Christ (12:10b-11). But the heavenly voice also warns that the dragon still needs to be driven from the other two cosmic realms, the earth and sea, and his rage will be especially intense because he knows his end is soon! (12:12).

12:13-18 Part two of the vision of the woman and the dragon

But what about the woman, whom John last saw in the desert, and how did she make her way from the heavens to the desert? The second half of the outer vision (12:13-18) provides an explanation. Unable to capture the woman's child, who was immediately taken up into heaven (12:5), the dragon is now in hot pursuit of the woman (12:13). But God rescues her, giving her two wings of an enormous bird, so that she can fly away to safety (12:14). Suddenly the great dragon becomes a huge water serpent, something like the mythical Leviathan, spewing a flood of water after her (12:15). Now God's creation comes to the woman's rescue: the earth comes alive, opening its mouth to swallow the river (12:16). Good news: the woman has escaped! One can almost imagine the dragon stomping away in fury!

At the conclusion of the vision, John observes that the dragon has turned his rage to the rest of the woman's children, the Christian believers (12:17). The reader is expected to understand, finally, the significance of the three and a half years (12:6, 14). Yes, it is the time that the woman is protected in the desert, but it is also the length of time that her children will suffer persecution. Half of seven, their persecution will be comprehensive but limited. In other words, there is reason for hope even in the midst of suffering.

But why did the author of the book of Revelation link these two visions together in this manner? Jewish tradition and Jewish apocalyptic literature in particular saw a direct connection between what was happening on earth and what was happening in the heavens. In fact, the rabbis had a saying, "As in heaven, so on earth." Thus this inner vision explains the source of the believers' persecution on earth, namely, the dragon and his angels who were thrown out of the heavenly realm, but it also promises that these evil powers will be defeated on earth just as quickly and dramatically as they were defeated in the heavens.

Given the high level of drama contained in these two visions, the reader should not be surprised that they ought to be interpreted symbolically rather than literally. We have already identified the woman's other offspring as the persecuted believers. Who, then, is the woman? John does not tell us her identity, but interpreters of the book of Revelation have advanced at least three possibilities. Some argue that the woman is Eve, because of allusions to Genesis 3:14-16, in which God curses the serpent, promising enmity between it and the woman and her offspring, and then tells the woman that her childbearing pain will intensify because of what she had done (see 12:2, 4, 9, 10).

Others argue that the woman is Mary, because the child that is snatched up to heaven is the messiah and the Lamb, by whose blood the believers are saved, that is, Jesus Christ (see 12:10-11). Still others argue that the woman represents the church, since her offspring are the persecuted believers (12:17).

The problem, of course, is that none of these identifications fit every detail of both visions. Perhaps the reader is expected to recall all three possibilities simultaneously, making these two visions a multilayered story of salvation.

Both of the visions described in Revelation 12 conclude with a reference to the dragon's fury being unleashed on earth and sea, thus anticipating the next two visions: the vision of the beast of the sea (13:1-10) and the vision of the beast of the land (13:11-18).

THE VISION OF THE BEASTS OF THE SEA AND THE LAND

Rev 13:1-18

13:1-10 The beast of the sea

John's next vision is of a beast emerging from the sea. In the ancient world the sea was seen as hostile and chaotic. The four great beasts of the book of Daniel also came from the sea (Dan 7:1-8). In fact, many of the descriptors of Revelation's beast from the sea are similar to those associated with the four beasts in Daniel. For example, Daniel's fourth beast has ten horns, which represent ten kings of the Greek empire (Dan 7:7-8, 23-24). In Revelation the diadems on the ten horns also represent kingship.

Other aspects of Revelation's beast of the sea (13:2) appear to relate to the first three of Daniel's beasts: the body of a leopard (cf. Dan 7:6), the feet of a bear (cf. Dan 7:5), and the head of a lion (cf. Dan 7:4). In the book of Daniel these three beasts represent three of the great empires of history—the Babylonian empire (winged lion), the Median empire (bear), and the Persians (leopard). Thus, given John's apparent familiarity with Daniel, we should conclude that Revelation's beast of the sea also symbolizes a very powerful empire. In John's historical context, this would be the Roman Empire (see also 6:1-8).

John describes the beast of the sea in considerable detail, but the details are to be understood metaphorically. Its seven heads (13:1) describe the

Revelation 13

fullness of power. The blasphemous name on its heads (13:1) probably refers to titles regularly given to the Roman emperors of John's day—"Lord," "Lord and God," and "Savior of the World"—all of which the Christian believer would have considered to be blasphemies against God. The blasphemies it utters (13:5) refer to its offenses against God and the Christians who worship God.

Regarding the detail about the beast's head seeming to have been "mortally wounded, but this mortal wound was healed" (13:3), some scholars conclude that the beast is the emperor Nero (d. A.D. 68), who committed suicide, leaving the empire in civil war for a year before Vespasian took the throne and restored the empire in A.D. 69. However, it is also likely that John is making a parody on the Lamb "that seemed to have been slain" (5:6). Thus, with much disdain, he writes that the people of the whole earth are completely enamored of the Roman Empire. They worship the Roman Empire, saying that there is no other like it and no one can stand against it, and they worship the dragon (i.e., Satan), from whom the Roman Empire gets its authority (13:3-4). But all this is so much foolishness! *God* is the one they should worship. And the Lamb, who gets its authority from God, is the one against whom no one can stand!

Worship of the dragon and the beast (13:4) is probably a reference to the emperor cult, in which people were obligated to offer sacrifices to the emperor in order to ensure the empire's prosperity. Christians who refused to participate were considered a threat to the empire. However, John reminds his readers that Rome has no power except what was given it by God. For this reason, John uses the passive forms of the verbs "to give" and "to permit." The beast, John says, "*was given* authority to act" (13:5; emphasis added), "*was also allowed* to wage war against the holy ones" (13:7; emphasis added), and "*was granted* authority over every tribe, people, tongue, and nation" (13:7). Thus John is asserting that God is sovereign over everyone and everything, even as the Roman Empire reigns over the whole world and God's holy ones are being killed by its emperor.

The holy ones, however, should be consoled by the fact that the time of their suffering is limited: Rome can act for only three and a half years, half of seven, the number of fullness (13:5). They should also be consoled by the fact that the names of the ones who worship the beast will *not* be found in the Lamb's book of life (13:8), while theirs most surely will be, as long as they remain faithful.

Thus John concludes this vision with a prophetic admonition directed to the Christian community. He begins with a riddle (13:10) that sounds like some kind of teaching on predestination, but most scholars agree that it is not; rather,

Revelation 13

it is a call for endurance and trust, no matter what the cost. If the Christian community opposes the beast (i.e., the Roman Empire) and refuses to worship it, they should expect suffering and even death, because it is an inevitable outcome of their opposition. However, that is not their concern. Whatever happens, their only response should be faithful perseverance (13:10).

13:11-18 The beast from the earth

Immediately following the vision of the beast from the sea, John receives a vision of a beast rising from the earth (13:11-18). Like the beast from the sea, this beast is related to the dragon. In fact, it *speaks* like the dragon (13:11). Further, it exercises all the authority of the first beast, which received *its* authority from the dragon (13:12). Therefore, if the first beast is the Roman Empire, then the second must be its representative, the emperor.

The narrator of John's vision makes clear that this beast is a deceiver. He has horns that make him look like a lamb, but he has the voice of the dragon, the embodiment of all that is evil (13:11). He works miracles like the prophets of Israel, even like Elijah, the prophet who could call down fire from heaven and who was expected to return in the end time (Rev 13:13-14; see 1 Kgs 18:38; 2 Kgs 1:10; and Rev 11:3-14 on the two witnesses who were prophets). In sum, he is a false prophet whose goal it is to deceive the whole world. Although John does not use the term, some scholars have called this beast the anti-Christ, because it gives the *appearance* of being the Christ ("anointed"), but clearly is not.

Again John uses the passive form of certain verbs to indicate that the beast acts with God's permission. Thus the narrator of this vision says that the beast "was allowed" to perform miracles (13:14) and give life to the image (i.e., statue) of the beast (13:15). In effect, John is saying that the deceptive activity of the beast is somehow part of God's plan. However, we should not interpret this to mean that God is the source of evil. Rather, John is asserting that God remains sovereign over all things, even over the emperor, despite appearances to the contrary.

John indicates that the stranglehold of the emperor extended beyond religion to politics and economics, since everyone was required to have the mark of the beast on their right hand and on their head (13:16). The mark on the head recalls the first-century A.D. practice of branding slaves on the forehead to show whose property they were. Thus the mark of the beast is most likely a reference to the official seal of the emperor, which was used to authenticate imperial documents and identify the emperor's property. The image of the emperor was also imprinted on all the coins of the empire, so a person could not even buy or sell without indirectly participating in

Revelation 13

the emperor cult (see 13:17). Again, the reader should not take this talk of branding literally. Rather, John intends that we treat it metaphorically and contrast this mark of the beast with the mark of the Lamb that was placed upon the forehead of God's holy ones (see 7:2-3). Either you belong to the Lamb or you belong to the beast! If you belong to the Lamb, you are protected from the catastrophes of the end time; but if you belong to the beast, you will suffer the same fate that he will suffer.

At the conclusion of this vision, John adds a note to his readers concerning the identity of the beast from the earth (13:18). To appreciate what John is saying here, we must imagine a community that already knows the identity of the beast and, together with John, shares a bit of "naughty" delight in talking about the beast behind his back! The practice in which John is engaged is called *gematria*. Jewish rabbis of the ancient world were skilled at it, but non-Jewish people in the Greco-Roman world enjoyed it too. It was a process of assigning numbers to letters of a word or a name and using the resulting number to designate something about the holder of that name.

Because Latin, Hebrew, and Greek do not have separate sets of symbols for numbers, people used the individual letters and combinations of letters to designate quantities. It became quite natural, then, to refer to a person by their number, particularly among friends who wished to share a "secret" that they wanted to keep from outsiders. People who already knew the name could very quickly discern the number, but those who did not would find it almost impossible to solve the riddle. Sometimes the number also has symbolic meaning, as in the case of 666. Six is one short of perfection or fullness and therefore means imperfection or evil. Thus John is saying to his audience, "Here is this beast who has deceived and enamored the whole world, but *we* know who he really is—he is evil itself!"

What, then, is the name of the beast? Since he appears to be one of the emperors of Rome, and presumably someone known to John, our choices have been narrowed considerably. Most scholars believe him to be Nero, since his Greek name and title, transliterated into Hebrew, adds up to 666: $N(50) + r(200) + o(6) + n(50) + Q(100) + s(60) + r(200)$, while his Latin name and title, transliterated into Hebrew, adds up to 616: $N(50) + r(200) + o(6) + Q(100) + s(60) + r(200)$, which is a variant reading found in some of the manuscripts (handwritten copies) of the book of Revelation. Nero was already deceased at the time of John's writing, but because of the legend associated with his departure and because he, like Domitian after him, also persecuted Christian believers, some have concluded that Domitian was Nero returned to life.

VISION OF THE LAMB AND IMMINENT JUDGMENT

Rev 14:1-20

14:1-5 Vision of the Lamb on Mount Zion

As a counterpoint to the visions of the dragon and its two beasts, John has another vision—this time of the Lamb standing on Mount Zion, also known as Jerusalem (14:1-5). Instead of the inhabitants of the world who wear the mark of the beast, John sees the 144,000—fullness upon fullness multiplied by a number too great to count—wearing the mark of the Lamb and his Father (14:1; cf. 13:16-17). These are the same 144,000 who were sealed in 7:1-8. In constructing this image, the author may have in mind Psalm 2: "I myself have installed my king / on Zion, my holy mountain" (Ps 2:6). In traditional Judaism this is the place where the remnant of Israel would be gathered together in the messianic age (Joel 3:5; Obad 17; Mic 4:6-8; Zeph 3:12-20).

As the vision proceeds, John hears sounds—something like rushing water, thunder, and harps (14:2)—that are usually associated with theophany (i.e., manifestation of God; cf. 1:15; 5:8; 15:2; 19:6). Further, the mention of the throne, the elders, and four living creatures (14:3) recalls the throne vision of Revelation 4, suggesting some direct connection between Zion (Jerusalem) and the heavenly throne room. Again, in contrast to the multitudes who worship the beast in the preceding vision (13:8), John sees the 144,000 singing a "new hymn" in praise of God and the Lamb (14:3). The "new hymn" is probably the same one sung by the heavenly court in 5:8-10. In it the heavenly host praised the Lamb, who is deemed worthy to break the seals on God's scroll because he redeemed all peoples and nations by his blood.

John observes that not everyone, but only the 144,000 who have been "ransomed from the earth" (14:3), can learn this song. They are the ones who were marked on their foreheads with the seal of God before the destructive forces were unleashed from the four corners of the world (7:3). Here, John adds, they "follow the Lamb wherever he goes" (14:4), most likely a reference to their perseverance, even to the point of suffering and death (14:3-4). Pure in every way, they are God's perfect sacrifice; they are the firstfruits, the first and best of the harvest, offered on behalf of all God's people (14:4-5). For persecuted Christians, this is the motivation for their faithful endurance: the opportunity to participate in the true heavenly liturgy.

The significance of the detail about the 144,000 who had not defiled themselves with sexual activity (14:4) is not altogether clear. Some scholars have suggested that this vision represents the gathering of God's army in anticipation of holy war, since soldiers who engaged in holy war were expected to abstain from sexual activity during military service. Others have argued that sexual abstinence is consistent with their role as priests in this heavenly liturgy. Still others have suggested that the virginal state of the 144,000 should be viewed as a metaphor for their refusal to participate in the emperor cult, since Jewish and early Christian writings often describe idol worship in terms of prostitution and adultery. Whether one or all of these meanings are intended, we can be quite sure that it should not be taken literally, so as to say that only celibate Christians are redeemed.

14:6-20 Visions of imminent judgment

Three more "mini" visions, or perhaps extensions of the previous vision, now follow in rapid succession (14:6-13, 14-16, 17-20). Together they represent the "good news" of God's coming judgment.

The first of these visions is introduced with the phrase "I saw another angel" (14:6), which will be repeated two more times before its end, as a second and third angel appear. The first angel flies into the midheaven announcing (literally, "evangelizing") an eternal gospel (literally, "good news"; the Greek word is *euangelion*) for all people (14:6). It is a call to repentance and an invitation to worship the one true God, who made the heavens, the earth, and the sea—the place from which the dragon was thrown down and the places where the beast of the earth and the beast of the sea currently reside, though not for long! The good news is that the time for God's judgment has come (14:7). The reader will recall that the great-winged vulture, who announced the three woes, also flew in the midheaven (see 8:13). It was understood to be the place that stretched across the entire created world.

A second angel appears with a prophetic message of doom for Babylon: the "great" city that made its peoples drunk on its enticements and practices of idol worship has fallen! (14:8). In 1 Peter 5:12 Rome is referred to as "Babylon," and there is every reason to suppose the same meaning is intended here.

The third angel appears with an admonition: whoever gives in to the enticements of the Roman Empire and participates in its cultic practices will also experience the full force of the wrath of God (14:9-10). Of whom is he speaking? Fellow Christians? This is certainly possible! One can probably imagine a situation in which a person decides to keep quiet and go along with the crowd rather than risk persecution or death. For this reason, John again calls his hearers to faithful endurance (14:12) by warning them what is in store if they fail in their perseverance (14:10-11). A heavenly voice adds authority to John's admonition with a beatitude: "Blessed are the dead who die in the Lord" (14:13). The Spirit confirms it with a second blessing:

the dead will be able to rest, knowing that their deeds (i.e., their witness to the faith) will follow them after death (14:13).

In the next vision John sees "one who looked like a son of man" seated on a white cloud (14:14). The crown on his head represents kingship. The sickle, necessary equipment for harvesting grain, is also a traditional symbol of God's judgment (see Isa 17:5; 27:12; Jer 51:33; Joel 3:13). The color white signals victory (14:14). Although the "one who looked like a son of man" is unnamed, we may safely conclude that he is Jesus Christ, because of the initial vision, in which he is revealed to be the risen Jesus (1:13). The imagery is borrowed from Daniel 7:9-14, a vision in which "one like a son of man" comes on the clouds and is presented before the "Ancient One" and given dominion over all nations and peoples. His will be an everlasting kingdom, in contrast to the kingdom of the fourth beast, who made war on the "holy ones" of God and reigned with terrifying strength, but only until the Ancient One arrived and pronounced judgment in favor of the "holy ones." In Daniel the fourth beast is the Greek empire and its king, Antiochus IV, who was notorious for his persecution of the Jewish people.

One can easily imagine John juxtaposing his own "one like a son of man," a heavenly warrior and deliverer of justice, against Rome and its emperor, represented by the great dragon and its beasts. In John's vision "one like a son of man" waits, poised for the harvest, until he hears the angel's command to begin the reaping (14:14-16). On first view, it might seem strange that Jesus Christ has to wait for the angel's command, but the angel is merely God's messenger (the Greek word *angelos* means "messenger"). It is God who is in charge! This harvest appears to refer to the gathering in of all humanity, because no distinction is made between righteous and wicked.

Another vision, also of judgment, follows immediately (14:17-20). In it John sees another angel wielding a sickle (14:17). The angel's job is to harvest the grapes of the earth, and his orders came from the angel in charge of the fire of the altar (14:18). The angel at the altar is the one who earlier offered up the prayers of the "holy ones" and then filled the censer with fire and threw it on the earth (8:3-5). Recall, also, that the souls of the martyrs have been resting under the altar, waiting for the day when God will vindicate them (6:9-10). Thus this vision is another response to the question raised by the martyred souls: "How long will it be . . . before you sit in judgment and avenge our blood on the inhabitants of the earth?" (6:10). They need not wait any longer because the time of judgment has come!

The angel's activity of harvesting the grapes and throwing them into the "great wine press of God's fury" (14:19) is a traditional metaphor for judgment. See, for example, Isaiah 63:1-6, Joel 4:13, and Jeremiah 25:30.

Although the narrator of the vision does not make it explicit, this judgment imagery is double-edged. For the owners and recipients of the fruits of the vineyard, harvest and winemaking are joyous events. But there can be no wine without first smashing the grapes and extracting their blood (i.e., juice). Therefore this harvest also involves suffering and pain.

John observes that God's wrath is so furious and God's judgment so comprehensive that the "blood" runs like a river, as deep as a horse's bridle and as far as two hundred miles (literally, 1,600 *stadia;* 14:20). Again, for the owner of the vineyard this is an astounding amount of wine, indicative of intensive and long-lasting joy! The Greek *stadion* (sing.) measures about 606 feet, so 1,600 *stadia* total approximately 183 miles. More important, however, are the symbolic meanings of this number. It is 40 multiplied by 40, with 40 symbolizing a period of transition or transformation. It is also 4 multiplied by 4 multiplied by 10 multiplied by 10, with 4 being the universal number and 10 representing fullness or completion. In other words, this judgment is wholly transformative and/or fully comprehensive, and God's power over evil is absolute.

VISIONS OF THE SEVEN BOWLS

Rev 15:1–16:21

John signals a transition to a new and important series of visions with the phrase "Then I saw in heaven another sign, great and awe-inspiring" (15:1). Elsewhere the word "sign" is used only of the woman enthroned in the heavens (12:1) and the great dragon (12:3). This third series of seven visions—the first was the opening of the seals (6:1–7:17), and the second the visions of the trumpets (8:1–9:19)—will be the last because, the reader is told, God's wrath is coming to completion in them (15:1).

15:2-8 Another vision of heavenly liturgy

Before these seven bowls of the seven plagues are unleashed, John is privileged to witness again the heavenly liturgy. The floor that looks like a sea of glass (15:2) is reminiscent of the throne vision in Revelation 4. The fact that it is mingled with fire (15:2) may indicate that God's judgment is about to be rendered, or it may signal that only those tried by fire—the persecuted—may enter. The latter view is supported by John's observation that the singers who hold God's harps are the ones who endured faithfully against the wicked enticements of the dragon and his two beasts (15:2-3). They were earlier identified as the 144,000 who were sealed with the name of God on their forehead (7:1-8; 14:1-5).

Revelation 16

The "song of Moses" (15:3) is an allusion to Exodus 15:1-18, the song that Moses and the Israelites sang in praise of God, who rescued them by unleashing the plagues on the Egyptians. John's version of the song is made up of phrases from throughout the Old Testament (Rev 15:3-4; see Ps 111:2; 139:14; Amos 4:13; Ps 145:17; Deut 32:4; Jer 10:7; Ps 86:9; Mal 1:11; Ps 98:2), making it a song in praise of God's justice and sovereignty. It also proclaims the goal of God's mighty deeds: that all God's peoples come together in worship.

The preparations for the release of the seven plagues are now underway. John sees the opening of the tent of witness, an allusion to the tent of meeting of the Exodus (15:5; see Exod 33:7-11). The seven angels who emerge (15:6) are wearing golden sashes, reminiscent of the priests of the temple, but also like the "one like a son of man" in Revelation's initial vision (see 1:6). Their white linen robes are a symbol of victory (see also 19:8, 14). They come out of the temple with seven plagues and then receive the implements of judgment—the bowls of the wrath of God—from one of the four living creatures who stand before the altar of God. The point of the vision is this: God is the source of these plagues. The smoke in the temple (15:8) suggests that God now inhabits it and will remain there until the seven angels complete their assigned task. This is why no one can enter the temple until the plagues are finished (15:9).

16:1-9 The first four bowl visions

The "loud voice" (16:1) that speaks from the temple, issuing the order to pour out the plagues, presumably is God's (see 15:8). Like the first four visions of the seals series (6:1-8) and the trumpets series (8:6-12), the pouring out of the first four bowls comes in rapid succession. Further, like the trumpets series, these visions recall the plagues of the Exodus. Thus the first bowl is poured out on earth, and people whose allegiance is with the dragon and its beasts develop boils and other skin diseases (16:2; see Exod 9:10-11). The second is poured into the sea, the sea turns to blood, and everything in it dies (16:3). The third is poured into the rivers and fresh water springs, and they, too, turn to blood (16:4-7; Exod 7:17-21).

Suddenly the angel of the waters (ancient peoples believed that there were heavenly beings in charge of the various elements of creation, like guardian angels) breaks out in a prayer in praise of God's justice (15:5). Those who killed the holy ones and prophets have received their just "reward," he says. They now have only blood to drink! (15:6). As this vision closes, the altar itself joins in the angel's prayer of praise. Of course, altars cannot talk, so the author may be using the literary technique of personification to refer to the angel of the altar or the souls of the martyrs who

Revelation 16

have been waiting *under* the altar for God to avenge their deaths (6:9-11). The altar's words, "Your judgments are true and just" (16:7), would suggest that the martyrs are now satisfied that God has answered their plea.

When the fourth bowl is poured out on the sun, scorching the people of the earth, John observes that its victims cursed the name of God (16:8-9). The language is reminiscent of the beast of the sea that blasphemes against God (13:1, 5-6) and also anticipates the description of the whore Babylon, who rides a beast covered in blasphemies (17:3). By cursing God the people identify themselves with the dragon and the beasts that get their authority from the dragon. However, the mention of repentance also recalls Pharaoh's response to the Exodus plagues: he expresses the desire to repent until the plague is removed and then returns to his obdurate behavior. Whatever the response of the people, the goal of God's wrath is clear: to call people to repentance and to worship of the one true God. These plagues are not simply gratuitous violence on God's part, but rather a tool for conversion. But the people do not repent or give God glory (16:9).

16:10-21 The last three bowl visions

The fifth bowl, which is poured upon the throne of the beast, results in darkness over its entire kingdom (16:10; cf. Exod 10:21). This is not the peaceful darkness of sleep, but a desperate darkness that drives people to great anguish, even to swearing against God, as their suffering from the earlier plagues is intensified. The narrator adds, "But they did not repent of their works" (16:11). As we shall see in Revelation 17–18, these people are the worshipers of Babylon (i.e., Rome), and their works are the activities that support the power of the beast, namely, politics, commerce, and cultic practices of the Roman Empire.

The sixth bowl is poured out in the Euphrates River, then the eastern border of the Roman Empire, and it dried up, so that armies from the East could enter the empire (16:12). John probably has in mind the Parthians, who were longtime enemies of the Romans (see also 6:1-2 and 9:14). Suddenly John sees unclean spirits emerge from the mouths of the dragon, the beast of the sea, and the beast of the land (here called "the false prophet" because of his deception, 16:13; cf. 12:3; 13:1, 11, 14). The narrator adds that they are "demonic" (that is, deceptive) spirits. John compares the demonic spirits to frogs, recalling the locust-scorpions in Revelation 9:1-9, which elicit feelings of disgust or dislike, but also suggesting the Exodus plague of frogs (Exod 7:25–8:15). The "kings of the whole world" (16:14) probably refers to the kings of the *Roman* world, as distinct from the kings of the East. As John describes it, the three unclean spirits are responsible for all the kings of the earth rallying to war; their assembly will mark the great day of God's justice and judgment (16:14).

The next statement is directed toward John's audience, the believing community, and presented as the words of Jesus: You will not know when or how I will come, so be alert and ready! (16:15). John's comment about being caught naked (16:15) should not be taken literally, but rather as a metaphor for the believers making themselves vulnerable to shame if they have not properly prepared for Jesus' return. In honor-shame cultures, one's honor is more valuable than any other possession a person might have.

The narrator concludes this vision by saying that the unclean spirits assembled the armies at Armageddon (16:16). In Hebrew, this is *har Megiddo*, which means "mountain of Megiddo." Strategically located between Mount Carmel and the Jordan River in the northern part of Israel, it was the entryway for invading armies from the north and east, and therefore the location of some especially fierce battles in Israel's history. However, for John, Armageddon is not so much a place but a symbol of the battle to end all battles!

Finally the seventh bowl is poured out into the air (16:17). The voice from the temple, the same voice that gave the command for the bowls to be poured out, shouts, "It is done," that is, the full measure of God's wrath is completed (16:17). Again John sees and hears the signs of theophany—thunder, lightning, earthquake, and the sounds that accompany them (16:18). As a result, the great city Babylon (i.e., Rome) was broken into three parts by the earthquake, people were pelted by enormous hailstones weighing a hundred pounds each, and the features of the land were so changed as not to be recognizable anymore (16:19-21). The storm and earthquake were fearful, that is, awesome and of catastrophic proportions! But the people did not repent. Rather, their hearts were hardened, so that they cursed God (16:21).

THE FALL OF BABYLON

Rev 17:1–18:24

Before the book's final series of visions, which describe the judgment of the world and the establishment of God's kingdom, Revelation provides a long interlude in which the judgment against the whore Babylon, that is, Rome, is described in great detail. This topic is not new to the readers of the book of Revelation. The seven bowl visions (16:1-21) that immediately precede this section are a final call to repentance for all who have fallen under the spell of the dragon, that is, Rome, and those who pay allegiance to her. However, Rome's fate was sealed already when the angel-prophet of Revelation 14:8 proclaimed, "Fallen, fallen is Babylon the great." These next two chapters are an elaboration of that prophecy.

17:1-18 Vision of the whore Babylon

The connection with the previous series of bowl visions is established in John's mind by the reappearance of one of the angels who held the seven bowls (17:1). The angel takes John to the wilderness, a place of safety in Revelation 12, but here it is also a vantage point from which he can see everything that is happening on the earth (17:3). From this place the angel invites John to view the verdict issued against the great harlot seated on many waters (17:1).

Although today's reader might be stymied by the metaphor of harlotry, John's readers likely understood that he was referring to the city of Rome. Prostitution and fornication (17:1-2) are metaphoric terms that were regularly used to describe idol worship and the material excesses associated with the Roman Empire (see 2:19-23). Likewise, the phrases "kings of the earth" and "the inhabitants of the earth" (17:2) are symbolic descriptors of those who have pledged allegiance to Rome.

The whore Babylon wears purple, a symbol of royalty, and scarlet, suggesting violence (17:4). The beast on which she rides is the beast of the sea (17:3; see 13:1), previously identified as the Roman Empire. However, now the beast is scarlet, perhaps recalling its connection to the red dragon of Revelation 12. Instead of blasphemous names on its heads (13:1), it now wears *many* blasphemous names *all over its body* (17:3). John continues to describe the harlot, saying that she has a name of mystery on her forehead—Babylon (17:5). The term *mystērion* usually refers to something that is secret or hidden, but in Revelation it also suggests an allegorical interpretation, making Babylon a metaphor for Rome.

The description of Rome as the one "who lives near the many waters" (17:1), who holds "a gold cup" in her hand (17:4), and whose inhabitants are drunk with the wine of her fornication (Rev 17:2), may be borrowed from Jeremiah's prophecy against Babylon (Jer 51:7, 13). Jeremiah describes Babylon's impending downfall as God's vengeance for the destruction of the temple (Jer 51:11). In the same spirit, the author of the book of Revelation attributes God's vengeance against Rome to its role in the death of the martyrs (17:6).

As John marvels over what he was seeing, one of the angels holding the seven bowls becomes the interpreter of his vision (17:6-7). The angel tells him that the beast is the one "who was and is *not* and is to rise" (17:8; author's translation), an obvious spoof on the name of God in the introduction of the book of Revelation: the one "who is and who was and who is to come" (1:4).

If we are correct in assigning Nero's name to the beast in Revelation 13, then the same should apply here. Thus John is saying that Nero was (i.e., he reigned), and is not (i.e., he died), and is to come (i.e., either he or a reign like his will return). See Revelation 13:3 and 13:14. This beast is about to rise from the abyss—the place with which it is regularly associated—and is going to perdition—a fate to which it is regularly assigned (17:8; see 11:7). The angel also tells John that the dwellers of the earth who do not have their names in the book of life will marvel over the beast (17:8), presumably because they pay allegiance to the beast and do not associate themselves with the Lamb.

The angel alerts John to pay careful attention to the next part of his interpretation, saying, "Here is a clue for one who has wisdom" (17:9; see 13:8). The "seven hills" are the seven hills on which Rome is seated (17:9). The reader might be tempted to think of the "seven kings" in historical terms, too, but the angel's riddle is vague, and the list of first-century Roman emperors does not correspond to the riddle. At a minimum, we can say that the five fallen kings describe a series of emperors who preceded the currently reigning emperor, the sixth king (17:10). The seventh king will reign for a limited time, and then an eighth will rise to the throne, who is like one of the seven (17:11). Scholars suggest that Nero (the beast personified) is the sixth king and that Domitian (A.D. 81–96) is the eighth king, whom second-century Roman historians described as a tyrant and a megalomaniac. However, little can be said beyond that. It is possible that the seven kings simply signify the full measure of kingship, since seven is the symbol of fullness.

The angel continues his interpretation, explaining that the "ten horns" are the ten kings still to come, who will have authority and be of one mind with the beast (17:12-13). For a short time they will make war on those who are faithful to the Lamb, but in the end the Lamb will be victorious, because he is sovereign over even the most powerful of kings. The ones who are with him need not fear, because they are called and chosen (17:14).

Finally, the angel explains that the "waters" are the peoples of the Roman Empire (17:15). Eventually, the beast and the ten kings who have authority with the beast will turn their hatred on Rome and shame her, devour her, and utterly destroy her (17:16). This is what evil does; it destroys everything, even its own. But as the beast and the kings allied with him rampage, God remains sovereign, because they are actually fulfilling God's purpose and will continue to do so until God's will is accomplished (17:17).

18:1-8 Babylon's fall

John's next vision is of an angel of great authority (18:1-3). The angel apparently originated from beside the heavenly throne, because his reflected glory lights up the earth (18:1). The angel's speech is a prophecy that is delivered in the form of a dirge (i.e., funeral song). The opening statement, "Fallen, fallen is Babylon" (18:2) recalls another angel's prophecy in Revelation 14:8, also against Rome. Rome's fornication involves both idolatry and material excess. The language and imagery of this dirge are similar to that found in Isaiah and Jeremiah (Isa 21:9; Jer 25:15, 27; 50:39).

In addition to the destruction of Rome, the angel prophesies that Rome's vassal kings (18:3) will suffer punishment because they participated in her fornication and will lament her passing (see 18:9-10). Likewise, the merchants of her empire (18:3) will pay a price; they have grown rich on her excess, so they, too, will grieve for her (see 18:11-17). A second voice urges God's people to leave Rome before they are drawn into her sinful ways (18:4; see Isa 48:20; Jer 50:8). Thus John's vision makes clear that sinful activity *will* result in punishment despite appearances to the contrary. Rome revels in her false glory and thinks herself a queen with no reason to mourn, but God remembers her wicked deeds and *in a single day* she will suffer double for her sins (18:5-7). Further, the intensity of God's vengeance will demonstrate that the One who judges is sovereign (18:8).

Finally, the angel prophesies that Rome's vassal kings, merchants, and seafarers will mourn over her destruction. Echoing the words of the prophet Ezekiel in his dirge over Tyre, the angel announces that Rome's vassal kings will weep and wail over the once powerful city, their terror rooted in the fact that they deserve the same fate, since they were wanton with her (18:9-10; see Ezek 26:16-17). Likewise, the merchants will mourn because no one buys Rome's riches anymore. All of her luxuries, excesses, and splendid dainties are destroyed, never to be restored (18:12-14; see Ezek 27:12-22). They fear her torment because they became wealthy on account of her (18:15; see Ezek 27:31-36). Finally, the captains of ships, sailors, and sea traders mourn and weep over Rome's burning, because they had grown rich from her wealth (18:17-19; see Ezek 27:30-34).

All three groups express terror over Rome's destruction, not in sympathy with Rome but because of their own self-interest. They understand that they will suffer because Rome suffers. Moreover, all three groups marvel over the swiftness of God's judgment—in a single hour! (18:10, 17, 19). Of course, John's audience would have heard this prophecy of doom as a message of hope, since it asserts unequivocally that God is just, and God's justice, when it comes, will be swift. The message of the prophecy is confirmed, at the conclusion of the lamentations, when John exhorts his hearers—the holy ones, apostles, and prophets—to rejoice because God has given judgment against Rome *on their behalf* (18:20).

Finally, John sees another angel described as "mighty" (18:21). This angel issues a prophecy of doom in both word and action. Taking a stone that resembled a great millstone used for grinding grain into flour, the angel threw it into the sea, where it quickly sank to the bottom. "With such force shall Babylon the great city be thrown down," the angel says, "and will never be found again" (18:21). Thus begins a litany whose antiphon is "No . . . will ever be heard in you again" (18:22-23).

What are these things that will no longer be seen or heard in Rome? They are the instruments of joy and merriment, the craftspeople that sustain the quality of life of the society (18:22), the grinding stones that help put bread on the table (18:22), the lights that brighten people's homes (18:23), and the bride and bridegroom whose marriage provides offspring for the future (18:23). As a literary technique, the litany booms like a solemn drumbeat or death knell: Rome will be no more! Finally, the mighty angel reveals the reason for this massive and pervasive destruction: the merchants deceived people with their sorcery and, more importantly, the blood of the martyrs was found in the great city that was Rome (18:24). In other words, God is about to avenge the death of his holy ones!

SEVEN VISIONS OF THE LAST THINGS
Rev 19:1–20:15

The book of Revelation concludes with a final series of visions that describe the judgment that is about to come upon the wicked and the reward that is promised to the righteous. All of these visions are presented in highly mythical language. Therefore, they should be interpreted as symbolic and not historical descriptions. However, the message is clear: God is just and God is sovereign. God will *indeed* vindicate the righteous and punish the wicked.

19:1-10 The heavenly liturgy

As a prelude to the visions of the last things, once again John is allowed to witness the heavenly liturgy (cf. 7:9-12; 14:1-5). The great multitude (19:1) described here is apparently the same as the great multitude who earlier stood before God's throne, dressed in white robes and with palm branches in their hands (cf. 7:9). They shout, "Alleluia," which translates "Praise Yhwh," and they sing a song of victory on account of God's true and just condemnation of the whore Babylon, i.e., Rome, and God's avenging of the death of the martyrs (19:2-3; cf. 6:10). Again, they shout "Alleluia" and affirm the final end of Rome by saying that the smoke from the city goes up forever and ever (19:3). John's mention of the twenty-four elders and the four living

Revelation 19

creatures who joined in worship of God, who is seated on the throne, again recalls the throne vision of Revelation 4.

Suddenly a voice from the throne calls everyone in heaven to offer praise to God (19:5), and the multitude responds with a sound so deafening that it resembles rushing water and thunder crashing (19:6). Again, they shout "Alleluia" and assert that God, the Almighty One, reigns as king (19:6), and they announce with great joy that it is time for the marriage of the Lamb. The bride, whose identity has not yet been revealed, has completed her wedding preparations (19:7). Her bridal gown, which is made of fine, costly, bright white linen (a type found only in Egypt), symbolizes her holiness (19:8). The gown *is given* (passive verb form) to her, meaning that it is a gift *from God* and God is the source or cause of her holiness. John adds that the bridal gown is the righteous deeds of the holy ones (19:8; cf. 15:6). Therefore, we can conclude that the bride is a metaphor for the church, and the holy ones are the members of the church. For a long time they waited under God's altar, demanding God's vengeance on those who killed them (6:9-11). Now they rejoice because the time of God's vindication has finally come (19:6-7).

John goes on to say that he heard the voice from the throne tell him to write the very words of God, "Blessed are those who have been called to the wedding feast of the Lamb" (19:9). This beatitude is about the establishment of God's kingdom, and being *the very words of God*, it carries divine authority. Elsewhere in the New Testament, imagery of a marriage feast is likewise associated with the coming of God's kingdom (Matt 7:11; 22:1-14; 25:1-13).

John falls down to worship the angel, but the angel stops him, telling him that he is not a deity. Rather, he is a fellow servant who holds the testimony of (i.e., concerning) Jesus (19:10). The Greek is difficult to translate into English here, but basically the angel is saying that he, like John himself and others like him, is a prophet who witnesses to Jesus by speaking his word (19:10; cf. 1:1-3). But they must worship only God! (19:10).

After this glorious vision of heavenly worship, John witnesses in rapid succession seven visions of vindication and final judgment. These are all cosmic in scope, embracing heaven and earth and even the space under the earth. The imagery is extremely graphic, but it should not be taken literally. Rather, using metaphorical language, John is asserting that God is sovereign and just and that God rewards the righteous and punishes the wicked.

19:11-16 Vision of the white horse and rider

In the first of seven concluding visions, John sees heaven opened, and again a white horse and rider appear. However, this time the rider is not the Parthian army that made war on Rome (6:2); this one is "Faithful and True" (19:11; cf. 3:14). Because he is described as having eyes of fire with a sword coming from his mouth (19:12, 15), the reader should conclude that the rider is the risen Jesus of the initial vision of this book (see 1:14, 16). He rides a beast of war, the horse, but his is a war of righteousness (19:11). The "many diadems" on his head (19:12) signify supreme kingship. Recall that the dragon wore seven diadems (12:3), and the beast wore ten (13:1). The "name . . . that no one knows" (19:12) means that he has absolute authority, and no one has ownership over him (19:12; cf. 14:1; 17:5), though later he is identified as "Word of God" (19:13), which symbolizes divine authority. The blood-washed robe (19:13) is a symbol of victory in battle (Isa 63:1-3; Wis 18:14-16), and "tread[ing] the wine press" (19:15) describes the wrath of . . . God on judgment day—God will crush the wicked so hard that their lifeblood will spurt out and run like a river! (see Isa 63:1-3). The heavenly army of the risen Jesus is also victorious, dressed in white linen robes (19:14), much like those of the bride in the preceding vision (cf. 7:9). These are the martyrs who had washed their robes in the blood of the Lamb and now no longer hunger or thirst or suffer grief (cf. 7:9-17).

19:17-18 Vision of the great supper of God

The second vision takes place in the midheaven (i.e., the sky). An angel standing in the sun invites all the birds of the sky to enjoy God's banquet (19:17). The banquet imagery is borrowed from Ezekiel's prophecy against Gog of the land of Magog (Ezek 39:17-20) and is typical of apocalyptic literature. However, for the novice reader, the imagery can be appalling! The birds are invited to dine on the flesh of kings, captains, soldiers, horses, and riders (19:18). Imagine the perverse delight of John's audience, thinking about how their persecutors would be eaten alive—banquet food for birds of prey! Thus God punishes the wicked.

19:19-21 Vision of the destruction of the beast and the false prophet

Without transition, suddenly John observes the beast and the kings of the earth gathering for battle against the Word of God and his army (19:19). This is the preparation for Armageddon (see 16:16). But the war is swift. The beast and the false prophet—the beasts of Revelation 13—are captured without incident, suggesting that they have little power when confronted by the risen Christ and the army of God (19:20). The lake of fire into which they are thrown symbolizes their final destruction (19:20). The slaying of the "rest" (19:21) explains how the kings, military officers, warriors, horses,

Revelation 19

and riders came to be table fare for God's banquet. Later they, too, will be thrown into the lake of fire (see 20:15).

20:1-10 The "thousand-year" visions

The fourth and fifth visions in this series are sandwiched together into an intercalation. The seer John begins by narrating the first part of the outer vision, then breaks away to describe the inner vision, and finally returns to complete the narration of the outer vision. The reader should think of the two visions as taking place at the same time. While the inner vision takes place in heaven, the outer vision spans all three realms of the created world.

In the outer vision (20:1-3, 7-10), the dragon (see Rev 12) is taken captive by the angel who descends from heaven with the key to the bottomless pit (see Rev 9). The angel hurls the dragon into the pit and seals it for a thousand years (20:2-3). Note the three other names by which the dragon is known: the ancient serpent, the devil, and Satan (20:2; cf. 12:9). The dragon's capture marks the end of his "short while" on earth (cf. 12:12). But this is not *the* end, for John is told that the dragon must be released for a little while after the thousand years are finished (20:3). The verb of necessity, *dei* in Greek, suggests that this is part of God's plan. Therefore God's holy ones should not be fearful.

Leaving the reader in suspense about the dragon, John abruptly shifts to the fifth vision (20:4-6), the thousand-year reign of Christ and those who had been martyred in his name. John sees thrones and, seated upon them, the ones who were given authority to judge (20:4). These are the souls of those who were martyred for their testimony to Jesus. God rewards them with resurrection so that they can share in Christ's reign (20:4). This, the reader learns, is the first resurrection (20:5). Those who enjoy the first resurrection are blessed because the second death (i.e., the general judgment, here associated with the lake of fire) will bring them no harm (20:6). Thus John asserts that God is just and God will reward the righteous.

Finally, John returns to the second half of the fourth vision (20:7-10). Satan is now released from his thousand-year bondage to gather his armies from the four corners of the earth (20:7). John's reference to Gog and Magog (20:8) comes from Ezekiel 38, in which the prophet rails against Gog, the king of Magog, who came from the far northern regions to wage war against Israel. The prophet promises that God's wrath will fall on Gog, and he and his armies will be utterly destroyed. Why? It is to show that God is great and holy and to make God known to the whole world! (Ezek 38:23). Here

John describes Magog not as Gog's kingdom but as a person who is in alliance with Gog. However, the message is the same as Ezekiel's: God is sovereign, and God will destroy the wicked.

With his vast armies coming from all over the world, Satan is ready to make war against God's people (20:8). John's use of the phrase "camp of the holy ones" (20:9) may be intended to recall the wilderness camp of the Israelites during the Exodus (e.g., Exod 19:16-17). The "beloved city" is Jerusalem (20:9). The holy ones are the members of the church (20:9). This is the battle of Armageddon, which John first mentioned in 16:14-16 and again in 17:14 and 19:11-21. The name is derived from the Hebrew *har Megiddo*, which means "mountain of Megiddo." Historically, it was the location of some of Israel's fiercest battles. Here it takes on cosmic and mythical proportions. The battle is swift and decisive! God intervenes on behalf of the holy ones, sending fire on the earth (20:9; cf. Ezek 38:22). Satan is thrown into the lake of fire, where the beast and the false prophet have already met their end (20:10).

20:11-15 Vision of judgment before God's throne

This throne vision has a link back to the fifth vision of the last things, in which the martyrs are described as seated on thrones in order to share judgment with the risen Christ (20:4), but it also recalls the throne vision of Revelation 4. Thus, as we arrive at the end of the book of Revelation, we have come full circle to a vision of the sovereign God seated on the throne of glory. Given the pervasiveness of the parallel theme of God's justice, the reader should not be surprised that this sixth (and second to the last) vision is one of judgment.

God's throne is white (20:11), signifying victory over the forces of evil. The earth and sky have fled (20:11), presumably because nothing tainted by evil can exist in this holy place, but also in anticipation of the final vision of this book, the New Jerusalem (see 21:1–22:5). Then John sees the dead as they emerge from the sea and the underworld (Hades) to stand before God, who will judge them based upon what is contained in the book of deeds and the book of life (20:12-13). Some, though not all, first-century Jews believed in a general resurrection of the dead at the end time, in which people would be judged on the basis of their deeds (see, for example, Dan 7:10). In this vision those whose names are not in the book of life are sentenced to the second death, the lake of fire (20:15). When the general judgment of human beings is complete, Death (personified; the consequence of evil) and Hades (the place of the dead) are also thrown into the lake of fire (20:14). John does not mention the fate of the holy ones, because they already enjoy resurrection

Revelation 20

with Christ (see 20:6). Thus John asserts God's power over the forces of evil and his justice in punishing the wicked. In sum, the slate has been wiped clean for the transformed *cosmos* (universe), which is about to appear.

VISION OF THE NEW JERUSALEM
Rev 21:1–22:5

The vision of the New Jerusalem is the seventh in this sequence of visions of the last things and the final vision of the book of Revelation. It can be divided into three parts based upon the three images used to describe this transformed universe: the bride and wife of the Lamb (21:1-8), the new temple (21:9-27), and the new creation (22:1-5).

21:1-8 The bride and wife of the Lamb

In the preceding vision (20:11-15), John narrated a scene in which the palette of God's creation has been wiped clean. Now he sees a *new* heaven and a *new* earth and the holy city, a *new* Jerusalem, coming out of heaven from God (21:1-2). The reader should notice that this vision is not about the coming of an otherworldly reality, but the restoration of a transformed *this-worldly* reality. John compares it to a bride who has prepared herself for her husband (21:2). The imagery is traditional. The prophets of the Old Testament used the bridal image to describe the restoration of the historical Jerusalem, when God's people would return from the Babylonian exile. See, for example, Isaiah 49:18: "Look about and see; / they are all gathering and coming to you. / As I live, says the LORD, / you shall be arrayed with them all as with adornments, / like a bride you shall fasten them on you." See also Isaiah 52:1 and Isaiah 61:10.

The voice that John hears explains the significance of the vision: this is God's dwelling, and the people who reside in this city are God's people (21:3). The relationship, which the voice describes, is *covenant*. The language is almost identical to that of Ezekiel: "I will make with them a covenant of peace . . . . My dwelling shall be with them; I will be their God, and they shall be my people" (Ezek 37:26-27). As narrated in the previous vision (20:11-15), the old order, dominated by the dragon, the beasts of the land and sea, Death and Hades, has passed away. Therefore there is no suffering or death in this new order (21:4). This, too, is traditional imagery for the restoration of Jerusalem. See, for example, Isaiah 25:7-8: "On this mountain . . . the Lord GOD will wipe away the tears from all faces."

Now God speaks: "They are accomplished," that is, "the transformation is complete" (21:6; see 21:5). God's declaration, "I [am] the Alpha and the

Omega" (the first and last letters of the Greek alphabet; 21:6), is an assertion of sovereignty over all things. Thus God promises to the thirsty (i.e., those who have committed themselves in covenant with God) the water of life *as a gift* and reaffirms his covenant with the holy ones (21:6-7). Again, the imagery is traditional. See, for example, Isaiah 55:1, 3: "All you who are thirsty, / come to the water! / You who have no money, / come, receive grain and eat; / . . . / I renew with you the everlasting covenant, / benefits assured to David." Other examples of water associated with life in the messianic age include Isaiah 41:17-18; Isaiah 44:3-4; Ezekiel 47:1-12; Zechariah 13:1; and Zechariah 14:8. The phrase to "the victor" (21:7) recalls the promises at the conclusion of the letters to the seven churches in Revelation 2–3. The reference to those who are doomed for the lake of fire (21:8) is a reminder that nothing evil can reside in this transformed city, the bride of the Lamb.

21:9-27 The new temple

When one of the angels of the seven plagues approaches John and invites him to see the bride of the Lamb (21:9), John is transported to a high mountain—most likely the location of the historical Jerusalem—where he can see the New Jerusalem coming out of heaven from God (21:10). In ancient Judaism the Jerusalem temple was the symbol of God's covenant, its worship center, and the place where God's glory resides on earth. Here John will use the temple as a metaphor for the New Jerusalem.

Again, the imagery is traditional. The new city is radiant with God's glory (21:11; cf. Isa 60:1-2; Ezek 43:2-5; Zech 2:5). Its cubic shape mirrors the holy of holies in Solomon's temple (21:16; cf. 1 Kgs 6:20; 2 Chr 3:8f.), and the plan of the temple, including its three gates on each of four walls, recalls Ezekiel's plan of the temple (21:12-13; cf. Ezek 41:21; 43:16; 45:1; 48:20). The twelve precious stones of the foundation of the walls (21:19) recall the high priest's breastplate, which was to have twelve stones representing the twelve tribes (cf. Exod 28:17-21). They also recall the promise of Jerusalem's restoration contained in both Tobit and Isaiah (Tob 13:15-17; Isa 54:11-12).

Some of the details of John's vision remind the reader that although the New Jerusalem is this-worldly, it also has a cosmic and mythical dimension. Its walls, for example, measure 144 cubits in height and thickness (21:17). A cubit was measured from the elbow to the tip of one's finger, approximately 18 inches, so 144 cubits is approximately 72 yards. More importantly, 144 is the total of 12 multiplied by 12, or perfection squared. Since the city walls were its first line of protection against attackers, this one is perfectly protected! The city itself measures four-square, 12,000 *stadia* on a side and

12,000 *stadia* high (21:16). A *stadion* measured approximately 606 feet, so 12,000 *stadia* is approximately 1,377 miles. A city this size is not feasible, but the symbolism is important. A four-square city, characterized by perfection (12) multiplied by a number too great to count (1,000), suggests one that is perfect in its dimensions, comprehensive, and all-inclusive. Consistent with this view of the city is the description of its walls being made of jasper, its streets paved in gold, and each of its gates crafted of a single pearl! (21:18, 21).

Other details in John's vision of the New Jerusalem are reminiscent of the throne vision of Revelation 4. For example, the city having the radiance of jasper (21:11) recalls the description of the One seated on the throne, who appeared "like jasper and carnelian" (4:3). Likewise, the names of the twelve tribes of Israel inscribed on the gates of the city (21:12) and the names of the twelve apostles inscribed on the foundation stones (21:14) recall the twenty-four elders who were situated on thrones surrounding the throne of God (4:4). Thus the reader should not be surprised when John announces that he saw no temple in the new city. God and the Lamb reside directly—that is, without the mediation of a temple—in the city (21:22). God's glory and the radiance of the Lamb provide the city's light, and because God is forever faithful, there is no need to fear danger because the city will never have darkness in it (21:23, 25). Moreover, God's radiance will attract all nations into the city, and nothing unclean will enter it (21:24, 26-27). In sum, the New Jerusalem is God's dwelling place on earth.

22:1-5 The new creation

In the third segment of this vision, the angel of the seven plagues takes John to see the river of the water of life coming out of the throne of God and the Lamb, which is now inside of the city (22:1). Again, the imagery is traditional. The river recalls the second creation story in Genesis, which provided the setting for God's creation of a human from the dust of the earth (cf. Gen 2:9-10), as well as Ezekiel's vision of a river of water flowing from the temple (Ezek 47:1-12) and Zechariah's vision of water coming from Jerusalem when God's day of judgment comes (Zech 14:8). John's observation that there is a tree of life on each side of the river (22:2) recalls the tree of life that God placed in the garden, also from the second creation story (cf. Gen 2:9). It is the same tree from which Adam and Eve were banished after their sin (Gen 3:22). In other words, John's vision of the New Jerusalem is paradise restored!

John further observes that these trees produce fruit twelve months of the year, and they have leaves that are good for healing of the nations (22:2). The language is closely related to that of the prophet Ezekiel: "Their leaves shall not fade, nor their fruit fail. Every month they shall bear fresh fruit, for they shall be watered by the flow from the sanctuary. Their fruit shall serve for food, and their leaves for medicine" (Ezek 47:12). The point of this part of the vision: God will provide all they need for nourishment and for well-being. John adds "for *the nations*," making the vision all-inclusive (emphasis added). John's observation that there is nothing accursed in the city (22:3) and no darkness (22:5) recalls an end-time prophecy about the lifting of the curse on Jerusalem, so that it can finally live in safety (cf. Zech 14:7-11). In sum, John's vision of the New Jerusalem is the establishment of a new creation, or better, a return to the first creation, before there was sin and evil in the world. It is a return to the Garden of Eden.

CONCLUDING MATERIALS

Rev 22:6-21

Revelation ends with a collection of warnings, beatitudes, and exhortations, some of which recall earlier sections of the book. Several refer to the prophetic character of the book.

The heavenly being who is speaking to John (22:6) appears at first to be one of the seven angels who hold the seven bowls (21:9). However, some of the later sayings in this section are clearly those of the risen Christ (e.g., 22:12-13). Perhaps we have sayings from a variety of sources, without regard to the identity of the speaker, collected together at the end of this document. The description of these words as "trustworthy and true" (22:6) is an assertion of their authenticity, as is the statement that God sent his angel to tell his prophets what must take place soon (22:6). John made a similar statement in the opening of the book (see 1:1).

The declaration "I am coming soon!" (22:7) most likely comes from the risen Christ (cf. 3:11). It will appear two more times in this section, in 22:12 and 22. The beatitude about keeping the message of this book is a short form of the first beatitude of the book of Revelation (1:3).

Now John speaks, identifying himself again as the recipient of the revelation (22:8; cf. 1:1, 9). He also recalls his encounter with the angel messenger in 19:10, with a few variations: "the brothers" of the earlier recollection are now "the prophets," and "the testimony concerning Jesus" is now "the message of this book."

This next saying is directed to John and most likely comes from the angel of verse 6. The command *not* to seal the words of the book (22:10) signals the immediacy of the end (cf. Dan 8:26). The saying about letting the wicked still act wickedly may sound like determinism, but since the book of Revelation allows for the possibility of repentance (see, for example, 14:6), that interpretation is unlikely. Instead, we should understand it as a warning not to be complacent but always to be ready, for the end is near.

The saying that begins "I am coming soon" (22:12) signals that the risen Christ is now speaking and that he brings rewards for believers according to their works. The attribution "Alpha and Omega" (22:13) is used elsewhere in the book of Revelation only for God (1:8; 21:6). The beatitude that follows, "Blessed are they who wash their robes . . . " (22:14), is most likely a recollection of 7:14, in which the angel explains to John the identity of the 144,000. The "tree of life" and the gates of the city are probably allusions to the vision of the New Jerusalem (21:24-27; 22:2). The saying about "dogs, the sorcerers, the unchaste . . . and all who love and practice deceit" (22:15) recalls those who are not allowed into the New Jerusalem, since it is the place where God and the Lamb reside (see 21:8, 27). It also suggests those who have made allegiance with the dragon and its beasts (see 13:6-8).

Jesus continues, providing further authentication for the book of Revelation, here called "testimony for the churches" (22:16). His authority to speak lies in the fact that he is the messiah: thus the reference to the root of David and the bright morning star (see Isa 11:1; Num 24:17).

The statement about the Spirit and the bride (22:17) has all the flavor of a call to worship, and some scholars have suggested that the author's liturgical allusion was intentional. The Spirit is the one who speaks to the churches through the prophets (see 2:7; 19:10). The bride is the New Jerusalem (see 21:2, 9). The one "who hears" is the one who reads and takes to heart the words of the book of Revelation. All say, "Come," addressed to the risen Jesus. He is the coming one. The invitation for the thirsty to come (22:17) is reminiscent of the promise made to the inhabitants of the New Jerusalem that they will have access to "the fountain of the water of life" (cf. 21:6).

The book ends with a warning to would-be editors not to add to, take away from, or otherwise alter the contents of this book (22:18). Certainly such things happened because ancient religious documents were considered to be community expressions of faith and recollections of larger oral or written traditions. Therefore, if a scribe found that something was missing or thought that a clarification of meaning was necessary, he would simply make the change. However, this warning might also serve to assure the reader that the content of the book is reliable, much like the statements of authenticity we have seen throughout this section. See, for example, 22:7, 12, and 20. In sum, whatever the involvement of the human author, the book of Revelation is reliable because God is its source (see 1:1).

Revelation 22

Once again Jesus promises, "I am coming soon!" (22:20), to which the author, on behalf of the readers, answers, "Amen," meaning, "So be it." Certainly this is a message of hope for the persecuted! However, the time is *coming;* it is not yet here. Therefore the author adds a prayer of petition, "Come, Lord Jesus" (in Aramaic *marana tha*).

Finally, the book ends as it began—with literary features of a letter. Thus we see a closing greeting, wishing the grace (i.e., gift) of Jesus on all (22:21). Amen. So be it!

www.ingramcontent.com/pod-product-compliance
Lightning Source LLC
Chambersburg PA
CBHW071849290426
44110CB00013B/1075